Direct 448 (ser.)

D0212224

REFERENCE
Not to be taken from this room

Kirtland Community College Library
3800 W. Four Mile Rd.
Grayling, MI 49738
989.275.5000 x1246

SALEM HEALTH

Psychology & Behavioral Health

SALEM HEALTH

Psychology & Behavioral Health

Volume 3
Hearing – Parental alienation syndrome (PAS)

Editor
Paul Moglia, PhD
South Nassau Communities Hospital
Oceanside, NY

SALEM PRESS
A Division of EBSCO Information Services, Inc.
IPSWICH, MASSACHUSETTS

GREY HOUSE PUBLISHING

Copyright © 2015 by Grey House Publishing and Salem Press, a division of EBSCO Information Services, Inc.

All rights reserved. No part of this work may be used or reproduced in any manner whatsoever or transmitted in any form or by any means, electronic or mechanical, including photocopy, recording, or any information storage and retrieval system, without written permission from the copyright owner. For information contact Grey House Publishing/Salem Press, 4919 Route 22, PO Box 56, Amenia, NY 12501.

∞The paper used in these volumes conforms to the American National Standard for Permanence of Paper for Printed Library Materials, Z39.48 1992 (R1997).

Some of the updated and revised essays in this work originally appeared in *Magill's Encyclopedia of Social Science: Psychology*, edited by Nancy A. Piotrowski, PhD (2003) and *Magill's Survey of Social Science: Psychology*, edited by Frank N. Magill (1993).

Publisher's Cataloging-In-Publication Data
(Prepared by The Donohue Group, Inc.)

Psychology & behavioral health / editor, Paul Moglia, PhD. – Fourth edition.

5 volumes : illustrations ; cm. -- (Salem health)

At head of title: Salem health.
Previously published as: Psychology & mental health.
Includes bibliographical references and index.
Contents: Volume 1. Ability tests-Community psychology -- volume 2. Comorbidity-Health psychology -- volume 3. Hearing-Parental alienation syndrome -- volume 4. Parenting styles-Sleep -- volume 5. Sleep apnea-Philip Zimbardo; Appendixes; Indexes.
    ISBN: 978-1-61925-543-2 (5-volume set)
    ISBN: 978-1-61925-810-5 (vol.1)
    ISBN: 978-1-61925-811-2 (vol.2)
    ISBN: 978-1-61925-812-9 (vol.3)
    ISBN: 978-1-61925-813-6 (vol.4)
    ISBN: 978-1-61925-814-3 (vol.5)

    1. Psychology, Applied--Encyclopedias. 2. Mental health--Encyclopedias. 3. Mental illness--Encyclopedias. 4. Medicine and psychology--Encyclopedias. I. Moglia, Paul. II. Title: Psychology and behavioral health III. Title: Salem health IV. Series: Salem health (Pasadena, Calif.)

BF636 .P86 2015
150.3

FIRST PRINTING
PRINTED IN THE UNITED STATES OF AMERICA

COMPLETE LIST OF CONTENTS

VOLUME 1

Publisher's Note. v
Editor's Introduction vi
Contributors viii

Ability tests 1
Abnormality: Biomedical models 6
Abnormality: Legal models 10
Abnormality: Psychological models 13
Achievement motivation 19
Addictive personality and behaviors. 22
Adler, Alfred. 25
Adlerian psychotherapy 26
Adolescence: Cognitive skills. 30
Adolescence: Cross-cultural patterns 34
Adolescence: Sexuality. 38
Adrenal gland. 41
Adult ADHD 44
Advertising. 46
Affiliation and friendship 49
Affiliation motive 54
African Americans and mental health 57
Ageism. 61
Aggression 64
Aggression: Reduction and control 67
Aging: Cognitive changes. 71
Aging: Physical changes. 76
Aging: Theories 79
Agoraphobia and panic disorders. 83
Air rage 86
Albee, George W. 88
Alcohol dependence and abuse 89
Allport, Gordon 92
Altered states of consciousness 93
Altruism, cooperation, and empathy 96
Alzheimer's disease 100
American Psychiatric Association 105
American Psychological Association 108
Amnesia and fugue 111
Analytic psychology: Jacques Lacan. 113
Analytic psychology: Carl Jung 118
Analytical psychotherapy. 121
Anger. 124
Anger management 127
Animal experimentation 129

Anorexia nervosa and bulimia nervosa 134
Antianxiety medications. 138
Antidepressant medications. 139
Antipsychotic medications. 141
Antisocial personality disorder. 142
Anxiety disorders 146
Aphasias. 150
Archetypes and the collective unconscious 154
Archival data 158
Artificial intelligence 161
Asperger syndrome 164
Asian Americans/Pacific Islanders and
    mental health. 168
Assessment 170
Assessment of the Hispanic community 173
Assimilative family therapy model 176
Assisted living 180
Attachment and bonding in infancy and
    childhood. 183
Attention 186
Attention-deficit hyperactivity
    disorder (ADHD). 190
Attitude-behavior consistency 193
Attitude formation and change 197
Attraction theories. 200
Attributional biases 205
Autism. 208
Autism spectrum disorder 211
Automaticity 214
Aversion therapy 217
Avoidant personality disorder. 218
Bad-Boy appeal 221
Bandura, Albert 223
Battered woman syndrome. 224
Beck, Aaron T. 226
Beck depression inventory (BDI). 227
Bed-wetting. 229
Behavior therapy 232
Behavioral addiction 237
Behavioral assessment 239
Behavioral economics 243
Behavioral family therapy. 246
Behaviorism. 249
Bilingualism. 253

Bilingualism and learning disabilities. 256
Binet, Alfred 258
Biofeedback and relaxation 259
Bipolar disorder 262
Biracial heritage and mental health 265
Birth: Effects on physical development 267
Birth order and personality 271
Blau, Theodore H. 274
Bobo doll experiment. 274
Body dysmorphic disorder 276
Borderline personality disorder 278
Brain damage. 281
Brain lateralization. 285
Brain structure. 288
Breuer, Josef 294
Brief therapy 295
Bronfenbrenner, Urie. 296
Bruner, Jerome. 297
Bullying 298
Bystander intervention. 299
Caffeine and mental health 304
California psychological inventory (CPI) 305
Cancer and mental health 307
Cannon, Walter Bradford. 310
Career and personnel testing. 311
Career occupational preference system
   (COPS) 315
Career selection, development, and change. 317

Case study methodologies 320
Causal attribution 323
Child abuse 327
Childhood disorders. 331
Childhood obesity 335
Children's depression inventory (CDI) 338
Children's mental health 339
Christian counseling 344
Chronic pain management: Psychological
   impact 347
Circadian rhythms. 350
Clinical interviewing, testing, and observation 354
Coaching 358
Codependency. 360
Cognitive abilities test (CogAT). 362
Cognitive ability: Gender differences 364
Cognitive behavior therapy (CBT). 367
Cognitive development: Jean Piaget 372
Cognitive dissonance. 375
Cognitive maps 379
Cognitive psychology 383
Cognitive social learning: Walter Mischel 388
Cognitive therapy (CT) 391
Collectivism. 395
College entrance examinations and cultural
   biases. 398
Community psychology 400

VOLUME 2

Comorbidity. 405
Complex experimental designs 407
Computer and internet use and mental health 410
Computer models of cognition. 412
Concept formation. 415
Conditioning 418
Conduct disorder. 424
Confidentiality. 426
Consciousness. 428
Consciousness: Altered states 432
Constructivist psychology 436
Consumer psychology 438
Cooperation, competition, and negotiation 441
Cooperative learning 444
Coping: Chronic illness 448
Coping: Social support. 452
Coping: Strategies 456

Coping: Terminal illness 459
Cosmetics and beauty 463
Couples therapy. 466
Creative reminiscence 470
Creativity. 474
Creativity and intelligence. 477
Creativity: Assessment. 479
Crisis intervention 482
Cross-cultural psychology 484
Crowd behavior 486
Cultural competence. 489
Culture and diagnosis 490
Culture-bound syndromes 492
Data description 495
Death and dying. 499
Deception and lying. 503
Decision making 504

Deductive reasoning 508
Defense mechanisms. 509
Defense reactions: Species-specific 511
Dementia. 514
Denial 517
Depression. 519
Depth and motion perception 525
Despair 528
Development 530
Developmental disabilities. 534
Developmental methodologies. 538
Developmental psychology. 542
Dewey, John. 546
Diagnosis 547
Dialectical behavioral therapy 551
Disability: Psychological impact. 553
Disaster psychology 557
Discipline 560
Dissociative disorders 563
Dix, Dorothea 566
Dog psychology 567
Dolphin psychology 570
Domestic violence 573
Down syndrome. 578
Dreams 581
Drive theory. 586
Drug therapies 589
DSM-5. 593
DSM-5: Controversies. 598
Dysgraphia. 602
Dyslexia 604
Dysphonia 607
Eating disorders. 610
Ebbinghaus, Hermann. 614
Ecological psychology 615
Educational psychology 618
Ego defense mechanisms. 621
Ego psychology: Erik H. Erikson 626
Ego, superego, and id. 631
Elder abuse 633
Elders' mental health 636
Electronic media and psychological impact 640
Elimination disorders. 645
Ellis, Albert 646
Emotional abuse 647
Emotional expression. 650
Emotional intelligence (EI) 653
Emotions 655
Encoding 659

Endocrine system and behavior 661
Endorphins 665
Environmental factors and mental health 668
Environmental psychology. 671
Environmental toxicology and mental health 675
Erikson, Erik H. 678
Ethology. 679
Evolutionary psychology. 682
Executive functions 685
Exercise addiction 688
Exercise and mental health 690
Existential psychology 692
Experimental psychology 695
Experimentation: Ethics and participant rights 698
Experimentation: Independent, dependent,
   and control variables 701
Eye movement desensitization and reprocessing
   (EMDR) 705
Eyewitness testimony. 707
Eysenck, Hans. 710
Facial feedback 712
Factitious disorders 715
Families and behavioral addictions 718
Families and substance abuse 721
Family dynamics 725
Family life: Adult issues 727
Family life: Children's issues 730
Family systems theory 733
Father-child relationship 736
Fear 739
Femininity 742
Feminist psychotherapy 744
Fetishes 747
Field experimentation 748
Field theory: Kurt Lewin 752
Fight-or-flight response 755
Flying phobia 757
Forensic psychology. 761
Forgetting and forgetfulness. 764
Forgiveness 768
Freud, Anna. 771
Freud, Sigmund. 772
Freudian psychology 773
Fromm, Erich 778
Frontotemporal dementia (Pick's Disease). 779
Gambling 782
Games and mental health 784
Gay, lesbian, bisexual, and transgender mental
   health. 786

Gender differences 789
Gender identity disorder 792
Gender identity formation 796
Gender roles and gender role conflicts 799
General adaptation syndrome (GAS) 802
General aptitude test battery (GATB) 805
Generalized anxiety disorder (GAD) 807
Genetics and mental health 808
Geriatric psychological disorders 812
Gesell, Arnold 816
Gestalt therapy 817
Giftedness 820
Gilligan, Carol 824
Gonads 825
Gossip 829

Grammar and speech 831
Gratitude 835
Grieving 837
Group decision making 840
Group therapy 844
Groups 847
Guilt 851
Habituation and sensitization 855
Hall, G. Stanley 858
Hallucinations 859
Hate crimes: Psychological causes and effects 861
Health insurance 864
Health maintenance organizations (HMOs) 866
Health psychology 868

VOLUME 3

Hearing 873
Help-seeking 876
Helping 879
Hierarchy of needs 882
Histrionic personality disorder (HPD) 884
Hoarding 886
Holland, John L. 889
Homelessness: Psychological causes and
   effects 892
Homosexuality 895
Hope 899
Hope and mental health 902
Hormones and behavior 903
Horney, Karen 908
Hospice 909
Hull, Clark L. 911
Human resource training and development 912
Humanistic psychology 915
Humanistic trait models: Gordon Allport 919
Hunger 922
Hypnosis 926
Hypochondriasis, conversion and somatization . . . 930
Hypothesis development and testing 934
Hysteria 938
Identity crises 942
Implosion 945
Imprinting 947
Impulse control disorders (ICD) 951
Incentive theory of motivation 954
Incompetency 957

Individual psychology: Alfred Adler 960
Inductive reasoning 964
Industrial and organizational psychology 965
Infant feeding 969
Infant sleep 971
Infidelity 974
Inhibitory and excitatory impulses 978
Insanity defense 982
Insomnia 983
Insomnia and sleep disorders 987
Instinct theory 990
Intelligence 993
Intelligence quotient (IQ) 997
Intelligence quotient (IQ) and measuring
   intelligence 999
Intelligence tests 1001
Interest inventories 1006
International Classification of Diseases (ICD) . . . 1010
Internet psychology 1011
Interpersonal attraction 1014
Intervention 1017
Interviewing 1018
Intimacy 1022
Introverts and extroverts 1025
James, William 1027
Jealousy 1028
Jung, Carl 1031
Jungian psychology 1032
Juvenile delinquency and development 1035
Kelly, George A. 1039

Kinesthetic memory. 1040
Kinsey, Alfred. 1043
Kleptomania. 1044
Kohlberg, Lawrence. 1045
Kraepelin, Emil 1046
Kübler-Ross, Elisabeth. 1047
Kuder occupational interest survey (KOIS) 1048
Lacan, Jacques. 1050
Language 1051
Latinos and mental health 1057
Law and psychology. 1060
Leadership. 1064
Learned helplessness. 1067
Learning. 1070
Learning disorders 1076
Lewin, Kurt 1079
Linguistics 1080
Little Albert study 1085
Lobotomy. 1087
Logic and reasoning. 1088
Long-term memory 1093
Lorenz, Konrad 1096
Love. 1097
Luminosity. 1101
Marijuana 1104
Marijuana dependence 1107
Marriage 1109
Marriage and family therapists. 1113
Masculinity 1117
Maslow, Abraham 1118
Masters, William H., and Virginia E. Johnson 1119
May, Rollo 1120
McGraw, Dr. Philip 1121
Media exposure and mental health 1123
Media psychology 1126
Meditation. 1131
Meditation and relaxation 1134
Memory. 1138
Memory: Animal research 1142
Memory disorders 1146
Memory: Empirical studies 1149
Memory: Enhancement 1152
Memory: Physiology. 1155
Memory: Sensory. 1159
Memory storage. 1164
Men's mental health 1168
Mental blocks 1172
Mental health parity 1176
Mental health practitioners 1177

Mental illness: Historical concepts 1180
Mental retardation. 1184
Midlife crisis 1189
Milgram experiment. 1191
Miller, Neal E., and John Dollard 1193
Millon, Theodore 1194
Mindfulness. 1197
Minnesota multiphasic personality inventory
    (MMPI). 1199
Misbehavior. 1201
Mischel, Walter 1205
Mood disorders 1206
Mood stabilizer medications 1210
Moral development 1211
Mother-child relationship 1215
Motivation. 1218
Motivation: Intrinsic and extrinsic. 1222
Motor development 1223
Multicultural disability competence 1226
Multicultural psychology 1230
Multiple intelligences 1232
Multiple personality. 1235
Munchausen syndrome and Munchausen
    syndrome by proxy 1238
Murray, Henry A. 1240
Music, dance, and theater therapy. 1241
Myers-Briggs personality type indicator 1245
Narcissistic personality disorder (NPD) 1248
Narcolepsy. 1249
National Institute of Mental Health (NIMH) 1253
Native Americans/Alaskan Natives and mental
    health. 1254
Nearsightedness and farsightedness 1256
Nervous system 1259
Neurons. 1262
Neuropsychology 1265
Neurotic disorders 1268
Neurotransmitters 1272
Nicotine dependence. 1273
Nonverbal communication and social cognition . . 1275
Nutrition and mental health 1279
Obesity 1284
Observational learning and modeling therapy 1286
Observational methods 1290
Obsessive-compulsive disorder 1293
Oedipus complex. 1298
Operant conditioning therapies 1299
Optimal arousal theory. 1302
Organizational behavior and consulting 1306

Pain 1309
Pain management 1312
Panic attacks 1316

Paranoia 1318
Parental alienation syndrome (PAS) 1321

VOLUME 4

Parenting and behavioral addictions 1325
Parenting styles 1328
Parkinson's disease 1331
Passive aggression 1334
Pattern recognition 1335
Pattern vision 1338
Pavlov, Ivan Petrovich 1341
Pavlovian conditioning 1342
Peabody individual achievement test (PIAT) 1346
Peak experiences 1347
Penis envy 1350
Person-centered therapy (PCT) 1352
Personal constructs: George A. Kelly 1356
Personality disorders 1359
Personality interviewing strategies 1363
Personality: Psychophysiological measures 1367
Personality rating scales 1371
Personality theory 1374
Personology theory: Henry A. Murray 1378
Pervasive developmental disorders 1381
Philosophy and psychology 1383
Phobias 1386
Physical development: Environment versus
    genetics 1389
Piaget, Jean 1393
Pinel, Philippe 1394
Pituitary gland 1395
Placebo effect 1398
Play therapy 1400
Pornography addiction 1403
Positive psychology 1406
Postpartum depression 1408
Post-traumatic stress (PTS) 1410
Power 1415
Prejudice 1418
Prejudice and stereotyping 1423
Prejudice reduction 1425
Prenatal physical development 1429
Problem-solving stages 1433
Problem-solving strategies 1436
Procrastination 1439
Profiling 1442

Projection 1445
Psychoanalysis 1449
Psychoanalytic psychology 1454
Psychoanalytic psychology and personality:
    Sigmund Freud 1458
Psychobiology 1461
Psychologically healthy workplace 1465
Psychology and film 1468
Psychology: Definition 1471
Psychology: Fields of specialization 1475
Psychology: History 1479
Psycho-oncology 1486
Psychopathology 1488
Psychopharmacology 1494
Psychosexual development 1498
Psychosomatic disorders 1502
Psychosurgery 1506
Psychotherapy: Children 1510
Psychotherapy: Effectiveness 1514
Psychotherapy: Goals and techniques 1518
Psychotherapy: Historical approaches 1521
Psychotic disorders 1525
Punishment 1528
Qualitative research 1532
Quality of life 1534
Quasi-experimental designs 1536
Race and intelligence 1541
Racism 1545
Radical behaviorism: B. F. Skinner 1548
Rape 1552
Rape and sexual assault 1556
Rational emotive therapy 1558
Reactive attachment disorder (RAD) 1563
Reality therapy 1565
Reality TV 1568
Recency effects 1571
Reflexes 1574
Reflexes in newborns 1577
Reinforcement 1580
Relaxation response: Herbert Benson 1584
Religion and psychology 1586
Religiosity 1590

Repressed memories 1594
Research ethics 1596
Reticular formation 1600
Retirement. 1603
Risk assessments 1606
Road rage. 1608
Rogers, Carl R.. 1610
Romantic addiction 1611
Rorschach, Hermann. 1613
Rorschach inkblots 1614
Rosenhan experiment 1616
Rule-governed behavior 1617
S-R theory: Neal E. Miller and John Dollard. 1622
Sadism and masochism 1625
Sampling 1628
Satir, Virginia 1632
Schizoid personality disorder (SPD) 1633
Schizophrenia: Background, types, and
    symptoms. 1635
Schizophrenia: High-risk children 1638
Schizophrenia: Theoretical explanations 1644
Schizotypal personality disorder. 1648
Scientific methods. 1650
Seasonal affective disorder. 1656
Self 1660
Self-actualization. 1665
Self-disclosure 1668
Self-efficacy. 1672
Self-esteem 1674
Self-help groups. 1677

Self-perception theory (SPT). 1679
Self-presentation 1683
Seligman, Martin E. P.. 1687
Selye, Hans 1688
Sensation and perception. 1689
Senses 1692
Separation and divorce: Adult issues 1695
Separation and divorce: Children's issues 1698
Separation anxiety 1701
Sex addiction 1704
Sex hormones and motivation 1706
Sexism 1709
Sexual abuse: Impact. 1713
Sexual behavior patterns 1715
Sexual dysfunction. 1719
Sexual harassment: Psychological causes and
    effects 1725
Sexual orientation 1727
Sexual predatory behaviors. 1731
Sexual variants and paraphilias 1734
Shift work 1738
Shock therapy 1742
Short-term memory 1746
Shyness 1749
Sibling relationships. 1751
Signal detection theory 1754
Skinner, B. F.. 1758
Skinner box 1759
Sleep 1760

VOLUME 5

Sleep apnea. 1767
Sleep disorders 1769
Sleep hygiene 1772
Smell and taste 1775
Social identity theory. 1778
Social learning: Albert Bandura 1782
Social networks 1786
Social perception. 1790
Social psychological models: Erich Fromm 1793
Social psychological models: Karen Horney. 1797
Social schemata. 1799
Social support and mental health. 1803
Sociopaths 1806
Speech disorders 1808
Speech perception 1812

Spirituality and mental health 1816
Split-brain studies 1818
Sports psychology 1822
Stanford-Binet test. 1826
Stanford prison experiment 1828
State-trait anxiety inventory (STAI) 1830
Statistical significance tests. 1832
Stepfamilies. 1836
Stimulant medications. 1838
Strategic family therapy. 1840
Stress: Behavioral and psychological responses . . . 1844
Stress: Physiological responses 1849
Stress-related diseases. 1852
Stress: Theories 1856
Strong interest inventory (SII) 1860

Structuralism and functionalism 1863
Stuttering. 1867
Substance abuse and Mental Health Services
    Administration 1872
Substance use disorders. 1874
Suicide. 1877
Sullivan, Harry Stack. 1881
Support groups. 1882
Survey research: Questionnaires and interviews . . 1885
Synaptic transmission 1888
Synesthesia 1892
Systematic desensitization 1895
Systems theories 1898
Taste aversion 1900
Teaching methods 1903
Teenage suicide 1908
Teenagers' mental health 1911
Temperature. 1916
Terrorism: Psychological causes and effects. 1919
Testing: Historical perspectives 1922
Testing, tests, and measurement 1925
Thematic apperception test (TAT). 1928
Thirst 1930
Thorndike, Edward L. 1932
Thought: Inferential. 1933
Thought: Study and measurement 1936
Thyroid gland. 1939
Tic disorders 1943
Time-out 1946
Tolman, Edward C. 1947
Touch and pressure 1948
Tourette's syndrome. 1951
Toxic environments and human development 1955
Transactional analysis (TA) 1958
Transgender psychology. 1962

Transtheoretical model 1965
Transvestism 1966
Twin studies. 1968
Type A behavior pattern. 1971
Verbal abuse. 1975
Victimization 1977
Violence and sexuality in the media. 1979
Violence by children and teenagers 1983
Violence: Psychological causes and effects 1985
Virtual reality. 1988
Vision: Brightness and contrast 1992
Vision: Color 1995
Visual system 1998
Watson, John B. 2002
Wechsler intelligence scale for children. 2003
Wellness. 2004
Within-subject experimental designs 2007
Women's mental health 2011
Women's psychology: Carol Gilligan 2016
Women's psychology: Karen Horney 2020
Women's psychology: Sigmund Freud 2023
Work motivation. 2027
Workforce reentry 2031
Workplace issues and mental health 2032
Yalom, Irvin D. 2037
Zimbardo, Philip 2039

Glossary. 2043
Bibliography. 2067
Website directory. 2122
Mediagraphy 2130
Organizations and support groups 2148
Category index. 2173
Subject index. 2198

Hearing

TYPE OF PSYCHOLOGY: Sensation and perception

Hearing, like vision, transmits information about things and events in the distance. Like smell, it can transmit information about things that cannot be seen. It impels people to take action that their lives may depend on, triggers emotional states, and makes spoken language possible. Hearing depends on sound waves made by the motion of objects.

KEY CONCEPTS

- Amplitude
- Complex waves
- Frequency
- Fundamental
- Harmonics
- Loudness
- Pitch
- Sound pressure level
- Timbre
- Wavelength

INTRODUCTION

Most things produce sound waves by vibrating or by moving quickly. All vibrations are similar in that they result from the basic physical properties of elasticity and inertia. For example, if one takes a rubber band and stretches it between thumb and forefinger and plucks one strand, the band, stretched into elastic tension and then released, accelerates as the elastic force stored in it by the pluck is changed to kinetic energy (movement). The elastic tension of the strand is fully spent and its velocity highest when it is at its midpoint of flight, where it was before it was plucked. The strand's inertia (tendency to keep moving) then carries it almost as far as did the pluck, but in the opposite direction, until this kinetic energy is stored again as potential energy in the elastic tension of the restretched strand. The process repeats itself rapidly, many times, until all the energy imparted to the strand has been lost in friction in the rubber and air molecules and, more important, by transferring kinetic energy to air molecules. It is this movement of air molecules that is the physical stimulus for the generation of sound. Thus, objects' elasticity and mass allow them to produce sound waves when energized. This is how musical instruments and the vocal apparatus of animals, including humans, work.

Sound waves move over distances through an elastic medium such as air. A violin string, like the rubber band, moves back and forth—but virtually continuously as it is being continually "replucked" by the bow. The vibrating string moves in air. Although originally distributed evenly, these gas molecules are compressed when the string moves one way against them and then are placed in a partial vacuum (a region of lower density of molecules) by the motion of the string in the opposite direction. The compressed particles push against the molecules just down the line, compressing them. Then, with their elastic energy transferred, they return to fill the space created initially by the opposite movement of the string. The just-compressed molecules now push against their neighbors before returning to fill the space created by their predecessors' reverse motion. Thus, there are two kinds of particle motion involved in a sound wave: a back-and-forth oscillation of compressed and rarefied air that remains essentially in place and a linear, continuous, outward movement of successive waves. The acoustic waves move outward from the vibrating object like waves in the ocean.

AMPLITUDE AND VIBRATION

Pressure wavefronts traveling in air like waves in the ocean provide the clearest example of what is meant by the amplitude of the wave. When a water wave reaches a barrier, it exerts a pressure against that obstruction proportional to its amplitude (like the force of waves against a jetty). The height (or depth) of a wave measured from the zero-reference of the average water level is the wave's amplitude. In air, an acoustic wave's amplitude is the maximum amount of compression (or rarefaction) of air molecules compared to the ambient atmospheric pressure. When this pressure wave reaches an object, it also exerts a force, although vastly weaker. Since the amplitude of a wave may be equated with the pressure created against an object in its path, such as an eardrum, the strength of a sound wave is referred to as its sound pressure level, or SPL. Sound pressure level is measured by the number of physical units of force, called dynes, that are exerted per square centimeter.

The amplitude of a wave determines how fast air molecules move back and forth in a very small space. A large wave will require that the particles move at a higher average velocity to complete a large back-and-forth displacement compared to a smaller one. However, the waves themselves move at the same speed for all sounds. This is called the speed of sound, and in air at room temperature it is approximately 335 meters per second (1,100 feet per second). Knowing this allows the determination of a sound wave's wavelength: the distance a wave travels in the time taken to complete one cycle (or the distance between any two corresponding points representing one full cycle of the wave).

The mass and elasticity of a vibrating object also determine how fast it vibrates. This rate of vibration determines the frequency of the sound wave, or how many times per second the air molecules move through one back-and-forth cycle. This value of cycles per second is expressed in units called Hertz (Hz). The range of sound wave frequencies audible to humans is roughly 20 to 20,000 Hertz.

When objects vibrate, their rate of movement back and forth is not linear. It is fastest at the vibration's midpoint and slows down to where the motion actually reverses and then accelerates again to maximum velocity at the midpoint. The movement is like that of a seat on a Ferris wheel, which rises and falls most quickly when it is at the "nine o'clock" and "three o'clock" positions, while its motion relative to the ground is greatest at "twelve o'clock" and "six o'clock." The mathematical function that describes these changes, and thus the changes in pressure or displacement over time that comprise the sound wave, is the sine function of an angle rotated through 360 degrees. The simplest sound wave (one that has only a single frequency) is a pure tone or sine wave. The instantaneous amplitude (the point in its 360-degree cycle) of such a wave is described by the phase angle of the wave. Thus, the peak of a wave is at 90 degrees and its trough occurs at 270 degrees. When sound waves reach the ear, they are funneled by the outer ear to the eardrum. The eardrum is elastic and is pushed by the sound wave's compression and pulled by its rarefaction. It then transfers, by a specialized lever and hydraulic system, the energy derived from the sound wave to a complex receptor mechanism located in the inner ear. This receptor system sends signals to the brain that tell it about the sound wave and that are heard as sound.

HEARING SOUNDS

In everyday life, however, pure sine waves are seldom heard, because vibrating objects rarely move only as a single piece. They normally have several integer subdivisions of themselves simultaneously vibrating at integer multiples, called harmonics, of their lowest frequency of vibration, called the fundamental. Each harmonic is produced at its own amplitude, determined by the physical

characteristics of the sound source. In addition to the vibrating material, which includes the elastic column of air in a wind instrument or organ pipe, the overall size and shape of the source also selectively serve to increase, reduce, or even eliminate specific harmonics by the effect of resonance. Thus normal sounds, even from a single source, are complex waves made up of several simultaneously occurring sine waves of different frequencies, amplitudes, and phase relationships. Sounds from several sources interact still further. Images of sound on an oscilloscope screen, or on the oscilloscope visualization of a computer sound player application, show that such pictures of sound waves are highly irregular, quite unlike the smooth and symmetrical undulations of a sine wave. Nonetheless, all vibrating objects emit sine waves; it is simply that they emit many of them at the same time.

The complexity of a sound wave, how many harmonics it contains and which ones, determines its timbre or quality. Typically, it is the fundamental (lowest) frequency that gives the sound its characteristic pitch. A low-frequency fundamental provides a low bass pitch; higher-frequency fundamentals produce higher midrange or, still higher, treble pitches. Thus, many different types of musical instruments, or many different singers, can produce the same note pitch, but sounds can be distinguished, one from another, by their characteristic timbre. For example, timbre can range from the very "smooth" sound of the flute, which has few harmonics and is close to a pure sine wave, through the "full" sound of a consonant piano chord, which has moderate, mostly even, harmonics, to the "rough" and "sharp" sound of a distorted, loud, metal-rock guitar, which has many, mainly odd, harmonics.

How the auditory system allows people to hear timbre is one of the astonishing properties of hearing. Although frequencies below a few hundred Hertz are relayed directly to the brain by a corresponding number of impulses in the auditory nerve, the processing of the full range of frequencies that form the more typical complex sound wave is much more complex. For example, it is easy to hear three individual notes struck separately on a keyboard. If one note is struck, then that note and another simultaneously, it is possible to keep track of the different sounds of the two notes even though they form a single harmony. Even when the three or four component notes of a chord are struck simultaneously, the complex sum of the underlying tones is not the only thing heard. Instead, the auditory system is able to extract each fundamental tone from the complex wave. This is based on the ability of the ear to analyze complex waves into their sine wave components, the possibility of which was formally established by the nineteenth century French mathematician and physicist Jean Fourier and applied to hearing by his German contemporary, the physicist Georg Ohm.

Indeed, this principle is applied to a common piece of modern sound reproduction electronics: the real-time spectrum analyzer. Many home and automotive sound systems, as well as computer sound player visualizations, have versions of this device. It displays the relative amplitude of several bands of frequencies, often at octave separation, as a constantly changing set of graphically presented columns, each column representing a range of frequencies and the height of each illuminated column indicating the amplitude of the frequencies displayed by that column. The ear performs the same function but on a vastly finer scale, using thousands of very finely tuned frequency detectors that are placed along the sound-sensitive membrane of the inner ear. Unlike the dedicated detectors displayed by stereos or computers, the ear can tell the difference between sounds that differ by only a few Hertz. Much of what humans hear, then, corresponds and is limited to the output of these individual detectors.

LOCALIZING A SOUND'S SOURCE

Not only is the ear a remarkable sound wave analyzer, but because the two ears are separated by a solid skull-width, a sound wave originating off to one side arrives at each ear at a very slightly different time (phase) and at a slightly different amplitude (weaker in the ear away from the sound source). The brain's computations are extremely sensitive to arrival time and phase differences that exist between the ears. The auditory system uses this information, along with small head movements, to let the listener perceive where the sounds seem to come from in the surrounding space, both in the natural environment and in multichannel sound reproduction environments, and to let attention be directed appropriately. The ability of the auditory system to use extremely small differences in the timing and amplitude of sound waves reaching the ear is the basis of the multichannel surround-sound reproduction used in movie theaters and home theater sound systems. By surrounding the listener with multiple sound sources, the system creates a realistic or even spectacular sense of ambience. The brain computes perceived locations completely surrounding the listener from the differing arrival times, phase re-

lationships, and amplitudes provided by the surround-sound sources, just as it does in nature.

The ability to analyze and locate sounds is more than equaled by the ear's incredible sensitivity and dynamic (amplitude) range. Sound waves whose pressure moves the eardrum only slightly more than the width of a hydrogen atom (the proverbial pin dropping) can be heard. The sound of a rock band, or loud sounds played through earphones, can be more than a million times greater. Because of the need to respond to such a large dynamic range the ear responds in a roughly logarithmic way, with the perceived loudness of a sound increasing linearly as the sound wave's amplitude leaps ahead exponentially (by ratios). Values along this large linear range are thus expressed by a logarithmic unit, the decibel (dB). The auditory system can also become fatigued or can actively reduce its sensitivity when exposed to extremely loud sounds (as when exposed to sound through headphones), making it easy to think that those sounds are less intense than they really are. Sustained exposure to high-amplitude sound waves can permanently damage the delicate receptor cells of the inner ear. This is another reminder that the sound wave is a physical pressure and can produce tissue damage just like any sufficient impact.

THE HISTORY OF UNDERSTANDING HEARING

The Greek philosopher Plato was one of the first thinkers to be struck by the fact that humans live in a subjective world of sensations, perceptions, and ideas, not the "real" world of objective physical phenomena. Psychology's preoccupation with "knowing one's self" is really an outgrowth of philosophy's attempt to understand this strikingly problematic gap between the subjective view from inside the self and the objective view from, as much as is ever possible, outside the self and in the world as it is.

It was not until the seventeenth century that scientists realized that sounds correspond to physical vibrations and not until late in the nineteenth century that the brilliant German physicist Hermann von Helmholtz developed a theory of how complex waves are analyzed into individual signals. Research into the relationship between physical states and their psychological counterparts was an important part of nineteenth century German science and became known as psychophysics. Psychophysics then became a major part of the research program of the first experimental psychology laboratory, established in 1879 by the father of modern psychology, Wilhelm Wundt. Along with the psychophysicists Ernst

Weber and Gustav Fechner, Wundt argued that lawful relationships between physical stimulation and subjective sensation showed that the scientific study of the mind was feasible.

People are often struck by the complexity of psychophysical research, but it is important to remember its roots. While the subjective beauty of great instrumental music and song can never be reduced to "nothing but vibrations," recognizing how such subjective sensory experience fits into the larger objective scheme of things provides a valuable self-awareness. This same rationale applies to all sensory modalities, but it even goes beyond the senses. Somewhat metaphorically, personality, values, interests, and psychological adjustment all can be understood as the way in which humans uniquely tune in, select, and respond to external stimuli. Understanding the way hearing is related to sound waves provides a valuable model for psychology's concern for making the subjective more objective.

BIBLIOGRAPHY

Coren, Stanley. *Sensation and Perception*. 6th ed. Hoboken, N.J.: John Wiley & Sons, 2004. This book is a particularly comprehensive and well-written survey of sensory processes. The section on audition contains many felicitous examples that make a complex topic accessible. Other chapters place the study of sound waves and hearing into a valuable general perspective.

Deutsch, Diana. *Ear and Brain: How We Make Sense of Sounds*. New York: Springer, 2003. This volume shows the nonspecialist how ear and brain interact to process sounds into forms that humans can hear and understand. A CD of sounds and samples that will help the reader understand the complex relationship between ear and brain is included.

Emanuel, Diana C., and Tomasz Letowski. *Hearing Science*. Philadelphia: Wolters Kluwer Health/ Lippincott Williams and Wilkins, 2009. This text covers all aspects of hearing science, with comprehensive coverage of acoustics, psychoacoustics, and anatomy. Suitable for those interested in speech pathology and audiology.

Gulick, W. Lawrence. *Hearing: Physiology and Psychophysics*. New York: Oxford University Press, 1971. A classic that is beautifully written, presenting difficult topics comprehensively but accessibly. All topics basic to the sense of hearing are included.

Levitin, Daniel J. *This Is Your Brain on Music: The Science of a Human Obsession*. New York: Plume, 2007. The author, a rock-musician-turned-neuroscientist, explains the science behind why people remain attached to the music they heard as teenagers, how those repetitive music snippets get stuck in the brain, and what composers know about appealing to listeners.

Van Bergeijk, W. A., J. R. Pierce, and E. E. David, Jr. *Waves and the Ear*. New York: Doubleday, 1960. Specifically written for the general reader and high school student, this is a good introduction to wave theory and hearing. Key research is simply and clearly presented with excellent figures and examples. Physiology and applications are also covered.

John Santelli

SEE ALSO: Brain structure; Hallucinations; Sensation and perception; Smell and taste; Touch and pressure; Visual system.

Help-seeking

TYPE OF PSYCHOLOGY: Social psychology

Few people who experience significant psychological distress seek professional help. Research has identified a number of factors that contribute to help-seeking behavior. These include demographic factors, patients' attitudes toward a service system that often neglects the special needs of racial and ethnic minorities, financial factors, and organizational factors. People most likely to be in need of help are least willing to seek it, and if they do seek help, they are least likely to benefit from it.

KEY CONCEPTS
- Acculturation
- Cultural heritage
- Demographics
- Mental illness
- Stigma
- Stigmatization

INTRODUCTION

According to a 2012 survey conducted by several national health and mental health organizations, including the Centers for Disease Control and Prevention (CDC) as well as the Substance Abuse and Mental Health Services Administration (Attitudes Toward Mental Illness: Results from the Behavioral Risk Factor Surveillance

System), over 26 percent of US adults in any given year have a diagnosable or self-reported mental disorder, while only 20 percent of those individuals receive treatment from mental health services. In other words, there are many with a diagnosable mental disorder who do not receive treatment for the disorder.

Help-seeking provides a critical step between the onset of mental health problems and the provision of help. Help-seeking is viewed as the contact between individuals and health care providers prompted by the effected person's efforts and his or her family and loved ones. Help-seeking has been defined as behavior that is designed to elicit assistance from others in response to a physical or emotional problem. There are three dimensions to help-seeking behavior, which include whether a person decides to seek help, at what time the person seeks help (delayed or prematurely), and the appropriateness of the help-seeking behavior. Societal attitudes and belief systems that are prevalent in any given group have a major impact on help-seeking behavior. Understanding patterns of when and why people seek help is fundamental to devising effective responses.

Evolving attitudes concerning mental illness have been monitored by nationally representative surveys since the 1950s to study how people cope with and seek treatment for mental illness if they become symptomatic. The 2012 CDC national survey, Attitudes Toward Mental Illness, tracked levels of public perception regarding the effectiveness of mental health treatment as well as public attitudes toward mental illness (stigma). The survey concluded that while over 80 percent of responding individuals belived that treatment of mental illness was effective, just over 50 percent of respondents felt that society was sympathetic toward the mentally ill. Stigmatization of mental illness is often a reason for inaction or refusal to engage in help-seeking behavior. According to the CDC, in 2011 just 20 percent of individuals over the age of eighteen with a diagnosed mental disorder or self-reported mental health condition saw a mental health provider. Not surprisingly, individuals from US states that had a high per capita expenditure for mental health services were not only more likely to seek and receive mental health treatment, but also reported a belief that mental health treatment was effective. Stigma interferes with the willingness of many people, even those who have a serious mental illness, to seek help.

BARRIERS TO SEEKING HELP

Most people with mental disorders do not seek treatment. The barriers to treatment include demographic factors, people's attitudes toward a service system that often neglects the special needs of racial and ethnic minorities, financial factors, and organizational factors.

Demographic factors also affect help-seeking behavior. African Americans, Latinos, and poor women are less inclined than non-Latino white females to seek treatment. L. K. Sussman, L. N. Robins, and F. Earls, in a 1987 study of differences in help-seeking behavior between African American and white Americans, found that common patient attitudes deter people from seeking treatment. These attitudes include not having enough time, fear of being hospitalized, thinking that they can handle it alone, thinking that no one can help, cost of treatment, and stigma. Cost is a major factor that predisposes people against seeking treatment, even people with health insurance because of the inferior coverage of mental health as compared with health care in general. Finally, organizational barriers to help-seeking include the fragmentation of services and unavailability of services. Racial and ethnic minority groups often perceive that services offered by the existing system will not meet their needs because helpers will not taking into account their cultural and linguistic practices.

Seeking treatment is a complex process that begins with the individual or individual's support system recognizing that thinking, mood, or behaviors are unusual and severe enough to require treatment; interpreting these symptoms as a medical or mental health problem; deciding whether or not to seek help and from whom; receiving care; and evaluating whether continuation of treatment is warranted.

A number of barriers deter racial and ethnic minority groups from seeking treatment. Many members of minority groups fear or feel ill at ease with the mental health system. Minority groups also may experience the system as a product of white, European culture. Clinicians often represent a white, middle-class orientation with biases, misconceptions, and stereotypes of other cultures.

Cultural heritages may also impart patterns of beliefs and practices that impact the willingness to seek help. Mental health issues may be viewed as spiritual concerns, and a number of ethnic groups, when faced with personal problems, therefore seek guidance from religious figures.

Asian Americans are less likely than whites, African Americans, and Latinos to seek help. Amy Okamura, a professor at the School of Social Work at San Diego State University, concludes that for many Asians and Pacific Islanders, it is more culturally appropriate to go to a doctor with physical symptoms that are a manifestation of mental and emotional problems. Furthermore, Asians and Pacific Islanders may first try to change their diet or use herbal medicine, acupuncture, or the services of a healer.

Julia Mayo, chief of the Clinical Studies Department of Psychiatry at St. Vincent's Hospital and Medical Center in New York, has found that often African Americans wait until they are in crisis and then go to emergency rooms for treatment rather than approach a white therapist. The practice of using the emergency room for routine care is generally attributed to lack of insurance. Cost and lack of insurance have been found to be barriers to treatment in the past.

In addition, level of acculturation, as measured by language preference, has been identified as an obstacle to seeking help; that is, people who do not speak English are less able to access formal help sources. For example, Asian international students were found to indicate a significant relationship between levels of acculturation and attitudes toward seeking professional psychological help. The most acculturated students were most likely to have positive attitudes toward seeking professional help. Several hypotheses, most of which assume a conflict between the psychotherapy process and the values of traditional East Asian culture, are offered to explain this pattern of underutilization of mental health services. For example, attitudes and beliefs about mental illness among Asians have been identified as influencing Asians' underutilization of psychotherapy. Examples of these attitudes and beliefs include the belief that seeking outside help for psychological problems will bring shame on one's family, that psychological problems are the result of bad thoughts and a lack of willpower, and that one must resolve problems of this type on one's own.

HELP-SEEKING PATTERNS AND MODELS

A number of factors seem to contribute to a person's willingness to seek help, including age, gender, availability of social support, expectations about help-seeking outcome, self-concealment tendencies, fear of psychological treatment, and type of psychological problem. Adults ask for help less often for intimate problems, for problems that are perceived as stigmatizing, and for problems that reflect personal inadequacy. Help is sought more often for problems that are regarded as serious and when

the cause of the problem is attributed to external causes. Help-seeking increases with age, and women have been found to seek help more often than men. Understanding patterns of help-seeking aids professionals in devising effective interventions for people in need.

Generally, people seek help based on the problem factors, such as the perceived normality of the problem, the perceived preventability of the problem, and the perceived cause of the problem. The level of pain or disability associated with the problem, the seriousness of the problem, and past positive history with help-seeking all contribute to one's decision to seek help.

Help-seeking behavior can be characterized by the following principles: The need for help arises from the help-seeker's situation; the decision to seek help or not to seek help is affected by many factors; people tend to seek help that is most accessible; people tend first to seek help or information from interpersonal sources, especially from people like themselves; help-seekers expect emotional support; and people follow habitual patterns in seeking help. Furthermore, people will go to anonymous sources of help if the personal cost of revealing a need is too much to go to an interpersonal source.

BIBLIOGRAPHY

Bergin, A. E., and S. L. Garfield. *Handbook of Psychotherapy and Behavior Change*. 4th ed. New York: John Wiley & Sons, 1994. Print.

Centers for Disease Control and Prevention, Substance Abuse and Mental Health Services Administration, National Association of County Behavioral Health and Developmental Disability Directors, National Institute of Mental Health, Carter Center *Mental Health Program. Attitudes Toward Mental Illness: Results from the Behavioral Risk Factor Surveillance System*. Atlanta: Centers for Disease Control and Prevention, 2012. Print.

Harris, Roma M., and Patricia Dewdney. *Barriers to Information: How Formal Help Systems Fail Battered Women*. Westport, Conn.: Greenwood Press, 1994. Print.

Karabenick, Stuart A. *Help Seeking in Academic Settings: Goals, Groups, and Contexts*. Mahwah, N.J.: Lawrence Erlbaum, 2006. Print.

Klaver, M. Nora. *Mayday! Asking for Help in Times of Need*. San Francisco: Berrett-Koehler, 2007. Print.

Leung, Kwok, Uichol Kim, Susumu Yamaguchi, and Yoshihisa Kashima. *Progress in Asian Social Psychology*. Vol. 1. New York: John Wiley & Sons, 1997. Print.

Lynch, John. *Overcoming Masculine Depression: The Pain Behind the Mask*. New York: Routledge, 2013. Print.

Stangor, Charles, and Chris Crandall. *Stereotyping and Prejudice*. New York: Psychology Press, 2013. Print.

Torrey, E. Fuller. *Out of the Shadows: Confronting America's Mental Illness Crisis*. New York: John Wiley & Sons, 1997. Print.

US Department of Health and Human Services. *Mental Health: A Report of the Surgeon General-Executive Summary*. Rockville, Md.: Author, 1999. Print.

US Department of Health and Human Services. *Mental Health: Culture, Race, and Ethnicity—A Supplement to Mental Health: A Report of the Surgeon General*. Rockville, Md.: Author, 2001.Print.

Zeidner, Moshe, and Norman S. Endler, eds. *Handbook of Coping: Theory, Research, Applications*. New York: John Wiley & Sons, 1996. Print.

Shelley A. Jackson

SEE ALSO: Addictive personality and behaviors; African Americans and mental health; Asian Americans/Pacific Islanders and mental health; Clinical interviewing, testing and observation; Confidentiality; Culture and diagnosis; Helping; Law and psychology; Mental health practitioners; Self-help groups; Social networks; Social support and mental health; Substance use disorders; Support groups.

Helping

TYPE OF PSYCHOLOGY: Developmental psychology; Motivation; Personality; Social psychology

Theories of helping behavior have attempted to explain why people offer physical and psychological assistance to others in both emergency and nonemergency situations. These theories have considered the roles of physiological arousal, judgments of costs and rewards, mood states, and attributions of responsibility in influencing helping behavior.

KEY CONCEPTS

- Arousal cost-reward model
- Attributions about responsibility
- Mood and helping
- Norm of reciprocity
- Prosocial behavior
- Self-help groups
- Spirituality

INTRODUCTION

Helping involves assisting in some way another person or animal in need. Helping behaviors can take a variety of forms. Some, such as carrying a book for a friend, require little effort. Others, such as jumping into a frozen lake to rescue a drowning stranger, are life-threatening. To explain helping behavior, researchers have studied many variables and have developed theories to organize them and account for their interrelationships.

AROUSAL COST-REWARD MODEL

In 1981, Jane Allyn Piliavin, John Dovidio, Samuel Gaertner, and Russell Clark introduced the arousal cost-reward model. This model assumes that witnessing the need or distress of another person is physiologically arousing. When one attributes the source of one's arousal to another person's distress, the arousal is sometimes experienced as emotionally unpleasant, and one becomes motivated to reduce it.

According to the arousal cost-reward model, a person will choose to engage in the arousal-decreasing response associated with the fewest net costs. Net costs are based on two types of rewards and costs associated with the helping situation: costs for not helping and rewards and costs for helping. Costs for not helping occur when no assistance is given and may include experiences such as feeling troubled because someone in need is continuing to suffer or receiving criticism from others for being callous. Costs for helping are direct negative outcomes that the potential helper might experience after offering help, such as loss of time, embarrassment, or injury. Helping, however, can also be associated with positive outcomes such as praise, gratitude, and feelings of self-worth.

Piliavin and her colleagues suggest that both types of costs influence the decision to help. When net costs are low, as the costs for not helping increase, helping in the form of direct intervention becomes more likely. If net costs for helping are high, however, direct intervention is unlikely regardless of potential costs for not helping. In this latter situation, a person may give indirect assistance (for example, call someone else to help). Alternatively, the person may deny responsibility for helping, reinterpret the situation as one in which help is not needed, or try to leave the scene altogether.

ATTRIBUTIONS OF RESPONSIBILITY

Philip Brickman and his colleagues argue that when one sees a person in need, one makes attributions about how responsible that person is for the problem he or she faces and also about how much responsibility that person should take for its solution. These attributions in turn influence one's judgment about who one thinks is best suited to deliver help, and, if one decides to offer help oneself, they influence its form. One may be most likely to offer direct assistance if one attributes little responsibility to that person for solving the problem—as when a child is lost in a shopping mall. In contrast, if one judges a person as responsible for solving his or her problem, as when a friend has a nasty boss, one may offer encouragement and moral support but not directly intervene. Thus, who one thinks should provide the remedy—oneself, experts, or the person who needs the help—depends on attributions that one makes about responsibility.

MOOD

One's mood may also influence one's decision to help someone who is in need. In general, people experiencing a positive mood, such as happiness, are more likely to offer help than are those in neutral moods. Using quantitative procedures for summarizing the results of thirty-four experimental studies, Michael Carlson, Ventura Charlin, and Norman Miller concluded that the best general explanation for why positive moods increase helpfulness is that they heighten sensitivity to positive reinforcement or good outcomes. This sensitivity includes both thinking more about good outcomes for oneself and increased thought about the goodness of behaving prosocially. This general summary incorporates many explanations that have been proposed for the relation between positive moods and helping, among them the mood maintenance and social outlook explanations.

Mood maintenance argues that one behaves more helpfully when happy because doing so prolongs one's good mood. The social outlook explanation points instead to the fact that positive moods are often the consequences of another person's behavior (for example, being given a compliment). Such actions by others trigger thoughts about human kindness, cooperativeness, and goodness. These thoughts, if still present when someone asks for help, make a person more likely to respond positively.

The effects of bad moods on helpfulness are more complex. Carlson and Miller also quantitatively summarized the effects found in forty-four studies concerned with the impact of various mood-lowering events on helpfulness. These studies included such diverse procedures for inducing negative moods as having subjects repeat depressing phrases, view unpleasant slides, imagine

sad experiences, and fail at a task. Two factors can apparently account for most of the findings on negative moods and helping. The first is whether the target of the mood-lowering event is the self or someone else; the second is whether the self or an outside force is responsible for the mood-lowering event. When one is responsible for imposing a mood-lowering event on another person and therefore feels guilty, helping is very likely. When one is responsible for an event that lowers one's own mood (as when one engages in self-harm) or when one witnesses another person impose a mood-lowering event on someone else (that is, when one experiences empathy), a positive response to a subsequent request for help is more likely, but not as much as in the first case. In contrast, when someone else is responsible for one's own negative mood—when one has been victimized—one's helpfulness tends to be inhibited.

THEORETICAL EXPLANATIONS

These explanations can be applied to a wide range of helping situations: reactions to both physical and psychological distress, situations in which helping appears to be determined by a rational consideration of costs and rewards, and situations in which the help offered seemingly is irrational and very costly.

One study on which the arousal cost-reward model was based suggests how consideration of costs and rewards might affect the decision to offer direct physical assistance. In this study, a man feigned collapse on the floor of a New York subway a few minutes after boarding the train and remained there until help was given. In some cases, the man smelled of alcohol and carried an alcohol bottle wrapped in a paper bag, giving the impression that drunkenness had caused his fall. In other instances, the man carried a cane, suggesting that he had fallen because of a physical impairment. Although many people offered assistance in both conditions, more people helped the man with the cane than the man who appeared to be drunk.

The different amounts of assistance in the two conditions may result from differences in perceived net costs. Potential helpers may have expected greater costs when the man looked drunk than when he appeared to be disabled. Helping a drunk may require more effort, invite more risk, and be more unpleasant than helping someone with a physical impairment. It may also be less intrinsically and extrinsically rewarding than helping someone with a physical impairment. Finally, costs for not helping may be lower in the case of the drunk than for the man with the cane. The drunk may be perceived as "only drunk" and therefore not really needy. Thus, the finding that more people helped the man with the cane is consistent with the hypothesis that helping increases as the net costs associated with the helping response decrease.

Although considerations of costs and rewards are important, it would be unrealistic to think that helping only occurs when net costs are low. People may engage in very costly helping behaviors when physiological arousal is especially high, such as in clear, unambiguous emergencies. The actions of an unknown passenger aboard an airplane that crashed into a frozen river illustrate this point. As rescuers in a helicopter attempted to pull people out of the water to safety, this passenger repeatedly handed the lowered life ring to other, more seriously injured passengers, even though these acts of heroism eventually cost him his life.

Much research on helpfulness has asked, When do people help? It is also important, however, to look at what type of help is given and how the person in need is expected to react to offers of assistance. The Brickman model, involving attributions of responsibility for the problem and its solution, does this. It also looks at more everyday forms of helping. According to Brickman, if one attributes responsibility for both the problem and its solution to the person in need, one is applying the moral model of helping. With this orientation, one may have the tendency to view the person in need as lazy and undeserving of help. In the subway example, people may not have helped the fallen drunk because they made such attributions. Although people who apply the moral model may not give direct assistance, they may sometimes support and encourage the person's own effort to overcome the problem.

If one sees people as responsible for their problem but not for its solution, then one is applying the enlightenment model. Criminals are held responsible for violating the law but are jailed because they are judged incapable of reforming themselves, and jail is believed to be rehabilitating as well as punishing. Discipline from those in authority is seen as the appropriate helping response, and submission to it is expected from the person receiving the "assistance."

The medical model applies when the person is seen as responsible for neither the problem nor its solution. This orientation is often taken toward the ill. Such situations call for an expert whose recommendations are to be accepted and fulfilled.

In the final combination of attributions of responsibility for a problem and its solution, the compensatory model, the person is not held responsible for having caused the problem. The problem may be judged to be caused by factors beyond the person's control, such as when an earthquake occurs. In this model, however, the person is held responsible for solving the problem. Helpers may provide useful resources but are not expected to take the initiative for a solution. In the case of an earthquake, the government may offer low-interest loans for rebuilding, but victims must decide whether to apply for one and rebuild their homes.

HISTORICAL BACKGROUND

Concern with helping behavior has its roots in early philosophy. Thinkers such as Aristotle, Socrates, Niccolò Machiavelli, and Thomas Hobbes debated whether humans are by nature good or bad, selfish or selfless. Most empirical psychological research on the topic, however, was only initiated after the 1950s. This was probably not coincidental. Many people were concerned with the atrocities of World War II and in the United States were concerned with rising crime rates. In response, psychologists not only began to investigate human cruelty but also gave increased attention to what could be done to offset it. Similarly, the emergence of the Civil Rights movement, with its emphasis on cooperation and harmony, probably further propelled the study of prosocial behavior. The term "prosocial behavior," or behavior intended to benefit other people, is sometimes used synonymously with "helping" and is sometimes meant to be a larger category that includes helping.

Early studies of helping behavior examined situational variables that influence the decision to help someone who is in physical distress. The arousal cost-reward model and the subway experiment characterize this type of work. Also important during this period were Alvin Gouldner's theorizing on the norm of reciprocity and subsequent empirical investigation of the norms governing helping behavior, such as Leonard Berkowitz's work in the 1960s. As social psychologists explored situational variables that influence helping, developmental psychologists examined the emergence of positive social behavior in children. Some, such as Jean Piaget and Lawrence Kohlberg, postulated distinct stages of moral development. Others focused on how people who model helping behavior influence children's subsequent behavior.

EXTENSIONS OF THE EARLIER RESEARCH

While research continues in all these areas, other questions also attract interest. Studies of people's responses to others' physical distress have been extended by research on how people respond to someone in psychological distress. Similarly, researchers have extended their interests in the potential helper to examine how the person in need of help is affected by seeking and receiving it.

Also important in understanding helping behavior has been the study of personality and how individuals differ in their tendency to help. Some of this work is related to research on norms, in that it looks at whether people develop a personal set of rules or standards that govern their helping behavior. Another approach, adopted by Margaret Clark and Judson Mills, has looked at how the relationship between the help requester and the help giver influences helpfulness. Research on helping now incorporates many different influences on the helping process, from individual to social to developmental factors. In the process, the applicability of the research findings has grown and has given rise to a broader understanding of the types of helping behavior that may occur, when they may occur, who might engage in them, and why.

BIBLIOGRAPHY

Batson, Charles Daniel. *The Altruism Question: Toward a Social-Psychological Answer.* Hillsdale, N.J.: Lawrence Erlbaum, 1991. Print.

Blumenthal, David R. *The Banality of Good and Evil: Moral Lessons from the Shoah and Jewish Tradition.* Washington, D.C.: Georgetown University Press, 1999. Print.

Brown, Stephanie L., Michael L. Brown, and Louis A. Penner. *Moving Beyond Self-Interest: Perspectives from Evolutionary Biology, Neuroscience, and the Social Sciences.* New York:Oxford UP, 2012. Print.

Brownell, Celia A., et al. "Socialization of Early Prosocial Behavior: Parents' Talk about Emotions Is Associated with Sharing and Helping in Toddlers." *Infancy* 18.1 (2013): 91–119. Print.

Clark, Margaret S., ed. *Prosocial Behavior.* Newbury Park, Calif.: Sage, 1991. Print.

Derlega, Valerian J., and Janusz Grzelak, eds. *Cooperation and Helping Behavior: Theories and Research.* New York: Academic Press, 1982. Print.

Dovidio, John F., Jane Allyn Piliavin, David A. Schroeder, and Louis A. Penner. *The Social Psychology of Prosocial Behavior.* Mahwah, N.J.: Lawrence Erlbaum, 2007. Print.

Fetchenhauer, Detlef, Andreas Flache, Abraham P. Buunk, and Siegwart Lindenberg, eds. *Solidarity and Prosocial Behavior: An Integration of Sociological and Psychological Perspectives.* New York: Springer, 2006. Print.

McMahon, Susan D., et al. "Aggressive and Prosocial Behavior: Community Violence, Cognitive, and Behavioral Predictors among Urban African American Youth." *American Journal of Community Psychology* (2012): 1–15. Web. 21 July 2013.

Oliner, Pearl M., and Samuel P. Oliner. *Toward a Caring Society: Ideas into Action.* Westport, Conn.: Praeger, 1995. Print.

Rushton, J. Philippe, and Richard M. Sorrentino, eds. *Altruism and Helping Behavior: Social, Personality, and Developmental Perspectives.* Hillsdale, N.J.: Lawrence Erlbaum, 1981. Print.

Schroeder, David A., Louis A. Penner, John F. Dovidio, and Jane A. Piliavin. *The Psychology of Helping and Altruism: Problems and Puzzles.* New York: McGraw-Hill, 1995. Print.

Staub, Ervin, Daniel Bar-Tal, Jerzy Karylowski, and Janusz Reykowski, eds. *Development and Maintenance of Prosocial Behavior: International Perspectives on Positive Morality.* New York: Plenum, 1984. Print.

Tiffany A. Ito and Norman Miller;
updated by Tanja Bekhuis

See Also: Aggression; Aggression: Reduction and control; Altruism, cooperation, and empathy; Bystander intervention; Crowd behavior; Moral development; Social perception; Social support and mental health.

Hierarchy of needs

Date: 1940s forward
Type of psychology: Motivation

Hierarchy of needs is the core organizing principle of Abraham Maslow's theory of human motivation. He first formulated this theory in the 1940's and elaborated on it in the 1950's and 1960's. His theory continues to be widely researched and has many applications.

KEY CONCEPT

- Basic needs
- Deficiency motivation
- Growth motivation
- Humanistic psychology
- Self-actualization

INTRODUCTION

The concept of a hierarchy of needs became the central organizing principle in Abraham Maslow's theory of human motivation. A research psychologist who began his career in the 1940's with a series of studies on motivation, culminating with his book *Motivation and Personality* (1954), Maslow greatly furthered the understanding of human motives. When Maslow began his research, psychology largely regarded hunger as the paradigm for all other motives and examined motivation through animal studies, behaviorist theory, or both. Maslow rejected these early theories as insufficient to account for the human dimensions of motivation. He supplemented experimental study with clinical evidence and redirected the focus from drives to goals and from isolated determinants to a sense of the person as an integrated and dynamic whole.

The most important aspect of Maslow's theory of motivation was the notion of a hierarchy of needs. Maslow first articulated this theory in his early works, including "A Theory of Human Motivation," which appeared in *Psychological Review* in 1943, and he would continue to develop his theory over time. He first identified and differentiated among various clusters of motives. The five clusters he identified were as follows:

- physiological needs
- safety needs
- belongingness or love needs
- esteem needs
- need for self-actualization

He noted that, in the order listed, the clusters formed a hierarchy from lower to higher motives. He pointed out that there is no final satiation point at which the person is no longer motivated, but rather that as a particular motivation is sufficiently gratified, another, higher motive will emerge more prominently. In Maslow's terms, the higher motives are therefore "prepotent" with regard to the lower ones. Furthermore, there is a basic directionality in the order in which each motivational cluster becomes prominent.

LATER DEVELOPMENTS

In 1955, following the success of his early studies, Maslow was invited to present his work at the prestigious Nebraska Symposium on Motivation. There he advanced his thesis by making a key distinction between deficiency motivation and growth motivation. The first four clusters of motives tend to be motivating precisely when they are lacking, when there is a deficit or empty hole that must be filled. In contrast, people who are very healthy psychologically have sufficiently gratified their basic needs. This does not mean they have obtained more in an objective sense, but rather that their experience is not structured by a sense of lack. With this experienced sense of sufficiency, healthy people are free to develop their motive toward self-actualization, which Maslow defined as an "ongoing tendency toward actualizing potentials, capacities and talents . . . of the person's own intrinsic nature." Thus self-actualization can be seen as a trend toward fulfillment and integration. He described thirteen specific observable characteristics of such self-actualizing people, including being more perceptive, more accepting of the self and others, more spontaneous, more autonomous, more appreciative, and more creative, and having a richer emotional life and more frequent peak experiences.

APPLICATIONS

As Maslow continued working, he began more and more to examine the lives of "self-actualizers," those people whom he identified as exemplary of being directed by self-actualizing motivation. He saw that a person's psychological life is lived differently when that individual is oriented not to the gratification of deficiency needs but to growth. This emphasis on growth soon became the focus of an emerging paradigm, known as humanistic psychology, studied by many other psychologists, including Carl R. Rogers. This emphasis on personal growth reoriented the study of psychology, focusing it not on issues of disease and negativity but rather on themes of personal enrichment and fulfillment, and of living an intrinsically meaningful life. Maslow's book *Toward a Psychology of Being* (1962) is one of the hallmarks of this movement, which swept beyond academic psychology into pop psychology.

Maslow's theory of motivation also influenced other disciplines, such as education and business. Mark Zimmeran's emotional literacy education project, for example, explicitly draws from Maslow's motivational theory. Research continues into the role of Maslow's hierarchy of needs in the fields of business, management, leadership, entrepreneurship, organizational development, and marketing. Issues such as optimally motivating workplace environments and incentives for employees continue to be particularly engaging topics for these studies. Though many of the specific applications often oversimplify Maslow's theory, the hierarchy of needs is still widely used, especially as the basis for management theories based on a vision of employees as most productive when synergistically and cooperatively engaged through opportunities for self-directed creativity rather than when subjected to authoritarian structures. Maslow himself considered this application important and contributed to it with his book Eupsychian Management: A Journal (1965). Maslow's position was that the more psychologically healthy people became, the more important such enlightened management would be for any competitive business.

BIBLIOGRAPHY

DeCarvalho, Roy Jose. *The Growth Hypothesis in Psychology: The Humanistic Psychology of Abraham Maslow and Carl Rogers.* San Francisco: Mellen Research UP, 1991. Print.

King, Daniel, and Scott Lawley. *Organizational Behavior.* Oxford: Oxford UP, 2013. Print.

Lowry, Richard. **A. H. Maslow: An Intellectual Portrait.** Monterey: Brooks/Cole, 1973. Print.

Moss, Donald, ed. *Humanistic and Transpersonal Psychology.* Westport: Greenwood, 1999. Print.

Stephens, Deborah C., ed. *The Maslow Business Reader.* New York: Wiley, 2000. Print.

Christopher M. Aanstoos

SEE ALSO: Adler, Alfred; Humanistic psychology; Incentive motivation; Maslow, Abraham; Motivation; Motivation: Intrinsic and extrinsic; Rogers, Carl R.; Self-actualization.

Histrionic personality disorder (HPD)

TYPE OF PSYCHOLOGY: Psychopathology

Histrionic personality disorder is characterized by excessive emotionality and attention seeking. Although researchers have found that it overlaps extensively with many other disorders, its causes and treatment remain controversial.

KEY CONCEPTS

- Antisocial personality disorder
- Borderline personality disorder
- Conversion symptoms
- Hysteria
- Personality disorders
- Somatization disorder

INTRODUCTION

Of all psychiatric conditions, personality disorders are perhaps the most controversial. Nevertheless, virtually all researchers agree that they are disorders in which maladaptive and inflexible personality traits cause impairment. Although some personality disorders are distinguished by the suffering they produce in affected individuals, others are distinguished by the suffering they inflict on others. Histrionic personality disorder (HPD) falls into the latter category.

HISTORY

HPD traces its roots to hysteria, from Greek hysterikos ("wandering womb"), a concept with origins in ancient Egypt and Greece. Hysteria was thought to be a state of excessive emotionality and irrational behavior in women caused by a migration of the uterus to the brain. Derogatory views of hysterical women continued throughout the Middle Ages, but in the centuries that followed, writers proposed that hysteria was not limited to women and was a condition of the brain rather than the uterus. In the late 1800's, French neurologist Jean Charcot used hypnosis to relieve conversion symptoms (deficits in sensory or motor function brought about by psychological factors) in hysterics. In doing so, Charcot approached hysteria as psychological rather than physiological in etiology. One doctor intrigued by the seeming efficacy of the new technique was the young Austrian neurologist Sigmund Freud. This early work with hysterical patients laid the groundwork for his theories of the unconscious.

Following World War II, a classification manual was developed by the American Psychiatric Association in an attempt to unify the array of diagnostic systems that were being used. This manual, the *Diagnostic and Statistical Manual of Mental Disorders* (DSM), has seen many versions and has remained standard in the mental health field. Hysterical personality was not included in the first DSM (1952, DSM-I) but is similar to the DSM-I description of "emotionally unstable personality."

DESCRIPTION

In 1958, two American psychiatrists, Paul Chodoff and Henry Lyons, delineated the primary characteristics of hysterical personality. Among these core features were vanity, theatrical behavior, and coy flirtatiousness. DSM-II (1968) introduced the primary diagnosis of hysterical personality, with "histrionic personality" in parenthesis. The DSM-III (1980) marked an official shift in the nomenclature to "histrionic personality," and "hysterical personality" was dropped completely.

The DSM-V (2013) describes the contemporary stance on the features of HPD, which have not changed significantly from the previous edition of the DSM. The essential feature is "pervasive and excessive emotionality and attention-seeking behavior." Their vivacious and energetic manner initially may charm new acquaintances. However, such characteristics often grow tiresome as it becomes apparent that these individuals' energy is directed primarily at gaining attention at any cost. They frequently use flamboyant displays of emotion, self-dramatization, and sexual suggestiveness to get attention. Their speech is often vague and tends toward global impressions without supporting details (for instance, they may declare enthusiastically that the film they just saw was wonderful but be unable to say why). Distorted interpersonal functioning is also characteristic of persons with HPD; they may accord relationships an unrealistic level of intimacy (such as introducing a casual acquaintance as "my dear friend") and are also easily influenced by others.

Many associated features of HPD (those that are not formally included in the diagnostic criteria) reflect the poor relationships experienced by these individuals; true emotional intimacy, whether with romantic partners or platonic friends, is often absent. They tend not to trust their partners and often manipulate them. Friends may become alienated by these individuals' constant demands for attention and sexually provocative behavior.

PREVALENCE AND DEMOGRAPHIC CORRELATES

Data from the general population indicate a prevalence rate of HPD of 2 to 3 percent. Higher rates, from 10 to 15 percent, are reported in clinical settings, with much of this variation probably attributable to differences in diagnostic measures used across studies. Although HPD has traditionally been viewed as a disorder of women, researchers in clinical settings have typically reported only a slight female predominance or, in some cases, approximately equal rates in men and women.

Although research examining cultural differences in HPD is scant, some researchers hypothesize that different social norms may produce disparate rates of this condition across cultures. For example, the impropriety of overt sexuality in Asian society could result in lower rates of HPD, whereas the spontaneous emotionality valued in Hispanic and Latin American society could lead to higher rates. Nevertheless, there are few systematic data addressing this possibility.

RELATIONS TO OTHER DISORDERS

Other personality disorders can be difficult to distinguish from HPD. Borderline personality disorder is classified by the same attention-seeking and manipulative behavior as HPD but differentiated from HPD by self-destructiveness, angry interpersonal relations, and persistent feelings of emptiness. Antisocial personality disorder and HPD both include reckless, seductive, and manipulative tendencies, but the former condition is distinguished by antisocial and often criminal acts. Persons with narcissistic personality disorder similarly strive for attention but usually as a means of validating their superiority rather than satisfying interpersonal and sexual needs. Dependent personality disorder is characterized by the same reliance on others for approval and guidance but tends to lack the theatrical behaviors of HPD.

Further complicating the diagnosis of HPD are its high rates of co-occurrence with other conditions. Among the conditions that overlap the most frequently with HPD are somatization disorder (characterized by multiple bodily complaints for which there is no discernible medical cause), dissociative disorders (characterized by disruptions in identity, memory, or consciousness), and dysthymic disorder (a chronic form of relatively mild depression).

CAUSES AND TREATMENT

Finally, little is known about either the causes or treatment of HPD. Although some authors, such as American psychiatrist C. Robert Cloninger, have argued that this condition is an alternative manifestation of antisocial personality disorder that is more common in women than in men, the evidence for this hypothesis is equivocal. Some psychodynamic theorists have conjectured that HPD stems from cold and unloving interactions with parents. Nevertheless, there is little research support for this hypothesis. Cognitive explanations of HPD typically focus on the underlying assumptions (such as, "Without other people, I am helpless") characteristic of this condition. It is not clear, however, whether these explanations provide much more than descriptions of the thinking patterns of individuals with HPD.

A variety of treatments for HPD have been developed. These treatments include behavioral techniques, which focus on extinguishing inappropriate (such as dependent, attention-seeking) behaviors and rewarding appropriate (that is, independent) behaviors, and cognitive techniques, which focus on altering irrational assumptions (such as the belief that one is worthless unless constantly showered with attention). Nevertheless, because no controlled studies have examined the efficacy of these or other techniques, it is not known whether HPD is treatable.

BIBLIOGRAPHY

Bornstein, Robert F. "Dependent and Histrionic Personality Disorders." *Oxford Textbook of Psychopathology,* ed. Theodore Millon, Paul H. Blaney, and Roger D. Davis. New York: Oxford UP, 1999. Print.

Chodoff, Paul, and Henry Lyons. "Hysteria, the Hysterical Personality, and 'Hysterical' Conversion." *American Journal of Psychiatry* 114 (1958): 734-740. Print.

O'Donohue, William T., Katherine Alexa Fowler, and Scott O. Lilienfeld, eds. *Personality Disorders: Toward the DSM-V.* Los Angeles: Sage, 2007. Print.

Pfohl, Bruce. "Histrionic Personality Disorder." *The DSM-IV Personality Disorders.* Ed. W. John Livesley. New York: Guilford, 1995. Print.

Sarkar, Jaydip, and Gwen Adshead. *Clinical Topics in Personality Disorder.* London: Royal College of Psychiatrists, 2012. Print.

Shapiro, David. "Hysterical Style." *Neurotic Styles.* New York: Basic, 2000. Print.

Veith, Ilza. Hysteria: *The History of a Disease.* Northvale: Aronson, 1993. Print.

Widiger, Thomas A. *The Oxford Handbook of Personality Disorders.* Oxford: Oxford UP, 2012. Print.

Katherine A. Fowler and Scott O. Lilienfeld

See Also: Antisocial personality disorder; Borderline personality disorder; Hypochondriasis, conversion, and somatization; Hysteria; Narcissistic personality disorder.

Hoarding

Type of Psychology: Clinical; Counseling; Psychopathology

Hoarding involves accumulation of animals and material goods (often of marginal value and utility) beyond the bounds of any reasonable need. When it involves acquisition of animals, hoarding can endanger health and sanitation. Compulsive hoarding has been associated with depression and poverty. Scarcity may be the original motive for hoarding, but the behavior can become compulsive to a degree that exceeds any degree of necessity. Hoarding may reach a level that inhibits usual household activities, such as cooking, bathing, and sleeping.

Key Concepts

- Animal hoarding
- Bibliomania
- Caching
- Delusional behavior
- Collecting
- Obsessive-compulsive disorder (OCD)

INTRODUCTION

Hoarders often prefer possessions to people. Hoarding is associated with obsessive-compulsive personality disorder (OCPD), obsessive-compulsive disorder (OCD), attention-deficit/hyperactivity disorder (ADHD), and depression. Occasionally, hoarding may be associated with eating disorders, including pica (the consumption of items that are not food), psychosis, and dementia. Hoarding also may occur with other forms of mental disorganization, such as "difficulty managing daily activities because of procrastination and trouble making decisions; moving items from one pile to another, without discarding anything; difficulty organizing items, sometimes losing important items in the clutter; shame or embarrassment" (Mayo Clinic, n.d.).

A study (Tolin, Frost, & Steketee, 2010) was conducted on 751 people who described their own hoarding. Of those surveyed, 70% said that hoarding began between ages 11 and 20. By age 40, 96% of the participants' behavior was firmly in place, after which it intensified. Investigators were interested in whether hoarders engaged in this form of behavior following traumatic experiences such as sexual aggression or abuse, including intercourse and physical punishment. The participants' testimonies generally supported this supposition.

The hoarder loses the abiliity to decide which possessions to keep and what to discard or give away; he or she may develop an attachment to items that most people find to be of little use or value. The hoarder may obsess over possible future uses for many similar items with litte attention to available space, health, or safety. They may object to disposing of items that are believed to have future value. Such compulsions may supercede objections of spouses, friends, and children. A hoarder may compile old magazines, junk mail, newspapers, scrap paper, old clothing, plastic and paper bags, memorable photographs, and even empty cardboard boxes.

Hoarding has only recently become a subject of serious study, having been first described as a diagnosable mental disorder in the fifth edition of the *Diagnostic and Statistical Manual of Mental Disorders (DSM-5)*. An estimated two to five percent of adults are afflicted in the United States (Pertusa et al., 2010). Although few exact methods exist to measure the number of people who are hoarders, anecdotal evidence, including media reports, seems to indicate an increase, especially among elderly adults. Hoarding also may be provoked or intensified by traumatic events in a person's life, including loss of employment or death of a family member. The possessions are said to fill a void created by the loss. Alcoholism may also be a factor..

Excessive hoarding in limited space may endanger safety and become dangerous in the event of a fire when debris composed of combustible materials, such as stacks of paper, blocks exits or accumulates near heat sources. Health also may be compromised by excretions from vermin and pets, as well as by the accumulation of organic debris, including food waste.

CACHING BY ANIMALS

Some animals also practice hoarding, or caching, most notably birds and rodents. One report in Omaha, Nebraska, described a very well-fed female rat that created a nest in a residential living-room couch. Before her eviction and trapping, this rat had accumulated more than 30 pounds of dog food from bowls in the nearby kitchen. The dog food had been accumulated at night, while the family was sleeping, by the stealthy and very careful rat, and was discovered only after it began spilling from the back of the couch. Several species of animals hoard food, but magpies have been known to steal and stash money and coins from humans, drawn by their shine.

HOARDING VIS A VIS COLLECTING

Some hoarding of food, water, and fuel is undertaken in anticipation of scarcity during times of war, civil unrest, and natural disaster. This type of stockpiling is usually rational. However, some "survivalists" stockpile food, weapons, and ammunition in anticipation of attacks that do not occur.

Hoarding is distinguished from collecting which usually involves a measure of planning and organization and involves goods with some market value. Collectors feel a sense of pride about their possessions, displaying them and taking part in social events. Collections are usually well organized, as opposed to the pell-mell nature of hoarding. Collectors seek specific items, such as stamps or model cars and categorize them.

BIBLIOMANIA: HOARDING OF BOOKS

A preference for certain types of possessions may develop. The urge to possess things also may lead to theft. For example, the disorderly accumulation of books has been called bibliomania. Persons who engage in bibliomania also may steal books. Stephen Blumberg, a bibliokleptomaniac, stole so many books that he became well-known for it. He said that he was trying to save books from being ignored in libraries. Bibliomaniacs may steal several copies or editions of the same title.

ANIMAL HOARDING

Those who hoard animals sometimes collect pets in the dozens or even hundreds, penning them inside or outside. Dogs, cats, and snakes, among others, have been objects of hoarding. The animal hoarder often lacks the capacity to care for a large number of animals, and may, at the same time, deny his or her inability. Animal hoarders thus engage in a form of delusional behavior, in other words, beliefs not consistent with reality. This denial is not usually expressed as direct cruelty to the animals. On the contrary, the hoarder may express affection for animals.

The American Society for the Prevention of Cruelty to Animals (ASPCA) has been told by hoarders that they are helping their animals. As with other forms of hoarding, the hoarder's possessions are viewed with affection. At the same time, dead pets may be cannibalized by survivors that have no other food. The hoarder genuinely cannot understand why lack of ability to care for of animals in large numbers may be viewed by other people as a form of abuse.

Photo: iStock

cooking. Refrigerators may be filled with rotting food and bathrooms with human and animal feces or bags of dirty diapers. Tubs and showers may be filled with such things to a point where they are useless for bathing. Window shades may be drawn to prevent anyone from seeing inside.

A 79-year-old woman died in Washington, D.C., during a row house blaze in conditions that firefighters said would suffocate a packrat which prevented them from reaching her before flames enveloped the home. In Southern California, nearly 50 firefighters fought a fire for two hours in a house packed with clutter that had to be hacked away.

DIAGNOSTIC CRITERIA

Criteria for a diagnosis of hoarding disorder are listed in the *Diagnostic and Statistical Manual of Mental Disorders (DSM-5)*, the standard desk reference for mental-health providers. Diagnostic criteria include

difficulty throwing out or parting with material things, regardless of actual value; a need to save these items or revulsion at the thought of discarding them; possessions crowding and cluttering living areas to the extent of making them unusable; and significant distress or problems functioning professionally or socially, among other areas.

Any attempt to decide what should be thrown away may provoke intense anxiety and indecsion for a hoarder. In the meantime, growing piles intensifythe problem. Hoarding may be related to and aggravated by compulsive buying, especially at a bargain price. A hoarder may become angry when his or her motives are questioned, it is implied that this sort of behavior is abnormal, or it is suggested that items seen as having sentimental value or being unique and irreplaceable are nothing but junk, robustly illustrating the old maxim that "one man's trash is another's treasure." Even the most mundane of objects may be invested with value as a reminder of a past event.

TREATMENT

Therapy has been recommended for advanced cases of hoarding. Treatment is challenged by the fact that many hoarders do not believe they have a problem. The possessions (especially animals) comfort the hoarder. Seizure of a hoarder's possessions spurs resentment and a rush to acquire more of them. Over protest, the hoarder may accept therapy and medication. Under therapy, a subject

Animal hoarding may stem from poor relationships with parents in childhood, including abuse and trauma. The ASPCA maintains hoarding prevention teams that work with hoarders to maintain a healthy number of pets. The Animal Defense Fund also provides online advice regarding mitigation of animal hoarding.

THE DISORDER DEVELOPS

Over time, the disorder becomes paramount in a hoarder's life. He or she will live with malfunctioning appliances or lack of heat and cooling rather than summon repair people into crowded, unsanitary, and unsafe living space. Disagreements with family over what is worth keeping may escalate into bitter arguments, divorce, separation, eviction, and loss of custody of children.

Hoarders have been known to acquire beds then fill them with other possessions so that they cannot be used for sleeping. Kitchens may be filled with broken appliances to a point where the space cannot be used for may be asked why he or she feels compelled to hoard and taught how to organize things and "de-clutter" living space.

Instruction in bathing and other forms of hygiene also may be included in therapy, along with advice regarding nutrition and socialization. Medication may include selective serotonin reuptake inhibitors (SSRIs), as well as anti-depressants such as Paxil, Zoloft, and Prozac. Individuals who hoard have been reported by therapists as showing low motivation and lack willingness to cooperate, procrastinating, and dropping out of therapy at the first opportunity, frustrating mental-health professionals, who find hoarding very difficult to deal with.

FAMOUS HOARDERS

Some hoarders have become famous for their behavior. An example is provided by two brothers, Homer Lusk Collyer (1881-1947) and Langley Wakeman Collyer (1885-1947). Living alone in Harlem, in New York City, the brothers amassed more than 140 tons of material goods – furniture, books, musical instruments, and much more. They set snares and booby traps before they were found dead by police amidst their accumulated goods on March 9, 1947. In 2009, E.L. Doctorow published *Homer & Langley,* a novel based on the lives of the Collyer brothers.

Hoarders also have been subject to reality television treatment in the United States and Great Britain with titles such as *Disaster Masters, A Life of Grime, Extreme Clutter, Clean Sweep, Stuffed: Food Hoarders,* and *Hoarding: Buried Alive.*

BIBLIOGRAPHY

Hoarding disorder definition. (2014, May 8). Retrieved from http://www.mayoclinic.org/diseases-conditions/hoarding-disorder/basics/definition/con-20031337 Basic advice for mental health professionals on hoarding and related disorders.

Neziroglu, F., Bubrick, J., & Yaryura-Tobias, J. (2004). *Overcoming Compulsive Hoarding: Why You Save & How You Can Stop.* Oakland, CA: New Harbinger. A self-help book for hoarders aiming to deal with the problem.

Pertusa, A., Frost, R.O., Fullana, M.A., Samuels, J., Steketee, G., Tolin, D., Saxena, S., Leckman, J.F., & Mataix-Cols, D. (2010). Refining the boundaries of compulsive hoarding: A review. *Clinical Psychology Review,* 30, 371-386. A compilation of the literature on hoarding.

Steketee, G., & Frost, R.O. (2006). *Compulsive Hoarding and Acquiring: Workbook.* New York, NY: Oxford University Press.

Tolin, D.F., Frost, R.O., & Steketee, G. (2007). *Buried In Treasures: Help for Acquiring, Saving, and Hoarding.* New York, NY: Oxford University Press. Advice for hoarders and their therapists.

Tolin, D.F., Meunier, S.A., Frost, R.O., & Steketee, G. (2010) "Course of Compulsive Hoarding and Its Relationship to Life Events". *Depression and Anxiety,* 27, 829-838. Results of a self-reported survey of 751 hoarders describes development of the disorder on an individual basis.

Bruce E. Johansen

SEE ALSO: Addiction; Behavior disorders; Obsessive compulsive disorders.

Holland, John L.

TYPE OF PSYCHOLOGY: Counseling; Educational; Organizational; Social

A key figure in the fields of career development and counseling psychology, Dr. John L. Holland (1919-2008) is best known for his theory of vocational personalities and work environments. His useful and applicable theory has had broad impact on a variety of fields by offering a way to measure and describe interests and personality. The "Holland hexagon," comprising realistic, investigative, artistic, social, enterprising, and conventional interests, is a commonly used framework in a wide array of counseling settings.

KEY CONCEPTS
- Career development
- Interests
- Personality
- Vocational psychology
- Career assessment

INTRODUCTION

In the offices of career counselors, academic advisers, and guidance counselors, a few key questions come up repeatedly: What are my interests? How do I find a career that best matches my personality? What careers would be a good fit for who I am? Counselors are often called upon to work with their clients on issues of career and workplace fit; they benefit from evidence-based, clear, and easy-to-use tools to help answer these questions. Dr. John L. Holland's theory of vocational personalities and work environments fits this need well. The "Holland hexagon," comprising realistic, investigative, artistic, social, enterprising, and conventional personality types, is a common framework in a wide array of counseling settings. According to the theory, the six types within the hexagon can describe both individuals and work environments. A match of a worker to a similar work environment leads to a good fit, or satisfaction on the part of both the worker and the supervisor. While the widespread use of Holland's model speaks to its accessibility, the theory holds up to research scrutiny as well.

In addition to his theory of vocational personalities and work environments, Dr. John Holland was known for the development of career assessments, including the Self-Directed Search (SDS), which can be used in career counseling settings to help clients determine their "Holland type," or vocational personality. Holland's consideration of the usefulness of his theory in applied settings is a major factor in its broad and varied use today.

BIOGRAPHY

Holland was born and raised in Omaha, Nebraska. He attended college locally at the Municipal University of Omaha (now University of Omaha), graduating in 1942 and enlisting in the Army immediately after. Majoring in psychology, mathematics, and French, Holland's roles in the military included psychological administration and interviewing. After three and a half years of service, Holland enrolled in graduate school at the University of Minnesota, completing his doctoral work in 1952.

Holland's career was characterized by a strong focus on applied psychology. From his contributions to scientific literature to the positions he held, he sought to provide a useful approach to career development and vocational counseling. He worked in applied settings for several years including the Western Reserve University counseling center (1950-1956), National Merit Scholarship Corporation (1957-1963), and the American College Testing Program (1963-1969). He joined the faculty at The Johns Hopkins University in 1969, where he spent the remainder of his career.

Holland first released his most well-known contribution to the field, the theory of vocational personalities and work environments, in 1959. Over the course of his academic career, he was a prolific contributor to scientific literature in interest measurement and vocational

psychology. Notably, he published the third edition of *Making Vocational Choices: A Theory of Vocational Personalities and Work Environments* in 1997, at the age of 77. Holland also provided many opportunities and tremendous personal support for junior colleagues who were eager to test and to understand the broad context of his theory. He received the American Psychological Association's Award for Distinguished Scientific Applications of Psychology in 2008.

THEORY OF VOCATIONAL PERSONALITIES AND WORK ENVIRONMENTS

Holland's theory of vocational personality and work environments follows the tradition of person-environment fit models where a match is sought between aspects of the individual and characteristics of the environment; a good match is likely to be accompanied by positive workplace outcomes such as job satisfaction, tenure, and satisfactory work performance. In particular, Holland's theory seeks to answer three common questions:

- What personal and environmental characteristics lead to satisfying career decisions, involvement, and achievement, and what characteristics lead to indecision, dissatisfying decisions, or lack of accomplishment?
- What personal and environmental characteristics lead to stability or change in the kind and level of work a person performs over a lifetime?
- What are the most effective methods for providing assistance to people with career problems?

To that end, Holland's model characterizes people by their level of similarity, or likeness, to each of six personality types: realistic, investigative, artistic, social, enterprising, and conventional. These types can be described as follows:

- Realistic: Characterized by technical and mechanical skills, a dogmatic and practical approach to work, and an interest in working outdoors, with machines, or with one's hands.
- Investigative: Characterized by scientific skills and interests, an intellectual and curious personality, and abilities in math and research.
- Artistic: Characterized by creative and imaginative traits and an interest and skill set in the arts, including visual and performing arts and creative writing.
- Social: Characterized by a sociable and agreeable demeanor, an interest in helping others in fields

such as teaching or counseling, and interpersonal skills.

- Enterprising: Characterized by interests in sales, law, and business, an extroverted, ambitious, and dominant personality, and leadership skills.
- Conventional: Characterized by a methodical and practical approach to work, strong clerical and organizational ability, and conservative values.

In Holland's model, individuals can exhibit different levels of similarity to multiple types. With a high degree of similarity, an individual would endorse many of that type's traits and characteristics. Additionally, work environments can also demonstrate their likeness to multiple types. Similarity between worker and workplace can be explored using Holland's model where "congruence" is predictive of fit. That is, an individual with similarity to the realistic type would tend to experience a fit with a work environment aligned with the realistic type more so than with a work environment aligned with the artistic or social type. However, given that both individuals and work environments can resemble multiple types at once, "congruence" is rarely a straightforward consideration. Holland introduced the concept of "differentiation" to describe how well an individual or work environment can be described by the six types. A highly differentiated type is best described by one type and not well described by the others. A less differentiated type may be described relatively equally by all types or none.

Though the theory's vocational personalities prove highly useful in counseling and placement settings, this is much more than a simple taxonomy at play. Holland proposed a hexagon of the aforementioned types in which the six types are arrayed in an order (RIASEC) that reflects the relations among the types. In Holland's earliest model, each type is equal distance from the two adjacent types (e.g., enterprising, which is located between social and conventional, is the same distance from social as it is from conventional). In this configuration, types adjacent to each other are the most likely to co-occur in an individual or a work environment, while types across the hexagon from each other are least likely to co-occur. For example, finding a work environment that combines realistic and investigative types, which are next to one another on the hexagon, would be relatively easy (e.g., engineer, forester, auto mechanic). Finding a work environment that combines artistic and conventional types, which are diametrically opposite to each other on the hexagon, would be more difficult. A person

who endorses types next to each other on the hexagon is said to have "consistent" interests, and, according to Holland, this individual is likely to experience greater ease in finding a work environment in line with her or his vocational personality.

Extensive research supports the hexagon configuration of interests (albeit an irregular hexagon rather than one that has an equal distance between types), both concerning the order of the six personality types and the level of similarity between types. The model holds in diverse populations and in countries around the world. In addition, a large body of work by Holland and others shows the ability of the model to predict occupational choice and membership, both in initial career choice and during transitions over the lifetime.

ASSESSMENTS

Holland developed a career assessment (i.e., interest inventory) to encourage application of his theory. The Self-Directed Search (SDS) is a questionnaire that assesses an individual's fit with the Holland typology based on interests, aspirations, skills, and participation in activities. The resulting report includes 1) a "summary code" of three letters corresponding to the three types that best describe the individual and 2) occupations, fields of study (college majors), and leisure activities that would match the individual's code. Holland developed alternate forms of the SDS that are appropriate for different populations including the E form, which can be used with children or those with limited reading skills, and the Career Explorer, which can be used with middle school or junior high students to start the career exploration process. Holland and his colleagues also developed several guides (e.g., *Dictionary of Holland Occupational Codes, Educational Opportunities Finder, Leisure Activities Finder,* and *Veterans and Military Occupations Finder*) that counselors and their clients can use to identify occupations and college majors that match the interests reflected by the client's "summary code." Several other interest inventories like the Strong Interest Inventory and the Career Assessment Inventory use scales representing Holland's six types on their profiles.

CAREER COUNSELING APPLICATIONS

Holland's theory and the RIASEC hexagon specifically have been used extensively in counseling and consulting contexts. Knowing their career "type" answers many questions for career counseling clients and provides a guide for seeking out additional information about the world of work. In addition, the model can be used in conjunction with other tools and theories to provide a more complete vocational picture. However, Holland's development of career types that incorporated information about interests, aptitudes, values, and personality provided a level of integration unique to the field at the time; still today, the six Holland types provide a holistic view of the career search and selection process.

BIBLIOGRAPHY

Gottfredson, G.D. (1999). "John L. Holland's Contributions to Vocational Psychology: A Review and Evaluation". *Journal of Vocational Behavior*, 55, 15-40. A summary of Holland's work and influence.

Gysbers, N.C., Heppner, M.J., & Johnston, J.A. (Eds.). (2014). *Career counseling: Holism, diversity, and strengths.* Alexandria, VA: American Counseling Association. A handbook describing the field of career counseling and several theories of career development and career decision-making including John Holland's.

Hansen, J.C. (2011). "Remembering John L. Holland, PhD". *The Counseling Psychologist*, 39 (8), 1212-1217. A eulogy for John Holland.

Holland, J.L. (1996). "Exploring Careers With a Typology: What We Have Learned and Some New Directions". *American Psychologist*, 51(4), 397-406. Holland's own summary of his theoretical and applied work.

Holland, J. L. (1997). *Making Vocational Choices: A Theory of Vocational Personalities and Work Environments* (3rd ed.). Odessa, FL: Psychological Assessment Resources. This book provides a comprehensive overview of Holland's theory of vocational personality types.

Weinrach, S.G. (1980). "Have Hexagon Will Travel: An Interview With John Holland". *The Personnel and Guidance Journal*, 58, 406-414. One of the first articles to describe the work of John Holland.

Jo-Ida C. Hansen and Kelly M. Jordan, MA

SEE ALSO: Adaptation; Professor; Psychologist; Research; University of Michigan.

Homelessness
Psychological causes and effects

TYPE OF PSYCHOLOGY: Developmental psychology; Psychopathology; Social psychology

Homelessness has deep psychological effects on individuals, especially children and adolescents. Furthermore, rates of mental illness among homeless people are estimated to be more than twice the rate for the general population. Homeless individuals are typically unable to access adequate mental health care and treatment, and in its absence, they often sink deeper into the social isolation and economic desperation that further hinders their ability to find safe and stable housing.

KEY CONCEPTS
- Antipsychotics
- Bipolar disorder
- Deinstitutionalization
- Depression
- Projects for Assistance in Transition from Homelessness
- Psychological trauma
- Schizophrenia
- Sleep problems

INTRODUCTION

According to the American Psychological Association, homelessness occurs when a person lacks a safe, stable, and appropriate place to live; both unsheltered and sheltered individuals can be considered homeless. The US Department of Housing and Urban Development estimated that on any given night in January 2013, approximately 610,042 people were homeless in the United States and an estimated 109,132 people were chronically homeless. Rates of mental illness among homeless individuals in the United States are much higher than rates for the general population. According to 2009 data from the US Substance Abuse and Mental Health Services Administration (SAMHSA), approximately 20 to 25 percent of the homeless population in the United States has a severe mental illness compared to 6 percent of the general population. Individuals with schizophrenia or bipolar disorder are particularly vulnerable to experiencing periods of homelessness. Serious mental illness without proper treatment and social support inhibits a person's ability to carry out essential aspects of daily life, disrupting their ability to maintain employment and housing.

One of the reasons for the high prevalence of mental illness among the homeless is the large-scale deinstitutionalization of mental hospital residents in the 1960s. The advent of antipsychotic medications for treating schizophrenia and bipolar disorder also contributed to the perceived decrease in need for continuous care;

mental hospitals started to release residents in large numbers with prescriptions for antipsychotics and other medications. However, these individuals often stopped taking their medications, either because of their prohibitive cost or because they did not feel they were necessary or helpful, resulting in the reemergence or exacerbation of their psychiatric symptoms. Community and mental health centers were originally intended to fill the vacuum, but funding cuts rendered them inadequate as a safety net.

Often, the psychiatric conditions and symptoms of individuals with mental illness make it difficult for them to obtain and maintain employment. Furthermore, the inability of many poor individuals with mental illness to support themselves financially and to obtain adequate treatment, as well as the lack of affordable housing in many communities, causes many individuals with mental illnesses to end up in shelters or on the streets. Homelessness often causes individuals with mental illness to enter a downward spiral of ever more desperate conditions, compounding their physical and mental health problems.

Some individuals who did not have preexisting mental diseases prior to becoming homeless may develop psychiatric disorders or symptoms after becoming homeless, triggered by the stress of living on the streets or in shelters. Homeless people are often the victims of crime, particularly theft and physical assault, with homeless women being especially vulnerable to sexual assault and rape. The trauma of such abuse can provoke the emergence of or exacerbate the symptoms of conditions such as depression, posttraumatic stress disorder, bipolar disorder, and schizophrenia, especially in individuals with a genetic predisposition. Homeless children often experience emotional and developmental problems; the negative effects of trauma from physical and sexual assault most likely have a greater effect on their psychological development than that of adults.

PSYCHOLOGICAL CAUSES

Mental illness interferes with individuals' ability to attend to essential aspects of daily life, including self-care, household management, and employment, placing individuals with mental illness at greater risk for experiencing periods of homelessness. Furthermore, poverty prevents many individuals with mental illness from obtaining adequate mental health care and treatment. However, although mental illness puts individuals at a greater risk

for becoming homeless, poverty and a lack of affordable housing remain the principal causes of homelessness.

As the economic situation of individuals with mental illness becomes more desperate, they face even more obstacles to obtaining and sustaining employment and housing. Many individuals with mental illness have other physical illnesses or mental conditions, including drug and alcohol addiction, diabetes, hypertension, and asthma, further hindering their ability to maintain employment. Mental illness can make it difficult for individuals to adequately care for comorbid conditions and other physical health problems. Individuals with mental disorders encounter more barriers to accessible housing than individuals without mental disorders through income deficits, stigma, and discrimination. Homelessness then exacerbates both physical and mental illnesses.

Contrary to popular belief, most homeless individuals with mental illness are willing to accept treatment services, although access to care remains difficult. People with schizophrenia and some forms of bipolar disorder may experience paranoia, hallucinations, and delusions, making them suspicious of outsiders' attempts to help them. However, according to the National Coalition for the Homeless, outreach programs have greater success when they establish a trusting relationship through continued contact with the people they are trying to help.

PSYCHOLOGICAL EFFECTS

Homelessness has definite psychological effects, ranging from the detrimental effects of disrupted sleep to the deep psychological trauma inflicted by chronic stress, instability, and exposure to violence. Sleep problems are rampant among homeless people living on the streets or in shelters, where there is constant noise, crowding, and interruption of sleep. On the severe end of negative effects, violent physical and sexual attacks are much more likely to be made on the homeless than on the general population. For example, a sexual assault is twenty times more likely to be made on a homeless woman than on a woman in the general population. These violent assaults result in considerable emotional and psychological trauma in survivors, often leading to posttraumatic stress disorder, anxiety, depression, suicide attempts, substance abuse and addiction, and further psychiatric symptoms. The death rate among the homeless is also three times greater than that of the general population, with many homeless people dying from preventable or treatable illnesses or from unprovoked violence. Homeless people with mental illness are even more vulnerable than other homeless individuals to violent attacks and death.

Another important consideration is the number of children and adolescents who are homeless. Homelessness has multiple significant psychological and developmental effects on children. Homeless preschoolers are more prone to developmental delays in language, motor skills, and social skills. Children who experience chronic stress due to poverty or homelessness have poorer concentration and memory, affecting their ability to learn. They also display more aggression and shyness, have sleep problems (often due to the noisy environment of the streets and in shelters), are more likely to exhibit aggressive behavior, have lower self-esteem, and experience more disruptions to their education. Homeless children are twice as likely to experience hunger as nonhomeless children; hunger has serious negative effects on children's physical, emotional, and cognitive development.

Some families consisting of women and children become homeless after escaping from child abuse, spousal abuse, or domestic violence. In addition to possible developmental problems, these children also have to struggle with the psychological trauma and aftereffects of abuse. A study of homeless and runaway adolescents suggests a link between domestic abuse and depression in these adolescents. Homeless adolescents are more likely to have health problems, including respiratory diseases and sexually transmitted diseases, as well as substance abuse problems, than their counterparts in the general population. The combination of developmental, psychological, and medical problems makes homeless adolescents extremely susceptible to poverty and homelessness in adulthood.

POTENTIAL SOLUTIONS

According to the US Department of Health and Human Services, most homeless individuals with mental illness do not require institutionalization but would benefit from a supported housing program that offers mental health care and treatment. However, the number of affordable housing and community treatment services is insufficient to accommodate all the homeless who suffer from mental diseases. Additional resources are urgently needed so that the mentally ill homeless can have access to continuous treatment and therapy. Additionally, making community activities and certain types of employment available to homeless individuals with mental illness may help break the vicious cycle of homelessness and unemployment. Programs that assist homeless individuals and

individuals with mental illness to find housing, such as the Projects for Assistance in Transition from Homelessness (PATH) program, need to be expanded to bring the these ndividuals into stable, safe housing where they can receive the adequate social support and treatment. Supplemental Security Income checks, which are the sole income source for some Americans with disabilities, currently fall far short of the amount required to cover rent and other necessities. Increasing this amount to keep up with rising living costs can help ease the situation for some of the homeless population. The Department of Health and Human Services has initiated a program to recruit homeless children and their families into the national Head Start program to provide much-needed education and other services via community and daycare programs. Studies have shown that preschool education and participation in the Head Start program improve preschoolers' development of various skills.

BIBLIOGRAPHY

Bao, W. N., L. B. Whitbeck, and D. R. Hoyt. "Abuse, Support, and Depression Among Homeless and Runaway Adolescents." *Journal of Health and Social Behavior* 41.4. (2000): 408–20. Print.

Darves-Bornoz, J. M., T. Lemperiere, A. Degiovanni, and P. Gaillard. "Sexual Victimization in Women with Schizophrenia and Bipolar Disease." *Social Psychiatry and Psychiatric Epidemiology* 30.2 (1995): 78–84. Print.

DiBiase, Rosemarie, and Sandra Waddell. "Some Effects of Homelessness on the Psychological Functioning of Preschoolers." *Journal of Abnormal Child Psychology* 23.6 (1995): 783–92. Print.

Farrell, Daniel. "Understanding the Psychodynamics of Chronic Homelessness from a Self Psychological Perspective." *Clinical Social Work Journal* 40.3 (2012): 337–47. Print.

Hodgetts, Darrin, Ottilie Stolte, and Shiloh Groot. "Towards a Relationally and Action-Oriented Social Psychology of Homelessness." *Social and Personality Psychology Compass* 8.4 (2014): 156–64. Print.

Poole, Rob, and Robert Higgo. *Mental Health and Poverty.* Cambridge: Cambridge UP, 2014. Print.

Roos, Leslie E., et al. "Relationship between Adverse Childhood Experiences and Homelessness and the Impact of Axis I and Axis II Disorders." *American Journal of Public Health* 103.S2 (2013): S275–S281. Print.

Tamara L. Roleff, ed. *The Homeless.* San Diego: Greenhaven, 1996. Print.

United States. Department of Housing and Urban Development. *The 2013 Annual Homeless Assessment Report (AHAR) to Congress.* N.p.: n.p., 2013. PDF file.

Ing-Wei Khor

SEE ALSO: Alcohol dependence and abuse; Antipsychotic medications; Assisted living; Bipolar disorder; Children's mental health; Depression; Domestic violence; Elder abuse; Elders' mental health; Hallucinations; Insomnia; Paranoia; Rape and sexual assault; Schizophrenia: Background, types, and symptoms; Sleep; Stress: Behavioral and psychological responses; Substance use disorders; Suicide; Teenagers' mental health.

Homosexuality

TYPE OF PSYCHOLOGY: Motivation

Sexuality is one of the most complex and individual attributes of the human psyche. There are four types of theories with regard to the development of sexual orientation, but none seems sufficient to explain the huge diversity to be found in sexual expression across ages and cultures.

KEY CONCEPTS
- Androgyny
- By-product model
- Gay
- Homophobia
- Homosexual
- Kin selection model
- Lesbian
- Parental manipulation model
- Transsexual
- Transvestite

INTRODUCTION
Theories on the origin and development of sexual orientation can be categorized into four groups: psychoanalytic, biological, social learning, and sociobiological theories. Psychoanalytic theories are based on the Freudian model of psychosexual stages of development, developed by Austrian psychiatrist Sigmund Freud. According to this model, every child goes through several stages, including the phallic stage, during which the child learns to identify with the same-sex parent. For boys, this is supposed to be particularly difficult, since it requires redefining the strong bond that they have had with their mother since birth. According to Freudian theorists, homosexuality is an outcome of the failure to resolve this developmental crisis: If a boy's father is absent or "weak" and his mother is domineering or overprotective, the boy may never come to identify with his father; for a girl, having a "cold" or rejecting mother could prevent her from identifying with the female role. However, Freud himself said in his original work that he felt most humans' natural inclinations were toward bisexuality.

THEORETICAL MODELS
Research has found that same-sex attracted individuals are, in fact, more likely to feel an inability to relate to their same-sex parent than are heterosexuals and to report that the same-sex parent was "cold" or "distant" during their childhood. Some studies have suggested, however, that this psychological distance between parent and offspring is found mostly in families with children who show cross-gender behaviors when very young and that the distancing is more likely to be a result of preexisting differences in the child than as a cause of later differences.

Biological studies over the years have suggested that same-sex attraction is found in almost all animal species that have been studied. Bonobo chimpanzees, dolphins, lions, sheep, penguins, and many other species have been extensively studied and shown to form continuing, same-sex preferences even if there is ample availability of opposite-sex members. Biological theories have also considered a genetic component, unusual hormone levels, or prenatal maternal effects on the developing fetus. Although there may be genes that predispose a person to preferring same-sex partners, no specific genes for homosexuality have thus far been discovered. Most scientists believe that it is a combination of biological events and social circumstances rather than one determining factor that result in same-sex preferences. Similarly, there are no consistent differences between levels of hormones in homosexual and heterosexual adults.

Some recent brain scan research does, however, show more similarity in the anatomy of the brains of heterosexual men and lesbians as well as between heterosexual women and gay men. The scans showed that key structures of the brain (in particular, the amygdala) governing mood, emotion, anxiety, and aggressiveness in gays and lesbians more closely resemble those in heterosexuals of the opposite sex. The possibility also remains that subtle fluctuations of testosterone during critical periods of fetal development may influence brain structures that regulate sexual arousal and attraction.

Social learning theory models suggest that homosexual orientation develops as a response to pleasurable homosexual experiences during childhood and adolescence, perhaps coupled with unpleasant heterosexual experiences. Many boys have homosexual experiences as part of their normal sexual experimentation while growing up. According to the model, some boys will find these experiences more pleasurable or successful than their experiments with heterosexuality and will continue to seek homosexual interactions. Why only certain boys find their homosexual experiences more pleasurable than their heterosexual experiences could be related to a variety of factors, including the child's age, family dynamics, social skills, and personality. Young girls are less likely to have early homosexual experiences but may have negative feelings toward heterosexuality as a result of experiences such as rape, abuse, or assault.

Sociobiological models are all based on the assumption that common behaviors must have evolved because they were somehow beneficial, or related to something beneficial, which helped the individuals who performed them to pass their genes to the next generation. From this perspective, homosexuality seems incongruous, but because it is so common, researchers have tried to find out how homosexual behavior might in fact increase a person's ability to pass on genes to subsequent generations. Theorists have come up with three possible explanations: the parental manipulation model, the kin selection model, and the by-product model.

The parental manipulation model of homosexuality suggests that homosexuals do not directly pass on more of their genes than heterosexuals, but that their parents do. According to this model, parents subconsciously manipulate their child's development to make him or her less likely to start a family; in this way, the adult child is able to contribute time, energy, and income to brothers, sisters, nieces, and nephews. In the end, the parents have "sacrificed" one child's reproduction in exchange for more grandchildren—or, at least, for more indulged, more evolutionarily competitive grandchildren.

The kin selection model of homosexuality is similar, but in it, the homosexual individual is not manipulated but sacrifices his or her own reproduction willingly (although subconsciously) in exchange for more nieces and nephews (that is, more relatives' genes in subsequent

generations). According to this model, individuals who are willing to make this sacrifice (no matter how subconscious) are either those who are not likely to be very successful in heterosexual interactions (and are thus not actually making much of a sacrifice) or those who have a particular attribute that makes them especially good at helping their families. As an analogy, theorists point out how, through much of human history, reproductive sacrifice in the form of joining a religious order often provided income, protection, or status for other family members.

The by-product model of homosexuality suggests that homosexuality is an inevitable outcome of evolved sex differences. According to this model, the facts that, overall, men have a higher sex drive than women and that, historically, most societies have allowed polygamy (where one man has more than one wife) will result in many unmated men who still have an urge to satisfy their high sex drive. Thus, men will become (or will at least act) homosexual when male partners are easier to find than female partners. This model is the one most likely to explain "facultative homosexuality," that is, homosexual behavior by people who consider themselves basically heterosexual.

SOCIAL CONTEXTS

Before the gay liberation movement of the 1970's, homosexuality was classified as a mental disorder. In the 1970's, however, when psychiatrists were revising the American Psychiatric Association's *Diagnostic and Statistical Manual of Mental Disorders* (2d ed., 1968, DSM-II), they removed homosexuality from the list of illnesses. The subsequent editions of the manual no longer list homosexuality as a disease. Homosexuality is not associated with disordered thinking or impaired abilities in any way. Therefore, counseling or therapy for the purpose of changing sexual orientation is not recommended. Even when sought, such therapy is rarely successful. On the other hand, many gays and lesbians, especially adolescents, do benefit from counseling, which provides information, support, and ways to cope with their sexuality. Many who complete a successful round of counseling are empowered, have a better self-image, and are better able to cope with a sometimes hostile society.

For men, sexual orientation seems to be fixed at an early age; most gay men feel as though they have always been homosexual, just as most heterosexual men feel as if they have always been heterosexual. In women, however, sexual orientation is less likely to be fixed early; some women change from a heterosexual to homosexual orientation (or vice versa) in adulthood. In such cases, sexual orientation may be more of a choice than the acting out of something preexisting in the psyche. Often women make such changes after they have left unhealthy or abusive relationships or have experienced some other sort of emotional or psychological awakening that changes their outlook on life. In these cases, counseling exclusively for the sake of changing sexual orientation is not recommended, but it may be appropriate for these women to seek help dealing with the other changes or events in their lives. Most women in these circumstances find that a same-sex, even lesbian, therapist is especially helpful, because she will be more likely to empathize with her client.

Many women who change sexual orientation in midlife already have children, and many who are lesbian from adolescence choose to have children by artificial insemination or by having intercourse with a male friend. Often, these women find that society does not support their parenting efforts, and they sometimes experience legal problems retaining custody rights over their children. Gay men, too, have had difficulty retaining parental rights or becoming foster or adoptive parents. Increasingly, however, states are allowing single or coupled homosexuals to adopt children.

According to psychological research, homosexuals are as good at parenting as heterosexuals and are equally effective at providing role models. Homosexuals are more likely than heterosexuals to model androgynyAndrogyny—the expression of both traditionally masculine and traditionally feminine attributes—for their children. Some research has shown that an androgynous approach is healthier and more successful in American society than an approach involving traditionally defined roles. For example, sometimes women need to be assertive on the job or in relationships, whereas traditionally men were assertive and women were passive. Similarly, men are less likely to experience stress-related mental and physical health problems if they have learned to express their emotions, something traditionally only women were supposed to do.

Neither modeling androgyny nor modeling homosexuality is likely to cause a child to become homosexual, and children reared by homosexual parents are no more likely to become homosexual than children reared by heterosexual parents. Similarly, modeling of androgyny or homosexuality by teachers does not influence the development of homosexuality in children and adolescents. Having an openly homosexual teacher may be a stimulus for a gay child to discover and explore more fully his or her own sexuality, but it does not create a same-sex attraction where it did not already exist.

Other variations in adult sexual expression, sometimes associated with, or confused with, homosexuality, are transvestism and transsexuality. Transvestism occurs when a person enjoys, or is sexually excited by, dressing in outfits traditionally associated with the opposite sex. Some gay men enjoy cross-dressing, and others enjoy acting overly feminine. The majority of homosexuals, however, do not do either; most transvestites are heterosexual. Transsexuality is different from both homosexuality and transvestism; it is categorized by a person's feeling trapped in a body of the wrong sex. Transsexuality, unlike homosexuality or transvestism, is considered a mental disorder. The *Diagnostic and Statistical Manual of Mental Disorders* (4th ed., 1994, DSM-IV) committee replaced the diagnosis of transsexualism with gender identity disorder. It is officially a form of gender dysphoria, or gender confusion. Transsexuals may feel as though they are engaging in homosexual activity if they have sexual relations with a member of the opposite sex. Some transsexuals decide to cross-dress and live as a member of the opposite sex. They may have hormone treatments and surgery to change into a member of the opposite sex. Transsexuality, unlike homosexuality or transvestism, is very rare.

THE HOMOSEXUAL SPECTRUM

The word "homosexual" is commonly used as a noun, referring to someone who is sexually attracted to and has sexual relations with members of the same sex. Most same-sex attracted people now prefer the term gay or lesbian and consider themselves a part of the gay, lesbian, bisexual, and transgendered (GLBT) community. The labels "homosexual" and "heterosexual" are misleading, however, as many people who call themselves homosexual have engaged in heterosexual activity; similarly, many people who call themselves heterosexual have at some time engaged in some sort of same-sex activity. Therefore, many sex researchers (sexologists) use a seven-point scale first devised for the Alfred Kinsey surveys in the 1940's, ranging from 0 (exclusively heterosexual) to 6 (exclusively homosexual). Others prefer to use the words "heterosexual" and "homosexual" as adjectives describing behaviors rather than as nouns.

Homosexual behavior has been documented in every society that sexologists have studied; in many societies, it has been institutionalized. For example, the ancient

Greeks believed that women were spiritually beneath men and that male-male love was the highest form of the emotion. In Melanesian societies, homosexual activity was thought to be necessary for young boys to mature into virile, heterosexual adults. In pre-Colombian South America, homosexual and transgendered relationships were quite common. The Spanish conquerors in the 1500's brutally burned and executed many native peoples who openly and shamelessly practiced same-sex relationships. Among North American natives, transgendered and homosexual men were prized as shamans and allowed to live in long-term same-sex unions. Homosexuality as an overall preference or orientation is harder to study, but it is thought that between 5 and 10 percent of adult men, and between 2 and 4 percent of women, have a predominantly homosexual orientation.

NEGATIVE CULTURAL STEREOTYPES

In Western culture, even though homosexual behavior has long been considered taboo or sinful under Christianity, a small number of religious organizations are allowing the ordination of ministers who are gay or lesbian and sanctioning same-sex unions. The GLBT community is gradually becoming viewed as people following an alternative lifestyle, and increasingly, the acts of its members are no longer universally condemned or judged to be completely incompatible with Judeo-Christian beliefs.

Many heterosexuals (especially men) still harbor prejudices regarding gays and lesbians, a phenomenon called homophobia. Some of this unwarranted fear, disgust, and hatred is attributable to the incorrect belief that many homosexuals are child molesters. The statistics actually show that more than 90 percent of pedophiles are heterosexual.

Another source of homophobia is the fear of acquired immunodeficiency syndrome (AIDS). This deadly, sexually transmitted disease is more easily transmitted through anal intercourse than through vaginal intercourse and thus at first spread more rapidly among homosexuals. However, after large populations of women became infected with the human immunodeficiency virus (HIV)—60 percent of cases in sub-Saharan Africa and 48 percent in the Caribbean are in women—the gay stigma attached to AIDS has lessened. Safe-sex practices have dramatically reduced transmission rates in homosexual communities, although new HIV cases among young homosexual men and blacks indicate that these groups may be having unprotected sex.

Sexologists have not been able to avoid the controversies surrounding their field, making the study of a difficult subject even harder. Research will continue, but fast and simple explanations are not likely. Sexuality, perhaps more than any other attribute of the human psyche, is personal and individual, and questions about sexual orientation, sexual development, and sexual behavior are all complex.

BIBLIOGRAPHY

Bagemihl, Bruce. *Biological Exuberance: Animal Homosexuality and Natural Diversity*. New York: St. Martin's Press, 1999. Fascinating account by a wildlife biologist who makes the case that some 450 species occasionally engage in homosexual behavior. Challenges the notion that all animal sexual behavior is driven by procreation.

Baird, Vanessa. *The No-Nonsense Guide to Sexual Diversity*. New York: Verso, 2001. A wide-ranging survey of cultural attitudes toward homosexuality throughout the world and over time. Provides a country-by-country survey of laws concerning homosexuality and addresses the rise in opposition to sexual nonconformism among religious fundamentalists.

Bell, Alan P., and Martin Weinberg. *Homosexualities: A Study of Diversity Among Men and Women*. New York: Simon & Schuster, 1978. This official Kinsey Institute publication presents the methods and results of the most extensive sex survey to focus specifically on homosexual behavior. Presents descriptions of homosexual feelings, partnerships, and lifestyles, based on intensive interviews with more than fifteen hundred men and women.

Brookey, Robert Alan. *Reinventing the Male Homosexual: The Rhetoric and Power of the Gay Gene*. Bloomington: Indiana University Press, 2002. Discusses recent attempts to identify a genetic component to sexual orientation and the cultural effect of such research on gay identity.

Coghlan, Andy. "Gay Brains Structured Like Those of the Opposite Sex." *NewScientist* 11 (2008): 13. Reports on brain scans that show that some physical attributes of the homosexual brain are similar to those found in the opposite sex.

Dean, Tim, and Christopher Lane, eds. *Homosexuality and Psychoanalysis*. Chicago: University of Chicago Press, 2001. Reviews the often-conflicted relationship between psychoanalytic theory and homosexuality. Covers the attitudes toward homosexuality found in the writings of Sigmund Freud, Melanie Klein, Wilhelm Reich, Jacques Lacan, and Michel Foucault, among others.

Garnets, Linda, and Douglas C. Kimmel, eds. *Psychological Perspectives on Lesbian and Gay Male Experiences.* New York: Columbia University Press, 1993. A collection of essays focusing on gay identity development, gender differences, ethnic and racial variations, long-term relationships, adult development, and aging.

Koertge, Noretta, ed. *Nature and Causes of Homosexuality: A Philosophic and Scientific Inquiry.* New York: Haworth Press, 1981. This volume is the third in the ongoing monograph series Research on Homosexuality, each volume of which was originally published as an issue of the Journal of Homosexuality. All volumes are valuable, although somewhat technical. This volume covers the nature and causes of homosexuality; others cover law, psychotherapy, literature, alcoholism, anthropology, historical perspectives, social sex roles, bisexuality, and homophobia.

Mondimore, Francis Mark. *A Natural History of Homosexuality.* Baltimore: Johns Hopkins University Press, 1996. A well-written, unbiased examination of the subject. The first half of the book reviews the history of homosexuality; the second contains an examination of the evidence for the biological bases for homosexuality.

Tripp, C. A. *The Homosexual Matrix.* 2d ed. New York: McGraw-Hill, 1987. Tripp covers fact, culture, and mythology, both historical and modern. A good representative of the gay liberation era books on homosexuality, most of the text is as valid as when it was written (though it clearly does not cover post-AIDS changes in homosexual culture and behavior).

Linda Mealey; updated by Robert Flatley

SEE ALSO: Adolescence: Sexuality; Attraction theories; Gender differences; Gender identity disorder; Gender identity formation; Gender roles and gender role conflicts; Kinsey, Alfred; Love; Physical development: Environment versus genetics; Psychosexual development; Sex hormones and motivation; Sexual behavior patterns; Sexual variants and paraphilias; Transvestism.

Hope

TYPE OF PSYCHOLOGY: Cultural; Existential; Humanistic; Social

Psychologists view hope as the result of a cognitive and emotional process of developing plans to meet important goals and having the willpower to pursue these plans, even in challenging times. Hope defined this way has been found to be related to mental and physical health and positive educational outcomes.

KEY CONCEPTS

- Cognitive behavioral therapy
- Positive psychology
- Willpower
- Waypower

INTRODUCTION

Hope has long been a topic of interest to scholars of religion, philosophy, and psychology. For the most part, hope has been seen as beneficial. Hope can encourage persistence in difficult times and comfort one in times of stress. Some scholars, however, have emphasized the negative side of hope, noting that false hope might have debilitating qualities. Recent psychological research has generally found hope to promote physical and psychological health.

In 1959, psychiatrist Karl Menninger addressed the topic of hope at the 115th annual meeting of the American Psychiatric Association, calling it "a basic but elusive ingredient in our daily work -- our teaching, our healing, our diagnosing." Since then, psychologists have attempted to develop meaningful theoretical analyses as well as conduct research on this topic. In the 1960s, psychologist Hobart Mowrer analyzed the emotion of hope as a form of secondary reinforcement. A secondary reinforcement is a neutral stimulus (such as a bell), which, when paired with a primary reinforcement (such as food to a hungry animal), takes on reinforcing qualities itself. Hope was viewed as the anticipation that rewards, or "good things," are coming, itself acquiring positive qualities. Psychologist Richard Lazarus viewed hope as an emotion important to coping with stress. He viewed hope as tied to goals in that the achievement of goals facilitates hope for the future, and this, in turn, encourages further goal directed action. Psychologist Ezra Stotland also viewed hope as arising from a template learned early in one's life that one can achieve important goals.

Building on these prior analyses, the most thorough psychological investigation of the concept of hope in recent years has been conducted by C. R. Snyder. Snyder defines hope as the combination of two factors. One, which he terms "waypower," is the belief that one can find ways to achieve one's important goals. The second, termed "willpower," is the ability to motivate oneself to engage in those activities in order to reach one's goals. Research conducted within this framework has found a number of beneficial effects of hope. People high in hope are more likely to graduate from college than people demonstrating a low amount of hope. People high in hope also have quicker recuperation after illness, better coping under stress, higher self-esteem, and higher perceived problem-solving ability than people low in hope.

THE HOPE THEORY OF C. R. SNYDER

The approach to hope most commonly found in current psychological research is based upon the theoretical analysis developed by psychologist C. R. Snyder. Snyder was one of many psychologists inspired by the positive psychology movement of the late 1990s. Rather than focus on the negative side of human experience, positive psychologists investigate positive emotions and experiences, such as flow, happiness, and forgiveness.

Snyder defines hope as "the perceived capability to derive pathways to desired goals, and to motivate oneself via agency thinking to use those pathways." People are able to anticipate the future and have goals and aspirations. People who are hopeful can envision plans of action designed to meet their important goals. This is what Snyder terms "waypower." At their best, people can devise multiple routes to their important goals, so that if one series of actions becomes blocked, other pathways are still available. For example, a young person who wishes to achieve a college degree may not have the financial resources to do so. Rather than despair, hope of achieving the goal can be facilitated by the plan to work full time and take college courses on a part time basis or attend a more affordable community college rather than a four-year institution or apply for scholarships and loans to pay for the college of his or her choice.

However, waypower by itself is not enough to sustain hope. According to Snyder, the second component that is required is willpower. One must, in addition to having a plan or plans for meeting a goal, have the discipline to motivate oneself to execute the plan or plans. This willpower is partially dependent on one's emotional set as one begins movement toward a goal. Having positive, self-encouraging emotions is important as one meets challenges in the pursuit of the goal. For example, a person who wishes to lose weight may have a variety of diet plans that would meet that goal, but if he or she cannot summon the discipline to execute those plans, or feels depressed in the face of the challenge of weight loss, hopelessness may ensue. If challenges are felt as potentially positive experiences, willpower is strengthened. In sum, both plans and the ability to monitor and motivate oneself to execute one's plans are required for one to have hope of meeting one's important goals. Plans without the motivation to follow through, or motivation without the ability to devise workable plans, lead to hopelessness.

In Snyder's theory, hope is conceived of as specific to a given situation. One may have hope in terms of some desirable outcomes, but not others, depending on one's skill at developing plans or "pathways" and at recruiting motivation to follow through with these plans. In that sense, hope may be considered a state, or a relatively temporary set of feelings and thoughts based on a particular situation or time. However, people may also vary in terms of how skilled they are at regulating their own behavior and devising plans across situations. In that sense, we may consider hope as a personality trait that is relatively consistent over time and situations. Some people may be generally hopeful, while others may generally be more prone to hopelessness.

RESEARCH ON SNYDER'S THEORY OF HOPE

Snyder and his colleagues developed the Hope Scale for Adults and the Hope Scale for Children. These scales have allowed them to assess hope, as their theory defines it, and study how it is associated with other aspects of people's lives. Hope has been found to be positively associated with other trait-like characteristics such as optimism, the perception of control, perceived problem-solving ability, high self-esteem, and positive feelings.

Hope has also been studied with respect to education. It has been found to predict grade point average and graduation from college, over and above preparation and intelligence. Hope also predicts grade point average in graduate school and in law school. Hope has also been found to be a predictor of divergent thinking, a component of creativity. Hope is also a significant predictor of a teacher's ability to persist in challenging circumstances.

There is evidence that physical and mental health may be improved with hope. Hope has been found to correlate positively with coping with debilitating health conditions such as arthritis, spinal cord injury, and blindness. People who are hopeful experience less pain and heal faster than people who are less hopeful. Hope has been found to be associated with greater success in mental health treatment, and interventions designed to increase hope have been applied in a number of medical and psychological settings.

HOPE IN CLINICAL SETTINGS

Hope is widely considered important for success in clinical settings, and a number of researchers and therapists have sought to explicitly increase hope as a part of their work with clients. Cognitive behavioral therapies are the most common strategies used to increase hope. The client may be helped to set explicit goals and develop strategies that incorporate sub-goals and self-monitoring as a way of developing pathways to achieve what Snyder calls "waypower." Helping clients counter their own self-defeating thoughts can increase willpower or motivation. Such interventions have been demonstrated to meet with success, particularly in brief interventions in experimental settings. As with teaching, hope is a quality that is helpful to therapists in reducing stress and maintaining persistence in their work.

RELATED CONCEPTS

Snyder's analysis of the characteristics of hope and hope's consequences is similar to a number of other concepts in positive psychology. One of these is optimism. Optimism, as described by psychologists Michael Scheier and Charles Carver, is an expectation that one will be able to achieve desirable goals. However, the concept of designing pathways to reach those goals is not explicit in their theory of optimism. Psychologist Martin Seligman developed an attributional analysis of optimism. He suggests that optimism can be learned by training that encourages one to attribute one's failures to causes that are temporary, specific to a given situation, and not personal. Such attributions encourage one to maintain motivation in challenging situations. Clearly these analyses overlap with Snyder's analysis of hope. Scales designed to measure hope and to measure optimism correlate substantially. However, statistical analyses have also found unique aspects of each of these concepts.

Snyder's analysis also overlaps with Albert Bandura's concept of self-efficacy. Bandura views self-efficacy as the belief that one is capable of reading one's goals. As with optimism, correlational studies find that measures of self-efficacy correlate positively with hope, but the two

are not identical concepts. Snyder suggests that the difference is that his analysis more fully explores the interplay of emotions with expectations than Bandura's.

ALTERNATIVE ANALYSES OF HOPE

Psychologist Anthony Scioli analyzes hope as an emotion with cognitive, spiritual, and social components. He describes people as having hope "blueprints" which include motives such as mastery, internal and social supports, psychological traits, faith systems, and expressions in terms of thoughts and feelings. Scioli's Adult Hope Test correlates substantially, but not completely, with tests of optimism and Snyder's Hope Scale for Adults. Like these other qualities, Hope as measured by Scioli is positively related to health.

Philosopher Adrienne Martin has also contributed to contemporary discussions of hope. She argues that hope may not always be positive, in that it can lead to passivity. She analyzes the cognitive and emotional processes involved in hoping for an outcome and argues that complex and sophisticated processes are required in order to develop and maintain hope. In effect, one has to suppress negative possibility in order to maintain hope. Martin also describes an interdependent quality of hope. Hope may be sustained as it is embedded in collective, social, and interpersonal relationships.

BIBLIOGRAPHY

Martin, A. (2014). *How We Hope: A Moral Psychology.* Princeton, NJ: Princeton University Press. A philosophical analysis of hope. The language is scholarly.

Scioli, A., & Biller, H. (2009). *Hope In The Age of Anxiety.* Oxford, UK: Oxford University Press. Psychologist Anthony Scioli's analysis of hope in an easily readable form. Further information can also be found at www.gainhope.com

Snyder, C. (1994). *The Psychology of Hope: You Can Get There From Here.* New York, NY: Free Press. The most popular psychological analysis of hope, written for a general audience.

Snyder, C. (2000). *Handbook of Hope Theory, Measures & Applications.* San Diego, CA: Academic Press. A thorough treatment of Snyder's theory of hope and its applications in a variety of settings including therapy and specific populations such as children and the elderly.

Susan E. Beers

SEE ALSO: Optimism; Positive emotion; Positive psychology; Prospective thinking; Self-esteem.

Hope and mental health

DATE: 1950's forward
TYPE OF PSYCHOLOGY: Cognition; Emotion; Motivation

Hope represents people setting goals, becoming aware of how to achieve them, and developing sufficient motivation to pursue them. Hope theories are based on emotion, cognition, or both. Mental health professionals use various scales to measure hope. The presence or lack of hope affects physical and emotional health.

KEY CONCEPTS

- Agency
- Cognition
- Emotion
- Expectations
- •Goals
- Hopelessness
- Motivation
- Pathways

INTRODUCTION

For centuries, people have contemplated the meaning of hope. Because hope is an abstract idea, definitions have varied according to diverse factors, including cultural, spiritual, and psychological needs to secure what people believe hope represents. The essence of hope frequently reflects wishes for accomplishments or objects that fulfill people or help them achieve behaviors compatible with societal demands. Secular and religious literature has depicted hope mostly with positive attributes, although some portrayals, such as the Pandora myth, hint of hope's ambiguities. Hope is often equated with resilience, while hopelessness is associated with despair. Until the mid-twentieth century, many psychology researchers resisted studying hope scientifically because they considered it difficult to define and quantify.

HOPE THEORIES

In 1959, Karl Menninger spoke about the need for psychiatrists to study and incorporate hope in therapy during his presidential presentation at an American Psychiatric Association meeting. Jerome Frank emphasized the importance of hope for effective psychotherapy in a 1968 *International Journal of Psychiatry* article. Hope theory

research, representing positive psychology, emerged throughout the latter half of the twentieth century. Erik H. Erikson hypothesized that hope, which he said started forming at birth, was essential for development of cognition. Ezra Stotland wrote *The Psychology of Hope* (1969), exploring his premise that people's expectations to meet valued goals influenced their experiences with hope.

By the 1980's, Sara Staats had stated that hope involved both emotion and cognition. At the University of Kansas, C. R. Snyder began developing a hope theory to assist his patients in recognizing ways to pursue their goals. In the 1990's, he outlined three components of hope. First, people identify goals, representing daily activities or more complicated endeavors. Next, people use their cognition skills to recognize pathways they can follow in pursuit of goals. Third, people need agency, demonstrating the motivation and perseverance required to engage in pathways, for goal resolution. All three cognitive elements are essential to Snyder's hope theory.

Obstacles, including negative emotions, attitudes, and experiences, affect whether people believe they can complete goals. People with high hope often pursue several goals simultaneously, express confidence in their abilities, and excel in school, athletics, or work. Hope also aids people to cope with such medical concerns as cancer. Imbalanced hope theory components can frustrate people who are unsure how to attain their goals or lack sufficient motivation. Although hope can empower people, psychology professionals recognize the absence of hope can impair mental health and result in depression.

In the early twenty-first century, research in hope theory has considered topics such as the positive or negative impact of unexpected events on hope. Emotions produced when people react to emergencies or other traumatic occurrences can motivate them to achieve goals such as fleeing danger or assisting injured people.

MEASURING HOPE

Mental health professionals use hope measurement to provide patients effective therapy that enhances existing hope or counters helplessness. In the April, 1975, Journal of Clinical Psychology, Richard Erickson, Robin Post, and Albert Paige introduced their Hope Scale, inspired by Stotland's scholarship. In this scale, people use a seven-point scale to respond to twenty goal statements. They also assign numerical values from one to one hundred to rate how attainable they perceive each goal to be.

During the 1980's, Staats developed the Expected Balance Scale (EBS) to evaluate adults' emotion-based hope with responses to a list of eighteen items, equally divided between negative and positive statements. Staats and Marjorie Stassen measured cognitive aspects with the Hope Index, which included sixteen items that people ranked in four categories: hope for themselves, hope for others, wishes, and expectations.

In the 1990's, Snyder developed several hope measurement tests. The Adult Dispositional Hope Scale consists of twelve statements to assess pathways and agency. The Children's Hope Scale (CHS), with six items quantified by a six-point scale, is for children age seven through sixteen. Snyder's Domain Specific Hope Scale focuses on relationship goals or other precise concerns. His Young Children's Hope Scale (YCHS) evaluated children age five to seven.

Other hope tests for adults include the Miller Hope Scale, created by nurses Judith Miller and M. J. Powers; the thirty-two item Herth Hope Index, designed by A. K. Herth; and the Nowotny Hope Scale, established by Mary Nowotny to assess hope in people enduring stress. Some psychologists observed patients' actions pursuing goals to measure hope. In the June, 1974, Archives of General Psychiatry, Louis Gottschalk described evaluating verbal samples for hope. Mary Vance devised the Narrative Hope scale in the 1990's to examine stories for references to pathways and agency. Hope measurement scales were frequently translated into Asian or European languages and adapted for compatibility with distinct cultures, such as a Norwegian version of the Herth Hope Index.

BIBLIOGRAPHY

Lopez, Shane J., C. R. Snyder, and Jennifer Teramoto Pedrotti. "Hope: Many Definitions, Many Measures." In Positive Psychological Assessment: A Handbook of Models and Measures, edited by Lopez and Snyder. Washington, D.C.: American Psychological Association, 2003. Summarizes hope theory developments and researchers' efforts to quantify hope. Diagram, tables, appendixes, bibliography.

Reading, Anthony. Hope and Despair: How Perceptions of the Future Shape Human Behavior. Baltimore: Johns Hopkins University Press, 2004. Psychiatrist Reading discusses cognitive, emotional, and physiological processes associated with hope and hopelessness. Figures, endnotes, bibliography.

Snyder, C. R., ed. Handbook of Hope: Theory, Measures, and Applications. San Diego, Calif.: Academic Press, 2000. Comprehensive source addresses gender, age, and ethnicity factors and how hope helps people recovery from injuries and helps relieve pain.

Snyder, C. R., Diane McDermott, William Cook, and Michael A. Rapoff. Hope for the Journey: Helping Children Through Good Times and Bad. Boulder, Colo.: Westview Press, 1997. Stresses storytelling's role in hope development. Discusses parents' and teachers' responsibilities. Appendices suggest children's literature with hope themes and provide a story version of the YCHS.

Snyder, C. R., Kevin L. Rand, and David R. Sigmon. "Hope Theory: A Member of the Positive Psychology Family." In Handbook of Positive Psychology, edited by Snyder and Shane J. Lopez. 2d ed. New York: Oxford University Press, 2005. Compares hope theory with optimism, self-efficacy, self-esteem, and problem-solving theories. Includes three measurement scales.

Elizabeth D. Schafer

SEE ALSO: Achievement motivation; Assessment; Attitude formation and change; Coping: Strategies; Emotional intelligence; Emotions; Erikson, Erik H.; Humanistic psychology; Personality rating scales; Positive psychology; Self-efficacy; Self-esteem; Spirituality and mental health.

Hormones and behavior

TYPE OF PSYCHOLOGY: Biological bases of behavior

Hormones are chemical messengers, usually of protein or steroid content, that are produced in certain body tissues and that target specific genes in the cells of other body tissues, thereby affecting the development and function of these tissues and the entire organism. By exerting their influences on various parts of the body, hormones can affect behavior.

KEY CONCEPTS

- Endocrine gland
- Hormone
- Human growth hormone (HGH)
- Hypothalamus
- Melatonin
- Oxytocin
- Pheromone

- Pituitary
- Steroid
- Vasopressin

INTRODUCTION

Cell-to-cell communication among the trillions of cells that make up multicellular animals relies primarily on the specialized tissues of the nervous and endocrine systems. These two systems are intricately connected, with the former having evolved from the latter during the past 500 million years of animal life. The endocrine system consists of specialized ductless glands located throughout the animal body that produce and secrete hormones directly into the bloodstream. Hormones are chemical messengers that usually are composed of protein or steroid subunits. The bloodstream transports the hormones to various target body tissues, where the hormones contact cell membranes and trigger a sequence of enzyme reactions that ultimately result in the activation or inactivation of genes located on chromosomes in the cell nucleus.

A gene is a segment of a chromosome that is composed of deoxyribonucleic acid (DNA). The DNA nucleotide sequence of the gene encodes a molecule of messenger ribonucleic acid (mRNA) which, in turn, encodes a specific protein for the given gene. If the control sequence of a gene is activated, then ribonucleic acid (RNA) and protein will be produced. If the control sequence of a gene is inactivated, then RNA and protein will not be produced. Hormones target the genes in specific cells to start or stop the manufacture of certain proteins. Within cells and the entire organism, proteins perform important functions. Therefore, hormones control the production of proteins by genes and, as a result, control many activities of the entire animal.

The nervous system, which in vertebrate animals has evolved to become more elaborate than the endocrine system, consists of billions of neurons (nerve cells) that conduct electrical impulses throughout the body. Neurons transmit information, contract and relax muscles, and detect pressures, temperature, and pain. Neuron networks are most dense in the brain (where there are 100 billion neurons) and spinal cord, where much of the electrical information is centralized, relayed, and analyzed. Neurons must communicate electrical information across the gaps, or synapses, that separate them. To accomplish this goal, the transmitting neuron releases hormones called neurotransmitters, which diffuse across the synapse to the receiving neuron, thereby instructing the receiving neuron to continue or stop the conduction of the electrical message. There are many different types of neurotransmitters, just as there are many different types of regular hormones.

NERVOUS SYSTEM-ENDOCRINE SYSTEM INTERACTIONS

The link between the nervous and endocrine systems lies in two glands located between the cerebrum and the brain stem, the hypothalamus and the hypophysis (the pituitary gland). Electrical impulses from neurons in the cerebral cortex may activate the hypothalamus to release hormones that activate the hypophysis to release its hormones, which in turn activate or inactivate other endocrine glands throughout the body. These glands include the thyroid, parathyroids, thymus, pancreas, adrenals, and reproductive organs. This entire system operates by negative feedback homeostasis so that, once information is transferred and specific bodily functions are achieved, nervous or hormonal signals travel back to the hypothalamus to terminate any further action.

Animal behavior occurs as a result of the actions of the nervous and endocrine systems. There is a complex interplay among these two body systems, the environment, and an individual's genetic makeup in terms of the cause-and-effect, stimulus-response events that constitute behavior. An animal receives external information via its special senses (eyes, ears, nose, mouth) and somatic sense organs (touch, pain, temperature, pressure). This external information travels along sensory neurons toward the brain and spinal cord, where the information is analyzed and a motor response to the external stimulus is initiated. Some of these motor responses will be directed toward the sense organs, locomotory muscles, and organs such as the heart and intestines. Other impulses will be directed toward the hypothalamus, which controls body cycles such as all endocrine system hormones, heart rate, sleep-wake cycles, and hunger.

When the hypothalamus releases the hormone corticoliberin, the pituitary gland (the hypophysis) releases the hormones thyrotropin (which activates the thyroid gland), prolactin (which stimulates milk production in the female breast), and growth hormone (which triggers growth in children and metabolic changes in adults). When the thyroid gland is activated, hormones such as thyroxine and triiodothyronine are released to accelerate cellular metabolism, an event that may occur in certain situations such as stress or fight-or-flight encounters.

If the pituitary gland releases adrenocorticotropic hormone (ACTH), the adrenal glands will be activated to release their hormones. The adrenal cortex produces and secretes a variety of hormones, such as aldosterone, which regulates the blood-salt balance directly and blood pressure indirectly; cortisol, which accelerates body metabolism; and androgens, or sex hormones. All of these are steroid hormones, which are involved in rapidly preparing the body for strenuous performance. Even more pronounced are the effects of the adrenal medulla, which produces and secretes the hormone neurotransmitters epinephrine and norepinephrine; these two hormones accelerate heart, muscle, and nerve action as well as stimulate the release of fat and sugar into the bloodstream for quick energy, all of which are extremely important for spontaneous activity such as fighting with or fleeing from enemies. The control of sugar storage and release from the liver by the pancreatic hormones insulin and glucagon also are important in this process.

THE EFFECTS OF HORMONES ON BEHAVIOR
The study of hormones and their effects on individual and group behaviors is of immense interest to psychologists. Hormones represent the biochemical control signals for much of animal and human behaviors. Understanding precisely how hormones affect individuals, both psychologically and physiologically, could be of great value in comprehending many different human behaviors, in treating abnormal behaviors, and in helping individuals cope psychologically with disease and stress. The hormonal control of behavior in humans and in many other animal species has been extensively studied, although much research remains to be performed. Hormones have been clearly linked to reproductive behavior, sex-specific behavioral characteristics, territoriality and mating behaviors, physiological responses to certain external stimuli, and stress.

The pineal gland, located in the posterior cerebrum, releases the hormone melatonin, which regulates the body's circadian rhythms and possibly its sexual cycles as well. Melatonin is normally synthesized and secreted beginning shortly after dusk throughout the night and ending around dawn. It thus corresponds with the individual's normal sleep-wake cycle. Melatonin may play an important role in humans adapting to shift work. It is promoted as a nutritional supplement to help people get a good night's sleep.

HORMONES AND REPRODUCTION
The most extensive research involving hormonal effects on behavior has been conducted on reproductive behavior. Among the most powerful behavior-influencing hormones are the pituitary gonadotropins luteinizing hormone (LH) and follicle-stimulating hormone (FSH). These two hormones target the reproductive organs of both male and female children and stimulate these organs to initiate sexual development and the production of sexual steroid hormones—estrogen and progesterone in women, testosterone in men. These sex hormones are responsible not only for the maturation of the reproductive organs but also for secondary sexual characteristics such as male aggression and female nesting behavior.

Reproductive patterns vary from species to species in occurrence, repetition of occurrence, and behaviors associated with courtship, mating, and caring for young. The achievement of reproductive maturity and reproductive readiness in a given species is subject to that species' circadian rhythm, a phenomenon regulated by hormones released from the hypothalamus, hypophysis, and pineal gland. These three endocrine glands are influenced primarily by the earth's twenty-four-hour rotation period and the twenty-eight-day lunar cycle. Furthermore, genetically programmed hormonal changes at specific times during one's life cycle also play a major role in the occurrence of reproductive behaviors.

In female vertebrates, LH, FSH, and estrogen are responsible for the maturation of the ovaries, the completion of meiosis (chromosome halving) and the release of eggs for fertilization, and secondary sexual characteristics. The secondary sexual characteristics involve physiological and closely related behavioral changes. In bird species, these changes include the construction of a nest and receptivity to dominant males during courtship rituals. In mammals, these same hormones are involved in female receptivity to dominant males during courtship. Physiological changes in mammals include the deposition of fat in various body regions, such as the breasts and buttocks, and increased vascularization (more blood vessel growth) in the skin. Females of most mammal and bird species go into heat, or estrus, one or several times per year, based on hormonally regulated changes in reproductive organs. Female humans follow a lunar menstrual cycle in which LH, FSH, estrogen, and progesterone oscillate in production rates. These hormonal variations influence female body temperature and behavior accordingly.

Male sexual behavior is controlled predominantly by testosterone produced in the testicles and male androgens produced in the adrenal cortex. These steroid hormones cause muscle buildup, increased hair, and aggressive behavior. As a consequence, such steroids are often used (illegally) by athletes to improve their performance. In a number of mammal and bird species, elevation of sex steroids causes increased coloration, which serves both as an attractant for females and as an antagonistic signal to competitor males. The aggressive behavior that is stimulated by the male sex steroid hormones thus plays a dual role in courtship and mating rituals and in territorial behavior, phenomena that are tightly linked in determining the biological success of the individual.

Pheromones are hormones released from the reproductive organs and skin glands. These hormones target the sense organs of other individuals and affect the behavior of these individuals. Sex pheromones, for example, attract males to females and vice versa. Other pheromones enable a male to mark his territory and to detect the intrusion of competitor males into his territory. Others enable an infant to imprint on its mother. Such hormones number in the hundreds, but only a few dozen have been studied in detail. Pheromones released by males serve as territorial markers, as is evidenced by most mammalian males spraying urine on objects in their own territory. Exchanges of pheromones between males and females are important stimulants for courtship and mating. In some species, the release of pheromones—or even the sight of a potential mate—will trigger hormonally controlled ovulation in the female. Furthermore, in several species, such as elephant seals and lions, the takeover of a harem by a new dominant male, a process that usually involves the murder of the previous male's offspring, stimulates the harem females to ovulate. The diversity of reproductive behaviors that is regulated by hormones seems to be almost as great as the number of species.

HORMONES AND STRESS

The fight-or-flight response is a hormone-controlled situation in which the body must pool all its available resources within a relatively short time span. The detection of danger by any of the special senses (sight, smell, hearing) triggers the hypothalamus to activate the pituitary gland to release adrenocorticotropic hormone, which causes the adrenal gland to release its highly motivating hormones and neurotransmitters. Many body systems are subsequently affected, especially the heart and circulatory system, the central nervous system, the digestive system, and even the immune system. One reason the fight-or-flight response is of major interest to psychologists is its link to stress.

Stress is overexcitation of the nervous and endocrine systems. It is caused by the body's repeated exposure to danger, excessive physical exertion, or environmental pressures that affect the individual psychologically. Stress is a major problem for humans in a fast-paced technological society. The physiological and behavioral manifestations of stress are very evident. There is considerable evidence that stress is associated with heart disease, cancer, weakened immune systems, asthma, allergies, accelerated aging, susceptibility to infections, learning disorders, behavioral abnormalities, insanity, and violent crime. The demands that are placed on individuals in fast-paced, overpopulated societies are so great that many people exhibit a near-continuous fight-or-flight response. This response, in which the body prepares for maximum physical exertion in a short time span, is the physiological basis of stress. It is not intended to be maintained for long periods of time; if it is not relieved, irreparable effects begin to accumulate throughout the body, particularly within the nervous system. Medical psychologists seek to understand the hormonal basis of physiological stress to treat stress-prone individuals.

HORMONES AND AGING

Another hormone that greatly influences human behavior and development is human growth hormone (HGH). This hormone is produced by the anterior pituitary (adenohypophysis) gland under the control of the hypothalamus. HGH production peaks during adolescence, corresponding to the growth spurt. Although it is produced throughout life, it declines with age in all species studied to date. In humans, HGH production tends to drop quickly beginning in the thirties so that by age sixty, HGH production is only about 25 percent of what it was earlier in life, and it continues to decline until death. The decrease in HGH production with age has been tied to thinning of skin and wrinkle formation, muscle wasting, sleep problems, cognitive and mood changes, decreased cardiac and kidney function, lessening of sexual performance, and weakening of bones, contributing to osteoporosis. Nutritional supplements including the amino acids arginine, lysine, and glutamine are being investigated as growth hormone releasers, which may then decrease signs of aging.

HORMONE TREATMENT OF HEALTH PROBLEMS

The ultimate goals of hormone studies are to arrive at an understanding of the physiological basis of behavior and to develop treatments for behavioral abnormalities. Synthetic hormones can be manufactured in the laboratory. Their mass production could provide solutions to many psychological problems such as stress, deviant behavior, and sexual dysfunction. Synthetic hormones already are being used as birth control mechanisms aimed at fooling the female body's reproductive hormonal systems.

Ongoing research focuses on the importance of many hormones, especially on understanding their functions and how they might be used in the treatment of common disorders. Two hormones produced by the hypothalamus and released by the posterior pituitary (neurohypophysis) gland are vasopressin (antidiuretic hormone) and oxytocin. Vasopressin keeps the kidneys from losing too much water and helps maintain the body's fluid balance. Variants of vasopressin that decrease blood pressure, identified by Maurice Manning, may lead to a new class of drugs to control high blood pressure. Oxytocin induces labor by causing uterine contractions and also promotes the production of milk for breastfeeding. Manning and Walter Chan are working to develop oxytocin receptor antagonists that may be used to prevent premature births.

THE PAST, PRESENT, AND FUTURE OF HORMONES

The activities of all living organisms are functionally dependent on the biochemical reactions that make up life itself. Since the evolution of the first eukaryotic cells more than one billion years ago, hormones have been used in cell-to-cell communication. In vertebrate animals (fish, amphibians, reptiles, birds, and mammals), endocrine systems have evolved into highly complicated nervous systems. These nervous systems are even evident in the invertebrate arthropods (crustaceans, spiders, and so on), especially among the social insects, such as ants. The endocrine and nervous systems are intricately interconnected in the control of animal physiology and behavior.

Psychologists are interested in the chemical basis of human behavior and therefore are interested in human and mammalian hormones. Such hormones control a variety of behaviors, such as maternal imprinting (in which an infant and mother bond to each other), courtship and mating, territoriality, and physiological responses to stress and danger. Animal behaviorists and psychologists study the connection between hormones and behavior in humans, primates, and other closely related mammalian species. They identify similarities in behaviors and hormones among a variety of species. They also recognize the occurrence of abnormal behaviors, such as antisocial behavior and sexual deviance, and possible hormonal imbalances that contribute to these behavioral anomalies.

Although the biochemistry of hormones and their effects on various behaviors have been established in considerable detail, numerous behaviors that are probably under hormonal influence have yet to be critically analyzed. Among them are many subtle pheromones that affect a person's interactions with other people, imprinting pheromones that trigger attraction and bonding between individuals, and hormones that link together a variety of bodily functions. These hormones may number in the hundreds, and they represent a challenging avenue for further research. Unraveling the relationships between hormones and behavior can enable researchers to gain a greater understanding of the human mind and its link to the rest of the body and to other individuals. These studies offer potential treatments for behavioral abnormalities and for mental disturbances created by the physiologically disruptive effects of drug use, a major problem in American society. They also offer great promise in the alleviation of stress, another major social and medical problem.

BIBLIOGRAPHY

Borer, Katarina T. *Exercise Endocrinology.* Champaign, Ill.: Human Kinetics, 2003. Begins with a discussion of the endocrine system and then looks at how it functions to control and regulate various functions of the body during exercise, including intense exercise. Looks at the effects of reproductive hormones on exercise as well.

Ellison, Peter T., and Peter B. Gray, eds. *Endocrinology of Social Relationships.* Cambridge, Mass.: Harvard University Press, 2009. Collection of essays on how the endocrine system and hormones influence aspects of human and animal relationships. Includes information on oxytocin, vasopressin, androgens, human mating, and fatherhood.

Kraemer, W. J., and Alan D. Rogol, eds. *The Endocrine System in Sports and Exercise.* Malden, Mass.: Blackwell, 2005. Collection of essays that looks at the principles and mechanism of endocrinology as related to sports and exercise. Contains several essays on growth hormone factors involved in exercise and examines how the endocrine system affects competition.

Lovallo, William R. *Stress and Health: Biological and Psychological Interactions.* 2d ed. Thousand Oaks, Calif.: Sage, 2005. Lovallo examines biological links between emotion and health. He looks at psychological stress and how it manifests physiologically and affects health and disease.

Neal, J. Matthew. *How the Endocrine System Works.* Malden, Mass.: Blackwell Science, 2001. A good general work on the endocrine system that has chapters on the major glands and discusses calcium and glucose metabolism as well as endocrine diseases.

Neave, Nick. *Hormones and Behaviour: A Psychological Approach.* New York: Cambridge University Press, 2008. Neave explains the endocrine system and how hormones can influence brain structure and function. He also presents a series of examples to show the influence of hormones on specific behaviors, including sexual determination, neurological differentiation, parental and aggressive behaviors, and cognition.

David Wason Hollar, Jr.;
updated by Robin Kamienny Montvilo

SEE ALSO: Adrenal gland; Emotions; Endocrine system; Gonads; Nervous system; Neurotransmitters; Pituitary gland; Sex hormones and motivation; Smell and taste; Stress: Physiological responses; Synaptic transmission; Thyroid gland.

Horney, Karen

BORN: September 16, 1885, Eilbek, near Hamburg, Germany
DIED: December 4, 1952, in New York, New York
IDENTITY: German-born American psychoanalyst
TYPE OF PSYCHOLOGY: Psychotherapy; Personality; Social psychology

Rebelling against traditional psychiatric theories of female motivation and behavior, Horney formulated theories dependent on social and environmental influences rather than sexual trauma.

Karen (Danielsen) Horney was born in Eilbek, a village near Hamburg, Germany. Determined to study medicine, she was among the first to be admitted to Hamburg's new, highly controversial girls' Gymnasium, a preparatory program to train women for admission to German universities. From 1906 to 1908, she studied medicine at Freiburg and Göttingen Universities, completing her work in Berlin. There she studied psychoanalysis with Karl Abraham, a follower of Sigmund Freud, and began to practice and teach. She married fellow student Oscar Horney in 1909. They had three daughters before separating in 1926. Alarmed by the rise of Adolf Hitler and the Nazi Party, she moved to the United States in 1932, becoming a citizen in 1938. She settled in New York, where she became a member of the New York Psychoanalytic Institute and a teacher at the New School for Social Research.

Although at first a disciple of Freud, Horney perceived the antifeminism of Freudian theory by the time of the 1937 publication of her book *The Neurotic Personality in Our Time.* She attacked that theory in *New Ways in Psychoanalysis* (1939), emphasizing the importance of environmental and social factors on personality development, as opposed to Freud's insistence that sexual conflicts were at the basis of psychological problems. Increasingly, she stressed the importance of the parent-child relationship. Not only must biological needs be met, she believed, but children must experience warmth and affection as well. The child who is not lovingly nurtured will develop hostility and distrust. This hostility may be projected onto the world in general or may be repressed to reappear as neurotic compliance or withdrawal.

Her theories brought her into conflict with the Freudian-dominated New York Psychoanalytic Institute, from which she was forced to resign in 1941. She then helped form the Association for the Advancement of Psychoanalysis and its *American Journal of Psychoanalysis.* Her later publications include *Self-Analysis* (1942), *Our Inner Conflicts* (1945), and *Neurosis and Human Growth* (1950), the posthumously published *Feminine Psychology* (1967), and many articles. The *Adolescent Diaries of Karen Horney* appeared in 1980.

In her last years, her interest turned to questions of faith. Shortly after a trip to Japan, where she studied Zen Buddhism, she was diagnosed with cancer, of which she died in 1952.

BIBLIOGRAPHY

Paris, Bernard J. *Karen Horney: A Psychoanalyst's Search for Self-Understanding.* New Haven, Conn.: Yale University Press, 1996. Traces the relationship between Horney's personal life and development of her thought; includes extensive bibliography.

Quinn, Susan. *A Mind of Her Own: The Life of Karen Horney.* New York: Other Press, 2003. Comprehensive general biography in the Radcliffe Biography series.

Solomon, Irving. *Karen Horney and Character Disorder: A Guide for the Modern Practitioner.* New York: Springer, 2006. An introduction to Horney's theories and how they apply to alleviating character disorders.

Betty Richardson

SEE ALSO: Ego, superego, and id; Freud, Sigmund; Freudian psychology; Personality theory; Psychoanalytic psychology; Psychoanalytic psychology and personality: Sigmund Freud; Women's psychology: Karen Horney; Children's mental health; Women's mental health.

Hospice

DATE: 1967 forward
TYPE OF PSYCHOLOGY: Developmental psychology

A hospice is a facility or program that provides physical and emotional comfort to dying individuals and their family and friends. Hospice services emphasize pain management rather than curative measures, involve a multidisciplinary team, and often allow the dying individual to stay at home with family.

KEY CONCEPTS
- Bereavement
- Dying
- Individualized care plan
- Life expectancy
- Palliative care
- Team approach
- Whole individual

INTRODUCTION

Hospice programs are designed for those who are dying or who have no reasonable hope of benefit from cure-oriented interventions. Hospice care typically starts when life expectancy is six months or less if the illness runs its normal course, but this type of care can continue longer than six months with physician certification. Hospice services can include home care, inpatient care, consultation, and bereavement follow-up. With a mission of palliative rather than curative care, hospice programs neither prolong life nor hasten death. The goal is to prolong the quality of life.

Hospice programs deal with whole individual, including the physical, emotional, social, and spiritual impact of the disease on the patient and the patient's friends and family. Hospice staff and volunteers offer specialized knowledge of medical care, including pain management. Most hospice care, about 75 percent, takes place within the dying person's home, the home or a friend or relative, a nursing home, or an assisted living facility. Other locations include residential hospice facilities or hospice units within hospitals.

Hospice care involves a multidisciplinary team, including physicians, nurses, pharmacists, social workers, physical and occupational therapists, and clergy. The team also includes family members and trained volunteers, who help with household chores and give family caregivers respite time. The team approach provides state-of-the-art care for pain and other distressing symptoms and emotional and spiritual support for the patient and family.

Before providing care, hospice staff members meet with the patient's personal physician and a hospice physician to discuss the patient's history, current physical symptoms, and life expectancy. Alternatively, families or patients can self-refer if the patient's physician is unavailable or unable to discuss the hospice program. After this initial meeting, hospice staff members meet with both the patient and family to discuss pain and comfort levels, support systems, financial and insurance resources, medications and equipment needs, and the hospice philosophy. Together, they develop an individualized care plan for the patient, and regularly review and revise this plan according to the patient's condition.

Hospice provides services to the family and friends of the dying individual. On average, about two family members per hospice death receive bereavement services, and they typically receive seven contacts (visits, phone calls, and mailings) in the year after the death.

HISTORY AND STATUS

Hospice programs trace their roots to age-old customs of hospitality and medieval religious institutions offering rest and support for weary travelers. In England, the modern hospice movement began in 1967 when Dame Cicely Saunders founded St. Christopher's Hospice in southeast London. In the United States, hospice care began in 1974 with a community-based home care program in New Haven, Connecticut.

From these roots, the hospice movement has grown tremendously. In 2006, the National Hospice and Palliative Care Organization (NHPCO) estimated that the United States had more than forty-five hundred hospices, including ones in all states and territories. These

---

HOSPICE RESOURCES

ORGANIZATIONS

National Hospice and Palliative Care Organization
http://www.nhpco.org
   Nonprofit membership organization for programs and professionals that provides statistics and research, as well as information about advance directives and locating a hospice.

Hospice Foundation of America
http://www.hospicefoundatiom.org
   Nonprofit organization that provides leadership in the development and application of hospice and its philosophy.

National Hospice Foundation
http://www.nationalhospicefoundation.org
   Foundation committed to leading global, philanthropic efforts to advance quality, compassionate, end-of-life care for all.

SCIENTIFIC JOURNALS
   • Annals of Long Term Care
   • American Journal of Hospice & Palliative Medicine
   • Caring
   • Clinical Journal of Oncology Nursing
   • Death Studies
   • Home Health Care Management and Practice
   • Hospice Management Advisor
   • Home Healthcare Nurse
   • International Journal of Palliative Nursing
   • Journal of Clinical Oncology
   • Journal of Medical Ethics
   • Journal of Pain Symptom and Management
   • Nursing Ethics
   • Omega: Journal of Death and Dying
   • Palliative Medicine
   • Psycho-Oncology
   • Supportive Care in Cancer

---

hospices served 1.3 million people in 2006, approximately 36 percent of all Americans who died that year. Of these patients, 56 percent were women, 64 percent were over the age of seventy-five, and 81 percent were white. The three diseases with the highest utilization rates were malignancies, nephritis or kidney disease, and Alzheimer's disease. In 2006, the average length of hospice service was fifty-nine days; the median, which represents what the most people actually experienced, was twenty-one days.

   Funding for hospice services is strong. The U.S. Congress enacted the Medicare Hospice Benefit in 1982, so most hospice programs are covered under Medicare. In addition, most states offer Medicaid coverage, and many private health insurance policies and health maintenance organizations (HMOs) cover hospice services. Unlike hospital funding, which is retrospective and fee-for-service, hospice funding is prospective and flat-rate. Hospice coverage includes physicians, nurses, and home health aides; medicine, medical appliances, and supplies; spiritual, dietary, and other counseling services; continuous home-care or inpatient care during crises; and around-the-clock on-call support.

BIBLIOGRAPHY

American College of Physicians. http:// www.acponline. org. Clinical practice guidelines on medical interventions that have been shown to relieve pain, breathing problems, and depression at the end of life.

Armstrong-Dailey, Ann, and Sarah Zarbock. *Hospice Care for Children*. 2d ed. London: Oxford University Press, 2001. Practical, highly readable information on end-of-life issues, focusing on children. Intended for a diverse audience of professionals and volunteers involved in hospice services.

Cairns, Moira, Marney Thompson, and Wendy Wainwright. *Transitions in Dying and Bereavement: A Psychosocial Guide for Hospice and Palliative Care*. Baltimore: Health Professions Press, 2003. Practical information about the needs of dying people and their families.

Forman, Walter B., Judith A. Kitzes, Robert B. Anderson, and Denice K. Sheehan, eds. *Hospice and Palliative Care: Concepts and Practice*. 2d ed. Sudbury, Mass.: Jones and Bartlett, 2003. Informative chapters on the history of hospice, the interdisciplinary team, reimbursement, settings, assessment, communication, ethics and legalities, spiritual issues, physical problems, cultural issues, and grief.

Marrelli, Tina M. *Hospice and Palliative Care Handbook: Quality, Compliance and Reimbursement.* St. Louis, Mo.: Mosby, 2004. Medical-surgical guidelines, practical advice regarding documentation, and sample forms for clinicians and managers.

Lillian M. Range

SEE ALSO: Assisted living; Cancer and mental health; Coping: Terminal illness; Death and dying; Elder abuse; Elders' mental health; Grieving; Health maintenance organizations; Pain; Pain management.

Hull, Clark L.

BORN: May 24, 1884, near Akron, New York
DIED: May 10, 1952
IDENTITY: American psychologist
PLACE OF DEATH: New Haven, Connecticut
TYPE OF PSYCHOLOGY: Learning; Motivation

Hull was a leading architect of learning theory and pioneered a quantitative description of the laws of behavior.

Clark L. Hull grew up on a farm in Michigan. He was educated in a one-room schoolhouse and passed the teacher's examination at the age of seventeen. After teaching school for a year, Hull continued his own education, spending one year in high school in West Saginaw and then two years at Alma Academy, where typhoid fever almost killed him. He then enrolled at Alma College but abandoned his plans for a career in mineral engineering when poliomyelitis left him paralyzed in one leg. He eventually graduated with a bachelor of arts degree in psychology from the University of Michigan in 1913. After teaching for a year in Richmond, Kentucky, Hull entered the graduate program in psychology at the University of Wisconsin. He earned a doctorate in 1918 for his dissertation on concept formation and was subsequently appointed to the Wisconsin faculty in the area of applied psychology. In 1929, Hull became a research professor at Yale, where he remained for the rest of his academic career. Hull was married to Bertha Iutzi.

While a faculty member at Wisconsin, Hull worked to improve psychological tests and measurements for assessing aptitude. He designed and built a device to help compute product-moment correlations for test validation. The results of this research formed the basis of his first book, *Aptitude Testing* (1928). Hull also pioneered the application of experimental and statistical methods to the study of hypnosis. He continued this research for a short time at Yale, summarizing his program in his second book, *Hypnosis and Suggestibility: An Experimental Approach* (1933).

At Yale, Hull began the task of making psychology an exact science. Influenced by his childhood instruction in geometry and the British physicist Sir Isaac Newton's *Philosophiae Naturalis Principia Mathematica* (1687), Hull used the hypothetico-deductive approach to develop testable principles, expressed mathematically, for his global theory of behavior. Hull's most important book, *Principles of Behavior* (1943), describes learning as the acquisition of stimulus-response habits reinforced by a reduction in drive (a biological need). With the psychologist Kenneth Spence, Hull developed the concepts of fractional anticipatory goal responses and incentive motivation to explain apparent instances of goal-directed behavior. Revisions to the theory were published in Hull's *Essentials of Behavior* (1951) and *A Behavior System* (1952). *Mathematico-Deductive Theory of Rote Learning* (1940), which Hull cowrote with several others, applied his principles to verbal learning.

At the time of his death in 1952, Hull's theory of learning, reinforcement, and motivation dominated research in psychology.

BIBLIOGRAPHY

Beach, Frank A. "Clark Leonard Hull: May 24, 1884-May 10, 1952." *Biographical Memoirs of the National Academy of Sciences* 33 (1959): 123-141. Print.

Bembenutty, Héfer. *Self-Regulated Learning.* San Francisco: Jossey-Bass, 2011. Print.

Bolles, Robert C. *Learning Theory.* 2d ed. New York: Holt, Rinehart and Winston, 1979. Print.

Harasim, Linda M. *Learning Theory and Online Technology.* New York: Routledge, 2012. Print.

Kimble, Gregory A. "Psychology from the Standpoint of a Mechanist: An Appreciation of Clark L. Hull." *In Portraits of Pioneers in Psychology*, edited by Gregory A. Kimble and Michael Wertheimer. Washington, D.C.: American Psychological Association, 1998. Print.

Klein, Stephen B. *Learning: Principles and Applications.* Thousand Oaks: Sage, 2012. Print.

Ormond, Jeanne Ellis Ormrod. *Human Learning.* Boston: Pearson, 2012. Print.

Ruth M. Colwill

SEE ALSO: Assessment; Learning; Motivation; Motivation: Intrinsic and extrinsic; Reinforcement; Testing: Historical perspectives.

Human resource training and development

TYPE OF PSYCHOLOGY: Motivation

Human resource training and development programs provide employees with the knowledge and skills they need to perform their jobs successfully. In an increasingly technical and complex world, training and development programs are vital for organizational survival.

KEY CONCEPTS
- Apprenticeships
- Computer-aided instruction (CAI)
- Job analysis
- Modeling
- Programmed instruction
- Role-playing
- Transfer of training

INTRODUCTION

The term "human resources" implies that human abilities and potential, such as aptitudes, knowledge, and skills, are as important to a company's survival as are monetary and natural resources. To help employees perform their jobs as well as they can, companies develop training and development programs.

Most employees must go through some form of training program. Some programs are designed for newly hired or recently promoted employees who need training to perform their jobs. Other programs are designed to help employees improve their performance in their existing jobs. Although the terms are used interchangeably in this discussion, the former type of program is often referred to as a "training program" and the latter as a "development program."

There are three phases to a training or development program. During the first phase, managers determine training needs. One of the best ways to determine these needs is with job analysis. Job analysis is a process that details the exact nature and sequencing of the tasks that make up a job. Job analysis also determines performance standards for each task and specifies the corresponding knowledge, skills, and aptitudes (potential) required to meet these standards. Ideally, job analysis is used as the basis for recruiting and selecting employees. Managers like to hire employees who already have the ability to perform the job; however, most employees enter an organization with strong aptitudes but only general knowledge and skills. Consequently, during the second phase of training, a method of training is designed that will turn aptitudes into specific forms of task-related knowledge and skills.

A long history of training and educational research suggests a number of guidelines for designing effective training programs. First, training is most effective if employees have strong intellectual potential and are highly motivated to learn. Second, trainees should be given active participation in training, including the opportunity to practice the skills learned in training. Practice will usually be most effective if workers are given frequent, short practice sessions (a method called distributed practice) rather than infrequent, long practice sessions (called massed practice). Third, trainees should be given continuous feedback concerning their performance. Feedback allows the trainee to monitor and adjust performance to meet training and personal standards.

One of the greatest concerns for trainers is to make certain that skills developed in training will transfer to the job. Problems with transfer vary greatly with the type of training program. In general, transfer of training will be facilitated if the content of the training program is concrete and behavioral, rather than abstract and theoretical. In addition, transfer is improved if the training environment is similar to the job environment. For example, a manager listening to a lecture on leadership at a local community college will have more difficulty transferring the skills learned in the classroom than will a mechanic receiving individual instruction and on-the-job training.

Once training needs have been analyzed and a training program has been implemented, the effectiveness of the training program must be measured. During the third phase of training, managers attempt to determine the degree to which employees have acquired the knowledge and skills presented in the training program. Some form of testing usually serves this goal. In addition, managers attempt to measure the degree to which training has influenced productivity. To do this, managers must have a performance evaluation program in place. Like the selection system and the training program, the performance evaluation system should be based on job analysis. Ideally, a third goal of the evaluation phase of training should be to examine whether the benefits of training, in terms of productivity and job satisfaction, warrant the cost of training. A common problem with training programs is that managers do not check the effectiveness of programs.

Training and development are integral parts of a larger human resource system that includes selection, performance evaluation, and promotion. Because employee retention and promotion can be considerably influenced by training, training and development programs in the United States are subject to equal employment opportunity (EEO) legislation. This legislation ensures that the criteria used to select employees for training programs, as well as the criteria used to evaluate employees once in training programs, are related to performance on the job. When managers fail to examine the effectiveness of their training programs, they cannot tell whether they are complying with EEO legislation. EEO legislation also ensures that if minority group members do not perform as well as majority group members in training, minorities must be given the opportunity for additional training or a longer training period. Minorities are given the additional time based on the assumption that their life experiences may not have provided them with the opportunity to develop the basic skills that would, in turn, allow them to acquire the training material as fast as majority group members.

ON-THE-JOB TRAINING

The most common form of training is on-the-job training, in which newly hired employees are put to work immediately and are given instruction from an experienced worker or a supervisor. On-the-job training is popular because it is inexpensive and the transfer of training is excellent. This type of training program is most successful for simple jobs not requiring high levels of knowledge and skill. On-the-job training is often used for food service, clerical, janitorial, assembly, and retail sales jobs. Problems with on-the-job training arise when formal training programs are not established and the individuals chosen to act as trainers are either uninterested in training or are unskilled in training techniques. A potential drawback of on-the-job training is that untrained workers are slow and tend to make mistakes.

An apprenticeship is a form of long-term training in which an employee often receives both on-the-job training and classroom instruction. Apprenticeships are one of the oldest forms of training and are typically used in unionized skilled trades such as masonry, painting, and plumbing. Apprenticeships last between two and five years, depending on the trade. During this time, the apprentice works under the supervision of a skilled worker, or "journeyman." Once a worker completes the training, he or she may join a trade union and thereby secure a position in the company. Apprenticeships are excellent programs for training employees to perform highly complex jobs. Apprenticeships offer all the benefits of on-the-job training and reduce the likelihood that training will be carried out in a haphazard fashion. Critics of apprenticeship programs, however, claim that some apprenticeships are artificially long and are used to keep employee wages low.

SIMULATION TRAINING

Although on-the-job training and apprenticeship programs allow employers to use trainees immediately, some jobs require employees to obtain considerable skill before they can perform the job. For example, it would be unwise to allow an airline pilot to begin training by piloting an airplane filled with passengers. Where employees are required to perform tasks requiring high levels of skill, and the costs of mistakes are very high, simulator training is often used.

In simulator training, a working model or reproduction of the work environment is created. Trainees are allowed to learn and practice skills on the simulator before they start their actual jobs. Simulators have been created for jobs as varied as pilots, mechanics, police officers, nuclear power plant controllers, and nurses. The advantage of simulator training is that trainees can learn at a comfortable pace. Further, training on simulators is less expensive than training in the actual work environment. For example, flight simulator training can be done for a fraction of the cost of operating a plane. An additional benefit of simulator training is that simulators can be used to train employees to respond to unusual or emergency situations with virtually no cost to the company for employee errors. A potential disadvantage of simulator training is the high cost of developing and maintaining a simulator.

These simulator training programs are used for technically oriented jobs held by nonmanagerial employees. Simulator training can also be used for managers. Two popular managerial simulations are in-basket exercises and business games. Here, managers are put in a hypothetical business setting and asked to respond as they would on the job. The simulation may last a number of days and involve letter and memo writing, telephone calls, scheduling, budgeting, purchases, and meetings.

Interpersonal skills training programs teach employees how to be effective leaders and productive group members. These programs are based on the assumption that an employee can learn how to be a good group participant or a good leader by learning specific behaviors. Many of the interpersonal skills programs involve modeling and role-playing. For example, videotapes of managerial scenarios are used to demonstrate techniques a manager might use to encourage an employee. After the manager has seen the model, he or she might play the role of the encouraging manager and thus be given an opportunity to practice leader behaviors. An advantage of role-playing is that people get the opportunity to see the world from the perspective of the individual who normally fills the role. Consequently, role-playing is a useful tool in helping members of a group in conflict. Role-playing allows group members to see the world from the perspective of the adversary.

PROGRAMMED INSTRUCTION

Programmed instruction is a self-instructed and self-paced training method. Training material is printed in a workbook and presented in small units or chapters. A self-administered test follows each unit and provides the trainee with feedback concerning how well the material has been learned. If the trainee fails the test, he or she rereads the material. If the trainee passes the test, he or she moves on to the next unit. Each successive unit is more difficult.

Programmed instruction has been used for such topics as safety training, blueprint reading, organizational policies, and sales skills. The advantage of programmed instruction is that trainees proceed at their own pace. Further, because training and tests are self-administered, employees do not feel much evaluation pressure. In addition, when units are short and tests are frequent, learners get immediate feedback concerning their performance.

Computers have increasingly replaced the function of the workbook. Computer-assisted instruction is useful because the computer can monitor the trainee's performance and provide more information in areas where the trainee is having trouble. A potential drawback of programmed instruction is that employees may react to the impersonal nature of training. Further, if the employees are not committed to the program, they may find it easier to cheat.

THE NEED FOR ONGOING TRAINING

Over the last two hundred years, there have been dramatic changes in both the nature of jobs and the composition of the workforce. Consequently, there have also been dramatic changes in the scope and importance of training. The history of formal employment training dates back thousands of years. Training programs were essential for jobs in the military, church, and skilled trades. Prior to the Industrial Revolution, however, only a small percentage of the population had jobs that required formal training. Training for the masses is a relatively new concept. At the beginning of the Industrial Revolution, the vast majority of workers lived in rural areas and worked on small farms. Training was simple and took place within the family. During the Industrial Revolution, the population started to migrate to the cities, seeking jobs in factories. Employers became responsible for training. Although early factory work was often grueling, the jobs themselves were relatively easy to learn. In fact, jobs required so little training that children were often employed as factory workers.

Since the Industrial Revolution, manufacturing processes have become increasingly technical and complex. Now, many jobs in manufacturing require not only lengthy on-the-job training but also a college degree. In addition, technology is changing at an ever-increasing pace. This means that employees must spend considerable time updating their knowledge and skills.

Just as manufacturing has become more complex, so has the process of managing an organization. Alfred Chandler, a business historian, suggests that one of the most important changes since the Industrial Revolution has been the rise of the professional manager. Chandler suggests that management used to be performed by company owners, and managerial skills were specific to each company. Today, managers work for company owners and are trained in universities. Because management functions are so similar across organizations, managers can take their skills to a wide variety of companies and industries.

In contrast to the increasingly technical nature of jobs, there has been an alarming increase in the number of illiterate and poorly trained entrants into the workforce. There has also been an increase in the number of job applicants in the United States who do not speak English. In response to these problems, many companies have begun to provide remedial training in reading, writing, and mathematics. Companies are thus taking the role of public schools by providing basic education. Training and development programs will continue to be essential to organizational survival. As the managerial and technological worlds become more complex, and as the number of highly skilled entrants into the workforce declines, companies will need to focus on both remedial training for new employees and updating the knowledge and skills of older employees. The use of the Internet for distance-learning training programs is expected to increase, offering opportunities for people in remote locations who traditionally have not had access to local training resources.

BIBLIOGRAPHY

Bandura, Albert. *Social Learning Theory.* Englewood Cliffs: Prentice, 1977. Print.

Biech, Elaine. *Developing Talent for Organizational Results: Training Tools from the Best in the Field.* San Francisco: Pfeiffer, 2012. Print.

Craig, Robert L., ed. *The ASTD Training and Development Handbook: A Guide to Human Resource Development.* 4th ed. New York: McGraw-Hill, 1996. Print.

Landy, Frank J., and Don A. Trumbo. "Personnel Training and Development: Concepts, Models, and Techniques." *Psychology of Work Behavior.* New York: McGraw-Hill, 2003. Print.

Latham, Gray P. "Human Resource Training and Development." *Annual Review of Psychology.* Vol. 39. Stanford: Annual Reviews, 1988. Print.

Moskowitz, Michael. *A Practical Guide to Training and Development: Assess, Design, Deliver, and Evaluate.* San Francisco: Pfeiffer, 2008. Print.

Noe, Raymond. *Employee Training and Development.* 4th ed. New York: McGraw, 2008. Print.

Sauser, William I., and Ronald R. Sims. *Managing Human Resources for the Millennial Generation.* Charlotte: Information Age, 2012. Print.

Wexley, K. N., and Gary P. Latham. *Developing and Training Human Resources in Organizations.* 3d ed. Upper Saddle River: Prentice, 2002. Print.

Wilson, John P. *International Human Resource Development: Learning, Education and Training for Individuals and Organizations.* 3d ed. London: Kogan. Print.

Derived from: "Human resource training and development." *Psychology and Mental Health.* Salem Press. 2009.

Daniel Sachau

See Also: Ability tests; Assessment; Bandura, Albert; Career and personnel testing; Career Occupational Preference System (COPS); Career selection, development, and change; Educational psychology; General Aptitude Test Battery (GATB); Industrial and organizational psychology; Intelligence tests; Interest inventories; Kuder Occupational Interest Survey (KOIS); Peabody Individual Achievement Test (PIAT); Race and intelligence; Scientific methods; Social learning: **Albert Bandura; Stanford-Binet** test; Strong Interest Inventory (SII); Survey research: Questionnaires and interviews; Testing: **Historical** perspectives; Wechsler Intelligence Scale for Children-Third Edition (WISC-III); Work motivation; Workforce reentry; Workplace issues and mental health.

Humanistic psychology

Type of psychology: Origin and definition of psychology

Humanistic psychology attempts to understand a person's experience precisely as it is lived. By respecting the reality of a person's own experiential viewpoint, humanistic psychologists can examine the actual meanings a situation has for the person. In doing so, humanistic psychology develops a comprehensive understanding of human nature and of psychological life in general..

Key Concepts
- Existence
- Existentialism
- Human science
- Intentionality
- Person-centered therapy
- Phenomenology
- Self-actualization

INTRODUCTION

Humanism became influential in psychology through a loosely knit movement that began in the 1950s and became a significant force in the 1960s. Humanistic psychology is not a single branch of psychology, focused on a particular content area, but a unique approach to all of psychology's content areas. Because humanistic psychology was not created around the work of one founder, it has avoided becoming dogmatic, but it suffers the corresponding disadvantage of having no unanimously inclusive doctrines. Nevertheless, humanistic psychology does offer a distinctive approach to psychological life, based on respect for the specifically human quality of human existence. In humanistic psychology, an existence is one's irreducible being in a world that is carved out by one's personal involvements. Fidelity to the full meaning of being human requires understanding human psychological life on its own terms, as it actually presents itself, rather than on models borrowed from other fields of inquiry. In contrast, traditional psychology assembled its foundational concept about human existence during the nineteenth century from such disciplines as physiology, biology, chemistry, and physics. These natural sciences share a common assumption about their subject matter—namely, that it is "matter," objective things that are completely determined by the causal impacts of other things in mechanical and lawful ways that can be explained, measured, predicted, and controlled.

CENTRAL TENETS

Humanistic psychology arose to counter the prevailing scientifically oriented beliefs within the field of psychology during the mid-twentieth century. It argues that the natural science model distorts, trivializes, and mostly neglects the real subject matter: human existence. When love is reduced to a biological drive and insight to a conditioned response, humanistic psychologists protest, psychology has lost contact with the real humanness of its subject matter. Their alternative approach includes four essential features.

First, integral to humanistic psychology is its appreciation of the person as a whole. Such a holistic emphasis holds that people cannot be reduced to parts (labeled processes, instincts, drives, conditioned responses) because the meaning of any part can only be understood in relation to the whole person. For example, a humanistic psychology of thinking also takes into account the thinker's feelings and motives, since it is the person as a whole who thinks, not only the brain or an information-processing system. Even the most seemingly isolated physiological events cannot be fully comprehended apart from the person's total existence. A study of women recently widowed, for example, showed that their bodies' immune systems weakened in the year after their husbands' deaths. This subtle yet profound way of embodying grief is best understood when the human body is grasped as a "bodying forth" of a whole existence and personal history.

A second essential feature of humanistic psychology concerns its notion of consciousness, which is informed by the phenomenological concept of intentionality.

Consciousness is seen as "intending" an object, meaning not the everyday sense of intending as a deliberate choice but rather that consciousness is always consciousness of something. Whereas traditional psychologies conceive of consciousness as a machine, a brain, or a container, or else dismiss it altogether, the concept of intentionality means that consciousness is fundamentally relational: it is an encountering and dwelling in one's world. For example, to be conscious of the room one is in means to be intertwined with it. To be immersed in a memory means to be there, in that remembered scene. This communion is reciprocal in the sense that the objects of consciousness are also implicated in this relation. It is neither objective stimulation nor variables that ordinary consciousness intends but a meaningful world, intended through one's own way of being with it. For example, a student driver is conscious of other cars as looming too close, whereas the consciousness of the race-car driver intends the spaces through which he or she could drive the car.

Third, this notion of consciousness leads to humanistic psychology's recognition of the irreducible reality of the person's own experience as the core of his or her psychological life. Rather than preconceiving a person's behavior from an outside point of view, humanistic psychology seeks to clarify its significance by understanding the behaving person's own viewpoint. In other words, behavior is seen as an expression of a person's involvement in a situation. For example, a man walking across a snow-covered frozen lake could not be said to be brave (or foolhardy) if he experienced it as a field instead.

A fourth essential constituent is a vision of human freedom. For humanistic psychology, a person unfolds his or her existence over time by responsibly owning and becoming who he or she is. This does not mean that the self is whatever a person wants to be; rather, one's own choice is to be the self that one authentically is. This choice, because one is free to make it or not, is also the source of anxiety, as people confront their own ultimate responsibility for what they will make of their lives. Terms such as "self-actualization" and "self-realization" depict this most crucial obligation of being human. Selfhood, in other words, is not simply what one has been given by environmental or genetic sources but rather a possibility to be owned and lived by transcending the given. Instead of determining the course of psychological life, the givens of one's existence must be freely engaged in the process of one's own authentic self-becoming.

CONTRIBUTIONS TO PSYCHOLOGY

Within psychology, the humanistic approach's most important applications have been in the areas of psychotherapy, personality theory, and research methods. Rollo May aptly described the humanistic idea of psychotherapy as helping patients experience their existence as real. Carl R. Rogers's person-centered therapy depicts the humanistic purpose: to assist clients in unblocking and experiencing their own self-actualizing tendencies. This is accomplished by nonjudgmentally clarifying and mirroring back to clients their own spontaneous expressions of self with genuine empathy and unconditional positive regard.

A second area of major application has been personality theory. Among the many who have contributed in this regard are Gordon Allport, Henry A. Murray, Charlotte Buhler, and James Bugental. The most famous are Rogers, May, and Abraham Maslow. They see personality as a tendency of self-actualizing: of "becoming" (May), of realizing one's possibilities for "full humanness" (Maslow), of being "fully functioning" (Rogers). They emphasize that the personality is oriented toward growth and is thus dynamic rather than static, yet they recognize that this process is unfinished and far from automatic. Rogers noted that "incongruence" between one's self-concept and one's actual self blocks actualizing tendencies. If a person experiences positive regard from significant others, such as parents, as being conditional (for example, "I love you because you never get angry" or "I'll love you if you always agree with me"), the effort to meet these conditions results in an "incongruence" between one's self-concept and the self one actually is being.

May stressed that to become self-actualized, one must be aware of oneself. Facing one's own being requires risk and commitment, based on one's capacities for love and will, courage and care. This "central distinguishing characteristic," the human capacity for self-awareness, can be blocked. People may evade the insecurity of this risk by not facing themselves, but the resulting deadening leads to boredom and a trivialization of life.

Maslow specified his conception of self-actualization in the context of his theory of motivation. He described a hierarchy of needs, extending from "deficiency needs" (physiological needs and safety) to "being needs" (belonging, love, self-esteem, and self-actualization). He considered growth motivation an inherent tendency of people to fulfill ever higher motives on this hierarchy.

A third application of the humanistic approach has been innovative methods for psychological research. These methods, known as human science, can be used to study human experience as it is actually lived in the world. Human science research is phenomenologically based, using data gathered by interviews and written descriptions, which are then analyzed qualitatively. The aim is not to reduce experience to the traditional operationally defined variables but to understand the essential structure of the person's actually lived experience.

CONTRIBUTIONS TO OTHER FIELDS
Humanistic innovations have been widely applied beyond psychology, in such areas as medicine, politics, feminism, law, religion, social action, international relations, and ecology. For example, former United States president Jimmy Carter used Rogers's techniques (in consultation with Rogers) during the successful Camp David peace talks he facilitated between Anwar Sadat of Egypt and Menachem Begin of Israel. The three areas in which humanistic psychology has had the widest impact are business management, education, and personal growth. In each, humanistic innovations derive from the basic point that the fully functioning person is one whose striving for self-actualization is unblocked.

Within management, humanistic psychology was an early contributor to the emerging field of organizational development. Rogers's person-centered approach was a key influence on the development of the human relations training for business managers conducted by the National Training Laboratory. In *Eupsychian Management: A Journal* (1965), Maslow provided a humanistic theory of management. He proposed that employees could be most productive if, through more democratic boss-worker relationships, they were given the opportunity to grow in terms of self-actualization and reach their highest human potential. (This book was translated into Japanese and was influential in the development of the managerial style that became characteristic of Japanese business.) Maslow's motivation hierarchy also was the basis for Douglas McGregor's well-known contrast between "theory X" (a traditional authoritarian managerial approach) and "theory Y" (a humanistic one proposing a more participative managerial style).

As humanistic psychology became more prevalent, it also had an impact on the adjoining field of education. Both Rogers and Maslow were severe critics of the prevailing system of education, in which learning had been reduced to the acquisition of skills, as if it were merely technical training. Disgusted by the extrinsic focus of education, they promoted the view that educators needed to foster students' intrinsic or natural sense of wonder, creativity, capacity for self-understanding, and growth toward their own self-actualization. Rogers's *Freedom to Learn: A View of What Education Might Become* (1969) became an influential summary of those views.

Beyond the professional fields of business and education, humanistic psychology affected the larger society most directly through spawning the human potential movement. In many "growth centers," the Esalen Institute in California being the most prominent, a wide assortment of services are offered. They include such techniques as sensitivity training, encounter groups, sensory awareness, and meditation. The length of time involved varies but is usually short, such as a weekend or a week. The aim is not treatment for psychologically disturbed persons but rather the facilitation of personal growth.

ROOTS AND EVOLUTION

Humanistic psychology's roots include European psychology and philosophy. Among its psychological predecessors are Kurt Goldstein's organismic theory, Karen Horney's self theory, and Erich Fromm's social analyses. Its philosophical heritage includes existentialism and phenomenology. Fearing the eclipse of the human in a world dominated by science, existentialism began with the recognition that "it is important . . . to hold fast to what it means to be a human being," as originally stated by Søren Kierkegaard in 1846. Beginning in the early twentieth century, Edmund Husserl, phenomenology's founder, articulated the key notion of the intentionality of consciousness. Husserl also fashioned a distinction between the natural sciences and the human sciences, made earlier by Wilhelm Dilthey, into a powerful critique of psychology's traditional scientific foundations. Later philosophers, particularly Martin Heidegger, Jean-Paul Sartre, and Maurice Merleau-Ponty, joined existentialism and phenomenology into a compelling philosophy of existence.

Existential phenomenology first affected the work of European psychologists, especially R. D. Laing, Jan Hendrik van den Berg, Viktor Frankl, Erwin Straus, Ludwig Binswanger, and Medard Boss. In the United States, May was influential in importing these European currents through his edited book of translated readings, *Existence: A New Dimension in Psychiatry and Psychology* (1958). In 1959, Duquesne University established a pioneering graduate program devoted to existential phenomenological psychology. In the 1960s, graduate programs in humanistic psychology were established at Sonoma State University and Saybrook Institute in California and at West Georgia College.

Much of the movement's early organizational work was done by Maslow, who, with Tony Sutich, launched the *Journal of Humanistic Psychology* in 1961. In 1963, Maslow, Sutich, and Bugental inaugurated the Association for Humanistic Psychology. Within psychology's main organization, the American Psychological Association, the Division of Humanistic Psychology was established in 1971 in response to a petition by its members. It began a journal, *The Humanistic Psychologist*.

EMERGENCE OF COGNITIVE PSYCHOLOGY

With the rapid pace of such developments, by the end of the 1960s humanistic psychologists saw themselves as a "third force": an alternative to behaviorism and psychoanalysis, the two dominant traditions in American psychology at that time. A naive optimism characterized their sense of the future; humanistic psychology has not succeeded in supplanting those traditions. What happened instead was the rise of cognitive psychology as the main challenger for dominance. Like humanistic psychology, the cognitive approach was formed during the 1950s to dispute traditional psychology's narrow focus on behavior as an objective, observable event, but it offered a more conventional alternative. While returning to the mind as a topic of psychology, it did so while retaining the traditional mechanistic view of mental life. In comparison, humanistic psychology's more fundamental proposal that psychology set aside its mechanistic assumptions altogether continues to cast it in the role of a less palatable alternative for most psychologists.

In other ways, however, the humanistic approach has been a victim of its own successes beyond psychology. Its applications to psychotherapy, management, and education are now so commonly known that they are scarcely recognized anymore as "humanistic." It appears that, for now at least, humanistic psychology has found greater integration beyond psychology than within it.

BIBLIOGRAPHY

Bugental, James F. T. *Intimate Journeys: Stories from Life-Changing Therapy.* San Francisco: Jossey, 1990. Print.

Grogan, Jessica. *Encountering America: Humanistic Psychology, Sixties Culture and the Shaping of the Modern Self.* New York: Harper, 2013. Print.

Hutchinson, Elizabeth D., ed. *Essentials of Human Behavior: Integrating Person, Environment, and the Life Course.* Thousand Oaks: Sage, 2012. Print.

Maslow, Abraham H. *Toward a Psychology of Being.* 3rd ed. New York: Wiley, 1999. Print.

May, Rollo. *Psychology and the Human Dilemma.* Princeton: Van Nostrand, 1967. Print.

Pfaffenberger, Angela H., Paul W. Marko, and Allan Combs, eds. *The Postconventional Personality: Assessing, Researching, and Theorizing Higher Development.* Albany: State U of New York P, 2011. Print.

Pollio, Howard R. *Behavior and Existence: An Introduction to Empirical Humanistic Psychology.* Monterey: Brooks, 1982. Print.

Rogers, Carl R. *On Becoming a Person: A Therapist's View of Psychotherapy.* Introd. Peter D. Kramer. New York: Houghton, 1995. Print.

Rowan, John, ed. *Ordinary Ecstasy: The Dialectics of Humanistic Psychology.* 3rd ed. Philadelphia: Taylor, 2001. Print.

Schneider, Kirk J., J. Fraser Pierson, and James F. T. Bugental, eds. *The Handbook of Humanistic Psychology: Theory, Research, and Practice.* 2nd ed. Thousand Oaks: Sage, 2015. Print.

Valle, Ronald S., and Steen Halling, eds. *Existential-Phenomenological Perspectives in Psychology: Exploring the Breadth of Human Experience.* New York: Plenum, 1989. Print.

Christopher M. Aanstoos

SEE ALSO: Abnormality: Psychological models; Allport, Gordon; Developmental psychology; Existential psychology; Gestalt therapy; Humanistic trait models: Gordon Allport; Maslow, Abraham; May, Rollo; Motivation; Motivation: Intrinsic and extrinsic; Murray, Henry A.; Person-centered therapy; Personology: Henry A. Murray; Play therapy; Rogers, Carl R.; Self-actualization; Self-efficacy; Workplace issues and mental health.

Humanistic trait models
Gordon Allport

TYPE OF PSYCHOLOGY: Personality

The humanistic trait model of Gordon Allport explains how a person's unique personal characteristics provide a pattern and direction to personality. It reveals the limitations of psychological theories that focus only on general rules of human behavior and provides insight into how to conduct in-depth study of individual dispositions.

KEY CONCEPTS
- Cardinal disposition
- Central dispositions
- Common traits
- Functional autonomy
- Idiographic or morphogenic study
- Nomothetic study
- Personal dispositions
- Proprium
- Secondary dispositions

INTRODUCTION
The humanistic trait model of Gordon Allport was based on his profound belief in the uniqueness of every personality, as well as his conviction that individuality is displayed through dominant personal characteristics that provide continuity and direction to a person's life. He saw personality as dynamic, growing, changing, and based on one's personal perception of the world. Like other humanists, Allport believed that people are essentially proactive, or forward moving; they are motivated by the future and seek tension and change rather than sameness. In addition, each individual possesses a set of personal dispositions that defines the person and provides a pattern to behavior.

Allport's approach is different from those of other trait theorists, who have typically sought to categorize personalities according to a basic set of universal, essential characteristics. Allport referred to such characteristics as common traits. Instead of focusing on common traits that allow for comparisons among many people, Allport believed that each person is defined by a different set of characteristics. Based on his research, he estimated that there are four thousand to five thousand traits and eighteen thousand trait names.

FUNCTIONAL AUTONOMY AND PERSONAL DISPOSITIONS
Most personality theorists view adulthood as an extension of the basic motives present in childhood. Consistent with his belief that personality is always evolving, Allport believed that the motivations of adulthood are often independent of the motivations of childhood, and he referred to this concept as functional autonomy.

For example, a person who plays a musical instrument during childhood years because of parental pressure may play the same instrument for relaxation or enjoyment as an adult. Although not all motives are functionally autonomous, many adult activities represent a break from childhood and are based on varied and self-sustaining motives.

According to this perspective, personality is based on concrete human motives that are represented by personal traits or dispositions. Human traits are seen as guiding human behavior, but they must also account for wide variability within a person's conduct from situation to situation. As a result, Allport distinguished between different types and levels of traits or dispositions. Common traits represent those elements of personality that are useful for comparing most people within a specific culture, but they cannot provide a complete profile of any individual person. In contrast, personal dispositions represent the true personality, are unique to the person, and represent subtle differences among persons.

Three kinds of personal dispositions exist: cardinal dispositions, central dispositions, and secondary dispositions. When a person's life is dominated by a single, fundamental, outstanding characteristic, the quality is referred to as a cardinal disposition. For example, Adolf Hitler's cruelty and Mahatma Gandhi's pacifism are examples of cardinal dispositions. Central dispositions represent the five to ten important qualities of a person that would typically be discussed and described in a thorough letter of recommendation. Finally, secondary dispositions are characteristics that are more numerous, less consistently displayed, and less important than central dispositions.

THREE ASPECTS OF THE PROPRIUM

Allport referred to the unifying core of personality, or those aspects of the self that a person considers central to self-identity, as the proprium. During the first three to four years of life, three aspects of the proprium emerge. The sense of a bodily self involves awareness of body sensations. Self-identity represents the child's knowledge of an inner sameness or continuity over time, and self-esteem reflects personal efforts to maintain pride and avoid embarrassment. Self-extension emerges between the fourth and sixth year of life; this refers to the child's concept of that which is "mine," and it forms the foundation for later self-extensions such as career and love of country. The self-image, which also emerges between ages four and six, represents an awareness of personal goals and abilities, as well as the "good" and "bad" parts of the self. The ability to see the self as a rational, coping being emerges between ages six and twelve and represents the ability to place one's inner needs within the context of outer reality. Propriate striving often begins in adolescence and focuses on the person's ability to form long-term goals and purposes. Finally, the self as

knower represents the subjective self and one's ability to reflect on aspects of the proprium.

IDIOGRAPHIC RESEARCH

From this humanistic trait framework, human personality can only be fully understood through the examination of personal characteristics within a single individual. The emphasis on individuality has significant implications for the measurement of personality and for research methods in psychology. Most psychological research deals with standardized measurements and large numbers of people, and it attempts to make generalizations about characteristics that people hold in common. Allport referred to this approach as nomothetic. He contrasted the study of groups and general laws with idiographic research, or approaches for studying the single person. Idiographic research, which is sometimes referred to as morphogenic research, includes methods such as autobiographies, interviews, dreams, and verbatim recordings.

One of Allport's famous studies of the individual appears in *Letters from Jenny* (1965), a description of an older woman's personality that is based on the analysis of approximately three hundred letters that she wrote to her son and his wife. Through the use of personal structure analysis, statistical analysis, and the reactions of various trained judges, Allport and his colleagues identified eight clusters of characteristics, including the following: artistic, self-centered, aggressive, and sentimental. Through revealing the central dispositions of a single individual, this study provided increased insight about all people. It also demonstrated that objective, scientific practices can be applied to the study of one person at a time.

PERSONAL ORIENTATIONS

Allport preferred personality measures designed to examine the pattern of characteristics that are important to a person and that allow for comparison of the strengths of specific characteristics within the person rather than with other persons. The *Study of Values* (3d ed., 1960), which was developed by Allport, Philip Vernon, and Gardner Lindzey, measures a person's preference for the six value systems of theoretical, economic, social, political, aesthetic, and religious orientations. After rank ordering forty-five items, the individual receives feedback about the relative importance of the six orientations within himself or herself. Consistent with the emphasis on uniqueness, the scale does not facilitate comparisons between people. Although the language of this scale is somewhat outdated, it is still used for value clarification and the exploration of career and lifestyle goals.

Allport's research also focused on attitudes that are influenced by group participation, such as religious values and prejudice. Through the study of churchgoers' attitudes, he distinguished between extrinsic religion, or a conventional, self-serving approach, and intrinsic religion, which is based on internalized beliefs and efforts to act on religious beliefs. Allport and his colleagues found that extrinsic churchgoers were more prejudiced than intrinsic religious churchgoers; however, churchgoers who strongly endorsed both extrinsic and intrinsic religion were even more prejudiced than either extrinsic or intrinsic religious church attenders. Allport also examined cultural, family, historical, and situational factors that influence prejudice.

AMALGAMATION OF APPROACHES

Allport provided theoretical and research alternatives at a time when a variety of competing approaches, including humanistic, psychoanalytic, and behavioral perspectives, were seeking preeminence in psychology. Allport found many existing theories to be limiting, overly narrow, and inadequate for describing the wide variations in human personality. As a result, he proposed an eclectic approach to theory that combined the strengths of various other perspectives. Instead of emphasizing a single approach, Allport thought that personality can be both growth-oriented and proactive, as well as reactive and based on instinctual processes. Through an eclectic approach, he hoped that the understanding of personality would become more complete.

Allport was also concerned that many of the existing theories of his time, especially psychoanalytic theories, virtually ignored the healthy personality. In contrast to Sigmund Freud, Allport strongly emphasized conscious aspects of personality and believed that healthy adults are generally aware of their motivations. Unlike Freud's notion that people are motivated to reduce the tension of instinctual drives, he believed that people seek the kind of tension that allows them to grow, develop goals, and act in innovative ways.

TRAIT APPROACHES

Like humanistic theorists Carl R. Rogers and Abraham Maslow, Allport identified vital characteristics of mature persons. His list of the characteristics of mature persons overlaps substantially with Maslow's enumeration of the qualities of self-actualizing persons and Rogers's

definition of the "person of tomorrow." Allport's list includes extension of the sense of self (identifying with events and persons outside oneself), emotional security, realistic perception, insight and humor, and a unifying philosophy of life.

Allport developed his theory at a time when other trait approaches that were based on nomothetic study were gaining prominence. Whereas Allport emphasized individual uniqueness, Raymond B. Cattell identified twenty-three source traits, or building blocks of personality, and Hans Eysenck identified three primary dimensions of extroversion, neuroticism, and psychoticism. Within the nomothetic tradition, later researchers have reexamined earlier nomothetic trait theories and have identified five primary common dimensions of personality: surgency (active/dominant persons versus passive/submissive persons), agreeableness (one's warmth or coldness), conscientiousness (one's level of responsibility or undependability), emotional stability(unpredictability versus stability), and culture (one's intellectual understanding of the world). Allport would have found these efforts to identify basic dimensions of personality to have limited usefulness for defining and understanding individual personality styles.

Criticisms of trait approaches that emphasize universal characteristics of people indicate that these approaches underestimate the role of situations and human variability and change across different contexts. Furthermore, those approaches that focus on general traits provide summaries and demonstrate trends about behavior but do not provide explanations for behavior.

The awareness that general trait approaches are inadequate for predicting behavior across situations has led to a resurgence of interest in the types of idiographic research methods proposed by Allport. Approaches to personality have increasingly acknowledged the complexity of human beings and the reality that individuals are influenced by a wide array of features that are often contradictory and inconsistent. Allport's emphasis on the scientific study of unique aspects of personality provided both the inspiration and a general method for examining the singular, diverse variables that define human beings.

BIBLIOGRAPHY

Allport, Gordon W. "An Autobiography." *A History of Psychology in Autobiography*, ed. Edwin Garrigues Boring and Gardner Lindzey. Vol. 5. New York: Appleton-Century-Crofts, 1967. Print.

Allport, Gordon W. *Becoming: Basic Considerations for a Psychology of Personality*. New Haven: Yale UP, 1983. Print.

Allport, Gordon W. *The Nature of Prejudice*. Cambridge: Perseus, 2003. Print.

Allport, Gordon W. *Pattern and Growth in Personality*. New York: Holt, 1970. Print.

Allport, Gordon W. *Personality and Social Encounter*. Chicago: U of Chicago P, 1981. Print.

Allport, Gordon W., Philip E. Vernon, and Gardner Lindzey. *Study of Values*. 3d ed. Boston: Houghton Mifflin, 1977. Print.

Berecz, John M. *Theories of Personality: A Zonal Perspective*. Boston: Pearson, 2009. Print.

Evans, Richard I. *Gordon Allport: The Man and His Ideas*. New York: Praeger, 1981. Print.

Maddi, Salvatore, and Paul Costa. *Humanism in Personology: Allport, Maslow, and Murray*. New Brunswick: AldineTransaction, 2008. Print.

Masterson, Jenny (Gove) [pseud.]. *Letters from Jenny*. 1965. Reprint. Ed. Gordon W. Allport. San Diego: Harcourt Brace, 1993. Print.

Nicholson, Ian A. M. *Inventing Personality: Gordon Allport and the Science of Selfhood*. Washington, DC: American Psychological Assn., 2003. Print.

Peterson, Christopher. *Personality*. 2d ed. San Diego: International Thomson, 1992. Print.

Carolyn Zerbe Enns

SEE ALSO: Allport, Gordon; Existential psychology; Freudian psychology; Gestalt therapy; Hierarchy of needs; Humanistic psychology; Maslow, Abraham; Personality interviewing strategies; Psychoanalytic psychology and personality: Sigmund Freud; Religion and psychology; Self-actualization.

Hunger

TYPE OF PSYCHOLOGY: Motivation

The psychological bases of hunger play an important role in the external and internal mediating forces that can affect and modify the physiological aspects of hunger..

KEY CONCEPTS
- Appetite
- Bingeing
- Deprivation
- Eating disorders
- External cues
- Homeostasis
- Hypothalamus
- Primary motives
- Satiety
- Set point

INTRODUCTION

Primary motives, or drives, are generated by innate biological needs that must be met for survival. These motives include hunger, thirst, and sleep. Hunger has been studied extensively, yet there is still uncertainty as to exactly how this drive works. A large body of research about the physiological analysis of hunger has led to the identification of important differences between physical hunger and psychological hunger.

Physical hunger theories assume that the body's physiological mechanisms and systems produce hunger as a need and that when this need is satisfied, the hunger drive is, for the time being, reduced. Psychologists have developed models and theories of hunger by analyzing its boundaries and restraint or regulation. The early findings on hunger-regulation mechanisms emphasized the biological state of the individual and his or her control over the hunger drive. If a person experiences hunger, consumption of food will continue until it is terminated by internal cues. This is referred to as regulation.

The individual learns to avoid hunger by reacting to the internal cues of satiety or fullness. The satiety boundary is characterized by feelings of fullness ranging from satisfaction to uncomfortable bloating. The normal eater learns to avoid transgressing far or often into the latter zone. Beyond the reaction to internal cues is a zone of indifference, in which the body is not subject to biological cues. Instead, hunger is influenced by social, cognitive, and psychological cues. These cues may be external or internalized and do not rely on satiety cues for restraint.

Eating past the point of satiety is referred to as counterregulation or, more commonly, as binge eating or compulsive eating. Because the inhibitors of hunger restraint are not physiological in this zone, the restraint and dietary boundaries are cognitively determined. The physical hunger mechanisms may send signals, but quite ordinary ideas such as "being hungry" and "not being hungry" must be interpreted or received by the individual. The person must learn to distinguish between bodily sensations that indicate the need for food and the feelings that accompany this need, such as anxiety, boredom, loneliness, or depression.

Thus, there are both internal cues and external cues that define hunger and lead an individual to know when and how much to eat. External cues as a motive for eating have been studied extensively, particularly in research on obesity and eating disorders such as binge behavior and compulsive overeating. External cues include enticing smells, locations such as restaurants or other kinds of social settings, and the social environment—what other people are doing. When external cues prevail, a person does not have to be hungry to feel hungry.

CHILDREN'S HUNGER

The awareness of hunger begins very early in life. Those infants who are fed on demand, whose cries of hunger determine the times at which they are fed, are taught soon after they can feed themselves that their eating must conform to family rules about when, what, and how much to eat to satisfy their hunger. Infants fed on a schedule learn even earlier to conform to external constraints and regulations regarding hunger. Throughout life, responding to hunger by feeding oneself is nourishing both physiologically and psychologically. Beginning in infancy, the sequences of getting hungry and being fed establish the foundations of the relationship between the physiological need or drive and the psychological components of feelings such as affiliation, interaction, calm, and security when hunger is satisfied.

In preschool and early school years, when children are integrating themselves into their social world, food acceptance and cultural practices are learned. Prior to the peer group and school environment, the family and media are usually the main vehicles of cultural socialization of the hunger drive. According to social learning theory, these agents will play an important role in the child's learning to interpret his or her level of hunger and in subsequent eating patterns, both directly and indirectly. The modeling behavior of children is also related to hunger learning.

Experiences of hunger and satiety play a central role in a person's relationship to hunger awareness, eating, and food. Some dispositions that influence hunger and eating behavior are long term (fairly stable and enduring), while other habits and attitudes may fluctuate. There are numerous theories about the relation between the hunger drive and other factors, such as genetic inheritance and activity level.

HUNGER AND THE BRAIN

A strictly physiological analysis claims that an individual's responses to hunger are caused by the brain's regulation of body weight. If the body goes below its predetermined "set point," internal hunger cues are initiated to signal the need for food consumption. External restraints, such as attempts to live up to ideal cultural thinness standards, also affect behavior and may result in restrained eating to maintain a body weight below the body's defined set point.

The idea of a body set point is rooted in the work of physiologist Claude Bernard, a pioneer in research based on the concept of homeostasis, or system balance in the body. Homeostasis has played a fundamental role in many subsequent investigations regarding the physiology of hunger and the regulatory systems involved in hunger satisfaction. Inherent in the set point theory is the concept of motivation, meaning that an organism is driven physiologically and behaviorally toward maintenance of homeostasis and the body's set point and will adapt to accommodate the systems involved in maintenance.

In addition, there appear to be two anatomically and behaviorally distinct centers located in the hypothalamus, one regulating hunger and the other regulating satiety. The area of the hypothalamus responsible for stimulating eating behavior is the lateral hypothalamus. The ventromedial hypothalamus is the area responsible for signaling the organism to stop eating. The lateral hypothalamus is responsible for establishing a set point for body weight.

In comparing hunger and satiety sensation differences, increased hunger and disturbed satiety appear to be two different and quite separate mechanisms. Imbalance or dysfunction of either the hunger mechanism or the satiety sensation can lead to obesity, overeating, binge eating, and other eating disorders. It appears that the way hunger is experienced accounts in part for its recognition. Whether hunger is experienced in context with other drives or becomes a compulsive force that dominates all other drives in life is a complex issue. The prevalence of eating disorders and the multitude of variables associated with hunger drives and regulation have provided psychologists with an opportunity to examine the ways in which hunger might take on different meanings. To a person who is anorexic, for example, hunger may be a positive feeling—a state of being "high" and thus a goal to seek. To others, hunger may produce feelings of anxiety, insecurity, or anger. In this case, a person might eat before feeling hunger to prevent the feelings from arising. People's ability to experience hunger in different ways provides psychologists with two types of hunger, which are commonly referred to as hunger and appetite.

Hunger and appetite are not the same. Actual physical need is the basis of true hunger, while appetite can be triggered by thought, feeling, or sensation. Physical need can be separate from psychological need, although they may feel the same to a person who is not conscious of the difference. Compulsive eaters are often unable to recognize the difference between "real" hunger and psychological hunger, or appetite. Although psychological hunger can be equally as motivating a need as stomach hunger, appetite (or mouth hunger) is emotionally, cognitively, and psychologically based and thus cannot be fed in the same way. Stomach hunger can be satisfied by eating, whereas "feeding" mouth hunger must involve other activities and behaviors, since food does not ultimately seem to satisfy the mouth type of hunger.

THE CULTURAL CONTEXT OF HUNGER

One approach to increasing understanding of hunger and its psychological components is to examine hunger in its cultural context. In American culture, the experience of hunger is inextricably tied to weight, eating, body image, self-concept, social definitions of fatness and thinness, and other factors that take the issue of hunger far beyond the physiological facts. Historian Hillel Schwartz has traced the American cultural preoccupation with hunger, eating, and diet by examining the cultural fit between shared fictions about the body and their psychological, social, and cultural consequences. Hunger becomes a broader social issue when viewed in the context of the culture's history of obsession with diet, weight control, and body image. The personal experience of hunger is affected by the social and historical context.

Eating disorders such as anorexia, bulimia, and compulsive overeating provide evidence of the complex relationship between the physiological and psychological components of hunger. Obesity has also been examined using medical and psychological models. The etiology of hunger's relationship to eating disorders has provided insight, if not consensus, by investigating the roles of hereditary factors, social learning, family systems, and multigenerational transmission in hunger as well as the socially learned eating patterns, food preferences, and cultural ideals that can mediate the hunger drive. Body image, eating restraint, and eating attitudes have been assessed by various methods. The focus of much of the research on hunger beyond the early animal experiments

has been on eating disorders. The findings confirm that hunger is more than a physiological need and is affected by a multitude of variables.

HUNGER REGULATION

The desire to regulate hunger has resulted in a wide variety of approaches and techniques, including professional diet centers, programs, and clinics; self-help books and magazines; diet clubs and support groups; self-help classes; and "diet doctors." Many people have benefited from psychotherapy in an effort to understand and control their hunger-regulation mechanisms. Group therapy is one of the most successful forms of psychotherapy for food abusers. Types of group therapy vary greatly and include leaderless support groups, nonprofessional self-help groups such as Overeaters Anonymous, and groups led by professional therapists.

Advantages of group support for hunger regulation include the realization that one is not alone. An often-heard expression in group therapy is "I always thought I was the only person who ever felt this way." Other advantages include group support for risk taking, feedback from different perspectives, and a group laboratory for experimenting with new social behaviors. Witnessing others struggling to resolve life issues can provide powerful motivation to change. Self-help and therapy groups also offer friendship and acceptance. Creative-arts therapies are other forms of psychotherapy used by persons seeking to understand and control their hunger-regulation mechanisms. Creative therapy may involve art, music, dance, poetry, dreams, and other creative processes. These are experiential activities, and the process is sometimes nonverbal.

A more common experience for those who have faced the issue of hunger regulation is dieting. Despite the high failure rate of diets and weight-loss programs, the "diet mentality" is often associated with hunger regulation. Robert Schwartz studied the elements of the diet mentality, which is based on the assumption that being fat is bad and being thin is good. Dieting often sets up a vicious cycle of failure, which deflates self-esteem, thus contributing to shame and guilt and to another diet. The diet mentality is self-defeating. Another key element to the diet mentality is the mechanism of self-deprivation that comes from not being allowed to indulge in certain foods and the accompanying social restrictions and isolation that dieting creates. Dieting treats the symptom rather than the cause of overeating.

Numerous approaches to hunger regulation share a condemnation of the diet mentality. Overcoming overeating; understanding, controlling, and recovering from addictive eating; and being "thin-within" are approaches based on addressing hunger regulation from a psychological perspective rather than a physiological one. These approaches share an emphasis on the emotional and feeling components of hunger regulation. They encourage the development of skills to differentiate between stomach hunger and mind hunger—that is, between hunger and appetite—and thereby to learn to recognize satiety as well as the reasons for hunger.

Behavior modification consists of a variety of techniques that attempt to apply the findings and methods of experimental psychology to human behavior. Interest in applying behavioral modification to hunger regulation developed as a result of the research on external cues and environmental factors that control the food intake of individuals. By emphasizing specific training in " stimulus control," behavior modification helps the individual to manage the environmental determinants of eating.

The first step in most behavior modification programs is to help the patient identify and monitor activities that are contributing to the specific behavior. In the case of an individual who overeats, this could involve identifying such behaviors as frequent eating of sweets, late-evening snacking, eating huge meals, or eating in response to social demands. Because most people have more than one stimulus for eating behavior, the individual then observes situational stimuli: those that arise from the environment in which eating usually takes place. Once the stimuli are identified, new behaviors can be substituted—in effect, behavior can be modified.

MODELS OF HUNGER

Early scientific interest in hunger research was dominated by medical models, which identified the physiological mechanisms and systems involved. One of the earliest attempts to understand the sensation of hunger was an experiment conducted in 1912, in which a subject swallowed a balloon and then inflated it in his stomach. His stomach contractions and subjective reports of hunger feelings could then be simultaneously recorded. When the recordings were compared to the voluntary key presses that the subject made each time he experienced the feeling of hunger, the researchers concluded that it was the stomach movements that caused the sensation of hunger. It was later found, however, that an empty stomach is relatively inactive and that the stomach con-

tractions experienced by the subject were an experimental artifact caused by the mere presence of the balloon in the stomach. Further evidence for the lack of connection between stomach stimuli and feelings of hunger was provided in animal experiments that resulted in differentiating the two areas of the hypothalamus responsible for stimulating eating behavior and signaling satiety—the "start eating" and "stop eating" centers.

Psychologist Stanley Schachter and his colleagues began to explore the psychological issues involved in hunger by emphasizing the external, nonphysiological factors involved. In a series of experiments in which normal-weight and overweight individuals were provided with a variety of external eating cues, Schachter found that overweight subjects were more attentive to the passage of time in determining when to eat and were more excited by the taste and sight of food than were normal-weight persons. More recently, the growth of the field of social psychology has provided yet another perspective on hunger, one that accounts for the situational and environment factors that influence the physiological and psychological states. For example, psychologists have examined extreme hunger and deprivation in case studies from historical episodes such as war, concentration camps, and famine in the light of the more recent interest in the identification and treatment of eating disorders.

There does not appear to be a consistent or ongoing effort to develop an interdisciplinary approach to the study of hunger. Because hunger is such a complex drive, isolating the factors associated with it poses a challenge to the standard research methodologies of psychology, such as the case study, experiment, observation, and survey. Each methodology has its shortcomings, but together the methodologies have produced findings that clearly demonstrate that hunger is a physiological drive embedded in a psychological, social, and cultural context.

Viewing hunger as a multidimensional behavior has led to an awareness of hunger and its implications in a broader context. Changing dysfunctional attitudes, feelings, thoughts, and behaviors concerning hunger has not always been seen as a choice. Through continued psychological research into the topic of hunger—and increasing individual and group participation in efforts to understand, control, and change behaviors associated with hunger—new insights continue to emerge that will no doubt cast new light on this important and not yet completely understood topic.

BIBLIOGRAPHY

Arenson, Gloria. *A Substance Called Food: How to Understand, Control and Recover from Addictive Eating.* 2nd ed. Blue Ridge Summit: TAB, 1989. Print.

Battegay, Raymond. *The Hunger Diseases.* Northvale: Aronson, 1997. Print.

Gould, Roger. *Shrink Yourself: Break Free from Emotional Eating Forever.* Hoboken: Wiley, 2007. Print.

Hirschmann, Jane R., and Carol H. Munter. *When Women Stop Hating Their Bodies: Freeing Yourself from Food and Weight Obsessions.* New York: Fawcett, 1995. Print.

Kristeller, Jean L., and Elissa Epel. "Mindful Eating and Mindless Eating: The Science and the Practice." *The Wiley Blackwell Handbook of Mindfulness.* Ed. Amanda Ie, Christelle T. Ngoumen, and Ellen J. Langer. Vol. 2. Malden: Wiley, 2014. 913–33. Print.

Nisbett, Richard E. "Hunger, Obesity, and the Ventromedial Hypothalamus." *Psychological Review* 79.6 (1972): 433–53. Print.

Schachter, Stanley, and Larry P. Gross. "Manipulated Time and Eating Behavior." *Journal of Personality and Social Psychology* 10.2 (1968): 98–106. Print.

Schwartz, Bob. *Diets Don't Work.* 3rd rev. ed. Houston: Breakthru, 1996. Print.

Schwartz, Hillel. *Never Satisfied: A Cultural History of Diets, Fantasies, and Fat.* New York: Anchor, 1990. Print.

Stewart, Charles T. *New Ideas about Eating Disorders: Human Emotions and the Hunger Drive.* New York: Routledge, 2012. Print.

Tribole, Evelyn, and Elyse Resch. *Intuitive Eating: A Revolutionary Program That Works.* 3rd ed. New York: St. Martin's, 2012. Print.

Young, John K. *Hunger, Thirst, Sex, & Sleep: How the Brain Controls Our Passions.* Lanham: Rowman, 2012. Print.

Robin Franck

SEE ALSO: Addictive personality and behaviors; Anorexia nervosa and bulimia nervosa; Drives; Eating disorders; Obesity; Self-help groups; Thirst.

Hypnosis

TYPE OF PSYCHOLOGY: Consciousness

Hypnosis is a trancelike altered state of consciousness in which the hypnotizable subject is typically more responsive to suggestions than is a waking subject. Hypnosis research has provided psychology with a number of useful theoretical insights into human cognition, as well as practical benefits in controlling pain and treating behavior disorders such as obesity, smoking, and sexual dysfunction.

KEY CONCEPTS
- Hypnotic analgesia
- Hypnotic anesthesia
- Hypnotic dissociation
- Hypnotic hypermnesia
- Hypnotic susceptibility
- Somnambulism

INTRODUCTION

Hypnosis derives its name from the Greek hypnos, which translates into English as "sleep." Hypnosis was so named by the Scottish physician James Braid, who noted the sleeplike features of the somnambulistic trance. Though hypnosis may appear to be a sleeplike state, several differences exist between hypnosis and sleep. First, hypnotic subjects will respond to suggestions from the hypnotist. Second, hypnotizable subjects exhibit a phenomenon known as waking hypnosis, in which they will open their eyes and behave as if awake yet continue to be under hypnosis. Last, brain-wave recordings in hypnosis reveal primarily an alpha pattern characteristic of a relaxed state, while those in sleep reveal theta and delta activity.

THEORETICAL PERSPECTIVES

If hypnosis is not a sleeplike state, how can it be characterized? Because two major theoretical views exist on hypnosis, the answer to that question is quite complex. From one perspective, hypnosis is an altered state of consciousness involving a trance state that is usually accompanied by heightened suggestibility. The primary feature of the hypnotic trance is the loss or suspension of a normal reality-testing orientation. Subjects become so absorbed in the hypnotist's words that they subjectively create the reality of those suggestions and limit their awareness of the environment to a very narrow range of external stimuli. Other qualitative dimensions of the hypnotic trance include a loss of volition, a sense of unreality, a diminished sense of identity, and physical relaxation.

A view of hypnosis as a trance state or an altered state of consciousness is represented by the neodissociation theory, which was developed by Ernest Hilgard in 1973. He was conducting studies on the anesthetic properties of hypnosis. Hilgard produced cold pressor pain in his subjects by placing one of their arms into a circulating pool of ice water, which resulted in reports of intolerable pain in approximately one minute. In contrast, when hypnotic subjects were given suggestions for limb anesthesia, they reported low levels of pain or the complete absence of pain. Yet if subjects were told to write down their experience, they reported the presence of pain. These results suggested a discrepancy between the subjects' oral and written reports of pain. Hilgard dubbed this phenomenon the "hidden observer" effect, because it was as though a hidden observer, who saw and felt everything, were present in the brain. According to Hilgard, the hidden observer effect suggests that the perceiver experiences pain at two levels. One level is experienced in immediate awareness and is subject to the effects of hypnotic analgesia (the use of hypnotic procedures to reduce or eliminate present pain) and anesthesia (the use of hypnotic procedures for preventing the occurrence of future pain). Subjects report a diminution in pain when this level of awareness is blocked by suggestions for pain relief. The second level of pain is dissociated from immediate awareness and maintains constant vigilance to detect the presence of pain. It is at the second level that the hidden observer operates in the brain. Because Hilgard's theory implies cognitive control of a stimulus event, it suggests that a trance or altered state of consciousness is operating during hypnosis.

The second major theoretical perspective emphasizes the importance of the social context in which hypnosis occurs, and it has been referred to as the social psychological theory. From this viewpoint, hypnotized subjects are not in a trance or an altered state of consciousness. Rather, they meet the implicit and explicit demand characteristics of hypnosis by enacting the role of a hypnotic subject. In other words, subjects simulate hypnotic behavior in response to their own preconceived notions and motivations, as well as those expectations conveyed by the hypnotist. T. R. Sarbin and W. C. Coe, in 1972, proposed several variables that influence hypnotic role enactment. They include the location of individual

participants in their proper roles, perceived congruence between self and role, accuracy of role expectations, possession of role-relevant skills, and the influence of the audience. If these factors are positive for the subject, hypnotic role enactment may be convincingly demonstrated to the audience and the subject.

Although both theories may explain hypnotic behavior, it is clear that not all subjects are simulating hypnosis to enact the role of a hypnotized subject. Measurements of hypnotic responsiveness indicate that hypnosis significantly increases suggestibility beyond that found in a waking state. If subjects were merely simulating hypnosis, hypnotic suggestibility would not exceed waking suggestibility. Clearly, hypnosis involves more than motivation to enact the role of a hypnotized subject.

HYPNOTIC RESPONSIVENESS AND SUSCEPTIBILITY

Measurements of hypnotic responsiveness are typically undertaken with two scales: the Harvard Group Scale of Hypnotic Susceptibility, Form A (HGSHS:A), and the Stanford Hypnotic Susceptibility Scale, Form C (SHSS:C). The HGSHS:A is used primarily as a screening device for large groups. Most of its suggestions are motor in nature, although some cognitive ones are included. The SHSS:C is usually administered to individuals and includes both cognitive and motor suggestions. Generally, the SHSS:C is considered to be a better measure of hypnotic susceptibility. Both scales include a sample of twelve total suggestions, with high hypnotizables defined as 9 to 12 on each scale, mediums as 4 to 8, and lows as 0 to 3.

Exactly what makes some people more hypnotizable than others is not entirely clear. Surprisingly, personality traits are not reliably correlated with hypnotic susceptibility. Instead, the following three cognitive variables seem to be more strongly related to hypnotic susceptibility: imaginative involvement, concentrated attention, and suspension of reality testing. In general, the higher a person scores on these three variables, the more hypnotizable that person tends to be. One thing is certain: There is no correlation between hypnotic susceptibility and strength of will. Although hypnosis reduces inhibitions and increases compliance to suggestions the subject considers to be acceptable, hypnotized subjects cannot be forced to perform acts that they would find morally reprehensible.

USE IN PAIN CONTROL

Among forms of altered consciousness, hypnosis may have the greatest practical utility. Hypnosis has been used to control pain, to treat behavior disorders, and to recover lost memories or enhance existing memories of eyewitnesses.

The use of hypnotic anesthesia has a long history, beginning with surgical amputation allegedly performed by the British physician W. S. Ward in 1842. Ward's report was strongly criticized at the time, but evidence suggests that it was legitimate. Another early report of hypnotic anesthesia use was provided by the nineteenth century Scottish physician James Esdaile, who was practicing in India at the time. Esdaile performed more than thirteen hundred operations on hypnotized subjects in the 1840's. Many of those surgeries involved the removal of scrotal tumors, which resulted in a recovery rate of only 50 percent for unanesthetized patients. With the use of hypnotic anesthesia, however, the mortality rate dropped to 5 percent. Esdaile's findings were also criticized by the British scientific community on the rather dubious and racist grounds that "native" assistants hypnotized the patients and that the patients actually liked to undergo operations.

The effectiveness of hypnotic anesthesia and analgesia has been examined in a number of wellcontrolled laboratory studies. Using cold pressor pain, Ernest and Josephine Hilgard demonstrated that hypnotic analgesia significantly reduces verbal reports of pain and increases pain tolerance levels as compared with a normal waking state. Reports of pain relief were correlated with hypnotic susceptibility levels; high hypnotizables tended to benefit more from hypnotic analgesia than did low hypnotizables.

Based on laboratory findings, three clinical procedures have been developed for using hypnosis to control pain. The first procedure involves giving the patient a direct suggestion that the painful body part is getting numb and can no longer feel any pain. If the patient requires a more concrete suggestion, the hypnotist may suggest that a local anesthetic is being injected into the shoulder. A second procedure is to alter the experience of pain by giving suggestions for its displacement to a less sensitive region of the body or by converting the pain into a less aversive experience. With diffuse pain, the patient may be told that the pain is diminishing in size to a small spot and being transferred to a less sensitive body region, where it can be converted into a tingling sensation. Finally, therapists use hypnotic anesthesia to

direct attention away from the pain and its source. For example, the patient may be told that the painful body part no longer exists. Alternatively, age regression to an earlier and happier experience may be employed, or the therapist may engage the patient in hypnotic fantasies. These two approaches presumably distract the patient's attention away from the pain.

BEHAVIOR DISORDERS TREATMENT

A second major field of application for hypnosis has been in the treatment of behavior disorders. Hypnotherapy has been used to treat a variety of behavior disorders, including smoking and obesity, both of which involve poor habit control. The use of hypnotherapy to alter bad habits may be successful because the strength of the habit is not in full force in an altered state of consciousness. In a normal waking state, the habit exerts its dominance over the patient's behavior and may be difficult to reshape or modify. In addition, the highly concentrated state of attention in hypnosis may allow patients to direct all of their resources to the task of altering the negative habit.

Hypnotherapy in the treatment of smoking and obesity seems to be more effective with several treatment sessions or with procedures for reinforcing the hypnotic suggestions on a daily basis. For example, in 1975, H. E. Stanton combined the following hypnotic procedures to treat overweight patients: direct suggestions to reduce food intake, ego-enhancing suggestions to improve self-esteem, self-hypnosis to reinforce the therapist's suggestions, and hypnosis audiotapes to provide additional support following the completion of formal treatment. The combined use of these hypnotic procedures resulted in marked weight loss among patients who completed the therapeutic process.

Although repeated hypnotherapy sessions appear to be most effective for treating behavior disorders, even one session may be useful. In 1970, Harold Spiegel used a competing-response hypnotic technique for the treatment of smoking. Subjects were told that cigarette smoke is a toxin to the body, that life is not possible without the body, and that life is possible only if one protects and treats the body well. The adverse effects of smoking were then placed in competition with the life process. The subjects could choose smoking, thereby threatening their lives, or they could choose to enhance life by abandoning the smoking habit. Although subjects were only exposed to one hypnotic session, 20 percent quit smoking. In 1970, using a total of five hypnotic sessions, Harold Crasilneck and James Hall reported a success rate of 75 percent. Many subjects do subsequently begin smoking again, but with a greater number of therapy sessions, the rate of recidivism declines.

Finally, hypnosis has been used to enhance recall of past events, which is termed hypnotic hypermnesia. A sensational example of hypnotic hypermnesia was reported in Chowchilla, California, in 1976. This incident involved the kidnaping of a group of children who were on a field trip. The bus, with all occupants aboard, was buried underground and kept there until a ransom was paid. The case was cracked by law-enforcement officials when the bus driver was able to recall under hypnosis the license plate of the car driven by the kidnappers. He was not able to do so in a normal waking state.

EVOLUTION OF PRACTICE

Franz Mesmer, an Austrian physician, is generally credited with the discovery of hypnosis. In his medical practice, Mesmer was sometimes confronted with patients who reported symptoms of physical illness but did not manifest any underlying physical pathology. To treat these seemingly incurable patients, Mesmer would pass magnets over the patients' bodies. In many cases, the patient would go into what Mesmer described as a "crisis," with trembling, twitching, intense pain at body regions associated with symptoms, and sometimes convulsions. After completion of the magnetic therapy, most patients would report a relief of symptoms. Eventually, Mesmer discovered that a cure could be wrought by simply passing his hands over the patient, usually accompanied by soft, soothing words.

One of Mesmer's students, Armand-Marie Jacques de Chastenet, the marquis de Puységur, disliked the rather violent and painful magnetic "crises" elicited in patients. While treating a young male patient, Puységur discovered that a peaceful, sleeplike state, resembling sleepwalking and talking in sleep, could be spontaneously induced. Because of its resemblance to these phenomena, he coined the term "artificial somnambulism" ("somnambulism" is now used as the scientific term for sleepwalking). Puységur later reproduced this trance state by suggesting it overtly.

It was left to the nineteenth century Scottish physician James Braid to incorporate artificial somnambulism into the mainstream of science. Braid made three i portant contributions. First, he scientifically demonstrated the existence of many somnambulistic phenomena and published his results. Second, Braid convinced the scientific establishment that the main effects of hypnosis

were a function of the subject's hypnotic susceptibility level and not attributable to the power of the magnetizer. Finally, Braid provided magnetic and somnambulistic phenomena with a new, more scientific sounding name. He coined the term "neuro-hypnology," which was shortened first to "hypnology" and later to the modern term "hypnosis."

In the twentieth century, Hilgard and his colleagues were instrumental in obtaining psychological recognition for hypnosis, especially as an altered state and as a method for controlling pain. Since the 1960's, hypnosis has been integrated into mainstream psychology, enjoying greater acceptance than ever before in areas such as cognitive and clinical psychology. The dissociative processes in hypnosis and the mechanisms by which hypnosis enhances cognitive functioning are especially important in cognitive psychology. In clinical psychology, hypnosis offers a host of practical applications for treating clients. Clinicians are also interested in the parallels between hypnotic dissociation (a hypnotic state in which thoughts, feelings, and perceptions are separated or dissociated from conscious awareness) and dissociative disorders, such as multiple personalities.

FUTURE RESEARCH

Future research will continue to examine the controversy that surrounds the fundamental nature of hypnosis—whether it induces a trance state or is simply role modeling, an instance of simulation. This controversy continues to fester, with no apparent end in sight to the heated debate. Additional research will also be needed to understand why some people are hypnotizable and others are not. Some cognitive and physiological correlates of hypnotizability have been discovered, but such correlations are only moderate in magnitude. Research into potential clinical applications of hypnosis will continue to be a central focus. Hypnotherapy is only in its infancy and will require much research to provide it with a solid scientific foundation. Finally, exploring the range of hypnotic effects on psychological and behavioral processes will continue to be a central concern among researchers. Only tightly controlled laboratory investigations will yield answers to questions such as what perceptual and cognitive processes are affected by hypnosis, how, and why.

BIBLIOGRAPHY

Hilgard, Ernest Ropiequet, and Josephine Rohrs Hilgard. *Hypnosis in the Relief of Pain.* Rev. ed. New York:

Brunner/Mazel, 1994. Provides a comprehensive review of the Hilgards' own research on hypnotic anesthesia and analgesia, as well as the research of others. Examines the physiological and psychological bases of pain and explores laboratory and clinical methods of controlling pain with hypnosis. Highly recommended for college students and advanced high school students.

Kirsch, Irving, Antonio Capafons, Etzel Cardena, and Salvador Amigo, eds. *Clinical Hypnosis and Self-Regulation: Cognitive-Behavioral Perspectives.* Washington, D.C.: American Psychological Association, 1999. A collection of papers, written for professionals. Argues that hypnosis is underused in clinical settings and attempts to show its benefits.

Pintar, Judith, and Steven Lynn. *Hypnosis: A Brief History.* Malden, Mass.: Wiley-Blackwell, 2008. Offers in-depth explanation of how hypnosis can be used to treat pain and anxiety; also describes how hypnosis can be dangerous in the hands of incompetent therapists.

Sheehan, Peter W., and Kevin M. McConkey. *Hypnosis and Experience: The Exploration of Phenomena and Process.* New York: Brunner/Mazel, 1996. An advanced treatise on hypnosis, focusing on the experiential analysis of hypnotic phenomena, such as ideomotor responses, age regression, hypnotic dreams and hallucinations, and posthypnotic amnesia. Because of its technical nature, this resource is recommended only for serious, advanced students.

Wallace, Benjamin, and Leslie E. Fisher. *Consciousness and Behavior.* 3d ed. Prospect Heights, Ill.:Waveland Press, 2003. A general textbook on consciousness containing an excellent, updated chapter on hypnosis. The chapter reviews theories and the history of hypnosis, describes ways of assessing hypnotic susceptibility, reviews research on basic hypnotic phenomena, and discusses practical applications of hypnosis. Highly recommended for high school and college students as well as for interested adults.

Watkins, John G., and Arreed Barabasz. *Advanced Hypnotherapy: Hypnodynamic Techniques.* New York: Routledge, 2008. This resource looks at the history of hypnosis and presents the latest research and techniques in the field.

Yapko, Michael D. *Treating Depression with Hypnosis: Integrating Cognitive-Behavioral and Strategic Approaches.* New York: Brunner/Mazel, 2001. Practical guidance to alleviating depression with hypnosis, written by a practicing psychotherapist.

Richard P. Atkinson

SEE ALSO: Amnesia and fugue; Attention; Automaticity; Consciousness; Consciousness: Altered states; Dissociative disorders; Meditation and relaxation; Multiple personality; Observational learning and modeling therapy; Pain management; Nicotine dependence.

Hypochondriasis, conversion and somatization

TYPE OF PSYCHOLOGY: Psychopathology

Conversion, hypochondriasis, and somatization are a group of mental disorders that are typically referred to as the somatoform disorders. The primary feature of these disorders, as their name suggests, is that psychological conflicts take on a somatic, or physical, form..

KEY CONCEPTS
- Cathartic method
- Conversion disorder
- Hypochonriasis
- Somatization disorder
- Somatoform disorders
- Somatoform pain

INTRODUCTION
Somatic symptom and related disorders, previously known as somatoform disorders, occur when a psychological conflict is expressed through a somatic, or physical, complaint. The main disorders in this category are somatic symptom disorder, illness anxiety disorder, conversion disorder, factitious disorder, and psychological factors affecting other medical conditions.

CONVERSION DISORDER
When an individual suffers from conversion disorder, also known as functional neurological symptom disorder, the psychological conflict results in some type of disability. Symptoms vary widely; some of the most common involve blindness, deafness, paralysis, and anesthesia (loss of sensation). For a diagnosis of conversion disorder to be made, medical examinations must show that there is nothing wrong physiologically with the individual. The handicap stems from a psychological or emotional problem.

In many instances, the handicap is thought to develop because it gives the person an unconscious way of resolving a conflict. For example, an adult who is feeling powerful yet morally unacceptable feelings of anger and rage may wish to strike his or her young child. Rather than carry out this dreadful action, this person will suddenly develop a paralyzed arm. The unacceptable emotional impulse is then "converted" (thus the term "conversion") into a physical symptom. When this happens, individuals will sometimes seem strangely unconcerned about their new physical disabilities. They will have what is known as *la belle indifférence* (beautiful indifference). Although most people would be quite upset if they suddenly became blind or paralyzed, conversion patients will often be rather calm or nonchalant about their disability, because their symptom unconsciously protects them from their desire to act on an unacceptable impulse.

ILLNESS ANXIETY DISORDER

The situation is somewhat different for individuals with illness anxiety disorder (formerly known as hypochondriasis), since individuals with this disorder do not experience a dramatic physical disability. Rather, they are preoccupied with anxieties about having or acquiring a serious illness. For a diagnosis of illness anxiety disorder to be made, the individual must suffer from minimal or no somatic symptoms; otherwise a diagnosis of somatic symptom disorder is considered more appropriate.

An individual with illness anxiety disorder often misinterprets ordinary physical symptoms as a sign of some extremely serious illness. Mild indigestion may be interpreted as a heart attack; a mild headache may be interpreted as a brain tumor. People with this disorder are usually quite interested in medical information and will keep a wide array of medical specialists at their disposal. Even after physician visits reveal that the patient does not suffer from some dreaded disease, the individual persists in this preoccupation.

SOMATIC SYMPTOM DISORDER

While the hypochondriac is typically afraid of having one particular disease, the individual with somatic symptom disorder will often have numerous medical complaints with no apparent physical cause. Somatic symptom disorder is also sometimes known as Briquet syndrome, after the physician of that name who described it in detail in 1859. A person suffering from somatic symptom disorder is not bothered by the fear of disease but rather by the actual symptoms that he or she reports. This individual will generally describe numerous aches and pains in a vague and exaggerated manner. The American Psychiatric Association's *Diagnostic and Statistical Manual of Mental Disorders: DSM-IV-TR* (rev. 4th ed., 2000)

stated the patient must have a history of pain related to at least four different sites or functions as well as at least two gastrointestinal symptoms, at least one sexual or reproductive symptom, and at least one symptom or deficit suggesting a neurological condition. However, the DSM-5 (2013) revised this to require a minimum of one somatic symptom resulting in significant disruption to everyday life, lasting more than six months, and causing a level of anxiety disproportionate to the seriousness of the symptom.

Like the hypochondriac, the somatizer will often seek out frequent, unnecessary medical treatment. The somatizer, however, will be a particularly difficult patient for the physician to handle. The somatizer will often present the physician with a long, vague, and confusing list of complaints. At times, it may seem as if the somatizer is actually developing new symptoms while talking to the physician. The dramatic and disorganized manner in which these patients describe their problems and their tendency to switch from one doctor to the next with great frequency make somatizers some of the most frustrating patients that medical professionals are likely to encounter.

It will also be difficult for even the most capable of medical professionals to work effectively with an individual who is suffering from somatic pain. Pain disorder is a relatively new diagnostic category, in which the individual experiences physical pain for which psychological factors are judged to have an important role in the onset, severity, exacerbation, or maintenance. Somatic pain is similar to conversion disorder, except that the individual experiences only pain rather than other types of disability or anesthesia. Because pain is a subjective sensory experience rather than an observable symptom, it is often quite difficult for physicians to determine whether pain is caused by psychological or physical factors. It is therefore very hard to diagnose somatic pain with any certainty.

PSYCHOLOGICAL FACTORS AFFECTING OTHER MEDICAL CONDITIONS

Psychological factors can also affect many real medical conditions, making the symptoms more severe or slowing recovery. This phenomenon was added to the Somatic Disorders chapter of the DSM-V under the name of Psychological Factors Affecting Other Medical Conditions (PFAMC). A diagnosis of PFAMC is made when an individual has a non-mental medical condition, such as asthma, migraine, fibromyalgia, diabetes, or heart disease, which is significantly aggravated by feelings of stress, anxiety, denial, or similar factors. However, the main cause of the symptoms must be physical; otherwise one of the other somatic disorders PFAMC has not been studied as much as some of the other somatic disorders, and its prevalence rate is unknown, but it can occur at any stage of life.

FACTITIOUS DISORDER

Factitious disorder is a condition in which a person deliberately creates or exaggerates symptoms of mental or physical illness in him- or herself or in another person, usually a child or an elderly or disabled adult under his or her care. The latter, formerly known as factitious disorder by proxy, is called factitious disorder imposed on another in the DSM-5. Factitious disorder with primarily physical symptoms is popularly known as Münchausen syndrome, although this is not an official diagnosis category.

Factitious disorder ranges widely in severity; some individuals with the disorder simply lie about symptoms, some falsify records or alter diagnostic tests in order to make themselves or others seem sick, and some go so far as to intentionally induce infections or injure themselves or others.

Little is known about which treatments for factitious disorder are most effective, although psychotherapy is generally considered more useful than medication. The disorder is not common, but is estimated to affect about 1 percent of patients admitted to hospitals.

THE CASE OF ANNA O.

The somatic symptom disorders, like all psychiatric diagnoses, are worth studying only when they can contribute to an understanding of the experience of a troubled individual. In particular, the somatic disorders are useful when they help show that although an individual may genuinely feel sick, or believe he or she has some physical illness, this is not always the case. There are times when a psychological conflict can manifest itself in a somatic form.

A classic example of this situation is a famous case of conversion disorder that was reported by Josef Breuer and Sigmund Freud in 1895. This case involved "Anna O.," a well-educated and extremely intelligent young Viennese woman who had rapidly become bedridden with a number of mysterious physical symptoms. By the time that Anna O. sought the assistance of Breuer, a prominent Austrian physician, her medical condition was quite serious. Both Anna O.'s right arm and her right leg

were paralyzed, her sight and hearing were impaired, and she often had difficulty speaking. She also sometimes went into a rather dreamlike state, which she referred to as an "absence." During these periods of absence, Anna O. would mumble to herself and appear quite preoccupied with disturbing thoughts.

Anna O.'s symptoms were quite troubling to Breuer, since she did not appear to suffer from any particular physical ailment. To understand this young woman's condition, Breuer encouraged her to discuss her symptoms at length, and he used hypnosis to explore the history of her illness. Over time, Breuer began to get Anna O. to talk more freely, until she eventually discussed some troubling past events. Breuer noticed that as she started to recall and discuss more details from her emotionally disturbing history, her physical symptoms began to go away.

Eventually, under hypnosis, Anna O. described what Breuer thought was the original trauma that had precipitated her conversion reaction. She indicated that she had been spending a considerable amount of time caring for her seriously ill father. After many days of patiently waiting at her father's bedside, Anna naturally grew somewhat resentful of the great burden that his illness had placed on her. These feelings of resentment were morally unacceptable to Anna O., who also experienced genuine feelings of love and concern for her father. One day, she was feeling particularly tired as she sat at her father's bedside. She dropped off into what Breuer describes as a waking dream, with her right arm over the back of a chair. After she fell into this trancelike state, Anna O. saw a large black snake emerge from the wall and slither toward her sick father to bite him. She tried to push the snake away, but her right arm had gone to sleep. When Anna O. looked at her right hand, she found that her fingers had turned into little snakes with death's heads.

The next day, when Anna O. was walking outside, she saw a bent branch. This branch reminded her of her hallucination of the snake, and at once her right arm became rigidly extended. Over time, the paralysis in Anna O.'s right arm extended to her entire right side; other symptoms began to develop as well. Recalling her hallucination of the snake and the emotions that accompanied it seemed to produce a great improvement in her condition. Breuer hypothesized that Anna O. had converted her original trauma into a physical symptom and was unable to recover until this traumatic memory was properly expressed and discussed. The way in which

Breuer treated Anna O. eventually became known as the cathartic method.

MIND AND BODY

Anna O.'s case and the development of the cathartic method eventually led to widespread interest in conversion disorders, as well as in the other types of somatic disorders. Many mental health professionals began to suspect that all the somatic disorders involved patients who were unconsciously converting unpleasant or unacceptable emotions into somatic complaints. The manner in which somatic patients could misinterpret or misperceive their bodily sensations, however, remained rather mysterious. For example, how can an individual who has normal vision truly believe that he or she is blind? Research conducted by the team of Harold Sackheim, Johanna Nordlie, and Ruben Gur suggested a possible answer to this question. Sackheim and his colleagues studied conversion patients who believed they were blind. This form of blindness, known as hysterical blindness, can be quite debilitating. Patients who develop hysterical blindness are generally unable to perform their usual functions and often report total loss of vision. When the vision of these patients was tested in an empirical fashion, an interesting pattern of results emerged. On each trial of a special visual test there were two time intervals, each of which was bounded by the sounding of a buzzer. During each trial, a bright visual target was illuminated during one of the intervals. Hysterically blind subjects were asked to report whether the visual target was illuminated during the first or the second interval. If truly blind subjects were to attempt this task, they should be correct by chance approximately 50 percent of the time. Most hysterically blind subjects were correct only 20 to 30 percent of the time, as if they were deliberately trying to demonstrate poor vision. A smaller number of hysterically blind subjects were correct on almost every trial, suggesting that they were actually able to see the visual stimuli before them.

Sackheim and his colleagues suggested that a two-state defensive reaction can explain these conflicting findings. First, the perceptual representations of visual stimuli are blocked from conscious awareness, so that subjects report that they are blind. Then, in the second part of the process, subjects continue to gain information from the perceptual representations of what they have seen. The performance of subjects on a visual task will then depend on whether the subjects feel they must deny access to the information that was gained during the second part of the visual process. If subjects believe that they must deny access to visual information, they will perform more poorly on a visual task than would be expected by chance. If subjects believe that they do not need to deny access to visual information, they will perform like a normal subject on a visual task. In other words, according to Sackheim and his colleagues, hysterically blind patients base their responses on the consequences of their behavior.

The way in which hysterically blind patients can manipulate their ability to see has led many scholars to question whether these patients are being truthful. Sackheim, Nordlie, and Gur, however, report that there are patients with lesions in the visual cortex (a part of the brain that processes visual information) who report that they are blind. These patients believe that they cannot see, even though they have normal eyes and can respond accurately to visual stimuli. They believe they are blind because they have trouble processing visual information. It is thus possible that an individual can have normal eyesight and still believe that he or she is blind. It is widely accepted in the psychological community that individuals with somatic disorders, aside from those with factitious disorder, truly and honestly believe that they have a physical symptom, even though they are actually quite healthy.

METAPHORICAL AND REAL ILLNESSES

The study of somatic disorders is an important area of concern for both medical professionals and social scientists. The somatic disorders are relatively common, and their great prevalence poses a serious problem for the medical establishment. A tremendous amount of professional energy and financial resources is expended in the needless medical treatment of somatic patients, who really suffer from emotional rather than physical difficulties. For example, when Robert Woodruff, Donald Goodwin, and Samuel Guze compared fifty patients with somatic symptom disorder with fifty normal control subjects in 1974, they found that the somatization patients had undergone major surgical procedures three times more frequently than had the normal controls. Since an effort was made to match the somatizing and control patients on the basis of their actual medical condition, one can assume that much of the surgery performed on the somatization patients was unnecessary.

On the other hand, there is also considerable evidence to indicate that many people who are genuinely ill are misdiagnosed with somatoform disorders. Charles

Watson and Cheryl Buranen published a follow-up study of somatization patients in 1979 which found that 25 percent of the patients actually suffered from real physical disorders. It seems physicians who are unable to explain a patient's puzzling medical problems may be tempted to label the patient prematurely with a somatic disorder. The diagnosis of a somatic disorder needs to be made with great caution, to ensure that a genuine medical condition will not be overlooked. There is also a need for further research into the causes and nature of the somatic disorders, so that they can be diagnosed in a more definitive fashion.

Further research is also needed to shed light on the ways in which somatic disorders can be treated. Most somatic patients are truly in need of assistance, for while their physical illness may be imaginary, their pain and suffering are real. Unfortunately, at this time, it is often difficult for mental health professionals to treat somatic patients effectively since these individuals tend to focus on their physical complaints rather than on their emotional problems. More research is needed on the treatment of somatoform patients so that they can overcome the psychological difficulties that plague them.

BIBLIOGRAPHY

Alloy, Lauren B., Neil S. Jacobson, and Joan Acocella. *Abnormal Psychology: Current Perspectives.* 9th ed. Boston: McGraw-Hill, 2005.

Breuer, Josef, and Sigmund Freud. *Studies in Hysteria.* Trans. James Strachey. New York: Penguin, 2004.

Comer, Ronald J. *Abnormal Psychology.* 8th ed. New York: Worth, 2013. Print.

Kirmeyer, L., and S. Taillefer. "Somatoform Disorders." *In Adult Psychopathology and Diagnosis,* edited by Samuel M. Turner and Michel Hersen. 5th ed. Hoboken: Wiley, 2007.

Larrabee, Glenn J., ed. *Forensic Neuropsychology: A Scientific Approach.* 2nd ed. New York: Oxford UP, 2012. Print.

Levenson, James L. *The American Psychiatric Publishing Textbook of Psychosomatic Medicine: Psychiatric Care of the Medically Ill.* 2nd ed. Washington, DC: American Psychiatric, 2011. Print.

Sackheim, Harold A., Johanna W. Nordlie, and Ruben C. Gur. "A Model of Hysterical and Hypnotic Blindness: Cognition, Motivation, and Awareness." *Journal of Abnormal Psychology* 88 (October, 1979): 474-489.

Sarason, Irwin G., and Barbara R. Sarason. *Abnormal Psychology: The Problem of Maladaptive Behavior.* 11th ed. Upper Saddle River: Prentice-Hall, 2008.

Waldinger, Robert J. *Psychiatry for Medical Students.* 3d ed. Washington, DC: American Psychiatric, 1997.

Steven C. Abell

SEE ALSO: Abnormality: Psychological models; Anxiety disorders; Breuer, Josef; Emotional intelligence; Health psychology; Pain; Pain management; Psychoanalytic psychology and personality: Sigmund Freud; Psychosomatic disorders; Stress-related diseases.

Hypothesis development and testing

TYPE OF PSYCHOLOGY: Psychological methodologies

A useful strategy for answering questions about behavior is to propose several possible answers (hypotheses), generate predictions based on these hypotheses, and collect information (data) to determine which hypothesis appears to have produced a correct prediction.

KEY CONCEPTS
- Experiment
- Falsifiability
- Hypothesis
- Prediction
- Specificity
- Testability

INTRODUCTION

All psychological research begins with observations of behavior, either informal, everyday observations or formal observations based on prior psychological research. Such observations frequently lead to questions. For example, many people drink beverages containing caffeine throughout the day. When asked why, these people often say that it helps them stay alert. Does caffeine really help people stay alert?

For every question one can ask, there are many possible answers. Caffeine might affect alertness at all dosages. It might only affect alertness at certain dosages or only in some situations. On the other hand, caffeine might decrease, not increase, alertness. Finally, one should not discount the possibility that caffeine has no effect on alertness and that the reported effects are placebo effects—that is, they might be caused by expectations about caffeine and not by caffeine itself.

In the language of science, the possible answers to questions are called hypotheses, and the procedure scientists employ to choose among these hypotheses is called hypothesis testing. Hypothesis testing, when used correctly, is a powerful tool for advancing knowledge because it provides a procedure for retaining hypotheses that are probably true and rejecting those that are probably false.

Scientists test hypotheses by making predictions and collecting information. A prediction is a statement of the evidence that would lead the scientist to accept a particular hypothesis. The hypothesis that caffeine maintains alertness leads to the prediction that people who ingest a measured dose of caffeine a given time before engaging in a task that requires alertness will perform better than people who do not ingest caffeine. An experiment could be conducted to test this hypothesis. An experiment is a set of controlled conditions used to test hypotheses. It contains at least one experimental group and one or more comparison, or control, groups.

ROLE OF PREDICTIONS

Hypothesis tests are only as good as the predictions generated. Good predictions tell the researcher what evidence to collect. To be a good test of the hypothesis, predictions must have three characteristics. The predictions must follow as a logical consequence from the hypothesis and the assumptions the researcher makes about the test situation. The hypothesis and its corresponding prediction must be testable, in the sense that the researcher could decide from the data whether a given prediction has been confirmed. Finally, it should be unlikely that a given prediction is confirmed unless the hypothesis on which it is based is correct.

If the prediction was not logically related to the hypothesis, a confirmation by the data would reveal nothing about the truth of the hypothesis. This logical relationship is complicated by the fact that rarely is it the case that a prediction can be generated solely from the hypothesis. To generate a prediction, a number of additional assumptions are usually required. It takes a certain amount of time for caffeine to enter the system and affect behavior; any behavioral effects will not be evident until the dosage reaches a certain level. The time it takes to detect the occurrence of a new object on a computer screen is a valid measure of alertness.

Although the prediction may logically follow from the hypothesis, it will not be confirmed if any of the assumptions are incorrect. Unfortunately, there is no foolproof way to avoid this problem. Researchers must carefully consider all assumptions they make.

The condition of testability means that it must be possible to decide on the basis of evidence whether the prediction has been confirmed. Testable predictions are falsifiable; that is, certain experimental outcomes would lead the researcher to conclude that the prediction and the hypothesis are incorrect. A prediction that is not potentially falsifiable is worthless. If researchers cannot conceive of data that would lead them to disconfirm a prediction, the prediction cannot be tested; all data would lead to confirmation.

The third condition, that it should be unlikely for a given prediction to be confirmed unless the hypothesis on which it is based is correct, is met when the hypothesis leads to a very specific prediction. Specificity is a characteristic of the hypothesis; if the hypothesis is specific, it should lead to a specific prediction. Hypotheses that meet the criterion of specificity tend to require fewer additional assumptions. Unfortunately, such hypotheses are rare in psychological research. Because of this lack of specificity, a single experiment rarely provides a definitive test of a hypothesis. As knowledge about behavior increases, the ability of psychologists to generate and test such hypotheses will no doubt improve.

TESTING STRATEGIES

Hypotheses are tested by comparing predictions to data. If the data confirm the prediction, then the researcher can continue to consider the hypothesis as a reasonable explanation for the phenomenon under investigation and a possible answer to the research question. If subjects react faster to new objects after ingesting caffeine, the investigator would conclude that caffeine affects alertness in this situation. If the data do not confirm the prediction, however, then the investigator would conclude that the hypothesis does not provide a correct explanation of the phenomenon and is not a correct answer to the research question. If subjects given caffeine perform similarly to those not given caffeine, then the researcher would conclude that caffeine does not have much, if any, effect on alertness in this experimental situation.

A useful strategy for testing hypotheses is to generate two hypotheses and attempt to show that if one is false, the other must be true. This can be accomplished if the hypotheses selected are mutually exclusive (they cannot both be true) and exhaustive (they are the only logical possibilities). When two hypotheses satisfy these conditions, demonstrating the truth or falseness of one of these hypotheses determines the status of the other: If one is probably true, the other must be probably false, and vice versa.

The conclusion drawn from a hypothesis test is that the hypothesis is either probably true or probably false—"probably" because it is possible that the wrong conclusion has been reached. The success of any hypothesis test depends on the logical connections among the hypothesis, assumptions, and prediction. Even when these connections are sound, however, different results might occur if the experiment were repeated again. Repeating the experiment and obtaining similar results increases the researcher's confidence in the data.

It is typically the case that a given experiment will not answer the research question unambiguously. By performing additional experiments with a variety of dosages, times, and tasks, researchers should discover the range of conditions under which caffeine affects alertness. Testing one hypothesis typically leads to more questions, and the cycle of asking questions, generating hypotheses, making predictions, collecting data, and drawing conclusions is repeated. Each round of hypothesis tests increases knowledge about the phenomenon in question.

GROUP BEHAVIOR RESEARCH

An excellent example of hypothesis testing was described by Bibb Latané and John M. Darley in their 1970 book *The Unresponsive Bystander: Why Doesn't He Help?* Latané and Darley became interested in this topic from reading newspaper accounts of people assaulted in the presence of bystanders who did little to assist the victims. The most famous of these was the murder of Kitty Genovese in the presence of thirty-eight neighbors who witnessed this event from their apartment windows; none of them intervened or even called the police. Latané and Darley asked the question, What determines in a particular situation whether one person will help another?

One of their hypotheses was that the number of people present is an important factor affecting how likely it is that someone will react to a dangerous situation. They also hypothesized that what a person does also depends on the behavior of other people at the scene. Latané and Darley predicted that people would be more likely to respond to an emergency when alone than when in the presence of others. They also predicted that what others who are present do affects a person's behavior.

To test this hypothesis, Latané and Darley solicited the participation of male college students to complete a questionnaire. Students went to a room in a university building where they worked on the task alone, along with two confederates of the experimenters, or with two other people who were also naïve subjects. After several minutes, smoke was introduced into the room through a small vent in the wall. The response measures were whether subjects would seek assistance, and, if they did, how long it took them to do so. If subjects did not respond after six minutes of sitting in a room that was filling with smoke, someone came in to get them.

The predictions and the experiments to test them were based on the above hypotheses and on assumptions about how subjects would view the test situation. Darley and Latané assumed that subjects would believe the emergency in the experiment was real and not contrived, and that subjects would perceive the situation as potentially dangerous.

Their predictions were confirmed by the data. Subjects were most likely to report the smoke when alone. When there were two passive confederates who acted in a nonchalant manner in the presence of the smoke, subjects were least likely to respond. Being in a group of three naïve subjects also inhibited responding, but not as much as when the other two people ignored the apparent danger.

The results of this experiment appear to provide rather convincing evidence for the correctness of Latané and Darley's hypotheses; however, the assumption that subjects would view the smoke as potentially dangerous is suspect. Postexperimental interviews revealed that some subjects did not perceive the smoke as potentially dangerous. Furthermore, the results of this experiment suggested additional questions to Latané and Darley: "Does the inhibitory effect of other people depend on the fact that in a three-person group, the subject is in a minority? What would happen if only one other person were present? Does the effect depend on the fact that the other people were strangers to the subject? What would happen if the subject were tested with a close friend?"

These questions were addressed in subsequent experiments. In each case, hypotheses were generated and predictions were derived and tested. Care was taken to make the dangerous situation as unambiguous as possible and not to give away the fact that it was contrived. The general results confirmed Latané and Darley's predictions and validated their hypotheses about bystander apathy.

EYEWITNESS TESTIMONY RESEARCH

For more than eighty years, psychologists have studied people's accuracy at describing events they have witnessed (eyewitness testimony). The history of this work is recounted by Gary Wells and Elizabeth F. Loftus in their edited volume *Eyewitness Testimony: Psychological Perspectives* (1984). Considerable evidence, collected in a wide variety of settings, demonstrates that people's recollections of an event can be influenced by postevent experiences such as interviews by the police and attorneys or the viewing of mug shots. This raises an interesting question: When people's recollection of an event is changed by postevent information, is the underlying memory changed, or is the original memory still intact but rendered temporarily inaccessible? In other words, does reporting of the event change following postevent experiences because the memory has changed, or because the new information blocks the ability to recall the event as originally experienced?

This is an example of an interesting question to which no satisfactory answer has yet been obtained—but not for lack of trying. The question suggests two mutually exclusive and exhaustive hypotheses: The underlying memory is changed by the postevent experience, so that what the person reports is not what he or she originally saw or heard, or the postevent experience has created a new memory that is in competition with the existing, original memory, and the new memory simply overwhelms the old memory. Both hypotheses lead to the prediction that postevent experiences will affect what a subject reports, but the second hypothesis leads to the additional prediction that the original memory can be teased out into the open under the right circumstances. The problem is how to do this in a convincing manner.

David Hall, Loftus, and James Tousignant reviewed the research on this question. They note that it is difficult, if not impossible, to disprove the hypothesis that both memories coexist. In some studies, what appear to be original memories seem to have been recovered but not always. The question as asked assumes an either-or situation (either the original unaltered memory still exists or it does not). Unfortunately, this question cannot be answered unambiguously with present knowledge and technology. On the other hand, the question of under what conditions recollections (as opposed to memories) are changed can be answered, because it leads to a number of testable predictions based on hypotheses about these conditions.

Clearly, not all questions lead to testable hypotheses and falsifiable predictions. When data support more than one hypothesis, or if the data are likely to occur even if the hypotheses are false, hypotheses have not been adequately tested. The hypotheses about the status of the original memory are an excellent illustration of this. Knowledge of the effects of postevent experiences was advanced by asking the more limited question that led to testable hypotheses. Scientific understanding advances when people ask the right question.

LABORATORY VERSUS FIELD EXPERIMENTATION

Laboratory experimentation, with its tight control over the variables that affect behavior, is the best way to test hypotheses. By randomly assigning subjects to conditions and isolating the variables of interest through various control procedures, researchers are afforded the opportunity to arrange situations in which one hypothesis will be confirmed to the exclusion of all other hypotheses. Unfortunately, laboratory experimentation is not always an appropriate way to test hypotheses.

When laboratory experimentation is neither possible nor appropriate, researchers can use field experiments, in which experimental methods are used in a natural setting. The inability to control the field setting, however, makes it more difficult to exclude some explanations for the data. Thus, the advantages and disadvantages of field experimentation must be weighed against those of the laboratory. The earliest research of Latané and Darley on bystander apathy involved field experimentation; however, they found it inadequate for rigorous hypothesis testing and moved their research to the laboratory.

ALTERNATE FORMS OF INQUIRY

Surveys and questionnaires can provide answers to some kinds of questions that experiments cannot: Do certain characteristics distinguish people with different attitudes or opinions on an issue? How many people have a given attitude or opinion? Do certain attitudes or opinions tend to occur together? Predictions can be made and tested with carefully designed surveys and questionnaires.

Archival data and case studies can be extremely useful sources for generating questions and hypotheses, but they are poor techniques for testing hypotheses. Both archival research and case studies can indicate relationships among various factors or events. Whether these relationships are causal or accidental cannot be determined by these methodologies; therefore, the only question that can be answered from archival data and case studies is whether certain relationships have been observed. An experiment is necessary to ascertain whether there is a causal connection.

Statistical significance tests are often part of hypothesis testing. Statistical hypotheses parallel research hypotheses; statistical hypotheses are about aspects of populations, while research hypotheses are about the subject of inquiry. Deciding which statistical hypothesis to accept tells the researcher which research hypothesis to accept. The logic of hypothesis testing in general applies to statistical significance tests.

Knowledge is advanced when research questions can be answered. Hypothesis testing, when used correctly, is a powerful method for sorting among possible answers to find the best one. For this reason, it is frequently employed by psychologists in their research.

BIBLIOGRAPHY

Giere, Ronald N. *Understanding Scientific Reasoning*. 5th ed. Belmont, Calif.: Thomson/Wadsworth, 2006. This readable book presents scientific reasoning from the point of view of a philosopher of science, with many examples from all areas of science, including psychology. Chapter 6, on testing theoretical hypotheses, and chapter 12, on causal hypotheses, provide several detailed examples of evaluating data.

Hall, David F., Elizabeth F. Loftus, and James P. Tousignant. "Postevent Information and Changes in Recollection for a Natural Event." *In Eyewitness Testimony: Psychological Perspectives*, edited by Gary L. Wells and Elizabeth F. Loftus. New York: Cambridge University Press, 1984. Discusses the hypotheses pertaining to the effects of postevent information on original memories, and why these hypotheses cannot be tested. Illustrates how questions about the conditions under which recollections change may be answered.

Latané, Bibb, and John M. Darley. *The Unresponsive Bystander: Why Doesn't He Help?* New York: Appleton-Century-Crofts, 1970. Latané and Darley describe why and how they performed their now-classic set of experiments on bystander apathy, clearly laying out for the reader their observations, questions, hypotheses, assumptions, predictions, experimental procedures, and conclusions.

Moore, K. D. *A Field Guide to Inductive Arguments*. 2d ed. Dubuque, Iowa: Kendall-Hunt, 1990. An excellent workbook for learning how to analyze arguments and evaluate evidence. Chapter 4, on hypothetical evidence, provides several interesting exercises on how to generate and test hypotheses.

Stanovich, Keith E. *How to Think Straight About Psychology*. 8th ed. Boston: Allyn & Bacon, 2007. Stanovich tries to undermine the misconceptions that many people have about the contributions of psychology to the scientific study of human behavior. Examples of hypothesis testing abound throughout the book.

Jerome Frieman

SEE ALSO: Animal experimentation; Case study methodologies; Data description; Experimentation: Independent, dependent, and control variables; Field experimentation; Placebo effect; Qualitative research; Scientific methods; Statistical significance tests; Survey research: Questionnaires and interviews.

Hysteria

TYPE OF PSYCHOLOGY: Personality; Psychopathology; Psychotherapy

Hysteria is an enigmatic condition that has been described for several millennia in the medical literature. Its manifestations have tended to change from era to era, perhaps reflecting the mores, social expectations, and medical knowledge of the day. Hysteria as an overarching category has disappeared from modern diagnostic systems, but its symptoms are still reflected in several disorders..

KEY CONCEPTS
- Attention seeking
- Gender roles
- Hypnosis
- Psychoanalysis
- Psychosomatic complaints
- Sexuality
- Social expectations
- Suggestibility

INTRODUCTION

The concept of hysteria has a rich history that dates back to early civilizations. Ancient Egyptian papyri provide the first medical records of hysteria. Egyptian physicians believed that the somatic and emotional problems of certain unstable women were caused by a migratory uterus. They prescribed the topical use of sweet- or foul-smelling herbs to entice or repel the uterus back to its original position. This theme of sexual etiology has pervaded theories of hysteria throughout the centuries.

GRECO-ROMAN VIEWS

There is considerable continuity between Egyptian and Greco-Roman views of hysteria. Hippocrates, often considered the founder of medicine, included the condition in the *Corpus Hippocraticum* (fifth to third centuries b.c.e.; *The Genuine Works of Hippocrates*, 1849), and solidified its connection with the uterus by assigning the appellation "hysteria," which is derived from the Greek term for the organ, "hystera." The Greeks were the first to connect hysteria with sexual activity; they believed that the condition occurred primarily in adult women deprived of sexual relations for extended periods, resulting in the migration of the uterus. Aromatic remedies were also prescribed by the Greeks, but the recommended remedy was to marry and, if possible, become pregnant. Some skeptics of the day denied the motility of the uterus. For example, the Roman physician Galen proposed that hysteria was instead caused by the retention of a substance analogous to sperm in the female, which was triggered by long-term abstinence.

THE DARK AGES

As the Middle Ages approached, magical thinking and superstition increased. Some Christian writers, especially Saint Augustine, condemned sex as the work of such unholy spirits as incubi, succubi, and witches. Numerous behavioral afflictions, particularly the peculiar and transient symptoms of hysteria, were viewed as the result of witchcraft. Many hysterics became victims of the witch craze, a long and dark chapter in Western history. *The Malleus Maleficarum* (c. 1486; *Malleus Maleficarum*, 1928), a manual whose title means "the witches' hammer," was written by two Dominican monks, Heinrich Kraemer and Jakob Sprenger. This book outlined the "telltale" signs of witchcraft, which were widely used and regarded as diagnostic by Middle Age inquisitors. Hysterical patients became both accusers, who came forth with complaints that spells had been cast on them, and confessors, who were willing to implicate themselves by weaving accounts of their participation in strange sexual rituals and witchcraft.

THE RENAISSANCE TO THE VICTORIAN ERA

With the arrival of the Renaissance, views on hysteria changed to accommodate natural causes. Medical writers of the day recognized the brain as the source of the affliction. As a result, hysteria soon became a topic of interest for neurologists. In addition, physicians suggested emotional contributions to hysteria, including melan-choly (which resembles modern depression). Largely as a result of the writings of physician Thomas Sydenham, hysteria came to be considered an affliction of the mind. At this time, some proposed a male analogue to hysteria termed "hypochondriasis".

Throughout history, the symptoms of hysteria have reflected prevailing sociocultural norms and expectations. In the nineteenth century, ideal women were physically and emotionally delicate, which was reflected in their greater susceptibility to hysteria and in the nature of their symptoms. Over time, infrequent but spectacular hysterical paroxysms gave way to milder chronic symptoms. Fainting spells, euphemistically called "the vapors," were accepted as a natural reaction of the vulnerable female to emotional distress. Some clinicians of this era considered hysteria a form of "moral insanity" and emphasized hysterical patients' penchant for prevarication, flamboyant emotional displays, and nearly constant need for attention. Others viewed hysterics with a patronizing compassion, as unfortunate victims of the natural weakness of femininity.

HYPNOSIS AND PSYCHOANALYTIC UNDERPINNINGS

Conceptions of hysteria were shaped substantially by the work of French neurologist Jean-Martin Charcot. Charcot emphasized the importance of suggestibility in the etiology of hysterical behavior; he found that under hypnosis, some hysterical patients' symptoms could be made to appear or disappear largely at will. Charcot was also the first to assign significance to a pathogenic early environment in producing hysterical episodes.

The young Austrian neurologist Sigmund Freud began his career by studying the blockage of sensation by chemicals. This interest extended to hysteria (known for its anesthetic symptoms), which brought him into contact with Viennese internist Josef Breuer. Breuer's account of the famous hysterical patient Anna O. and her treatment provided the early foundations of psychoanalytic theory. Breuer found that, under hypnosis, Anna recalled the psychological trauma that had ostensibly led to her hysteria. Moreover, he found that her symptoms improved or disappeared after this apparent memory recovery. Freud studied hypnosis under Charcot and extended Breuer's concepts and treatments to develop his own theory of hysteria. He reintroduced sexuality into the etiology of hysteria, particularly the notion of long-forgotten memories of early sexual trauma. Freud himself eventually concluded that most or all of these "recovered" memories were fantasies or confabulations, a view shared by many modern memory researchers.

CURRENT STATUS

The term "hysteria" has long been regarded as vague and needlessly pejorative, and it is no longer a part of the formal diagnostic nomenclature. The broad concept of hysteria was splintered with the appearance of the third edition of the *Diagnostic and Statistical Manual of Mental Disorders (DSM-III)* in 1980 and is currently encompassed by a broad array of conditions, including somatic disorders, dissociative disorders, and histrionic personality disorder. The separation of somatic from dissociative disorders in the current diagnostic system is controversial, because these two broad groupings of disorders often covary substantially with one another. Some researchers have argued that somatic and dissociative disorders should be reunited under a single broad diagnostic umbrella.

Somatic disorders are a group of ailments in which the presence of physical symptoms suggests a medical condition but in which the symptoms are involuntarily psychologically produced. Somatic symptom disorder, conversion disorder, illness anxiety disorder (formerly known as hypochondriasis), and factitious disorder are the major conditions in this group.

Dissociative disorders are characterized by disruptions in the integrated functioning of consciousness, memory, identity, or perception. Dissociative amnesia, dissociative fugue, dissociative identity disorder (formerly multiple personality disorder), and depersonalization/derealization disorder belong to this category. The causes of some dissociative disorders, particularly dissociative identity disorder, are controversial, as some writers maintain that these conditions are largely a product of inadvertent therapeutic suggestion and prompting. This controversy has been fueled by the fact that diagnoses of dissociative identity disorder have become much more frequent.

Histrionic personality disorder (HPD), formerly hysterical personality disorder, is the most direct descendent of the concept of hysteria. This disorder involves excessive emotionality and attention-seeking behaviors and is often a correlate of somatic and perhaps dissociative disorders. Due to its roots in diagnoses of hysteria and the fact that it is more commonly diagnosed in women, HPD remains controversial. While the claim that it is used to pathologize normal female behavior is widely regarded to be untrue, there is a somewhat better-respected theory that HPD is not actually distinct from antisocial

personality disorder, but is the result of societal factors causing antisocial personality disorder to manifest differently in women. There was some speculation in the psychological community that the two disorders would be merged in the DSM-5, but HPD remains a separate diagnosis.

A paucity of behavior-genetic studies leaves the relative contribution of genetic and environmental factors to somatic and dissociative disorders a mystery. The precise sociocultural expressions of hysteria are also unclear. Many authors have suggested that hysteria has been manifested in a plethora of different conditions over time and across cultures, including dissociative identity disorder, somatoform disorders, purported demonic possession, mass hysteria, and even such religious practices as glossolalia (speaking in tongues). According to these authors, such seemingly disparate conditions are all manifestations of a shared predisposition that has been shaped by sociocultural norms and expectancies. "Hysteria" as a diagnostic label is no longer accepted, but its protean manifestations may be here to stay.

BIBLIOGRAPHY

Bartholomew, Robert E., Robert J. M. Rickard, and Glenn Dawes. *Mass Hysteria in Schools: A Worldwide History since 1566.* Jefferson: McFarland, 2014. Print.

Bollas, Christopher. *Hysteria.* New York: Routledge, 2000. Print.

Chodoff, Paul, and Henry Lyons. "Hysteria, the Hysterical Personality, and 'Hysterical' Conversion." *American Journal of Psychiatry* 114 (1958): 734-740. Print.

Hustvedt, Asti. *Medical Muses: Hysteria in Nineteenth-Century Paris.* New York: Norton, 2011. Print.

Kraemer, Heinrich Institoris, and Jakob Sprenger. *Malleus Maleficarum.* Trans. Montague Summers. New York: Blom, 1970. Print.

Pickren, Wade E., and Alexandra Rutherford. *A History of Modern Psychology in Context.* Hoboken: Wiley, 2010. Print.

Sarkar, Jaydip, and Gwen Adshead. *Clinical Topics in Personality Disorder.* London: Royal College of Psychiatrists, 2012. Print.

Scull, Andrew. *Hysteria: The Disturbing History.* Oxford: Oxford UP, 2011. Print.

Shapiro, David. "Hysterical Style." *Neurotic Styles.* New York: Basic, 2000. Print.

Spanos, Nicholas P. *Multiple Identities and False Memories: A Sociocognitive Perspective.* Washington,

DC: American Psychological Assn., 1996. Print.

Veith, Ilza. *Hysteria: The History of a Disease.* Northvale: Aronson, 1993. Print.

Widiger, Thomas A. *The Oxford Handbook of Personality Disorders.* Oxford: Oxford UP, 2012. Print.

Yarom, Nitza. *The Matrix of Hysteria: Psychoanalysis of the Struggle Between the Sexes Enacted in the Body.* New York: Routledge, 2005. Print.

Katherine A. Fowler and Scott O. Lilienfeld

SEE ALSO: Amnesia and fugue; Breuer, Josef; Dissociative disorders; Freud, Sigmund; Freudian psychology; Histrionic personality disorder; Hypnosis; Hypochondriasis, conversion, and somatization; Multiple personality; Munchausen syndrome and Munchausen syndrome by proxy; Neurotic disorders; Psychoanalytic psychology and personality: Sigmund Freud; Women's psychology: Sigmund Freud; Women's mental health.

I

Identity crises

TYPE OF PSYCHOLOGY: Developmental psychology; Personality

Identity crises are states of conflict during which a person may suffer from role disorientation and question his or her self-perception. Psychoanalytical theorist Erik H. Erikson coined the term "identity crisis," which is an integral component of his identity development model. Identity crises are experienced throughout the life span and are viewed as often necessary processes in healthy psychosocial development.

KEY CONCEPTS
- Eight stages of psychosocial identity development
- Emerging adulthood
- Four status model of identity
- Identity achievement
- Identity development theory
- Identity diffusions
- Identity foreclosure
- Identity moratorium
- Midlife crisis
- Psychosocial theory

INTRODUCTION
The foundation for theories involving identity crises and the importance of these crises in human development is Erik H. Erikson's eight stages of identity development. The identity development theory, also called the psychosocial theory, creates a blueprint for how personality is expressed and how a person becomes integrated with others. The theory involves the role of social interaction between the self and others as each individual undergoes the process of socialization. In each stage of identity development, a person encounters a conflict or crisis that needs to be resolved to successfully navigate through the stage. During an identity crisis, a person experiences intensive self-reflection and exploration. Erikson describes a crisis as the process of resolving conflict regarding a person's colliding desires for both individuality and communal belonging. The approach people take toward resolving a crisis will ultimately develop into a pattern, which Erikson considered the cornerstone of identity development.

Erikson proposed a sequential stage theory to explain identity development. He believed that prior stages of development (specifically identity) or construction influence later stages of development and that the ability to move through the stages is influenced by stages of physical maturation, such as puberty. However, completion of a stage was not necessary to move on to another stage, and development did not come to fruition at the end of adolescence. Erikson felt that identity development and the accompanying crises continued throughout a person's life span.

THE STAGES
The first stage of psychosocial development and later identity development is trust versus mistrust. During this stage, which Erikson associated with infants up to one year old, babies learn to trust their caregivers and the support, both emotional and physical, that they provide. At this point in human development, people are at their most vulnerable; to survive, they must rely on others. Children begin to identify with their caregivers' actions toward them, which creates a model for their own caregiving later in life. According to Erikson, the crisis arises as babies mature and their mothers begin to resume their prior roles, including that of wife. The mothers must begin to alter their responses to their babies' needs while maintaining their trust. This conflict is evident in the process parents go through to help their babies sleep through the night. Parents may be told not to respond to every cry to help the baby self-regulate and maintain a sleep routine. Babies must learn that fewer responses are not an indication of abandonment. Successful completion of this stage is the formulation of a model of trust and security in future interactions.

The second stage, autonomy versus shame or doubt, covers children aged two to three. As children gain the physical ability to move on their own, they begin to want more control; however, they simultaneously doubt their capabilities and fear that their parents will retain too much control over them. These conflicting fears create doubt in children. This conflict can be seen in children who want to touch and explore their surroundings but hesitate to leave the side of their caregivers. If the conflict between a desire for self-control and parental control is not resolved, low self-esteem may develop.

Erikson suggested that in the third stage, initiative versus guilt (ages three to six), children begin to explore who they are and the ways they identify with their parents. Specifically, Erikson speculated that during this stage, children develop the foundation for understanding gender roles. For example, during this stage, children may find themselves favoring one parent over the other. Although the favoring may be a way for children to start to understand gender roles (such as what each parent does), children may also feel guilt for not evenly distributing their attention and affection.

In Erikson's fourth stage, the industry versus inferiority stage of development (ages six to twelve), he considered the role of the environment. The stage begins when children enter elementary school, where learning is focused on concrete tasks such as classifying objects and recognition of patterns and orders. Children rely on concrete evidence, such as performance in an academic, artistic, or athletic domain, to define who they are. Erikson suggested that children begin to believe that what they produce is used to determine and evaluate them. However, during this time, children also become aware of the social inequalities (such as race, ethnicity, and socioeconomic background) that influence who they will be. The developing of this awareness coincides with the onset of puberty, which also contributes to children's progression into the next stage of development.

ADOLESCENCE AND BEYOND

The fifth of Erikson's stages, the identity versus role confusion (about thirteen to eighteen years of age), is one of the most studied. For Erikson, this period marks the transition from childhood to adulthood and is characterized by the adolescents' continual need to explore the roles they may want to assume. This stage also marks a shift from relying solely on parents for identification cues; youths begin to identify more with their peer groups and any activities, religion, and social-political movements with which they may be involved. However, Erikson proposed that to ward off role confusion, adolescents may be overzealous in their identification with and endorsement of social group leaders, which can lead to total self-conformity. Therefore, the goal of identity development during adolescence is to integrate various identities into a unified whole. This need for integration and the fear of permanent identity diffusion are the result of puberty changes and growing social pressure from peers and the larger community. Integration is considered the successful outcome of identity crisis resolution in adolescence.

Stages six through eight were structured around Erikson's belief that people emerge from adolescence into young adulthood with an intact identity. In these stages, therefore, the focus shifts from finding the self to becoming intimate with other people. Erikson refers to stage six as intimacy and solidarity versus isolation. During this stage, the conflict or crisis is about learning to coexist in a partnership. However, if individuals do not have intact identities, they will be unable to experience intimacy or commit for fear that they might lose themselves.

During middle adulthood, people enter into the seventh stage, characterized by generativity versus self-absorption or stagnation. Erikson assumed that people would be raising children and would therefore develop a need to impart knowledge to their offspring. People may suffer from self-absorption or lack of psychological growth if not given the opportunity to share their knowledge with others. The generative crisis is the foundation for research regarding the midlife crisis. This stage contains a bias toward having children, which reflects the time in which the theory was developed.

The eighth stage, during late adulthood, is called integrity versus despair. This period is when people reflect on their lives; if people are happy and at peace with their pathways through development, they will have integrity and will therefore not fear death.

EXPANSIONS ON IDENTITY DEVELOPMENT

Using Erikson's identity development theory as a frame, in 1966, Canadian developmental psychologist James Marcia developed an identity status model based on the use of exploration and commitment in developing an identity. This model deconstructs identity acquisition into four critical statuses. Although the statuses appear hierarchical in organization, they should not be considered stages because no clear sequence exists. The four statuses are identity foreclosure, identity diffusion, identity moratorium, and identity achievement. During each status, people may encounter an identity crisis or confusion, which will prompt them to reconcile the conflict and possibly result in the transition to another status.

Foreclosed statuses are characterized by high levels of commitment and low levels of exploration or agency.

In a foreclosed status, identity is ascribed or given to the person. Identity is made up of the ready-made goals and values of an authority figure or society that are accepted by the person. During this status, the people are highly susceptible to peer-group pressure. Erikson described people in this status when he talked about the need for adolescents to quickly conform to the characteristics of a group.

Diffusion refers to a status in which people have no complexity or purpose and high levels of apathy. Prior research suggests that prolonged diffusion past adolescence can result in maladaptive outcomes, such as drug abuse and sexual risk taking. It is during this status that people are incredibly vulnerable to persuasion and have the least amount of agency. This status is often considered a starting point for identity searching.

Marcia's moratorium status is considered very brief yet functional; it is both intensely stressful and overwhelming. In this status, people are in full-blown identity crisis and cannot commit to any single identity. However, the noncommittal person in moratorium status can become a very open-minded individual. Researcher Harold Grotevant suggests that the moratorium status describes most identity development in adolescence, the period in which alternatives to a current identity and the values and beliefs that are attached are explored. Adolescents seek out alternatives in an effort to resolve the pressures they may be encountering. The moratorium status also marks a shift away from acceptance of ascribed (given) identities and identifications.

Identity achievement is thought to be the endpoint for adolescence and identity crisis or confusion. During this status, the core identity has emerged as a result of successful integrations; adolescents are able to commit to values and goals they have chosen. Researchers suggest identity achievement is the most beneficial status for self-esteem, which is another aspect of identity. Adolescents with higher reported self-esteem are more likely to have reported an identity achievement status.

Although Marcia's typology is one of the most influential post-Erikson expansions, critics fear this narrowed focus negates the important role of context in identity development and the ensuing crisis. Critics such as E. P. Schachter suggest that there is underlying universality to Erikson's identity development theory, in that the process to resolve a crisis will remain the same regardless of the sociocultural and sociohistorical frames. For example, achievement identity may be considered the ultimate status for functioning in one society, but foreclosure may be the desired identity status in another society. Renewed interest in the resolution of identity crises has spurred more in-depth examinations of developmental stages beyond adolescence.

BEYOND THE ADOLESCENT IDENTITY CRISIS
Research by American psychologist Jeffery J. Arnett has uncovered a distinct period of exploration and understanding that separates adolescence from adulthood. Emerging adulthood has also been viewed as a prolonged period of high identity exploration and low identity commitment—in other words, a state of persistent moratorium. The normative expectations of this distinct period revolve around identity exploration and the resolution of conflict. However, emerging adulthood and the conflicts encountered are not universal concepts but rather the by-products of cultural construction in Western late-modern societies such as the United States. Arnett defines this period as a time for constant transition and change, and because one-third of emerging adults in the United States are attending college, development during this time often begins to take place during a time of semiautonomy. Semiautonomy implies that although the majority of college students do not live with their families, they still rely on some forms of family financial and social support. An example of semiautonomy is a student who rents an apartment and may have a part-time job but whose parents still pay for his or her medical insurance and health care.

Research on how people conceptualize this period has found that a majority of individuals aged eighteen to twenty-five do not identify themselves as adolescents but do not see themselves as full-fledged adults either. Closer examination as to why individuals have this subjective sense of emerging adulthood has revealed that the criteria that these individuals use to infer a transition to adulthood are financial independence and accepting responsibility for the self. The adherence to these criteria can be a source of conflict resulting in crisis. By enrolling in college, these students are granted the ability to exist in a paradoxical universe, where an emerging adult with a previously stable identity configuration is given permission to revert back into a state of exploration. During this period, personal expectations and social-role expectations collide, allowing a stronger integrated and achieved identity to emerge before adulthood. However, again the assumption is that the achieved identity status is the desired goal.

One of the most commonly cited types of crisis after adolescence and emerging adulthood is the midlife crisis, which usually occurs between the ages of forty and sixty. Experts believe that rapid role changes and expectations, such as facing new limitations because of physical deterioration or reflecting on one's disappointing professional status, bring on psychological distress. A person suffering from a midlife crisis may exhibit personality and behavioral changes, such as a low mood, self-absorption, or depression. The underlying assumption behind midlife crises is that aging is an intensely stressful event that spurs an overwhelming period of self-reflection and possible regret. It has also been suggested that middle age is a time during which people must contend with their own mortality, which echoes the original conflicts of identity posited by Erikson. However, as other major life events such as marriage, parenthood, and career establishment have been taking place later and later, the expectation of having a midlife crisis wanes.

CONCLUSION

Although an identity crisis is often thought of as typically occurring in either adolescence or middle adulthood, it is actually a normative process experienced throughout a person's life. The belief in normative crises is a major contribution of Erikson's original identity development theory. An identity crisis or process of conflict resolution is a necessary aspect of psychosocial development. It is not always stressful and cannot be assumed to lead to the person's engaging in maladaptive behaviors. Future research should focus on how society and or culture may influence the onset and type of crisis experienced, the factors that assist people during their crises and how these factors may be a function of the culture and society to which the person belongs, and whether identity crises are universal.

BIBLIOGRAPHY

Andersson, Matthew A. "Identity Crises in Love and at Work: Dispositional Optimism as a Durable Personal Resource." *Social Psychology Quarterly* 75.4 (2012): 290–309. Print.

Arnett, Jeffery J. *Emerging Adulthood: The Winding Road from Late Teens through the Twenties.* New York: Oxford UP, 2004. Print.

Dunlop, William L., and Lawrence J. Walker. "The Life Story: Its Development and Relation to Narration and Personal Identity." *International Journal of Behavioral Development* 37.3 (2013): 235–47. Print.

Erikson, Erik H. Identity: Youth and Crisis. New York: Norton, 1994. Print.

Grotevant, Harold D. "Toward a Process Model of Identity Formation." *Journal of Adolescent Research* 2.3 (1987): 203–22. Print.

Hirschi, Andreas. "Vocational Identity Trajectories: Differences in Personality and Development of Well-Being." *European Journal of Personality* 26.1 (2012): 2–12. Print.

Kroger, Jane. *Identity Development: Adolescence through Adulthood.* 2nd ed. Thousand Oaks: Sage, 2007. Print.

Research Network on Successful Midlife Development (MIDMAC). http://midmac.med.harvard.edu/

Schachter, E. P. "Identity Constraints: The Perceived Structural Requirements of a 'Good' Identity." *Human Development* 45.6 (2002): 416–33. Print.

Wethington, Elaine. "Expecting Stress: Americans and the 'Midlife Crisis.'" *Motivation and Emotion* 24.2 (2000): 85–103. Print.

Buffie Longmire Avital

SEE ALSO: Adolescence: Cognitive skills; Aging: Cognitive changes; Erikson, Erik H.; Gender identity formation; Gender roles and gender role conflicts; Midlife crises; Personality theory; Self-esteem; Teenagers' mental health.

Implosion

TYPE OF PSYCHOLOGY: Learning; Psychological methodologies; Psychopathology

Implosion is a behavior therapy that incorporates principles of Pavlovian conditioning and psychodynamic concepts. It is used in the treatment of fears, phobias, and anxiety disorders and was developed by the psychologist Thomas G. Stampfl in the late 1950s.

KEY CONCEPTS

- Exposure technology
- Extinction
- Hypothesized cues
- Pavlovian fear conditioning
- Prolonged/intense exposure therapy

INTRODUCTION

Implosion, along with in vivo and imaginal flooding, is categorized as a prolonged/intense exposure therapy. It is used in the treatment of fears, phobias, anxiety disorders, and negative emotional reactions such as anger. The therapist asks the client to imagine exaggerated, horrifying scenes that are constructed from the client's report of stimuli that evoke fear or anxiety, supplemented by the therapist's list of hypothesized cues. The therapist helps the client maintain a high level of fear or anxiety regarding these scenes until the anxiety response spontaneously subsides (implodes).

There are two types of hypothesized cues. One type consists of stimuli not reported by the client but inferred by the therapist to be related to the client-reported cues. The other type consists of cues that are identified by the therapist based on psychoanalytic theory. The therapist validates these hypothesized cues by observing the client for emotional responses, such as sweating, restlessness, facial flushing, or negative comments, during their presentation. Hypothesized cues that do not elicit signs or reports of discomfort are discarded by the therapist. Cues that elicit strong emotional responses are expanded and repeated. Hypothesized cues are considered to be more potent than client-reported cues because of their presumed greater proximity to the original traumatic episode.

During therapy, the client is instructed to "lose" him- or herself in the scenes described by the therapist, which are embellished with graphic and sometimes surreal imagery. For example, a snake-phobic subject might be asked to imagine being stalked and swallowed by a monster snake or having millions of tiny snakes slithering up his or her nose and into the mouth and ears. The therapist also probes for evidence of unresolved inner conflicts, such as anxiety about sex, through interviews with the client about childhood experiences and relationships. Relevant themes, as suggested by psychoanalytic theory, are incorporated into new scenes for the client to visualize and act out. Scene presentation is also dynamic, with material evolving on the basis of client feedback. For example, a client who was being treated for impotence spontaneously recalled an episode when his first-grade teacher ridiculed him for not being able to write the number six in front of the class. This memory was incorporated into a subsequent implosion session by the therapist.

The supposition underlying implosion therapy is that continuous and inescapable exposure to a stimulus that elicits fear or anxiety in the absence of reinforcement or negative consequences will eventually weaken the anxiety-eliciting power of the stimulus. This principle

derives from classical studies of Pavlovian fear conditioning in which a neutral stimulus (conditioned stimulus) that predicts an aversive stimulus (unconditioned stimulus) acquires the ability to elicit a conditioned fear response. This learned fear response can be extinguished by subsequently presenting the conditioned stimulus without the unconditioned stimulus. Subsequent research has shown that extinction involves new learning rather than unlearning and that this new learning is specific to the extinction context. Psychologist Mark E. Bouton, a pioneer of the view that Pavlovian extinction is context dependent, has discussed its implications for exposure-based therapies in general.

Intense/prolonged exposure therapy is rapid and advantageous for clients who want immediate relief. Ethical considerations have been raised about the extreme level of discomfort that clients experience when undergoing implosion or flooding and the possibility that treatment may exacerbate a client's anxiety. Clients may have to imagine a disturbing scene for more than an hour and rehearse the scenes outside of the therapeutic setting. A 1980 survey of exposure therapists, however, revealed serious negative side effects in only 9 of 3,493 clients (0.26 percent).

HISTORY AND EVALUATION OF IMPLOSION

Implosion was developed by the psychologist Thomas G. Stampfl in 1957 and outlined in a series of papers coauthored with psychologist Donald J. Levis from 1966 to 1969. Freudian psychodynamic concepts guide identification of hypothesized anxiety-eliciting stimuli; principles of Pavlovian and instrumental conditioning are invoked to explain acquisition, maintenance, and extinction of anxiety reactions. Stampfl and his colleagues claimed high success rates using this unique integrated approach and reported marked changes in symptomatology within one to fifteen one-hour sessions. Despite such reports, growth in the use of implosion was slow, a situation that psychologist Robert H. Shipley blamed on uncertainty about the technique and concern about its potential for worsening a client's condition.

A 1973 review by psychologist Kenneth P. Morganstern was highly critical of exposure-therapy research. Case studies did not control for spontaneous remission of symptoms. Laboratory (analogue) studies tended to use mildly phobic subjects with little potential relevance to clinical populations. Moreover, experimental confounds made it impossible to draw any firm conclusions about the relative efficacy of implosion, flooding, and systematic desensitization. While exposure therapy has since gained widespread acceptance, the distinction between implosion and flooding is often blurred, and the terms are frequently used synonymously to refer to prolonged/intense exposure to anxiety-eliciting stimuli.

EXPOSURE THERAPY

Exposure therapies have gained recognition as efficient and effective treatments for post-traumatic stress disorders (PTSD). A 1998 study reported that eighteen of twenty-four infants were successfully treated with flooding for post-traumatic feeding disorders and that treatment prognosis correlated with four behavioral measures, including passive refusal to swallow food and not chewing/sucking/moving food placed in the mouth for more than five seconds. Success has also been reported for treating veterans with combat trauma and victims of physical and sexual assault.

Advances in technology have allowed therapists to use virtual reality or computer-simulated exposure to replace in vivo exposure, which is not always practical, affordable, or safe. A 2007 review reported positive results of virtual reality exposure for combat veterans and a victim of the September 11, 2001, terrorist attacks. Whether this approach will come to replace implosion or imaginal flooding will depend on the outcome of studies using well-controlled, robust randomized trials with clinically identified populations and long-term follow-ups.

BIBLIOGRAPHY

Abramowitz, Jonathan S., Brett J. Deacon, and Stephen P. H. Whiteside. *Exposure Therapy for Anxiety: Principles and Practice.* New York: Guilford, 2011. Print.

Bouton, Mark E. "Context and Ambiguity in the Extinction of Emotional Learning: Implications for Exposure Therapy." *Behaviour Research and Therapy* 26.2 (1988): 137–49. Print.

Gregg, Lynsey, and Nicholas Tarrier. "Virtual Reality in Mental Health." *Social Psychiatry & Psychiatric Epidemiology* 42.5 (2007): 343–54. Print.

Morganstern, Kenneth P. "Implosive Therapy and Flooding Procedures: A Critical Review." *Psychological Bulletin* 79.5 (1973): 318–34. Print.

Neudeck, Peter, and Hans-Ulrich Wittchen, eds. *Exposure Therapy: Rethinking the Model—Refining the Method.* New York: Springer, 2012. Print.

Shipley, Robert H. "Implosive Therapy: The Technique." *Psychotherapy: Theory, Research, and Practice* 16.2 (1979): 140–47. Print.

Sisemore, Timothy A. *The Clinician's Guide to Exposure Therapies for Anxiety Spectrum Disorders: Integrating Techniques and Applications from CBT, DBT, and ACT.* Oakland: New Harbinger, 2012. Print.

Spiegler, Michael D., and David C. Guevremont. *Contemporary Behavior Therapy.* 5th ed. Belmont: Wadsworth, 2010. Print.

Ruth M. Colwill

SEE ALSO: Anger; Anxiety disorders; Aversion therapy; Behavior therapy; Eye movement desensitization and reprocessing; Fear; Freudian psychology; Pavlovian conditioning; Phobias; Post-traumatic stress disorder; Systematic desensitization; Virtual reality.

Imprinting

TYPE OF PSYCHOLOGY: Learning

Imprinting is an endogenous, or inborn, animal behavior by which young mammals and birds learn specific, visible physical patterns to associate with important concepts such as the identification of one's mother, navigation routes, and danger. The phenomenon, which relies primarily on visual cues and hormonal scents, is of high survival value for the species possessing it..

KEY CONCEPTS

- Conditioning
- Critical period
- Endogenous behavior
- Ethology
- Exogenous behavior
- Imprinting
- Pheromone
- Plasticity
- Visual cues
- Vocal cues

INTRODUCTION

Imprinting is an important type of behavior by which an animal learns specific concepts and identifies certain objects or individuals that are essential for survival. Imprinting events almost always occur very early in the life of an animal, during critical periods or time frames when the animal is most sensitive to environmental cues and influences. The phenomenon occurs in a variety of species, but it is most pronounced in the homeothermic (warm-blooded) and socially oriented higher vertebrate species, especially mammals and birds.

Imprinting is learned behavior. Most learned behavior falls within the domain of exogenous behavior, or behavior that an animal obtains by its experiences with fellow conspecifics (members of the same species) and the environment. Imprinting, however, is predominantly, if not exclusively, an endogenous behavior, which is a behavior that is genetically encoded within the individual.

An individual is born with the capacity to imprint. The animal's cellular biochemistry and physiology will determine when in its development the imprinting will occur. The only environmental influence of any consequence in imprinting is the object of the imprint during the critical period. Ethologists, scientists who study animal behavior, debate the extent of endogenous and exogenous influences on animal behavior. Most behaviors involve a combination of both, although one type may be more pronounced than the other.

The capacity for an animal to imprint is genetically determined and, therefore, is inherited. This type of behavior is to the animal's advantage for critical situations that must be correctly handled the first time they occur. Such behaviors include the identification of one's parents (especially one's mother), the ability to navigate, the ability to identify danger, and even the tendency to perform the language of one's own species. Imprinting behaviors generally are of high survival value and hence must be programmed into the individual via the genes. Biological research has failed to identify many of the genes that are responsible for imprinting behaviors, although the hormonal basis of imprinting is well understood. Most imprinting studies have focused on the environmental signals and developmental state of the individual during the occurrence of imprinting.

MATERNAL IMPRINTING

These studies have involved mammals and birds, warm-blooded species that have high social bonding, which seems to be a prerequisite for imprinting. The most famous imprinting studies were performed by the animal behaviorists and Nobel laureates Konrad Lorenz and Nikolaas Tinbergen. They and their many colleagues detailed analyses of imprinting in a variety of species, in particular waterfowl such as geese and ducks. The maternal imprinting behavior of the newborn gosling or duckling on the first moving object that it sees is the most striking example of imprinting behavior.

The maternal imprint is the means by which a newborn identifies its mother and the mother identifies its young. In birds, the newborn chick follows the first moving object that it sees, an object that should be its mother. The critical imprinting period is within a few hours after hatching. The chick visually will lock on its moving mother and follow it wherever it goes until the chick reaches adulthood. The act of imprinting not only allows for the identification of one's parents but also serves as a trigger for all subsequent social interactions with members of one's own species. As has been established in numerous experiments, a newborn gosling that first sees a female duck will imprint on the duck and follow it endlessly. On reaching adulthood, the grown goose, which has been raised in the social environment of ducks, will attempt to behave as a duck, even to the point of mating. Newborn goslings, ducklings, and chicks can easily imprint on humans.

In mammals, imprinting relies not only on visual cues (specific visible physical objects or patterns that an animal learns to associate with certain concepts) but also on physical contact and smell.

Newborn infants imprint on their mothers, and vice versa, by direct contact, sight, and smell during the critical period, which usually occurs within twenty hours following birth. The newborn and its mother must come into direct contact with each other's skin and become familiarized with each other's smell. The latter phenomenon involves the release of special hormones called pheromones from each individual's body. Pheromones trigger a biochemical response in the body of the recipient individual, in this case leading to a locked identification pattern for the other involved individual. If direct contact between mother and infant is not maintained during the critical imprinting period, then the mother may reject the infant because she is unfamiliar with its scent. In such a case, the infant's life would be in jeopardy unless it were claimed by a substitute mother. Even in this situation, the failure to imprint would trigger subsequent psychological trauma in the infant, possibly leading to aberrant social behavior in later life.

BIRD MIGRATION AND DANGER RECOGNITION

Although maternal imprinting in mammal and bird species is the best-documented example of imprinting behavior, imprinting may be involved in other types of learned behavior. In migratory bird species, ethologists have attempted to explain how bird populations navigate from their summer nesting sites to their wintering sites and back every year without error. Different species manage to navigate in different fashions. The indigo bunting, for example, navigates via the patterns of stars in the sky at night. Indigo bunting chicks imprint on the celestial star patterns for their summer nesting site during a specific critical period, a fact that was determined by the rearrangement of planetarium stars for chicks by research scientists.

Further research studies on birds also implicate imprinting in danger recognition and identification of one's species-specific call or song. Young birds of many species identify predatory birds, such as hawks, falcons, and owls, by the outline of the predator's body during flight or attack and by special markings on the predator's body. Experiments also have demonstrated that unhatched birds can hear their mother's call or song; birds may imprint on their own species' call or song before they hatch. These studies reiterate the fact that imprinting is associated with a critical period during early development in which survival-related behaviors must become firmly established.

HUMAN IMPRINTING

Imprinting is of considerable interest to psychologists because of its role in the learning process for humans. Humans imprint in much the same fashion as other mammals. The extended lifetime, long childhood, and great capacity for learning and intelligence make imprinting in humans an important area of study. Active research on imprinting is continually being conducted with humans, primates, marine mammals (such as dolphins, whales, and seals), and many other mammals, as well as with a large variety of bird species. Comparisons among the behaviors of these many species yield considerable similarities in the mechanisms of imprinting. These similarities underscore the importance of imprinting events in the life, survival, and socialization of the individual.

With humans, maternal imprinting occurs much as with other mammals. The infant and its mother must be in direct contact during the hours following birth. During this critical period, there is an exchange of pheromones between mother and infant, an exchange that, to a large extent, will bond the two. Such bonding immediately following birth can occur between infant and father in the same manner. Many psychologists stress the importance of both parents being present at the time of a child's delivery and making contact with the child during the critical hours of the first day following birth. Familiarization

is important not only for the child but for the parents as well because all three are imprinting on one another.

Failure of maternal or paternal imprinting during the critical period following birth can have drastic consequences in humans. The necessary, and poorly understood, biochemical changes that occur in the bodies of a child and parent during the critical period will not occur if there is no direct contact and, therefore, no transfer of imprinting pheromones. Consequently, familiarization and acceptance between the involved individuals may not occur, even if intense contact is maintained after the end of the critical period. The psychological impact on the child and on the parents may be profound, perhaps not immediately, but in later years. Studies on this problem are extremely limited because of the difficulty of tracing cause-and-effect relationships over many years when many behaviors are involved. There is some evidence, however, that indicates that failure to imprint may be associated with such things as learning disabilities, child-parent conflicts, and abnormal adolescent behavior. Nevertheless, other cases of imprinting failure seem to have no effect, as can be seen in tens of thousands of adopted children. The success or failure of maternal imprinting in humans is a subject of considerable importance in terms of how maternal imprinting affects human behavior and social interactions in later life.

Different human cultures maintain distinct methods of child rearing. In some cultures, children are reared by family servants or relatives from birth onward, not by the mother. Some cultures wrap infants very tightly so that they can barely move; other cultures are more permissive. Child and adolescent psychology focuses attention on early life experiences that could have great influence on later social behavior. The success or failure of imprinting, along with other early childhood experiences, may be a factor in later social behaviors such as competitiveness, interaction with individuals of the opposite sex, mating, and maintenance of a stable family structure. Even criminal behavior and psychological abnormalities may be traceable to such early childhood events.

EXPERIMENTS

Imprinting studies conducted with nonhuman mammals and bird species are much easier than those with humans because the researcher has the freedom to conduct controlled experiments that test many different variables, thereby identifying the factors that influence an individual animal's ability to imprint. For bird species, a famous experiment is the moving ball experiment.

A newly hatched chick is isolated in a chamber within which a suspended ball revolves around the center of the chamber. The researcher can test not only movement as an imprinting trigger but also other variables, such as critical imprinting time after hatching, color as an imprinting factor, and variations in the shape of the ball as imprinting factors. Other experiments involve switching eggs between different species (for example, placing a duck egg among geese eggs).

For mammals, imprinting has been observed in many species, such as humans, chimpanzees, gorillas, dolphins, elephant seals, wolves, and cattle. In most of these species, the failure of a mother to come into contact with its newborn almost always results in rejection of the child. In species such as elephant seals, smell is the primary means by which a mother identifies its pups. Maternal imprinting is of critical importance in a mammalian child's subsequent social development. Replacement of a newborn monkey's natural mother with a "doll" substitute leads to irreparable damage; the infant will be socially and sexually repressed in its later encounters with other monkeys. These and other studies establish imprinting as a required learning behavior for the successful survival and socialization of all birds and nonhuman mammals.

BIOLOGY AND BEHAVIOR

Animal behaviorists and psychologists attempt to identify the key factors that are responsible for imprinting in mammalian and avian species. Numerous factors, including vocal cues (specific sounds, frequency, and language that an animal learns to associate with certain concepts) and visual cues, are probably involved, although the strongest two factors appear to be direct skin contact and the exchange of pheromones that are detectable by smell. The maternal imprinting behavior is the most intensively studied imprinting phenomenon, though imprinting appears to occur in diverse behaviors such as mating, migratory navigation, and certain forms of communication.

Imprinting attracts the interest of psychologists because it occurs at critical periods in an individual's life; because subsequent developmental, social, and behavioral events hinge on what happens during the imprinting event; and because imprinting occurs at the genetic or biochemical level. Biochemically, imprinting relies on the production and release of pheromones, molecules that have a specific structure and that can be manufactured in the laboratory. The identification and mass production of these pheromones could possibly produce treatments for some behavioral abnormalities.

As an endogenous (instinctive) form of learning, imprinting relies on the highly complex nervous and endocrine systems of birds and mammals. It also appears limited to social behavior, a major characteristic of these species. The complex nervous systems involve a highly developed brain, vocal communication, well-developed eyes, and a keen sense of smell. The endocrine systems of these species produce a variety of hormones, including the pheromones that are involved in imprinting, mating, and territoriality. Understanding the nervous and endocrine regulation of behavior at all levels is of major interest to biological and psychological researchers. Such studies may prove to be fruitful in the discovery of the origin and nature of animal consciousness.

Imprinting may be contrasted with exogenous forms of learning. One type of exogenous learning is conditioning, in which individuals learn by repeated exposure to a stimulus, by association of the concept stimulus with apparently unrelated phenomena and objects, or by a system of reward and punishment administered by parents. Other exogenous learning forms include habituation (getting used to something) and trial and error. All learned behaviors are a combination of endogenous and exogenous factors.

BIBLIOGRAPHY

Beck, William S., Karel F. Liem, and George Gaylord Simpson. Life: *An Introduction to Biology*. 3rd ed. New York: Harper, 1991. Print.

Chaffee, Dalton W., Hayes Griffin, and R. Tucker Gilman. "Sexual Imprinting: What Strategies Should We Expect to See in Nature?" *Evolution* 67.12 (2013): 3588–99. Print.

Jablonka, Eva, and Marion J. Lamb. *Evolution in Four Dimensions: Genetic, Epigenetic, Behavioral, and Symbolic Variation in the History of Life*. Rev. ed. Cambridge: MIT P, 2014. Print.

Klopfer, Peter H., and Jack P. Hailman. *An Introduction to Animal Behavior: Ethology's First Century*. 2nd ed. Englewood Cliffs: Prentice, 1974. Print.

Manning, Aubrey, and Marian Stamp Dawkins. *An Introduction to Animal Behaviour*. 6th ed. New York: Cambridge UP, 2012. Print.

Raven, Peter H., et al. *Biology*. 10th ed. New York: McGraw, 2014. Print.

Schneider, Susan M. *The Science of Consequences: How They Affect Genes, Change the Brain, and Impact Our*

World. Amherst: Prometheus, 2012. Print.

Thornton, Stephanie. *Understanding Human Development: Biological, Social and Psychological Processes from Conception to Adult Life*. New York: Palgrave, 2008. Print.

Town, Stephen. "The Effects of Social Rearing on Preferences Formed during Filial Imprinting and Their Neural Correlates." *Experimental Brain Research* 212.4 (2011): 575–81. Print.

Wallace, Robert A., Gerald P. Sanders, and Robert J. Ferl. *Biology: The Science of Life*. 4th ed. New York: Harper, 1996. Print.

Wilson, Edward O. *Sociobiology: The New Synthesis*. 25th anniv. ed. Cambridge: Belknap, 2000. Print.

David Wason Hollar, Jr.

SEE ALSO: Defense reactions: Species-specific; Ethology; Father-child relationship; Genetics and mental health; Hormones and behavior; Instinct theory; Learning; Lorenz, Konrad; Mother-child relationship; Reflexes; Reflexes in newborns.

Impulse control disorders (ICD)

TYPE OF PSYCHOLOGY: Emotion; Sensation and perception; Social psychology; Stress

Impulse control disorders are represented by destructive behaviors resulting from the inability to control urges to act irresponsibly.

KEY CONCEPTS

- Destruction
- Disruption
- Exhilaration
- Gratification
- Irresistibility
- Pleasure
- Relief
- Spontaneity
- Tension

INTRODUCTION

Impulse control disorders are characterized by spontaneous behavior that satisfies a person's urges to feel tension-induced exhilaration. Mental health authorities attribute impulse control disorders to neurological or environmental causes that are aggravated by stress. People with impulse control disorders have an intense craving for instant gratification of specific desires and are usually unable to ignore temptations that tend to cause negative results. Pressure increases these people's impulsive urges until they become irresistible, and they feel pleasure and relief when yielding control to enjoy appealing yet unacceptable activities. They are compelled to engage in destructive, sometimes violent behaviors. Most people with impulse control disorders feel no guilt or remorse for their actions.

People who have impulse control disorders repeatedly indulge in a behavioral pattern of impulsivity, disrupting their lives. Their family and employment roles are often impaired. They frequently face legal ramifications for their recurrent impulsive behavior. People suffering from impulse control disorder often experience associated anxiety, stress, and erratic sleeping cycles.

For centuries, people have been aware of behavior associated with modern impulse control disorders. By 1987, the revised third edition of the American Psychiatric Association's *Diagnostic and Statistical Manual of Mental Disorders (DSM-III-R)* defined impulse control disorders as representing mental disorders that involve uncontrollable impulsive behavior that can potentially result in danger and harm to the affected person or other people. According to this classification, individuals with impulse control disorders are unable to resist urges to engage in this behavior despite feeling tension prior to impulsive activity. During the impulsive behavior, the person usually experiences sensations of release, titillation, and then satisfaction.

The 1994 DSM-IV assigned codes to six types of impulse control disorders not elsewhere classified: pathological gambling (312.31), kleptomania (312.32), pyromania (312.33), intermittent explosive disorder (312.34), trichotillomania (312.39), and impulse control disorder not otherwise specified (312.30). These classifications were retained in the text revision, DSM-IV-TR, published in 2000.

The DSM-V, published in 2013, added two childhood disruptive behavior disorders, oppositional defiant disorder and conduct disorder, to the category of impulse control disorders, and renamed the category as a whole "disruptive, impulse-control, and conduct disorders." Additionally, gambling disorder, previously considered an impulse disorder, was moved to the addiction category following research which established that impulsivity was not significantly higher in those who gambled compulsively than those who did not and that gambling, for those with this disorder, activated reward centers in the brain similar to those activated by addictive substances. Trichotillomania, meanwhile, was moved to the category of obsessive-compulsive and related disorders.

Sometimes impulse control disorders are associated with other mental illnesses, such as bipolar disorders, impulse control disorders or behaviors including road rage.

Patients are often identified with an impulse control disorder while undergoing treatment for another psychological problem. Some mental health professionals attribute behaviors classified as impulse control disorders to types of different mental conditions. Impulse control disorders are distinguished by being primarily characterized by people's absence of control over potentially damaging impulses.

RISKY IMPULSIVENESS

In 2002 it was estimated that shoplifters steal approximately thirteen billion dollars of merchandise from stores in the United States every year. While many of these thieves are criminals, impoverished people, substance abusers, or teenagers responding to a dare, some thieves have kleptomania. This impulse control disorder is characterized by people submitting to urges to steal items that are not essential to sustain their lives or for the purpose of generating revenues. Instead, kleptomaniacs, usually women, steal to experience thrilling sensations of fear. The threat of being caught, arrested, and prosecuted does not discourage most kleptomaniacs. Occasionally, people with kleptomania experience guilty feelings and discreetly return stolen items. Some mental health professionals state that kleptomaniacs have an addictive-compulsive disorder, not an impulse control disorder.

The DSM-V describes kleptomania as a pattern of impulsive stealing with the motive to achieve emotional release, then enjoyment. Therapists evaluate whether patients steal because of specific manic episodes or because they suffer from an antisocial personality or conduct disorder. A kleptomania diagnosis is made when patients continually steal unnecessary objects, do not steal because they are delusional, are not motivated by a resentful need to retaliate against businesses, and report feelings of tension, relief, and gratification.

People who have pyromania repeatedly set fires to experience similar emotions. The DSM-V defines pyromania as recurrent acts of arson for personal enjoyment. Pyromaniacs, usually men, cannot control impulses to spark fires because they are intrigued by the flames, the emergency response to fires, and the resulting destruction. Some children experience a temporary fascination with setting fires that might reveal other psychological problems. Therapists rule out manic episodes, antisocial personality and conduct disorders, delusional behavior, intoxication, and retardation before diagnosing patients with pyromania.

Behaviors associated with pyromania include anxious feelings prior to a deliberate fire setting that culminate in excitement. Patients are usually obsessed with fire and related equipment. They often collect information about disastrous fires, learn about firefighting techniques, and eagerly discuss fires. Sometimes pyromaniacs indulge in pleasurable emotions by remaining at fire scenes to watch emergency personnel while delighting in the damage they have caused. Pyromaniacs do not set fires to make political statements, commit retaliatory sabotage, seek insurance money, or destroy criminal evidence.

Pyromania and kleptomania are both very rare disorders, affecting less than 1 percent of the population, according to the DSM-V.

CHILDHOOD BEHAVIOR DISORDERS

Conduct disorder (CD) is a disorder in which a child or adolescent routinely behaves in an antisocial manner, violating major social norms or the rights of other people without remorse or empathy for those they may have harmed. CD tends to present differently according to gender; boys with CD often engage in physical and verbal aggression, while girls engage in more covert behavior, such as stealing or lying. This may contribute to CD being diagnosed more often in males than in females. CD is often viewed as a precursor to antisocial personality disorder, which cannot be diagnosed before the age of eighteen.

Oppositional defiant disorder (ODD) is a childhood disorder in which the child shows a pattern of conflict with others, especially authority figures such as parents or teachers. The symptoms of the disorder are divided into three categories: angry mood, argumentative behavior, and vindictiveness. A child with ODD may act specifically to annoy others, pick fights, seek revenge when others behave in ways he or she doesn't like, blame others for his or her mistakes, or refuse to comply with rules or requests. A diagnosis of ODD is made when a child exhibits such behavior consistently over a six-month period and with a greater severity than is usual for the age group.

Both ODD and CD are commonly comorbid with attention deficit-hyperactivity disorder, and ODD may also be comorbid with other issues, such as depression. According to the DSM-V, a child with CD cannot be diagnosed with ODD and vice versa, although there is some dispute among clinicians about this rule.

INTERMITTENT EXPLOSIVE DISORDER

Intermittent explosive disorder is a violent form of impulsive control disorder. Patients repeatedly act out excessive aggressive impulses and often cause harm to the people and objects they attack. Sometimes property is destroyed. Physically destructive behavior is not required for a diagnosis of intermittent explosive disorder, however; nondistructive physical aggression and verbal aggression are considered sufficient as of the publication of the DSM-V. Based on the DSM-V classification, therapists examine patients for possible medication reactions, medical problems such as Alzheimer's disease or head injuries, and mental conditions such as psychotic, borderline personality, or attention-deficit hyperactivity disorders. Mental health professionals establish an intermittent explosive disorder diagnosis based on whether recurring aggressive behavior exceeds appropriate response to any stimuli and patients seem out of control.

People with intermittent explosive disorder frequently face legal charges of domestic violence, assault, and property destruction. Many patients do not feel guilty and refuse to accept responsibility for their attacks. They usually blame their victims, who they claim provoked them. Various forms of stress such as perceived insults and threats and fear of not having demands fulfilled also are offered as justification for intermittent explosive disorder assaults. Researchers have determined that some people with intermittent explosive disorder have irregularities in brain wave activity or chemistry.

TREATMENT

Psychotherapy and pharmacotherapy are the usual treatments for impulse control disorders. Based on a psychological evaluation, therapists choose treatment methods suitable for each patient and applicable to specific undesirable behaviors. Medication, outpatient therapy, and hospitalization at public or private facilities are options to treat impulse control disorders. Treatment success varies. Many kleptomaniacs are secretive about their behavior and only encounter therapists because of court orders following arrests. The 1990 Americans with Dis-

abilities Act does not recognize impulse control disorders as disabilities.

Some researchers suggest that selective serotonin reuptake inhibitors (SSRIs) can minimize impulses to steal, althought they do not cure kleptomania. Therapists use behavior modification techniques to develop alternative behaviors and motivations to replace destructive impulses and responses. Patients learn to revise irrational thinking patterns with cognitive therapy. Anger management methods help some people with intermittent explosive disorder, while neurofeedback aids others to manage stress and develop self-control.

BIBLIOGRAPHY

Barkley, Russell A. *Defiant Children: A Clinician's Manual for Assessment and Parent Training*. New York: Guilford, 2013. Print.

Gaynor, Jessica, and Chris Hatcher. *The Psychology of Child Firesetting: Detection and Intervention*. New York: Brunner, 1987. Print.

Goldman, Marcus J. *Kleptomania: The Compulsion to Steal—What Can Be Done?* Far Hills: New Horizon, 1998. Print.

Grant, Jon E., and Marc N. Potenza. *The Oxford Handbook of Impulse Control Disorders*. Oxford: Oxford UP, 2012. Print.

Hollander, Eric, and Dan J. Stein, eds. *Impulsivity and Aggression*. New York: Wiley, 1995. Print.

Maees, Michael, and Emil F. Coccaro, eds. *Neurobiology and Clinical Views on Aggression and Impulsivity*. New York: Wiley, 1998. Print.

Matthys, Walter, and John E. Lochman. *Oppositional defiant Disorder and Conduct Disorder in Childhood*. Chichester: Wiley-Blackwell, 2010. Print.

Webster, Christopher D., and Margaret A. Jackson, eds. *Impulsivity: Theory, Assessment, and Treatment*. New York: Guilford, 1997. Print

Elizabeth D. Schafer

SEE ALSO: Addictive personality and behaviors; Aggression: Reduction and control; Anger; Antidepressant medications; Bipolar disorder; Domestic violence; Drug therapies; Elder abuse; Endocrine system; Endorphins; Kleptomania; Misbehavior; Nervous system; Neurotransmitters; Optimal arousal theory; Psychopharmacology; Road rage; Substance use disorders.

Incentive theory of motivation

TYPE OF PSYCHOLOGY: Motivation

Incentive motivation is a determinant of behavior from without, in contrast to drive motivation, which is a determinant from within. Both jointly determine the quality and quantity of behavior. Each motivation can energize behavior alone, however, and the relative importance of each differs for different behaviors.

KEY CONCEPT
- Achievement motivation
- Anticipatory goal responses
- Brain reward mechanism
- Crespi effect
- Expectancy theory
- Intracranial self-stimulation

INTRODUCTION

Motivation refers to a group of variables that determine what behavior—and how strong and how persistent a behavior—is to occur. Motivation is different from learning. Learning variables are the conditions under which a new association is formed. An association is the potential for a certain behavior; however, it does not become behavior until motivation is introduced. Thus, motivation is necessary to convert a behavioral potential into a behavioral manifestation. Motivation turns a behavior on and off.

Incentive motivation is an attracting force, while drive motivation is an expelling force. Incentive is said to "pull" and drive to "push" an individual toward a goal. The attracting force originates from the reward object in the goal and is based on expectation of the goal object in certain locations in the environment. The expelling force originates from within organisms as a need, which is related to disturbances in homeostasis in the body. The two forces jointly determine behavior in a familiar environment. In a novel environment, however, there is not yet an expectation; no incentive motivation is yet formed, and drive is the only force to cause behavior. The organism can be expected to manifest various responses until the goal-oriented responses emerge.

Once the organism achieves the goal, the reward stimuli elicit consummatory responses. Before the organism reaches the goal, the stimuli that antedate the goal would elicit responses; these are termed anticipatory goal responses. The anticipatory responses are based on the associational experience among the goal stimuli, the goal responses, and the situational stimuli present prior to reaching the goal. The anticipatory responses and their stimulus consequences provide the force of incentive motivation. Incentive refers to the expected amount of reward given certain behavior.

Though drive motivation and incentive motivation jointly determine behaviors, the importance of each differs for different behaviors. For example, bar-pressing behavior for drinking water by an animal in a Skinner box normally requires both drive motivation, induced by water deprivation, and the incentive motivation of a past experience of getting water. Under special conditions, however, the animal will press the bar to drink water even without being water deprived. In this case, drinking is no longer related to drive. This type of drinking is called nonhomeostatic drinking. Drinking a sweet solution, such as one containing sugar or saccharin, does not require any deprivation, so the behavior to get sweet solutions is based on incentive motivation alone. Under normal conditions, sexual behavior is elicited by external stimuli, so sexual drive is actually incentive motivation elicited from without.

BEHAVIOR AND INCENTIVES

Two experiments will illustrate how the concept of incentive motivation may be applied to explain behavior. Carl J. Warden of Columbia University conducted a study that is regarded as a classic. A rat was placed in the start box of a short runway, and a reward (food) was placed in its goal box at the other end. The food-deprived animal had to cross an electrified grid on the runway to reach the goal. When the animal reached the goal, it was repeatedly brought back to the start box. The number of times the animal would cross the grid in a twenty-minute period was recorded. It was found that the longer the food deprivation, the more times the animal crossed the grid, for up to about three days without food, after which the number decreased. The animal crossed only about two times with no food deprivation; however, the number increased to about seventeen at three days of food deprivation, then decreased to about seven at eight days without food. When the animal was water deprived, the animal crossed the grid about twenty times to the goal box containing water at one day without water. When the reward was an infant rat, a mother rat crossed about twenty times. A male rat crossed about thirteen times to a female rat after being sex deprived (without a female companion) for one day. A female rat in heat crossed thirteen times to a male rat. Even without any object in the goal box, the animal crossed about six times; Warden attributed this to a "novelty" reward. The reward variable in this experiment was the goal object, which was manipulated to fit the source of the drive induced by deprivation or hormonal state (as in an estrous female). The rat, placed in the start box, was induced by the goal.

CRESPI EFFECT

The second study, conducted by Leo P. Crespi, established the concept of incentive motivation as an anticipatory response. He trained rats in a runway with different amounts of food and found that the animals reached different levels of performance. The speed of running was a function of the amount of reward: The more the food in the goal box, the faster the animal would run. There were three groups of rats. Group 1 was given 256 food pellets (about a full day's ration) in the goal box; the animals would run at slightly over 1 meter (about 3.28 feet) per second after twenty training trials. Group 2 was given 16 pellets, and their speed was about 76 centimeters (2.5 feet) per second. Group 3 was given only 1 pellet, and the speed was about 15 centimeters (6 inches) per second.

When the speed became stable, Crespi shifted the amount of food. The rats in all groups were now given 16 pellets. The postshift speed eventually, but not immediately, settled to near that of the group originally given 16 pellets. An interesting transitional effect of so-called incentive contrast was observed. Immediately after the shift from the 256-pellet reward to the 16-pellet reward, the animal's speed was much lower than the group continuously given the 16-pellet reward. Following the shift from the 1-pellet to the 16-pellet reward, however, the animal's speed was higher than the group continuously given the 16-pellet reward. Crespi called these the elation effect and the depression effect, or the positive contrast effect and the negative contrast effect, respectively. Clark L. Hull and K. W. Spencer, two of the most influential theorists of motivation and learning, interpreted the Crespi effect as evidence of anticipatory responses. They theorized that the goal response had become conditioned to the runway stimuli such that the fractional goal responses were elicited. Because the responses occurred before the goal responses, they were anticipatory in nature. The fractional goal responses, along with their stimulus consequence, constitute the incentive motivation that would energize a learned associative potential to make it into a behavior.

MANIPULATION OF MOTIVATION

Incentive motivation has been manipulated in many other ways: the delay of reward presentation, the quality of the reward, and various partial reinforcement schedules. In relation to the delay variable, the sooner the reward presentation follows the responses, the more effective it is in energizing behavior, although the relationship is not linear. In the case of partial reinforcement, when the subject received a reward only part of the time, behavior was shown to be more resistant to extinction than when reward was delivered every time following a response; that is, following withdrawal of the reward, the behavior lasted longer when the reward was given only part of the time than when the reward was given every time following the response. The quality of the reward variable could be changed by, for example, giving a monkey a banana as a reward after it had been steadily given raisins. In Warden's experiment, the various objects (water, food, male rat, female rat, or rat pup) placed in the goal box belong to the quality variable of incentive. Another incentive variable is how much effort a subject must exert to obtain a reward, such as climbing a slope to get to the goal versus running a horizontal path.

INTRACRANIAL SELF-STIMULATION

The term " reinforcer" usually indicates any stimulus that would result in increasing the probability or magnitude of a response on its presentation following that response. When the response has reached its maximum strength, however, a reinforcer can no longer increase it; nevertheless, it has a maintenance effect. Without it, the response would soon cease. A reward reinforces and maintains a response. It is believed that the rewarding effects are mediated by the brain; the mechanism that serves as the substrate of the effects has been studied.

In a breakthrough experiment in this line of study, in 1954, James Olds and Peter Milner reported that a rat would press a bar repeatedly to stimulate certain areas of its brain. (If the bar press resulted in stimulation of certain other areas of the brain, the rat would not repeat the bar press.) Thus, this particular brain electrical stimulation has a rewarding effect. The phenomenon is termed intracranial self-stimulation. The rewarding effect is so powerful that the hungry animal would rather press the bar to stimulate its brain than eat. It has also been shown that animals will press a bar to self-inject cocaine, amphetamine, morphine, and many other drugs. The rewarding effect is so powerful that if rats or monkeys are given access to a bar that allows continuous self-administration of cocaine, they often die of an overdose. It is now known that the neurotransmitter involved in this rewarding effect, as well as in the rewarding effect of food, is dopamine, acting at the nucleus accumbens, a part of the limbic system in the brain. Addictions and drug-directed behaviors can be understood better because of studies related to the brain reward mechanism. This mechanism is defined as the rewarding effect of various stimuli, such as food, cocaine, and intracranial self-stimulation, as related to dopamine activity in the brain. Whether incentive motivation is mediated by the same brain mechanism can also be studied.

ACHIEVEMENT MOTIVATION

In humans, achievement motivation can be measured to predict what a subject would choose to do given tasks of different difficulty as well as how persevering the subject will be when he or she encounters failure. Achievement motivation is related to past experiences of rewards and failures to obtain a reward, so it becomes an incentive motivation of anticipating either success or failure to obtain a reward. Fear of failure is a negative motivational force; that is, it contributes negatively to achievement motivation. Those people with a strong fear of failure will choose easy tasks to ensure success, and on encountering failure they will give up quickly.

Unless an individual anticipates or believes that the effort will lead to some desired outcome, the person will not expend much effort. Expectancy theory states that how much effort a person will expend depends on the expected outcome of the effort. If the expected outcome is positively correlated to the effort, the person will work as hard as possible. In a classroom setting, effort can be evaluated from a student's attendance, note taking, and discussions with classmates or teachers. The expected outcome would be to earn a particular grade, as well as perhaps to obtain a scholarship, make the dean's list, obtain a certain job, gain admission to graduate school, or gain respect from peers and parents. Unless the effort is perceived to be related to the outcome, little effort will be expended.

If one is expecting a big reward, one would work harder than if the reward were small. An Olympic gold medal is worth harder work than a school gold medal is. Anyone can affect other people's behavior with proper incentive; behavior can be manipulated to promote learning in students and promote productivity in industry. The way incentive is used to promote productivity distinguishes the free enterprise system based on a market economy from a socialist society of controlled economy which is not based on market force. In a socialist economy, one's reward is not based on the amount of one's economic contribution; it is based on the degree of socialistic behavior. One's political background, in terms of family, loyalty to the party, and "political consciousness," are the things that matter most. It is difficult or impossible to predict, under this kind of reward situation, what kinds of activities will be reinforced and maintained. The expected outcome of an individual's effort or behavior is the incentive motivation; teachers and managers must understand it to promote desired learning and production. For example, an employee will be motivated to perform certain tasks well by a pay raise only when he or she perceives the relationship between the effort and the raise. A student will be motivated to study only when he or she sees the relationship between the effort and the outcome.

RELATIONSHIP TO PLEASURE

The concepts of incentive, reward, and reinforcement originated with the concept of pleasure, or hedonism. The assumption that a major motivation of behavior is the pursuit of pleasure has a long history. Epicurus, a fourth century b.c.e. Greek philosopher, asserted that pleasure is good and wholesome and that human life should maximize it. Later, Christian philosophers asserted that pleasure is bad and that if a behavior leads to pleasure it is most likely bad as well. John Locke, a seventeenth century British philosopher, asserted that behavior is based on maximizing anticipated pleasure. Whether a behavior would indeed lead to pleasure was another matter. Thus, Locke's concept of hedonism became a behavioral principle. Modern incentive motivation, based on anticipation of reward, has the same tone as Locke's behavioral principle. Both traditions involve the concepts of incentive and of reinforcement being a generator of behaviors.

There is a danger of circularity in this line of thought. For example, one may explain behavior in terms of it resulting in obtaining a reward, then explain or define reward in terms of behavior. There is no new understanding to be gained in such circular reasoning. Fortunately, there is an independent definition of the rewarding effect, in terms of the brain mechanism of reward. If this mechanism is related to pleasure, there could also be a definition of pleasure independent of behavior. Pleasure and reward are the motivating force, and anticipation of them is incentive motivation. Because it attracts people toward their sources, by manipulating the sources, the behavior can be predictably altered.

BIBLIOGRAPHY

Bolles, Robert C. *Theory of Motivation*. 2d ed. New York: Harper, 1975. Print.

Comer, Ronald J., and Elizabeth Gould. *Psychology Around Us*. Hoboken: Wiley, 2013. Print.

Crespi, Leo P. "Quantitative Variation of Incentive and Performance in the White Rat." *American Journal of Psychology* 55.4 (1942): 467–517. Print.

Deckers, Lambert. *Motivation: Biological, Psychological, and Environmental*. 3d ed. Boston: Allyn, 2009. Print.

Green, Russell. *Human Motivation: A Social Psychological Approach*. Pacific Grove: Brooks, 1995. Print.

Kohn, Alfie. *Punished by Rewards: The Trouble with Gold Stars, Incentive Plans, A's, Praise, and Other Bribes*. Boston: Houghton, 1999. Print.

Liebman, Jeffrey M., and Steven J. Cooper, eds. *The Neuropharmacological Basis of Reward*. Oxford: Oxford UP, 1989. Print.

Logan, Frank A., and Douglas P. Ferraro. *Systematic Analyses of Learning and Motivation*. New York: Wiley, 1978. Print.

Olds, James, and Peter Milner. "Positive Reinforcement Produced by Electrical Stimulation of Septal Area and Other Regions of Rat Brain." *Journal of Comparative and Physiological Psychology* 47 (1954): 419–427. Print.

Ryan, Richard M. *The Oxford Handbook of Human Motivation*. Oxford: Oxford UP, 2012. Print.

Shah, James Y., and Wendi L. Gardner, eds. *Handbook of Motivation Science*. New York: Guilford, 2008. Print.

Warden, Carl John. *Animal Motivation: Experimental Studies on the Albino Rat*. New York: Columbia UP, 1931. Print.

Sigmund Hsiao

SEE ALSO: Achievement motivation; Drives; Educational psychology; Hull, Clark L.; Motivation; Motivation: Intrinsic and extrinsic; Sex hormones and motivation; Skinner box; Work motivation.

Incompetency

TYPE OF PSYCHOLOGY: Cognition; Psychopathology

Incompetency refers to a state of diminished mental functioning such that a person is judged unable to give voluntary and informed consent to psychiatric hospitalization, undergo a medical procedure, participate in research, or, in legal contexts, stand trial, waive constitutional rights, enter a plea, or be executed. Among the conditions that affect mental capacity are mental retardation, mental illness, and the progressive dementia seen in older adults. Juveniles are also seen as having diminished competency based on cognitive immaturity. Although specialized measures of mental capacity are available, no widely accepted, standardized method exists to establish competency.

KEY CONCEPTS

- Competency
- Informed consent
- Medical decision-making capacity
- Mental capacity
- Situation-specific decision-making capacity
- Treatment-specific decision-making capacity

INTRODUCTION

The terms "incompetency" and "incompetence" refer to a state of diminished mental functioning that, for example, precludes an individual from giving informed consent to go undergo a particular medical procedure. Other contexts in which the issue of incompetency—or its obverse, competency—might arise include competence to consent voluntarily to psychiatric hospitalization, competence to give informed consent to participate in research, and competence in right-to-die issues, such as requesting physician-assisted suicide. In legal contexts, situations requiring determination of whether an individual has the requisite mental abilities for competent decision making include competence to execute a will, competence to enter a plea, competence to stand trial, competence to waive Miranda and other constitutional rights, competence to waive death sentence appeals, and competence to be executed.

Psychologists and other mental health professionals rarely use the terms "incompetency" and "incompetent" because they imply a global deficit that has little practical meaning or application. Alzheimer's disease patients, for example, are at risk for autonomy-restricting interventions, including institutionalization and guardianship. As greater attention is paid to preserving individual rights, increased emphasis is placed on identifying, in functional terms, specific mental tasks and skills that people retain and lose. "Mental capacity" is the term used to describe the cluster of mental skills that people use in their everyday lives. It includes memory, logic and reasoning, the ability to calculate, and the mental flexibility to shift attention from one task to another. Describing a person's ability or mental capacity to perform particular tasks, such as remembering to pay bills or calculating how much change is owed, enables professionals to assess vulnerability more effectively and develop suitable treatment and service plans.

Medical decision-making capacity is defined as the ability to give informed consent to undergo a particular medical test or intervention or the ability to refuse such intervention. Capacity may extend to the question of disclosure of sensitive confidential information or an individual's permission to participate in research. When a legal determination of competency has not been made, decisional capacity is used to describe an individual's ability to make a health care decision.

CONDITIONS AND FACTORS AFFECTING MENTAL CAPACITY

Among the conditions that affect mental capacity are mental retardation, mental illness, and the progressive dementia seen in older adults. There are also a variety of other medical conditions that can interfere with mental capacity—for example, the encephalopathy seen in patients with advanced liver disease. It should be noted that capacity can and will vary over time, either as a disease process progresses, as in a dementing illness, or as clinical conditions wax and wane, as in a patient with a bipolar disorder. In the case of delirium, for example, a patient may be capable of participating in treatment decisions in the morning but incapable of making a decision at a later point in that day. A variety of factors, some of which are treatable, may contribute to mental decline. These include poor nutrition, depression, and interactions among medications.

Mental, or decision-making, capacity is also treatment- or situation-specific. For example, a person may have the ability to agree to a diagnostic procedure, yet be unable to comprehend fully the consequences of accepting a particular medication or surgical intervention. When assessing capacity, one is determining whether an individual is capable of deciding about a specific treatment or class of treatments rather than making a global determination of incompetence. A person will sometimes be found to have the capacity to make some decisions and yet not others, especially when more complex information must be presented and understood.

THE ROLE OF THE MENTAL HEALTH PRACTITIONER

Psychologists and other mental health practitioners are often asked to evaluate a person's cognitive functioning to determine whether the individual is competent, for example, to execute a will or to assign power of attorney. For individuals obviously in mental decline, the role of the psychologist is to determine whether it is appropriate to appoint a guardian to manage the person's financial affairs and to make medical decisions regarding long-term care. To determine treatment decision-making capacity, the psychologist assesses the individual's understanding of the disorder and the recommended treatment, appreciation of the situation and treatment choices, ability to reason and evaluate options and consequences of choices, and ability to express a choice.

Given the lack of consensus on both the exact criteria and the method for assessing mental competency, it is important that psychologists undertake a broad examination to determine an individual's ability to make decisions affecting his or her own welfare. A competency evaluation begins with a review of the person's medical and psychological records and history, with information being supplied by family members as well as the individual being evaluated. Following the record review, the individual is seen for a clinical interview, which includes several measures of orientation, short-term memory, and reasoning ability.

Following the clinical interview, psychological testing is administered for an objective assessment of cognitive functioning. The psychologist then offers an expert opinion, based on the evaluation, regarding whether the person is capable of making decisions regarding his or her welfare and finances.

This process is also done retrospectively at times, for example, to determine if an individual was competent when the person's last will was executed. The competency evaluation has been characterized as an iterative process in which the clinician is both assessing and attempting to maximize the individual's capacity and autonomy.

INSTRUMENTS FOR MAKING ASSESSMENTS

Although there is no definitive assessment instrument or battery of instruments that should be used to determine competency, a variety of commonly used instruments are available to the psychologist. Personality tests such as the Minnesota Multiphasic Personality Inventory-2 (MMPI-2) and the Personality Assessment Inventory (PAI), can be used to assess both abnormal and normal personality traits. The Wechsler Adult Intelligence Scale-IV (WAIS-IV) can be used to assess overall intelligence. If organic brain damage is suspected, the Luria-Nebraska, a neuro-psychological test, can be administered.

There are a variety of instruments that are specifically designed to look at competency issues, including Capacity to Consent to Treatment Instrument (CCTI), the MacArthur Competency Assessment Tools, the Competency Screening Test (CST), the Competency to Stand Trial Assessment Instrument(CAI), the Interdisciplinary Fitness Interview-Revised (IFI-R), the Georgia Court Competency Test (GCCT), the Evaluation of Competency to Stand Trial-Revised (ECST-R), the Aid to Capacity Evaluation, and the Competence Questionnaire (CQ), for which versions for pediatric medical patients and children in the juvenile justice system have been developed. The reliability and validity of all these instruments varies, and many of them were developed for very specific subjects. This must be kept in mind when they are employed in an evaluation.

COMPETENCY IN THE LEGAL CONTEXT

Often, forensic mental health professionals are called on to make a determination regarding a person's competency in a legal context. Psychologists may be asked to determine a person's competency to stand trial, to waive rights, to enter a plea, or to be executed. This deals specifically with whether the person was cogent of his or her actions and the results of those actions. This question may revolve around present-time actions or actions in the past. Assessing competency in the past can be particularly difficult. The psychologist's report would include psychiatric, medical, and substance abuse history, as well as results from mental status and psychological testing. A key part of the evaluation is the determination of the defendant's ability to understand the proceedings. Within the legal system, competency of adults is assumed, and the burden of proof rests on the individual questioning competency. Competency evaluations are often required for children in the juvenile justice system, and young children are assumed to not be competent.

The courts recognize a difference between competency and credibility in a court of law. An individual may be deemed to be incompetent, meaning that they have diminished capacity to understand; however, they may still be a credible witness, meaning that they can still relate (often to a judge or jury) events that have occurred. An individual may not be aware of what it means to waive rights, yet may still be able to tell the jury his or her whereabouts at the time a crime was committed.

BIBLIOGRAPHY

Arias, Jalayne J. "A Time to Step In: Legal Mechanisms for Protecting Those with Declining Capacity." *American Journ. of Law & Medicine* 39.1 (2013): 134–59. Print

Grisso, T., and P. S. Applebaum. *Assessing Competence to Consent to Treatment: A Guide for Physicians and Other Health Professionals.* New York: Oxford UP, 1998. Print.

Grisso, T., G. Vincent, and D. Seagrave, eds. *Handbook of Mental Health Screening and Assessment in Juvenile Justice.* New York: Guilford, 2005. Print.

Grisso, T., et al. "Juveniles' Competence to Stand Trial: A Comparison of Adolescents' and Adults' Capacities as Trial Defendants." *Law and Human Behavior* 27 (2003): 333–63. Print.

Looman, Mary. "Establishing Parental Capability as a Legal Competency in Child Maltreatment Cases." *Annals of the American Psychotherapy Association* 13.2 (2010): 45–52. Print.

O'Donnell, Philip C., and Bruce Gross. "Developmental Incompetence to Stand Trial in Juvenile Courts." *Journ. of Forensic Sciences* 57.4 (2012): 989–96. Print.

Sachs, G. A. "Assessing Decision-Making Capacity." *Topics in Stroke Rehabilitation* 7.1 (2000): 62–64. Print.

Schopp, Robert F. *Competence, Condemnation, and Commitment: An Integrated Theory of Mental Health Law.* Washington: APA, 2001. Print.

Allyson Washburn;
updated by Ayn Embar-Seddon O'Reilly
and Allan D. Pass

SEE ALSO: Abnormality: Legal models; Aging: Cognitive changes; Alzheimer's disease; Brain damage; Coping: Terminal illness; Death and dying; Decision making; Dementia; Juvenile delinquency; Law and psychology; Mental retardation.

Individual psychology
Alfred Adler

TYPE OF PSYCHOLOGY: Personality

Individual psychology is the personality theory that was developed by Alfred Adler after he broke from Freudian psychoanalytical ideas. Adler emphasized the importance of childhood inferiority feelings and stressed psychosocial rather than psychosexual development..

KEY CONCEPTS

- Compensation
- Inferiority
- Masculine protest
- Private logic
- Social interest
- Style of life

INTRODUCTION

Individual psychology is the name of the school of personality theory and psychotherapy developed by Alfred Adler, a Viennese general-practice physician turned psychiatrist. The term "individual" has a dual implication: It implies uniqueness (each personality exists in a person whose distinctiveness must be appreciated); also, the personality is an indivisible unit that cannot be broken down into separate traits, drives, or habits that could be analyzed as if they had an existence apart from the whole.

The essence of a person's uniqueness is his or her style of life, a unified system that provides the principles that guide everyday behavior and gives the individual a perspective with which to perceive the self and the world. The style of life is fairly stable after about age six, and it represents the individual's attempt to explain and cope with the great problem of human existence: the feeling of inferiority.

ROLE OF INFERIORITY

All people develop a feeling of inferiority. First of all, they are born children in an adult world and realize that they have smaller and weaker bodies, less knowledge, and virtually no privileges. Then people start to compare themselves and realize that there are other people their own age who are better athletes, better scholars, more popular, more artistically talented, wealthier, more socially privileged, more physically attractive, or simply luckier. If one allows the perception of one's own self-

worth to be influenced by such subjective comparisons, then one's self-esteem will be lowered by an inferiority complex.

Adler believed that since one's style of life is largely determined early in life, certain childhood conditions make individuals more vulnerable to feelings of inferiority. For example, children born into poverty or into ethnic groups subjected to prejudice may develop a heightened sense of inferiority. Those children with real disabilities (learning or physical disabilities, for example) would also be more susceptible to devaluing their own worth, especially when others are excessively critical or mocking.

ROLE OF EARLY FAMILY LIFE

Adler looked inside the family for the most powerful influences on a child's developing style of life. Parents who treat a child harshly (through physical, verbal, or sexual abuse) would certainly foster feelings of inferiority in that child. Similarly, parents who neglect or abandon their children contribute to the problem. (Adler believed that such children, instead of directing their rage outward against such parents, turn it inward and say, "There must be something wrong with me, or they would not treat me this way.") Surprisingly, Adler also believed that those parents who pamper their children frustrate the development of positive self-esteem, for such youngsters conclude that they must be very weak and ineffectual to require such constant protection and service. When such pampered children go out into the larger world and are not the recipients of constant attention and favors, their previous training has not prepared them for this; they rapidly develop inferior feelings.

The impact of the family on the formulation of one's style of life also includes the influence of siblings. Adler was the first to note that a child's birth order contributes to personality. Oldest children tend to be more serious and success-oriented, because they spend more time with their parents and identify more closely with them. When the younger children come along, the oldest child naturally falls into a leadership role. Youngest children are more likely to have greater social skills and be creative and rebellious. Regardless of birth order, intense sibling rivalries and comparisons can easily damage the esteem of children.

INDIVIDUAL INTERPRETATION OF CHOICE

Adler was not fatalistic in discussing the possible impact on style of life of these congenital and environmental forces; he held that it is neither heredity nor environment that determines personality but rather the way that individuals interpret heredity and environment. They furnish only the building blocks out of which the individual fashions a work of art: the style of life. People have (and make) choices, and this determines their own development; some people, however, have been trained by life to make better choices than others.

All individuals have the capacity to compensate for feelings of inferiority. Many great athletes were frail children and worked hard to develop their physical strength and skills. Great painters overcame weak eyesight; great musicians overcame poor hearing. Given proper encouragement, people are capable of great accomplishments.

DEVELOPMENT OF SOCIAL INTEREST

The healthy, normal course of development is for individuals to overcome their feelings of inferiority and develop social interest. This involves a feeling of community, or humanistic identification, and a concern with the well-being of others, not only one's own private feelings. Social interest is reflected in and reinforced by cooperative and constructive interactions with others. It starts in childhood, when the youngster has nurturing and encouraging contacts with parents, teachers, and peers.

Later, the three main pillars of social interest are friends, family, and career. Having friends can help overcome inferiority, because it allows one to be important in the eyes of someone else. Friends share their problems, so one does not feel like the only person who has self-doubt and frustration. Starting one's own family reduces inferiority feeling in much the same way. One feels loved by spouse and children, and one is very important to them. Having an occupation allows one to develop a sense of mastery and accomplishment and provides some service to others or to society at large. Therefore, those people who have difficulty establishing and maintaining friendships, succeeding as a spouse or parent, or finding a fulfilling career will have less opportunity to develop a healthy social interest and will have a greater susceptibility to lingering feelings of inferiority.

PRIVATE LOGIC

The alternatives to developing social interest as a way of escaping from feelings of inferiority are either to wallow in them or to explain them away with private logic. Private logic is an individual's techniques for coping with the feeling of inferiority by unconsciously redefining himself or herself in a way not compatible with social interest. Such individuals retreat from meaningful interpersonal relationships and challenging work because it might threaten their precariously balanced self-esteem. Private logic convinces these individuals to seek a sham sense of superiority or notoriety in some way that lacks social interest.

One such approach in private logic is what Adler termed masculine protest (because Western patriarchal culture has encouraged such behavior in men and discouraged it in women). The formula is to be rebellious, defiant, even violent. Underlying all sadism, for example, is an attempt to deny weakness. The gangster wants more than money, the rapist more than sex: they need a feeling of power to cover up an unresolved inferiority feeling. The prostitute wants more than money; she needs to have the power to attract and manipulate men, even though she herself may be totally dependent on her pimp or on drugs.

USE IN CHILD DEVELOPMENT STUDIES

Adler's theory, like Sigmund Freud's psychoanalysis and B. F. Skinner's radical behaviorism, is a flexible and powerful tool for understanding and guiding human behavior. The first and foremost applications of individual psychology have been in the areas of child rearing, education, and guidance. Because the first six years of life are formative, the contact that children have during this time with parents, teachers, siblings, and peers will influence that child's later decisions in the direction of social interest or private logic. Adlerians recommend that parents and teachers be firm, fair, and, above all, encouraging. One should tell children that they can overcome their disabilities and praise every progress toward accomplishment and social interest. One should avoid excessive punishments, for this will only convince children that others are against them and that they must withdraw into private logic.

After World War I, the new Social Democratic government of Austria gave Adler the task of developing a system of youth guidance clinics throughout the nation. Each child age six to fourteen was screened, then counseled, if necessary. In the 1920s, the rates of crime and mental disorders among young people declined dramatically.

USE IN ELDER STUDIES

A second example of the applicability of Adler's theory occurs at the other end of the life cycle: old age. Late life is a period in which the incidence of mental disorders, especially depression, increases. This can be understood in terms of diminished opportunity to sustain social interest and increased sources of inferiority feeling.

Recall that social interest has three pillars: career, friends, and family. Traditionally, people retire from work at about age sixty-five. Elders who do not develop satisfying new activities (especially activities that involve a sense of accomplishment and contribution to others) adjust poorly to retirement and tend to become depressed. Old friends die or move into retirement communities. Sometimes it is harder to see and talk with old friends because of the difficulty of driving or using public transportation as one ages, or because one or one's friends become hard of hearing or experience a stroke that impairs speech. By far the greatest interpersonal loss in later life is the loss of a spouse. When adult children move away in pursuit of their own lives, this may also give an elder the perception of being abandoned.

Conditions that can rekindle old feelings of inferiority abound in later life. Real physical inferiorities arise. The average elder reports at least two of the following chronic conditions: impaired vision, impaired hearing, a heart condition, stroke, or arthritis. The United States is a youth- and body-oriented culture that worships physical attractiveness, not wrinkles and fat. Some elders, especially those who have had the burdens of long-term illness, feel inferior because of their reduced financial resources.

USE IN STUDYING PREJUDICE

A third area of application is social psychology, especially the study of prejudice. Gordon Allport suggested that those who exhibit racial or religious prejudice are typically people who feel inferior themselves: They are trying to feel better about themselves by feeling superior to someone else. Typically, prejudice against African Americans has been greatest among whites of low socioeconomic status. Prejudice against new immigrants has been greatest among the more poorly skilled domestic workers. Another example of prejudice would be social class distinctions. The middle class feels inferior (in terms of wealth and privilege) to the upper class. Therefore, the middle class responds by using its private logic to demean the justification of wealth: "The rich are rich because their ancestors were robber barons or because they themselves were junk bond traders in the 1980s." The middle class feels superior to the lower class, however, and again uses private logic to justify and legitimize that class distinction: "The poor are poor because they

are lazy and irresponsible." To solidify its own identity as hardworking and responsible, the middle class develops a perception of the poor that is more derogatory than an objective analysis would permit.

The most telling application of the theory of individual psychology to prejudice occurred in the first part of the twentieth century in Germany. The rise of Nazi anti-Semitism can be associated with the humiliating German defeat in World War I and with the deplorable conditions brought about by hyperinflation and depression. Adolf Hitler first blamed the Jews for the "November treason" that stabbed the German army in the back. (This private logic allowed the German people to believe that their defeated army would have achieved an all-out victory at the front had it not been for the Jewish traitors back in Berlin.) All the problems of capitalism and social inequality were laid at the feet of Jewish financiers, and every fear of rabble-rousing Communists was associated with Jewish radicals. Since everything bad, weak, cowardly, or exploitive was labeled "Jewish," non-Jewish Germans could believe that they themselves were everything good. The result of the institutionalization of this private logic in the Third Reich led to one of the most blatant examples of masculine protest that humankind has witnessed: World War II and the Holocaust.

USE IN INTERPERSONAL RELATIONS

A fourth application is associated with management and sales. Management applies interpersonal relations to subordinates; sales applies interpersonal relations to prospective customers. Adler's formula for effective interpersonal relations is simple: Do not make the other person feel inferior. Treat workers with respect. Act as if they are intelligent, competent, wise, and motivated. Give subordinates the opportunity and the encouragement to do a good job, so that they can nurture their own social interest by having a feeling of accomplishment and contribution. Mary Kay Ash, the cosmetics magnate, said that she treated each of her employees and distributors as if each were wearing a sign saying "make me feel important." A similar strategy should apply to customers.

FREUD'S INFLUENCE

The idea of the inferiority complex bears some similarity to the writings of many previous thinkers. Nineteenth century French psychologist Pierre Janet came closest by developing a theory of perceived insufficiency as a root of all neurosis. American psychologist William James spoke of an innate craving to be appreciated. Adler's emphasis on the individual's capacity for compensation (a defense mechanism for overcoming feelings of inferiority by trying harder to excel) and on masculine protest has parallels in the writings of philosopher Friedrich Nietzsche.

Yet the optimistic, simplified, psychosocial approach of Adler can only be understood as a reaction to the pessimistic, esoteric, psychosexual approach of Freud. Adler was a respected general practitioner in Vienna. He heard his first lecture on psychoanalysis in 1899 and was fascinated, although he never regarded himself as a pupil or disciple of Freud. He was invited to join the Vienna Psychoanalytic Society and did so in 1902, but he was never psychoanalyzed himself. By the end of the decade, he had become president of the society and editor of its journal. As Adler's own theories developed, and as he voiced them within the psychoanalytic association, Freud became increasingly defensive.

Adler came to criticize several underpinnings of psychoanalytic theory. For example, he suggested that the Oedipus complex was merely the reaction of a pampered child, not a universal complex. Adler saw dysfunctional sexual attitudes and practices as a symptom of the underlying neurosis, not as its underlying cause. When Adler would not recant his heresy, the Vienna Psychoanalytic Society was split into a Freudian majority and an Adlerian minority. For a brief period, the Adlerians retained the term "psychoanalysis," only later defining their school as individual psychology.

Freud's influence on Adler can be seen in the emphasis on the importance of early childhood and on the ideas that the motives that underlie neurosis are outside conscious awareness (private logic) and that it is only through insight into these motives that cure can be attained. It is largely in Adler's reaction against Freud, however, that Adler truly defined himself. He saw Freud as offering a mechanistic system in which individuals merely react according to instincts and their early childhood environment; Adler believed that individuals have choices about their futures. He saw Freud as emphasizing universal themes that are rigidly repeated in each patient; Adler believed that people fashion their unique styles of life. Adler saw Freud as being focused on the intrapsychic; Adler himself emphasized the interpersonal, social field.

Although Freud's personality theory has been the best remembered, Adler's has been the most rediscovered. In the 1940's, holistic theorists such as Kurt Lewin and Kurt Goldstein reiterated Adler's emphasis on the individual's subjective and comprehensive approach to perceptions.

In the 1960s, humanistic theorists such as Abraham Maslow and Carl R. Rogers rediscovered his emphasis on individuals overcoming the conditions of their childhood and striving toward a self-actualization and potential to love. In the 1980s, cognitive theorists such as Albert Ellis, Aaron T. Beck, and Martin E. P. Seligman emphasized how individuals perceive and understand their situation as the central element underlying psychopathology.

STRENGTHS AND WEAKNESSES

An evaluation of individual psychology must necessarily include some enumeration of its weaknesses as well as its strengths. The positives are obvious: The theory is easy to comprehend, optimistic about human nature, and applicable to the understanding of a wide variety of issues. The weaknesses would be the other side of those very strengths. If a theory is so easy to comprehend, is it not then simplistic or merely a reformulation of common sense? This may explain why so many other theorists "rediscovered" Adler's ideas throughout the twentieth century. If a theory is so optimistic about human potential, can it present a balanced view of human nature? If a theory is flexible and broad enough as to be able to explain so much, can it be precise enough to explain anything with any depth? Although everything in individual psychology fits together as a unified whole, it is not always clear what the lines of reasoning are. Does excessive inferiority feeling preclude the formulation of social interest, or does social interest assuage inferiority feeling? Does inferiority feeling engender private logic, or does private logic sustain inferiority feeling? At different times, Adler and Adlerians seem to argue both sides of these questions. The Achilles' heel of individual psychology(and of psychoanalysis) is prediction. If a given child is in a situation that heightens feelings of inferiority, will that child overcompensate effectively and develop social interest as an adult, or will private logic take over? If it does, will it be in the form of self-brooding or masculine protest?

Although the fuzziness of Adlerian concepts will preclude individual psychology from being a major force in academic psychology, it is safe to predict that future theorists will again rediscover many of Adler's concepts.

BIBLIOGRAPHY

Adler, Alfred. *The Practice and Theory of Individual Psychology.* New York: Routledge, 1999. Print.

Bottome, Phyllis. *Alfred Adler: A Biography.* New York: Putnam, 1939. Print.

Carlson, Jon, and Michael Maniacci. *Alfred Adler Revisited*. New York: Routledge, 2012. Print.

Dreikurs, Rudolf. *Fundamentals of Adlerian Psychology*. Chicago: Alfred Adler Inst., 1989. Print.

Ellis, Albert, Mike Abrams, and Lidia Dengelegi Abrams. *Personality Theories: Critical Perspectives*. Los Angeles: Sage, 2009. Print.

Ganz, Madelaine. *The Psychology of Alfred Adler and the Development of the Child*. New York: Routledge, 1999. Print.

Mozak, Harold, and Michael Maniacci. *A Primer of Adlerian Psychology: The Analytic-Behavioral-Cognitive Psychology of Alfred Adler*. New York: Brunner/Mazel, 1999. Print.

Sweeney, Thomas. *Adlerian Counseling: A Practitioner's Approach*. 5th ed. New York: Routledge, 2009. Print.

Yang, Julia, Alan P. Milliren, and Mark Blagen. *The Psychology of Courage: An Adlerian Handbook for Healthy Social Living*. New York: Routledge, 2010. Print.

T. L. Brink

SEE ALSO: Adler, Alfred; Adlerian psychotherapy; Birth order and personality; Cognitive psychology; Ego psychology: Erik H. Erikson; Elders' mental health; Erikson, Erik H.; Family systems theory; Freud, Sigmund; Hull, Clark L.; Humanistic psychology; James, William; Maslow, Abraham; Power; Psychoanalytic psychology; Psychoanalytic psychology and personality: Sigmund Freud; Seligman, Martin E. P.

Inductive reasoning

TYPE OF PSYCHOLOGY: Cognition

Inductive reasoning is the form of logic in which specific examples are used to come to a generalization. People use inductive reasoning to understand their lives and how to function in a situation. Conclusions reached by inductive reasoning are often erroneous because people have used the wrong examples.

KEY CONCEPTS

- Deductive reasoning
- Fallacy
- Generalization
- Inference
- Logic

INTRODUCTION

Inductive reasoning is a form of logic in which specific examples form the basis of a generalization. Facts are collected and then classified to determine patterns, from which an inference is drawn and a generalization is made. Unlike deductive reasoning, inductive reasoning does not always lead to a true statement, no matter how many true statements precede it. Because of the infinite number of examples that exist and the observer's limited experiences, conclusions drawn from inductive reasoning can form the basis of hypotheses but are not likely to yield a true statement.

People tend to use inductive reasoning to evaluate what is happening in their lives and in their relations with other people. In this area, most conclusions are false because they are based on a finite number of observations and people's own life experiences, which are limited. In essence, people examine their experiences and identify a number of patterns for situations. An example might be an adolescent who is being raised by a mother who is a drug addict and cannot be trusted to follow through on what she promises. The adolescent might have two friends who are also being raised by similarly untrustworthy drug-addicted parents. Based on these specific observations, the adolescent would then make the generalization that all parents cannot be trusted. Of course, this generalization is not true, although it might be true of many parents in the adolescent's neighborhood.

Inductive and deductive reasoning are part of the philosophy of logic. Logic is a way of presenting arguments and then demonstrating the proof of the arguments using deductive or inductive reasoning, or other methods. The philosophy of logic studies reasoning, probability, and arguments that lead to demonstrating the cause of an occurrence. In addition, logic includes the study of fallacies, validity, and paradoxes.

APPLICATIONS

Inductive reasoning is used in many areas. It is used in geometry, where a number of examples of a shape, such as a triangle, are studied and then used to make a generalization about the characteristics of all triangles. These generalizations form a hypothesis, which is then proven in a theorem. Another application of inductive reasoning is the game of chess. Different chess strategies have been developed and published, and a chess player might observe the moves of his or her opponent and identify them as a strategy known as the Caro-Kann defense. Accordingly, the chess player would then use another strategy to outsmart the Caro-Kann defense.

Inductive reasoning is used in economics when agencies use identified patterns of behavior in the economic system to determine how to proceed in investing or what interest rate to charge for loans. Archaeology is another area in which inductive reasoning is used. Archaeologists search for relics and other artifacts from past societies and then use their findings to describe the behavior and societal structure of ancient peoples. Inductive reasoning is also used in astronomy when scientists study the elements of our solar system and make generalizations about other possible solar systems, or when they make generalizations about the physical characteristics of other planets within our solar system based on examples from Earth. Obviously, in these examples, the use of inductive reasoning has a high likelihood of leading to false conclusions.

HISTORY
Inductive reasoning began in the Greek classical period. Aristotle, Thales, Pythagoras, and other philosophers described reasoning patterns. Aristotle wrote about logic, primarily deductive reasoning, although he also described inductive reasoning. Eighteenth-century Scottish philosopher David Hume was the first person to state that inductive reasoning is rarely true. He argued that people's everyday reasoning depends on repeated patterns of existence rather than deductively valid arguments. In the mid-nineteenth century, German mathematician and philosopher Gottlob Frege began the study of mathematics and logic, in which he was followed by philosophers such as Alfred North Whitehead and Bertrand Russell. In the twentieth century, philosophers Karl Raimund Popper and David Miller questioned the validity of inductive reasoning and its use in science.

BIBLIOGRAPHY
Arthur, W. Brian. "Inductive Reasoning and Bounded Rationality." *American Economic Review* 84.2 (1994): 406–11. Print.

Baum, Robert. *Logic*. 4th ed. New York: Oxford UP, 1996. Print.

Feeney, Aidan, and Evan Heit, eds. *Inductive Reasoning: Experimental, Developmental, and Computational Approaches*. New York: Cambridge UP, 2007. Print.

Kalish, Charles W., and Jordan T. Thevenow-Harrison. "Descriptive and Inferential Problems of Induction: Toward a Common Framework." *The Psychology of Learning and Motivation*. Ed. Brian H. Ross. Vol. 61. Waltham: Academic, 2014. 1–39. Print.

Pine, Ronald C. *Essential Logic: Basic Reasoning Skills for the Twenty-First Century*. New York: Oxford UP, 1996. Print.

Schulz, Kathryn. *Being Wrong: Adventures in the Margin of Error*. New York: Ecco, 2011. Print.

Shenefelt, Michael, and Heidi White. *If A, Then B: How the World Discovered Logic*. New York: Columbia UP, 2013. Print.

Walton, Douglas. *Informal Logic: A Pragmatic Approach*. 2nd ed. New York: Cambridge UP, 2008. Print.

Woods, John. *Errors of Reasoning: Naturalizing the Logic of Inference*. London: College, 2013. Print.

Christine M. Carroll

SEE ALSO: Cognitive psychology; Decision making; Deductive reasoning; Logic and reasoning.

Industrial and organizational psychology

TYPE OF PSYCHOLOGY: Social psychology

Industrial and organizational psychology applies psychological research methods and theories to issues of importance in work organizations. From its beginnings as psychology applied to a few personnel topics, it has expanded to deal with almost all aspects of work, changing as they have.

KEY CONCEPTS
- Experimentation
- Fairness in work settings
- Field research
- Industrial psychology
- Organizational psychology
- Scientific method

INTRODUCTION
Industrial and organizational psychology (often shortened to I/O psychology) is a somewhat deceptive title for the field. Even when industrial psychology alone was used to label it, practitioners were involved with issues and activities far beyond solving industrial problems— for example, designing procedures for selecting salespeople, advertising methods, and reducing accidents on public transportation. "Organizational" suggests the ap-

plication of knowledge to organizations, but the intended meaning is closer to "the study of forces that influence how people and their activities at work are organized."

In colleges and universities, I/O psychology is a long-recognized discipline. Graduate programs leading to the MA and, more commonly, PhD degrees in this field are most typically offered within psychology departments, sometimes in collaboration with departments of business; occasionally they are offered by business departments alone. In most cases, students working toward graduate degrees in I/O psychology first study a wide range of psychological topics, then study, in even greater detail, those that make up the I/O specialty. The study of research methods, statistical tools for evaluating findings, motivation, personality, and so on forms a base from which psychological testing, interviewing, job analysis, and performance evaluation are studied in depth.

EVOLUTION OF STUDY

Psychologists were certainly not the first to study work settings and suggest changes or even the first to apply the scientific method to the enterprise. For example, Frederick Winslow Taylor and Frank Gilbreth were industrial engineers who considered workers not too different from cogs in the machines also involved in industry. Their time and motion studies sought to discover how workers could most efficiently carry out their parts of the enterprise. Although their conclusions are often now cited as examples of inhumane manipulation of workers for companies' benefits, Taylor and Gilbreth envisioned that both workers and employers were to gain from increases in efficiency. Not surprisingly, most of what industrial engineering studied was appropriated by industrial psychology and remains part of I/O psychology—usually under the designations of job design and human factors engineering in the United States, or the designation ergonomics elsewhere.

Early psychologists had an advantage over the others studying and offering advice about work. They were popularly identified as people experts, and for the many problems thought to be based on human characteristics or limitations, their expertise was acknowledged even while it was very modest. The advantage of being expected to make valuable contributions was put to good use, and within the first two decades of the twentieth century, industrial psychology became a recognized discipline with the ability to deliver most of what was expected of it.

Ironically, wars materially aided the early development of industrial and organizational psychology. World War I provided psychologists unprecedented opportunities to try intelligence testing on a very large scale and to develop and implement a very large personnel program. Robert Yerkes directed the intelligence testing of more than one million men between 1917 and 1919, and Walter Dill Scott and Walter Van Dyke Bingham interviewed and classified more than three million men before the war ended.

Testing, interviewing, and classification were also part of industrial psychologists' efforts during World War II, and many other lines of research and application were also pursued. For example, human factors engineering, which emphasized machine design tailored to the people who would use the device, was greatly advanced by the necessity that people be able to control aircraft and other sophisticated weapons.

Following each war, some of the psychologists who had successfully worked together chose to continue to do so. Major consulting firms grew out of their associations and remain a source of employment for many I/O psychologists.

METHODS OF RESEARCH

Industrial and organizational psychology borrowed much from many other areas of psychology during its growth and has retained the strong research orientation common to them, along with many of the research methods each has developed and many of the findings that each has generated. Bringing psychological methods to work settings where experts from many other disciplines are studying some of the same problems results in conflicts, but it also produces a richness of information beyond the scope of any one of the disciplines.

In most cases, the most feasible approach to data collection for I/O psychologists is field research, an approach in which evidence is gathered in a "natural" setting, such as the workplace; by contrast, laboratory research involves an artificial, contrived setting. Systematic observation of ongoing work can often give a psychologist needed information without greatly disturbing the workers involved. Generally, they will be told that data are being gathered, but when the known presence of an observer likely would change what is being studied, unobtrusive methods might be used. Information from hidden cameras, or observations from researchers pretending to be workers and actually engaging in whatever must be done, can be used when justified.

Again, studying within the actual work setting, I/O psychologists may sometimes take advantage of natural experiments, situations in which a change not deliberately introduced may be studied for its effect on some important outcome. If, for example, very extreme, unseasonable temperatures resulted in uncontrollably high, or low, temperatures in an office setting, a psychologist could assess the effects on employee discomfort, absenteeism, or productivity.

Still, studying within the actual work setting, an I/O psychologist may arrange a quasi-experiment, a situation in which the researcher changes some factor to assess its effect while having only partial control over other factors that might influence that change. For example, the psychologist might study the effects of different work schedules by assigning one schedule to one department of a company, a second schedule to a second department, and a third schedule to a third department. The departments, the people, and the differences in the work itself would prevent the strategy from being a true experiment, but it still could produce some useful data.

An experiment, as psychology and other sciences define it, is difficult to arrange within work settings, but it may be worth the effort to evaluate information gathered by other methods. In the simplest form of experiment, the researcher randomly assigns the people studied into two groups and, while holding constant all other factors that might influence the experiment's outcome, presents some condition (known as an independent variable) to one group of subjects (the experimental group) and withholds it from another (the control group). Finally, the researcher measures the outcome (the dependent variable) for both groups.

Carrying out a true experiment almost always requires taking the people involved away from their typical activities into a setting obviously designed for study (usually called the laboratory, even though it may bear little resemblance to a laboratory of, say, a chemist). The need to establish a new, artificial setting and the need to pull workers away from their work to gather information are both troublesome, as is the risk that what is learned in the laboratory setting may not hold true back in the natural work setting.

Correlational methods, borrowed from psychometrics, complement the observational and experimental techniques just described. Correlation is a mathematical technique for comparing the similarity of two sets of data (literally, to determine their co-relation). An important example of the I/O psychologist's seeking information on relationships is found in the process of hiring-test validation, answering the question of the extent to which test scores and eventual work performance are correlated. To establish validity, a researcher must demonstrate a substantial relationship between scores and performance, evidence that the test is measuring what is intended.

APPLICATIONS IN THE WORKPLACE

Industrial and organizational psychology, as the term implies, focuses on two broad areas; Linda Jewell and Marc Siegall, in their *Contemporary Industrial/Organizational Psychology* (3d ed., 1998), demonstrate this by their arrangement of topics. Industrial topics include testing; job analysis and evaluation; recruitment, selection, and placement of applicants; employee training and socialization; evaluation of employee job performance; job design; working conditions; health and safety; and motivation. Organizational topics include a company's social system and communication, groups within organizations, leadership, and organizational change and development. Topics of overlap of the two areas include absenteeism, turnover, job commitment, job satisfaction, employee development, and quality of work life.

Testing in I/O psychology most often is done to assess people's aptitudes or abilities as a basis for making selection, placement, or promotion decisions about them. It may also be used for other purposes—for example, to judge the quality of training programs. The tests used range from ones of general aptitude (IQ, or intelligence quotient, tests) through tests of specific aptitudes, interests, and personality, although use of IQ and personality tests remains controversial. Aptitude for success in academically related activity (as might be related to one's IQ) is often of only modest importance in work settings, but the folk wisdom "the best person is the most intelligent person" can lead to giving IQ tests routinely to applicants. Personality is a troublesome concept within psychology. Tests of it can be useful to clinicians working with mental health issues but are rarely useful as bases for employment-related decisions. When outcomes from personality testing are specific enough to be useful—for example, when they reveal serious personality problems—the same information is usually obtainable from reviews of work history or from interviews.

Along with other procedures related to making decisions about people in work settings, testing is often targeted as being unfair to some groups—for example, African Americans or women. If the use of a particular test results in decision making that even suggests unfair discrimination, companies must have available solid evidence that this is not the case if they choose to continue using the test.

Job analysis determines what tasks must be carried out in a job. It serves as the major basis for deciding what skills successful job applicants must have or what training to provide unskilled applicants. The evaluation of job performances of individual employees must be based on what they should be doing, revealed by job analysis. Dismissal, retention, promotion, and wage increases may all be related to job analysis information. It is also a basis for job evaluation, the determining of what is appropriate pay for the job, although evaluation often must also be based on the availability of applicants, average wages in a geographic area, and other factors.

Recruiting, selecting, and placing refer to sequential steps in filling positions. Although some companies can let prospective employees come to them, many prefer actively to seek applicants. Recruiting may involve little more than announcing that a position is open or as much as sending trained representatives to find promising people and encourage them to apply for work. At least two considerations make vigorous recruiting attractive. First, it is often possible for companies to reduce training costs greatly by finding already-proficient applicants. Second, when minority-group employees are needed to achieve fair balance in an organization, recruiting can often focus on, for example, African Americans or women.

Although training may be unnecessary if a company is able to hire already-skilled people, training is generally advantageous after hiring and periodically over a worker's tenure. Promotion may be based on success in training, or training may follow promotion based on other considerations. Although "training" suggests the development or enhancement of job skills, it often also includes socialization, the bringing of new employees into the "family" of the company and the teaching of values, goals, and expectations that extend beyond carrying out a specific work assignment. Job design, working conditions, health and safety, and motivation are usually given separate chapters in texts, but often in work settings they must be considered as a set. For example, if a job, as designed, forces or even encourages workers to put their health or safety at risk, their working conditions are unsatisfactory, and when they recognize the nature of the situation, their motivation is likely to be impaired.

LEGAL AND ETHICAL REQUIREMENTS
When industrial psychologists of the early twentieth century recommended hiring or promotion, designed training, or carried out any other of their responsibilities, they had only to satisfy their employers' demands. Since the late 1960s, I/O psychologists have also had to satisfy legal and ethical requirements pertaining to a host of problem areas such as racism, sexism, age discrimination, and discrimination against the handicapped. More than good intentions are necessary here. The psychologists must work to balance the societal demands for fairness in work settings (the basing of decisions about workers' hiring, salary, promotion, and so on entirely on work-relevant considerations and not on race, sex, age, or other personal characteristics) and the practical interests of employers, sometimes having to endure criticism for even the most ingenious of solutions.

For example, if an employer finds the company must increase its number of Latino workers, vigorous recruiting is an excellent first step, yet it may prove expensive enough to aggravate the employer. If recruiting is not successful because would-be applicants doubt the employer's sincerity, both they and the employer will be unhappy. If recruiting is successful in generating interest, but many interested individuals are unqualified, providing them special training could be a reasonable solution. Applicants might feel it degrading, however, to be required to undergo more training than others before them, or the employer might balk at the extra cost involved.

The first industrial psychologists needed little more than solid training in their discipline to achieve success. Their successors need, beyond training in a discipline that has enlarged enormously, the talents of diplomats.

BIBLIOGRAPHY
Anderson, Neil, Deniz S. Ones, and Handan Kepir Sinangil, eds. *Handbook of Industrial, Work, and Organization Psychology*. 2 vols. Thousand Oaks: Sage, 2002. Print.

Cartwright, Susan. *Managing Health at Work: Practical Lessons from Organizational Research*. Oxford: Blackwell, 2009. Print.

Hilgard, Ernest Ropiequet. *Psychology in America: A Historical Survey*. San Diego: Harcourt, 1987. Print.

Jewell, Linda N., and Marc Siegall. *Contemporary Industrial/Organizational Psychology*. 3d ed. Belmont: Wadsworth, 1998. Print.

Muchinsky, Paul M. *Psychology Applied to Work: An Introduction to Industrial and Organizational Psychology*. 10th ed. Summerfield: Hypergraphic, 2012. Print.

Rogelberg, Steven, ed. *Blackwell Handbook of Research Methods in Industrial and Organizational Psychology.* Malden: Blackwell, 2004. Print.

Rosenzweig, Mark R., and Lyman W. Porter, eds. *Annual Review of Psychology.* Stanford: Annual Reviews. Print.

Silzer, Rob, and Rich Cober. "Shaping the future of Industrial-Organizational Psychology Practice." TIP: *The Industrial-Organizational Psychologist* 49.1 (2011): 81–88. Print.

Spector, Paul E. *Industrial and Organizational Psychology: Research and Practice.* Hoboken: Wiley, 2008. Print.

Steelman, Lisa, et al. "Making History: The Evolution of The Industrial-Organizational Psychologist." *TIP: The Industrial-Organizational Psychologist* 50.4 (2013): 15–28. Print.

Harry A. Tiemann, Jr.

SEE ALSO: Ability tests; Achievement motivation; Career and personnel testing; Group decision making; Human resource training and development; Leadership; Organizational behavior and consulting; Work motivation; Workforce reentry; Workplace issues and mental health.

Infant feeding

TYPE OF PSYCHOLOGY: Biological bases of human behavior; Clinical; Counseling; Cultural; Developmental; Family; Social

Infant feeding has a profound influence on human development and growth, and it is particularly important in the early stages of child development. Some areas that may be related to infant feeding include physical growth, behavioral development, social development, psychosocial development, intellectual development, and cognitive development. The interplay of infant feeding and attachment styles may have long-lasting effects, and potential disparities between breastfeeding and formula feeding may factor into individuals' developmental trajectories across psychological contexts.

KEY CONCEPTS
- Breastfed
- Formula-fed
- Zone of proximal development (ZPD)
- Intelligence quotient (IQ)
- Attachment styles
- John Bowlby

INTRODUCTION
Soon after the birth of a child, the process of infant feeding plays a central role in his or her development and growth. The practice of infant feeding has been observed across an array of cultures, and records of breastfeeding date early as 2,000 B.C. Emily Stevens, Thelma Patrick, and Rita Pickler suggest that around this time wet nurses, or a woman who breastfeeds another person's child, began to be used for feeding children. Also, in Israel there are records of breastfeeding dating back to 2,000 B.C., where it was considered a religious obligation. Since this early era, what is understood about breastfeeding and its relatedness to human development has progressed, and the available alternatives to breastfeeding have been developed further. Currently, the most prominent alternative to breastfeeding is formula feeding, and this may be a method of infant feeding used by mothers who may be unable to breastfeed or may not prefer to breastfeed their child. Whether breastfed or formula-fed, it is important to discern that infant feeding plays a crucial function in children's earliest stages of development. Infant feeding relates to the physical growth, intellectual growth, and attachment style of the child, and the observed differences between infants who are breastfed and infants who are formula-fed vary across these different contexts.

PHYSICAL, BEHAVIORAL, SOCIAL, AND PSYCHO-SOCIAL DEVELOPMENT
In terms of physical growth, infant feeding is critical because it directly relates to the infant's caloric intake, and more broadly it may be related to the infant's behavior and day-to-day functioning. Peter Wright suggests that breastfeeding may minimize the risk of rapid weight gain as compared to formula feeding, and this may be due to the nature of the infant dictating their feeding during breastfeeding as opposed to the mother dictating the amount which is provided. Behaviorally, infants may differ in their ability to breastfeed, and R.F. Drewett suggests that low intake may be a result of a child's motor problem or a problem with the mother's production of breast milk.

Drewett highlights the notion that the energy derived from infant feeding is largely used for expenditure and not actual physical growth. Infants' crying and sleeping patterns may be closely tied to feeding, and Drewett cites that breastfed infants are less likely to sleep through the night as compared to bottle-fed infants. Interestingly, Peter Wright argues that infant feeding is one of the earliest examples of the zone of proximal development

(ZPD), a Vygotskian theory that emphasizes the importance of scaffolding and pursuing potentially challenging behaviors or tasks with the support of those who are better equipped. Additionally, ZPD as it is related to infant feeding may be influential of how the child begins to organize his or her world, and the interaction of infant cues and parent's responsiveness may be another integral part of this construct.

INTELLECTUAL AND COGNITIVE DEVELOPMENT

Somewhat controversially, it has been posited that intellectual and cognitive development differs for breast-fed infants as compared to formula-fed infants. In a meta-analysis investigating breastfed infants and cognitive outcomes, James Anderson, Bryan Johnstone, and Daniel Remley found that across 20 studies infants who were breastfed had enhanced cognitive development as compared to those who were formula-fed, and these differences were seen through childhood and adolescence. Echoing these findings, Jean Golding, Imogen Rogers, and Pauline Emmett discussed findings that may detail an association between breastfed infants and mental abilities, specifically that breastfed infants may have higher IQs than infants who are formula-fed. Research conducted by Ruth Feldman and Arthur Eidelman found that low-birth-weight premature infants who received an abundance of breast milk had better neurodevelopmental gains than those who did not receive a significant amount of breast milk. At six months old (corrected age) these premature infants had higher mental skills than premature infants who did not receive as much breast milk.

Ann Reynolds alludes to research which has suggested breastfed children have better neurodevelopmental outcomes and higher IQs than infants who are formula-fed, warning that the causality of these findings must be scrutinized. Due to the inability to test these questions experimentally, confounding factors including socioeconomic status, parental IQ, bonding and attachment styles, maternal well-being, gestational age, and birth weight may be influencing these outcomes more than the differences arising between breastfeeding and formula-feeding infants. One major confounding question is whether the nutrients in breast milk themselves may be related to these beneficial gains or whether the physical closeness and tactile intimacy that occurs during breastfeeding may be more influential on later intellectual and cognitive development. This aspect of infant feeding is an ongoing debate, and research continues to yield new findings that contribute to the understanding of how different approaches to infant feeding may be related to different intellectual and cognitive development.

ATTACHMENT

There is a storied history of psychoanalytic research interested in love and dependency as it relates to breastfeeding; however, most of this research has been discounted in favor of work pioneered by Mary Ainsworth and John Bowlby. As mentioned previously, infant feeding and caregivers' responsiveness to infant cues, especially when an infant is signaling for the need to be fed, may impact the development of the child's attachment style. Famed psychologist Mary Ainsworth argued that an infant's behavior, and the responsiveness of caregivers to these behavioral cues, may influence an infant's perception of control over environment. The attachment behaviors resulting from these types of feeding interactions may have long-lasting implications. Forming a close and intimate bond between mother and child is not unique to mothers who choose to breastfeed, as Marshall Klaus, John Kennell, and Phyllis Klaus reason that physical and emotional closeness may be accomplished through formula-feeding. This relationship is bidirectional, and as the infant's hunger is satiated, the mother may also feel personally fulfilled or satisfied for being able to provide for her child. John Bowlby reiterates this sentiment when expressing the importance of face-to-face time for the caregiver and infant which can occur during feeding. Although fathers or male caregivers may be unable to breastfeed their child, a similar intimacy between father and infant may be achieved through kangaroo care. This practice of having skin-to-skin contact with an infant may be beneficial for the well-being of infants, and this practice may be utilized during periods of feeding.

PROBLEMS WITH FEEDING

Despite the positive characteristics and outcomes of infant feeding, there are some instances in which infant feeding may be problematic or harmful for the child. Gillian Harris mentions that negative feeding behaviors or refusal to feed may stem from problems within the interaction between caregiver and infant, or it may also be the result of a cognitive model in which infants' understanding of the feeding process may be inadequate. In the interaction model, an emphasis on improving the caregiver-infant relationship may improve these feeding problems. For the cognitive model, imitative processes may be especially salient for success, and classical conditioning could be one method to circumvent these issues. One other problem that may arise from infant feeding and the consumption of breast milk is the transmitting of teratogens. Some teratogens and harmful toxic agents, including mercury, may be passed through breast milk. Although the risk of mercury is low, breast milk may carry other teratogens that may be harmful to the infant's growth and development, and instances where the mother may be at risk for having breast milk containing teratogens should consult a professional about using formula in place of breastfeeding.

BIBLIOGRAPHY

American Academy of Pediatrics. (2014). *Infant food and feeding.* Retrieved from http://www.aap.org/en-us/advocacy-and-policy/aap-health-initiatives/HALF-Implementation-Guide/Age-Specific-Content/Pages/Infant-Food-and-Feeding.aspx Provides resources and extensive information about infant feeding and breastfeeding.

Bacchi, C. (2003). *Fear of Food: A Diary of Mothering.* Australia: Spinifex Press. A mother's firsthand account of her child's feeding behaviors and patterns over the first two years of his life. This includes accounts of breastfeeding and the keeping of feeding logs.

Carey, W. B., Crocker, A. C., Coleman, W. L., Elias, E. R., & Feldman, H. M. (2009). *Developmental-behavioral pediatrics* (4th ed.). Philadelphia, PA: Saunders/Elsevier. Includes a comprehensive chapter on infant feeding. Details infant feeding differences across cultures, parental perceptions of feeding problems, and issues with spitting up.

Klaus, M. H., Kennell, J. H., & Klaus, P. H. (1995). *Bonding: Building the Foundations of Secure Attachment and Independence.* Reading, MA: Addison-Wesley. Discusses infant bonding and attachment, allotting some discussion to the topic of breastfeeding and infant feeding and how this relates to forming a relationship between caregiver and infant.

St. James-Roberts, I., Harris, G., & Messer, D. (1993). *Infant Crying, Feeding and Sleeping: Development, Problems and Treatments.* UK: Harvester Wheatsheaf. Over the course of three chapters, the authors discuss infant feeding in great depth from various perspectives. The authors draw heavily on the intellectual differences that may be a result of differences in infant feeding, the behavioral development of the infant, infants' use of signaling and cues to engage caregivers, and mothers' beliefs about infant feeding

and their infant's behavior. The interplay between infant feeding, sleeping, and crying is a constant theme throughout the literature.

Andrew P. Minigan and Molly B. Connelly

SEE ALSO: Bottle feeding; Breast feeding; Childrearing; Eating behavior; Infant development; Mother-child relationship.

Infant sleep

TYPE OF PSYCHOLOGY: Biological bases of human behavior; Child; Clinical; Counseling; Cross-cultural; Developmental; Family; Social

According to Merriam-Webster, sleep is the natural, periodic suspension of consciousness during which the powers of the body are restored. Sleep plays a critical role in brain development in infants and young children. During sleep, the body works to support healthy brain function and maintain physical health.

KEY CONCEPTS
- Infant sleep patterns
- Attachment
- Self-regulation
- Parental concerns
- Cultural beliefs

INTRODUCTION

One of the major concerns of parents of newborns is their infant's sleeping routines. From the first few months to a year of the newborn's life, sleeping patterns may not be well established and parents often find this a troublesome period for the baby's comfort level and the parents' personal adjustment to sleep deprivation. Sleep is not only a critical feature for the baby's brain growth and physical development, but the newborn also becomes familiar with its bodily functions and rhythms, thus leading to an improved sleep/wake cycle. Because parents and the newborn are unfamiliar with each other, they are often learning about each other seemingly "on the fly." Newborns are learning to adjust to the "outside" world of getting their breathing, sucking, and swallowing pattern organized in order to nurse or be fed. They are unaware that there is a difference between night and day (i.e., sleep/wake cycle), and their circadian rhythms have not yet been established. (Our activity cycle lasts twenty-four hours; many living things, including humans, follow a circadian rhythm that is generated by an internal clock that is synchronized to light-dark cycles.) Additionally, the newborn's physiological system is becoming synchronized. During the first or second month, babies may sleep from 45-75 minutes at one time which does not provide the parents the long and sound sleep to which they were accustomed prior to the newborn's arrival. All newborns and infants are different so though a newborn may sleep through the night at six weeks, not all babies will do so.

IMPORTANCE OF SLEEP

"…[A] mother's ability to attune, regulate, and appropriately respond to an infant has significant relational and developmental implications" (Snyder, Shapiro, & Treleaven, 2012, 709).

Signs that a baby may be sleepy are often present; however, parents are new to picking up on the subtle clues that their baby may be giving. If a parent notices the baby rubbing his or her eyes, crying, or becoming fussy, these may be signs of needing to settle quietly for a nap or bedtime. Sometimes babies may become overtired and have great difficulty in quieting so it is important to become attuned to the baby's communicative attempts.

Typically babies sleep anywhere from 10-16 hours a day; however, a sleep/wake cycle may take months to develop into a routine. During the first few months, however, they may only sleep for two to four hours at any given time. This is due to their need to be fed every three hours or so. Just like any new baby, the routine when very young is eat, sleep, cry/wake, change diaper, eat, sleep, cry/wake, change and so on.. All babies are different, and parents should not become concerned if their baby does not exactly "match" what experts or other parents may say. Around six months, the periods of sustained sleep may begin to lengthen as the baby has formed the sleep/wake cycle. Parents should take cues from the baby to get some rest when the baby is down for a nap during the day or asleep for the night. In the first few months, attention to a newborn's needs and the clues indicated by movements, facial signs, and feel of the body (relaxed or tense) are all ways a newborn communicates needs. As the baby's brain matures over the first few months, a sleep pattern should start to emerge.

FEEDING

Sleep 'til you're hungry, eat 'til you're sleepy. —Author Unknown

Tiny babies mean tiny stomachs, causing babies to feel hungrier more often. Infants who are nursed are able to digest and use breast milk more efficiently and therefore are hungrier within shorter periods of time. Formula is often more difficult to digest and takes longer to be metabolized so babies may sleep or nap for longer periods of time. The medical field does, however, recommend breastfeeding for the first six months to a year for maximum benefit of breast milk. Infants at three months are sleeping typically for a total of 15 hours throughout the day and are awake to nurse/be fed and be changed. As little bodies continue to develop, the sleep-wake patterns will change. Infants will not require the same amount of sleep as when a newborn, and they will be able to sleep for longer periods of time between physiologically needing to wake to be fed or changed. Feeding is a cultural practice influenced by family traditions and values and lifestyle choices. Breastfeeding versus bottle-feeding is controversial in many cultures.

If the infant pulls away from the bottle it may indicate lack of hunger or the need to take a break. Breastfed infants may need more frequent, shorter feedings than formula fed infants because the body breaks down and uses breast milk more easily. Breastfeeding infants receive antibodies from the milk which support a stronger immune system, resulting in fewer ear infections, allergies, and respiratory and intestinal illnesses. Most important is the fact that the feeding experience provides a wonderful opportunity to get to know the infant. It is a care-giving situation that allows development of a loving, secure relationship with the infant and a supportive environment for the infant's developing brain.

CRYING

A baby's developing brain is significantly influenced by interactions with the world around him or her and especially by relationships with the adults who care for him or her. Crying may be nature's way of helping ensure that babies receive enough interaction – holding, snuggling, talking, and singing –that helps the brain develop. Perhaps we do not know what the brain is learning from this wonderful attention, but we do know that children grow up more secure and competent when their parents respond to their cries with loving attention (www.zerotothree.org).

Crying is one important way babies communicate their feelings and needs. Learning what a baby's cries mean may take time. Thinking about the situation when the crying occurs may help parents identify the specific need the baby is trying to share. Parents might ask themselves, When was the last time I changed the diaper? Is this room too noisy? When was the last feeding? Sometimes crying follows a pattern or routine of the baby. For instance, the baby may cry during the mid-morning or mid-afternoon. This might indicate that the baby is tired and ready to be placed in the crib for a nap. It is often normal for a newborn to cry frequently during the first three months of life. In fact, some may cry up to two hours a day. Sometimes babies experience "colic" (sometimes due to having a temporary lactose intolerance that affects one in five babies). Digestive upset may also be caused by gas, air, over-stimulation, or an immature digestive system.

Be patient. Learn a baby's cues and how to soothe a baby takes time and some trial and error. Parents are often torn between letting their baby cry when going to bed or comfortingtheir baby. There certainly are a lot of opinions from well-meaning family members and friends, but this decision is ultimately the parents. Even if successful, many parents find it difficult and too stressful to demand a baby fall asleep this way. WebMD discusses a method known as "progressive watching" or "graduated extinction" for the crying to sleep approach during bedtime routines. This method is the Ferber method, named after a physician at the Children's Hospital in Boston. Although controversial, Dr. Ferber does not recommend trying this method with babies under five or six months old. (See Črnčec, Matthey, & Nemth, 2010, under Sources For Further Study.)

CRIB ENVIRONMENT

A baby should always be placed on the back when being put down to sleep. This will lower the risk of sudden infant death syndrome (SIDS). Important also is following safety standards for the crib environment. Have a firm mattress covered with a well-fitting crib sheet. Do not include soft objects, toys, crib bumpers, loose blankets, pillows, sheepskin, or pillows. Dress the baby lightly, do not use a blanket, and keep the room at a comfortable temperature.

SLEEPING ROUTINES
People who say they sleep like a baby usually don't have one.
– Leo J. Burke

Parents should not wait until their baby is fully asleep to put him or her down in the crib. If the baby begins to be drowsy, place him or her on the back in the crib so that the baby may learn to fall asleep on his or her own. This will support thebaby in learning how to "self-regulate" or self-sooth. In this way, babies may not need to be rocked to sleep or rocked if they wake up during the night. Parents should begin talking more softly to the baby when preparing for a night of sleep or a nap. Ensure that the lighting in the bedroom is soft or subdued to support the transition from a light to dark environment.

Swaddling newborns may help them transition from the womb to the outside world more easily. When not swaddled, babies' twitches or jerky movements may unfortunately startle them from sound sleep. Learn the right techniques of swaddling to ensure that the baby is safe and secure.

Photo: iStock

CO-SLEEPING

Some cultures and parenting philosophies include infants sleeping in the parental bed. While this certainly may be considered providing a close, secure, and warm environment for sleeping, a note of extreme caution would be advised when considering this type of sleeping arrangement. This practice is controversial as it has both proponents and those who are in strong opposition to the practice for safety reasons.

BIBLIOGRAPHY

About Health. http:www/about.com/health__Brazelton, T. B., & Sparrow, J. D. (2006). *Touchpoints* (2nd ed.). Cambridge, MA: Da Capo Press.

Cooper, N. (2014). *The Baby Sleeping Bible: The Ultimate Guide To Solving Your Child's Sleeping Problems* (Kindle ed.). San Francisco, CA: Amazon Digital Services.

Črnčec, R., Matthey, S., & Nemth, D. (2010). "Infant Sleep Problems and Emotional Health: A Review of Two Behavioral Approaches. *Journal of Reproductive and Infant Psychology,* 28(1), 4-54. Article compares two approaches to supporting infants' developing a sleep routine. One approach is behavioral in nature (extinction) and one is an immediate-responding approach to the baby's inability to go to sleep.

Healthy Children. http://www.healthychildren.org

Snyder, R., Shapiro, S., & Treleaven, D. (2012). "Attachment Theory and Mindfulness". *Journal of*

Child and Family Studies, 21, 79-717. DOI 10.1007/s10826=11-09522-8 Support for new mothers in developing the early mother-infant relationship and using mindfulness (non-judgmental, present-moment awareness) is discussed. Beneficial effects of mindfulness on healthy attachment is recognized.

Sparrow, J. (2013). "Newborn Behavior, Parent-infant Interaction, and Developmental Change Processes: Research Roots of Developmental, Relational, and Systems-Theory-Based Practice". *Journal of Child and Adolescent Psychiatric Nursing,* 26, 180-185. Suggestions for change in processes in organizations, systems, and communities after examining potential applications of Touchpoints' core elements of shared mission, common language, and consensus of action.

WebMD. www.webmd.com/parenting/baby/sleep-naps-12/nighttime

ZERO TO THREE.

http://www.zerotothree.org/child-development/brain-development/baby-brain-map.html

Robin A. Wells

SEE ALSO: Childrearing; Circadian rhythms; Infant development; Sleep wake cycle.

Infidelity

TYPE OF PSYCHOLOGY: Clinical; Counseling; Family; Psychopathology; Psychotherapy; Social

Infidelity can be defined as any endeavor which breaks an explicit or implicit agreement between individuals who are in an intimate relationship and which also results in damage to the trust in that relationship. Some examples of promises that people make related to intimacy in relationships are marriage vows, privately expressed face-to-face verbal agreements between lovers, and agreements made in written form, such as love notes, emails, and chats. Although the topic of infidelity has a tendency to make many people uncomfortable, it is a fairly common occurrence and happens across cultures. One survey of counselors working with couples found infidelity to be the most frequently reported reason that couples come to therapy. Infidelity happens for a range of reasons, presents in a range of ways, and can have different impacts on individuals and relationships.

KEY CONCEPTS

- Infidelity
- Intimacy
- Attachment
- Emotional infidelity
- Sexual infidelity
- Internet infidelity
- Cybersex

INTRODUCTION

Infidelity happens when one or more partners who have agreed to be intimately exclusive are unfaithful to that agreement, resulting in an erosion of trust. Infidelity can be classified as emotional or sexual and can also combine varying degrees of the two. Affairs can take many different forms, ranging from a one night stand to long-term casual philandering to a full-scale emotional and sexual affair. Further, people who commit acts of infidelity hold different perspectives on their actions and people in relationships respond to infidelity in a variety of ways.

An affair can shatter a relationship, even a relationship in which there is already substantial discontent. Couples counseling has the potential to facilitate the healing process when applying interventions that focus on the affair along with other concerns that are present in the relationship. When couples are committed to change and are open to exploring new ideas and learning new coping mechanisms in response to infidelity, there is the potential for success in therapy.

High on the list of actions that constitute infidelity is sexual intimacy outside of the relationship agreement. Intimacy means different things to different people and sex carries different weight in terms of intimacy for different people. Further, sexual interactions and sex with people other than a person's partner will hold different meanings for different people. However, perceived infidelity is broadly understood as a threat to an established relationship that undermines the stability of the relationship. This said, infidelity also can be interpreted many ways and can incorporate varying degrees of sexual or emotional involvement. For example, a person who engages in a one night stand may frame that event as a superficial chance encounter. This perspective contrasts with a person who maintains a relationship that spans years and involves strong emotional commitment and daily deception. Some individuals begin an affair knowing that the affair will devastate the relationship and so commit infidelity as a means of ending the relationship; other people state that they believe their relationship is healthy and they also want to have an occasional liaison. Some people interpret infidelity as a signal to end the relationship, whereas other people see it as an invitation to explore a deeper intimacy than they had known before. While one partner in a relationship may be able to accept his or her partner engaging in brief romances under particular circumstances as long as certain rules are observed, another partner may find even a flirtation to be intolerable. The context and underlying dynamics of the relationship are essential components to explore in therapy.

Many clinicians who work with people in intimate relationships find that helping clients determine how to get past the affair and cope, as well as how to heal and move on, is a vital part of their practice. Some common, overarching goals are to support the couple working to get over the discovery and betrayal, understand how the infidelity came about, help partners accept mutual responsibility, and facilitate a decision regarding whether the partners will stay together.

ETIOLOGY
Infidelity is typically conceptualized as rooted in the relationship, not in sex. Focusing entirely on the event of the affair has the potential to limit therapeutic progress.

Thus, treatment addresses the underlying issue(s). For example, some partners in relationships engage in infidelity in an effort to fulfill emotional needs. For others with high levels of insecurity and self-doubt, infidelity provides opportunities for confirmation of attractiveness and self-worth. In these cases, it is essential that those underlying needs be explored in therapy.

Sometimes partners will suppress negative feelings to avoid being upset and unsatisfied constantly. Ultimately, warm and positive feelings are at risk for being shut down as well. The relationship may be at a standstill. When this happens, the partners are still vulnerable and will connect with people who fulfill the needs that are left unmet in their primary relationship. When negative feelings build up between partners, infidelity becomes a way of balancing the hostility felt toward a partner or a way of getting even for the perceived injuries inflicted by the partner. Infidelity is less likely to occur in relationships when everything is going well. This supports the contention that an affair can be treated as a symptom of problems rather than the problem itself.

Over time, unresolved conflicts will often build while dissatisfaction increases. Unresolved problems may be related to the need for increased communication, the tendency for one partner to take a dominant role, an unmet need for affection, or a need for more active social opportunities and increased companionship. Sexual affairs are more likely to occur when sexual intimacy in the relationship is unsatisfactory, monotonous, or infrequent.

For example, sometimes a single person who is ambivalent about getting married will initiate infidelity with a person who is married. The single individual may seek intimate partners who are already in committed relationships because he or she feels "safer" knowing that he or she will not be expected to make an enduring commitment. In this situation, the single person can shirk the responsibilities associated with being in a committed relationship but at the same time is able to access the benefits of having an intimate partner.

Affairs can also happen because a person finds sexual variety enticing or enjoys a sense of competition, in which case the unavailability of a married person increases the sense of challenge. Some partners are attracted to infidelity because they seek the thrill of illicit sex.

INFIDELITY AND GENDER
Research suggests that men become more upset than women when partners commit sexual infidelity. Women, on the other hand, become more upset than men when

they experience emotional infidelity. Men perceive sexual infidelity as a greater risk to their relationship while women, in general, are more threatened by emotional attachment outside their relationship. Research has shown that these gender differences in the impact of different types of infidelity and relational jealousy are also comparable to online infidelity, suggesting that the impact of Internet infidelity is similar to that of conventional infidelity.

INTERNET INFIDELITY

The proliferation of Internet use has impacted how people interact with one another. People are increasingly able to hold relationships that exist in varying degrees through Internet channels. The existence of online infidelity is one consequence of this trend. Like other forms of infidelity, Internet infidelity has the potential to create feelings of betrayal and a decreased desire for intimacy with the partner who has stepped outside the relationship and may cause the partner who has been betrayed to engage in negative self-evaluation in comparison with the online fantasy partner. Several recent studies report that online infidelity has become a more frequent reason cited for divorce.

How do we define online infidelity? At this time there is no widely recognized definition, but the literature indicates two basic categories of online infidelity. The first category includes individuals who participate in cybersex online; the second category includes individuals who have formed a close emotional attachment with someone online. The term cybersex has come to refer to online sexual activity wherein two or more people participate in online interactions for the purpose of sexual pleasure. In addition to these characteristics, several researchers indicate that secrecy is one important characteristic of online infidelity.

CLINICAL PERSPECTIVES ON INFIDELITY

Clinicians hold different theoretical perspectives on infidelity. Some clinicians view adult intimate partnerships through the lens of attachment theory. In this context, infidelity represents the potential for the attachment bond between intimate partners to be damaged.

Some clinicians refer to infidelity as a form of attachment injury. Attachment injuries occur in response to betrayal or abandonment at a moment of intense need or vulnerability. This results in a violation of trust. Attachment injuries are challenging to address in therapy and often create a significant barrier to relationship

repair that hyper-activates the deceived spouse's attachment needs and fears. In so doing, the attachment injury generates a crisis that must be addressed and resolved for the relationship to return to a healthy state.

One study found that practicing clinicians who treat infidelity typically go through a series of steps, which include the following:

1. building physical boundaries,
2. constructing psychological boundaries,
3. exploring accountability, trust, and emotions,
4. developing client understanding of etiology of the affair,
5. assessing the couple's background and willingness to work for change,
6. assessing the potential existence of unique circumstances, and
7. moving toward forgiveness.

POTENTIAL PITFALLS FOR BEGINNING PRACTITIONERS

When working with clients who have disclosed infidelity, empirical research suggests that therapists are at risk for a number of pitfalls. These include disclosing the affair without notice, thinking that all affairs are the same, permitting countertransference to be a barrier to the counseling relationship, providing treatment for the infidelity while ignoring the context of the relationship's troubles, and overlooking the messages communicated through the affair itself. Counselors who are new to working with intimate relationships will benefit from seeking supervision and consultation to avoid these pitfalls.

Infidelity represents a betrayal of a partner's trust and a disruption in relationship continuity. Further, an affair creates a sense of unrest in the relationship and invokes feelings of shame. These factors can produce a number of challenges for the clinician during treatment. Couples counselors can help partners handle the feelings of crisis that arise when an affair is disclosed. Because this can involve a fair amount of stress, clinician reactions may involve anxiety as well as concerns regarding whether they are competent to work with couples experiencing infidelity. Again, supervision and consultation are essential to support a clinician's work with clients. Ultimately, the counselor is responsible for avoiding the temptation to overly blame the offending partners but is also responsible for holding them accountable for their behavior. Similarly, the clinician maintains a balance between expecting too much change of the partners (and thereby creating a barrier to successful therapy) and encouraging the couple to explore the underlying relationship dynamics that lead to the crisis.

BIBLIOGRAPHY

Becker, D. V., Sagarin, B. J., Guadagno, R. E., Millevoi, A., & Nicastle, L. D. (2004). "When The Sexes Need Not Differ: Emotional Responses To The Sexual and Emotional Aspects of Infidelity." *Personal Relationships*, 11, 529-538. This is an empirical study which suggests that the jealous response to emotional infidelity best distinguishes women from men. Further, women along with those participants in a serious, committed relationship reported significantly stronger emotional responses to infidelity in comparison with men and those individuals not in a committed relationship.

Bell, S. K., & Widener University. (2009). "A Critical Review of Couple Therapy Models That Address Infidelity: Identifying Common Themes and Introducing a Multimodal Integrative Approach". This dissertation describes and evaluates seven couple therapy models for dealing with infidelity. It also presents a multimodal, integrated approach.

Buss, D. M., Larsen, R. J., Westen, D., & Semmelroth, J. (1992). "Sex Differences In Jealousy: Evolution, Physiology, and Psychology." *Psychological Science*, 3, 251–255. This seminal article describes three separate studies designed to test the hypothesis that sex differences in jealousy emerged in humans as responses to the respective problems in adaptation faced by each sex. In Study 1, men and women chose whether a partner's sexual infidelity or emotional infidelity would cause them more distress. Study 2 documented physiological responses while subjects imagined separately emotional infidelity and sexual infidelity. Study 3 evaluated the effect of being in a committed intimate partnership on the stimulation of jealousy. Each of the studies demonstrated significant gender differences, thereby confirming a correlation between gender and jealousy activation.

Carlson, J.. (2011). *Rebuilding Trust Through Integrative Therapy*: (Session 4 of 6). Washington, DC: American Psychological Association. This is a video demonstration of a session in which a clinician works with a couple who discloses infidelity.

Cherlin, A. J. (2009). *The Marriage-Go-Round: The State of Marriage and the Family in America Today*. New York, NY: Knopf. This book examines the status of marriage in the United States. It explores the cultural evolution of marriage and places marriage in a religious and legal context. .

Confidentiality, Secrets, and How to Deal With Affairs [Video file]. (2012). Psychotherapy Networker. Esther Perel demonstrates a therapeutic approach to infidelity that challenges conventional wisdom about rebuilding trust and intimacy after an affair by challenging the contention that there is a victim and offender in every affair. Perel works with couples to transform rather than traumatize the relationship.

Couples Counseling: Session One [Video file]. (2010). Psychotherapy.net. This is the first in a series of six videos focusing on a couple who has disclosed infidelity. The series was created by Richard Schwartz who developed the Internal Family Systems Model of family therapy which he demonstrates.

Guadagno, R. E., & Sagarin, B. J. (2010). "Sex Differences in Jealousy: An Evolutionary Perspective on Online Infidelity." *Journal of Applied Social Psychology*, 40, 10. Based on the evolutionary psychological explanation for differences in jealousy according to gender, this empirical study examined whether sex differences in jealousy would generalize to online infidelity.

Hertlein, K. M., & Piercy, F. P. (2012). "Essential Elements of Internet Infidelity Treatment". *Journal of Marital and Family Therapy*, 38, 257-70. This article reports the results of an empirical qualitative study conducted on how practicing therapists treat Internet infidelity.

Peluso, P. R. (2007). *Infidelity: A Practitioner's Guide To Working With Couples in Crisis*. New York, NY: Routledge. This book is a collection of contributions on infidelity from a range of disciplines and backgrounds, including couple and family therapy, evolutionary psychology, research on intimate relationships, and cyberstudies.

Schneider, J. P. (2000). "Effects of Cybersex Addiction On The Family: Results of a Survey". *Sexual Addiction & Compulsivity*, 7, 31-58. In this empirical quantitative study, 91 women and three men aged 24-57 completed a brief survey regarding the serious adverse consequences of their partner's cybersex involvement.

Whisman, M. A., Dixon, A. E., & Johnson, B. (1997). "Therapists' Perspectives of Couple Problems and Treatment Issues in Couple Therapy". *Journal of Family Psychology*, 11, 361-366. Empirical quantitative study in which couple therapists completed a survey of couple problem areas and therapeutic issues encountered in couple therapy. Results suggested that lack of loving feelings, power struggles, communication, extramarital affairs, and unrealistic expectations were the most frequent, challenging, and damaging struggles couples brought to therapy.

Laurie Bonjo

SEE ALSO: Behavior; Deception; Interpersonal interaction; Love; Marital relations; Marriage; Relationships.

Inhibitory and excitatory impulses

TYPE OF PSYCHOLOGY: Biological bases of behavior

Two types of processes occur in neurons: those that excite the cell to react to a stimulus and those that inhibit the cell. Cells receive many impulses of both types and must integrate the incoming messages to determine what response should be produced.

KEY CONCEPTS

- Action potential
- Axon
- Dendrite
- Depolarization
- Excitability
- Ion channel
- Neurotransmitter
- Postsynaptic potential
- Resting membrane potential
- Synapse

INTRODUCTION

An unstimulated neuron—one that is neither receiving nor transmitting an impulse—maintains a difference in ions on either side of its cell membrane. While many positively charged potassium (K+) ions are present within the cytoplasm of a cell, proteins and other large molecules located there carry more numerous negative charges, making a negative net charge inside the membrane. Large numbers of positively charged sodium ions (Na+) are located on the outside of the cell in the intercellular space, giving it a net positive charge. Thus, in a resting neuron, there is a positive charge on the outside of the cell membrane and a negative charge on the inside. This charge difference is called the resting membrane potential. It is usually expressed as 70 millivolts, meaning that the inside of the cell is seventy thousandths of a volt more electrically negative than the outside.

The resting membrane potential is maintained by active transport of ions across the cell membrane. Sodium and potassium ions move across the membrane by diffusion, with sodium leaking into the cell and potassium leaking out. These ions are said to be moving down their concentration gradients, going from an area of higher concentration of each ion to an area of lower ion concentration. Such movement occurs passively, without the addition of energy by the cell. If this movement were allowed to continue uninterrupted, the resting potential would be lost fairly quickly, as the ions would reach equilibrium where they would be at the same concentration on both sides of the membrane. This is prevented from happening by the active transport process of the sodium-potassium pump. Active transport is a means of moving materials across the cell membrane from an area of lower concentration to an area of higher concentration. It cannot occur by diffusion, but requires the input of energy from the cell, released by breakage of a molecule by adenosine triphosphate (ATP), the energy currency of the cell. The sodium-potassium pump is a protein that spans the cell membrane and acts as a channel through which both sodium and potassium are pushed against their concentration gradients by the cell's energy. Much of the ATP made by every cell is used to run this pump and maintain the resting potential, not only in neurons but in all other cells as well. The sodium-potassium pump moves two potassium ions into the cell and three sodium ions out of the cell for each ATP molecule broken.

PROCESS OF INFORMATION TRANSMISSION

The electrical difference between the sides of the cell membrane is particularly important in neurons, since it is through a change in this difference that a message is passed along the surface of a single neuron. In this information transmission, an electrical impulse passes down an excited, activated neuron's axon (the single fiberlike extension of a neuron that carries information away from the cell body toward the next cell in a pathway) to the "output" end of the cell, the axon terminal. There the electrical impulse causes tiny vesicles or sacs filled with a chemical called a neurotransmitter to move to the cell membrane and fuse with it, emptying the contents of the vesicles into the space between cells, which is called a synapse. The cell that releases its chemical messengers at the synapse is the presynaptic neuron, and the cell that receives the message is the postysynaptic neuron. The message of the neurotransmitter is received by the second cell when the chemical binds to a protein receptor on the surface of the postsynaptic cell, usually on a dendrite (a branching extension of a neuron through which information enters the cell) or the cell body. This message may be interpreted as an excitatory stimulus or as an inhibitory stimulus. Either kind of stimulus causes a change in the properties of the receptor and of the postsynaptic cell to which it belongs, generally by changing the permeability of the cell's membrane.

EXCITATORY STIMULATION

When the stimulus is excitatory, the charge difference on the two sides of the membrane is at first lowered. A threshold level of electrical charge is reached, about 55 millivolts, and an action potential—a rapid change in electrical charges on a neuron's cell membrane, with depolarization followed by repolarization, leading to a nerve impulse moving down an axon—is generated, followed by the firing of the neuron. A self-propagating wave of depolarization results from an excitatory stimulus that causes the neuron to reach threshold. Depolarization can be defined as a shift in ions and electrical charges across a cell membrane, causing loss of resting membrane potential and bringing the cell closer to the action potential. Special proteins called sodium gates open in the cell membrane, forming a channel that allows sodium ions from outside the cell to flow rapidly down their concentration gradient into the cell's interior. As the net charge inside the cell becomes positive, the charge outside the cell becomes negative. There is a sharp rise, then a decline of the charge within the cell, called a spike, that reaches as high as 35 millivolts with the inflow of sodium ions. The action potential that results from this entry of ions acts according to the all-or-none law. A neuron will either reach the threshold and respond completely or will not reach the threshold and will not respond at all; there is no partial response. After sodium ions rush into the cell, the sodium gates close and the potassium gates open, allowing potassium ions to flow out of the cell, restoring the negative charge inside the cell. The sodium-potassium pump then must reestablish the relative ion concentrations across the membrane, necessitating a period in which the cell cannot respond to an excitatory impulse, called the absolute refractory period.

INHIBITORY STIMULATION

When the message imparted by the neurotransmitter is inhibitory, a different response occurs in the postsynaptic neuron. Instead of depolarizing the membrane by changing the membrane potential from 70 to 55 milli-

volts, the inhibitory message causes hyperpolarization, raising the difference in charge between the inside and outside of the membrane. The interior of the cell becomes more negative, reaching 80 millivolts or more, thus inhibiting the generation of an action potential in that cell. The inhibitory impulses help prevent the chaos that would result if excitatory impulses were firing with nothing to regulate the chain of stimulation. They also help fine-tune sensory perceptions; they can make sensations more exact and sensitive by blocking the firing of neurons around a specific point, such as the precise place on the skin that a touch is felt.

ROLE OF NEUROTRANSMITTERS

Transmission of information in the form of electrochemical messages is the job of the entire nervous system. This information movement can be understood through the study of neurotransmitters. Different parts of the nervous system show the action of many different chemicals that either excite or inhibit the passage of information by means of generation of an action potential in a postsynaptic neuron. The response of the postsynaptic neuron that leads to firing of an action potential is called an excitatory postsynaptic potential (EPSP). If such firing is instead prevented, the response is called an inhibitory postsynaptic potential (IPSP). Together these are referred to as postsynaptic potentials (PSPs).

An important aspect of the generation of these excitatory and inhibitory postsynaptic potentials is that they may be cumulative, with numerous different presynaptic cells sending different messages to the same postsynaptic cell. The messages may all be the same, leading to summation of the information. This would allow a neuron to fire even if each individual excitatory PSP is unable to reach threshold by itself, since the effect can be additive over time (temporal summation, with several messages received from the same cell in a short time) or over space (spatial summation, with several axons sending impulses at the same time). Inhibitory PSPs also have a cumulative effect, but the result of several of these would be to make it harder for the neuron to reach threshold and the development of an action potential. Alternatively, the messages coming into a neuron from several different presynaptic cells might be conflicting, some excitatory and others inhibitory. In this case, the postsynaptic cell would act like a computer and integrate the information from all presynaptic cells to determine whether the net result allows threshold to be reached. If threshold is achieved, the cell fires and a nerve impulse is generated.

If threshold is not achieved, the cell does not fire, but it will be brought closer to the action potential by reduction of the voltage difference across the membrane. Since development of an action potential is an all-or-none response, no matter how the threshold is reached the same level of information passage will result. Behavior of an individual organism thus results from the actions of each separate neuron in determining the net balance of incoming information and determining whether an action potential is reached.

FOUR TYPES OF NEUROTRANSMITTERS

Neurotransmitters are the chemical messengers that act in the nervous system to excite or inhibit the postsynaptic neurons. At least four neurotransmitters have been studied in detail: acetylcholine, norepinephrine, dopamine, and serotonin. Other transmitter substances have also been examined, such as the amino acids glutamate, aspartate, gamma-aminobutyric acid (GABA), and glucine. From these studies it has been shown that the interpretation of the message lies within the postsynaptic neuron, since the same neurotransmitter may be either inhibitory or excitatory, depending on the tissues in which it is found.

Acetylcholine, for example, is found in both the brain and the peripheral nervous system. Since the peripheral nerves are more accessible to study, more is known about the activities of acetylcholine there than in the brain. Two types of cholinergic receptors (those for acetylcholine) are found in the peripheral nervous system, called muscarinic and nicotinic receptors. Acetylcholine has an excitatory effect on nicotinic receptors, as in causing the contraction of skeletal muscles, but an inhibitory effect on the muscarinic receptors, as in slowing the heartbeat. This neurotransmitter is also believed to cause excitation of tissues in the brain and in autonomic ganglia. In the cerebral cortex, acetylcholine is thought to be involved in cognitive processes, while in the hippocampus it appears to be linked to memory; in the amygdala, it seems to help control emotions.

Norepinephrine, dopamine, and serotonin are monoamines, neurotransmitters that act by means of a second messenger system to produce a postsynaptic response. In this system, cyclic adenosine monophosphate (cAMP) is produced within the cell when a neurotransmitter binds to its receptor, and the cAMP opens the ion channels (a pathway through the cell membrane, controlled by gates and used for passage of ions during electrical impulse generation) that cause excitation or inhibition to

be produced. This causes a longer-lasting effect on the postsynaptic neuron, and the neurotransmitters that use this system are apparently involved in long-term behaviors that include memory, emotion, and motivation.

Like acetylcholine, norepinephrine is formed in both the brain and the peripheral nervous tissues, while dopamine and serotonin have been localized to brain tissues only. In the peripheral nervous system, norepinephrine interacts with two kinds of adrenergic receptors on muscle cells, the alpha and beta receptors. Alpha receptors are found on blood-vessel cells, where an excitatory effect results from binding norepinephrine. Beta receptors are seen in the lungs, heart, and intestines, tissues in which norepinephrine has different effects. Binding of the neurotransmitter to beta receptors in cardiac tissue causes excitation, while binding to lung and intestinal receptors inhibits their activities. It is still unclear how the same kind of beta receptor can have different responses in different tissues to the same chemical message. In the brain, a diffuse system of neurons produces norepinephrine, so its effects are widespread, affecting emotion, learning, memory, and wakefulness.

Dopamine is produced by cells found in the substantia nigra, the hypothalamus, and the ventral tegmental areas of the brain, where abnormal levels cause profound behavioral disorders. The related monoamine, serotonin, has distribution and behavioral effects similar to those of norepinephrine. In the upper regions of the brain, the presence of serotonin stimulates higher sensory states and sleep, while reduced levels are associated with severe depression. Since most of the effects of raised or lowered quantities of these mood-altering neurotransmitters seem to cause depression and psychoses, their study has been of great interest. Many of the drugs that have been found to elevate mood clinically act by enhancing or interfering with the action of these neurotransmitters. Through their control of excitation and inhibition of the neural impulse, neurotransmitters control an incredibly complex system of neural interconnections and neuroneffector cell interactions. If this system were under less strict control, behavioral chaos would result, as it does in certain psychiatric and psychological disorders. Applications of knowledge in this area of behavioral research may eventually lead to the ability to control such disorders chemically.

RESEARCH ON SQUID AXONS

Studies on the mechanisms of action of the neuron have been ongoing since the 1930s in giant axons of the squid nervous system. Discovered by J. Z. Young, these axons are so large that a single cell can be dissected out and examined in the laboratory. Much of what is known about the human nervous system's response to excitatory and inhibitory stimuli comes from pioneering work done on these marine mollusks. K. C. Cole and coworkers developed a voltage clamp system of electronic feedback to maintain a constant membrane potential at a chosen voltage level. The axons are penetrated by tiny electrodes and used to measure how electrical transmission occurs in different areas of the neuron across the cell membrane. A later development is the whole cell patch recording, used to examine a small area of the neuron's cell membrane with ion channels more or less intact. A classic series of papers published by Andrew Huxley and Alan Hodgkin in 1952 explained the regulation of electrical conductance along the neural membrane, including movement of ions across the sodium and potassium channels after excitatory stimulation. Huxley and Hodgkin received a Nobel Prize in 1963 for their work on squid axons.

EFFECT OF DRUGS AND TRANSMITTER SUBSTANCES

Another way that excitatory and inhibitory responses are studied is with the muscarinic and nicotinic cholinergic receptors, which are inhibited from working by the actions of the drugs muscarine (from poisonous mushrooms) and nicotine (from tobacco). The drugs mimic the action of acetylcholine on these different kinds of molecules on target tissues. Less is known about the effects of acetylcholine on brain tissues, but this area of research is getting widespread attention because of the evidence that the neurotransmitter appears to be related to the development of Alzheimer's disease. Acetylcholine deficiency in the nucleus basilis is a general finding at autopsy in patients with this disease of aging, which is accompanied by loss of memory and intellectual ability and by profound personality changes.

Behavioral disturbances, including depression and mania, are also caused by abnormally high or low concentrations of norepinephrine in the brain. Some of the drugs used to treat depression are able to do so by controlling the levels of norepinephrine and thus the stimulation of excitatory and inhibitory pathways in the brain. Dopamine is associated with Parkinson's disease, in which there is an abnormally low level in the substantia nigra of the brain, and the condition can be treated by increasing the amount of dopamine and by slowing its

breakdown in this region. In addition, an abnormally high level of dopamine in other parts of the brain has been associated with causing schizophrenia, suggested by the fact that drugs which block the actions of dopamine also reduce the behavioral aberrations seen in this disease. Since brains of patients with these diseases are studied at autopsy and not during the actions that cause the behaviors, it is difficult to tell what actually occurs at the synapses and whether actions are attributable to inhibition or excitation of particular neurons.

Other transmitter substances include amino acids and neuropeptides, but less information has been gathered on these chemicals, and less is known about their activities in the nervous system and behavior. Glutamate and aspartate are amino acids that are thought to be the main excitatory chemicals in use in the brain, while GABA and glycine are inhibitory. GABA is thought to be the most widespread neurotransmitter in the brain, particularly in functions involving movement. Neuropeptides include endorphins, but the mechanisms by which they act are less well known. It is thought that certain cells are able to produce and release both a neurotransmitter such as dopamine and a neuropeptide, giving the nervous system more versatility and complexity in its decision-making capabilities. Perhaps both excitation and inhibition may be handled by the same cell at different times in its regulation of behavioral activities.

BIBLIOGRAPHY

Carlson, Neil R. *Physiology of Behavior.* 10th ed. Boston: Allyn, 2009. Print.

Heilman, Kenneth M., and Edward Valenstein. *Clinical Neuropsychology.* 5th ed. New York: Oxford UP, 2012. Print.

Jones, H. Royden, Ted M. Burns, Michael J. Aminoff, and Scott L. Pomeroy. *The Netter Collection of Medical Illustrations: Nervous System.* 2nd ed. Philadelphia: Saunders, 2013. Print.

Kolb, Bryan, and Ian Q. Whishaw. *Fundamentals of Human Neuropsychology.* 6th ed. New York: Worth, 2009. Print.

Levitan, Irwin B., and Leonard K. Kaczmarek. *The Neuron: Cell and Molecular Biology.* 3d ed. New York: Oxford UP, 2002. Print.

López-Muñoz, Francisco, and Cecilio Alamo. "Historical Evolution of the Neurotransmission Concept." *Journal of Neural Transmission* 116.5 (2009): 515–33. Print.

Ornstein, Robert, and Richard F. Thompson. *The Amazing Brain.* 1984. Reprint. Boston: Houghton,

1991. Print.

Restak, Richard M. *The Mind*. Toronto: Bantam, 1988. Print.

Tortora, Gerard J., and Nicholas P. Anagnostakos. *Principles of Anatomy and Physiology*. New York: Wiley, 2008. Print.

Jean S. Helgeson

SEE ALSO: Endorphins; Nervous system; Neurons; Neurotransmitters; Nicotine dependence; Synaptic transmission.

Insanity defense

TYPE OF PSYCHOLOGY: Psychopathology; Psychotherapy

Legal insanity is a status achieved by convincing the trier-of-fact in a legal proceeding that a defendant did not possess the requisite mind-set, or mens rea, for his or her criminal behavior. It remains one of the most controversial aspects of mental health law, especially to the public. It is an important concept because mental health professionals are often required to evaluate and/or give expert testimony regarding the insanity of a criminal defendant.

KEY CONCEPTS

- Civil aspects of insanity defense
- Competency determination
- Expert testimony
- Insanity and criminal culpability

INTRODUCTION

The insanity defense is a legal provision that protects those who are sufficiently incapacitated because of mental illness or defect from being held criminally liable for their acts. It is a legal idea that reflects the humanistic belief of society and the criminal law community that criminal sanctions should be imposed only on those violations of law that are committed willfully, purposefully, knowingly, wantonly, or recklessly, as is usually required by statutory criteria.

The focus of insanity defense is on the mental state of the defendant at the time the crime was committed, not the mental state at the time of trial. A defendant's mental status at the time of trial is the focus of competency evaluation. The competency determination process is concerned with the ability of defendants to understand and participate in their own legal defense.

The insanity defense can be traced as far back as the reign of the English king Henry III (1207-1272), who granted pardons to those he judged insane. By the sixteenth century, the courts in England had so frequently and consistently adopted insanity as a defense that it became a well-established defense in criminal cases whenever the facts of the case permitted. In 1800 Hadfield, a soldier who had suffered very severe head injuries in battle, was acquitted of the crime of attempting to assassinate the king because he was judged to be insane. In 1849 Edward Oxford was also acquitted of attempting to assassinate Queen Victoria on the ground of insanity. When, in 1843, Daniel M'Naghten was also acquitted on insanity grounds after murdering Edward Drummond, a major controversy arose over insanity defense. That controversy led to the first legislative insanity test requiring that the defendant must either not know the nature of the act or not know the wrongfulness of the act.

In the United States, the insanity defense remains established yet controversial. While the Supreme Court has ruled on various occasions that the execution of an insane criminal defendant is unconstitutional, jurisdictions remain divided over procedural, evidentiary, and dispositional aspects of the insanity defense. Fortunately, the number of times and cases in which insanity defense is asserted remains far fewer than the public perceives. The dispute over which mental disease or defect a defendant can use for the insanity defense remains almost as strong as was the case two hundred years ago.

INSANITY DEFENSE TESTS

Over the years, four different insanity tests have emerged, and they remain in use in one form or another in all jurisdictions. The four are the Durham test, the American Bar Association's Model Penal Code test, the M'Naghten test, and the irresistible impulse test. To establish a defense on the grounds of insanity under the Durham test the defendant's lawyer must clearly and convincingly prove that at the time of the crime, the defendant's mental disease made it impossible for him or her to know the nature and quality of the act he or she was committing. The defendant did not know that what he or she was doing was wrong, and the act is a product of mental dysfunctionality.

To establish a defense of insanity under the Model Penal Code test it must be clearly and convincingly shown that as a result of mental disease or defect, the defendant substantially lacked the capacity to appreciate the criminality or wrongfulness of his or her conduct or to conform to the requirements of law.

To establish a defense of insanity under the M'Naghten test, it must be clearly and convincingly shown that because of his or her mental disease or defect, the defendant was incapable of forming the guilty intent or mind-set required by the crime.

To establish a defense of insanity under the irresistible impulse test, Irresistible impulse rule it must be clearly and convincingly shown that the defendant had a mental disease and that his or her action is an irresistible result of the disease.

THE PRACTITIONER AND INSANITY DEFENSE

For mental health professionals, it should suffice to know that all forms and variations of these tests seek to defeat the presumption of the defendant's sanity at the time the crime was committed, either because the crime was a product of mental dysfunction or the dysfunction made it impossible for the defendant to know the wrongfulness of his or her behavior. Critical for mental health professionals is that the legal viability of their expert testimony in any jurisdiction may depend on which test of insanity that jurisdiction uses. Many jurisdictions have made and are making evidentiary changes to streamline and simplify their insanity defense trials to conform with the Insanity Defense Reform Act of 1984, requiring that a defendant bear the burden of establishing his or her insanity by "clear and convincing evidence." Some jurisdictions have gone further, instituting bifurcated procedures in which the defendant's criminal responsibility is determined after a much-simplified determination of guilt or innocence. This makes it possible for an "insane" defendant to be found guilty of a crime and the evidence of insanity considered during the dispositional phase of the case. In such jurisdiction, for example, John Hinckley, who attempted to assassinate President Ronald Reagan in 1981, would be found guilty of attempted murder because the evidence showed he did commit the act, but before his sentencing, evidence of his insanity would be introduced to determine the nature of his sentencing or responsibility.

In civil cases, defendants are usually held legally responsible for their injury to others or to property. This means that even if the defendant's harmful action is a product of mental disease or defect or if, as a result of the disorder, the defendant could not understand the wrongfulness of the action, he or she would still be found liable of the action. The focus of civil actions is generally to compensate the plaintiff for the wrong or loss he or she suffered. However, should a civil case be based on a wrongdoing in which intent is necessary to prove culpability, the mentally disabled defendant may not be found guilty or responsible. Mental health professionals need to remember that insanity for civil or criminal defense is defined by law, not by mental health diagnosis. Psychiatric diagnosis is only one of the factors generally taken into consideration in reaching a legal definition of insanity. Mental health expert testimonies about a defendant's sanity or insanity are subject to cross-examination.

BIBLIOGRAPHY

Ewing, Charles Patrick. *Insanity: Murder, Madness, and the Law.* New York: Oxford University Press, 2008. This resource examines ten murder cases in which defendants used the insanity defense, showing how some were successful in their plea and why others were rejected.

Packer, Ira K. *Evaluation of Criminal Responsibility.* New York: Oxford University Press, 2009. Offers guidelines for assessing mental health in a forensic setting and suggests effective approaches for criminal, civil, and juvenile/family cases.

Reisner, Ralph. *Law and the Mental Health System: Civil and Criminal Aspects.* 4th ed. St. Paul, Minn.: West, 2004. A textbook on mental health laws and systems. The text carefully and clearly selects, reviews, and presents legal cases that define the landscape of mental health law.

Wulach, James S. *Law and Mental Health Professionals: New Jersey.* Washington, D.C.: American Psychological Association, 1999. A comprehensive review of New Jersey laws and legal procedures that affect mental health professionals.

C. Emmanuel Ahia

SEE ALSO: Forensic psychology; Incompetency; Law and psychology.

Insomnia

TYPE OF PSYCHOLOGY: Consciousness

Insomnia is a complaint of poor, insufficient, or non-restorative sleep; it may be experienced for a few nights or for a lifetime. Daytime functioning is often affected. Insomnia may be caused by an underlying physiological or psychological disorder or by substance abuse, but it can also occur independently of these factors.

KEY CONCEPTS

- Chronotherapy
- Circadian rhythm
- Persistent psychophysiological insomnia (PPI)
- Polysomnography
- Primary insomnia
- Transient insomnia

INTRODUCTION

Insomnia is defined as the perception that a person's sleep is inadequate or abnormal. The person with insomnia may report difficulty falling asleep, a short sleep time, frequent awakenings, and nonrestorative sleep. The daytime symptoms of insomnia include fatigue, excessive daytime sleepiness (EDS), mood changes, and impaired mental as well as physical functioning. Insomnia can be caused by conditions such as stress, anxiety, depression, substance abuse, medical illness, or other sleep disorders, but it may occur in some patients without any known underlying disorders. The occurrence of insomnia increases with age; one study estimates that approximately 50 percent of people between the ages of sixty-five and seventy-nine experience trouble sleeping. A 2004 study indicated that this is most likely related to the pain and discomfort associated with chronic disease. Treatment options such as the use of eszopiclone (Lunesta), zolpidem (Ambien), sedative-hypnotics, and behavioral interventions have been studied, each noting various degrees of success (although sedatives were found to sometimes increase adverse effects).

TYPES OF INSOMNIA

The American Academy of Sleep Medicine (AASM) recognizes two general types of insomnia. Classified on the basis of the duration of the period in which the person experiences insomnia, these two types are transient insomnia and primary insomnia. Transient insomnia is seen when a person has had a history of normal sleep but experiences a period of insomnia that lasts less than three weeks; the patient returns to normal sleep after the insomnia period. The insomnia period is usually tied to a specific experience or situation, and it is believed that there are two common processes that are involved in transient insomnia. The first involves central nervous system arousal and any condition that may cause such arousal, whether it is psychological or environmental. There is no clear physiological disorder associated with this condition, but some research suggests that individuals who are likely to be aroused by stress may be more

vulnerable to this type of insomnia than other people. Some sleep researchers indicate that emotional disturbance may play a role in up to 80 percent of transient insomnia cases.

A second process involved in transient insomnia results from people having a sleep-wake schedule that is not aligned with their own circadian (twenty-four-hour) rhythms. Biological rhythms control many bodily functions, such as blood pressure, body temperature, hormonal activity, and the menstrual cycle, as well as the sleep-wake cycle. Insomnia can be caused by a sleep-wake cycle that is misaligned with the circadian rhythm, such as that which occurs when people travel across many time zones or engage in shift work. Circadian rhythm disorders can last for periods of more than six months, in which case the problem would be considered chronic.

Primary insomnia is diagnosed when the patient's insomnia is not secondary to problems such as depression, anxiety, pain, or some other sleep disorder, and it lasts for a period longer than three weeks. Two types of primary insomnia are persistent psychophysiological insomnia (PPI) and insomnia complaints without objective findings. PPI is commonly known as learned, or behavioral, insomnia, as it is caused or maintained by maladaptive learning—that is, by the occurrence of sleep-incompatible behaviors, such as caffeine intake before bedtime. PPI is diagnosed when the patient demonstrates sleep difficulties that are verified in a sleep laboratory and are then traced to their behavioral causes. Figures vary, but approximately 15 percent of those patients diagnosed as having insomnia probably have PPI. One common feature of PPI is excessive worrying about sleep problems. Great efforts are made to fall asleep at night, which are unsuccessful and lead to increased sleep difficulty; however, the patient may fall asleep quite easily when not trying to fall asleep.

THEORIES OF INSOMNIA

One theory concerning how persistent psychophysiological insomnia can develop suggests that some people have a poor sleep-wake cycle, which makes it more difficult for them to overcome sleep-inhibiting behavior. For example, it is possible for people to become so anxious concerning their poor sleep that even the thought of their own bedrooms causes them stress, which further increases their sleep problems and creates a cycle of increasingly difficult sleep. This cycle would eventually end for persons with normal sleep cycles, but it is much easier for these events to disrupt those who already have the poor sleep-wake cycle suggested by this theory. Although PPI may begin in response to stress or an emotional situation, it should again be noted that in PPI this type of learning or behavior plays the major role in the insomnia complaint.

Most patients with insomnia will exhibit irregular sleep patterns or polysomnographic findings when tested in a sleep laboratory; however, there are those who complain of insomnia yet show no irregular sleep patterns. In the past, these people were viewed as having "pseudoinsomnia," and they were sometimes suspected of complaining of poor sleep as an excuse for being lazy. Those who have insomnia complaints without objective findings do not show any physiological or psychological disorder and do not exhibit any sleep-incompatible behaviors, yet they commonly respond to treatment of their insomnia as would a verified insomnia patient.

One study found that insomnia was associated with anxiety, depression, psychiatric distress, and medical illness in 47 percent of the cases. The medical and psychiatric disorders, as well as the pharmacological substances, that can cause insomnia are extremely numerous. James Walsh and Roger Sugerman note three theories that attempt to explain the occurrence of insomnia in psychiatric disorders and that may prove helpful in understanding the process. The first suggests that insomnia results from a psychological disturbance that goes unresolved and leads to arousal that prevents sleep. The second states that neurochemical abnormalities may be the cause of insomnia in psychiatric disorders. The final theory asserts that affective (emotional) disorders may disturb the biological rhythms that control sleep.

DIAGNOSING INSOMNIA

The importance of a greater understanding of the mechanisms of sleep and insomnia can be appreciated by everyone. Everyone knows that when one feels sleepy, it is difficult to concentrate, perform simple tasks, or be patient with other people. If the sleep disorder is present in an individual over a protracted length of time, it can become virtually intolerable.

The general consensus developed from population-based studies as of 2014 is that approximately 30 percent of the adult population of the United States experience one or more symptoms of insomnia. However, the National Institute of Health found in 2005 that if diagnostic requirements included impaired functioning during the day as a result of the insomnia symptoms, this number declined to 10 percent. Still, many adults experience at least some difficulty sleeping in their lifetimes.

Insomnia may have drastic effects on behavior during the day. Fatigue, excessive daytime sleepiness, mood changes, and impaired mental and physical functioning are all frequently caused by insomnia. Difficulties in the workplace, as well as increased health problems, may also be associated with insomnia.

Diagnosis of insomnia depends on an accurate evaluation of the circumstances surrounding the complaint. The clinician must take many things into account when diagnosing each particular case, as insomnia may be the result of any number of factors in the patient's life. Questions concerning behavior should be asked to determine if the insomnia is caused by sleep-incompatible behaviors. Polysomnographic testing in a sleep laboratory may be necessary to determine which type of insomnia the patient has.

TREATMENT OPTIONS

Once properly diagnosed, insomnia may be treated in a number of ways, all of which depend on the type of insomnia. The typical treatment for sleeping problems tends to be the prescription of sleeping pills. A 2005 study found that adults aged twenty to forty-four doubled their use of prescription sleep aids, while among adolescents aged ten to nineteen, the increase in usage was 85 percent between 2000 and 2004. The treatment of transient insomnia may involve small doses of a short-acting drug, including benzodiazepines such as diazepam (Valium) or lorazepam (Ativan); Z-drugs such as zaleplon (Sonata), zolpidem (Ambien), and zopiclone (eszopiclone analogue Lunesta); or nonbenzodiazepines, such as indiplon. Simply counseling or educating patients concerning situations that may increase their sleep problems is frequently found to be effective. If the transient insomnia is caused by disruptive sounds in the sleeping environment (such as snoring or traffic noise), devices that mask the noise may be used. Using earplugs and placing a fan in the room to mask the noise are two simple examples of this method. If the sleep disturbance is associated with misaligned circadian rhythms, the person's bedtime may be systematically adjusted toward either an earlier or a later hour, depending on what time the individual normally goes to sleep. Strict adherence to the adjusted sleep-wake schedule is then necessary for the individual to remain on a regular schedule. This method is referred to as chronotherapy.

Peter Hauri suggests that treatment of persistent psychophysiological insomnia should typically involve aspects of three domains: sleep hygiene, behavioral treatment, and the use of hypnotics. Methods involving sleep hygiene focus on educating the patient concerning proper sleep habits. Hauri states that the goal is for the patient to avoid all stimulating or arousing thoughts. This is done by focusing on or engaging in monotonous or nonstimulating behaviors at bedtime such as reading or listening to pleasant music.

Behavioral methods include performing relaxation therapy, limiting sleep time to a few hours per night until the patient is able to use the time in bed as true sleeping time, and using stimulus control therapy. This method requires patients to get out of bed whenever they are not able to sleep. The process is aimed at reducing the association between the bedroom and the frustration with trying to go to sleep. Auricular acupuncture also has been found successful in the treatment of insomnia.

The use of hypnotic medications is indicated in patients who have such a need for sleep that they "try too hard" and thus become aroused by their efforts. In 2005, the Food and Drug Administration approved ramelteon (Rozerem) for the treatment of long-term insomnia. As with transient insomnia, a small dose of a short-acting drug is suggested to break this cycle of frustration.

The treatment for patients who exhibit no objective polysomnographic findings is similar to that for patients with any other type of insomnia. These patients also tend to respond to behavioral, educational, and pharmacological methods.

SLEEP RESEARCH

The discovery of the methods used to monitor electrical activity in the human brain during the late 1920's essentially ushered in the modern era of sleep research. With this development, sleep stages were discovered, which eventually led to a greater understanding of what takes place in both normal and abnormal sleep.

In *Sleep: A Scientific Perspective* (1988), A. Michael Anch, Carl P. Browman, Merrill M. Mitler, and James K. Walsh state that most insomnia research before 1980 treated insomniacs as one group, with little attention paid to differences such as duration of the disorder, causal factors, or the nature of certain study groups, such as the elderly, women, or ethnic minorities. Although specifying types of insomnia limits the ability to generalize findings, these authors note that the inclusion of different types of insomnia in studies eventually increased knowledge of the psychology of sleep and insomnia.

Much has been learned that allows doctors and psychologists to treat the different types of insomnia more effectively. The myth of the "cure-all" sleeping pill has been replaced with a more sophisticated approach, which includes educational and behavioral practices. Medications are still used, but treatment options have increased so that clinicians are not as limited in their choices.

As the study of sleep disorders has developed in terms of scientific sophistication, researchers have been able to learn the importance that sleep holds in day-to-day functioning. They have also discovered how detrimental sleep loss or disruption of the sleep-wake cycle can be. Aiding in the discoveries have been scientific developments in neurobiology, behavioral medicine, physiology, and psychiatry that allow analysis of the mechanisms in normal and abnormal sleep. It is hoped that as scientists gain a further understanding of insomnia through research, they will also understand, more generally, the true purpose of sleep.

BIBLIOGRAPHY

Anch, A. Michael, Carl P. Browman, Merrill M. Mitler, and James K. Walsh. *Sleep: A Scientific Perspective.* Englewood Cliffs: Prentice-Hall, 1988. Print.

Berntson, Gary G., and John T. Cacioppo. *Handbook of Neuroscience for the Behavioral Sciences.* Hoboken: Wiley, 2009. Print.

Green, Gayle. *Insomniac.* Berkeley: U of California P, 2008. Print.

Krakow, Barry. *Sound Sleep, Sound Mind: Seven Keys to Sleeping Through the Night.* Hoboken: Wiley, 2007. Print.

Kryger, Meir H. *A Woman's Guide to Sleep Disorders.* New York: McGraw-Hill, 2004. Print.

Kryger, Meir H., Thomas Roth, and William C. Dement, eds. *Principles and Practice of Sleep Medicine.* 5th ed. Philadelphia: Elsevier, 2011. Print.

Morin, Charles M., and Colin A. Espie. *The Oxford Handbook of Sleep and Sleep Disorders.* Oxford: Oxford UP, 2012. Print.

Nicholson, Anthony N., and John Marks. *Insomnia: A Guide for Medical Practitioners.* Boston: MTP, 1983. Print.

Poceta, J. Steven, and Merrill M. Mitler, eds. *Sleep Disorders: Diagnosis and Treatment.* Totowa: Humana Press, 1998. Print.

Summers-Bremmer, Eluned. *Insomnia: A Cultural History.* London: Reaktion, 2008. Print.

Swanson, Jenifer, ed. *Sleep Disorders Sourcebook.* 2d ed. Detroit: Omnigraphics, 2005. Print.

Alan K. Gibson

See Also: Aging: Physical changes; Circadian rhythms; Depression; Narcolepsy; Post-traumatic stress disorder; Sleep; Sleep apnea.

Insomnia and sleep disorders

Type of psychology: Behavioral medicine; Biological bases of human behavior; Clinical; Counseling; Developmental; Family; Health; Psychopathology; Social

Sleep disorders are a group of disorders that affect the quantity or quality of sleep. They often cause severe daytime consequences including chronic sleepiness, fatigue, impairments in cognitive functioning such as attention, concentration and memory, and mood difficulties including depression and anxiety. Sleep disorders may be physiological or psychological in nature.

Key Concepts:
- Fatigue
- Insomnia
- Sleepiness

INTRODUCTION

Although most individuals have experienced a bad night of sleep, individuals with a sleep disorder regularly have a disturbance in either or both, their sleep quality and quantity, and consequently suffer from severe daytime impairments. Certain sleep disorders have well-determined causes and evidence-based treatments that are highly effective, while others have causes that are less clear and treatments dependent on the individual's experience. The following presents information regarding five of the most common sleep disorders: insomnia, sleep-disordered breathing, narcolepsy, restless legs syndrome, and circadian rhythm disorders.

INSOMNIA

Insomnia has been commonly defined as the experience of having difficulty falling asleep, staying asleep, waking too early, or waking feeling unrefreshed that leads to daytime consequences. These daytime consequences may include daytime sleepiness, fatigue, irritability, feelings of depression or anxiety, difficulty concentrating, or impaired memory. According to the *Diagnostic and Statistical Manual of Mental Disorders* (DSM-5), these symptoms are typically present for 30 minutes or more for at least 3 days per week for 3 months or longer. An episode of insomnia may be provoked by an obvious trigger, such as a drastic change in personal or professional environment including marriage, divorce, death, change in career, or new child, medical illnesses, or certain types of medication. However, there may also be no identifiable trigger. Treatment for insomnia can take many forms, including medication sleep aids, or psychological therapies such as cognitive-behavioral therapy for insomnia, an evidence-based treatment that has shown very high efficacy and effectiveness in treating symptoms of insomnia.

SLEEP-DISORDERED BREATHING

Sleep-disordered breathing is a term for a collection of disorders that disrupt sleep as a result of multiple, brief periods of cessation of breathing. Obstructive sleep apnea, one of the more common forms of sleep-disordered breathing, occurs when the soft palette in the throat relaxes and blocks the airway during sleep. When this happens, breathing becomes difficult and sometimes impossible. When breathing is prevented, it triggers the individual to awaken in order to gasp for breath. These awakenings are often so brief that the individual is not even aware that breathing has stopped, or that they have been awake. Once breathing has resumed, the individual typically falls back asleep immediately, and the cycle begins again. According to the American Academy of Sleep Medicine, while mild sleep apnea is defined as 5-15 apneas, or cessations of breath, per hour, the most severe cases of sleep apnea can result in the individual waking more than 30 times per hour. This fragmentation of sleep can lead to both physiological and psychological consequences, including increased blood pressure and incidence of cardiovascular disease, chronic daytime sleepiness, fatigue, difficulty with attention, concentration, memory, and depression.

Although the exact causes of obstructive sleep apnea are not completely understood, rates of sleep apnea increase with increased age and weight. Additionally, because the relaxation of the muscles in the throat has been implicated in the manifestation of the disorder, an overall decrease in muscle tone within the body can result in the onset of sleep apnea. Physicians have established a brief measure used to determine the likelihood of having

Photo: iStock

NARCOLEPSY

Narcolepsy is a disorder that affects the regulation of the sleep/wake cycle producing excessive daytime sleepiness. Symptoms can, but do not always, include cataplexy, hypnogogic hallucinations and sleep paralysis. Cataplexy, one of the diagnostic symptoms of narcolepsy, is defined as a sudden loss of muscle tone prompted by strong emotion such as laughter or sadness. The loss of muscle tone can range from mild to severe weakness in limbs, with potentially complete loss of tone resulting in collapse. Hypnogogic hallucinations are visual or auditory perceptions in the absence of real stimuli which typically occur while the individual is falling asleep or waking up. Sleep paralysis, the last of the "tetrad of narcolepsy" is the phenomenon whereby the individual experiences the inability to move upon waking.

sleep apnea. The STOP-BANG includes questions with regard to snoring, tiredness, observations of cessation of breath during sleep, increased blood pressure, BMI score, age, neck circumference and gender. Although measures like the STOP-BANG are useful in identifying potential sleep apnea patients, formal diagnosis can only be made following an overnight sleep study including polysomnography.

Various treatments, including oral appliances, surgery and continuous positive airway pressure, have been developed for sleep apnea, and can be selected according to the comfort of the patient. Oral appliances are fitted by dentists and help re-align the jaw in order to keep the airway more open during sleep. Oral surgery can also be performed to reduce the size of the soft palette including the uvula, although the long term effectiveness of the treatment has been debated. To date, the most common and effective treatment for sleep apnea is the use of continuous positive airway pressure, or CPAP. CPAP is a device worn typically over the nose and mouth that utilizes pressurized air to keep the soft palette in place in order to keep the airway open. In order to be effective, however, the patient must continue to use CPAP throughout the course of the disorder.

The cause of narcolepsy is now considered to be mainly genetic. Although the cause is genetic, diagnosis of narcolepsy does not rely on genetic testing. Instead, a combination of sleep measures is utilized including overnight polysomnography and the Multiple Sleep Latency Test (MSLT). The MSLT consists of an individual coming to a sleep laboratory during the day. Individuals are then given the opportunity to nap, every two hours, after having had a full night of sleep, the night before. Technicians monitor polysomnography to look for the signs and symptoms of narcolepsy, sleep onset latency, or how fast the individual falls asleep, and REM latency, or how fast the individual takes to begin REM sleep. Because of the excessive daytime sleepiness associated with the disorder, individuals with narcolepsy will typically show very fast sleep onset latency, and will enter REM faster than healthy individuals.

Treatment for narcolepsy involves treating each of the presenting symptoms separately. One can manage excessive sleepiness by utilizing stimulants, stimulant-like medications or napping regimens. Additionally, symptoms of cataplexy can be treated with two classes of antidepressant medications, tricyclics or selective serotonin reuptake inhibitors (SSRI's). Although there is no known cure for narcolepsy, successfully managing daytime sleepiness and cataplexy can allow an individual to lead a relatively asymptomatic life.

RESTLESS LEGS SYNDROME

Restless legs syndrome (RLS) is a disorder affecting the muscles in the legs during rest or at night, in the period just prior to sleep. According to the American Academy of Sleep Medicine, RLS results in an irresistible urge to move one's legs in order to reduce or eliminate painful or uncomfortable sensations in the legs. During the night, many individuals with RLS will experience periodic limb movements (PLM), where one will move their legs during sleep causing sleep fragmentation and disruption. The occurrence of PLM can be detected objectively using overnight polysomnography, but is not necessary for diagnosis. Although there are genetic factors that contribute to RLS, many cases have been found to be associated with iron deficiency. Certain types of medications may also lead to increased incidence or worsening of RLS.

Treatment of RLS can vary according to the severity of the disorder. In cases where iron deficiency is noted, iron supplements may alleviate or prevent symptoms. For more severe cases, or those that may not respond to treatment with iron, medications such as dopaminergic agents may improve both daytime symptoms and sleep quality. However, there are significant side effects associated with these types of medications, and they should not be used for the long-term management of RLS.

CIRCADIAN RHYTHM DISORDERS

Two of the most researched and common circadian rhythm disorders are advanced sleep phase syndrome (ASPS) and delayed sleep phase syndrome (DSPS). These two disorders, although manifesting at different times of day, are conceptually similar, in that they are disorders that prevent individuals from going to sleep or waking up at their preferred time. Individuals with ASPS feel excessively sleepy early in the evening, and as a result fall asleep and wake up earlier than they prefer. In contrast, individuals with DSPS, do not feel sleepy at their desired bedtime, and instead go to bed and wake up much later than preferred.

Treatment of circadian rhythm disorders, ASPS and DSPS, utilizes a variety of methods including chronotherapy, light therapy, or the use of melatonin supplements. Chronotherapy is the use of scheduled sleep/wake times in order to alter natural body rhythms. Chronotherapy can be used to treat ASPS and DSPS by moving scheduled bedtimes and wake times later, by an hour or more every day, until the preferred bed time can be achieved. As treatment for DSPS, chronotherapy involves moving the bedtime completely around the clock, eventually allowing one to achieve an "earlier" bedtime. This form of chronotherapy, however, may not be appropriate for all individuals since it can be very disruptive to a work or school schedule. Light therapy consists of the utilization of a light box which emits bright light. Bright light suppresses melatonin onset, which causes sleepiness and prompts sleep onset. With regard to ASPS, if melatonin is suppressed at night, sleep onset may occur later, at a more preferred time. In contrast, when light therapy is used in the morning, sleepiness may be decreased, allowing the individual to wake earlier, at a more preferred wake time. Lastly, as treatment for DSPS, melatonin supplements can be taken in the evening to mimic the naturally occurring process by which melatonin entrains the sleep/wake cycle, allowing sleep to occur earlier.

BIBLIOGRAPHY

Allen, R. P., Picchietti, D., Hening, W. A., Trenkwalder, C., Walters, A. S., & Montplaisi, J. (2003). "Restless Legs Syndrome: Diagnostic Criteria, Special Considerations, and Epidemiology: A Report From the Restless Legs Syndrome Diagnosis and Epidemiology Workshop at the National Institutes of Health". *Sleep Medicine*, 4(2), 101-119. The seminal paper describing the causes, treatments, and significance of restless legs syndrome.

Dauvilliers, Y., Arnulf, I., & Mignot, E. (2007). "Narcolepsy with Cataplexy". *The Lancet*, 369(9560), 499-511. A scientific article thoroughly describing narcolepsy with cataplexy.

Hening, W., Allen, R., Earley, C., Kushida, C., Picchietti, D., & Silber, M. (1999). "The Treatment of Restless Legs Syndrome and Periodic Limb Movement Disorder". An American Academy of Sleep Medicine Review. *Sleep*, 22(7), 970-999.

Mellinger, G. D., Balter, M. B., & Uhlenhuth, E. H. (1985). "Insomnia and its Treatment: Prevalence and Correlates". *Archives of general psychiatry*, 42(3), 225-232. A scientific report describing an epidemiological sample of insomnia patients and selected treatments.

Sack, R. L., Auckley, D., Auger, R. R., Carskadon, M. A., Wright Jr, K. P., Vitiello, M. V., & Zhdanova, I. V. (2007). "Circadian Rhythm Sleep Disorders: Part I, Basic Principles, Shift Work and Jet Lag

Disorders An American Academy of Sleep Medicine Review: An American Academy of Sleep Medicine Review". *Sleep*, 30(11), 1460. &

Sack, R. L., Auckley, D., Auger, R. R., Carskadon, M. A., Wright Jr, K. P., Vitiello, M. V., & Zhdanova, I. V. (2007). "Circadian Rhythm Sleep Disorders: Part II, Advanced Sleep Phase Disorder, Delayed Sleep Phase Disorder, Free-running Disorder, and Irregular Sleep-wake Rhythm: An American Academy of Sleep Medicine review. *Sleep*, 30(11), 1484. This two-part review describes circadian rhythm disorders in detail.

Young, T., Peppard, P. E., & Gottlieb, D. J. (2002). "Epidemiology of Obstructive Sleep Apnea: A Population Health Perspective". *American Journal of Respiratory and Critical Care Medicine*, 165(9), 1217-1239. A highly-cited study examining the incidence, health consequences and treatment of obstructive sleep apnea.

Jennifer R. Goldschmied and Patricia J. Deldin

See Also: Circadian rhythm; Health; Sleep wake cycle; Wellness.

Instinct theory

Type of psychology: Motivation

Until the early decades of the twentieth century, when behaviorism, which rejected instincts, became the dominant theoretical model for psychology, instinct theory was often used to explain both animal and human motivation. As behaviorism faded, aspects of instinct theory returned to psychology—modernized, but still recognizable as parts of the oldest theory of motivation..

Key Concepts
- Behaviorism
- Instinct
- Motivation
- Reflex
- Scientific method
- Tropism

INTRODUCTION

When instinct theory was incorporated into the new scientific psychology of the late nineteenth century, it was already centuries old. In its earliest form, instinct theory specified that a creature's essential nature was already established at birth and that its actions would largely be directed by that nature. A modern restatement of this notion would be that, at birth, creatures are already programmed, as computers are, and that they must operate according to their programs. Charles Darwin's theory of evolution through natural selection, first published in 1859, led to great controversy in the late nineteenth and early twentieth centuries. It also fostered speculation that if humans were evolved from earlier forms and were therefore more closely related to other animals than had once been believed, humans might have instincts, or inherited behaviors, that other animals were observed to have. In 1908, William McDougall, one of the main early instinct theorists, suggested a list of human instincts that included such varied behaviors as repulsion, curiosity, self-abasement, and gregariousness. Many researchers came up with their own lists of human instincts; by the 1920s, more than two thousand had been suggested.

A computer program can be printed out and studied, but an instinct in the original sense cannot so easily be made explicit. At best, it can be inferred from the behavior of an animal or person after other explanations for that behavior have been discounted; at worst, it is simply assumed from observing behavior. That a person has, for example, an instinct of argumentativeness could be assumed from the person's arguing; arguing is then "explained" by declaring that it comes from an instinct of argumentativeness. Such circular reasoning is unacceptable in scientific analysis, but it is very common in some early scientific (and many modern popular) discussions of instinct.

VARIATIONS IN THEORY

As is often the case with ideas that have long been believed by both scientists and the general public, instinct theory has separated into several theories. The earliest form was accepted by Aristotle, the ancient Greek philosopher and scientist. He stated in his *Politics* that "a social instinct is implanted in all men by nature" and that "a man would be thought a coward if he had no more courage than a courageous woman, and a woman would be thought loquacious if she imposed no more restraint on her conversation than the good man." The first statement declares an inherent quality of people; the second, inherent qualities of men and women. Very likely, Aristotle's beliefs were based on careful observation of people around him—a good beginning, but not a sufficient basis for making factual comments about people in general.

Aristotle's views were those of a scientist of his day. Centuries later, a scientist would not hold such views, but a layperson very well might. Over the many centuries since Aristotle expressed his views on instinct theory, "popular" versions of it have been more influential than the cautious versions offered by later scientists.

HISTORIC MISINTERPRETATIONS

Modern science reaches conclusions based, to the greatest extent possible, on evidence gathered and interpreted along lines suggested by theories. Traditional instinct theory is especially weak in suggesting such lines; usually it put early psychologists in the position of trying to support the idea that instinct had caused a behavior by demonstrating that nothing else had caused it. Rather than supporting one possibility, they were attempting to deny dozens of others. Even worse, they were forcing thought into an "either-or" pattern rather than allowing for the possibility that a behavior may be based on inherited influences interacting with learned ones.

For example, to try to evaluate the possibility that people are instinctively afraid of snakes, one might first find a number of people who are afraid of snakes and then attempt to establish that those people had never had an experience that might have caused them to learn their fear, such as being startled or harmed by a snake or even being told that snakes are dangerous. Such a task is all but impossible, almost guaranteeing that a researcher will conclude that there are several ways that the fear could have been learned, so an instinct explanation can be discounted. The fact that people who fear snakes can learn not to fear them can be offered as further evidence that they had learned their original fear—not a particularly compelling argument, but a good enough approach for a researcher who wants to discount instinct.

When behaviorism became the predominant theoretical stance of psychology in the 1920s, the problems with instinct as an explanation of motivation were "resolved" simply by sidestepping them. Instincts were discarded as unscientific, replaced by concepts such as needs, drives, and motives. Dropping the term "instinct" from the vocabulary of psychology did not eliminate the behaviors it had originally labeled, either for lower animals or for people, but it did separate even further the popular views of instinct from the scientific ones.

REEMERGENCE OF HUMAN NATURE RESEARCH

Instinct theory's purpose in psychology's infancy was the same as it had once been in the distant past: to explain the motivations of a variety of species, from the simplest creatures up to humans. Unfortunately, it had also served other purposes in the past, purposes that often proved unwelcome to early behavioral scientists. To declare people superior to other animals, or men superior to women, or almost any target group better or worse than another was not a goal of psychology.

Worse than the heritage of centuries of misuse of the concept of instinct was the accumulation of evidence that instincts, defined at the time as completely unlearned behaviors, were limited to simple creatures and were virtually nonexistent in people. Psychology and related sciences all but eliminated instinct as a motivational concept for decades. However, they could not avoid bringing back similar notions; the term "instinct" was gone, but what it tried to explain was not. For example, in the 1940s, social psychologists working to find alternatives to the belief that aggression is instinctive in humans proposed that frustration (goal blocking) is a major cause of aggression. When pressed to explain why frustration led to aggression, many indicated that this is simply part of human nature. Some years later, it was demonstrated that the presence of some sort of weapon during a frustrating experience enhanced the likelihood of aggression, apparently through a "triggering effect." Instinct as a concept was not invoked, but these ideas came very close.

Even closer was the work of another group of scientists, ethologists, in their explanations of some animal behaviors. Evaluating what might be thought a good example of instinct in its earliest definition, a duckling following its mother, they demonstrated that experience with a moving, quacking object is necessary. In other words, learning, albeit learning that was limited to a very brief period in the duckling's development, led to the behavior. Many other seemingly strong examples of instinct were demonstrated to be a consequence of some inner predisposition interacting with environmental circumstances. A new, more useful rethinking of the ancient concept of instinct had begun.

INSTINCTIVE INFLUENCES

A 1961 article by Keller and Marian Breland suggested that instinct should still be a part of psychology, despite its period of disgrace. While training performing animals, they had witnessed a phenomenon they termed "instinctive drift." (Although other terms, such as "species-specific behavior," were at that time preferred to "instinct," the Brelands stated their preference for the original label.) Instinctive drift refers to the tendency of a creature's trained behavior to move in the direction of inherited predispositions.

When the Brelands tried to teach pigs to place coins in a piggy bank, they found that although the pigs could easily be taught to pick up coins and run toward the bank, they could not be stopped from repeatedly dropping and rooting at them. Raccoons could be taught to drop coins in a container but could not be stopped from "dipping" the coins in and rubbing them together, a drift toward the instinctive washing of food. Several other species presented similar problems to their would-be trainers, all related to what the Brelands willingly called instinct.

Preparedness is another example of an instinct/ learning relationship. Through conditioning, any creature can be taught to associate some previously neutral stimulus with a behavior. Dogs in Ivan Petrovich Pavlov's laboratory at the beginning of the twentieth century readily learned to salivate at the sound of a bell, a signal that food would appear immediately. While some stimuli can easily serve as signals for a particular species, others cannot. It seems clear that animals are prepared by nature for some sorts of learning but not for others. Rats can readily be trained to press a lever (a bar in a Skinner box) to obtain food, and pigeons can readily be trained to peck at something to do so, but there are some behaviors that they simply cannot learn to serve that purpose.

Taste aversions is yet another example of an instinctive influence that has been well documented by modern psychology. In people and other animals, nausea following the taste of food very consistently leads to that taste becoming aversive. The taste/nausea combination is specific; electric shock following a taste does not cause the taste to become aversive, nor does a visual stimulus followed by nausea cause the sight to become aversive. Researchers theorize that the ability to learn to detect and avoid tainted food has survival value, so it has become instinctive.

LIMITATIONS AND MISUSE OF THEORY

In popular use, belief in instincts has confused and hurt people more than it has enlightened or helped them. Instinct theory often imposes a rigid either-or form on people's thinking about human motivation. That is, people are encouraged by the notion of instinct to wonder if some behavior, such as aggression, is either inherent in people or learned from experience. Once one's thoughts are cast into such a mold, one is less likely to consider the strong likelihood that a behavior has multiple bases, which may be different from one person to the next. Instead of looking for the many possible reasons for human aggression, some related to inherent qualities and some related to learned qualities, one looks for a single cause. Intently focusing on one possibility to the exclusion of all others often blinds people to the very fact that they are doing so. Searching for "the" answer, they fail to recognize that their method of searching has locked their thinking onto a counterproductive track.

Instinct theory has been invoked to grant humans special status, above that of other animals. Generally, this argument states that humans can reason and rationally control their actions, while lower animals are guided solely by instincts. At best, this argument has been used to claim that humans are especially loved by their God. At worst, the idea that lower animals are supposedly guided only by instinct was used by philosopher René Descartes to claim that animals were essentially automatons, incapable of actually feeling pain, and that therefore they could be vivisected without anesthesia.

Instinct theory has also been used to support the claim that some people are more worthy than other people. Those with fewer "base instincts," or even those who by their rationality have overcome their instincts, are supposedly superior. Acceptance of such ideas has led to very real errors of judgment and considerable human suffering. For example, over many centuries, across much of the world, it was believed that women, simply by virtue of being female, were not capable of sufficiently clear thinking to justify providing them with a formal education, allowing them to own property, or letting them hold elected office or vote. Anthropologist Margaret Mead, in her 1942 book *And Keep Your Powder Dry: An Anthropologist Looks at America,* reports a reversal of the claim that women inherently lack some important quality. Young women in her classes, when told the then-prevailing view that people had no instincts and therefore they had no maternal instinct, became very upset, according to Mead, believing that they lacked something essential. Many minority racial or ethnic groups have suffered in similar fashion from claims that, by their unalterable nature, they are incapable of behaving at levels comparable to those in the majority.

Instinct theory has been used to suggest the absolute inevitability of many undesirable behaviors, sometimes as a way of excusing them. The ideas that philandering is part of a man's nature or that gossiping is part of a woman's are patently foolish uses of the concept of instinct.

BIBLIOGRAPHY

Barrett, Deirdre. *Supernormal Stimuli: How Primal Urges Overran Their Evolutionary Purpose.* New York: Norton, 2010. Print.

Bering, Jesse. *The Belief Instinct: The Psychology of Souls, Destiny, and the Meaning of Life.* New York: Norton, 2011. Print.

Birney, Robert Charles, and Richard C. Teevan, eds. *Instinct: An Enduring Problem in Psychology.* Princeton: Van Nostrand, 1961. Print.

Breland, Keller, and Marian Breland. "The Misbehavior of Organisms." *American Psychologist* 16.11 (1961): 681–84. Print.

Cofer, Charles Norval, and M. H. Appley. *Motivation: Theory and Research.* New York: Wiley, 1967. Print.

Hilgard, Ernest Ropiequet. *Psychology in America: A Historical Survey.* San Diego: Harcourt, 1987. Print.

Pinker, Steven. *The Language Instinct: How the Mind Creates Language.* New York: Harper, 2007. Print.

Portegys, Thomas E. "Discrimination Learning Guided by Instinct." *International Journal of Hybrid Intelligent Systems* 10.3 (2013): 129–36. Print.

Spink, Amanda. *Information Behavior: An Evolutionary Instinct.* Heidelberg: Springer, 2010. Print.

Sun, L. *The Fairness Instinct: The Robin Hood Mentality and Our Biological Nature.* Amherst: Prometheus, 2013. Print.

Wallenstein, Gene V. *The Pleasure Instinct: Why We Crave Adventure, Chocolate, Pheromones, and Music.* Hoboken: Wiley, 2009. Print.

Watson, John B. *Behaviorism.* New York: Norton, 1925. Print.

Weiten, Wayne. *Psychology: Themes and Variations.* 9th ed. Belmont: Wadsworth, 2013. Print.

Harry A. Tiemann, Jr.

SEE ALSO: Aggression; Aggression: Reduction and control; Behaviorism; Conditioning; Defense reactions: Species-specific; Drives; Ethology; Genetics and mental health; Imprinting; Learning; Motivation; Motivation: Intrinsic and extrinsic; Reflexes; Skinner box; Taste aversion.

Intelligence

TYPE OF PSYCHOLOGY: Intelligence and intelligence testing

Intelligence is a hypothetical concept, rather than a tangible entity, that is used by psychologists and other scientists to explain differences in the quality and adaptive value of the behavior of humans and, to some extent, animals. Its meaning and the theoretical models used to explore it are as varied as the field of psychology itself.

KEY CONCEPTS
- Cognitive psychology
- Correlation
- Factor
- Factor analysis
- Heritability

INTRODUCTION

The idea that human beings differ in their capacity to adapt to their environments, to learn from experience, to exercise various skills, and in general to succeed at various endeavors has existed since ancient times. Intelligence is the attribute most often singled out as responsible for successful adaptations. Up to the end of the nineteenth century, notions about what constitutes intelligence and how differences in intelligence arise were mostly speculative. In the late nineteenth century, several trends converged to bring about an event that would change the way in which intelligence was seen and dramatically influence the way it would be studied. That event, which occurred in 1905, was the publication of the first useful instrument for measuring intelligence, the Binet-Simon scale, which was developed in France by Alfred Binet and Théodore Simon.

Although the development of intelligence tests was a great technological accomplishment, it occurred, in a sense, somewhat prematurely before much scientific attention had been paid to the concept of intelligence. This circumstance tied the issue of defining intelligence and a large part of the research into its nature and origins to the limitations of the tests that had been devised. In fact, the working definition of intelligence that many psychologists have used either explicitly or implicitly in their scientific and applied pursuits is the one expressed by Edwin Boring in 1923, which holds that intelligence is whatever intelligence tests measure. Most psychologists realize that this definition is redundant and inadequate in that it erroneously implies that the tests are perfectly accurate and able to capture all that is meant by the concept. Nevertheless, psychologists and others have proceeded to use the tests as if the definition were true, mainly because of a scarcity of viable alternatives. The general public has also been led astray by the existence of "intelligence" tests and the frequent misuse of their results. Many people have come to think of the intelligence quotient, or IQ, not as a simple score achieved on a particular test, which it is, but as a complete and stable measure of intellectual capacity, which it most definitely is not. Such misconceptions have led to an understandable resistance toward and resentment of intelligence tests.

CHANGING DEFINITIONS

Boring's semifacetious definition of intelligence may be the best known and most criticized one, but it is only one among many that have been offered. Most experts in the field have defined the concept at least once in their careers. Two of the most frequently cited and influential definitions are the ones provided by Binet himself and by David Wechsler, author of a series of "second-generation" individual intelligence tests that overtook the Binet scales in terms of the frequency with which they are used. Binet believed that the essential activities of intelligence are to judge well, to comprehend well, and to reason well. He stated that intelligent thought is characterized by direction, knowing what to do and how to do it; by adaptation, the capacity to monitor one's strategies for attaining a desired end; and by criticism, the power to evaluate and control one's behavior. In 1975, almost sixty-five years after Binet's death, Wechsler defined intelligence, not dissimilarly, as the global capacity of the individual to act purposefully, to think rationally, and to deal effectively with the environment.

In addition to the testing experts (psychometricians), developmental, learning, and cognitive psychologists, among others, are also vitally interested in the concept of intelligence. Specialists in each of these subfields emphasize different aspects of it in their definitions and research.

Representative definitions were sampled in 1921, when the *Journal of Educational Psychology* published the views of fourteen leading investigators, and again in 1986, when Robert Sternberg and Douglas Detterman collected the opinions of twenty-four experts in a book entitled *What Is Intelligence? Contemporary Viewpoints on Its Nature and Definition*. Most of the experts sampled in 1921 offered definitions that equated intelligence with one or more specific abilities. For example, Lewis Terman equated it with abstract thinking, which is the ability to elaborate concepts and to use language and other symbols. Others proposed definitions that emphasized the ability to adapt or learn. Some definitions centered on knowledge and cognitive components only,

whereas others included nonintellectual qualities, such as perseverance.

In comparison, Sternberg and Detterman's 1986 survey of definitions, which is even more wide ranging, is accompanied by an organizational framework consisting of fifty-five categories or combinations of categories under which the twenty-four definitions can be classified. Some theorists view intelligence from a biological perspective and emphasize differences across species or the role of the central nervous system. Some stress cognitive aspects of mental functioning, while others focus on the role of motivation and goals. Still others, such as Anne Anastasi, choose to look on intelligence as a quality that is inherent in behavior rather than in the individual. Another major perspective highlights the role of the environment, in terms of demands and values, in defining what constitutes intelligent behavior. Throughout the 1986 survey, one can find definitions that straddle two or more categories.

A review of the 1921 and 1986 surveys shows that the definitions proposed have become considerably more sophisticated and suggests that, as the field of psychology has expanded, the views of experts on intelligence may have grown farther apart. The reader of the 1986 work is left with the clear impression that intelligence is such a multifaceted concept that no single quality can define it and no single task or series of tasks can capture it completely. Moreover, it is clear that to unravel the qualities that produce intelligent behavior, one must look not only at individuals and their skills but also at the requirements of the systems in which people find themselves. In other words, intelligence cannot be defined in a vacuum.

New intelligence research focuses on different ways to measure intelligence and on paradigms for improving or training intellectual abilities and skills. Measurement paradigms allow researchers to understand ongoing processing abilities. Some intelligence researchers include measures of intellectual style and motivation in their models.

FACTOR ANALYSIS

The lack of a universally accepted definition has not deterred continuous theorizing and research on the concept of intelligence. The central issue that has dominated theoretical models of intelligence is the question of whether it is a single, global ability or a collection of specialized abilities. This debate, started in England by Charles Spearman, is based on research that uses the correlations among various measures of abilities and, particular, the method of factor analysis, which was also pioneered by Spearman. As early as 1904, Spearman, having examined the patterns of correlation coefficients among tests of sensory discrimination and estimates of intelligence, proposed that all mental functions are the result of a single general factor, which he later designated g. Spearman equated g with the ability to grasp and apply relations. He also allowed for the fact that most tasks require unique abilities, and he named those s, or specific, factors. According to Spearman, to the extent that performance on tasks was positively correlated, the correlation was attributable to the presence of g, whereas the presence of specific factors tended to lower the correlation between measures of performance on different tasks.

By 1927, Spearman had modified his theory to allow for the existence of an intermediate class of factors, known as group factors, which were neither as universal as g nor as narrow as the s factors. Group factors were seen as accounting for the fact that certain types of activities, such as tasks involving the use of numbers or the element of speed, correlate more highly with one another than they do with tasks that do not have such elements in common.

Factor-analytic research has undergone explosive growth and extensive variations and refinements in both England and the United States since the 1920s. In the United States, work in this field was influenced greatly by Truman Kelley, whose 1928 book *Crossroads in the Mind of Man* presented a method for isolating group factors, and L. L. Thurstone, who by further elaboration of factor-analytic procedures identified a set of about twelve factors that he designated as the "primary mental abilities." Seven of these were repeatedly found in a number of investigations, using samples of people at different age levels, that were carried out by both Thurstone and others. These group factors or primary mental abilities are verbal comprehension, word fluency, speed and accuracy of arithmetic computation, spatial visualization, associative memory, perceptual speed, and general reasoning.

ORGANIZATIONAL MODELS

As the search for distinct intellectual factors progressed, their number multiplied, and so did the number of models devised to organize them. One type of scheme, used by Cyril Burt, Philip E. Vernon, and others, is a hierarchical arrangement of factors. In these models, Spearman's g factor is placed at the top of a pyramid and the specific factors are placed at the bottom; in between, there are one or more levels of group factors selected in terms of their breadth and arranged according to their interrelationships with the more general factors above them and the more specific factors below them.

In Vernon's scheme, for example, the ability to change a tire might be classified as a specific factor at the base of the pyramid, located underneath an intermediate group factor labeled mechanical information, which in turn would be under one of the two major group factors identified by Vernon as the main subdivisions under g—namely, the practical-mechanical factor. The hierarchical scheme for organizing mental abilities is a useful device that is endorsed by many psychologists on both sides of the Atlantic. It recognizes that very few tasks are so simple as to require a single skill for successful performance, that many intellectual functions share some common elements, and that some abilities play a more pivotal role than others in the performance of culturally valued activities.

Another well-known scheme for organizing intellectual traits is the structure-of-intellect (SOI) model developed by J. P. Guilford. Although the SOI is grounded in extensive factor-analytic research conducted by Guilford throughout the 1940s and 1950s, the model goes beyond factor analysis and is perhaps the most ambitious attempt to classify systematically all the possible functions of the human intellect. The SOI classifies intellectual traits along three dimensions—namely, five types of operations, four types of contents, and six types of productions, for a total of 120 categories ($5 \times 4 \times 6$). Intellectual operations consist of what a person actually does (for example, evaluating or remembering something), the contents are the types of materials or information on which the operations are performed (for example, symbols, such as letters or numbers), and the products are the form in which the contents are processed (for example, units or relations). Not all the 120 categories in Guilford's complex model have been used, but enough factors have been identified to account for about one hundred of them, and some have proved very useful in labeling and understanding the skills that tests measure. Furthermore, Guilford's model has served to call attention to some dimensions of intellectual activity, such as creativity and interpersonal skills, that had been neglected previously.

COMPETENCE AND SELF-MANAGEMENT

Contemporary theorists in the area of intelligence have tried to avoid the reliance on factor analysis and existing tests that have limited traditional research and have tried different approaches to the subject. For example, Howard Gardner, in his 1983 book *Frames of Mind: The Theory of Multiple Intelligences*, starts with the premises that the essence of intelligence is competence and that there are several distinct areas in which human beings can demonstrate competence. Based on a wide-ranging review of evidence from many scientific fields and sources, Gardner designated seven areas of competence as separate and relatively independent "intelligences." In his 1993 work *Multiple Intelligences*, Gardner revised his theory to include an eighth type of intelligence. This set of attributes comprises verbal, mathematical, spatial, bodily/ kinesthetic, musical, interpersonal, intrapersonal, and naturalist skills.

Another theory is the one proposed by Robert Sternberg in his 1985 book *Beyond IQ: A Triarchic Theory of Human Intelligence*. Sternberg defines intelligence, broadly, as mental self-management and stresses the "real-world," in addition to the academic, aspects of the concept. He believes that intelligent behavior consists of purposively adapting to, selecting, and shaping one's environment and that both culture and personality play significant roles in such behavior. Sternberg posits that differences in IQ scores reflect differences in individuals' stages of developing the expertise measured by the particular IQ test, rather than attributing these scores to differences in intelligence, ability, or aptitude. Sternberg's model has five key elements: metacognitive skills, learning skills, thinking skills, knowledge, and motivation. The elements all influence one another. In this work, Sternberg claims that measurements derived from ability and achievement tests are not different in kind; only in the point at which the measurements are being made.

INTELLIGENCE AND ENVIRONMENT

Theories of intelligence are still grappling with the issues of defining its nature and composition. Generally, newer theories do not represent radical departures from the past. They do, however, emphasize examining intelligence in relation to the variety of environments in which people actually live rather than to only academic or laboratory environments. Moreover, many investigators, especially those in cognitive psychology, are more interested in breaking down and replicating the steps involved in information processing and problem solving than they are in enumerating factors or settling on a single definition of intelligence. These trends hold the promise of

moving the work in the field in the direction of devising new ways to teach people to understand, evaluate, and deal with their environments more intelligently instead of simply measuring how well they do on intelligence tests. In their 1998 article "Teaching Triarchically Improves School Achievement," Sternberg and his colleagues note that teaching or training interventions can be linked directly to components of intelligence. Motivation also plays a role. In their 2000 article "Intrinsic and Extrinsic Motivation," Richard Ryan and Edward Deci provide a review of contemporary thinking about intrinsic and extrinsic motivation. The authors suggest that the use of motivational strategies should promote student self-determination.

The most heated of all the debates about intelligence is the one regarding its determinants, often described as the nature-nurture controversy. The nature side of the debate was spearheaded by Francis Galton, a nineteenth century English scientist who had become convinced that intelligence was a hereditary trait. Galton's followers tried to show, through studies comparing identical and nonidentical twins reared together and reared apart and by comparisons of people related to each other in varying degrees, that genetic endowment plays a far larger role than the environment in determining intelligence. Attempts to quantify an index of heritability for intelligence through such studies abound, and the estimates derived from them vary widely. On the nurture side of the debate, massive quantities of data have been gathered in an effort to show that the environment, including factors such as prenatal care, social-class membership, exposure to certain facilitative experiences, and educational opportunities of all sorts, has the more crucial role in determining a person's level of intellectual functioning.

Many critics, such as Anastasi (in a widely cited 1958 article entitled "Heredity, Environment, and the Question 'How?'") have pointed out the futility of debating how much each factor contributes to intelligence. Anastasi and others argue that behavior is a function of the interaction between heredity and the total experiential history of individuals and that, from the moment of conception, the two are inextricably tied. Moreover, they point out that, even if intelligence were shown to be primarily determined by heredity, environmental influences could still modify its expression at any point. Most psychologists now accept this "interactionist" position and have moved on to explore how intelligence develops and how specific genetic and environmental factors affect it.

BIBLIOGRAPHY

Alloway, Tracy Packiam, and Ross Alloway. *Working Memory: The Connected Intelligence.* New York: Psychology Press, 2013. Print.

Fancher, Raymond E. *The Intelligence Men: Makers of the IQ Controversy.* New York: W. W. Norton, 1987. Print.

Flynn, James R. *What Is Intelligence? Beyond the Flynn Effect.* New York: Cambridge University Press, 2009. Print.

Gardner, Howard. *Frames of Mind: The Theory of Multiple Intelligences.* New York: Basic Books, 2004. Print.

Gardner, Howard. *Multiple Intelligences: The Theory in Practice.* New York: Basic Books, 2006. Print.

Guilford, Joy Paul. *The Nature of Human Intelligence.* New York: McGraw-Hill, 1967. Print.

Kaufman, Scott Barry. *Ungifted: Intelligence Redefined.* New York: Basic, 2013. Print.

Martinez, Michael E. *Future Bright: A Transforming Vision of Human Intelligence.* New York. Oxford UP, 2013. Print.

Murdoch, Stephen. *IQ: A Smart History of a Failed Idea.* Hoboken, N.J.: John Wiley & Sons, 2007. Print.

Ryan, R. M., and E. L. Deci. "Intrinsic and Extrinsic Motivation." *Contemporary Educational Psychology* 25(2000): 54–67. Print.

Sternberg, Robert J. *Successful Intelligence.* New York: Plume, 1997. Print.

Sternberg, Robert J.*The Triarchic Mind: A New Theory of Human Intelligence.* New York: Viking Penguin, 1989. Print.

Sternberg, Robert J., B. Torff, and E. L. Grigorenko."Teaching Triarchically Improves School Achievement." *Journal of Educational Psychology* 90 (1998): 374–84. Print.

Vernon, Philip Ewart. *Intelligence: Heredity and Environment.* San Francisco: W. H. Freeman, 1979. Print.

Susana P. Urbina; updated by Ronna F. Dillon

SEE ALSO: Ability tests; Binet, Alfred; Cognitive psychology; College entrance examinations; Concept formation; Creativity and intelligence; Emotional intelligence; Giftedness; Intelligence quotient (IQ); Intelligence tests; Logic and reasoning; Mental retardation; Multiple intelligences; Race and intelligence; Stanford-Binet test; Testing: Historical perspectives; Wechsler Intelligence Scale for Children- Third Edition (WISC-III).

Intelligence quotient (IQ)

DATE: Early 1900s forward
TYPE OF PSYCHOLOGY: Intelligence and intelligence testing

Intelligence quotient, referred to as IQ, is a general term used to reflect one's mental or cognitive ability. More specifically, it refers to one's ability to engage in abstract thinking or reasoning, capacity to acquire knowledge, and problem-solving ability. IQ is typically measured by comparing one's performance on a standardized measure of intelligence with the performance of similar-aged individuals.

KEY CONCEPTS

- Cognitive ability
- Mental quotient

INTRODUCTION

Alfred Binet and Théodore Simon in France designed the first formal test of intelligence, called the Binet-Simon scale, in 1905. Theirs was an age-based test in that items passed by a majority of children at a particular age were assigned to that age level. For instance, if the majority of nine-year-olds passed a particular item, that item was assigned to the nine-year age level.

William Stern first coined the term "mental quotient" in 1912. Mental quotient was derived by dividing mental age, as assessed by performance on a test such as the Binet-Simon, by chronological age, which yielded a ratio. Children with a ratio of greater than 1 were ahead of their age in mental development, whereas children with a ratio of less than 1 were behind their age in mental development.

In 1916, Lewis Terman published the Stanford Revision and Extension of the Binet-Simon scale, subsequently referred to as the Stanford-Binet. With the publication of the Stanford-Binet, Terman changed the term "mental quotient" to "intelligence quotient," and he changed Stern's ratio to a whole number by multiplying the ratio by 100. For example, if a person performed at the seventy-eight-month level on the Stanford-Binet (mental age) and was seventy-two months old (chronological age), his or her intelligence quotient was estimated to be 108.

CHANGE IN IQ SCORE COMPUTATION

Shortly after the publication of the Stanford-Binet, fair criticism began to emerge regarding the age-based format of the tests. The alternative suggested was a points-based test for assessing IQ. Tests that use a points-based format assign points based on correctness, quality, and sometimes swiftness of responding. These points are then converted to standard scores, which are then converted into IQ scores. David Wechsler, in the 1930s, was the first to design an intelligence test based on the points format. Current versions of his scales include the Wechsler Preschool and Primary Scales of Intelligence-III (WPPSI-III), the Wechsler Intelligence Scale for Children-III (WISC-III), and the Wechsler Adult Intelligence Scale-III (WAIS-III); these are the most widely used tests of intelligence. Each of the Wechsler scales actually yields three difference intelligence quotients: Verbal IQ, Performance IQ, and a Full Scale IQ that is a combination of the Verbal and Performance IQs.

INTERPRETATION OF IQ SCORES

IQ scores typically have a mean of 100 and a standard deviation of 15. This means that average intelligence is considered to be any score between 90 and 109. IQs from 110 to 119 are considered to be high average, while scores that range from 80 to 89 are considered to be low average. Scores that fall in the 120 to 129 range are labeled superior, while scores of 130 and above are regarded as very superior. In some instances, individuals who score above 130 are labeled as intellectually gifted. Scores in the 70 to 79 range are considered borderline scores. Those who score below 70 are usually further assessed to determine if a diagnosis of intellectual disability is appropriate.

FACTORS THAT INFLUENCE IQ

The environmental factors that seem to impact IQ the most include family income, parental education level, parental occupation, and the home atmosphere, which includes the degree to which the parents press for achievement and language development and the provisions they make for their child's general learning. Although the exact degree to which genetics influences IQ is unclear, estimates are that about 30 to 50 percent of IQ is accounted for by a person's genotype.

USES OF IQ SCORES

One of the primary uses of IQ scores is to assist with the diagnosis and classification of children for special education services. Outside of education, IQ scores have been used to screen applicants for jobs, to help determine the most appropriate job placement within an organi-zation, to assist with vocational counseling, and as part of a complete psychological assessment battery. Relatedly, IQ scores obtained between the ages of three and eighteen have been found to be a significant predictor of educational and occupational success as an adult.

CHANGES IN CONCEPTUALIZATION OF INTELLIGENCE

Early conceptualizations of intelligence were that one primary underlying cognitive ability permeated all other cognitive skills. Later, researchers have proposed the existence of a number of essential cognitive abilities that should be reflected in the intelligence quotient and have designed tests to measure these different cognitive abilities. For instance, Jagannath Das suggested that the intelligence quotient should reflect a person's ability to process information simultaneously and sequentially, while Raymond B. Cattell proposed that the two factors that make up intelligence are fluid intelligence and crystallized intelligence. These are two of several possible examples of how the conceptualization of intelligence and the abilities that comprise intelligence have changed.

BIBLIOGRAPHY

Block, Ned J., and Gerald Dworkin. *The IQ Controversy.* New York: Random, 1976. Print.

Gellman, Ellen. *School Testing: What Parents and Educators Need to Know.* Westport: Praeger, 1995. Print.

Herrnstein, Richard, and Charles Murray. *The Bell Curve.* 1994. New York: Free, 2010. Print.

Hunt, Earl. "The Role of Intelligence in Modern Society." *American Scientist* 83.4 (1995): 356+. Print.

Kaneshiro, Neil K. "IQ Testing." *MedlinePlus.* US National Library of Medicine, 16 May 2014. Web. 27 May 2014.

Kush, Joe. *Intelligence Quotient: Testing, Role of Genetics and the Environment and Social Outcomes.* Hauppage: Nova, 2013. Digital file.

Nisbett, Richard E. "Schooling Makes You Smarter: What Teachers Need to Know about IQ." *American Educator* 37.1 (2013): 38–39. Print.

Sattler, Jerome M. *Assessment of Children.* 5th ed. San Diego: Sattler, 2006. Print.

T. Steuart Watson

SEE ALSO: Ability tests; Assessment; Binet, Alfred; Creativity: Assessment; Intelligence; Intelligence tests; Race and intelligence; Stanford-Binet test; Wechsler Intelligence Scale for Children-Third Edition (WISC-III).

Intelligence quotient (IQ) and measuring intelligence

TYPE OF PSYCHOLOGY: Cognitive; Developmental; Neuropsychology; Psychometrics

Early references to intelligence in literature can be found as far back as the ancient Greeks and Chinese. The measurement of intelligence began in its most rudimentary form when scientists attempted to identify those characteristics thought to contribute to the concept of intelligence. While initially, intelligence was viewed as being composed of various physical characteristics, such as head circumference and muscle strength, modern measures now focus on specific areas dealing with measurable human characteristics including abstract reasoning, memory, and spatial abilities.

KEY CONCEPTS

- Hypothetical construct
- Intelligence
- Normal distribution
- Norm referenced
- Standard deviation
- Standardized

INTRODUCTION

Because the concept of intelligence is considered to be hypothetical,, those wishing to measure intelligence had to develop theories to explain their ideas of what constitutes intelligence. Once areas were identified, tasks could then be developed to measure these areas. For example, because memory was often considered to be an indicator of intelligence, tasks were developed to measure this area. Auditory memory was often measured by having an individual repeat a series of numbers or words back to the examiner, while visual memory tasks sometimes required an individual to look at a picture for a specific period of time and remember later what he or she saw.

The concept of the Intelligence Quotient (IQ) was created after intelligence tests were developed. It is the score derived from the test administration that describes a person's overall abilities. Early test developers utilized a ratio IQ score that was obtained by dividing an individual's mental age score obtained from the test administration

by that person's chronological age. Because this often resulted in a number with a decimal point, the result was then multiplied by 100. Thus, an individual with a physical age of 20 years, who obtained a mental age score of 25 years, would have a ratio IQ of 125 (IQ = 25/20 X 100 = 125). Current intelligence tests no longer use ratio IQ scores which poses problems with interpretation, especially between individuals of different ages. Instead, a standard score is derived from testing that has a mean of 100 and a standard deviation of 15. This score is obtained by comparing the individual's score to those scores obtained in the norming sample. This technique allows for comparisons to be made between individuals of differing ages and over time.

INTELLIGENCE

While definitions of intelligence vary widely, most include some form of abstract reasoning and problem-solving abilities. Also frequently found in definitions are the concepts of spatial ability, memory, speed and accuracy, and learning and planning. Current intelligence tests generally consist of numerous subtests which are believed to tap into these areas. The scores obtained on the subtests combine to provide an intelligence quotient.

IQ scores in individuals older than eight years of age tend to be very consistent, suggesting that people generally cannot change their scores dramatically by studying or taking courses. Scores are determined through the interaction of both genetic and environmental factors. While genetic factors may set boundaries for an individual's abilities, environmental factors can determine where an individual will fall within those boundaries. For example, an individual born with superior intellectual abilities and raised in an enriching environment is likely to score well on an IQ test. Conversely, a person with similar genetic make-up but raised in an impoverished environment may never display his or her true potential. Studies performed on twins who were raised together and twins who were raised apart support this interaction of genetics and environment. Twins who were raised together showed less variation in their IQ scores than twins raised apart.

IQ scores are normally distributed and can be graphed on a normal or bell-shaped curve. The average IQ score is 100, meaning that 50% of scores fall above and below this score. The standard deviation, which indicates how far a score is from the mean, is 15. A person who obtains an IQ score of 85 would be considered one standard below the mean, while a score of 130 would be two standard deviations above. As scores deviate further from the mean, there are fewer scores. For example, 68% of all IQ scores fall within one standard deviation on either side of the mean. However, only 26% of scores fall between one and two standard deviations and only 4% fall between two and three standard deviations.

IQ scores are also categorized by ranges. While different intelligence tests tend to have slightly different classification names, the ranges themselves are consistent. For example, classifications used on instruments developed by prolific test developer Dr. David Wechsler include the following ranges: Average 90-109, High Average 110-119, Superior 120-129, Very Superior 130 and above, Low Average 80-89, Borderline 70-79, and Extremely Low 69 and below. These ranges are helpful when attempting to interpret test results.

THE HISTORY OF INTELLECTUAL ASSESSMENT

While at some level, humans have always attempted to assess the abilities of others, whether it be for self-preservation or scientific discovery, it was not until the beginning of the 20th century that the first modern intelligence test was developed. In 1905, Alfred Binet and Theodore Simon were recruited by the French government to develop an instrument to determine which children should be provided an education and which should be dismissed from school. The Binet-Simon test included numerous tasks that measured verbal skills and provided a mental age score. It became quite popular and, in 1916, was brought to the United States by Lewis Terman, a professor at Stanford University. After revisions designed to have the instrument reflect American culture, Terman introduced the Stanford-Binet Intelligence Scale. The measure was widely accepted and the idea of intellectual assessment gained a strong foothold in American society. The fifth edition of the Stanford-Binet is currently in use today.

In 1939, David Wechsler published the first of his many intelligence tests, the Wechsler-Bellevue Intelligence Scale. While the Stanford-Binet provided a single overall score, Wechsler felt that intelligence included both verbal and performance (nonverbal) components. Thus, he developed an instrument that provided three separate IQ scores: Verbal IQ, Performance IQ, and Full Scale IQ, the combination of both verbal and performance. The instrument was very popular, and Wechsler went on to develop other instruments including the Wechsler Adult Intelligence Scale (WAIS), the Wechsler Intelligence Scale for Children (WISC), and the Wechsler Preschool

and Primary Scale of Intelligence (WPPSI). These instruments became the most widely used instruments of their kind and are available today in their most current revisions: WAIS-IV, WISC-V, and the WPPSI-III.

Recent trends in the development of intelligence tests have focused on the growing popularity of CHC Theory, based on the works of Raymond Cattell, John Horn, and John Carroll. This theory is well documented and supported empirically and consists of three levels or strata: Stratum I - Narrow Abilities, Stratum II - Broad Abilities, and Stratum III - General Ability. The most popular intelligence instrument, based on CHC Theory, is the Woodcock-Johnson IV, Tests of Cognitive Ability (WJ-IV Cog). As the name states, this instrument uses the term "cognitive abilities" which is steadily gaining favor over the term intelligence. The WJ-IV Cog consists of 18 individual subtests that make up the Narrow Abilities. The individual subtests combine with other subtests to provide Broad Ability scores that are called Cluster scores. Finally, the Cluster scores combine to provide the General Ability score, which is often viewed as an intelligence quotient.

IQ TEST CONSTRUCTION

While early IQ tests were often developed with little consideration for statistical properties and standardization, today's instruments represent the capstone of test development. They are very valid, meaning that they measure what they report to measure, and are quite reliable in that they measure consistently over time. When an IQ test is developed, the first step is to identify the theoretical background to be used as its basis. For example, the WJ-IV Cog adheres to CHC Theory. Numerous theories of intelligence exist, and test developers often modify theories or expand on them for test development purposes.

Once a theory has been adopted, experts develop subtests and individual items to measure the components of the theory. Items go through extensive review and modification by the developer until a specific set of subtests and items are chosen for inclusion in the instrument. The test is then administered to a representative sample of our national population. This sample generally includes thousands of individuals who are selected on the basis of such characteristics as age, sex, socio-economic status, education level, and geographic location. Information obtained from this sample, known as the norming sample, is then evaluated to establish the statistical qualities of the instrument. The information is also used to evaluate test items and make modifications where necessary. Once the test is fully developed, studies are conducted to compare the new instrument with already published instruments currently thought to be valid for the purpose of intellectual assessment. If scores on the newly developed instrument are similar to scores on the existing instruments, the authors can state that their instrument is valid for the measurement of intelligence. Future research, performed by practitioners who use the instrument along with researchers in universities and other institutions, will further establish the usefulness of the new test instrument.

USES OF IQ TESTS

Intelligence tests are used for a broad range of purposes in our society as they are capable of predicting success in a wide variety of areas and fields. Probably the most prolific use of IQ tests can be found in the preschool through 12th grade educational setting. With the passage of such laws as The Education of All Handicapped Children Act in 1979 and the Individuals with Disabilities Education Improvement Act of 2004, schools use IQ tests to identify students with educational needs and then provide programming for them. These laws not only state that all children must be educated to the fullest of their abilities, but also that they be classified for funding purposes. IQ tests help determine, for example, which students have learning disabilities or which may be intellectually disabled. IQ tests are used to determine initial eligibility for services progress made in a remedial program, and eligibility for future services.

Intelligence tests are also used in a host of other settings including the workplace, mental health facilities, the armed services, and research environments. In the past 25 years, employers have increasingly used IQ assessments as part of the employment application process. Research has shown that there is a correlation between IQ scores and job performance and that applicants with higher IQs generally perform better than those with lower IQs. Employers also use test instruments to make promotional decisions as well as changes in placements. IQ tests have long been used in the profession of mental health for classification and treatment purposes and in the armed services to classify large numbers of individuals and assign training options. Finally, researchers in a wide variety of fields use intelligence tests in their studies for numerous purposes including subject placement, response to treatment, and classification.

BIBLIOGRAPHY

Flanagan, D.P., & Harrison, P.L. (2005). *Contemporary Intellectual Assessment: Theories, Tests, and Issues.* (2nd ed.). New York, NY: GuilfordPress. A comprehensive review of intellectual tests and assessment of intelligence for individuals from preschool through adult.

Gregory, R.J. (1998). *Foundations Of Intellectual Assessment.* Boston, MA: Allyn & Bacon. This text deals specifically with the intellectual assessment of adults and covers intelligence tests appropriate for this group.

Gregory, R.J. (2006). *Psychological testing: History, principles, and applications* (5th ed.). Boston, MA: Allyn & Bacon. The author covers a gamut of topics pertaining to various types of assessment including tests for assessing specific populations and consideration of race in the testing process.

Mackintosh, N.T. (2011). *IQ and Human Intelligence* (2nd ed.). New York, NY: Oxford University Press. This book provides information on a broad range of topics pertaining to intelligence and intelligence tests including test development, factors impacting intellectual development, and the role of social factors in intelligence.

Sattler, J.M. (2008). *Assessment of Children: Cognitive Foundations* (5th ed.). San Diego, CA: Sattler. The definitive source for information pertaining to intellectual assessment. Included are extensive reviews of numerous intelligence tests along with information pertaining to history, theory, and practice.

Gene Johnson

SEE ALSO: Measurement; Psychometrics; Testing.

Intelligence tests

TYPE OF PSYCHOLOGY: Intelligence and intelligence testing

Individual intelligence tests are used by psychologists to evaluate a person's current cognitive ability and prior knowledge. The intelligence testing movement has a long history, including the development of numerous group and individual tests to measure one aspect of a person's overall intelligence, which frequently changes over time.

KEY CONCEPTS

- Age norm
- Cognition

- Intelligence
- Intelligence quotient (IQ)
- Mentally gifted
- Mentally handicapped
- Percentile
- Performance tests
- Sensorimotor tests
- Verbal tests

INTRODUCTION

Although means for measuring mental ability date as far back as 2000 BCE, when the ancient Chinese administered oral tests to determine a candidate's fitness for carrying out the tasks of civil administration, the modern intelligence test has its origins in the nineteenth century, when Jean-Étienne-Dominique Esquirol drew a clear distinction between mentally deranged people, or "lunatics," and intellectually disabled people, deemed "idiots." Esquirol believed that it was necessary to devise a means of gauging "normal" intelligence so that deviations from an agreed-on norm could be ascertained, and he pointed out that intellectual ability exists on a continuum extending from idiocy to genius. His work coincided with studies in Europe and the United States that were designed to develop a concept of intelligence and to fashion a means of testing this capacity. Work done by Sir Francis Galton in the United Kingdom on hereditary genius, by James McKeen Cattell in the United States on individual differences in behavior, and by Hermann Ebbinghaus in Germany on tests of memory, computation, and sentence completion culminated in the 1905 Binet-Simon scale, created by Alfred Binet and Théodore Simon.

It was the first practical index of intelligence measurement as a function of individual differences. This test was based on the idea that simple sensory functions, which had formed the core of earlier tests, are not true indicators of intelligence and that higher mental processes had to be included.

THE BINET TESTS

French psychologist and educator Binet founded the first French psychological laboratory. He was a pioneer in the study of individual differences in abilities and introduced intelligence tests that were quickly accepted and widely used in Europe and the United States. His work stemmed from a commission from the minister of education in Paris, who gave him the task of devising a way to distinguish between idiocy and lunacy, as Esqui-

rol had defined them, and normal intelligence, so that handicapped students could be given special instruction. Binet and Simon used many items that had been developed by earlier examiners; the key advances they made were to rank items in order of difficulty and to register results in terms of age-based cognitive development. Their scale reflected the idea that intelligence was a combination of faculties—judgment, practical sense, and initiative—and contained measures related to memory, reasoning ability, numerical facility, and object comparison.

Binet and Simon's work demonstrated the feasibility of mental measurement, assessing intelligence for the first time in general terms rather than measuring its component parts. Binet revised the test in 1908, and another revision was published in 1911, the year of his death. Advances in his basic design led to the development of tests that could be used for all children (not only those considered mentally limited) in assessing their "mental quotient," a ratio adapted by Lewis Terman of Stanford University. It was obtained by dividing mental age (as determined through scores on a test) by chronological age. Terman renamed it the intelligence quotient (IQ), and his 1916 version of the Binet-Simon scale became known as the Stanford-Binet test, the most common intelligence test administered in the United States. It was revised and updated in 1937, 1960, 1972, and 1986, when a point-scale format was introduced for the first time.

THE WECHSLER TESTS

Binet's test depended on an age scale; that is, the questions that were answered correctly by a majority of ten-year-old children were assigned to the ten-year age level of intelligence. A more sophisticated version of the test devised by Robert Yerkes depended on a point scale for scoring; this format was fully developed by David Wechsler. While the Binet-Terman method used different tests for different age groups, Wechsler worked toward a test to measure the same aspect of behavior at every age level. The goal of his test was to measure intelligence in a holistic (encompassing the larger whole of personality) fashion that did not depend on the verbal skills that the Stanford-Binet tests required. Wechsler thought of intelligence as a multifaceted complex of skills, the total of an effective intellectual process; he wanted his test to show the way intelligent people behaved as a consequence of an awareness of the results of their actions. He thought that those actions would be more rational, worthwhile (in terms of social values), and meaningful than those of less intelligent people.

Wechsler's first test (the Wechsler-Bellevue Intelligence Scale) was published in 1939, and it awarded points for each answer depending on the level of sophistication of the response. The test consisted of six verbal subjects (information, comprehension, arithmetic, similarities, vocabulary, and digit span) and five performance subtests (picture completion, picture arrangement, block design, object assemblies, and digit symbols). The division into verbal and performance skills permitted the calculation of three intelligent quotients: a verbal IQ based on the sum of the verbal tests, correlated with norms of age, a performance IQ based on the sum of performance tests, and a full-scale IQ derived from the sum of all the answers. The test was standardized on a sample of adults, and it could be used to test individuals who had linguistic or sensorimotor handicaps. The pattern of scores on the separate tests could also be used to diagnose learning disability or, in some situations, clinical disorder or dysfunction.

The original test was limited by the sample used for standardization, but the 1955 Wechsler Adult Intelligence Scale (WAIS) provided a basis for testing adults from the ages of sixteen to seventy-five. Further revision in the standard scale (including the WAIS-R, 1981) updated the test to coincide with changes in cultural experience. In addition, a Wechsler Intelligence Scale for Children (WISC) was designed to cover ages five to fifteen in 1949 and was revised (WISC-R) in 1974 to cover ages six to sixteen. In 1991, another revision (WISC-III) was introduced. Subsequent modifications also led to a test suitable for preschool children, the Wechsler Preschool and Primary Scales of Intelligence (WPPSI) of 1967, which covered ages four to six and a half and included mazes, animal figures, and geometric designs. This test was revised in 1981 (WPPSI-R) to extend its range over three years to seven years, three months. Further adjustments have also been made to account for a candidate's sociocultural background in a test called the System of Multicultural Pluralistic Assessment (SOMPA, 1977).

Recent definitions of intelligence have resulted in further development of testing instruments. Raymond Cattell's proposal that intelligence could be divided into two types—fluid (or forming) and crystallized (fixed)—led to a test that used figure classification, figure analysis, and letter and number series to assess the essential nonverbal, relatively culture-free aspects of fluid intelligence; it used vocabulary definition, abstract word analogies, and general information to determine the skills that depend on exposure to cultural processes inherent in crystallized intelligence. Other theories, such as Jean Piaget's idea that intelligence is a form of individual adaptation and accommodation to an environment, led to the development of a test that measures mental organization at successive ages.

USES OF INTELLIGENCE ASSESSMENT

There was a tendency at various times to regard intelligence assessment as an answer to questions of placement and classification in almost every area of human experience. The most effective and scientifically valid uses of tests, however, have been in predicting performance in scholastic endeavor, in revealing disguised or latent ability to assist in career counseling, in determining the most appropriate developmental programs for handicapped or mentally handicapped individuals, in locating specific strengths and weaknesses in an individual, in measuring specific changes associated with special programs and forms of therapy, and in comparing a child's mental ability with other children observed in a similar situation to establish a profile of cognitive skills.

One of the most widespread and effective uses of intelligence tests is the determination of possible problems in a child's course of basic education. As reported by Lewis Aiken in *Assessment of Intellectual Functioning* (1987), a typical case involved an eight-year-old boy with a suspected learning disability. He was given the WISC-R test in 1985, and his full-scale IQ was figured to be 116, placing him in the high average classification. This provided an assessment of general intelligence and scholastic aptitude. His verbal IQ was 127, placing him in the ninety-seventh percentile, indicative of exceptional verbal comprehension. This suggested that he could reason very well, learn verbal material quickly, and process verbal information effectively. His performance IQ of 98 placed him in the average category, but the magnitude of the difference between his verbal and performance IQs is very unusual in children of his age. It pointed to a need for additional interpretive analysis, as well as further study to reveal the reasons behind the discrepancy. Close scrutiny of the test results showed that low scores on the arithmetic, digit span, and coding subtests might indicate a short attention or memory span, poor concentration, or a lack of facility in handling numbers. While no absolute conclusions could be drawn at this point, the results of the test could be used in conjunction with other procedures, observation, and background information to determine an appropriate course of action.

INTELLIGENCE AND GUIDANCE

Another common use of an intelligence test is to help an examinee determine specific areas of ability or aptitude that might be useful in selecting a career route. As reported in Aiken, a college senior was given the Otis-Lennon School Ability Test (O-LSAT, Advanced Form R) just before her twenty-second birthday. She planned to enroll in a program in a graduate business school and work toward a master of business arts degree. The O-LSAT is designed to gauge general mental ability, and it includes classification, analogy, and omnibus (a variety of items to measure different aspects of mental functioning) elements. The omnibus includes verbal comprehension, quantitative reasoning, and the ability to follow directions. The examinee was able to complete the test in thirty-five minutes and used the remaining allotted time to check her answers. Her raw score (number of items answered correctly) was 64 (out of 80), her school ability index was 116—which approximated her IQ—and her percentile rank among candidates in the eighteen-plus range was 84. These scores were in the average range for college seniors, indicating an overall intellectual ability that could be classified as "high average" in terms of the general population. Of the sixteen items answered incorrectly, a superficial analysis pointed toward some difficulty with nonverbal reasoning, but no conclusions could be reached without further examination in this area. There was no significant pattern of errors otherwise, and the random distribution offered no additional guide to areas of weakness. The initial conclusion that was drawn from the test was that a career in business was appropriate, and that with hard work and the full application of her intellectual abilities, she would be able to earn an M.B.A. at a reputable university.

A particularly important application of intelligence assessment is the identification and guidance of a child with advanced intellectual abilities. In a case reported in Jerome M. Sattler's *Assessment of Children* (1988), a three-year-old boy was tested repeatedly from that age until his sixth birthday. This procedure required the implementation of the Stanford-Binet Form L-M, the WPPSI, and the Peabody Individual Achievement Test (PIAT) for grade equivalents. The Stanford-Binet scores were 127 (at age three), 152, 152, and 159+ (with a linear extrapolation to 163). During his first test he was anxious and did not give long verbal responses, but the range of his scores indicated a very superior classification. He did not cooperate with the examiner on the WPPSI vocabulary and animal subtests (the examiner believed that

he was not interested), but his performance at age four placed him in the superior range. On the PIAT, he was consistently above average, earning a grade equivalent above 4.0 at the age of six, with a grade equivalent of 7.4 (his highest score) in mathematics; the average grade equivalent for age six is 1.0.

As Sattler points out, the case illustrates "a number of important principles related to testing and assessment." In the largest sense, it illustrates the way different tests measuring general intelligence may yield different results (although all pointed toward superior mental development). The same test may also yield different scores at different age levels. The child's motivation (among other factors) may also play an important part in his results. More specifically, since the boy showed more interest in reading at age three and mathematics at age six, the test could not be considered a useful predictor of later interest, although an interest in solving perceptual-logical problems remained consistent throughout. Finally, since the parents had kept a detailed record of the boy's early development in a baby book, the rich history recorded there was corroborated by the test results that reaffirmed their initial suspicions that the boy was unusually gifted. During his first year in school, he tended to play alone and had frequent minor tantrums that affected his performance in school subjects. When he became accustomed to the social process of school life, however, he was able to demonstrate the ability that his parents had observed at home and that the initial tests validated.

DEFINITIONS OF INTELLIGENCE

While intelligence tests of some sort appeared in human history as early as the Old Testament book of Judges (7:3–7, 12:6), which indicates that early Jewish society used questions and observations in personnel selection, the intelligence test as it is known today can be traced to Renaissance Europe. In 1575 the Spanish physician Juan Huarte wrote *Examen de Ingenios,* a treatise concerning individual differences in mental ability with suggestions for appropriate tests. His work, and that of other investigators and theorists, was the result of the rise of a middle class with aspirations to productive employment. Previously, the aristocracy had controlled everything, and fitness for a position was determined by lineage. Once this monarchical rule began to break down, other means were necessary for determining who was fit for a particular occupation and what might be the most productive use of a person's abilities. When it became apparent that royal blood was no guarantee of competence, judgment, or mental acuity, the entire question of the origins of intelligence began to occupy members of the scientific community. For a time, the philosophy of empiricism led scientists toward the idea that the mind itself was formed by mental association among sense impressions, and sensorimotor tests were particularly prominent. As the results of these tests failed to correlate with demonstrations of mental ability (such as marks in school), however, other means were sought to measure and define intelligence. The interest in intelligence testing in the nineteenth century was an important aspect of the development of psychology as a separate scientific discipline, and the twin paths of psychometric (that is, the quantitative assessment of an individual's attributes or traits) and statistical analysis on one hand and philosophical conjecture concerning the shape and operation of the mind on the other were joined in experimentation concerning methods of assessing intelligence.

From their first applications in France as a diagnostic instrument, intelligence tests have been used to help psychologists, educators, and other professionals plan courses of action to aid individuals suffering from some mental limitation or obstacle. This role has been expanded to cover the full range of human intellectual ability and to isolate many individual aspects of intelligence in myriad forms. The profusion of tests has both complicated and deepened an understanding of how the mind functions, and the continuing proposition of theories of intelligence resulted in an increasingly sophisticated battery of tests designed to assess and register each new theory.

MODERN TESTING

In addition, technological developments, particularly the growing use of computers, permit a wider use of flexible testing in which the decision about what item or task to present next depends on the previous answer. Computers are also useful in "number crunching," so that such basic components of a test system as norms, derived scores, and reliability and validity coefficients (the basic statistical material behind the calculation of scores) can be assembled more quickly and efficiently. Computers also make it possible to administer tests at multiple sites simultaneously when an individual examiner's presence is not necessary. Nevertheless, the human capacity for judgment and analysis in the interpretation of results remain crucial to test procedures.

Intelligence testing is likely to continue as a primary means of predicting educational or vocational performance, but tests designed to measure the mind in terms of its ability to process information by shifting strategies in response to a changing environment are likely to become more prevalent. The proliferation of more detailed, separate sets of norms for different groups (age, sex, ethnic origin, and so on) is likely to continue. Also, the relationship between intelligence per se and behavioral attitudes that seem to resemble aptitude rather than personality measures is part of the heredity-environment controversy that will continue. Finally, advances in studies on the neurophysiological bases of intelligence will be reflected in tests responsive to a growing understanding of the biochemical aspects of cognition. As an operating principle, though, professionals in the field will have to be guided by a continuing awareness that intelligence testing is only one aspect of understanding a person's total behavior and that the limitations involved in the measuring process must be understood to avoid incorrect or inappropriate diagnoses that might prove harmful to an individual.

Howard Gardner postulated a theory of multiple intelligences that focuses on a symbol system approach combining both factor analytic and information-processing methodology. He included seven dimensions of intelligence: verbal and linguistic, mathematical and logical, visual and spatial, body and kinesthetic, musical and rhythmical, interpersonal and intrapersonal, and environmental. The concept of types of intelligence is not new. L. L. Thurstone developed a test of eight scales named the Primary Mental Abilities test. Edward L. Thorndike identified several types of intelligence: abstract, social, and practical. Sternberg used informational processing and cognitive theory in his model of intelligence and identified three different types of information-processing components: metacomponents, performance components, and knowledge-acquisition components. He saw metacomponents as the higher-order control processes used to oversee the planning, monitoring, and evaluation of task performance.

BIBLIOGRAPHY

Gardner, Howard. Multiple Intelligences: New Horizons. Rev. ed. New York: Basic, 2010. Digital file.

Goldstein, Gerald, and Michael Hersen, eds. Handbook of Psychological Assessment. 3d ed. New York: Pergamon, 2000. Print.

Herrnstein, Richard, and Charles Murray. The Bell Curve. 1994. New York: Free, 2010. Print.

Jensen, Arthur. The "G" Factor: The Science of

Mental Ability. Westport: Praeger, 1998. Print.

Kampaus, Randy W. Clinical Assessment of Child and Adolescent Intelligence. 2d ed. New York: Springer, 2005. Print.

Kaneshiro, Neil K. "IQ Testing." MedlinePlus. US National Library of Medicine, 16 May 2014. Web. 27 May 2014. Kush, Joe. Intelligence Quotient: Testing, Role of Genetics and the Environment and Social Outcomes. Hauppage: Nova, 2013. Digital file.

Nisbett, Richard E. "Schooling Makes You Smarter: What Teachers Need to Know about IQ." American Educator 37.1 (2013): 38–39. Print.

Sternberg, Robert J., ed. Handbook of Human Intelligence. Cambridge: Cambridge UP, 2010. Print.

Leon Lewis and James R. Deni;
updated by Robert J. Drummond

SEE ALSO: Ability tests; Assessment; Binet, Alfred; Career and personnel testing; College entrance examinations; Creativity: Assessment; Ebbinghaus, Hermann; General Aptitude Test Battery (GATB); Human resource training and development; Intelligence; Intelligence quotient (IQ); Interest inventories; Peabody Individual Achievement Test (PIAT); Race and intelligence; Scientific methods; Stanford-Binet test; Survey research: Questionnaires and interviews; Testing: Historical perspectives; Wechsler Intelligence Scale for Children-Third Edition (WISC-III).

Interest inventories

TYPE OF PSYCHOLOGY: Personality

Interest inventories are questionnaires that have been developed for the purpose of assessing an individual's patterns of interest in or preference for a variety of activities. Most commonly, the interest inventory is designed to assist a person in making decisions about future educational and career directions.

KEY CONCEPTS
- Criterion group
- Holland's typology
- Inventory
- Reference group
- Trait-factor approach
- Validity

INTRODUCTION

Since the inception of the interest inventory in the late 1920s, its development in the context of educational and vocational counseling has expanded considerably. The interest inventory is a questionnaire-type device designed to measure the intensity and breadth of an individual's interests. Most often, the specific interests measured by an inventory relate to a variety of vocational and avocational activities. The term "interest" refers to a very specific aspect of human behavior. An interest is an enduring trait, a predilection for a particular activity, avocation, or object. It is a special attitude that engages the individual and motivates him or her to move toward the object of interest.

An interest inventory is distinct from both an achievement test and an aptitude test. An achievement test measures an individual's current ability to perform a particular task. An aptitude test measures potential or capacity for performing that task in the future. An interest inventory, on the other hand, measures a person's liking for a particular task without reference to the individual's actual ability to perform the task or potential for doing so in the future. For example, a high school student may show a high interest in the field of nursing. This interest alone, however, does not mean that he or she has any current nursing skills, nor does it indicate that the student has the mental ability, physical stamina, or emotional makeup for success in the nursing field.

What then is the rationale for examining patterns of interest? First, interest in a particular activity provides some motivation for engaging in that activity. Therefore, when one identifies areas of interest, one is also identifying areas in which a person might have the degree of motivation necessary for following through on that activity. Second, the scores obtained from an interest inventory are helpful in pointing out which groups of persons an individual most resembles. Finally, it has been shown that there is some relationship between a person's domain of interest and the occupational field that that person may eventually choose.

The construction of an interest inventory may be empirically based (that is, based on observation of factual information) or theory-based (based on systematic principles concerning occupational categories). Some inventories have utilized a combination of these approaches. In its development, the empirically based inventory would be administered to various criterion groups of successful persons representing particular occupations. The inventory would also be given to a reference group, a large group representing people in general. The items on the inventory that set apart a particular criterion group from the larger reference group would then become part of the scale for that occupation. A person would be considered to have a high score on a particular occupational scale if he or she has interests that closely match the criterion group's interests.

Other inventories are simply based on occupational theory. One well-known theory that has been utilized in the construction of interest surveys was first set forth in John L. Holland's 1992 publication *Making Vocational Choices: A Theory of Careers*. The theory involved the categorization of occupations into the following six types: realistic, investigative, artistic, social, enterprising, and conventional. Other occupational categories have also been devised and used as the bases for interest inventory construction and scoring. Interest inventories also differ on the basis of the format used in the construction of the items. Some inventories ask the individual to indicate the degree of interest he or she has in a particular activity, whereas others use a forced-choice format, asking the testee to make an either/or choice between two activities.

POPULAR INVENTORIES

In their book *Career Guidance and Counseling Through the Life Span* (1996), Edwin L. Herr and Stanley H. Cramer reviewed some commonly used interest inventories. Some of the inventories, such as the well-known Strong Interest Inventory (SII), the Career Assessment Inventory (CAI), and the Vocational Preference Inventory (VPI), yield results based on Holland's six general occupational themes. Others, such as the Career Occupational Preference System (COPS) and the Vocational Interest Inventory (VII), are constructed around Anne Roe's eight occupational groups.

Interest inventories also differ in terms of their intended use. The Interest Determination, Exploration, and Assessment System (IDEAS) was developed for grades six through twelve; the Geist Picture Interest Inventory (GPII) is intended for culture-limited and educationally deprived populations; and the Kuder Occupational Interest Survey (KOIS) is designed for high school students and adults. The scope of occupations explored is another variable. The Minnesota Vocational Interests Inventory (MVII) deals with skilled occupations, while the COPS, Form P, deals with professional occupations. Some inventories are hand scored, while others are scored by computer. Tests such as the SII can be computer administered as well. Some of the inventories are designed to be used in conjunction with the Dictionary of Occupational Titles, published by the US Employment Service, or the

OCCUPATIONAL OUTLOOK HANDBOOK

Occupational Outlook Handbook, published by the U.S. Department of Labor, Bureau of Labor Statistics, and available online. The KOIS and the Ohio Vocational Interest Inventory (OVII) are two such examples.

There are various ways to judge the relative value or dependability of these measurement devices. First of all, one must consider the reliability of the inventory. Interests are human traits with a somewhat enduring quality. They are not expected to change radically over a short period of time. The reliability of the inventory is a measurement of how stable scores on the inventory would be if the inventory were administered to the same person over a period of time.

A second consideration in determining the value of an inventory is its validity. Though there are many ways to approach test validity, the aim is to determine if the inventory is really measuring interests as opposed to some other trait. Studies are often undertaken to see if scores on one interest inventory are consistent with scores on another interest inventory that is considered to be a valid measure. Another test of validity involves giving the interest inventory to persons in that occupation to see if their interest scores emerge in the direction expected. Information about the specific reliability and validity of a particular interest inventory is reported in the manual developed for its use.

Of particular concern in evaluating an interest inventory is the possibility of sex-role bias. The extent to which an interest inventory is constructed to perpetuate stereotypical male and female roles is a major issue. The SII, for example, attempted to use both male and female criterion groups for each occupation on the inventory. This posed some problems, such as finding sufficient numbers of males or females in certain occupations. Care was also taken in revisions to eliminate inappropriate references to gender; for example, "policeman" was changed to "police officer."

INVENTORY USES

Interest inventories are typically used in educational and vocational counseling. Most interest inventories are devised to assist a person in pinpointing possible career options. This entails assessing not only his or her interests in terms of particular careers but also interests related to college majors. Often an interest inventory will be helpful in determining where an individual's interests lie in relation to larger clusters of occupational groupings. Interest inventories are also used by researchers in obtaining information about the vocational interests of specific groups for the purpose of planning and implementing career training programs and noting overall occupational trends.

The following case study serves as an illustration of the practical use and interpretation of the interest inventory. It includes a student profile based on the KOIS and the recommendations that a counselor might make to this student in the light of the results obtained.

"John" is a seventeen-year-old adolescent in his junior year of high school. He is enrolled in a college preparatory program and has often verbalized at least a tentative interest in following in the footsteps of his father, who works in commercial real estate appraisal. His grades in art and drafting classes indicate that he has a propensity for visual thinking and illustration. John would be the first to admit, however, that his interests are very practical in nature, and he is not drawn toward philosophical debates. John's entire class was administered the KOIS through the counseling and guidance department of his school. The tests are computer-scored, and results are distributed to the students during individual appointments with the school counselor.

John's KOIS report form indicates that his results appear to be dependable. His interests in ten vocational activities are ranked in order of his preference for each. As compared with other males, his top interests, which are literary, persuasive, artistic, and mechanical, are average in intensity. The two areas ranked least interesting to John are social service and musical. John's patterns of interest as compared with men in many different occupations are most consistent with auto salesperson, photographer, travel agent, buyer, retail clothier, radio station manager, and real estate agent. Furthermore, John shows an interest pattern most similar to men in the following college majors: business administration, physical education, economics, and engineering.

John's counselor reminds John that the KOIS measures interests, not aptitudes or other personal variables that are part of a successful career match. The counselor observes that John's KOIS profile does accentuate some of the areas of interest to which John has alluded during his high school years. She notes that on the KOIS there were several indications that John might like an occupation related to business and sales.

As a follow-up to the KOIS, the counselor points out that John could benefit from exploring various school programs that offer the college majors that surfaced on his report form. She encourages John to talk to college representatives about his particular interests. She suggests that John look into some of the occupations that appeared on his KOIS report and possibly utilize such resources as the US Department of Labor's Guide for Occupational Exploration in learning about working conditions, employment prospects, promotion opportunities, and related occupational opportunities. The counselor also encourages John to talk with persons working in those general areas of employment that appeared on his KOIS. Exploration of other careers in the same job families as those which appeared on his report form might also prove beneficial. For John, the KOIS is probably the most beneficial in providing him with the impetus for continued career exploration.

The counselor, in perusing all the scores of the junior class members with whom she is working, may note overall patterns of interest appearing in the KOIS report forms. This information may lead her to make certain provisions for those interests in the school's career awareness program, in the type of invited speakers, and in the kinds of college and training program representatives invited to make presentations at the school.

While John was given the opportunity to take an interest inventory in high school, there are other situations in which a person may do so. Professional career counselors offer such opportunities to interested parties through college and university career centers and vocational rehabilitation services, in workshops for those planning second careers, and in private practice settings.

VOCATIONAL COUNSELING

Interest inventories can be situated in the overall context of vocational counseling, a field whose origins stemmed from the focus on job productivity and efficiency that arose during the Industrial Revolution. Frank Parsons is credited with laying the foundation for the field of career development. In his book *Choosing a Vocation* (1909), Parsons articulated a conceptual framework for career decision making. He emphasized that career decision making must be based on a clear understanding of one's personal attributes (such as aptitudes, interests, and resources) as related to the requirements of the job field. Parsons's theory provided the theoretical backdrop for the more scientifically oriented trait-factor approach to vocational counseling that would soon follow.

Getting displaced American workers back on the job was a major impetus in vocational counseling after the Great Depression of the 1930s. During that era, the University of Minnesota became a center for the development of new assessment devices to measure individual differences, and researchers there designed instruments that became part of test batteries used in counseling centers around the country. E. G. Williamson's work in career counseling research led to the publication of the *Dictionary of Occupational Titles by the U.S. Employment Service in 1939*. D. G. Paterson and J. G. Darley were also prominent among those psychologists who developed what is referred to as the "Minnesota point of view," or trait-factor theory.

TRAIT FACTOR THEORY

This trait factor approach has been the basis for many of the interest inventories that have been devised. Attempts were made to match the personal traits (in this case, interests) of the individual with the requirements of particular careers and job environments. The interest inventories have been the most widely used.

The most popular interest inventory is the Strong Interest Inventory. The first version of the SII was published in 1927 by Edward K. Strong, Jr., from Stanford University; this inventory has been in use ever since. At that time it was known as the Strong Vocational Interest Blank, a project on which Strong worked tirelessly, revising and improving it until his death in 1963. In that same year, David P. Campbell at the University of Minnesota Center for Interest Measurement Research assumed the task of continuing to update Strong's work. Along with Jo-Ida Hansen, Campbell produced the interest inventory that was redesignated the Strong-Campbell Interest Inventory in its fourth (1985) edition. The 1997 edition, however, was published under the name of the Strong Interest Inventory, and subsequent versions of the inventory have retained that name.

Probably the most common alternative to the SII is the Kuder Occupational Interest Survey, which was first published by G. Frederic Kuder as the Kuder Preference Record. Differences can be noted between the KOIS and the SII in terms of their technical construction and scales.

Although many interest inventories have been devised since the idea was first conceived, most of these inventories have focused on interests in career activities and related college majors. The 1970's, however, brought about the notion of inventories designed to measure leisure interests. Richard N. Bolles, in his book *The Three Boxes of Life* (1981), indicated that, in addition to meaningful work, people need to engage in the pursuit of two other "boxes," that of learning/education and that of leisure/playing. This more holistic approach may be more evident in the interest inventories yet to be developed.

BIBLIOGRAPHY

Bolles, Richard. *What Color Is Your Parachute?* Rev. ed. Berkeley: Ten Speed, 2007. Print.

Bringman, Wolfgang. *A Pictorial History of Psychology.* Chicago: Quintessen, 1997. Print.

Capuzzi, David, and Mark D. Stauffer. *Career Counseling: Foundations, Perspectives, and Applications.* 2nd ed. New York: Routledge, 2012. Print.

Farr, J. Michael, and Lavern Lidden. *Guide to Occupational Exploration.* 3d ed. Indianapolis: JIST, 2001. Print.

Farr, J. Michael, Lavern Lidden, and Lawrence Shatkin. *Enhanced Occupational Outlook Handbook.* 7th ed. Indianapolis: JIST, 2009. Print.

Graham, John R., and Jack A. Naglieri, eds. *Assessment Psychology.* Vol. 10. Hoboken: Wiley, 2012. Print.

Handbook of Psychology. Gregory, Robert. Psychological Testing: History, Principles, and Applications. 7th ed. Boston: Pearson, 2007. Print.

Herr, Edward, and Stanley Kramer. *Career Guidance and Counseling Through the Life Span.* 5th ed. New York: Harper, 1996. Print.

Sacks, Peter. *Standardized Minds: The High Price of America's Testing Culture and What We Can Do to Change It.* Cambridge: Perseus, 2000. Print.

Wood, Chris, and Danica G. Hays. *A Counselor's Guide to Career Assessment Instruments.* 6th ed. Columbus: NCDA, 2013. Print.

Zunker, Vernon. *Career Counseling: Applied Concepts of Life Planning.* 7th ed. Pacific Grove: Brooks, 2006. Print.

Karen M. Derr; updated by Robert J. Drummond

SEE ALSO: Ability tests; Career Occupational Preference System (COPS); Career and personnel testing; Career selection, development, and change; Kuder Occupational Interest Survey (KOIS); Strong Interest Inventory (SII); Testing: Historical perspectives; Work motivation; Workplace issues and mental health.

International Classification of Diseases (ICD)

DATE: 1903 forward

TYPE OF PSYCHOLOGY: Biological bases of behavior; Psychopathology

Development of an international classification of diseases, beginning in the early twentieth century, provided a systematic method of organizing a statistical summary of organic disorders. Many of these illnesses have an impact on the biological basis for behavioral disorders.

KEY CONCEPTS

- Alphanumeric coding scheme
- Morbidity or mortality statistics
- Psychiatric and behavioral disorders
- Zymotic

INTRODUCTION

An understanding of the mathematical principles that underlay the existence and spread of disease in populations had its origins within the Royal Society of London during the seventeenth century. Founded in 1662, the Royal Society included among its members John Graunt, a local tradesman. Graunt collected and organized bills of mortality from local parishes, which represented the first complete listing of causes of morbidity and mortality in local populations. Descriptions were simplistic compared with data collected now; nevertheless, the principle that information about disease could be statistically compiled would lead to further refinements and increasing accuracy. In 1836 the establishment of the Registrar-General's Office in London provided a central clearinghouse for compilation of such statistics. In particular, under the leadership of William Farr, compiler of statistical abstracts and finally superintendent, the office represented the first complete centralized bureau for analysis of disease in a population.

Farr initially divided diseases into five classes, three of the major groups being zymotic or infectious diseases; developmental diseases, such as those related to age or nutrition; and violent diseases. While some of Farr's conclusions are obviously outdated, the separation of behavioral disease from those with clearly contagious characteristics represented an early attempt to distinguish the two.

The major impetus to categorizing morbidity or mortality statistics was the increasing level of information gathering within individual European countries. The development of the germ theory of disease provided a means of diagnosis for individual illnesses; as noted in several studies of the history of information technology, such growing medical statistics were a part of the larger quantification of everyday life in many of these Western countries.

As noted by information technologist Geoffrey Bowker, the International Statistical Institute (IST) during its 1891 meeting in Vienna established a committee under the auspices of Jacques Bertillon, chief of statistical works in Paris, to develop a system for the categorization of illnesses. At its meeting in Chicago two years later, the committee presented a system that was immediately adopted by the larger institute and that was implemented by most countries. The classification became known as the International Classification of Diseases, or ICD; the first system became known as ICD-1. The initial listing included two hundred categories, the number of lines present on the paper used by Bertillon's committee during its deliberations.

PERIODIC REVISION

As further refinements in research into diagnosis or understanding of disease came about, it was quickly clear that the original categories of illness would be insufficient as a universal classification system. Meetings at approximately ten-year intervals addressed such changes and resulted in significant revisions. The first major revision occurred in 1909 (ICD-2), the second in 1920 (ICD-3), and so on. Following World War I, the League of Nations became the governing body that dealt with the classification system.

At the International Health Conference that met in New York in 1946, the World Health Organization was charged with supervision of the system, including any necessary revisions; the result was ICD-6, which included nonfatal diseases such as those found in psychiatric disorders. In the years since, there have been periodic changes and revisions in that classification system; the ICD-10 was published in 1992, with the next revision slated for publication in 2017. The full name of the publication is now The *International Statistical Classification of Diseases and Related Health Problems,* although the common acronym of ICD is still used. The number of classifications has ballooned to more than 14,400, with national Clinical Modifications sometimes including even more; the US clinical modification for the ICD-10, for example, has over 68,000.

With development of computer technology, the use of numeric codes became standard in ICD classification. Among other changes, such a numeric system allowed for the encoding of more than just a single underlying cause of death on death certificates; contributing causes could also now be included. The result was a more accurate rendering of disorders affecting an individual.

ICD CLASSIFICATION AND BEHAVIORAL DISORDERS

ICD classification represents to a significant degree a classification system for causes of death. Its primary function is to track the changes in diagnosis and spread of disease in populations for epidemiological purposes. However, among the illnesses that have been included in the revisions since World War II are those that represent psychiatric and behavioral disorders.

The changes in the coding scheme in ICD-10 represents the most significant revision in the area of mental illnesses. In ICD-9, numeric codes numbered 001-999 were utilized. For the ICD-10 system, an alphanumeric scheme was adopted, which used a letter followed by a two-numeral character (A00-Z99). For example, Alzheimer's disease as a cause of death has been classified as G30 in the ICD-10 coding system. The coding of mental disorders increased from thirty categories in ICD-9 (290-319) to one hundred categories in ICD-10 (F00-F98). Each "family" of disorders represents a particular form or cause. For example, F00-F09 includes only disorders with an organic basis. F10-F19 includes "Mental and behavioral disorders due to psychoactive substance abuse," and so on.

Some of these categories are further subdivided to allow for divisions within the form of the illness. For example, the category F60 represents "Specific personality disorders." The category is subdivided into ten levels on the basis of specific forms or diagnoses of such disorders: F60.0 represents "Paranoid personality disorder," F60.1 represents "Schizoid personality disorder," and so on.

BIBLIOGRAPHY

Andrews, Gavin. "Should Depression Be Managed as a Chronic Disease?" *In British Medical Journal* 322.7283 (2001): 419–421. Print.

Bowker, Geoffrey. "The History of Information Infrastructures: The Case of the International Classification of Disease." *Information Processing and Management* 32.1 (1996): 49–61. Print.

Bowker, Geoffrey. "The Kindness of Strangers: Kinds and Politics in Classification Systems." *Library Trends* 47.2 (1998): 255–292. Print.

Ferenc, Debra P. *Understanding Hospital Billing and Coding*. St. Louis: Elsevier, 2011. Print."

International Classification of Diseases (ICD)." *World Health Organization*. World Health Org, 2014. Web. 20 May 2014.

Killewo, J. Z. J., Kris Heggenhougen, and Stella R. Quah. *Epidemiology and Demography in Public Health*. Sand Diego: Academic, 2010. Print.

Lilienfeld, David, and Paul Stolley. *Foundations of Epidemiology*. New York: Oxford UP, 1994. Print.

World Health Organization. *The International Statistical Classification of Diseases and Related Health Problems*. Rev. 10th ed. Geneva: Author, 1992.

Richard Adler

SEE ALSO: Culture and diagnosis; Diagnosis; *Diagnostic and Statistical Manual of Mental Disorders (DSM)*.

Internet psychology

TYPE OF PSYCHOLOGY: Learning; Origin and definition of psychology; Psychological methodologies; Psychopathology; Psychotherapy

Internet psychology refers to the study of human behavior taking place on the World Wide Web and related global electronics communications networks.

KEY CONCEPTS
- Asynchronous
- Boundaries
- Bulletin board
- Chat room
- Online learning environment
- Psychological distance
- Telemedicine

INTRODUCTION

The Internet is an electronic computer-based network facilitating communication among vast numbers of individuals, groups, businesses, and governments. Internet psychology is a new area in psychology that touches on earlier work in the areas of addiction, communication, learning, teaching, and the provision of therapeutic services. Foundational work in each of these areas of study, based mostly in face-to-face interactions, will provide a standard beside which Internet-related behavior will be compared.

Internet psychology has blossomed both as a result of the large numbers of individuals using the technology and as a result of its unique social interaction features. For instance, in comparison to everyday social interactions, the Internet allows for communication to flow from single individuals to large numbers of other individuals instantaneously. Further, this ability is shared by all individuals on the Internet, whether they are located in major urban areas or in remote locales. The Internet also allows for both asynchronous (meaning not at the same time) and simultaneous communication among individuals. Such features allow individuals to communicate when it is most convenient for them and also in such a way as to reach others whom they might not otherwise meet because of their locales.

One asynchronous Internet-based technology is an electronic bulletin board, an online location where information can be posted by individuals so that anyone who later visits the location can see the message posted. The original message poster may then receive a message back, in the form of another message left in the same place or as a private message sent directly to the original poster. What is unusual about an electronic bulletin board in comparison to everyday communication, however, is that other individuals may join in and have other conversations in and around the original conversation without the knowledge of the original poster. For an outsider observing such an interaction, there would be no way to determine the true identity of the individual participants, nor would there be a way for the outsider to know if everyone listed as participating in the conversation has read or otherwise processed the interaction in its entirety. Even more psychologically interesting is that the individuals in the conversation have no way of knowing how many others visiting the bulletin board might be paying attention to their communications and not responding, a practice commonly called lurking.

Similar to bulletin boards, other technologies, such as chat rooms, provide virtual locations where information can be communicated simultaneously, sometimes described as "in real time," and where it is publicly on view. Chat rooms also raise issues about anonymity and uncertainty as to who might be observing one's conversation. Rather than communicating in a somewhat timeless environment, as on a bulletin board, many people may communicate at the same time in a chat room, much like being at a party or large social gathering. The only differences are that no one has immediate physical contact or cues, everyone can see what everyone else is saying, and the conversation is preserved in writing in the chat room for a period of time. Also, to the extent that the conversations are preserved, there may be more time to analyze communications among individuals.

In both of these types of communications, the issue of boundaries, or how information and relationships are defined and limited, also may be perceived as and function in a way that is more fluid than in face-to-face interactions. Further, boundaries may be more vulnerable to intrusion from uninvited others because most communications are publicly observable. In many online environments, anyone can communicate with everyone all at once, people can communicate anything they want to, and everyone can respond all at once. As a result, communications can be overwhelmingly positive or negative due to the sheer number of responses one might receive. Also, communications may be jarring because of their content.

This reaction is attributable to another feature of Internet-based communications related to anonymity: psychological distance, the social proximity that individuals feel to others. It is something like a perceived safety or danger zone for interactions that have psychological consequences, such as emotional responses. In Internet-based communication, because of anonymity and because social interactions are computer mediated, where individuals may never see or hear each other, psychological distance can be great and have behavioral consequences in communication. While some Internet users may respond to such an environment by opening up emotionally and allowing themselves to be more vulnerable to others in expressing feelings or thoughts, other users might become more extreme and aggressive in terms of how they pursue communications and what they express.

These aspects of Internet-based communications are only a few of many that are interesting to psychologists. Other examples include the effect of this type of remote communication on existing social networks and the formation of new social networks; group cohesion in online groups; the efficacy of online support groups; the development of online social skills; the psychological states of individual participants over time; and the relationship between online and "real-life" communications.

IMPORTANCE

The Internet affects many different kinds of social behavior, including work communications, organizational behavior, dating behavior, everyday social communications, learning and teaching, and even health care. In terms of positive effects, the Internet allows for many benefits. One major benefit is that individuals in remote locations can participate actively in wide social, learning, and business networks, perhaps more so than they could if they were limited to their own locales. This may lead to increased transmission of new science, learning, and social data into such remote areas. It may also lead to decreased feelings of isolation in the individual participants as well as increased opportunities for such individuals.

One opportunity is Internet-based learning. In an online learning environment, individuals in remote locations can access educational opportunities that might otherwise be unavailable to them without traveling great distances. Similarly, such technologies allow for financial savings on intellectual resource acquisition and dispensation, as such resources can be made available to all needing it in one spot on the Internet. This same advantage translates into being able to reach a larger number of trainees than might typically be able to attend training because of time, geographic, or financial constraints. Finally, because the learning takes place online, where interactions and Web-related behavior can be tracked, new information about how trainees seek information, integrate it, and draw conclusions may be discerned, ultimately contributing to advances in teaching.

Another benefit for individuals in remote locations where health care providers are scarce is Internet-based medicine, such as telemedicine, or medical care provided at a distance. Such technologies can be invaluable in saving lives through prevention and informational or supportive treatments that complement face-to-face medical care. Such services may include health-care-related Web sites providing information, assessments, discussion lists for support, chat rooms devoted to individual health care topics, contact information for providers, and even an alternative means of sending messages to health care providers, such as through e-mail. Such Web sites are valuable not only to individual clients but also to their families, treatment providers, and others involved in health care, such as trainees and researchers.

Some of the positive aspects of the Internet also have drawbacks. For instance, rapid and instantaneous communication is good if the information communicated is good. If, however, it has errors or is vague or phrased in a way that is ambiguous in terms of its social tone, it could create conflict and social discomfort for all receiving the message, as well as for the sender.

Another negative aspect that has received attention is what some call Internet addiction. In this syndrome, individuals are judged as being dependent on their use of the Internet. Such dependence might be characterized by any of the following features: a desire to use the Internet more and more; using it more than intended; feeling a strong desire to cease using it or reduce the time spent using it; reducing or giving up other social behaviors to use the Internet; finding that personal Internet use is creating problems in other life activities because they have been neglected; and continued use despite knowledge of psychological or other problems caused or exacerbated by the Internet usage. Finally, "addicted" individuals who do not have access to the Internet may experience feelings of withdrawal. The term "addiction" has been used to describe this condition because many of these features are similar to those defining substance abuse and dependence problems. In terms of the potential scope of the problem, according to research conducted by Keith J. Anderson and published in the *Journal of American College Health* (2001), as many as 10 percent of college students may experience some feelings of dependence on the Internet.

CONTEXT

The Internet appears to be firmly in place in modern society as a major social, educational, and health-related resource. In 1998, the Office for the Advancement of Telehealth was established by the Health Resources and Service Administration of the U.S. Department of Health and Human Services. This office is devoted to the advancement of telehealth and Internet-based medicine to improve public health service and research. Estimates suggest that, each year, more than sixty million people search for health information online, including searches for mental health information. In addition, communications technologies improve daily, reaching more homes. By 2012, for example, 78.9 percent of all households in the United States had a personal computer, and 74.8 percent of all households had access to the Internet at home, according to the US Census Bureau. In this same time period, many workplaces gained an online presence to conduct their business and communicate with their employees. Universities followed suit, using the Internet to host class materials, classes, and even academic conferences.

Understanding the psychology of the Internet remains a critical task. As Internet-based technologies work their way into more settings, the effects of this technology will need to be assessed for their impact on the individuals using the technology and the organizational structures hosting this type of communications network. In addition, it must be kept in mind that the Internet is an international communications medium. Like the telephone and the television, it can spread information anywhere that the technology is installed. Unlike these earlier technological advances, it is capable of transmitting far more information, more rapidly and to more people. The implications of such transmissions remain to be evaluated. As C. A. Bowers suggests in *Let Them Eat Data* (2000), these communications may have costs that are yet to be recognized.

BIBLIOGRAPHY

Agger, Ben. *Oversharing: Presentations of Self in the Internet Age.* New York: Routledge, 2012. Print.

American Psychological Association. *DotCOMSense.* Washington: Author, 2000. Print.

Anderson, Keith J. "Internet Use Among College Students: An Exploratory Study." *Journ. of American College Health* 50.1 (2001): 21–26. Print.

Bauer, Jeffrey C., and Marc A. Ringel. *Telemedicine and the Reinvention of Healthcare.* New York: McGraw, 1999. Print.

Birnbaum, Michael H., ed. *Psychology Experiments on the Internet.* San Diego, Calif.: Academic Press, 2000. Print.

Bowers, C. A. *Let Them Eat Data: How Computers Affect Education, Cultural Diversity, and the Prospects of Ecological Sustainability.* Athens: U of Georgia P, 2000. Print.

Gackenbach, Jayne. *Psychology and the Internet: Intrapersonal, Interpersonal, and Transpersonal Implications.* 2d ed. San Diego: Academic Press, 2007. Print.

Joinson, Adam, Katelyn McKenna, Tom Postmes, and Ulf-Dietrich Reips. Oxford *Handbook of Internet Psychology.* New York: Oxford UP, 2009. Print.

Kiesler, Sara, ed. *Culture of the Internet.* Mahwah: Erlbaum, 1997. Print.

Manjikian, Mary. *Threat Talk: The Comparative Politics of Internet Addiction.* Burlington: Ashgate, 2012. Print.

Rosen, Larry D., Nancy A. Cheever, and L. Mark Carrier. *iDisorder: Understanding Our Obsession with Technology and Overcoming Its Hold on Us.* New York: Palgrave, 2012. Print.

Wallace, Patricia M. *The Psychology of the Internet.* Cambridge: Cambridge UP, 2001. Print.

Weiss, Robert, and Jennifer P. Schneider. *Untangling the Web: Sex, Porn, and Fantasy Obsession in the Internet Age.* New York: Alyson, 2006. Print.

Wolfe, Christopher R., ed. *Learning and Teaching on the World Wide Web.* San Diego: Academic Press, 2001. Print.

Young, Kimberly S. *Caught in the Net: How to Recognize the Signs of Internet Addiction.* New York: Wiley, 1998. Print.

Nancy A. Piotrowski

SEE ALSO: Addictive personality and behaviors; Affiliation and friendship; Attitude formation and change; Computer and Internet use and mental health; Consumer psychology; Coping: Chronic illness; Coping: Social support; Coping: Strategies; Coping: Terminal illness; Emotional expression; Groups; Health psychology; Help-seeking; Intimacy; Learning; Media psychology; Self-disclosure; Self-help groups; Selfpresentation; Social identity theory; Social networks; Social perception; Social support and mental health; Support groups; Teaching methods.

Interpersonal attraction

TYPE OF PSYCHOLOGY: Clinical; Evolutionary; Social

When two individuals are brought together by one or a number of factors and positively evaluate each other, they experience interpersonal attraction. These factors may be proximity and familiarity, attractive characteristics, brain chemistry, similarity, social exchange, a sense of equity, or instrumentality.

KEY CONCEPTS
- Brain chemistry
- Equity
- Instrumentality
- Physical attractiveness
- Proximity
- Similarity
- Social exchange

INTRODUCTION

Interpersonal attraction refers to the factors that impel two people to meet and to stay together. Two people experience interpersonal attraction when they have a positive emotional evaluation of each other and want to be with each other.

Photo: iStock

There are many theories that explain why certain couples fall in love or why certain people interact and become friends. Below is an exploration of seven factors studied by scientists. These studies explain our attraction to those who live or work near us, are physically attractive, arouse us, are similar to us, reward us, or have the ability and motivation to help us achieve our goals.

PROXIMITY AND FAMILIARITY

People who see each other and interact regularly are the most likely to establish some level of meaningful relationship. Familiarity creates opportunities for this attraction. For example, people who live close to each other or in other ways interact with each other tend to be attracted to each other. Sometimes interaction is not even necessary. The mere exposure effect predicts that the more a person sees something, the more he or she will like it. Male students who were exposed to a woman in a course tended to rate that woman as more attractive as the number of classes that woman attended increased, despite having no recollection of having ever seen the woman.

ATTRACTIVE CHARACTERISTICS

Both men and women use physical attractiveness when selecting a sexual partner, although men tend to put more of a premium on physical attractiveness when se-

lecting a potential marital partner. Certain physical aspects are considered especially attractive. Research has shown that women prefer symmetry in both the face and body of males. They view symmetrical men as dominant, powerful, and wealthy as well as potentially better sexual partners and spouses. Women also attribute more dominance to men who have traditionally masculine facial features. As for symmetry in women, men prefer this as well and see these women as fertile, attractive, and healthy as well as potentially better sexual partners and spouses. In addition, according to evolutionary psychologists, men in 33 different countries stated they preferred a mate whose body was physically attractive. This finding is consistent with the tendency for men throughout the ages to view physical attractiveness, especially a waist-hip ratio of .70, as a signal of health and fertility.

When it comes to the first few minutes of sizing up a potential partner, both men and women rely mainly on physical attractiveness, according to scientists who studied three-minute meetings (a la speed dating). Moreover, people overgeneralize from appearance, assuming that those who are attractive on the outside are also nicer on the inside, a phenomenon that has been termed the "what-is-beautiful-is-good-stereotype." In fact, these judgments occur during the first 100 milliseconds of viewing a person's face. Not only is an individual judged for attractiveness, but he or she is also judged on likeability, trustworthiness, competence, and aggressiveness. However, what constitutes physical attractiveness may not be as uniform as the above studies suggest for people have a sense of their own beauty and will seek out someone who matches their conception of beauty and their conception of their own attractiveness. It is a process of social comparison combined with a personal valuing of certain attributes independent of social standards.

Although people use physical attractiveness when choosing a sexual relationship, other factors become more important when seeking a long-term relationship. In a recent study, both sexes ranked warmth, kindness, and intelligence as the most desirable traits when choosing a mate.

BRAIN CHEMISTRY

When two people are sexually attracted to each other, a rapid release of chemicals (neurotransmitters) are released in their brains, according to neuroscientists. By increasing the availability of the neurotransmitter, dopamine, nature sustains the interest two people might have with another, increasing the chances of procreation. Dopamine creates a feeling of reward every time an individual iswith the object of passion. Another chemical, phenylethylamine (PEA) floods the brain when we experience "love at first sight," and this chemical causes even more dopamine to be released. When the lovers are not with each other, they experience withdrawal and crave to have the closeness again. They also obsess about the loved one, due to changes in the neurotransmitter, serotonin. As the relationship progresses, other brain chemicals are also involved.

SIMILARITY

People who are similar tend to be attracted to each other. This similarity can be in values, interests, opinions, social desirability, and physical attractiveness. There is a saying that "opposites attract" but the social psychology literature demonstrates similarity is what holds people together. Furthermore, perceived, rather than actual, similarity has the main effect. One study found that couples' similarity in physical attractiveness rather than the degree of physical attractiveness predicted their going out on a second date. Another study found that those that saw themselves as most similar in attractiveness reported being the most deeply in love nine months later. It seems perceived similarity is an important factor in interpersonal attraction because this similarity validates

people's beliefs and views of themselves. This social comparison in terms of similarity bolsters self-esteem. Thus, people with a low comparison level experience stronger attraction to others because their standards for receiving an ego boost from another are lower. For example, studies have shown that physically unattractive people not only tend to have lower standards for a potential partner, but they also tend to view potential partners as more attractive.

SOCIAL EXCHANGE

People are attracted to others who satisfy various needs, in other words, those who are rewarding. These needs may be pleasure, anxiety reduction, or self-esteem. For example, a person with a sense of humor gives pleasure to others in both romance and friendship. Additionally, studies have shown that help managing anxiety through social contact with another person who experiences the same anxiety-provoking situation is rewarding. Other studies have shown that people who boost another's self-esteem, either by agreeing with his or her views or by allowing an association with a high status person, are also perceived as rewarding.

According to social exchange theory, people then assess a possible relationship in terms of the rewards and costs as well as a social comparison of whether this relationship is better than another relationship they could have. A person might value a relationship with a friend who plans fun activities even though the friend sometimes forgets to invite that person. This is a more gratifying relationship than that with people who are not fun. In a romantic relationship, a woman might reward a man with her beauty and feel rewarded by that man's wealth, while both of them put up with each other's occasional outbursts.

People are also attracted to others who like them. In keeping with this reciprocity effect, men are attracted to women who are easy for them to get but hard for other men to get. Thus, people are attracted to others who like them, but only if this liking makes them feel special.

EQUITY

Equity theory goes beyond social exchange theory to explain attraction based on an assessment of equity in the exchange. Men and women may say they want a partner who is more desirable than they are, but they end up choosing partners similar to their own social worth. The socially desirable characteristics used in matches to create equity are not just physical attractiveness but include income, social status, intelligence, attractive personality, compassion, and ability to be agreeable. Thus, one desirable characteristic can be traded for another. Furthermore, those couples who perceived their relationship to be equitable were happiest and had the longest-lasting relationships. It is the perception that one is getting as much as one deserves in the relationship that holds the relationship together.

INSTRUMENTALITY

People are attracted to and approach other people who might help them achieve their goals while avoiding those who cannot help them. A person is selected to help with a currently activated goal but then may be discarded when not instrumental in achieving other goals. Furthermore, those people selected must have both the ability and willingness to help others achieve their goals. For example, if a person wants to exercise on a more regular basis, he or she will select someone in the social network who may be instrumental to achieving this goal. Thus, the concept of instrumentality explains one of the motivations behind attraction to various members of a social network. It addresses more than just the reward value in a relationship and recognizes that people value different rewards at different times. In fact, some researchers have declared that the interpersonal facilitation of one's goal pursuits is the main reason why close relationships exist.

BIBLIOGRAPHY

Berscheid, E. & Walster, E. (1978). *Interpersonal Attraction* (2nd ed.). Reading, MA: Addison-Wesley. Although this book was published decades ago, it is still one of the best sources of information about the proximity, similarity, social exchange, and equity of interpersonal attraction. It also explains the process of romantic love.

Hendrick, S. (2004). *Understanding Close Relationships*. Boston, MA: Pearson. This book describes attraction in friendship and in romantic love and is a good source of scientific references for these topics.

Young, L., & Alexander, B. (2014). *The Chemistry Between Us: Love, Sex, and The Science Of Attraction*. New York, NY: Penguin Books. A neuroscientist and popular science writer describe the chemistry that draws people together and keeps them together.

Beverly B. Palmer

See Also: Attraction; Attractiveness; Interpersonal relationships; Relationships; Sex.

Intervention

Type of psychology: Psychopathology; Psychotherapy

In the field of psychology, "intervention" is a term used to convey actions, therapeutic or experimental, to effect change. In many ways, the field of psychology is best known for its interventions in clinical treatment and research; therefore, this concept is a foundational one for the field.

Key Concepts
- Addiction
- Experimental conditions
- Methodology
- Placebo
- Psychopathology
- Psychotherapy
- Research design
- Substance use

INTRODUCTION

The word "intervention" is derived from the word "intervene," which means to come in between in a way that causes change. It is a term that is used in many professions, including medicine, nursing, education, and law enforcement. The term is also used in the mental health field in several ways; one applies to clinicians and one applies to researchers. Across all professions, however, interventions are designed to be specific actions to deal with specific problems. In mental health, the typical target of intervention is psychopathology.

Among clinicians, the term "intervention" is generally used to refer to any application of a specific psychotherapy plan or technique. For instance, a clinician planning to work with a client who is depressed might describe the chosen intervention to combat the depression as a cognitive behavior therapy. Thus the therapy described was the way in which the therapist intended to make changes happen on the identified problem.

Researchers in mental health also use the term "intervention" but in a slightly different way. Those who do clinical research might also be looking to compare one treatment to another type of treatment or placebo (also known as an innocuous or inactive treatment). To discuss such research plans, professionals use special language that describes the mechanics of research methodology. Part of research methodology for any research project is the specific design chosen. In this case, where a researcher was comparing a treatment to a placebo condition, the methodology language would call this design a two-group comparison of intervention versus control, or, sometimes, treatment versus placebo. As such, among professionals working in mental health, the term "intervention" has at least two meanings. One is related to general clinical work. The second is related more to research. In some areas of mental health, the word also has specific implications. In the treatment for addictive behavior, for instance, intervention has a precise meaning.

USE IN ADDICTIONS AND SUBSTANCE USE TREATMENT

Beginning treatment for addiction generally requires that one either enter treatment voluntarily or otherwise be remanded to such care for legal reasons. Mental health professionals prefer that clients enter treatment voluntarily. Occasionally this does not happen because the person suffering fails to recognize the problem. With substance use and other problems related to addiction, this happens frequently because the range of problems demanding treatment can extend from mild to severe. With less-severe problems, social pressure to encourage a person to seek help might be scant. As problems become more severe and the presence of an addiction becomes more pronounced, however, social pressure to seek help does increase. Sometimes, family members and significant others may conclude that a loved one needs help before the loved one recognizes the problem. If the individual does not seek help, then others may seek out qualified professionals to help them perform an intervention.

Traditionally and predominantly used in the addictions field, the intervention approach expanded after the mid-1980s to address a wide range of self-destructive behaviors. In this technique, the attempt to effect change usually occurs in a circumscribed period of time and in a planned locale. These procedures should not be attempted without serious study and even consultation. In some cases, interventions can be simple, firm conversations that set boundaries with the intent of helping the person to change. In others, more sophisticated strategies may be needed, involving more people. In the latter case, the concerned party often enlists the help of professionals, usually called interventionists, to help them prepare for the event. Preparation typically involves

identifying individuals whom the addicted person knows well and who have seen the effects of the addiction on that person's life. These individuals then convene for a structured confrontation that stresses concern for the welfare and safety of the confronted individual. The desired end result is usually for the person to decide to enter treatment.

BIBLIOGRAPHY

Clough, Peter, and Cathy Nutbrown. *A Student's Guide to Methodology.* 3d ed. London: Sage, 2012. Print.

Corsini, Raymond J., and Danny Wedding. *Current Psychotherapies.* 10th ed. Belmont: Brooks-Cole, 2014. Print.

Health Library. "Intervention Trial." *Health Library.* EBSCO Information Services, 2014. Web. 27 May 2014.

Jay, Jeff, and Debra Jay. *Love First: A Family's Guide to Intervention.* 2d ed. Center City: Hazelden, 2008. Print.

Johnson, Vernon E. *Intervention: How to Help Someone Who Doesn't Want Help.* Center City: Hazelden, 2009. Digital file.

Mayo Clinic. "Intervention: Help a Loved One Overcome Addiction." *Mayo Clinic Diseases and Conditions: Mental Illness.* Mayo Foundation for Medical Education and Research, 23 Aug. 2011. Web. 27 May 2014.

Meier, Scott T. *Measuring Change in Counseling and Psychotherapy.* New York: Guilford, 2008. Print.

Nancy A. Piotrowski

SEE ALSO: Addictive personalities and behaviors; Alcohol dependance and abuse; Denial; Group therapy; Substance use disorders.

Interviewing

TYPE OF PSYCHOLOGY: Behavioral medicine; Clinical; Consulting; Counseling; Educational; Family; Forensic; Health; Organizational; Psychotherapy; School; Social

An interview involves communication between at least two persons. Each contributor impacts and is impacted by the responses of the other. The practice of interviewing is central to the work done in many mental health settings. Interviews may be conducted for a variety of intended purposes and can be structured, semi-structured, or un-

structured to best serve the purpose of the interview. The goals of a particular interview relate to the context in which that interview is conducted. Ethical clinical interviewing encompasses care for the client while working to achieve the goals of the interview. Some practitioners refer to interviewing as a conversation with a purpose.

KEY CONCEPTS:

- Case history interview
- Crisis interview
- Diagnostic interview
- Interview purpose
- Mental status interview
- Rapport
- Structured interviews
- Termination interview

INTRODUCTION

Clinical interviewing is the foundation for practically all work conducted in the helping professions. There are a number of distinct advantages that contribute to the widespread use of clinical interviewing. Interviews are inexpensive to conduct, are multidimensional in that they tap into both verbal and nonverbal behaviors, are both portable and flexible, and facilitate the development of a therapeutic rapport.

Due to these advantages, the clinical interview has become the most widely used method of preliminary clinical assessment and provides a basic context for almost all other psychological assessments and treatments. The concept that interviews are a "conversation with a purpose" is an important starting point. The interviewer is purposeful and accepts responsibility for keeping the interview on track and moving toward the goal. In this sense, the interviewer's awareness is different than a typical conversation partner and the flow of the discourse is usually more goal-oriented than a typical conversation.

Besides having a purpose, there are some other points that distinguish interviews from conversations. For example, a conversation usually happens without a central theme, the participants' roles are typically not defined, and the conversation begins and ends according to the will of the participants rather than a pre-established start and end time in a pre-determined place. By contrast, interviews typically incorporate some efforts directed at achieving a specific purpose or intended goal. In addition, interviews usually integrate an awareness of defined roles between participants, i.e., interviewer and interviewee. The establishment of defined roles in the clinical

interview is an essential step in crafting an effective therapeutic alliance between the client and the practitioner.

RAPPORT

A clinical interview incorporates an alliance between the interviewer and the interviewee to facilitate the goal of data collection. The practitioner's ability to gather information about the client requires that the client and the clinician are able to build a relationship in which the client is able to trust the interviewer. The process of establishing this relationship is referred to as building a rapport. Along with the goal of rapport-building, most interviews have in common the goal of collecting information about the interviewee's current situation, beliefs, feelings, and/or attitudes as skillfully as possible.

Building rapport is essential for conducting a clinical interview. Rapport refers to the relationship between patient and clinician. It includes a positive atmosphere along with mutual understanding of the purpose of the interview. A strong rapport can provide the clinician with leverage by which to achieve the goals of the interview. Although a comfortable atmosphere will not guarantee a productive interview (a warm, yet poorly prepared interviewer may make the interviewee feel at home but may not reach established goals), lack of attention to atmosphere and warmth can inhibit the development of trust. Clinicians from nearly every theoretical orientation agree that developing trust and rapport as a means of building a positive, collaborative alliance with clients is essential in the early stages of a therapy.

TYPES OF INTERVIEWS

There are two primary distinguishing factors which shape every interview. First, every interview is shaped by its purpose. Next, the interview is shaped by its relative degree of structure. Some interview purposes are best served by a structured interview; others will be more effectively served by semi-structured or unstructured interviews. A structured interview requires the interviewer to use a pre-determined series of questions or prompts to elicit information from the interviewee. A semi-structured interview is more flexible, allowing the interviewer to use variable means to collect data from the interviewee, shifting questions and prompts according to what works best in a given situation. An unstructured interview may be focused on a particular theme but allows for the questions and prompts to be spontaneously developed during the course of the interview. In addition to purpose and degree of structure, interviews have other shaping characteristics. For example, interviews can be more or less formal. Some interviews are more or less focused on information seeking versus information giving. Interviews may incorporate a focus on the past, present, or future. Further, interviews are shaped by the developmental status of the client. It is also important to note that the focus of a series of interviews with one client may shift according to the stage of treatment or other factors pertaining to the needs of the client.

Some examples of clinical interviews include these: intake interviews, mental status interviews, case history interviews, diagnostic interviews, and termination interviews. The purpose of an *intake interview* is to report the circumstances which led the client to seek help. A *mental-status interview* evaluates the appearance, mood, speech and thoughts of the interviewee. A *diagnostic interview* evaluates criteria for clinical diagnosis. The goal of a *case history interview* is to determine the antecedents to the client's current state. A *crisis interview* occurs in relation to a traumatic event. *Termination interviews* prepare interviewees for conclusion of services. It is important to be aware that more than one of the following forms of interviews may be administered to the same client. For example, a client may complete an intake interview when first admitted for treatment. The client may later be provided a mental status examination, a case history interview, and a diagnostic interview in preparation for treatment or at intervals throughout treatment to evaluate treatment effectiveness. At the successful completion of treatment, the client might also be provided a termination interview. With this in mind, a brief typology of interviews typically used in psychotherapy follows.

INTAKE INTERVIEWS

The primary purpose of an intake interview is to gather information related to the immediate concerns that prompted the client to seek treatment. For example, during an intake, the interviewer may ask about when the presenting problem became a complaint and who defined it as such. The interviewer may probe to see what the client believes about the origin of the problem or symptoms. An intake interview might also include questions about any action the client has already taken to solve the problem. The interviewer may assess any biases or distorted thinking the client has about the problem. The interviewer may inquire about medical problems and any medication the client takes regularly as well as any substance abuse concerns. In addition to the primary purpose of collecting information, the intake interview

allows the clinician to assess whether they possess the necessary competencies to work with the client, given their presenting concerns. The intake interview can also provide clinicians an opportunity to ask clients about their expectations for treatment and to offer information about available options.

MENTAL STATUS INTERVIEW

A mental status exam (MSE) provides information that forms the basis for understanding and conceptualizing the client's concerns. Several areas are addressed in a mental status interview or exam. In an MSE, the interviewer assesses the interviewee's appearance, behavior, psychomotor activity, and speech. Reports from an MSE typically include information regarding whether the client is alert, oriented to place and time, and dressed appropriately for the weather. The interviewer also assesses the interviewee's affect and mood along with the interviewee's attitude toward the interviewer. Other areas of consideration are the interviewee's attention, concentration, memory, cognition, reliability, judgment, and capacity for insight. Among other things, a mental status interview is an opportunity to evaluate and document client perceptual disturbances.

DIAGNOSTIC INTERVIEW

There are several features which distinguish a diagnostic interview from other forms of interviewing. The purpose or goal of a diagnostic interview is to arrive at a clinical diagnosis using specific diagnostic criteria. The interviewer typically uses standard, structured questions to determine whether diagnostic criteria are met. Most diagnostic interviews use an initial question based on broad criteria. This question is designed to let the interviewer to "skip" the related questions if the broad criteria are not met. Criteria are frequently coded as present, subthreshold, or absent.

CASE HISTORY INTERVIEW

A case history interview aims to collect a detailed personal and social history that is as complete as possible. The goal is to provide a broad historical and developmental context in which the client and problem are situated. Related to this goal, case history interviews typically collect a broad range of information. Case history interviews may include family/parental, environmental, religious/spiritual, educational, sexual, medical, and/or psychopathological concerns. The interviewer is attentive to concrete facts such as dates, times, and events as well as the client's relevant thoughts and feelings.

CRISIS INTERVIEW

The purpose of a crisis interview is to assist the client or the family with an immediate crisis. The first goal in a crisis interview is always to identify the problem and assess the safety of the individual(s) involved. Crisis interviewers work under the assumption that individuals in crisis are unable to use previously developed coping mechanisms to manage their response to a traumatic event. Crisis interviewers work with clients to re-stabilize and seek new coping strategies. Work done with clients in a crisis interview is not meant to be long term, so interviewers typically provide referrals for longer term treatment.

TERMINATION INTERVIEW

In clinical terms, the word *termination* refers to the last phase of therapy. Though often underappreciated, termination can be an important piece of the therapeutic puzzle. For some clients, termination can be profoundly healing, meaningful, and transformative. Frequently, clients have come to therapy with concerns that include an element of loss. In the termination phase, therapy provides a venue through which clients can examine how they experience, process and cope with feelings associated with loss. When it is time for clients to begin termination, clinicians and clients can collaboratively evaluate the work that has been accomplished in therapy. They can celebrate the progress that has been made, have a conversation about goals that weren't reached and explore any disappointments with the process. For many clients, reminiscing and building an overview of therapy is gratifying because it helps the client put therapy into perspective.

BIBLIOGRAPHY

Fowler, J. C., & Perry, J. C. (2005). Clinical tasks of the dynamic interview. *Psychiatry*, 68(4), 316-36. Explores five broad purposes and tasks associated with a psychodynamic interview

Ivey, A. E., Ivey, M. B., Zalaquett, C. P., & Quirk, K. (2012). *Essentials of intentional interviewing: Counseling in a multicultural world.* Belmont, CA: Brooks/Cole Cengage Learning. Basic textbook breaks down interviewing skills into discrete elements and assists reader in learning to predict client reactions to interviewing techniques.

Jones, K. D. (2010). "The Unstructured Clinical Interview". *Journal of Counseling and Development* : JCD, 88(2), 220-226. Provides information about how to conduct an unstructured diagnostic interview.

McConaughy, S. H. (2005). *Clinical Interviews For Children and Adolescents: Assessment To Intervention.* New York: Guilford Press. Textbook on interviewing children and adolescents as well as their teachers and parents using multi-method assessment.

McDowell, T. (2000). *Practice Evaluation as a Collaborative Process: A Client's and a Clinician's Perceptions of Helpful and Unhelpful Moments In a Clinical Interview.* Smith College Studies in Social Work, 70(2), 375. Provides process commentary on an actual interview to highlight what clinician and client deemed useful or not during the interview.

Murphy, B. C., & Dillon, C. (2015). *Interviewing in Action in a Multicultural World.* Australia: Thomson/Brooks Cole. Textbook supports the importance of culturally competent relationship building to the development of client-clinician relationships.

Norcross, J. C., & Lambert, M. J. (2011). "Psychotherapy Relationships That Work II". *Psychotherapy*, 48(1), 4–8. doi: 10.1037/a0022180 Discusses elements of evidence-based researchtherapeutic relationship, the centrality of the therapy relationship, and its interdependence with treatment methods.

Prout, T. P. D. (2014). *Essential Interviewing and Counseling Skills: An Integrated Approach to Practice.* Springer Publishing Company. Textbook dedicated to the development of clinical interviewing skills which encompasses both theory and practice from a diverse array of theoretical schools and practice orientations.

Sommers-Flanagan, J., & Sommers-Flanagan, R. (2014). *Clinical Interviewing.* Hoboken, N.J: Wiley. A basic guide to effective interviewing which includes focus on multicultural competency, emphasis on evidence-based practice, attention to diagnosis and treatment planning, and case examples.

Stuart, A. L., Pasco, J. A., Jacka, F. N., Brennan, S. L., Berk, M., & Williams, L. J. (2014). "Comparison of Self-Report and Structured Clinical Interview in The Identification of Depression". *Comprehensive Psychiatry,* 55(4), 866-869. doi:http://dx.doi.org/10.1016/j.comppsych.2013.12.019 An empirical study which suggests that simple self-report methods can be used to identify depression with some degree of confidence but are not as trustworthy as interviews.

Vanderploeg, R. D., Groer, S., & Belanger, H. G., (2012). "Initial developmental process of a VA semistructured clinical interview for TBI identification". *Journal of Rehabilitation Research and Development,* 49(4), 545-56. Describes the six-step developmental methodology and presents the process underwent in developing a semi-structured interview for identifying traumatic brain injury (TBI)as well as the resulting semistructured interview and accompanying manual.

Wright, K. M., Adler, A. B., Bliese, Paul D., & Eckford, R.D. (2008). "Structured Clinical Interview Guide for Postdeployment Psychological Screening Programs". *Military Medicine,* 173(5), 411-21. Provides information about structured post-deployment interviews conducted in the United States military. Post-deployment interviews are an example of a termination interview which includes assessment of post-deployment mental health intended for use in follow-up assessment and care.

Laurie Bonjo

SEE ALSO: Clinical methods; Insight; Interpersonal relationships.

Intimacy

TYPE OF PSYCHOLOGY: Social psychology

Intimacy describes a special quality of emotional closeness between two people. It involves mutual caring, trust, open communication of feelings and sensations, as well as an ongoing interchange of information about significant emotional events. Self-disclosure is a critical ingredient of intimacy.

KEY CONCEPTS
- Difficulties in intimacy
- Intimacy and sexuality
- Intimacy and well-being
- Risk
- Self-identity
- Vulnerability

INTRODUCTION

Intimacy is the opening of oneself to another person so that the two individuals can share with each other their innermost thoughts and feelings that are usually kept hidden from other people. The word "intimacy" derives from intimus, the Latin term for "inner" or "inmost." It denotes a kind of sharing that comes from within and inspires thoughts of closeness, warmth, and shared affection. Intimacy also involves getting close enough to another person that he or she can see not only one's positive qualities and strengths but also one's hidden faults and weaknesses. Authentic closeness between two persons requires that both of them step out of their traditional roles, dispense with their usual facades, and try to become their true selves. Intimacy with another person is, therefore, a combination of individual identity and mutual sharing. In a healthy intimacy, two individuals move into a relationship with each other, sharing common interests without losing their separate identities. Interpersonal exchange in intimate relationships is an end in itself rather than a means to achieving any other goal.

Intimacy, by its very nature, is elusive, subjective, and intensely private. An important basis of intimacy is the sharing of private thoughts and feelings through self-disclosure. Such self-disclosure involves the sharing of both pleasant and unpleasant feelings and emotions. There appears to be something uniquely intimate about sharing personal pain. It is also considered intimate to share feelings of love, caring, attraction, and closeness, as well as well as hopes, joys, accomplishments, and pride. The sharing of joyous experiences and cherished memories is considered to be as intimate as that of unpleasant experiences and long-suppressed secrets. In addition, intimacy refers not just to the act of self-disclosure but also to the interpersonal interaction in which self-disclosure is validated and reciprocated.

Nonverbal behaviors are as important to intimacy as are verbal expressions. Sex is cited as the most frequent example, but other examples include being with another person in an atmosphere of comfort and ease; handholding; hugging; sharing excitement, joy, and laughter; and doing things together. Other examples include sharing the touch, taste, and smell of cherished objects. Feeling good in the presence of each other, touching each other in silence, having a quiet dinner together, and silently sharing excitement and anticipation are some other examples that illustrate intimacy.

Intimacy also denotes a special type of feeling that is often described in terms of warmth, closeness, and love. Intimacy can thus refer to individual behavior (such as self-disclosure), to interactions between two partners, to types of relationships, and to specific feelings. Intimate partners experience a unique sense of exuberance, warmth, and vitality. Sometimes they waver, intermittently feeling both closeness and distance. At other times, there can be a simultaneous experience of both closeness and distance.

SELF-IDENTITY

A positive and realistic sense of self is a prerequisite for healthy intimacy. Intimacy requires a full awareness of one's own feelings, thoughts, and values and the ability to bring that awareness into a relationship with another. As one becomes aware of one's own self-identity and self-understanding, one is able to move into a relationship with another individual who also maintains a somewhat similar sense of healthy self-identity. Intimacy involves being able to share worlds while maintaining one's own boundaries. It requires being honest with oneself and one's partner, even during those times when one is not focused on sharing or is in some other way preoccupied.

A person who is aware of his or her own needs and is willing to explore his or her own limitations and potentialities will allow another to do the same. This may, at times, lead to conflicts. Variations in emotional expression, the nature of attention, and the quality of communication are bound to occur in a relationship from time to time and are unavoidable. The truly intimate partners are able to handle such occasional turmoil with graceful acceptance and mutual respect.

Healthy intimacy is notable for an ability to maintain a solid, self-sustained sense of identity while remaining emotionally engaged with another. The sense of self in a person involved in an intimate relationship is very resilient. Such a person is able and willing to differ with another and still maintain his or her unique identity, expressed through thoughts, feelings, values, vulnerabilities, strengths, desires, and fantasies. A person with a healthy sense of self can tolerate multiple, distinct, and coequal realities. Such people can be themselves in the presence of others, and can accept others being themselves.

A less-than-healthy relationship is marked by blurred or indistinct boundaries. In such relationships, a person pays an inordinate amount of attention to the other individual to monitor his or her actions and, more important, reactions. Even minor differences can be anxiety producing and/or threatening. One attempts to deny, minimize, or rapidly smooth differences out of existence. Contact with a partner is neither solid nor comfortable because the closeness causes anxiety about losing one's self, whereas separateness creates anxiety about losing the other person. If the self-identity is shaky or insecure,

there is an inability to maintain proper boundaries and, in turn, a resistance to really "letting in" another person—whether emotionally or intellectually. In extreme cases, contact with the partner's differing reality is so difficult that it may give rise to an illusion of an alternate reality or a sense of no connection whatsoever.

An alternative to this sort of distortion is to allow both oneself and one's partner to be transparent and visible. When separateness is maintained, the option to know another person exists. One's self is solid enough to withstand the risks that accompany intense emotional involvement—the inevitability of misunderstanding, disappointment, disapproval, conflict, rejection, and even loss. In a paradoxical sense, one can only have as good a relationship as one is willing to lose. This is one of the key dynamics that largely determines how much emotional intensity and intimacy a person is capable of handling.

RISK AND VULNERABILITY

Being intimate with another individual necessitates risk and vulnerability through self-disclosure. Intimacy inherently feels risky because one goes out to the edge of individual expression without being certain how the other person will respond. Whereas closeness affirms and sustains a relationship, intimacy reveals and affirms individuality, and, in the process, changes the nature and quality of a relationship. A person who is able to maintain individuality in the midst of togetherness can reap the rewards of both closeness and intimacy. If not, one swings between compulsive togetherness and reactive individuality.

Intimate relationships evolve gradually and naturally. The more valued the relationship, the more there is to lose. One feels more anxiety in being intimate in the sense of being honestly and fully oneself. There is always some amount of tension between closeness and intimacy. The paradox of closeness and intimacy is that the only way to really have either is to be willing at times to sacrifice closeness for the sake of intimacy.

INTIMACY AND SEXUALITY

Although intimacy is commonly thought of in connection with sex, sex is not a necessary component of intimacy. Satisfying intimate relationships in themselves are the most important source of people's happiness. Intimacy is a very important ingredient in the quality of love and sex. A high degree of intimacy between two lovers or spouses contributes to the happiness, emotional stability, and sexual enrichment of both. All activities are more enjoyable and life is richer and more colorful when shared with an intimate partner. Sexual experiences are more pleasurable if the partners know each other intimately, when they are completely open and vulnerable, when they can trust each other to care about each other's feelings, and when they take pleasure in each other's pleasure.

INTIMACY AND WELL-BEING

Humans are social animals, and without intimate relationships they risk loneliness and depression. The availability of intimate relationships is an important determinant of how well people master life's crises. Satisfying intimate relationships are a very important source of most people's happiness. An intimate involvement with a special someone provides a person with a purpose and meaning in life and seems to promote a sense of overall well-being. Intimate relationships have been shown to buffer people from the pathogenic effects of stress. People in intimate relationships have fewer stress-related symptoms and faster recoveries from illnesses. Intimate partners confide in each other, which has been shown to carry its own health benefits. Individual well-being and intimate relationships appear to be closely intertwined. People in satisfied intimate relationships have been shown to be less vulnerable to the negative outcomes of stress than those who lack such relationships.

DIFFICULTIES IN INTIMACY

People may find it difficult to develop and maintain intimacy in two different ways: They are compulsively searching for intimacy but are unable or unwilling to invest time and energy in developing meaningful intimate relationships, or they are afraid of losing their identity and, therefore, purposefully avoid intimate relationships.

Some people harbor unrealistic expectations about intimacy and closeness. Such people are always looking for instant intimacy, even at the cost of compromising their basic values. They tend to share secrets instantly and pour out their life stories in search of establishing immediate contact and emotional intensity. In doing so, they often end up surrendering their personal boundaries in a relationship. This tendency to lose the sense of self and define oneself through the response of others is called emotional fusion. In such a fusion, the boundaries of self become quite vague, and the person is unable to withstand much pressure or disagreement from another. Holding a distinct, self-defined position can be a very frightening experience for such a person. In such

relationships, partners try to merge their internal experiences into a single common reality. As a result, each person's well-being gets inextricably linked to the other's experience and wishes. Both focus on the other, trying to ensure consensus and avoid defining their own reality.

A person with fear of intimacy is basically afraid of losing ego boundaries. There is a lack of interest in and motivation for becoming intimate with others. In most cases, such disturbance in the capacity to form intimate interpersonal relationships stems from early adverse experiences within one's family. Such a person has an active fear of closeness, suffers from self-doubts, and actively distrusts others. He or she has a very low self-image and is easily susceptible to loneliness and depression. Such a person sees himself or herself as undeserving of the love and support of others, is afraid to trust others, and has an unrealistic fear of dependence. When a person is repeatedly unable to share inner thoughts and feelings with a single other person in a sustained manner, he or she may experience emotional isolation.

BIBLIOGRAPHY

Brehm, Sharon S. *Intimate Relationships*. 5th ed. New York: McGraw, 2008. Print.

Brown, Norman, M., and Ellen S. Amatea. *Love and Intimate Relationships*. Philadelphia: Brunner, 2000. Print.

Carlson, Jon, and Len Sperry, eds. *The Intimate Couple*. Philadelphia: Brunner, 1999. Print.

Firestone, Robert W., and Joyce Catlett. *Fear of Intimacy*. Washington: APA, 2000. Print.

Halling, Steen. *Intimacy, Transcendence, and Psychology: Closeness and Openness in Everyday Life*. New York: Palgrave, 2008. Print.

Horstman, Judith. *The Scientific American Book of Love, Sex, and the Brain: The Neuroscience of How, When, Why, and Who We Love*. San Francisco: Jossey-Bass, 2012. Print.

Levine, Suzanne Braun. *How We Love Now: Sex and the New Intimacy in Second Adulthood*. New York: Viking, 2011. Print.

Paludi, Michele Antoinette. *The Psychology of Love*. Santa Barbara: Praeger, 2012. Print.

Prager, Karen J. *The Psychology of Intimacy*. New York: Guilford, 1995. Print.

Sternberg, Robert J., and Karin Weis, eds. *The New Psychology of Love*. New Haven: Yale UP, 2008. Print.

Tulsi B. Saral

SEE ALSO: Affiliation and friendship; Affiliation motive; Attachment and bonding in infancy and childhood; Attraction theories; Codependency; Couples therapy; Emotional intelligence; Father-child relationship; Jealousy; Love; Mother-child relationship; Narcissistic personality disorder; Risk assessment; Self-disclosure; Self-esteem.

Introverts and extroverts

TYPE OF PSYCHOLOGY: Emotion; Personality

The extroversion-introversion dimension has been included in nearly every major taxonomy of personality traits since the middle of the twentieth century. The hypothesized dimension of extroversion is applied to persons who tend to direct their energies outward and to derive gratification from the physical and social environment. The dimension of introversion is applied to individuals whose primary concerns are their own thoughts and feelings. Most theorists today believe that extroversion and introversion exists not as singular types but rather as a collection of different patterns of behavior in that many individuals exhibit aspects of both.

KEY CONCEPTS
- "Big Five"
- Extroversion
- Introversion
- Libido
- Trait

INTRODUCTION
Traditionally, Western philosophy has conceived of two main ways of fulfilling human potential: vita activa and vita contemplativa. Vita activa represented one's being through action, while vita contemplativa represented solitary reflection. The term "introversion" first appeared in the seventeenth century in a purely descriptive sense of turning one's thoughts inward in spiritual contemplation.

Theoretical conceptualizations of extroversion and introversion have gradually and consistently evolved since the 1920s. Today, they are found in nearly every widely used personality inventory. Extroverts are often described by such adjectives as adventurous, assertive, sociable, and talkative. Introverts are often described as being quiet, reserved, and unsociable. Although the constructs of extroversion and introversion are intangible and thus difficult to determine, many personality inventories have been developed to attempt to do so. Most individuals could be located at some point on a broad continuum rather than labeled as clearly an extrovert or an introvert.

PERSONALITY THEORIES
The concepts of introversion and extroversion in their modern psychological sense were introduced by Carl Jung introversion and extroversion in 1910 and were possibly the best-known parts of his system. Jung viewed extroversion-introversion as a bipolar personality dimension along which people can be divided into types, characterized by outward-directedness on one extreme and inward-directedness on the other extreme. Jung did not view introversion and extroversion specifically as personality traits, but rather as different attitudes or orientations. Jung believed that attitudes of extroversion and introversion determine much of people's perception and reaction to the surrounding world.

Extroversion for Jung was the preference for active interaction with others and the environment. Introversion for Jung was characterized by the habitual attitude that preferred introspection and solitary activity. According to Jung, introversion was an orientation inward toward the self.

An important way in which Jung differed from Sigmund Freud was in his conception of the nature of libido. Rather than viewing it exclusively as sexual energy, Jung perceived it as a broad and undifferentiated life energy. In a narrower perspective, libido became the fuel that energized the psyche or personality. It is through this psychic energy that the important psychological activities of perceiving, thinking, and feeling are carried out. As such, the libido could be directed externally toward the outside world (extroversion) or internally toward the self (introversion). Although everyone has the capacity for either attitude, one of them becomes dominant for each individual. At the same time, the nondominant attitude exists and also has the capability of influencing one's behavior. According to Jung, a person is not exclusively extrovert or introvert.

Jung's proposal of extroversion and introversion as two personality types emerged as a single dimension in the analyses of personality as provided by Hans Eysenck in 1947. Eysenck, a German-born British psychologist, is credited with popularizing the terms "introvert" and "extrovert." Eysenck established two dominant factors as being important dimensions of personality, the introversion-extroversion dimension and the neuroticism-stability dimension.

Factor analysis, widely accepted since the 1980s, identified five fundamental dimensions of human personality known as the "Big Five": extroversion, agreeableness, conscientiousness, neuroticism, and openness to experience or intellect. Extensive interest is focused on this five-factor model of personality. Paul Costa and Robert R. McCrae emphasize the Big Five personality theory in their NEO Personality Inventory, which is an extension of their earlier three-factor model (neuroticism, extroversion, and openness).

PRACTICAL APPLICATIONS

An important issue in life-span development is the stability-change issue, which addresses whether an individual can develop into a different personality type or whether there is a tendency for people to remain older renditions of their earlier years. Costa and McCrae concluded that there is considerable stability in the five personality factors, one of which is extroversion.

Some additional areas of research give interesting practical applications of the extroversion-introversion dimension. First is the question of the heritability of the extroversion-introversion variable. Eysenck believed that individual differences in extroversion-introversion were based in biology, although he had little evidence to support this. Since that time, however, a great deal of research has appeared to support his view for the genetic source of introversion/extroversion. A second question is the potential difference between introverts and extroverts in their preference for arousal. Researchers have found that introverted individuals could be characterized as operating at a near-optimal arousal level and are more sensitive to stimulation. The extrovert, however, is always seeking additional stimulation from the environment. A third area of consideration is the question of whether greater happiness can be predicted for introverts or extroverts. Researchers find that extroverts report higher levels of subjective well-being than do introverts.

BIBLIOGRAPHY

Buettner, Dan. "Are Extroverts Happier than Introverts? Insight into Differences between Two Personality Types." *Psychology Today*. Sussex, 14 May 2012. Web. 20 May 2014.

Burger, Jerry M. *Personality*. 8th ed. Belmont: Wadsworth, 2011. Print.

Cain, Susan. *Quiet: The Power of Introverts in a World That Can't Stop Talking*. New York: Crown, 2012. Print.

Cervone, Daniel, and Pervin, Lawrence A. *Personality: Theory and Research*. 12th ed. Hoboken: Wiley, 2013. Print.

Dembling, Sophia. *The Introvert's Way: Living a Quiet Life in a Noisy World*. New York: Penguin, 2012. Print.

Friedman, Howard S., and Miriam W. Schustack. *Personality: Classic Theories and Modern Research*. Boston: Allyn, 2009. Print.

Hogan, Robert, John Johnson, and Stephen Briggs, eds. *Handbook of Personality Psychology*. San Diego: Academic, 1997. Print.

McAdams, Dan P. *The Person: An Integrated Introduction to Personality Psychology*. 5th ed. Hoboken: Wiley, 2009. Print.

Lillian J. Breckenridge

SEE ALSO: Analytical psychology: Carl Jung; Eysenck, Hans; Jung, Carl; Jungian psychology; Neurotic disorders; Personality theory.

J

James, William

BORN: January 11, 1842, in New York, New York
DIED: August 26, 1910, in Chocorua, New Hampshire
IDENTITY: American psychologist
TYPE OF PSYCHOLOGY: Biological bases of behavior; Consciousness; Emotion; Sensation and perception

James popularized a pragmatic approach to psychological issues and a pluralistic view of human experience; he believed that all humans are different and that their varying experiences are equally deserving of respectful study.

William James was oldest son of independently wealthy philosopher Henry James, Sr., and Mary Walsh James. The parents moved their five children from house to house and country to country, unsuccessfully seeking an ideal environment and educational system. The children suffered from lifelong illnesses and depression. In 1861, William James entered Harvard University's Lawrence Scientific School; in 1869, he received a degree from Harvard Medical School. He never practiced. In 1871, he was hired to teach comparative physiology at Harvard. He taught there until 1907, instructing in many aspects of physiology, anatomy, philosophy, and psychology. He lectured extensively in the United States and abroad and produced numerous papers and reviews for both specialized and popular publications.

His first major work was *The Principles of Psychology* (1890). Mind, he argued, is simply a process, a stream of consciousness, constantly changing. What the individual perceives from this stream depends on many things, among them emotions, physical stimuli, and prior experiences. No two persons' perceptions of reality are exactly alike. In such a pluralistic universe, no experiences should be rejected out of hand as invalid. Thus, James's 1896 Lowell Lectures included such subjects as hypnotism, multiple personality, and demoniac possession, and he was involved in psychical investigations. He attacked exploitation of others—lynching and American colonization of the Philippines—and attracted then-unconventional students including W. E. B. Du Bois, Harvard's first African American graduate.

His belief in the right to religious belief is recorded in *The Will to Believe, and Other Essays in Popular Philosophy* (1897), but his rejection of rigid dogma is recorded in his most popular work, *The Varieties of Religious Experience* (1902). Other major works include *Psychology: Briefer Course* (1892; abridgment of *Principles of Psychology*), *Talks to Teachers on Psychology* (1899), *A Pluralistic Universe* (1909), *The Meaning of Truth: A Sequel to "Pragmatism"* (1909), and the posthumous *Essays in Radical Empiricism* (1912). In *Pragmatism: A New Name for Some Old Ways of Thinking* (1907), he argued that action must be evaluated, not by some single absolute standard, but by the usefulness of its consequences and its consistency with facts.

BIBLIOGRAPHY

Fisher, Paul. *House of Wits: An Intimate Portrait of the James* Family. New York: Henry Holt, 2008. Most readable of the several family biographies, it focuses on emotions, illnesses, alcoholism, and possible homosexuality, primarily of Henry and Alice James. Provides valuable historical background. Bibliography.

Richardson, Robert D. *William James: In the Maelstrom of American Modernism*. Boston: Houghton Mifflin, 2006. Densely packed with information, this volume cannot be quickly read, but a detailed index and clear writing style ensure that information can be quickly located and understood. Chronology and family genealogy.

Simon, Linda. *Genuine Reality: A Life of William James*. New York: Harcourt Brace, 1998. Focuses on experiences that led to James's method of making sense of human experience. Lengthy bibliography and family genealogy.

Betty Richardson

SEE ALSO: Attitude formation and change; Consciousness; Emotions; Sensation and perception.

Jealousy

TYPE OF PSYCHOLOGY: Social psychology

Jealousy is the experience of perceiving that one's relationship is threatened; it is influenced by cultural expectations about relationships, self-esteem, and feelings of possessiveness. Jealousy is a common source of conflict, and it can have a destructive impact on relationships.

KEY CONCEPTS
- Dispositional
- Dyadic
- Patrilineage
- Possessiveness
- Socialization

INTRODUCTION

Jealousy is not a single emotion; it is most likely a complex of several emotions whose central theme is the fear of losing to someone else what rightfully belongs to one. In personal relationships, jealousy focuses on fear of losing the partner; the partner is seen as a possession whose ownership is in jeopardy. Whether the threat is real or imaginary, it endangers the jealous person's self-esteem as well as the relationship. Theorists argue that three elements are central to the emotional experience of jealousy: an attachment between two people, valued resources that are exchanged between them, and an intrusion on this attachment by a third person seen to be supplanting the giver or receiver of resources.

Early theories of jealousy suggested that the jealous person fears losing possession; later conceptualizations, however, have specified that jealousy is a fear not of loss of possession but of loss of control. The intrusion of a third party also threatens the cohesiveness of the attachment, dividing partners into opponents. Insofar as the relationship has been integrated into each partner's identity, the intruder threatens not only what the jealous person has but also who he or she is. Most researchers conclude that the experience of jealousy is itself a damaging and destructive relationship event. Emotional bonds are reduced to property rights. Jealousy involves the manipulation of feelings and behaviors, and it can erupt in anger or cause depression. The positive aspects of jealousy are few, but they are identifiable: It intensifies feelings, provides information about the partners, can trigger important discussions between them, and can enhance the jealous person's self-concept.

Research on jealousy has several origins. Anthropologists have long observed dramatic cultural variations in the causes and expressions of jealousy. Psychologists have noted that jealousy has no consistent emotional expression or definition: For some people, jealousy is a version of anger; for others, it resembles sadness, depression, or fear. When research on close relationships began to develop in the 1960s and 1970s, jealousy was found to help explain the dynamics of power and conflict in intimacy. Early research produced the counterintuitive findings that jealousy hinders rather than enhances romantic relationships, and that its roots are not in intimacy but in possessiveness. Jealousy was eventually found to be an aspect of self-esteem and defensiveness rather than a quality of intimacy or dyadic (pertaining to a couple) communication.

Jealousy is more likely when a relationship is intensely valued by someone; the more important it is, the more dangerous would be its loss. Social norms do not support the expression of some forms of jealousy; for example, most cultures do not tolerate expressing jealousy of one's own children. Inexpressible jealousies may be displaced onto the more tolerated forms, such as a couple's sexual relationship. Sexual attraction or behavior is often the focus of jealousy, even though sexual interaction may not be the most valued aspect of a relationship. For example, one gender difference that has been identified in the experience of jealousy in heterosexual relationships is that while men focus on sexual infidelity or intrusion, women express greater jealousy about the emotional attachment between a partner and a rival.

DISPOSITIONAL FACTORS

Dispositional factors in jealousy include feelings of personal insecurity, a poor self-image, and deficient education. Jealous people appear to be unhappy even before they identify a target for their dissatisfaction. Describing oneself as "a jealous person" is related to a negative attributional style; a self-described jealous person sees his or her jealous reaction as stable and uncontrollable, and thus as unlikely to change. Developmental research suggests that jealous emotions originate in childhood when the child's exclusive attachment to the mother outlives the mother's intense bond to the child. Childhood jealousy also manifests itself in rivalry with one's other parent or with siblings, implying that jealousy assumes that love is a finite resource that cannot be shared without diminishment. A common theme in jealousy research is the jealous person's sense of dependence on the threatened relationship, as well as the conviction that he or she is somehow lacking. Before an intrusion appears or is imagined, therefore, a jealous person may already feel inadequate, insecure, and threatened.

Jealousy is also related to possessiveness—the desire to maintain and control a person or resource. Thus, the central issue of relationship jealousy is not love but power and control. Relatively powerful people (in most societies, men rather than women) feel less possessive than those not in power. Circumstances can trigger possessiveness: In all types of relationships studied, one partner feels more possessive when he or she fears that the other might have a meaningful interaction with a third person.

CULTURAL VARIATIONS

Cultural and subcultural norms determine the forms and incidences of jealousy. For both men and women, jealousy is related to the expectation of exclusiveness in a relationship. For men in particular, jealousy is related to gender role traditionalism (adherence to traditional standards of masculinity) and dependence on their partners' evaluations for self-esteem. For women, jealousy is related to dependence on the relationship. With these gender role expectations, individuals decide whether they are "obligated" to feel jealous when the circumstances indicate a threat to self-esteem or intimacy.

Cultures vary widely in the standards and degree of jealousy attached to sexual relationships. Jealousy is rare in cultures that place few restrictions on sexual gratification and do not make marriage or progeny important to social recognition. In contrast, high-jealousy cultures are those that place great importance on control of sexual behavior and identification of patrilineage (the tracing of ancestry by means of the father's family). Cultural researchers conclude that jealousy is not inborn but learned through socialization to what is valued in one's culture. For example, a cultural norm commonly associated with jealousy is monogamy. In monogamous cultures, alternative liaisons are condemned as wrong, and jealousy is seen as a reasonable, vigilant response. In such contexts a double standard is promoted, separating jealousy from envy, a covetous feeling about material property. While envy and greed are considered unacceptable, jealousy is justified as a righteous defense of intimate territory.

JEALOUSY-INDUCING TECHNIQUES

Despite the negative form and consequences of jealousy in most relationships, it is popularly associated with intensity of romantic commitment. Researchers have found that individuals who score high in measures of romanticism believe that jealousy is a desirable reaction in a partner. Perhaps because jealousy is mistakenly believed to strengthen intimacy (although research indicates that it has the opposite effect), some individuals may seek to induce jealousy in their partners. Researchers have found that women are more likely than men to induce jealousy with an expectation of renewed attention or greater control of the relationship. Five jealousy-inducement techniques have been identified: exaggerating a third person's appeal, flirting with others, dating others, fabricating another attachment, and talking about a previous partner. Theorists speculate that the gender difference in jealousy inducement reflects the imbalance of power in male-female relationships. Provoking jealousy may be an attempt to redress other inequities in the relationship.

VARIATIONS IN REACTIONS

Reactions to jealousy vary by age, gender, and culture. Young children may express rage in tantrums or attack the interloping sibling. Research has identified six common responses made by jealous children: aggression, identification with the rival (for example, crying or acting cute like a new baby), withdrawal, repression or feigning apathy, masochism (exaggerating pain to win attention), and creative competition (with the possible outcome of greater self-reliance).

Gender differences in adult jealous reactions include self-awareness, emotional expression, focus of attention, focus of blame, and restorative behavior. When jealous, men are more likely to deny such feelings, while women more readily acknowledge them. Men express jealousy in rage and anger, while women experience depression and fear (that the relationship may end). Men are more likely to blame the third party or the partner, while women blame themselves. Men engage in confrontational behavior and focus on restoring self-esteem. Women intensify possessiveness and focus on strengthening the relationship. In general, these gender differences reflect different sources of jealousy and different emotional and social implications. For most men, a relationship is regarded as a personal possession or resource to be protected with territorial aggression. For most women, a relationship is an extension of the self, a valued opportunity but not a personal right, whose loss is feared and defended with efforts to secure the bonds of attachment. The focus of postjealousy behavior is guided by the resource that is most damaged or threatened by the episode: For men, this is the role of the relationship in supporting self-esteem; for women, it is the health and security of the relationship.

Cultural differences in reacting to jealousy range from extreme violence to dismissive inattention. A jealous Samoan woman might bite her rival on the nose, while a New Mexican Zuñi wife might refuse to do her straying husband's laundry. Cultures may overtly or tacitly condone violence incited by jealous passion. Jealousy has been cited as a justifying factor in many forms of social violence: family murder and suicide, spouse abuse, divorce, depression, and criminal behavior. Despite cultural stereotypes of women as more prone to jealousy, a review of murders committed in a jealous rage has revealed that men are much more likely to commit murder because of feelings of jealousy.

MANAGING JEALOUSY

Researchers have identified positive, constructive approaches to managing jealous experiences. Three broad coping strategies have been identified: self-reliance, self-image improvement, and selective devaluing of the loved one. In the first case, self-reliance involves controlling expressions of sadness and anger, and forging a tighter commitment with one's partner. In the second, one's self-image can be enhanced by making positive social comparisons and identifying and developing one's good qualities. Finally, jealousy can be reduced and the threat eliminated if one convinces oneself that the loved person is not so important after all. These approaches are all popular, but they are not equally effective. Researchers comment that self-reliance works best, selective devaluing is less effective, and self-bolstering does not appear to be effective at all.

LESSONS FROM RESEARCH

Jealousy has gained attention as a social problem because of its implications in criminal behavior and domestic violence. Increases in the rate of domestic assault and murder have warranted a closer examination of the cultural assumptions and stereotypes that support jealous rage and depression. Educational programs to address self-esteem, especially in young children and adolescents, are focusing on jealousy as a symptom of pathology rather than a normal or healthy emotional experience.

Consistent discoveries of cultural differences in patterns of jealous experience have supported the view that jealousy, like many other "natural" relationship phenomena, is learned and acquired through socialization and experience. Thus, jealousy research is contributing to the "demystification" of close relationships—attraction and attachment are not seen as mysterious or fragile processes, but as learned behavior patterns that can be both understood and modified. Jealous individuals can thus be taught to derive their sense of self-esteem or security from more stable, self-controlled sources. Jealousy can be explained as the unhealthy symptom of a treatable complex of emotions, beliefs, and habits. Its contributions to relationship conflict and personal distress can be reduced and its lessons applied to developing healthier attitudes and behaviors. However, a 2013 jealousy research study conducted by the Karolinska Institute of Sweden found that genetics plays a significant role in how and when jealousy manifests.

BIBLIOGRAPHY

Brehm, Sharon S. *Intimate Relationships*. 6th ed. New York: McGraw, 2012. Print.

Buss, David M. *The Dangerous Passion*. New York: Free, 2000. Print.

Clanton, Gordon, and Lynn G. Smith, eds. *Jealousy*. 3rd ed. Washington, DC: UP of America, 1998. Print.

Dandurand, Cathy, and Marie-France Lafontaine. "Jealousy and Couple Satisfaction: A Romantic Attachment Perspective." *Marriage and Family Review* 50.2 (2014): 154–73. Academic Search Alumni Edition. Web. 21 May 2014.

Mattingly, Brent, Diane Whitson, and Melinda Mattingly. "Development of the Romantic Jealousy-Induction Scale and the Motives for Inducing Romantic Jealousy Scale." *Current Psychology* 31.3 (2012): 263–81. Business Source Alumni Edition. Web. 21 May 2014.

Mehta, Vinita. "Who's More Jealous: Men or Women?" *Psychology Today*. Sussex, 28 Aug. 2013. Web. 21 May 2014.

Salovey, Peter, ed. *The Psychology of Jealousy and Envy*. New York: Guilford, 1991. Print.

Walum, Hasse, et al. "Sex Differences in Jealousy: A Population-Based Twin Study in Sweden." *Twin Research and Human Genetics: The Official Journal of the International Society for Twin Studies* 16.5 (2013): 941–47. MEDLINE with Full Text. Web. 21 May 2014.

White, Gregory L., and Paul E. Mullen. *Jealousy: Theory, Research, and Clinical Strategies*. New York: Guilford, 1989. Print.

Wurmser, Léon, and Heidrun Jarass, eds. *Jealousy and Envy: New Views about Two Powerful Feelings*. New York: Analytic, 2008. Print.

Ann L. Weber

SEE ALSO: Attraction theories; Culture and diagnosis; Emotional expression; Emotions; Gender differences; Intimacy; Love; Power; Self-esteem; Sibling relationships; Violence: Psychological causes and effects.

Jung, Carl

BORN: July 26, 1875, in Kesswil, Switzerland
DIED: June 6, 1961, in Küsnacht, Switzerland
IDENTITY: Swiss psychiatrist
TYPE OF PSYCHOLOGY: Personality; Psychopathology; Psychotherapy

Jung is one of the founders of modern psychoanalytic theory.

As a young boy, Carl Jung developed an avid interest in superstition, mythology, and the occult. He attended the University of Basel for medical training in 1895. After earning a medical degree in 1900, Jung was employed as an assistant staff physician at the Burghölzli Mental Hospital. In 1902, he wrote his dissertation on occult phenomena and earned a degree in psychiatry from the University of Zurich.

In 1905, Jung was appointed as the senior staff physician at the Burghölzli Mental Hospital and also became a lecturer on the medical faculty at the University of Zurich. He was instrumental in developing the concept of the autonomous complex and the technique of free association. After he met Sigmund Freud in Vienna in 1907, the two men became close friends and worked together on the advancement of psychoanalytical theories. In 1910, Jung was selected as the first president of the International Psychoanalytic Association.

By 1912, Jung believed that Freud was placing too much emphasis on sexual instincts in human behavior. Their friendship ended in 1913. Jung believed not only in the biological drives but also in metaphysical or spiritual aspirations as an integral part of human individuality. In formulating his theory of the collective unconscious, Jung included patterns of human thought that he called archetypes, which developed through heredity and included spiritual yearnings. He suggested that therapy was a way to bring people into contact with their collective unconscious.

Jung also developed a groundbreaking personality theory that introduced the classification of psychological types into introverts and extroverts. He explained human behavior as a combination of four psychic functions—thinking, feeling, intuition, and sensation—and proposed the concept of individuation,Individuation which is the lifelong process of "self-becoming." Jung coined the term "synchronicity" as an explanation for extrasensory events that were typically deemed occult. He made significant contributions to the understanding of dreams as well as the language and importance of myths and symbols.

Jung published many important works, including *Über die Psychologie der Dementia praecox: Ein Versuch* (1907; *The Psychology of Dementia Praecox*, 1909), *Wandlungen und Symbole der Libido* (1912; *The Psychology of the Unconscious*, 1915), *Psychologische Typen* (1921; *Psychological Types*, 1923), and *Synchronizität als ein Prinzip akausaler Zusammenhange* (1952; *Synchronicity: An Acausal Connecting Principle*, 1955). Honorary doctorates were awarded to Jung from many notable universities, including Harvard. In 1934, he founded the International General Medical Society for Psychotherapy and became its first president. He was awarded the Literature Prize of the city of Zurich in 1932, was made an Honorary Member of the Swiss Academy of Sciences in 1943, and was named the Honorary Citizen of Küsnacht in 1960.

BIBLIOGRAPHY

Blisker, Richard. *On Jung*. Belmont, Calif.: Wadsworth/Thomson Learning, 2002. Insightful work on the life and contributions of Jung to the development of analytic psychology.

Schoeni, William J., ed. *Major Issues in the Life and Work of C. G. Jung*. Lanham, Md.: University Press of America, 1996. Discusses Jung's life and his contributions to Jungian psychology and psychoanalysis.

Shamdasani, Sonu. *Cult Fictions: C. G. Jung and the Founding of Analytical Psychology*. New York: Routledge, 1998. An accurate, revealing account of the history of the Jungian movement in the development of analytical psychology.

Young-Eisendrath, Polly, and Terence Dawson, eds. *The Cambridge Companion to Jung*. 2d ed. New York: Cambridge University Press, 2008. This updated edition of fifteen essays assesses Jung's legacy and shows how his theories apply to modern psychoanalysis.

Includes chronology, bibliography, and glossary.

Alvin K. Benson

SEE ALSO: Analytical psychology: Carl Jung; Archetypes and the collective unconscious; Dreams; Introverts and extroverts; Jungian psychology; Personality theory.

Jungian psychology

DATE: 1912 forward
TYPE OF PSYCHOLOGY: Consciousness; Memory; Personality

Jungian psychology refers to the school of psychology originating with Carl Jung, which attempts to uncover the deep forces underlying human behavior by reconciling the conscious life of the individual with the person's unconscious. A process of psychoanalytical dialogue is used to make the person aware of the symbols of common human experiences, often found in dreams, to achieve positive changes in the individual's personality and behavior.

KEY CONCEPTS
- Anima/animus
- Archetype
- Collective unconscious
- Complexes
- Extroversion/introversion
- Persona
- Personal unconscious
- Self-realization
- Shadow
- Synchronicity

INTRODUCTION
Jungian psychology, also termed analytical psychology, is based on the concept of the collective unconscious and the need for individuals to achieve healthy psychological growth by balancing opposing forces within the personality. This school of psychology stems from the ideas of the Swiss psychiatrist Carl Jung, who early in his career was a close associate of Sigmund Freud. It was termed analytical psychology by Jung to distinguish it from psychoanalysis, a school of psychology founded by Sigmund Freud.

While agreeing with Freud that each individual had a personal unconscious filled with traumas and emotional drives derived from that person's life experiences, Jung introduced a deeper and much more universal consciousness, which he called the collective unconscious. The collective unconscious was derived from experiences dating back to even prehuman evolutionary forms and filled with archetypes (primordial images) that steered human behavior. Such symbols and images could be found throughout history in mythology, art, religion, and dreams. These images cut across time and cultures and were a sort of genetic inheritance for all humans.

Neurosis resulted from blockage of an individual's consciousness from the greater archetypal world. Such disharmony could have negative consequences such as the development of depression or phobias. Jung's basic premise was that the personal unconscious was a vital part of the human psyche and that communication between the conscious and unconscious parts of the psyche was necessary for wholeness. In addition, Jung believed that dreams were one of the main places where the unconscious could find expression.

According to Jung, during the first half of life, individuals establish their own separate identities, often at odds with the larger society. They seek material things, are sexually driven, and are most concerned about benefitting their own children. During this phase, individuals are normally extroverted. They tend to be outgoing and socially oriented. A gradual shift, however, emerges as an individual approaches the age of forty. In this second phase, individuals feel a greater identity with humanity and are more open to collective unconscious. They can experience thoughts and feelings beyond their own individual life, seek answers to the larger questions of life, and attain a higher spiritual plane. In this phase, individuals are introverted. They seek ideas instead of people and withdraw to reflect.

The two distinct phases of life were part of the process of self-realization. To achieve this self-realization, men and women had two separate guides. Jung defined the anima as the unconscious feminine component of men, an inner voice that leads them to their irrational self. Housed in the irrational self are the two basic psychic functions of sensing and intuition. Its counterpart, the animus, was the masculine component in women that led to the rational part of their nature. Residing in the rational part are the other two basic psychic functions of thinking and feeling.

Jung viewed this journey to know the greater self as being at the heart of all major religions and as part of a spiritual development necessary for individual mental wellness. The problem was that these opposite tendencies working within an individual were often difficult to reconcile. He viewed dreams as a compensating factor aiding the reconciliation process to balance opposing forces within the personality. A complicating factor was that Jung viewed all individuals as having shadows. A shadow was an unconscious complex containing repressed aspects of the conscious self. Often a shadow contained the aspects that the individual repressed because they were opposite to the identifications made by the conscious self. Therefore, a kind and gentle person might have harsh and violent aspects of the self repressed in the shadow. Often an individual's shadow appeared in dreams. Meanwhile, the type of person presented to the outside world, termed by Jung to be the persona, is merely the mask a person wears to make a particular impression on others. It is superficial and artificial, conforming to particular demands made by society. It is made up of things such as professional titles and job roles, which have little to do with individual psychological development.

To intervene in the process of normal psychological growth when problems arose, Jung developed techniques to be used by the therapist. Jungian (analytical) psychoanalysis placed the patient in a chair beside an analyst so that they could interact and maintain a dialogue. The aim was to connect patients with their unconscious minds as a source of healing as well as a springboard toward continued psychological growth. In short, by stimulating communication between the conscious and unconscious parts of the human mind, the therapist could stimulate within the individual self-realization and a sense of wholeness.

EARLY HISTORY

Jung was born the only son of a Protestant minister. Many other relatives on both his maternal and paternal side were clergymen, and it was intended that Carl follow a similar path. He attended the University of Basel from 1894 to 1900, and while fascinated by early Christian literature and religion as well as archaeology, he ultimately decided to study medicine. It was during this time that Sigmund Freud's influential work *Die Traumdeutung* (1900; *The Interpretation of Dreams*, 1913) was published. Toward the end of his studies, Jung decided to specialize in the new field of psychiatric medicine. On graduation, Jung interned at the Burghölzli Asylum, which was a psychiatric hospital in Zurich directed by Eugen Bleuler, a leading proponent of the new field of psychoanalysis.

At the hospital, Jung was intrigued by the irrational responses of inmates to simple word stimuli. Awarded his doctor of medicine degree in 1902, Jung continued his research. The results were published in *Studien zur Wort-Association* (1906; *Studies in Word-Association*, 1918), in which he tried to show how words could open repressed psychic groupings in individuals. He termed these groupings "complexes."

A copy of his book was sent to Freud, the leading psychiatrist of the day. This resulted in the two psychiatrists forming a collegial relationship characterized by voluminous correspondence and close collaboration. They worked together and even traveled together in 1911 to the United States to popularize the techniques used in psychoanalysis. The tight relationship ended shortly after Jung published his major work, *Wandlungen und Symbole der Libido* (1912; *The Psychology of the Unconscious*, 1915).

The Psychology of the Unconscious made it clear that Jung had a markedly different view than Freud on the nature of the unconscious. In particular, Jung believed that Freud overestimated the role of childhood sexual conflicts in causing neurosis. Instead, Jung downplayed childhood and stressed lifelong psychological development. Jung's paper, presented at the Fourth International Psychoanalytical Congress, held in September, 1913, at Munich, introduced his new concepts of introverted and extroverted personality types and allied concepts, which horrified Freud. It was the last time the two would meet.

In 1911, before the publication of his work, Jung was elected president of the International Psychoanalytical Society and was viewed as a possible successor to Freud. By 1914, after a two-year break with Freud, Jung resigned from the society. Freud had steered psychiatry toward being established as an empirical science. Jung wanted to integrate into psychiatry an understanding of unconscious realms beyond direct individual experience and an appreciation for the role played by spirituality. His split with Freud did not diminish Jung's stature in the growing field of psychoanalysis. He attracted many students from Europe and the United States, who returned home to popularize what was now termed analytical psychology.

MATURATION OF IDEAS

The break with Freud and the trauma of World War I caused Jung to undergo a nonproductive period of introspection and reflection in the midst of a nervous breakdown. In 1921, he published *Psychologische Typen* (*Psychological Types*, 1923), a highly developed version of concepts introduced in his 1913 paper. The landmark study defined two personality types (extrovert and introvert) and two sets of functions (sensing versus intuitive and thinking versus feeling). Because all took place in either a rational or irrational framework, the end result was Jung's identification of sixteen different types of people. Jung's categories ultimately became the basis for the famous Myers-Briggs Type Indicator, a test that categorized people according to personality type.

During the 1920's, Jung became a world traveler. He journeyed to North Africa, the mountains of Kenya, and New Mexico to study the Pueblo Indians. Jung was seeking not tourist sites but rather archetypes common to primitive peoples that had commonalities with belief systems of more advanced societies. His travels, which were part anthropological and part spiritual in nature, culminated in 1937 with a long visit to India.

Jung's observations were translated first into a collection of essays entitled *Modern Man in Search of a Soul* (1933), then into a lecture series at Yale University on psychology and religion. A major theme of the lectures was that the systematic scrutiny of dreams, art, mythology, and religious beliefs led to a more in-depth understanding of the human psyche. Jung reasoned that it was from archetypes instilled in individuals through the process of evolution that individuals interpreted their own life experiences and developed their own behavior patterns. Jung used archetypal figures such as mother, father, God, hero, wise old man, trickster, and outcast; these became complexes containing both good and bad characteristics and were firmly established in the individual's unconscious since early childhood. Therefore, the mother complex would set off positive symbols such as the earth and goddesses or negatives ones such as witches and dragons. Animals such as the snake and lion, plants such as the lotus and rose, and even objects such as the philosopher's stone and Holy Grail also formed archetypes, as did major events such as birth, marriage, initiation, and death. Jung found that ultimately the self is the major archetype and that the definition of self was always incomplete. However, full development in life necessitated the establishment of psychic harmony and finding a balance between opposing forces. Life's journey for Jung was to meet the self and meet the divine.

Jung's own intellectual journey continued into old age. In 1951, at the age of seventy-six, he developed the important concept of synchronicity, which was defined as the experience of two or more events with unrelated causes occurring together in a meaningful manner. Jung argued in *Synchronizität als ein Prinzip akausaler Zusammenhange* (1952; *Synchronicity: An Acausal Connecting Principle*, 1955) that because of the existence of archetypes and the collective unconscious, which influence perception, events can be grouped by their meaning because of their coincidence in time. His final work was published in 1963, two years after his death. *Erinnerungen, Träume, Gedanken* (with Aniela Jaffé, 1962; *Memories, Dreams, Reflections,* 1963) was autobiographical in nature, relating Jung's childhood, his personal life, and exploration into the psyche. It related his self-growth and his quest to find himself and God.

IMPACT

Jung founded the school of analytical psychology. He authored twenty volumes of works and wrote more than two hundred papers. His followers were numerous, first founding clubs devoted to his thoughts in the 1920's and 1930's, then training institutes after World War II. The first training institute, the Society of Analytical Psychology, was established in London in 1945 by Gerhard Adler, Michael Fordham, and Edward Bennett. Three years later, the Carl Gustav Jung Institute was established in Zurich. During the 1960s and thereafter, training institutes spread worldwide. In the United States, training institutes can be found in New York, San Francisco, Los Angeles, and other major cities. Training and certification is a lengthy process taking four to eight years. Analytical psychology is the subject of French and German scholarly journals and *The Journal of Analytical Psychology*, published since 1955.

Many thousands of therapists internationally practice Jungian psychology. The movement has grown to include at least four major schools of thought. The Classical School, headquartered in Zurich, consists of orthodox Jungists. They try to apply the theories and procedures put forth by Jung in his major works and by his close followers such as Marie-Louise von Franz, Carl Meier, and Edward F. Edinger. The Developmental School, headquartered in London, incorporates many ideas from Freudian psychoanalysis and seeks to merge them with Jungian concepts to find a balanced approach. A leading figure in this movement was Michael Fordham. The Process School seeks to develop an increased awareness of the unconscious using a wide variety of individual and group experiences including physical experiences. It is associated with the Zurich-trained Jungian analyst Arnold Mindell.

The fourth and least structured is the Archetypal School. It is mainly interested in myths, how they relate to the self, and in continuing the quest for continued discovery of what constitutes the archetypal makeup of the human psyche. The continued popularity of this search raises a basic paradox about Jung. Although Jung was a psychiatrist trying to use analytical psychology to help his patients by using the unconscious mind as a means of healing, his writings drew interest from a wide variety of people including theologians, mythologists, literary writers and critics, artists, and filmmakers. It is in this area that Jung has had a far greater impact than Freud. Jung heavily influenced the scholar Mircea Eliade, who wrote numerous studies on myths and chaired the history of religion department at the University of Chicago for almost thirty years. He also had a major influence on Joseph Campbell, whose books on myths became best sellers and the basis for the internationally popular 1987 television series about mythology. Other theorists dealing extensively with myth and deeply influenced by Jung are Erich Neumann, Marie-Louise von Franz, and James Hillman.

Critics of Jungian psychology focus on his theory of the collective unconscious, claiming that it is overly general and based on ethnically narrow evidence drawn from a cross-section of Indo-European cultures. They also point to gender bias in drawing symbols from overwhelmingly male experiences. Jungian psychology is also denounced as nonempirical in its linkage of myths to patients' dreams. However, Jung's theories of personality, his division of people into extroverts and introverts, and his personality classifications of thinking, feeling, sensing, and intuiting, which are based on empirical observations, are widely accepted. They are widely used by psychologists today particularly in the form of the Myers-Briggs Type Indicator, which, after more than fifty years, continues to be the most trusted and widely used assessment for identifying individual personality differences and uncovering new ways to work and interact with others.

BIBLIOGRAPHY

Aziz, Robert. C. G. *Jung's Psychology of Religion and Synchronicity*. Albany: State U of New York P, 1990. Print.

Cambray, Joseph. *Analytical Psychology: Contemporary Perspectives in Jungian Analysis*. New York: Routledge, 2004. Print.

Campbell, Joseph, ed. *The Portable Jung*. New York: Penguin, 1976. Print.

Jung, C. G., William McGuire, and Sonu Shamdasani. *Introduction to Jungian Psychology: Notes of the Seminar on Analytical Psychology Given in 1925*. Princeton: Princeton UP, 2012. Print.

Miller, Jeffrey C. *The Transcendent Function: Jung's Model of Psychological Growth Through Dialogue with the Unconscious*. Albany: State U of New York P, 2004. Print.

Noll, Richard. *The Jung Cult: Origins of a Charismatic Movement*. New York: Free Press, 1997. Print.

Papadopolous, Renos K. *Handbook of Jungian Psychology: Theory, Practice, and Applications*. New York: Routledge, 2006. Print.

Quenk, Naomi L. *Essentials of Myers-Briggs Type Indicator Assessment*. New York: Wiley, 2009. Print.

Stein, Murray. *Jungian Psychoanalysis: Working in the Spirit of C. G. Jung*. Chicago: Open Court, 2010. Print.

Stevens, Anthony. *Jung on Jung*. Princeton: Princeton UP, 1999. Print.

Wehr, Gerhard. *Jung: A Biography*. Boston: Shambahla, 2001. Print.

Withers, Robert. *Controversies in Analytical Psychology*. New York: Routledge, 2003. Print.

Irwin Halfond

SEE ALSO: Analytical psychology: Jacques Lacan; Analytical psychology: Carl Jung; Analytical psychotherapy; Archetypes and the collective unconscious; Dreams; Freud, Sigmund; Freudian psychology; Introverts and extroverts; Jung, Carl; Lacan, Jacques; Myers-Briggs Type Indicator (MBTI); Personality rating scales; Personality theory; Psychoanalytic psychology; Religion and psychology.

Juvenile delinquency and development

DATE: 1899–

TYPE OF PSYCHOLOGY: Developmental psychology; Social psychology

The term juvenile delinquency refers to criminal actions committed by individuals who are not yet considered to be adults. However, the juvenile justice system deals with three types of young people: juvenile criminal offenders, status offenders, and children in need of services.

KEY CONCEPTS

- Balanced and restorative justice
- Children in need of services
- Juvenile justice system
- Resiliency
- Status offenders
- Waiver to adult court

INTRODUCTION

The first juvenile court was founded in Cook County, Chicago, in 1899. Before that time, children over the age of seven were treated as adults in criminal court. They were tried as adults, sentenced as adults, and served their time in adult facilities. The juvenile court sought to act in the best interest of the child and had the goal of keeping children out of the adult criminal justice system. Early reformers saw the adult criminal system as being harmful to young people and actually being responsible for turning youthful offenders into hardened criminals. These reformers felt that juveniles, because of their age, could be rehabilitated and become contributing citizens.

The juvenile court systems that were established in jurisdictions throughout the United States were very different from the criminal courts that tried adult cases. Unlike criminal courts, juvenile courts do not have the burden of establishing proof beyond a reasonable doubt. The lesser standard of preponderance of evidence is used. Juvenile courts are not open to the public for inspection. This shields the juveniles from the detrimental effects of being known as an offender. The juvenile court process is not meant to be an adversarial process but, much like therapeutic jurisprudence in the adult system, is meant to work toward the outcome that is in the best interest of the juvenile. Historically, the judge has acted more as a parent toward the wayward juvenile than as a judge handing out sentences.

Initially, the granting of even limited constitutional rights was seen as anathema to the juvenile system. However, while juvenile court judges were supposed to look out for the best interests of the juveniles who came into their courtrooms, this was not always what transpired. There were serious problems with the protection and care that juvenile courts gave. Juveniles were often punished more harshly than adults would be for similar actions. Many young people were given punishments based more on their ethnicity, race, and socioeconomic status than on the offense that had been committed. By the 1960s, it was clear to many that the juvenile system did not look after the interests of all juveniles equally

and the Supreme Court, through a series of landmark decisions, extended some (although not all) due process rights to juveniles.

TYPES OF JUVENILES IN THE SYSTEM

The juvenile court system handles three types of juveniles: juvenile criminal offenders, status offenders, and children in need of services. Juvenile criminal offenders are juveniles who have committed actions that would be criminal even for an adult, such as theft, robbery, rape, or murder. In some cases, juvenile cases may be waived, or transferred, to adult court. There are four ways this can occur: judicial waiver (the judge has the power to waive the juvenile to adult court), statutory exclusion (certain offenses are automatically waived to adult court), direct file (prosecutor may request that the case be waived to adult court), and demand waiver (the juvenile's attorney may request that the case be waived to adult court). The demand waiver is most often done so that the juvenile has access to all constitutional protections afforded to adults. About half of the states place the lower age limit for transfer to adult court at fourteen or fifteen years of age. A significant portion of the remaining states have no lower age limit for transfer to adult court, and children as young as ten and eleven have been tried as adults. However, there are problems with transferring juveniles to adult court. Juveniles who are transferred to adult court have higher rates of recidivism than those who remain in the juvenile court. Juveniles who are sent to adult correctional institutions are more likely to be victimized while incarcerated. Once a juvenile is in the adult system, rehabilitation is far less likely.

Status offenders have engaged in behavior that is not allowed because of their age, such as skipping school or running away—actions that would not be illegal for an adult. It is important for the system to deal with status offenders in a different manner than juvenile criminal offenders. If possible, formal processing of these juveniles and contact with juvenile criminal offenders should be avoided.

Children in need of services (also referred to as children in need of supervision and children in need of protection) are not delinquent but rather have been victims of neglect or abuse and come into the system to be protected. Abuse can take a variety of forms, from sexual to physical to emotional. The majority of all cases of child abuse consist of instances of neglect. Neglect can take many forms, including failure to provide food, shelter, clothing, education, or medical needs.

TREATING JUVENILE OFFENDERS

The earlier intervention can begin with a juvenile, the better. Too often, juveniles are not referred for treatment until they have committed several serious offenses; by then rehabilitation is a much more difficult task. The best approach focuses on prevention at one of three stages: before any sort of negative behavior, after some minor negative behavior has occurred but before serious delinquent behavior, and after serious delinquent behavior has begun.

Programs may be geared toward youths in general and may focus on building strengths and resiliency. These aim at helping youths to be the best they can be and to never engage in delinquent behavior. Resiliency research looks at ways to make delinquency less likely by helping young people to focus on their strengths rather than their deficits. Programs can help young people develop skills in academics, sports, and the arts.

Prevention programs may focus on young people who have committed less serious offenses, often status offenses—skipping school or running away. The goal is to prevent any more serious delinquent behavior from occurring. Research has shown that the single most predictive factor in later delinquency is school failure. Interventions designed to help young people succeed in school, reduce truancy, and remain in school can be highly successful. Juveniles who run away, especially female juveniles, often do so to avoid abuse within the home. Programs should address these girls' unique needs and not necessarily return them to the abusive environment from which they came or criminalize their behavior.

Prevention programs can address the needs of the juvenile offender who has already engaged in serious delinquent behavior. These programs must be comprehensive and consistent, providing counseling, sanctions and supervision. Because of their age and the importance of the family unit to the lives of juveniles, the family should be actively involved in interventions.

Juvenile justice agencies and practitioners have moved toward a model of balanced and restorative justice. This model balances the rehabilitation of the offender with concern for the safety and well-being of the victim and the community. Balanced and restorative justice sees crime as a break in the relationship that society has with the offender. The goal of the balanced and restorative justice approach is to rehabilitate and reintegrate the offender into the community. Offenders must take responsibility for their actions and repair the harm caused by their crime.

MYTHS OF JUVENILE DELINQUENCY

Not only the general public but also many criminal justice students believe that juvenile crime rates are rising and spiraling out of control. In fact, there was a steady increase in juvenile crimes until the mid-1990s, at which time the rates began to fall. According to statistics from the Office of Juvenile Justice and Delinquency Prevention, from 1996, when it peaked, to 2011, the juvenile arrest rate declined 48 percent.

While juvenile crime rates were rising in the early 1990s, many people feared that younger and younger juveniles were committing more and more violent and serious crimes. However, even as juvenile crime rates were on the rise, most juvenile offenses were property crimes and not violent offenses. One outcome of this myth was that it became more common to waive juveniles to adult court.

A common misconception is that waiver to adult court is used to process only the most serious and violent juvenile offenders. Statistically, however, more than half of juvenile offenders who are subject to waiver have committed property crimes and not violent offenses. Far from serving as a deterrent to these or other juveniles, being sent to an adult facility increases the likelihood of recidivism.

BIBLIOGRAPHY

Ellis, Rodney A., and Karen M. Sowers. *Juvenile Justice Practice: A Cross-Disciplinary Approach to Intervention.* Thousand Oaks: Sage, 2001. Print.

Farrington, David P., and Rolf Loeber. *From Juvenile Delinquency to Adult Crime: Criminal Careers, Justice Policy, and Prevention.* New York: Oxford UP, 2012. eBook Collection (EBSCOhost). Web. 21 May 2014.

Fuller, John Randolph. *Juvenile Delinquency: Mainstream and Crosscurrents.* Upper Saddle River: Prentice, 2009. Print.

Greenwald, Ricky. *Trauma and Juvenile Delinquency: Theory, Research, and Interventions.* Hoboken: Taylor, 2014. eBook Collection (EBSCOhost). Web. 21 May 2014.

Howell, J. C. *Preventing and Reducing Juvenile Delinquency: A Comprehensive Framework.* Thousand Oaks: Sage, 2003. Print.

Office of Juvenile Justice and Delinquency Prevention. http://ojjdp.ncjrs.org.

Ryan, Joseph P., Abigail B. Williams, and Mark E. Courtney. "Adolescent Neglect, Juvenile Delinquency, and the Risk of Recidivism." *Journal of Youth and*

Adolescence 42.3 (2013): 454–65. MEDLINE Complete. Web. 21 May 2014.

Sharp, P. M., and B. W. Hancock. *Juvenile Delinquency: Historical, Theoretical, and Societal Reactions to Youth.* 2d ed. Upper Saddle River: Prentice, 1998. Print.

Sickmund, M., Sladky, A., and Kang, W. "Easy Access to Juvenile Court Statistics: 1985–2010." *National Center for Juvenile Justice.* National Juvenile Court Data Archive, 2013. Web. 21 May 2014.

Ayn Embar-Seddon O'Reilly and Allan D. Pass

SEE ALSO: Adolescence: Cognitive skills; Bullying; Child abuse; Children's mental health; Family life: Children's issues; Teenagers' mental health.

K

Kelly, George A.

BORN: April 28, 1905
DIED: March 7, 1967
IDENTITY: American theorist and leader in clinical psychology
BIRTHPLACE: Perth, Kansas
PLACE OF DEATH: Waltham, Massachusetts
TYPE OF PSYCHOLOGY: Personality; Psychotherapy

Kelly was the founder of the psychology of personal constructs.

George A. Kelly's early years of education largely consisted of homeschooling from his parents and were followed by his earning degrees in a wide variety of fields. He studied physics and mathematics at Park College, Kansas (BA, 1926), educational sociology at the University of Kansas (MA, 1928), education at Edinburgh University in Scotland (BEd, 1930), and psychology at the University of Iowa (PhD, 1931). His first professional position was at Kansas State College in 1931, where he stayed until entering the US Navy in 1943. After the end of World War II in 1945, he spent a year at the University of Maryland, and then became professor and director of the clinical psychology training program at Ohio State University. From 1965 to 1967, he held the Riklis Chair of Behavioral Science at Brandeis University.

Kelly's views are not easily assimilated into other approaches to psychology, for he was an independent and original thinker. In his massive two-volume *Psychology of Personal Constructs* (1955), he treated persons as if they were scientists trying to develop a theory (test hypotheses) about the world in which they lived. He tried to understand individuals not from their current environment or past history, but from their subjective or interpretative viewpoint—the hypotheses they had constructed about what was happening to them.

An individual's theory (constructs or interpretations of the real world) was ever-changing, and no one construct was useful for more than a limited range of circumstances or time. For Kelly, individuals were not merely passive victims of the past (as with psychodynamic psychology) or of the current environment (as with behaviorism) but were active and responsible individuals who could change the circumstances they faced by reinterpreting them. Kelly developed a technique for assessing constructs, thereby permitting many applications to personality theory, psychotherapy, business, and education.

Kelly was also a pioneer in developing psychological services for rural areas, a leader in the establishment of psychologists as independent practitioners, and a central figure in the planning of the most widely used clinical training model (the Boulder Model). He died of a heart attack in 1967. The threads of his contributions may be found in the contemporary perspective called constructionism. His influence continues with each issue of the *Journal of Constructionist Psychology*.

BIBLIOGRAPHY
Caputi, Peter, Heather Foster, and Linda L. Viney, eds. *Personal Construct Psychology: New Ideas*. Hoboken: Wiley, 2006. Print.
Caputi, Peter, Linda L. Viney, Beverly M. Walker, and Nadia Crittenden, eds. *Personal Construct Methodology*. Malden: Wiley, 2012. Print.
Fransella, Fay. *George Kelly*. Thousand Oaks: Sage, 1995. Print.
Mischel, Walter. "Looking for Personality." *A Century of Psychology as Science*. Ed. Sigmund Koch and David Leary. Washington, DC: American Psychological Assn., 1992. Print.
Neimeyer, Robert R., and Thomas T. Jackson. "George A. Kelly and the Development of Personal Construct Psychology." *Pictorial History of Psychology*. Ed. Wolfgang G. Bringman, Helmut E. Luck, Rudolf Miller, and Charles E. Early. Chicago: Quintessence, 1997. Print.

Terry J. Knapp

SEE ALSO: Constructivist psychotherapy; Personal constructs: George A. Kelly; Personality theory.

Kinesthetic memory

TYPE OF PSYCHOLOGY: Cognition; Developmental psychology; Learning; Memory; Sensation and perception; Social psychology

Kinesthetic memory refers to how muscles remember movements and is an essential for normal motor activity and learning.

KEY CONCEPTS
- Body
- Cerebellum
- Learning
- Memory
- Motor movement
- Muscle
- Retention
- Sensation
- Sequences

INTRODUCTION

Movement is central to sustaining life and fostering learning. Humans learn by kinesthetic, visual, or auditory methods, known as modalities, of processing sensory information. Each learning style engages a specific part of the brain to acquire, process, and store data. Educators develop teaching objectives compatible with students' learning styles. Although the majority of people, approximately 65 percent, tend to learn best with visual memory, and 20 percent learn best through auditory memory, the 15 percent of humans who function best with kinesthetic memory usually retain information longer according to Bettina Lankard Brown for the Educational Resources Information Center (1998).

Kinesthetic memories are primarily stored in the cerebellum. This part of the brain has less risk for injury than the neocortex and hippocampus, which are involved in visual and auditory learning processes. Although kinesthetic memory is basic to the motions involved in writing, it is often ineffective for people attempting to comprehend academic topics. Kinesthetic types of learning are more suitable for mastering physical movements in sports and dance and in performance control such as playing instruments or singing.

Kinesthetic memory is fundamental to motor activity. Muscles in people and animals recall previous movements according to how body parts such as joints, bones, ligaments, and tendons interact and are positioned.

This innate memory of relationships and sequences is the basis of motor skills such as writing or riding a bicycle. Because the brain relies on kinesthetic memory, it does not have to concentrate on how to move body parts. Instead, the brain can be focused for more complex thought processes and enhancement or refinement of movements.

Proprioception, the unconscious knowledge of body placement and a sense of the space it occupies, benefits from kinesthetic memory. Bodies are able to coordinate sensory and motor functions because of proprioception so that reflexes in response to stimuli can occur. These innate motor abilities help most organisms to trust that their bodies will behave as expected.

People have been aware of elements of kinesthetic memory since the late nineteenth century. Teacher Anne Sullivan used tactile methods to teach Helen Keller words. Keller, who was blind, deaf, and mute, touched objects, and kinesthetic sensations guided her to remember meanings. Educators have recognized the merits of kinesthetic learning to assist students, both children and adults, with reading difficulties. Kinesthetic memory has also been incorporated into physical therapies.

MEASURING MEMORY

Kinesthetic memory is crucial for people to function proficiently in their surroundings. Measurement of kinesthetic memory is limited by clinical tools and procedures. Researchers are attempting to develop suitable tests to comprehend the role of kinesthetic memory in maintaining normal motor control for physical movement. Psychologists Judith Laszlo and Phillip Bairstow designed a ramp device that measures motor development and kinesthetic acuity in subjects' upper extremities but not in specific joints. Kinesthetic acuity is how well people can describe the position of their body parts when their vision is obscured.

Some investigators considered Laszlo and Bairstow's measurement method insufficient to examine some severely neurologically impaired patients, and it was revised to gauge nervous system proprioceptive deficiencies. Researchers at the University of Michigan-Flint's Physical Therapy Laboratory for Cumulative Trauma Disorders adjusted ramp angles of laboratory devices in an attempt to create a better kinesthetic testing tool.

Kinesthetic studies examine such variables as gender and age and how they affect perception and short- and long-term kinesthetic memory. Results are applied to create more compatible learning devices and techniques that enhance information retention and recollection. Researchers sometimes assess how vibration of tendons and muscles or anesthesia of joints affects movement perceptions. Studies evaluate how kinesthetic stimuli affect awareness of size, length, and distance.

Kinesthetic memory tests indicate that kinesthetic performance varies according to brain characteristics and changes. Some tests involve tracing patterns at intervals during one week. Subjects are evaluated for how accurate their perceptions and memory of the required movements are from one testing session to the next. Such studies have shown that as people age, their kinesthetic memory capabilities decline. Mental health professionals seek treatment for brain injuries that result in ideomotor apraxia, a memory loss for sequential movements, and ideational apraxia, the breakdown of movement thought.

INTELLECTUAL APPLICATIONS

Some educational specialists hypothesize that people with dyslexia might lack sufficient kinesthetic memory to recognize and form words. Some dyslexia treatments involve strengthening neural pathways with physical activity to reinforce kinesthetic memory. As a result, some processes become instinctive and the brain can concentrate on understanding academic material and behaving creatively.

Teachers can help students acquire cursive handwriting skills by practicing unisensory kinesthetic trace techniques. Touch is the only sense students are permitted to use with this method, which develops kinesthetic memory for future writing. Blindfolded students trace letters with their fingers in a quiet environment. They repeat these hand and arm movements to form letters, then words. Muscular memories of these movements and body positions improve motor control for writing.

Kinesthetic-tactile methods are applied with some visual and auditory learning styles. In 1943 Grace Fernald introduced her method, VAKT, which used visual, auditory, kinesthetic, and tactile tasks simultaneously during stages of tracing, writing, and pronouncing. Margaret Taylor Smith established the Multisensory Teaching Approach (MTA). Beth Slingerland created the Slingerland Approach, which integrates all sensory learning styles, including kinesthetic motor skills.

Memorization is a fundamental part of musical activities. Singers rely on kinesthetic memory of throat muscles to achieve their desired vocal range and performance.

Musicians develop kinesthetic memory skills by practicing pieces without visual cues to avoid memory lapses due to performance anxiety. Panic or nervousness can disrupt kinesthetic memories unless performers develop methods to deal with their fears or excitement.

Studies indicate that kinesthetic memory provokes signals that influence people's memory. In particular, one study investigated how cues acquired during a learning process affect how people retain memories. Researchers focused on how people interacted with computers, specifically how the use of a pointing device, such as a mouse, and touchscreens affected retention of information viewed on computer screens. Pressing touchscreens, for instance, to control information contributed to increased spatial memory.

BODY INTELLIGENCE

Kinesthetic memory guides children to develop control over their bodies. Jay A. Seitz, of York College/City University of New York, emphasizes that conventional intellectual assessments of children ignore bodily-kinesthetic intelligence. He argues that kinesthetic education, particularly in the mastery of aesthetic movements, is essential to balance traditional Western formal education, which focuses on cognitive linguistic and logical-numerical skills. Many educators consider those skills superior to other means of expressing intelligence. Seitz states that kinesthetic skills such as those developed by dance have significant cognitive aspects that can enhance academic curricula and children's intellectual growth.

Jean Piaget stressed that movement is an important factor in children's early learning development. Infants' sensorimotor experiences provide foundational knowledge for speech. Harvard University professor Howard Gardner built on Piaget's premise by focusing on how people become skilled in coordinating their movements, manipulating items, and managing situations competently, what he terms bodily kinesthetic intelligence.

Kinesthetic memory is one of three main cognitive skills associated with bodily kinesthetic intelligence. Muscle memory allows people to use their bodies artistically to perform desired motion patterns, imitate movements, and create new nonverbal physical expressions. Motor logic and kinesthetic awareness supplement kinesthetic memory and regulate neuromuscular organization and presentation in such physical forms as rhythmic movement sequences and posture. Muscles and tendons have sensory receptors that aid kinesthetic awareness.

Seitz investigated how people use gestures to think and to express themselves. He emphasized that movement is the product of intellectual activity and can be recorded in kinesic language such as choreography, which describes dance sequences. Seitz conducted a qualitative and quantitative analysis of formal and informal dance classes to determine how children use kinesthetic sense and memory and motor logic to learn increasingly complicated dance routines. He noted that children aged three to four years have awareness of movement dynamics such as rhythm and balance.

After being taught simple choreography such as a butterfly-shaped pattern, children were asked to repeat the pattern five minutes later for a kinesthetic memory test. They were also asked to demonstrate a possible final gesture to a pantomime, such as pretending to throw a ball, as a motor logic test. The children were also shown pictures of people, structures, or items and asked to use their bodies to show what movements they associated with the images. All tests were videotaped to assess how children copied, created, or finished movements or the degree to which they failed.

Some children who lack motor skill competence have developmental coordination disorder (DCD), which was first classified in the fourth edition of the *Diagnostic and Statistical Manual of Mental Disorders* (1994, DSM-IV) and is included in the fifth edition, DSM-5. Authorities disagree whether DCD is caused by kinesthetic or visual perceptual dysfunction. Some tests reveal that children who have DCD might not kinesthetically rehearse memories they acquire visually. Laszlo and Bairstow developed kinesthetic sensitivity tests to assess subjects' motor skills in processing information such as the position and movement of limbs. Kinesthetic perceptual problems result in clumsy movements. Therapists advocating the kinesthetic training approach encourage children to practice movements and develop better body awareness to refine motor skills.

THERAPY

Kinesthetic memory contributes to physical fitness and the prevention of injuries. Researchers in the fields of kinesiology and biomechanics study how people move and incorporate kinesthetic concepts. Many athletes participate in Prolates, or progressive Pilates, which is a kinesthetically based conditioning program designed to achieve balance of muscle systems and body awareness of sensations and spatial location. Prolates practitioners view the human body as a unified collection of connected parts that must smoothly function together to achieve coordination, flexibility, and efficiency and to reduce stress.

This exercise program develops the mind-body relationship with movement visualization and concentration skills practice so people can instinctively sense how to fix athletic problems using appropriate muscles instead of repeatedly rehearsing mechanics. Prolates requires participants to achieve control of their center of gravity during diverse movements, thus refining kinesthetic memory. Athletes automatically adjust their physical stance when details about muscles are conveyed to the brain by proprioceptors, which are enhanced by Prolates.

Aquatic proprioceptive neuromuscular facilitation (PNF) is a movement therapy. This treatment helps fibromyalgia sufferers learn appropriate movement patterns to replace damaging behaviors such as clenching teeth, raising shoulders, and other excessive and unconscious muscle contractions and tensions that people use to deal with chronic pain and emotional stimuli. They also learn more efficient breathing techniques.

Erich Fromm encouraged the use of visual kinesthetic dissociation (V/KD), which is a therapy designed to help patients attain detachment from kinesthetic memories acquired traumatically, through physical abuse or rape. Therapists initiate V/KD by asking patients to act as observers, not participants, as though they are watching a movie, not acting in it, as they recall the traumatic experiences in their imagination. By paying attention to visual and auditory cues, patients gradually release kinesthetic memories. Sometimes, therapists ask the patients to play the scenes backward to reinforce nonkinesthetic memories and develop sensations of being empowered and competent.

BIBLIOGRAPHY

Crawley, Sharon J. *Remediating Reading Difficulties.* 6th ed. New York: McGraw, 2012. Print.

Floyd, R. T. *Manual of Structural Kinesiology.* 18th ed. New York: McGraw, 2012. Print.

Jamison, Lynette, and David Ogden. *Aquatic Therapy Using PNF Patterns.* Tucson: Therapy Skill Builders, 1994. Print.

Laszlo, Judith I., and Phillip J. Bairstow. *Perceptual Motor Behavior: Developmental Assessment and Therapy.* New York: Praeger, 1985. Print.

Messing, Lynn, and Ruth Campbell, eds. *Gesture, Speech, and Sign.* Oxford: Oxford UP, 2004. Print.

Seitz, Jay A. "I Move . . . Therefore I Am." *Psychology Today* 26.2 (1993): 50–55. Print.

Sheets-Johnstone, Maxine. "Kinesthetic Memory: Further Critical Reflections and Constructive Analyses." *Body Memory, Metaphor, and Movement.* Eds. Sabine C. Koch, Thomas Fuchs, Michela Summa, and Cornelia Muller. Vol. 84. Amsterdam: Benjamins, 2012. 43–72. Print.

Wing, Alan M., Patrick Haggard, and J. Randall Flanagan, eds. *Hand and Brain: The Neurophysiology and Psychology of Hand Movements.* San Diego: Academic, 1996. Print.

Elizabeth D. Schafer

See Also: Brain structure; Depth and motion perception; Memory; Memory: Animal research; Memory: Empirical studies; Memory: Physiology; Memory: Sensory; Memory storage; Motor development; Sensation and perception.

Kinsey, Alfred

Born: June 23, 1894, in Hoboken, New Jersey
Died: August 25, 1956, in Bloomington, Indiana
Identity: American sexologist and zoologist
Type of psychology: Psychological methodologies

Kinsey's survey research in human sexuality revealed the diversity of sexual behavior and helped launch a sexual revolution.

Alfred Kinsey grew up in an extremely restrictive Methodist family. His father forbade dating, and Kinsey's keen interest in sexuality may have stemmed from the frustration that this produced. After earning his bachelor's degree at Bowdoin College, Kinsey did graduate work in entomology at Harvard. After earning his doctorate, Kinsey was employed at Indiana University as a professor in zoology. In 1938, a group of female students, perhaps at Kinsey's request, petitioned the university to offer a course on marriage and the family. The university president chose Kinsey to teach the course. He later claimed that his study of human sexuality was fueled by the paucity of data that he encountered while teaching the course.

Kinsey began to gather sexual histories from students and, with funding from external sources, established the Institute for Sexual Research in 1942. He and his colleagues then began extensive surveying, questioning several thousand persons over the next few years. The surveys were conducted orally, with the interviewers asking direct, memorized questions in a rapid fashion. Kinsey developed techniques designed to improve honesty and establish rapport with participants; he often altered his speech habits, dress, and behavior to match those of his interviewees.

The surveys became the basis of Kinsey's most famous work, *Sexual Behavior in the Human Male* (1948), which sold nearly 500,000 copies and offended the staid sexual attitudes of the time. The book and its companion, *Sexual Behavior in the Human Female* (1953), presented data and discussion of previously taboo topics such as masturbation, homosexual behavior, and oral sex. Kinsey's research indicated that such behaviors were far more common than expected. For example, he reported that more than 90 percent of males and 58 percent of adult females had engaged in masturbation. About half of surveyed females admitted to premarital sex. Critics validly objected that his sample, while large, was biased, with college-educated whites being overrepresented. Kinsey also endured many personal attacks and threats from conservative groups. The Rockefeller Foundation terminated its funding of his institute in 1954. Kinsey's death may have been hastened by the relentless attacks.

Kinsey is still a controversial figure. There is considerable evidence that Kinsey did engage in several homosexual affairs and that he encouraged his wife to have sexual encounters with other men. To some, these revelations arouse suspicion concerning his data and threaten the integrity of his work. However, many other sexologists have reported findings that generally support Kinsey's work.

BIBLIOGRAPHY

Christenson, Cornelia V. *Kinsey: A Biography.* Bloomington: Indiana University Press, 1971. Written by a colleague of Kinsey, this book includes many personal insights.

Gathorne-Hardy, Jonathan. *Sex the Measure of All Things: A Life of Alfred C. Kinsey.* Bloomington: Indiana University Press, 2004. An exhaustively researched effort that argues that Kinsey was a diligent and reputable researcher despite his atypical sexual life

Jones, James H. *Alfred C. Kinsey: A Public/Private Life.* New York: W. W. Norton, 2004. Often questions Kinsey's scientific integrity and the validity of his work.

Charles H. Evans

SEE ALSO: Gay, lesbian, bisexual, and transgender mental health; Homosexuality; Sadism and masochism; Sexual behavior patterns; Sexual dysfunction; Sexual variants and paraphilias; Survey research: Questionnaires and interviews.

Kleptomania

TYPE OF PSYCHOLOGY: Cognition; Psychopathology

Kleptomania is an impulse control disorder wherein an individual is unable to resist the repetitive impulse to steal objects that the individual does not need. Although associated with depression and anxiety, kleptomania has no clear causes or treatments.

KEY CONCEPTS

- Behavioral therapy
- Chemical imbalance theory
- Covert sensitization
- Impulse control disorder
- Psychotherapy

INTRODUCTION

Kleptomania is one of five impulse control disorders (ICDs) that also include pyromania (compulsively setting fires), pathological gambling, trichotillomania (pulling out one's hair), and intermittent explosive disorder, which involves incidents of aggression toward other people. An estimated 1 to 3 percent of the world's population suffers from one of these disorders; more women than men develop kleptomania, although fewer than 5 percent of shoplifters are believed to suffer from kleptomania.

Perceptions of impulsive control disorders, or impulsive behaviors, and their origins have changed dramatically throughout history. The Greek doctor Hippocrates believed they were caused by an excess of yellow bile, a bodily fluid thought to produce impulsiveness. German Protestant Reformation leader Martin Luther exhorted his congregation to shun impulses, presumed to be harmful, while the founder of modern psychology, Sigmund Freud, insisted that impulses are common to all individuals and, as such, are neither good nor bad. Most of the research on impulse control disorders was carried out in the early twentieth century, and the third edition of the *Diagnostic and Statistical Manual of Mental Disorders* (1980, DSM-III), a record of all known mental and psychological disorders, began to list impulse control disorders among them.

The manual's criteria for diagnosing kleptomania are specific: individuals repeatedly fail to resist impulses to steal items for no material gain; great irritation occurs before individuals begin the theft; individuals feel pleasure, gratification, or relief as they commit the theft; individuals do not steal to express anger or vengeance; and the individuals who steal are not diagnosed with antisocial personality disorders.

However, the causes of kleptomania are far less defined. Although early views of kleptomania generally held that those with the disorder were seemingly "normal" people with impulses to steal, more recent research indicates that kleptomania or any impulse control disorder is not a lone disorder. Women make up 80 percent of the total number of known kleptomaniacs, and many of their medical records document troubled histories of depression, self-loathing, and suicidal tendencies. Others show patterns of early pain, emotional loss, and identity confusion, although it is not known how these traumas connect with kleptomania.

In the pursuit of causes for kleptomania, attention is directed toward the chemical makeup of the brain. Brain chemistrykleptomaniaThe chemicals serotonin, norepinephrine, and dopamine are neurotransmitters that influence judgment and feelings, so any imbalance in the levels of these chemicals can produce impulsivity. Also, genetic research has determined that impulsivity tends to extend through an entire family.

TREATMENT

Treatment of kleptomania is difficult because most kleptomaniacs are never arrested or come forward for treatment. Families inhibit identification or treatment of the family member out of shame and efforts to maintain secrecy; and many victims who begin treatment often drop out before any real benefits are achieved. Also, because most kleptomaniacs or people with other impulse control disorders suffer from additional psychological disorders, no single medication is available for treatment of any impulse control disorder.

Because depression, anxiety, and mood swings usually accompany kleptomania, antidepressants are most commonly prescribed for it in an effort to relieve the depression and self-loathing that prompts the act of stealing. Selective serotonin reuptake inhibitors (SSRIs), less harmful in the case of an overdose, are prescribed with increasing frequency in cases of impulse control disorders, as are mood stabilizers, which can have serious side effects. However, most medications have mixed results

DSM-IV-TR CRITERIA FOR KLEPTOMANIA (DSM CODE 312.32)

Recurrent failure to resist impulses to steal objects that are not needed for personal use or for their monetary value

Increasing sense of tension immediately before committing the theft

Pleasure, gratification, or relief at the time of committing the theft

Stealing is not committed to express anger or vengeance and is not in response to a delusion or a hallucination

The stealing is not better accounted for by Conduct Disorder, a Manic Episode, or Antisocial Personality Disorder

for kleptomania, with the best results attributed to a combination of therapies.

Behavioral therapy attempts to alter behavior by helping the patient learn to avoid participation in detrimental activity. As individuals are rewarded by positive behavior, they are punished by negative behavior. Aversion therapy pairs various forms of discomfort with the impulse to steal, for example, patients snap a rubber band against their wrist as thoughts of stealing increase. Covert sensitization, or the process of encouraging the patient at the time of impulse to think the situation through, including the possibilities of traumatic experiences, such as being arrested and spending time in jail has been reported to be somewhat effective.

Painful or unpleasant consequences imagined by the victim frequently counter the theft impulses. Because most victims of kleptomania are beset by other issues and conflicts, the most beneficial treatment seems to be psychotherapy. In conversations with a trusted therapist, a patient may reveal a history of emotional turmoil that could provide some understanding of or key to the patient's impulses.

BIBLIOGRAPHY

Cupchick, Will. *Why Honest People Steal or Commit Other Acts of Theft: Assessment and Treatment of "Atypical Theft Offenders."* Bangor, Maine: Booklocker, 2002. Examines the relationship between theft and personal loss, stress, illness, and manipulation.

Grant, Jon E. *Impulse Control Disorders: A Clinician's Guide to Understanding and Treating Behavioral Addictions.* New York: W. W. Norton, 2008. Discusses various aspects concerning impulse control disorders, including their relation to drugs and alcohol, treatment, the role of family, and legal issues.

Grant, Jon E., S. W. Kim, and Gregory Fricchione. *Stop Me Because I Can't Stop Myself: Taking Control of Impulsive Behavior.* New York: McGraw-Hill, 2004. Provides information on how to recognize children, adolescents, and elderly people who may be victims of impulse control disorders, how family and friends can help, and available treatments.

McIntosh, Kenneth, and Phyllis Livingston. *Youth and Impulse Control Disorders: On the Spur of the Moment.* Broomall, Pa.: Mason Crest Books, 2007. Concerns high-school students who find impulsive activities, including shoplifting and setting fires, irresistible.

Shulman, Terrence Daryl. *Something for Nothing: Shoplifting Addiction and Recovery.* West Conshohocken, Pa.: Infinity, 2003. Analyzes the difference between kleptomania and shoplifting addiction along with various types of shoplifters.

Mary Hurd

SEE ALSO: Antidepressant medications; Aversion therapy; Behavior therapy; Impulse control disorders; Psychotherapy: Goals and techniques.

Kohlberg, Lawrence

BORN: October 25, 1927
DIED: c. January 17, 1987
IDENTITY: American developmental psychologist
BIRTHPLACE: Bronxville, New York
PLACE OF DEATH: Boston, Massachusetts
TYPE OF PSYCHOLOGY: Developmental psychology

Kohlberg is best known for studying the moral development of children.

Lawrence Kohlberg was born to Alfred and Charlotte Kohlberg. He attended and graduated from Andover Academy. In the fall of 1945, Kohlberg traveled to war-torn Europe with the Merchant Marines and was much affected by the plight of Jewish refugees. Thereafter, Kohlberg volunteered on a ship smuggling Jewish refugees to British-controlled Palestine. The British navy seized the ship and imprisoned the crew. Eventually, Kohlberg escaped and returned to the United States. This early experience helped lay the groundwork for his abiding interest in moral dilemmas (for example, obeying the law versus doing what seemed morally right).

In 1948, Kohlberg entered the University of Chicago, tested out of several classes, and earned his bachelor's degree in a single year. He began his dissertation research on moral development in the mid-1950s, presenting moral dilemmas to boys between the ages of eleven and sixteen. A well-known dilemma concerns a man named Heinz whose wife is dying of cancer. Heinz cannot afford a life-saving drug, and faces the dilemma of whether he should break into a pharmacy to steal the drug. After presenting each dilemma to the boys, Kohlberg would ask whether the action taken was okay, and then ask additional questions to determine the moral reasoning behind their answers. Kohlberg received his doctorate in psychology in 1958.

Based on his research, Kohlberg posited his well-known theory of moral development. It consists of six sequential stages grouped in pairs at three levels: preconventional level (punishment-obedience stage, personal reward stage), conventional level (good boy-nice girl stage, law and order stage), and postconventional level (social contract stage, universal ethical principle stage). Development proceeds sequentially from an egocentric orientation at the bottom to one based on universal "truths" at the top.

Kohlberg worked at Yale University (1959-1961), the Institute for Advanced Study (1961-1962), and the University of Chicago (1962-1968). In 1968, he joined the faculty of Harvard University, and there he remained. Beyond his groundbreaking work in the study of moral development, Kohlberg did research and published in a variety of areas, including moral education, "just communities," ego development, sex-role development, socialization, egocentric speech, and using childhood behavior to predict later mental health.

Conducting cross-cultural research in Belize in the early 1970s, Kohlberg acquired a parasitic infection that caused him to suffer dizziness, nausea, and depression the rest of his life until his apparent suicide in 1987. His legacy is his well-known work in the area of moral development and, more broadly, his rich and varied contributions to the field of child development.

BIBLIOGRAPHY

Crain, William. *Theories of Development: Concepts and Applications*. 5th ed. Upper Saddle River: Pearson, 2005. Print.

Gibbs, John C. *Moral Development and Reality: Beyond the Theories of Kohlberg, Hoffman, and Haidt*. Oxford: Oxford UP, 2014. Print.

Kohlberg, Lawrence. *The Psychology of Moral Development: The Nature and Validity of Moral Stages*. New York: Harper, 1984. Print.

Rest, James, Clark Power, and Mary Brabeck. "Lawrence Kohlberg (1927-1987)." *American Psychologist* 43 (1988). Print.

Russell N. Carney

SEE ALSO: Children's mental health; Development; Developmental psychology; Moral development; Teenagers' mental health.

Kraepelin, Emil

BORN: February 15, 1856
DIED: October 7, 1926
IDENTITY: German psychiatrist
BIRTHPLACE: Neustrelitz, Germany
PLACE OF DEATH: Munich, Germany
TYPEOFPSYCHOLOGY: Emotion;Personality;Psychopathology; Social psychology

Kraepelin developed a classification system for mental illness and identified bipolar disorder and schizophrenia.

Emil Kraepelin was taught the value of hard work by his father, a Prussian schoolteacher. Kraepelin began studying medicine in 1874 at the University of Leipzig, then studied at the University of Würzburg. In 1877 he met experimental psychologist Wilhelm Wundt and studied with him from 1882 to 1883, pursuing a better understanding of the effects of drugs, alcohol, and fatigue on the human mind. Between 1878 and 1882, he assisted Bernhard von Gudden at the psychiatric asylum of Munich County. In 1882 he was appointed as the senior assistant under Paul Flechsig at the psychiatric hospital at Leipzig University.

In an effort to improve his financial situation, Kraepelin wrote his first edition of *Compendium der Psychiatrie* (1883; compendium of psychiatry), which focused on a workable model for classifying mental illnesses. He divided mental disorders into two categories, those caused by external conditions (exogenous), and those related to biological disorders (endogenous). He believed that exogenous disorders, such as fear of spiders and depression, could be treated, while endogenous disorders, such as brain damage and genetic defects, were incurable.

After serving as a senior assistant at the asylum at Leubus (1884), as the head of the ward for mentally ill patients at the general hospital in Dresden, Germany (1885), and as a professor of psychiatry at Dorpat (Estonia) University (1886–1891), he accepted a position as a professor of psychiatry at Heidelberg University. In his sixth edition of the Compendium (1899), Kraepelin distinguished between bipolar disorder (also called manic-depressive disorder) and schizophrenia. After many years of clinical studies and thousands of cases, he concluded that bipolar disorders were treatable but that schizophrenia was incurable. During the same period of time, he also published many papers on the harmful psychological effects of alcohol.

In 1903, Kraepelin accepted a job as a professor of psychiatry at Munich University. In 1909, he and one of his former students, Alois Alzheimer, classified a disorder that became known as Alzheimer's disease. Kraepelin spent a great deal of time designing and preparing the German Psychiatric Research Institution that opened in Munich in 1917. In 1922, he became the director of the institution. Kraepelin's classification system of mental disorders greatly influenced subsequent classifications by other psychiatrists. His fundamental concepts continue to be valid working principles in modern psychiatric research.

BIBLIOGRAPHY

Hersen, Michel, Alan E. Kazdin, and Alan S. Bellack, eds. *The Clinical Psychology Handbook*. 2d ed. New York: Pergamon, 1991. Print.

Kring, Ann M., et al. *Abnormal Psychology*. Hoboken: John Wiley, 2012. Print

McWilliams, Nancy. *Psychoanalytic Case Formulation*. New York: Guilford, 1999. Print.

Psychiatry: *Past, Present, and Prospect*. New York: Oxford UP, 2014. Print

Read, John, and Jacqui Dillon. *Models of Madness: Psychological, Social, and Biological Approaches to Psychosis*. London: Routledge, 2013. Print.

Shrout, Patrick E., and Susan T. Fiske, eds. *Personality Research, Methods, and Theory*. Hillsdale, N.J.: Lawrence Erlbaum, 1995. Print.

Alvin K. Benson

SEE ALSO: Alzheimer's disease; Bipolar disorder; Diagnosis; Schizophrenia: Background, types, and symptoms; Schizophrenia: High-risk children; Schizophrenia: Theoretical explanations.

Kübler-Ross, Elisabeth

BORN: July 8, 1926, in Zurich, Switzerland
DIED: August 24, 2004, in Scottsdale, Arizona
IDENTITY: Swiss-American psychiatrist
TYPE OF PSYCHOLOGY: Emotion; Psychotherapy; Stress

Kübler-Ross was a pioneer in methods for treating grief associated with dying and death.

Elisabeth Kübler-Ross was the first born of triplet girls to Ernst and Emmy Villiger Kübler. She enjoyed hiking with her family in the Swiss mountains near Furlegi and developed a deep appreciation for nature and life. During her public schooling, Kübler-Ross developed an intense interest in science and decided that she would eventually pursue a medical career.

After Germany invaded Poland in 1939, Kübler-Ross helped Polish refugees who were sent to Swiss hospitals. In 1945, she joined the International Volunteers for Peace and worked along the Swiss-French border and in Sweden. She traveled to Poland in 1948 and worked as a nurse and a camp cook. She decided that her life's work would be devoted to healing human minds and bodies, with a focus on a humanistic perspective of death and dying.

In 1951, she entered the University of Zurich Medical School and graduated with a medical degree in pediatrics in 1957. The following year, she married fellow medical student Emanuel Robert Ross, a native of New York. After they moved to New York City, Kübler-Ross obtained a three-year residency in psychiatry at Manhattan State Hospital. She was appalled at the inhumane treatment received by patients who were dying in psychiatric hospitals and vowed to do something about it.

In 1962, Kübler-Ross and her husband accepted positions at the University of Colorado School of Medicine in Denver. She became an instructor at Colorado General Hospital in 1963. In 1965, they moved to Chicago, where Kübler-Ross accepted a position at the University of Chicago Medical School as an assistant professor of psychiatry and assistant director of psychiatric consultation and liaison services. She worked with nurses and doctors to provide better counseling for the dying.

Kübler-Ross's work with the dying led to her classic book *On Death and Dying* (1969), which is considered the master text on the subject. It includes a grief-cycle model consisting of emotional states that all individuals tend to go through when faced with death or dying. The five stages of the cycle, though not always sequential, are denial, anger, bargaining, depression, and acceptance. In 1977, she founded Shanti Nilaya, a healing center for the dying and their families, in Escondido, California. She also cofounded the American Holistic Medical Association. Kübler-Ross published twenty books and received numerous awards for her contributions to psychiatry.

BIBLIOGRAPHY

Gill, Derek L. T. *Quest: The Life of Elisabeth Kübler-Ross*. New York: Harper & Row, 1980. Discusses the life of Kübler-Ross and her contributions to the study of coping with dying and death, and the associated grieving.

Wanzer, Sidney H., and Joseph Glenmullen. *To Die Well: Your Right to Comfort, Calm, and Choice in the Last Days of Life*. Cambridge, Mass.: Da Capo Press, 2007. Examines the grieving process that accompanies death and dying, including the contributions of Kübler-Ross. Includes index and bibliography.

Welch, Fern Stewart, ed. *Tea with Elisabeth*. Güllesheim, Germany: Silberschnur Verlag, 2007. A tribute paid to Kübler-Ross from leaders in hospice care, colleagues, family, and friends that includes memories and anecdotes.

Alvin K. Benson

SEE ALSO: Coping: Terminal illness; Death and dying; Denial; Elders' mental health; Grieving; Hospice.

Kuder occupational interest survey (KOIS)

DATE: 1939 forward
TYPE OF PSYCHOLOGY: Intelligence and intelligence testing

Career interest surveys such as the KOIS have been developed to assist people in making career placement decisions. KOIS purports to assess self-reported abilities, interests, and other characteristics and correlates them with characteristics or traits of jobs, occupations, college ma-

jors, and careers. These selections can outline a direction that an individual can use to make better decisions.

KEY CONCEPTS

- Career
- Interest inventory
- Job choice
- Self-efficacy

INTRODUCTION

The Kuder Occupational Interest Survey is an inventory originally developed by G. Frederic Kuder and has been in use since 1939. The earliest version was the Kuder Preference Record-Vocational (KPR-V) survey. This measurement of vocational interest was primarily for use in vocational placement and job choice. Individuals identify items according to most-liked and least-liked preferences. This is accomplished using forced-choice items that differentiate among three activities that might be preferred as a career choice. The goal of the survey is not to suggest specific jobs or occupations, but rather to determine broad interest areas. These are Outdoor, Mechanical, Computational, Scientific, Persuasive, Artistic, Literary, Musical, Social Science, or Clerical. Later, the Kuder General Interest Survey (KGIS) was developed as a revision of the KPR-V, designed for sixth through twelfth grades, using simpler language. The KOIS provides scores with reference to specific occupational groups in addition to the broad interest areas noted above. Scores are used to identify 109 specific occupations and 40 college majors.

The scores can also be converted to a common reporting system known as the Holland system (using the R-I-A-S-E-C sequence). The Holland system consists of six concepts, arranged in a hexagon indicating relative positioning: Realistic (R), Investigative (I), Artistic (A), Social (S), Enterprising (E), and Conventional (C). To emphasize nontraditional occupations for men and women, a series of new scales have been added to the KOIS.

TECHNICAL ASPECTS

The report received as a result of completing the KOIS is divided into four sections. The first section summarizes the dependability of the results by analyzing their consistency. The report can suggest the dependability of the results for the individual who completed the KOIS. The second section rank-orders interest patterns in comparison to a normative sample of both men and women. This allows either gender to make a comparison directly.

The third section ranks the test taker in relation to men and women who are employed in different occupations and are satisfied with their career choices. The fourth section of the report matches patterns of interest to those of students who have selected different college majors. These sections match interest patterns corresponding to occupations and career choices such as lawyers, personnel managers, and physicians. College major interest patterns include history, English, and political science.

Psychometric properties for the KOIS are very good. For instance, short-term reliability is a property of an instrument that indicates that the score of a test taker will tend to be the same over time (that is, test-retest reliability). Short-term reliability of the KOIS is between .80 and .95, and there is evidence indicating the scores may be stable for as long as thirty years.

Predictive validity is an important concept for career instruments and tests such as the KOIS. Predictive validity indicates that the results of a test score can "predict" the career choice. Although the test scores cannot actually predict behavior, it is possible to match up (correlate) a score with career choice, job placement, and college major made by a person at a later date. This type of validity gives credibility to the test. In the case of the KOIS, predictive validity is very high. While job placement and KOIS scores of students in high school match up well, student scores and choice of college major match up better.

CRITIQUE

One useful aspect of the KOIS is how self-efficacy influences confidence for takers' knowledge of themselves when the results of the KOIS are made known to them. Additionally, self-efficacy for specific occupational tasks has been demonstrated. Research indicates that there is a difference between expectations of various groups and the types of occupations, careers, or jobs chosen. This type of information is particularly useful for guidance decisions for high-school and college students. Refine-

ments published in 1985 reflect continuing development of this type of information.

For individuals to enter an appropriate career, they must begin to identify specific interests and the relative importance of those interests. Some individuals will need little guidance in making career choices; others will need the guidance of a survey instrument such as the KOIS. In the more than seventy-five years since the introduction of the first interest inventory (the Carnegie Interest Survey) millions of people have received important information to use in decision making. Caution is always expressed by the authors of these inventories that no decision should be made solely on the basis of the results determined by one inventory alone.

BIBLIOGRAPHY

Anastasi, Anne, and Susan Urbina. *Psychological Testing.* 7th ed. Upper Saddle River: Prentice Hall, 1997. Print.

Capuzzi, David, and Mark D. Stauffer. *Career Counseling: Foundations, Perspectives, and Applications.* 2nd ed. New York: Routledge, 2012. Print.

Graham, John R., and Jack A. Naglieri, eds. *Assessment Psychology.* Vol. 10. Hoboken: Wiley, 2012. Print.

Handbook of Psychology. Pajares, Frank, and Timothy C. Urdan. *Self-Efficacy Beliefs of Adolescents.* Greenwich: Information Age, 2006. Print.

Rottinghaus, Patrick J. "Thirty-Year Stability and Predictive Validity of Vocational Interests." *Journal of Career Assessment* 15.1 (2007): 5–22. Print.

Daniel L. Yazak

SEE ALSO: Ability tests; Assessment; Career and personnel testing; Career Occupational Preference System (COPS); College entrance examinations; General Aptitude Test Battery (GATB); Human resource training and development; Intelligence tests; Interest inventories; Race and intelligence; Scientific methods; Self-efficacy; Strong Interest Inventory (SII); Survey research: Questionnaires and interviews; Testing: Historical perspectives; Workplace issues and mental health.

L

Lacan, Jacques

BORN: April 13, 1901, in Paris, France
DIED: September 9, 1981, in Paris, France
IDENTITY: French psychoanalyst and philosopher
TYPE OF PSYCHOLOGY: Psychotherapy

Lacan was a pioneering psychoanalyst who emphasized the relationship between language and the unconscious.

Jacques Lacan earned his baccalaureate degree from the Collège Stanislas, a Jesuit school in Paris. He began his clinical training in 1927 at Sainte-Anne's Hospital. Lacan received a diploma in forensic psychology in 1931 and doctorat d'état in 1932 for his dissertation on paranoid psychosis and personality.

In 1936, Lacan presented his paper "Le Stade du Miroir" (The Mirror Stage) at the fourteenth International Psychoanalytical Congress. In this seminal essay, Lacan argued that the child's ego only begins to emerge between the ages of six and eighteen months, when it first sees and identifies with its own reflection in a mirror and begins to conceive of itself as a separate, unified being. The apparent completeness of the reflected image gives the otherwise helpless child a sense of mastery over its own body. The ego is therefore the effect of an alienating identification based on a lack of completeness in the body of the child. Lacan concluded from this that psychoanalysis should reassess its focus on the patient's ego and turn its attention back to the unconscious because of what he later termed "the falsifying character of the ego."

In the mirror stage, according to Lacan, the child also enters the "language system," characterized by absence, lack, and separation because language names things that are not immediately present ("signifieds") and substitutes words ("signifiers") for them. It is through what Lacan calls the "linguistic chain" that desire seeks to recover its original, though illusory, unity. This is also the beginning of socialization, says Lacan. The child is now exposed to the linguistic world of prohibitions characterized by the figure of the father, or what Lacan calls "the father's æno.'" Lacan was heavily influenced by structuralist thinkers such as the anthropologist Claude Lévi-Strauss and linguists Ferdinand de Saussure and Roman Jakobson. Lacan's chief claim, based on his readings of Saussure and Jakobson, is that the unconscious is "structured like a language."

Lacan's *Écrits* (2 vols., 1966-1971; *Écrits: A Selection*, 1977) were based on transcripts of lectures given over a number of years. The multivolume *Le Séminaire de Jacques Lacan* (20 vols., 1973-1981; *The Seminar of Jacques Lacan*, 1988), edited by Jacques-Alain Miller, contains some of Lacan's most accessible material, including *Quatre Fondamentaux de la Psychanalyse* (1973), translated as *The Four Fundamental Concepts of Psychoanalysis* (1978). Lacan dissolved his École Freudienne de Paris in 1980 and died a year later, leaving behind a body of work that continues to influence psychoanalytic studies, philosophy, and literary and cultural theory.

BIBLIOGRAPHY

Dor, Joel. *Introduction to the Reading of Lacan: The Unconscious Structured Like a Language.* New York: Other Press, 1998. A clearly written and accessible introduction. Includes a useful bibliography.

Evans, Dylan. *An Introductory Dictionary of Lacanian Psychoanalysis.* London: Routledge, 2001. Evans defines more than two hundred technical terms in their historical contexts.

Fink, Bruce. *A Clinical Introduction to Lacanian Psychoanalysis: Theory and Technique.* Cambridge, Mass.: Harvard University Press, 1999. A practicing psychoanalyst clearly introduces Lacan in theory and in clinical practice. Includes an extensive bibliography.

Gerard O'Sullivan

SEE ALSO: Analytic psychology: Jacques Lacan; Children's mental health; Language; Psychoanalytic psychology; Psychoanalytic psychology and personality: Sigmund Freud.

Language

TYPE OF PSYCHOLOGY: Cognition; Language

Language is a system of arbitrary symbols that can be combined in conventionalized ways to express ideas, thoughts, and feelings. Various theories and models have been constructed to study, describe, and explain language acquisition, language processing, and its relation to thought and cognition.

KEY CONCEPTS
- Displacement
- Grammar
- Language faculty
- Linguistic relativity
- Morphology
- Phonology
- Pragmatics
- Semantics
- Syntax
- Universal grammar

INTRODUCTION

Language is a system of arbitrary symbols that can be combined in conventionalized ways to express ideas, thoughts, and feelings. Language has been typically seen as uniquely human, separating the human species from other animals. Language enables people of all cultures to survive as a group and preserve their culture. The fundamental features of human language make it extremely effective and very economical. Language uses its arbitrary symbols to refer to physical things or nonphysical ideas; to a single item or a whole category; to a fixed state or to a changing process; to existent reality or to nonexistent fiction; to truths or to lies.

Language is systematic and rule-governed. Its four component subsystems are phonology, semantics, grammar, and pragmatics. The phonological system uses phonemes (the smallest speech sound units capable of differentiating meanings) as its building blocks to form syllables and words through phonemic rules. For example, /m/ and /n/ are two different phonemes because they differentiate meaning as in /mēt/ (meat) versus /nēt/ (neat), and "meat" has three phonemes of /m/, /ē/, and /t/ placed in a "lawful" order in English to form one syllable. The semantic system makes language meaningful. It has two levels: Lexical semantics refers to the word meaning, and grammatical semantics to the meaning derived from the combinations of morphemes (the smallest meaning units) into words and sentences. "Beds," for example, has two morphemes, "bed" as a free morpheme means "a piece of furniture for reclining or sleeping," and "s" as a bound morpheme means "more than one."

The grammatical system includes morphology and syntax. Morphology specifies rules to form words (for example, prefixes, suffixes, grammatical morphemes such as "-ed," and rules to form compound words such as "blackboard"). Syntax deals with rules for word order in sentences (such as, "I speak English," but not "I English speak"). Furthermore, the syntax of human language has four core elements, summarized in 1999 by Edward Kako as discrete combinatorics (each word retains its general meaning even when combined with other words), category-based rules (phrases are built around word categories), argument structure (the arguments or the participants involved in an event, labeled by verbs, are assigned to syntactic positions in a sentence), and closed-class vocabulary (the grammatical functional words, such as "the," "on," or "and," are usually not open to addition of new words).

The fourth subsystem in human language is the pragmatic system. It involves rules to guide culture-based, appropriate use of language in communication. For example, people choose different styles (speech registers) that they deem appropriate when they talk to their spouses versus their children. Other examples include the use of contextual information, inferring the speaker's illocutionary intent (intended meaning), polite expressions, conversational rules, and referential communication skills (to speak clearly and to ask clarification questions if the message is not clear).

Language is creative, generative, and productive. With a limited number of symbols and rules, any language user is able to produce and understand an unlimited number of novel utterances. Language has the characteristic of displacement; that is, it is able to refer to or describe not only items and events here and now but also items and events in other times and places.

LANGUAGE ACQUISITION AND DEVELOPMENT

Views on language acquisition and development are diverse. Some tend to believe that language development follows one universal path, shows qualitatively different, stage-like shifts, proceeds as an independent language faculty, and is propelled by innate factors. Others tend to believe in options for different paths, continuous changes through learning, and cognitive prerequisites for language development.

A Universal Pathway in Language Development. Stage theories usually suggest a universal path (an invariant sequence of stages) for language development. A typical child anywhere in the world starts with cooing (playing with the vowel sounds) at two to three months of age, changes into babbling (consonant-vowel combinations) at four to six months, begins to use gestures at nine to ten months, and produces first words by the first birthday. First word combinations, known as telegraphic speech (content word combinations with functional elements left out, such as "Mommy cookie!"), normally appear when children are between 1.5 and 2.5 years. Meanwhile, rapid addition of new words results in a vocabulary spurt. Grammatical rules are being figured out, as seen in young children's application of regular grammatical rules to irregular exceptions (called over-regularization, as in "I hurted my finger"). Later on, formal education promotes further vocabulary growth, sentence complexity, and subtle usages. Language ability continues to improve in early adulthood, then remains stable, and generally will not decline until a person reaches the late sixties.

Different Pathways in Language Development. Although the universal pattern appears true in some respects, not all children acquire language in the same way. Analyses of young children's early words have led psychologists to an appreciation of children's different approaches to language. In her 1995 book *Individual Differences in Language Development*, Cecilia Shore analyzed the different pathways of two general styles (sometimes termed analytic versus holistic) in the four major language component areas.

In early phonological development, holistic babies seem to attend to prosody or intonation. They tend to be willing to take risks to try a variety of sound chunks, thus producing larger speech units in sentence-like intonation but with blurred sounds. Analytic babies are phonemic-oriented, paying attention to distinct speech sounds. Their articulation is clearer.

In semantic development, children differ not only in their vocabulary size but also in the type of words they acquire. According to Katherine Nelson (cited in Shore's work), who divided children's language acquisition styles into referential versus expressive types, the majority of the referential babies' first words were object labels ("ball," "cat") whereas many in the expressive children's vocabulary were personal-social frozen phrases ("Don't

do dat"). In Shore's opinion, the referential babies are attracted to the referential function of nouns and take in the semantic concept of object names; the expressive children attend more to the personal-social aspect of language and acquire relational words, pronouns, and undifferentiated communicative formulaic utterances.

Early grammatical development shows similar patterns. The analytical children are more likely to adopt the nominal approach and use telegraphic grammar to combine content words but ignore the grammatical inflections (such as the plural "-s"). The holistic children have a tendency to take the pronominal approach and use pivot-open grammar to have a small number of words fill in the frame slots (for instance, the structure of "all-gone [. . .]" generates "allgone shoe," "allgone cookie," and so on). The units of language acquisition might be different for different children.

In the area of pragmatic development, children may differ in their understanding of the primary function of language. Nelson has argued that the referential children may appreciate the informative function of language and the expressive children may attend to the interpersonal function of language. The former are generally more object-oriented, are declarative, and display low variety in speech acts, whereas the latter are more person-oriented, are imperative, and display high variety in speech acts.

Convenient as it is to discuss individual differences in terms of the two general language acquisition styles (analytic versus holistic), it does not mean that the two are necessarily mutually exclusive—children actually use both strategies, although they might use them to different extents at different times and change reliance patterns over time.

THEORIES OF LANGUAGE DEVELOPMENT

With an emphasis on language performance (actual language use in different situations) rather than language competence (knowledge of language rules and structure), learning theories contend that children learn their verbal behavior (a term suggested by the behaviorist B. F. Skinner in 1957 to replace the vague word of "language") primarily through conditioning and imitation, not maturation. Classical conditioning allows the child to make associations between verbal stimuli, internal responses, and situational contexts to understand a word's meaning. It also enables the child to comprehend a word's connotative meaning—whether it is associated with pleasant or unpleasant feelings. Operant conditioning shapes the child's speech through selective reinforcement and punishment. Adults' verbal behaviors serve as the environmental stimuli to elicit the child's verbal responses, as models for the child to imitate, and as the shaping agent (through imitating their children's well-formed speech and recasting or expanding their ill-formed speech).

Nevertheless, learning theories have difficulty explaining many phenomena in language development. Imitation cannot account for children's creative yet logical sayings, such as calling a gardener "plantman," because there are no such models in adult language. Shaping also falls short of an adequate explanation, because adults do not always correct their children's mistakes, especially grammatical ones. Sometimes they even mimic their children's cute mistakes. Furthermore, residential homes are not highly controlled laboratories—the stimulus-response-consequence contingencies are far from perfect.

The Nativist Perspective. The nativist perspective, turning to innate mechanisms for language development, has the following underlying assumptions: language is a human-species-specific capacity; language is "unlearnable" because it is impossible for a naïve and immature child to figure out such a complex linguistic system from an imperfect, not very consistent, highly opaque, and frequently ambiguous language environment; and there is a common structural core in all human languages. In 1965, linguist Noam Chomsky posited an innate language-acquisition device (LAD), with the universal grammar residing in it, to explain children's rapid acquisition of any language and even multiple languages. LAD is assumed to be a part of the brain, specialized for processing language. Universal grammar is the innate knowledge of the grammatical system of principles and rules expressing the essence of all human languages. Its transformational generative grammar consists of rules to convert the deep structure (grammatical classes and their relationships) to surface structure (the actual sentences said) in the case of production, or vice versa in the case of comprehension. Equipped with this biological endowment, children need only minimal language exposure to trigger the LAD, and their innate knowledge of the universal grammar will enable them to extract the rules for the specific language(s) to which they are exposed.

Evidence for the nativist perspective can be discussed at two levels: the linguistic level (language rules and structure) and the biological level. At the linguistic level, people are sensitive to grammatical rules and linguistic structural elements. For example, sentences in the active voice are processed more quickly than sentences in the passive voice, because the former type is closer to the deep structure and needs fewer transformation steps than the latter type. Click insertion studies (which insert a click at different places in a sentence) and interrupted tape studies (which interrupt a tape with recorded messages at different points) have shown a consistent bias for people to recall the click or interruption position as being at linguistic constituent boundaries, such as the end of a clause. After a sentence has been processed, what remains in memory is the meaning or the gist of the sentence, not its word-for-word surface structure, suggesting the transformation from the surface structure to the deep structure.

Around the world, the structure of creolized languages (invented languages), including the sign languages invented by deaf children who have not been exposed to any language, is similar and resembles early child language. Young children's early language data have also rendered support. In phonology, habituation studies show that newborns can distinguish between phonemes such as /p/ and /b/. Most amazingly, they perceive variations of a sound as the same if they come from the same phoneme, but different if they cross the boundary into a different phoneme (categorical speech perception). In semantics, babies seem to know that object labels refer to whole objects and that a new word must mean the name of a new object. If the new word is related to an old object whose name the child already knows, the word must mean either a part or a property of that object (the mutual exclusivity hypothesis). In the domain of grammar, Dan Isaac Slobin's 1985 cross-cultural data have shown that young children pay particular attention to the ends of words and use subject-object word order, probably as a function of their innate operating principles. By semantic bootstrapping, young children know that object names are nouns and that action words are verbs. By syntactic bootstrapping, they understand a word's grammatical class membership according to its position in a sentence. Even young children's mistaken over-regularization of grammatical rules to exceptions demonstrates their success in rule extraction, since such mistaken behavior is not modeled by adults.

The Neural Storehouse. At the biological level, human babies seem to be prepared for language: They prefer the human voice to other sounds and the human face to other figures. Some aspects of the language developmental sequence appear to be universal—even deaf children, despite their lack of language input, start to coo and babble at about the same ages as hearing children and later develop sign combinations that are very similar to telegraphic speech. Children's language environment is indeed quite chaotic, yet it takes them only four to five years to speak their mother tongue like an adult without systematic, overt teaching. Furthermore, a critical or sensitive period seems to exist for language acquisition. Young children are able to pick up any language or a second language effortlessly, with no accent or grammatical mistakes. After puberty, people generally have to exert great efforts to learn another language, and their pronunciation as well as grammar typically suffers. Reinforced language teaching in postcritical years was not successful in the cases of "Victor" (a boy who had been deserted in the wild) and "Genie" (a girl who had been confined in a basement). Kako's 1999 study—a careful analysis of the linguistic behavior of a parrot, two dolphins, and a bonobo—led him to conclude that no nonhuman animals, including the language-trained ones, show all the properties of human language in their communication, although he respectfully acknowledges all the achievements in animal language training. Language is unique to human beings.

Although the neural storehouse for the universal grammar has not been pinpointed yet, cognitive neuroscience has delivered some supportive evidence. Infants' brains respond asymmetrically to language sounds versus nonlanguage sounds. Event-related potentials (ERPs) have indicated localized brain regions for different word categories in native English speakers. Research suggests possible specific brain structures that had registered a detailed index for nouns. Brain studies have confirmed the left hemisphere's language specialization relative to the right hemisphere, even among very young infants. Broca's area and Wernicke's area are housed in the left hemisphere. Damage to Broca's area results in Broca's aphasia, with a consequence of producing grammatically defective, halting, telegram-like speech. When Wernicke's area is damaged, speech fluency and grammatical structure are spared but semantics is impaired. This linguistic lateralization pattern and the linguistic consequences of brain injuries are also true of normal and aphasic American Sign Language users.

However, the nativist perspective is not immune to criticism. The universal grammar cannot adequately explain the grammatical diversity in all human languages. The growth spurts in brain development do not correspond to language development in a synchronized manner. The importance of social interaction, contextual factors, and formal education for knowledge and pragmatic usage of complex rules, subtle expressions, speech acts, and styles has been neglected in nativist theories.

Dissatisfied with this nature-nurture dichotomy, interactionist theories try to bring the two together. They recognize the reciprocal influences, facilitating or constraining, dependent or modifying, among multiple factors from the biological, cognitive, linguistic, and social domains. For instance, the typical prenatal and postnatal mother-tongue environment will eventually wean the infants' initial ability to differentiate the speech sounds of any language and, at the same time, sharpen their sensitivity to their native language. Deaf children's babbling does not develop into words as does that of hearing children. Babies deprived of the opportunity of social interaction, as seen in the cases of "Victor" and "Genie," will not automatically develop a proper language. It is in the dynamic child-environment system that a child acquires language.

LANGUAGE AND COGNITION

Cognitive Development and Language Acquisition. Cognitive theorists generally believe that language is contingent on cognitive development. The referential power in the arbitrary symbols assumes the cognitive prerequisite of understanding the concepts they signify. As a cognitive interactionist, Jean Piaget believed that action-based interaction with the world gave rise to the formation of object concepts, separation of self from the external world, and mental representation of reality by mental images, signs, and symbols (language). Language reflects the degree of cognitive maturity. For example, young children's immature egocentric thought (unable to understand others' perspectives) is revealed in their egocentric speech (talking to self)—children seem to show no realization of the need to connect with others' comments or to ascertain whether one is being understood. Older children's cognitive achievements of logical thinking and perspective-taking lead to the disappearance of egocentric speech and their use of socialized speech for genuine social interaction. Although language as a verbal tool facilitates children's interaction with the world, it is the interaction that contributes to cognitive development. Piaget gave credit to language only in the later development of abstract reasoning by adolescents.

In L. S. Vygotsky's social-functional interactionist view, language and cognition develop independently at first, as a result of their different origins in the course of evolution. Infants use practical/instrumental intelligence

(intelligence without speech), such as smiling, gazing, grasping, or reaching, to act on or respond to the social world. Meanwhile, the infants' cries and vocalizations, though they do not initially have true communicative intent (speech without thinking), function well in bringing about adults' responses. Adults attribute meaning to infants' vocalizations and thus include the babies in the active communicative system, fostering joint attention and intersubjectivity (understanding each other's intention). Such social interactions help the infants eventually complete the transition from nonintentional to intentional behavior and to discover the referential power of symbols, thus moving on to verbal thinking and later to meaningful speech. Externalized speech (egocentric speech) is a means for the child to monitor and guide his or her own thoughts and problem-solving actions. This externalized functional "conversation with oneself" (egocentric speech) does not disappear but is internalized over time and becomes inner speech, a tool for private thinking. Thus, in Vygotsky's theory, language first develops independently of cognition, then intersects with cognition, and contributes significantly to cognitive development thereafter. Language development proceeds from a global, social functional use (externalized speech) to a mature, internalized mastery (inner speech), opposite to what Piaget suggested.

Linguistic Relativity. Linguistic relativity refers to the notion that the symbolic structure and use of a language will shape its users' way of thinking. The Sapir-Whorf hypothesis, also known as linguistic determinism, is a strong version. According to anthropologist John Lucy, writing in 1997, all the variations of linguistic relativity, weak or strong, share the assumption that "certain properties of a given language have consequences for patterns of thought about reality. . . . Language embodies an interpretation of reality and language can influence thought about that reality." Many researchers have tested these claims. Lera Boroditsky, for example, in a 2001 study, examined the relationship between spatial terms used to talk about time and the way Mandarin Chinese speakers (using vertical spatial metaphors) and English speakers (using horizontal spatial metaphors) think about time. The findings suggested that abstract conceptions, such as time, might indeed be subject to the influence from specific languages. On the other hand, the influence between language and thought might be more likely bidirectional than unidirectional. Many examples from the civil rights movement or the feminist movement, such as the thought of equality and bias-free

linguistic expressions, can be cited to illustrate the reciprocal relationships between the two.

Language Faculty as a Module. There have been debates over whether language is a separate faculty or a part of general cognition. Traditional learning theories are firm in the belief that language is a learned verbal behavior shaped by the environment. In other words, language is not unique in its own right. By contrast, nativist theorists insist on language being an independent, innate faculty. Chomsky even advocates that, being one of the clearest and most important separate modules in the individual brain, language should be viewed internally from the individual and therefore be called internal language or "I-language," distinct from "E-language" or the external and social use of language. Nativists also insist on language being unique to humans, because even higher-order apes, though they have intelligence (such as tool using, problem solving, insights) and live a social life, do not possess a true language.

The view of language as an independent faculty has received support from works in cognitive neuroscience, speech-processing studies, data associated with aphasia (language impairment due to brain damage), and unique case studies. Specific word and grammatical categories seem to be registered in localized regions of the brain. Some empirical studies have suggested that lexical access and word-meaning activation appear to be autonomic (modular). As noted, Broca's aphasia and Wernicke's aphasia display different language deficit symptoms. In 1991, Jeni Yamada reported the case of Laura, a person with an IQ score of just 41 when she was in her twenties. Her level of cognitive problem-solving skill was comparable to that of a preschooler, yet she was able to produce a variety of grammatically sophisticated sentences, such as "He was saying that I lost my battery-powered watch that I loved; I just loved that watch." Interestingly, Laura's normal development in phonology, vocabulary, and grammar did not protect her from impairment in pragmatics. In responding to the question, "How do you earn your money?," Laura answered, "Well, we were taking a walk, my mom, and there was this giant, like, my mother threw a stick." It seems that some components of language, such as vocabulary and grammar, may function in a somewhat autonomic manner, whereas other parts, such as pragmatics, require some general cognitive capabilities and social learning experiences.

Cognitive psychologists hold that language is not a separate module but a facet of general cognition. They caution people against hasty acceptance of brain localization as evidence for a language faculty. Arshavir Blackwell and Elizabeth Bates (1995) have suggested an alternative explanation for the agrammaticality in Broca's aphasia: grammatical deficits might be the result of a global cognitive resource diminution, rather than just the damaged Broca's area. In 1994, Michael Maratsos and Laura Matheny criticized the inadequate explanatory power of the language-as-a-faculty theory pertaining to the following phenomena: comprehension difficulties in Broca's aphasia in addition to grammatical impairment; semantically related word substitutions in Wernicke's aphasia; the brain's plasticity or elasticity (the flexibility of other parts of the brain adapting to pick up some of the functions of the damaged parts); and the practical inseparability of phonology, semantics, syntax, and pragmatics from one another.

Some information-processing models, such as connectionist models, have provided another way to discuss language, not in the traditional terms of symbols, rules, or cognitive capacity, but in terms of the strengths of the connections in the neural network. Using computer modeling, J. L. McClelland explains that knowledge is stored in the weights of the parameter connections, which connect the hidden layers of units to the input units that process task-related information and the output units that generate responses (performance). Just like neurons at work, parallel-distributed processing, or many simultaneous operations by the computer processor, will result in self-regulated strength adjustments of the connections. Over extensive trials, the "learner" will go through an initial error period (the self-adjusting, learning period), but the incremental, continual change in the connection weights will give rise to stage-like progressions. Eventually, the machine gives rule-like performance, even if the initial input was random, without the rules having ever been programmed into the system. These artificial neural networks have successfully demonstrated developmental changes or stages in language acquisition (similar to children's), such as learning the past tense of English verbs.

As a product of the neural network's experience-driven adjustment of its connection weights, language does not need cognitive prerequisites or a specific language faculty in the architecture (the brain). Although emphasizing learning, these models are not to prove the tabula rasa (blank slate) assumption of traditional behaviorism, either, because even small variations in the initial artificial brain structure can make qualitative differences in language acquisition. The interaction between the neural structure and environment (input cues and feedback patterns) is further elaborated in dynamic systems models. For example, Paul van Geert's dynamic system, proposed in 1991, is an ecosystem with heuristic principles modeled after the biological system in general and the evolutionary system in particular. The system space consists of multiple growers or "species" (such as vocabulary and grammatical rules) in interrelated connections. Developmental outcome depends on the changes of the components in their mutual dependency as well as competition for the limited internal and external resources available to them.

CONCLUSION

As Thomas M. Holtgraves said in 2002, "It is hard to think of a topic that has been of interest to more academic disciplines than language." Language can be analyzed at its pure, abstract, and symbolic structural level, but it should also be studied at biological, psychological, and social levels in interconnected dynamic systems. Continued endeavors in interdisciplinary investigations using multiple approaches will surely lead to further understanding of language.

BIBLIOGRAPHY

American Speech-Language-Hearing Association. "Activities to Encourage Speech and Language Development." *American Speech-Language-Hearing Association.* American Speech-Language-Hearing Association, 1997–2014. Web. 28 May 2014.

Blackwell, Arshavir, and Elizabeth Bates. "Inducing Agrammatic Profiles in Normals: Evidence for the Selective Vulnerability of Morphology Under Cognitive Resource Limitation." *Journal of Cognitive Neuroscience* 7.2 (1995): 228–257. Print.

Boroditsky, Lera. "Does Language Shape Thought? Mandarin and English Speakers' Conceptions of Time." *Cognitive Psychology* 43.1 (2001): 1–22. Print.

Chomsky, Noam. *Aspects of the Theory of Syntax.* 1965. Cambridge: MITP, 2007. Print.

Chomsky, Noam. "Language from an Internalist Perspective." *The Future of the Cognitive Revolution.* Eds. David Johnson and Christina E. Erneling. New York: Oxford UP, 1997. Print.

Daniels, Harry, ed. *An Introduction to Vygotsky.* 2d ed. New York: Routledge, 2005. Print.

Gleason, Jean Berko, and Nan E. Bernstein, eds. *Psycholinguistics.* 2d ed. Fort Worth: Harcourt, 2011. Print.

Hoff, Erika. *Language Development*. 5th ed. Belmont: Wadsworth, 2014. Print.

Holtgraves, Thomas M. *Language as Social Action: Social Psychology and Language* Use. New York: Routledge, 2011. Print.

Kako, Edward. "Elements of Syntax in the Systems of Three Language-Trained Animals." *Animal Learning & Behavior* 27.1 (1999): 1–14. Print.

Lloyd, Peter, and Charles Fernyhough, eds. *Lev Vygotsky: Critical Assessments, Volume II: Thought and Language*. New York: Routledge, 1999. Print.

Lucy, John A. "Linguistic Relativity." *Annual Review of Anthropology* 26 (1997): 291–312. Print.

McClelland, J. L. "A Connectionist Perspective on Knowledge and Development." *Developing Cognitive Competence: New Approaches to Process Modeling*. Eds. Tony Simon and Graeme S. Halford. Hillsdale: Erlbaum, 1995. Print.

Matatsos, Michael, and Laura Matheny. "Language Specificity and Elasticity: Brain and Clinical Syndrome Studies." *Annual Review of Psychology* 45 (1994): 487–516. Print.

Nelson, Amy. "Delayed Speech or Language Development." *KidsHealth*. Nemours Foundation, July 2013. Web. 28 May 2014.

Owens, Robert E. *Language Development: An Introduction*. 8th ed. Harlow: Pearson, 2014. Print.

Piaget, Jean. *The Language and Thought of the Child*. Trans. Marjorie and Ruth Gabain. 3d ed. N.p.: Routledge, 2013. Print.

Shore, Cecilia M. *Individual Differences in Language Development. Individual Differences and Development*. Vol. 7 Ed. Robert Plomin. Thousand Oaks: Sage, 1995. Print.

Van Geert, Paul. "A Dynamic Systems Model of Cognitive and Language Growth." *Psychological Review* 98.1 (1991): 3–53. Print.

Yamada, Jeni E. *Laura: A Case for the Modularity of Language*. Cambridge: Bradford, 1999. Print.

Ling-Yi Zhou

SEE ALSO: Aphasias; Bilingualism; Brain damage; Brain structure; Grammar and speech; Linguistics; Nonverbal communication; Speech disorders; Speech perception; Stuttering; Thought: Inferential.

Latinos and mental health

TYPE OF PSYCHOLOGY: Multicultural psychology; Psychopathology; Psychotherapy

Latinos, the largest minority group in the United States, are culturally and racially diverse. The experiences of Latinos differ widely based on their citizenship status, socioeconomic class, language skills, and many other factors, which also affect the population's mental health. The scientific study of mental health issues among Latinos is relatively new but has been influenced historically by negative and stereotypic views of Latinos.

KEY CONCEPTS
- Acculturation
- Acculturative stress
- Hispanic
- Latino
- Multiculturalism

INTRODUCTION

Roughly 17 percent of the United States population—about 53 million people—identified themselves as Hispanic or Latino in 2012, according to the US Census Bureau. Latinos are an ethnically and racially diverse group made up of people descended from a number of countries, including Mexico, Puerto Rico, Cuba, El Salvador, Guatemala, Nicaragua, Peru, Chile, Argentina, and several other Central and South American nations. In 2010, according to the Pew Research Center's Hispanic Trends Project, Mexican Americans made up the largest percentage of the US Hispanic population (63 percent), followed by Puerto Ricans (9.2 percent).

The term "Hispanic" refers to those persons having Spanish ancestry and was first used in the United States Census in the 1970s. The term "Latino" is derived from American Spanish and is embraced by many in the Latino community because it refers to their Latin and American heritage. The US government officially adopted the term "Latino" in 1997 and used it to replace the designation of Hispanic on the census forms. Not all Latinos use this term to self-identify. Although "Latino" is becoming the preferred terminology for referring to this group, the terms "Latino" and "Hispanic" are often used interchangeably. Neither term refers to a racial category because Latinos come from diverse racial and ethnic backgrounds. However, society often treats Latinos as both an ethnic minority and a racial group.

Like members of racial groups, Latinos are often subjected to discrimination.

Latinos are a growing segment of the population. By the first decade of the twenty-first century, they had become the largest ethnic minority group in the United States. They represent 50.5 percent of US population growth since 2000. This is partially attributed to higher birthrates. Latinos are also a young population. According to the Pew Research Center, the Latino population in 2012 had a median age of 27 years compared with 37.6 years for the population as a whole. About one-third of the Latino population was under the age of eighteen in 2012, compared with about one-fourth of the total population. According to the US Bureau of the Census, in 2009, more than half of Latinos (62.7 percent) were native-born Americans, and 37.3 percent were foreign-born.

The history of Latinos in the United States varies by group. For example, the Mexican War (1846–48) ended with the Treaty of Guadalupe Hidalgo, by which Mexico gave Texas, California, New Mexico, Nevada, and parts of Colorado, Arizona, and Utah to the United States. Most of the Mexicans who owned land in these areas lost it and ended up working for the new white landowners. The resulting tension between the United States and Mexico has never been fully resolved. Many Mexicans migrated to the United States from the early 1920s to 1940s to work on railroads, mines, and farms. They were paid less than their white counterparts and were often forced to live in segregated housing.

Puerto Rico became a territory of the United States in 1898 as a result of the Spanish-American War, but Puerto Ricans were not allowed to become citizens of the United States until 1917. The federal government mandated that English was to be the language used in schools, although few Puerto Ricans spoke English at the time. Puerto Ricans began emigrating to the United States in the 1940s and 1950s to find employment and better economic opportunities. They were actively discriminated against by American society and not viewed as US citizens. Puerto Rico became a commonwealth in 1952.

Most Cubans came to the United States as a result of political unrest in Cuba. The Spanish ruled Cuba for more than four hundred years, but the US government was also interested in Cuba because of its proximity. Cuba's exports were highly desirable and included tobacco, sugar, and molasses. In 1848, the United States offered to buy Cuba from Spain, but the Spanish were not interested in selling. The United States briefly occupied Cuba from 1898 to 1902, when Cuba gained its independence from Spain. US-Cuban relations deteriorated after World War II, and reached a low point when Fidel Castro seized power in 1959 and Cuba became a communist nation. Cubans left their home country for political reasons in three distinct waves from the 1960s through the 1980s.

Although the majority of Latinos in the United States are native born, a significant number—about two in five—are immigrants. Many undocumented Latinos leave their home countries to work in the United States. Historically, Latinos have faced discrimination in the United States. They frequently have menial jobs, are mistreated, and are generally viewed negatively. These negative influences have affected the way in which mental illness in Latinos has been viewed, diagnosed, and treated.

LATINO MENTAL HEALTH

Latino mental health is influenced by multiple factors, including immigrant versus nonimmigrant status, the absence or presence of a familial support system, acculturative stress (psychological stress associated with adapting to a new cultural group and new cultural values), socioeconomic status, access to health care and other basic resources, and exposure to trauma. Mental health issues may manifest differently in native-born than in immigrant Latinos. Immigrant Latinos have been found to experience fewer mental disorders than their native-born Latino counterparts do. Higher rates of affective disorders, anxiety disorders, and chemical use and dependency have been found among native-born Latinos than in immigrants.

Acculturation refers to the level of competency an individual from another culture or ethnic group gains in a second culture. Becoming acculturated, however, does not mean abandoning the original culture. Usually, the old and new culture and values are blended. Research suggests that as Latinos from various backgrounds become more acculturated, they often experience a decline in mental health. This can be the result of stressful experiences during the process of acculturation, such as loss of a familial support system, discrimination by society, intergenerational conflict, loss of Latino cultural values, devaluation of Latino cultural values by society, feelings of isolation, and attempts at developing a bicultural identity as an American and a Latino. Latinos who have a supportive family tend to cope more effectively with acculturative stress. Additionally, having a positive view of being Latino has been demonstrated to be a protective factor against some of the negative consequences of discrimination.

Other stressors contributing to mental health issues for some Latinos are a lack of adequate health insurance and health care, inadequate knowledge of the health care system, inadequate English language skills, family members living in different countries, and limited access to educational resources. Additionally, undocumented immigrants experience the constant threat of deportation. It is important to note that the experiences of non-immigrant Latinos and immigrant Latinos may differ significantly.

Scientific study of Latino mental health is relatively new. Previous models of Latino mental health were negatively influenced by the view that cultural differences were negative and pathological. Mental health professionals have come to embrace the differences model of mental health, which promotes acceptance of cultural differences and seeks to incorporate a more culturally sensitive view in the diagnosis and treatment of mental illnesses. This model examines how social, cultural, political, and economic factors affect mental illness. This model has ushered in psychology's fourth force, multiculturalism. Appropriate models of treatment for this population and longitudinal statistical data regarding mental health disorders among Latinos need to be examined through empirical study. Additionally, the field needs more Latino mental health professionals, who could positively affect empirical analysis of this population and the treatment of mental health issues among it.

CONTRIBUTING SOCIOECONOMIC FACTORS

It is important to understand the social, political, and economic factors that influence Latinos in the United States. These factors significantly affect the types of mental distress experienced by this population. Although most Latinos are not poor, a disproportionate number are impoverished relative to their numbers in the population. According the Pew Research Center, about 25 percent of Latino families—compared with about 16 percent of American families as a whole and 11 percent of non-Hispanic whites—lived in poverty in 2012. Latinos also have higher unemployment rates (2.3 percent) when compared with whites (0.9 percent). There is a correlation between socioeconomic status and diagnosed mental health disorders. Higher rates of mental illness are correlated with poverty, rates of violence, and little attention to mental health treatment. Approximately 29

percent of Latinos do not have health insurance, which limits their access to adequate health care, according to the Pew Center. These demographic conditions significantly affect rates of mental illness within the Latino population.

Latino utilization of mental health services varies. Immigrant Latinos use mental health services less than their nonimmigrant counterparts do. Latinos are more likely to seek mental health services from clergy or general health care practitioners and far less likely to seek services from mental health professionals. However, when community-based mental health resources are available, Latinos are more likely to use these services.

RATES OF MENTAL ILLNESS

According to the National Alliance on Mental Illness, Latinos are identified as a high-risk group for depression, anxiety, and substance abuse. Latino women have a higher rate of depression (46 percent) than Latino men (19.6 percent). Rates of mental illness, especially substance abuse, among US-born and long-term US residents are higher than those in recently immigrated Latinos.

Latino youth are more likely than white or African American youths to have experimented with alcohol and binge drinking. Latino youth also are more likely than their counterparts in other ethnic groups to consider or to commit suicide. Finally, domestic violence is also an issue faced by this population, although specific rates are not known.

HEALTH DISPARITIES

Latinos are diagnosed with diabetes and cardiovascular disease at significantly higher rates than those of their white counterparts. These medical conditions have been linked to genetic factors as well as the high levels of stress often experienced by Latinos. According to the US Centers for Disease Control, in 2009, stroke was the fourth leading cause of death among male and female Latinos. In addition, although Latinos make up only 17 percent of the US population, they accounted for approximately 21 percent of all new infections with the human immunodeficiency virus (HIV) in 2010. HIV and AIDS have been found to contribute to depressive symptoms and other mental health issues in this population.

BIBLIOGRAPHY

Atkinson, Donald R., ed. *Counseling American Minorities*. 6th ed. Boston: McGraw, 2004. Print.

Buki, Lydia P., and Lissette M. Piedra. *Creating Infrastructures for Latino Mental Health.* New York: Springer, 2011. Print.

Cabrera, Natasha J., Francisco Villarruel, and Hiram E. Fitzgerald. *Latina and Latino Children's Mental Health.* Santa Barbara: Praeger/ABC-CLIO, 2011. Print.

Chabran, Richard, and Rafael Chabran, eds. *The Latino Encyclopedia.* 6 vols. Tarrytown: Cavendish, 1996. Print.

Kanellos, Nicolás, and Claudio Esteva-Fabregat. *Handbook of Hispanic Cultures in the United States.* 4 vols. Houston: Arte Público, 1994. Print.

Organista, Kurt C. *Solving Latino Psychosocial and Health Problems: Theory, Practice, and Populations.* Hoboken,: Wiley, 2007. Print.

Sher, Leo, and Alexander Vilens. *Immigration and Mental Health: Stress, Psychiatric Disorders and Suicidal Behavior Among Immigrants and Refugees.* Hauppauge: Nova Science, 2011. Print.

Smith, Robert L., and R. Esteban Montilla, eds. *Counseling and Family Therapy with Latino Populations: Strategies That Work.* New York: Routledge, 2007. Print.

Katherine M. Helm

SEE ALSO: Bilingualism; Bilingualism and learning disabilities; Community psychology; Cross-cultural psychology; Culture and diagnosis; Diagnosis; Language; Prejudice; Suicide.

Law and psychology

TYPE OF PSYCHOLOGY: Cognition; Social psychology

The legal decisions made by juries are intended to be uncontaminated by evidence not presented within the court case. Jury behavior and the preconceived ideas that jurors carry into the courtroom reflecting their attitudes, opinions, and personal experiences have been recognized as standard components of trial preparation.

KEY CONCEPTS
- Advocacy
- Attitudes
- Communicative ability
- Credibility
- Jury research
- Memory and retention
- Perception
- Salience

INTRODUCTION

The study of psychology and law, specifically decision making by a jury, is a subset of social psychology. A man might be sitting in his living room watching television when, all of a sudden, a police officer knocks on his door, asks him to step outside, and then informs him that he is being arrested on suspicion of burglary. He claims that he is innocent, but six months later he finds himself on trial for this crime in front of a jury. Should it make any difference to the jury whether he has a good or bad character, whether he is attractive or unattractive, or whether he is white, black, or Latino? The US legal system is designed to yield objective, unbiased decisions based on a set of rules and procedures intended to focus on evidence presented at the trial. Yet Clarence Darrow, one of America's most famous lawyers, bluntly saw it otherwise: "Jurymen seldom convict a person they like, or acquit one that they dislike. The main work of the trial lawyer is to make a jury like his client, or, at least, to feel sympathy for him; facts regarding the crime are relatively unimportant." Research in the field of forensic psychology confirms Darrow's 1933 statement by indicating that human beings do not always conform to such idealistic principles as complete objectivity. Though moral character, lifestyle, attractiveness, race, and related factors have little, if anything, to do with the evidence presented in a given case, research shows that they nevertheless affect the outcome of both real and simulated trials.

The field of psychology and law is continually expanding. Research has focused on such topics as jury selection and jury functioning, social influence as it occurs in the courtroom, the deterrence value of capital punishment and the length of jail sentences, the validity of expert witnesses, and the effect of memory on eyewitness identifications. These areas of psychological application to the legal arena provide a wealth of information that not only will make people aware of potential problems within the judicial system but also will, it is hoped, help provide solutions to the make system as unbiased and objective as possible.

In trying to persuade a jury, a lawyer must discover jury preferences concerning the verdict or the issue to be decided in the case even before the jury is impaneled. Thus, the voir dire examination in which prospective jurors are questioned on their biases or prejudices is of extreme importance. Psychologists have shown in jury research that people decide between alternative explanations of someone else's behavior by using attitudes already established. These attitudes concern the behavior under evaluation and the person being judged. This psychological insight about the importance of prior attitudes is the basis for trial strategy in general and for specific persuasion strategies and techniques in individual cases. The main objective of jury attitude research is to identify attitudes and values that determine which case facts or issues jurors will find most salient, how they will perceive the evidence gathered on those issues, and how those perceptions are likely to influence their decisions about the case. Moreover, in most research on juror decision making, it was found that jurors' decisions tend to be determined by groups or clusters of attitudes related to the decision.

An example of a powerful but supposedly irrelevant variable is the moral character or lifestyle of the person on trial. A study by David Landy and Elliot Aronson in 1969 provided support for this claim when people acting as jurors in a simulated courtroom read facts about a negligent homicide case in which a pedestrian was run over and killed on Christmas Eve. Mock jurors read either positive or negative character descriptions of the defendant. In the positive character case, the defendant was described as a widowed insurance adjuster going to spend Christmas Eve with his son and daughter-in-law. In the negative character case, the defendant was described as a janitor, twice divorced, possessing a criminal record, going to spend Christmas Eve with his girlfriend. Mock jurors were asked to judge whether the defendant was guilty or innocent and, if guilty, to decide how many years he should spend in jail. When the person on trial was described as having a positive character, mock jurors sentenced him to two years in jail; when he was described as having a negative character, they sentenced him to five years in jail. This clearly suggests that the lifestyle and moral character of people on trial do dramatically influence jury decisions.

The attractiveness of the person on trial has also been found to affect the verdict reached by jurors. Michael Efran in 1974 wondered whether physical attractiveness might bias students' judgments of another student who was accused of cheating. He had college students act as school jurors. Students received a photograph of the fellow student and a written description of the cheating case. All students read the same case description. Half had an attractive photograph attached, whereas the other half saw an unattractive photograph. Those with the attractive photograph attached judged the student to be less guilty than did those with the unattractive photograph. For those found guilty of the crime, more severe

sentencing was recommended for the less attractive photograph group. Evidence that attractiveness affects jury decision making is found not only in simulated, but also in real court cases. John Stewart in 1980 asked observers to rate the attractiveness of seventy-four male defendants tried in Pennsylvania. When he later examined the court records, he found that the more attractive defendants received the lighter sentences. Once convicted, the more attractive defendants were twice as likely to avoid prison as those who were less attractive.

Although attractiveness often helps, there are circumstances under which good looks can actually hurt a person on trial. In 1975, Harold Sigall and Nancy Ostrove found that when mock jurors judged a woman accused of stealing $2,200 they were more lenient in their sentencing decisions when she was attractive than when she was not. When she was said to have swindled the money by charming a middle-aged man into making a phony investment, however, the beautiful defendant was sentenced more severely than her less-attractive counterpart. Apparently, people react quite negatively toward someone who uses his or her appearance to commit a crime.

The race of the person on trial also seems to affect the jury decision process. Stewart found that nonwhite defendants were more likely to be convicted than were whites for comparable crimes. Further, the convicted were much more likely to be sent to prison if they were nonwhite than if they were white. Louis Cohen, Laura Gray, and Marian Miller in 1990 had white students act as mock jurors in a burglary case. They all read the same burglary case, but the race of the person on trial varied among black, Latino, and white. When the defendant was black or Latino, a more severe sentence was awarded than when the defendant was white. Although the race of the defendant should theoretically be irrelevant to a court case, it does, in fact, appear to affect the verdict.

Much of the psychology associated with legal decision making is centered on trial tactics or strategy. The key to courtroom persuasion is understanding what jurors feel, know, and believe and providing them with information consistent with those predispositions. Jury persuasion is really strategy that depends on a trial lawyer's ability to conceive, formulate, and convey information with which a jury will agree. This technique demands sophisticated insight into the complexities of human psychology combined with instincts, judgment, and oratory skills. Lawyers must act as advocates, shaping the argument in a fashion most favorable to their position. The ideas or premises jurors bring with them into the courtroom constitute what psychologists call cognitive structures. Cognition pertains to what people know; cognitive structures consist of what people think they know. Jurors are found to be inflexible because their cognitive structures act as a mechanism through which they admit information consistent with what is already there. Therefore, most jurors strive to reach verdicts that do not conflict with their cognitions (beliefs, attitudes, opinions, or values) at the beginning of the trial. Jurors' perceptions of the trial process and their ultimate decisions are largely determined by their preexisting cognitions, which interpret, distort, or reinforce the information presented during the trial. In short, jurors view the evidence presented at the trial through their own value systems and the predisposed beliefs that they bring with them into the courtroom.

ATTITUDES AND VALUE SYSTEMS

The main objective of jury attitude research is to identify attitudes and values that determine which facts or issues in the case the jurors will find most salient, how they will perceive the evidence presented to substantiate those issues, and how those perceptions are likely to influence their decisions about the case. Most psychologists agree that attitudes consist of three components: affect, cognition, and behavior. Affect refers to a person's emotions, feelings, and "gut instincts" about something. Cognition refers to perceiving, thinking about, and interpreting information related to an object, person, or event. Behavior refers to the intention to act in ways that are consistent with an attitude. These three components are closely related. Attitude formation is acquired over time in three ways: It is learned from others, it is developed through experience, or it is the product of self-observation. Attitude salience refers to the strength with which attitudes are held. The way to determine what attitudes jurors hold and the salience of these attitudes is to undertake pretrial research focusing on what kinds of jurors hold which attitudes, their composition, and salience.

Attitudes linked to people's key values play a significant role in shaping how they react to events both inside and outside the courtroom, including how jurors think and feel about the entire trial process and their decisions. Most attitudes are developed over a lifetime of experience with parents, friends, colleagues, teachers, books, television, and other direct and indirect sources. Attitudes vary in the intensity with which they are held, depending on how closely they relate to some underlying

core value. These attitudes are the best predictors of behavior because people tend to act in ways consistent with their values.

Juror profiles based on demographics such as gender, income, age, education, religion, and political preference are desirable because they are readily observable factors. Attitude and personality, however, are said to be better predictors of juror behavior. Affective jurors decide on an emotional rather than a rational basis. They are impulsive decision makers, who often base their decisions on what they see and hear rather than waiting until all the facts have been gathered. They tend to reformulate information until it fits into their previously held worldview or set of conclusions based on how they feel about the matter at issue. They often draw conclusions without reviewing the facts or analyzing witness testimony. Affective jurors are generally deeply devoted to religious principles or philosophies of life. They are often not college educated and conduct business based on how they "feel," what they believe, and what "ought to be." Cognitive jurors are orderly and logical decision makers. They seek information and are organized and fastidious. They are methodical list makers who seek out facts and information. They are often college-educated and rely on detailed instruction and precision.

KEYS TO PERSUASION

Understanding what jurors feel, know, and believe and providing them with messages consistent with these predispositions are keys to persuasion in the courtroom. What jurors see and hear in the courtroom depends on what meaning they attach to the information provided and its relevance according to their value systems. Jurors are not computers or automatons that store information and then later retrieve it verbatim. Rather, jurors store information according to their own ideas of its importance. As a general proposition, it is agreed that jurors tend to remember best the information heard first (primacy) and last (recency). Therefore, jurors tend to retain information presented at the beginning and the end of the trial better than information presented during the middle. Jurors generally argue deductively, from the general to the particular, fitting facts to premises as they are received.

Lawyers attempt to reinforce, change, or create some specific attitude, opinion, or behavior in jurors favorable to the position they are advocating. It is a dynamic process involving the relationship between those who attempt to persuade and their audience. For lawyers to be persuasive, they must adjust their strategies and tactics to the characteristics of the jury.

Jury decisions tend not to be completely objective, and factors irrelevant to the evidence presented in the case are often considered. That is, the character, physical attractiveness, and ethnicity of the defendant, as well as other factors such as attitude similarity between the jurors and the person on trial, all seem to impact the jury's decision-making process, despite the fact that justice should be blind to these extraneous variables.

Although lawyers make use of their clients' attractiveness, dressing and grooming them appropriately for a court appearance, the idea of a trial as a beauty contest is not an appealing one. Means of diminishing the impact of physical attractiveness on legal decisions need to be established. Some researchers have proposed that attractiveness has been found to be less powerful if a sufficient amount of factual information is presented to the jury, if the judge explicitly reminds the jury of the basis on which the verdict should be reached, and if the jury is presented with transcripts of the testimony rather than being directly exposed to those who testify. These same factors should diminish the subjective impact of race as well.

Words should be free of double or multiple meanings. A. Daniel Yarmey points out that the testimony "Mr. Brown shot Mr. Jones" depends on the witness's perception, memory, and communications process and ability to relate what was seen and heard. Memory and language overlap. In another example, Yarmey points out that a witness who testifies to "seeing a black face" is drawing on questions of eyesight, how much light was present, the witness's distance from the scene, other persons present, physical features, an interpretation of what constitutes "blackness," and other such variable factors. For a jury to accept eyewitness testimony, the credibility of the eyewitness is always at issue. This is also apparent during expert testimony, when the lay jury is asked to determine the relative merit of often technical evidence. Credibility is often a deciding factor, coupled with other considerations. Other factors affecting eyewitness performance include the duration of the event, a stress or fear factor, the age of the witness, the length of the retention interval, postevent information, and the method of questioning. A lawyer who asks a witness to relate "what happened" and then asks questions is often more successful than the lawyer who attempts to draw out facts one by one.

BIBLIOGRAPHY

Bradshaw, Brad. *The Science of Persuasion: A Litigator's Guide to Juror Decision-Making.* Chicago: American Bar Association, Criminal Justice Section, 2011. Print.

Costanzo, Mark, and Daniel Krauss. *Forensic and Legal Psychology: Psychological Science Applied to Law.* New York: Worth, 2012. Print.

Greene, Edie, and Kirk Heilbrun. *Wrightman's Psychology and the Legal System.* 8th ed. Belmont: Wadsworth, 2014. Print.

Hastie, Reid, Steven D. Penrod, and Nancy Pennington. *Inside the Jury.* Union: Lawbook Exchange, 2002. Print.

Kassin, Saul M., and Lawrence S. Wrightsman. *The American Jury on Trial: Psychological Perspectives.* New York: Hemisphere, 1988. Print.

Landy, David, and Elliot Aronson. "The Influence of the Character of the Criminal and His Victim on the Decisions of Simulated Jurors." *Journal of Experimental Social Psychology* 5 (1969): 141–52. Print.

Loftus, Elizabeth F., and James M. Doyle. *Eyewitness Testimony.* 4th ed. Newark: LexisNexis, 2007. Print.

Loftus, Elizabeth F., and Katherine Ketcham. *Witness for the Defense.* New York: St. Martin's, 1992. Print.

Nemeth, C. J. "Jury Trials: Psychology and Law." *Advances in Experimental Social Psychology.* Ed. Leonard Berkowitz. New York: Academic Press, 1981. Print.

Ross, David Frank, J. Don Read, and Michael P. Toglia, eds. *Adult Eyewitness Testimony: Current Trends and Developments.* New York: Cambridge UP, 2007. Print.

Taylor, Lawrence. *Eyewitness Identification.* Charlottesville: Michie, 1982. Print.

Vinson, Dr. Donald E. *Jury Persuasion: Psychological Strategies and Trial Techniques.* 3d ed. Little Falls: Glasser LegalWorks, 1996. Print.

Yarmey, A. Daniel. *The Psychology of Eyewitness Testimony.* New York: Free Press, 1979. Print.

Amy Marcus-Newhall; updated by Marcia J. Weiss

SEE ALSO: Attraction theories; Attributional biases; Eyewitness testimony; Forensic psychology; Group decision making; Juvenile delinquency; Memory; Prejudice; Racism; Social perception.

Leadership

TYPE OF PSYCHOLOGY: Social psychology

Leadership involves a complex set of interactions between an individual and a group. The conclusion of extensive research on leadership is that good leaders come in many forms; there is no one best type of leader. Effective leadership has been shown to depend on characteristics of the group and its environment as well as those of the leader.

KEY CONCEPTS

- Consideration
- Contingency theory
- Initiating structure
- Leader-matching training
- Least-preferred coworker
- Transformational leadership

INTRODUCTION

Much of the behavior of individuals is shaped and influenced by other people. Someone who has relatively more influence over others—for better or worse—can be called a leader. This influence can arise naturally through personal interactions, or it may be attributed to a structuring of relationships whereby one person is designated as having power over, or responsibility for, the others.

CONSIDERATION VERSUS INITIATING STRUCTURE

In general, theories of leadership make a distinction between two broad types of behavior. One type, often called consideration, revolves around the leader's relationship with the group members. The leader who exhibits this type of behavior shows warmth, trust, respect, and concern for the group members. Communication between the leader and the group is two-way, and group members are encouraged to participate in decision making. The second type of leader behavior concerns initiating structure. This construct refers to a direct focus on performance goals. The leader who is high in initiating structure defines roles, assigns tasks, plans work, and pushes for achievement.

Over the years, theorists differed in their views on the optimal mix of consideration and initiating structure in their conceptions of the ideal leader. Those advocating a human-relations approach saw leadership success resulting from high consideration and low initiating structure. Others, however, argued for the intuitive appeal of

a leader being high on both dimensions. Research soon revealed that there was no single best combination for every leader in every position.

CONTINGENCY THEORY

One approach to the study of leadership, Fred Fiedler's contingency theory, is founded on the assumption that effective leadership depends on the circumstances. Every leader is assumed to have either a work focus or a worker focus. This is measured by the "least-preferred coworker" scale. By asking people a series of questions about the person with whom they have worked least well, the procedure permits an evaluation of the degree to which one can keep work and relationships separate.

Three characteristics of a situation are deemed important in determining which style will work best. First and most important is the quality of the relations between the leader and members of the group. To assess leader-member relations, a leader is asked to use a five-point scale to indicate extent of agreement or disagreement with statements such as "My subordinates give me a good deal of help and support in getting the job done." After scoring the leader's responses to such items, the leader-member relations are characterized as "good" or "poor."

The second most important feature of a situation is the amount of task structure. A situation is classified as "high" or "low" depending on the leader's rating of the frequency with which various statements are true. The statements ask whether there is a quantitative evaluation of the task, whether roles are clearly defined, whether there are specific goals, whether it is obvious when the task is finished, and whether formal procedures have been established.

According to contingency theory, the third—and least important—characteristic of a situation is the degree of power inherent in the leader's position. Position power is assessed by asking questions such as whether the leader can affect the promotion or firing of subordinates and if the leader has the necessary knowledge for assigning tasks to subordinates. As with the other features, there are two types of position power, strong or weak.

In summary, there are eight possible types of situations, according to contingency theory: every possible combination of leader-member relations (good vs. poor), task structure (high vs. low), and position power (strong vs. weak). These eight combinations vary along a continuum from high situational control (good leader-member relations, high task structure, and strong position power) to low situational control (poor leader-member relations, low task structure, and weak position power). Fiedler notes that the match between situation and leader orientation is critical for effective leadership. He recommends an emphasis on task performance in the three situations with the highest situational control and in the one with extremely low situational control. For the remaining four situations, the theory suggests that a group will perform best if the leader has an employee-oriented style and is motivated by relationships rather than by task performance.

TRANSFORMATIONAL LEADERS

Using an alternative perspective, Bernard Bass conceptualizes leadership as a transaction between followers and their leader. He sees most leadership as characterized by recognizing what followers want and trying to see that they get what they want—assuming that the followers' behavior warrants it. In short, the leader and followers exchange rewards and promises of rewards for the followers' cooperation. A minority of leaders are able to motivate their followers to accomplish more than they originally expected to accomplish. This type of leader is called "transformational." A transformational leader affirms the followers' beliefs about the values of outcomes; moves followers to consider the interests of the team, organization, or nation above their own self-interests; and raises the level of needs that followers want to satisfy. Among those who may be called transformational leaders are Alfred Sloan, for his reformation of General Motors; Henry Ford, for revolutionizing US industry; and Lee Iacocca, for revitalizing the Chrysler Corporation. Although transformational leadership has been found in a wide variety of settings, the research on its effectiveness has been almost exclusively conducted by Bass and his colleagues.

GENDER AND CULTURAL DIFFERENCES IN LEADERSHIP

There has been much speculation about the differences between men and women in their leadership abilities. Psychologists examine these differences by performing controlled studies. In two field studies of leadership in the United States Military Academy at West Point, Robert Rice, Debra Instone, and Jerome Adams asked participants (freshmen) in a training program to evaluate their squad leaders (juniors and seniors). The program consisted of two parts. First there was a six-week period of basic training covering military protocol, tradition, and skill (such as weapon use and marching). The second part was a field training program covering combat-oriented tasks (such as fabricating bridges, driving tanks, directing artillery fire, and conducting reconnaissance exercises). About 10 percent of the leaders in each program were women. The participants' responses on questionnaires showed the men and women to be comparable in terms of their success as leaders and in the nature of their leadership styles. This conclusion is in agreement with the observations of real operational leadership roles at the academy.

Although sex differences in leadership effectiveness appear to be minimal, there appear to be other group characteristics that are important determinants of leadership behavior. For example, in 1981 Frank Heller and Bernhard Wilpert reported different influence styles for managers from different countries. They determined the extent to which senior and subordinate managers involved group members in decisions. At one extreme, managers made decisions without explanation or discussion. At the other extreme of influence, they delegated decisions, giving subordinates complete control. Their data indicated that participation was emphasized in nations such as Sweden and France, but not in Israel. The United States was somewhere in the middle.

LEADERSHIP STYLE RESEARCH

Regardless of the extent to which there are differences among various groups of people, it is clear that there remain individual differences in leadership style. What are the implications for attempts to improve leadership effectiveness if there is no single best leadership style for all situations? One approach is to select the leader who exhibits those characteristics that are most appropriate for the situation.

Another approach, promoted by Fiedler and colleagues, is to engineer the situation to match the characteristics of the leader. That is, people cannot change the extent of task performance or employee orientation in their leadership styles, but they can change the characteristics of their situations. The program to accomplish this uses a self-taught learning process. First the person fills out a questionnaire designed to assess leadership style. Then the characteristics of that individual's situation, leader-member relations, task structure, and position power are measured. Finally, the person is taught to change the situation to mesh with his or her personality. This might involve such tactics as influencing the supervisor to alter position power or redesigning work to modify task structure. A test of this process was conducted by Fiedler and Martin Chemers in 1984 at Sears, Roebuck, and Company. They implemented eight hours of leader-matching training in two of five randomly selected stores. The other stores had equivalent amounts of training discussions. Subsequent rates of the managers on eight performance scales used by Sears showed those who had received the leader-matching training to be superior on every performance dimension.

ASSESSING LEADERSHIP TYPES

There have been other applications of leadership research that recommend that the leader choose the appropriate behavior. Victor Vroom and Philip Yetton urge leaders to adopt one of four leadership types. The autocratic leader solves the problem independently, with or without information from subordinates. A consultative leader shares the problem with individual subordinates or with the group and obtains ideas and suggestions that may or may not influence the final decision. A group leader shares the problem with an individual, and together they find a mutually agreeable solution, or with a group that produces a consensus solution that the leader implements. A delegatory leader gives the problem to a single subordinate, offering relevant information but not exerting any influence over the subordinate's decision.

Which of the above four types of leadership is advocated depends on the answers to a series of questions about the need for a quality solution, the amount of information available to the leader and subordinates, the structure of the problem, and attitudes of subordinates. The questions are arranged in a decision tree, so that at each step the leader answers "yes" or "no" and then proceeds to the next step. Vroom has developed a training program based on this model. It has several components. First is an explanation of the theory. Trainees practice using the theory to describe leader behavior and deciding how they would handle various hypothetical situations. Then trainees take part in simulated leadership situations and receive feedback on both their actual behavior and the leader behavior that is prescribed by the theory. Finally, there are small-group discussions about the experience. The goal is for trainees to learn how and when to adopt new leadership patterns. Reactions of participants to the program tend to be highly favorable.

LEADER BEHAVIOR RESEARCH

Concerns about leadership are evident in nearly every aspect of society. Problems such as illiteracy, inferior education, and environmental destruction are routinely attributed to misguided leadership, ineffective leadership, or an absence of leadership. Within organizations, leaders are held accountable for the work of their subordinates and the ultimate success of the organization. Because of its obvious importance, psychologists have pursued the study of leadership with the goal of developing explanations about the factors that contribute to effective leadership.

One popular conception of leadership is that it is a personality trait. If so, people vary in the extent to which they have leadership abilities. It would also be logical to expect that people in positions of leadership will have different personality characteristics from those who are followers. Yet surprisingly, the results of a large number of studies comparing the traits of leaders and followers have revealed only a few systematic differences. For example, those who are in positions of leadership appear to be, on average, slightly more intelligent and self-confident than followers; however, the magnitude of such differences tends to be small, so there is considerable overlap between leaders and followers. One problem in using this evidence to conclude that individual differences in personality determine leadership is that the traits noted may be the result, rather than the cause, of being in a position of leadership. For example, a person who, for whatever reason, is in a position of leadership may become more self-confident.

This research suggests that there are many factors besides personality that determine the ascent to a position of leadership. This is not so surprising if one considers that groups vary in many ways, as do their leadership needs. Thus there is no clear "leadership type" that is consistent across groups. For this reason, psychologists have tended to abandon the study of leadership as a personality characteristic and pursue other approaches. The advent of an emphasis on leader behavior occurred at Ohio State University in the 1950s. Ralph Stogdill, Edwin Fleischman, and others developed the constructs of leader consideration and initiating structure. These constructs have proved to be useful in several theories of leadership and have been important in attempts to improve leader effectiveness, particularly in organizational settings.

In addition to academic settings, applied settings have been important in the history of leadership research. Studies conducted by the oil company Exxon in an attempt to improve leadership effectiveness led to the independent development of the managerial grid by Robert Blake and Jane Mouton. The two important dimensions of leader behavior that emerged from this work are concern for people and concern for production.

BIBLIOGRAPHY

Bass, Bernard M. *Bass and Stogdill's Handbook of Leadership*. 3d ed. New York: Free Press, 1990. Print.

Bass, Bernard M.. *Leadership and Performance Beyond Expectations*. New York: Free Press, 1985. Print.

Brady, Chris, and Orrin Woodward. *Launching a Leadership Revolution: Mastering the Five Levels of Influence*. New York: Business Plus, 2008. Print.

Day, David V., and John Antonakis. *The Nature of Leadership*. 2d ed. Thousand Oaks: SAGE, 2012. Kellerman, Barbara. *The End of Leadership*. New York: Harper Business, 2012. Print.

Kouzes, James M., and Barry Z. Posner. *The Leadership Challenge*. 4th ed. San Francisco: Jossey, 2008. Print.

Smith, Blanchard B. "The TELOS Program and the Vroom-Yetton Model." *In Crosscurrents in Leadership*. Ed. James G. Hunt and Lars L. Larson. Carbondale: Southern Illinois UP, 1979. Print.

Williams, Pat, and Jim Denney. *Leadership Excellence*. Uhrichsville: Barbour, 2012. Print.

Yukl, Gary A. *Leadership in Organizations*. 5th ed. Englewood Cliffs: Prentice, 2001. Print.

Janet A. Sniezek

SEE ALSO: Behavioral assessment; Crowd behavior; Group decision making; Groups; Human resource training and development; Personality rating scales; Power.

Learned helplessness

TYPE OF PSYCHOLOGY: Learning

The concept of learned helplessness, first observed in laboratory animals, has been applied to humans in various situations, particularly those experiencing depression. The theory states that feelings of helplessness are often learned from previous experience, and it should also be possible to unlearn them..

KEY CONCEPTS

- Attribution
- Helplessness
- Learning
- Personality
- Self-concept

INTRODUCTION

The concept of learned helplessness originated with experiments performed on laboratory dogs by psychologist Martin E. P. Seligman and his colleagues. Seligman noticed that a group of dogs in a learning experiment were not attempting to escape when they were subjected to an electric shock. Intrigued, he set up further experiments using two groups of dogs. One group was first given electric shocks from which they could not escape. Afterward, even when these dogs were given shocks in a situation where they could avoid them, most of them did not attempt to escape. By comparison, another group, which had not first been given inescapable shocks, had no trouble jumping to avoid the shocks. Seligman also observed that even after the experiment, the dogs that had first received the unavoidable shocks seemed to be abnormally inactive and had reduced appetites.

After considerable research on the topic, Seligman and others correlated this "learned" helplessness with depression. It seemed to Seligman that when humans or other animals feel unable to extricate themselves from a highly stressful situation, they perceive the idea of relief to be hopeless and thus give up. The belief that they cannot affect the outcome of events no matter what force they exert on their environment seems to create an attitude of defeat. Actual failure eventually follows, thereby reinforcing that belief. It seems that the reality of the situation is not the crucial factor; what matters is the perception that the situation is hopeless.

ATTRIBUTIONAL STYLE QUESTIONNAIRE

As research continued, Seligman discovered that exposure to uncontrollable negative situations did not always lead to helplessness and depression. Moreover, the results yielded no explanation of the loss of self-esteem frequently seen in depressed persons. To refine their ability to predict helpless attitudes and behavior, Seligman and his colleagues developed a measuring mechanism called the attributional style questionnaire. The attributional style questionnaire involves twelve hypothetical events, six bad and six good.

Subjects are told to imagine themselves in the situations and to determine what they believe would be the major cause of the situation if it were to happen to them. After they complete the test, their performance is rated according to stability versus instability, globality versus specificity, and externality versus internality. An example of stable, global, internal perceptions would be a feeling of stupidity for one's failure; an unstable, specific, and external perception might consider luck to be the cause of the same situation. The questionnaire has been used by some industries and corporations to identify people who may not be appropriate for certain positions requiring assertiveness and a well-developed ability to handle stress. It has also been used to identify individuals who may be at high risk for developing psychosomatic disorders so that early intervention can be implemented.

Perhaps the primary significance of learned helplessness is its model of how a person's perception of a life event can influence that person's behavior, thus affecting his or her life and possibly the lives of others. Seligman believes that the way people perceive and explain the things that happen to them may be more important than what actually happens. These perceptions can have serious implications for a person's mental and physical health.

PERCEPTIONS OF HELPLESSNESS

The human mind is so complex and the cognitive process so unknown that perception is one of the most confusing frontiers facing social scientists. Why do people perceive situations as they do, often in ways far different from how they actually transpire? If a person is convinced that an event occurred the way he or she remembers it, then it becomes that person's reality. It will be stored that way and may be retrieved that way in the future—perhaps blocking opportunities for positive growth and change because the memory is based on an inaccurate perception.

If children are taught that they are "stupid" because they cannot understand what is expected of them, for example, then they may eventually stop attempting to understand: They have learned that their response (trying to understand) and the situation's outcome are independent of each other. If such helpless feelings are reinforced, the individuals may develop the expectation that no matter what they do, it will be futile. They will then develop a new feeling—helplessness—that can be generalized to a new situation and can interfere with the future. Various studies have indeed shown that many people have been "taught" that no matter what their response, the outcome will be the same—failure—so there is no reason to try to do anything.

ROLE IN VICTIMIZATION

One example of this can be demonstrated in the area of victimized women and children. Some women's shelters and refuges have programs to retrain battered women and children in addition to protecting them. Efforts are made to teach them how to change their perceptions and give them new feelings of potency and control. The goal is to teach them that they can have an effect on their environment and have the power to administer successful positive change. For many women, assertiveness training, martial arts classes, and seminars on how to make a strong positive statement with their self-presentation (such as their choice of clothes) become matters of survival.

Children are in a much more vulnerable situation, as they must depend on adults to survive. For most children in the world, helplessness is a reality in many situations; they do not, in fact, have much control over what happens to them, regardless of the response they exhibit. Adults, whether they are parents, educators, church leaders, or older siblings, have the responsibility of being positive role models to help children shape their perceptions of the world. If children are allowed to express their feelings, and if their comments are listened to and considered, they can see that they do have some power over their environment and can break patterns of learned helplessness.

A therapist has described "Susan," a client who as a child lived with the belief that if she argued or asserted her needs with her parents, they would leave her. In the past, if she had done so, her parents would often get into a fight, and one would temporarily leave. Susan became the "perfect" child, never arguing or seeming to be ungrateful; her perception was that if she asserted her needs, she would be abandoned, and if she then begged the parent who remained to tell the absent parent that she was sorry and would never do it again, that parent would return. In reality, her parents did not communicate well and were using their child as an excuse to get angry with each other and leave. The purpose was to punish the other adult, not to hurt the child.

When Susan became an adult, she became involved with a man who mistreated her, both physically and emotionally, but always begged forgiveness after the fact. She always forgave him, believing that she had done something wrong to deserve his harsh treatment in the first place. At her first session with a therapist, she was reluctant to be there, having been referred by a women's shelter. She missed her second session because she had returned to her lover, who had found her at the shelter. Eventually, after a cycle of returns to the shelter, the therapist, and her lover, Susan was able to break free and begin the healing process, one day at a time. She told the therapist repeatedly that she believed that no matter what she did, the outcome would always be the same, and she would rather be with the man who abused her but paid attention to her than be alone. After two difficult years of concentrating on a new perception of herself and her environment, she began to experience actual power in the form of positive effectiveness on her life. She became able to see old patterns before they took control and to replace them with new perceptions.

Another example of the power that perceptions of helplessness can have concerns a man, "John," who, as a young boy, was very attached to his father and used to throw tantrums when his father had to leave for work. John's mother would drag him to the kitchen and hold his head under the cold-water faucet to stop his screaming. It worked, but John grew up with an impotent rage toward his mother and disappointment in his father for not protecting him. He believed that no matter how he made his desires known, his feelings would be drowned, as they had been many years before. As a teenager, John grew increasingly violent, eventually getting into trouble. He did not realize that his family was dysfunctional and did not have the necessary skills to get better.

John was never able to believe in himself, even though, fueled by raw rage and little confidence, he triumphed over his pain and terror to achieve an advanced education and a black belt in martial arts. He even made a career of teaching others how to gain power in their lives and how to help nurture the spirit of children. Yet after all this, he still does not have much confidence in his abilities. He is also still terrified of water, although he forces himself to swim.

MIND-BODY RELATIONSHIP

Research has provided validity for the suspected link between how a person perceives and influences his or her environment and that person's total health and effectiveness. There is significant evidence that the mind and body are inseparable, and one can influence the other to the point of either breakdown or healing. Leslie Kamen, Judith Rodin, and Seligman have corroborated the idea that how a person explains life situations (a person's explanatory style) seems to be related to immune-system functioning. Blood samples were taken from a group of older persons who had been interviewed about life changes, stress, and health changes. Those whose interviews revealed a pessimistic or depressive explanatory style had a larger percentage of suppressor cells in their blood. Given that suppressor cells are believed to

undermine the body's ability to fight tumor growth, these discoveries suggest a link between learned helplessness (as revealed by attitude and explanatory style) and susceptibility to diseases.

Studies have also been conducted to determine whether learned helplessness and explanatory style can predict illness. Results, though inconclusive, suggest that a person's attitude and perception of life events do influence physical health some twenty to thirty years later and can therefore be a valuable predictor and a tool for prevention. Particularly if an illness is just beginning, a person's psychological state may be crucial to healing.

NEW RESEARCH DIRECTIONS

The concepts of helplessness and hopelessness versus control over life situations are as old as humankind. The specific theory of learned helplessness, however, originated with the experiments conducted by Seligman, Steven F. Maier, and J. Bruce Overmier at the University of Pennsylvania in the mid-1960s. The idea that helplessness could be learned has opened the door to many exciting new approaches to disorders formerly considered personality or biologically oriented, such as psychosomatic disorders, victimization by gender, depression (the "common cold" of mental disorders), and impaired job effectiveness.

The idea that they actually do have an effect on their environment is of tremendous importance to people suffering from depression. Most such people mention a general feeling of hopelessness, implying that they feel powerless over their reactions and behavior, which makes the journey out of depression seem overwhelming. Research-based evidence has shown that people do have the power to influence their perceptions of their environment and therefore change their reactions to it.

If the research on perception and learned helplessness is accurate, a logical next step is to find out how explanatory style originates and how it can be changed. Some suspected influences are how a child's first major trauma is handled, how teachers present information to be learned (as well as teachers' attitudes toward life events), and parental influence. Perhaps the most promising aspect of the research on learned helplessness is the idea that what is learned can be unlearned; therefore, humans really do have choices as to their destiny and quality of life. Considerable importance falls on those who have a direct influence on children, because it is they who will shape the attitudes of the future.

BIBLIOGRAPHY

Applebee, Arthur N. *The Child's Concept of Story: Ages Two to Seventeen.* Chicago: U of Chicago P, 1978. Print.

Bammer, Kurt, and Benjamin H. Newberry, eds. *Stress and Cancer.* Toronto: Hogrefe, 1981. Print.

Coopersmith, Stanley. *The Antecedents of Self-Esteem.* San Francisco: Freeman, 1967. Print.

Hooper, Nic, and Louise McHugh. "Cognitive Defusion versus Thought Distraction in the Mitigation of Learned Helplessness." *Psychological Record* 63.1 (2013): 209–17. Print.

Klein, Stephen B. *Learning: Principles and Applications.* 7th ed. Thousand Oaks: Sage, 2015. Print.

Klemm, W. R. *Mental Biology: The New Science of How the Brain and Mind Relate.* Amherst: Prometheus, 2014. Print.

Lieberman, David A. *Human Learning and Memory.* New York: Cambridge UP, 2012. Print.

Peterson, Christopher, Steven F. Maier, and Martin E. P. Seligman. *Learned Helplessness: A Theory for the Age of Personal Control.* New York: Oxford UP, 1993. Print.

Seligman, Martin E. P. *Flourish: A Visionary New Understanding of Happiness and Well-Being.* New York: Free, 2011. Print.

Seligman, Martin E. P. *Helplessness: On Depression, Development, and Death.* San Francisco: Freeman, 1975. Print.

Seligman, Martin E. P. *What You Can Change and What You Can't: The Complete Guide to Successful Self-Improvement.* 1993. New York: Vintage, 2007. Print.

Vollmayr, Barbara, and Peter Gass. "Learned Helplessness: Unique Features and Translational Value of a Cognitive Depression Model." *Cell & Tissue Research* 354.1 (2013): 171–78. Print.

Frederic Wynn

SEE ALSO: Battered woman syndrome; Causal attribution; Child abuse; Cognitive maps; Conditioning; Depression; Domestic violence; Learning; Observational learning and modeling therapy; Seligman, Martin E. P.; Stress: Theories.

Learning

TYPE OF PSYCHOLOGY: Biological bases of behavior; Learning; Motivation

Learning refers to a change in behavior as a result of experience. Learning is studied in a variety of species in an attempt to uncover basic principles. There are two major types of learning: classical (Pavlovian) conditioning and operant (instrumental) conditioning. Exposure to uncontrollable aversive events can have detrimental effects on learning. Consequences can be successfully used to develop a variety of behaviors, including even random, unpredictable performance. Learning produces lasting changes in the nervous system.

KEY CONCEPTS
- Classical conditioning
- Contingency
- Law of effect
- Learned helplessness
- Operant conditioning
- Shaping

INTRODUCTION

Learning has been of central interest to psychologists since the beginning of the field in the late 1800's. Learning refers to changes in behavior that result from experiences. The term "behavior" includes all actions of an organism, both those that are directly observable, such as typing at a keyboard, and those that are unobservable, such as thinking about how to solve a problem. Psychologists studying learning work with a variety of species, including humans, rodents, and birds. Nonhuman species are studied for a variety of reasons. First, scientists are interested in fundamental principles of learning that have cross-species generality. Second, the degree of experimental control that can be obtained with nonhumans is much higher than with humans. These controlled conditions make it more likely that any effect that is found is due to the experimental manipulations rather than to some uncontrolled variable. Third, studying the learning of nonhumans can be helpful to animals. For example, a scientist might need to know the best way to raise an endangered giant condor so it is more likely to survive when introduced to the wild.

There are two major types of learning. Classical conditioning (also called Pavlovian `conditioning, after Russian physiologist Ivan Petrovich Pavlov) involves the transfer of control of reflexes to new environmental stimuli. For example, when a person gets a glaucoma test at an optometrist's office, a puff of air is delivered into the eyes, which elicits blinking. After this experience, putting one's head into the machine elicits blinking. The glaucoma-testing machine now elicits the reflex of blinking, before the air puff is delivered.

Operant conditioning, also called instrumental conditioning, involves the regulation of nonreflexive behavior by its consequences. American psychologist Edward L. Thorndike was a pioneer in the study of operant conditioning, publishing his work about cats escaping from puzzle boxes in 1898. Thorndike observed that over successive trials, movements that released a latch, allowing the animal to get out of the box and get some food, became more frequent. Movements not resulting in escape became less frequent. Thorndike called this the law of effect: responses followed by satisfaction would be strengthened, while responses followed by discomfort would be weakened. The study of operant conditioning was greatly extended by American behaviorist B. F. Skinner, starting in the 1930's.

In the 1960's, American psychologists Martin E. P. Seligman, Steven F. Maier, J. Bruce Overmier, and their colleagues discovered that the controllability of events has a large impact on future learning. Dogs exposed to inescapable electric shock became passive and failed to learn to escape shock in later situations in which escape was possible. Seligman and his colleagues called this phenomenon learned helplessness because the dogs had learned that escape was not possible and gave up. The laboratory phenomenon of learned helplessness has been applied to the understanding and treatment of human depression and related conditions.

In the 1970's, some psychologists thought the use of rewards (such as praise or tangible items) was harmful to motivation, interest, and creativity. Beginning in the 1990's, however, American Robert Eisenberger and Canadian Judy Cameron, conducting research and analyzing previous studies, found that rewards generally have beneficial impacts. Rewards appear to have detrimental effects only when they are given regardless of how the person or animal does. Furthermore, the work of Allen Neuringer and his colleagues has shown that, contrary to previous thinking, both people and animals can learn to behave in random, unpredictable ways.

The changes in behavior produced by learning are accompanied by changes in physiological makeup. Learning is associated with changes in the strength of connections between neurons (nerve cells in the brain), some quite long-lasting. Eric R. Kandel and his colleagues have documented the changes in physiology underlying relatively simple learning in giant sea snails, progressing to more complex behaviors in mammals. Similar physiological changes accompany learning in a variety of organisms, highlighting the continuity of learning across different species.

CLASSICAL CONDITIONING

Classical conditioning was first systematically investigated by Pavlov beginning in the late 1800's and into the 1900's. Classical conditioning involves the transfer of control of an elicited response from one stimulus to another, previously neutral, stimulus. Pavlov discovered classical conditioning accidentally while investigating digestion in dogs. A dog was given meat powder in its mouth to elicit salivation. After this process had been repeated a number of times, the dog would start salivating before the meat powder was put in its mouth. When it saw the laboratory assistant, it would start to salivate, although it had not initially salivated at the sight. Pavlov devoted the rest of his long career to the phenomenon of classical conditioning.

In classical conditioning, a response is initially elicited by an unconditioned stimulus (US). The US is a stimulus that elicits a response without any prior experience. For example, the loud sound of a balloon bursting naturally causes people to blink their eyes and withdraw from the noise. The response that is naturally elicited is called the unconditioned response (UR). If some stimulus reliably precedes the US, then over time it, too, will come to elicit a response. For example, the sight of an overfull balloon initially does not elicit blinking of the eyes. Because the sight of the balloon predicts the loud noise to come when it bursts, however, eventually people come to blink and recoil at the sight of an overfull balloon. The stimulus with the new power to elicit the response is called the conditioned stimulus (CS) and the response elicited by the CS is called the conditioned response (CR).

Classical conditioning occurs with a variety of behaviors and situations. For example, a person who was stung by a wasp in a woodshed may now experience fear on approaching the building. In this case, the woodshed becomes a CS eliciting the CR of fear because the wasp's sting (the US) elicited pain and fear (the UR) in that place. To overcome the classical conditioning, the person would need to enter the woodshed repeatedly without incident. If the woodshed was no longer paired with the painful sting of the wasp, over time the CR would extinguish.

Many phobias are thought to arise through classical conditioning. One common successful treatment is systematic desensitization, in which the person, through progressive steps, gradually faces the feared object or situation until the fear CR extinguishes. Classical conditioning has also been recognized as the culprit in food aversions developed by people receiving chemotherapy treatments for cancer. In this case, the food becomes a CS for illness (the CR) by being paired with the chemotherapy treatment (the US) that later elicits illness (the UR). Using more advanced principles of classical conditioning learned through research with nonhumans, people are now able to reduce the degree of aversion that occurs to regular meals, thus preventing the person from developing revulsions to food, which would further complicate the treatment of the cancer by introducing potential nutritional problems.

OPERANT CONDITIONING

Operant conditioning (also called instrumental conditioning) involves the regulation of voluntary behavior by its consequences. Thorndike first systemically studied operant conditioning in the late 1800's. He placed cats in puzzle boxes and measured the amount of time they took to escape to a waiting bowl of food. He found that with increasing experience, the cats escaped more quickly. Movements that resulted in being released from the box, such as stepping on a panel or clawing a loop in a string, became more frequent, whereas movements that were not followed by release became less frequent. This type of operant learning is called trial-and-error learning, because there is no system to teach the behavior. Instead, the organism makes many mistakes, which become less likely over time, and sometimes hits on the solution, which then becomes more likely over time.

Beginning in the 1930's, Skinner greatly extended and systematized the study of operant conditioning. One of his major contributions was to invent an apparatus called the operant chamber, which provided a controlled environment in which behavior was automatically recorded. In the operant chamber, an animal, such as a rat, would be able to make an arbitrary response, such as pressing a small lever on the side of the chamber with its paws. The apparatus could be programmed to record the response automatically and provide a consequence, such as a bit of food, to the animal. There are several advantages to this technique. First, the chamber filters out unplanned

sights and sounds that could disturb the animal and affect ongoing behavior. Second, the animal is free to make the response at any time, and so response rate can vary over a wide range as a result of any experimental manipulations. This range means that response rate is a sensitive measure to detect the effects of changes the experimenter makes. Third, the automatic control and recording means that the procedure can be repeated exactly the same way in every experimental session and that the experimenter's ideas about what should happen cannot influence the outcome. The operant conditioning chamber is used extensively today in experiments investigating the learning of a variety of species from different perspectives.

One major technique to teach new behavior is called shaping. Shaping refers to providing a consequence for successive approximations to a desired response. For example, to teach a child to tie shoelaces, a parent might start by crossing the laces, forming the loops and crossing them, and having the child do the last part of pulling the loops tight. The parent would then praise the child. The parent could then gradually have the child do more and more of the task, until the whole task is successfully completed from the start. This type of approach ensures that the task is never too far out of reach of the child's current capabilities. Shaping takes place when young children are learning language, too. At first, parents and other caregivers are overjoyed at any approximation of basic words. Over time, however, they require the sounds to be closer and closer to the final, precisely spoken performance. Shaping can be used to teach a wide variety of behaviors in humans and nonhumans. The critical feature is that the requirement for the reward is gradually increased, in pace with the developing skill. If for some reason the behavior deteriorates, then the requirement can be lowered until the person is once again successful, then proceed again through increasing levels of difficulty. In order for any consequence to be effective, it should occur immediately after the behavior and every time the behavior occurs.

REINFORCERS AND PUNISHERS

In operant conditioning, there are four basic contingencies that can be used to modify the frequency of occurrence of nonreflexive behavior. A contingency refers to the relation between the situation, a behavior, and the consequence of the behavior. A reinforcement is a consequence that makes a behavior more likely in the future, whereas a punishment is a consequence that makes a behavior less likely in the future. Reinforcements and punishments come in positive and negative forms. A positive consequence is the presentation of a stimulus or event as a result of the behavior, and a negative consequence is the removal of a stimulus or event as a result of the behavior. Correctly used, the terms positive and negative refer only to whether the event is presented or removed, not whether the action is judged good or bad.

A positive reinforcment is a consequence that increases the future likelihood of the behavior that produced it. For example, if a parent were to praise a child at dinner for eating properly with a fork, and as a result the child used the fork properly more often, then praise would have served as a positive reinforcement. The vast majority of scientists studying learning recommend positive reinforcement as the best technique to promote learning. One can attempt to increase the desired appropriate behavior through positive reinforcement, rather than focusing on the undesired or inappropriate behavior. If the appropriate behavior becomes more frequent, then chances are that the inappropriate behavior will have become less frequent as well, because there are only so many things that a person can do at one time.

A negative reinforcement is a consequence that increases the future likelihood of the behavior that removed it. For example, in many cars, a buzzer or bell sounds until the driver puts on the seat belt. In this case, putting on the seat belt is negatively reinforced by the removal of the noise. Another example of negative reinforcement occurs when a child is having a tantrum in a grocery store until given candy. The removal of the screaming would serve as a negative reinforcement for the parent's behavior: In the future when the child was screaming, the parent would probably be more likely to give the child candy. Furthermore, the parent is providing positive reinforcement for screaming by presenting a consequence (candy) for a behavior (screaming) that makes the behavior more likely to occur in similar situations in the future. This example should make clear that reinforcement is defined in terms of the presentation or removal of an event increasing the likelihood of a behavior in the future, not in terms of intentions or opinions. Most parents would not consider the behavior inadvertently created and maintained in this way to be "positive."

Positive punishment refers to the presentation of an event that decreases the likelihood of the behavior that produced it. For example, if a person touches a hot stove, the pain that ensues makes it much less likely that the person will touch the stove under those conditions in the future. In this case, the behavior (touching the stove) produces a stimulus (pain) that makes the behavior less frequent. Negative punishment, on the other hand, refers to the removal of an event that decreases the likelihood of the behavior that produced it. For example, if a birdwatcher walking through the woods makes a loud move that causes all of the birds to fly away, then the watcher would be less likely to move like that in the future. In this way, watchers learn to move quietly to avoid disturbing the birds they are trying to observe.

Negative reinforcement, positive punishment, and negative punishment all involve what is called aversive control. An aversive stimulus is anything that an organism will attempt to escape from or try to avoid if possible. Aversive control refers to learning produced through the use of an aversive stimulus. For example, parents sometimes use spanking or hitting in an attempt to teach their child not to do something, such as hitting another child. This type of approach has been shown to have a number of undesirable outcomes, however. One problem is that the appropriate or desired alternative behavior is not taught. In other words, the child does not learn what should be done instead of what was done. Another problem is that the use of aversive stimuli can produce aggression. Humans and nonhumans alike often respond to painful stimuli with an increased likelihood of aggression. The aggression may or may not be directed toward the person or thing that hurt them. Additionally, the use of aversive control can produce avoidance—children who have been spanked or hit may try to stay away from the person who hurt them. Furthermore, through observation, children who have been spanked may be more likely to use physical harm to others as an attempted solution when they encounter conflict. Indeed, corporal punishment (the use of spanking or other physical force intended to cause a child to experience pain, but not injury, for the purpose of correction) has been linked to many undesirable outcomes for children, some of which extend well into adulthood. Beginning in the 1970's, American psychologist Murray Straus and his colleagues investigated the impact of corporal punishment on children. Their findings indicated that the use of corporal punishment is associated with an increase in later antisocial behavior as a child, a decrease in cognitive development relative to children who are not spanked, and an increased likelihood of spousal abuse as an adult, in addition to several other detrimental outcomes.

LEARNED HELPLESSNESS

As Seligman, Maier, and Overmier discovered, exposure to uncontrollable aversive events can have profound impacts on future learning, a phenomenon called learned helplessness. In learned helplessness, an organism that has been exposed to uncontrollable aversive events later has an impaired ability to learn to escape from aversive situations and even to learn new, unrelated behaviors. The phenomenon was accidentally discovered in laboratory research with dogs. Seligman and his colleagues found that dogs that were exposed to electrical shocks in a harness, with no possibility of escape, later could not learn to escape shocks in a shuttle box in which they had only to jump to the other side. Disturbingly, they would lie down and whimper, not even trying to get away from the completely avoidable shocks. Dogs that had not been exposed to the uncontrollable shocks learned to escape in the shuttle box rapidly. More important, dogs exposed to the same number and pattern of shocks, but with the ability to turn them off, also had no trouble learning to escape in the shuttle box. In other words, it was the exposure to uncontrollable shocks, not just shocks, that produced the later deficit in escape learning. Moreover, the dogs that had been exposed to uncontrollable aversive events also had difficulties learning other, unrelated, tasks. This basic result has since been found many times with many different types of situations, species, and types of aversive events. For example, learned helplessness has been shown to occur in dogs, cats, mice, rats, gerbils, goldfish, cockroaches, and even slugs. Humans show the learned helplessness phenomenon in laboratory studies as well. For example, people exposed to an uncontrollable loud static noise later solved fewer anagrams (word puzzles) than people exposed to the same amount and pattern of noise but who could turn it off.

Learned helplessness has major implications for the understanding and treatment of human depression. Although certainly the case with people is more complex, animals that have developed learned helplessness in the laboratory show similarities to depressed people. For example, they have generalized reduced behavioral output. Similarly, early on researchers discovered that learned helplessness in rats could be prevented by treatment with antidepressant medication. Furthermore, exposure to uncontrollable aversive events produces deficiencies in immune system function, resulting in greater physical ailments, in both animals and people. In people, serial combinations of uncontrollable aversive events, such as sudden and unexpected loss of a spouse or child, being laid off from a job, or losing a home to fire, can result in the feeling that one is powerless and doomed. These feelings of helplessness can then produce changes, such as decreased interest in life and increased illness, which further compound the situation. Fortunately, there are effective treatments for learned helplessness. One solution already mentioned is antidepressant medication, which may work in part because it overcomes the physiological changes produced by the helpless experience. Additionally, therapy to teach effective coping and successful learning experiences can reverse learned helplessness in people and laboratory animals.

LEARNED CREATIVITY AND VARIABILITY

Beginning in the 1970's, some psychologists began to criticize the use of rewards to promote learning. Tangible rewards as well as praise and attention, they argued, could interfere with creativity, problem-solving ability, motivation, and enjoyment. Fortunately, these concerns were allayed in the 1990's by careful research and examination of previous research, most notably that of Eisenberger and Cameron. Together, they analyzed the results of more than one hundred published studies on the effects of rewards and found that, in general, rewards increase interest, motivation, and performance. The only situation in which rewards had detrimental effects was when they were offered independently of performance. In other words, giving "rewards" regardless of how the person does is bad for morale and interest.

Furthermore, several aspects of performance previously thought to be beyond the domain of learning, such as creativity and even randomlike behavior, have been demonstrated to be sensitive to consequences. Children can learn to be creative in their drawing, in terms of the number of novel pictures drawn, using rewards for novelty. Similarly, as shown by the work of American psychologist Allen Neuringer and his colleagues, people and animals alike can learn to engage in strings of unpredictable behavior that cannot be distinguished from the random sort of outcomes generated by a random number generator. This finding is particularly interesting given that this novel behavior has been found to generalize to new situations, beyond the situation in which the learning originally occurred. Learned variability has been demonstrated in dolphins, rats, pigeons, and humans, including children with autism. Learning to be creative and to try new approaches has important implications for many aspects of daily life and problem solving.

BIOLOGICAL BASES OF LEARNING

The features of learning do not occur in a vacuum: They often produce lasting, physiological changes in the organism. The search for the physical underpinnings of learning has progressed from relatively basic reflexes in relatively simple organisms to more complex behaviors in mammals. Beginning in the 1960's, Kandel and his colleagues started to examine simple learning in the large sea snail Aplysia. This snail was chosen as a model to study physiological changes in learning because its nervous system is relatively simple, containing several thousand neurons (nerve cells) compared to the billions of neurons in mammals. The neurons are large, so researchers can identify individual cells and monitor them for changes as learning progresses. In this Nobel Prize-winning work, Kandel and his colleagues outlined many of the changes in the degree of responsiveness in connections between neurons that underlie classical conditioning processes. The same processes have been observed in other species, including mammals, and the work continues to expand to more complex behavior. This research shows the commonality in learning processes across species and emphasizes the progress in understanding the physical basis that underlies learning.

BIBLIOGRAPHY

Branch, Marc N., and Timothy D. Hackenberg. "Humans Are Animals, Too: Connecting Animal Research to Human Behavior and Cognition." *In Learning and Behavior Therapy*, edited by William O'Donohue. Boston, Mass.: Allyn & Bacon, 1998. The authors explain the relevance of work with nonhumans to humans. Includes a discussion of the effects of explicit rewards on motivation and the phenomenon of learning without awareness. This book chapter is clearly written and understandable to the interested nonprofessional reader.

Carroll, Marilyn E., and J. Bruce Overmier, eds. *Animal Research and Human Health: Advancing Human Welfare Through Behavioral Science*. Washington, D.C.: American Psychological Association, 2001. This comprehensive book contains descriptions of the application of research with animals to a variety of human conditions, including anxiety, stress, depression, drug abuse, aggression, and a variety of areas of learning. Also contains a section on the ethics of using animals in behavioral research and a list of additional readings.

Eisenberger, Robert, and Judy Cameron. "The Detrimental Effects of Reward: Myth or Reality?" *American Psychologist* 51, no. 11 (1996): 1153-1166. This journal article in the premier publication of the American Psychological Association provides an analysis of more than one hundred studies and finds that rewards generally are not detrimental, but in fact beneficial, to motivation, interest, and enjoyment of a task. Although the article contains advanced statistical techniques, they are not critical to the understanding of the findings.

Mazur, James E. *Learning and Behavior*. 6th ed. Upper Saddle River, N.J.: Prentice Hall, 2006. This best-selling introduction to the topic of learning and behavior assumes no prior knowledge of psychology. The reading is straightforward though sometimes challenging as it covers the basics of classical and operant conditioning, biological bases of learning and behavior, and applications to complex human learning situations.

Overmier, J. Bruce, and V. M. LoLordo. "Learned Helplessness." *In Learning and Behavior Therapy*, edited by William O'Donohue. Boston: Allyn & Bacon, 1998. Scholarly, complete discussion of the history of research in learned helplessness, thorough description of the phenomenon, up to current controversies and debates in this area. Contains information on the physiological underpinnings of learned helplessness and the application of this research to human depression. Includes large reference section with classic papers in this area of research.

Seligman, Martin E. P. *Learned Optimism*. New York: Random House, 2006. This book by one of the pioneers in the area describes the basic research underlying the proposed therapeutic approach to address problems with learned helplessness. Contains scales to assess the reader's degree of optimism and scientifically based recommendations to change problematic behavior. Written for a broad audience.

Skinner, B. F. *Science and Human Behavior*. 1953. Reprint. Delray, N.J.: Classics of Medicine Library, 2000. This classic work by Skinner was designed to bring the study of human learning to a wide audience. Describes the application of science to human problems. Reviews basic learning principles before discussing their application to a variety of wide-ranging human issues.

Straus, Murray A., and Denise A. Donnelly. *Beating the Devil out of Them: Corporal Punishment in American Families and Its Effects on Children.* New Brunswick, N.J.: Transaction, 2001. This thought-provoking book by one of the foremost experts on family violence is written for a broad audience. Discusses the prevalence of spanking and other forms of corporal punishment. Outlines the short-term and long-term impacts of spanking on children, including increased aggression, criminality, and depression. Includes a discussion of benefits of alternative child-rearing strategies.

Amy L. Odum

SEE ALSO: Ability tests; Achievement motivation; Assessment; Cognitive ability: Gender differences; Cognitive development: Jean Piaget; Computer models of cognition; Concept formation; Cooperative learning; Dyslexia; Educational psychology; Giftedness; Human resource training and development; Imprinting; Intelligence; Intelligence quotient (IQ); Language; Logic and reasoning; Memory; Mental retardation; Observational learning and modeling therapy; Pavlovian conditioning; Problem-solving stages; Problem-solving strategies; Race and intelligence; Seligman, Martin E. P.; Teaching methods; Thought: Study and measurement.

Learning disorders

TYPE OF PSYCHOLOGY: Psychopathology

Learning disorders (LD) are the disorders usually first diagnosed in infancy, childhood, or adolescence. Because they affect the academic progress of numerous students, they have attracted the attention of clinicians, educators, and researchers from varied disciplines. Substantial progress has been made in the assessment and diagnosis of learning disorders, but questions regarding etiology, course, and treatment of the disorder continue to challenge investigators.

KEY CONCEPTS

- Disorder of written expression
- Dyslexia
- Learning disabilities
- Learning disorder not otherwise specified
- Mathematics disorder
- Phonological processing
- Reading disorder

INTRODUCTION

Learning disorders (LD) is a general term for clinical conditions that meet four diagnostic criteria, as specified by the fifth edition of the *Diagnostic and Statistical Manual of Mental Disorders* (DSM-5), published in 2013 by the American Psychiatric Association. Those criteria include an individual displays symptoms of a learning disorder for more than six months, despite efforts to provide additional or specifically targeted instruction; the person's achievement in an academic domain (such as reading) is substantially below that expected given his or her age, schooling, and level of intelligence, and this learning disturbance interferes significantly with academic achievement or activities of daily living that require specific academic skills; the symptoms manifest during the individual's school-age years or young adulthood; and intellectual disorders, sensory problems, adverse learning conditions, and other potential causes have been ruled out. Earlier editions of the DSM listed four subcategories of learning disorders: reading disorder, mathematics disorder, disorder of written expression, and learning disorder not otherwise specified (NOS). However, the DSM-5 groups all learning disorders under the category of specific learning disorder. Specific learning disorder encompasses all varieties of learning disorders, including problems in reading, writing, and mathematics.

A variety of statistical approaches are used to produce an operational definition of academic achievement that is "substantially below" expected levels. Despite some controversy about its appropriateness, the most frequently used approach defines "substantially below" as a discrepancy between achievement and intelligence quotient (IQ) of more than two standard deviations (SD). In cases where an individual's performance on an IQ test may have been compromised by an associated disorder in linguistic or information processing, an associated mental disorder, a general medical condition, or the individual's ethnic or cultural background, a smaller discrepancy (between one and two SDs) may be acceptable. In general, the DSM-5 has moved somewhat away from the use of IQ tests in diagnosis, instead encouraging a greater focus on assessments that take environmental and other factors into account.

Differential diagnosis involves differentiating learning disorders from normal variations in academic achievement; scholastic difficulties due to lack of opportunity, poor teaching, or cultural factors; and learning difficulties associated with a sensory deficit. In cases of autism spectrum disorder, communication disorders, or mild intellectual disability, an additional diagnosis of learning disorder is given if the individual's academic achievement is substantially below the expected level given the individual's schooling and intelligence.

The term learning disorders was first applied to a clinical condition meeting these three criteria in the DSM-IV, published in 1994. Earlier editions of the DSM used other labels such as learning disturbance, a subcategory within special symptom reactions in DSM-II (1968). In DSM-III (1980) and DSM-III-R (1987), the condition was labeled academic skills disorders and listed under specific developmental disorders; furthermore, the diagnosis was based only on academic achievement substantially below the norm. The LD condition is also known by names other than those used in the psychiatric nomenclature, most frequently as learning disabilities, which may manifest in an imperfect ability to listen, think, speak, read, write, spell, or do mathematical calculations in children whose learning problems are not primarily the result of visual, hearing, or motor handicaps, mental retardation, emotional disturbance, or environmental, cultural, or economic disadvantage. Specific learning disorders are also commonly referred to by other names, such as dyslexia (reading disorder), dyscalculia (mathematics disorder), or dysgraphia (disorder of written expression). Empirical evidence about prevalence, etiology, course of the disorder, and intervention comes mainly from subjects identified as having dyslexia or learning disabilities.

PREVALENCE

Prevalence rates for learning disorders vary, depending on the definitions and methods of determining the achievement-intelligence discrepancy. According to a 2014 report by the National Center for Learning Disabilities (NCLD), approximately 5 percent of public school students in the United States have been diagnosed with a learning disorder; in addition, other children who fit the DSM-5's criteria may not yet have been officially diagnosed. The prevalence rate for specific subsets of specific learning disorder is more difficult to establish because many studies simply report the total number of learning disorders without separating them according to subcategory. According to the NCLD report, specific learning disorder with impairment in reading is the most common, followed by impairment in mathematics. Disorder of written expression alone is rare; it is usually associated with the other categories of specific learning disorder.

The NCLD report further states that male students are significantly more likely to be diagnosed with a learning disability than female students; as of 2014, two-thirds of diagnosed students were male. LD often coexists with another disorder, usually language disorders, communication disorders, or attention-deficit hyperactivity disorder (ADHD).

ETIOLOGY

There is strong empirical support for a genetic basis of reading disorders or dyslexia from behavior genetic studies. John C. DeFries and his colleagues indicate that heredity can account for as much as 60 percent of the variance in reading disorders or dyslexia. As for the exact mode of genetic transmission, Lon R. Cardon and his collaborators, in two behavior genetic studies, identified chromosome 6 as a possible quantitative trait locus for a predisposition to develop reading disorder. The possibility that transmission occurs through a subtle brain dysfunction rather than autosomal dominance has been explored by Bruce Pennington and others.

The neurophysiological basis of reading disorders has been explored in studies of central nervous dysfunction or faulty development of cerebral dominance. The hypothesized role of central nervous dysfunction has been difficult to verify despite observations that many children with learning disorders had a history of prenatal and perinatal complications, neurological soft signs, and electroencephalograph abnormalities. In 1925, neurologist Samuel T. Orton hypothesized that reading disorder or dyslexia results from failure to establish hemispheric dominance between the two halves of the brain. Research has yielded inconsistent support for Orton's hypothesis and its reformulation, the progressive lateralization hypothesis. However, autopsy findings of cellular abnormalities in the left hemisphere of dyslexics that were confirmed in brain-imaging studies of live human subjects have reinvigorated researchers. These new directions are pursued in studies using sophisticated brain-imaging technology.

Genetic and neurophysiological factors do not directly cause problems in learning the academic skills. Rather, they affect development of neuropsychological, information-processing, linguistic, or communication abilities, producing difficulties or deficits that lead to learning problems. The most promising finding from research on process and ability deficits concerns phonological processing—the ability to use phonological information (the phonemes or speech sounds of one's language)—in processing oral and written language. Two types of phonological processing, phonological awareness and phonological memory (encoding or retrieval), have been studied extensively. Based on correlational and experimental data, there is an emerging consensus that a deficit in phonological processing is the basis of reading disorder in a majority of cases.

ASSESSMENT

Assessment refers to the gathering of information to attain a goal. Assessment tools vary with the goal. If the goal is to establish the diagnosis, assessment involves the individualized administration of standardized tests of academic achievement and intelligence that have norms for the child's age and, preferably, social class and ethnicity. To verify that the learning disturbance is interfering with a child's academic achievement or social functioning, information is collected from parents and teachers through interviews and standardized measures such as rating scales. Behavioral observations of the child may be used to supplement parent-teacher reports. If there is a visual, hearing, or other sensory impairment, it must be determined that the learning deficit is in excess of that usually associated with it. The child's developmental, medical, and educational histories and the family history are also obtained and used in establishing the differential diagnosis and clarifying etiology.

If LD is present, then the next goal is a detailed description of the learning disorder to guide treatment. Tools will depend on the specific type of learning disorder. For example, in the case of dyslexia, E. Wilcutt and Pennington suggest that the achievement test given to establish the achievement-intelligence discrepancy be supplemented by others such as the Gray Oral Reading Test, a timed measure of reading fluency as well as of reading comprehension. Still another assessment goal is to identify the neuropsychological, linguistic, emotional, and behavioral correlates of the learning disorder and any associated disorders. A variety of measures exist for this purpose. Instrument selection should be guided by the clinician's hypotheses, based on what has been learned about the child and the disorder. Information about correlates and associated disorders is relevant to setting targets for intervention, understanding the etiology, and estimating the child's potential response to intervention and prognosis.

In schools, identification of LD involves a multi-disciplinary evaluation team, including the classroom teacher, a psychologist, and a special education teacher or specialist in the child's academic skill deficit (such as reading). As needed, input may be sought from the child's pediatrician, a speech therapist, an audiologist, a language specialist, or a psychiatrist. A thorough assessment should provide a good description of the child's strengths as well as weaknesses that will be the basis of effective and comprehensive treatment plans for both the child and the family. In school settings, these are called, respectively, an Individualized Education Plan (IEP) and an Individual Family Service Plan (IFSP).

TREATMENT

Most children with LD require special education. Depending on the disorder's severity, they may learn best in a one-to-one setting, small group, special class, or regular classroom plus resource room tutoring.

Treatment of LD should address both the disorder and associated conditions or correlates. Furthermore, it should include assisting the family and school in becoming more facilitative contexts for development of the child with LD. Using neuropsychological training, psychoeducational methods, behavioral or cognitive behavioral therapies, or cognitive instruction, singly or in combination, specific interventions have targeted the psychological process dysfunction or deficit assumed to underlie the specific learning disorder; a specific academic skill such as word attack; or an associated feature or correlate such as social skills. Process-oriented approaches that rose to prominence in the 1990s are linguistic models aimed at remediating deficits in phonological awareness and phonological memory and cognitive models that teach specific cognitive strategies that enable the child to become a more efficient learner. Overall, treatment or intervention studies during the last two decades of the twentieth century and at the beginning of the twenty-first century are more theory-driven, built on prior research, and rigorous in methodology. Many studies have shown significant gains in target behaviors. Transfer of training, however, remains elusive. Generalization of learned skills and strategies is still the major challenge for future treatment research, and LD remains a persistent or chronic disorder.

BIBLIOGRAPHY

American Psychiatric Association. *Diagnostic and Statistical Manual of Mental Disorders: DSM-5.* Washington: American Psychiatric Association, 2013. Print.

American Psychiatric Association. "Specific Learning Disorder." *American Psychiatric Association*. APA, 2013. Web. 5 June 2014.

Brown, F. R., H. L. Aylward, and B. K. Keogh, eds. *Diagnosis and Management of Learning Disabilities*. San Diego: Singular, 1996. Print.

Harwell, Joan M., and Rebecca Williams Jackson. *The Complete Learning Disabilities Handbook* . 3rd ed. San Francisco: Jossey-Bass, 2008. Print.

Lerner, Janet W., and Beverley Johns. *Learning Disabilities and Related Mild Disabilities: Characteristics, Teaching Strategies, and New Directions* . Boston: Houghton, 2009. Print.

Lyon, G. Reid. "Treatment of Learning Disabilities." *Treatment of Childhood Disorders*. Ed. E. J. Mash and L. C. Terdal. New York: Guilford, 1998. Print.

National Center for Learning Disabilities. *The State of Learning Disabilities*. New York: NCLD, 2014. Print.

Sternberg, Robert J., and Louise Spear-Swerling, eds. *Perspectives on Learning Disabilities*. Boulder: Westview, 1999. Print.

Felicisima C. Serafica

SEE ALSO: Aphasias; Attention-deficit hyperactivity disorder; Brain structure; Children's mental health; Cognitive ability: Gender differences; Dyslexia; Educational psychology; Forgetting and forgetfulness; Intelligence; Intelligence tests; Language; Logic and reasoning; Memory; Memory storage; Speech disorders; Teaching methods.

Lewin, Kurt

BORN: September 9, 1890, in Mogilno, Prussia (now in Poland)
DIED: February 12, 1947, in Newtonville, Massachusetts
IDENTITY: Jewish refugee to America from Nazi Germany, social psychologist
TYPE OF PSYCHOLOGY: Social psychology

Lewin originated the concept of field theory to explain how human behavior interacts with the environment in which the behavior occurs. He utilized action research, a form of research that integrates the pursuit of knowledge with action on social issues.

Kurt Lewin was born in Prussia to a middle-class Jewish family. The family moved to Berlin, Germany, when Lewin was fifteen years old. He studied the theory of science at the University of Berlin, where he completed his doctorate in 1914 under the influence of Carl Stumpf and the emerging Gestalt psychology, an orientation that focuses on "wholes" rather than the parts that make up the whole. He was injured in combat while serving in the German army in World War I, and he wrote "War Landscape" (1917), an initial description of field theory, during his recovery.

He returned to lecture at the Psychological Institute at the University of Berlin. He encouraged social action on important issues such as democracy in government and social organizations. Women were included in his research circle at a time when many scholars excluded them.

Lewin was invited to the United States to present at the International Congress of Psychologists at Yale in 1929. He presented a film that depicted the "field forces" at work on a child learning a new behavior, and he interested many psychologists in his ideas. Field theory suggests that behavior is a function of the totality of interdependent facts and circumstances that exist at the time the behavior occurs.

The presentation led to an invitation to serve as a visiting professor at Stanford University in 1930. Adolf Hitler's rise to power and increasing anti-Semitism in Germany led Lewin to accept a temporary appointment at Cornell University and then a faculty position at the University of Iowa and the Child Welfare Research Station, where he stayed until 1945. He published his first major work, *A Dynamic Theory of Personality,* in 1935.

Lewin consulted and conducted research for the United States during World War II regarding public policy issues. He developed action research, a study of the conditions and effects of types of social action that were used to facilitate social change. He was interested in minority issues and relations between groups of people, which led to the establishment of the Research Center for Group DynamicsResearch Center for Group Dynamics at the Massachusetts Institute of Technology, and action research, which gave birth to a type of group process known as the T-group or sensitivity group. Such groups used feedback, disconfirmation of a person's existing beliefs, and participant observations to motivate change.

Lewin died in 1947 at the age of fifty-six. The posthumous publication of *Resolving Social Conflicts* (1948) provided a collection of papers he wrote during his time in the United States.

BIBLIOGRAPHY

Bargal, David, Martin Gold, and Miriam Lewin. *The Heritage of Kurt Lewin: Theory, Research, and Practice.* New York: Plenum, 1992. An overview of Lewin's work and influence.

Lewin, Miriam A. "Kurt Lewin: His Psychology and a Daughter's Recollections." *In Portraits of Pioneers in Psychology*, edited by Gregory A. Kimble and Michael Wertheimer. Vol. 3. Washington, D.C.: American Psychological Association, 1998. Chapter in a series on key people in psychology, written by Lewin's daughter.

Perecman, Ellen, and Sara R. Curran, eds. *A Handbook for Social Science Field Research: Essays and Bibliographic Sources on Research Design and Methods.* London: Sage, 2006. Essays from noted scholars in the arena of field research comment on such topics as ethnography, oral history, surveys, and ethics. Includes helpful and extensive bibliography.

Mark Stanton

SEE ALSO: Field theory: Kurt Lewin; Gestalt therapy; Personality theory; Social support and mental health.

Linguistics

TYPE OF PSYCHOLOGY: Cognition; Language

Linguistics, the scientific study of the structure of language, is a close companion of cognitive psychology. The linguist Noam Chomsky changed the way psychologists view language. He sees language as a complex, partly innate system of abstract rules. Linguists and psychologists sometimes disagree about exactly how language is learned and used. They use different kinds of evidence to support their theories of language.

KEY CONCEPTS

- Chimpanzee language
- Deep structures
- Grammatical rules
- Grice's cooperative principle of conversation
- Language acquisition
- Linguistics
- Morphology
- Performance versus competence
- Phonology
- Pragmatics
- Semantics
- Surface structures
- Syntax

INTRODUCTION

Linguistics, the scientific study of the structure of language, is a field in its own right, but it makes contact with psychology at every turn. Linguists address speech perception, language development, and language comprehension, while cognitive psychologists (psychologists who study human thought) study memory for exact wording, the relationship of language and thought, and language disorders, among other topics.

The work of linguists (especially that of Noam Chomsky in the 1960s) has been instrumental in launching American cognitive psychology by drawing attention to the importance of abstract rules that characterize behavior, the distinction between performance and competence, and the distinction between "surface" behaviors and the "deep" structural basis of those behaviors. It might be said that, before Chomsky, the best theory of language structure had amounted to the art of drawing diagrams of sentences.

The best psychological account of how people learn language had been B. F. Skinner's behaviorist account. The behaviorists refrained from theorizing about invisible processes within the mind, so they limited their accounts to physically observable events, namely imitation, practice, and reinforcement. They used general principles of learning to account for all behaviors, so their theories applied to mice and pigeons as well as to humans.

CHOMSKY'S THEORY

Chomsky developed a theory of grammar that changed these assumptions forever. Linguistics no longer consisted of mere structural descriptions, but a set of rules with the (theoretical) capacity to generate all and only well-formed utterances of any given human language; linguists hoped to discover rules that were accurate reflections of the process of using language. Chomsky set the standard of "explanatory adequacy" for a linguistic theory, by which he meant that the theory could account for actual psychological processes in the use of language, not merely describe what language is like. Thus, Chomsky's revolutionary ideas about linguistics were also revolutionary ideas about psychology.

He argued that the rules of language are so complex that humans could not possibly learn them, especially not young children with no training in linguistic theory, who are exposed to confusingly faulty examples of language every day. Yet normal four-year-old children across the world effortlessly master all the basic complexities of their native languages, despite the lack of formal (or even much informal) language training. If children do not consciously learn the rules they master, they must have those rules programmed into their brains by genetics.

Chomsky did not claim that any particular language is programmed genetically into human beings. Rather, he claimed that all human languages are more similar to each other than they seem at first glance. All languages share a common core of principles, and it is this core grammar, or set of "linguistic universals," that is thought to be genetically programmed. He suggested that language (in its full complexity) is uniquely human, and the only reason humans are capable of it is that they have genetically engineered language modules in their brains (presumably, he was referring to the famous Wernicke's and Broca's areas in the left cerebral cortex).

Chomsky's claims made a dramatic impact on American psychology. Chomsky's arguments against Skinner's behaviorist account of language learning through imitation, practice, and reinforcement were seized by the scientific community and have become the generally accepted view of language acquisition. Although learning through imitation, practice, and reinforcement can pretty well account for vocabulary acquisition (though there are many who would claim that behaviorism fails in even that area), the acquisition of syntactic structure (correct word order) and of morphology (word formation, such as past tenses and plurals) cannot be understood without referring to the abstract rules underlying those abilities. Research confirms the claim that rule discovery, not rote imitation, and internal organization, not external reinforcement, best account for how young children develop language skills.

Although developmental psychologists have for the most part joined hands with linguists in rejecting behavioral accounts of language learning, the claims that Chomsky made about a genetically programmed core grammar have not fared as well in mainstream cognitive psychology. Most (but not all) psychologists working in the area suggest that what humans have genetically programmed is not anything so rigid as a core grammar, but rather a set of strategies for learning language. Psychologists also cite Katherine Snow's discovery that toddlers are not exposed to confusingly faulty examples of language (as Chomsky claimed), but that, in fact, parents generally use simplified, overly clear and correct language when addressing their young ones. Thus, language is learned through well-designed social interactions (an idea with which the great Russian scholar Lev Vygotsky would have been quite comfortable).

There has been considerable enthusiasm in efforts to disprove Chomsky's claim that language is unique to humans. In fairness to Chomsky, he never claimed that other animals could not communicate, only that those communications were not based on the complex, abstract, unlearnable, genetically programmed core grammar of human language. No one has ever challenged that version of Chomsky's claim. Researchers have, however, trained chimpanzees and gorillas to communicate with American Sign Language (ASL) or other artificial, rule-based language systems. Primates have had much more success with these systems than most people would have anticipated. They have learned vocabularies of several hundred words and have used those words in sentences for personal communication in ways that are unarguably "linguistic." The success has been so impressive and surprising that it is occasionally overlooked that there remain many serious differences between chimp language and human language, not the least of which is the level of complexity: All chimp language has been easily learnable, and no human language is.

The debate between Chomsky and his critics rages on. Chomsky still has some points about language complexity and universals that have been by and large ignored rather than improved on by current psychological theory. Chomsky in his turn has never felt compelled to modify his theory in the face of psychological research. In many ways, mainstream cognitive psychologists have lost contact with the person who won them their license to defy behaviorist theory.

BASIC LINGUISTIC CONCEPTS

Linguistic theory has come to make several basic distinctions among the various aspects of language that can be studied. Each aspect is a system of rules. The job of each rule system is to create. The rules create (or generate) all the possible (well-formed) utterances of a language. Any structures that cannot be generated by the rules are not well formed and are therefore considered illegal or anomalous. These rules are not the kind one goes to school to learn. Rather, they are the rules that every speaker of the language already knows. Every time one says something, one uses these rules without even thinking about them, or realizing they are there. In fact, people are so unaware of these rules, which they all use, that it takes a great deal of clever effort for linguistic researchers to figure out what the rules are, and there still is not agreement on the subject.

Phonology. Phonology refers to the system of distinctive sounds (or phonemes) used in a language. Phonemes are not to be confused with letters of the alphabet. A letter may stand for a sound (a phoneme), but then a letter may stand for several different phonemes (the letter c stands for at least three: cat, ceiling, and ancient) and several different letters can stand for the same phoneme (cat, kite, quiche). Every language has a somewhat different set of phonemes. Not many languages other than English have the phonemes for th (either, ether), but then English lacks the trilled r that is common in other languages.

The various sounds of a language can be categorized by their distinctive features, that is, by the characteristics they have that make them recognizably different from other sounds of the language. For example, linguists use the term "plosive" to refer to consonants that are abrupt (such as b, d, and k) or not smooth (such as m, s, and w), and they use the term "labial" to describe phonemes made with the lips (such as b, m, and w) and "velar" to describe phonemes made at the back of the throat (such as k and g). Where English distinguishes between only two labial plosives (b and p) some languages distinguish between four (they have two different b's and two different p's). That means, where English has only two possible rhymes with the word dig that begin with a labial plosive (big and pig), there are other languages that could have four different rhymes.

Not only does a language's phonology determine which sounds are and are not legal (and distinctive) in the language, but also it determines how sounds can be combined to make syllables. For example, even though all of the sounds in the syllable ngoh are completely legal in English, at least in isolation, English phonology does not allow ng at the beginning of syllables, nor h at the end (though there are languages that allow both).

Morphology. Morphology refers to the system of morphemes, that is, root words, prefixes, and suffixes). Morphemes such as "book," "hate," "-ful," and "anti-" are the smallest units of language that have meaning. (Phonemes are smaller, but they do not have any particular meaning.) Morphemes are not to be confused with words, because some morphemes (prefixes and suffixes) are less than words, and some words (such as "homework" and "uncooked") consist of several morphemes.

Morphological rules govern how morphemes may be combined to form words. For example, English morphology requires that the past tense morpheme "-ed" not stand on its own, but must appear at the end of a verb (never a noun: talk/talked but not apple/appled). Morphology also specifies exceptions to the rules (such as "make" + "-ed" = "made"). Morphophonemics are rules that govern how sounds change when morphemes are combined ("leaf" + "s" = "leaves").

Syntax. Syntax is the language's system of word combination. Syntax governs what words must appear together and what words cannot, as well as the order in which they must appear. Syntax is close to what most people mean by the word "grammar." The syntax of English allows "The door opened" but not "Opened door the." Syntax does not simply allow and disallow certain word orders; it also specifies the relationship among those words. However, there is not always agreement among theorists about exactly how syntax does this.

For instance, "I opened the door with the key" and "The key opened the door" and "The door opened" refer to essentially the same event, even though all three sentences have a different subject ("I," "the key," and "the door" each take turns "opening"). Some theories of syntax (such as case grammars) attempt to account for these relationships and some theories ignore these relationships as coincidental, or at least as the job of semantics, not of syntax.

Other theories consider the relationships between such sentences as "I kicked the ball" (active voice), "The ball was kicked by me" (passive voice), and "Did I kick the ball?" (yes/no question) to be the responsibility of syntactic theory. Such theories (for example, Chomsky's earlier theories of syntax) suggest that all three of these sentences are derived from the same kernel sentence (or deep structure), namely, "I kick+ed the ball." According to such theories, the deep structure is then transformed into one of the three (surface) sentences by different rules of transformation. Thus, there would be a transformational rule for passive voice, a transformational rule for forming questions, and even a very simple transformational rule for forming active sentences. Chomsky's more recent theories have abandoned relating these three sentences to each other (and so have abandoned the related transformations), yet he uses newly defined transformational rules to account for other things, such as the placement of "did" in "Did I kick the ball?" and "whom" in "Whom shall I give the money to?"

Although the details are still controversial, most syntactic theories claim that word order is governed by at least two kinds of rules: phrase structure rules and transformational rules. The phrase structure rules determine how the deep structure (kernel sentence) is organized, and the transformational rules determine how these deep phrase structures are rearranged to form surface structures (what is actually said out loud). People are not aware of using any of these rules; they just do it.

What is the point in a theory claiming that one or the other set of transformational rules is used by the language? It is hoped that once linguists have settled on the correct set of rules, they will be able to explain such oddities as why, as a person thumbs through Mary's pictures of her children, saying "Who is that a picture of?" is syntactically acceptable, but "Who is that Mary's picture of?" is not. So far, no theory has been able to account for all such examples of acceptable versus unacceptable utterances. This is despite decades of research by the best minds the field of linguistics has to offer. Yet every normal four-year-old speaker of English knows these rules—though they cannot state these rules, they can follow them to create a natural-sounding sentence. How is it that average four-year-olds can do effortlessly in a few years what teams of brilliant professionals cannot do in many decades? No wonder Chomsky believed these rules are not learned, but genetically programmed.

Semantics and Pragmatics. Semantics is the meaning system of a language. This includes the meaning both of individual words (for example, "father" means "male parent") and of sentences (take a list of word meanings from a sentence and come up with the point of the statement). Semantic rules state that sentences such as "Colorless green ideas sleep furiously" are nonsense (not well formed). Theories of semantics are fundamental to psychological theories of concept formation and text comprehension and memory.

Pragmatics is the system of whatever rules of language are not covered by the other systems. It includes the rules of language usage and style. Some sort of pragmatic rule tells us that "Howdy, my lord" is not acceptable, even though it is syntactically and semantically well formed. Conversational rules are pragmatic rules. When a person wishes to end a phone conversation, it is acceptable to say, "Gosh, look at the time" or "Well, it sure has been nice talking to you. Do call again," but it appears as rude to say simply, "Please stop talking." Evidently, yet another rule of pragmatics is at work.

H. P. Grice suggests that pragmatic rules allow more to be said than is actually spoken. According to Grice, anyone who engages in a conversation must agree to be conversationally cooperative, even if one's purpose is to be oppositional and uncooperative. One can be uncooperative in dozens of other ways, but if one is conversationally uncooperative, the conversation simply ends. By conversationally cooperative, Grice means that people try to be clear, succinct, relevant, and (except where they are purposely trying to deceive) truthful. Grice points out that any time people say something that obviously violates this cooperative principle, by being flagrantly unclear, wordy, irrelevant, or untruthful, they are sending an implied message. Sarcasm, for example, is accomplished by saying something obviously false, such as "I simply love being publicly humiliated." This sarcastic comment breaks the cooperative principle of truthfulness. By so doing, it not only lets the hearer know that the speaker hates being humiliated, but it does so better than does the corresponding nonsarcastic statement "I simply hate being publicly humiliated." Grice suggests that when people make such obvious violations of the cooperative principle, the hearer can infer that they did it on purpose, for effect, and can usually even figure out for what effect it was done. By counting on their listeners to figure out why they have done this, speakers can get a point across without coming right out and saying it.

THE SIGNIFICANCE OF AN UTTERANCE

The meaning of a person's statement is not purely a matter of semantics, but of pragmatics as well. Linguists have identified a variety of types of meaning conveyed by language.

Propositional content is the set of claims made by a declarative sentence (and if the sentence is a question or command, the claims made by the corresponding declarative sentence). Thus "You eat cake," "Do you eat cake?" and "Eat cake!" all have the same propositional content, namely the claim that "eating" is performed by "you" on an object of the type "cake." There can be multiple propositions in a single sentence: "The tall, dark stranger thought the statement I made was clever" includes the propositions that (1) the stranger is tall; (2) the stranger is dark; (3) I made a statement; (4) the statement was clever; (5) the stranger thought so.

The speaker is not committed to the truthfulness of every proposition in the utterance. The stranger may have thought the speaker's statement was clever, but the speaker need not agree. Furthermore, each proposition constitutes a description of some part of the common universe. One of the jobs of semantic theory is to determine the conditions under which such a description would be true (these are called truth conditions). Propositions are understood in terms of their truth conditions and in terms of their relationships to other propositions.

Thematic structure is a specification of which parts of a conversation are new, or to be emphasized, and which parts are old (given) information that the speaker can safely assume is already understood by the listener. To communicate, the speaker must use both old and new information: new, to tell listeners something they did not already know; old, to help listeners figure out where the new information fits in with what they already know, so they can relate to it. In the following examples, the same sentence is used, but a different word is emphasized. The emphasis indicates that the emphasized material is new, perhaps even unexpected, whereas the unemphasized material is treated as old, already known material.

> *John* ate the cake. (Answers the question, Who ate the cake?)

> John *ate* the cake. (Answers the question, What did John do to the cake?)

> John ate the *cake*. (Answers the question, What did John eat?)

> John ate *the* cake. (Answers the question, Which cake did John eat?)

Presupposition is an assumption that one must make before one can understand the proposition being stated. The assumption is not directly stated, but the statement makes no sense if the presupposition is not made. For example, "Did you ever stop beating your wife?" presupposes that "you" have been beating "your wife," whether the answer to the question is yes or no, and "You left your car unlocked" presupposes "you" have a car.

Entailment is a logical conclusion that must be drawn if the stated proposition is taken to be true. The entailment is not directly stated, nor is it presupposed, but once one accepts the proposition, one must accept the entailment if one is to be logical. "Marty has ten dollars" entails that Marty has more than three dollars.

Implicature is the conclusion one draws when the speaker conveys it by flagrantly breaking Grice's cooperative principle.

Illocution is the form of a sentence, whether it is declarative (a statement), imperative (a command), or interrogative (a question). Illocutionary force is the direct or implied impact of a statement, regardless of its illocution. For example, the sentence "Could you open the window?" has the illocution of a question, but it has the illocutionary force of a request (something akin to "Please open the window").

SPEECH ACTS AND INDIRECT SPEECH ACTS

Sometimes an utterance is more than just an utterance: It actually does something. When the justice of the peace says, "I now pronounce you husband and wife," the very words cause the couple in question to become husband and wife. When a person says "I promise to stop," that person thereby makes a promise. Any time an utterance does the thing it says it is doing, whether it be promising, commanding, asking, refusing, or whatever, that is a direct speech act. If an utterance accomplishes the same thing, but without coming right out and stating that it is doing so, that is an indirect speech act. "I won't do it again" is an indirect promise, since the speaker never actually said it was a promise.

There are many more kinds of meaning attached to utterances, but these serve as an introduction to the variety that linguists have identified.

EVIDENCE FOR EVALUATING LINGUISTIC THEORY

Both linguists and psychologists have debated about the nature of human language and language processes for decades. Linguists and psychologists use different kinds of data for testing their claims about language. For the most part, linguists use language judgments (of whether a given utterance is acceptable or not) to confirm or refute a proposed rule or rule system. That is, they ask native speakers of a language to judge whether this or that utterance is well formed. Linguists focus on the idealized competence of a speaker and try to avoid performance issues (such as whether an otherwise perfectly good utterance is too difficult to produce or comprehend).

Psychologists, on the other hand, use subjects' performance at perceiving, remembering, interpreting, and utilizing language as clues about human language abilities. They tend to consider idealized rules that overlook actual performance to be less satisfying.

Nonetheless, psychologists are indebted to linguists for proposing an impressive array of linguistic structures and abilities, which psychologists have then taken and tested, using their own methods. Often this endeavor is referred to as testing the psychological reality of a linguistic construct. Basically, the psychology researcher is trying to find out if the rules and structures that linguists have come up with using linguistic research methods will actually make a difference in how long a subject takes to react or how accurately a subject perceives or how well a subject remembers various words, phrases, sentences, or paragraphs. If the pattern of reaction times or of memory errors is consistent with the proposed linguistic rule (or structure), then that rule (or structure) is said to have demonstrated psychological reality.

Some linguistic rules (such as phrase structure rules) have had demonstrable psychological reality. When researchers presented clicks in the middle of a sentence, participants heard the clicks as if they happened between phrase structure boundaries (say, between the subject and predicate of a sentence) even when the clicks occurred well before (or after) the actual boundary. The fact that people's hearing is altered by the presence of phrase structure boundaries shows that those phrase structures are actually influencing their behavior and are thus psychologically real.

On the other hand, some linguistic rules (such as the passive transformation) have failed to demonstrate any psychological reality. Sentences that were more complex (because they included an extra transformation) took participants no longer to process than simpler sentences. This finding suggests that the so-called complex sentence was not in fact more complex, as far as the research participants were concerned. The supposed extra transformation had no impact on the participants and is thus concluded to have no psychological reality.

BIBLIOGRAPHY

Carnie, Andrew. *Syntax: A Generative Introduction.* 2d ed. Malden,: Blackwell, 2007. Print.

Chomsky, Noam. "Review of B. F. Skinner, Verbal Behavior." *Language* 35 (1959): 26–57. Print.

Chomsky, Noam. *Syntactic Structures.* The Hague: Mouton, 1957. Print.

Davis, Flora. *Eloquent Animals: A Study in Animal Communication.* New York: Coward, 1978. Print.

Fromkin, Victoria, and Robert Rodman. *An Introduction to Language.* 8th ed. Boston: Thomson, 2007. Print.

Grice, H. P. "Logic and Conversation." *Speech Acts*, ed. P. Cole and J. L. Morgan. New York: Academic, 1975. Print.

Harley, Trevor A. *The Psychology of Language: From Data to Theory.* 4th ed. Hove: Psychology, 2014. Print.

Harley, Trevor A. *Talking the Talk: Language, Psychology, and Science.* Hove: Psychology, 2010. Print.

Hudson, Grover. *Essential Introductory Linguistics.* Malden: Blackwell, 2002. Print.

Levelt, Willem J. M. *A History of Psycholinguistics: The Pre-Chomskyan Era.* Oxford: Oxford UP, 2014. Print.

Searle, John R. *Speech Acts: An Essay in the Philosophy of Language.* New York: Cambridge UP, 2005. Print.

Skinner, B. F. *Verbal Behavior.* 1957. Reprint. Acton: Copley, 1992. Print.

Victor K. Broderick

SEE ALSO: Bilingualism; Bilingualism and learning disabilities; Brain damage; Brain structure; Grammar and speech; Language; Nonverbal communication; Speech disorders; Speech perception; Stuttering; Thought: Inferential.

Little Albert study

DATE: 1920
TYPE OF PSYCHOLOGY: Emotion; Learning

The Little Albert study was intended to provide data with respect to the premises that an infant can be conditioned to fear a previously neutral stimulus by pairing the stimulus with one that arouses fear or avoidance, that the fear would generalize to other stimuli, and that the fear would be retained over a period of time. Despite the modest findings of the study and its limitations, the study has generated much interest in conditioning and related work since its publication.

KEY CONCEPTS
- Avoidance
- Classical conditioning
- Experimentation
- Fear
- Psychopathology

INTRODUCTION

John B. Watson and Rosalie Rayner's Little Albert study involved attempted conditioning of an infant known as Albert B. Some researchers see the work as way to explore classical conditioning as a mechanism of change in emotional behavior in young children, while other researchers view the work as a way to advance understanding in psychopathology. The study, however, must be viewed in light of the early nineteenth century methodology employed as well as the study's modest results.

Perhaps as interesting as the study itself is the historical pattern created by psychologists' accounts of the work. In the years since the publication of the Little Albert study, its methods and results have been described many times. Some researchers believe that the study's importance and its theoretical offerings have been overstated in the literature. In 1979, Ben Harris proposed possible causes for these alleged overstatements, and he discussed the changing interpretations of the Little Albert study. Any examination of the Little Albert study must deal with the manner in which changes in psychological theory have influenced psychologists' interpretations of such research endeavors.

METHOD

he Little Albert study was designed to test the premises that an infant can be conditioned to fear an animal that appears at the same time as a loud sound that was previously identified to arouse fear in the infant, that the fear would generalize to other animals or inanimate objects, and that such fears would persist over a period of time. On pretesting, nine-month-old Albert was shown to display no fear when observing certain live animals as well as several inanimate objects. In contrast, he showed fear through crying and avoidance when the experimenter struck a steel bar with a hammer near him (the unconditioned stimulus in this work).

Two months after pretesting, Albert was shown a white rat, and anytime Albert touched the rat, he was exposed to the sound of the hammer hitting a steel bar. After seven trials, Albert cried and demonstrated avoidance on presentation of the rat—the conditioned stimulus—in the absence of the loud noise. The experimenters sought to test for generalization after five days by presenting the rat along with other small animals and objects. The authors reported that Albert appeared to show a strong fear response to the rat and certain other small animals, a "negative" response to some human hair and a bearded mask, and a "mild" response to some white cotton.

After five additional days, Watson attempted to recondition Albert to the rat by one trial of rat and noise pairing and to condition Albert directly to fear the previously presented rabbit and dog. On moving Albert to a different room for testing, the child was said to demonstrate a "slight" reaction to the rat, rabbit, and dog. Watson again subjected Albert to noise and rat pairing, but the dog barked in the middle of the session, rendering the session particularly problematic. After thirty-one days, Albert was said to show "fear" when touching a mask, a sealskin coat, the rat, a dog, and a rabbit. At the same time, however, he initiated contact with the coat and the rabbit. Albert's avoidance behaviors coupled with gestures of interest are difficult to interpret, making it hard to draw conclusions regarding persistence of conditioned responses.

From Watson and Rayner's report, it is difficult to conclude that the child developed a rat phobia or that Albert responded interpretably toward the stimuli. Theoretical limitations are apparent. Also, methodological advances necessary to permit more objective and reliable assessments of emotional responses had not yet been developed. The stimuli were of a limited nature, and the data came from only one participant. Watson and Rayner never repeated the study with other subjects, and the results have never been successfully replicated. Despite the theoretical and methodological limitations of the Little Albert study, persistent interest in the work is reflected in its continued citation in psychology textbooks as well as in the public's interest in the relationship between fear and emotional well-being.

SUMMARY

The methods and findings of the Little Albert study must be understood in the context of the early history of experimental psychology. According to Harris, repeated retelling of the Little Albert study may have adversely affected the accuracy of the details of the study. Later researchers may have a tendency to reconcile findings to unify support for some theories. In addition, when a particular research endeavor is cited frequently, the consequence may be enhanced attributions of the magnitude of reported effects.

BIBLIOGRAPHY

Harris, Ben. "Whatever Happened to Little Albert?" *American Psychologist* 34. 2 (1979): 151–160. Print.

Jones, Mary Cover. "A Laboratory Study of Fear: The Case of Peter." *Pedagogical Seminary* 31 (1924): 308–315. Print.

Marks, Isaac Meyer, and David Mataix-Cols. "Diagnosis and Classification of Phobias: A Review." *Phobias*, ed. by Mario Maj et al. Hoboken: Wiley, 2004. Print.

Rolls, Geoff. *Classic Case Studies in Psychology*. 2nd ed. New York: Routledge, 2013. Print.

Todd, James T., and Edward K. Morris, eds. *Modern Perspectives on John B. Watson and Classical Behaviorism.* Westport: Greenwood, 1994. Print.

Watson, J. B., and R. Rayner. "Conditioned Emotional Reactions." *Journal of Experimental Psychology* 3 (1920): 1–14. Print.

Ronna F. Dillon and Amber D. Dillon

SEE ALSO: Behaviorism; Conditioning; Experimentation: Independent, dependent, and control variables; Fear; Phobias; Watson, John B.

Lobotomy

DATE: 1935 forward
TYPE OF PSYCHOLOGY: Psychopathology

Lobotomy describes several different surgical procedures that all result in the deliberate destruction of brain tissue located just behind the forehead. The procedure was primarily performed on individuals suffering from severe mental disturbances such as schizophrenia or chronic depression.

KEY CONCEPTS

- Freeman-Watts standard lobotomy
- Leukotome
- Prefrontal leukotomy
- Psychosurgery
- Transorbital procedure

INTRODUCTION

The surgical procedure referred to as a lobotomy was initially proposed by physicians who believed that severe emotional and cognitive disturbances were caused by aberrant neural connections in the brain. It was hypothesized that destruction of this abnormal brain tissue could lead to clinical improvements for major psychiatric disturbances. The lobotomy was used, in part, because there were relatively few treatment alternatives to improve the condition of people who suffered from severe psychiatric conditions such as schizophrenia.

Gottlieb Burckhardt, in 1890, is credited as being one of the first surgeons to perform a psychosurgery procedure on mental patients to address symptoms such as agitation and hallucinations. Others, such as Ludvig Puusepp, in 1910, began to operate more specifically on the frontal lobes of the brain to help a group of patients suffering from manic-depression psychosis. The results of the surgeries were mixed, and Puusepp, like Burckhardt, concluded that the dangerous procedure was not worth the risks to patients.

Years later, in 1935, Portuguese physician and neurologist António Egas Moniz, working with surgeon Pedro Almeida Lima, revived the psychosurgery debate by performing a prefrontal leukotomy. This type of lobotomy involved drilling holes on each side of the top of the head, near the frontal areas, and then inserting a leukotome, a needle that contains a small circular wire that can be deployed. Once the leukotome was in position, the wire was released and the instrument was twisted to cut the white matter of the brain, which contains primarily nerve connections from the frontal lobes to other areas of the brain. In 1949, Egas Moniz became the first physician from Portugal to be awarded the Nobel Prize for Physiology or Medicine for his work on the development of the lobotomy.

MOVEMENT AWAY FROM PREFRONTAL LEUKOTOMY

One year after Egas Moniz and Lima's initial prefrontal leukotomy, American physician Walter Jackson Freeman II and surgeon James Watts began to modify the medical procedures. Freeman and Watts did away with the leukotome and started to drill holes on each side of the head, near the temples. A blunt spatula was then inserted and waved toward the top and back and toward the bottom of the head, effectively severing the neural connections between the frontal lobes and the thalamus. This procedure came to be known as the Freeman-Watts standard lobotomy. This procedure was believed to be more precise in its ability to selectively destroy connections between the frontal cortex and the thalamus and to produce better clinical results. However, Freeman still did not like the fact it was a time-consuming surgery that involved drilling into the cranium and required an operating room.

In 1946, Freeman began to popularize a new version of the lobotomy called the transorbital procedure. Although this procedure had its beginnings in Italy in the late 1930s, Freeman altered the way that brain tissue would be destroyed. Freeman's procedure involved taking a sharp metal instrument (he first used an ice pick) and placing it under the patient's eyelid. A mallet would then be used to tap the instrument until it broke through the thin bone behind the eye socket. The instrument was then inserted a couple of inches into the head and moved back and forth. Freeman perfected this procedure to the point that he could train another physician to complete it in ten minutes, without the use of a surgical room. This simple transorbital procedure made it possible for lobotomies to be performed on a far larger number of patients. Although Freeman himself performed about thirty-five hundred lobotomies during his career, it is believed that tens of thousands of lobotomies were performed worldwide.

TREATMENT EFFECTIVENESS

Of Egas Moniz's first twenty patients, fourteen were reported to have recovered or to have substantially improved. The remaining six were believed to have shown some improvement in that they had had more severe symptoms (hallucinations and delusions) before the surgery. Egas Moniz was criticized because he followed his patients for only a few days after the surgery. One follow-up study that was conducted twelve years later revealed that the results were not as positive as initially reported.

Freeman reported that patients, with the exception of those who were suffering from chronic schizophrenia and a limited number of other types of psychosis, generally benefited from the procedure. Follow-up studies have found that it is difficult to determine who will benefit from a lobotomy and what kinds of detrimental effects the procedure will have on emotions and cognition. Also, proselytizers of the procedure overstated the positive outcomes. By the mid-1950s, the introduction of antipsychotic medication such as chlorpromazine (Thorazine) had begun to transform the lives of residential psychiatric patients to the point that lobotomies became seldom used.

BIBLIOGRAPHY

Culliton, B. J. "Psychosurgery: National Commission Issues Surprisingly Favorable Report." *Science* 194 (1976): 299–301. Print

El-Hai, Jack. *The Lobotomist: A Maverick Medical Genius and His Tragic Quest to Rid the World of Mental Illness.* Hoboken: Wiley, 2007. Print.

Finger, Stanley. *Origins of Neuroscience: A History of Explorations into Brain Function.* New York: Oxford UP, 2001. Print.

Johnson, Jenell. "Thinking with the Thalamus: Lobotomy and the Rhetoric of Emotional Impairment." *Journal of Literary and Cultural Disability Studies* 5.2 (2011): 185–200. Print.

Raz, Mical. "Interpreting Lobotomy—The Patients' Stories." *Psychologist* 27.1 (2014): 56–59. Print.

Raz, Mical. *The Lobotomy Letters: The Making of American Psychosurgery.* Rochester: U of Rochester P, 2013. Digital file.

Valenstein, Elliot S. *Great and Desperate Cures: The Rise and Decline of Psychosurgery and Other Radical Treatments for Mental Illness.* New York: Basic, 1986. Print.

Valenstein, Elliot S., ed. *The Psychosurgery Debate: Scientific, Legal, and Ethical Perspectives.* San Francisco: Freeman, 1980. Print.

Bryan C. Auday

SEE ALSO: Abnormality: Biomedical models; Antipsychotic medications; Brain structure; Psychobiology; Psychosurgery; Psychotic disorders; Schizophrenia: Background, types, and symptoms; Schizophrenia: Theoretical explanations.

Logic and reasoning

TYPE OF PSYCHOLOGY: Cognition

Logic and reasoning are essential elements of the human mind and underlie many daily activities. Although humans may not follow the prescriptions of formal logic precisely, human reasoning is nevertheless often systematic. Study of the structures and processes involved in the use of logic and reasoning provides insight into both the human mind and the possible creation of intelligent machines.

KEY CONCEPTS

- Atmosphere hypothesis
- Availability
- Belief-bias effect
- Confirmation bias
- Deductive reasoning
- Gambler's fallacy
- Heuristic
- Inductive reasoning
- Representativeness
- Syllogism

INTRODUCTION

Logical and reasoning tasks are typically classified as either deductive or inductive. In deductive reasoning, if the premises are true and a valid rule of inference is used, the conclusion must be true. In inductive reasoning, in contrast, the conclusion can be false even if the premises are true. In many cases, deductive reasoning also involves moving from general principles to specific conclusions, while inductive reasoning involves moving from specific examples to general conclusions.

Cognitive psychologists study deductive reasoning by examining how people reason using syllogisms, logical arguments comprising a major and a minor premise that lead to a conclusion. The premises are assumed to be true; the validity of the conclusion depends on whether a proper rule of inference is used. The classic example of deduction is as follows:

All men are mortal.

Socrates is a man.

Socrates is a mortal.

A more modern (and more controversial) example of deduction might be:

Abortion is murder.

Murder should be illegal.

Abortion should be illegal.

The second example prompts a distinction between "truth" and "validity." Even though the second syllogism is logically valid, it may or may not be true. Broadly speaking, truth refers to content (that is, applicability of the conclusion to the real world), and validity refers to form (that is, whether the conclusion is drawn logically). It is thus possible to have a valid argument that is nevertheless untrue. For a clearer example, consider this syllogism:

All dinosaurs are animals.

All animals are in zoos.

All dinosaurs are in zoos.

The conclusion is valid but is not true, because one of the premises (all animals are in zoos) is not true. Even though a valid rule of inference was applied and a valid conclusion was drawn, the conclusion is not true. If a valid conclusion has been drawn from true premises, however, the argument is called "sound."

With inductive reasoning, the validity of the conclusion is less certain. The classic example of induction is as follows:

Every crow I have seen in my life up to this time has been black.

All crows are black.

Other examples of induction include a child who begins to say "goed" (from "go") instead of "went," a detective piecing together evidence at the scene of a crime, and a stock analyst who, after observing that prices have fallen during the past two Septembers, urges clients to sell in August. In all these cases, a conclusion is drawn based on evidence observed before the conclusion. There remains the possibility, however, that additional evidence may render the conclusion incorrect. It does not matter how many positive instances (for example, black crows, September stock declines) have been observed; if one counterexample can be found (a white crow, a September stock rise), the conclusion is incorrect.

HEURISTICS

The study of induction spans a variety of methods and topics. In this article, most of the consideration of induction involves cases in which people rely on heuristics in their reasoning. Heuristics involve rules of thumb that yield ballpark solutions that are approximately correct and can be applied across a wide range of problems.

One common heuristic is representativeness, which is invoked in answering the following questions: What is the probability that object A belongs to class B, event A originates from process B, or that process B will generate event A? The representativeness heuristic suggests that probabilities are evaluated by the degree to which A is representative of B, that is, by the degree to which A resembles B. If A is representative of B, the probability that A originates from B is judged to be high; if A does not resemble B or is not similar to B, the probability that A originates from B is judged to be low.

A second heuristic is availability, which is invoked in judgments of frequency; specifically, people assess the frequency of a class by the ease with which instances of that class can be brought to mind. Factors that influence the ability to think of instances of a class, such as recency, salience, number of associations, and so forth, influence availability in such a way that certain types of events (such as recent and salient) are more available. For example, if several people one knows have had car accidents recently, one's subjective probability of being in a car accident is increased.

RULES OF INFERENCE

Before examining how people reason deductively, two rules of inference must be considered: modus ponens (the "method of putting," which involves affirming a premise) and modus tollens (the "method of taking," which involves negating a premise). Considering P and Q as content-free abstract variables (much like algebraic variables), modus ponens states that given "P implies Q" and P, one can infer Q. In the following example, applying modus ponens to 1 and 2 (in which P is "it rained last night" and Q is "the game was canceled"), one can infer 3.

1. If it rained last night, then the game was canceled.

2. It rained last night.

3. The game was canceled.

Modus tollens states that given "P implies Q" and ~Q (read "not Q"; "~" is a symbol for negation), one can infer "~P." Applying modus tollens to 1 and 4, one can infer 5.

4. The game was not canceled.

5. It did not rain last night.

In general, people apply *modus ponens* properly but do not apply *modus tollens* properly. In one experiment, four cards showing the following letters or numbers were placed in front of subjects:

E K 4 7

Subjects saw only one side of each card but were told that a letter appeared on one side and a number on the other side. Subjects judged the validity of the following rule by turning over only those cards that provided a valid test: If a card has a vowel on one side, then it has an even number on the other side. Turning over E is a correct application of *modus ponens*, and turning over 7 is a correct application of *modus tollens* (consider P as "vowel on one side" and Q as "even number on the other side"). Almost 80 percent of subjects turned over E only or E and 4, while only 4 percent of subjects chose the correct answer, turning over E and 7. While many subjects correctly applied *modus ponens*, far fewer correctly applied

modus tollens. Additionally, many subjects turned over 4, an error called affirmation of the consequent.

When stimuli are concrete, reasoning improves. In an analogous experiment, four cards with the following information were placed before subjects:

beer Coke 16 22

One side of each card showed a person's drink; the other side showed a person's age. Subjects evaluated this rule: If a person is drinking beer, that person must be at least nineteen. In this experiment, nearly 75 percent of the subjects made the correct selections, showing that in some contexts people are more likely to apply *modus tollens* properly.

When quantifiers such as "all," "some," and "none" are used within syllogisms, additional errors in reasoning occur. People are more likely to accept positive conclusions to positive premises and negative conclusions to negative premises, negative conclusions if premises are mixed, a universal conclusion if premises are universal (all or none), a particular conclusion if premises are particular (some), and a particular conclusion if one premise is general and the other is particular. These observations led to the atmosphere hypothesis, which suggests that the quantifiers within the premises create an "atmosphere" predisposing subjects to accept as valid conclusions that use the same quantifiers.

INFLUENCE OF KNOWLEDGE AND BELIEFS

Prior knowledge or beliefs can influence reasoning if people neglect the form of the argument and concentrate on the content; this is referred to as the belief-bias effect. If a valid conclusion appears unbelievable, people reject it, while a conclusion that is invalid but appears believable is accepted as valid. Many people accept this syllogism as valid:

All oak trees have acorns.

This tree has acorns.

This tree is an oak tree.

Consider, however, this logically equivalent syllogism:

All oak trees have leaves.

This tree has leaves.

This tree is an oak tree.

In the first syllogism, people's knowledge that only oak trees have acorns leads them to accept the conclusion as valid. In the second syllogism, people's knowledge that many types of trees have leaves leads them to reject the conclusion as invalid.

BIASES IN REASONING

A common bias in inductive reasoning is the confirmation bias, the tendency to seek confirming evidence and not to seek disconfirming evidence. In one study, subjects who were presented with the numbers (2, 4, 6) determined what rule (concept) would allow them to generate additional numbers in the series. In testing their hypotheses, many subjects produced series to confirm their hypotheses—for example, (20, 22, 24) or (100, 102, 104)—of "even numbers ascending by 2," but few produced series to disconfirm their hypotheses—for example, (1, 3, 5) or (20, 50, 187). In fact, any ascending series (such as 32, 69, 100,005) would have satisfied the general rule, but because subjects did not seek to disconfirm their more specific rules, they did not discover the more general rule.

Heuristics also lead to biases in reasoning. In one study, subjects were told that bag A contained ten blue and twenty red chips, while bag B contained twenty blue and ten red chips. On each trial, the experimenter selected one bag; subjects knew that bag A would be selected on 80 percent of the trials. The subject drew three chips from the bag and reasoned whether A or B had been selected. When subjects drew two blues and one red, all were confident that B had been selected. If the probability for that sample is actually calculated, however, the odds are 2:1 that it comes from A. People chose B because the sample of chips resembles (represents) B more than A, and they ignored the prior probability of 80 percent that the bag was A.

In another experiment, subjects were shown descriptions of "Linda" that made her appear to be a feminist. Subjects rated the probability that Linda was a bank teller and a feminist higher than the probability that Linda was a bank teller. Whenever there is a conjunction of events, however, the probability of both events is less than the probability of either event alone, so the probability that Linda was a bank teller and a feminist was actually lower than the probability that she was only a bank teller. Reliance on representativeness leads to overestimation of the probability of a conjunction of events.

Reliance on representativeness also leads to the gambler's fallacy. This fallacy can be defined as the belief that if a small sample is drawn from an infinite and randomly distributed population, that sample must also appear randomly distributed.

Consider a chance event such as flipping a coin (H represents "heads," T represents "tails"). Which sequence is more probable: HTHTTH or HHHHHH? Subjects judge that the first sequence is more probable, but both are equally probable. The second sequence, HHHHHH, does not appear to be random, however, and so is believed to be less probable. After a long run of H, people judge T as more probable than H because the coin is "due" for T. A problem with the idea of "due," though, is that the coin itself has no memory of a run of H or T. As far as the coin is concerned, on the next toss there is 0.5 probability of H and 0.5 probability of T. The fallacy arises because subjects expect a small sample from an infinitely large random distribution to appear random. The same misconceptions are often extended beyond coin-flipping to all games of chance.

In fallacies of reasoning resulting from availability, subjects misestimate frequencies. When subjects estimated the proportion of English words beginning with R versus words with R as the third letter, they estimated that more words begin with R, but, in fact, more than three times as many words have R as their third letter. For another example, consider the following problem. Ten people are available and need to be organized into committees. Can more committees of two or more committees of eight be organized? Subjects claimed that more committees of two could be organized, probably because it is easier to visualize a larger number of committees of two, but equal numbers of committees could be made in both cases. In both examples, the class for which it is easier to generate examples is judged to be the most frequent or numerous. An additional aspect of availability involves causal scenarios (sometimes referred to as the simulation heuristic), stories or narratives in which one event causes another and which lead from an original situation to an outcome. If a causal scenario linking an original situation and outcome is easily available, that outcome is judged to be more likely.

EVOLUTION OF STUDY

Until the twentieth century, deductive logic and the psychology of human thought were considered to be the same topic. The mathematician George Boole entitled his 1854 book on logical calculus *An Investigation of the Laws of Human Thought*. This book was designed "to investigate the fundamental laws of those operations of the mind by which reasoning is performed." Humans did not always seem to operate according to the prescriptions of logic, but such lapses were seen as the malfunctioning of the mental machinery. When the mental machinery functioned properly, humans were logical. Indeed, it is human rationality, the ability to think logically, that for many thinkers throughout time has separated humans from other animals (for example, Aristotle's man as rational animal) and defined the human essence (for example, René Descartes's "I think, therefore I am").

As a quintessential mental process, the study of reasoning is an integral part of modern cognitive psychology. In the mid-twentieth century, however, when psychology was in the grip of the behaviorist movement, little attention was given to such mentalistic conceptions, with the exception of isolated works such as Frederic C. Bartlett's studies of memory and Jerome Bruner, Jacqueline J. Goodnow, and George A. Austin's landmark publication A Study of Thinking (1956), dealing with, among other topics, induction and concept formation. The development of the digital computer and the subsequent application of the computer as a metaphor for the human mind suggested new methods and vocabularies for investigating mental processes such as reasoning, and with the ascendancy of the cognitive approach within experimental psychology and the emergence of cognitive science, research on human reasoning has become central in attempts both to understand the human mind and to build machines that are capable of independent, intelligent action.

INVOLVEMENT OF COMPUTERS
In the latter part of the twentieth century, there were attempts to simulate human reasoning with computers and to develop computers capable of humanlike reasoning. One notable attempt involved the work of Allen Newell and Herbert Simon, who provided human subjects with various sorts of problems to solve. Their human subjects would "think out loud," and transcripts of what they said became the basis of computer programs designed to mimic human problem solving and reasoning. Thus, the study of human logic and reasoning not only furthered the understanding of human cognitive processes but also gave guidance to those working in artificial intelligence. One caveat, however, is that even though such transcripts may serve as a model for computer intelligence, there remain important differences between human and machine "reasoning." For example, in humans, the correct application of some inference rules (for example, *modus tollens*) depends on the context (for example, the

atmosphere hypothesis or the belief-bias effect). Furthermore, not all human reasoning may be strictly verbalizable, and to the extent that human reasoning relies on nonlinguistic processes (such as imagery), it might not be possible to mimic or re-create it on a computer.

After being assumed to be logical or even being ignored by science, human reasoning is finally being studied for what it is. In solving logical problems, humans do not always comply with the dictates of logical theory; the solutions reached may be influenced by the context of the problem, previous knowledge or belief, and the particular heuristics utilized in reaching a solution. Discovery of the structures, processes, and strategies involved in reasoning promises to increase the understanding not only of how the human mind works but also of how to develop artificially intelligent machines.

BIBLIOGRAPHY
Halpern, Diane F. *Thought and Knowledge: An Introduction to Critical Thinking.* 4th ed. Hillsdale: Erlbaum, 2003. Print.
Holland, John H., et al. *Induction: Processes of Inference, Learning, and Discovery.* Reprint. Cambridge: MIT Press, 1989. Print.
Holyoak, Keith James, and Robert G. Morrison. *The Oxford Handbook of Thinking and Reasoning.* Oxford: Oxford UP, 2012. Print.
Johnson, Robert M. *A Logic Book: Fundamentals of Reasoning.* 5th ed. Belmont: Wadsworth, 2007. Print.
Johnson-Laird, Philip Nicholas. *Mental Models.* Cambridge: Harvard UP, 1983. Print.
Kahneman, Daniel, Paul Slovic, and Amos Tversky, eds. *Judgment Under Uncertainty: Heuristics and Biases.* New York: Cambridge UP, 2007. Print.
Kelley, David. *The Art of Reasoning.* 3d ed. New York: Norton, 1998. Print.
Manktelow, Kenneth Ian. *Thinking and Reasoning: An Introduction to the Psychology of Reason, Judgment and Decision Making.* Hove: Psychology Press, 2012. Print.
Ribeiro, Henrique Jales. *Inside Arguments: Logic and the Study of Argumentation.* Newcastle upon Tyne: Cambridge Scholars, 2012. Print.
Sternberg, Robert J., and Talia Ben-Zeev. *Complex Cognition: The Psychology of Human Thought.* New York: Oxford UP, 2001. Print.
Weizenbaum, Joseph. *Computer Power and Human Reason II.* New York: Freeman, 1997. Print.

Timothy L. Hubbard

SEE ALSO: Artificial intelligence; Computer models of cognition; Concept formation; Decision making; Deductive reasoning; Inductive reasoning; Pattern recognition; Problem-solving stages; Problem-solving strategies; Thought: Inferential; Thought: Study and measurement.

Long-term memory

TYPE OF PSYCHOLOGY: Memory

The study of long-term memory investigates the mechanisms of information retention and retrieval in relatively permanent storage. Without the capacity for long-term memory, learning would be impossible, as would nearly every facet of human intelligence.

KEY CONCEPT

- Encoding
- Episodic memory
- Levels-of-processing model
- Mnemonics
- Procedural memory
- Semantic memory
- Sensory memory
- Short-term memory
- Storage

INTRODUCTION

William James, in his famous work *The Principles of Psychology* (1890), was one of the first to make the distinction between short-term memory and long-term memory, which he called primary and secondary memory. James believed that secondary (long-term) memory was the only true memory, because it possessed two important characteristics that are absent from primary memory: remembered events seem to belong to the past, and their recollection is brought about by appropriate cues. Another early memory researcher was Hermann Ebbinghaus, who introduced the use of nonsense syllables (meaningless sets of two consonants and a vowel) in investigating the nature of long-term memory. Ebbinghaus systematically studied forgetting of information from long-term memory and found that most forgetting occurs during the first nine hours after learning, and especially during the first hour. After that, forgetting continues, but at a much slower rate. He also discovered that much forgetting from long-term memory is caused by interference from other, previously learned material (proactive interference) or by interference created by learning new material (retroactive interference).

Psychologists today generally propose a three-stage theory of memory: sensory memory, short-term memory, and long-term memory. When information first enters through one of the senses, it is retained briefly (for less than a second, generally) in sensory memory. Even though this information fades very rapidly, through processes such as selective attention, some of the information is processed further. The next processing stage is referred to as short-term, or working, memory. Information is retained in this stage for about twenty to thirty seconds, but through the use of rehearsal, items can be maintained in short-term memory indefinitely. Short-term memory has a limited capacity; it can hold about five to nine items at a time.

Information can reach long-term memory by several methods. Items that are particularly meaningful or that have a high emotional content are usually directly encoded into long-term memory. The use of a type of rehearsal called elaborative rehearsal, which involves thinking about how new material relates to information already stored, is also an effective method for transferring items from short-term memory to long-term memory. Unlike short-term memory, storage in long-term memory appears to be relatively permanent, and the capacity of long-term memory appears to be virtually unlimited.

In 1972, Fergus Craik and Robert Lockhart suggested that long- and short-term memory do not necessarily represent distinct stages of memory. They proposed what has come to be known as the levels-of-processing model, which holds that differences in how long or how well something is remembered depend on the degree or depth to which incoming information is mentally processed. The depth of processing for incoming information is related to how much it is thought about, organized, and related to one's existing knowledge. Thus, long-term memory, in their view, simply represents information that has been processed to a greater depth. This model has been very influential and has stimulated a tremendous body of research.

CLASSIFYING LONG-TERM MEMORY

Another influential theorist, Endel Tulving, proposed a classification scheme that distinguishes three aspects of long-term memory: procedural memory, episodic memory, and semantic memory. Procedural memory, also called skill memory, represents knowledge of how to do something. This can involve motor skills, such as knowing how to swing, or cognitive skills, such as reading and writing. Episodic memory is the memory of events from one's personal past. One's recollection of where one was last Saturday night or what one had for dinner yesterday would represent information from episodic memory. Semantic memory represents a person's knowledge of the world not tied to a specific event in one's life. This type of general knowledge includes definitions of words, facts such as the name of the first president of the United States, and relationships between concepts. Although some researchers have questioned the need for these distinctions among types of memory, there is evidence that supports this classification scheme. Many people who suffer from amnesia (partial or total loss of memory), for example, usually are unable to remember specific incidents or facts about their lives (episodic memory), yet their general knowledge (semantic memory) and knowledge of how to do things (procedural memory) remain intact. Also, studies involving monitoring of blood-flow patterns in the brain reveal different patterns when one is thinking about personal experiences versus impersonal facts. The frontal region of the brain appears to be more active during retrieval from episodic memory, and the posterior regions have a greater degree of activation during semantic retrieval.

ENCODING, STORAGE, AND RETRIEVAL

Researchers have also attempted to understand the nature of three basic processes associated with long-term memory: encoding, storage, and retrieval. Encoding concerns how information is put into memory; storage refers to the maintenance of information in memory; retrieval refers to the recovery of information from memory. Forgetting can represent a failure of any of these processes. Researchers are interested in the specific mental operations that are involved in each of these operations. Successful encoding of information into long-term memory is usually based on the meanings of the items. This is in contrast to short-term memory, which primarily involves an acoustic coding of information. Acoustic codes can also be used in long-term memory, but the dominant or preferred code involves meaning.

As mentioned above, the capacity of long-term memory appears to be virtually unlimited, and storage relatively permanent, although some storage loss probably does occur. Experimental evidence indicates that storage processes usually require some time for items to be placed in long-term memory. This process is referred to as consolidation. If a disruption (such as

electroconvulsive shock) occurs shortly after information is encoded, the information will be lost from storage. Sometimes, information is definitely stored in one's long-term memory but one still cannot recall it (for example, the name of an old friend whom one has not seen for some time). Usually, this represents a retrieval failure. Retrieval of information from long-term memory has sometimes been compared to searching for an item stored in an attic. The success of the search process depends on knowing where to look. The retrieval of information stored in long-term memory is usually initiated by some stimulus, referred to as a retrieval cue. Such cues provide information that can aid in the recall of stored material. Factors associated with encoding can also aid in retrieval. For example, organizing information at the time of encoding will increase the chances of successful retrieval. Retrieval will also be facilitated if the context in which information is encoded is similar to that in which it will be retrieved. Many studies have even shown that the psychological state (for example, the drug state or mood state) that one is in during the time information is encoded can act as a retrieval cue at the time of recall. This is referred to as state-dependent memory. Thus, if one was depressed when one learned material, one will more easily recall that material when one is in that same state again.

EYEWITNESS TESTIMONY RESEARCH

Investigations of the nature of long-term memory have led to findings that have proved useful in many areas of psychology and in other fields. Elizabeth F. Loftus and other researchers have done extensive research on the accuracy of long-term memory in eyewitness testimony. Loftus found that juries tend to rely heavily on eyewitness testimony, but she also found that the reliability of the memories of eyewitnesses was not very high.

When episodic information is stored in long-term memory, it is constantly being affected by material stored in semantic memory, including beliefs, prejudices, expectancies, inferences, and so on. What is stored in memory is not a simple copy of experiences but rather a construction that a person has created based on material already stored in long-term memory. People frequently fill in gaps in their memory with appropriate bits and pieces of their general knowledge of human situations and activities. These changes occur without their awareness; a memory of an event might seem accurate yet may have been changed dramatically. Loftus showed that the memory of witnesses could be affected by the type of question asked or by the specific wording of a question. In one experiment, subjects were shown a film of a traffic accident and then were asked questions about it. A question about the speed of the vehicles was asked in two different ways: "How fast were the cars going when they smashed into each other?" and "How fast were the cars going when they hit each other?" Subjects who were asked the "smashed" question not only estimated greater speeds but also one week later had memories of many details (such as broken glass) that were not in the film.

Another study, done on television station WNBC in New York, allowed viewers to witness a simulated crime in which they could closely see the assailant's face for 3.5 seconds. They were then asked to pick out the criminal from a lineup of six men through a special telephone number. Eighty-six percent of the 2,145 viewers who phoned in either "recognized" the wrong man or decided that the guilty man was not in the lineup. Overall, the performance was at the level that would be expected by chance alone. This type of research has led to modifications in some courtrooms, such as clearer instructions to jurors that are more easily remembered (jurors are usually not allowed to take notes, so they have to rely wholly on long-term memory).

MNEMONIC TECHNIQUES

Understanding the nature of long-term memory has led to the development of many mnemonic techniques: strategies to help improve memory. Two mnemonic systems that are particularly useful for remembering ordered sequences of unrelated items (such as grocery lists) are the method of loci (loci is Latin for "places") and the peg-word system. In the method of loci, the first step is to think about a set of familiar geographic locations, such as the rooms in one's house. The next step is to form a mental image of each item on the list in one of these locations, that is, one word in each room in the house. Whenever one wants to remember the list, one takes a mental walk through the house and collects the items in each room.

Use of the peg-word system requires the memorization of a list of words that will serve as memory pegs for the list to be remembered. One popular example of a peg-word list is: "One is a bun, two is a shoe, three is a tree, four is a door, five is a hive, six is a stick, seven is heaven, eight is a gate, nine is a hive, and ten is a hen." Once this list is learned, mental images are created between each new item to be remembered and the previously learned peg word. For example, if the first item on a grocery list is

coffee, one might image coffee being poured over a bun. If the second item is milk, one might image a milk carton being kicked by a shoe. This might seem cumbersome, but it works. With both the method of loci and the peg-word system, particularly vivid images seem to produce the best results.

LEARNING TECHNIQUES

The study of long-term memory has also led to the development of techniques for improving the learning of more complex material. In general, the more that items are elaborated on during the encoding, the more easily they can subsequently be recalled or recognized. This is true because the more connections are established between items, the larger the number of retrieval possibilities. Therefore, if one wants to remember some fact, one should expand on its meaning. Questions about the causes and consequences of an event, for example, are particularly effective elaborations because each question sets up a meaningful connection, or retrieval path, to the event.

The more organized the material is during the process of encoding, the more easily the material will be retrieved later. Massive amounts of information can be stored and retrieved, if only it is properly organized. For example, remembering textbook material can be facilitated by not only outlining a chapter but also sketching a hierarchical tree that pictures the relations between chapter headings and subheadings.

A formal strategy developed for remembering textbook material is the SQ3R method. SQ3R stands for "survey, question, read, recite, and review." Before reading a chapter, one should survey, or skim, the material, looking for section headings and key ideas. Next, one should question or ask oneself what subject will be covered before one reads each section. As one reads the text, one should continue thinking about the question and how topics are connected. Next, one recites to oneself the major points at the end of each section. Finally, one reviews all the material after one has read to the end of the chapter. This method encompasses most of the principles by which material can be effectively encoded, stored, and retrieved from long-term memory.

EVOLUTION OF STUDY

The study of long-term memory has continued in psychology since the pioneering work of James and Ebbinghaus in the late nineteenth century. It was clear even during those early efforts that a distinction could be made between the temporary storage of information in short-term, or working, memory, and the relatively permanent nature of long-term memory.

During the early part of the twentieth century, however, the study of memory fell into disfavor during the era in which psychology was dominated by the behaviorist movement. Behaviorists believed that if psychology was to be a science, it had to limit its investigations to phenomena that are directly observable and measurable. Memory was viewed as a subjective element that was not amenable to experimental investigation.

It was not until the development of the computer, around the time of World War II, that the experimental study of memory again achieved respectability in academic psychology. The computer offered an objective model of how information might be stored and processed in human memory. Since that time, developments in computer science and in the psychological study of memory have progressed in tandem, with breakthroughs in one area providing insights into the other. The computer model is still very much a part of the study of memory, with new theories of memory often modeled as computer programs. In many ways, the study of memory was responsible for experimental psychology shifting from a focus exclusively on overt behavior to the "cognitive revolution," in which mental functions are studied directly.

The study of long-term memory in the future will likely focus more on understanding how processes related to memory have their physiological basis in the functioning of the brain. Locating where memories are stored in the brain has long eluded psychologists. Most now believe that memory is distributed over the entire surface of the cerebral cortex rather than located at a particular spot. It is also known from the study of amnesiacs that brain structures such as the hippocampus and amygdala appear to be involved in the consolidation of new material in long-term memory. As knowledge of neurotransmitters (chemicals involved in the sending of messages from one brain cell to another) expands, the role that they play in memory may also become more apparent.

BIBLIOGRAPHY

Baddeley, Alan D. *Your Memory: A User's Guide*. London: Carlton, 2004. Print.

Bransford, John. *Human Cognition: Learning, Understanding, and Remembering*. Belmont: Wadsworth, 1989. Print.

Fedoseev, Lazar M., and Arseni K. Alexandrov. *Long-Term Memory: Mechanisms, Types and Disorders*. New York: Nova Science, 2012. Digital file.

Höchsler, Christian, ed. *Neuronal Mechanisms of Memory Formation: Concepts of Long-Term Potentiation and Beyond*. New York: Cambridge UP, 2005. Print.

Loftus, Elizabeth F., et al. *Eyewitness Testimony: Civil and Criminal*. 5th ed. New Providence: LexisNexis, 2013. Print.

Neath, Ian. *Human Memory: An Introduction to Research, Data, and Theory*. Belmont: Wadsworth, 2006. Print.

Neisser, Ulric, and Ira E. Hyman, eds. *Memory Observed: Remembering in Natural Contexts*. 2d ed. New York: Worth, 2000. Print.

Parkin, Alan J. *Memory and Amnesia: An Introduction*. N.p.: Taylor, 2013. Digital file.

Schweppe, Judith, and Ralf Rummer. "Attention, Working Memory, and Long-Term Memory in Multimedia Learning: An Integrated Perspective Based on Process Models of Working Memory." *Educational Psychology Review* 26.2 (2014): 285–306. Print.

Vitevitch, Michael S., et al. "Complex Network Structure Influences Processing in Long-Term and Short-Term Memory." *Journal of Memory and Language* 67.1 (2012): 30–44. Print.

Oliver W. Hill, Jr.

SEE ALSO: Ebbinghaus, Hermann; Encoding; Eyewitness testimony; Forgetting and forgetfulness; James, William; Kinesthetic memory; Memory; Memory: Empirical studies; Memory: Physiology; Memory: Sensory; Memory storage; Short-term memory.

Lorenz, Konrad

BORN: November 7, 1903, in Vienna, Austro-Hungarian Empire (now in Austria)
DIED: February 27, 1989, in Altenburg, Austria
IDENTITY: Austrian ethologist
TYPE OF PSYCHOLOGY: Biological bases of behavior; Motivation

Lorenz was a pioneer in the field of ethology, the study of animal behavior in natural surroundings. His studies support the position that instinct is a major determinant of animal (including human) behavior.

Konrad Lorenz was born in Vienna, the capital of the Austro-Hungarian Empire. He attended an excellent Viennese private school, the Schottengymnasium, where he became fascinated by natural history in general and Darwinist theory in particular. Lorenz continued that interest during summer vacations at the family estate in Altenberg, Austria, where he closely observed instinctive behavior, including imprinting, in greylag geese.

In 1922, Lorenz entered Columbia University in New York, and he completed his medical studies at the University of Vienna in 1928. He did not immediately practice medicine, however; instead, he worked with a noted comparative anatomist, Ferdinand Hochstetter, at the Vienna Anatomical Institute, and in 1933 he received his Ph.D. in zoology at the University of Vienna.

In 1939, Lorenz became the chair of the psychology department at the University of Königsberg. In 1941, however, he was drafted into the German army, and from 1942 to 1944 he served as a psychiatrist and neurologist in a military hospital. Early in 1944 he was transferred to the eastern front, where Soviet forces captured him. From that point until his release in 1948, he served as a doctor in Soviet prison camps. His experiences in captivity produced a heightened interest in the causes of human aggression and resulted in a key work, *The Natural Science of the Human Species: An Introduction to Comparative Behavioral Research: The "Russian Manuscript"* (1944-1948) (1996).

Following repatriation, Lorenz continued his ethological work with help from the Austrian Academy of Sciences and, later, in association with the Max Planck Institute. In 1973, his work in genetic programming won international recognition when he became a corecipient of the Nobel Prize in Physiology or Medicine. In 1982, he became a director in the Konrad Lorenz Institute, which was affiliated with the Austrian Academy of Sciences. Lorenz died on February 27, 1989, in Altenburg, Austria.

Lorenz's work underlined the importance of instincts and viewed significant aspects of human behavior as refinements of cruder instinctual mechanisms clearly seen in other living creatures. His *Er redete mit dem Vieh, den Vögeln, und den Fischen* (1949; *King Soloman's Ring*, 1952) is a classic on animal behavior, and his *Das Sogenannte Böse* (1963; *On Aggression*, 1966), perhaps his most important work, identifies the instinctual underpinnings of human values. Lorenz's work on fixed action patterns and behavior triggers has gained wide general acceptance. However, his views remain controversial in some quarters, for his deterministic leanings have sometimes been equated with Nazi positions on race.

BIBLIOGRAPHY

Burkhardt, Richard W. *Patterns of Behavior: Konrad Lorenz, Niko Tinbergen, and the Founding of Ethology.* Chicago: University of Chicago Press, 2005. Chronicles the history of ethology and work of Lorenz and Tinbergen, whose pioneering research made legitimate this study of behavioral science.

Evans, Richard I. *Konrad Lorenz: The Man and His Ideas.* New York: Harcourt Brace Jovanovich, 1976. An excellent introduction that contains conversations with Lorenz, several of his essays, and a list of his publications.

Gould, James L. *Ethology: The Mechanisms and Evolution of Behavior.* New York: W. W. Norton, 1982. This work places Lorenz in context of the emerging field of ethology, describes his main experiments, and clearly presents his conclusions.

Nisbett, Alec. *Konrad Lorenz.* London: Dent, 1977. A good general biography of Lorenz, containing a chronology and numerous photographs.

Michael J. Fontenot

SEE ALSO: Animal experimentation; Ethology; Imprinting

Love

TYPE OF PSYCHOLOGY: Social psychology

Love is a mixture of passion, intimacy, and commitment. Studying these components of love, psychologists have identified how people fall in love, stay in love, and fall out of love.

KEY CONCEPTS
- Companionate love
- Evolutionary psychology
- Intermittent reinforcement
- Liking
- Passionate love
- Perceptual accentuation
- Principle of equity
- Romantic love

INTRODUCTION

According to psychologist Robert Sternberg, love can be considered to have three main components: passion, intimacy, and commitment.

Passion is sexual arousal and an intense desire to be with another person; it is expressed through hugging, kissing, and sexual intimacy. Intimacy is a feeling of closeness and connectedness and is expressed through communication and doing things to support the other person. Commitment is a decision that one loves the other person and wants to maintain that love over time. Commitment is often expressed through fidelity, and the institution of marriage makes one's commitment legally binding.

The amount of love that one feels depends on the strength of these three components. The kind of love one feels depends on the mixture of these components. One might have a commitment to a partner but feel little passion; or one might be passionately in love but not be able to communicate the deep feelings that go with intimacy. The amount or kind of love one partner experiences in a relationship might not be the same as the other partner's experience. Misunderstandings often result, for example, when one partner thinks the relationship contains commitment and the other partner sees the relationship as only a passionate one. Finally, a loving relationship can change over time. In marriage, the passion may fade over the years, while intimacy and commitment bloom.

PASSIONATE LOVE

Passionate love is the kind of love sometimes described as "love at first sight." It occurs suddenly, and one feels as if one has fallen into love. Passionate love is a state of sexual arousal without the intimacy and commitment components. One knows that one is passionately in love when one is always daydreaming about the other person, longs to be constantly with the other person, and feels ecstatic when with the other person. Passionate love thrives on unavailability. As in unrequited love, either the loved one does not reciprocate the intensity of the lover's affections or the lovers cannot get together as often as they wish. Being loved is reinforcing, and some psychologists say that passionate love may survive only under conditions of intermittent reinforcement, where uncertainty about when one will be reinforced plays a major role. Romeo and Juliet's passionate love, for example, was inflamed by the prohibitions of their feuding families.

In passionate love, partners idealize each other. They engage in perceptual accentuation, or seeing what they want to see. Only the good features of each other are noticed and enhanced. The more the partners live in the illusion of their ideals, the more intense is the passionate love. Passionate love really is "blind."

Most people think of passionate love as being true love, and many people think that passionate love is the only kind of love; they expect passionate love to last forever. Despite their expectations (and wishes), passionate love does not last. Indeed, passionate love appears to last a maximum of two and a half years. After that time, according to Charles Hill, Zick Rubin, and Letitia Paplau, almost one-half of dating couples report having broken up. As partners become more familiar with each other, illusions are shattered and the passion wanes. Unfortunately, some people believe that this is the end of love.

ROMANTIC LOVE

For many people, however, love does persist—in the form of romantic love. Romantic love is passionate love with the added component of intimacy. The romantic ideal, which has existed since the medieval time of courtly love, looks much like passionate love. It contains the belief that love is fated and uncontrollable, strikes at first sight, transcends all social boundaries, and mixes agony and ecstasy. This ideal is very much alive today; it is reflected in romance novels, motion pictures, and advertisements. Psychologists have found that this type of love is a poor basis for marriage, which requires steady companionship and objectivity. If a relationship is to survive, romantic passion is not enough.

Rubin has shown that there is a type of romantic love that contains intimate communication and caring. In his study, loving feelings of dependency, exclusivity, and caring were contrasted with the type of liking that exists in friendship. Men, more than women, tended to blur the distinction between liking and loving. Both sexes, though, often experience liking the person they are in love with. Rubin also noticed that one can tell if two people are "in love" simply by observing them: Partners who are strongly in love exhibit more mutual eye contact than partners who are weakly in love.

Intimacy without passion or a long-term commitment is experienced as liking. One feels closeness, bondedness, and warmth toward the other—as one does in friendship. There is a willingness to let the other person see even the disliked parts of oneself and a feeling of being accepted when these parts are disclosed. Intimacy includes open communication, acceptance, and the sharing of oneself and one's resources. There is a high degree of trust in intimate relationships.

COMPANIONATE LOVE

When commitment is added to intimacy, one experiences what psychologists Ellen Berscheid and Elaine Walster call companionate love. There is a deep attachment that is based on extensive familiarity with the loved one. Companionate love often encompasses a tolerance for the partner's shortcomings, along with a desire to overcome difficulties and conflicts in a relationship. There is a commitment to the ongoing nurturing of the relationship and to an active caring for the partner, even during rough times. Marriages in which the physical attraction has waned but intimate caring and commitment have increased are characterized by this type of love. When researchers asked couples who had been married for at least fifteen years what kept their relationships alive, they put long-term commitment at the top of the list. The romantic passion that brings a couple together is not the force that keeps them together. Each partner must trust that the other is committed to nurturing support, acceptance, and communication in the relationship.

ATTRACTION

Psychologists have used theories and laboratory studies to answer the basic question, "Why do some people have a happy love life while others have unhappy relationships?" Part of the answer comes from the partner one chooses.

One may think that opposites attract, but psychologist Donn Byrne has shown that people are attracted to those who are similar to them in attractiveness, interests, intelligence, education, age, family background, religion, and attitudes. Researchers have noted what is called a "matching phenomenon" when choosing romantic partners. This phenomenon is described as a tendency to choose partners who are a good match to ourselves in attractiveness and other traits. Studies have shown that those who were a good match in physical attractiveness were more likely to be dating longer than couples who were not well matched, and that married couples are more closely matched in attractiveness than couples who are casually dating. Furthermore, Rubin and his associates have found that dating couples who eventually broke up were less well matched in age, educational ambitions, intelligence, and physical attractiveness than those who stayed together.

Another factor that is extremely important in predicting attraction is proximity. Studies have shown that most people marry someone who lives in the same neighborhood or works at the same job; and it is not simply a matter of physical proximity, but a matter of how often one crosses paths with the potential mate that determines the likelihood of romantic involvement. Overall, people tend to like and be attracted to those who have the potential to reward them. People tend to be attracted to those who are similarly attractive, who share their opinions and attitudes, whom they have grown accustomed to meeting, and with whom they have shared positive experiences.

LOVE IN RELATIONSHIPS

After one finds a partner, whether one is happy or unhappy in love depends on the relationship one creates. According to Cindy Hazan and Philip Shaver, both adults and teenagers recreate the same type of relationship they experienced with their parents during childhood. Secure lovers create an intimate relationship that is neither excessively dependent nor independent. They bring a secure sense of self and an interest in developing the independence of their partner into the relationship. Avoidant lovers are overly independent. They get nervous when their partner gets too close because they do not trust the other person completely. Anxious-ambivalent lovers are too dependent; they often worry that their partner does not really love them or will not want to stay with them. Thus, many lovers end up playing out the script that they were taught as children.

Men often follow a different script from that followed by women when they are in love. Men tend to choose a partner on the basis of physical attractiveness, while women emphasize interpersonal warmth and occupational status. Romance involves both passion and affection; men, however, tend to get hooked into the passion first, while women tend to want the affection as a prerequisite to sex. As the relationship matures, men want the affection as much as the sex, and women get equally excited by sexual stimuli as do men. Who, then, one might ask, are the real romantics? Men agree with more of the statements about romantic love; they fall in love more quickly; and they hold on to a waning affair more so than do women. After the breakup of a relationship, a man feels more lonely, obsessed with what went wrong, and depressed than does a woman.

Indeed, men and women may inhabit different emotional worlds. Men and women both want intimacy, but they express themselves differently. Men are more likely to be doers and women to be talkers. For example, a man will wash a woman's car or bring her flowers to show he loves her, while a woman will tell a man how much she loves him. When asked what causes an emotion such as love, men will say it is something in the world outside themselves, such as seeing an attractive woman. Women, on the other hand, will attribute being in love to positive interactions with others or to internal factors such as moods. These socially learned differences between men and women in their styles of intimacy are often a source of tension between them. Women sometimes want men to talk more, while men will want women to stop talking. Finally, some men will sacrifice intimacy because they fear loss of independence, while some women sacrifice independence because they fear a loss of intimacy.

HISTORY OF RESEARCH ON LOVE

Psychologists have approached the topic of love from a variety of perspectives. In the early 1900s, clinical psychologists looked at love mainly in terms of its sexual component. For example, Sigmund Freud defined love as sublimated sexuality. By the middle of the twentieth century, humanistic psychologists such as Abraham Maslow, Erich Fromm, and Carl R. Rogers saw love as including the empathy, responsibility, and respect that is characteristic of friendship. Next, there was an attempt to measure love as distinct from friendship, with Rubin creating his liking and loving scales.

Since love involves emotions, motivations, and cognitions, Walster and Berscheid drew on the earlier work of Stanley Schachter and Jerome Singer to devise a multifactor explanation of love called the two-factor theory. They theorize that love arises when a person is physiologically aroused and labels that arousal as love. For example, being in a dangerous situation creates physiological arousal, and, if one is with an attractive partner, one could feel that the sweating palms and pounding heart mean that one is falling in love. Researchers have found that men approached by an unknown, attractive woman as they crossed a dangerous bridge were more likely to ask her out and indicate attraction than men approached by the woman while crossing a sturdy, safe bridge. Studies show that watching scary movies, riding on roller coasters, and exercising are all arousing activities that increase the likelihood that people will be attracted to one another.

Social psychologist Byrne tried to explain both the passionate feeling and the friendship feeling as arising from the reinforcement one gets from one's lover. People like, and love, people who give them rewards, whether the reward is sexual gratification or a feeling of being needed.

Although many social psychologists have focused on separate concepts, such as interpersonal attraction, social exchange, and cognitive consistency, to explain love, Sternberg combined all these concepts in his triangular theory of love. Sternberg contends that liking and loving are interrelated phenomena and that there are different types of love that develop from different combinations of liking and loving. Sternberg's theory explains the difference between a partner's love for his or her child and lovers' love for each other.

Historically, conceptions of love have been tied to economic conditions and to social role definitions. One example of these economic conditions is the Industrial Revolution, which moved men out of the fields and into the factories. Women also moved—from the fields into the home. Men's social role was to produce; women's was to love (provide nurturance and intimacy). These roles created societal expectations for the nature of love. Thus, one's expectations determine whether one will be satisfied or disappointed with love. For example, Western society often expects a woman to define herself in terms of her relationship with a man; love is closely linked to sex and marriage. Yet women live longer than men, which often means that a woman will be living without a man in her later years. Women can retain society's expectations or can change their expectations so that they can connect with others on a basis other than traditional concepts of love. Psychologists will continue to investigate changing expectations about loving relationships.

BIBLIOGRAPHY

Buss, David M. *The Dangerous Passion*. New York: Free Press, 2000. Print.

Fisher, Helen. *Why We Love: The Nature and Chemistry of Romantic Love*. New York: Holt, 2005. Print.

Fromm, Erich. The Art of Loving. New York: Harper, 1956. Print.

Horstman, Judith. *The Scientific American Book of Love, Sex, and the Brain: The Neuroscience of How, When, Why, and Who We Love*. San Francisco: Jossey-Bass, 2012. Print.

Jolly, Alison. *Lucy's Legacy: Sex and Intelligence in Human Evolution*. Cambridge: Harvard UP, 2001. Print.

Paludi, Michele Antoinette. *The Psychology of Love*. Santa Barbara: Praeger, 2012. Print.

Person, Ethel S. *Dreams of Love and Fateful Encounters*. Washington: American Psychiatric, 2007. Print.

Rubin, Zick. *Liking and Loving*. New York: Holt, 1973. Print.

Shaver, P., C. Hazan, and D. Bradshaw. "Love as Attachment: The Integration of Three Behavioral Systems." *The Psychology of Love*. Ed. Robert J. Sternberg and Michael L. Barnes. New Haven: Yale UP, 1988. Print.

Sternberg, Robert J. *Love Is a Story: A New Theory of Relationships*. New York: Oxford UP, 1999. Print.

Wright, Robert. *The Moral Animal: The New Science of Evolutionary Psychology*. London: Abacus, 2005. Print.

Young, Larry, and Brian Alexander. *The Chemistry Between Us: Love, Sex, and the Science of Attraction*. New York: Current, 2012. Print.

Beverly B. Palmer; updated by Michelle Murphy

SEE ALSO: Affiliation and friendship; Affiliation motive; Attraction theories; Emotional intelligence; Emotions; Gender differences; Hierarchy of needs; Intimacy; Jealousy; Maslow, Abraham; Motivation; Self-actualization; Separation and divorce: Adult issues; Social perception; Social psychological models: Erich Fromm.

Luminosity

TYPE OF PSYCHOLOGY: Cognitive; Developmental; Educational; Geri-psychology; Neuropsychology

Summary: Luminosity is a computerized brain training program designed to assess and enhance cognitive ability. Luminosity is a commercial product distributed online, but is also used as a learning tool in colleges and universities across the country. In research, it has been tested as a clinical tool to help decrease cognitive decline and increase neuroplasticity and the formation of new neural connections. Although more research needs to be done on its effectiveness, brain training programs like Luminosity may be helpful as a rehabilitation tool, as well as a tool to foster peak performance in the healthy brain.

KEY CONCEPTS:
- Brain training programs
- Neuroplasticity
- Cognitive decline
- Visual attention
- Working memory

INTRODUCTION

Computerized brain training programs are designed to assess and enhance cognitive ability; much like personal trainers may assess or enhance one's physical ability. Numerous brain training products have been produced for personal and clinical use, and can be delivered online, via specialized software, or through gaming devices. Brain training programs are based upon evidence that living in a cognitively rich environment can increase neuroplasticity and strengthen certain structures in the brain. When an individual performs a task that is cognitively novel, the brain responds by forming new neural connections.

There are three basic purposes for brain training. The first purpose is for rehabilitation. Brain training programs are used in hospitals, psychiatric centers, nursing homes, and doctors' offices for the purpose of assisting in recovery from psychiatric or neurological problems. The second purpose is for brain maintenance and learning. Many colleges and universities across the nation use computerized brain training software in order to enhance students' knowledge about brain structure, function, and cognitive processes. Consumers of brain training programs use the training in order to maintain their neural strength. Finally, brain training programs can be used for peak performance purposes. The brain is a muscle, and the more it is used, the more neural connections are made. Brain training programs allow consumers a chance to play games and experience different situations, with the hope that new neural connections can be created. Peak performance users believe that brain training assists individuals in getting the most out of their brain, so that they can get the most out of their lives.

LUMINOSITY

Over the past several years, brain training programs have increased in popularity. Luminosity, a computer based online brain training program, is reported to have over 50 million subscribers in 180 countries. These subscribers pay a monthly or yearly fee to access brain strengthening games created by neuroscientists hired by Luminosity.

A paid subscription to Luminosity allows the user access to fifty-five games, focusing on 5 key areas. These areas are speed, memory, attention, flexibility, and problem solving. Before initial paid registration, Luminosity asks users about aspects of the five key areas they would like to improve. Then, from those responses, plus factoring in the individuals age, Luminosity builds a personalized brain training program for the user. Initially, "fit tests" provide a baseline of brain function. Then, games are introduced, which expose the user to gradually increasing levels of challenge. As scores increase, the program adapts by introducing new levels or more difficult games. Periodic assessments gauge individual improvement.

RESEARCH ON BRAIN TRAINING USE IN CHILDREN

Although Luminosity states that the consumer version of its program is not meant for users under the age of 13, numerous researchers have used Luminosity in clinical experiments with children and adolescents. Currently, Luminosity is being tested as a tool to increase working memory in students with Attention Deficit Disorder. Tests are also being done on Luminosity as a cognitive training tool for children with high lead levels in their blood. Another study is focusing on using Luminosity to increase levels of motivation and academic achievement in adolescents.

In 2014, Luminosity announced the launching of LumiKids, a "digital playground" application for children age two and up. LumiKids is currently in application form only, and provides interactive training in cognitive, motor, and social – emotional skills.

RESEARCH ON BRAIN TRAINING USE IN ADULTS

Hardy, Drescher, Saker, Kellett, and Scanlon (2011) did a study on 23 participants with a mean age of 54 using the Luminosity brain training program. Specifically, the 23 person group was split into two. The experimental group was given brain training twenty minutes per day for five weeks, focusing on visual attention and working memory. The control group was given no brain training whatsoever. At the end of the study, the trained group performed significantly better than the control group on previously untrained measures of visual attention and working memory.

Another study, the Iowa Healthy and Active Minds Study (IHAMS), focused on the effect of brain training programs on cognitive function in six hundred eighty one participants aged 50 and older. Participants who engaged in ten hours of brain training using online software (as opposed to those who trained on 10 hours of computerized crossword puzzles) improved drastically in cognitive function as measured by neuropsychological testing. This improvement was seen one year after the initial brain training as well, in both younger and older participants. Research has also been done on using Luminosity as an intervention to increase levels of executive functioning in those who have received chemotherapy; as well as a strengthening tool for individuals who need work regulating emotions.

RESEARCH ON BRAIN TRAINING USE AND THE ELDERLY

In the January 2014 issue of the *Journal of the American Geriatrics Society*, the now famed Advanced Cognitive Training for Independent and Vital Elderly (ACTIVE) study was presented. This National Institute of Health (NIH) funded study is the largest study on cognitive brain training ever performed. Within the ACTIVE study, 2,832 participants aged 65 and older were divided into four groups: Memory, Reasoning, Speed of Processing, and a control group. All groups with the exception of the control group participated in 10 sixty to seventy minute brain training sessions over five to six weeks. Subjects were post tested immediately following the sessions, and at one, three, five, and ten years later. All experimental groups showed a marked improvement in cognitive ability immediately after the training. During the follow up period, all experimental groups reported less difficulty in performing everyday tasks such as preparing meals, paying bills, dressing, and using the telephone. At the 10-year follow up, over 70% of the Reasoning and Speed of Processing group members were still performing Reasoning and Speed of Processing tasks above their baseline scores as compared to the control group. There was no difference after 10 years in memory performance between the Memory group and the control group. Researchers see this as encouraging, as even a small increase in quality of life of the elderly due to brain training would be a huge gain for older individuals as well as their caregivers.

A smaller 2014 study by Mayas, Parmenteier, Andres and Ballesteros used 27 healthy older adults, split into two groups. The experimental group received twenty 1-hour brain training sessions using Luminosity. Upon comparison after the sessions, the experimental group showed less distractibility and a higher level of alertness as compared to the control group, illustrating that brain training really could increase cognitive performance in older adults. Many studies like the Mayas et al. study continue to be performed, as brain training may quite possibly have not only a positive effect on healthy adults, but also a positive effect on adults demonstrating varying rates of cognitive decline.

THE FUTURE OF COMPUTERIZED BRAIN TRAINING PROGRAMS LIKE LUMINOSITY

Most of us end up doing similar activities every day. When activities are repeated, the brain tends to depend on similar neural pathways. To change, the brain must be exposed to new experiences so that it can work in new ways. Of course, individuals can go out and expose themselves to novel experiences and new hobbies, possibly increasing neural activity and creating new neural pathways. However, research illustrates that brain training programs like Luminosity can also assist with increasing cognitive ability and neuroplasticity in commercial and research based clients. The question remains, though, as to whether the tasks worked on in Luminosity can effectively transfer to increased brain power in the real world. Currently, the National Institute of Health has invited researchers to more rigorously test brain training programs and how they may deter cognitive decline in the elderly and other sensitive populations. Time and research will tell if computerized brain training programs are a trend, or if they can be utilized effectively in personal as well as clinical settings.

BIBLIOGRAPHY

Hardy, J. L., Drescher, D., Sarkar, K., Kellett, G., & Scanlon, M. (2011). "Enhancing Visual Attention and Working Memory With A Web-Based Cognitive Training pProgram". *Mensa Research Journal*, 42(2), 13–20. A small study on the effect of brain training using Luminosity, specifically focused on visual attention and working memory skills. Participants of the study who used Luminosity performed significantly better than the control group on previously untested measures of visual attention and working memory.

Luminosity (n.d.) Retrieved from www.luminosity.com. Computerized brain training website used to assess and strengthen cognitive ability. Used for personal, educational, and clinical purposes.

Mayas, J., Parmentier, F.B.R., Andres, P., Ballesteros, S. (2014). "Plasticity of Attentional Functions In Older Adults After Non-Action Video Game Training: A Randomized Control Trial". *PLosOne*. Retrieved from http://www.ncbi.nlm.nih.gov/pmc/articles/PMC3960226/. A study of 27 older adults, split into two groups. The group that received Luminosity brain training for twenty one hour sessions experienced increased levels of alertness and lower levels of distractibility as compared to the control group.

Parker-Pope, T. (2014, March 10). "Do Brain Workouts Work? Science Isn't Sure". Retrieved from http://well.blogs.nytimes.com/2014/03/10/do-brain-workouts-work-science-isnt-sure/?_r=0. Questions whether brain training is a true clinical resource, or a money making trend.

Rebok, G.W., Ball, K., Guey, L.T., Jones, R.N., Kim, H.Y., Kim, J.W. Marsiske, M., Morris, J.N., Tennstedt, S.L., Unverzagt, F.W., Willis, S.L. (2014). "Ten-Year Effects of The Advanced Cognitive Training for Independent and Vital Elderly: Cognitive Training Trail on Cognition and Everyday Functioning In Older Adults." *Journal of the American Geriatrics Society*, 62, 16 – 24. Also known as the ACTIVE study. Largest study of cognitive brain training ever performed. All groups provided with brain training showed marked improvement in cognitive ability immediately after training. Ten years later, those in the Reasoning and Speed of Processing groups were still performing above their baseline on computerized brain training measures.

Wolinsky, F.D., VanderWeg, M.W., Howren, M.B., Jones, M.P., Martin, R., Luger, T.M., Duff, K., Dotson, M.M. (2011). "Interim Analysis From A Randomized Controlled Trial to Improve Visual Processing Speed In Older Adults: The Iowa Healthy and Active Minds Study. *BMJ Open*. Retrieved from http://bmjopen.bmj.com/content/1/2/e000225.full.pdf+html. This study, known as the IHAMS study, tested the effects of 10 hours of brain training on the overall cognitive functioning of participants aged 50 and above. Those who engaged in brain training (as opposed to working on computerized crossword puzzles) performed significantly better on basic neurological tests.

Gina Riley

SEE ALSO: Illumination; Luminance; Phototopic stimulation; Psychophysics; Visual perception.

M

Marijuana

TYPES OF PSYCHOLOGY: Addiction, clinical, psychopathology, social psychology

Summary: Marijuana has been cultivated for approximately 14,000 years and is used worldwide for medicinal and recreational purposes. The active chemical in marijuana binds to receptor sites in the brain and affects the human motivation and reward systems resulting in potential for addiction. Marijuana is the most frequently consumed illicit drug in the United States. It has long been associated with counterculture movements but is gaining more widespread acceptance as of late. Current trends toward legalization of marijuana by 25 states in the US are contrasted with continued prohibition by the federal government.

KEY CONCEPTS:
- Cannabis Sativa
- delta-9-tetrahydracanabinol (Δ9-THC)
- Effects of marijuana
- Marijuana subculture
- Medical marijuana

INTRODUCTION

Marijuana is the leaves, stems, and seeds of the Cannabis Sativa plant. Most commonly known for its mind altering properties and addictive potential, marijuana also has a long history of use in medicine and in social settings world-wide. Currently, marijuana production results in a multi-billion dollar industry, most of which is illegal and unregulated. Currently, four states allow recreational and medical marijuana use and an additional 21 allow only medical use, while the remaining 25 states prohibit the growing, use, distribution, and sale of it entirely.

HISTORY

Marijuana and the closely-related hemp plant (Cannabis Sativa L) are thought to be some of humanity's oldest cultivated crops. Marijuana evolved in present day Mongolia and Southern Serbia around 12,000 BC and has since been cultivated for its psychoactive and medicinal properties, as well as for religious and recreational use. Cultivation and use of marijuana spread to Eastern and Southern Asia and to Europe around 2,000 BCE. Marijuana arrived in South America in the 16th century when Angolan slaves and Portuguese sailors brought it from Africa. Marijuana was largely introduced to the United States beginning in 1910 by immigrants fleeing the violent Mexican Revolution. A trend of legal prohibition quickly followed, beginning with an El Paso, Texas, city ordinance in 1914 and culminating with the federal Marijuana Tax Act of 1937. In 1970, the federal government declared marijuana a "Schedule 1" drug, meaning that it has no recognized medial use and there is no safe level of consumption.

CHEMICAL STRUCTURES

Marijuana contains a chemical called delta-9-tetrahydracanabinol (Δ9-THC) which is largely responsible for its psychoactive properties. Common hemp also contains Δ9-THC, however in such low quantities that it is not considered psychoactive. Δ9-THC is one of at least 60 cannabinoids, a class of chemicals unique to the marijuana plant. Recent innovations in breeding and growing of marijuana plants have resulted in Δ9-THC concentrations of 20% or more, although concentrations still vary widely among strains. These days, a typical marijuana cigarette—or joint—contains approximately 150-200mg of Δ9-THC. By comparison, the hemp plant contains less than 1% Δ9-THC.

Marijuana is typically consumed by smoking. Because Δ9-THC is lipid soluble it can also be eaten; however absorption and the related onset of psychoactive effects are slower. When smoked, Δ9-THC quickly enters the blood stream via the lungs, crosses the blood-brain barrier, and finds its way to cannabinoid-1 (CB1) receptors in the brain. CB1 receptors are also found in the spinal cord and throughout the central peripheral nervous system. Recent research suggests CB2 receptors in the central nervous system also moderate the action of cannabinoids. In this way Δ9-THC interacts with the action of the endogenous cannabinoids (or endocannabinoids) which are natural ligands for the CB1 receptors, such as anandamide. Once in the body Δ9-THC is stored in fat cells, from which it is slowly released over several weeks or months. Eventually, Δ9-THC is cleared from the body through urine and feces.

The psychoactive properties of marijuana are mainly a result of Δ9-THC. The effects of Δ9-THC on CB1 receptors in the mesocorticolimbic dopaminergic pathway are thought to be responsible for its addictive properties as well as the tolerance and withdrawal syndrome experienced by regular users. CB1 receptors in this area are associated with motivation and reward systems in the brain; hence the action of Δ9-THC may be associated with an antimotivational syndrome and the rewarding properties of marijuana.

EFFECTS
Marijuana is the most widely used illicit drug in the United States; approximately 25 million Americans report having used it in the last year and about 6% of the US population uses it regularly. About 10% of those who try marijuana will proceed to become daily marijuana smokers and approximately 4% of the US population has meet criteria for cannabis dependency* at some point in their lifetime. After smoking marijuana, acute effects generally come on within a few minutes and last a few hours. Effects are dose-dependent. The more one consumes the more effects one feels. Likewise, regular users can develop tolerance to the effects, making it necessary to use more marijuana to obtain the same effects. Regular users who stop using marijuana experience a withdrawal syndrome related to the absence of the drug in the body. Withdrawal may last 1-2 weeks and is characterized by irritability, insomnia, weight loss, anxiety, sweating, shakiness, depressed mood, chills, fever, and headaches.

Marijuana is most well-known for creating mild to intense euphoria and altering perceptual experiences. For instance, marijuana may cause an altered sense of time and space, heightened aesthetic experiences, increase perception of emotions, and intensify desires for sensual experiences such as eating and sex. Marijuana's ability to cause a diminished perception of pain has long been useful in medical settings. Marijuana may also enhance creativity, lead to introspective states and heightened curiosity, and trigger positive emotions such as empathy. Marijuana can also be associated with uncomfortable mental states of anxiety and paranoia, drowsiness, and impaired short-term memory. Effects vary greatly depending on the potency of the drug and the user's experience, tolerance, and expectations.

Because marijuana is usually smoked its greatest negative health impact is on the pulmonary and cardiovascular systems. Marijuana smoke is said to have even higher concentrations of carcinogens than tobacco smoke, therefore frequent marijuana smokers are at higher risk for related health problems. Regular marijuana smokers have poor lung function compared to non-smokers and tobacco-only smokers. The most common health consequence of regular marijuana smoking is bronchitis. Lung cancer risk is also increased among marijuana smokers. Animal research suggests that marijuana may impair reproductive capacity but these findings have yet to be consistently replicated in humans.

SOCIAL FACTORS
Marijuana has been long been associated with subcultures such as jazz musicians in the 1930s and artists and writers of the beat culture of the 1950s. While the production and sale of hemp was briefly promoted during WWII it was effectively prohibited again soon after. With the 1960s marijuana was associated with hippies, Vietnam War protests, and the women's and civil rights movements. Laws restricting the possession and sale of marijuana have long been seen as attempts to control the associated subcultures, while users saw the drug as relatively safe way to express a rejection of mainstream values. Currently mainstream acceptance of the safety and medical usefulness of marijuana is growing.

The increasing mainstream acceptance of marijuana, though far from universal, has changed the sociology of the marijuana subculture. What was counterculture and porously hidden has become more open and easily accessible. For instance, marijuana subculture is characterized by a specific and unique language of argot, or slang, which can now be easily heard on MTV or popular hip-hop and rap albums. Marijuana subculture is also linked to a rich variety of symbols, stories, and rituals. These factors help marijuana users identify one another and facilitate obtaining and sharing the drug. Having evolved in the climate prohibition it is unclear how these cultural trappings will translate to medically sanctioned and legal recreational use.

Recently a new culture of legitimate marijuana growers and distributers is emerging. This includes growers who have been in the business for some time and are currently enjoying a friendlier legal climate as well as entrepreneurs new to the business. All are eager to cash in on this potentially lucrative new market; many work tirelessly and invest millions to navigate the stringent restrictions and application processes required to obtain distribution licenses. Tobacco companies are also involved and have even conducted some of the medical marijuana research and advocated for legalization in order to be able to market and sell marijuana for a profit.

MEDICAL MARIJUANA AND LEGALIZATION

The legal status of marijuana is a reflection of attitudes about its use. In 1996 California became the first state to allow the use of marijuana for medical purposes and an additional 24 states have followed suit since. In 2012 Colorado became the first state to allow recreational marijuana use, followed by Washington, Oregon, and Alaska. In general, states with higher numbers of marijuana smokers are more likely to have medical or recreational use laws. Likewise, legalizing marijuana for medical or recreational use indicates social approval which in turn makes use more likely. State laws allowing the use of marijuana for medical or recreational purposes are in conflict with federal laws which still prohibit it.

Although marijuana remains illegal at the federal level, the current U.S. policy has been one of non-interference in instances where users abide by state regulations. This requires that state statutes are clear and address the possible risks of legal medical and recreational marijuana use, and that citizens abide by them. When this is not the case, the federal government can and does intervene. Federal prosecution of marijuana growers and users has been more likely in states with less clear and stringent regulations such as Montana and California, while federal prosecution in states with clearer and stronger regulations–including Arizona, Colorado, and Vermont–have been sparse.

Marijuana has a long history of use in medicine. Marijuana can diminish the perception of pain and has historically been used as an anesthetic as well as to treat migraines and insomnia, increase stamina, and help with a host of other ailments. Currently, state laws provide for the availability of marijuana to residents of 25 states by prescription. It is used to reduce nausea and enhance appetite in cancer patients undergoing chemotherapy, or to combat weight loss and waiting associated with cancer, HIV, and other illnesses. Marijuana can also be used in treatment of multiple sclerosis, glaucoma, and epilepsy.

There is currently much debate about whether the pros of medical marijuana outweigh the cons. Clearly, marijuana can help many individuals with serious ailments. At the same time, concerns about drivers being under the influence, risk of children and adolescents gaining access to marijuana, and the risk of iatrogenic addiction are all on the forefront of public debate. Proponents of marijuana legalization argue that marijuana is relatively very safe, especially when compared to legal drugs such as alcohol and tobacco. Tax revenue from legal medical and recreational marijuana sales has already begun to assist states in financing important capital improvements and strengthen education systems. Law enforcement officials once busy with marijuana arrests are free to focus on arguably more dangerous crimes, although some worry that that marijuana arrests are an important part of early intervention in the career of a criminal. Ultimately it is too soon to tell the final impact of the recent trend toward legalization, however it is clear that legalization is under way and can be expected in more states in the future.

*Since the publication of the DSM-5 in August 2013 the diagnosis of cannabis dependency is no longer in use. Research conducted prior to this date and ongoing at the time of publication is based on DSM-IV-TR criterion for marijuana dependency. See the section on Marijuana Dependency for further details.

BIBLIOGRAPHY:

www.mmp.org The website of the Marijuana Policy Project provides updated information regarding legal status of marijuana in each of the 50 states and the science behind efforts to legalize marijuana for medical and recreational use.

Robinson, R. (1996) *The Great Book Of Hemp: The Complete Guide to the Environmental, Commercial, and Medicinal Uses of the World's Most Extraordinary Plant*. Rochester, VT: Park Street Press. This volume describes the many uses of hemp and marijuana throughout history and looks at the current hemp and marijuana industries.

Johnson, B. D., Bardhi, F., Sifaneck, S. J., & Dunlap, E. (2006). "Marijuana Argot as Subculture Threads: Social Constructions By Users In New York City." *British Journal of Criminology*, 46(1), 46-77. This extensive description of the slang used by members of the marijuana subculture in NYC explains the development and role of such language in drug subcultures in general. The article concludes with a glossary of over 180 slang terms in the vernacular at the time of writing.

Warf, B. (2014). "High Points: An Historical Geography of Cannabis". *Geographical Review*, 104(4) 414-438.

Warf gives a detailed history of the cultivation of marijuana and hemp including its spread through Asia, Europe, Africa, and to the Americas. Various uses for marijuana in medicine and religious ceremonies over the years are documented, as well as historical attempts at prohibition.

Elizabeth M. Nielson

SEE ALSO: Cannabis; Drugs; Marijuana legalization; Marijuana usage; Smoking.

Marijuana dependence

TYPE OF PSYCHOLOGY: Addiction; Biological bases of human behavior; Clinical; Psychopathology; Social

Marijuana is the most widely used illicit drug in the US, and probably in the world. At present, although it is still prohibited at the federal level 25 states have approved its use for medical purposes and four for recreational purposes. Marijuana is hence becoming more widely available and socially sanctioned of late. Marijuana use can lead to cannabis use disorder, an addictive disorder in which the individual experiences clinically significant impairment or distress in relation to the use of marijuana. How the recently increased legal and social approval of marijuana use will affect rates of cannabis use disorder and its treatment are as yet unclear. Prevalence, risk factors, and behavioral and pharmacological treatments for cannabis use disorder are discussed.

KEY CONCEPTS

- Addiction treatment
- Cannabis use disorder
- Co-occurring disorders
- Δ9-Tetrahydracannabinol
- Psychological and physical symptoms

INTRODUCTION

Marijuana is the leaves, stems, and seeds of the plant cannabis sativa. It is the most widely used illicit drug. It is estimated that about 25 million Americans have used marijuana in the last year, and that over four million meet criterion for a cannabis use disorder at any given time. In most cases marijuana causes relatively brief and mild intoxication. Addiction to marijuana is diagnosed as a cannabis use disorder, and can range from moderate to severe depending on the number of criteria met.

Chronic use can effect motivational and reward systems, leading to addiction. For chronic users, ceasing marijuana use can result in a withdrawal syndrome not unlike nicotine withdrawal in intensity and duration. Several treatments exist including behavioral and pharmacological therapies.

DIAGNOSIS

Cannabis Abuse and Cannabis Dependence were initially listed as a diagnosis in the *Diagnostic and Statistical Manual – III* (DSM-III) published by the American Psychiatric Association in 1980. Prior to 1980, a diagnosis of drug addiction would have been made with a specification of marijuana as the drug. The DSM-III notes that – at the time of publication – tolerance and withdrawal related to marijuana use had not been established, so unlike other drugs, cannabis dependence was to be diagnosed based on level of impairment and not the presence of tolerance and withdrawal. The Abuse and Dependence diagnostic categories were carried through the DSM-IV with only minor changes. Although these terms are no longer in use, they and their related criterion were used as standards in research until the publication and adoption of the DSM-5 started in 2013.

In the years since the DSM-III scientists have established that tolerance and withdrawal do exist in cases of chronic marijuana use, and that these play a complex role in the addictive cycle. With the publication of the DSM-5 the diagnostic system changed to conceptualize cannabis use disorders on a continuum. In addition to using marijuana in a way that results in clinically significant impairment or distress, the patient must meet at least two of eleven criteria. Tolerance to the drug, and a withdrawal syndrome upon stopping use of the drug are two of the listed criterion.

ACUTE INTOXICATION

Marijuana intoxication is usually relatively mild and short. It can include feelings of euphoria, levity, and relaxation. Marijuana intoxication is accompanied by distorted perceptual experiences, for instance, the user may experience a distorted sense of time or distance. Users may experience a decreased sensation of pain as marijuana alters the perception of pain. Negative effects may include paranoia, drowsiness, difficulty concentrating, and increased appetite. Panic is not uncommon during acute marijuana intoxication: 40% of marijuana users report that they have experienced panic related to their marijuana use at some time. When used for medical purposes marijuana is often used for its acute effects of decreased perception of pain, decrease nausea, and to induce appetite.

PREVALENCE AND EPIDEMIOLOGY

Cannabis use disorders have high prevalence rates, reflective of the widespread use of marijuana. Approximately 8.6% of the population of the United States has used marijuana in the past year, and about 10% of those who try marijuana will go on to develop a Cannabis Use Disorder. Based on DSM-IV criteria, about 3.4% of youth ages 12 - 17 and 1.5% of adults meet criterion for a cannabis use disorder. Rates of cannabis use disorders are higher in males and younger adults than in females and older adults. There are also differences in rates of cannabis use disorders between racial and ethnic groups in the US.

COURSE OF ADDICTION

Marijuana contains over 60 chemicals called cannabinoids which are unique to the cannabis plant family. The cannabinoids found in marijuana are similar to the endogenous cannabinoid (or endocannabinoid) anandamide, which occurs naturally in the human brain that they can bind to existing cannabinoid receptors. The chemical responsible for marijuana's psychoactive effects is one of these cannabinoid compounds: Δ9-Tetrahydracannabinol, or Δ9-THC. Cannabinoid 1 receptors are found throughout the human brain, spinal cord, and peripheral nervous system, but it is in the brain that Δ9-THC's action at these receptor sites causes its psychoactive properties.

Marijuana is usually consumed by smoking in a small pipe or marijuana cigarette. When smoked, Δ9-THC quickly enters the bloodstream through the capillaries of the lungs and reaches the brain within seconds. Marijuana can also be eaten and the Δ9-THC absorbed into the blood stream through the gastrointestinal system. When eaten the effects of marijuana are slower to commence and longer-lasting. As users develop tolerance and require more of the drug to obtain effects they may change their smoking methods by using paraphernalia that will cool the smoke so it can be held longer in the lungs, use pressurized devices to force smoke deeper into the lungs, or vaporize marijuana so that the smoke will not cause irritation that requires quick exhalation.

Most cannabis users start as adolescents or young adults. Most illicit drug users start with a licit drug, such as alcohol or tobacco before trying marijuana or other illicit drugs however some follow an alternative sequence, trying marijuana first. Marijuana is often the first illicit drug tried because of its perceived safety and wide availability. Other risk factors include having family members who use drugs, having low academic performance, and engaging in other deviant behaviors. It is unclear how these patterns will be affected by the legalization of marijuana for recreational and medical use.

Potential for addiction is dose-dependent, with higher doses and more frequent use leading to higher likelihood of addiction. Likewise, due to refined plant breeding and growing practices, marijuana is increasing in potency and is now estimated to be 15-20 times stronger than it was in the 1960's. As Δ9-THC levels in marijuana has increased, the potential for addiction has risen, and the tolerance and withdrawal have become more prominent in maintaining cannabis use disorders.

PSYCHOLOGICAL SYMPTOMS

Adolescent and young adult users of marijuana often display an array of anti-social behaviors of which marijuana use is just one. Indeed, marijuana has long been associated with counterculture movements and used to repudiate mainstream societal values of hard work and achievement. Many young users will continue use despite disapproval and some consequences from their families or schools. If cannabis use progresses young people will often experience loss of interest in pro-social activities (such as after-school clubs or sports), a drop in grades, and truancy.

Cannabis use can cause cognitive problems and loss of motivation for goal-directed activity. In the short-term, marijuana use impairs cognitive and psychomotor performance, especially in relation to complex or demanding tasks. In some cases, reduced cognitive function can be found months after marijuana use is stopped, however it is unclear if marijuana use has caused these impairments or exacerbated existing cognitive problems. In cases of chronic use antimotivational syndrome may occur, in which the individual seems depressed and lethargic and is unable to find motivation for daily activities that once seemed rewarding.

PHYSIOLOGICAL SYMPTOMS

Because marijuana is usually smoked, the most significant consequence to physical health is respiratory problems, especially bronchitis. Compared to regular tobacco smokers, lung function of marijuana-only smokers is significantly worse. Marijuana smokers are also at increased risk of lung cancer. Some animal research suggests that marijuana impairs the immune and reproductive systems; however these effects have not been consistently established in humans.

TREATMENTS

Reflecting the high prevalence of cannabis use disorders in the general population people seeking to quit smoking marijuana are often seen in treatment settings. Among those who meet criteria for cannabis use disorder there are also high rates of alcohol use disorder and tobacco use disorder. Cannabis use can be seen as a secondary problem; however it is likely an integral part of the picture for those who meet criteria for multiple diagnoses and requires treatment in its own right.

Cannabis use disorders are not easily treated. Research shows that most promising treatments are those already applied to other types of substance use disorders such as Motivational Interviewing and Cognitive Behavioral Therapies. Longer duration treatments seem more promising for cannabis use disorders than brief interventions, such as two-session Motivational Enhancement Therapy. Voucher incentives may also help produce positive outcomes in treatment of cannabis use disorders.

One classic theory of drug addiction is that it is driven by negative reinforcement when the drug user suffers withdrawal symptoms which are relieved by taking more of the drug. Several pharmacological interventions under investigation for cannabis use disorders, some of which may alleviate this withdrawal so that further marijuana use is no longer negatively reinforced. Researchers have noted that administering synthetic Δ9-THC (dronabinol, Marinol®) will reduce symptoms of marijuana withdrawal. Other medications may be able to block the psychoactive effects of marijuana, such that further use is not rewarded. Although several medications are under investigation, none are as-yet approved for the treatment of cannabis use disorders.

CO-OCCURRING DISORDERS

Marijuana users have higher rates of other mental disorders than are found in the general population. An estimated 33% of adolescents with cannabis use disorder also meet criterion for an internalizing disorder (such as a mood disorder) and an estimated 60% meet criterion for an externalizing disorder (such as conduct disorder). In adults who have met the criterion for cannabis use disorder at some point in the past year, 11% meet criterion for depressive disorder, 24% for an anxiety disor-

der, and 13% for bipolar I disorder. Personality disorders are also common among this group, with 30% meeting criterion for antisocial, 19% for obsessive-compulsive, and 18% for paranoid personality disorders. These co-occurring diagnoses will need to be taken into account when planning treatment for individuals with cannabis use disorders.

BIBLIOGRAPHY

American Psychiatric Association (2013) "Cannabis Use Disorders", in *Diagnostic and Statistical Manual of Mental Disorders*, 5th Ed, Washington, DC. The most recent edition of the DSM gives full diagnostic criterion and an explanation of how these apply to cannabis use disorders. These criteria represent a change from the categorical diagnoses of cannabis abuse and cannabis dependence found in the previous edition.

National Institute on Drug Abuse: Marijuana http://www.drugabuse.gov/publications/research-reports/marijuana/letter-director NIDA's main informational page on marijuana includes information about its addictive potential and use in medical settings.

Panagis, G., Mackey, B., & Vlachou, S. (2014). "Cannabinoid Regulation of Brain Reward Processing With an Emphasis on the Role of CB1 Receptors: A Step Back Into the Future", *Frontiers in Psychiatry*, 5(92), 1-19. An overview of how the Δ9-THC in marijuana interacts with the brain's existing endocannabinoids and their respective receptors to create addiction to marijuana, and implications for treatment.

Elizabeth M. Nielson

SEE ALSO: Addiction; Drug addiction; Marijuana usage; Smoking; Substance abuse.

Marriage

TYPE OF PSYCHOLOGY: Clinical; Counseling; Cross-cultural, Family; Psychotherapy; Social

Marriage is a relational commitment people are drawn to make for a variety of reasons. A short-term relationship has been a common version of marriage for millennia in response to environmental pressures. This marital dynamic contrasts the 21st century reality that offers a more stable environment conducive to longevity of both life and marriage. The marital relationship can serve as a platform for couples to gain greater personal growth and maturity, which provides couples with positive reasons to stay to-gether and grow together.

KEY CONCEPTS
- Attachment
- Interpersonal relationships
- Long-term marriage
- Marriage
- Maturity

INTRODUCTION

Marriage has been a key factor of societal organization for millennia and people have been drawn to commit to marriage for a variety of reasons. In earlier decades, motivations for marriage stemmed from procreation and families joining their resources together. Marriages tend-ed to end through the death of one of the spouses, and the average marriage prior to the turn of the 20th century was about 15 years. In part due to increases in longevity, greater personal resources, and gender equality, marriag-es are increasingly ending through divorce. Currently, more than half of all marriages end in divorce, and the divorce rate increases exponentially as people remarry. These statistics shed light on the increased cultural con-cern to understand the changing landscape of the mari-tal relationship. In addition, research has demonstrated that people in Western cultures are marrying later for a variety of reasons, typically after reaching a level of in-dividual stability. Research has evaluated the impact of marriage on well-being, factors influencing marital sat-isfaction, and ways to decrease divorce in couples. This research is valuable for the field in understanding the multi-causal phenomenon of marital satisfaction, but it appears there has been a paradigm shift in motivations for marriage in recent decades. In addition to marriage serving the purpose of extended family partnerships and an environment for child rearing, marriage can be an avenue for personal growth. Therefore, a discussion of marriage as a mode for maturity offers couples positive reasons to stay together and grow together.

Healthy marriages experience changes throughout the relationship. Part of creating a successful marriage is maintaining the healthy relationship through the in-evitable transitions. During situations of change and conflict, couples have the opportunity to deepen their marital relationship and love. While many factors influ-ence why couples divorce, a variety of factors are also present that contribute to the creation of a healthy, lasting relationship.

MARITAL SATISFACTION

Martial satisfaction is often used as a means to assess the overall quality of a romantic relationship. Psycho-logical research has sought understanding of the factors contributing to satisfaction because the concept is one of the strongest predictors of overall life satisfaction. Marital satisfaction is complex and requires understand-ing of the biological, psychological, and social factors. Participation in leisurely activities as a couple, person-ality characteristics, social similarities, and interaction style, including communication skills, all correlate with marital satisfaction.

Research has found that couples with greater shared leisurely interests are less likely to pursue individual leisure activities. When couples pursue activities both partners enjoy, it is likely both partners will experience pleasure in the joint interaction and consequently in their relationship. Furthermore, couples that engage in activities that bring both partners enjoyment create greater overall connection and increased marital satisfac-tion. Marital companionship also relates to the concept of compatibility. Compatibility suggests that if a couple possesses a combination of social similarities they are more likely to experience relational harmony. Social similarities like similarities religion, values, social class, education, and ethnicity are modestly linked to happi-ness in day-to-day living; therefore, they also contribute to marital satisfaction. In addition to marital compan-ionship and social similarities, spousal interaction, in-cluding communication style, is a key predictor of satis-faction. Interaction and communication skills are strong predictors of the stability and quality of a relationship and can provide information on the future course of a relationship. The most significant determinant of marital satisfaction is debated among specialists, although lei-sure activities, compatibility, personality characteristics, and communication interactions are the most widely re-searched variables.

ATTACHMENT

Attachment is a key concept for understanding inter-personal relationships since it explains some of the en-vironmental factors that influence the lens people use to view the world. Children express both physical and emotional needs, and caregivers can respond to those needs in a variety of ways. Parent-child interaction early in life creates an attachment bond that is either secure or insecure. A person with a secure attachment indicates that caregivers were responsive, available, trustworthy and safe. Secure attachment tends to indicate a stronger ability to form healthy relationships since earlier needs were met in a healthy manner and appropriate interpersonal relationship strategies were demonstrated. These early relationship patterns provide for the understanding of future relationships.

Research suggests that attachment styles established in childhood significantly contribute to couples' marital satisfaction. For couples who feel safe and secure in their marital relationship, indicating a secure attachment, marital satisfaction is higher. While people develop their attachment style in childhood, a person can work on becoming securely attached even if they enter adulthood with insecure attachment. When an individual matures in life, both the individual and corresponding relationships can grow as a result. Attachment influences the type of interpersonal relationships individuals seek. In terms of partner compatibility, it is typical for people to find a partner who has the same attachment style. This commonality allows each person to relate in an innate manner, which is comforting because conflicting attachment styles can create greater initial turmoil. Lastly, research suggests that individuals with secure attachment tend to think more positively regarding romantic love, possess positive relationship expectations, report greater relationship satisfaction, and have a lower divorce rate. These findings can have a significant impact on relationships and the development of an enduring marriage as it relates to a long-term commitment.

ENDURING MARRIAGE

Healthy marital relationships possess a variety of intrapersonal, interpersonal, and environmental factors including, strong support system, self-confidence, and healthy communication skills. For millennia, the ideal marriage has been based on serial monogamy sequenced through the death of the other spouse. Humans have adapted to the environmental pressures of early life-ending experiences of disease, accident, illness, famine and war by switching the preference of mate over time. This historical modality contrasts with the current 21st Century reality that offers a more stable environment conducive to longevity of both life and marriage. This dissonance between adaptive serial monogamy and newly acquired longevity has resulted in social disequilibrium evidenced by high divorce rates, premarital cohabitation, and the avoidance of marriage altogether. Divorce, infidelity, and cohabitation are maladaptive methods utilized to adapt to the changes in marriage and artificially induce serial

monogamy. They are maladaptive because they negatively influence society and culture, leading to fragmented resources, which in turn leads to higher poverty rates for single parent families, inconsistent role models for child development and destabilized modern economies which are grounded in the traditional nuclear family. Therefore, the current approach to understanding marital relationships needs to be revised to account for present day dynamics.

Pinsof proposed reconceptualizing marriage from a biopsychosocial perspective, assuming divorce is the new reality. The new adaptation emphasized shifting society to accept the new reality of serial monogamy, which is organized around procreation. However, instead of focusing primarily on the biological bases of marriage, another method of reconceptualization would focus on the relational foundation as a means of addressing the current environmental changes. The marital relationship may act as an incubator that provides a platform for spouses to achieve greater personal maturity. Over time, a new marriage model may be created that represents enduring monogamy and reflects the current reality. This model, emphasizing marriage as a vehicle for maturity, provides couples with positive reasons to remain in the relationship and grow together. This systemic approach accounts for the understanding that each partner influences the other since they are part of a system that is continually responding to changes in the dynamics and striving for equilibrium. This integration of growth and relational factors, including attachment, development, companionship, and love may promote non-serial, enduring monogamy. Marriage now becomes a method of self-fulfillment that meets basic needs while providing opportunities for self and couple enhancement.

MATURITY AND GROWTH

Recognizing the constraints of the new marital environment, identifying a foundation that is relationally focused can address societal limitations. When an individual works with the relational environment of the marriage to enhance personal well-being and identity, the incorporation of taking control over personal needs and supporting others creates a healthy independence between partners. It is evident that people change from decade to decade, which is ultimately one of the key challenges in long-term marriages because individual changes cause for adjustments in the relational system.

Across lifetime, couples experience a transition from a focus on promotion to prevention. This theory describes how the young adult years are often focused on promotion, which incorporates more risk-taking behaviors with the intention of seeing their goals as a way of advancement, chance-taking, and positive thinking. This focus often causes increased mistakes and decreased follow-through. Over time, the focus in marriage shifts from taking every opportunity to seeking greater security. The shift to prevention incorporates a greater focus on making commitments where it is certain failure will not occur, which causes individuals to be conservative and thorough with planning. These orientations can be applied to the marital relationship as well because earlier in life relationships are about trying out different people and exploring the relational world. Over time, people become more focused on the safety, trust, and companionship of a partner and without safety seeking needs met, the relationship may not be appropriate. Additionally, in later stages of life, couples may become more focused on the negative consequences and risks of divorce, which affects the choices couples may make when evaluating their relationship. While individual transition and development occurs, couples also experience transitions between relational stages.

Research suggests that couples experience various developmental stages in the lifecycle of their marriage including honeymoon, early employment and/or child rearing, empty nest, retirement, and widowhood. Each stage comes with changes and challenges. Part of what can be particularly rewarding in marital relationships is the ability to develop mature love over time that solidifies and surpasses all these transitions. Knowing that significant periods of transition will occur is healthy, otherwise dynamics may lead to concerns about lost love or the possible need for divorce. In reality, it may be a normal transition and finding ways to reconcile the differences or changes will bring new stability back to the relationship. The honeymoon period is often laced with chemically mediated romance and an emphasis on the partner's positive traits to the point that difficult traits are not bothersome. Over time, every couple leaves this stage and enters the employment/child-rearing stage, and research suggests this is the most difficult stage for couples with a significant decrease in marital satisfaction often occurring. The relational system changes with the entrance of new people into the family as well as numerous other factors. Once couples move through this stage, they report increases in satisfaction. While the empty nester stage can be a period of grieving, it also provides the couple with space for reconnection. For couples that remain together for many years, the stage of retirement provides new challenges that often include an increase in time together. Marriage requires work and its evolution over time requires continual processing, but the work can provide a valuable outcome of a rewarding marriage laced with mature love. Understanding transitions are a normal part of life allows couples the opportunity to better recognize the novelty within their partner as change occurs during the lifetime of their relationship. A focus on the novelty as a positive factor allows couples to grow as an individual with the support of their spouse, which ultimately can enrich the marital relationship.

BIBLIOGRAPHY

Fisher, H. (1994). *Anatomy of Love: A Natural History of Mating, Marriage, and Why We Stray.* New York, NY: Ballantine Books. Anthropologist who explains the history and future of human relationships, love, and the role of sex.

Gottman, J. M., & Silver, N. (2002). *The Seven Principles For Making Marriage Work.* New York: Crown Publishers. Information regarding developing healthy and lasting relationships and contains questionnaires and exercises to enhance a relationship.

Johnson, S. (2008). *Hold Me Tight: Seven Conversations For a Lifetime of Love.* New York, NY: Little, Brown and Company. Information and exercises to understand the role of attachment and emotions in relationships and how understanding both concepts can enhance a relationship. This content is based off of Emotionally Focused Therapy, which is one of the evidence-based treatments in couples therapy.

Johnson, S. (2013). *Love Sense: The Revolutionary New Science of Romantic Relationships.* New York, NY: Little, Brown and Company. Explores the scientific research surrounding the concept that humans are meant to be in life-long marriages as well as the physical and psychological benefits of love.

Schnarch, D. (2009). *Passionate Marriage: Sex, Love, and Intimacy In Emotionally Committed Relationships.* New York, NY: W. W. Norton & Co. Explores the role of intimacy in relationships and tools for achieving greater intimacy in your relationships.

Schnarch, D. (2011). *Intimacy and Desire: Awaken the Passion In Your Relationship.* New York, NY: Beaufort Books. Discusses the normal occurrence of sexual desire and intimacy issues in couples and provides strategies to use sexual difficulties to strengthen a relationship.

Tashiro, T. (2014). *The Science of Happily Ever After.*

Ontario, Canada: Harlequin Enterprises Limited. Presents the scientific research regarding decision-making strategies used for identifying a partner and how to make more informed partner choices.

Heather L. Lucas and John W. Thoburn,

SEE ALSO: Family; Family dynamics; Interpersonal relationships; Love; Relationships; Sex.

Marriage and family therapists

TYPE OF PSYCHOLOGY: Clinical; Counseling; Consulting; Developmental; Family; Psychotherapy; Social

Marriage and family therapy is a specific profession in the mental health field which focuses on understanding problems based on a relational and systemic worldview. Marriage and family therapists are licensed professionals who do clinical psychotherapy with individuals, couples, and families. They treat all mental health issues.

KEY CONCEPTS:
- Counseling theory
- Introduction
- Law and ethics
- Marriage and family therapy (MFT)
- Therapeutic supervision

WHAT IS A MARRIAGE AND FAMILY THERAPIST?
Most of us are familiar with the applied psychology and social work professions, however marriage and family therapy is not as well known. This is probably because the marriage and family therapy (MFT) field is still relatively new. MFT is unique in its focus on working with clients in a relational manner. This means that often MFT's will see more than one person at a time for therapy, either a couple or an entire family. The MFT profession holds a belief that no one is an island. Everyone is impacted by their relationship with others, and it is not possible to work on people without exploring these relationships. MFT takes a systemic approach that explores the interactions, feedback loops, and circular impact of problems.

HISTORY
The family therapy movement began in the 1950's, when psychologists started to gain insight into the impact of families on psychological disorders and struggles. Pri-

or to this, all therapy and mental health was focused solely on the individual, also known as the identified patient. It was believed that this individual may have a personal defect or internal flaws specific to them until child psychologists began to recognize the profound impact parents, families, and other relationships have on an individual's mental health. Following World War II, researchers found evidence that families were greatly influenced by those coming home from the war. The schizophrenogenic mother was a theory coined in the beginning of the creation of marriage and family therapy; this described a mother who through passive and cold interactions created confused and inadequate children leading to schizophrenia. Although this was later dismissed as the reason causing schizophrenia it did begin the thought process of family impact on mental health disorders. Family therapy progressed looking deeper into relational dynamics, feedback loops, and explored ideas of how to create healing in people's lives. Among others, the originators of family therapy include Gregory Batson (double binds), Murray Bowen (intergenerational), Jay Haley and Don Jackson (furthered explored schizophrenia), John Bowlby (attachment), Nathan Ackerman, Carl Whitaker, Virginia Satir (experiential), and Salvador Minuchin (structural family therapy).

UNDERLYING PHILOSOPHY
The overall philosophy of the marriage and family therapy field revolves around the emphasis put on people as relational beings. All humans are impacted by the relationships in their lives or even the absence of relationships. Marriage and family therapy views problems as a systemic collection of experiences that have influenced the person's way of functioning. This worldview is different from other mental health professions, as problems and people are often viewed through a more individualistic and possibly deficit based perspective. Clients may notice the difference in the questions, direction and interventions marriage and family therapists will use to create goals, process information, and help create change.

Marriage and family therapist utilize different theories than other helping professions, which have all been created in reaction to the original Family Systems Theory. Family Systems Theory was expanded into Intergenerational Family Therapy created by psychiatrist Murray Bowen, in the 1960's while working with schizophrenic patients and their families. He changed his approach from focusing on internalized issues of the patient to explore the relational impact of them and their families. Bowen focused his theory on understand the family of origin impact on people where the goal of therapy was to increase awareness of patterns in order to help clients increase functioning. Following the Family Systems Theory many other theories have emerged either expanding this belief or introducing a new perspective. These theories include the following: Structural Family Therapy, Strategic Family Therapy, Humanistic (Experiential/Satir and Gestalt Therapy), Object Relations (Attachment), Narrative Therapy, Emotional Focused Therapy, and Solution Focused Therapy. All of these theories originate from a systemic approach. They vary in how they understand how change happens. For example, Structural Family Therapy focuses on the relationships and patterns in the family and believes that change happens through altering the structure of the family. Narrative Therapy focuses on how meaning is developed through experiences in our lives creating a problem storyline, and believes that change happens through insight around the meanings and working to find alternative and preferred meaning in one's life.

Cognitive Behavioral Therapy and Psychodynamic theory are also used by MFT's; however, they were not originally developed as a systemic theory. MFT's also incorporate approaches that reflect the most current,

evidence-based approaches to therapy such as Eye Movement Desensitization Reprocessing (EMDR) and Trauma Focused Cognitive Behavioral Therapy.

EDUCATION AND TRAINING

Marriage and family therapy is a specific form of psychotherapy involving viewing clients and their problems through a relational perspective. MFT's begin with entering a Masters level program, which is generally 2-3 years in length. To be accepted into a graduate program, the individual must already have a bachelor's degree. This degree may be in psychology, nursing, social work, education or other counseling related fields. If the applicant does not have a bachelor's degree in a helping profession, they may be required to complete additional coursework before being considered. They will have the option to go to marriage and family therapy doctorate programs or may choose to go clinical psychology or counseling doctorate programs. However, unlike other mental health professions, having a master's degree in MFT will allow for licensure, owning a private practice, and affords the ability to supervise others. According to the Federal government, marriage and family therapy has been recognized as a core mental health profession. Other mental health professions in this category in-

Photo: iStock

clude psychiatry, psychology, social work and psychiatric nursing.

After completing a MFT graduate program students go into an intern or trainee phase of their learning. This is regulated on a state to state basis. During the intern phase the professional is required to work in the field seeing clients and needs to keep track of counting their own clinical, supervision, client advocacy and other professional development hours. All of the 50 states recognize the MFT profession and administer the licensure according to their own state regulations. For example, in California, registered interns are required to have 3000 clinically supervised hours. The supervisor is a licensed professional (at least 2 years) who has completed the approved supervisor requirements and is responsible for overseeing the cases and signing documentation. In New York State graduates have a limited permit and are required to do 1500 clinically supervised hours before they are eligible to sit for the licensing exam. The American Association of Marriage and Family Therapy provides standards of the profession that all of the state licensure aim to meet. This association accredits universities that meet the high standards of the profession. Often it will take approximately 2-4 years after the degree to complete the requirements to sit for the licensing exam.

All of the states require interns to complete relational hours which are distinctive to this specialty. Interns must see a large amount of couples and families to get their hours. Due to the emphasis on the relational and systemic approach of MFT these hours are very important. Working relationally can be a challenge for mental health professionals since the Diagnostic and Statistical Manual (DSM), which serves as the guideline for understanding mental health disorders is individual based. Marriage and family therapists see problems as less within the individual client or patient and more as resulting from the system of relationships like those most often found in families. Since this is not the norm in how American culture explains and understands personal issues, learning to think systemically requires a learning curve for MFTs. In more recent years there has been some shift in this viewpoint, as the DSM now includes some relational disorders and other mental health professionals are opening up their theories and interventions to include some systems ideas.

SUPERVISION

Perhaps more than other clinical specialties, the MFT profession focuses on supervision. Supervisors are ex-

pected to fill a combination of roles that includes supportive, didactic, therapeutic, as well as serving as the gate keepers of the profession. Although supervisors cannot act as the trainee's actual therapist, there is often a therapeutic-like relationship of support and learning. Supervisors have a large impact on the philosophy and the practice of their interns. They must share their supervision philosophy to provide transparency in their approach. Supervision may be provided for the interns at their place of employment or on some occasions interns are responsible for seeking out and paying for their own supervision. The intern must be in supervision the entire time they are counting hours towards their licensure. The supervisor is the one who is overseeing all of the clinical cases and it is their job to ensure clients are receiving the appropriate care. Supervisors are also seen as the gatekeepers for the profession, as it is their responsibility to make sure that the intern's follow the main ethical standard of doing no harm. They provide feedback for the intern on their abilities, successes and where they need improvement. It is also possible for a supervisor to provide feedback that an intern may not be appropriate for the profession.

Live supervision is also common to the MFT profession and highly prized. A supervisor either watches the intern's therapy sessions on video, through a one way mirror or actually sits in on the sessions. Although this can be a stressful experience for interns, it also yields a large amount of feedback. Supervision in other fields such as social work or psychology often is done through case consultations. The professional reports back to the supervisor about what happened in the session and what they feel worked and what did not. Case consultations are also used by MFT supervisors, however live supervision provides all the details of the session that can be left out or overlooked in the session. For example, if a supervisor is watching a session they have the ability to pick up on non-verbal cues such as eye contact, body language and tone. Since non-verbal communication represents a huge portion of expression, these elements are extremely important in understanding clients. Therefore the added value of live supervision is that it provides much more information for the supervisor than simply being told about the therapeutic process.

LAW AND ETHICS

The practice of marriage and family therapy is governed through state laws and the ethics code of the profession. There is an ethical code written by the American Association of Marriage and Family Therapy which includes all the expectations of how therapists should behave and how to ensure that they do no harm to their clients. The code of ethics is not only taught in training programs but is highly tested on the licensing exams and is also required to be part of a continuing education post licensure. The laws of marriage and family therapy vary slightly from state to state. These laws include information of mandated reporting, where clinicians are required to break confidentiality to report suspected abuse, suicidality and homicidally. Licensed professionals are required to keep current on the changing legal and ethical codes of the field.

PRACTICE

Marriage and family therapists have the ability to practice in many different settings. Among these include private practice, hospitals, community clinics, substance abuse treatment centers, residential facilities or nursing homes. Most of the agencies that hire mental health professionals will consider MFT's for the position. There are a few agencies that may be behind on this since MFT is still seen as a newer field than social work and psychology. Marriage and family therapist who possess a doctoral degree will also be considered for academic jobs at universities. On a rare occasion even MFT's with only a master's degree may be able to do some adjunct teaching at most universities. Marriage and family therapists at a master's level are also able to own their own private practice. This is different from psychology, since psychologists must have a doctorate to own a practice.

Salary for marriage and family therapist will vary depending on the state and the setting of where they work. Community based agencies often pay the lowest salary while MFT's in private practice or private facilities will tend to make the most. It is also very common to find MFT's who work at a combination of these settings. Lower income for MFT's is around $30,000 annually while higher incomes can reach $80,000 or more. Median income for marriage and family therapist's continues to grow in the United States.

CHOOSING A HELPING PROFESSIONAL

When looking to choose a mental health professional there a few things to keep in mind to help you make an educated decision. Psychologists, marriage and family therapists, and social workers all provide therapy. Psychologists are often the professionals that will do psychological testing and will all have their doctoral degrees. This means that they can offer an expertise in the testing professionand may also be more expensive to see in a private practice. Social workers often work in mental health care agencies and have more of a focus on case management and obtaining resources. Social workers can also advance their degrees to get a doctorate or become licensed clinical social workers, which you will also find in working in private practice. Marriage and family therapists will most likely be master's level clinicians, and their entire training and education experience is around doing therapy therefore they often have more experience in seeing clients right out of school. Whereas psychologist and social workers can focus on other avenues of mental health in their training, such as case management or testing, MFT's focus primarily on doing therapy. Again, this will vary based on the individual as some psychologists will focus their training mostly on doing therapy. There will be a difference in the theoretical approach these professionals take based on their education, training and also their personality. Overall regardless of which helping professional you choose to see it is very important to find a person who will be a good fit with you and your needs. Therapists are just people and you will not get along with all of them solely because they are therapists. If you do not feel that the therapist's style is a good fit for you, try another.

BIBLIOGRAPHY

Brown, Jenny. (2008, September). "Is Bowen Theory Still Relevant in the Family Therapy Field?" *Journal of the Counsellors and Psychotherapists Association of NSW Inc* 3. Retrieved from http://www.familysystemstraining.com/papers/is-bowen-theory-still-relevant.html This source discusses the history of MFT, the impact of Bowen Theory and the current theories uses in the field.

Corey, G., Corey, M. S., & Callanan, P. (2011). *Issues and Ethics In the Helping Professions* (8th ed.). Cole, Belmont, CA This book covers all of the ethical codes that are held by the American Association of Marriage and Family Therapists, discussing in detail the understanding and intention of each code.

Goldenberg, H., & Goldenberg, I. (2008). *Family therapy: An overview* (7th ed.). Thomson Higher Education, Belmont, CA. This book provides an overview of the history of marriage and family therapy and information of all the systemic theories this field utilizes.

Todd, T. C., & Strom, C. L. *The Context, Complete Philosophy, Systemic and Supervisor Pragmatics.* (2002). Authors Choice Press, Lincoln, NE. This source covers the meaning behind systems theory and the importance of supervision on the MFT field. It provides information about the role, focus and responsibility of supervisors.

Kimberly Ortiz

SEE ALSO: Childrearing; Divorce; Dysfunction; Family dynamics; Family relations; Family therapy; Relationships.

Masculinity

TYPE OF PSYCHOLOGY: Developmental psychology

Masculinity refers to masculine traits or characteristics that are capable of being transformed in line with historical and cultural change. Responding to challenges, male reevaluation of masculinity frequently results in confusion and disillusionment.

KEY CONCEPTS
- Feminist movements
- Hegemonic man
- Male identity
- Manliness
- Men's movements

INTRODUCTION

Masculinity, or manhood, is a construct shaped by historical and ideological processes that results in many different masculinities. Not historically fixed or based on biology, masculinity is a dynamic progression that projects male identity as constantly changing through its contacts with various institutions and ideologies. Although strength and dominance have always been male attributes, variations in male identity are apparent, for example, from prehistoric hunters, to Greek warriors, to the Christian devout of the Middle Ages, to twenty-first century business executives.

The idea of masculinity, as opposed to manliness, or a man exhibiting an upright character, emerged near the beginning of the twentieth century as the dominant male attributes of the Victorian era began to fade with the advent of a new, more aggressive society. In the United States, manly self-restraint and respectability began to be perceived by mainstream men as inadequate to combat the surge of immigrants determined to prove their vitality and manhood. Also, the rise of women activists, suffragettes, or those merely seeking advancement was perceived to threaten manhood, creating an urge among many men to reclaim their former dominance. Men began to form restrictive groups and associations that championed specific ideas of masculinity. During this time, the Boy Scouts organization was begun as a way to remove boys periodically from female influences and "teach them how to be men."

Despite the potential for change in male identity that exists naturally in the day-to-day lives of individuals, families, and communities, the force possibly most resistant to change is the construction of the hegemonic man in the media. Depictions of men in advertisements present images of masculinity that suggest power and control. Male characters in war or action films are depicted as aggressive and violent, and frequently mistreat women, children, homosexuals, and minorities. Men's magazines tout hegemonic masculinity in the form of physically attractive leaders who are in control of their environment as well as their own destiny. These images undermine more conservative masculine identities in children and teenagers, and also prove detrimental to men who are uncomfortable with such portrayals.

STATUS

Although studies in masculinity were largely an outgrowth of the feminist movement, whose attacks on male privilege eventually transformed ideas concerning manhood, evidence suggests that men had previously staged a rebellion against the predominant view of men as the mainstay of the family. Author Barbara Ehrenreich insists that the launch of *Playboy* magazine in 1953 was designed to indicate male dissatisfaction with the image of the man as a "breadwinner"; she also maintains that the feminist movement of the 1970s was really an assault on the men's revolt.

Some men had already begun fighting the inequity of divorce courts, both in the financial realm and that of child custody, which favored the mother. A large number of men were already pursuing men's liberation. However, although the impact of the feminist movement led many men either to angrily refute feminist charges or to engage in pro-feminist activities to make amends for their past behavior, others took part in a men's movement that included writing and reading books on masculinity and its history, and joining various organizations for the benefit of fathers who had lost custody of their children, men unable to express their feelings, men alienated from the company of men, men who feared women, and men concerned with the effects of "traditional" views of masculinity on their sons, as well as gay liberation groups.

In some cases, violence has been the result of changing masculinity roles. The lack of positive father-son relationships has been blamed for incidents of youth violence and rage, including school shootings. While the emergence of the gay liberation movement allowed homosexual men to pursue lives that redefined masculinity, some heterosexual men saw these public avowals of homosexuality as a threat to their own masculinity and retreated into homophobia, a traditional male trait. As a result, some men engaged in acts of violence toward gay men and lesbians.

A major masculinity crisis exists in the area of men's health, largely the result of unvoiced notions of strength and toughness that undermine men's well-being. Ideals of masculinity seem to place low priority on maintaining health, eating a proper diet, eliminating harmful habits, reducing stress, or moderating risk taking. In the United States, men's life expectancy is about five years less than women's; their rate of completed suicide is almost four times that of women; and their rate of accidental death, compared with that of women, is shockingly high.

BIBLIOGRAPHY

Bly, Robert. *Iron John: A Book about Men.* Cambridge: Da Capo, 2004. Print.

Connell, R. W. *Masculinities.* 2nd ed. Berkeley: U of California P, 2005. Print.

Kimmel, Michael S. *Manhood in America: A Cultural History.* 3rd ed. New York: Oxford UP, 2011. Print.

Kimmel, Michael, Jeff R. Hearn, and R. W. Connell, eds. *Handbook of Studies on Men and Masculinities.* Thousand Oaks: Sage, 2004. Print.

Lotz, Amanda D. *Cable Guys: Television and Masculinities in the Twenty-First Century.* New York: NYU P, 2014. Print.

Newkirk, Thomas. *Misreading Masculinity: Boys, Literacy, and Popular Culture.* Portsmouth: Heinemann, 2002. Print.

Noble, Jean Bobby. *Masculinities without Men? Female Masculinity in Twentieth-Century Fictions.* Seattle: U of Washington P, 2005. Print.

Reeser, Todd W. *Masculinities in Theory: An Introduction.* Malden: Wiley, 2010. Print.

Mary Hurd

SEE ALSO: Femininity; Gender differences; Gender identity formation; Gender roles and gender role conflicts; Men's mental health.

Maslow, Abraham

BORN: April 1, 1908
DIED: June 8, 1970
BIRTHPLACE: Brooklyn, New York
PLACE OF DEATH: Menlo Park, California
IDENTITY: American psychologist
TYPE OF PSYCHOLOGY: Motivation; personality

Maslow is considered a father of humanistic psychology and is remembered particularly for his theory describing a hierarchy of human needs and motivations.

Abraham Maslow was born the first of seven children to Jewish immigrants from Russia. Though uneducated themselves, Maslow's parents pushed him to excel academically and encouraged him to go into law. He married his first cousin, Bertha Goodman, and they eventually had two daughters.

Maslow studied law at the City College of New York, but after three semesters transferred to Cornell University, and later to the University of Wisconsin to study psychology. He received his bachelor's degree in 1930, a master's degree in 1931, and a doctorate in 1934, all in psychology from the University of Wisconsin. Maslow worked for a time at Columbia, then served on the faculty of Brooklyn College from 1937 to 1951, and was professor and chairman of the psychology department at Brandeis University from 1951 to 1969.

Maslow was an articulate and prolific scholar; an author of more than twenty books and close to one hundred articles. His books included *Motivation and Personality* (1954), *Toward a Psychology of Being* (1962), *Religions, Values, and Peak-Experiences* (1964), and *The Farther Reaches of Human Nature* (1971). He cofounded the *Journal of Humanistic Psychology* and is considered a father of humanistic psychology.

His theory of a hierarchy of human needs has been particularly influential. Maslow proposed that human needs and motivations could be construed in a hierarchy, often pictured as a pyramid with five levels, from bottom to top: basic physiological needs such as hunger and thirst, safety needs, needs for love and belonging, needs for self-esteem, and a need for self-actualization. In this hierarchy, lower, more basic needs must be met before higher needs emerge. The uppermost need, self-actualization, Maslow saw as a need for personal growth and self-fulfillment.

In recognition of his many contributions to psychology, Maslow was elected president of the American Psychological Association for 1967-1968. Maslow moved to California in 1969 and served as resident fellow of the Laughlin Institute while semiretired. He died of a heart attack on June 8, 1970.

BIBLIOGRAPHY

Berecz, John M. *Theories of Personality: A Zonal Perspective.* Boston: Allyn, 2009. Print.

Feist, Jess, and Gregory J. Feist. *Theories of Personality.* 8th ed. Boston: McGraw-Hill Higher Education, 2012. Print.

Hergenhahn, B. R. *An Introduction to the History of Psychology.* 6th ed. Belmont: Wadsworth/Cengage Learning, 2009. Print.

Hoffman, Edward. *The Right to Be Human: A Biography of Abraham Maslow.* Rev. ed. New York: McGraw-Hill, 1999. Print.

Schultz, Duane, and Sydney Schultz. *Theories of Personality.* 10th ed. Belmont: Wadsworth/Cengage Learning, 2013. Print.

John W. Engel

SEE ALSO: Allport, Gordon; Hierarchy of needs; Motivation; Motivation: Intrinsic and extrinsic; Rogers, Carl R.

Masters, William H., and Virginia E. Johnson

BORN: December 27, 1915
BIRTHPLACE: Cleveland, Ohio
DIED: February 16, 2001
PLACE OF DEATH: Tucson, Arizona

BORN: February 11, 1925
BIRTHPLACE: Springfield, Missouri

IDENTITY: American researchers of human sexual response
TYPE OF PSYCHOLOGY: Emotion; Sensation and perception; Social psychology

Masters and Johnson were pioneers in the scientific study of sexual arousal and the treatment of sexual problems.

William H. Masters attended public schools in Kansas City and in Lawrenceville, New Jersey. In 1938, he earned a bachelor's degree from Hamilton College in New York. After receiving his medical degree in gynecology from the University of Rochester in 1943, he began laboratory studies of sexual behavior in 1954 while on the faculty of Washington University in St. Louis, Missouri.

A precocious child, Virginia E. Johnson was allowed to skip several grades during her public schooling. She studied piano and voice and read extensively. She studied psychology and sociology at Drury College and at the University of Missouri, joining Masters as a research associate in 1957. At that time, scientists knew little about human responses to sexual stimulation. Masters and Johnson used motion pictures, electrocardiograms, electroencephalograms, polygraph-like instruments, and other scientific equipment to record the human body's physiological responses to sexual stimulations in men and women who volunteered to engage in sexual activity.

In 1964, Masters and Johnson established the Reproductive Biology Research Foundation in St. Louis, Missouri. In 1973, they became codirectors of the Masters and Johnson Institute in St. Louis. Their research stirred up a great deal of controversy. Many critics called them immoral and accused them of dehumanizing sex.

In 1966, the results of their research were published in Human Sexual Response, which described the physiological responses during four phases of erotic arousal for males and females. Although written in technical language for physicians and other health scientists, the book became a best seller. After counseling hundreds of married couples about problems dealing with sexual performance, Masters and Johnson published *Human Sexual Inadequacy* in 1970. It dealt with the treatment of sexual problems, including impotence, premature ejaculation, and frigidity. It is considered by many experts to be the first comprehensive study of the physiology and anatomy of human sexual activity under laboratory conditions. Masters and Johnson were married in 1971.

Homosexuality in Perspective, a report on the clinical treatment of the sexual problems of homosexuals, appeared in 1979. Although they received much criticism for their views, Masters and Johnson claimed an ability to change the sexual preference of homosexuals who wished to change. More controversy was sparked by their 1988 publication of *Crisis: Heterosexual Behavior in the Age of AIDS*, wherein they forecast an epidemic spread of acquired immunodeficiency syndrome (AIDS) among heterosexuals. After their divorce in 1993, Masters and Johnson continued their research collaboration.

BIBLIOGRAPHY

Drucker, Donna J. *The Machines of Sex Research: Technology and the Politics of Identity, 1945–1985.* Dordrecht: Springer, 2014. Print.

Fox, Stuart Ira. *Human Physiology.* 11th ed. Dubuque: McGraw-Hill, 2009. Print.

Mader, Sylvia S. *Human Reproductive Biology.* 3d ed. Dubuque: McGraw-Hill, 2005. Print.

Maier, Thomas. *Masters of Sex: The Life and Times of William Masters and Virginia Johnson, the Couple Who Taught America How to Love.* New York: Basic, 2009. Print.

Robinson, Paul. *The Modernization of Sex.* Ithaca: Cornell University Press, 1989. Print.

Alvin K. Benson

SEE ALSO: Gay, lesbian, bisexual, and transgender mental health; Gender identity formation; Homosexuality; Kinsey, Alfred; Sex hormones and motivation; Sexual behavior patterns; Sexual dysfunction; Sexual variants and paraphilias; Survey research: Questionnaires and interviews.

May, Rollo

BORN: April 21, 1909, in Ada, Ohio
DIED: October 22, 1994, in Tiburon, California
IDENTITY: American psychologist
TYPE OF PSYCHOLOGY: Psychotherapy

May, a psychotherapist and author, introduced and popularized existential psychology in the United States.

Rollo May was raised in Michigan and graduated from Oberlin College in 1930 with a degree in English. He taught for three years at the American College in Greece. While in Europe, May attended seminars by psychoanalyst Alfred Adler. After returning to the United States, May became a counselor at Michigan State University (then college). He found his interest in the profound aspects of human existence growing and therefore pursued the study of theology at the Union Theological School, from which he graduated in 1938. Subsequently, May attended Columbia University, earning a doctorate in counseling psychology in 1944. His dissertation was completed under the mentorship of Paul Tillich and was published as *The Meaning of Anxiety* (1950). With it, and his next book, *Man's Search for Himself* (1953), May charted a lifelong course to understand the human dilemma of living in an age of anxiety, alienation, and self-estrangement.

These inquiries led May to examine the work of existential therapists and scholars in Europe such as Ludwig Binswanger and Medard Boss, whose incorporation of the insights of existential-phenomenological philosophy was creating a new approach to psychology and psychiatry. In bringing these insights to an American audience with his coedited collection Existence: A New Dimension in Psychiatry and Psychology (1958; edited with Ernest Angel and Henri F. Ellenberger), May became the father of Existential psychologyexistential psychology in the United States. By "existential," May meant a psychology concerned with the profound dimensions of human existence.

A key innovation for May was to revise psychology's understanding of psychopathology. For May, psychological suffering was rooted in the alienation of the person from his or her own self, stemming from the failure to become the self. This loss of selfhood or centeredness yields anxiety, an anxiety May noted had become epidemic, beginning in the 1950's. For him, this epidemic revealed the cost of living in a cultural age that is so disintegrated that it makes it hard to attain personal integration of the self. May proposed that it is this predicament that propels each person to search for the self, which can be found by attuning oneself authentically (within not without) via courage and creativity.

May's own work analyzed such themes as paradox, anxiety, tragedy, alienation, freedom, responsibility, love, will, innocence, power, creativity, and the roles of myth and beauty in life. He published these studies in widely popular books: *Psychology and the Human Dilemma* (1967), *Love and Will* (1969), *The Courage to Create* (1975), *Freedom and Destiny* (1981), and *The Cry for Myth* (1991).

BIBLIOGRAPHY

Reeves, Clement. *The Psychology of Rollo May.* San Francisco: Jossey-Bass, 1977. A philosophical analysis of May's books up to 1977, with commentary by May.

Review of Existential Psychology and Psychiatry 24 (1999). This issue, devoted to Rollo May, includes both biographical studies and six lectures by May.

Schneider, Kirk J., and Rollo May. *The Psychology of Existence.* New York: McGraw-Hill, 1995. Some of May's papers, along with those of many other foremost existential psychologists, on an integrative clinical perspective.

Christopher M. Aanstoos

SEE ALSO: Anxiety disorders; Existential psychology; Self.

McGraw, Dr. Philip

TYPE OF PSYCHOLOGY: Clinical; Counseling; Family; Psychotherapy; Social

"Dr. Phil" McGraw is a television talk show host and former clinical psychologist. Initially, he became well known for his frequent appearances on The Oprah Winfrey Show, and he is now known for his own widely syndicated psychologically-oriented television program, The Dr. Phil Show, which he both hosts and produces.

KEY CONCEPTS

- Cognitive behavioral therapy
- Emotional and behavioral issues
- Forensic psychology
- Pop psychology
- Television talk shows

Dr. Philip McGraw is a television personality, author, producer, and former clinical psychologist. He received his Ph.D. from the University of North Texas and worked in his father's clinical psychology practice for several years. He then went on to invest in many business ventures, including a trial consulting firm called Courtroom Sciences, Inc. During his tenure at CSI, he consulted for Oprah Winfrey, who later catapulted him into fame as a lifestyle and relationship expert on *The Oprah Winfrey Show*. After four years as a weekly guest, he launched his own show, *The Dr. Phil Show*. This syndicated talk show focuses on emotional, psychological, relational, family, and behavioral health issues and usually features guest professionals whose expertise illuminates the concerns at hand. Often guests, who present a problem which serves as the theme of the show, are offered the opportunity of professional, licensed intervention and treatment. *The Dr. Phil Show* has received 27 Emmy nominations, and is one of the most popular talk shows in television history.

EARLY YEARS

Philip Calvin McGraw was born September 1, 1950, in Vinita, Oklahoma, to Anne Geradine Stevens and Joseph McGraw. His mother was a housewife, and his father was an equipment supplier for the oil industry. His father later went on to become a licensed clinical psychologist. McGraw attended the University of Tulsa for a short time on a football scholarship, transferring to Midwestern State University in Texas where he received a B.A. in psychology. He then went on to receive his M.A. and Ph.D. at the University of North Texas (formally North Texas State University) in clinical psychology. His doctoral dissertation focused on the management of pain in patients with rheumatoid arthritis.. McGraw later completed one year of postdoctoral work in forensic psychology at the Wilmington Institute in Dallas, Texas. He was licensed as a clinical psychologist in the state of Texas until 2006.

MID CAREER

After graduate school, McGraw worked within his father's clinical psychology practice, counseling clients using cognitive behavioral therapy. In the early 1980s, he met Thelma Box, and together, they created what is now known as the "Pathway Seminars," a series of personal growth and self empowerment seminars that they presented live. These seminars focused on using individual strengths to pave a path to success and taught individuals to continue with the methods they found to be most sucessful. The "Pathway Seminars" are important because many of the tenets became the basis for Dr. Phil's later television career and books.

CSI

In 1989, McGraw became involved in a new business venture with a well-known Kansas attorney, Gary Dobbs. They called their venture Courtroom Sciences, Inc., or CSI, and branded themselves as a trial consulting firm, focusing on witness preparation and juror selection. It was through his work at CSI that McGraw met Oprah Winfrey, and the two became personal and professional friends.

In 1996, mad cow disease was given much attention in health-related media, and Winfrey focused on this disease on a segment of her long running show. During the segment, Winfrey interviewed Howard Lyman, a rancher turned vegetarian. Lyman made a comment about the safety of beef, and Oprah then stated that his comment "stopped me cold from eating another burger." Texas beef producers were in an uproar regarding the statement, and Paul Engler, a Texas cattle owner, sued Winfrey, her production studio, and Howard Lyman. Winfrey's lawyer in that suit hired Courtroom Sciences, Inc., to prepare her for the trial, and McGraw traveled to Chicago to help Winfrey. Winfrey and McGraw bonded during this time, forming a close personal and professional relationship that exists to this day.

After successfully defending against the suit, Winfrey asked Dr. Phil to appear on her show as a lifestyle and personal growth coach. His first appearance, April 10, 1998, met mixed reviews. Oprah featured McGraw a second time, and audiences warmed to him. Between 1998 and 2002, Dr. Phil became a weekly guest on The Oprah Winfrey Show and an icon within pop culture, widely considered an expert on mental health, relationships, and personal growth.

BOOKS

Dr. Phil's popularity created an opening for his entrance into the writing world. Since 1998, he has authored more than 13 books and workbooks, seven of which were number one on the *New York Times* bestseller list. Some of his most popular titles include: *Life Strategies: Doing What Works, Doing What Matters* (1999); *The Ultimate Weight Solution: The 7 Keys to Weight Loss Freedom* (2003); *Family First: Your Step-by-Step Plan for Creating a Phenomenal Family* (2005); *Love Smart: Find the One You Want—Fix the One You Got* (2006); and *Life Code: The New Rules for Living in the Real World* (2012).

THE DR. PHIL SHOW

In 2002, McGraw was given the opportunity to host his own show, The Dr. Phil Show, with Oprah Winfrey's full support. The show, produced by Paramount, focuses on the stories of those with emotional, behavioral, and relationship-based issues, with Dr. Phil facilitating the discussion and dispensing advice. The Dr. Phil Show quickly became the number one show in its time slot and has since received 27 Emmy nominations. As of January 2015, it remains one of the top rated syndicated talk shows in the United States. McGraw describes his show as an educational and entertainment based platform, designed to discuss, but not treat, mental health issues. Guests on The Dr. Phil Show are frequently referred to aftercare with licensed professionals within their own communities. This focus on aftercare assists guests with the issues they may have while also exposing the show's television audience to the benefits of psychological intervention.

The Dr. Phil Show has not been immune to controversy. In 2008, Dr. Phil showed up at Cedars Sinai Medical Center in Los Angeles, California, to talk to singer Britney Spears, who was under an involuntary psychiatric hold at the time. He later made statements to the media regarding her condition leading to a complaint being filed against McGraw with the California Board of Psychology. Later that same year, *The Dr. Phil Show* was under scrutiny again, this time because a producer of the show allegedly posted $30,000 bail for a Florida teen, who, along with several other girls, was accused of beating another girl and posting a video of the act on the Internet. The producer posted bail because *The Dr. Phil Show* hoped to air a special segment regarding the incident. That show was scrapped immediately after allegations regarding the incident were publicized.

CRITICISMS AND ACCOLADES

Critics of Dr. Phil will state that he treads a fine line between educating the public and dispensing medical advice, especially considering he has not been licensed to practice clinical psychology since 2006. Critics also point out his quick advice and "one liners" are not helpful to the therapeutic process. Real change takes time and effort. Other psychologists disagree, stating that Dr. Phil has normalized the process of therapy, specifically cognitive behavioral therapy, for present and future clients. The American Psychological Association (APA) presented Dr. Phil with a Presidential Citation in 2006, with APA president Dr. Gerald Koocher stating, "Your work has touched more Americans than any other living psychologist."

THE DOCTORS

Dr. Phil continues to be one of the most highly recognized doctors of psychology in history. He continues his work on *The Dr. Phil Show* while also writing books and workbooks, guest starring on television shows, and promoting several different products and new businesses. He also successfully created, with his son Jay, a Dr. Phil spin off show called *The Doctors,* starring Dr. Travis Stork. *The Doctors* is a syndicated talk show similar to *The Dr. Phil Show,* focusing on a panel of four medical doctors who discuss medical issues such as infertility, surgery, pediatric concerns, and obesity.

PERSONAL LIFE

Currently, McGraw lives in Beverly Hills, California, with his wife, Robin McGraw. They have been married since 1976. Together, they run the Dr. Phil Foundation, a non-profit foundation focused on supporting the varied needs of children and families. Dr. Phil and Mrs. McGraw have two children, Jay, and Jordan. They also have two grandchildren from Jay's marriage to model Erica Dahm.

BIBLIOGRAPHY

Dembling, S., & Guiterrez, L. (2005). *The Making of Dr. Phil: The Straight Talking True Story of Everyone's Favorite Therapist.* Hoboken, NJ: John Wiley & Sons. The first published biography of Dr. Phil McGraw, focusing on his birth to his current status as an award winning television talk show host, businessman, and producer.

McGraw, P. (1999). *Life Strategies: Doing What Works, Doing What Matters.* New York, NY: Hyperion. Dr. Phil's first book, outlining ten strategies that can change one's life. These strategies are very similar to the strategies presented in the "Pathway's Seminars" that he and Thelma Box created in the 1980s.

McGraw, P. (2012). *Life Code: The New Rules For Living In The Real World.* Los Angeles, CA: Bird Hill Books. Dr. Phil's most recent book, focusing on new "life rules" for a new generation.

Meyers, L. (2006 October). "Behind the Scenes of the 'Dr. Phil' show". *Monitor on Psychology,* 63. Retrieved from http://www.apa.org/monitor/oct06/drphil.aspx. This article is a brief, behind the scenes look at The Dr. Phil Show. It also summarizes comments made during his presidential address at the 2006 convention of the American Psychological Association.

Parker – Pope, T. (2008, January 10). "Do The Rules Apply to Dr. Phil?" Retrieved from http://well.blogs.nytimes.com/2008/01/10/do-the-rules-apply-to-dr-phil/. This blog posting focuses on the ethical issues related to Dr. Phil's visit to Britney Spears' bedside while she was placed on involuntary psychiatric hold at Cedar Sinai Hospital in Los Angeles.

Gina Riley

Media exposure and mental health

DATE: 1970s forward

TYPE OF PSYCHOLOGY: Cognition; Developmental psychology; Psychopathology; Social psychology

Media exposure is increasingly prevalent, but its impact is still not completely understood. Research indicates that the quantity, content, and context of media exposure influence the psychological, social, and behavioral development of children and adolescents. Violent media exposure affects behavior and social interactions of both children and young men, and media exposure to female standards of beauty affects women's and adolescent girls' attitudes toward their bodies and to gender roles.

KEY CONCEPTS

- Aggression
- Cyberbullying
- Eating disorders
- Hostile social information processing
- Social isolation
- Violence

INTRODUCTION

Because children and adolescents are in the process of developing cognitive, social, and behavioral traits, media exposure typically has a greater effect on the psychological, cognitive, and social health of young people than of adults. Studies have found both positive and negative effects of media, including television, video games, and the Internet, on children. Media can be educational for children, expanding their general knowledge and improving their cognitive skills. However, the exposure of children and adolescents to media can promote aggressiveness, early (and risky) sexual behavior, desensitization to the pain of others, anxiety, sleep problems, attention problems, and reduced literacy.

Excessive media exposure, in the form of television viewing or recreational computer use, has been associated with increased social isolation in children and adolescents. In particular, children's viewing of violent television programs appears to be closely linked to decreased social interaction with peers. In young men, exposure to violent media has been associated with uncooperative behavior, negative affect, and hostile social information processing. Exposure to violent media has also been shown to interact with violence in the home and community of these men to further increase hostile social information processing.

For both women and adolescent girls, images of unrealistically thin and large-bosomed "desirable" women and the depiction of women as sex objects in the media may negatively affect self-esteem and their attitudes toward their bodies. In some individuals, this can result in eating disorders such as anorexia nervosa and bulimia nervosa. Some women and girls may also undergo multiple plastic surgeries, including liposuction and breast enhancement, in an attempt to achieve the "perfect" figure.

Whatever the effects of media exposure on the mental and cognitive health of children and adults, these issues will only become more pressing as digital devices that play videos, games, and television shows become more ubiquitous. Intervention and treatment for the psychological disturbances caused by media exposure include parental monitoring and control of media content to which children are exposed, and cognitive behavior therapy for women and adolescent girls with body issues and eating disorders.

TELEVISION VIEWING

Children and adolescents are exposed to an unprecedented quantity and diversity of media. Because they are undergoing cognitive, social, and behavioral development, they are also more vulnerable to being affected by media exposure. Many young people spend several hours a day watching television or using a computer. In the United States, children spend an average of twenty-seven hours per week watching television. In the 2011 Youth Risk Behavior Survey conducted on high school students by Centers for Disease Control and Prevention researchers, just over 32 percent of students said they watched television for three or more hours per school day. The highest percentage of students viewing three or more hours of television was found among African American high school students (more than 54 percent), with Latino students having the next highest percentage (almost 38 percent), and white students having a lower percentage (less than 26) than either Latino or black students.

The impact of television watching on children's behavior has been studied by various researchers. Some researchers have found that television viewing has no effect on the amount of time a child spends socializing with other children. Other researchers, however, assert that television viewing displaces the time a child would normally spend socializing with other children and interacting with family members. Other studies have found that children viewing a lot of television, especially programs with violent content, had increased antisocial behavior and decreased positive social behaviors. These negative social behaviors increase the likelihood of social isolation and make it more difficult for children to develop successful peer relationships. This negative effect can also trigger a vicious cycle whereby children who watch more television become more socially isolated, which makes them watch even more television to compensate for their lack of social interactions, which further increases their social isolation.

A study conducted by researchers at the Center on Media and Child Health at Harvard Medical School

revealed that the content (violent or nonviolent) and the context (with friends or without friends) of television viewing is important in determining how much time children spend socially interacting with their peers. According to the study, the amount of time spent viewing violent television programs had a negative impact on the amount of time children spent with their friends in nontelevision-related social activities. Each extra hour of viewing resulted in a 12.1 percent decrease in peer social time in six- to eight-year-olds and a 9.8 percent decrease in nine- to twelve-year-olds. Viewing violent television programs also increased aggressiveness and violent behavior in children.

Although this link between viewing violent television programs and aggressive behavior has been discussed since the 1970s, meta-analyses were not performed until the 1990s. These later studies suggest that aggressive behavior induced by viewing violent television programs may be caused by simple mimicking behavior, arousal of angry emotions that erupt later in response to subsequent events, or observational learning from violence portrayed as normal behavior that gets rewarded. Viewing of nonviolent television programs, in contrast, did not affect time spent socially interacting with peers. Interestingly, if children watched television with friends, they were more likely to spend time with friends in nontelevision-related social activities. For six- to eight-year-olds, one more hour of viewing television with friends led to 59 minutes of additional time spent in nontelevision-related social activities. For nine- to twelve-year-olds, this number increased slightly to 62 minutes.

COMPUTER USE

In the 2011 Youth Risk Behavior Survey on high school students, 31 percent of students used a computer for activities not related to school work (including computer or video games) for three or more hours per school day, and increase from 25 percent in 2007. The highest percentage of children using a computer for three or more hours per school day was found among Asian American high school students (42 percent), with African American students having the next highest percentage (38), and white students having the lowest percentage (28).

Potential problems of Internet use include the possibility of encountering disturbing content, including images and videos, as well as exposure to cyberbullying. Children who use the Internet are also vulnerable to sexual predators who may pose as children or friendly adults on social networking sites and arrange to meet in person.

Cyberbullying, or online harassment, is a growing problem and involves the embarrassment or intimidation of others, for example, through the online posting or instant messaging of rude, humiliating, or threatening messages. Online harassment is a problem for both those doing the harassment and those being harassed. One study reported that approximately 15 percent of children were online harassers. These children tended to have poor caregiver-child relationships and were much more likely to engage in delinquent behavior and substance abuse and to themselves be victims of traditional bullying.

Many children are also exposed to video games on a regular basis. It is well documented that playing violent video games increases aggressive behavior, including the tendency to act out physically by, for example, hitting, kicking, choking, or wrestling. Children playing these games are more likely to act aggressively when they fail to get what they want. They are imitating behavior that was rewarded in their video games. Children who spend a lot of time playing video games or using the computer are more likely to become socially isolated and withdrawn. Some solutions that parents can use to counteract the negative effects of video games are restricting the types of games their children play, not allowing video game systems and televisions in their children's bedrooms, and encouraging their children to interact and participate in activities with other children. When selecting appropriate video games for children, it is important for parents to research the games themselves, because studies have found that video game ratings sometimes do not accurately reflect the amount of violence actually present in games. Even video games given seemingly innocuous ratings such as E (Everyone) and T (Teen) often contain significant violence and substance use.

CELL PHONE USE

The excessive use of cell phones has been linked to mental health problems. One study found an association between addictive cell phone use and poor self-esteem. Another study found that teenagers with the heaviest cell phone use were more likely to be depressed and anxious. The number of cases of bullying via text messaging and instant messaging, particularly among girls, is increasing. These forms of cyberbullying can cause psychological and emotional distress in recipients. Incoming calls, text messages, and e-mails throughout the night may disrupt sleep and result in sleepiness and decreased concentration the next day. According to the Pew Research Center, in 2013 about 78 percent of teenagers in the United States had a cell phone, and almost half of those were smartphones; therefore, understanding the mental, social, and behavioral impact of teen cell phone use is essential.

Violence depicted in television programs, films, and video games can have a strong effect on the behavior of young men. One model of how violence provokes aggression suggests that exposure to violence in the media may affect the internal state of an individual, including cognition (in the form of proviolent attitudes), affect (anger), and arousal (manifesting as high blood pressure). In a study of young male undergraduates aged eighteen to twenty-one years, subjects either played a violent video game, *Grand Theft Auto III,* or a nonviolent game, *The Simpsons: Hit and Run.* The young men who played the violent game exhibited raised blood pressure, more negative (angry) affect, and more hostile social information processing. These young men also had more permissive attitudes toward alcohol and marijuana use, and tended to be less cooperative during a subsequent task. When the backgrounds of the young men were taken into account, the subjects from homes and communities with higher levels of violence showed higher systolic blood pressure and more hostile social information processing following exposure to media violence. The researchers hypothesized that young men with higher exposure to violence in the home and community may have more difficulty interpreting ambiguous social cues as nonhostile after being primed for hostile thoughts by exposure to media violence. Regardless of the level of violence in the backgrounds of the young men, however, they were all susceptible to raised blood pressure and the exhibition of negative affect, hostile social information processing, uncooperative behavior, and more permissive attitudes toward substance use.

MEDIA'S DEPICTION OF WOMEN

The portrayal of women in the mainstream media can have a powerful effect on the attitudes of women and adolescent girls toward their bodies. Women in the media are often narrowly depicted as young and thin, as sex objects, or in the traditional, subservient mold. There is an overwhelming emphasis on the importance of physical beauty and attractiveness in all forms of media, including television programs, films, magazines, newspapers, and music videos, as well as print and television advertisements. The media mostly portray a standard of beauty according to which a woman must be young, thin, and shapely.

Studies in college-age women have linked media exposure to eating disorders such as anorexia and bulimia. Women who are at high risk for an eating disorder often are dissatisfied with their bodies, compare their physical appearance with that of others, and exhibit perfectionism, a compulsion to be thin, and feelings of ineffectiveness. These women frequently show a high degree of internalization of media messages about physical beauty. Interventions such as media literacy programs, which involve cognitive behavior therapy, can decrease some of these symptoms and reduce the risk of eating disorders in high-risk women.

Adolescent girls are especially vulnerable to the influence of media messages. Prime-time television programs most favored by adolescents convey the message that physical beauty is important for attracting partners and for success in life. Another detrimental message common in all forms of media is that a major role of women is to appear attractive to men; their appearance, body size, and weight are continually the subject of comments. Adolescent girls may easily internalize these messages of the supposedly ideal girl or woman and the traditional role of women as sexual objects who are subservient to men. One study looking at African American adolescent girls' response to media exposure showed that girls who were more exposed to music and music videos containing gender stereotypes expressed more traditional views about gender roles. Girls who identified with the female characters in television shows and music videos were also more likely to echo traditional views of gender and assign high importance to physical attractiveness.

BIBLIOGRAPHY

Bickham, David S., and Michael Rich. "Is Television Viewing Associated with Social Isolation? Roles of Exposure Time, Viewing Context, and Violent Content." *Archives of Pediatrics & Adolescent Medicine* 160.4 (2006): 387–92. Print.

Boyd, Danah. It's *Complicated: The Social Lives of Networked Teens.* New Haven: Yale UP, 2014.

Brady, Sonya S., and Karen A. Matthews. "Effects of Media Violence on Health-Related Outcomes among Young Men." *Archives of Pediatrics & Adolescent Medicine* 160.4 (2006): 341–47. Print.

Center on Media and Child Health, Harvard Medical School. http://www.cmch.tv/.

Coughlin, Janelle W., and Cynthia Kalodner. "Media Literacy as a Prevention for College Women at Low- or High-Risk for Eating Disorders." *Body Image* 3.1 (2006): 35–43. Print.

Eaton, Danice K., et al. "Youth Risk Behavior Surveillance—United States, 2007." *Centers for Disease Control and Prevention Morbidity and Mortality Weekly Report* 57.SS04. (2008): 1–131. Print.

Gordon, Maya K. "Media Contributions to African American Girls' Focus on Beauty and Appearance: Exploring the Consequences of Sexual Objectification." *Psychology of Women Quarterly* 32 (2008): 245–56. Print.

SafetyNet. American Academy of Pediatrics. http://safetynet.aap.org/.

Shifrin, Donald. "Effect of Media on Children and Adolescents: It's about Time." *Archives of Pediatrics & Adolescent Medicine* 160.4 (2006): 448–50. Print.

Teens and Technology 2013. Pew Research Center, 13 Mar. 2013. PDF file.

Turkle, Sherry. *Alone Together: Why We Expect More from Technology and Less from Each Other.* New York: Basic: 2011. Print.

Ing-Wei Khor

SEE ALSO: Adolescence: Cognitive skills; Aggression; Anger; Anorexia nervosa and bulimia nervosa; Attitude formation and change; Behavior therapy; Bobo doll experiment; Body dysmorphic disorder; Children's mental health; Computer and Internet use and mental health; Developmental psychology; Eating disorders; Internet psychology; Misbehavior; Teenagers' mental health; Violence and sexuality in the media; Violence by children and teenagers; Violence: Psychological causes and effects; Women's mental health.

Media psychology

DATE: 1970s forward
TYPE OF PSYCHOLOGY: Emotion; Language; Learning; Personality; Sensation and perception; Social psychology; Stress

Media psychology is a field of study that addresses the role of psychology in information dissemination and as a cultural form of entertainment and an influential molder of popular opinion concerning societal psychological issues.

KEY CONCEPTS

- Accessibility
- Ethics
- Expertise
- Influence
- Information
- Media consultants
- Newsworthiness
- Perceptions
- Sensationalization
- Technology

INTRODUCTION

Media psychology emerged as an applied psychological discipline concurrently with the rise in popularity of such talk shows as *Donahue* on television and radio in the 1970s. Mental health professionals have contributed their expertise and knowledge to a variety of media, including newspapers, magazines, television, movies, radio, cell phones, and the Internet. Technology advancements have expanded the influence of psychology to more people globally.

Media psychologists serve as media consultants, preparing specific programming or articles about significant issues, such as depression, or topics suddenly newsworthy, such as school violence. Many host or appear on television and radio programs to discuss mental health issues and advise listeners. Other mental health professionals concentrate on media-oriented careers, writing self-help books and screenplays or serving as columnists for national, regional, or local publications. Scholars analyze how the media depicts psychological issues, such as mental illness, and influence people's perceptions of themselves and others.

Mental health professionals are concerned with how psychological issues are portrayed in the media. Beginning in the 1950s, newspaper advice columnists such as *Dear Abby* and *Ann Landers* assumed the role of amateur mental health authorities, and they have been followed by many others. Culturally, people tend to find such amateur psychological input appealing, accessible, and comforting. Similarly, many talk show hosts who lack professional credentials also often act as if they are psychologically knowledgeable. They unrealistically expect psychology to serve as a sensational entertainment tool to address media-popular disorders such as anorexia nervosa in an attempt to score high ratings. Hosts have minimal awareness of the complexities and subtleties of the topics they are discussing, nor do they understand suitable therapeutic treatments for their guests.

Professional psychologists worry that such popular psychology is damaging not only to the people involved but also to the mental health profession. From 1953 to 1981, the American Psychological Association (APA) outlined prohibitions in its ethical principles against psychologists offering superficial or sensational services that were unrelated to professional contexts. Some psychologists ignored professional suggestions and began participating in media opportunities before 1992, when the APA loosened its restrictions. New guidelines permitted psychologists to comment about psychological issues or advise people who were not patients in some circumstances understood to be through media outlets.

PROFESSIONALISM

The Association for Media Psychology (AMP) was organized in 1982 and issued guidelines to regulate professional conduct. Five years later, the APA established the Society for Media Psychology and Technology (Division 46) to focus on media psychology issues. Media psychology has many facets. Primarily, the field investigates how media influences human behavior. Division 46's purpose is also to assist mental health professionals and journalists to provide the public with timely, useful, and accessible psychological information that addresses concerns and crises through the mass media.

The division's website, quarterly newsletter the Amplifier, and listserv provide forums for professionals to discuss their ideas, research, and concerns regarding the impact of media on human behavior. Those electronic resources also provide contacts for media to consult experts. Two professional periodicals, *Media Psychology* and the online *Journal of Media Psychology*, also address issues specific to media psychology.

Division 46's goal is to communicate essential information about psychology based on members' experiences in their practices and research. Professionals are urged to use media to educate people about psychology. Collaboration with communication experts is encouraged to enhance the delivery techniques of ideas to audiences. Both psychologists and journalists strive to devise informative, accurate, professional, yet entertaining presentations. Mental health professionals participate in workshops specializing in media training and ethics. Outreach programs with journalists help educate them about professional ethics, standards, and credentials so that they will consult a legitimate mental health professional instead of contacting a self-help celebrity who lacks substantial formal training. Division 46 emphasizes the need for mental health professionals to observe the APA's ethical standards and guidelines while interacting with media.

Mental health professionals distribute information in a variety of modes. Some individuals present speeches and participate in public campaigns concerning issues related to mental health such as substance abuse. A public information committee in the APA has functioned since 1979, and the APA public affairs department alerts media to available media psychologists and releases monthly news packages of interesting items related to its research-based journals. The APA science media relations specialist focuses on placing psychological news in science media.

The division specifically seeks to establish theoretical paradigms to study and practice media psychology internationally, such as how mass media influences the public and how effective it is at distributing psychological information. Many researchers design surveys to study how people react to media presentations, such as coverage of the controversial 2000 US presidential election and analysis of the stock market. Media psychologists collaborate with professionals in other psychological fields to examine specific issues, such as how the media portrays marriage and family relationships.

At California State University, Los Angeles, Stuart Fischoff, who founded the Department of Psychology's Media Psychology Research Institute (MPRI), initiated the first media psychology classes and laboratory in the United States and developed a master's program specializing in media psychology. The forty-five units required for graduation include sixteen units of broadcasting and communications courses to supplement psychology class work. Each student prepares a thesis investigating some aspect of media psychology.

ETHICS

Radio and television psychology have become subdisciplines of psychology. Audiences seek to be entertained and to acquire advice and information. Many mental health professionals support and encourage this form of media psychology but insist that radio and television psychiatrists should strive to be broadcast educators instead of psychotherapists. They can advise listeners but not diagnose them. The AMP developed ethical guidelines relevant to Federal Communications Commission (FCC) rules for mental health professionals. Prior to a

media appearance, professionals should watch or listen to a broadcast to determine what their roles as guests will be and if the show is professionally appropriate and not exploitative and sensationalized. If a professional declines an invitation, he or she should explain to the show's producers what is ethically problematic. Above all else, media psychologists should retain their integrity and standards.

Because media psychology is constantly evolving and expanding in response to new technology and formats, peer discussion is crucial to maintain ethical standards. Some state boards of examiners in psychology, such as the one in Louisiana, issue opinions that restrict state mental health professionals' participation in media activities to prevent harming the public. State regulations usually require that media psychology professionals base their comments on accurate psychological resources, do not exploit patients, and clarify that they have not established a personal psychological relationship with anybody who receives their information in any form of public delivery. Most important, media psychologists are not to place entertainment over ethical psychological practices.

Mental health professionals participating in media are urged to avoid exploitative relationships. In particular, psychologists on call-in broadcasts must insist that calls are screened off the air before publicly conversing with callers. Also, the screeners should use a process approved by mental health experts, not show producers or hosts, and be adequately trained to refer callers to mental health resources and crisis and support groups as necessary. Professionals must require media to provide callers disclaimers that explain that on-air interaction is not a substitute for therapy and that it is not private and any disclosures will become public information. Also, callers are warned that there may be a delay when they are placed on hold before their call is aired or that their call might not be broadcast because they will be referred to other forms of assistance. The professional should also insist that an on-air disclaimer emphasize that information on the show is presented in a limited format and should not be considered adequate therapy.

In many cases, mental health professionals might be asked about a subject outside of their specialty area, about which they have limited knowledge. They should recognize the limitations of talk show formats and not advise callers to make impulsive, life-changing decisions. Media psychology professionals also need to be alert for callers' and show personnel's unique ethnic, cultural, or special interests, which might influence those people's psychological perceptions, expectations, and agendas.

PSYCHOLOGY VIA MEDIA

Media psychologists strive to tell audiences about psychological topics in concise passages without using complicated jargon. Mental health professionals provide essential psychological assistance during times of crisis, such as after the September 11, 2001, terrorist attacks.

Media psychologists volunteered with the APA/American Red Cross Disaster Response Network. These professionals helped comfort audiences, especially children, counseled survivors, and suggested how to cope with emotional shocks, tragedies, and trauma. Publicity also addressed people's fear of flying after the hijackings. Media professionals also try to explain the psychological aspects of traumatic violent actions such as murders and school shootings. Their knowledge can also be used to develop violence intervention and prevention programs for public presentation.

Media used to distribute psychology information range from local to international forums. Information tends to address issues relevant to a broad audience and is often created to be appealing and familiar, such as publicizing the therapeutic role of pets in people's lives. Print is a popular medium, whether in the form of books, pamphlets, or articles appearing in newspapers, magazines, newsletters, or mass mailings. Media psychologists deliver public lectures and perform demonstrations of methods. Often such presentations are recorded on audio or video tapes or broadcast on radio or television programs. Many broadcasts are interactive events among professionals, guests with problems, and audiences. Computer software and the Internet, including chat rooms and message boards, have provided innovative forums to disseminate media psychology information quickly and broadly.

Mental health professionals use media to address their interests and concerns for legislation and community services concerning mental health. Media psychology also has valuable applications to marketing and consumer and political psychology. Psychologists often comment in the media about controversial court trials that involve psychological issues such as battered women, violent children, or mental illnesses. Often, different psychologists present contrasting perceptions of defendants and witnesses during a trial, particularly when assessing the reliability of childhood memories of abuse or trauma.

FORENSIC PSYCHOLOGY

Forensic psychology is appealing to the media and to the public, who want to understand why people might commit shocking crimes, but the media often sensationalize information instead of presenting psychological data factually and unemotionally. Media psychologists study the role of psychologists in legal reporting. They are concerned about the ethical ramifications of mental health professionals publicly discussing people they have not evaluated and with privacy and confidentiality issues regarding the people being analyzed in the press.

Some media psychologists are celebrities, such as Ruth Westheimer, John Gray, James Dobson, Barbara De Angelis, and Phil McGraw. Others have high-profile positions as consultants on morning news shows or as magazine columnists while also teaching or practicing in their communities. Several serve as staff psychologists for reality television shows. Some media psychologists host regional television shows on local access channels. On *Dr. Carol Goldberg and Company* in New York, viewers learn about the psychology profession during interviews with psychologists who discuss social concerns such as parenting.

EXPERTS VERSUS AMATEURS

Talk shows need psychology professionals to legitimize programs. Media psychologists often encounter disrespect for their expertise, especially on shows such as Jerry Springer and Maury, which encourage tabloid techniques such as ambushes, revenge-seeking, hostility, and exhibitionism. Audiences often prefer receiving psychological advice from flashy, entertaining people who lack academic credentials but offer easy answers and quick fixes. The sensationalism inherent in many public talk show forums encourages an adversarial relationship with mental health professionals. Cal State's Stuart Fischoff, who frequently appeared as an authority on major talk shows, exposed their exploitative and damaging nature. Fischoff noted that most shows were manipulated to present a biased message that would attract large audiences and that producers expected invited authorities to approve this spin publicly even if it was contrary to their research and beliefs.

According to Fischoff, most talk show formats impede mental health goals. Invited experts are expected to perform by providing entertaining comments in brief, simple sound bites and to summarize complex situations in short time periods averaging thirty seconds. Usually, they can only make general remarks and are often interrupted by hosts or audience members who want to promote their views. Media psychologists only briefly encounter guests and do not develop a therapist-patient relationship in which they acquire sufficient information about the person for professional analysis. Most guests are not seeking help but want the expert's validation, approval, and acceptance and the exposure to millions of viewers who might identify with them in some way. Some shows, such as Oprah, purposefully attempt to educate guests but sometimes succumb to ratings stunts.

Experts are discouraged from engaging in profound, original discourse. Audience members are encouraged to consider themselves equals to psychological experts, and personal experiences are valued more than clinical experiences and academic training. Shows are formulaic, and experts are expected to conform. Many media psychologists appear on talk shows solely for self-promotion. Occasionally guests sue shows for suffering they claimed was inflicted on them, and media psychologists are consulted to evaluate and testify whether the plaintiffs were traumatized.

Media consultants often are frustrated by how some journalists distort and fabricate psychological information. For example, the media often perpetuate stories about syndromes and disorders that lack factual verification by clinical trials and research. Uncritical reporting and hype result when the press is intrigued by sensational descriptions that have no scientific basis. For example, some media depicted psychotherapy negatively in their skewed coverage of false memory syndrome related to childhood abuse described in legal testimony. By concentrating on controversial psychotherapists and clinics, the media caused the public to lose confidence in mental health professionals, sparking a temporary backlash.

Media psychologists urge reporters to aspire to be accurate, fair, and responsible in their coverage of psychological issues. Reporters often do not comprehend who is an expert on a subject and showcase people whose personal experiences are equated with expertise. Media personnel often have insufficient familiarity with social science research methodology to understand why some data or statements are flawed. Psychologists may choose not to appear as experts on media, concerned that they might inadvertently veer from APA principles because of host pressure and editing. Most media psychologists strive to be responsible and to avoid having their comments misused and deceptively presented. In contrast, the nonexperts touting pop psychology often detrimentally influence media and public knowledge through their

ignorance, and psychology is often mistakenly comprehended as a pseudoscience because of these amateurs.

MEDIA IMPACT AND DEPICTIONS

Media psychologists research how media impact individuals and society. The role of the media in possibly provoking violence is a controversial topic. Most researchers agree that data analyzed according to accepted methodology reveal that media in the form of television, movies, video games, music, and other modes do not cause people to become violent. Instead, violence is triggered by other factors, mainly environmental, such as peer group pressure. Other media psychologists insist that violence and media are connected and testify to legislative bodies about controlling children's access to violent forms of entertainment. Many journalists ignore the scientific findings and experts' testimony that argue against a media link to causing violence and instead emphasize accounts that suggest that media provokes violence. Other research topics include how stereotypes and clichés in media influence cultural attitudes toward groups such as women and foreigners and processes such as aging.

Media psychology is concerned with how mental health professionals are depicted by popular culture. Psychologists, psychiatrists, and therapists have been characters in television programs such as *The Bob Newhart Show* and *Frasier* and films such as *Silence of the Lambs* (1991) and *Analyze This* (1999). Soap operas often have a psychiatrist character, such as Dr. Marlena Evans on *Days of Our Lives,* whose career is pivotal to plots. Therapy and support groups are the focus of plots and settings.

The APA's Division 46 established a media watch committee to monitor how media portray psychologists, psychiatrists, and therapists. The committee's rating system evaluates how television programs emphasize mental health authorities as being professional and ethical, respecting laws and therapist-patient confidentiality, or stress if a character is behaving contrary to professional standards. Media psychologists criticize entertainment that stereotypes psychologists, such as depicting male therapists as extremely competent or evil, while demeaning female psychologists as ineffective and primarily sexual objects.

The Golden Psi Award has been presented to producers of television shows, including *Law & Order, Once and Again, The Sopranos,* and *Chicago Hope,* who have responsibly and realistically presented mental health issues and competent, intelligent, and compassionate characters. Descriptions of psychologically related issues on those shows demonstrate accurate knowledge of disorders and comprehension of physiological development and social dynamics relevant to mental health. Characters are identified by their credentials or discredited for not being suitably trained as mental health professionals.

BIBLIOGRAPHY

Brewer, Gayle. *Media Psychology*. New York: Palgrave, 2011. Print.

Crigler, Ann N., ed. *The Psychology of Political Communication*. Ann Arbor: U of Michigan P, 1998. Print.

Dill, Karen E. *The Oxford Handbook of Media Psychology*. New York: Oxford UP, 2013. Print.

Fischoff, Stuart. "Confessions of a TV Talk Show Shrink." *Psychology Today* 28.5 (Sept./Oct., 1995): 38–45. Print.

Fox, Ronald E. "The Rape of Psychotherapy." *Professional Psychology: Research and Practice* 26.2 (1995): 147–55. Print.

Giles, David. *Psychology of the Media*. New York: Palgrave, 2010. Print.

Henricks, William H., and William B. Stiles. "Verbal Processes on Psychological Radio Call-In Programs: Comparisons with Other Help-Intended Interactions." *Professional Psychology: Research and Practice* 20.5 (1989): 315–21. Print.

Kirschner, Sam, and Diane Kirschner, eds. *Perspectives on Psychology and the Media*. Washington: APA, 1997. Print.

Klonoff, E. A. "A Star Is Born: Psychologists and the Media." *Professional Psychology: Research and Practice* 14.6 (1983): 847–54. Print.

Levy, David A. "Social Support and the Media: Analysis of Responses by Radio Psychology Talk Show Hosts." *Professional Psychology: Research and Practice* 20.2 (1989): 73–78. Print.

McCall, Robert B. "Science and the Press: Like Oil and Water?" *American Psychologist* 43.2 (1988): 87–94. Print.

Schwartz, Lita Linzer, ed. *Psychology and the Media: A Second Look*. Washington: APA, 2000. Print.

Trend, David. *The Myth of Media Violence: A Critical Introduction*. Malden: Blackwell, 2007. Print.

Elizabeth D. Schafer

See Also: Disaster psychology; Media exposure and mental health; Research ethics; Violence and sexuality in the media; Violence: Psychological causes and effects.

Meditation

Type of Psychology: Biological bases of human behavior; Health

Meditation, a practice of focusing and calming the mind, has been found to be beneficial in reducing stress and anxiety. Research has begun to determine the neurological correlates of meditation practice. A number of psychological therapies make use of meditation, and it is being applied in educational settings.

Key Concepts:
- Mindfulness
- Transcendental Meditation
- Meditative health benefits
- Spirituality and meditation.

INTRODUCTION

The term "meditation" sometimes is used synonymously with thinking or reflection, as in Descartes' philosophical meditations, but often meditation is used to describe mental exercises performed as spiritual practices. These generally involve focusing attention on the breath, particular phrases, or images. Spiritually based meditation includes (but is not limited to) Centering prayer in Christianity, Meditative Kabbalah in Judaism, and Sufi Meditation in Islam. Buddhist meditation techniques developed as spiritual practices, but in the West they have come to have applications separate from spirituality. These include the alleviation of stress, fostering of physical and mental health, and self-awareness and personal development.

Some of the earliest scientific research on health benefits of meditation was conducted in the 1960s on Transcendental Meditation (TM). This form of meditation, associated with the Maharishi Mahesh Yogi, uses a mantra (word or sound) as the focus of meditation. Some of the research on TM was conducted at Harvard University by cardiologist Dr. Herbert Benson. In 1975, Dr. Benson and Miriam Klipper published the book, *The Relaxation Response*, describing a secular version of meditation designed to reduce stress.

Research continued, and in 1979 psychologist Jon Kabbat-Zinn founded the Stress Reduction Clinic, and later the Center for Mindfulness in Medicine, Health Care and Society, at the University of Massachusetts Medical School. There he worked with patients using Mindfulness Based Stress Reduction (MBSR), a combination of a variety of meditation techniques, to reduce stress and pain. His work was described in the 1990 book *Full Catastrophe Living: Using the Wisdom of Your Body and Mind to Face Stress, Pain and Illness*. In recent years research into the effects of meditation has grown dramatically and applications of meditation to therapy and education have become common.

PRACTICING MEDITATION

Meditation involves the practice of focusing and calming the mind. The most common technique that may be used to this end is awareness of breath. The meditator assumes an attentive but relaxed posture, and then focuses on the sensation of the breath, either at the nostrils or in the abdomen. As thoughts arise, and this may happen soon and often, one gently brings one's attention back to the breath. Psychologist Jack Kornfield in his book, *A Path with Heart*, describes the process as analogous to training a puppy. One may tell the puppy to "stay," but at first he cannot stay long without wandering. One keeps gently placing the puppy where one wants, and over a period of gentle urging, the puppy masters this ability.

Although the breath is the most common focus of concentration in meditation practices, some practices use a mantra, a word or phrase that is internally repeated or vocally chanted. A visualization or an external visual object like a candle or flower may also be used to focus attention. Also used are "body scans," walking meditations and yoga that emphasize focused attention to sensations within the body. Whichever object is used, the process of returning the mind to the object of concentration when it wanders remains the same.

The concentrative forms of meditation as described above generally are used to introduce one to meditative practices. Other forms may be taught concurrently, or subsequently, to concentration. Mindfulness, or Insight Meditation, generally begins with a focus on the breath, but it also has a strong emphasis on non-judgment and acceptance. Mindfulness Meditation forms the foundation for the Mindfulness Based Stress Reduction practices and a family of other mindfulness practices used in a variety of settings, including hospitals, psychological therapy settings, and schools.

Lovingkindness (Metta) meditation is a practice in which one mentally recites phrases of good will, e.g., "be happy", "be healthy" for oneself, and then for others in a widening circle of humanity. Its intention is to increase compassion, both for oneself and for others. One may find variations of compassion or loving kindness meditation in a variety of secular, as well as religious, settings.

Meditation can be challenging for the novice meditator. There are many books and audio recordings available to help one begin on one's own, but learning meditation can be greatly facilitated by finding a class or teacher to support and instruct one's practice. Fortunately, classes in meditation are widely available in places of worship, gyms, continuing study programs and independent study groups.

SCIENTIFIC RESEARCH ON MEDITATION

Meditation has its origins in spirituality, but is now of particular interest to those wishing to improve psychological and physical health. Decades of research have left little doubt that meditation can be of benefit in the alleviation of stress and anxiety. Other firm conclusions

Photo: iStock

concerning the possible benefits of meditation are difficult to draw, as various forms of meditation are examined in different studies, with a variety of practitioners and a variety of outcome variables.

A number of researchers have examined the physiological effects of meditation. Foremost among these is Richard Davidson of the University of Wisconsin. Davidson has emphasized the ability of the mind to change itself as the result of experience. For example, he has found that meditators with more than 10,000 hours of practice experience sustained attention, but show less activation in attention related areas in the brain than novice meditators. They seem to be able to sustain attention with less effort than novices. They also seem to be both more mindful and less reactive to sensory stimuli, as indicated by imaging of the amygdala and insular cortex, two areas of the brain associated with arousal. In other research, after an eight-week training program in mindfulness, participants experienced an enhanced positive response to an influenza vaccine, in comparison with participants who did not have meditation training.

Research involving the Shamatha project, a longitudinal study involving experienced meditators centered at the University of California, Davis, has found evidence for lowered cortisol, a stress hormone, in meditators as opposed to control participants. Research with participants in this project, has found increased telomerase activity, which is a measure of cell viability.

Much research has suggested that there are psychological benefits of meditation, but the specific nature and potency of these benefits has not been clear. Neither has the "active ingredient" that accounts for these benefits, as the experience of meditation is confounded with specific methods, teachers, and participant characteristics. Meta-analyses, which statistically combine the results of many individual studies are helpful in overcoming some of the difficulties of assessing individual studies, but they too are dependent upon the particular subset of studies included in the meta-analysis.

A meta-analysis of the results of studies using kindness based meditation (including loving kindness meditation and compassion meditation) found that meditators reported less depression and more compassion, self-compassion, and positive emotions than control groups of participants. Other meta-analyses examining a variety of meditative techniques in non-clinical populations found widespread positive effects on emotional variables such as lowered anxiety, increased positive emotions, and decreased neuroticism.

In summary, there is evidence that meditation can produce positive outcomes in terms of stress reduction. Relatively short-term meditators can experience relaxation and increased compassion from meditation, and long-term meditators may experience stronger health benefits mediated by brain changes that occur with practice.

PSYCHOTHERAPEUTIC USES OF MEDITATION

A number of popular meditation teachers are also mental health professionals, and meditation has become a tool therapists use to relieve their own stress and enhance their compassion and understanding of clients. A number of therapeutic techniques that use meditation taught to clients have also been developed. Mindfulness Based Stress Reduction (MBSR) was one of the earliest forms of therapy that made meditation a major component of the therapeutic process.

Other therapies include Mindfulness Based Cognitive Therapy (MBCT), developed by Jon Teasdale, Zindal Segal and Mark Williams, Acceptance and Commitment Therapy (ACT), developed by Steven C. Hayes, Kelly G. Wilson and Kirk Strohasl, and Dialectical Behavior Therapy (DBT), developed by Marcia Linehan. Each of these combines mindfulness practice with techniques from cognitive and behavioral therapy. Mindfulness Based Cognitive Therapy is based on the MBSR techniques, but is designed specifically to help people who experience repeated episodes of depression to recognize the emotional and cognitive components that lead to depression and develop a sense of distance from those self-defeating emotions and thoughts as they stay in the present moment. Research confirms that patients with three or more instances of depression relapse can benefit from Mindfulness Based Cognitive Therapy.

Acceptance and Commitment Therapy (ACT) is a combination of behavioral and cognitive therapies with mindfulness principles. The goal is to help the client examine his or her language for describing experience, while staying actively present in the current moment. The increase in flexibility that can result from this practice has helped treat a variety of psychological difficulties, including depression, anxiety and addiction.

Dialectical Behavior Therapy (DBT) was initially developed to help clients with actively self-harming behaviors. The therapy is based on mindfulness, in which the client is affirmed and accepted while also learning that specific behaviors are harmful and cannot be allowed. Mindfulness practice, development of coping skills, and group and individual therapy sessions form the body of DBT.

Mindfulness based meditation has been integrated into a variety of mental health treatments. In some it serves as the primary treatment, and in others it serves as an adjunct to behavioral and cognitive therapeutic methods.

MEDITATION IN THE SCHOOLS

Mindfulness meditation has been applied to education at all levels. A number of studies have demonstrated that it increases empathy and reduces stress in nursing and medical students, and general graduate and undergraduate populations.

Mindfulness interventions have also been instituted for teachers and students in the primary and secondary schools. Individual studies have found that such interventions may be particularly helpful for anxiety, and may reduce stress and aggressive responses in children. Mark Greenberg, the Founding Director of The Prevention Research Center for the Promotion of Human Development at the University of Pennsylvania, has conducted and reviewed much of this literature. Although he finds the results encouraging, much more research needs to be done.

BIBLIOGRAPHY

The Mind's Own Physician: A Scientific Dialogue With The Dalai Lama On The Healing Power of Meditation. (2012). Oakland, CA: New Harbinger Publications. A presentation of the thirteenth Mind And Life Institute's Conference with the Dalai Lama, with a variety of scientific presentations on research on meditation.

Davidson, R., & Begley, S. (2012). The Emotional Life of Your Brain: How Its Unique Patterns Affect The Way You Think, Feel, and Live--and How You Can Change Them. New York: Hudson Street Press. Neuroscientist Richard Davidson describes six emotional styles, and how mental practices can help change them.

Rechtschaffen, D. (2014). The Way of Mindful Education: Cultivating Well-Being In Teachers and Students. New York, NY: W. W. Norton and Co. How school teachers may use mindfulness practice for themselves and to help their students.

Salzberg, S. (2011). Real Happiness: The Power of Meditation: A 28-day Program. New York: Workman Pub. Salzberg provides a thorough introduction to meditative techniques, including the practice of lovingkindness.

Zinn, J. (1990). Full Catastrophe Living: Using The Wisdom of Your Body and Mind To Face Stress, Pain, and Illness. New York, N.Y.: Delacorte Press. Describes the basis of Mindfulness Based Stress Reduction.

Susan E. Beers

SEE ALSO: Alternative therapy; Attention; Consciousness; Mindfulness; Relaxation; Wellness.

Meditation and relaxation

DATE: 1910s–

TYPE OF PSYCHOLOGY: Consciousness

Psychologists regard meditation and relaxation techniques as possible means for reducing stress, improving mental and physical health, and expanding conscious awareness. Some of these techniques may help psychology fulfill its goals of developing the mental potential of individuals and improving social behavior.

KEY CONCEPTS
- Consciousness
- Guided imagery
- Mindfulness
- Progressive relaxation
- Self-actualization
- Systematic desensitization
- Transcendental meditation

INTRODUCTION

Forms of meditation have been practiced in many cultures throughout the ages. Traditionally, meditation techniques have been used to cultivate self-realization or enlightenment, in which higher levels of human potential are said to be realized. Traditional meditation techniques as well as modern techniques of relaxation are often used today for more limited purposes—to combat stress and specific problems of physical and mental health. There is also growing interest, however, in the greater purpose of meditation to achieve higher states of human development.

TECHNIQUES

The various techniques of meditation practiced today derive from diverse sources. Some, such as yoga and Zen Buddhism, come from ancient traditions of India and other Asian countries, having been introduced in the West by traditional teachers and their Western students. Others originate in Western traditions such as Christianity. Some relaxation techniques taught today were adapted from these traditions, whereas others were invented independently of meditative traditions. For example, Edmund Jacobson introduced a progressive relaxation technique in 1910 and advocated its use to the medical profession and the public for more than fifty years. His research found progressive relaxation helpful for a variety of stress-related problems. Jacobson's rather elaborate procedure, which could require up to six months of training, was adapted and shortened by Joseph Wolpe in his book *Psychotherapy by Reciprocal Inhibition* (1958). Later, Douglas A. Bernstein and Thomas D. Borkovec, in *Progressive Relaxation Training: A Manual for the Helping Professions* (1973), further adapted progressive relaxation. These programs require a qualified therapist to teach the relaxation technique. A different approach, autogenic training, derived from self-hypnotic techniques by Johannes Schultz, has been used widely, especially in Europe, since the 1930s.

The approaches of various meditation techniques differ greatly. Most techniques involve sitting quietly with the eyes closed. In some techniques, however, the eyes are kept open, or partially open, as in Zazen practice of Zen Buddhism. Other "meditative" techniques, among them tai chi and hatha-yoga, involve physical movement. Techniques of meditation may be classified according to the way in which mental attention is used during the practice. In some techniques, one focuses or concentrates attention on a specific thought, sensation, or external object. Such concentration techniques train the mind to ignore extraneous thoughts and sensations to remain quiet and focused, as in the Theravadin Buddhist tradition's second stage of practice. Other techniques, such as mindfulness or insight meditation, allow the mind to experience all thoughts and perceptions without focusing on a specific object. In these techniques, the goal is to remain aware of the present moment without judging or reacting to it. Both concentration and mindfulness techniques may be employed in different Buddhist practices. In another approach, contemplative meditation, one thinks about a philosophical question or a pleasant concept such as "love," contemplating the meaning of the thought. This technique is employed, for example, in some Christian practices to produce tranquillity in the mind.

Relaxation techniques take various forms. In progressive relaxation (PR), muscles are consciously tensed and relaxed in a systematic manner. PR is often combined with pleasant mental imagery in a directed manner called guided imagery to produce physical relaxation and a calm mind. Relaxation strategies are often employed in programs of systematic desensitization relaxation techniques to reduce stress responses to frightful or anxiety-producing situations. Autogenic training, another major approach to relaxation, employs an adaptation of self-hypnosis to change the body's functioning. This self-regulation can be very effective, as can biofeedback, which uses scientific instruments to reveal specific physiologic information. While observing signals from the instruments, one consciously manipulates bodily functions to achieve more normal states. In clinical settings, biofeedback is more effective when combined with relaxation and psychotherapeutic techniques than when used alone. Relaxation techniques such as these produce physical and mental relaxation and give the individual some control over physiological processes such as breathing and heart rate. They also result in lower levels of stress hormones such as adrenaline.

Though often confused with these approaches, transcendental meditation, commonly called TM, involves different mechanics. In TM, one uses a sound without meaning, selected for its soothing influence on the mind. This process does not involve concentration, because the sound is used effortlessly. This use of a sound allows one's awareness to shift from the surface level of thinking to subtler levels of the thinking process, and ultimately to transcend thinking and experience a state of silent, restful alertness without thoughts, bodily sensations, or emotions. This inner wakefulness is called transcendental consciousness or pure consciousness. TM is taught in accord with the ancient Vedic tradition of India. Each tradition of meditation has its own understanding of the goals of long-term practice. Though the theme of gaining pure consciousness is shared by several meditative traditions, it cannot be assumed that all techniques of meditation produce the same results.

POTENTIAL BENEFITS

There has been considerable controversy over the years about whether meditation and relaxation techniques differ significantly in the relaxation they produce or in the cumulative effects of their long-term practice. The use of meta-analysis—statistical comparison of the results of many studies—has produced interesting results in this area. Meta-analyses can reveal trends not observed in individual studies and can control for effects of such variations in methods as sample size, study period, and observer bias by combining results from different sources. Because meditation techniques differ and because most meditation studies have been done on TM, these meta-analyses have tended to focus on potential differences between TM and relaxation.

In the mid-1980s, some researchers asked whether simply relaxing with the eyes closed would produce the same level of physiological rest as meditation. A meta-analysis of thirty-one studies showed significantly deeper rest during TM than during eyes-closed rest as indicated by breath rate, basal skin resistance (a measure of stability of the autonomic nervous system), and plasma lactate (a chemical in the blood related to stress).

Individuals practice meditation or relaxation techniques for many different reasons, particularly for relief from anxiety and stress. Both scientific research and anecdotal evidence on some of these techniques indicate that they may produce significant benefits to physical and mental health and to the quality of life as a whole.

APPLICATIONS

People often use relaxation techniques to relieve specific problems. For example, progressive relaxation has been demonstrated to reduce high blood pressure, headaches, insomnia, and anxiety; to improve memory; to increase internal locus of control (being in control of oneself); and to facilitate positive mood development in some people. When used in conjunction with muscle biofeedback, progressive muscle relaxation (PMR) has been effective in treating alcoholism. Autogenic training has also been shown to be effective in many of these areas. These techniques find wide application in psychologists' offices, in hospitals, in schools, and in institutions. For example, medical practitioners teach relaxation techniques to patients for pain management and anxiety reduction, for the control of asthma symptoms, and for treating migraine headaches. Studies have also shown that relaxation improves the concentration abilities of severely intellectually disabled adults and increases academic performance among grade school children.

Of the various meditation techniques, transcendental meditation is the most widely practiced in the West. The standardized method of teaching and uniform method of practicing TM make it particularly suitable for scientific study, and more than five thousand studies have delineated the effects of TM. In a study of health insurance

statistics published in 1987 in *Psychosomatic Medicine*, for example, two thousand TM meditators showed 50 percent less serious illness and use of health care services than did nonmeditators over a five-year period. Risk factors for disease, such as tobacco and alcohol use, high blood pressure, and high cholesterol levels, also have been found to decrease among TM meditators. In 1994, psychologist Charles Alexander found that TM proved to be an effective treatment for substance dependence.

There is also some evidence suggesting that meditation is more effective than relaxation techniques. For example, a meta-analysis of 144 independent findings published in the *Journal of Clinical Psychology* in 1989 indicated that the effect of TM on reducing trait anxiety (chronic stress) was approximately twice as large as that produced by progressive relaxation, other forms of relaxation, or other forms of meditation. This was the case even when researchers statistically controlled for differences among studies in subject expectancy, experimenter bias, or quality of research design.

Although meditation is usually considered an activity that affects only the individual practitioner, studies have been performed that suggest that the influence of meditation can extend beyond the meditator to the environment. Such findings are controversial, with many scientists summarily dismissing the possibility of any correlation between meditation and external events. Respected journals have published such studies, however, because the methodologies used were deemed scientifically sound. More than forty studies have found improvements in social conditions and prosperity when a small proportion of the population involved practices TM. For example, in 1999, British researchers Guy Hatchard, Ashley Deans, Kenneth Cavanaugh, and David Orme-Johnson reported that crime rates in Merseyside, England, dropped by 13 percent when the local TM group grew to a certain size. This drop in crime was sustained for the following four years of the study.

MEDITATION AND THE SCIENCE OF PSYCHOLOGY

The field of psychology was born with the hope that it would someday provide a complete account of human nature. William James, the founder of American psychology, in seeking ways to promote psychological growth, attempted to study elevated states of consciousness and suggested that meditation might be a means to cultivate their development. Few psychologists pursued this direction, however, until advances in bioengineering and the introduction of standardized forms of meditation and relaxation allowed psychologists to study consciousness in the laboratory.

Studies of self-actualization conducted by Abraham Maslow also renewed interest in meditation. According to Maslow, self-actualizing persons are individuals who display high levels of creativity, self-esteem, capacity for intimacy, and concern for the well-being of the world community. They seem to have mastered living happily in a complex world. Maslow believed that self-actualization was the pinnacle of psychological development, and he found that some adults spontaneously had "peak" or transcendental experiences. Sometimes these experiences produced abrupt changes in people's self-perception and significantly advanced their psychological development. Recognizing that meditation might produce such transcendental experiences, Maslow strongly encouraged research on meditation as a means for developing self-actualization.

With the recent development of appropriate scientific methods, alternative states of consciousness such as meditation and relaxation have once again become the focus of much research. Meditation and relaxation are the subject of thousands of studies each year. These studies investigate a wide range of psychological variables, from social development and self-actualization to brain activity.

The various types of meditation are based in ancient systems of philosophy or religion and therefore have ultimate purposes beyond those of strictly psychological approaches to personal development. Whereas self-actualization typically refers to the development of one's unique individual self, Vedic philosophy describes the potential for realizing a transcendental self in the growth of "higher states of consciousness" beyond self-actualization. Through repeated transcendence, one is said to experience this transcendental self as a limitless field of intelligence, creativity, and happiness at the source of the individual mind. In higher states of consciousness, the transcendental self comes to be fully realized and permanently maintained in daily life. In the Vedic tradition, the enlightened are said to enjoy freedom from stress and to find life effortless and blissful.

BIBLIOGRAPHY

Alexander, Charles N., and Ellen J. Langer, eds. *Higher Stages of Human Development: Perspectives on Adult Growth*. New York: Oxford UP, 1990. Print.

Austin, James H. *Zen and the Brain: Toward an Understanding of Meditation and Consciousness*. Cambridge: MIT P, 1998. Print.

Gackenbach, Jayne, Harry Hunt, and Charles N. Alexander, eds. *Higher States of Consciousness: Theoretical and Experimental Perspectives*. New York: Plenum, 1992. Print.

Fontana, David. *The Meditation Handbook: The Practical Guide to Eastern and Western Meditation Techniques*. London: Watkins, 2014. eBook Collection (EBSCOhost). Web. 21 May 2014.

Hagen, Steve. *Meditation Now or Never*. New York: Harper, 2007. Print.

Jacobson, Edmund. *You Must Relax*. 5th ed. New York: McGraw, 1978. Print.

Kabat-Zinn, J. *Wherever You Go, There You Are: Mindfulness Meditation in Everyday Life*. New York: Hyperion, 2005. Print.

Kornfield, Jack. *The Wise Heart: A Guide to the Universal Teachings of Buddhist Psychology*. New York: Bantam, 2008. Print.

Lichstein, Kenneth L. *Clinical Relaxation Strategies*. New York: Wiley, 1988. Print.

Mahesh Yogi, Maharishi. *On the Bhagavad-Gita: A New Translation and Commentary*. New York: Penguin, 1986. Print.

Murphy, Michael, and Steven Donovan. *The Physical and Psychological Effects of Meditation*. San Rafael: Esalen Institute, 1988. Print.

Tang, Yi-Yuan, Michael I. Posner, and Mary K. Rothbart. "Meditation Improves Self-Regulation over the Life Span." Annals of the New York Academy of Sciences 1307.1 (2014): 104–111. *Academic Search Alumni Edition*. Web. 21 May 2014.

Weber, Joseph. *Transcendental Meditation in America: How a New Age Movement Remade a Small Town in Iowa*. Iowa City: U of Iowa P, 2013. eBook Collection (EBSCOhost). Web. 21 May 2014.

Charles N. Alexander and David Sands;
updated by Cynthia McPherson Frantz

SEE ALSO: Biofeedback and relaxation; Consciousness; Consciousness: Altered states; Creativity and intelligence; Endocrine system; Environmental factors and mental health; James, William; Maslow, Abraham; Nervous system; Self-actualization; Stress: Physiological responses; Stress-related diseases.

Memory

TYPE OF PSYCHOLOGY: Memory

Theories of memory attempt to identify the structures and explain the processes underlying the human memory system. These theories give coherence to an understanding of memory and suggest new research needed to extend knowledge about learning and memory.

KEY CONCEPTS
- Episodic memory
- Iconic memory
- Long-term memory
- Memory trace
- Schemas
- Semantic memory
- Sensory memory
- Short-term memory

INTRODUCTION

Human memory is among the most complex phenomena in the universe. A Russian newspaper reporter once flawlessly recalled a list of fifty unrelated words he had studied for only three minutes fifteen years before. On the other hand, as everyone knows from personal experience, the memory system is also capable of losing information presented only seconds in the past. Errors in memory create so many problems that it seems imperative to know all that is possible about human memory. For that, a theory is needed.

A scientific theory is a systematic way to understand complex phenomena that occur in nature. A theory is judged to be useful insofar as its claims can be supported by the findings of empirical tests, especially experimentation, and insofar as it leads to further research studies. A theory is not right or wrong; it is simply a tool to describe what is known and to suggest what needs further study.

Three major forms of memory are generally described: short-term, long-term, and sensory memory. Short-term memory represents the temporary retention of newly acquired information. Generally, short-term memory lasts no longer than about twenty seconds. This is useful for short-term tasks, such as the recall of speech during discussions or discourse with another person. Short-term memory is rapidly lost, sometimes referred to as a process of decaying. Alan Baddeley, a major researcher in the field of memory, has suggested that a concept of working memory may be substituted for short-term.

Repeat stimulation, or rehearsal, may transfer short-term memory into that of long-term.

Long-term memory involves storage of information over longer periods of time, potentially as long as the life of the individual. Some researchers into the subject consider long-term memory to include two major areas: episodic and semantic. Episodic memory addresses events that have a temporal relationship with a person's life. This may include recall of when events or information appeared. Semantic memory represents the concepts or skills, represented in part by learning, that people acquire through the course of their lives.

Sensory memories are those that can be retrieved as a result of sensory stimuli. For example, a particular odor may result in the recall of events from the past. The unusual smell of a cleaning solution may cause the recall of a college dormitory from years past. This form of recall has been called olfactory memory. The image of a flower may result in the memory of a teenage boyfriend. Such a visual stimulus is sometimes referred to as iconic memory.

Theories of memory have been important to psychology for a long time, often occupying the time and interest of researchers throughout their careers. Memory, which is always connected to learning, Learning is defined as the mental process of preserving information acquired through the senses for later use. The cognitive approach to memory places emphasis on mental processes, which result in the ability to comprehend or recall what is learned. The basis is found in changes that occur in the regions of the brain, such as the hippocampus, associated with memory. In a sense, memory is the record of the experiences of a lifetime. Without it, a person could not re-experience the past; everything at every moment would be brand-new. A person could not even recognize the face of a loved one or learn from any experience. A person would thus have a greatly reduced chance for survival and would have no sense of personal identity. Memory is, in short, critical to functioning as a human being.

ASSOCIATIONISM, COGNITIVE THEORY, AND NEUROPSYCHOLOGY

The goal of a theory of memory is to explain the structures (hardware) and the processes (software) that make the system work. Explaining how such a complex system works is a massive undertaking. The attempts have taken the form of large-scale theories, which seek to deal with all major operations of the memory systems. The major theories of memory are associationism and theories from cognitive psychology and neuropsychology. The theories differ primarily in views of the retention and retrieval functions of memory. They also differ in terms of their conception of memory as active or passive.

Associationism, the oldest of the three, is the theory that memory relies on forming links or bonds between two unrelated things. This theory stems from the work of Hermann Ebbinghaus, who started the use of laboratory methods in the study of memory in the late nineteenth century. According to this theory, the ability to remember depends on establishing associations between stimuli and responses (S-R). Establishing associations depends on the frequency, recency, and saliency of their pairing. If these bonds become very strong, the subject is said to have developed a habit. Associationism also assumes the existence of internal stimuli that produce behavioral responses. These responses then become stimuli for other unobservable internal responses, thus forming chains. In this way, complex physical behaviors and mental associations can be achieved. Associationists tend to view the memory system as essentially passive, responding to environmental stimuli.

Cognitive theory emphasizes studying complex memory in the real world; it is concerned with the ecological validity of memory studies. Most of this work stems from the research of Sir Frederic C. Bartlett, who was not satisfied with laboratory emphasis on "artificial memory," but rather chose to study what he called meaningful memory. Meaningful memory, he said in his book *Remembering: A Study in Experimental and Social Psychology* (1932), is a person's effort to make sense of the world and to function effectively in it. Cognitive psychology recognizes subjective experiences as inescapably linked to human behavior. It centers on internal representation of past experiences and assumes that intentions, goals, and plans make a difference in what is remembered and how well it is remembered. The focus in memory research is on semantic memory—the knowledge of words, categories, concepts, and meanings located in long-term memory. People have highly complex networks of concepts, which helps account for their behavior in the real world. These networks are called schemas. New experiences and new information are viewed in light of old schemas so that they are easier to remember. Cognitive theory emphasizes how the individual processes information, and it uses the computer as its working model of memory.

Neuropsychology has contributed the third major theory of memory. Although psychology has always recognized the connection between its concerns and those of biology and medicine, the technology now available has made neuropsychological analysis of brain structure and functioning possible. Karl Lashley was an early researcher who sought to find the location of memory in the brain. He ran rats through mazes until they had learned the correct pathway. His subsequent surgical operations on experimental rats' brains failed to show localization of memory.

The search for the memory trace, the physiological change that presumably occurs as a result of learning, continued with Donald O. Hebb, who had assisted Lashley. The brain consists of billions of nerve cells, which are connected to thousands of other neurons. Hebb measured the electrical activity of the brain during learning, and he discovered that nerve cells fire repeatedly. He was able to show that an incoming stimulus causes patterns of neurons to become active. These cell assemblies discovered by Hebb constitute a structure for the reverberating circuits, a set of neurons firing repeatedly when information enters short-term memory. This firing seems to echo the information until it is consolidated in long-term memory. Other researchers have found chemical and physical changes associated with the synapses and in the neurons themselves during learning and when the learning is consolidated into long-term memory. The discovery of the memory trace, a dream of researchers for a long time, may become a reality. Neuropsychology sees memory as a neural function controlled by electrical and chemical activity.

CLINICAL APPROACHES TO MEMORY DISORDERS

Human memory is so important to daily life that any theory that could explain its structures and processes and thus potentially improve its functioning would be invaluable. Memory is inextricably tied to learning, planning, reasoning, and problem solving; it lies at the core of human intelligence.

None of the three theories is by itself sufficient to explain all the phenomena associated with memory. Over the years, a number of ideas have been developed in the attempt to improve memory functioning through passive means. Efforts to induce learning during sleep and to assess memory of patients for events taking place while under anesthesia have had mixed results but on the whole have not succeeded. Memory enhancement through hypnosis has been attempted but has not been shown to be very effective or reliable. Pills to improve memory and thereby intelligence have been marketed but so far have not been shown to be the answer to memory problems. Research has begun on the possibility that certain drugs (such as tacrine) may interactively inhibit memory loss in people afflicted with certain kinds of dementia (for example, Alzheimer's disease). Work in neuropsychology has shown the influence of emotion-triggered hormonal changes in promoting the memory of exciting or shocking events (such as one's first kiss or an earthquake). This has led to an understanding of state-dependent memory: Things learned in a particular physical or emotional state are more easily remembered when the person is in that state again. This helps explain the difficulties in remembering events that took place when a person was intoxicated or depressed. In fact, heavy use of alcohol may result in significant memory loss. A person may not even remember having injured someone in a car accident. Although not fully researched, it may be that certain kinds of memory are mood-congruent. Perhaps memories of events that occurred when a person was in a certain mood may become available to the person only when that mood is again induced.

More active means for memory improvement have met with greater success. Associationist theory has demonstrated the value of the use of mnemonics, devices or procedures intentionally designed to facilitate encoding and subsequent recall. The use of rhymes, acronyms, pegwords, and the like enables people to recall factual information such as the number of days in each month ("Thirty days hath September . . . "), the names of the Great Lakes (the acronym HOMES), and the colors of the visible spectrum (ROY G. BIV). Visual cues, such as tying a string around one's finger or knotting one's handkerchief, are traditional and effective ways to improve prospective memory. Cognitive psychology has demonstrated the importance of emotional factors—how and why something is learned—to the effectiveness of memory. It has provided the research base to demonstrate the effectiveness of study strategies such as the SQ3R (survey, question, read, recite, review) technique. Cognitive theory has also shown that metamemory, a person's knowledge about how his or her memory works, may be important for the improvement of memory.

In clinical settings, much research has been concerned with memory impairment as a means to test the applicability of theories of memory. Head injuries are a common cause of amnesia in which events immediately prior to an accident cannot be recalled. Damage to the hippocampus, a part of the brain that is vital to memory, breaks down the transfer of information from short-term to long-term memory. One dramatic case concerns "H. M.," a patient who had brain surgery to control epileptic seizures. After surgery, H. M.'s short-term memory was intact, but if he was momentarily distracted from a task, he could not remember anything about what he had just been doing. The information was never transferred to long-term memory. Such patients still remember information that was stored in long-term memory before their operation, but to them everyday experiences are always strangely new. They can read the same paragraph over and over, but each time the material will be brand-new. In H. M.'s case, it was discovered that his intelligence as measured by standardized tests actually improved, yet he was continually disoriented and unable to learn even the simplest new associations. Intelligence tests are made to measure general information, vocabulary, and grammatical associations; these things were stored in H. M.'s long-term memory and were apparently not affected by brain surgery. In cases less dramatic than H. M.'s, damage to particular areas of the brain can still have devastating effects on the memory. Damage can be caused by accidents, violent sports activity, strokes, tumors, and alcoholism. Alzheimer's disease is another area to which research findings on memory may be applied. In this fatal disease, a patient's forgetfulness increases from normal forgetting to the point that the patient cannot remember how to communicate, cannot recognize loved ones, and cannot care for his or her own safety needs.

Associationism, cognitive psychology, and neuropsychology can each explain some of the structures and processes involved in these and other real-world problems, but it seems as though none of the theories is sufficient by itself. Memory is such a complex phenomenon that it takes all the large-scale theories and a number of smaller-scale ones to comprehend it. The truth probably is that the theories are not mutually exclusive but rather are complementary to one another.

PHYSIOLOGICAL BASIS OF MEMORY

Theories of learning and memory have been of great concern to philosophers and psychologists for a long time. They have formed a major part of the history of psychology. Each of the theories has been ascendant for a time, but the nature of theory building requires new conceptions to compensate for perceived weaknesses in currently accepted theories and models. Associationism was the principal theory of memory of stimulus-response psychology, which was dominant in the United States until the mid-1950s. Cognitive psychology evolved from Gestalt psychology, from Jean Piaget's work on developmental psychology, and from information-processing theory associated with the computer, and was extremely important during the 1970s and 1980s. Neuropsychology developed concurrently with advanced technology that permits microanalysis of brain functioning. It has resulted in an explosion of knowledge about how the brain and its systems operate.

Formation of memory seems to involve two individual events. Short-term memory develops first. Repeated rehearsal transfers this form of memory into long-term storage. At one time, it was believed both these forms of memory involved similar events in the brain. However, experimental models have shown such a theory to be incorrect. Two experimental approaches have addressed this issue: the separation of memory formation involving "accidental" or intentional interference with brain function, and development of an animal model for the study of memory.

Electroshock treatment of depression in humans has been shown to interfere with short-term memory formation. However, these persons are still perfectly able to recall the memory of earlier events stored within long-term memory. Accidental damage to temporal lobes of the brain does not appear to interfere with short-term memory but may inhibit the ability to recall events from the past.

The experimental use of an animal model in the study of memory formation was developed by Eric R. Kandel at Columbia University. Kandel has used the sea slug *Aplysia* in his study of memory. The advantage of such a model is its simplicity—instead of the approximately one trillion neurons that make up the nervous system of humans, *Aplysia* contains a "mere" twenty thousand.

Using a variety of stimuli on the animal and observing its response, Kandel has shown that the physiological basis for short-term memory differs from that of long-term. Specifically, short-term memory involves stimulus to only a small number of individual neurons. Long-term memory involves de novo (new) protein synthesis in the affected cells and formation of extensive neural circuits. Kandel was awarded the Nobel Prize in Physiology or Medicine in 2000 for this work.

MEMORY RETRIEVAL

The basis for memory recall remains an active area of study. Memory retrieval can be of two types: recognition

and recall. In recognition, the individual is presented with information that had been previously learned. The subject remembers he or she has already observed or learned that information. In effect, it is analogous to seeing a movie or book for the second time. In recall, information is reproduced from memory, as in response to a question. The physiological basis for retrieval probably involves the activation of regions of the brain that were involved in the initial encoding.

BIBLIOGRAPHY

Baddeley, Alan D. *Human Memory: Theory and Practice.* Rev. ed. Hove, East Sussex, England: Psychology Press, 2005. Print.

Collins, Alan, ed. *Theories of Memory.* Mahwah: Erlbaum, 1994. Print.

Holcomb, Orval, and Dannie M. Hendrix. *Psychology of Memory.* New York: Nova Science, 2012. Digital file.

Kandel, Eric. "The Molecular Biology of Memory Storage: A Dialogue Between Genes and Synapses." *Science* 294 (2001): 1030–1038. Print.

Kellogg, Ronald Thomas. *Fundamentals of Cognitive Psychology.* 2d ed. Los Angeles: Sage, 2012. Print.

Klingberg, Torkel. *The Learning Brain: Memory and Brain Development in Children.* New York: Oxford UP, 2013.

Neisser, Ulric. *Cognition and Reality: Principles and Implications of Cognitive Psychology.* San Francisco: Freeman, 1981. Print.

Norman, Donald A. *The Psychology of Everyday Things.* New York: Basic, 2008. Print.

Nyberg, Lars, et al. "Reactivation of Encoding-Related Brain Activity During Memory Retrieval." *Proceedings of the National Academy of Sciences of the United States of America* 97 (2000): 11,120–121,124. Print.

Weisberg, Robert W., and Lauretta Reeves. *Cognition: From Memory to Creativity.* Hoboken: Wiley, 2013. Digital file.

R. G. Gaddis; updated by Richard Adler

SEE ALSO: Alzheimer's disease; Artificial intelligence; Brain structure; Concept formation; Ebbinghaus, Hermann; Encoding; Forgetting and forgetfulness; Kinesthetic memory; Long-term memory; Memory: Animal research; Memory: Empirical studies; Memory: Physiology; Memory: Sensory; Memory storage; Short-term memory.

Memory
Animal research

TYPE OF PSYCHOLOGY: Biological bases of behavior; Memory

Research with nonhuman animals has significantly contributed to an understanding of the basic processes of memory, including its anatomy and physiology. Important brain regions, neurotransmitters, and genes have been identified, and this information is now being used to further understand and treat human memory disorders.

KEY CONCEPTS

- Anterograde amnesia
- Engram
- Experimental brain damage
- Genetic engineering
- Hippocampus
- Prefrontal cortex
- Retrograde amnesia
- Stroke

INTRODUCTION

Nonhuman animals have been used as subjects in memory research since the earliest days of psychology, and much of what is known about the fundamental processes of memory is largely based on work with animals. Rats, mice, pigeons, rabbits, monkeys, sea slugs, flatworms, and fruit flies are among the most commonly used species. The widespread use of animals in psychological research can be attributed to the ability to systematically manipulate and control their environments under strict laboratory conditions and to use procedures and invasive techniques, such as surgery and drugs, that cannot ethically be used with humans. A typical memory research protocol involves training animals on any of a variety of learning paradigms and concurrently measuring or manipulating some aspect of the nervous system to examine its relationship to memory.

Although learning is closely related, a distinction should be drawn between learning and memory. Learning is defined as a relatively permanent change in behavior as a result of experience. Memory is the underlying process by which information is encoded, stored, and retrieved by the nervous system. Contemporary learning and memory paradigms are based on the principles of classical and operant conditioning first established by the early behaviorists: Ivan Petrovich Pavlov, Edward L. Thorndike, John B. Watson, and B. F. Skinner. These learning paradigms can be used to examine different types of memory and to explore the underlying brain mechanisms that may mediate them. For classical conditioning, widely used paradigms include eyeblink conditioning, taste-aversion learning, and fear conditioning. For operant conditioning, memory for objects, spatial memory, context discrimination, and maze learning are among the most frequently used procedures. Two other very simple forms of learning, habituation, the gradual decrease in response to a stimulus as a result of repeated exposure to it, and sensitization, the gradual increase in response to a stimulus after repeated exposure to it, are both simple forms of nonassociative learning also extensively used in animal memory research.

Researchers have at their disposal a number of techniques that allow them to manipulate the nervous system and assess its functions. Historically, experimental brain damage has been one of the most widely utilized procedures. This technique involves surgically destroying (known as lesioning) various parts of the brain and assessing the effects of the lesion on memory processes. Pharmacological manipulations are also frequently used and involve administering a drug known to affect a specific neurotransmitter or hormonal system thought to play a role in memory. Functional studies involve measuring brain activity while an animal is actually engaged in learning. Recordings can be made from individual brain cells (neurons), groups of neurons, or entire anatomical regions. Beginning in the late 1990s, genetic engineering began to be applied to the study of animal memory. These procedures involve the direct manipulation of genes that produce proteins suspected to be important for memory.

By combining a wide variety of memory paradigms with an increasing number of ways to manipulate or measure the nervous system, animal research has been extremely useful in addressing several fundamental questions about memory, including the important brain structures involved in memory, the manner in which information is stored in the nervous system, and the causes and potential treatments for human memory disorders.

HE ANATOMY OF MEMORY

One of the first questions about memory to be addressed using animals was its relationship to the underlying structure of the nervous system. American psychologist Karl Lashley was an early pioneer in this field in the mid-twentieth century; his main interest was in finding what was then referred to as the engram, the physical location in the brain where memories are stored. Lashley trained rats on a variety of tasks, such as the ability to learn mazes or perform simple discriminations, and then lesioned various parts of the cerebral cortex (the convoluted outer covering of the brain) in an attempt to erase the memory trace. Despite years of effort, he found that he could not completely abolish a memory no matter what part of the cortex he lesioned. Lashley summed up his puzzlement and frustration at these findings in this now well-known quote: "I sometimes feel, in reviewing the evidence on the localization of the engram, that the necessary conclusion is that learning just is not possible."

While the specific location of the brain lesion did not appear important, Lashley found that the total amount of brain tissue removed was critical. When large lesions were produced, as compared to smaller ones, he found that memories could be abolished, regardless of the location in the cortex where they were made. This led Lashley to propose the concepts of mass action and equipotentiality, which state that the cortex works as a whole and that all parts contribute equally to complex behaviors.

Further research has generally supported Lashley's original conclusions about the localization of the engram. However, better memory tests and more sophisticated techniques for inducing brain damage have revealed that certain brain regions are more involved in memory than others, and that different brain regions are actually responsible for different types of memory. For example, classical conditioning, which is the modification of a reflex through learning, appears primarily to involve the brain stem and cerebellum, which are two evolutionarily old brain structures. Specific circuitry within these structures that underlies a number of forms of classical conditioning has been identified.

In the rabbit, a puff of air blown into the eye produces a reflexive blinking response. When researchers repeatedly pair the air puff with a tone, the tone itself will eventually come to elicit the response. The memory for this response involves a very specific circuit of neurons, primarily in the cerebellum. Once the response is well learned, it can be abolished by lesions in this circuit. Importantly, these lesions do not affect other forms of memory. Similarly, taste-aversion learning, a process by which animals learn not to consume a food or liquid that has previously made them ill, has been shown to be mediated by a very specific circuit in the brain stem, specifically the pons and medulla. Animals with lesions to the nucleus of the solitary tract, a portion of this circuit in

the medulla where taste, olfactory, and illness-related information converge, will not readily learn taste aversions.

More complex forms of learning and memory have been shown to involve more recently evolved brain structures. Many of these are located in either the cortex or the limbic system, an area of the brain located between the newer cortex and the older brain stem. One component of the limbic system believed to be heavily involved in memory is the hippocampus. One of its primary functions appears to be spatial memory. Rats and monkeys with damage limited to the hippocampus are impaired in maze learning and locating objects in space but have normal memory for nonspatial tasks. Additionally, animals that require spatial navigation for their survival, such as homing pigeons and food-storing rodents (which must remember the location of the food that they have stored), have disproportionately large hippocampi. Moreover, damage to the hippocampus in these species leads to a disruption in their ability to navigate and to find stored food, respectively.

One area of the cortex that has been shown to be involved in memory is the prefrontal cortex. This area has been implicated in short-term memory, which is the ability to temporarily hold a mental representation of an object or event. Monkeys and rats that received lesions to the prefrontal cortex were impaired in learning tasks that required them to remember briefly the location of an object or to learn tasks that required them to switch back and forth between strategies for solving the task. Studies involving the measurement of brain function have also demonstrated that this area of the brain is active during periods when animals are thought to be holding information in short-term memory.

While experimental brain damage has been one of the predominant techniques used to study structure/function relationships in the nervous system, difficulty in interpretation, an increased concern for animal welfare, and the advent of more sophisticated physiological and molecular techniques have led to an overall decline in their use.

THE MOLECULES OF MEMORY

While lesion studies have been useful in determining the brain structures involved in memory, pharmacological techniques have been used to address its underlying chemistry. Pharmacological manipulations have a long history in memory research with animals, dating back to the early 1900s and the discovery of neurotransmitters. Neurotransmitters are chemical messengers secreted by neurons and are essential to communication within the nervous system. Each neurotransmitter, of which there are more than one hundred, has its own specific receptor to which it can attach and alter cellular functioning. By administering drugs that either increase or decrease the activity of specific neurotransmitters, researchers have been able to investigate their role in memory formation.

One neurotransmitter that has been strongly implicated in memory is glutamate. This transmitter is found throughout the brain but is most highly concentrated in the cerebral cortex and the hippocampus. Drugs that increase the activity of glutamate facilitate learning and improve memory, while drugs that reduce glutamate activity have the opposite effect. The neurotransmitter dopamine has also been implicated in memory formation. In small doses, drugs such as cocaine and amphetamine, which increase dopamine activity, have been found to improve memory in both lower animals and humans. Moderate doses of caffeine can also facilitate memory storage, albeit by a less-well-understood mechanism. Other neurotransmitters believed to be involved in memory include acetylcholine, serotonin, norepinephrine, and the endorphins.

Research with simpler organisms has been directed at understanding the chemical events at the molecular level that may be involved in memory. One animal in particular, the marine invertebrate Aplysia californica, a species of sea slug, has played a pivotal role in this research. Aplysia have very simple nervous systems with large, easily identifiable neurons and are capable of many forms of learning, including habituation, sensitization, and classical conditioning. Canadian psychologist Donald O. Hebb, a former student of Lashley, proposed that memories are stored in the nervous system as a result of the strengthening of connections between neurons as a result of their repeated activation during learning. With the *Aplysia*, it is possible indirectly to observe and manipulate the connections between neurons while learning is taking place. Eric R. Kandel of Columbia University has used the *Aplysia* as a model system to study the molecular biology of memory for more than thirty years. He demonstrated that when a short-term memory is formed in the *Aplysia*, the connections between the neurons involved in the learning process are strengthened by gradually coming to release more neurotransmitters, particularly serotonin. When long-term memories are formed, new connections between nerve cells actually grow. With repeated disuse, these processes appear to reverse themselves. Kandel's work has suggested that memory (what Lashley referred to as the engram) is represented in the nervous system in the form of a chemical or structural change, depending on the nature and duration of the memory itself. For these discoveries, Kandel was awarded the Nobel Prize in 2000.

Modern genetic engineering techniques have made it possible to address the molecular biology of memory in higher mammals (predominantly mice) as well as invertebrates. Two related techniques, genetic knockouts and transgenics, have been applied to the problem. Genetic knockouts involve removing, or "knocking out," a gene that produces a specific protein thought to be involved in memory. Frequently targeted genes include those for neurotransmitters or their receptors. Transgenics involves the insertion of a new gene into the genome of an organism with the goal of either overproducing a specific protein or inserting a completely foreign protein into the animal. Neurotransmitters and their receptors are again the most frequently targeted sites. A remarkable number of knockout mice have been produced with a variety of short- and long-term memory deficits. In many ways, this technique is analogous to those used in earlier brain lesion studies but is applied at the molecular level. Dopamine, serotonin, glutamate, and acetylcholine systems have all been implicated in memory formation as a result of genetic knockout studies. Significantly, researchers have also been able to improve memory in mice through genetic engineering. Transgenic mice that overproduce glutamate receptors actually learn mazes faster and have better retention than normal mice. It is hoped that in the future gene therapy for human memory disorders may be developed based on this technique.

ANIMAL MODELS OF HUMAN MEMORY DISORDERS

Animal research has many practical applications to the study and treatment of human memory dysfunction. Many types of neurological disorder and brain damage can produce memory impairments in humans, and it has been possible to model some of these in animals. The first successful attempt at this was production of an animal model of brain-damage-induced amnesia.

It had been known since the 1950s that damage to the temporal lobes, as a result of disease, traumatic injury, epilepsy, or infection, could produce a disorder known as anterograde amnesia, which is the inability to form new long-term memories. This is in contrast to the better-known retrograde amnesia, which is an inability to remember previously stored information. Beginning in the late 1970s, work with monkeys, and later rats, began to identify the critical temporal lobe structures that, when damaged, produce anterograde amnesia. These structures include the hippocampus and, perhaps more important, the adjacent, overlying cortex, which is known as the rhinal cortex. As a result of this work, this brain region is now believed to be critical in the formation of new long-term memories.

Memory disorders also frequently develop after an interruption of oxygen flow to the brain (known as hypoxia), which can be caused by events such as stroke, cardiac arrest, or carbon monoxide poisoning. There are a variety of animal models of stroke and resultant memory disorders. Significantly, oxygen deprivation produces brain damage that is most severe in the temporal lobe, particularly the hippocampus and the rhinal cortex. Using animal models, the mechanisms underlying hypoxic injury have been investigated, and potential therapeutic drugs designed to minimize the brain damage and lessen the memory impairments have been tested. One potentially damaging event that has been identified is a massive influx of calcium into neurons during a hypoxic episode. This has led to the development of calcium blockers and their widespread utilization in the clinical treatment of complications arising from stroke.

Alzheimer's disease is probably the best-known human memory disorder. It is characterized by gradual memory loss over a period of five to fifteen years. It typically begins as a mild forgetfulness and progresses to anterograde amnesia, retrograde amnesia, and eventually complete cognitive dysfunction and physical incapacitation. One pathological event that has been implicated in the development of Alzheimer's disease is the overproduction of a protein known as the amyloid-beta protein. The normal biological function of this protein is not known, but at high levels it appears to be toxic to neurons. Amyloid-beta deposits are most pronounced and develop first in the temporal and frontal lobes, a fact that corresponds well with the memory functions ascribed to these areas and the types of deficits seen in people with Alzheimer's disease. The development of an animal model has marked a major milestone in understanding the disorder and developing a potential treatment. Mice have been genetically engineered to overproduce the amyloid-beta protein. As a result, they develop patterns of brain damage and memory deficits similar to humans with Alzheimer's disease. The development of the Alzheimer's mouse has allowed for a comprehensive investigation of the genetics of the disorder as well as

providing a model on which to test potential therapeutic treatments. Limited success for potential treatments has been obtained with an experimental vaccine in animals. This vaccine has been shown to reduce both brain damage and memory deficits. As with most experimental drugs, application to the treatment of human Alzheimer's disease is many years away.

BIBLIOGRAPHY

Anagnostopoulos, Anna V., Larry E. Mobraaten, John J. Sharp, and Muriel T. Davisson. "Transgenic and Knockout Databases: Behavioral Profiles of Mouse Mutants." *Physiology and Behavior* 73 (2001): 675–89. Print.

Cohen, Neil J., and Howard Eichenbaum. *Memory, Amnesia, and the Hippocampal System*. Cambridge: MIT P, 1995. Print.

Duva, Christopher A., Thomas J. Kornecook, and John P. J. Pinel. "Animal Models of Medial Temporal Lobe Amnesia: The Myth of the Hippocampus." *Animal Models of Human Emotion and Cognition*. Ed. Mark Haug and Richard E. Whalen. Washington, DC: American Psychological Association, 1999. Print.

Gaidos, Susan. "Memories Lost and Found: Drugs that Help Mice Remember Reveal Role for Epigenetics in Recall." *Science News* 27 July 2013: 24–28. Print.

Hurley, Dan. "Where Memory Lives." Discover 33.3 (2012): 30–37. Print.

Kiefer, Steven W. "Neural Mediation of Conditioned Food Aversions." *Annals of the New York Academy of Sciences* 443 (1985): 100–109. Print.

Martinez, Joe L., and Raymond P. Kesner. *Neurobiology of Learning and Memory*. 2nd ed. Boston: Academic, 2007. Print.

Morgan, Dave, et al. "A Peptide Vaccination Prevents Memory Loss in an Animal Model of Alzheimer's Disease." *Nature* 408 (2000): 982–85. Print.

Squire, Larry R., and Eric Kandel. *Memory: From Mind to Molecules*. 2nd ed. Greenwood Village: Roberts, 2009. Print.

Tang, Ya-Ping, et al. "Genetic Enhancement of Learning and Memory in Mice." *Nature* 401 (1999): 63–69. Print.

Thompson, Richard F. "The Neurobiology of Learning and Memory." *Science* 233.13 (1986): 941–47. Print.

Tulving, Endel, and Fergus I. M. Craik, eds. *The Oxford Handbook of Memory*. New York: Oxford UP, 2005. Print.

Wilson, A., and Jonathon Crystal. "Prospective Memory in the Rat." *Animal Cognition* 15.3 (2012): 349–58. Print.

Christopher A. Duva

SEE ALSO: Animal experimentation; Artificial intelligence; Brain structure; Concept formation; Encoding; Forgetting and forgetfulness; Habituation and sensitization; Kinesthetic memory; Long-term memory; Memory: Empirical studies; Memory: Physiology; Memory: Sensory; Memory storage; Research ethics; Short-term memory.

Memory disorders

TYPE OF PSYCHOLOGY: Clinical; Developmental; Health; Neuropsychology

Since the late 19th century, memory disorders have been researched from various perspectives. By the late 20th century, a resurgence of memory research and the advent of more advanced technologies better equipped psychologists and neuroscientists to study the neurological perspective of the human brain and human memory. These breakthroughs have led to a more extensive understanding of memory disorders including amnesia and dementia.

KEY CONCEPTS

- Alan Baddeley
- Amnesic syndrome
- Dementia
- Hermann Ebbinghaus
- Korsakoff's syndrome
- Long-Term memory
- Short-Term memory

INTRODUCTION

When exploring the history of memory disorders research, it is essential to consider both neurological and psychological aspects of the topic of memory. Alan Parkin states that by the Middle Ages it had been discovered that memory capacities were derived from the brain. Parkin goes on to explain it was not until the late 19th century when neurological research extended its focus toward memory disorders. Namely, Carl Wernicke and Sergei Korsakoff pioneered the study of amnesic syndromes with their research of patients who were incapable of acquiring or learning new information.

Similar to other psychological disciplines, memory research has a storied history. According to Alan Baddeley, experimental studies interested in human memory date back to 1879 when Hermann Ebbinghaus began his landmark research. Ebbinghaus tested his own capacity to learn and remember novel stimuli (nonsense syllables) while also accounting for the demand and ability to re-learn content which was forgotten. Although it may be suggested Ebbinghaus failed to detail a theoretical paradigm to complement his findings investigating the human memory, he was paramount in establishing memory research as a topic that may be researched objectively and experimentally.

Baddeley details that Ebbinghaus' work was met with some opposition and critiques which argued Ebbinghaus' work was too simplified and ignored the everyday utilities that the human memory may serve. These concerns regarding Ebbinghaus' experimental human memory research were voiced by Frederic Bartlett in his 1932 book *Remembering*. Bartlett focused on bridging the gap between human memory laboratory research and more naturalistic designs that may be reasoned as more crucial to understanding how the human memory functions. Further, Bartlett's work drew upon the idea of schemata, or the concept that ongoing learning builds upon previous experiences and memories. Interestingly, in the years following the publication of *Remembering*, Bartlett's work was somewhat ignored as the field of memory favored an Ebbinghaus approach to research; however this orientation toward the Ebbinghaus tradition began to shift in the late 1960s and early 1970s. One of the most prominent psychologists that influenced this shift was Ulric Neisser whose 1967 book *Cognitive Psychology* and 1976 book *Cognition and Reality: Principles and Implications of Cognitive Psychology* challenged the direction memory research had taken the previous 30 years. Thereafter, research concerning the human memory has more adequately approached the nuances and complexities that the topic presents, and this progression may be posited to be the result of integrating both Ebbinghaus and Bartlett inspired research within the discipline.

MEMORY CONCEPTS

It is pivotal to understand the concepts of working, short-term, and long-term memory as well as semantic memory, episodic memory, and procedural memory when examining research related to memory disorders. Although there are additional concepts that are pertinent to the current topic, these may be considered the most central.

Joseph LeDoux attributes William James as the psychologist who first presented the idea that memory may exist in either a "temporary form" or "persistent form." Additionally, LeDoux cites experimental work conducted by Muller and Pilzecker as seminal research evidencing the existence of short-term memory and long-term memory. Nelson Cowan describes long-term memory as "a vast store of knowledge and a record of prior events." Cowan goes on to describe short-term memory as information that is available for a shorter span of time, and it may be argued that some but not all of this information may exist unconsciously or implicitly. Contrasting short-term and long-term memory, capacity (i.e., amount), and duration (i.e., time) varies across the two types of memory. Addressing working memory, Cowan cites work by George Miller and colleagues from 1960 which explained working memory is used for planning and executing behavior. Cowan further delineates that some modern definitions and conceptual designs for working memory integrate short-term and long-term memory functions within the model for working memory.

Another conceptual distinction for semantic, episodic, and procedural memory must be clarified. Daniel Schacter explains the difference between these three memory systems, describing episodic memory as an individual's recollection of his or her own experiences, semantic memory as an individual's memory for "general knowledge of facts and concepts," and procedural memory as the "acquisition of skills or procedures." Schacter asserts that there is a general consensus amongst psychologists and researchers regarding the features and the existence of these three types of memory.

AMNESIC SYNDROME

In his specifying of overarching characteristics, Alan Parkin lists five features which discern general commonalities across amnesic syndrome. Parkin suggests that short-term memory, semantic memory, and procedural memory will remain intact, a "severe and permanent anterograde amnesia is present," and retrograde amnesia will manifest but may differ across diagnoses. Importantly, anterograde amnesia alludes to instances when new information may not be acquired, and retrograde amnesia refers to instances when an individual is unable to recall information or knowledge of experiences that occurred before the onset of amnesia. Parkin states that rather than memory and its overall function breaking down gradually over time, amnesic syndrome more closely reflects impairments and failures of certain specific memory capacities.

As alluded to previously, amnesic syndrome tends to impair long-term memory, and this is especially evident in amnesic individuals' failure to encode or learn new information, and their inability to reminisce on previous life experiences. With this said, the complexities of amnesic syndrome and how symptoms may differ in individuals is still being explored by psychological researchers. One main source of amnesic syndrome research has stemmed from individuals who present severely impeded memories and have been diagnosed with Korsakoff's syndrome. Baddeley explains that Korsakoff's syndrome may derive from alcoholic conditions and poor dieting, and this may contribute to a vitamin deficiency which ultimately results in amnesic symptoms. Parkin also proposes that Korsakoff's syndrome is caused by a thiamine deficiency which thereafter leads to hemorrhaging. It is known that Korsakoff's syndrome is often the cause of diencephalic (the region of the brain where hemorrhaging occurs) amnesia, and this may result in an individual's inability to accurately contextualize his or her experiences.

As Parkin warns, although the amnesia literature has been dominated by patients diagnosed with Korsakoff's syndrome, there are many other types of amnesic diagnoses. Alluding to this, he points to research that has found amnesia may be associated with two unique parts of the brain (the mid-line diencephalon and the medial temporal lobe region). For instance, another type of amnesia that has been studied at length is temporal lobe amnesia. A now famous case study by Milner and colleagues studying an amnesic named in the psychological literature as "H.M." is one example of research investigating the impact of temporal lobe amnesia. Baddeley also points toward seminal temporal lobe research from a 1966 study by Drachman and Arbit. This study examined temporal lobe amnesia using an Ebbinghaus style methodology, and the researchers found that amnesic patients performed similarly to non-amnesic participants on short-term memory tasks, but amnesic patients did not perform as well as non-amnesic participants on long-term memory tasks. There are many other types of amnesias (e.g., focal retrograde amnesia, source amnesia) which present unique symptoms and neurological underpinnings in comparison to the amnesic syndromes previously discussed. It is important to consider the differences across amnesic diagnoses, but it is just as critical to keep in mind that individuals who are diagnosed with a similar amnesic syndrome may vary in their behavior and experiences with amnesia.

DEMENTIA

Another psychological category connected with memory disorders is dementia and its interrelated diagnoses. Kathryn Bayles and Cheryl Tomoeda cite that 24 million individuals are currently diagnosed with dementia (and mild cognitive impairment), and they also suggest that this number may reach 42 million people by 2020. Although dementia includes an impairing of an individual's communicative processes, the information presented here will focus on the impact dementia may have on the human memory in addition to the diagnoses which may exist with dementia. It is also important to note that the communicative deficits may be partially linked to the deterioration of memory systems.

Considering memory systems for those diagnosed with dementia, Bayles and Tomoeda posit that the severity and the onset of memory impairments may affect memory systems dissimilarly. One example would be research which indicates during early stages of their disease individuals with Alzheimer's disease are subject to impeded working and declarative memory (specifically, episodic memory). In contrast, Bayles and Tomoeda say that conditioning, motor procedural, and habit memory remain mostly intact for Alzheimer's disease patients. In fact, memory measures and performance are strong predictors of Alzheimer's disease according to Bayles and Tomoeda. Illustrating another perspective of how memory systems may be damaged for those who have dementia, during Parkinson's disease nondeclarative and working memory tend to be impaired, but declarative memory typically functions at a normal capacity. For those diagnosed with dementia and Lewy body disease, working memory and episodic memory are two memory systems which are primarily harmed. One other disease which deserves mention is Huntington's disease. This inherited disease always includes the onset of dementia, and semantic, episodic, visual, verbal, and motor procedural memory are all affected. Similar to amnesic syndromes, despite some generalities across diseases there is no ubiquitous dementia experience, and how memory systems are altered changes on a case-by-case basis.

TREATMENT

How the effects of memory disorders are mitigated and how patients diagnosed with amnesia, dementia, or other memory ailments are treated will continue to de-velop as researchers and scientists learn more about the construction and function of human memory. According to Parkin, despite the possibility that an amnesic may accept his or her memory deficits (e.g., this is not uncommon for Korsakoff's syndrome patients), others may be more prone to frustration and depression as a result of their deteriorating memory. Parkin suggests potential helpful ways to lessen the effects of memory loss consist of using external memory cues or aids, the instillation and practice of memory strategies (e.g., mnemonics), and use of domain-specific knowledge methods which may improve a targeted area of difficulty. In regards to those with dementia, Bayles and Tomoeda allude to the medical application of appreciating how memory systems are impacted for different dementias, and how treatments should focus on utilizing and strengthening the memory systems that remain most functional. Ideally, treatments for memory disorders will continue to progress and improve as the scientific understanding of memory advances.

BIBLIOGRAPHY

Baddeley, A. D. (1976). *The Psychology of Memory.* New York, NY: Basic Books. A highly influential publication in the field of memory research. Baddeley's work provides an overview of the history of memory research and then delves into the concepts and components of memory as well as its limitations. Also, Baddeley provides a closing chapter providing accounts of exceptional or extraordinary memory.

Bayles, K. A., & Tomoeda, C. K. (2014). *Cognitive-Communication Disorders of Dementia: Definition, Diagnosis, and Treatment* (2nd ed.). San Diego, CA: Plural. This recent publication provides detailed analyses of dementia and the diseases it tends to accompany. How dementia influences cognition and communication is assessed across a bevy of diseases including Alzheimer's disease, Down syndrome, and Parkinson's disease.

Parkin, A. J. (1997). *Memory and Amnesia: An Introduction* (2nd ed.). Oxford, UK: Blackwell. Deliberating over the scope of memory and amnesia, Parkin provides a rich perspective of memory and amnesia from a psychological and neurological view. The work also encompasses the assessment and treatment of memory disorders pertaining to amnesia and dementia.

Roediger III, H. L., Dudai, Y., & Fitzpatrick, S. M. (Eds.). (2007). *Science of Memory: Concepts.* New York, NY: Oxford University Press. Spanning 16 core concepts, the leading researchers in the field of memory provide a wide array of topical analyses via succinct essays.

Schacter, D. L. (2001). *The Seven Sins of Memory: How The Mind Forgets and Remembers*. New York, NY: Houghton Mifflin Harcourt. According to Schacter, it appears our memories are prone to make mistakes and errors regularly. In this poignant work, Schacter writes how memory failures may affect our everyday lives and asserts that these may actually be "by-products of otherwise adaptive properties of memory."

Andrew P. Minigan

SEE ALSO: Alzheimer's disease; Amnesia; Brain trauma; Dementia; Neurodegenerative diseases; Neuropsychology; Neuroscience.

Memory
Empirical studies

TYPE OF PSYCHOLOGY: Memory

Researchers have investigated a variety of experimental variables to understand better the structure of the memory storage system and the processes of remembering and forgetting. Key variables studied include the type of materials to be remembered, such as words, sentences, or pictures; the order of presentation; and the order of recall.

KEY CONCEPTS
- Episodic memory
- Long-term memory
- Recall
- Recognition
- Rehearsal
- Semantic memory
- Sensory memory
- Short-term memory

INTRODUCTION
A number of testing procedures have been devised to determine how much a person can remember. Much information about short-term memory has been obtained through a set of recall tasks in which the subject is presented with items to be recalled. Basically, the short-term memory system is of limited capacity; information is maintained by continued attention and rehearsal (the repetition of memory items). The information in short-term memory may be lost through displacement by in-

coming information or lost through decay with time; information in short-term memory can also be transferred to long-term memory. The experimental design can be modified to examine different aspects of short-term memory.

RECALL AND RECOGNITION TESTS
In the free recall technique, subjects are presented with items at a fixed rate of presentation; several trials take place, in which the order of presentation is randomized. Recall refers to the retrieval of information from memory, with or without clues.

The important feature of free recall is that subjects are allowed to remember the items in whatever order they wish. In ordered recall tasks, the subjects can report the items in any order, but they must also identify the position of their presentation. The oldest of all the techniques that involve learning a list of items is serial recall, or serial learning. In serial learning, the subject is shown one word from a list at a time, for a limited amount of time, such as two seconds per word. The second time that the list is presented, it is presented one word at a time, and the subject's task is to remember the upcoming word in the series. In some experimental procedures, the list is repeated until the subject can accurately remember every item. In others, the list is presented a fixed number of times.

In probe recall tasks, by comparison, the subject is required to recall particular elements in a sequence of items. A common example of this is the paired-associate technique of list learning, in which subjects are shown pairs of items. The first item in the pair is called the stimulus, and the second is called the response. Recall is tested by showing the stimulus item only, requiring the subject to remember the response. The paired-associate and serial learning techniques both allow the experimenter to have considerable control, in that subjects have only one possible correct response, a limited time in which to make it, and a specific cue to aid in recall.

In another variation of list learning, called distractor recall, a subject is presented with a set of stimulus items, one item at a time. Each item is presented for a fixed period of time. Once each item has been presented a single time, a short period may follow during which the subject is asked to do an irrelevant task. The purpose of the irrelevant task is to create a delay between presentation of the stimulus items and the test to minimize the subject's mental repetition of the items. One such task would be to require the subject to count backward, such as by threes (986, 983, 980, and so on), from a predetermined starting point. Finally, the subject is given a test to determine how many of the original items are remembered.

In general, it is more difficult to test recognition than to test recall. Recall, at least when lists of words are used, is easily scored. When recognition (noticing that information is familiar) is tested, however, the old items must be mixed with new items so that the subjects can indicate which they have seen before. One method of testing recognition is to present the old item with one or more new items and require the subject to select one which he or she believes to be the old item. In such tests, the proportion of items correctly identified as having been seen before decreases as the number of alternatives increases. Accuracy also decreases if the alternatives are similar to the originally presented items. Even when recall is perfect, the time required to produce a response varies. Latency in giving a response can also provide information about the memory processes when performance is close to perfect, making the amount recalled an inappropriate measure. Even when recall is less than perfect, time latencies can reveal underlying differences in memory processes.

TESTING LONG-TERM MEMORY

Experimental tests have also been designed to study long-term memory. Long-term memory refers to the storage area that holds permanent memories and is unlimited in capacity. There is overlap between short-term memory and long-term memory, so a test that requires subjects to recall a list of words will include an assessment of both short-term and long-term memory. For example, words at the end of the list will be in short-term storage, while words at the beginning of the list might have entered long-term storage. Two major forms of long-term memory are episodic memory and semantic memory. Episodic memory involves information about where and when some event occurred. In contrast, semantic memory contains stores of words and coded categorical information.

Researchers seeking to determine the characteristics of long-term memory present subjects with tasks that require decisions about the meaning of words. In a semantic decision task, the subject is asked to decide whether the word is a member of a particular category; the phrase "Tigers are felines" might be presented, and the subject would be asked for a true/false decision. In a lexical decision task, the subject decides whether a string of letters forms a word.

MEMORY ORGANIZATION RESEARCH

A number of studies have been described that are concerned with short-term and long-term memory. Memory research has also included diverse studies of the effects of prior activities, everyday activities, sensory modalities, perfect memories, pathological memory losses (caused by surgery, amnesia, or drug usage), and old age on memory.

Memory experiments have been conducted using materials such as cards, pencils, paper, and stopwatches. More complex techniques control the speed of presentation with computers programmed to present material visually or verbally; there are appropriate response-recording keys for voice response or finger press, which analyze the recall correctness as well as the speed of response. Experiments on memory have been conducted with animals, such as pigeons, rats, and primates, as well as with humans.

Laboratory studies of long-term memory organization are of particular interest for real-world applications. Many of these studies use categorized lists of words. The lists often consist of words from the same natural category, such as dog, cat, horse, and sheep from the category "animal." A list might contain forty words with eight words from five categories. Subjects remember categorized lists better than uncategorized ones. Categorized lists are also remembered better when they are presented in blocks rather than when presented randomly. Blocked presentation refers to the fact that all items from a particular category are presented one after another, and then items from another category are presented. In comparison, with random presentation, the items from different categories are completely mixed in the presentation order. Blocked presentation is much more organized than random presentation. The superior memory for blocked presentation suggests the important role that organization plays in memory.

A further indication of the importance of organization is the finding that people actively rearrange randomly presented lists. That is, even though items from various categories are presented in random order, subjects tend to group the items into their appropriate categories at recall. That is, the items are recalled by category in spite of having been presented randomly. Examining the order of recall led researchers to the realization that learning and memory are influenced by the active strategies of the subject and by the properties of the learning material that allow organization to take place. When the lists consist of a set of items from a limited number of semantic categories (for example, marine animals and means of transportation) scattered throughout the list, words from each category tend to be recalled together. A number of researchers in cognitive psychology have used these principles for real-world applications. For example, knowing that people tend to recall information in these ways, educators who write textbooks can organize information in ways that will enhance the human memory system. In addition, understanding human memory helps human-factors psychologists devise techniques for the display of information on computer screens (computer interfaces) that make computer presentations more compatible with the way people learn and remember. Furthermore, in this technological age, people commonly need to search through large amounts of information to find what they are seeking. Using what is known about memory, psychologists are working to devise systems for searching large databases, such as computerized card catalogs in libraries, that work in conjunction with the way people search their own memories.

The importance of the relationships among separate elements has also been illustrated with nonverbal materials. It has been shown, for example, that simple line drawings of parts of the face are difficult to recognize when presented separately. The same drawings, however, are quickly recognized when presented in the context of a face. Additional information is provided by the context—the face, in this case—which aids the recognition of each separate element. Organization in the form of relationships among elements is important to the process of storing information in memory. This research has applications in the area of artificial intelligence. It is helping scientists to program computers to recognize human handwriting, fingerprints, and other complex stimuli.

BIOLOGICAL ASPECTS OF MEMORY

Studies on memory that are of a biological nature have also helped psychologists who are concerned with determining how specific parts of the brain are related to the processes underlying the various types of memory. For example, both external and internal stimuli are perceived by an organism as experiences. The organism converts these experiences to a form that the nervous system can understand; they must be stored in an electrical or molecular form in the brain. An understanding of the biological processes involved has helped psychologists devise tests that are used to assess memory deficits. A memory deficit might be caused by a head injury, tu-

mor, or disease such as Alzheimer's disease. Researchers continue to search for clues that will help people with memory deficits to overcome those deficits by means of drug therapy or surgical repair.

EVOLUTION OF RESEARCH

Plato thought of memory as something like a block of wax. Aristotle considered the heart to be of primary importance in the memory process. Other ancient Greeks argued that the brain was the seat of memory. Although thinkers have been interested in memory for thousands of years, it was not studied experimentally until fairly recently. Research on human memory was greatly influenced by the work of European psychologists more than a century ago.

The first controlled experiments on memory were conducted in Europe by Hermann Ebbinghaus in 1885. Ebbinghaus was engrossed in finding out how much verbal material that was well learned would be saved by his own memory over a period of time. He served as his own subject. The number of trials required to relearn a list, compared to the time to learn either a new list or the list when it was first acquired, provided a measure of the saving in learning. This experimental method has rarely been used since his time.

In 1890, William James, an American, included a chapter on memory in his renowned book on psychology. Frederic C. Bartlett, in 1932, began a tradition of studying how memories change over time. After Bartlett's time, the primary experimental strategy became to have subjects learn lists of items, such as nonsense syllables, nouns, or adjectives. The concentration on list learning comes from the early theoretical background, which assumed that memory was built from associations. Behaviorists, such as B. F. Skinner, elaborated on memory as one of many parameters involved in learning; they treated the learning process as the association of responses to stimuli. Repeated exposure to stimuli and responses could strengthen the association between them; forgetting was thought to be a weakened association.

Since the advent of the information-processing approach in psychology in the 1960s, a large number of theories and models of memory have been proposed, including the dual-process theory, the levels-of-processing theory, the neurobiological two-phase model, and the neurobiological four-phase model. The experiments that have been conducted on memory have emerged from these unique theoretical approaches. No matter what the theoretical approach, a constant problem facing the psychologist who studies memory is the need to conduct tests using situations that are similar enough to daily life so that the results can be generalized beyond the laboratory, while allowing enough control to be maintained so that scoring can accurately show the effect of the experimental variables.

BIBLIOGRAPHY

Alloway, Tracy Packiam, and Ross Alloway. *Working Memory: The Connected Intelligence.* New York: Psychology Press, 2013. Print.

Baddeley, Alan D. *Human Memory: Theory and Practice.* Rev. ed. Hove: Psychology Press, 2005. Print.

Cowan, Nelson. *Attention and Memory: An Integrated Framework.* New York: Oxford UP, 1998. Print.

Fernyhough, Charles. *Pieces of Light: How the New Science of Memory Illuminates Stories We Tell About Our Pasts.* New York: Harper, 2013. Print.

Klingberg, Torkel. *The Learning Brain: Memory and Brain Development in Children.* New York: Oxford UP, 2013. Print.

Lachman, Roy, Janet L. Lachman, and Earl C. Butterfield. *Cognitive Psychology and Information Processing: An Introduction.* Hillsdale: Erlbaum, 1979. Print.

Neath, Ian. *Human Memory: An Introduction to Research, Data, and Theory.* Belmont: Wadsworth, 2006. Print.

Tulving, Endel, and Fergus I. M. Craik, eds. *The Oxford Handbook of Memory.* New York: Oxford UP, 2005. Print.

Deborah R. McDonald

SEE ALSO: Artificial intelligence; Brain structure; Concept formation; Ebbinghaus, Hermann; Elders' mental health; Encoding; Forgetting and forgetfulness; James, William; Kinesthetic memory; Longterm memory; Memory; Memory: Animal research; Memory: Physiology; Memory: Sensory; Memory storage; Short-term memory.

Memory
Enhancement

TYPE OF PSYCHOLOGY: Clinical; Cognitive; Counseling; Developmental; Neuropsychological

Memory enhancement may be defined as the improvement of retrieval from long-term memory through the use of either external or internal memory strategies. External strategies place a cue in the physical environment to prompt memory, and include such practical techniques as using a day planner, placing ones briefcase by the door, or setting a timer. In contrast, internal memory strategies are systematic mental techniques that aid memory by re-coding and storing information in a more memorable way. These include mnemonic techniques such as first-letter mnemonics, the keyword method, the face-name mnemonic, the pegword method, and the method of loci.

KEY CONCEPTS

- Face-name mnemonic
- Letter-based mnemoni
- Keyword method
- Long-term memory
- Method of loci
- Mnemonic strategies
- Pegword method

INTRODUCTION

Before introducing specific strategies for enhancing memory, it is important to differentiate two types of memory. In their classic "box model" of information processing, Atkinson and Shiffrin (1968) described several components, including short-term and long-term memory. Short–term memory refers to what the individual is currently thinking about. It is temporary in nature, and information is held in this "box" only briefly unless it is rehearsed. Contemporary memory theorists frequently use the term "working memory" as a replacement for the short-term designation. Rehearsal in short-term memory (essentially, one's consciousness) can take two forms: maintenance rehearsal (e.g., mentally saying something over and over to ourselves) or elaborative rehearsal (e.g., connecting new information to prior knowledge, perhaps by using a mnemonic strategy). Both maintenance and elaborative rehearsal can help transfer information from short-term memory into more permanent, long-term memory.

Individuals who complain of losing their train of thought mid-sentence, or of forgetting what they were seeking after walking into a closet, are referring to problems with their "here and now" short-term memory. In contrast, when someone complains that they cannot remember a former classmate's name, or what they did last weekend (or last night, for that matter), they are referring to problems with retrieval from long-term memory.

Retrieval from long-term memory (i.e., remembering) can be enhanced by the use of either external or internal, mental strategies. Again, external strategies place a cue of some sort in the physical environment to prompt memory. On the other hand, internal memory strategies are elaborative, cognitive techniques that facilitate storage and retrieval of information from long-term memory.

EXTERNAL MEMORY AIDS

In today's world, external memory strategies abound. Beyond time-worn, practical techniques such as making a list or using a pill box with designated days of the week, electronic devices such as computers or smart phones can serve to cue us to do things at certain times -- and perhaps obviate the need for memorizing some information because the answer is literally at our fingertips by way of an internet search engine, such as Google. Today, GPS (Global Positioning System) devices direct us to locations so that we may not need to remember directions (or use a paper copy of a map). Yet, at times, we still need to remember things without relying on physical cuing systems. In this regard, internal memory strategies can be used to enhance memory.

INTERNAL MEMORY STRATEGIES

One way to move information from short-term memory (our consciousness) to long-term memory is to use simple rote rehearsal. For example, mentally saying something over and over to oneself can be a useful memory strategy. Further, retrieval practice, such as testing oneself with flash cards, has been found to improve memory.

Another way to store information effectively in long-term memory is to do something extra with the information, such as applying a mnemonic strategy. Mnemonics are systematic mental techniques that recode and store information in a way that aids retrieval. Worthen and Hunt (2011) list four basic processes that underlie effective mnemonic strategies: elaboration, organization, distinctiveness, and mental imagery. Thus, mnemonic techniques may help make information more memorable by: (a) elaborating upon it, (b) systematically organizing the to-be-remembered information, (c) making the information more distinctive, and (d) using mental imagery to connect otherwise unrelated information. Several of the more well-known mnemonic strategies are now described.

LETTER-BASED MNEMONICS

Acronyms, and other letter-based mnemonics, are probably the most widely used type of mnemonic strategy. For example, a student of first aid may learn the acronym "RICE" to help cue the four steps in treating a fracture: rest, immobilize, cold, and elevate. Or, a student in a science class may learn "ROY G. BIV" in order to re-member the colors of the spectrum in order: red, orange, yellow, blue, indigo and violet. And, the strategy can take the form of a rhyming sentence, such as in learning "On old Olympus' towering tops, a Finn and a German viewed some hops" to cue memory for the 12 cranial nerves in order (e.g., olfactory, optic, oculomotor, trochlear, trigeminal, etc.). In the latter two, the letter-based mnemonics cue not only the particular words, but also convey their fixed orders. However, although popular with students, individual letters are sometimes rather weak prompts for the to-be-remembered words. And, as illustrated with the cranial nerves, there is the problem of having multiple names starting with the same letter (e.g., the initial three "o's").

THE KEYWORD METHOD

Among mnemonic strategies, the keyword method has received the most attention from researchers -- and for good reason. This versatile strategy can be applied whenever one wishes to improve paired-associate verbal learning (e.g., learning a foreign word and its meaning, or a part of the brain and it's function). For example, say that one wanted to remember that the part of the brain called Broca's Area is involved in the production of speech. First, the unfamiliar name "Broca" is recoded as more familiar keyword that resembles it, such as "broken." Second, the keyword is interacted with "production of speech" by way of an interactive mental image. For example, one might "imagine that a talking doll is broken, so that it cannot talk." Having interacted with the material in this manner, upon seeing the name "Broca's Area," retrieval proceeds as follows: "Broca" > "broken" > mental image involving the talking doll > talking (or the production of speech).

Further, using what is termed a "dual-keyword" approach, one can associate two unfamiliar names or terms. For example, to associate states and their capitals, consider Kansas, whose capital is Topeka. Keywords for Kansas and Topeka are then selected, such as can (for Kansas) and top (for Topeka). Then, one can combine the two by way of an interactive mental image, such as "a tin can (Kansas) with a top (Topeka) spinning on top of it." Further, encoding the information by way of interactive imagery yields good associative symmetry. That is, retrieval works well in either direction. For example, the retrieval path may proceed as follows: Kansas > "can" > mental image of can with top spinning on it > "top" > Topeka. Or, retrieval may proceed as follows: Topeka

> "top" > mental image of can with top spinning on it > "can" > Kansas.

THE FACE-NAME MNEMONIC

Many of us find remembering people's names (when prompted by their faces) to be difficult. For this task, memory improvement books often recommend the face-name mnemonic (e.g., Higbee, 1993). As with the keyword method, the face-name mnemonic first involves recoding the person's name as a keyword (or name clue). Second, the strategy requires the identification of a prominent feature of the person. Finally, the name clue is connected with the prominent feature by way of an interactive mental image. For example, consider the actress Julianne Moore who is known for her striking red hair. First, her name "Julianne" can be recoded as a keyword or name clue, such as "jewels." Then, "jewels" are tied to her prominent red hair by way of an interactive mental image. For example, one might "imagine her beautiful red hair covered with sparkling jewels (Julianne)." Then, upon seeing her, remembering proceeds as follows: beautiful red hair > mental image of her red hair covered with sparkling jewels > jewels > Julianne. One can use the technique to remember first or last names, as desired.

THE PEGWORD METHOD

Like the first-letter mnemonics described earlier, the pegword method is a mnemonic strategy that enhances memory for an ordered list of items. It involves first learning an easily-memorized list of concrete pegwords that rhyme with numbers, and is often presented as follows: one is a bun, two is a shoe, three is a tree, four is a door, five is a hive, and so forth. Once the list of number-cued pegwords is memorized, the next step is to interact each to-be-remembered item with its corresponding pegword. For example, consider a back-to-school shopping list that includes pencils, paper, crayons, scissors, and glue. One then forms a mental image of each item interacting with a pegword. For example, you might imagine (a) a hamburger bun skewered with sharpened pencils, (b) a shoe stuffed with paper, (c) a tree with lots of colorful crayons hanging from its branches, (d) prying open a door with a pair of scissors, and (e) pouring glue down a bee hive. Once the items have been encoded in this fashion, one simply goes down the list of numbers to cue each of the desired items. For example, one > bun > image of bun skewered with pencils > pencils; then two > shoe > image of shoe stuffed with paper > paper, and so

forth. Although the order of this particular list may not be important, there are situations where remembering things in order is important – and this strategy preserves that order.

THE METHOD OF LOCI

The method of loci is a technique that traces its origin to ancient Greece ("loci" means "places" in Latin). Like first-letter mnemonics and the pegword method, the method of loci is designed to store and enhance retrieval of a list of items in a fixed order. First, a well-known set of locations are identified such as one might consecutively pass on a walk in some location (e.g., a park, through one's home, etc.). For example, perhaps a walk through a local park passes a gate, a bench, a bird bath, and so forth. Second, the to-be-remembered items are "placed" in these locations – optimally by way of interactive mental images. Using the same back-to-school list as above, we might imagine: the gate closing on and breaking a pencil, the bench covered with paper, a bird bath filled with loose, colorful crayons, and so forth. Having stored the items in these locations, we then retrieve them by taking a mental walk down that familiar path or route. Each location serves to prompt the interactive mental image, and the image cues the desired item.

BIBLIOGRAPHY

Henner, M., & Henner, L. (2012). *Total Memory Makeover: Uncover Your Past, Take Charge Of Your Future*. New York: Gallery Books. Memory advice based on the experience of Marilu Henner, an actress with an extremely rare ability called "superior autobiographical memory."

Higbee, K. L. (1993). *Your Memory: How It Works and How to Improve It* (3rd ed.). New York: Prentice-Hall. Professor Higbee's book is one of the best on the topic.

Levin, J. R. (2015). *Mnemonic Strategies and Techniques: Components of Mnemonic Techniques, Varieties and Uses of Mnemonic Techniques, Educational Applications of Mnemonic Techniques*. An excellent explanation of mnemonic strategies by Professor Levin, who has conducted extensive research in this area. His article is available online at: http://education.stateuniversity.com/pages/2241/Mnemonic-Strategies-Techniques.html

Lorayne, H., & Lucas, J. (1974). *The Memory Book*. New York: Ballantine. Written by professional mnemonist Harry Lorayne and former basketball player Jerry Lucas, it remains a classic on the topic of memory improvement.

McPherson, F. (2000). *The Memory Key: Unlock the Secrets to Remembering.* New York: Barnes and Noble. A practical book on memory improvement .

Worthen, J. B., & Hunt, R. R. (2011) *Mnemonology: Mnemonics for the 21st Century.* New York: Psychology Press. A scholarly, yet readable, explanation of mnemonic strategies within the broader context of memory processes.

Russell N. Carney

SEE ALSO: Healthy diet; Hippocampus; Meditation; Nootropics; Sleep health; Temporal lobe.

Memory
Physiology

TYPE OF PSYCHOLOGY: Biological bases of behavior

In the early 1990s, scientists developed a better understanding of the molecular basis of memory. Specific genes conserved through evolution allowed for analysis at the level of the gene in determining which proteins are involved in memory formation. Application of this information has resulted in better means of detection of memory dysfunction, as well as improved treatments.

KEY CONCEPTS
- Consolidation
- Dendrite
- Electroencephalography
- Evoked potential
- Hippocampus
- Lesion
- Neuron
- Neurotransmitter
- Synapse

INTRODUCTION
Investigations of the biological basis of memory have proceeded simultaneously at many different levels: individual neurons and synapses, systems of neurons, whole brains, and whole behaving organisms. Isolated cells, slabs of brain tissue, live invertebrates (such as sea slugs), nonhuman vertebrates (often rats), and even awake human patients have been studied. Several strategies have been used to reveal the location of and mechanisms underlying the engram, or memory trace. In one approach, after an animal subject has learned a task very well, lesions are made in specific regions of the brain. If only memory of the task is impaired, the damaged structure is implicated in the memory process.

Trauma, stroke, disease, and even deliberate surgery may produce "natural" lesions in human patients. Resultant amnesia, or memory loss, can be correlated with the damaged structures using magnetic resonance imaging (MRI), positron emission tomography (PET), computed tomography (CT), and other scanning techniques, and with behavioral performance on standardized psychological and neuropsychological tests.

Another approach is to record changes in the nervous system that occur at the same time as a memory process. If such changes occur only when memory is formed, then they may play a role in the process. Such functional changes in the human (and animal) brain may be seen using single-cell or multicell electrophysiology, electroencephalography, and evoked-potential electrical recording techniques. Researchers have studied memory formation by looking at the chemical composition of the brain (for example, neurotransmitters and protein synthesis).

Finally, various techniques may be used to disrupt the memory formation (consolidation) process shortly before or after a subject has learned a task (that is, started to develop permanent memories). Successful disruption may point to the underlying nature of the process. For example, formation of permanent memories can be prevented by giving direct electrical stimulation to the amygdala (a specific brain area associated with emotion and motivation) or enhanced by stimulation of the reticular formation (associated with alertness and waking), suggesting different roles for these areas.

Neuropsychology, a specialty combining clinical neurology and behavioral analysis, has used both "natural" and experimental lesion techniques to explore memory processes. According to some researchers, for the purposes of neuropsychological analysis, memory should be divided into two categories: declarative and procedural. Declarative memories are facts that one can consciously recollect, while procedural memories are skills or operations that one does not have to think about consciously and that are not linked to a particular time or place. Brain damage does not usually impair procedural knowledge. Global permanent anterograde amnesia (inability to form new permanent memories) and temporary retrograde amnesia(inability to remember past events) for declarative knowledge, however, have been correlated consistently with bilateral (left and right side) lesions of both cortical (the highest and most newly evolved) and subcortical (the lower and older) regions of the brain. Memory problems of chronic alcoholics (Wernicke-Korsakoff syndrome), demented patients (Alzheimer's disease), and patients with some strokes and aneurysms have all been associated with damage to these areas.

Deficits in long-term memory produced by temporal cortex lesions (lesions of the lateral brain area) depend on the type of material that is presented: Left lesions interfere with verbal material, while right lesions interfere with nonverbal material. It does not matter by what sensory modality the material was presented or what modality was used to test for its retention. By contrast, lesions of the frontal cortex (the largest and most forward brain area) interfere with only certain components of memory: memory for the order of things and events, short-term memory for the location of things in space, normal resistance to distraction during learning, and the ability to learn new material without being confused by old material. Unusual and discrete types of amnesia can result from damage to other specific cortical areas, such as the parietal, posterior temporal, and occipital lobes. For example, people may be unable to remember and recognize colors, faces, the names of objects, or the location of an object in the environment.

In contrast to this whole-brain approach, neurobiological investigations have focused on short-, intermediate-, and long-term cellular memory mechanisms. The sensory memory, the shortest memory, persists for about 0.5 second and depends on the activity of reverberating circuits. These circuits are loops of interconnected neurons arranged so that stimulating one will activate each successive one, including, eventually, the first one again. The net effect of this arrangement is that the entire loop stays active—and the memory trace of the initial stimulation persists—long after the initial stimulation has ended.

Other, more enduring memories, lasting from days to years, are thought to reside in synaptic (neuron-to-neuron) connections and to result from neuronal plasticity—the creation of new synaptic connections or increased capacity or efficiency of old ones. Many mechanisms for this have been proposed. One possibility is that learning causes neurons to sprout new terminals and make new connections directly (this is termed synaptic turnover or reactive synaptogenesis). Another possibility is that learning liberates blocked connections, which can then respond to incoming signals (the Calpain-Fodrin

theory). Dendritic branching may also be important. If memories are stored in synaptic connections, brains with thickly branched dendrites could store more memories than those with thinly branched dendrites. It is known, for example, that brains of healthy elderly people have more dendritic branches than brains of younger people or of adults with some types of memory disorders. Moreover, animals raised in stimulating learning environments develop more branches and a greater brain mass than do less stimulated control animals. Learning-induced changes in the shape of dendrites may also promote memory: Stubby ones transmit information more readily than long, thin ones.

Among the most important proponents of animal models in the elucidation of the physiological basis for memory has been Eric Kandel. Kandel, a professor at Columbia University in New York, was awarded the Nobel Prize in Physiology or Medicine in 2000 for his discoveries in the molecular basis for memory. Kandel has carried out much of his work studying the nervous system in the sea slug *Aplysia*. This organism contains relatively few nerve cells (approximately twenty thousand); its neural circuitry is simple by comparison with more evolved organisms such as human beings (containing approximately one trillion nerve cells), and thus it serves as an ideal laboratory animal in the study of memory. Behavioral changes in the animal may involve fewer than one hundred nerve cells.

Kandel tested various forms of stimuli on the organism and observed changes in the responding gill withdrawal reflex as the basis for "memory." Since the reflex would remain for various periods of time, it represented a primitive form of memory. An amplification of the synapses connecting sensory nerve cells to motor neurons could be detected as a molecular response to stimuli and represented memory development.

If the stimulus was weak, a form of "short-term memory" would develop. In this case, the reflex lasted only a short period of time. If the stimulus was stronger, "memory" would last for weeks. At the molecular level, the basis for memory was found to be the relative levels of neurotransmitters that would be released at the synapses. Short-term memory was represented by calcium, which originated from specific ion channels, with resultant release of higher levels of neurotransmitters at the synapses. Kandel found phosphates were joined to certain channel proteins, resulting in amplification of the response.

Formation of long-term memory had an analogous mechanism utilizing phosphorylation reactions. The concentration of an enzyme, protein kinase A (PKA), also involved in phosphorylation of protein targets, was increased in neurons following higher levels of stimuli.

Activity of this enzyme was related to formation of a second molecule within the cell, cyclic adenosine monophosphate (cAMP). The result of increasing the activity of PKA and cAMP was to stimulate the cell to increase levels of proteins in the synapse, with the effect of increasing function of that synapse. Another key protein activated by cAMP was called the cAMP response element binding protein (CREB). If synthesis of new proteins was blocked using drugs, no long-term memory would result. Kandel summarized his work in the statement that all memory is "located in the synapse."

ROLE OF NEUROTRANSMITTERS

The brain and body produce a number of substances that have the ability to modify memory in everyday life.

Catecholamines, brain neurotransmitters released during emotional states, seem to facilitate memory storage, and damage to brain structures that secrete catecholamines impairs memory. Stress-produced hormones from the pituitary and adrenal glands can also alter memory formation. Even the endorphins, the body's own morphinelike substances released during stress and involved in pain reduction, may play a modulatory role. Drugs can also influence memory function by altering nervous system activity. For example, stimulants of the central nervous system, such as amphetamine, can enhance memory formation, while depressants of the system, such as barbiturates and morphine, can interfere with it.

Kandel believes that the neurotransmitter serotonin is particularly important in regulating activity of both cAMP and PKA, thereby playing a critical role in memory. Addition of serotonin resulted in an increase in excitability of the synapses, similar to that of adding cAMP directly. Serotonin itself was found to cause an increase in cAMP levels.

The same neurotransmitter, serotonin, was found to be involved in development of both short-term and long-term memory. When a synapse is activated by serotonin, a signal results that activates cAMP and the CREB protein. Newly synthesized proteins move to the terminals of the cells. Only those synapses bound by serotonin undergo development and growth.

The different forms of memory are the result of different forms of stimuli. Short-term memory results from a synapse-specific increase in the level of neurotransmitter. Preexisting proteins are modified (phosphorylated), and synaptic connections involve a relatively small number of neurons. In contrast, long-term memory results from activation of a protein pathway and requires new protein synthesis. In addition, significantly more connections are formed with other nerve synapses.

UNDERSTANDING MEMORY LOSS

Sometimes an anecdotal observation leads to new understanding of human behavior. Schizophrenia is a severe mental illness, characterized by thought disorder and incoherent speech, that has been extremely resistant to cure and treatment. By chance, the Italian psychiatrist Ugo Cerletti, practicing in the late 1930s, observed that electric shock applied to the heads of pigs in the local slaughterhouse made the pigs easier to manage. This inspired him to apply a small voltage to the temples of one of his schizophrenic patients in the hope that improvement would result. Nothing appeared to change, so he announced his intention to increase the voltage. At this point, to Cerletti's amazement, the patient protested loudly and with perfectly coherent speech. Encouraged by this improvement, Cerletti gave another shock. This time, unfortunately, the patient became unconscious because of a massive brain seizure and, on awakening, experienced retrograde amnesia—he was unable to recall what had happened to him in the recent and sometimes distant past.

Following this, shock treatment, or electroconvulsive therapy (ECT), became quite popular for treating schizophrenia and was tried for every sort of mental illness. It became clear over the years, however, that only patients with mood disorders (particularly certain severely depressed patients) showed consistent benefits. In suicidal patients, ECT became the life-saving treatment of choice.

Transient and even permanent memory loss associated with ECT was largely ignored by clinicians, but this amnesiac effect became the focus of experimental research with animals. In a typical experiment, rats were trained on a simple learning task. Electroconvulsive shock—electrical shock to the brain—was given either immediately or at various intervals after training. Memory for the task was then tested a day or so later. Memory was poorest if the shocks were given right after training. This observation led to the conclusion that memory does not form instantaneously but takes time to "consolidate," a major development in memory research. Further investigation determined that, in animals, the body convulsions produced by the shocks were not themselves responsible for the retrograde amnesiac effects. Moreover, a variety of brain structures were found to produce amnesia without seizures. Indeed, stimulation of one structure (the hippocampus) disturbed long-term memory, while stimulation of another (the reticular formation) interfered with short-term memory, indicating different roles for each in the memory process.

This consolidation-disruption research strategy has become one of the major approaches used by memory investigators. Experimental work such as this has also led to improvements in ECT: Shocks are given to a smaller brain region; voltages are lower and better controlled (although seizures are still produced); muscle relaxants and sedatives are administered to avoid the hazards of convulsions; drugs are given to minimize heart-rate and blood-pressure changes; and oxygen is given to lessen memory loss.

The interplay between clinical and experimental work is also seen in research on Alzheimer's disease, a slowly debilitating and life-threatening disease that affects 6 percent of the adult population. Once thought to be an inevitable consequence of aging, or senility, caused by multiple "ministrokes," it is now recognized as a distinct and specific disorder. It begins insidiously, with difficulties of concentration, followed by increasing troubles with problem solving, speaking, learning, and remembering. Patients become apathetic and disoriented; even the ability to recognize loved ones is eventually lost.

Much of psychology's meager understanding of the basis for the memory impairment associated with this disease has come from basic research with animals. For example, studies of patients and animals with lesions in the hippocampus suggested early that this was an important site for memory formation but not for permanent storage. The hippocampus also contains mechanisms for neural plasticity. This is significant because postmortem studies of Alzheimer's patients' brains have revealed a selective loss of cells going to the hippocampus and cells in the neocortex, the highest brain area. Many researchers believe that both the number and shape of dendrites and the growth of synaptic endings are important for memory formation. The number of dendrites is reduced in Alzheimer's patients. Moreover, even normal cells contain abnormal strands (neurofibrillary tangles) inside and tangled masses (neuritic plaques) outside the nerve cells.

Basic animal research has also shown that acetylcholine, an important brain neurotransmitter, plays an important modulatory role in memory. Drugs that interfere with acetylcholine function can produce some symptoms of dementia (cognitive impairment, including memory deficits) in normal human subjects. Moreover, if acetylcholine neurons are transplanted from fetal (still-developing) rat brains to the brains of old rats, the old rats regain some of their youthful ability to learn and remember. In view of these findings, it is significant that both acetylcholine and the enzyme needed to make it (choline acetyltransferase) are reduced in Alzheimer's patients. Indeed, the greater the reduction, the worse the patient's symptoms. This observation, coupled with results from animal studies, has encouraged clinicians to treat the memory and other cognitive problems of Alzheimer's patients with drugs that enhance acetylcholine function—so far, however, with limited success.

RESEARCH AND MEMORY

During the 1880s, the fact that learning, memory, and forgetting operate according to laws was revealed by Hermann Ebbinghaus's laboratory investigations in *Über das Gedächtnis* (1885; *Memory*, 1913). Human amnesia and its implications for memory organization were chronicled by Theodule-Armand Ribot in *Les Maladies de la mémoire* (1881; *The Diseases of Memory*, 1883). Sergei Korsakoff first documented alcohol-induced amnesia (Korsakoff syndrome), and the psychologist William James, in his classic work *The Principles of Psychology* (1890), distinguished primary and secondary memory, key concepts in the search for the engram, or memory trace.

The search for a mechanism began in earnest in the 1930s with the systematic experimental animal (as opposed to purely clinical and correlational) studies in the neuropsychology laboratory of Karl Lashley. Using lesions, he attempted to localize memory in particular brain structures, but he failed. This led him to conclude that the brain is equipotential: that the memory engram is distributed throughout the brain or is at least distributed equally throughout functional subunits of the brain.

Donald O. Hebb, who proposed the notion of reverberating circuits in the 1940s, was one in a long line of researchers who, in opposition to Lashley, believed that memory would be found in specific neural circuits. The role of the middle temporal cortex, in particular, was inadvertently revealed by William Scoville in the 1950s. In an effort to eradicate epileptic seizures in his now-famous patient H. M., he performed a bilateral temporal lobe resection. This resulted in permanent anterograde amnesia. Some researchers now propose that both distributed and localized accounts of memory are valid. That is, memory, in the general sense, may be distributed widely throughout the brain, but different areas may store different components of memory. The anatomical details of this theory remain to be worked out.

Rapid advances in computer-based neural network techniques seem to hold particular promise for yielding useful models of how memory works. Data from basic research on cellular memory mechanisms are translated into mathematical formulations. These in turn are transformed into computer programs that simulate or mimic the observed function of selected subsets of neural nets. Comparing the behavior of computer-simulated nets to actual nets permits refinement of the hypothesized mechanisms. Ideas emerging from this work—for example, the notion of parallel distributed processing (PDP)—will provide work for neurobiologists for years to come.

The possible role played by memory suppressor genes is among the newest areas of research into the regulation of memory. Most prior research centered on positive control of memory formation at the molecular level—the activation of genes for formation of neural circuits and resultant memory. Kandel has also found evidence for a negative control, using the products of memory suppressor genes. Products of these genes inhibit development of the synapse and prevent memory formation.

If indeed such regulation exists, pharmacological agents targeted at suppressor proteins might serve to increase development of memory. This would provide additional targets for reversal, or at least slowing, of the memory loss associated with neurodegenerative illnesses such as Alzheimer's disease.

BIBLIOGRAPHY

Abel, Ted, Kelsey Martin, Dusan Bartsch, and Eric Kandel. "Memory Suppressor Genes: Inhibitory Constraints on the Storage of Long-Term Memory." *Science* 279 (1998): 338–41. Print.

Allman, William F. *Apprentices of Wonder: Inside the Neural Network Revolution.* New York: Bantam, 1990. Print.

Carlson, Neil R. *Foundations of Physiological Psychology.* 7th ed. Boston: Allyn, 2008. Print.

Eichenbaum, Howard, and Neal Cohen. *From Conditioning to Conscious Recollection: Memory Systems and the Brain.* New York: Oxford UP, 2004.
Print.

Kandel, Eric. "The Molecular Biology of Memory Storage: A Dialogue between Genes and Synapses." *Science* 294.5544 (2001): 1030–38. Print.

Radvansky, Gabriel A. *Human Memory.* 2nd ed. Boston: Allyn, 2011. Print.

Sweatt, J. David. *Mechanisms of Memory.* 2nd ed. Boston: Elsevier, 2010. Print.

Taylor, Annette Kujawski, ed. *Encyclopedia of Human Memory.* Santa Barbara: Greenwood, 2013. Print.

Nancy Oley; updated by Richard Adler

SEE ALSO: Aging: Cognitive changes; Alzheimer's disease; Brain structure; Dementia; Ebbinghaus, Hermann; Elders' mental health; Memory: Animal research; Neuropsychology; Parkinson's disease; Shock therapy; Synaptic transmission.

Memory
Sensory

TYPE OF PSYCHOLOGY: Memory; Sensation and perception

Sensory memory captures information acquired through the senses and retains it for a brief time. This allows the important information to be selected and processed further by other memory systems.

KEY CONCEPTS

- Echoic memory
- Iconic memory
- Information-processing model
- Informational persistence
- Long-term memory
- Memory decay
- Partial-report technique
- Short-term memory
- Visible persistence
- Whole-report technique
- Word superiority effect

INTRODUCTION

Human senses—such as sight, smell, touch, and hearing—pick up information about the surrounding physical world. Once this information is received, it must be converted by the senses into a code that is transmitted to the brain and eventually interpreted. Sensory memory plays a critical role in this process of transforming the outside world into an inner psychological experience. The sensory-memory system stores information acquired through the senses for a brief time to allow other memory systems to screen and select which parts of the message will be kept for further processing. Depending on the particular sense modality, the duration that items can be held ranges from 0.25 to 2 seconds. Thus, one primary characteristic of this system is that its retention is very brief.

One important question concerns how much information can fit into sensory memory. Sensory memory has a larger capacity than short-term memory, which can hold five to nine bits of information, but a smaller capacity than long-term memory, which is limitless. A third, and somewhat controversial characteristic, of sensory memory is that the information it holds is believed to be "precategorical." That is, the information has not been significantly altered, categorized, or processed but is believed to be represented in a form that is nearly identical to its original copy. However, research by Phil Merikle published in 1980 weakened this third distinction of sensory memory from other memory systems.

Merikle performed one experiment in which he demonstrated that subjects could pick out a group of letters from any array of letters and numbers that were held in sensory memory. Merikle's research provided evidence that information in sensory memory is susceptible to at least some processing. This assumes that the test stimuli were held in sensory memory and never transferred into short-term memory. If the information had been transferred, this second memory system could have been responsible for the ability to select out a group of letters from a group of letters and numbers.

Each sense modality is believed to have its own distinct sensory memory with its own unique characteristics. Much more is known about visual and auditory sensory memory than any of the other senses, simply because the vast majority of research has focused on these two systems. Ulric Neisser coined the terms " iconic memory" and " echoic memory" to refer to these separate systems.

ICONIC MEMORY

Much of what is known about iconic memory has come from an experimental procedure originally used by George Sperling in 1959. He wanted to find out how much information could be seen during a rapid, brief exposure of stimuli. To answer this question he presented subjects, using specialized equipment, with a matrix of

twelve letters (four letters placed in three rows) for the duration of 50 milliseconds (0.05 seconds). After asking the subjects to recall as many of the letters as they could, Sperling found that, on average, they named about four items. More important, he noticed that his subjects insisted that they had seen more than four items but had forgotten the others. Sperling concluded that perhaps more of the letters were originally seen but the subjects held them for such a brief time that some of the items were lost through memory decay as the subjects called out the letters.

To explore this possibility further, Sperling altered his experimental procedure. Rather than have subjects call out items from anywhere within the matrix of letters—called the whole-report technique—he presented the test subjects with a tone signal that immediately followed the presentation of letters. He used the tone to cue the subjects to call out only items from one row of the matrix. For example, a high tone would signal that the top row should be recalled. Using this partial-report technique, Sperling found that the subjects recalled three to four letters, despite the fact that they did not know in advance which row they would be asked to report. This level of performance was nearly identical to the previously used whole-report technique and led Sperling to infer that the subjects saw approximately nine items. He based this conclusion on the fact that three items were recalled from a row that was not determined until after the display was shown. Since it did not matter which row was signaled for recall, Sperling found that, on average, three letters were seen from each of the three rows. Subjects did not call out all nine letters because of the short duration of the memory trace.

Sperling's research provided empirical support for the existence of a brief sensory register. Not only did he find the capacity of sensory memory, but also, by delaying the presentation of the tone during the partial-report technique, he learned about its duration. He found that information in sensory iconic memory lasted only about 250 milliseconds (0.25 seconds). Sperling published his findings in the 1960 *Psychological Monographs* article, "The Information Available in Brief Visual Presentations."

By the late twentieth century, many researchers referred to iconic memory as visual sensory memory and established two types of its persisting visual information, known as visible persistence and informational persistence. In visible persistence, neurons and photoreceptors influence how images briefly remain then fade, somewhat like what a person sees when a flashbulb illuminates a dark room. In contrast, informational persistence refers to information that remains available and does not fade after stimuli occur. The partial-report method developed by Sperling relies on this type of visual sensory memory, which researchers further differentiate into two types according to information decay, organization, and categorical factors.

ECHOIC MEMORY AND OTHER SENSES

Echoic memory has been ingeniously studied using a similar method as iconic memory tests. Subjects are aurally presented with different letter combinations simultaneously to the right ear, left ear, and both ears (for a total of nine items) using special headphones. Subjects then receive visual cues to recall only the items presented to one ear. When this partial-report technique was compared to the whole-report method, the results paralleled what was found with iconic memory. Subjects recalled more items using the partial-report technique, which indicated an echoic memory was present. Most believe that the duration of echoic memory is considerably longer than iconic memory, somewhere between 2 and 3 seconds.

By the early twenty-first century, researchers concentrated on specific auditory sensory memory investigations. Elisabeth Glass, Steffi Sachse, and Waldemar von Suchodoletz emphasized the importance of young children's ability to store auditory information in short-term memory for cognitive development associated with learning and language problems. In 2005, French scientists Julien Besle, Alexandra Fort, and Marie-Hélène Giard published findings in *Experimental Brain Research,* hypothesizing that auditory sensory memory sometimes interacts with visual information. A 2006 *Journal of Cognitive Neuroscience* article addressed timbre and auditory sensory memory.

Researchers also investigated the role of touch in sensory memory. Some experiments that tested subjects with tactile stimuli resembled those conducted for iconic and echoic memory. Displays contained from one to six stimuli that were touched simultaneously against subjects' arms or legs, and subjects stated how many stimuli they felt or commented about stimuli positions on the display. Textures of food and drink influence memory more than tastes. In tests, participants fasted prior to eating a breakfast consisting of yogurt, biscuits, and a drink. By nighttime, they were presented those same food types but prepared in five different textures, to test their memory to remember which version they had consumed.

Subjects did not recall foods because they liked their taste but because the foods were creamy or crispy.

The role of smell in sensory memory has received less attention than other senses from researchers. Frank R. Schab and Robert G. Crowder edited *Memory for Odors* (1995), the first monograph focusing on that subject. They criticized much of the existing olfactory memory research as too narrow and for not incorporating sufficient memory theory. Schab and Crowder urged scientists to consider how odors were stimuli to store and retrieve memories and to differentiate how smell varied from other sensory-memory types. A 2006 *Neural Computation* article reported scientists' observations of neurons in honeybees' brains when antennal lobes, similar to olfactory bulbs in vertebrates, were exposed to odor stimuli. The study attempted to comprehend how olfactory sensory memory functioned.

An important issue that has received some attention concerns the reasons why sensory memory is necessary. In 1989, Margaret Matlin pointed out that humans live in a world in which their senses are overwhelmed with stimulation that can change in an instant. A memory system that can rapidly absorb information from this abundance of varied sensory stimuli, and retain it for even a brief time, allows subsequent memory systems to perform more in-depth analyses. In this way, information deemed to be unimportant can be discarded, while information regarded as important can advance to the next processing stage, short-term memory.

USES OF SENSORY MEMORY

ensory memory plays an integral role in a variety of psychological processes. For example, someone who has just returned from Europe might show a friend some of the pictures she has taken. One of these pictures shows her in Rome standing next to a large piece of stone called Trajan's column. The process of pattern recognition gives the friend the ability to recognize her as well as the other objects in the picture. For this to occur, the visual system must receive information from the picture by attending to it; then, this information is temporarily stored in iconic memory. At this point, an interaction occurs between information held in sensory memory and memories of previous experience held in long-term memory. As mentioned earlier, information in iconic memory must be acted upon quickly or else it will be lost. Decision rules must be applied at this stage to determine which pieces of information are relevant and deserving of more complex processing. One way meaningful information can be identified occurs through a process of matching information stored in long-term memory with the contents of iconic memory. One friend can recognize the other in the picture because he "knows" what she looks like. Specifically, he has detected unique features, such as her eyes or the shape of her nose, that tell him for certain that the person in the picture is his friend. Pattern recognition does not end with identifying the friend, but extends to all the other objects in the picture. Although numerous theories have been put forth to explain pattern perception, a common component of many of these theories is the important role sensory memory plays.

In 1981, the notion of a sensory memory was used by Robert Solman and colleagues to explain the phenomenon of the word superiority effect: People who are briefly presented with a letter (T) and then asked to choose which letter they have just seen from a set of two letters (D, T) do not perform as well as when they are presented with a word (CART) and have to choose the correct word from a set (CARD, CART). Basically, subjects are better able to discriminate the letter T from D when it is embedded in a word. Solman and colleagues believe that one possible explanation for the word superiority effect is that words are stored longer than individual letters in sensory memory. Thus, the longer the words are retained in iconic memory, the more easily subjects can remember the correct response in a subsequent recall test.

Henry Ellis and Reed Hunt, in their book *Fundamentals of Human Memory and Cognition* (4th ed., 1989), describe how research into sensory memory can be used to help solve an important problem associated with a learning disability. They mention a particular reading problem called specific reading disability, which prevents children from reading normally. One unusual characteristic of this reading disorder is that in its early stages, no other intellectual abilities are affected. Once a child matures to the age of approximately twelve years, academic performance in other areas such as mathematics begins to deteriorate. It is not known what causes the specific reading disability.

Ellis and Hunt mention that some believed that children with the reading problem did not see the same perceptual images as normal readers. The perceptual deficit hypothesis theory assumes the root of this problem to be perceptual in nature. One unfortunate aspect of the perceptual deficit hypothesis was that it implied the problem was occurring at the most basic level of the visual system: the sense receptors. If this were true, then no amount of training, practice, or learning strategies could possibly help overcome the disability.

In 1977, Frederick Morrison and his colleagues performed an experiment using a group of sixth-graders to test this hypothesis. Half the children in the group were normal readers, while the other half was poor readers with reading disabilities. Morrison believed that if the problem were caused by a perceptual abnormality, it would become evident after looking at the precise nature of the information held in the sensory memory. By conducting an experiment similar to the one performed by Sperling, Morrison tested the contents of the perceptual stimuli in iconic memory for both the normal and poor readers to find out if they differed.

Morrison found that good readers and poor readers performed equally well on a recognition task for information in sensory memory. This finding was contrary to the prediction made by the perceptual deficit hypothesis. Morrison found that good readers began to outperform poor readers only after the cue that started the recognition test was delayed by at least 300 milliseconds. This revealed that the problem that caused the reading disability was occurring at a higher level of information processing rather than at the sensory-memory stage.

INVESTIGATION HISTORY

The notion that humans possess a brief visual sensory storage was first proposed by Wilhelm Wundt as early as 1899. Although he did not have access to the sophisticated equipment needed to demonstrate experimentally the existence of this memory system, perhaps he saw evidence for it by making the following observation: If a hand-held candle is moved rapidly in a circular path in a darkened room, one can see what appears to be a brightly lit ring. Despite the fact that the flame of the candle does not occupy every position on this circle continuously, an illusion occurs whereby one can still "see" the flame after it has moved. This phenomenon occurs as a result of visual sensory memory. Possibly, Wundt proposed a brief visual register after seeing evidence for it with common, everyday examples such as this.

In 1958, Donald Broadbent proposed a theory of attention that incorporated the concept of a sensory register. The sensory register, as Broadbent saw it, was a temporary short-term store for information received by the senses. Information from different senses was transmitted on separate channels. A selective filter was believed to act on the information in the sensory store by conducting a rudimentary analysis of its contents to determine which information should be processed more thoroughly. The notion of a brief sensory store was an integral part of Broadbent's theory, as well as of other theories of attention which were developed later.

In 1960, when Sperling discussed his results, which provided empirical support for a sensory memory, the scientific community readily embraced them. By 1968, Richard Atkinson and Richard Shiffrin had incorporated sensory memory into their information-processing theory of memory. The Atkinson and Shiffrin theory evolved into one of the most significant and influential models of human memory devised to that time. Sensory memory, according to their model, was viewed as the first stage in a series of information-processing stages. Sensory memory captured and briefly held information while control processes determined which information would be transferred to short-term memory and eventually to long-term memory.

Although at times the concept of a sensory memory has been challenged, it continued to be a pivotal psychological construct for the understanding of many perceptual and learning processes. In the late twentieth century and early twenty-first century, psychologists initiated new sensory-memory research or returned to previous investigations (to determine if results retained credibility decades later), altered methods, or utilized advanced computerized and testing technologies. Despite scientific journals publishing these innovative sensory-memory findings, many textbooks presented outdated and inaccurate information which simplified sensory memory instead of discussing its complexities.

Sensory memory researchers explored and presented novel insights and suggested theories for future investigations. Many researchers sought to comprehend neural activity associated with sensory memory. Several experiments contemplated the effect of blinking on iconic memory. Referring to predecessors' efforts in this field, Mark W. Becker and University of California, San Diego Department of Psychology colleagues tested subjects' visual sensory memory in terms of noticing changes in arrays. The researchers reported in 2000 that that they had determined that a blank interstimulus interval (ISI) placed between the initial array viewed and an altered array lowered participants' detection of changes. If the ISI contained a cue identifying where the change occurred, more subjects noticed the change.

Laura E. Thomas and David E. Irwin, visual sensory-memory experts at the University of Illinois, also studied how blinking affected cognitive processes (2006). In a partial-report iconic-memory test, they displayed arrays with letters for subjects to view during specified durations measured by milliseconds. Thomas and Irwin eliminated other factors, such as lighting fluctuations, to determine blinking was the main impediment affecting how subjects' iconic memory functioned. They introduced the concept of cognitive blink suppression, referring to how blinking interfered with cognition. Thomas and Irwin acknowledged that neural disruptions and reduced area VI activity in brains might also disrupt iconic memory.

Christian Keysers and his colleagues studied neurophysiological aspects of iconic memory (2005). They arranged viewings of rapid serial visual presentation (RSVP) images, using ISI at lengths as long as 93 milliseconds in some RSVP tests and as short as zero in others. Test subjects included humans and macaque monkeys. During ISI, neurons in the temporal cortex of the subjects' brains kept responding to stimuli they experienced before ISI occurred despite the absence of stimuli in ISI. As a result, the researchers hypothesized that temporal cortex neurons were important to iconic memory.

In addition to iconic-memory studies, researchers considered other factors that might affect sensory memory, including aging, Huntington's and Alzheimer's diseases, genetics, alcoholism, and affect. Some investigators studied how blindness and deafness affected people's sensory memory. Researchers at the University of California, Irvine Center for the Neurobiology of Learning and Memory examined the relationship of stress hormones and memory. Subjects with post-traumatic stress disorder presented interesting research possibilities because sensory experiences associated with what people saw, heard, touched, or smelled when traumatized shaped their memories.

BIBLIOGRAPHY

Becker, Mark W., Harold Pashler, and Stuart M. Anstis. "The Role of Iconic Memory in Change-Detection Tasks." *Perception* 29 (2000): 273–286. Print.

Caclin, Anne, et al. "Separate Neural Processing of Timbre Dimensions in Auditory Sensory Memory." *Journal of Cognitive Neuroscience* 18.12 (2006): 1959–1972. Print.

Galán, Roberto F., et al. "Sensory Memory for Odors Is Encoded in Spontaneous Correlated Activity Between Olfactory Glomeruli." *Neural Computation* 18.1 (2006): 10–25. Print.

Gallace, Alberto, Hong Z. Tan, Patrick Haggard, and Charles Spence. "Short Term Memory for Tactile

Stimuli." *Brain Research* 1190 (2008): 132–142. Print.

Glass, Elisabeth, Steffi Sachse, and Waldemar von Suchodoletz. "Development of Auditory Sensory Memory from Two to Six Years: An MMN Study." *Journal of Neural Transmission* 115.8 (2008): 1435–1463. Print.

Keysers, Christian, Dengke K. Xiao, Peter Földiák, and David I. Perrett. "Out of Sight but Not Out of Mind: The Neurophysiology of Iconic Memory in the Superior Temporal Sulcus." *Cognitive Neuropsychology* 22.3/4 (2005): 316–332. Print.

Kuhbander, Christof, Stephanie Lichtenfeld, and Reinhard Pekrun. "Always Look on the Broad Side of Life: Happiness Increases the Breadth of Sensory Memory." *Emotion* 11.4 (2011): 958–964. Print.

Luck, Steven J., and Andrew Hollingsworth, eds. *Visual Memory.* New York: Oxford UP, 2008. Print.

Matlin, Margaret W. *Cognition.* 8th ed. Hoboken: Wiley, 2013. Print.

Mojet, Jos, and Egon Peter Köster. "Sensory Memory and Food Texture." *Food Quality and Preference* 16.3 (2005): 251–266. Print.

Spachtholz, Philipp, Christof Kuhbandner, and Reinhard Pekrun. "Negative Affect Improves the Quality of Memories: Trading Capacity for Precision in Sensory and Working Memory." *Journal of Experimental Psychology: General* (14 Apr. 2014): n.pag. Digital file.

Thomas, Laura E., and David E. Irwin. "Voluntary Eyeblinks Disrupt Iconic Memory." *Perception & Psychophysics* 68.3 (2006): 475–488. Print.

Vlassova, Alexandra, and Joel Pearson. "Look before You Leap: Sensory Memory Improves Decision Making." *Psychological Science* 24.9 (2013): 1635. Print.

Bryan C. Auday; updated by Elizabeth D. Schafer

SEE ALSO: Attention; Hearing; Kinesthetic memory; Long-term memory; Memory: Empirical studies; Pattern recognition; Sensation and perception; Senses; Short-term memory; Smell and taste; Touch and pressure; Visual system.

Memory storage

TYPE OF PSYCHOLOGY: Memory

The distinction between episodic and semantic memory provides a useful tool for classifying memory phenomena and methods of measuring memory performance. Separate types of memory models have been proposed for each, but debate continues as to whether episodic and semantic memories constitute distinct memory systems. Special cases of memory such as photographic memory and flashbulb memory provide insight into how the brain consolidates memory.

KEY CONCEPTS
- Anterograde amnesia
- Autobiographical memory
- Episodic memory
- Flashbulb memory
- Photographic memory
- Prospective memory
- Repisodic memory
- Retrospective memory
- Semantic memory

INTRODUCTION

The capacity to recall important details and events is at the heart of human existence. People's identities are merged with who they are, whom they know, and what they have accomplished. The concept of memory has fascinated scientists and psychologists for centuries. Accounts of individuals with superior memory skills, such as those with apparent photographic memories, have further produced interest in the topic of memory. Conversely, the idea of memory loss, especially as a person ages, both frightens and fascinates almost everyone.

Hermann Ebbinghaus is considered to be a pioneer in the experimental investigation of the properties of human memory. After acquiring his doctoral degree, Ebbinghaus set up a laboratory in Berlin, where he formally investigated the concept of memory and forgetting through experimentation. One of his notable concepts was the serial-position effect, wherein the first and last few items in a series are recalled better than the middle items (the primacy effect and the recency effect, respectively). He also described and published his findings on the forgetting curve, in which he described how quickly information is forgotten. Ebbinghaus's work spurred on the field of experimental psychology, and his concepts continue to be discussed and debated.

Another key historical figure in describing memory was Endel Tulving Tulving pointed out that up to 1972, most memory research followed in the tradition of Ebbinghaus, focusing on verbal learning tasks concerned with the accuracy of a subject's performance in remembering personally encountered events (such as the word "bed" in a list). Tulving considered these tasks to be tapping episodic memory.

In 1972, Tulving proposed a distinction between two parallel and partially overlapping memory systems, one for personal experiences and the other for general knowledge of the world. Episodic memory stores personal recollections of episodes or events that one has encountered at a particular time and place. Examples of episodic memories would include remembering such things as one's first airplane trip, eating cereal for breakfast this morning, and seeing the word August on a list recently learned in an experiment. Semantic memory stores shared factual information about language and the world, but without reference to when it was learned. For example, knowledge that a Boeing 747 is a type of airplane, that cereal is a common breakfast food, and that August has thirty-one days is all stored in semantic memory.

In his 1983 book, *Elements of Episodic Memory,* Tulving lists twenty-eight differences between episodic and semantic memory. Among them are the source of information (sensation versus comprehension), organization (temporal versus conceptual), emotional content (more important versus less important), vulnerability to forgetting (great versus small), and method of testing in the laboratory (recall of particular episodes versus general knowledge).

Since the early 1970s, memory research has expanded to include tasks designed to uncover the content and organization of information in semantic memory. Some tests assess factual and linguistic knowledge acquired over years of study and experience. Examples include the verbal and quantitative sections of college entrance examinations. A variety of new methods has also been developed to investigate how factual and lexical information is structured and interrelated in long-term memory. For example, subjects have been asked to generate lists of category members, in which the first and most often mentioned instances are interpreted to be the prototypical or best examples available in memory. In a fragment-completion task, the strength of memory traces is indexed by how much of a picture or printed word can be erased from memory and still be identified.

Several semantic memory tasks rely on reaction time as their dependent measure. In a lexical decision task, shorter reaction times to decide whether a string of letters composes a word provide a measure of the item's strength or current level of activation. Similarly, in a semantic verification task, the time to decide whether a sentence is true (for example, "A tomato is a vegetable") can be interpreted to indicate the strength of the stated fact or the semantic distance "traveled" between the two named concepts to verify or negate the statement. A robust semantic memory phenomenon is priming, which refers to the activation of associations in a memory network. For example, in a lexical decision experiment, subjects identify nurse as a word more quickly if it is preceded by the semantically related word doctor than by the unrelated word table or the nonword batel. This finding suggests that concepts with similar or shared meanings are stored close to one another in a semantic network, so that accessing one tends to highlight the others.

MEMORY MODELS

Memory models based on episodic tasks have focused on the transition of information from acquisition to storage. One of the most renowned models of memory was the multistore model of Richard Atkinson and Richard Shiffrin. This model distinguished between preattentive sensory registers: a limited-capacity, short-term store (STS) and a semantically organized, long-term store (LTS). Of critical interest were the coding processes used to transfer information from STS to LTS. This model gained popularity for some time, but later experimentation identified weaknesses in the model. For example, the famous case study of KF yielded a patient with an extremely limited STS, yet his long-term recall of stories and word lists remained intact. This finding could not be adequately explained by the multistore model of memory. More recently, Fergus Craik and Robert Lockhart proposed a levels-of-analysis model to account for the increasing trace duration of episodic memories. Both of these models were developed to explain the accumulation of memory phenomena from traditional list-learning experiments.

By contrast, semantic memory models have focused exclusively on the organization and retrieval of information already stored in long-term memory (LTM). For example, Lance Rips, Edward Shoben, and Edward Smith proposed a feature-comparison model, in which semantic information is coded as lists of necessary (defining) and descriptive (characteristic) features.

According to this model, subjects verify statements by searching the stored features of the named concepts, looking for matches. Fast reaction times are associated with close matches (resulting in a decision of "true") or the apparent absence of matches (with a decision of "false"). Their model explains why subjects verify sentences with considerable overlap between concepts (for example, "A robin is a bird") or none at all (for example, "A robin is a fish") more quickly than sentences with concepts that have only a few shared features (for example, "A penguin is a bird"). It also accounts for either fast, "false-alarm" errors or slow, correct decisions, when many shared features suggest at first glance that a false statement is true (for example, "A whale is a fish").

Another model originally proposed by Alan Baddeley and Graham Hitch in 1974 described the components of short-term memory. In this model, Baddeley and Hitch described three major features including a central executive, phonological loop, and visuo-spatial sketch pad. Essentially, the phonological loop is dedicated to rehearsal of verbally based information and the visuo-spatial sketch pad rehearses visual information. Both these components are slaves to the central executive (CE), which functions like the chief executive officer of the system. The CE manages the flow of information to the other components. For example, the CE prioritizes which slave system will be active and incorporates meta-cognitive (higher order) strategies that facilitate memory. In 2000, Baddeley added a third slave system, the episodic buffer, which serves as a link between short-term and long-term memory. The episodic buffer explains why numbers such as 1492 or 1867 might be easier to remember than other numbers.

EPISODIC AND SEMANTIC MEMORIES

An issue of critical importance is how information gets from episodic into semantic memory. Marigold Linton has suggested that as the number of experiences with a particular type of event increases, memories of the specific episodes become confused and eventually cannot be distinguished, but the strength of its generalized trace in semantic memory increases. These contrasting functions were suggested by the results of Linton's study of her own memory. Every day for six years, she recorded at least two events from her own life, then periodically tested her ability to remember those specific events. She found that memories of unique events, especially those with high emotional content, were often retained intact in episodic memory, whereas repeated events were transformed into generalized, abstracted memories or facts in semantic memory. Overall, her memories of personal events were forgotten at a rate of about 5 percent a year, in a nearly linear fashion.

A class of episodic memories that do not appear to erode over time has been called flashbulb memories. For example, Roger Brown and James Kulik reported that nearly all the adults they interviewed reported vivid personal memories of where they were, what they were doing, how they heard about it, and their own subsequent feelings and actions when they received the news of President John F. Kennedy's assassination in 1963. Previous generations of Americans have reported similar memories regarding the attack on Pearl Harbor in 1941, whereas other subjects have reported flashbulb memories for the September 11, 2001, terrorist attacks.

The clarity of people's memories for these and similar important historical and personal episodes has suggested to Ulric Neisser that they constitute a special case of episodic memories that are reflected on, repeated to others, and rehearsed countless times. What is finally remembered is a combination of the original episode, other generic information about the event drawn from semantic memory (for example, recalled facts reported by the news media), and the subtle changes that appear with each repetition. Neisser calls these repisodic memories, and he offers another example in the case of John Dean's testimony at the Senate's Watergate hearings in 1973. Dean had practiced the presentations he made to Richard Nixon in the Oval Office, subsequently rehearsed his memories of those conversations many times, and kept a scrapbook of newspaper accounts of the unfolding tale. By comparing Dean's sworn statements to the tape recordings of the actual White House conversations, Neisser confirmed that Dean's repisodic memory was essentially correct in retaining the gist of the whole chain of events, even though it did not faithfully report the individual encounters.

ACCESSING PERSONAL MEMORIES

Clearly, people's personal and generic memories are often intertwined, as they recall a compromise between what was and what must have been. From the outset, episodic memories are fashioned by an individual's pre-existing knowledge of the world, which is necessary to make sense of experience. As noted above, semantic memories often reflect generalizations constructed from many similar episodes. As people search their memories, the retrieval process often assumes the characteristics of problem solving. For example, in answering the question "What were you doing at 2:00 p.m. on the third Monday in September five years ago?," people's retrieval strategy would depend on some abstract factual information from semantic memory (for example, determining that one was a sophomore in high school that year and would have been in school, in an afternoon biology class). One might then reason that since mid-September is early in the semester, one was probably studying some introductory biological concept such as evolution. That insight then cues an episodic memory of Mr. Brown, the biology teacher, blaming evolution for the football team's loss in their opening game the previous Saturday night.

Autobiographical memories provide a link to one's personal past and help one maintain a coherent sense of self. For elderly persons who may be struggling to preserve their self-respect, keeping access to personal memories can be extremely important. Sharan Merriam has reported that providing cues such as old photographs and objects from the past, as part of a technique known as reminiscence therapy, has proved successful with disoriented persons, as it assists them in remembering who they are. Fortunately, even among those patients suffering dense anterograde amnesia (the inability to enter new information into memory), most retain access to autobiographical memories of events that occurred before the onset of amnesia.

PROSPECTIVE VERSUS RETROSPECTIVE MEMORY

Baddeley and Arnold Wilkins have suggested that the episodic-semantic distinction can be meaningfully applied to prospective memory (remembering to perform some act in the future) as well as to retrospective memory (remembering events experienced in the past). An example of a prospective episodic task is remembering to carry out some infrequently performed action on a fixed time schedule, such as recalling to take medication four times a day over the course of a week. In this case, the reference is personal, the organization is temporal, and the occasion of first learning and establishing this intention to act can still be recalled. By contrast, an example of a prospective semantic task is remembering an action sequence of overlearned steps, such as those involved in cooking with a memorized recipe. The reference is cognitive, the organization is cognitive, and the origin of this habitual sequence probably can no longer be recalled.

DEBATE IN RESEARCH

Douglas Hintzman has noted that authors in various fields had applied labels to capture the essence of the episodic-semantic distinction before Tulving's landmark article in 1972. In philosophy, Henri Bergson distinguished between pure and habit memory, and Don Locke contrasted personal memory with factual memory. In literature, Arthur Koestler differentiated between picturestrip and abstractive memory. Neurologist Wilder Penfield distinguished between experiential record and concepts. In psychiatry, Ernest Schactel defined autobiographical memory (memory for information and events related to the self from an individual's past) versus practical memory, and Robert Reiff and Martin Scheerer focused on remembrances versus memoria. Since the 1970s, however, Tulving has been the main standard-bearer of the dichotomy.

Although its heuristic value for classifying memory phenomena and methods has gone relatively unchallenged, Tulving's claim for episodic and semantic memories as separate systems has engendered considerable debate. Attempts to validate this position have relied on experimental demonstrations of dissociation, or cases in which a variable affects performance in an episodic task differently than it affects performance in a semantic task. Research using functional imaging studies (for example, functional magnetic resonance imaging, or fMRI) have, in general, not supported the distinction proposed by Tulving. These studies have suggested that multiple regions of the brain work together in the formation of new memories. Therefore, the process of memory consolidation is much more complex than originally hypothesized.

A notable outcome of Tulving's original argument was to shift attention in memory research away from episodic list learning and toward the structure of long-term semantic knowledge. However, there has been a growing interest in personal episodic, or autobiographical, memory. These are precisely the kinds of recollections that Ebbinghaus sought to exclude from the study of memory, considering them too personal and difficult to verify. Any comprehensive theory of memory, however, will need to account for the full range of interdependent memories, from highly personal accounts to abstract facts.

OTHER MEMORY TOPICS

Injury or damage to specific brain regions have been informative about the process of memory. Specifically, disruption to a person's stream of consciousness has predictive value for the recovery of a patient following head trauma. Loss of memory before the event is called retrograde amnesia, whereas loss of memory of events following the event is called anterograde amnesia. Typically, the longer the time period of amnesia after the accident, the more likely there will be permanent impairment of brain functioning. Disruption to an individual's memory, especially short-term memory, is a common outcome of many neurological and cardiovascular illnesses or injuries. This reflects the brain's vulnerability to memory loss following trauma.

An interesting although controversial topic relates to what is commonly described as photographic memory. Also called eidetic memory, persons with this rare ability are said to have an extraordinary capacity to recall precise details. Classic experiments determine that these individuals can study a detailed picture for thirty seconds and then maintain a complete visual image of the picture. It is believed that historical figures including Napoleon and Theodore Roosevelt may have had this capacity. In rare cases, extraordinary memory capacity has been identified in individuals with developmental disabilities such as autism.

BIBLIOGRAPHY

Baddeley, Alan D. *Human Memory: Theory and Practice.* Rev. ed. Hove: Psychology, 2005. Print.

Bauer, Patricia J. *Remembering the Times of Our Lives: Memory in Infancy and Beyond.* New York: Psychology, 2013. Print.

Carruthers, Mary J. *The Book of Memory: A Study of Memory in Medieval Culture.* Rpt. New York: Cambridge UP, 1993. Print.

Emilien, Gerard, et al. *Memory: Neuropsychological, Imaging, and Psychopharmacological Perspectives.* New York: Psychology, 2004. Print.

Kahana, Michael Jacob. *Foundations of Human Memory.* New York: Oxford UP, 2012. Print.

Neisser, Ulric, and Ira E. Hyman, eds. *Memory Observed: Remembering in Natural Contexts.* 2nd ed. New York: Worth, 2000. Print.

Taylor, Annette Kujawski, ed. *Encyclopedia of Human Memory.* 3 vols. Santa Barbara: ABC-CLIO, 2013. Print.

Tulving, Endel. *Elements of Episodic Memory.* London: Oxford UP, 1983. Print.

Tulving, Endel. "How Many Memory Systems Are There?" *American Psychologist* 40.4 (1985): 385–98. Print.

Tulving, Endel, and Fergus I. M. Craik, eds. *The Oxford Handbook of Memory.* New York: Oxford UP, 2000. Print.

Thomas J. Thieman; updated by Martin Mrazik

SEE ALSO: Amnesia and fugue; Aphasias; Brain structure; Elders' mental health; Encoding; Forgetting and forgetfulness; Long-term memory; Memory; Memory: Empirical studies.

Men's mental health

TYPE OF PSYCHOLOGY: Biological bases of behavior; Developmental psychology; Emotion; Psychotherapy; Social psychology; Stress

Gender roles inform almost all human interactions. In the case of mental health, gender politics, especially the role of societal expectations when it comes to masculinity, can prove to be detrimental. The concept of men's mental health takes as its fundamental basis the idea that men and women are different creatures when it comes to psychology.

KEY CONCEPTS

- Aging
- Gender identity politics
- Gender roles
- Help-seeking behavior
- Masculinity
- Socialization
- Suicide

INTRODUCTION

Researchers who study the mental health of men will ultimately find themselves becoming conversant on various issues, most of which share the problem of gender identity politics as their root cause. Both academicians and clinicians study diverse aspects of men's mental health, including male development and theories of masculinity. Contemporary perspectives of masculinity do not always focus solely on men who conform to the expectations associated with traditional masculinity; rather some of the later theories examine and describe the increasing number of men in modern Western societies who actively eschew traditional masculine values and choose not to engage in traditionally rigid male role behavior.

Such studies not only examine the individuated behaviors and beliefs of the liberated man, but also question the extent of societal support and acceptance of the changes in gender identity. In short, men who identify with both masculine and feminine roles risk social sanctions because they either choose to disregard gender norms or are unable to fit the idealized male image as reflected in hegemonic culture.

MENTAL HEALTH AND HEALTH ISSUES

Generally, some of the more often discussed issues in men's mental health include normal childhood development and psychopathology, adolescent impulsivity (including neurodevelopment), male depression, workplace anxiety disorders, substance abuse, sexual health issues (erectile dysfunction, premature ejaculation, and male orgasmic disorder), emotional issues related to partner health, and aging—especially its relationship to depression and suicide. Other popular issues among theorists in the discipline include studies of antisocial personality, conduct, and post-traumatic stress disorders; fathering, as it is related to mental health; masculinity, gender identity, and the family unit (marriage and divorce included); propensities toward aggression, violence, and domestic abuse; issues stemming from culture, ethnicity, and race; homosexuality; and help-seeking behavior, which includes overcoming stigmas and barriers to mental health treatment. Also of note are the problems introduced by men's body image concerns.

HELP-SEEKING

Generally speaking, most clinicians find that male clients who seek out therapy do so because their hand has been forced. For example, they may have been referred for treatment in response to excessive alcohol consumption or substance-related abuse, such as driving under the influence (DUI) citations or arrests for domestic violence. In some cases, the spouse has demanded that undesired behaviors must be stopped or curtailed. Similar to their avoidance of seeking medical help (the grin-and-bear-it syndrome associated with traditional masculinity), men typically eschew therapy because talking about their feelings is viewed as at best weak, and at worst completely nonmasculine, contrary to the male robust image. As a result, they place both their physical and mental health at risk. Men who exhibit self-destructive behavior may seek therapy as a result of a physician's referral, but the irony is that the behaviors that lead to men being referred to therapy (for example, excessive anger, uncontrollable competitiveness, or sexual harassment in the workplace) are often seen as socially desirable, even essential, because these behaviors define masculinity. In fact, Morley D. Glicken found that "the involuntary nature of a man's use of therapy is complicated by the fact that men often view therapy as feminizing and their resistance to the process can be considerable."

Gender issues can become problematic, because at a very early age, boys are constantly barraged with the message that they are essentially different from girls. They may receive these messages from their parents; however, even parents who attempt to encourage boys to be sensitive and to recognize the feminine traits that are part of their masculinity can find themselves facing the same negative influence of strict adherence to gender identity, for their sons receive messages of male expectations from peers, from older boys, from sports exposure (including from their coaches), and from various media outlets. In essence, boys, especially those involved in sport, make pain what Glicken calls "a pledge of manliness." This stands in contrast to women, who as girls are taught to always express their emotions.

MASCULINITY AND GENDER ROLES

It is particularly tragic that the masculine sense of independence stands in the way of counseling or therapy, for men generally have few other support systems—and a very limited number of friends. The problem is that male clients often feel uncomfortable revealing their emotional problems and insecurities to a therapist. Traditional maleness usually involves some embracing of self-sufficiency, which can lead to aloneness or loneliness, both part and parcel of the unwritten code of masculinity. Yet some theorists argue that issues of men and masculinity have rarely been considered in relation to the theory and practice of person-centered therapy, arguing that the trappings of modern society make this focus more essential.

Scholars and clinicians have expressed the need for a male-sensitive approach in the mental health and psychotherapeutic domains, especially given the ongoing research that indicates the need for a diverse range of seemingly competing theories pertaining to the nature and basis of male gender identity in the Western world. Some theories emphasize the biological aspects of masculinity, with lengthy discussions of the underlying sexual (physiological) differences between men and women, while others look at psychodynamics, sociological pressures (especially the role of relationships), and even power structure issues. Although the traditional idea of masculinity is basically hegemonic, consisting of varying beliefs, tropes, role definitions, and practices, at any given time, alternative constructs of maleness are recognized as valid, making it even more complex for clinicians involved in therapeutic work with men, thereby calling for an ongoing dialogue. What some academicians refer to as a crisis in masculinity also contributes to gender identity issues; these crises usually involve radical questioning of the meaning of masculinity, and they occur during periods of significant ideological, economic, and social tension, producing a culture wherein traditional masculinity is seen as less valid. However, because new definitions need to be firmly established, these periods may be more confusing than they are enlightening.

Another fundamental dialogue exists between theorists who argue that young men inherit what is called innate maleness at birth and that their masculinity is predetermined, and those who posit that men are born tabula rosa and are socialized into maleness. Gender role strain theory argues that masculinity and femininity are socially constructed and are relative, so that the contemporary understanding of gender roles tends to be contradictory, despite consistent themes. These contradictions inherent in modern masculinity ideology can have the negative impact of creating a sense of trauma in young men when it comes to issues of socialization. In some cases, male teens and young adults will over-conform, adopting extreme, perhaps even toxic versions of traditional male traits. Some theorists argue that ultimately this can lead to the male propensity toward violence and other unhealthy practices.

Academicians who focus on male gender-role development (with special emphasis on early developmental struggles) theorize that even though male children are masculine at conception, they possess the same innate feminine emotional and psychological traits. It is only through the deidentification with the mother that they begin the stages of repression, and if the father subscribes to traditional roles of masculinity, which would dictate that men are breadwinners, sacrificing familial interaction for professional advancement, the male child is left without a parental figure with whom to identify. Hence, boys learn about masculinity through negation, by inferring what it means to not be feminine. Daniel J. Levinson and associates have found that these restrictive notions of the male role are present throughout most of adulthood, tending to be modified in middle age, perhaps due to healthy relationships. Toward middle age, men begin to integrate both male and female definitions of their roles, becoming more nurturing. Men at this stage of life also seem to be more concerned about the quality of relationships.

INTERPERSONAL RELATIONSHIPS
Relationships seem to be at the forefront of men's mental health issues. Problems such as role in the family unit and sexual dysfunction are omnipresent in the literature.

Of the latter, researchers and practitioners have found that there is a direct association between emotional health and sexual function in men. In addition to the physical reasons for erectile dysfunction (hypertension, for example), therapists have also identified psychological contributing factors, such as general fatigue, depression, and prolonged stress. Because male arousal disorder can also result from combined factors, it is possible that a man with a medical condition of insufficient severity to cause dysfunction could experience dysfunction after a slight emotional trauma—which by itself would not have caused difficulty. Because of this complexity, therapists and academicians use various methods to study the causes of male arousal disorder, such as determining organic, psychological, and relational etiologies, and have found that eclectic therapeutic approaches raise the success rate.

When studying the male role in the modern family unit and how it affects the mental health of men, researchers begin with the acknowledgement that the reliance on the standards of a hegemonic patriarchy serves as the primary source of difficulty in relationship adjustment. Despite the actual change over time of the male role in family function and structure, societal pressure continues to prioritize and aggrandize the idea of the traditional, heterosexual, two-parent family in which the man is the primary means of financial support. This, of course, inadequately reflects reality, where a broad spectrum of manifestations of the family unit are observed; this inconsistency between expectations and reality results in the majority of contemporary families first appearing to be dysfunctional and then perhaps becoming so as a self-fulfilling prophecy. The main problem with the gender-role expectations that promote male dominance is that patriarchal values often promote inequitable gender expectations, which by extension sanctions female subordination. As female partners in the family unit are perceived principally responsible for both the relationship itself, for the well-being of the family, and for domestic upkeep, familial conflict is likely to ensue. Theorists therefore must examine the basis for the continual adherence to patriarchal standards to determine methods to ameliorate resulting difficulties. On the individual level, therapists work with men who find themselves being torn between societal expectations and the realities of their family units by helping them understand the necessity and inevitability of shifting gender roles.

AGGRESSION AND MASCULINITY

Another prevalent issue in men's mental health is the reliance on aggression as a coping technique, which can lead to violence and possibly even domestic abuse. Because men, as young children, are taught, perhaps even in good faith (to protect themselves from bullies, for example) to fight, as they age, boys are faced with the decision to either eschew physical methods of settling differences or continue to use violence to cope. Unfortunately, many male young adults lack effective strategies to deal with anger and frustration; therefore, they will adopt behaviors such as throwing items, banging on materials that frustrate them, or punching inanimate objects. Sandra P. Thomas found that men, in general, were no more comfortable with the emotion of anger than were women. As a result, some men feel shame concerning their inability to cope without violence, so they withdraw altogether. In worst-case scenarios, they self-isolate, which endangers relationships.

DEPRESSION

Problems such as anger management issues and self-isolation, as well as other issues, make depression one of the biggest mental health concerns for men. In England, for example, researchers have found that heart disease, sexual dysfunction, and other chronic conditions can lead to serious emotional problems such as depression, and that conversely, men who are depressed are three times more likely to develop long-term illnesses such as heart disease. The same study found that although an equal number of men and women are affected by mental health problems, twice as many women are diagnosed and treated. As Rosemary L. Hopcroft and Dana Burr Bradley noted in 2007, generally, in developed countries, the sex difference in depression and symptoms of depression is well documented. In the United States, women are more likely to report symptoms of depression than men at all ages, with a peak in the sex difference in late middle age. Psychiatric epidemiology has consistently shown that with the notable exception of substance abuse, women have higher rates of nonpsychotic disorders and report depression, as compared with men, at a 2:1 ratio. However, a growing body of scholarship in men's studies has focused on sociological and artifact explanations, purporting that the traditional male role, associated with self-reliance and stoicism, actually results in men's depression often being undetected and untreated. Psychiatrist Martin Kantor argues that the signs and symptoms of depression differ between men and women and that clinicians, looking for the classic signs of depression in women, may miss the diagnosis in men. He identifies the major inconsistency in diagnosis as being a result of the failure to recognize the male depressive equivalents—the indirect actions that men use to display depression. For example, depressed men do not appear tearful; rather, they have a tendency to become irritable or develop psychosomatic symptoms, or, as Kantor theorizes, deny their depression and shift into hypomania.

SUICIDE

Sam V. Cochran and Fredric E. Rabinowitz argued that far too many depressed men ultimately commit suicide and that the number rises dramatically with age. In the United States, suicide rates for men in all age groups are higher than for women; in fact, men are four times as likely to kill themselves as women, according to the American Foundation for Suicide Prevention. When dealing with suicidal men, therapists often watch for suicide equivalents, since suicidality can be subtle, even sometimes symbolic. Suicide equivalent behaviors include actions such as inadequate care of one's physical health, suffering from professional or occupational block, workaholism, hypomania, substance abuse (especially addiction to alcohol, cocaine, and oxycodone), and self-defeating neuroses. At-risk men will often express suicidal thoughts (which may or may not evolve into suicidal behavior), although some depressed men may hide their intentions. In cases in which suicidal thoughts become threats, clinicians are forced to determine the seriousness of the claim. Suicidal attempts will range from those that are symbolic or gestural (which are usually used to manipulate an individual or group) to those that signal a sincere desire to end one's life.

Of particular concern to many researchers in the field is the fact that many men, responding to what they feel is a cultural imperative to be traditionally masculine, view help-seeking as showing weakness and therefore avoid therapy. This behavior is endemic among certain cultures. A 2007 study found that rural men not only lead a life that presents more challenges that statistically increase the risk of mental illness, but also are most likely to not seek professional help. Researchers have found that, generally speaking, one of the biggest dilemmas for psychotherapeutic practitioners is getting men (of all ethnicities, cultures, and ages) to actually attend counseling or psychotherapy. Statistics show that men are far less likely than women to seek help in the form of therapy;

service statistics verify this, showing a preponderance of female clients. The reasons for this phenomenon are varied, but the overarching theme seems to be that male reticence to seek counseling is a reflection of the masculine emphasis on self-sufficiency, part of a wider refusal to ask for help until absolutely necessary. If one examines the act of help-seeking through the lens of traditional gender-role identity, the resulting portrayal of therapy would be that it denotes vulnerability and weakness, in other words, failure. Therefore many men, especially young men, avoid services offering help, working out psychological and emotional problems themselves, or using unhealthy coping mechanisms, such as substance abuse, resorting to violence, or ending their own lives. Therapy is not even viewed as an option by these types of men. To offset the negative help-seeking behavior of men, clinicians are developing a better model. Group discussions about health are one viable alternative, and men seem to respond positively. Also, responding to studies that indicate that men are less likely to report pain while in the presence of a female clinician, practitioners are steering male patients towards male therapists.

BIBLIOGRAPHY

Berger, Joshua L., et al. "Men's Reactions to Mental Health Labels, Forms of Help-Seeking, and Sources of Help-Seeking Advice." *Psychology of Men and Masculinity* 14.4 (2013): 433–43. PsycARTICLES. Web. 22 May 2014.

Cochran, Sam V., and Fredric E. Rabinowitz. *Men and Depression: Clinical and Empirical Perspectives.* San Diego: Elsevier, 2000. Print.

Edwards, Tim. *Men in the Mirror: Men's Fashion, Masculinity, and the Consumer Society.* London: Cassell, 1997. Print.

Glicken, Morley D. *Working with Troubled Men: A Contemporary Practitioner's Guide.* Mahwah: Erlbaum, 2005. Print.

Grant, Jon E., and Marc N. Potenza. *Textbook of Men's Mental Health.* Washington, DC: American Psychiatric, 2007. Print.

Haddad, Mark. "Promoting Mental Health in Men." *Nursing Standard* 27.30 (2013): 48–57. Academic Search Complete. Web. 22 May 2014.

Hopcroft, Rosemary L., and Dana Burr Bradley. "The Sex Difference in Depression across Twenty-Nine Countries." *Social Forces* 85.4 (2007): 1483–1507. Print.

Judd, Sandra J. *Men's Health Concerns Sourcebook.* Detroit: Omnigraphics, 2013. eBook Collection (EBSCOhost). Web. 22 May 2014.

Levinson, Daniel J., et al. *The Seasons of a Man's Life.* New York: Ballantine, 1988. Print.

Rabinowitz, Fredric Eldon, and Aaron B. Rochlen. *Breaking Barriers in Counseling Men: Insights and Innovations.* New York: Routledge, 2014. eBook Collection (EBSCOhost). Web. 22 May 2014.

Thomas, Sandra P. "Anger: The Mismanaged Emotion." *Medical and Surgical Nursing* 12.2 (2003): 103–110. Print.

Anthony J. Fonseca

SEE ALSO: Aggression; Aging: Cognitive changes; Anger; Depression; Father-child relationship; Femininity; Gender differences; Gender identity formation; Gender roles and gender role conflicts; Helpseeking; Masculinity; Suicide.

Mental blocks

TYPE OF PSYCHOLOGY: Biological bases of human behavior; Health, Neuropsychology

A mental block is a sudden disruption in performance such as when speaking a new language, when asked to recall something from the past, when writing an essay or homework assignment, when in a class or training program and you go blank, or such as when you are in a stressful social situation such as on a date or performing in front of other people. Mental blocks are common and can be avoided, overcome and even eliminated.

KEY CONCEPTS
- Diaphragmatic breathing
- Information overload
- Mental block vs. panic attack
- Performance anxiety
- Retrieval problems
- Unconscious resistance

INTRODUCTION

The term "mental block" has been around for many years and utilized to describe a number of different phenomena. Often, a person is unable to recall an event, or something of importance or relevance. Sometimes, psychologists who align themselves with Freudian psychoanalytic theory would refer to this as "unconscious resistance" referring to some defense mechanism. There are several hypotheses regarding this phenomenon, and each will be described briefly.

One explanation for the mental block is simply that there are memory problems. Some people have a well-developed memory, and do not need to write things down to remember them. Other individuals do not have a large capacity or storage space and thus, while they may have learned something, or been introduced to someone, they may not have learned or repeated the information adequately in order to have learned the information.

Other individuals have difficulty with the construct of the mental block because of apprehension or anxiety. There may be some fear or trepidation about some issue, or there may simply be a concern about appearing foolish or not too bright. Anxiety can take many different forms to result in a mental block. The fear may be so overwhelming that all psychic energy is devoted to attempting to cope with the situation. Some individuals have better coping skills than others, and have learned how to deal with a highly anxious situation. Some individuals take a deep breath, relax, and try to make associations so as to be able to deal with the mental block and be able to adjust accordingly.

There is performance anxiety which may result in a mental block in terms of not knowing what to do in a certain situation. There is free floating anxiety which refers to the fact that some people are in a constant state of stress or anxiety. There is pervasive fear or anxiety, due perhaps to some event or trauma. There is even anticipatory anxiety which refers to the fact that some individuals become anxious because they are aware that there is a pending event which is going to elicit anxiety and they despise this feeling.

Some mental blocks could be described as retrieval problems. In such instances, there is no anxiety, but simply a sincere attempt to try to recall a person's name or some other bit of information. Often this is referred to as the tip of the tongue phenomenon. The person literally works at trying to reconstruct some information, or form some association so that they are able to piece together some data or information so as to be able to recall or retrieve certain information. This type of mental block varies by age, as some individuals have a more difficult time recalling or retrieving information learned many years ago. Some individuals have a mental block when asked to recall a specific place or time or event that occurred many years ago. Many items simply fade with the passage of time if they are not mentally reviewed. Other events fade and decay as they are simply not very relevant or linked to anything of critical importance or anchored to another important event.

Information overload refers to efforts to learn or memorize or master too much material in too brief a period. People need a certain amount of time to assimilate and accommodate new information. When asked to recall the information and they cannot, they may be described as having a mental block. They may have been inundated with too many new people to meet, or procedures to learn, or confronted with having to learn a new foreign language in too brief a time.

For some, coping with mental blocks may require simple relaxation. This alleviates the stress and frustration that further exacerbates the situation. Some may utilize a piece of paper and pencil in an attempt to reconstruct the needed information, or to provide links and clues for future use. Many musicians carry a tape recorder with them so that they can preserve the melody that they want to use.

Some individuals may experience a mental block more than others as they may have a low frustration tolerance. They believe that everything should be simple, easy and facile. They become exasperated, frustrated, and this does not facilitate the retrieval of the desired information.

Writers may often have a mental block or writer's block at various stages of the writing process. Some authors have difficulty beginning a piece they are attempting to write, and others may have difficulty resolving a literary situation involving plot or characters.

There is little empirical research on the phenomenon of mental block. It could also be that the individual experiencing a mental block has not slept well, or has not eaten for a while or is simply having a stressful day.

We all have mental blocks at one time or another. They may be referred to by different names, such as brain freeze. At a presidential debate, Texas Governor Rick Perry attempted to recall three departments that he would eliminate if elected president. He was able to recall two, but was not able to remember the third. It may have been the television cameras, or it may have been his lack of preparation that caused what has been termed his brain freeze. Others may refer to it as the tip of the tongue phenomenon. The expectation of a presidential candidate is that he would be able to rattle off a good deal of information quite fluidly. While some people are able to keep large amounts of information handy, not all people are as facile with their retrieval of the information.

HOW A MENTAL BLOCK DIFFERS FROM A PANIC ATTACK

Mental blocks and panic attacks are often confused as being the same. They are distinctly different experiences. When a person experiences a mental block, he or she feels annoyed or frustrated but can usually recover quickly and carry on as before the block in a matter of minutes. A mental block is not triggered by anything happening in the present or anything from the past. Research is inconclusive regarding a specific cause for a mental block.

By contrast, when a person experiences a panic attack, typically, he or she has an elevated heartbeat, chest pains, a sense of lightheadedness, difficulty breathing, and may begin to sweat profusely. They feel as if something terrible is about to happen that cannot be stopped. Some fear that they are going to die. A panic attack can last for a few minutes or days. The attacks are usually triggered by a previous event or trauma.

What a mental block and a panic attack have in common is that both experiences are instantaneously disruptive to a person cognitive performance. In addition, both are often overcome or eliminated by some of the same recovery strategies such as deep breathing exercises, visualization, or psychotherapy.

RECOGNIZING A MENTAL BLOCK

Sometimes a sudden mental block is due to not being able to change perspective or an unwillingness to see things differently when other points of view are presented. It means being stuck in an old paradigm that no longer works. When a person working with others gets mentally stuck being right about their point of view while making others feel they are wrong, he or she stops being reasonable. It is as if they are driven to be right and will not let up until others agree. Unfortunately, such a mental block often results in a negative standstill, leaving co-workers or significant others feeling frustrated and exasperated. Sometimes the block is so intense that the person may become hostile and out of control all the while feeling extremely uncomfortable and clueless as to what is driving the intensity of their reaction. Here, an unrecognized mental block is the problem.

One strategy that is helpful to escape the constraints of such a mental block is to examine constrictive thinking such as being too logical or wanting to do something the way it has always been done even if it doesn't work. In this instance you need to be more flexible with rules. It might mean that you have to raise your voice, be assertive, and

speak firmly to someone even when it is not your style to do so. It may even mean conceding that someone is right. Maybe the problem is that you are being too practical or afraid to let go of being right.

Sometimes people seem as if they are just tolerating a bad situation such as not being able to leave home over night because he or she has pets at home to care for. Perhaps another view is that they have a mental block about what to do so they just do nothing. Such mental blocks are common. Just having someone else to help generate multiple, viable solutions can usually break the binds of the mental block which will lead to smart, sensible, satisfying answers to the problem. Recognizing when one is experiencing a mental block regarding an issue is key to overcoming the block.

OVERCOMING MENTAL BLOCKS IN THE COLLEGE CLASSROOM

College students report that they often experience a mental block when it comes to absorbing material being presented in class during a lecture. Such a mental block could result in daydreaming, not taking notes, looking down throughout the lecture, feeling lightheaded or dizzy and unable to concentrate. Such unpleasant feelings often result in students avoiding the class and procrastinating to the point that assignments and studying for exams are completed at the last minute resulting in poor quality work as well as physical and emotional problems due to the stress from the pressure caused by procrastination.

Some tips for avoiding a mental block while in the classroom include nodding positively to comments during class, paying close attention to whoever has the floor, and writing notes. When you understand something, paraphrase what the teacher said so as to condense it. If you do not understand something, write down word for word what the teacher is saying. Through body language, let the teacher or other students know when you agree with them. Say to yourself, "Ok. That is right. I got it," or "That's what I thought" while following along in class

It also helps to avoid mental blocks by participating each day in the whole class experience. Do what it takes to stay up to date with assignments by completing all homework on time. If you need help, get help. Ask a fellow student or friend to help when you do not understand something. Keep your mind clear. Remind yourself that you are in this class on this day because you are going to be a speech pathologist, a probation officer, a physician, a psychologist, a special education teacher, nurse, journalist, or a forensic crime investigator and every class you take will prepare you for that. Be ready for anything in class. Concentrate on learning new material that day. Such strategies can eliminate mental blocks and save time and energy by really putting yourself in your class while you are in it and learning the class material at the same time that everyone else in the class is learning it.

STRATEGIES FOR OVERCOMING MENTAL BLOCKS

Some mental blocks require a quick, immediate reaction in the moment to overcome the block. Such blocks include difficulty recalling something specific while under pressure, performance anxiety, information overload, or a brain freeze. When experiencing such a block, immediately take a deep breath in and slowly out. Then repeat. Continue breathing slowly. Say to yourself, "Everything is ok." Smile. Try to recall the last thing you said or did before the block. If needed, ask for help remembering where you left off. Just relax. The key to the immediate reversal is deep breathing through your nose with your mouth closed and relaxing your mind. Be kind and accepting of yourself. Hopefully the block will pass quickly.

Sometimes a mental block is due to fatigue, lack of sleep, dehydration or not enough brain fuel food. A person can become sleepy and tired when dehydrated so keep water near and drink fluids in intervals throughout the day rather than just when thirsty. Taking 10-15 minute power naps can be refreshing and result in an alert state. Brain fuel food such as crackers, cheese and orange juice are good to have with you while studying or while taking an exam.

A relaxation strategy that is highly effective in overcoming a mental block involves relaxing muscles that have become tense due to stress. The exercise is called The Calm Exercise. First, say the word CALM to yourself over and over very slowly. If you are able, close your eyes so you can better concentrate. Begin relaxing your chest, shoulders, and torso. Close your mouth. Breathe slowly through your nose. Notice tense areas and just relax those muscles. Uncross your legs and let go of all tension in your legs and lastly, let your jaw drop slowly. Repeat this for 30 to 60 seconds or for as long as you need to. The key is repeating the word calm over and over, relaxing your muscles, breathing only through your nose, and relaxing your jaw. With practice, you can learn to relax and calm yourself on command.

Some strategies for writers to use when feeling hijacked by a mental block or you just want to reset an unwanted rut, try some refreshing things such as spinning in your chair or taking a shower, going for a walk or drive, exercising, playing with your pet, playing an instrument, or relaxing. If still stuck, ask for help.

Practicing and mastering diaphragmatic breathing is the best defense for avoiding and quickly eliminating mental blocks. It can be done several different ways. One way is by putting one hand over your chest bone, the other just above your belt line. Your diaphragm is located between your hands. This allows you to use your hands as a simple biofeedback device. You want to concentrate on expanding the diaphragm as much as is comfortable while inhaling and completely deflating it when exhaling. Begin by closing your mouth, breathing in deeply and slowly through your nose for about 5 seconds. Next, breathe out deeply and slowly through your mouth allowing the air to fully escape. Repeat this procedure for 30-60 seconds or as long as needed to get you to a calm and clear state. With practice, you will be able to breathe this way on a regular basis, keeping your body and mind in an alert, calm and balanced state so that you can be a more happily productive person without fear of a mental block.

Researchers and scholars are still investigating variants of the mental block or tip of the tongue phenomenon to see if there are differences in terms of word retrieval problems, name retrieval, information retrieval, difficulties retrieving information under test like conditions, or interpersonal conditions (such as a party) or a vocational instance (meeting a client and not recalling his or her name) and variations on this phenomenon.

BIBLIOGRAPHY

http://www.columbia.edu/cu/psychology/metcalfe/PDFs/Schwartz_Metcalfe_inPress.pdf   This is an excellent article by Schwartz and Metcalfe with an overview of the entire phenomenon from various perspectives.

http://www.nextavenue.org/article/2013-05/how-beat-tip-tongue-syndrome This is an excellent piece discussing coping strategies to deal with mental blocks, and difficulties noted as " tip of the tongue " phenomenon.

http://129.237.66.221/P800/Burke1991.pdf   This article specifically addresses word finding failures in young and old adults.

http://mercercognitivepsychology.pbworks.com/w/page/32859313/Tip-of-the-Tongue%20Phenomenon

June Shepherd and Michael Shaughnessy

SEE ALSO: Cognitive ability; Consciousness; Memory; Memory recall; Repression.

Mental health parity

TYPE OF PSYCHOLOGY: Biological bases of behavior; Psychopathology; Psychotherapy

Mental health parity is a health care policy endorsed by the U.S. government through Public Law 110-343, which states that mental health care coverage must be equitable to physical health care coverage. Research indicates that a connection exists between mental and physical well-being; therefore, comprehensive, integrated insurance coverage that accounts for all aspects of health care is in the best interest of both the public and employers.

KEY CONCEPTS
- Addiction
- Integrated care
- Mental health
- Out-of-network costs
- Parity
- Substance use disorders

INTRODUCTION

In 2008, the Paul Wellstone and Pete Domenici Mental Health Parity and Addiction Equity Act was approved as part of the US legislation known as Public Law 110-343, the Emergency Economic Stabilization Act of 2008. Also known as the Mental Health Parity Act, this legislation prohibited health insurers from restricting mental health care and addiction treatment and required such to be equal to what is offered for physical health care. The intention was to establish functional equality for treatment for these different types of problems.

In this law, mental health care referred to services for mental health conditions, while addiction treatment referred to services for substance-use disorders, conditions known as substance abuse and substance dependence. Thus, insurers could not charge higher co-pays or deductibles and could not impose lower-frequency-of-treatment and number-of-visits or days-of-coverage

limits on mental health and addiction benefits in comparison to other medical services. In addition, if the health plan provided coverage for medical or surgical services through providers not normally associated with the health plan—a policy known as out-of-network costs—it also had to do so for mental health and addiction. Finally, in accordance with this law, insurers could not require federal update coinsurance or set higher out-of-pocket limits for these services than for other medical or surgical expenses within the health plan.

This law was created because the intentions of the previously passed Mental Health Parity Act (MHPA), signed into law on September 26, 1996, had been circumvented through restrictions on specific terms related to service not covered in the law. The design of the 2008 law was to correct such problems. This law, however, did not mandate that health plans provide mental health or addiction coverage; it only required that if such services were provided, they had to be done so in a way that demonstrated equality with the physical health care benefits. Small businesses that employed between two and fifty employees were exempt for compliance with this law.

Treatment for mental health and addictions created significant cost-offset savings on future health care, meaning that if money was spent on treatment for problems when they were diagnosed, it would be saved in the end by preventing new or worsening problems. Furthermore, research indicated an association between treatment for such problems and improved workplace functioning and productivity. Given this fact, the 2008 law was created without the expectation of required coverage for mental health and addiction because of the cost savings and other benefits. The lawmakers assumed that mental health and addictive benefits would be offered because they were not only valuable benefits to employees but also financially wise investments for employers.

QUALITY HEALTH CARE EQUALS INTEGRATED HEALTH CARE

True health is a combination of physical and mental well-being and a freedom from addictions. Numerous sources related to psychophysiology and the interactions among health, stress, and psychological processes point to the importance of integrative health care. Further, epidemiology from around the world demonstrates that comorbidity, the condition in which a person has multiple disorders, frequently includes mixes of physical, mental, and addiction-related problems. When considering that stress also affects health and may exacerbate other conditions, the interdependence of successful treatment of and attention to all these factors is underscored. As such, common sense dictates that good health care should allow for integration of and consistent attention to each of these aspects of health in the provision of treatment. Arbitrarily setting financial limits or other barriers could detract from the overall effectiveness and quality of care. Thus, from a mental health perspective, mental health parity laws became a logical outcome of the literature on and history of mind-body interactions.

BIBLIOGRAPHY

Andersen, Ronald, Thomas H. Rice, and Gerald F. Kominski. *Changing the US Health Care System: Key Issues in Health Services Policy and Management*. San Francisco: Jossey-Bass, 2007. Print.

Chatterjee, Anjan, and Martha J. Farah. *Neuroethics in Practice*. Oxford: Oxford UP, 2013. Print.

Hugdahl, Kenneth. *Psychophysiology: The Mind-Body Perspective*. Cambridge: Harvard UP, 2001. Print.

Kelly, Timothy A. *Healing the Broken Mind: Transforming America's Failed Mental Health System*. New York: New York UP, 2009. Print.

Lovallo, William R. *Stress and Health: Biological and Psychological Interactions*. 2d ed. Thousand Oaks: Sage, 2004. Print.

"The Mental Health Parity and Addiction Equity Act of 2008." *United States Department of Labor*. United States Department of Labor, 29 Jan. 2010. Web. 13 May 2014.

Mueser, Kim T., Douglas L. Noordsy, Robert E. Drake, and Lindy Fox. *Integrated Treatment for Dual Disorders: A Guide for Effective Practice*. New York: Guilford, 2003. Print.

Sapolsky, Robert M. *Why Zebras Don't Get Ulcers*. 3d ed. New York: Holt, 2004. Print.

Shally-Jensen, Michael. *Mental Health Care Issues in America: An Encyclopedia*. Santa Barbara: ABC-CLIO, 2013. Print.

World Health Organization. *Integrating Mental Health Care into Primary Care: A Global Perspective*. Geneva: World Health Org., 2008. Print.

Nancy A. Piotrowski

SEE ALSO: Assessment; Diagnosis; Environmental factors and mental health; Health insurance; Health maintenance organizations; Law and psychology; National Institute of Mental Health; Stress: Behavioral and psychological responses; Stress-related diseases; Substance use disorders; Workplace issues and mental health.

Mental health practitioners

TYPE OF PSYCHOLOGY: Psychotherapy

Mental health practitioners are professionals who are involved in the treatment of psychological and emotional disorders. They include clinical psychologists, counseling psychologists, psychiatrists, and psychiatric social workers; their professional preparations differ considerably, but their contributions are all essential.

KEY CONCEPTS

- Assessment
- Behavioral medicine
- Brain dysfunction
- Diagnosis
- Electroconvulsive therapy (ECT)
- Forensic psychology
- Neuropsychology
- Psychotherapy

INTRODUCTION

Since the beginning of the twentieth century, there has been a growing concern about mental health. Studies have indicated that approximately one out of every five persons in the United States will experience a psychological disorder severe enough to warrant professional help. Given the magnitude of this problem, the question emerges as to who will provide the kind and amount of treatment needed for this large number of individuals.

Mental health practitioners have emerged from different fields of endeavor. The field of medicine produced psychiatrists; the field of psychology produced clinical psychologists and counseling psychologists; and the field of social work produced psychiatric social workers. In some states, such as California, legislation created special mental health practitioners called marriage, family, and child counselors to fulfill the needs that were not met by these large professional groups.

TYPES OF PRACTITIONERS

Psychiatrists are those individuals who have completed four years of college and four years of medical school, including one year of internship. After completion, they continue their studies in a residency in psychiatry for approximately three years and learn the skills of a practicing psychiatrist. This is generally done in a mental hospital or clinic, under the supervision of other psychiatrists. On completion, they may choose to take an examination that will award them the status of being certified. This status recognizes that a psychiatrist has demonstrated a level of competence that meets professional standards.

As a physician, the psychiatrist can perform all the medical functions that any physician can perform. In terms of the mental health setting, this means that the psychiatrist's activities can involve the administration of different types of drugs that are designed to alter the way a patient feels, thinks, or behaves. The psychiatrist conducts psychotherapy and is concerned about any physical conditions that might make the patient's psychological disposition more serious. The psychiatrist may use other biological treatments, such as electroshock therapy, in the treatment of severe depression and is qualified to supervise the care of patients requiring long-term hospitalization.

The clinical psychologist emerges from the tradition of psychology rather than that of medicine, with a background in theories of behavior and the ways in which behavior may be changed. After completing four years of undergraduate study—usually, but not necessarily, in psychology—the student studies two more years to obtain a master's degree in psychology and completes a master's thesis, which provides evidence of research capabilities. This is followed by three more years working toward a PhD degree and the completion of an internship in a mental health setting. After completion of these academic requirements, a psychologist is eligible to take the state licensing examination, which usually requires an oral and a written test. In some states, such as California, the psychologist is required to complete an additional year of supervised experience after receiving a PhD before becoming eligible for the licensing examination. After passing the examination for licensing, the psychologist is then able to offer services to the public for a fee. Many clinical psychologists choose to go into private practice, that is, to provide services to private patients in their own offices. About a quarter of all psychologists in the United States list private practice as their primary setting of employment. Other clinical psychologists work in settings such as hospitals, mental health clinics, university counseling centers, and other human service agencies.

After five years of clinical experience, the psychologist may apply for certification by the American Psychological Association. Obtaining certification requires passing written and oral tests as well as an on-site peer examination of clinical skills. Those who succeed are awarded the title of Diplomate in Clinical Psychology. This same award is given in other areas, such as counseling psychology, school psychology, industrial and organizational psychology, and neuropsychology. Board certification clarifies for the general public that the psychologist has demonstrated better-than-average clinical skills and is recognized as such by his or her professional peers. Fewer than 10 percent of all clinical psychologists have been awarded the status of diplomate. This is a useful guide, therefore, for persons who are uncertain about whom to see for therapy or assistance. Most telephone directories will designate the diplomate status of individuals, since the American Psychological Association requires that they identify themselves as such.

The counseling psychologist, much like the clinical psychologist, is required to obtain a PhD and complete an internship in counseling psychology. Counseling psychologists work in the mental health profession by providing services to those individuals, or couples, who are under stress or crisis but who continue to be functional. These are individuals who have functioned well in their lives but are meeting particularly difficult situations and require professional help to adjust to or overcome the stresses of the moment. These situations could involve loss of job, marital conflict, divorce, separation, parent-child or other family conflicts, prolonged physical illnesses, or academic difficulties. Counseling psychologists may either be in private practice or be employed by a university counseling center, where they provide services exclusively to college students.

A fourth type of mental health worker is the psychiatric social worker. This person completes four years of undergraduate study in the social or behavioral sciences, then completes two additional years of study in a school of social work. Social workers may choose different areas of specialty; the mental health worker usually concentrates in psychiatric social work. This involves recognizing the social environment of the patient and altering it in ways that will reduce stress and help maintain the gains that the patient may have achieved in treatment. The social worker becomes involved with issues such as vocational placements, career choice, and family stresses and is the link between the patient and the outside world. Social workers who are licensed may have their own private practices and may offer counseling and psychotherapy as a form of treatment.

TYPICAL ACTIVITIES

Surveys conducted by the American Psychological Association indicate that clinical psychologists spend most of their professional time with therapy, diagnosis and assessment, and teaching and administration. These categories constitute approximately 70 percent of their daily activity. Additional activities involve research and consultation with other agencies or professionals. Forty percent of their daily activity, however, is devoted to providing direct clinical services to patients either through psychotherapy or psychological testing.

Almost all practicing clinical psychologists engage in some type of diagnosis or assessment. These assessments usually involve the administration of psychological tests, which include intelligence tests, vocational tests, personality tests, attitude tests, and behavioral repertoires. The purpose of the testing is to assess the patient's current status, to determine any disabling conditions, to assess the patient's psychological strengths that can be used in therapy, and to determine treatment recommendations that are specific to the patient's particular problem. Usually these results are discussed with the patient, and a plan of treatment or therapy is recommended by the psychologist and agreed on by the patient.

Because there are more than two hundred forms of psychotherapy or behavioral interventions, it is the responsibility of the psychologist to determine which of these procedures is best for the patient, taking into consideration the patient's age, physical status, psychological and emotional condition, and the length of time the disorder has been present. Psychologists should have a good knowledge of the research literature, which would tell them which of these many therapeutic approaches is best for the particular clients with whom they are working at the time.

In the course of private clinical work, the clinical psychologist is likely to meet a variety of different types of cases. These clients may be referred for treatment by other mental health workers, hospitals, insurance plans, ministers, or prior patients.

Clients vary as to the severity of their disorders. Some are very seriously disturbed, such as schizophrenic adults who are not receiving treatment in the community and are homeless. They often require hospitalization that provides a complete plan of treatment. Clients with drug or alcohol problems who have had long-standing difficulties with these substances may also require partial hospitalization. The clinical psychologist often acts as the principal or cooperating therapist who plans and participates in the treatment program. Because many clinical psychologists have hospital privileges that allow them to admit their patients to a hospital facility, this procedure is used with severely disturbed persons who are a danger to themselves or to others.

Those psychologists who work principally in private practice tend to see clients who have problems adjusting but who do not require hospitalization. These clients often seek therapy to reduce excessive symptoms of anxiety, depression, or intrusive thoughts that affect their daily lives. Other clients seek help in relationships with others to solve marital, parent-child, employee-supervisor, or sexual conflicts. The clinical psychologist in private practice meets the needs of these clients by providing the best means of resolving these conflicts.

Because psychologists deal with human behavior, they are often involved in many other facets of human activity that require their expertise. For example, psychologists are called on to testify in court on questions of sanity, in custody cases, and, occasionally, as expert witnesses in criminal cases. Other psychologists are involved in sports psychology, helping athletes to develop the best psychological and emotional conditions for maximum performance. Still others work in the area of neuropsychology, which deals with patients who have experienced head injuries. Psychologists are asked to assess the extent of the injury and to find those areas that could be used to help the patient recover lost skills. Other psychologists specialize in treating of children who have been sexually or physically abused, in providing drug or alcohol counseling, in working in prisons with juvenile delinquents, or in working with patients who have geriatric disorders.

Some psychologists are involved in full- or part-time teaching at a university. These clinical psychologists not only continue their own clinical practices but also help prepare undergraduate and graduate students through direct classroom instruction or through supervision of their intern or field experiences.

DEVELOPMENTS IN THE FIELD

The field of psychology that deals mainly with emotional and psychological adjustment is called clinical psychology. This field began to take root during World War I, when psychologists were asked to screen military recruits for emotional problems and to assess intellectual abilities so that recruits could be placed in appropriate military positions. During World War II, clinical psychologists assumed an even greater role by developing psychological tests that were used in the selection of undercover agents. They were also asked to provide psychotherapy for soldiers who had emotional or neurological disorders.

Following World War II, clinical psychologists became heavily involved in the development and construction of psychological tests to measure intelligence, interest, personality, and brain dysfunction. Psychologists also became more involved in providing psychotherapy. Today, more psychologists spend their time providing psychotherapy than performing any other single activity.

Clinical psychology today regards itself as an independent profession, separate from the field of psychiatry, and sees itself rooted in the discipline of general psychology with the added clinical skills that make its practitioners uniquely capable of providing services to the general public. It is likely that clinical psychologists will continue to move in the direction of independent practice, focusing on new areas such as behavioral medicine, neuropsychology, forensic psychology, and pharmacotherapy. The latter trend is seen in the states of New Mexico and Louisiana, which allow psychologists with appropriate training to prescribe psychotropic drugs. Other states are actively considering legislation in this area.

BIBLIOGRAPHY

American Psychological Association. *Graduate Study in Psychology*, 2013. Washington: Author, 2013. Print.

American Psychological Association. *Psychology as a Health Care Profession*. Washington: Author, 1980. Print.

Gerig, Mark S. *Foundations for Clinical Mental Health Counseling: An Introduction to the Profession*. 2nd ed. Upper Saddle River: Pearson, 2014. Print.Linden, Wolfgang, and Paul L. Hewitt. Clinical Psychology: A Modern Health Profession. Boston: Prentice, 2012. Print.

Saccuzzo, Dennis P., and Robert M. Kaplan. *Clinical Psychology*. Boston: Allyn, 1984. Print.

Sternberg, Robert J., ed. Career Paths in Psychology: Where Your Degree Can Take You. 2nd ed. Washington: APA, 2007. Print.

Gerald Sperrazzo

SEE ALSO: Behavior therapy; Behavioral family therapy; Brief therapy; Clinical interviewing, testing, and observation; Cognitive behavior therapy; Cognitive therapy; Community psychology; Couples therapy; Diagnosis; Diagnostic and Statistical Manual of Mental Disorders (DSM); Existential psychology; Gestalt therapy; Group therapy; Health maintenance organizations; Health psychology; Music, dance, and theater therapy; Observational learning and modeling therapy; Person-centered therapy; Play therapy; Psychoanalytic psychology; Psychology: Fields of specialization; Psychotherapy: Children; Psychotherapy: Effectiveness; Psychotherapy: Goals and techniques; Psychotherapy: Historical approaches; Rational emotive therapy; Reality therapy.

Mental illness
Historical concepts

TYPE OF PSYCHOLOGY: Psychopathology

Throughout history, humans have tried to explain the abnormal behavior of people with mental disorders. From the ancient concept of demoniacal possession to modern biopsychosocial models, beliefs regarding the cause of mental disorder have influenced the way communities treat those variously labeled mad, insane, or mentally ill.

KEY CONCEPTS
- Asylum
- Biopsychosocial model of mental disorders
- Deinstitutionalization
- Demoniacal possession
- Humoral imbalance
- Lobotomy
- Madness
- Moral treatment
- Phenothiazines

INTRODUCTION

People are social creatures who learn how to behave appropriately in families and in communities. What is considered appropriate, however, depends on a host of factors, including historical period, culture, geography, and religion. Thus, what is valued and respected changes over time, as do sociocultural perceptions of aberrant or deviant behavior. How deviancy is treated depends a great deal on the extent of the deviancy—is the person dangerous, a threat to self or to the community, in flagrant opposition to community norms, or is the person just a little odd? How the community responds also depends on its beliefs as to what causes aberrant behavior. Supernatural beliefs in demons, spirits, and magic were common in preliterate societies; in the medieval Western world, Christians believed that the devil was in possession of deranged souls. Hence, the mad were subjected to cruel treatments justified by the idea of routing out demons or the devil. For centuries, the prevailing explanation for madness was demonic possession.

Prior to the nineteenth century, families and communities cared for the mad. If they were unmanageable or violent, the mad were incarcerated in houses of correction or dungeons, where they were manacled or put into straitjackets. If a physician ever attended someone who was deemed mad by the community, it was to purge or bleed the patient to redress a supposed humoral imbalance. Most medical explanations before the advent of scientific medicine were expressed in terms of the four humors: black and yellow bile, blood, and phlegm. Imbalances usually were treated with laxatives, purgatives, astringents, emetics, and bleeding. In the late eighteenth century, however, understanding moved from the holistic and humoral to the anatomical, chemical, and physiological. Views of humans and their rights also changed enormously around this time as a consequence of the American and French Revolutions.

During the nineteenth and twentieth centuries, madhouses were first replaced by more progressive lunatic asylums and then by mental hospitals and community mental health centers. In parallel fashion, custodians and superintendents of madhouses became mad-doctors or alienists in the nineteenth century and psychiatrists, psychologists, and counselors of various kinds in the twentieth century. Similarly, the language changed: Madness was variously called lunacy, insanity, derangement, or alienation. The contemporary term is mental disorder. These changes reflect the rejection of supernatural and humoral explanations of madness in favor of a disease model with varying emphases on organic or psychic causes.

EARLY VIEWS OF MADNESS

One of the terrible consequences of the belief in supernatural possession by demons was the inhumane treatment in which it often resulted. An example is found in the book of Leviticus in the Bible, which many scholars believe is a compilation of laws that had been handed down orally in the Jewish community for as long as a thousand years until they were written down, perhaps about 700 b.c.e. Leviticus 20:27, in the King James version, reads, "A man or a woman that hath a familiar spirit . . . shall surely be put to death: they shall stone him with stones." The term "familiar spirit" suggests demonic possession, and death was the response for dealing with demons in their midst.

There were exceptions to the possession theory and the inhumane treatment to which it often led. Hippocrates, who lived around 300 b.c.e. in Greece and who is regarded as the father of medicine, believed that mental illness had biological causes and could be explained by human reason through empirical study. Although Hippocrates found no cure, he did recommend that the mentally ill be treated humanely, as other ill people would be treated.

The period of Western history that is sometimes known as the Dark Ages was particularly dark for the mad. Folk belief, theology, and occult beliefs and practices of all kinds often led to terrible treatment. Although some educated and thoughtful people, even in that period, held humane views, they were in the minority regarding madness.

EIGHTEENTH AND NINETEENTH CENTURY VIEWS

It was not until what could be considered the modern historical period, the end of the eighteenth century, that major changes took place in the treatment of the insane. Additionally, there was a change in attitudes toward the insane, in approaches to their treatment, and in beliefs regarding the causes of their strange behaviors. One of the pioneers of this new attitude was the French physician Philippe Pinel. Pinel was appointed physician-in-chief of the Bicêtre Hospital in Paris in 1792. The Bicêtre was one of a number of "asylums" that had developed in Europe and in Latin America over several hundred years to house the insane. Often started with the best of intentions, most of the asylums became hellish places of incarceration.

In the Bicêtre, patients were often chained to the walls of their cells and lacked even the most elementary amenities. Under Pinel's guidance, the patients were freed from their confinement—popular myth has Pinel removing the patients' shackles personally, risking death if he should prove to be wrong about the necessity for confinement, but in fact it was Pinel's assistant Jean Baptiste Pussin who performed the act. Pinel also discarded the former treatment plan of bleeding, purging, and blistering in favor of a new model that emphasized talking to patients and addressing underlying personal and societal causes for their problems, using medical treatments such as opiates only as a last resort. Talking to his patients about their symptoms and keeping careful notes of what they said allowed Pinel to make advances in the classification of mental illnesses as well.

This change was occurring in other places at about the same time. After the death of a Quaker in Britain's York Asylum, the local Quaker community founded the York Retreat, where neither chains nor corporal punishment were allowed. In America, Benjamin Rush, a founder of the American Psychiatric Association, applied his version of moral treatment, which was not entirely humane as it involved physical restraints and fear as therapeutic agents. Toward the middle of the nineteenth century, American crusader Dorothea Dix fought for the establishment of state mental hospitals for the insane. Under the influence of Dix, thirty-two states established at least one mental hospital. Dix had been influenced by the moral model, as well as by the medical sciences, which were rapidly developing in the nineteenth century. Unfortunately, the state mental hospital often lost its character as a "retreat" for the insane.

The nineteenth century was the first time in Western history that a large number of scientists turned their attention to abnormal behavior. For example, the German psychiatrist Emil Kraepelin spent much of his life trying to develop a scientific classification system for psychopathology. Sigmund Freud attempted to develop a science of mental illness. Although many of Freud's ideas have not withstood empirical investigation, perhaps his greatest contribution was his insistence that scientific principles apply to mental illness. He believed that abnormal behavior is not caused by supernatural forces and does not arise in a chaotic, random way, but that it can be understood as serving some psychological purpose.

MODERN MEDICINES

Many of the medical and biological treatments for mental illness in the first half of the twentieth century were frantic attempts to deal with very serious problems—attempts made by clinicians who had few effective therapies to use. The attempt to produce convulsions (which often did seem to make people "better," at least temporarily) was popular for a decade or two. One example was insulin shock therapy, in which convulsions were induced in mentally ill people by insulin injection. Electroshock therapy was also used. Originally it was primarily used with patients who had schizophrenia, a severe form of psychosis. Although it was not very effective with schizophrenia, it was found to be useful with patients who had depressive psychosis. Now known as electroconvulsive therapy, it continues to be used in cases of major depression or bipolar disorder which are resistant to all other treatments. Another treatment sometimes

used, beginning in the 1930's, was prefrontal lobotomy. Many professionals today would point out that the use of lobotomy indicates the almost desperate search for an effective treatment for the most aggressive or the most difficult psychotic patients. As originally used, lobotomy was an imprecise slashing of the frontal lobe of the brain.

The real medical breakthrough in the treatment of psychotic patients was associated with the use of certain drugs from a chemical family known as phenothiazines. Originally used in France as a tranquilizer for surgery patients, their potent calming effect attracted the interest of psychiatrists and other mental health workers. One drug of this group, chlorpromazine, was found to reduce or eliminate psychotic symptoms in many patients. This and similar medications came to be referred to as antipsychotic drugs. Although their mechanism of action is still not completely understood, there is no doubt that they worked wonders for many severely ill patients while causing severe side effects for others. The drugs allowed patients to function outside the hospital and often to lead normal lives. They enabled many patients to benefit from psychotherapy. The approval of the use of chlorpromazine as an antipsychotic drug in the United States in 1955 revolutionized the treatment of many mental patients. Individuals who, prior to 1955, might have spent much of their lives in a hospital could now control their illness effectively enough to live in the community, work at a job, attend school, and be a functioning member of a family.

In 1955, the United States had approximately 559,000 patients in state mental hospitals; seventeen years later, in 1972, the population of the state mental hospitals had decreased almost by half, to approximately 276,000. Although all of this cannot be attributed to the advent of the psychoactive drugs, they undoubtedly played a major role. The phenothiazines had finally given medicine a real tool in the battle with psychosis. One might believe that the antipsychotic drugs, combined with a contemporary version of the moral treatment, would enable society to eliminate mental illness as a major human problem. Unfortunately, good intentions go awry. The "major tranquilizers" can easily become chemical straitjackets; those who prescribe the drugs are sometimes minimally involved with future treatment. In the late 1970s, the makers of social policy saw what appeared to be the economic benefits of reducing the role of the mental hospital, by discharging patients and closing some mental hospitals. However, they did not foresee that large numbers of homeless psychotics would live in the streets as a consequence of deinstitutionalization. The plight of the homeless during the early part of the twenty-first century continues to be a serious, national problem in the United States.

DISORDER AND DYSFUNCTION

The twentieth century saw the exploration of many avenues in the treatment of mental disorders. Treatments ranging from classical psychoanalysis to cognitive and humanistic therapies to the use of therapeutic drugs were applied. Psychologists examined the effects of mental disorders on many aspects of life, including cognition and personality. These disorders affect the most essential of human functions, including cognition, which has to do with the way in which the mind thinks and makes decisions. Cognition does not work in "ordinary" ways in the person with a serious mental illness, making his or her behavior very difficult for family, friends, and others to understand. Another aspect of cognition is perception. Perception has to do with the way that the mind, or brain, interprets and understands the information that comes to a person through the senses. There is a general consensus among most human beings about what they see and hear, and perhaps to a lesser extent about what they touch, taste, and smell. The victim of mental illness, however, often perceives the world in a much different way. This person may see objects or events that no one else sees, phenomena called hallucinations. The hallucinations may be visual—for example, the person may see a frightening wild animal that no one else sees—or the person may hear a voice accusing him or her of terrible crimes or behaviors that no one else hears.

A different kind of cognitive disorder is delusions. Delusions are untrue and often strange ideas, usually growing out of psychological needs or problems of a person who may have only tenuous contact with reality. A woman, for example, may believe that other employees are plotting to harm her in some way when, in fact, they are merely telling innocuous stories around the water cooler. Sometimes people with mental illness will be disoriented, which means that they do not know where they are in time (what year, what season, or what time of day) or in space (where they live, where they are at the present moment, or where they are going).

In addition to experiencing cognitive dysfunction that creates havoc, mentally ill persons may have emotional problems that go beyond the ordinary. For example, they live on such an emotional "high" for weeks or months at a time that their behavior is exhausting both to

themselves and to those around them. They may exhibit bizarre behavior; for example, they may talk about giving away vast amounts of money (which they do not have), or they may go without sleep for days until they drop from exhaustion. This emotional "excitement" seems to dominate their lives and is called mania. The word "maniac" comes from this terrible emotional extreme.

At the other end of the emotional spectrum is clinical depression. This does not refer to the ordinary "blues" of daily life, with all its ups and downs, but to an emotional emptiness in which the individual seems to have lost all emotional energy. The individual often seems completely apathetic. The person may feel life is not life worth living and may have anhedonia, which refers to an inability to experience pleasure of almost any kind.

TREATMENT APPROACHES

Anyone interacting with a person suffering from severe mental disorders comes to think of him or her as being different from normal human beings. The behavior of those with mental illness is regarded, with some justification, as bizarre and unpredictable. They are often labeled with a term that sets them apart, such as "crazy" or "mad." There are many words in the English language that have been, or are, used to describe these persons—many of them quite cruel and derogatory. Since the nineteenth century, professionals have used the term "psychotic" to denote severe mental illness or disorder. Interestingly, one translation of psychotic is "of a sickness of the soul" and reflects the earlier belief regarding the etiology, or cause, of mental illness. This belief is still held by some therapists and pastoral counselors in the twenty-first century. Until the end of the twentieth century, the term "neurosis" connoted more moderate dysfunction than the term "psychosis." However, whether neurosis is always less disabling or disturbing than psychosis has been an open question. An attempt was made to deal with this dilemma in 1980, when the DSM-III officially dropped the term "neurosis" from the diagnostic terms.

The contemporary approach to mental disorder, at its best, offers hope and healing to patients and their families. However, much about the etiology of mental disorder remains unknown to social scientists and physicians.

In 1963, President John F. Kennedy signed the Community Mental Health Act. Its goal was to set up centers throughout the United States offering services to mentally and emotionally disturbed citizens and their families, incorporating the best that had been learned and that would be learned from science and from medicine. Outpatient services in the community, emergency services, "partial" hospitalizations (adult day care), consultation, education, and research were among the programs supported by the act. Although imperfect, it nevertheless demonstrated how far science had come from the days when witches were burned at the stake and the possessed were stoned to death.

When one deals with mental disorder, one is dealing with human behavior—both the behavior of the individual identified as having the problem and the behavior of the community. The response of the community is critical for the successful treatment of disorder. For example, David L. Rosenhan, in a well-known 1973 study titled "On Being Sane in Insane Places," showed how easy it is to be labeled "crazy" and how difficult it is to get rid of the label. He demonstrated how one's behavior is interpreted and understood on the basis of the labels that have been applied. (The "pseudopatients" in the study had been admitted to a mental hospital and given a diagnosis—a label—of schizophrenia. Consequently, even their writing of notes in a notebook was regarded as evidence of their illness.) To understand mental disorder is not merely to understand personal dysfunction or distress, but also to understand social and cultural biases of the community, from the family to the federal government. The prognosis for eventual mental and emotional health depends not only on appropriate therapy but also on the reasonable and humane response of the relevant communities.

BIBLIOGRAPHY

American Psychiatric Association. *Diagnostic and Statistical Manual of Mental Disorders: DSM-5.* 5th ed. Washington, DC: American Psychiatric Assn., 2013. Print.

Berrios, German E., and Roy Porter. *A History of Clinical Psychiatry: The Origin and History of Psychiatric Disorders.* New Brunswick: Athlone, 1999. Print.

Chung, Man Cheung, and Michael Hyland. *History and Philosophy of Psychology.* Chichester: Wiley, 2012. Print.

Frankl, Viktor Emil. *Man's Search for Meaning.* New York: Washington Square, 2006. Print.

Freud, Sigmund. *The Freud Reader.* Ed. Peter Gay. 1989. Reprint. New York: Norton, 1995. Print.

Grob, Gerald N. *The Mad Among Us: A History of the Care of America's Mentally Ill.* New York: Free Press, 1994. Print.

Porter, Roy. *The Greatest Benefit to Mankind: A Medical History of Humanity.* New York: Norton, 1999. Print.

Porter, Roy. *Madness: A Brief History.* New York: Oxford UP, 2003. Print.

Robinson, Daniel N. *An Intellectual History of Psychology.* 3d ed. Madison: U of Wisconsin P, 1995. Print.

Rosenhan, David L. "On Being Sane in Insane Places." *Science* 179 (January 19, 1973): 250–258. Print.

Rudnick, Abraham. *Recovery of People with Mental Illness: Philosophical and Related Perspectives.* Oxford: Oxford UP, 2012. Print.

Shiraev, Eric. *A History of Psychology: A Global Perspective.* Thousand Oaks: Sage, 2011. Print.

Torrey, E. Fuller, and Judy Miller. *The Invisible Plague: The Rise of Mental Illness from 1750 to the Present.* New Brunswick: Rutgers UP, 2007. Print.

Wallace, Edwin R., and John Gach. H*istory of Psychiatry and Medical Psychology: With an Epilogue on Psychiatry and the Mind-Body Relation.* New York: Springer, 2008. Print.

James Taylor Henderson; updated by Tanja Bekhuis

SEE ALSO: Abnormality: Biomedical models; American Psychiatric Association; American Psychological Association; Dix, Dorothea; Lobotomy; Pinel, Philippe; Psychology: Fields of specialization; Psychology: History; Psychosurgery; Psychotherapy: Historical approaches; Schizophrenia: Background, types, and symptoms; Schizophrenia: Theoretical explanations; Thought: Study and measurement.

Mental retardation

TYPE OF PSYCHOLOGY: Developmental psychology

Mental retardation occurs about three times per thousand births and usually indicates an intelligence quotient (IQ) of less than 70. Variations in severity may allow some individuals to be virtually independent and capable of retaining simple jobs, whereas more severely affected persons may require lifetime institutional care. The causes of mental retardation are numerous, with many having a clearcut underlying genetic basis, others implicating environmental factors, and still others with no known cause.

KEY CONCEPTS

- Congenital
- Down syndrome
- Fetal alcohol syndrome

- Fragile X syndrome
- Idiopathic
- Intelligence quotient (IQ)
- Mental retardation
- Phenylketonuria
- Teratogens

INTRODUCTION

The term "mental retardation" conjures up different meanings for different people. A useful definition is provided by the American Association on Mental Retardation: "Mental retardation is a particular state of functioning that begins in childhood and is characterized by limitation in both intelligence and adaptive skills." Mental retardation reflects the "fit" between the capabilities of individuals and the structure and expectations of their environment. It is characterized by significantly subaverage intellectual functioning, existing concurrently with related limitations in two or more of the following applicable adaptive skill areas: communication, home living, community use, health and safety, leisure, self-care, social skills, self-direction, functional academics, and work. It is evident that deficits in intelligence and adaptive skills will be related to the complexity of the society in which the individual lives.

Degrees of severity of mental retardation have been determined based on intelligence quotient (IQ) scores. The four levels of severity (with some overlap) are mild retardation (IQ range 50-70), moderate retardation (IQ range 35-55), severe retardation (IQ range 20-40), and profound (IQ range less than 20 or 25). Rather than use a classification based on the severity level, a classification based on the type and intensity of support needed also is now in practice: intermittent, limited, extensive, or pervasive. Persons with mild retardation usually are capable of living with some degree of independence in the community and can usually work successfully at simple jobs. The great majority—85 percent—of cases of mental retardation fall into this category. The remaining 15 percent of cases are at the moderate, severe, and profound levels, with only approximately 1-2 percent at the profound level. These last three levels are sometimes grouped together as severe. Profoundly affected individuals require constant care and supervision.

Several causes of mental retardation are becoming known, although in many cases it may not be possible to ascribe mental retardation in a family member to a specific cause. Just because a disorder is congenital (present at birth) does not necessarily imply that the disorder is genetic. Agents that are capable of affecting the developing fetus such as alcohol, mercury, infections, maternal

---

DSM-IV-TR CRITERIA FOR MENTAL RETARDATION

Significantly subaverage intellectual functioning:
- for children and adults, IQ of approximately 70 or below
- for infants, clinical judgment of significantly subaverage intellectual functioning

Concurrent deficits or impairments in adaptive functioning (effectiveness in meeting standards expected for age and cultural group) in at least two of the following areas:
- communication
- self-care
- home living
- social/interpersonal skills
- use of community resources
- self-direction
- functional academic skills
- work

- leisure
- health
- safety

Onset before age eighteen

DSM code based on degree of severity reflecting level of intellectual impairment:
- Mild Mental Retardation (DSM code 317): IQ level
- of 50-55 to approx. 70
- Moderate Mental Retardation (DSM code 318.0):
- IQ level of 35-40 to 50-55
- Severe Mental Retardation (DSM code 318.1):
- IQ level of 20-25 to 35-40
- Profound Mental Retardation (DSM code 318.2):
- IQ level below 20 or 25
- Mental Retardation, Severity Unspecified (DSM
- code 319): IQ level untestable

phenylketonuria, and many other substances may lead to mental retardation. Many single-gene disorders and chromosomal abnormalities produce mental retardation as part of their syndromes, or disorders characterized by multiple effects. A large-scale study of severely mentally retarded patients institutionalized in Wisconsin, summarized by Sarah Bundey in 1997, indicated that 11.8 percent of the cases were due to chromosomal abnormality, 6.5 percent to singlegene defects, 16.3 percent to multiple congenital anomaly syndromes, 14.7 percent to central nervous system malformations such as hydrocephalus, 32.1 percent to central nervous system dysfunction due to perinatal or unidentified prenatal causes including cerebral palsy, 8.5 percent to infectious disease, 3.9 percent to postnatal brain damage, and 1.2 percent to infantile psychosis; 5.0 percent were unclassified. It was noted that the number of patients with Down syndrome was low since they were admitted less frequently. Other surveys have shown that Down syndrome accounts for about one-third of mentally retarded patients.

ETIOLOGY

Although some cases of mental retardation are idiopathic (without a specific known cause), many known causes account for many of the cases of mental retardation. The difficulties in identifying factors involved in mental and behavioral disorders are seen clearly in the study of children exposed prenatally to radiation following the Chernobyl nuclear plant accident in 1986, as reported by S. Igumnov and V. Drozdovitch. The children who had been exposed to radiation displayed borderline intellectual functioning and emotional disorders to a greater degree when compared with a control group. Other unfavorable social-psychological and sociocultural factors included a low educational level of the parents and problems associated with relocation from the contaminated areas.

Similar complications are seen in the work of M. S. Durkin and colleagues on prenatal and postnatal risk factors among children in Bangladesh. The study screened more than ten thousand children from both rural and urban areas. Significant predictors of serious mental retardation included maternal goiter and postnatal brain infections. Consanguinity also was a significant factor in the rural areas. For less severe mental retardation, maternal illiteracy, maternal history of pregnancy loss, and small size for gestational age at birth were significant independent risk factors.

It is convenient to separate the known causes of mental retardation into the two categories of genetic and acquired or environmental. However, many cases of mental retardation may be a result of the interaction of several genes and the environment, in which case the disorder is said to be multifactorial.

GENETIC CAUSES

Approximately one thousand genetic disorders are associated with mental retardation, and the number increases regularly. If mental retardation is associated with other conditions or features, it is syndromic; if it is the only primary symptom, it is said to be nonspecific. In general, a genetic involvement is more likely to be found in severe forms of mental retardation than it is in milder forms. A few examples of chromosomal and single-gene disorders leading to mental retardation will be discussed as representative examples.

Chromosomal Disorders. Down syndrome was first described by John Langdon Down in 1866, and although heredity was suspected in its etiology, it was not until 1959 that it was discovered that Down syndrome patients had one extra chromosome, for a total of forty-seven instead of the normal forty-six. Down syndrome occurs at a frequency of about one in one thousand births and is the single most important cause of mental retardation. The great majority of Down patients have three chromosomes number 21 instead of two (a condition called trisomy 21). The physical features associated with Down syndrome are easily recognizable: short stature, a short neck with excessive loose skin, thick lips, epicanthal folds of the eye, malformed ears, poor muscle tone, and a flattened facial profile. Major physical problems include heart and kidney defects, deafness, and gastrointestinal blockages. Developmental milestones are delayed, and mental retardation is common. Intelligence varies considerably, with an aver-age IQ of 50 and only a small percentage of patients approaching the lower end of the normal range. It is essential that parents and educators assess the capabilities of each child and provide an educational environment that maximizes achievement.

Although Down syndrome is genetic in the sense that it results from an imbalance in the genetic material—an extra chromosome— it is not hereditary in the sense that it does not run in families. The incidence of Down syndrome also shows a striking increase with maternal age, increasing dramatically (one in fifty births) in women giving birth beyond age thirty-five.

Other cases involving an extra chromosome or a missing chromosome, particularly if the missing chromosome is one of the autosomes, usually lead to spontaneous abortion. A normal human has twenty-two pairs of autosomes and one pair of sex chromosomes— XX if a female, XY if a male. The few that survive have severe malformations, including those of the brain, and are likely to have severe mental retardation. Malformations as a result of abnormalities involving the sex chromosomes are usually less severe. Females with an extra X chromosome (XXX) tend to have lower IQs than their siblings. Males with an extra X chromosome (XXY), a condition called Klinefelter syndrome, usually are not mentally retarded but may develop psychosocial problems. Males with an extra Y chromosome (XYY) may have speech, language, and reading problems.

Single-Gene Disorders. Fragile X syndrome is the second most common genetic cause of mental retardation. It is the most common inherited form of mental retardation. As is true of other disorders due to sex-linked recessive genes, more males are affected than are females. The frequency of fragile X males is about 1 in 1,000; for females, it is about 1 in 2,500. It is estimated that up to 8 percent of the males in institutions for mental retardation have a fragile X chromosome. Grant R. Sutherland and John C. Mulley in 1996 provided a useful review of the characteristics of fragile X syndrome. Features include a prominent forehead and jaws; prominent, long, and mildly dysmorphic ears; hyperextensible finger joints; enlarged testes (macroorchidism); and mitral value prolapse. About 80 percent of fragile X males have mental retardation. Most of them have moderate retardation, but some are only mildly retarded. They tend to have better verbal than spatial abilities. They show speech abnormalities such as echolalia (compulsively repeating the speech of others). In general, they tend to be hyperactive. Only about one-half of girls with the fragile X chromosome are affected, and limited studies of females estimate that perhaps up to 7 percent of female mental retardation is caused by fragile X syndrome. The specific gene involved in fragile X syndrome has been identified: The syndrome is caused by an expanded triplet repeat, a form of mutation in which deoxyribonucleic acid (DNA) nucleotides are repeated a number of times.

Phenylketonuria (PKU) is one of the inborn errors of metabolism that results in mental retardation if left untreated. PKU is a disorder of amino acid metabolism in which individuals cannot metabolize normally the amino acid phenylalanine because they are deficient in the liver enzyme phenylalanine hydroxylase. As a result, phenylalanine and other metabolites accumulate in the blood. At birth, children are normal, but clinical features gradually appear during the first twelve months. Some affected persons have a "mousy" odor about them because of the excretion of phenylacetic acid. They tend to have light skin and hair, seizures, mental retardation, and other neurologic symptoms. PKU occurs in about one in fourteen thousand births and once accounted for about 1 percent of severely retarded individuals in institutions. Some interesting variations in the incidence of PKU are seen among different populations. In Turkey, a very high incidence is seen, 1 in 2,600 births, whereas in Japan the rate is only 1 in 143,000 births. The disorder is inherited as autosomal recessive, and most of the affected children are born to parents who are not affected.

PKU represents the prototype of genetic disorders for which newborn screening can be done: Babies with high blood levels of phenylalanine can be identified and treatment can begin immediately. Dietary management of phenylalanine levels does not correct the underlying gene defect, but it keeps the levels sufficiently low that adverse effects on the brain and nervous system do not occur and mental retardation is avoided. It is thought necessary to maintain the special diet through the adolescent years. It also is necessary for women with PKU who become pregnant to resume a diet low in phenylalanine to prevent high intrauterine levels from affecting the developing fetus, even though the latter may not be genetically "programmed" to inherit PKU. Untreated patients with PKU have mean IQs around 50, whereas treated patients will have IQs close to normal.

ENVIRONMENTAL CAUSES

Numerous cases of mental retardation are a result of damage to a fetus during pregnancy. Other problems may arise during birth or after birth. Physical or chemical agents that cause an increase in congenital defects are known as teratogens. Since teratogens affect embryos and fetuses directly, the effects are not likely to produce heritable changes. A woman who uses or is exposed to various teratogens during pregnancy runs the risk of producing a child with a developmental malformation. Potential teratogens include alcohol, drugs, viral infections, radiation, diabetes mellitus, malnutrition, and environmental toxins.

Since its initial clinical delineation in 1973, fetal alcohol syndrome has been noted as a major cause of mental retardation in countries where alcohol is consumed regularly. Estimates indicate that it may be responsible for as many as one to three cases of mental retardation out of every thousand births. Fortunately, fetal alcohol syndrome is easily preventable through abstinence from alcohol during pregnancy. Children affected with fetal alcohol syndrome have a characteristic facial appearance, with a small skull, upturned nose, thin upper lip, underdeveloped upper jaw, epicanthal folds, and a long philtrum (the vertical groove on the median line of the upper lip). There is growth retardation, which has its onset prenatally and continues during the postnatal period with some catch-up growth taking place thereafter. Head and brain size remain well below normal. Children show developmental delays, attention deficits, hyperactivity, and mental deficiency. Although the average IQ of children with fetal alcohol syndrome is low, 60 to 65, there is considerable variation, with some children having normal or nearnormal intelligence but experiencing learning disorders. Severe physical defects found in many of these children include cardiac and skeletal defects.

Although it is evident that the risk of fetal alcohol syndrome is related to the amount and timing of the alcohol consumed by the pregnant woman, an exact close relationship has been difficult to establish. Even with moderate consumption (one to two ounces of absolute alcohol), the serious effects of

fetal alcohol syndrome have been observed in approximately 10 percent of births. Many physicians now recommend that women practice total abstinence from alcohol during the entire pregnancy.

PREVENTION AND TREATMENT

Although it is not possible to treat some underlying causes of mental retardation, many of the genetic and teratogenic cases can be prevented through genetic counseling, prenatal diagnosis, and education to alert people of the risk to developing fetuses of teratogens such as alcohol. It also is essential to have an accurate diagnosis of the cause and nature of the problems associated with individual cases of mental retardation for parents to be able to undertake the best possible intervention program for their children.

Newborn screening programs can detect certain disorders that will lead to mental retardation, including PKU, congenital hypothyroidism, galactosemia, maple syrup urine disease, and other inherited metabolic disorders. Prenatal testing (such as amniocentesis and chorionic villi sampling) can be used to detect chromosomal disorders, including Down syndrome and several hundred single-gene disorders that may lead to severe physical or mental disorders in children. Neural tube defects can be detected prenatally by testing the amniotic fluid for elevated levels of alpha-fetoprotein. Most of the cases of prenatal testing are done for individuals in which there is a reason to suspect that the fetus is at an increased risk for a particular genetic disease or birth defect. These risks include increased maternal age, birth of a previous child with a disorder, and a family history of a disorder. Genetic counseling also is used to aid a couple in understanding genetic risks before a pregnancy has commenced, however, most mentally retarded children are born to parents with no history of mental retardation.

BIBLIOGRAPHY

Baroff, George S., and J. Gregory Olley. *Mental Retardation: Nature, Cause, and Management*. 3d ed. Philadelphia: Brunner-Routledge, 1999. This textbook presents information on the biological and psychological causes of mental retardation and its management.

Beirne-Smith, Mary, James R. Patton, and Richard F. Ittenback. *Mental Retardation*. 7th ed. Upper Saddle River, N.J.: Prentice Hall, 2006. A comprehensive book that deals with historical, biological, psychological, and sociological aspects of mental retardation.

Burack, Jacob A., Robert M. Hodapp, and Edward Zigler, eds. *Handbook of Mental Retardation and Development*. New York: Cambridge University Press, 1998. This handbook provides comprehensive information emphasizing the developmental aspects of mental retardation.

Durkin, M. S., et al. "Prenatal and Postnatal Risk Factors for Mental Retardation Among Children in Bangladesh." *American Journal of Epidemiology* 152, no. 11 (2000): 1024-1033. This study examines the role of different factors in causing mental retardation in rural and urban children.

Igumnov, S., and V. Drozdovitch. "The Intellectual Development, Mental, and Behavioural Disorders in Children from Belarus Exposed in Utero Following the Chernobyl Accident." *European Psychiatry* 15, no. 4 (2000): 244-253. The authors report borderline intellectual functioning and emotional disorders in children exposed in utero to fallout from Chernobyl, along with factors thought to contribute (such as relocation).

McKusick, Victor A. *Mendelian Inheritance in Man*. 12th ed. Baltimore: Johns Hopkins University Press, 1999. This book is a comprehensive catalog of human genes and genetic disorders, including mitochondrial genes.

Rimoin, David L., J. Michael Connor, and Reed E. Pyeritz. *Emery and Rimoin's Principles and Practice of Medical Genetics*. 5th ed. New York: Churchill Livingstone, 2007. This voluminous book includes several chapters dealing with mental and behavioral disorders.

Donald J. Nash

SEE ALSO: Birth: Effects on physical development; Down syndrome; Intelligence; Intelligence quotient (IQ); Prenatal physical development; Thought: Study and measurement.

Midlife crisis

TYPE OF PSYCHOLOGY: Developmental psychology; Personality; Psychological methodologies; Psychopathology; Psychotherapy; Social psychology; Stress

Midlife crisis describes a period of self-doubt and searching between the ages of thirty and sixty. It is a cultural phenomenon and has no formal diagnosis. First identified formally by Carl Jung in the 1930's, midlife crisis received a great deal of popular attention during and after the 1970's. People in many traditional and non-Western cultures experience such changes less frequently and often deal with them as ordinary changes in a cycle of life.

KEY CONCEPTS

- Depression
- Empty-nest syndrome
- Insomnia
- Menopause
- Rites of passage

INTRODUCTION

Midlife crisis (also known as the midlife transition) in Western societies often involves a period of self-doubt that can afflict people during the midst of life, usually during their forties (but as early as their thirties or as late as age sixty). Self-doubts often involve the passage of youthful ambitions and hopes, as the recognition dawns that certain career and romantic goals are no longer attainable, along with the anticipation of old age and its limitations. When a midlife crisis afflicts women, it is sometimes related to menopause, which is often called the change of life.

Less than 10 percent of people experience severe enough psychological problems during a midlife crisis to seek some sort of counseling. Although the condition has never been formalized as a diagnostic category, a minority of those who believe they are afflicted with it may require psychotherapy. Although rare, some manifestations of midlife crisis can be severe and may include suicide attempts.

HISTORY OF THE IDEA

About the same time that Sigmund Freud, founder of psychoanalysis, argued that adulthood was a largely stable state bereft of important changes, a lesser-known author, French folklorist Arnold van Gennep, in *The Rites of Passage* (1909), described ancient ceremonies that celebrated an individual's transitions as passages of life. He saw such changes not as crises, but as opportunities for a person to accumulate new knowledge and, thus, new status in society. Western society lacks rituals that guide most people through life's transitions.

The idea that people may experience dramatic psychological changes in midlife was first introduced to the theory of psychology during the 1930's by the Swiss psychologist Carl Jung. Jung compared midlife to noon in a diurnal cycle. About "noon" in the cycle of life, he theorized, significant change is most likely to take place in the human psyche. Jung did not see midlife as a time of crisis, however, but one in which people could rediscover qualities that had been underdeveloped or neglected during the first half of life.

Since the 1970's, the concept has received copious popular attention that provoked academic research, indicating that most people experience a midlife crisis in a mild way. At that time, Gail Sheehy's popular book *Passages: Predictable Crises of Adult Life* (1976) enhanced discussion of midlife crisis in much of the Western, industrial world.

CAUSES AND CONSEQUENCES

Midlife crisis may be intensified by the death of a family member or lover, or career-related stress. Midlife crisis in men is more likely to be triggered by work-related issues, but menopause in a partner can contribute to a man's yearning for a younger partner, contributing to marital infidelity. Such crises also tend to last longer in men (three to ten years), than in women (two to five years). Midlife concerns for women are more likely to involve changes related to menopause, children leaving home, or demands related to caring for live-in parents and children at the same time. However, the midlife profile of an increasing number of women in the workforce may more closely resemble that of men.

People, ideas, and possessions that once brought excitement and joy may be rejected as boring and out-of-date. A sense of excitement may be sought in unusual (and sometimes risky) adventures. A spouse may be rejected as an impediment to a new life; formerly enduring love may be questioned, as those who experience midlife changes (usually men, in this case) seek new, hopefully passionate, intimate relationships.

Men who define their self-worth according to job performance may be more prone to midlife crisis if they lose a job in middle age. Women, who are more likely to define self-worth through human (especially family) relationships, may feel inadequate when these change, even through ordinary stages of life, such as when children grow up and leave home, contributing to empty-nest syndrome. Some women cope with such losses by going back to school or taking jobs.

Midlife crisis is often characterized by a person's search for a dream that is difficult to define (and, therefore, to attain). At the same time, life to date may be characterized as without meaning, a state of mind that sometimes leads to depression (a chronic lack of interest in life). Symptoms of serious depression may be accompanied by striking changes in eating habits, insomnia, fatigue, anxiety, nonspecific aches and pains, irritability, and even thoughts of or attempts at suicide. Midlife crisis may be more intense for people who at other ages have had low self-esteem, have repressed interpersonal conflict, feel inadequate, and have been emotionally distant. People who easily experience shame and rejection may find such experiences amplified at middle age.

Remorse regarding onset of aging can contribute, most often in Anglo-American men, to abuse of alcohol and other drugs, acquisition of luxury goods symbolic of youth (most notably items of personal adornment, such as tattoos, body piercings, flashy clothing, and jewelry), as well as other consumer goods symbolic of youth, such as motorcycles.

CROSS-CULTURAL ATTRIBUTES

Some critics contend that midlife crisis is more of a psychological urban legend than a reality. People experience identity concerns at other ages (most notably adolescence), and concern about aging is hardly unique to middle life. Major life changes, such as a divorce or loss of a job, can provoke acute psychological reaction at any age. For the majority of people who do not experience a pronounced midlife crisis, the years thirty to sixty can be a time of general happiness and achievement that may be recalled in old age as "the good old days." Some critics argue that the very popularity of the term "midlife crisis" may prompt some people in that age group to elevate ordinary anxieties to a psychological condition.

Midlife passages may be more stressful in societies in which people (such as ethnic minorities in the United States) must negotiate more than one culture in their daily lives. Stereotypes in the media complicate such situations. Ethnic traditions often come into conflict with mainstream values, creating additional anxieties. Such anxieties often bring people to more avid practice of traditions involving rituals that help define cultural expectations.

In many cultures, the attainment of middle age is not usually accompanied by unusual psychological stress and turmoil. Therefore, midlife crisis has been recognized as a cultural construct specific to technologically advanced Western societies. Self-doubt in the midst of life has been studied cross-culturally, and it has been found to be most intense in people with Anglo-American or European heritage. It is less frequent, and less intense, in Japan and India. The cultural obsession with youth that is prevalent in Western cultures probably contributes to a feeling of letdown after youth has passed.

People in several indigenous cultures believe that people change throughout their lives. Traditional stories (including some origin stories) allow for such changes. In *Drawing from the Women's Well: Reflections on the Life Passage of Menopause* (1992), Joan Borton describes traditional rites of passage that honor menopause as a positive passage through a stage of life. Here, and elsewhere in many indigenous cultures, storytelling is instructive in negotiating life's passages. In Western cultures, by contrast, stories are often relegated to childhood.

In *The Fountain of Age*, published in 1993 when she was seventy-two years old, feminist author Betty Friedan argues that looking at midlife as a decline from youth is a societal construct that demeans aging, whereas many traditional cultures esteem their elders. Friedan asserts that people continue to develop throughout life.

Many traditional stories told by indigenous groups center on a protagonist beset by conflict, anxiety, and adversity. The Haudenosaunee (Iroquois) Confederacy's origin story, which relates in mythical form historical events roughly a thousand years ago (1142 C.E., according to research by Barbara Alice Mann and Jerry Fields of the University of Toledo), features the conversion of a formerly remarkably evil man (Tadadaho) to wisdom and political leadership at an advanced age. In the Iroquois origin story, the Peacemaker (Deganawidah) and his aid Hiawatha overcome Tadahaho's evil genius and convert him to help found a confederacy of peace that replaced a history of bloodletting among the five Iroquois nations.

CONCLUSION

Whether it is real or imagined (or a combination), change in midlife, if properly understood and managed, need not result in depression or fractured relationships. It can result in profound personal redefinition and growth, leading to a richer later life. The shedding of old identifies often leads to the forging of new ones. Today many psychologists have come to agree that life's major struggles do not end in childhood and adolescence; redefinition extends to the end of life, and crisis, or transition, at midlife or even later can be part of such a change. The idea first posited by Freud that adulthood is a "mature" or stable state of life when large-scale change ceases is no longer common intellectual currency.

BIBLIOGRAPHY

Colarusso, Calvin A. *Fulfillment in Adulthood: Paths to the Pinnacle of Life.* New York: Plenum Press, 1994. A view of midlife transition as a developmental stage in the cycle of life.

Polden, Jane. *Regeneration: Journey Through Mid-life Crisis.* New York: Continuum, 2002. A popular treatment of midlife transition by an author who believes it to be a stage of growth, not a crisis.

Sharp, Daryl. *The Survival Papers: Anatomy of a Midlife Crisis.* Toronto, Ont.: Inner City Books, 1988. A case study of midlife transition, No. 35 in Studies in Jungian Psychology by Jungian Analysts.

Sheehy, Gail. *Passages: Predictable Crises of Adult Life.* New York: E. P. Dutton, 1976. A popular book that turned midlife crisis into a household phrase during the 1970's.

Shek, D. T. L. "Midlife Crisis in Chinese Men and Women." *Journal of Psychology* 130 (1995): 109-119. Study of midlife transition in Chinese culture.

Bruce E. Johansen

SEE ALSO: Abnormality: Psychological models; Ageism; Aging: Cognitive changes; Aging: Physical changes; Aging: Theories; Culture and diagnosis; Culture-bound syndromes; Men's mental health; Women's mental health.

Milgram experiment

DATE: 1961-1962
TYPE OF PSYCHOLOGY: Social psychology

Stanley Milgram designed and conducted an interesting and original experiment designed to measure the extent to which ordinary persons would inflict pain on others when instructed to do so by an authoritative figure. The experiments were highly controversial because participants were put in potentially stressful and embarrassing situations without their informed consent.

KEY CONCEPT

- Aggression
- Authority
- Behaviorism
- Conformity
- Ethics in human experiments
- Obedience

INTRODUCTION

Stanley Milgram is widely acknowledged to have been one of the most innovative and creative experimental social psychologists in the history of the discipline. Raised in a Jewish family during the Great Depression and World War II, Milgram was influenced by stories he heard about the Nazi persecutions of European Jews. After graduating in political science at Queen's University, he did graduate work in Harvard's social relations department, where he studied under Gordon Allport and Solomon Asch. His doctoral dissertation was devoted to a comparative study of conformity in Norway and France.

After he received his PhD in 1960, Milgram was appointed assistant professor of psychology at Yale University. During his first year at Yale, he conducted pilot studies of obedience with small groups of students. About this time, he conceptualized the framework for his famous obedience experiments. Influenced by accounts of mass participation in Nazi atrocities, his goal was to measure the willingness of average citizens to obey a person who had institutionalized authority. After receiving a grant from the National Science Foundation, Milgram conducted the experiments from July, 1961, to May, 1962. His first publication reporting the results of the experiments appeared in the *Journal of Abnormal and Social Psychology* in 1963, and his major book, *Obedience to Authority: An Experimental View*, was published eleven years later.

THE EXPERIMENTS

Each of Milgram's obedience experiments involved three people: a supervisor, a learner, and a teacher. Milgram's initial experiments were made with only men. Milgram employed and trained the supervisor and the learner, both of whom were actors. The third person in each session, the teacher, was an individual who had responded to an advertisement calling for volunteers to assist in a psychological study for a small fee. The teacher was uninformed about the true nature of the experiment. When the uninformed volunteer and actor entered the lab, the supervisor explained to them that the purpose of the experiment was to determine whether punishment in the form of electrical shocks would promote learning.

The supervisor had the two men select slips of paper to decide their respective roles. The slips, however, were arranged so that the unsuspecting volunteer would always take the role of teacher. The supervisor then seated the teacher in front of a large and impressive apparatus containing a series of levels marked from 15 volts to 450 volts. In most versions, the learner was strapped to a chair in a different room. After hearing that the shocks were painful but not dangerous, the teacher was instructed to give the learner a long multiple-choice test of word associations. Whenever the learner's response was incorrect, the teacher's duty was to administer a shock, increasing the voltage in 15-volt increments for each wrong answer. Although no shocks were actually delivered, the learner would cry out as if in pain when the 150-volt stage was reached, and he screamed louder until the shocks reached 315 volts, after which he would make no more sounds.

When a participant said he wanted to halt the experiment, the supervisor would reply with one of the following four directives: "Please continue!" "The experiment requires that you continue!" "It is absolutely essential that you continue!" and "You have no other choice; you must go on!" If the participant refused to continue, the experiment was stopped. Otherwise, it continued until the teacher had administered three successive shocks marked 450 volts. At the end of every experiment, the teacher was introduced to the learner and shown that the learner was unharmed. There was no attempt made to assure volunteers who gave high-voltage shocks that their behavior was not shameful or unusual.

In the first set of experiments, 65 percent of forty participants continued until the 450-volt shock. None of the participants insisted on stopping before the 300-volt stage. Milgram conducted nineteen variations of the experiments. In the tenth experiment, when the experiments took place in a modest office building in Bridgeport, Connecticut, continuation to the highest shock dropped to 47.5 percent. In the eighth experiment, he found that the use of women participants did not significantly change the result. When the physical proximity between teacher and learner increased, obedience significantly decreased. When a teacher was joined with other actor-teachers, full conformity reached about 90 percent.

IMPACT AND REACTION

The Milgram experiment raised a number of serious ethical issues. Without their informed consent, participants were put in extremely stressful conditions, with the real possibility that a person with a heart condition might have suffered significant harm. Some participants, moreover, were embarrassed by their own conduct in rendering fake shocks. In answer to his critics, Milgram argued that there was no evidence that any significant harm had occurred and that he had protected each participant's confidentiality. He also pointed to a survey indicating that 84 percent of participants said that they were "glad" or "very glad" to have been part of the experiment. Some even reported that the experiments had made them more ethically sensitive about the dangers of unquestionable obedience to authority.

The ethical controversy surrounding Milgram's experiments was one of several reasons why the American Psychological Association formulated its principles for research with humans and required approval of proposed experiments by institutional review boards (IRBs) in the early 1970s. Congress in 1974 enacted legislation mandating both informed consent and the use of IRBs. Although variations on Milgram's experiments were conducted a number of times in the United States and other countries throughout the 1960s and early 1970s, after the establishment of these regulations, social psychologists were no longer able to replicate the Milgram experiment in its entirety. In 2006, however, social psychologist Jerry M. Burger obtained permission to conduct a partial replication, stopping at 150 volts, the point at which the actor-learner began to scream in pain. Burger's results were similar to those recorded by Milgram, finding that approximately 67 percent of male participants and 73 percent of female participants continued administering shocks up to the 150-volt level.

BIBLIOGRAPHY

Blass, Thomas. *The Man Who Shocked the World.* New York: Basic, 2004. Print.

Blass, Thomas, ed. *Obedience to Authority: Current Perspectives on the Milgram Paradigm.* Mahwah: Erlbaum, 2000. Print.

Burger, Jerry M. "Replicating Milgram: Would People Still Obey Today?" *American Psychologist* 64.1 (2009): 1–11. Print.

Milgram, Stanley. *Obedience to Authority: An Experimental View.* New York: Harper, 2009. Print.

Miller, Arthur G. *The Obedience Experiments: A Case Study of Controversy in Social Science.* New York: Praeger, 1986. Print.

Sales, Bruce D., and Susan Folkman, eds. *Ethics in Research with Human Participation.* Washington, DC: Amer. Psychological Assn., 2005. Print.

Slater, Lauren. *Opening Skinner's Box: Great Psychological Experiments of the Twentieth Century.* New York: Norton, 2005. Print.

Smeulers, Alette, and Fred Grünfeld. *International Crimes and Other Gross Human Rights Violations: A Multi- and Interdisciplinary Textbook.* Leiden: Nijhoff, 2011. Print.

Thomas Tandy Lewis

SEE ALSO: Animal experimentation; Experimentation: Ethics and subject rights; Research ethics.

Miller, Neal E., and John Dollard

MILLER, NEAL E.
BORN: August 3, 1909
DIED: March 23, 2002
BIRTHPLACE: Milwaukee, Wisconsin
PLACE OF DEATH: Hamden, Connecticut
IDENTITY: American psychologist, social learning theorist

DOLLARD, JOHN
BORN: August 29, 1900
DIED: October 8, 1980
BIRTHPLACE: Menasha, Wisconsin
PLACE OF DEATH: New Haven, Connecticut
IDENTITY: American sociologist, social psychologist

TYPE OF PSYCHOLOGY: Learning; Personality; Psychotherapy

Miller and Dollard were pioneers in the scientific study of personality who integrated neobehaviorism with psychoanalysis and established the first social learning theory.

Psychologist Neal E. Miller and sociologist John Dollard began their long-lasting and influential collaboration while members of the Yale University Institute of Human Relations. Their first major publication together, which included several coauthors, was *Frustration and Aggression* (1939). This work stimulated a wide range of studies on aggression.

Their next major book, *Social Learning and Imitation* (1941), introduced the first fully articulated social learning theory, including the proposition that models constitute an important determinant of behavior. Unlike many personality theories at the time, Dollard and Miller's propositions were well grounded in experimentation, including research with laboratory animals. Their 1950 book *Personality and Psychotherapy: An Analysis in Terms of Learning, Thinking, and Culture* offered a remarkable synthesis of neobehavioral learning theory and psychoanalysis.

Dollard earned an undergraduate degree from the University of Wisconsin in 1922 and his PhD in sociology from the University of Chicago in 1931. He joined Yale University that same year as an assistant professor of anthropology and was trained in psychoanalysis while a research fellow in Berlin. He joined the Institute of Human Relations as a sociologist and, as further evidence of his academic range and depth, from 1948 until his retirement in 1969 served as professor of psychology. In addition to his work with Miller, Dollard is highly regarded for his 1937 book *Caste and Class in a Southern Town*.

Miller earned a BS from the University of Washington, an MA from Stanford in 1932, and a PhD in psychology from Yale in 1935, where he worked under Clark L. Hull, the famous neobehaviorist. He traveled Europe as a research fellow and received psychoanalytic training in Vienna. Miller subsequently joined the Institute of Human Relations at Yale and began his renowned collaboration with Dollard. He conducted research for the U.S. Army Air Force from 1942 to 1946, but he returned to Yale and became the James Rowland Angell Professor of Psychology in 1952. He received the Warren Medal for outstanding research in psychology from the Society of Experimental Psychologists in 1957, was elected to the National Academy of Sciences in 1958, and was recognized for Distinguished Scientific Contributions by the

American Psychological Association (APA) in 1959. He was elected president of the APA in 1961 and received the National Medal of Science in 1964. Miller moved to Rockefeller University in 1966 to head the laboratory of physiological psychology, where he helped pioneer the field of health psychology, conducting research on such topics as biofeedback and the voluntary control of autonomic nervous system processes. The APA honored him again in 1983 with the Distinguished Professional Contributions to Knowledge Award and in 1991 with the Outstanding Lifetime Contribution to Psychology Award.

BIBLIOGRAPHY

Ellis, Albert, Mike Abrams, and Lidia Abrams. *Personality Theories: Critical Perspectives*. Los Angeles: Sage, 2009. Print.

Gilkeson, John S. *Anthropologists and the Rediscovery of America, 1886–1965*. Cambridge: Cambridge UP, 2010. Print.

Hergenhahn, B. R., and Matthew Olsen. *An Introduction to Theories of Personality*. 7th ed. Upper Saddle River: Pearson, 2007.

Miller, Neal E. "Obituary: John Dollard (1900–1980)." *American Psychologist* 37.5 (1982): 587–588.

Phares, E. Jerry, and William F. Chaplin. *Introduction to Personality*. 4th ed. New York: Longman, 1997.

Jay W. Jackson

SEE ALSO: Behaviorism; Conditioning; Habituation and sensitization; Hull, Clark L.; Operant conditioning therapies; Pavlovian conditioning; Phobias; Reflexes; S-R theory: Neal E. Miller and John Dollard.

Millon, Theodore

TYPE OF PSYCHOLOGY: Assessment; Biography; Personality

Theodore Millon, PhD, DSc (1928-2014) was a psychologist whose theories helped to define how scientists think about personality disorders, and who developed a series of widely used personality tests.

KEY CONCEPTS:

- Antisocial personality disorder
- Borderline personality disorder
- Paranoid personality disorder
- Personality disorder

INTRODUCTION:

Over a very productive career in which he wrote or co-wrote 30 books and more than 100 book chapters and scientific papers, Theodore Millon (surname pronounced Mil-lon) synthesized a great deal of descriptive information into a set of standardized types of personality disorders, such as borderline, antisocial, and paranoid. In doing so, he helped establish personality disorders as an important area of clinical practice and research. The most famous of his inventories is the Millon Clinical Multiaxial Inventory (MCMI), now it its third edition, (MCMI-III). Millon also developed similar tests for other groups, such as college students, adolescents, and medical patients. All these tests are 175 or fewer true-false questions that can be hand- or computer-scored; they are often included in intake screening, outcome measurement, or research, at community agencies, mental health centers, college counseling programs, general and mental hospitals, courts, and private practice offices.

Born in Brooklyn, New York, Theodore Millon was the only child of emigrates from Eastern Europe (Lithuania, Poland, Russia). His ancestry included many Jewish scholars, and his first language was Yiddish; he did not begin to learn English until the first grade and spoke with a Yiddish accent that took over a decade to fade.

Although his father operated a small clothing manufacturing business, the Millon family strongly valued education. Millon did well in school. For college, after starting as an accounting major, he earned a bachelor's degree in psychology, physics and philosophy from City College of New York (CUNY) in 1945 and a master's degree in psychology from there in 1947. At CUNY, he was highly involved in student activities, met his wife, and got to meet regularly with influential people, including art historian, Meyer Schapiro, and anthropologist, Margaret Mead. He earned a PhD in personality/social psychology from the University of Connecticut in 1953.

In 1954, in his first post-graduate school job as Assistant Professor at Lehigh University in Pennsylvania, as part of an abnormal psychology course, Millon took students on a field trip to the local mental hospital, Allentown State. Conditions at this 2,200-bed hospital were appalling. That same fall, one contender for governor, George Leader, criticized previous administrations for providing inadequate care for Pennsylvania's citizens, especially the mentally ill. Millon wrote Leader a detailed, 5-page letter asking him to visit the revolting institution. Leader did so, accompanied by reporters, photographers, and Millon. Leader won the election, and Millon was appointed to a newly developed Board of Trustees for the hospital. This board elected him to be its president, a position he retained for 10 years. In his involvement with this mental hospital, Millon sometimes walked incognito through the halls, slept there, and talked to patients and staff. What he learned became the motivation for his work on personality disorders and the basis for *Modern Psychopathology*, published in 1969, a textbook that introduced his biosocial learning theory.

In 1969, Millon moved to Chicago to be the chief psychologist at the Neuropsychiatric Institute of the University of Illinois Medical Center. While there, he became involved in the task force that developed the *Diagnostic and Statistical Manual-III* (DSM-III; American Psychiatric Association, 1980), which in the United States was at the time, the universal standard for establishing psychiatric diagnoses. As the only expert in the field of personality disorders, and a psychologist on a team composed mostly of psychiatrists, he played a central role in the development of the personality disorders section of the Manual. Millon was also on the developmental task force for the DSM-IV. Although the DSM is now in its fifth edition (published in 2013), it retains the same ten personality disorders that appeared in earlier versions.

While in Chicago in the 1970s, Millon began to develop a test of personality disorders, the Millon Clinical Multiaxial Inventory (MCMI). Later, he participated in developing similar inventories for adolescents, preadolescents, medical patients, college students, and normal populations. Millon thought that normal and abnormal traits lie along a continuum with no sharp dividing line between the two. For example, the person who is shy has much in common with a person with avoidant personality disorder. The difference is that the shy person can adapt to the environment in a healthy way, whereas the avoidant personality person is so inflexible he or she cannot adapt to the environment in a healthy way.

The MCMI has been translated into several languages and is used in cross-cultural research. Derived from his taxonomy and personality theory, it assumes that all people have a personality that influences what kind problems they experience, how severe these problems are, how they express symptoms, and what kinds of treatments are most likely to be effective. Thus, the MCMI requires the person completing it to know something about his or her personality, behavior, and symptoms and be willing to report it honestly. The MCMI is one of the most widely used and researched objective measures of assessing personality in history, behind only the Minnesota Multiphasic Personality Inventory in both clinical and research use.

Millon designed the MCMI to be user friendly. Written at an 8th-grade reading level, it usually takes people about 20 to 30 minutes to answer its 175 true-false questions (for example, "As a teenager, I got into lots of trouble because of bad school behavior."). He also was responsive to new research, and developed newer versions of the MCMI when he thought that new information warranted revisions. The newest version, the MCMI-III, changed 95 of the original items, was published in 1994 and updated in 2008, and includes personality disorders as well as clinical syndromes.

Although personality disorders are long-standing, originating in childhood, and resistive to treatment, Millon was optimistic that they could be treated. The 14 disorder in the MCMI-III are schizoid, avoidant, depressive, dependent, histrionic, narcissistic, antisocial (aggressive or sadistic), compulsive, negativistic (passive-aggressive or masochistic), schizotypal, borderline, and paranoid. The MCMI provides a score on each of these disorders, so gives a complex picture of personality.

In contrast to personality disorders, clinical syndromes are considered to be responses to life events, so can be treated relatively more easily. Millon included these clinical syndromes in the MCMI-III: anxiety, somatoform (psychological problems reflected in physical symptoms), bipolar (formerly termed manic-depression), dysthymia (chronic depression), alcohol dependence, drug dependence, posttraumatic stress disorder (PTSD), thought disorder, major depression, and delusional disorder. The MCMI also includes some scales that indicate the person's response style when taking the test, such as overly reserved or overly disclosing; scores on these scales might influence or even invalidate all other scores.

Millon's focus was on people who have psychiatric disorders, and the MCMI has several uses for them. It can serve as a screening device or as part of a test battery, for example, at a mental health clinic or health department, to identify those with emotional and interpersonal difficulties that may require more intensive evaluation or professional attention. The MCMI profile includes suggestions for therapeutic management. Thus, it can be used by psychologists, counselors, psychiatrists, social workers, or anyone licensed and trained in the use of assessment instruments. But, it is not designed for everyone. Rather, it is specifically for persons in the midranges of severity, rather than those whose difficulties are either close to normal (e.g., those in workers compensation lawsuits, spouses of patients) or markedly clinically severe (e.g., those who are acutely psychotic, or those with chronic schizophrenia).

Millon designed other tests as well. The college students test helps counselors identify, predict, and understand many psychological issues common among college and university students. It might be used at a college counseling center as part of an initial intake, a way to measure counseling progress, or an indication of treatment outcome. It includes three important areas of college student functioning. First, personality scales offer a rich portrait of the student's characteristic manner of thinking, feeling, and behavior (including introverted, dejected, needy, sociable, confident, unruly, conscientious, oppositional, denigrated, and borderline). Second, expressed concerns are problems that would cause students to seek mental health treatment (including dissatisfaction and unhappiness with life circumstances, identity quandaries, family problems, peer alienation, romantic distress, academic concerns, career confusion, abuse, living arrangement problems, finances, and spiritual doubts). Third, clinical signs are problem areas like suicidal thoughts and intentions, depressive outlook, anxiety, posttraumatic stress, eating disorders, out-of-control anger, attention deficits, obsessions and compulsions, alcohol abuse, and drug abuse.

Millon developed two tests for adolescents, one for adolescents in general and the other for adolescents in a clinical setting. Both are at a sixth-grade reading level and written in language that teenagers use. Although usually administered individually, there are no special conditions or instructions beyond those printed on the test booklet itself. Thus, like other versions of Millon's tests, they lend themselves well to group settings.

Millon designed a test for medical patients, developed in 2001, to assess aspects of personality that might be especially relevant to treatment and adjustment to illness. It includes psychiatric indications, coping styles, stress moderators, treatment prognostics, and management guides. Its 165 questions are computer-scored and automatically corrected for response style such as over-reporting or under-reporting symptoms.

In 1977, after serious heart surgery and his wife's colon cancer, Millon moved to sunnier climate to become the Clinical Psychology Director at the University of Miami, where he taught and supervised clinical psychology graduate students for more than 20 years.

Though initially planning to cut back on work activities, he also accepted a part-time visiting professorship at the Psychiatry Department of Massachusetts's General Hospital of Harvard Medical School, and later transferred to its affiliated McLean Hospital. In this time period, he co-founded the International Society for the Study of Personality Disorders (with Niels Strandbygaard and Erik Simonsen) and the *Journal of Personality Disorders* (with Allen Frances).

Millon has been described as voluble and gifted in his vocabulary, which at times gave his writing a very imaginative quality and quite expansive perspective. Among many honors, he was professor emeritus at both Harvard Medical School and the University of Miami, and in 2008 received the American Psychological Association's Gold Medal Award for Lifetime Achievement.

BIBLIOGRAPHY

Millon, Theodore. (1981, revised in 2011). *Disorders of Personality. DSM-III, Axis 11. York: Wiley. Disorders of Personality.* Links the personality disorders found in the DSM-III with their historical and theoretical antecedents.

Millon, Theodore. (2002). "A Blessed and Charmed Personal Odyssey". *Journal of Personality Assessment*, 79, 171– 194. Part of a special series on autobiographies, this article is written in a flowery style, but gives personal information about family, education, and major influences.

Millon, Theodore. (2004). *Masters of the Mind: Exploring the Story of Mental Illness from Ancient Times to the New Millennium.* This warm and well informed historical discussion of the history of mental health summarizes the contributions of nearly 400 philosophers, theorists, researchers, and clinicians, including such notables as Hippocrates, Freud, and Rogers. It includes about 90 portraits drawn by Millon or his daughter. Not particularly easy reading, but great for academics or students.

Trigone, R., Joloshy, Theo, and Strack, Stephen. (2014). "Theodore Millon (1928-2014)". *American Psychologist*, 69, 552. A thoughtful obituary written by three people who were colleagues, collaborators, and friends.

Lillian M. Range

SEE ALSO: *Diagnostic and Statistical Manual of Mental Disorders*; Harvard; Millon clinical multiaxial inventory;

Passive-aggressive personality disorder; Personality disorders; Psychologist.

Mindfulness

TYPE OF PSYCHOLOGY: Biological bases of human behavior; Comparative; Cultural; Health; Occupational; and Social

Mindfulness is an essential component of Buddhist philosophy. As mindfulness has entered the mainstream, it has been integrated into psychotherapy practice to treat numerous conditions including anxiety, depression, attention deficit, obesity, chronic pain, and substance abuse. Jon Kabat-Zinn, a molecular biologist, studied mindfulness under some of the most well-known Buddhist meditation teachers, and developed the Mindfulness-Based Stress Reduction Clinic at the University of Massachusetts School of Medicine. Mindfulness is a key component of Dialectical Behavior Therapy, Acceptance & Commitment Therapy, and Mindfulness-Based Cognitive Therapy, and has become a major area of study for researchers.

KEY CONCEPTS:

- Acceptance & Commitment Therapy (ACT)
- Buddhism
- Dialectical Behavior Therapy (DBT)
- Jon Kabat-Zinn
- Mindfulness-Based Cognitive Therapy (MBCT)
- Mindfulness-Based Stress Reduction (MBSR)
- Mindfulness meditation

INTRODUCTION

Mindfulness is the English translation of the word "sati," in Pali, an Indo-Aryan language which is indigenous to the Indian subcontinent (India, Pakistan, Bhutan, Bangladesh, Nepal, Sri Lanka). Known as one of the seven factors of enlightenment in Buddhist tradition, the word sati means "to remember." The Abhidhammattha-Sangha, a Buddhist text, explains sati as a mental state that signifies attentiveness to and awareness of the present. Buddhist teachings on mindfulness describe it primarily as a tool that individuals can use to realize enlightenment in themselves. Mindfulness allows people to simply experience the moment they are in.

The Satipatthana Sutta, one of the most widely studied discourses in Buddhist tradition, outlined four foundations of mindfulness: mindfulness of body, mindfulness of feelings/sensations, mindfulness of mind/consciousness, and mindfulness of mental objects. The Buddha described the four foundations of mindfulness as a path to achieving freedom, and are fundamental in the practice of Buddhist meditation. They are usually taught one at a time. Mindfulness of body is often introduced by having practitioners experience their own breath. This is in contrast to thinking about breath. Rather, it is the experience and awareness of breath which is central to mindfulness practice. Mindfulness of feelings/sensations includes awareness of both emotions and bodily sensations. In mindfulness meditation, the practitioner is taught to observe, or watch, emotions and sensations come and go. Emotions are observed and acknowledged, but not held onto. Mindfulness of mind is awareness of mental states and thoughts, and involves teaching the practitioner to simply observe and notice mental states as transient events. Freedom from suffering is achieved when individuals notice that thoughts and emotions, and in particular painful thoughts and emotions, naturally dissipate. Mindfulness of mental objects is awareness of the surrounding world, and the idea that the world is experienced as it is perceived by the individual.

MINDFULNESS & PSYCHOLOGY

All individuals have the capacity to become mindful, and as a result, mindfulness is often referred to as a practice. As mindfulness has become part of the mainstream, its definition has expanded. Depending on who is talking about mindfulness, it might be described as a mental state to be achieved, or, as a set of skills to be learned.

Jon Kabat-Zinn was introduced to meditation while he was a molecular biology Ph.D. student at the Massachusetts Institute of Technology. He studied meditation under Buddhist teachers, Thich Nhat Hanh and Seung Sahn, and worked to integrate their teachings with his science background. In 1979, he founded the Stress Reduction Clinic at the University of Massachusetts Medical School, where he adapted Buddhist teachings to develop an eight-week Mindfulness-Based Stress Reduction (MBSR) program. Over the years, Kabat-Zinn has become internationally recognized as one of the most foremost experts in mindfulness. He has written countless books on the topic, and his MBSR program has been adopted in clinics across the country. MBSR is also available as an online, self-guided video coursed which can be accessed through the University of Massachusetts Medical School website.

According to Kabat-Zinn, mindfulness means paying attention in a particular way, on purpose, in the present moment, non-judgmentally. He has spoken of mindful-ness as a path to healing; as coming to terms with things as they are, so that individuals can optimize their poten-tial. Kabat-Zinn has commented on the human tendency to want to distract oneself from the present moment, often so that unpleasant moments do not have to be ex-perienced. Mindfulness encourages people to simply no-tice and observe what is happening, both internally and externally. It is not about changing an experience, getting to a better mental space, or trying to alter one's feelings. Rather, it is simply about being where you are, and be-coming more aware of your experience in that particular moment in time. Over time, unpleasant experiences be-come more tolerable, and pleasant experiences that have perhaps gone unnoticed, become more fully integrated into consciousness.

While Kabat-Zinn has been a strong proponent of meditation as a way of learning to become more mindful, it is not the only way to learn mindfulness. One can be mindful at any moment, anywhere. For example, one can be mindful while eating, walking, listening, talking, sit-ting, and dancing. Kabat-Zinn has published numerous meditations over the years, most of which are widely available on the internet and in his many books. One of his most well-known meditations is the raising con-sciousness exercise, available in his book, *Coming to Our Senses*. In this exercise, practitioners are invited to explore, examine, observe, experience, and taste a raisin with all senses, with curiosity, and with awareness of thoughts, emotions, and bodily sensations.

There is a growing body of research literature which has examined the efficacy of mindfulness-based stress reduction programs. Research has generally focused on clinical populations; people suffering from depres-sion, chronic pain, and other psychological and physical problems. In general, the research on MBSR has been favorable and supported the use of MBSR as a way to help people reduce pain, anxiety, depression, and better manage stress.

THE THIRD WAVE OF BEHAVIOR THERAPY
Jon Kabat-Zinn is responsible for bringing mindfulness into the American mainstream and encouraging its inte-gration into psychotherapy practices. Over the years, the benefits of mindfulness have been observed and empiri-cally studied, and psychologists have developed specific treatments that have integrated mindfulness with behav-ior therapy. These treatments have become part of what is known as the third wave of behavior therapy.

Marsha Linehan, a psychologist and researcher at the University of Washington, integrated mindfulness with traditional behavior therapy and created Dialectical Behavior Therapy (DBT), a widely-used skills-based pro-gram for the treatment of borderline personality disorder, depression and suicidal behavior. Mindfulness is consid-ered the backbone of DBT, and it is the foundation upon which all other skills are built. For this reason, mindful-ness is integrated into all other skills, and re-taught sev-eral times throughout the program. Linehan talks about "core mindfulness," which she describes as learning to control your mind. DBT teaches mindfulness as being made up of the "what skills" and "how skills." The what skills include: observation, description, and participa-tion. The how skills include: non-judgmentally, one-mindfully, and effectively. In observation, the individual is invited to non-judgmentally observe what is happening both internally and externally. When describing, in-dividuals are invited to non-judgmentally express what they have observed. Participation invites people to fully throw themselves into what they are doing and focus on one activity at a time. Being non-judgmental involves sticking to the facts of what has been observed. The goal is to help people label their experience based on what they observed, described, and experienced, rather than their feeling about it (e.g. it is brown vs. it is ugly). One-mindfully means doing one thing at a time, which en-courages focus on the present moment experience. Being effective means doing what works. It involves being aware of what is happening in the moment and doing what is needed at the time. At the present time, DBT is the only evidenced-based treatment which has been shown to successfully treat individuals with borderline personality disorder.

Acceptance and Commitment Therapy (ACT) was developed by psychologists Steven C. Hayes and Kirk D. Strosahl. ACT is a mindfulness-based treatment that integrates acceptance and commitment strategies with behavior therapy. ACT is an empirically-supported treat-ment that has been shown to be effective in the treat-ment of anxiety, depression, chronic pain, psychosis, dia-betes, obesity, and other conditions.

Like in DBT, mindfulness is considered the foun-dation of ACT, and has been conceptualized as having three components: defusion, acceptance, and contact with the present moment. Defusion refers to letting go of unhelpful thoughts and beliefs. Acceptance means acknowledging that individuals must make space for unpleasant emotions, by allowing them to come and go.

Contact with the present moment means being curious about the moment that you are currently experiencing, and engaging with it fully.

Mindfulness-Based Cognitive Therapy (MBCT) is primarily used in the treatment of depression. It was developed by John Teasdale, Mark Williams, and Zindel Segal. MBCT is a hybrid of traditional cognitive behavior therapy and mindfulness, and is built on the idea that people who are depressed tend to have automatic negative thoughts, and attach negative judgments to their experiences. Mindfulness helps individuals become more aware of their automatic thoughts, and to simply observe them as transient events, rather than holding onto them. As individuals become more aware of their automatic thoughts, they develop the capacity to move from a perspective of reaction, to a perspective of reflection. MBCT is in part based on Jon Kabat-Zinn's eight-week Mindfulness-Based Stress Reduction program and echoes much of the theory put forth in Kabat-Zinn's program. The creators of MBCT developed it with the intention of helping people who have suffered from repeated bouts of depression. The MBCT program is taught over the course of eight-weeks, where participants are encouraged to use guided meditations to help them cultivate a more mindful way of living.

MINDFULNESS & NON-CLINICAL POPULATIONS

While mindfulness has garnered the attention of the psychological community as a useful tool for helping people achieve relief from psychological and physical conditions, it can also be practiced by non-clinical populations. The benefits of mindfulness can be experienced by all people, as all individuals at some point experience distress. By becoming more present in their daily lives, and aware of both their internal and external experiences, people can learn to deal with problems more effectively, and take greater pleasure in the good things that often go unnoticed.

BIBLIOGRAPHY

Gunaratana, B. (2005). *Mindfulness in Plain English: 20th Anniversary Edition*. Somerville: Wisdom Publications. Provides an easy to read introduction to mindfulness and meditation.

Gunaratana, H. (2012). *The Four Foundations of Mindfulness in Plain English*. Boston: Wisdom Publications. A practical guide that discusses the four foundations of mindfulness in a way that is easy to understand.

Kabat-Zinn, J. (2013). *Full Catastrophe Living: Using the Wisdom of Your Body and Mind to Face Stress, Pain, and Illness*. New York: Bantam Books Trade Paperbacks. Discusses how mindfulness-based experiences can be used to combat stress and pain.

Kabat-Zinn, J. (2012). *Mindfulness for Beginners: Reclaiming the Present Moment--and Your Life*. Boulder, CO: Sounds True. An essential book that provides an overview and introduction to various aspects of mindfulness, and how it can be used to reduce stress.

Nhâ´t, H. (2008). *The Miracle of Mindfulness: The Classic Guide to Meditation By the World's Most Revered Master*. London: Rider. A collection of practical mindfulness exercises that can be used to introduce mindfulness into everyday life.

Nhâ´t, H., & Ellsberg, R. (2001). *Thich Nhâ´t Hanh: Essential Writings*. Maryknoll, NY: Orbis Books. A collection of essays from one of the foremost experts on mindfulness.

Melissa Otero

SEE ALSO: Awareness; Buddhism; Intention; Meditation; Relaxation; Self awareness.

Minnesota multiphasic personality inventory (MMPI)

DATE: 1943 forward
TYPE OF PSYCHOLOGY: Personality; Psychopathology

The Minnesota Multiphasic Personality Inventory is the most widely used and researched personality assessment instrument in clinical practice. It is primarily used to aid in the diagnosis and assessment of the major psychological disorders.

KEY CONCEPTS

- Clinical scales
- Normative sample
- Psychological test
- Psychopathology
- Restandardization
- Validity scales

INTRODUCTION

The Minnesota Multiphasic Personality Inventory (MMPI/MMPI-2) was developed during the late 1930s, reaching publication in 1943. The authors of the test were Starke R. Hathaway, a psychologist, and J. C. McKinley, a physician to whom Hathaway reported at the University of Minnesota Hospitals. The test was originally developed to aid in the assessment of adult psychiatric patients, both to describe the type and severity of their disturbance and to measure patient change over time. It quickly grew in popularity to become the most widely used and researched psychological test ever published.

Three characteristics distinguished the MMPI from the psychological tests of the 1930s. First, it was developed as a broadband test, that is, a multiphasic test that would assess a number of personality attributes in a single administration. Most personality tests up to that time were more narrow in their focus. Second, this was the first personality test to use an empirical method of selecting test questions. This procedure involved selecting test items that differentiated between persons making up a normal population and persons in the clinical group of interest (such as individuals diagnosed with schizophrenia, depression, or other psychiatric disorders) at a statistically significant level. Third, the MMPI incorporated validity scales, or measures of test-taking attitude that identified tendencies to either underreport or overreport psychopathology.

RESTANDARDIZATION

An important limitation of the original MMPI had to do with its normative sample, or the reference group used to represent the normal population (in contrast to the clinical groups). The original normal reference group consisted primarily of a rural, all white, eighth-grade-educated population who were visiting patients at the University of Minnesota Hospital. Over time, a number of criticisms were made that this group, predominantly Scandinavian in origin, was not representative of the broader United States population. Other problems with the MMPI also developed, including outdated test item content, poorly worded items, or item content objectionable to contemporary test takers (for instance, questions regarding religious beliefs or bodily functions). In response to such concerns, an MMPI restandardization project was begun in 1982, culminating in the publication of the MMPI-2 in 1989. Comparison of the restandardized normal sample to 1990 census data by ethnicity, age, and education indicated that the new normative group was significantly more representative of the United States population than were the original norms, with the exception that well-educated persons were overrepresented. The MMPI-2 also incorporated additional validity measures and newly developed scales reflecting contemporary clinical problems.

DESCRIPTION OF THE TEST

The MMPI-2 is an objectively scored, standardized questionnaire consisting of 567 self-descriptive statements answered as either "true" or "false." Responses can be either hand- or computer-scored and are summarized on a profile sheet. Interpretation is based on both the configuration of scales on the profile sheet and demographic variables characterizing the test-taker. The basic profile sheet is made up of nine validity measures and ten traditional clinical scales. Fifteen additional "content" scales can also be scored, as well as potentially hundreds of supplementary and research scales. The validity scales measure test-taking attitudes, including such characteristics as consistencies in response patterns and tendencies to exaggerate or minimize psychological problems. The clinical scales are labeled both by a number and with traditional psychiatric diagnostic labels such as depression, paranoia, and schizophrenia. The specific MMPI scale labels may be misleading in that some diagnostic labels are outdated (such as "psychasthenia" or "hysteria"). In addition, the scales do not effectively differentiate diagnostic groups (for instance, an elevation on the paranoia scale is not exclusive to persons with a paranoia diagnosis). It has thus become standard practice to refer to profiles by characteristic scale numbers (such as a "49" profile) and to interpret them according to relevant research rather than by scale labels. The fifteen content scales reflect the client's endorsement of test items whose content is obvious and descriptive of particular problem areas such as anxiety, health concerns, or family problems. The many supplementary scales measure a wide range of concerns, ranging from addiction proneness to post-traumatic stress disorder to marital distress. The MMPI-2 is appropriate for use only with those aged eighteen years and older. A shorter version of the test, the MMPI-A, is available for use with fourteen- to eighteen-year-old adolescents.

Although the MMPI-2 is still widely administered, there is a revised version published in 2008 known as the MMPI-2 Restructured Form (MMPI-2-RF). The MMPI-2-RF is 338 questions long and scores test-takers on a set of clinical scales which has been altered to better reflect the current understanding of the psychological issues covered by the test.

BIBLIOGRAPHY

Ben-Porath, Yossef S. *Interpreting the MMPI-2-RF.* Minneapolis: U of Minnesota P, 2012. Print.

Butcher, James N., ed. *Basic Sources on the MMPI-2.* Minneapolis: U of Minnesota P, 2000. Print.

Butcher, James N., ed. *International Adaptations of the MMPI-2.* Minneapolis: U of Minnesota P, 1996. Print.

Butcher, James N., and Carolyn L. Williams. "Personality Assessment with the MMPI-2: Historical Roots, Internatinoal Adaptations, and Current Challenges." *Applied Psychology: Health and Well-Being* 1.1 (2009): 105–35. Print.

Butcher, James N., and John R. Graham. *Development and Use of the MMPI-2 Content Scales.* 3d ed. Minneapolis: U of Minnesota P, 2007.

Caldwell, Alex B. "What Do the MMPI Scales Fundamentally Measure? Some Hypotheses." *Journal of Personality Assessment* 76.1 (2001): 1–17. Print.

Dahlstrom, W. G., D. Lachar, and L. W. Dahlstrom. *MMPI Patterns of American Minorities.* Minneapolis: U of Minnesota P, 1986. Print.

Framingham, Jane. "Minnesota Multiphasic Personality Inventory (MMPI)." *Psych Central.* Psych Central, 2011. Web. 20 May 2014.

Friedman, A. F., R. Lewak, D. S. Nichols, and J. T. Webb. *Psychological Assessment with the MMPI-2.* Mahwah: Erlbaum, 2001. Print.

David W. Brokaw

SEE ALSO: Beck Depression Inventory (BDI); California Psychological Inventory (CPI); Children's Depression Inventory (CDI); Clinical interviewing, testing, and observation; Depression; Diagnosis; Personality interviewing strategies; Personality: Psychophysiological measures; Personality rating scales; State-Trait Anxiety Inventory (STAI); Thematic Apperception Test (TAT).

Misbehavior

TYPE OF PSYCHOLOGY: Learning

The association between misbehavior and learning has been addressed by psychoanalytic theorists as well as social learning theorists; both have shed light on the social conditions that precipitate misbehavior, particularly in children.

KEY CONCEPTS
- Goals of misbehavior
- Imitation
- Modeling
- Recognition reflex
- Social learning

INTRODUCTION

Behavior is called misbehavior when it is found to be outside the range of what is acceptable to others. Unacceptable behaviors include noncompliance, defiance, destructiveness, and aggression. Those who determine what constitutes misbehavior are typically adults, and those whose actions are labeled misbehavior are usually children, although sometimes they are other adults.

Both psychoanalytic theorists and social learning theorists relate misbehavior to the individual's interpretation of social experiences. A secondary conclusion by theorists in both camps is that misbehavior is purposeful and goal directed. According to both theoretical orientations, the link between social experiences and misbehavior is bridged by an emphasis on the cognition of the individual. What separates the two theoretical views is the role each attributes to human consciousness. The psychoanalytic explanation of why a person misbehaves emphasizes unconscious motivation, whereas social learning theorists assign a larger role to conscious cognitive processes.

DREIKURS'S CONTRIBUTIONS

Rudolf Dreikurs (1897–1972), an early student and colleague of Alfred Adler, was a strong supporter of Adler's school of individual psychology. From the time of his arrival in the United States until his death in 1972, Dreikurs worked to popularize Adler's views. Adler, who believed that the goal of psychology is to educate the whole community toward more effective social living, developed an innovative counseling approach for restricted audiences. This approach focused on a community of committed parents, teachers, and other adults working together toward the fostering of social responsibility in children. This effort resulted in the opening of a number of child guidance centers in Vienna and elsewhere in Europe. Dreikurs participated in the child guidance centers in Vienna and was well known throughout Europe before the fascist governments gained power. After escaping to the United States by way of Brazil in 1939, he established a practice in Chicago and thereafter had a profound impact on parent education in the United

States. Dreikurs placed considerable emphasis on the process by which a person is socialized within the family. By emphasizing this process, Dreikurs provided a basis for understanding how the family atmosphere is played out in the socialization process and how the socialization process contributes to children's misbehavior. Dreikurs's major contributions to Adler's approach consist of the refinement of open-centered family counseling concepts, demonstration of the multiple-therapist concept long before it was presented in the general psychology literature, and the development of a system of democratic conflict resolution to be used in the family, or in any other setting in which people live and interact with one another.

DREIKURS'S FOUR GOALS OF MISBEHAVIOR
Based on his clinical work, Dreikurs discovered four goals that he believed guide all forms of misbehavior: attention, power, revenge, and a display of inadequacy. According to Dreikurs, these goals derive from children's private logic—what they think of themselves, others, and life, and the goals they set for themselves. These four categories of misbehavior are seen as goals in that the misbehavior achieves something for the individual.

Children who misbehave to obtain attention have learned from previous social experiences that certain unacceptable behaviors gain attention from others, even though the attention is typically negative. Those who misbehave with the goal of power have discovered a way of gaining a type of power by misbehaving. Individuals whose misbehavior derives from the goal of revenge are those whose bids for attention and power have been met with such negative consequences that they are motivated to seek revenge. Finally, people who misbehave with a goal of displaying inadequacy are those who do not try, are often seen as lazy, are unkempt, or appear to be unmotivated. These individuals have given up trying to gain attention or power and feel powerless to seek revenge.

The concept of the four goals of misbehavior is premised on the assumption, reflecting the theorizing of Adler, that people are social creatures whose behavior is purposeful and whose primary desire is to belong. Thus, the four goals of misbehavior are actually underlying goals, each of which is believed to aid people in the quest for belonging. However, misbehavior does not secure belonging and acceptance within a family or group because it generally alienates people. In recognition of this, Dreikurs emphasized that the goals of misbehavior are mistaken goals. Even though people may be able to observe keenly, accurately, and carefully what goes on

around them, they often misinterpret events, draw mistaken conclusions, and make faulty decisions based on their interpretations and conclusions. This is particularly true of children, whose cognitive understanding of the world differs from that of adults.

RECOGNIZING UNDERLYING GOALS
Although misbehaving people, particularly children, are generally unaware of the mistaken goals underlying their misbehavior, observers can learn to recognize these underlying goals by observing the effects the misbehavior has on others. As noted by Dreikurs, what people are inclined to do in response to another person's misbehavior is generally consistent with the goal underlying that misbehavior. Reactions that correspond to and reflect mistaken goals are giving undue attention, engaging in power struggles, seeking retaliation, or giving up in despair. According to this model, observers can discern the goals of those misbehaving, although the individuals acting out may be unaware of why they are doing so. The key to discerning the goal of misbehaving people is to take notice not only of their behavior but also of others' reactions to their behavior.

Even though the method for recognizing Dreikurs's mistaken goals of misbehavior is clear and simple, the application of this process in decreasing a child's (or an adult's) misbehavior is a bit more complicated. First, if a person is attempting to discern the underlying goal motivating a child's misbehavior, the person must carefully note not only that child's misbehavior but also how others (including the self) respond to that behavior. This may require several observations. In observing responses, it is necessary to watch not only for actual responses but also for what people are inclined to do in reaction to the misbehavior.

If people typically respond to the misbehavior in question by giving attention (positive or negative) to the child who is misbehaving, then it is logical to assume that attention is the underlying goal (even if people do not actually give attention each instance). If people are inclined to become angry (lose control) in response to misbehavior, there is a good chance that power is the underlying goal. It is important to remember that when people respond to misbehavior by losing control, power is ceded to the misbehaving child.

If people have a tendency to feel hurt by a misbehaving child, the misbehavior is probably motivated by a goal of revenge. The misbehaving child is responding to feelings of pain and hurt by behaving in ways designed to inflict pain on others, though not necessarily the person or persons responsible for inflicting the pain and hurt. This is a critical point, because it emphasizes the necessity not only of observing how the observer interacts with the child but also of taking into consideration interactions that child has had with others.

If people tend to give up in despair in response to the misbehaving child, a display of inadequacy is likely to be the underlying goal of the child. The misbehaving child has learned, through repeated experiences, that attempts to gain positive attention or power have been relatively fruitless. Rather than continuing to be exposed to painful evaluations and criticisms, the child displays a lack of motivation, causing others to give up in despair, and the child displaying inadequacy is spared the pain of negative evaluation and humiliation.

FOCUS ON AGGRESSION

Social learning theorists also emphasize the process by which a child is socialized within the family. In stressing the relevance of this process to misbehavior, they have addressed various aspects of misconduct. The type of misbehavior that has received the most attention from social learning theorists is aggression, particularly in children. According to this theory, aggressiveness is learned from observing and imitating models. These models include parents who rely on physical punishment as well as other punitive methods of discipline, aggressive siblings and peers, and aggressive models on television. When parents display aggressiveness by the use of physical punishment or verbal attacks, they provide children with a very clear model of aggressive behavior. Children learn from this model that the best way to get people to do what they want is to behave aggressively toward them. Those children who have been exposed to parental models of aggression are more likely to use aggression with siblings and peers. If the aggressive children's victims fight back, their aggressive acts will not be reinforced; however, if victims cry or run away, the apparent success reinforces the aggressive acts. Furthermore, other children witnessing the aggression learn that aggression brings reinforcement. In addition to parental, peer, and sibling models of aggression, children are exposed to aggressive models on television that demonstrate vicarious reinforcement for aggression.

STRATEGIES FOR MANAGING MISBEHAVIOR

Applications of misbehavior theory focus on managing the undesirable behaviors by focusing on their conse-

quences. Dreikurs's method for decreasing misbehavior consists of three strategies: changing responses to the misbehavior so that the unacceptable behavior does not achieve the goal that it is designed to achieve; assisting the misbehaving person in becoming aware of the underlying goal motivating the misbehavior; and making deliberate efforts to assist a person prone to misconduct in achieving a sense of belonging, so that he or she does not resort to misbehavior to satisfy this need.

The first strategy (changing responses to misbehavior) is simple and straightforward in theory but somewhat more difficult in application. The challenge is for people to respond differently from the way they are inclined to respond to misbehavior. Specifically, this strategy consists of not giving attention to misbehavior designed to attract attention, not reacting angrily or losing control in response to behavior designed to provoke such a response, not focusing on or exposing hurt feelings in response to misbehavior intended to avenge, and not giving up in despair at a person's display of inadequacy.

The second part of the approach (assisting the misbehaving person in becoming aware of the underlying goal motivating the misbehavior) can sometimes be accomplished simply by calling the person's attention to what appears to be the underlying goal. An example of this would be to say (to a child), "Do you think that you knock over your sister's blocks to get my attention?" The purpose of this strategy is to assist individuals in becoming conscious of why they behave in ways that others consider unacceptable. If this strategy is to be successful, it must be done in a way that does not communicate a value judgment or sound reproachful. If individuals are not suffering the sting of disapproval, they may be assisted in understanding why they misbehave (which often troubles the person displaying this behavior as much as it does those who are exposed to it). Dreikurs referred to this awareness as the recognition reflex. In emphasizing the value of the recognition reflex for assisting people in understanding what motivates their misbehavior, Dreikurs pointed out that this tactic is more effective with children than with adolescents and adults, who have had more time to build stronger defense mechanism s.

The third strategy (assisting the misbehaving person in achieving the goal of belonging without resorting to misconduct) is based on an appreciation of everyone's need for attention and power. This understanding suggests an effective approach for decreasing misbehavior by providing sufficient attention to the individual and recognizing the person's need for power.

The strategy of providing attention is uncomplicated. Positive attention should be freely given at any time except when misbehavior is occurring. Therefore, one does not wait for some specified behavior to occur to show attention. Depending on the level of misconduct in which that person is engaging, this could be a long wait. Meanwhile, the misbehavior will probably continue. It is suggested, instead, that attention be generously bestowed in a variety of ways. This could be as casual as recognizing that person's entrance into the room, noticing personal things about that person (haircut, clothes, mood, and so on), and showing interest in ideas, concerns, and questions generated by the person. Based on the relationship one has with the person exhibiting misbehavior, one may choose to design a more structured method of delivering attention, such as engaging the person in projects that provide an opportunity for a large amount of feedback and considerable dialogue.

To decrease misbehavior motivated by power needs, it is important to monitor closely experiences of the individual, which may diminish the person's sense of power, while simultaneously making deliberate efforts to assist that person in appropriate efforts to gain power. In the case of children misbehaving with an underlying goal of power, one is likely to find that power-assertive methods of discipline are being used with the child. Excessively strict, harsh methods of control, including the use of physical punishment, weaken a child's sense of power and contribute to the likelihood of misbehavior based on power needs. It is reasonable to conclude that anyone engaging in misbehavior with the goal of power has been exposed to some type of experience that contributed to the person's sense of powerlessness.

While monitoring experiences that diminish a person's sense of power is necessary, it is not sufficient for decreasing misbehavior. People with a lowered sense of power also require experiences designed to assist them in regaining a feeling of power. According to Dreikurs, the most appropriate group arrangement for meeting the power needs of all individuals within the group is one based on democratic relations. Although this arrangement is based on the concept of equality, it does not assign identical responsibilities and privileges to all group members but rather recognizes that all members have equal worth. Decisions affecting group members are made with the needs and well-being of all members in mind. Furthermore, input from all members is encouraged to the degree that it is feasible.

SOCIAL LEARNING APPROACH

The application of the social learning approach to misbehavior focuses on discovering environmental consequences that influence behavior and taking steps to change these consequences, thereby decreasing misbehavior. The misconduct of primary interest to social learning theorists has been aggressiveness. According to their model, because aggressiveness is maintained or increased through the consequence of reinforcement, the recommended approach for dealing with this type of misbehavior is fourfold: Limit exposure to aggressive models in real life and on television; provide models who behave responsibly and considerately rather than cruelly or impulsively; be certain that aggression is not reinforced; and reinforce behavior that is incompatible with aggression.

The influence of models on the behavior of individuals was first demonstrated by the work of Albert Bandura in 1962. Since then, social learning theory has been invoked to explain a variety of behaviors. This theoretical approach gets its name from the emphasis it places on social variables as determinants of behavior and personality. Foremost in Bandura's analysis of learning is the role of imitation, which has its conceptual foundation in operant conditioning.

According to social learning theorists, most of a person's learning comes from actively imitating, or modeling, the actions of others. The term "modeling" is used interchangeably with terms such as "observational learning" and "vicarious learning" to mean that people add to their repertoire of actions by seeing or hearing someone else perform the behavior rather than carrying out the behavior themselves.

Bandura's views regarding imitation are reflected in the chief contributions of social learning theory, which consist of an explanation of the way a person acquires a new behavior never attempted before, the identification of the steps involved in the process of learning from models, and explanations of the way consequences influence future actions and of the development of complex behavior.

BIBLIOGRAPHY

Bandura, Albert. *Social Learning Theory.* Englewood Cliffs: Prentice, 1977. Print.

Brooks, Jane. *The Process of Parenting*. 9th ed. Boston: McGraw, 2013. Print.

Dreikurs, Rudolf, Pearl Cassel, and Eva Dreikurs Ferguson. *Discipline without Tears: How to Reduce Conflict and Establish Cooperation in the Classroom*. Rev. ed. Mississauga: Wiley, 2004. Print.

Epstein, Michael, et al. *Reducing Behavior Problems in the Elementary School Classroom*. Washington: National Center for Education Evaluation and Regional Assistance, 2008. Print.

Flicker, Eileen, and Janet Andron Hoffman. *Guiding Children's Behavior: Developmental Discipline in the Classroom*. New York: Teachers College P, 2006. Print.

Kern, Roy M., and William L. Curlette. "Individual Psychology: A Rich and Viable Theory for the Present and the Future." *Journal of Individual Psychology* 69.4 (2014): 277–79. Print.

Olson, Matthew H., and B. R. Hergenhahn. *An Introduction to Theories of Learning*. 9th ed. Upper Saddle River: Pearson, 2012. Print.

Thomas, R. Murray. *Comparing Theories of Child Development*. 6th ed. Belmont: Wadsworth, 2005. Print.

Phyllis A. Heath

SEE ALSO: Aggression; Aggression: Reduction and control; Attention-deficit hyperactivity disorder; Bandura, Albert; Cognitive social learning: Walter Mischel; Conduct disorder; Mischel, Walter; Parenting styles; Punishment; Radical behaviorism: B. F. Skinner; Reinforcement; Skinner, B. F.; Social learning: Albert Bandura.

Mischel, Walter

BORN: February 22, 1930
BIRTHPLACE: Vienna, Austria
TYPE OF PSYCHOLOGY: Personality
IDENTITY: Austrian-born U.S. clinical psychologist and personality theorist

Mischel, with Yuichi Shoda, developed a dynamic theory of personality that is an alternative to the traditional, trait-based view.

Walter Mischel and his family fled the Nazi regime in 1938 and eventually immigrated to Brooklyn, New York. He earned a BA in psychology from New York University in 1951 and an MA in clinical psychology from City College of New York in 1953. While a graduate student, he worked as a social worker in the slums of Manhattan. Because the methods of psychoanalysis seemed to have little utility when applied to social work, he sought a more empirically grounded doctoral program. He attained a PhD in clinical psychology in 1956 at Ohio State University, where he studied social learning theory with Julian B. Rotter and personal construct psychology with George A. Kelly. Both men greatly influenced Mischel's subsequent scholarly development.

At Harvard University, he reviewed the empirical research and concluded that most of the studies did not support the prevailing ideas about personality. He levied this serious criticism in a monograph titled *Personality and Assessment* (1968), which was at first disparaged. However, a long debate ensued that revolved around the personality paradox, a term coined by Daryl Bem and Andrea Allen. At the time, most theorists believed that traits or dispositions characterized a relatively stable personality structure. However, the paradox was that observed behavior was not consistent in a variety of situations. Mainstream psychologists believed that measurement error accounted for the inconsistent data. Mischel believed that the problem was not with flawed measures but with flawed thinking about the nature of personality. The search for the locus of personality consistency and a desire to understand better the organization of personality were major themes for the rest of Mischel's career.

In 1973, he wrote an important paper titled "Toward a Cognitive Social Learning Reconceptualization of Personality." He replaced traits with person variables and considered behavior in context. For example, a person may be shy in some settings and not in others. In 1995, Mischel and Yuichi Shoda wrote "A Cognitive-Affective System Theory of Personality: Reconceptualizing Situations, Dispositions, Dynamics, and Invariance in Personality Structure" that resolved the personality paradox. The surprising resolution was that intra-individual profiles or patterns of responses in a variety of settings were consistent.

Mischel won many awards for his creative work. In 1982, he received the Distinguished Scientific Contribution Award of the American Psychological Association, and he held an endowed chair in psychology at Columbia University. He has served as president of the Association for Psychological Science and the Association for Research in Personality and as editor of the respected journal *Psychological Review*. In 2011 he received the University of Louisville Grawemeyer Award in psychology.

BIBLIOGRAPHY

Baumeister, Roy F., and John Tierney. *Willpower: Rediscovering the Greatest Human Strength*. New York: Penguin, 2011. Print.

Cervone, Daniel, and Walter Mischel, eds. *Advances in Personality Science*. New York: Guilford, 2002. Print.

Lehrer, Jonah. "Don't! The Secret of Self-Control." *New Yorker*. Condé Nast, 18 May 2009. Web. 8 May 2014.

Mischel, Walter, Yuichi Shoda, and Ozlem Ayduk. *Introduction to Personality: Toward an Integrative Science of the Person*. 8th ed. Hoboken: Wiley, 2008. Print.

Pervin, Lawrence A., Richard W. Robins, and Oliver P. John, eds. *Handbook of Personality: Theory and Research*. 3rd ed. New York: Guilford, 2008. Print."Walter Mischel." American Psychologist 38, no. 1 (1983): 9–14. Print.

Tanja Bekhuis

SEE ALSO: Cognitive psychology; Cognitive social learning: Walter Mischel; Kelly, George A.; Personality theory.

Mood disorders

TYPE OF PSYCHOLOGY: Psychopathology

The diagnosis of a mood disorder requires the presence or absence of a mood episode: major depressive episode, manic episode, or hypomanic episode. The mood disorders include major depressive disorder, persistent depressive disorder, bipolar I disorder, bipolar II disorder, and cyclothymic disorder. The mood disorders can be specified with seasonal pattern, rapid cycling, or peripartum onset.

KEY CONCEPTS
- Bipolar I disorder
- Cyclothymic disorder
- Depressive episode
- Dysthymic disorder
- Hypomanic episode
- Major depressive disorder
- Manic episode
- Postpartum onset
- Rapid cycling
- Seasonal pattern

INTRODUCTION

Descriptions of mood disorders can be found in ancient texts such as the Bible and writings of the ancient Greek physician Hippocrates. Aulus Cornelius Celsus, a medical writer, described melancholia as a depression caused by "black bile" in about 30 CE

Mood disorders are characterized predominantly by a disturbance in mood. Although earlier editions of the American Psychiatric Association's *Diagnostic and Statistical Manual of Mental Disorders* (DSM) grouped a wide variety of disorders under the heading of mood disorders, the fifth edition of the DSM (DSM-5), published in 2013, divides them into two categories: depressive disorders and bipolar and related disorders. Both categories include disorders characterized by mood epidodes, which include major depressive episode, manic episode, and hypomanic episode.

In a major depressive episode, a person experiences depressed mood for a period of at least two weeks. For the diagnosis of a depressive episode, the person must experience at least four of the following symptoms: changes in appetite or weight, sleep, and psychomotor activity; decreased energy; feelings of worthlessness or guilt; difficulty concentrating; or recurrent thoughts of death or suicide. There is significant impairment in occupational or social functioning.

In a manic episode, a person experiences an abnormally elevated or irritable mood for at least one week. In addition, the person must experience at least three of the following symptoms: inflated self-esteem, decreased need for sleep, pressured (loud, rapid) speech, racing thoughts, excessive planning of or participation in multiple activities, distractibility, psychomotor agitation (such as pacing), or excessive participation in activities that may lead to negative consequences (such as overspending). There is severe impairment in social or occupational functioning, or there are psychotic features. The DSM-5 emphasizes that manic episodes typically feature changes in energy level and activity.

A hypomanic episode is characterized by a period of at least four days of abnormally elevated or irritable mood. The affected person must experience at least three of the following symptoms: inflated self-esteem, decreased need for sleep, pressured speech, flight of ideas, increased involvement in goal-directed activities, psychomotor agitation, or excessive participation in activities that may lead to negative consequences. The hypomanic episode is differentiated from the manic episode by less severe impairment in social or occupational functioning and a lack of psychotic features.

The fourth edition of the DSM also described the characteristic of a mixed episode, in which a person displays symptoms of both manic and major depressive episodes nearly every day for a period of one week. However, the American Psychiatric Association determined that such episodes are exceedingly rare and opted to eliminate the category from the DSM-5, replacing it with the "mixed features" specifier, which refers to episodes that are predominantly of one type but have some features of another.

Depressive disorders include major depressive disorder, characterized by one or more major depressive episodes, and persistent depressive disorder, which involves at least two years of depressed mood with symptoms that do not meet the criteria for a major depressive episode. Bipolar and related disorders include bipolar I disorder, which features one or more manic or mixed episodes with major depressive episodes; bipolar II disorder, characterized by one or more major depressive episodes with at least one hypomanic episode; and cyclothymic disorder, represented by at least two years of hypomanic episodes and depressive symptoms that do not meet the criteria for a major depressive episode.

MAJOR DEPRESSIVE DISORDER

Major depressive disorder, often known simply as depression, involves disturbances in mood, concentration, sleep, activity, appetite, and social behavior. A major depressive episode may develop gradually or appear quite suddenly, without any relation to environmental factors. The symptoms of major depressive disorder will vary among individuals, but there are some common symptoms. People with major depressive disorder may have difficulty falling asleep, sleep restlessly or excessively, and wake up without feeling rested. They may experience a decrease or increase in a desire to eat. They may crave certain foods, such as carbohydrates. They may be unable to pay attention to things. Even minor decisions may seem impossible to make. A loss of energy is manifested in slower mental processing, an inability to perform normal daily routines, and slowed reaction time. Sufferers may experience anhedonia, an inability to experience pleasure. They lose interest in activities they used to enjoy. They ruminate about failures and feel guilty and helpless. People with major depressive disorder tend to seek negative feedback about themselves from others. They see no hope for improvement and may be thinking

of death and suicide. In adolescents, depression may be manifested in acting out, anger, aggressiveness, delinquency, drug abuse, poor performance in school, or running away. Depression is a primary risk factor in suicide, one of the leading causes of death among young people in the United States.

There is probably no single cause of major depressive disorder, although it is primarily a disorder of the brain. A chemical dysfunction and genetics are thought to be part of the cause. Neural circuits, which regulate mood, thinking, sleep, appetite, and behavior, do not function normally. Neurotransmitters are out of balance. One neurotransmitter implicated in depression is serotonin.

It is thought that in major depressive disorder there is a reduced amount of serotonin available in the neural circuits (specifically, in the synapse). This results in reduced or lacking nerve impulse. In many patients with the disorder, the hormonal system that regulates the body's response to stress is overactive. Stress, alcohol or drug abuse, medication, or outlook on life may trigger depressive episodes.

Cognitive theories of depression state that a negative cognitive style, such as pessimism, represents a diathesis (a predisposition) that, in the presence of stress, triggers negative cognitions such as hopelessness. Negative cognitions increase the person's vulnerability to depression. Some common precipitants of depression in vulnerable people include marital conflict, academic or work-related difficulty, chronic medical problems, and physical or sexual abuse.

In most cases, medication, psychotherapy, or both are the treatment of choice. Treatment depends on the severity and pattern of the symptoms. With treatment, the majority of people with major depressive disorder return to normal functioning.

Antidepressant drugs influence the functioning of certain neurotransmitters (serotonin, which regulates mood, and norepinephrine, which regulates the body's energy). Tricyclic antidepressants act simultaneously to increase both these neurotransmitters. This type of antidepressant has often intolerable side effects, such as sleepiness, nervousness, dizziness, dry mouth, or constipation. Monoamine oxidase inhibitors (MAOIs) increase levels of these same neurotransmitters plus dopamine, which regulates attention and pleasure. MAOIs can cause dizziness and interact negatively with some foods. Selective serotonin reuptake inhibitors (SSRIs) have fewer side effects but can cause nausea, insomnia or sleepiness, agitation, or sexual dysfunction. Aminoketones increase norepinephrine and dopamine, with agitation, insomnia, and anxiety being common side effects. Selective norepinephrine reuptake inhibitors (SNRIs) increase levels of norepinephrine and can cause dry mouth, constipation, increased sweating, and insomnia. The selective serotonin reuptake inhibitor and blockers (SSRIBs) increase serotonin and elicit the fewest side effects (nausea, dizziness, sleepiness). Herbal remedies, such as St. John's wort, may act like SSRIs. Some drugs blunt the action of a neurotransmitter known as substance P. Other drugs reduce the level and effects of a stress-sensitive brain chemical known as corticotropin-releasing factor (CRF). The hypothalamus, the part of the brain that manages hormone release, increases production of CRF when a threat is detected. The body responds with reduced appetite, decreased sex drive, and heightened alertness. Persistent overactivation of this hormone may lead to depression. The effects of antidepressants are caused by slow-onset adaptive changes in neurons. They may take several weeks to have a noticeable effect.

Psychotherapy works by changing the way the brain functions. Cognitive behavioral therapy helps patients change the negative styles of thinking and behaving associated with depression. Therapies teach patients new skills to help them cope better with life, increase self-esteem, cope with stress, and deal with interpersonal relationships. There is evidence that severe depression responds most favorably with a combination of medication and psychotherapy.

Electroconvulsive therapy (ECT), or shock therapy, is an effective treatment for major depressive disorder. The treatment, first developed in 1934, produces a seizure in the brain by applying electrical stimulation to the brain through electrodes placed on the scalp. ECT reduces the level of CRF. The treatment is usually repeated to obtain a therapeutic response. Common, yet short-lived, side effects include memory loss and other cognitive deficits.

PERSISTENT DEPRESSIVE DISORDER

Persistent depressive disorder comprises the disorders formerly known as chronic major depressive disorder and dysthymic disorder. It is characterized as a mild, chronic depression lasting at least two years. Some people with persistent depressive disorder also develop major depressive disorder, a state called double depression. The disorder is more prevalent in women than in men. Essentially, dysthymic disorder is a low-grade, chronic depression. Diagnosis of dysthymic disorder requires the impairment of physical and social functioning. Treatment may include cognitive and behavioral therapy as well as pharmacotherapy, especially SSRIs.

BIPOLAR DISORDER

In 1686, Théophile Bonet, a French pathologist, described a mental illness he called maniaco-melancholicus. In 1854, Jules Falret, a French physician, described folie circulaire, distinguished by alternating moods of depression and mania. In 1899, Emil Kraepelin, a German psychologist, described manic-depressive psychosis, later described as bipolar disorder.

There is a genetic link to bipolar disorder, and individuals who have a least one parent with the disorder are significantly more likely to develop it themselves. An increased level of calcium ions is found in the blood of patients with bipolar disorder. There is also a lowered blood flow in the brain, as well as slower overall metabolism. Some research suggests that bipolar disorder may be caused by disturbed circadian rhythms and related to disturbances in melatonin secretion.

The DSM-5 divides bipolar disorder into bipolar I disorder, bipolar II disorder, and cyclothymic disorder. Bipolar I disorder is characterized by the occurrence of one or more manic episodes and one or more major depressive episodes; episodes may also have mixed features. Bipolar II disorder is characterized by the occurrence of one or more major depressive episodes accompanied by at least one hypomanic episode. Cyclothymic disorder is a chronic, fluctuating mood disturbance involving periods of hypomanic episodes and periods of major depressive episodes.

Treatment options include psychotherapy and medication. Mood stabilizers, such as lithium and divalproex sodium, are the most commonly used medications. Lithium is a naturally occurring substance that increases serotonin levels in the brain. Side effects can include dry mouth, high overdose toxicity, nausea, and tremor. Divalproex sodium increases gamma-aminobutyric acid (GABA) in the brain. Neurotransmitters trigger either "go" signals that allow messages to be passed on to other cells in the brain or "stop" signals that prevent messages from being forwarded. GABA is the most common message-altering neurotransmitter in the brain. Possible side effects of divalproex sodium include constipation, headache, nausea, liver damage, and tremor. Olanzapine increases levels of dopamine and serotonin. Side effects include drowsiness, dry mouth, low blood pressure, rapid heartbeat, and tremor. Anticonvulsants are also widely prescribed. Carbamazepine, for example, increases

GABA and serotonin. Possible side effects include blurred vision, dizziness, dry mouth, stomach upset, or sedation. In the case of severe mania, patients may take a tranquilizer or a neuroleptic (antipsychotic drug) in addition to the mood stabilizer. During the depressive episode, the person may take an antidepressant, although some antidepressants are known to intensify symptoms in some patients. ECT may also be helpful during severe depressive episodes.

SPECIFIERS FOR MOOD DISORDERS

Specifiers allow for a more specific diagnosis, which assists in treatment and prognosis. A peripartum onset specifier can be applied to a diagnosis of major depressive disorder, or bipolar I or II disorder, if the onset is during pregnancy or within four weeks after childbirth. Symptoms include fluctuations in mood and intense (sometimes delusional) preoccupation with infant well-being. Severe ruminations or delusional thoughts about the infant are correlated with increased risk of harm to the infant. The mother may be uninterested in the infant, afraid of being alone with the infant, or may even try to kill the child (infanticide) while experiencing auditory hallucinations instructing her to do so or delusions that the child is possessed. Postpartum mood episodes severely impair functioning, which differentiates them from the "baby blues" that affect many women within ten days after birth.

The seasonal pattern specifier can be applied to bipolar I or II disorder or major depressive disorder. Occurrence of major depressive episodes is correlated with seasonal changes. In the most common variety, depressive episodes occur in the fall or winter and remit in the spring. The less common type is characterized by depressive episodes in the summer. Symptoms include lack of energy, oversleeping, overeating, weight gain, and carbohydrate craving. Light therapy, which uses bright visible-spectrum light, may bring relief to patients with a seasonal pattern to their mood disorder.

The rapid cycler specifier can be applied to bipolar I or II disorder. Cycling is the process of going from depression to mania, or hypomania, and back or vice versa. Cycles can be as short as a few days or as long as months or years. Rapid cycling involves the occurrence of four or more mood episodes during the previous twelve months. In extreme cases, rapid cyclers can change from depression to mania and back or vice versa in as short as a few days without a normal mood period between episodes..

BIBLIOGRAPHY

American Psychiatric Association. *Diagnostic and Statistical Manual of Mental Disorders: DSM-5.* Washington: American Psychiatric Association, 2013. Print.

American Psychiatric Association. "Highlights of Changes from DSM-IV-TR to DSM-5." *DSM-5 Development.* American Psychiatric Association, 2013. Web. 5 June 2014.

Copeland, Mary Ellen. *The Depression Workbook: A Guide for Living with Depression and Manic Depression.* Oakland: New Harbinger, 2002. Print.

Court, Bryan L., and Gerald E. Nelson. *Bipolar Puzzle Solution: A Mental Health Client's Perspective.* Philadelphia: Taylor, 1996. Print.

Cronkite, Kathy. *On the Edge of Darkness.* New York: Dell, 1994. Print.

Cutler, Janis L. *Psychiatry.* 3rd ed. New York: Oxford UP, 2014. Print.

Dowling, Colette. *You Mean I Don't Have to Feel This Way? New Help for Depression, Anxiety, and Addiction.* New York: Macmillan, 1991. Print.

Gold, Mark S. *The Good News About Depression: Breakthrough Medical Treatments That Can Work for You.* New York: Bantam, 1995. Print.

Gordon, James. *Unstuck: Your Guide to the Seven-Stage Journey Out of Depression.* New York: Penguin, 2008. Print.

Ingersoll, Barbara D., and Sam Goldstein. *Lonely, Sad, and Angry.* New York: Doubleday, 1996. Print.

Moreines, Robert N., and Patricia L. McGuire. *Light Up Your Blues: Understanding and Overcoming Seasonal Affective Disorders.* Washington: PIA, 1989. Print.

Nelson, John E., and Andrea Nelson, eds. *Sacred Sorrows: Embracing and Transforming Depression.* New York: Tarcher, 1996. Print.

Radke-Yarrow, Marian. *Children of Depressed Mothers.* New York: Cambridge UP, 1998. Print.

Thompson, Tracy. *The Beast: A Journey Through Depression.* New York: Penguin, 1996. Print.

Williams, Mark, John Teasdale, Zindel Segal, and Jon Kabat-Zinn. *The Mindful Way Through Depression: Freeing Yourself from Chronic Unhappiness.* New York: Guilford, 2007. Print.

Elizabeth M. McGhee Nelson

SEE ALSO: Antidepressant medications; Bipolar disorder; Depression; Drug therapies; Genetics and mental health;

Mood stabilizer medications; Postpartum depression; Seasonal affective disorder; Shock therapy; Teenagers' mental health.

Mood stabilizer medications

DATE: 1949 forward
TYPE OF PSYCHOLOGY: Psychopathology

Although the term "mood stabilizers" is clinically imprecise, these medications remain an essential part of treatment for several mood and thought disorders.

KEY CONCEPTS

- Anticonvulsants
- Bipolar disorder
- Carbamazepine
- Lithium
- Valproic acid

INTRODUCTION

Typically, most medications used to treat bipolar disorder and related mood disorders—such as cyclothymia—are popularly called mood stabilizers. A more clinically precise use of the term would refer only to medications that decrease mania, alleviate depression, and provide long-term protection against relapse. Given this qualification, the most commonly used mood stabilizers are lithium and two anticonvulsants, valproic acid (Depakote, Depakene, Depakon) and carbamazepine (Tegretol, Carbatrol).

HOW THEY WORK

Central nervous system medications work by regulating the effects of a group of chemicals used to relay signals throughout the brain. In simple terms, neurotransmitters relay signals after being released into the physical gaps between a neuron and its neighbors. In these gaps, neurotransmitters stimulate receptors on neighboring cells, which prompts processes within those cells. One of these processes, for example, is the production of secondary chemicals, called second messengers.

Although precisely how lithium works is unknown, it is believed either to alter the synthesis of neurotransmitters associated with altered moods, or to decrease the production of second-messenger chemicals. Valproic acid and carbamazepine appear to work by decreasing the excitability of neurons or by increasing the effectiveness of a neurotransmitter associated with calm, tranquillity, and relaxation.

LITHIUM

Lithium is a naturally occurring element and in various formulations is the drug of choice for treating euphoric mania. In this mood state, people experience increased energy and decreased need for sleep, impaired judgment and impulse control, irritable moods, and in extreme cases delusions or hallucinations.

As a mood stabilizer, lithium reduces elation, grandiosity, irritability, and anxiety. It also helps control insomnia, agitation, threatening or assaultive behavior, and distractibility. Although it is not otherwise useful in the depressive phases of bipolar disorder, lithium reduces suicidal thinking. Besides bipolar disorder, lithium has been used in schizoaffective disorder and schizophrenia, as well as in impulse control disorders involving unplanned outbursts of violence and rage.

Like all other mood stabilizers, lithium takes effect only after accumulating in the blood to certain levels, called the therapeutic window. When the level is too low, lithium will not have a notable effect; if the level is too high, the person taking it will experience toxicity. Reaching a therapeutic level with lithium usually takes between seven days and two weeks. At therapeutic levels, lithium's most common side effects include gastrointestinal upset, fine tremors, increased urination, and fatigue. Some of these side effects go away on their own, others can be easily treated. Potential long-term side effects include weight gain and cognitive dulling.

Unfortunately, lithium has a narrow therapeutic window, meaning that dosages must be carefully adjusted to avoid toxicity. Even with recommended blood tests, toxicity is sometimes detected symptomatically. Low toxicity is often indicated by nausea and vomiting, diarrhea, thirst, slurred speech, and muscle weakness. Severe toxicity is signaled by coarse hand tremors, confusion, hyperactive muscles and reflexes, cardiac problems, and loss of coordination. Extreme toxicity is marked by seizures, coma, cardiac arrhythmia, circulatory collapse, and death as a result of pulmonary failure.

Maintaining a therapeutic lithium level can be difficult with certain environmental or lifestyle conditions. When hot weather, strenuous exercise, or prolonged diarrhea leads to dehydration, the kidneys retain lithium, which can lead to toxicity. Adequate water intake usually prevents this. Moreover, other drugs—such as ibuprofen—can raise lithium levels.

People with dementia and neurological disorders do not respond well to lithium. Likewise, it is contraindicated for people with brain damage, myasthenia gravis, or cardiovascular, renal, or thyroid disease. Further, lithium is contraindicated in women who are breast feeding or who are pregnant or become pregnant. The Food and Drug Administration (FDA) recommends avoiding lithium during pregnancy, especially the first trimester. Several studies have demonstrated a link between lithium and fetal damage, including severe cardiac problems and deformation.

THE ANTICONVULSANTS

In the 1980s, scientists discovered that a number of medications used to treat epilepsy demonstrated remarkable efficacy in bipolar disorder. Many anticonvulsants are now used for manic or depressed moods, although only two of them have been approved by the FDA for treating bipolar disorder.

Valproic Acid. In 1995, valproic acid (Depakote, Depakene, Depakon) became the first anticonvulsant approved by the FDA for the treatment of mania. It has become the preferred medication over lithium for most types of bipolar disorder. Generally speaking, valproic acid works faster, has a wider therapeutic window, and fewer overall side effects.

Like lithium, gastrointestinal distress is a common side effect with valproic acid, except in formulations with enteric coatings. More serious side effects include potential damage to the liver and the pancreas, as well as decreased platelet counts. Most significantly, valproic acid is harmful to the human fetus and is absolutely contraindicated in pregnant women.

Carbamazepine. Carbamazepine (Tegretol, Carbatrol) received FDA approval in 2005. Some side effects include visual disturbances, ataxia, vertigo, and other neurological side effects. Although these side effects are common, they are usually transient. More significantly, carbamazepine has been associated with decreased white blood cell count and decreased platelet count. Hence, blood cell counts must be monitored in patients using the drug. Further, carbamazepine can accelerate the metabolism of other medications, including oral contraceptives, blood thinners, and certain kinds of antidepressants. As a result, doses of these other medications must be reevaluated.

BIBLIOGRAPHY

Albers, Lawrence J., Rhoda K. Hahn, and Christopher Reist. *Handbook of Psychiatric Drugs.* Blue Jay: Current Clinical Strategies, 2011. Print.

Griswold, Kim S., and Linda F. Pessar. "Management of Bipolar Disorder." *American Family Physician* 62.6 (15 Sept. 2000): 1343–53. Print.

Harris, Margaret, et al. "Mood-Stabilizers: The Archeology of the Concept." *Bipolar Disorders* 5.6 (December 2003): 446–52. Print.

Kalikow, Kevin T. *Kids on Meds: Up-To-Date Information About the Most Commonly Prescribed Psychiatric Medications.* New York: Norton, 2011. Print.

Lehne, Richard. "Drugs for Bipolar Disorder." *Pharmacology for Nursing Care.* 5th ed. St. Louis: Saunders, 2004. Print.

Plunkett, Jeanette M. *Bipolar Disorder: Causes, Diagnosis and Treatment.* New York: Nova, 2011. Print.

Stahl, Stephen M. *Essential Pharmacology of Antipsychotics and Mood Stabilizers.* Cambridge: Cambridge UP, 2002. Print.

Suppes, Trisha, and Ellen B. Dennehy. *Bipolar Disorder.* Kansas City: Compact Clinicals, 2005. Print.

Young, L. Trevor. "What Exactly Is a Mood Stabilizer?" *Journ. of Psychiatry and Neuroscience* 29.2 (March 2004): 87–88. Print.

Michael R. Meyers

SEE ALSO: Antianxiety medications; Antidepressant medications; Antipsychotic medications; Bipolar disorder; Depression; Drug therapies; Hallucinations; Impulse control disorders; Mood disorders; Psychopharmacology.

Moral development

TYPE OF PSYCHOLOGY: Developmental psychology

Moral development is the process of internalizing society's rules and principles of right and wrong. The achievement of morality is necessary to maintain a stable social order. Acquiring morals is a sequential process linked to a person's stage of moral reasoning and cognitive understanding.

KEY CONCEPTS
- Cognitive development
- Empathy
- Moral development
- Moral rules
- Morality
- Social order

INTRODUCTION

Morality is a set of standards that a person has about the rightness and wrongness of various kinds of behavior. Moral development is the way in which these sets of standards change over a period of time and experiences. Without moral rules—obligatory social regulations based on the principles of justice and welfare for others—society would be chaotic and without order. Most societies, for example, agree that certain behaviors (such as murder and theft) are wrong, and most people follow these moral principles. Not everyone has the same way of reasoning about the morality of a situation, however, as seen in the following two scenarios from the work of psychologist Jean Piaget.

A little boy named John is in his room. He is called to dinner, and he goes into the dining room. Behind the door on a chair is a tray with fifteen cups on it. John does not know this; when he goes in, the door knocks against the tray, and all fifteen cups are broken. There is another boy, named Henry. One day when his mother is out he tries to get some jam from the cupboard. He climbs onto a chair but cannot reach it; he knocks over a cup. The cup falls down and breaks.

When asked which of the above two boys is more naughty, most adults would immediately reply that Henry is more guilty. Conversely, a child between six and ten years of age usually will say that John is more guilty. The differences between the two scenes consist of both the amount of damage done and the intentions of the two children. It is obvious that children and adults do not view the situations in the same way.

INFLUENCE OF FREUD AND PIAGET

Human morality has been an issue in philosophy since the days of Aristotle; psychology primarily began to study the topic in the early twentieth century. At this time, both Sigmund Freud and Piaget addressed the issue of children's moral development.

Freud proposed that children around four years of age assimilate the morals and standards of their same-sex parent, resulting in the onset of the child's superego, which is the storehouse for one's conscience. Thus, children have a rudimentary sense of right and wrong based on the morals of their parental figure. Since Freud's concept was based on his theory of psychosexual development, it was discredited by his European colleagues for most of his lifetime. Thus, his theory of moral acquisition has not generally been the basis of research on the development of morality.

Piaget began observing children when he was giving intelligence tests in the laboratory of Alfred Binet. He observed that children do not reason in the same way that adults do. Thus, by questioning Swiss schoolchildren about their rules in a game of marbles, Piaget adapted his theory of cognitive development to moral development. Lawrence Kohlberg elaborated on Piaget's theory by studying children's as well as adults' reasoning concerning moral dilemmas. Kohlberg is still generally considered the leading theorist of moral development.

STAGES OF MORAL DEVELOPMENT

According to Piaget and Kohlberg, moral judgments are related to the stage of cognitive development from which a person is operating when making these judgments. According to Piaget's theory, the development of morality includes several stages. People cannot progress to higher stages of moral development until they have also progressed through higher stages of cognitive understanding. Cognition refers to the mental processes of thinking, reasoning, knowing, remembering, understanding, and problem solving. During the premoral stage (through five years of age), children have little awareness of morals. As children grow, they learn about cooperative activity and equality among peers. This cognitive knowledge leads to a new respect for rights and wrongs. At this stage (age six to ten), children cannot judge that Henry is more guilty than John, because they are not capable of understanding the differences in the children's intentions. The only understanding is of the degree of damage done. Therefore, the number of cups broken is the basis for the judgment of the wrongness of the act, regardless of the actor's good or bad intentions.

Finally, as children develop, they learn that rules can be challenged and are able to consider other factors, such as a person's intentions and motivation. Once this shift in perception occurs, children's moral development will progress to a higher stage.

ROLE OF REASONING

Kohlberg expanded Piaget's theory by investigating how people reasoned the rightness or wrongness of an act and not how people actually behaved. For example, Kohlberg proposed the following moral dilemma. A man named Heinz had a wife who was dying from a disease that could be cured with a drug manufactured by a local pharmacist. The drug was expensive to make, but the druggist was charging ten times the amount it cost. Heinz could not afford the drug and pleaded with the man to discount the drug or let him pay a little at a time. The druggist refused, so Heinz broke into the pharmacy and stole the drug for his wife. Should Heinz have stolen the drug?

By listening to people's reasoning concerning Heinz's actions, Kohlberg proposed that there are three levels (of two stages each) of moral reasoning. The first level is called the preconventional level; in this stage, a person's feelings of right and wrong are based on an external set of rules that have been handed down by an authority figure such as a parent, teacher, or religious figure. These rules are obeyed to avoid punishment or to gain rewards. In other words, people at this stage of moral reasoning would not steal the drug—not because they believed that stealing was wrong, but rather because they had been told not to and would fear being caught and punished for their action.

The second level of moral reasoning is the conventional level, at which judgments of right and wrong are based on other people's expectations. For example, at this level there are two substages. One is known as the good boy/nice girl orientation, in which morality is based on winning approval and avoiding disapproval by one's immediate group. In other words, people may or may not steal the drug based on what they believe their peers would think of them. The second substage is called the law and order orientation, under which moral behavior is thought of in terms of obedience to the authority figure and the established social order. Social order refers to the way in which a society or culture functions, based on the rules, regulation, and standards that are held and taught by each member of the society. The "laws" are usually obeyed without question, regardless of the circumstances, and are seen as the mechanism for the maintenance of social order. A person operating from this stage would say that Heinz should not steal the drug because it was against the law—and if he did steal the drug, he should go to jail for his crime.

The third level of moral reasoning is called the postconventional orientation. At this stage, the person is more concerned with a personal commitment to higher principles than with behavior dictated by society's rules. Disobeying the law would be in some instances far less immoral than obeying a law that is believed to be wrong, and being punished for the legal disobedience would be easier than the guilt and self-condemnation of disobeying the personal ethical principles held by that person. For example, many civil rights workers and Vietnam War conscientious objectors were jailed, beaten, and shunned from mainstream society, but those consequences were far less damaging to them than transgressing their own convictions would have been.

According to Kohlberg, the preconventional stage is characteristic of young children, while the conventional stage is more indicative of the general population. It has been estimated that only about 20 percent of the adult population reach the postconventional stage. Thus, the course of moral development is not the same for everyone. Even some adults operate at the preconventional level of moral reasoning. Education, parental affection, observation and imitation, and explanations of the consequences of behavior are factors in determining the course of moral development in a child.

ROLE-PLAYING
Moral development is a progression from one stage to a different, higher stage of reasoning. One cannot proceed to a higher stage of morality without the accompanying cognitive understanding. Thus, if a child thinks that John, who broke fifteen cups, is more guilty than Henry, who broke one cup, then merely telling the child that Henry's intentions were not as good as John's, and therefore John is not as guilty, is not going to change the child's perceptions. The child's understanding of the situation must be actively changed. One way of doing this is through role-playing. The child who thinks that John is more guilty can be told to act out the two scenes, playing each of the two boys. By asking the child questions about his or her feelings while going through each of the scenes, one can help the child gain empathy (the capacity for experiencing the feelings and thoughts of other people) for each of the characters and gain a better understanding of intentions and actions. Once the child has the cognitive understanding of intentions, he or she is then able to reason at a higher level of moral development.

In other words, in trying to elevate someone's moral reasoning, the first goal is to elevate his or her cognitive understanding of the situation. This can also be done by citing similar examples within the person's own experience and chaining them to the event at hand. For example, if last week the child had accidentally broken something, asking the child how he or she remembers feeling when that event happened will remind the child of the emotions experienced at the time of the event. The child must then associate the remembered emotions with the situation at hand. This can be accomplished by asking questions, such as "Do you think that John might have felt the same way as you did when you broke the vase?" or "How do you think John felt when the cups fell down? Have you ever felt the same?" If one merely tells the child that John felt bad, the child may or may not comprehend the connection, but if one asks the child to reason through the situation by having empathy for John, then the child is more likely to progress to the next stage of moral reasoning.

This type of empathetic role-playing can be very important in trying to change deviant behavior. If a child is stealing, then having the child imagine or play a role in a situation where he or she is the one being stolen from is the quickest way for the child to change his or her judgments of the rightness or wrongness of the situation. Punishment may deter the behavior, but it does not result in a change in cognitive understanding or moral reasoning.

In addition to changing moral reasoning powers, this type of role-playing is also more likely to aid the child from an understimulated home environment. The child whose social environment includes many incidents of undesirable behaviors or who lacks examples of positive behaviors must be stimulated in ways that appeal to current cognitive understanding but that show ways of thinking that differ from current examples in his or her life.

STUDY OF SOCIAL COGNITIONS

Other areas of psychological research are concerned with the topic of children's social cognitions,Cognition which subsumes the topic of morals and considers other issues such as empathy, attribution, and motivations. One area that has come to light is the issue of the effect of the emotions on cognitions and their contribution to moral judgments. For example, it has been shown that people in a good mood are more likely to help than those in a bad mood. Expanding on this premise, other research has demonstrated that even the way people perceive an object or situation is closely linked to their psychological or emotional states at the time. Even concrete perceptions can be changed by a person's state of being. One example is that people who are poor actually judge the size of a quarter to be larger than do people who are rich.

As cognitive theories begin to consider the interactive components that emotions have in cognitions, new methods of study and new theoretical predictions will change the way cognitive psychologists study such areas as problem solving, decision making, reasoning, and memory. Each of these areas is independently related to

the study of moral development and should affect the way psychologists think about how people acquire and think about morality within society.

In addition, as society increases in sophistication and technology, new issues will emerge that will strain old theories. Issues that are particular to new generations will result in new ways of thinking about morality that were not faced by past generations. The direction that moral development goes is ultimately highly dependent on the problems of the current society.

BIBLIOGRAPHY

Duska, Ronald F., and Mariellen Whelan. *Moral Development: A Guide to Piaget and Kohlberg.* New York: Paulist Press, 1975. Presents Jean Piaget's theory and its implications for Lawrence Kohlberg's expansion into his own theory of moral development. All of the moral stories used by Piaget and Kohlberg in their research are replicated in this book. Also includes research findings and ways in which to apply these theories to everyday situations in teaching children. This book can be read easily by the high school or college student.

Gilligan, Carol, Janie Victoria Ward, and Jill McLean Taylor, eds. *Mapping the Moral Domain: A Contribution of Women's Thinking to Psychological Theory and Education.* Cambridge, Mass.: Harvard Graduate School of Education, 1988. A collection of essays presenting the contribution of women's studies to Kohlbergian theories of moral development.

Killen, Melanie, and Judith Smetana. *Handbook of Moral Development.* Mahwah, N.J.: Lawrence Erlbaum, 2006. This book covers the wide range of theories being studied in the field of moral development, with chapters on conscience, stages of moral development, social justice, emotions, and community service.

Nucci, Larry P. *Education in the Moral Domain.* New York: Cambridge University Press, 2001. Brings together theoretical and practical approaches to creating a classroom environment that nurtures moral development in children.

Reed, Donald R. C. *Following Kohlberg: Liberalism and the Practice of Democratic Community.* South Bend, Ind.: University of Notre Dame Press, 1998. Offers a comprehensive overview of Kohlberg's research, from an empirical and psychological perspective as well as a more abstract philosophy.

Rich, John Martin, and Joseph L. DeVitis. *Theories of Moral Development.* 2d ed. Springfield, Ill.: Charles C Thomas, 1996. Presents a range of psychologists' theories on moral development, including Sigmund Freud, Alfred Adler, Carl Jung, and David Sears. In addition, it places moral development within the framework of higher education and relates it to a life-span perspective. Certain sections of the book would be difficult for a novice student to follow; however, in terms of a summary review of theoretical positions, the book is a handy reference.

Shumaker, David M., and Robert V. Heckel. *Kids of Character: A Guide to Promoting Moral Development.* Westport, Conn.: Praeger, 2007. The authors contend that with the decrease in importance of religious institutions and the increase in two-working-parent families, children are losing ground in character development. This resource offers the latest research in this field and practical suggestions for giving children the guidance they need.

Donna Frick-Horbury

SEE ALSO: Adolescence: Cognitive skills; Binet, Alfred; Birth order and personality; Cognitive ability: Gender differences; Cognitive development: Jean Piaget; Crowd behavior; Development; Developmental psychology; Gilligan, Carol; Juvenile delinquency; Kohlberg, Lawrence; Women's psychology: Carol Gilligan.

Mother-child relationship

TYPE OF PSYCHOLOGY: Developmental psychology

The mother-child relationship is a process of attachment that begins at birth and is usually in place by one year of age. Attachments can be either secure or insecure and are based primarily on the mother's response to the child. However, infants participate in the synchrony of the attachment relationship.

KEY CONCEPTS

- Ambivalent attachment
- Avoidant attachment
- Biological preparedness
- Critical periods
- Disorganized attachment
- Ethological theory of attachment
- Resistant attachment
- Secure attachment
- Separation anxiety

INTRODUCTION

John Bowlby was one of the first psychologists to be interested in studying attachment patterns in mother and child. He became involved in this when he was working with juvenile thieves and noticed that all such youths had experienced a disruptive relationship with their mothers when they were infants or young children. His studies led him to formulate his theory of attachment, which is considered the most comprehensive of its kind. Bowlby's theory is based on the ethological principle that some behaviors are biologically programmed for optimal adaptability to the environment, which in turn increases the probability for survival. According to Bowlby, infants' behaviors are biologically programmed to insure attachment to a primary caretaker, and attachment is an optimal strategy for survival.

ETHOLOGICAL THEORY OF ATTACHMENT

Mother-child relationships begin as an interactive dance in which each party responds to the other with a set of behaviors meant to result in a synchronized pattern of love. According to the principles of Bowlby's ethological theory of attachment, all infants are born into the world biologically prepared to respond to attachment behaviors from a primary caretaker. At birth, infants have a set of limited responses, each of which elicits a specific response in an adult. For example, the cries of newborn babies will trigger milk flow in their mothers or increase the physiological arousal of any adult, which in turn increases the probability that the child's needs will be met. Other examples include the fact that a newborn can recognize its mother's voice, will grasp a finger placed in its hand, and will calm down when touched. In turn, an adult is likely to respond to these behaviors with loving and tender caresses and words. As the interactions grow and mature, the patterns of attachment become more canalized until, at about one year old, a child can be classified into one of several attachment patterns.

ATTACHMENT TYPES

Attachment is a pattern of parent-child interactions that determines the overall relationship between the child and its mother or father. Children can have a secure attachment to one or both parents, or they can have an insecure attachment. Bowlby determined that children who are securely attached view their mothers as "secure bases" to which they will return when feeling anxious or threatened.

The attachment classification was enhanced by Mary Ainsworth when she determined that one way to view differences in attachment security was to purposefully expose a baby to a environment that may be distressing. She devised the laboratory procedure of the strange situation, where infants and mothers were placed into a room full of toys. During a specified time period, the mother left and returned several times. The baby was left either with a stranger or alone. The child's response to the separation and its reunion behaviors to the mother showed several differences in the child's behaviors dependent on its pattern of maternal attachment. This procedure has become the standard operation used to measure attachment and has revealed a great deal about attachment in both the infant and older child.

SECURE ATTACHMENT

In a secure attachment, infants tend to explore the environment more freely and are able to separate from their mothers without too much distress. On reunion, secure children are always happy to see their mothers and respond in a positive way. These children are also able to share their toys with strangers and be comforted by strangers if left alone. As children grow, those with a secure attachment tend to be happier and more stable, have more friends, do better in school, have higher motivation and achievement mastery, be more empathetic and more moral, and more likely to be a leader in school.

Secure attachment begins primarily with mothers responding in a nurturing and gentle manner. They are quick to comfort a crying child, show affection, are sympathetic, and smile at their children frequently. In the context of discipline, they are less likely to nag or punish, especially spank, and are more likely to reinforce positive behavior than focus on negative behavior. When a child does something wrong, this mother will explain to the child why the behavior was wrong and what the consequences are in a context that the child will understand. The mother encourages, helps, nurtures, and disciplines in a firm but gentle manner.

INSECURE ATTACHMENT

There are at least two kinds of insecure attachment. Even though it is called insecure attachment, it is still an attachment. The bonding is not as strong or stable as a secure attachment and there are different consequences. Insecure attachment occurs because the infant has a need to protect himself or herself from some unpleasant parental situation and the only way to do that is to direct its attention away from the parent. All infants have a need for affection and love. If they seek out the mother, for example, and reach out or smile at her and the mother does not respond, the child's emotional needs are not met and he or she feels distress and anxiety. If this happens enough times, the child learns to expect rejection and a conflict arises between the child's needs and expectations. The child learns to avoid this unpleasant situation by directing attention away from the parent. Thus, the attachment that forms is not one where the child is certain that the parent will respond to his or her needs or make him or her feel secure. The child's emotional development hardwires in the brain differently from the secure child. Thus, the insecure child's emotional responses will be different also.

Generally, the two most widely recognized types of insecure attachment are avoidant attachment and resistant attachment. Children who form a resistant attachment pattern have found that the mother is inconsistent in her response to the child's need. In some situations the mother is available and helpful, while at other times she is unresponsive or unavailable and may even use abandonment as a means of controlling the child. According to Ainsworth, this results in the child having a severe emotional response when separated from the mother, and separation anxiety results in clinging and anxious behavior. However, when the mother returns, the child will resist any overtures of contact that the mother might make and does not easily calm down. The child may even show signs of anger or aggressive behavior toward the mother. About 10 to 15 percent of American infants show this pattern. Ainsworth refers to this type of attachment as ambivalent. Because the mother sometimes shows positive reactions to the child, the child does not totally disengage and still desires contact with the mother. Thus, these children show a mixture of desire for and rejection of the mother. They will be intimate one second and hostile the next. If the mother joins them after a separation, these children will focus on the toys or tasks at hand and will greet the mother briefly but distantly.

The second pattern of insecure attachment is avoidant. An avoidantly attached infant does not expect the mother to respond in a helpful manner, and the child learns that he or she may even be rebuffed when approaching the mother for protection or comfort. The mother of this child is usually rejecting of the child and shows little affection to the child. To protect himself or herself, the child distances from the mother and is not distressed during parental separation. When the mother returns, the child avoids the mother and does not greet her positively or affectionately. As the child ages, he or she attempts to live without love and support from others by becoming emotionally self-sufficient. About 20 percent of American babies show this type of attachment.

An avoidant attachment can also occur with the mother who shows too much attention to a child, who overreacts to everything, who is too exuberant in responses of even a positive expression, or who is too possessive or protective of the child. This overreactive response is too overwhelming for the child, who will react by directing attention away from the mother and thus become insecurely attached.

Photo: iStock

Another pattern of insecure attachment is disorganized/disoriented attachment. This attachment illustrates the most severe pattern of insecurity for the child. When young, these children display confused, contradictory behaviors toward the mother when reunited with her. For example, they may approach her but their facial expressions will relate no element of pleasure. In fact, these children more likely will display a flat, unemotional, or depressed expression. As these children age, their behavior toward their mother changes, responding to their mother at reunion with either a controlling or a dominating attitude, possibly trying to humiliate or reject the parent. They may also respond with an attitude of role-reversal, where the parent is treated as if he or she had become the child.

ATTACHMENT STABILITY

Although attachment patterns for the most part are stable over the life span, attachment patterns can be changed. It is never too late to forge a secure attachment. However, the emotional patterns of the child tend to be hardwired during early development and some of the child's emotional responses will be automatic. The critical period is thought to be within the first three years of life. In other words, when a parent comforts a hurt child, there is a corresponding neural loop that goes from the emotional centers of the brain to the cerebral cortex of the brain and reduces anxiety. When this occurs enough times there is an automatic response in the brain that allows the child to comfort himself or herself. However, if the child is hurt and seeks comfort but gets instead a rebuke or even more physical pain, then the brain wires up differently so that physical hurts are associated with emotional hurts or vice versa. This does not necessarily indicate that the brain neural networks are abnormal, but they are different from children whose parents meet their emotional needs. There is still much research that needs to be done before it can be said for sure that the neural pattern is irrevocable, but some things can be changed.

BIBLIOGRAPHY

Ainsworth, Mary, et al. *Patterns of Attachment: A Psychological Study of the Strange Situation.* Hillsdale: Erlbaum, 1978. Print.

Bowlby, John. *Attachment and Loss.* 2nd ed. New York: Basic, 1999. Print.

Bowlby, John. *A Secure Base: Parent-Child Attachment and Healthy Human Development.* London: Routledge, 1988. Print.

Chen, Fu, et al. "The Role of Emotion in Parent-Child Relationships: Children's Emotionality, Maternal Meta-Emotion, and Children's Attachment Security." *Journal of Child and Family Studies* 21.3 (2012): 403–10. Print.

Holmes, Jeremy. *John Bowlby and Attachment Theory.* 2nd ed. London: Routledge, 2013. Print.

Karen, Robert. *Becoming Attached*. New York: Oxford UP, 1998. Print.

Main, Mary, and Donna Weston. "Avoidance of the Attachment Figure in Infancy: Descriptions and Interpretations." *The Place of Attachment in Human Behavior*. Ed. Colin Murray Parkes and J. S. Hinde. London: Tavistock, 1982. 31–59. Print.

Mooney, Carol Garhart. *Theories of Attachment: An Introduction to Bowlby, Ainsworth, Gerber, Brazelton, Kennell, and Klaus*. St. Paul: Redleaf, 2010. Print.

Donna Frick-Horbury

SEE ALSO: Archetypes and the collective unconscious; Attachment and bonding in infancy and childhood; Child abuse; Children's mental health; Elder abuse; Family life: Adult issues; Family life: Children's issues; Family systems theory; Father-child relationship; Gender identity formation; Oedipus complex; Parental alienation syndrome; Parenting styles; Separation and divorce: Adult issues; Separation and divorce: Children's issues; Sibling relationships; Stepfamilies.

Motivation

TYPE OF PSYCHOLOGY: Biological bases of behavior; Emotion; Learning; Memory; Motivation; Social psychology

Central to the study of psychology is motivation, which is fundamentally concerned with emotion, personality, learning, memory, and with gaining an understanding of how behavior is most effectively activated, organized, and directed toward the achievement of goals.

KEY CONCEPTS

- Activation theory
- Behavioral approach
- Cognitive approach
- Hedonistic theory
- Humanistic approach
- Hydraulic model
- Incentive theory
- Pavlovian conditioning
- Psychodynamic approach
- Teacher expectations

INTRODUCTION

Research in motivation is pivotal to such fields as educational psychology, social psychology, behavioral psychology, and most other subareas of psychology. Motivation is centrally concerned with the goals people set for themselves and with the means they take to achieve these goals. It is also concerned with how people react to and process information, activities directly related to learning. People's motivation to process information is influenced by two major factors: the relevance of the topic to the person processing the information, which affects their willingness to think hard about the topic; and the need for cognition, or people's willingness to think hard about varied topics, whether they are directly relevant to them or not. The relevance of a topic is central to people's motivation to learn about it.

For example, if the community in which a person lives experiences a severe budgetary crisis that will necessitate a substantial increase in property taxes, every resident in that community, home owners and renters alike, is going to be affected directly or indirectly by the increase. Because this increase is relevant to all the residents, they will, predictably, be much concerned with the topic and will likely think hard about its salient details. If, on the other hand, a community in a distant state faces such a crisis, residents in other communities, reading or hearing about the situation, will not have the motivation to do much hard thinking about it because it does not affect them directly.

The second category of motivation rests in the need of some individuals for cognition. Their inherent curiosity will motivate them to think deeply about various topics that do not concern them directly but that they feel a need to understand more fully. Such people are deliberative, self-motivated thinkers possessed of an innate curiosity about the world that surrounds them. They generally function at a higher intellectual level than people who engage in hard thinking primarily about topics that affect them directly. One of the aims of education at all levels is to stimulate people to think about a broad variety of topics, which they will do because they have an inherent curiosity that they long to satisfy.

EARLY CONCERNS WITH MOTIVATION

During the late nineteenth century, Austrian psychoanalyst Sigmund Freud developed theories about motivation that are usually categorized as the psychodynamic approach. He contended that people have psychic energy that is essentially sexual or aggressive in its origins. Such energy seeks results that please, satisfy, or delight. This pleasure principle, as it was called, had to function within the bounds of certain restraints, identified as the reality principle, never violating the demands of people's conscience or of the restraints or inhibitions that their self-images imposed. In Freudian terms, the superego served to maintain the balance between the pleasure principle and the reality principle. In *Beyond the Pleasure Principle* (1922), Freud reached the conclusion that all motivation could be reduced to two opposing sources of energy, the life instinct and the death instinct.

Heinz Hartmann went a step beyond Freud's psychodynamic theory, emphasizing the need for people to achieve their goals in ways that do not produce inner conflict, that are free of actions that might compromise or devastate the ego. More idealistic was Robert White, who denied Freud's contention that motivation is sexual or aggressive in nature. White contended that the motivation to achieve competence is basic in people. Everyone, according to White, wishes to be competent and, given proper guidance, will strive to achieve competence, although individual goals and individual determinations of the areas in which they wish to be competent vary greatly from person to person.

Such social psychologists as Erik H. Erikson, Carl Jung, and Karen Horney turned their attention away from the biological and sexual nature of motivation, focusing instead on its social aspects. They, like Freud, Hartmann, and White before them, sought to understand the unconscious means by which psychic energy is distributed as it ferrets out sources of gratification.

THE BEHAVIORISTS

The behavioral approach to motivation is centrally concerned with rewards and punishments. People cultivate behaviors for which they are rewarded. They avoid behaviors that experience has shown them will result in pain or punishment. B. F. Skinner was probably the most influential behaviorist. Many educators accepted his theories and applied them to social as well as teaching situations.

Clark L. Hull, working experimentally with rats, determined that animals deprived of such basic requirements as food or punished by painful means, such as electric shock, develop intense reactions to these stimuli. John Dollard and Neal Miller extended Hull's work to human subjects. They discovered that the response elicited by these means depends on the intensity of the stimulus, not on its origin. The stimuli employed also evoke previously experienced stimulus-response reactions, so that if subjects are hurt or punished following a volitional act, they will in future avoid such an act. In other words, if the negative stimuli are rapidly reduced, the responses

that immediately preceded the reduction are reinforced. These researchers concluded that physiological needs such as hunger are innate, whereas secondary drives and the reaction to all drives, through conditioning, are learned.

Ivan Petrovich Pavlov demonstrated the strength of conditioned responses in his renowned experiments with dogs. He arranged for a bell to sound immediately before the dogs in his experiment were to be fed. The dogs came to associate the sound of a bell with being fed, a pleasurable and satisfying experience. Eventually, when Pavlov rang the bell but failed to follow its ringing with feeding, the dogs salivated merely on hearing the sound because they anticipated the feeding to which they had become conditioned. Over time, the motivation to satisfy their hunger came to be as much related to hearing the bell as it was to their actually being fed. Pavlovian conditioning is directly related to motivation, in this case the motivation to satisfy hunger.

KONRAD LORENZ'S HYDRAULIC MODEL

Freud argued that if instinctive urges are bottled up, they will eventually make the individual ill. They demand release and will find it in one way or another as the unconscious mind works to direct the distribution of people's psychic energy.

Konrad Lorenz carried this notion a step beyond what Freud had postulated, contending that inherent drives that are not released by external means will explode spontaneously through some inherent releasing mechanism. This theory, termed Lorenz's hydraulic model, explains psychic collapses in some people, particularly in those who are markedly repressed.

Erich Fromm carried Freud's notions about the repression of innate drives one step beyond what Lorenz espoused. Fromm added a moral dimension to what Freud and Lorenz asserted by postulating that humans develop character as a means of managing and controlling their innate physiological and psychological needs. He brought the matter of free will into his consideration of how to deal in a positive way with innate drives.

THE HEDONISTIC THEORY OF MOTIVATION

Hedonism emphasizes pleasure over everything else. The hedonistic theory of motivation stems from Freud's recognition of the pleasure principle, which stipulates that motivation is stimulated by pleasure and inhibited by pain.

Laboratory experiments with rats demonstrated un-equivocally that, given a choice, rats work harder to get food that tastes good to them than to get food that is nutritious. Indeed, laboratory animals will take in empty calories to the point of emaciation as long as the food that contains such calories tastes good. It is thought that hedonistic motivation is directly related to pleasure centers in the brain, so that organisms work both consciously and unconsciously toward stimulating and satisfying these pleasure centers.

THE INCENTIVE THEORY OF MOTIVATION

Alfred Adler, the Austrian psychologist who founded the school of individual psychology, rejected Freud's emphases on sex and aggression as fundamental aspects of motivation. Breaking from Freud, who had been among his earliest professional associates, Adler contended that childhood feelings of helplessness led to later feelings of inferiority. His means of treating the inferiority complex, as this condition came to be known, was to engage his patients in positive social interaction. To do this, he developed an incentive theory of motivation, as articulated in his two major works, *Praxis und Theorie der Individual psychologie* (1920; *The Practice and Theory of Individual Psychology*, 1924) and *Menschenkenntnis* (1927; *Understanding Human Nature*, 1927).

Adler's theory focused on helping people to realize the satisfaction involved in achieving superiority and competence in areas in which they had some aptitude. The motivation to do so is strictly personal and individual. Adler's entire system was based on the satisfactions to be derived from achieving a modicum of superiority. The incentive approach views competence as a basic motivation activated by people's wish to avoid failure. This is a reward/punishment approach, although it is quite different from that of the behaviorists and is in essence humanistic. The reward is competence; the punishment is failure. Both factors stimulate subjects' motivation.

THE ACTIVATION THEORY OF MOTIVATION

Drive reductionists believed that if all of an organism's needs are fulfilled, that organism will lapse into a lethargic state. They conclude that increasing needs will cause the organism to have an increased drive to fulfill those needs. Their view is that the inevitable course that individual organisms select is that of least resistance.

Donald O. Hebb, however, takes a more sanguine view of motivation, particularly in humans. In his activation theory, he contends that a middle ground between lethargy at one extreme and incapacitating anxiety at the other produces the most desirable level of motivation. This theory accounts for states of desired arousal such as that found in such pursuits as competitive sports.

The drive reductionists ascribe to the reward/punishment views of most of the behaviorists, who essentially consider organisms to be entities in need of direction, possibly of manipulation. The drive inductionists, on the other hand, have faith in the innate need of organisms to be self-directive and to work individually toward gaining competence. Essentially they accept the Greek ideal of the golden mean as a guiding principle, which has also been influential in the thinking of such humanistic psychologists.

THE HUMANISTIC APPROACH TO MOTIVATION

Abraham Maslow devised a useful though controversial hierarchy of needs required to satisfy human potential. These needs proceed from low-level physiological needs such as hunger, thirst, sex, and comfort, through such other needs as safety, love, and esteem, finally reaching the highest level, self-actualization. According to Maslow, human beings progress sequentially through this hierarchy as they develop. Each category of needs proceeds from the preceding category, and no category is omitted as the human develops, although the final and highest category, self-actualization, which includes curiosity, creative living, and fulfilling work, is not necessarily attained or attainable by all humans.

The humanists stipulate that people's primary motives are those that lead toward self-actualization, those that capitalize on the unique potential of each individual. In educational terms, this means that for education to be effective, it must emphasize exploration and discovery over memorization and the rote learning of a set body of material. It must also be highly individualized, although this does not imply a one-on-one relationship between students and their teachers. Rather than acting as fonts of knowledge, teachers become facilitators of learning, directing their students individually to achieve the actualization of the personal goals that best suit them.

Carl R. Rogers traced much psychopathology to conflicts between people's inherent understanding of what they require to move toward self-actualization and society's expectations, which may run counter to individual needs. In other words, as many people develop and pass through the educational system, they may be encouraged or required to adopt goals that are opposed to those that are most realistic for them. Humanistic views of human development run counter to the views of most of the psychodynamic and behaviorist psychologists concerned with learning theory and motivation as it relates to such theory.

COGNITIVE APPROACHES TO MOTIVATION

The research of Kurt Lewin in the subjective tension systems that work toward resolution of problems in humans along with his research, done in collaboration with Edward C. Tolman, that emphasizes expectancies and the subjective value of the results of actions has led to a cognitive approach to motivation. Related to this research is that of Leon Festinger, whose theory of cognitive dissonance stipulates that if people's beliefs are not in harmony with each other, they will experience a discomfort that they will attempt to eliminate by altering their beliefs.

People ultimately realize that certain specific behaviors will lead to anticipated results. Behavior, therefore, has a purpose, but the number of goals related to specific behaviors is virtually infinite. People learn to behave in ways that make it most likely to achieve expected results.

Robert Rosenthal and Lenore Jacobson demonstrated that teacher expectations have a great deal to do with the success of the students with whom they work. Their experiment, detailed fully in *Pygmalion in the Classroom* (1968), relates how they selected preadolescent and adolescent students randomly and then told the teachers of those students that they had devised a way of determining which students were likely to show spurts of unusual mental growth in the coming year.

Each teacher was given the names of two or three students who were identified as being on the brink of rapid intellectual development. The researchers tested the students at the end of the school year and found that those who had been designated as poised on the brink of unusual mental development tested above the norm even though they had been selected randomly from all the students in the classes involved. In this experiment, teacher motivation to help certain students succeed appears to have been central to those students' achieving goals beyond those of other students in the class.

BIBLIOGRAPHY

Boekaerts, Monique, Paul R. Pintrich, and Moshe Zeidner, eds. *Handbook of Self-Regulation.* San Diego: Academic Press, 2007. Print.

Elliot, Andrew J., and Carol S. Dweck, eds. *Handbook of Competence and Motivation.* New York: Guilford, 2007. Print.

Ferguson, Eva Dreikurs. *Motivation: A Biosocial and Cognitive Integration of Motivation and Emotion.* New York: Oxford UP, 2000. Print.

Glover, John A., Royce R. Ronning, and Cecil R. Reynolds, eds. *Handbook of Creativity.* New York: Plenum, 1989. Print.

Greenwood, Gordon E., and H. Thompson Fillmer. *Educational Psychology: Cases for Teacher Decision-Making.* Columbus: Merrill, 1999. Print.

Kendrick, Douglas T., Steven L. Neuberg, and Robert B. Cialdini, eds. *Social Psychology: Unraveling the Mystery.* 4th ed. Boston: Pearson, 2007. Print.

Kreitler, Shulamith. *Cognition and Motivation: Forging an Interdisciplinary Perspective.* New York: Cambridge UP, 2013. Print.

Lawler, Edward E., III. *Rewarding Excellence: Pay Strategies for the New Economy.* San Francisco: Jossey, 2000. Print.

Lesko, Wayne A., ed. *Readings in Social Psychology: General, Classic, and Contemporary Selections.* 7th ed. Boston: Pearson, 2009. Print.

Reeve, Johnmarshall. *Understanding Motivation and Emotion.* 5th ed. Hoboken: Wiley, 2009. Print.

Rosenthal, Robert, and Lenore Jacobson. *Pygmalion in the Classroom.* New York: Holt, 1968. Print.

Sinnott, Jan D. *Positive Psychology: Advances in Understanding Adult Motivation.* New York: Springer, 2013. Print.

Tracy, Brian. *Motivation.* New York: American Management Assoc., 2013. Print.

Wagner, Hugh. *The Psychobiology of Human Motivation.* New York: Routledge, 1999. Print.

Wong, Roderick. *Motivation: A Biobehavioural Approach.* New York: Cambridge UP, 2000. Print.

R. Baird Shuman

SEE ALSO: Achievement motivation; Adler, Alfred; Affiliation motive; Behaviorism; Conditioning; Drives; Ego, superego, and id; Freud, Sigmund; Fromm, Erich; Hull, Clark L.; Incentive motivation; Lewin, Kurt; Lorenz, Konrad; Maslow, Abraham; Miller, Neal E., and John Dollard; Motivation: Intrinsic and extrinsic; Pavlov, Ivan Petrovich; Pavlovian conditioning; Punishment; Reinforcement; S-R theory: Neal E. Miller and John Dollard; Work motivation.

Motivation
Intrinsic and extrinsic

TYPE OF PSYCHOLOGY: Biological bases of behavior; Motivation; Social psychology

Motivation, both intrinsic and extrinsic, is integral to all human behavior, both in developing new behaviors and in attempting to create changes in behavior.

KEY CONCEPTS
- Achievement goal
- Ego orientation
- Punishment
- Rewards
- Self-efficacy
- Task orientation

INTRODUCTION

Motivation is an integral part of human behavior. It is an important determinant in why a person may pursue a particular activity. Intrinsic motivation is something internal, either primal (such as the need to eat) or learned (such as the knowledge of healthful eating). Extrinsic motivation is something external and may be both positive (such as rewards) or negative (such as punishment). Repeated exposure to extrinsic motivation may help create an intrinsic motivation. For example, students who are motivated to learn to receive good grades may develop a desire to learn.

The simplest goal for using motivation in behavior change is to create a habit. An early example is the experiment by Russian physiologist Ivan Petrovich Pavlov. Ringing a bell (extrinsic motivation) and then providing food (extrinsic motivation) resulted in the dog salivating in anticipation of eating the food (intrinsic motivation). Removing the middle step after the behavior was set did not change the salivation reaction to the bell. This is also seen in humans and is related to the primal need to eat for survival. A difference between human and animal behavior related to motivation is that humans can translate a behavior to other situations. People often eat for pleasure, not just hunger or need. When realtors suggest that homeowners bake cookies before an open house, they are making use of humans' ability to translate behaviors. The salivation habit activated when potential buyers smell the cookies is associated with positive memories, which translates to a positive reaction to the house.

MOTIVATION IN THE EDUCATIONAL SETTING

In the 1970s, much of educational psychology revolved around using motivation theory to achieve high performance. Government agencies demanded high achievement in exchange for funding. Early research on how motivation affected student outcomes consistently showed that high self-efficacy was related to positive outcomes. Students with high self-efficacy are confident in their ability to succeed even when obstacles or barriers are present. Teachers encouraged self-efficacy by removing failure as an option.

Soon educators and researchers realized that a false sense of self-efficacy was being created. Educational psychology saw the emergence of achievement goal theories, which held that students needed to be goal directed and that goals should guide decision making and behavior within the context of achievement. If the goal was to develop competence, goal theory suggests that the perception of ability becomes a central variable. Students have to be able to differentiate the concepts of luck, task difficulty, and effort from ability. The terms used to suggest this orientation are "task" and "ego." When a student is task oriented, all actions are aimed at achieving mastery, learning, or perfecting a task (true self-efficacy). When a student follows an ego-oriented goal, the student perceives success when he or she can perform better than peers, and the perceived level of success is highest when the student believes natural ability, not effort, to have been responsible for that success (false self-efficacy).

Research has suggested that if students are task oriented, they are more likely to persevere to the point of mastery, whereas ego-oriented students are competitive toward other students and the goal of their efforts is to be better than the other students while expending little or no effort. Relating this back to motivation, the task-oriented students are experiencing intrinsic motivation as they pursue learning for learning's sake. The ego-oriented students are experiencing extrinsic motivation; they are primarily interested in their class standing and care little how they achieve the grade. This can lead to behavior that might not be morally acceptable, such as cheating.

MOTIVATION IN PROFESSIONAL SETTINGS

Extrinsic motivation, often in the form of money, is a strong influence in many professional settings. For example, the emphasis in professional sports is increasingly on winning, which is tied to salaries, jobs, and other possible remuneration such as product endorsements and sponsorships. Winning or losing the Super Bowl or the

World Series can mean a difference of millions of dollars, and in some cases, the jobs of players and coaches. This show-me-the-money attitude is not limited to the sports world. In the everyday workplace, researchers have shown that extrinsic financial compensation is a stronger motivator for performance among workers than the intrinsic motivation provided by a pleasant environment or job satisfaction.

Because extrinsic motivation has been shown to increase worker performance, many companies have cut back on intrinsic rewards and concentrated on purely extrinsic rewards for their employees. This, in turn, causes employees to focus even more on extrinsic rewards. This can have the effect of employees choosing business options that will maximize their money-making potential by furthering their career rather than options that will promote the company's well-being. Professional athletes, who probably became proficient in their sports through a love of the sport and of physical activity, eventually associate excellence in sports with extrinsic rewards such as money. This can lead, among other things, to bad decisions regarding when to play with an injury or other health issue. Many of these athletes gradually lose the intrinsic rewards they received from playing their sport, and therefore, when they retire, they often stop being active, gain weight, and suffer from the same lifestyle-related diseases as do their relatively inactive peers.

BIBLIOGRAPHY

Deci, Edward L., and Richard M. Ryan. *Intrinsic Motivation and Self-Determination in Human Behavior.* New York: Plenum, 1985. Print.

Kreitler, Shulamith. *Cognition and Motivation: Forging an Interdisciplinary Perspective.* New York: Cambridge UP, 2013. Print.

McClelland, David. *Human Motivation.* Cambridge: Cambridge UP, 1987. Print.

Roberts, Glyn C., ed. *Advances in Motivation in Sport and Exercise.* Chicago: Human Kinetics, 2001. Print.

Sinnott, Jan D. *Positive Psychology: Advances in Understanding Adult Motivation.* New York: Springer, 2013. Print.

Tracy, Brian. *Motivation.* New York: American Management Assoc., 2013. Print.

Urdan, T. C. "Achievement Goal Theory: Past Results, Future Direction." *Advances in Motivation and Achievement.* Ed. M. L. Maehr and R. P. R. Pintrich. Vol. 10. Greenwich: JAI, 1997. Print.

Wong, Roderick. *Motivation: A Biobehavioural Approach.* New York: Cambridge UP, 2000. Print.

Wendy E. S. Repovich

SEE ALSO: Achievement motivation; Conditioning; Motivation; Pavlov, Ivan Petrovich; Punishment; Reinforcement.

Motor development

TYPE OF PSYCHOLOGY: Developmental psychology

Motor development refers to the development of voluntary control over one's body and its parts, as in crawling, walking, reaching, and grasping. Motor development parallels brain growth and development and is influenced by both biological and environmental factors..

KEY CONCEPTS

- Central nervous system
- Cephalo-caudal development
- Cerebral cortex
- Fine motor movements
- Gross motor movements
- Mass-to-specific development
- Maturation
- Proximo-distal development

INTRODUCTION

Motor development refers to the development of motor skills, or voluntary control over the body and its parts. Gross motor development refers to the development of skills or behaviors that involve the large muscle masses and large body movements (such as crawling, walking, running, and throwing), whereas fine motor development refers to the development of small muscle movements, usually in reference to the hands (as in grasping, writing, and fastening buttons). Motor skills develop rapidly during the early years of life and follow a predictable sequence of stages.

Motor development proceeds according to three developmental principles: from head to toe (cephalo-caudal development), from the center of the body to the body's periphery (proximo-distal development), and from large to small muscle control, with actions becoming more refined and directed (mass-to-specific development). Cephalo-caudal development is illustrated by the fact that infants gain control over their heads and shoulders before their legs. Proximo-distal development is shown by young children gaining control over their arms before their hands and fingers, and mass-to-specific development is illustrated by the fact that infants reach for an object with both arms extended before they can reach out with one arm at a time.

The development of both gross and fine motor skills depends on the maturation (development attributable to one's genetic timetable and not to experience) of the nervous system. Voluntary movements develop as the cortex, which is the outer layer of the brain, matures. Whereas the cortex is barely functioning at birth, the "lower" parts of the brain—such as the brain stem and the midbrain—that control basic, nonthinking functions such as breathing, heartbeat, digestion, and reflexes are mature at birth. This is part of the reason that newborns have only reflexive, involuntary movements during the first few months of life. Voluntary control over the body develops gradually as connections between the muscles and the higher brain centers such as the cortex become established. The parts of the brain concerned with posture and balance also develop gradually over the first year of life; they contribute to infants being able to sit up, stand, and then walk.

The gradual acquisition of fine and gross motor skills has a number of important implications for a child's social, cognitive, and personality development. The development of fine motor skills allows infants to examine and experiment with objects, explore their environment, and even communicate with others by showing objects or by pointing. Gross motor milestones provide children with a new and progressively complex perspective of the world, more opportunities to explore and learn about the physical and social environment, and increasing degrees of independence—which have implications for children's developing sense of mastery and competence. These motor milestones in turn affect parents' interactions with, and treatment of, their increasingly independent children.

SEQUENCES OF DEVELOPMENT

Gross motor and fine motor skills follow a specific sequence of development. Gross motor (or locomotor) development eventually results in a young child being able to walk and run. To reach this point, a child must first develop control of his or her head, sit up, and then develop enough balance and strength to stand. By approximately two months of age, most infants can lift their heads, and by three to four months of age they are usually able to roll over. At five or six months they can sit up, and by seven to nine months they usually begin crawling.

Infants may be able to stand while holding on to an object at six months, pull themselves to standing between eight and ten months, and walk independently at around twelve to fourteen months. By eighteen months of age, toddlers are usually able to run, walk backward, throw a ball, and climb stairs; between twenty-four to thirty-six months, they may be able to ride a tricycle. From two to six years of age, children continue to refine their movements. For example, a two-year-old's awkward gait and poor balance change by three years of age to a more stable and balanced gait, allowing the child to hop, jump, and run back and forth. By four years of age, children's walking movements are similar to adults', allowing them to move easily up and down stairs and even to hop on one foot. By age five, children are well coordinated, have good balance, and are able to move skillfully and gracefully while walking, running, climbing, and throwing.

Fine motor development eventually results in refined eye-hand coordination, which will enable a child to write. To achieve this, children must first be able to reach, grasp, and manipulate objects voluntarily and possess refined finger (especially thumb-to-index-finger) control. At birth, no voluntary control exists. By three months of age, babies begin to make poorly directed swiping movements with their entire arms (fists closed). At around four months, infants use an open-handed, scooping movement with a slightly better aim; by five months, infants can reach and grasp objects with both hands, holding the object in the center of the palm by all fingers. Between nine and ten months, infants can hold objects by the palm and middle fingers in a palmar grasp. The ability to use the thumb and index finger together (pincer grasp) typically develops between nine and fifteen months. Infants who have developed this skill usually enjoy practicing it and will pick up tiny objects such as lint or bugs from the floor. By eighteen months of age, toddlers are able to hold crayons and to open drawers and cupboards; by twenty-four months, the development of full thumb-to-index-finger control makes it easier for them to turn doorknobs, unscrew lids, scribble, and feed themselves. By age three, children may be able to put some puzzle pieces together. They also have better control when using forks and can begin to dress themselves. (The ability to lace shoes, fasten buttons, and pull zippers, however, generally does not appear until age six or seven.) By age four or five, eye-hand coordination and fine motor skills improve. Children may be able at this time to print large letters that look pieced together; they are typically placed anywhere on a piece of paper. Many can print their first names and a few numbers by age five. From age six on, hand movements become more fluid and refined; writing is characterized by more continuous strokes and is less choppy.

Although the sequence of stages of motor development is uniform in normal individuals, there is wide variation among individuals in the ages at which certain skills are acquired. This normal variation is attributable to both biological and environmental factors, including maturation, heredity, neurological maturity, health, activity level, experience, and nutrition.

ROLE OF BIOLOGICAL MATURATION

Learning to walk, achieving bowel and bladder control, and even learning to read and write are not physiologically possible until the child's nervous and motor systems are sufficiently developed. Although normal experience (such as that offered by an average home environment) appears to be necessary for normal motor development, biological maturation places limits on what can be achieved through experience or practice. In fact, efforts by parents or other adults to teach or push young children to learn particular skills before they are maturationally ready may actually be harmful to their development.

Learning to walk, for example, requires central nervous system maturity, postural balance, muscular and skeletal strength, and well-developed sight and hearing. Studies have suggested that practicing the early walking reflex in infants to speed up their learning to walk may actually be harmful, because it may interfere with the development of the "higher" (cortical) areas of the brain that gradually take over the control of mature, independent walking. Early walking movements, which are evident between birth and three months of age, are actually a reflex that is controlled by the "lower" parts of the brain that control involuntary behavior. In addition, other studies have found that using walkers (seats on frames with wheels) too early or too often may damage infants' hip sockets.

Toilet training is also dependent on nervous system maturation. The neurons (nerve cells) controlling bowel and bladder movements mature at about the same time that children generally achieve voluntary control, around eighteen to twenty-four months of age. Bowel control is achieved before bladder control, and girls typically achieve bowel and bladder control before boys do.

Being able to ride a tricycle (which usually occurs around age three) or a bicycle (which typically occurs by age six or seven) also requires that a certain level of muscle strength, posture, and balance be achieved before these skills are possible. Catching a ball is usually too difficult and complex for four-year-olds because it requires timing, distance perception, quick reactions, and coordinated movements of the arms, hands, eyes, and body. A successful way of playing "catch" with children of this age is to roll the ball on the ground.

Fine motor skills (such as pouring juice from a pitcher, writing with a pencil, assembling a puzzle with many small pieces, cutting food with a knife and fork, or fastening small buttons) develop more slowly than gross motor skills during infancy and early childhood and are therefore more difficult for young children to master. Children lack the motor control necessary to complete these tasks successfully because the central nervous system is not completely developed at this age—the parts of the brain governing fine motor coordination take years to mature fully.

Reading and writing also depend on maturational readiness. Reading requires focused attention, controlled coordination between the eye muscles and the brain, and a certain level of nervous system maturity. Children younger than six years of age usually are not physiologically capable of moving their eye muscles slowly and deliberately across lines of small letters. They also have a difficult time sustaining controlled and systematic focusing and are farsighted. Writing, on the other hand, depends on the eyes, brain, and small muscles of the fingers working together. As nervous system maturation progresses, greater fine motor control is achieved, and children's hand strokes become more fluid and continuous during the school-age years.

Finally, hand preference ("handedness") is also biologically based. Hand preference in reaching, grasping, and writing may be found even in infancy. Hand preference appears to be determined partly by heredity but also by the organization of the brain, with structural and functional differences between the left and right sides of the brain evident at birth. Most children develop hand preferences by age three or four, with the majority (85 to 90 percent) showing a right-hand preference. It may, however, take some children several years after this to solidify their hand preference. Forcing children to change their handedness may create a number of problems, including stuttering and other language problems, fine motor skill deficits, and emotional problems.

EVOLUTION OF RESEARCH

Early interest in motor development focused primarily on outlining the sequence of stages of motor development, identifying approximate ages at which these milestones occur, and speculating about the relative contributions of biology and the environment to motor development. These themes mirror two principal concerns of developmental psychology: the sequence of stages of development and the influence of biology versus experience on development.

Interest in, and observations of, early motor development date back at least to the eighteenth century. The earliest accounts of children's development, known as "baby biographies," were detailed descriptions of the developmental sequence of behavior during the early years of life. A more methodical approach to outlining behavioral milestones began around the early 1900s, when normative studies (studies investigating the typical performance of children at different ages) were undertaken. In 1911, for example, Arnold Gesell founded the Yale Clinic of Child Development and constructed norms for such motor skills as grasping, crawling, swimming, standing, and walking. His norm charts were used throughout most of the twentieth century.

The general conclusion of Gesell and others during the 1930s and 1940s was that motor development is under biological control; however, studies have since shown that severe environmental deprivation can retard motor development and that environmental improvement by age two is necessary for infants to recover fully. Most researchers today believe that both maturation and experience play important roles in the course of motor development.

Although there was interest in motor development during the first half of the twentieth century, this interest declined somewhat from the 1950s until the 1980s. During this lull, however, motor development was still considered an integral part of Jean Piaget's well-known theory of cognitive development in young children. Whereas motor development was originally viewed as the gradual acquisition of isolated skills, motor skill acquisitions are currently viewed as parts of a complex, interrelated motor system that parallels brain growth and development. It is likely that future research will continue to examine these issues as well as the relationship of motor development to cognition, language acquisition, and social development.

BIBLIOGRAPHY

Bremmer, Gavin, and Theodore D. Wachs, eds. *The Wiley-Blackwell Handbook of Infant Development.* Vol. 1. Malden: Blackwell, 2010. Print.

Fitzgerald, Hiram E., et al. "The Organization of Lateralized Behavior During Infancy." *Theory and Research in Behavioral Pediatrics.* Vol. 5. Ed. Hiram E. Fitzgerald, B. Lester, and M. Yogman. New York: Plenum, 1991. Print.

Gabbard, Carl P. *Lifelong Motor Development.* 5th ed. San Francisco: Pearson, 2008. Print.

Gallahue, D. L. *Motor Development and Movement Experiences.* New York: Wiley, 1976. Print.

Haywood, Kathleen. *Life Span Motor Development.* 5th ed. Champaign: Human Kinetics, 2009. Print.

Payne, V. G., and L. D. Isaacs. *Human Motor Development: A Lifespan Approach.* 7th ed. Boston: McGraw-Hill, 2008. Print.

Piper, Martha C., and Johanna Darrah. *Motor Assessment of the Developing Infant.* Philadelphia: Saunders, 1994. Print.

Rosenblith, Judy F., and Judith E. Sims-Knight. *In the Beginning.* 2nd ed. Newbury Park: Sage, 1992. Print.

Sugden, David, and Michael G. Wade. *Typical and Atypical Motor Development.* London: Mac Keith, 2013. Print.

Zelazo, Philip David. *The Oxford Handbook of Developmental Psychology.* Vol. 1. New York: Oxford UP, 2013. Print.

Laura Kamptner

SEE ALSO: Birth: Effects on physical development; Cognitive development: Jean Piaget; Development; Developmental psychology; Physical development: Environment versus genetics; Prenatal physical development; Reflexes in newborns.

Multicultural disability competence

TYPE OF PSYCHOLOGY: Clinical; Counseling; Cross-cultural; Developmental; Health; Rehabilitation; School; Social

Multicultural disability competence (MDC) has not been heavily researched in the field of psychology. Characteristics of diversity researched in the past have included other members of minority groups (e.g., racial/cultural groups, sexual orientation, gender/expression, social economic status, age, and religion). People with disabilities are characterized by having physical, mental, emotional, behavioral, psychiatric, intellectual, or sensory impairments which may limit their ability to participate in life activities attributed to attitudinal and structural barriers within the environment. The importance of studying MDC has increased as the numbers of persons with disabilities continue to rise in the population.

KEY CONCEPTS

- Attitudes
- Knowledge of cultural diversity
- Practice accessibility
- Skills
- Social model of disability
- The therapeutic conversation

INTRODUCTION

In the United States, there are approximately 51 million people who have one or more identified disabilities (*Annual Disability Statistics Compendium*, 2010). Additionally, as the United States population grows older, advances in healthcare are helping individuals who sustain traumatic injuries to survive the injury. These factors, and a general population growth due to increased birth and immigration rates, could result in individuals with disabilities becoming the largest growing minority group in the country (*Annual Disability Statistics Compendium*). MDC as a category of diversity can be expected to present more frequently in psychotherapy, and all practicing psychologists should possess the knowledge, attitudes, and skills to work effectively with these clients. Topics such as disability-related social implications, disability adjustment, and disability acceptance are therapeutic conversation hallmarks that a psychologist should broach in the appropriate manner and format. Clients with disabilities (CWDs), like everyone, are interested in life achievements such as work, love, and recreational play, and it may be challenging to obtain because of stigma, discrimination, and inaccessibility of facilities constructed in an abled-bodied world. The challenges presented by disability can also negatively affect the overall psychological and emotional well-being of CWDs and such possible impact should be explored in psychotherapy. Thus, in order to work effectively with any client, especially with a CWD, the psychologist must be aware of his or her views or preconceived notions regarding the impact of disability on life goals and therefore making it necessary for the CWDs to select the psychologist who comprise the knowledge regarding disability related topics and attitudes.

THE THERAPEUTIC CONVERSATION

It is 9:00 a.m. and you are a new client in an independent psychotherapy practice. When you scheduled your appointment you mentioned to the licensed psychologist that you were Client-J, and you further mentioned that you had a presenting issue of depression and has felt depressed approximately one year. Client-J enters the office, and the psychologist noticed that Client-J uses a wheelchair and she speaks with a slight accent. Client-J reports to the psychologist that she is depressed because she was diagnosed with multiple sclerosis and it has caused her to lose function in her lower extremities.

Client-J is a thirty-five year old, single, Caribbean American, lesbian, non-practicing Roman Catholic, unemployed female who now has added the diversity domain area of disability to her identity composition. How should the psychologist begin the initial assessment with this client? It is important for the CWDs to recognize that the psychologist is thinking about her knowledge, attitudes, and skills associated with disability as she begins to assess the clinical case.

KNOWLEDGE

Knowledge is defined as acquiring information and insight about different cultures including traditions, customs, values, and historical perspectives (Artman & Daniels, 2010). Thus, the psychologist in question should begin from a multicultural framework that takes into consideration all the diversity domain areas that comprises the client. One must not assume that one domain area holds more salience compared to another. Instead, it is the psychologist's responsibility to determine which domains, if any, hold importance from the client's view.

The concept of disability has always been viewed as a medical phenomenon. The medical model posits CWDs to have deficits, loss, and functional limitations attributed to their disability. Therefore, the CWD is relegated to live in an inaccessible environment which is handicapping for them; they are viewed as objects of pity, charity, and ridicule; and are deemed to have low social status due to their inability to achieve gainful employment opportunities when compared to their peers without disabilities.

When working with Client-J, a psychologist with MDC will consider the social model of disability. This model emphasizes empowerment, resources, and unequal access attributed to disability. Client-J has decision-making power, resources, and options despite her disability status. Client-J requires the social removal of environmental barriers including attitudinal and physical barriers that could prevent the achievement of social gains despite her disability.

Psychologists with MDC learn about the community resources available to provide comprehensive support to CWDs (e.g., disability rehabilitation and habilitation programs, disability-specific service organizations, independent living centers, disability legislation, and literature detailing the history of the disability movement in the United States). This is done in hope to gain insight to the struggles and levels of discrimination/oppression that faced this minority group.

ATTITUDES

Client-J reports that she is having difficulty adjusting to her disability. Prior to her diagnosis, she was working as a dancer, engaged in a committed relationship with a partner who enjoyed traveling, lived in a small walk-up, brownstone building in one of the boroughs of New York City, and overall had a positive attitude about her life. Since her diagnosis, her partner left her, she had to move to a more accessible low income building, resigned from her job, and further reports feelings of dependency, isolation, depression, sadness, and hopelessness. Client-J said, "My life sucks, and I don't think that my life will ever be good again. I am in this chair and the world is looking down at me. I am poor, black, gay, and disabled. What can I do now as a disabled person?"

Do you agree that her life sucks as a CWD? What is your personal belief on disability? Are you, too, afraid of acquiring a disability? MDC requires the psychologist to reflect on their perceptions and attitudes pertaining to disability. Attitudes are defined as the awareness of personal biases, the comprehension of ableism (viewing the world as an abled-bodied person), and having limited knowledge/training on disability.

Psychologists with MDC skills face their biases by acknowledging the language, attributions, and attitudes they hold regarding CWDs. Language usage can reflect negative views regarding disability. Psychologists with MDC skills are reminded to use person-first language when working with CWDs (Artman & Daniels, 2010). For instance, you shouldn't refer to the CWD as client is wheel bound or schizophrenic. Instead use client uses a wheelchair or person with schizophrenia. Additionally, statements such as "You are so brave to handle your

disability," sets a power struggle between the person who is abled-bodied compared to the CWD. Psychologists with MDC skills reflect empathy, understanding, and compassion for the CWD in addressing all of their issues in psychotherapy.

SKILLS

Client-J states her feelings of dependency, isolation, depression, sadness, and hopelessness. The psychologist is engaging in an initial assessment with her. Is she depressed? Does she have suicidal ideation? Is this part of the disability conceptualization model associated with adjustment and/or acceptance? What are the MDC skills needed here? How will it help the psychologist to treat this case?

Skill is defined as enhancing exposure, awareness, knowledge, and training associated with disability. It is important for psychologist to broach disability related topics in a professional manner. CWDs might and might not mention the disability during the presenting issue phase of the session. Psychologists with MDC skills are prepared for this fact and thus, should ask the client if they think that the disability could be factoring into the presenting issue in psychotherapy. Psychologists with MDC skills will ask questions that do not put the client on the defensive. For example, if the client is blind, asking "Were you blind since birth?" may not be the best way to broach the topic. However, another approach might be: "Do you think that your blindness and/or social implications of your blindness are contributing to what brings you to therapy?" The essential point here is that it is important to have the discussion even if the disability may not be the reason for treatment.

Psychologists with MDC skills are aware of disability related Countertransference. This may result from the psychologist being apprehensive about their own vulnerability to disability, and witnessing visual and auditory signs of disability (Artman & Daniels, 2010). Signs include disability related aids and devices (e.g., mobility canes, crutches, hearing aids, etc.), disfigurement, scarring, amputations, burns, coughing, drooling, toileting needs, intellectual processing, and speech impairments (Artman & Daniels). Skills development will assist the psychologist to consider disability when conducting initial assessments, diagnostic evaluation, and testing. Also, depression and anger regarding lack of accommodations and discrimination received in an abled-bodied world may be justified, and not attributed to pathology (Artman & Daniels). If lack of MDC becomes a problem, supervision and case transfer is recommended. The CWD should not receive treatment that diminish their potential in the areas of educational and employment objectives, intimate relationships, and recreational play. This is why it is important for CWDs to recognize the skills needed for MDC and make the appropriate decision when selecting a clinician who comprise these desired skills.

Psychologists with MDC skills are too concerned about the practice of disability etiquette in psychotherapy. This is something that can be discussed with the client. For example, if you have a CWD who is blind, making a statement like "See you next week!" may not be offending. It really depends on the CWD level of disability awareness and adjustment (Artman & Daniels, 2010). This can be determined by developing a working alliance with the client and having those therapeutic conversations in an open and professional manner.

PRACTICE ACCESSIBILITY
The following recommendations are given to psychologists with MDC skills as they try to make their practice inclusive for CWDs. First, psychologists with MDC skills consider the building and location accessibility where they work. Disability legislation has been developed to include modifications on structure design to include CWDs (Americans with Disabilities Act of 1990; ADA-Amendments Act, 2008). Building accessibility can consists of ensuring designated parking spots, usable ramps, working elevators and/or stair gliders, hallways and offices that are cluttered free to ensure the mobility for a person who uses a wheelchair or a person with low or no vision, good interior and/or exterior lighting for persons with low vision, brail markings, and accessible restrooms.

Second, when developing the psychotherapy milieu, some adjustment is needed for CWDs. For instance, proxemics may have to be modified (Artman & Daniels, 2010). A CWD who uses a wheelchair may need some room in the office to transfer from the wheelchair to the office chair. Artman and Daniels described that Some CWDs may not be able to sit for the entire session, and may need to stand, walk around the room, or lie down. They also mentioned that some CWDs may need to have office lighting altered depending on their visual problems, migraines, or light sensitivity issues. Additionally, they recommend that some CWDs with temperature sensitivities may require some accommodations in this area, and fans or blankets could be utilized if the psychologist is unable to regulate the temperature in the office. Finally, they advise that the use of potpourri, candles, room deodorizers, and wearing heavy fragrances should be limited because some CWDs may have allergies, respiratory disorders, and chemical sensitivities.

Third, when scheduling appointments for CWDs, psychologists with MDC skills consider the type of disability and how it is impacted by time of day, temperature, and extreme seasonal conditions (Artman & Daniels, 2010). For example, CWDs who are sensitive to extreme heat might prefer their appointment to be schedule during the coolest point of the day (e.g., early morning, or late evening). CWDs may use public transit or para-transit services and time slots should factor in if they arrival time might be late or early.

Fourth, psychologists with MDC skills consider how they advertise to their patients. They incorporate user friendly websites, client recruitment flyers, and ads. Standard printed information may not be accessible to CWDs with visual, cognitive, and/or reading disabilities. A better option is adapted Websites that take into account the use of assistive technology that incorporates access for all users with and without disabilities (Artman & Daniels, 2010). Additionally, psychologists who want to serve CWDs who are deaf, hard of hearing, or have speech impairments should establish a TTY number and make sure that all staff in the office are able to use it.

When dispensing consent forms, handouts, and publications to CWDs with visual and/or reading limitations, an alternative format will be needed. Providing a print font in 16–18 point with black letters on a white background can be quite helpful to provide contrast (Artman & Daniels, 2010). Also, printed information can be recorded clearly on to smart phones, digital recorders, tape, or directly read aloud to the CWD while in session. Psychologists who provide homework or suggested reading can give this to the CWD in a disk for viewing in the home with screen reading software or other assistive technology (Artman & Daniels, 2010).

In developing advocacy skills, psychologists with MDC skills can teach these skills to CWDs through improvement of self-esteem, self-image, and assertiveness training. Psychologists with MDC skills can exemplify these skills by encouraging an accessible office environment; by including disability as a diversity domain area through their professional associations; by encouraging authors and publishers of assessment tools to make these tools accessible to CWDs; by including disability concerns and resources in their lectures; by advocating for the inclusion of disability issues in the curriculum; and by advocating for students with disabilities to be enrolled in graduate programs (Artman & Daniels, 2010).

Because CWDs are the largest growing minority group in the United States, it is quite possible that psychologists will serve this population in psychotherapy. Having a diagnosis of a disability can be life-changing. Some of these changes could create psychological problems and adaptations. For more information regarding the psychological impact of disability on a CWD, please refer to the chapter on psychological impact of disability available in this volume.

Additionally, vocational dreams and aspirations, hopes of having romantic and familial interests with significant partners, and relationships with social peers can be present in the life of a CWD. CWDs may bring these concerns to psychotherapy, and it is critical for a psychologist to have a high level of MDC to work with them. The psychologist must demonstrate the knowledge, attitudes, and skills that are needed. Preconceived notions and beliefs regarding disability must be dealt with by the psychologist through exposure to disability, supervision, and training to become more culturally competent in this domain area. It is critical for CWDs to be informed about the importance of MDC skills in order to make appropriate choices and decisions when selecting a psychotherapist for psychiatric treatment.

BIBLIOGRAPHY

Americans with Disabilities Act Amendments Act of 2008, P. L., 110-325. (September 25, 2008). Title 42, U. S. C. A. 12101 et seq: U. S. Statutes at Large, 104, 378. This was a follow-up disability legislation amendment act from the original disability act which was the Americans with Disabilities Act of 1990. This was one of the first comprehensive disability legislation passed in the United States for all persons with disabilities from all age ranges that included provisions for equal opportunity and access for persons with disabilities to employment, public services consisting of architectural and design including new construction, public accommodations, telecommunications, and other miscellaneous provisions.

Annual Disability Compendium Disability Statistics. Retrieved January 26, 2011, from the Disability Compendium Web site: http://www.disabilitycompendium.org/pdf/Compendium2010.pdf, 2010. This is a follow-up annual disability statistics manual which states the disability utilization rates including number of persons in the United States with disabilities, social services utilization rates, engaging in employment, education, recreational activities, etc. It is an academic comprehensive look at disability statistics in the United States.

Artman, L. K., and Daniels, J. A. "Disability and Psychotherapy Practice: Cultural competence and practical tips." *Professional Psychology: Research and Practice,* 41(5) 2010. This article is a helpful guide to assist in understanding how psychologists can use competency skills in disability to ensure that their CWDs will feel assured that their therapist is competent to work with this population.

Loy, B. A., and Rowan, L. "JAN Technical Series: Tips For Designing Accessible Websites." Retrieved from http://askjan.org/media/webpages.html 2009. This document discussed the format that psychologists could employ for text descriptions for visual material, captioning, Web navigation, and resources associated with how to get a website reviewed for accessibility purposes.

Pope, K. (n.d.). "Accessibility & Disability Information & Resources in Psychology Training & Practice". Retrieved from http://kpope.com. This Website provides disability information regarding guidelines on disability etiquette, resources, training, and other referral information pertaining to a CWD.

Sharon McLennon Wier

SEE ALSO: Cross cultural differences; Cross cultural treatment; Cultural sensitivity; Multiculturalism; Sociocultural factors.

Multicultural psychology

DATE: 1960's forward
TYPE OF PSYCHOLOGY: Social psychology

Multicultural psychology assumes that cultural contexts govern a person's attitudes toward the self and others in the same and different cultural groups. For that reason, this field of psychology emphasizes the interplay between culture and mind and the influence of cultural contact.

KEY CONCEPTS

- Fourth force
- Interplay between mind and culture
- Multiculturalism

- Qualitative research methods
- Universality
- Worldview

INTRODUCTION

Multicultural psychology is the study of human behavior as it occurs when people from multiple cultural groups encounter one another within the same context. This field emphasizes understanding how recurrent contact between people from different cultures shapes behavior, cognition, and affect.

Those who study multicultural psychology stress the interplay between mind and culture. Psychological processes are assumed to be learned and to occur in cultural contexts, which, narrowly considered, are characterized by race, ethnicity, or nationality. This characterization can be broadened to include ethnographic, demographic, status, and affiliation identities. From this, it can be inferred that people belong to multiple and overlapping cultures. In this field, it is assumed that cultural contact and the characteristics, values, and behaviors that are associated with cultures govern all aspects of human behavior, including a person's perception of the self, other people, and things. This perception is called a worldview. It is the aim of multicultural psychology to strengthen the understanding of how cultural contact produces different worldviews and the reasons and ways in which groups influence one another as a function of power and status.

The culture-centered perspective of multicultural psychology conflicts with perspectives common in much of psychology that emphasize the universality of mental processes. This may explain why psychology was slow to embrace the study of multicultural issues. However, the United States is a multicultural society, in which people from different backgrounds live and work together on a daily basis, creating a need for the inclusion of factors related to culture in the study of psychology.

HISTORY

Multicultural psychology as its own discipline gained considerable attention in the 1960s and 1970s, when psychologists began to recognize the importance of understanding issues of culture in diverse communities and advocated for research examining the influence of culture and ethnicity on all aspects of human behavior. It was during the 1970s that the study of gender gained inclusion in multicultural psychology. Soon after, the scope was again broadened to include the worldview of lesbian, gay, and bisexual individuals. The understanding of this worldview contributed in part to the removal of homosexuality as a mental disorder in the American Psychiatric Association's *Diagnostic and Statistical Manual of Mental Disorders* (DSM), beginning with the third edition (1980).

Some early efforts within the field of multicultural psychology depended on traditional quantitative research methods that used Western constructs and psychological instruments to study differences between cultural groups. White populations were treated as the standard against which minority groups were measured. From a multicultural perspective, this makes little sense. For example, if a researcher wants to understand how Confucian teachings influence some parenting practices, a white comparison group is not necessary. As a result of the implicit power dynamic, researchers failed to recognize how groups influence one another and how stereotyping, prejudice, and discrimination shape the worldviews of people of color and women. To correct the notion that other cultures were inferior to white culture, researchers in the 1980s and 1990s began to use qualitative research methods, such as observation and interviews, to gain a more accurate understanding of how culture governs human behavior and to develop an understanding of behaviors in their cultural context.

STATUS IN THE TWENTY-FIRST CENTURY

In spite of resistance from researchers who have attempted to develop universal principles of human behavior, the multicultural perspective in psychology has gained acknowledgment for its inclusion of culture-centered research and the emphasis it places on acquiring culturally appropriate skills in applied psychological practices, education, and organizations. Its emphasis on understanding one's own culture, understanding other worldviews, and developing appropriate interpersonal skills has had a transformative effect on how researchers and practitioners approach various fields of psychology, including testing, communication, social processes, health, counseling, and education. This led Paul Pedersen, a long-time contributor to multicultural psychology, to suggest that the growing perspective of multicultural psychology is the "fourth force" in psychology. Like the first three forces—psychoanalysis, behaviorism, and humanism—multicultural psychology has changed, and continues to change, the way people think about all aspects of human behavior.

BIBLIOGRAPHY

Davis-Russell, Elizabeth, ed. *The California School of Professional Psychology Handbook of Multicultural Education, Research, Intervention, and Training.* San Francisco: Jossey, 2002. Print.

Jackson, Yolanda K., ed. *Encyclopedia of Multicultural Psychology.* Thousand Oaks: Sage, 2006. Print.

Leong, Frederick T. L., ed. *APA Handbook of Multicultural Psychology.* Washington: APA, 2013. Print.

Locke, Don C. *Increasing Multicultural Understanding: A Comprehensive Model.* Thousand Oaks: Sage, 1998. Print.

Mio, Jeffery Scott, Lori A. Barker, and Jaydee Tumambing. *Multicultural Psychology: Understanding Our Diverse Communities.* 3rd ed. New York: Oxford UP, 2012. Print.

Nagayama Hall, Gordon C.. *Multicultural Psychology.* 2nd ed. Upper Saddle River: Prentice, 2010. Print.

Anne M. W. Kelly

SEE ALSO: African Americans and mental health; Asian Americans/Pacific Islanders and mental health; Cross-cultural psychology; Cultural competence; Culture and diagnosis; Culture-bound syndromes; Gay, lesbian, bisexual, and transgender mental health; Latinos and mental health; Native Americans/Alaskan Natives and mental health; Prejudice; Qualitative research; Racism.

Multiple intelligences

DATE: 1983 forward

TYPE OF PSYCHOLOGY: Intelligence and intelligence testing; Learning

The theory of multiple intelligences was proposed by a Harvard professor of cognition and education in 1983. The theory has major implications on the best ways for children to learn and has been successfully implemented in schools around the world.

KEY CONCEPTS
- Bodily-kinesthetic intelligence
- Intelligence quotient (IQ)
- Interpersonal intelligence
- Intrapersonal intelligence
- Linguistic intelligence
- Logical-mathematical intelligence
- Musical intelligence
- Naturalistic intelligence
- Spatial intelligence

INTRODUCTION

The first attempt to measure and quantify intelligence was made by Alfred Binet at the beginning of the twentieth century. He was asked to devise a test to identify children who would have trouble succeeding in school. This test has evolved into the standard intelligence quotient (IQ) test given today. Other tests of intelligence, such as the SAT Reasoning Test, were developed over the years for more specialized purposes. The SAT, for example, was designed to predict which students would be most successful in college. Howard Gardner, Howard-Gardner believed that these intelligence tests examined only two aspects of the spectrum of human intelligence, linguistic and mathematical ability, and ignored several other areas of intelligence that humans possess.

The theory of multiple intelligences (MI theory) was proposed by Gardner in 1983. He identified a number of categories of intelligence based on his consideration of intelligence as a biopsychological construct. For Gardner, an intelligence has to have a biological origin in a specific, identifiable part of the human brain, and it must provide a way for a human to solve significant problems. Each intelligence has a definite core operation or set of operations and must be activated by information that comes from the environment or originates internally. The first seven intelligences outlined by Gardner were logical-mathematical, linguistic, musical, bodily-kinesthetic, spatial, interpersonal, and intrapersonal intelligences; he later added naturalistic.

THE TYPES OF INTELLIGENCES

Logical-mathematical intelligence is one of the two intelligences assessed by the IQ and SAT tests. The linguistics areas in the frontal and temporal lobes of the brain perform logical deduction, and areas in the parietal and frontal lobes perform numerical calculations, the two parts of this intelligence. How these two parts of the brain work together to develop a solution to a logical-mathematical problem is not yet understood. Some people, known as savants, can perform amazing mathematical calculations but have very low capabilities in other intelligences. Logical-mathematical intelligence is very necessary to human information processing as it is the intelligence that solves myriad problems.

Linguistic intelligence is the other intelligence assessed by the IQ and SAT tests. Broca's area in the brain produces grammatical sentences. A person with damage to this area can understand spoken language but cannot respond. Linguistic intelligence is the intelligence that facilitates complex communication among humans.

Musical intelligence gives humans the ability to react emotionally to and to make music. Certain parts of the right hemisphere of the brain allow humans to perceive and produce music. People who suffer damage to this part of the brain develop amusia, or loss of musical ability. Musical intelligence was important to early humans because it enabled them to recognize birdsongs and calls of other animals and possibly provided a means of communication.

Bodily-kinesthetic intelligence is the ability to make purposeful, specialized bodily movements such as throwing a ball or dancing. Movement is controlled by both hemispheres of the brain in the motor cortex. The right hemisphere of the brain controls the left side of the body and vice versa. Apraxia, or the loss of the ability to perform learned or planned movements, occurs in persons with damage to the motor cortex. The capability of humans to perform specialized body movements, paired with sophisticated use of tools, has made it possible for humans to develop and move through an amazingly complex technological environment.

Spatial intelligence gives humans the ability to navigate, to visualize objects from different angles, and to use space well. Spatial processing occurs in the posterior part of the right cerebral cortex. If this area is damaged, a person loses the ability to navigate around familiar places, to recognize pictures or faces, or even to perceive fine details. Sight is not a requirement for spatial intelligence; blind individuals are capable of very sophisticated spatial reasoning.

Interpersonal intelligence is the ability to perceive differences among other humans, especially their motivations, intentions, desires, moods, and traits. This intelligence is highly useful for people who work with others, such as clergy, therapists, salespersons, and judges. The frontal lobes of the brain appear to have an important role in interpersonal knowledge. Pick's disease, which damages the frontal lobes, causes a loss of ability to relate socially to others.

Intrapersonal intelligence gives humans the ability to understand their emotions and to use this understanding to appropriately control their behavior. The frontal lobes also play an important role in this intelligence. Injury to the lobes can cause a person to become indifferent and apathetic. An extreme lack of intrapersonal intelligence

is seen in autistic children who seem to have no concept of "self."

These seven intelligences are the original ones proposed by Gardner in 1983. Since then, many people have suggested other possible intelligences, but Gardner has added only one more intelligence, naturalistic.

Naturalistic intelligence was added by Gardner several years after he described the first seven intelligences. This intelligence provides people with the ability to recognize differences between plants, animals, geological formations, meteorological phenomena, and other aspects of nature. Biological evidence of this intelligence comes from brain-damaged people who lose the ability to recognize living things but still can identify inanimate and manufactured items. This intelligence would have been very important to the first humans as it would have helped them identify predators, prey, and edible and medicinal plants.

Other intelligences that have been proposed to Gardner include humor, cooking, sexual, and spiritual intelligences but none of these has met Gardner's criteria. One aspect of spiritual intelligence that remains a possible candidate is existential intelligence, an individual's ability to consider the "big questions" of human existence. However, so far, no specific area of the brain controlling consideration of existential issues has been identified.

EXPRESSION AND ASSESSMENT
All humans have different strengths and ranges of intelligences. Whether the various intelligences work separately or are in some ways codependent has not been determined. However, Gardner has found that individuals can be generalists or specialists, characteristics that allow persons to be "lasers" and "searchlights." People who are lasers generally use one or possibly two intelligences almost to the exclusion of the others. Examples of famous lasers are Wolfgang Amadeus Mozart, Albert Einstein, Charles Darwin, William Shakespeare, and Mario Andretti. Searchlights have strengths in several intelligences but do not have a single, very strong intelligence. Searchlights are good at keeping track of many different details, multitasking, and monitoring. Politicians; business executives; presidents of universities, corporations, and countries; and athletic coaches are examples of people who are searchlights. Gardner has proposed that autistic individuals are "involuntary" lasers and that those with attention-deficit disorders are "in-

voluntary" searchlights. Both lasers and searchlights are critical to the smooth functioning of a society.

Although there are many assessments that individuals can use to determine which of their intelligences are stronger or weaker, Gardner has strongly resisted developing any type of assessment that could be used to quantitatively scale each type of intelligence. Gardner does recognize the existence of different abilities within an intelligence and developed a "giftedness matrix" to describe these differences. He classifies someone as possessing "giftedness" if that person has a high biopsychological potential to excel at something, and "prodigiousness" as an extremely high form of giftedness. These rankings refer to the person's potential to excel, whereas "expert" is used to describe an individual who, after working for a long time in a certain area, masters the area.

EDUCATION AND BEYOND

Multiple intelligences theory can be used to help Educationmultiple intelligenceseducators reach their goals by allowing them to structure education in various ways so that students with strengths in different intelligences can have the subject matter presented to them in the best format for them to learn it. Multiple intelligences theory is not an educational goal unto itself, but rather a way of understanding how children learn. Once educational goals have been outlined for a particular school, multiple intelligences theory can help educators develop ways to present information and materials to harmonize with the students' intelligences.

Gardner has proposed three roles that could be useful in an educational program based on multiple intelligences theory. The assessment specialist would obtain information about each child and present the evaluations to teachers and parents to aid them in determining the best methods of teaching the child. The student-curriculum broker would match students with curricula that, along with a basic required curriculum, would be a good fit to the child's multiple intelligences profile. The broker could also help the child enter sections of the required courses that are taught in a manner that would be congruent with the child's abilities. The school community broker would show students various vocational (and avocational) possibilities that might be good matches for their various multiple intelligences profiles.

Multiple intelligences theory can be useful in the workplace. Most people gravitate to jobs that they enjoy doing and have an aptitude for, which is usually the result of their having intellectual strengths in those areas.

However, using multiple intelligences profiles of individuals who will be making up a team can help determine if the intelligences will constrain or hinder the group's work, if one person's intelligences will compensate for others' weaknesses, and if the individuals will catalyze each other to produce better work than any of them could do alone. Knowing whether individuals are lasers or searchlights can help determine the best positions for them; for example, lasers would be better suited for occupations such as proofreaders or production inspectors, while searchlights make good division managers and even chief executive officers.

BIBLIOGRAPHY

Armstrong, Thomas. *Multiple Intelligences in the Classroom.* 2d ed. Alexandria, Va.: Association for Supervision and Curriculum Development, 2000. An in-depth explanation of how to incorporate multiple intelligences into the classroom. Armstrong includes a discussion of both naturalistic and existential intelligences along with the original seven intelligences. Index.

Gardner, Howard. *Frames of Mind: The Theory of Multiple Intelligences.* New York: Basic Books, 2004. The original, seminal work by Gardner describing his theory of multiple intelligences. Index.

_____. *Multiple Intelligences: New Horizons.* New York: Basic Books, 2006. An update on Gardner's theory, a discussion of the eighth intelligence, and an examination of actual applications of his theory to education as well as recommendations of how to use his theory. Index.

Lazear, David. *Eight Ways of Teaching: The Artistry of Teaching with Multiple Intelligences.* 4th ed. Tucson, Ariz.: Zephyr Press, 2003. The author clearly explains intelligence-focused lessons and how to create them. This edition includes an example that incorporates all eight intelligences into a single learning experience. Index.

Martin, Joyce. *Profiting from Multiple Intelligences in the Workplace.* Aldershot, England: Gower Press, 2004. An application of multiple intelligences theory to the workplace to evaluate the abilities of individual workers and to combine these abilities into efficient teams. Index.

Polly D. Steenhagen

SEE ALSO: Ability tests; Assessment; Binet, Alfred; Creativity and intelligence; Emotional intelligence; General Aptitude Test Battery (GATB); Human resource training and development; Intelligence; Intelligence quotient (IQ); Intelligence tests; Race and intelligence; Stanford-Binet test; Workplace issues and mental health.

Multiple personality

TYPE OF PSYCHOLOGY: Psychopathology

Multiple personality is the name of abnormal behavior in which a person behaves as if under the control of distinct and separate parts of the personality at different times. It is most probably caused by severe childhood abuse and responds to long-term psychotherapy that addresses the past abuse and the resulting symptoms of dissociation.

KEY CONCEPTS
- Alternate personality
- Dissociation
- Dissociative identity disorder
- Integration
- Repression

INTRODUCTION

Multiple personality has had considerable research and clinical attention focused on it since the early 1980's, and this interest has increased significantly. However, multiple personality was known and studied even prior to the famous Sigmund Freud, the Austrian psychiatrist and founder of psychoanalysis. Well-known French psychologists Pierre Janet and Alfred Binet, among others, had written about it in the late nineteenth century, prior to Freud's writings. With the rise of psychoanalysis in the early twentieth century, the study of multiple personality and dissociation waned dramatically for many years. Two famous multiple personality cases in the United States were popularized by books and then films: *The Three Faces of Eve* in 1957 and *Sybil* in 1973.

In 1980, multiple personality disorder (MPD) was officially sanctioned as a legitimate psychiatric disorder by its inclusion in the third edition of the *Diagnostic and Statistical Manual of Mental Disorders* (DSM-III) published by the American Psychiatric Association. The official diagnostic label was changed in the fourth edition, DSM-IV, to dissociative identity disorder (DID), though it is still commonly known as multiple personality.

CAUSE

Research has shown that multiple personality is most probably caused by severe childhood abuse, usually both physical and sexual. Psychotherapists who specialize in treating disorders caused by trauma hypothesize that the human mind or personality divides to cope with the terror of the trauma. It is as if one part of the mind handles the abuse to protect another part of the mind from the pain. This splitting of consciousness is a psychological defense called dissociation. Instead of memory, bodily sensation, emotions, and thoughts all being associated with an experience (which is the normal process of human experience), these aspects lose their association and seem to separate. A common example would be that a person who was sexually abused as a child loses the memory of those events and may have no recall of them until later in adulthood. In this case, the whole experience is dissociated. For example, in multiple personality, a so-called alternate personalities ("alter" for short) named Ann experienced the abuse, while alter Jane, who deals with normal, everyday living, was not abused. Thus, Jane has no memories of abuse. A variation is that only certain aspects of the experience are dissociated, so that, for instance, the abused person has the memory that the sexual abuse happened but has no emotions regarding the pain and trauma of it. Freud coined the term "repression" to describe the process by which emotions that are too threatening to be admitted into consciousness are pushed into the unconscious.

DIAGNOSIS

Several well-researched psychological tests and structured interviews aid in diagnosing a client. For a formal diagnosis of DID, the DSM-IV-TR states that the following four criteria must be present: two or more distinct identities or personality states (each with its own relatively enduring pattern of perceiving, relating to, and thinking about the environment and self); at least two of these identities or personality states recurrently take control of the person's behavior; there is an inability to recall important personal information that is too extensive to be explained by ordinary forgetfulness; and the disturbance is not due to the direct physiological effects of a substance (such as blackouts due to alcohol, drugs, or seizures).

The central paradox of multiple personality is that it is both real and not real at the same time. It is not real in that the mind or personality does not literally split. There is only one brain and one body. It is a creation of a person's

DSM-IV-TR CRITERIA FOR DISSOCIATIVE IDENTITY DISORDER (DSM CODE 300.14)

Presence of two or more distinct identities or personality states (each with its own relatively enduring pattern of perceiving, relating to, and thinking about the environment and self)

At least two of these identities or personality states recurrently take control of the person's behavior

Inability to recall important personal information too extensive to be explained by ordinary forgetfulness

Disturbance not due to the direct physiological effects of a substance (such as blackouts or chaotic behavior during alcohol intoxication) or a general medical condition (such as complex partial seizures); in children, the symptoms are not attributable to imaginary playmates or other fantasy play

imagination. At the same time, however, the person with DID experiences very real separations and is not faking them. The perceived separate parts must be dealt with as if they were separate while teaching them the reality that they must live in the same body and jointly suffer the consequences of the actions of any one part.

Multiple personality often goes unrecognized for several reasons. First, it has only received considerable attention since the early 1980's. Second, it was wrongly thought to be extremely rare, so psychotherapists were previously taught that they would probably never see a case of it. Third, the trauma that causes DID produces so many symptoms, such as depression, anxiety, hearing voices, and mood changes, that it is wrongly diagnosed as schizophrenia, bipolar disorder, or something else. Fourth, there is skepticism about its validity as a true diagnosis.

Alters can be categorized in various ways. Some are victims who took most of the abuse. Some are persecutors who identified with the abuser and try to control other alters internally. Some are functioning alters who handle work or school. Alters may believe they are the opposite sex and can see themselves as almost any age. Some may know a great deal about other alters. Others may only know of themselves and have no knowledge that others even exist.

Because at least some alters are usually dissociated from other alters, the person with DID will typically experience time loss. Time loss when one alter has had control of the body and a different alter takes control who does not know what has happened previously. Dissociation is

experienced in degrees. When it is present to a lesser degree, DID patients hear voices inside their heads. They are hearing alters talking. This may scare them when they first experience it, or it may be so normal for them that they mistake these voices for their own thoughts.

TREATMENT

Clinical experience and research have shown that this disorder is treatable to full remission, and therefore the prognosis is more hopeful than with some other psychiatric disorders. The negative side of treatment is that it takes a long time, usually five to seven years and in some cases longer. The guidelines for treatment established by the International Society for the Study of Dissociation call for psychotherapy two to three times a week for several years.

The initial goal of psychotherapy is stabilization, to stop any destructive behaviors such as suicide or other forms of self-harm. The intermediate goal is to become aware of the alters, counsel their individual needs, and then bring about cooperation and communication between alters to make daily functioning more effective. The long-range goal is to bring about the integration of all split personalities into one unified personality. Integration is the combining of all aspects of the self, even the ones that may seem destructive or feel great pain. The goal is not to get rid of certain alters, as every part is an aspect of the self and needs to be integrated into the self.

Part of treatment consists of recounting and processing the memories of abuse. Ignoring past abuse is not helpful. However, this memory work needs to be done slowly and carefully, going at a pace that does not overwhelm the client. One goal is to keep the client functioning as normally as possible in daily life. Mistakes have been made by therapists who go too fast, too far, and who focus on talking about memories without addressing other needs, such as helping clients stabilize, encouraging cooperation and communication of alters, gradually integrating alters, teaching toleration of uncomfortable emotions, and instilling new coping mechanisms other than dissociating. The therapist should not suggest to the client that he or she was abused but should let the client discover this on his or her own.

Hypnosis may be used as part of the treatment, but it is not required. Experienced trauma therapists talk easily with the various alters and usually learn to recognize the different parts with little trouble. The switch between alters most often but not always is subtle and not dramatic. Psychiatric medications are often used as an adjunct to talking therapy, to help with the symptoms accompanying DID such as depression and anxiety. Since DID is a disorder caused by personal experience, it is not cured by medications.

What does not work is ignoring or denying the presence of alters, focusing only on the present and ignoring the past, trying to get rid of so-called bad alters, and exorcising alters who are psychological entities. Obviously, a person with DID will succeed best in counseling with a psychotherapist who is experienced and has specialized training in the treatment of trauma disorders.

IMPACT

People who suffer from multiple personality are adults who live with a coping mechanism that worked well to survive the horrors of abuse in childhood but is not working as well in a normal adult environment. All patients with DID suffer to some extent, which usually drives them to find relief. Some of these forms of relief are healthy, such as psychotherapy, and some may be unhealthy, such as addictions used to drown the painful feelings.

Some people with multiple personality appear to function normally and may not even know themselves that they have more than one personality. They may be able to function at a very high level at a job, for instance, while those close to them sense things are not normal. They may function normally for years and then have a crisis that seems to develop very rapidly. Other people with DID have trouble functioning normally and have a long history of psychological problems. These people may be unable to work to support themselves and need multiple hospitalizations. It is common for someone with DID to function at an extremely high level in one area or at one time and conversely to function at a very low level in another area or at another time. This leaves those around them puzzled and confused.

CONTROVERSY

Unfortunately, there is controversy regarding multiple personality. Some critics inside and outside the mental health profession claim that it is not a legitimate psychiatric disorder, perhaps because the idea of having multiple personalities and repressed memories-Repressed memories does not make common sense to them. They may believe that this disorder is created by people seeking attention through being dramatic, caused by incompetent therapists suggesting this diagnosis to their clients, or used by people wanting an excuse for irresponsible or even criminal behavior. Some of these critics also attack the concept of recovered memories of child sexual abuse. They believe this profound loss of memory is not real and that these recovered memories are actually false memories that serve the same purposes mentioned above.

The result is that the trauma field has tended to become polarized into true believers and extreme skeptics. Trauma experts with a balanced view will admit that some memories are inaccurate, that some clients labeled as having DID have indeed been misdiagnosed for the reasons the critics offer, and that some therapists do a poor job. However, these experts argue that the research base and clinical evidence supporting the existence of a distinct diagnosis called DID is strong and that the repression of memories of childhood abuse is real.

BIBLIOGRAPHY

Cohen, L., J. Berzhoff, and M. Elin, eds. *Dissociative Identity Disorder: Theoretical and Treatment Controversies*. Northvale, N.J.: Jason Aronson, 1995. This book gives the differing views regarding the controversies around DID. Each chapter offers both sides of the position on the topic at hand. It is somewhat technical.

Hocking, Sandra J. *Living with Your Selves: A Survival Manual for People with Multiple Personalities*. Rockville, Md.: Launch Press, 1992. This is a self-help book written by and for someone who has multiple personality. It contains helpful and accurate information.

Hyman, Jane Wegscheider. *I Am More than One*. New York: McGraw-Hill, 2007. This book is a fascinating collection of personal stories by women who have DID, showing how they have coped and thrived with the condition.

Putnam, Frank. *Diagnosis and Treatment of Multiple Personality Disorder*. New York: Guilford, 1989. A leading textbook meant for professionals written by an expert at the National Institute of Mental Health.

Ross, Colin A. *Dissociative Identity Disorder: Diagnosis, Clinical Features, and Treatment of Multiple Personality*. New York: John Wiley & Sons, 1997. Perhaps the leading textbook on DID. Everything you wanted to know and more by an international psychiatric expert.

It is written for the professional, though it is very readable. It also contains the author's psychological test called the DDIS to help diagnose DID.

_____. *The Osiris Complex: Case Studies in Multiple Personality Disorder.* Toronto, Ont.: University of Toronto Press, 1994. This international expert writes an interesting and readable book for both lay and professional audiences giving specific cases with details that illustrate features of DID.

Sinason, Valerie. *Attachment, Trauma and Multiplicity: Working with Dissociative Identity Disorder.* New York: Brunner-Routledge, 2002. This resource covers the controversies involved in a diagnosis of DID and offers clinical accounts of sufferers.

Dennis Bull

SEE ALSO: Child abuse; Dissociative disorders; Hallucinations; Hypnosis; Personality disorders; Repressed memories.

Munchausen syndrome and Munchausen syndrome by proxy

DATE: 1951 forward
TYPE OF PSYCHOLOGY: Psychopathology

Munchausen syndrome is the most severe form of factitious disorder, in which people simulate or produce mental or physical symptoms to benefit from playing the role of the ill person. Munchausen syndrome by proxy describes a condition in which individuals deliberately produce physical or mental symptoms in another person under their care.

KEY CONCEPTS
- Child abuse
- Factitious disorder
- Malingering
- Munchausen syndrome
- Munchausen syndrome by proxy

INTRODUCTION
Munchausen syndrome is often used interchangeably with factitious disorder; however, Munchausen syndrome describes a specific form of factitious disorder. Factitious disorders are characterized by the deliberate creation or simulation of physical or psychological symptoms.

In 1951, physician Richard Asher identified a pattern of patients who were fabricating medical histories and symptoms. He termed it Munchausen syndrome after Baron Münchhausen, an eighteenth century Prussian cavalry officer who created fantastical stories about his exploits.

Munchausen syndrome represents the most severe form of factitious disorder, in which individuals complain of serious physical symptoms although they are aware that they are fabrications. It differs from malingering, in which patients deliberately report nonexisting symptoms, in its motivation. Malingerers seek specific rewards such as time off from work or monetary benefits; people with Munchausen syndrome are motivated by internal needs such as a desire for approval or attention.

The serious symptoms reported by those with Munchausen syndrome often result in multiple hospitalizations, and individuals may travel between hospitals or engage in "doctor shopping" to earn a desired diagnosis. Patients usually describe their symptoms in dramatic detail; they can be highly knowledgeable about symptoms, terminology, and procedures. However, they may become vague when questioned. They often eagerly accept recommendations for invasive procedures and may display multiple surgical scars. In extreme cases, individuals may sabotage their laboratory samples or aggravate existing symptoms. If they are hospitalized, few friends visit, and patients are reluctant to have medical professionals query prior medical providers. Tests often reveal no medical causes for the reported symptoms. After initial tests are negative, patients with Munchausen syndrome often will report that their previous symptoms are gone, but new ones have appeared. After medical professionals have failed to substantiate reported symptoms, patients are either released or diagnosed with Munchausen syndrome. If confronted, patients may deny the diagnosis of Munchausen syndrome or suddenly discharge themselves, only to seek another opinion.

MUNCHAUSEN SYNDROME BY PROXY
In 1977, pediatrician Roy Meadow reported that one mother poisoned her child with salt and another injected her own blood into her baby's urine. He termed this behavior Munchausen syndrome by proxy. Munchausen syndrome by proxy describes a condition in which caregivers create symptoms or actual illness in a person under their care. The caregiver is usually the mother, and the victim typically a child under the age of six; however, cases have occurred in which adults create or lie about

illnesses in their elderly parents. The caregiver ensures that the child experiences afflictions that warrant medical attention and presents the child to medical authorities while claiming not to know how symptoms began. Rarely, those with Munchausen syndrome by proxy may be medical professionals who create symptoms in their patients.

Individuals with Munchausen syndrome by proxy may use their child's illness as a way to gain sympathy. Their hospitalized child gets them attention from medical professionals, and they may use this as a way to earn praise for their devotion to the child's care, often developing friendships with medical personnel. These caregivers may have previously experienced Munchausen syndrome themselves, but when they make their child ill, they learn that they can receive psychological rewards for playing the "hero" role.

Individuals with Munchausen syndrome by proxy may exacerbate a child's condition by lying about symptoms, altering samples, feeding the child contaminated or poisoned food, or injecting the child with bacteria, causing symptoms such as gastrointestinal upset or infection. The child may improve while hospitalized but relapse after discharge.

When confronted, individuals with Munchausen syndrome by proxy may become depressed and suicidal. Some respond with anger and hastily remove the child from medical care. Since Munchausen syndrome by proxy has a victim, it is considered a form of abuse and is a criminal offense. It is estimated that approximately 10 percent of victims of Munchausen syndrome by proxy die. In some cases, the child learns that sickness gains him or her attention and manifests Munchausen syndrome in adulthood. It has been recognized that children and adolescents may falsify their own illnesses and have Munchausen syndrome rather than be victims of Munchausen syndrome by proxy.

POSSIBLE CAUSES AND TREATMENTS

There are no reliable statistics on the prevalence of the disorders because of the inherent dishonesty involved. Individuals with these disorders may visit various hospitals, making any statistics suspect. The causes of both are also not known, but theories center on existing mental or personality disorders or a major life stress as possible origins. In some instances, the impulse to cause illness stems from rage, jealousy, or the desire to control others. Individuals with Munchausen syndrome may have had childhood illnesses that required extensive hospitalization or may have experienced family disturbances or abuse. Munchausen syndrome is associated with low self-esteem and severe emotional disturbances. It is very difficult to treat and often requires years of therapy. The patients' first goal is to acknowledge that they are lying. Psychotherapy aids in working through underlying psychological issues. Family therapy might be indicated to teach family members not to reward "sick" behavior on the part of the patient. In Munchausen syndrome by proxy, the first concern is the victim's safety. Psychotherapists, law enforcement, foster care organizations, and social workers all may be involved in treatment.

BIBLIOGRAPHY

Feldman, Marc. *Playing Sick? Untangling the Web of Munchausen Syndrome, Munshausen Syndrome by Proxy, Malingering, and Factitious Disorder.* New York: Routledge, 2004. The author has an extensive background in forensic psychology and presents sixty-five relevant cases with tips on how to recognize and treat them.

Gregory, Julie. *Sickened: The True Story of a Lost Childhood.* New York: Bantam Books, 2004. The author, the adult child of a woman with Munchausen syndrome by proxy, was subjected to operations until she was an adult, even though she had no true illness other than malnutrition. Gregory recounts her efforts to save herself.

Lasher, Louisa J., and Mary S. Sheridan. *Munchausen by Proxy: Identification, Intervention, and Case Management.* New York: Haworth Maltreatment and Trauma Press, 2004. Discusses the syndrome, how to identify and document it, and the proper steps to protect the victim, as well as the court's role.

Olsen, Gregg. *Cruel Deception: A Mother's Deadly Game, a Prosecutor's Crusade for Justice.* New York: St. Martin's True Crime, 2005. Account of a mother whose daughter died suddenly of suspected sudden infant death syndrome (SIDS) and whose newborn son then developed the same symptoms. Details the criminal aspects of Munchausen syndrome by proxy, including trial and aftermath.

Shaw, R., et al. "Factitious Disorder by Proxy: Pediatric Condition Falsification." *Harvard Review of Psychiatry* 16 (July, 2008): 215-224. This comprehensive overview of Munchausen syndrome by proxy discusses definitions and causes, and gives information on assessment, legal issues, and treatment.

Eugenia M. Valentine

SEE ALSO: Child abuse; Deception and lying; Factitious disorders; Family life: Children's issues; Mother-child relationship.

Murray, Henry A.

BORN: May 13, 1893
DIED: June 23, 1988
BIRTHPLACE: New York, New York
PLACE OF DEATH: Cambridge, Massachusetts
IDENTITY: American physician and psychologist
TYPE OF PSYCHOLOGY: Personality

Murray is well known as the developer of personology, the integrated study of the individual from physiological, psychoanalytical, and social viewpoints and the primary developer of the Thematic Apperception Test (TAT). In addition, his concept of motivation has had a major influence on the theories of psychology.

Henry A. Murray entered Harvard University in 1911 as a history major. However, in 1915 he entered the Columbia College of Physicians and Surgeons in New York, earning a degree in medicine in 1919.

In 1925, Murray first met the Swiss psychiatrist Carl Jung, who had a lasting influence on his work. Drawing on the writings of Herman Melville, the author of the novel *Moby Dick* (1851), Murray began to develop his theory of personality, using Melville as a case study. Though never published, the biography of Melville, according to Murray, had a major influence on the scholars of that time. Also during this period, Murray's published articles and book chapters introduced the application of Jung's "depth psychology" to the American community of scholars.

After earning his Ph.D. in 1927, Murray became an instructor at Harvard under Morton Prince, a psychopathologist who had founded the Harvard Psychological Clinic. Murray became an assistant professor at Harvard in 1929, associate professor in 1937, and professor of clinical psychology in 1948. Murray continued his work with the Harvard Psychological Clinic after the death of Prince, and with the assistance of a neuropsychiatrist colleague, Stanley Cobb, Murray moved the focus of the clinic from experimental research in hypnosis and multiple personality to Freudian and Jungian psychoanalysis. He also introduced these subjects into the Harvard curriculum. Under the umbrella of personology, Murray and his interdisciplinary research team studied single individuals on a variety of levels. With his staff, Murray published *Explorations in Personality: A Clinical Study of Fifty Men of College Age* in 1938. For decades, this remained the principal text for personality theory.

As interest in the newly emerging field of psychoanalysis grew in the 1930s, two important projective techniques introduced systematic ways to study unconscious motivation: the Rorschach or inkblot test, developed by the Swiss psychiatrist Hermann Rorschach, and the Thematic Apperception Test (TAT), developed by Murray and C. D. Morgan, an American psychologist. Both of these tests are frequently included in contemporary personality assessment. The TAT, an important tool in clinical psychology, requires the subject to tell stories about a series of pictures from which interpretations are made by the therapist.

Murray served in the Army from 1943 until 1948, selecting personnel for the Office of Strategic Services, later known as the Central Intelligence Agency (CIA), and training agents in the United States and abroad. After his discharge from the Army as a lieutenant colonel, Murray joined Gordon Allport in the newly established department of social relations at Harvard. There, with anthropologist Clyde Kluckhohn, he began studying personality in society and, from the viewpoint of the dyadic interaction, the idea that a relationship between two people could be viewed as a single system with equal input from both partners. He also studied the role of mythology in personality and in society. At this time, Murray was best known for his development of a human motivational system of social needs. He described behavior as a function of the interaction of individual needs, such as a need for achievement or a need for affiliation, and the "press" of the environment.

Murray held numerous honorary doctorates and was a member of the American Academy of Arts and Sciences. He retired from Harvard in 1962 as a professor emeritus. Murray died in Cambridge, Massachusetts, in 1988, at the age of ninety-five. In his memory, Radcliffe College established the Henry A. Murray Research Center for the Study of Lives.

BIBLIOGRAPHY

Mumford, Lewis, and Henry A. Murray. *In Old Friendship: The Correspondence of Lewis Mumford and Henry A Murray, 1928-1981.* Ed. Frank G. Novak. Syracuse: Syracuse UP, 2007. Print.

Murray, Henry A. *Explorations in Personality: 70th Anniversary Edition.* New York: Oxford UP, 2008. Print.

Robinson, Forrest G. *Love's Story Told: A Life of Henry A. Murray.* Cambridge: Harvard UP, 1992. Print.

Schneidman, Edwin S., ed. *Endeavors in Psychology: Selections from the Personology of Henry A. Murray.* New York: Harper, 1981. Print.

Mary E. Carey

SEE ALSO: Allport, Gordon; Jung, Carl; Personology: Henry A. Murray; Rorschach inkblots; Thematic Apperception Test (TAT).

Music, dance, and theater therapy

DATE: 1920s forward
TYPE OF PSYCHOLOGY: Psychotherapy

Music, dance, and theater therapies utilize various media such as movement and creative expression to accomplish the desired therapeutic goals; these therapies reflect a focus on the therapeutic value of artistic experiences and expression.

KEY CONCEPTS
- Adaptive patterns
- Creativity
- Developmental task
- Improvisation
- Movement therapy
- Philosophical models

INTRODUCTION

Music, dance, and theater therapies employ a wide range of methods to accomplish the goal of successful psychotherapy. "Psychotherapy" is a general term for the wide variety of methods psychologists and psychiatrists use to treat behavioral, emotional, or cognitive disorders. Music, dance, and theater therapies are not only helpful in the observation and interpretation of mental and emotional illness but also useful in the treatment process. Many hospitals, clinics, and psychiatrists or therapists include these types of therapy in their programs. They are not limited to hospital and clinical settings, however; they also play important roles in a wide variety of settings, such as community mental health programs, special schools, prisons, rehabilitation centers, nursing homes, and other settings.

Music, dance, and theater therapies share a number of basic characteristics. The therapies are generally designed to encourage expression. Feelings that may be too overwhelming for a person to express verbally can be expressed through movement, music, or the acting of a role. Loneliness, anxiety, and shame are typical of the kinds of feelings that can be expressed effectively through music, dance, or theater therapy. These therapies share a developmental framework. Each therapeutic process can be adapted to start at the patient's physical and emotional level and progress from that point onward.

Music, dance, and theater therapies are physically integrative. Each can involve the body in some way and thus help develop an individual's sense of identity. Each therapy is inclusive and can deal with either individuals or groups and with verbal or nonverbal patients in different settings. Each is applicable to different age groups (children, adolescents, adults, the elderly) and to different diagnostic categories, ranging from mild to severe. Although music, dance, and theater therapies share these common characteristics, however, they also differ in important respects.

DANCE THERAPY

Dance therapy does not use a standard dance form or movement technique. Any genre, from ritual dances to improvisation, may be employed. The reason for such variety lies in the broad spectrum of persons who undergo dance therapy: Neurotics, psychotics, schizophrenics, the physically disabled, and geriatric populations can all benefit from different types of dance therapy. Dance therapy may be based on various philosophical models. Three of the most common are the human potential model, the holistic health model, and the medical model. The humanistic and holistic health models have in common the belief that individuals share responsibility for their therapeutic progress and relationships with others. By contrast, the medical model assumes that the therapist is responsible for the treatment and cure.

Dance therapy is not a derivative of any particular verbal psychotherapy. It has its own origin in dance, and certain aspects of both dance and choreography are important. There are basic principles involving the transformation of the motor urge and its expression into a useful, conscious form. The techniques used in dance therapy can allow many different processes to take place. During dance therapy, the use of movement results in a total sensing of submerged states of feeling that can serve to eliminate inappropriate behavior. Bodily integration is another process that can take place in dance therapy. The patient may gain a feeling of how parts of the body are connected and how movement in one part of the body affects the total body. The therapist can also help the patient become more aware of how movement behavior reflects the emotional state of the moment or help the patient recall earlier emotions or experiences. Dance therapy produces social interaction through the nonverbal relationships that can occur during dance therapy sessions.

MUSIC THERAPY

Music therapy is useful in facilitating psychotherapy because it stimulates the awareness and expression of emotions and ideas on an immediate and experiential level. When a person interacts musically with others, he or she may experience (separately or simultaneously) the overall musical gestalt of the group, the act of relating to and interacting with others, and his or her own feelings and thoughts about self, music, and the interactions that have occurred. The nonverbal, structured medium allows individuals to maintain variable levels of distance from intrapsychic (within self) and interpersonal (between people) processes. The abstract nature of music provides flexibility in how people relate to or take responsibility for their own musical expressions. The nonverbal expression may be a purely musical idea, or it may be part of a personal expression to the self or to others.

After the activity, the typical follow-through is to have each client share what was seen, heard, or felt during the musical experience. Patients use their musical experiences to examine their cognitive and affective reactions to them. It is then the responsibility of the music therapist to process with the individual the reactions and observations derived from the musical experience and to help the person generalize them—that is, determine how they might be applied to everyday life outside the music therapy session. Group musical experiences seem to stimulate verbal processing, possibly because of the various levels of interaction available to the group members.

THEATER THERAPY

Theater therapy, or drama therapy, uses either role-playing or improvisation to reach goals similar to those of music and dance therapy. The aims of the drama therapy process are to recognize experience, to increase one's role repertoire, and to learn how to play roles more spontaneously and competently.

The key concepts of drama therapy are the self and roles. Through role taking, the processes of imitation, identification, projection, and transference take place. Projection centers on the concept that inner thoughts, feelings, and conflicts will be projected onto a relatively ambiguous or neutral role. Transference is the tendency of an individual to transfer his or her feelings and perceptions of a dominant childhood figure—usually a parent—to the role being played.

Photo: iStock

USES AND GOALS OF PSYCHOTHERAPIES

New approaches and applications of music, dance, and theater therapies have been and are being developed as these fields grow and experiment. The goal of theater or drama therapy is to use the universal medium of theater as a setting for psychotherapeutic goals. Opportunities for potential participants include forms of self-help, enjoyment, challenge, personal fulfillment, friendship, and support. The theater setting helps each individual work with issues of control, reality testing, and stress reduction.

David Johnson and Donald Quinlan conducted substantial research into the effects of drama therapy on populations of schizophrenics. Their research addressed the problem of the loss of the self and the potential of drama therapy in recovering it. They found that paranoid schizophrenics create more rigid boundaries in their role-playing, while nonparanoid schizophrenics create more fluid ones. They concluded that improvisational role-playing is an effective means to assess boundary behaviors and differentiate one diagnostic group of schizophrenics from another. Subtypes of schizophrenia diagnosis, however, are no longer included in the American Psychiatric Association's *Diagnostic and Statistical Manual of Mental Disorders*, which was published in its fifth addition in 2013.

Drama therapy has also been used in prison environments to institute change and develop what has been termed a therapeutic community. The Geese Theatre Company, founded in the United States in 1980, works to change the institutional thinking, metaphors, responses, and actions unique to the prison environment, to allow both staff and prisoners to change and convert prisoner images and metaphors. The therapists found that drama therapy, or role-play, intensifies the affect necessary to challenge beliefs. The method requires strong support from the staff and the institution. Drama therapy, they point out, provides an unexpected format, action-based, and driven by people in relationship with one another. Their work in prison settings in both Australia and Romania helped in continuing development of process and principles for transforming prison cultures into effective therapeutic communities.

Dance therapy has been found to be extremely useful in work with autistic children as well as with children with minimal brain dysfunction (MBD). The symptoms of a child with MBD may range from a behavioral disorder to a learning disability. Though the symptoms vary, and some seem to vanish as the child matures, the most basic single characteristic seems to be an inability to organize internal and external stimuli effectively. By helping the child with MBD to reexperience, rebuild, or experience for the first time those elements on which a healthy body image and body scheme are built, change can be made in the areas of control, visual-motor coordination, motor development, and self-concept.

The goals of dance therapy with a child with MBD are to help the child identify and experience his or her body boundaries, to help each child master the dynamics of moving and expressing feelings with an unencumbered body, to focus the hyperactive child, to lessen anxiety and heighten the ability to socialize, and to strengthen the self-concept.

Music therapy has been used successfully with patients who have anorexia nervosa, an eating disorder that has been called self-starvation. Anorexia nervosa represents an attempt to solve the psychological or concrete issues of life through direct, concrete manipulation of body size and weight. Regardless of the type or nature of the issues involved, which vary greatly among anorectic clients, learning to resolve conflicts and face psychological challenges effectively without the use of weight control is the essence of therapy for these clients. To accomplish this, anorectics must learn to divorce their eating from their other difficulties, stop using food as a tool for problem solving, face their problems, and believe in themselves as the best source for solving those problems. Music therapy has provided a means of persuading clients to accept themselves and their ability to control their lives, without the obsessive use of weight control, and to interact effectively and fearlessly with others.

Many health professionals have acknowledged the difficulty of engaging the person with anorexia in therapy, and music has been found to work well. Because of its nonverbal, nonthreatening, creative characteristics, music can provide a unique, experiential way to help clients acknowledge psychological and physical problems and resolve personal issues.

Music and dance therapies are being used to improve quality of life for older victims of dementias, including Alzheimer's disease. The number of cases of Alzheimer's is expected to increase as the population ages. It has been found that both music and movement can be used to reach these patients when other methods fail. The keys to this therapy include song preference of the client and the use of music specific to the client's life and youth. This music has been most effective if presented live, using the same rhythms and syncopations as the original music. Such therapy can be used to support and encourage behaviors that allow patients with dementia access to a higher quality of life, and to the expression of feelings and enjoyment.

Dynamic play therapy is another approach that combines concepts and techniques of drama and dance improvisation. It has been used in clinical settings involving foster, adoptive, and birth families with troubled children. This type of family play therapy emerged from sessions that often included adult caretakers of foster children and addressed specific problems concerning abuse and family-related expressive activities.

INTERDISCIPLINARY RELATIONSHIPS

The interdisciplinary sources of dance, music, and drama therapies bring a wide range of appropriate research methodologies and strategies to the discipline of psychology. These therapies tend to defy conventional quantification. Attempts to construct theoretical models of these therapies draw on the disciplines of psychology, sociology, medicine, and the arts. There is no unified approach to the study and the practice of these therapies.

Dance therapy has its roots in ancient times, when dance was an integral part of life. It is likely that people danced and used body movement to communicate long before language developed. Dance could express and reinforce the most important aspects of a culture. Societal values and norms were passed down from one generation to another through dance, reinforcing the survival mechanism of the culture.

The direct experience of shared emotions on a preverbal and physical level in dance is one of the key influences in the development of dance or movement therapy. The feelings of unity and harmony that emerge in group dance rituals provide the basis of empathetic understanding between people. Dance, in making use of natural joy, energy, and rhythm, fosters a consciousness of self. As movement occurs, body sensations are often felt more clearly and sharply. Physical sensations provide the basis from which feelings emerge and become expressed. Through movement and dance, preverbal and unconscious material often crystallizes into feeling states of personal imagery. It was the recognition of these elements, inherent in dance, that led to the eventual use of dance or movement in psychotherapy.

Wilhelm Reich was one of the first physicians to become aware of and use body posturing and movement in psychotherapy. He coined the term "character armor" to describe the physical manifestation of the way an individual deals with anxiety, fear, anger, and similar feelings. The development of dance into a therapeutic modality, however, is most often credited to Marian Chace, a former dance teacher and performer. She began her work in the early 1940s with children and adolescents in special schools and clinics. In the 1950s and 1960s, other modern dancers began to explore the use of dance as a therapeutic agent in the treatment of emotional disturbances.

There is a much earlier history of music therapy; the use of music in the therapeutic setting dates back to the 1700s. The various effects of different types of music on emotions were recognized. Music could be used to restrain or inflame passions, as in examples of martial, joyful, or melancholic music. It was therefore concluded that music could also have positive healing effects, although these would vary from person to person. Early research showed music therapy to be useful in helping mental patients; people with physical disabilities; children with emotional, learning, or behavioral problems; and people with a variety of other difficulties. Music could be used to soothe and to lift the spirits, but it required experimentation and observation.

Although its theatrical roots are ancient, drama or theater therapy is still in early stages of professional development. The field developed out of clinical experience in the 1920s, and its use and its value as a psychotherapeutic tool is well documented. As a profession, drama therapy now requires the articulation and documentation of theories and methods as well as intensive case studies as support. Four challenges have been identified for the field: to develop new university programs and to increase the supply of students, to expand opportunities for advanced learning and to use mentors to help internalize a professional identity, to produce books and texts to attract new students and to establish the field academically, and to participate with other creative arts therapy organizations to protect legislatively professional interests and the needs of clients. All these forms of therapy can thus be best understood in terms of their backgrounds, relationships, and individual contributions to therapeutic applications in both mental and physical healing.

BIBLIOGRAPHY

Gilroy, Andrea, and Colin Lee, eds. *Art and Music: Therapy and Research*. New York: Routledge, 1995. Print.

Grocke, Denise E., Tony Wigram, and Cheryl Dileo.

Receptive Methods in Music Therapy: Techniques and Clinical Applications for Music Therapy Clinicians, Educators, and Students. Philadelphia: Kingsley, 2007. Print.

Johnson, David Read, and Renee Emunah, eds. *Current Approaches in Drama Therapy.* Springfield: Charles C. Thomas, 2009. Print.

Kirkland, Kevin H. *International Dictionary of Music Therapy.* New York: Routledge, 2013. Print.

Landy, Robert J. *Drama Therapy: Concepts and Practices.* 2d ed. Springfield: Charles C. Thomas, 1994. Print.

Payne, Helen. *Dance Movement Therapy: Theory, Research, and Practice.* 2d ed. New York: Routledge, 2006. Print.

Pinson, Joe. *Involving Senior Citizens in Group Music Therapy.* Philadelphia: Kingsley, 2013. Print.

Schneider, Erwin H., ed. *Music Therapy.* Lawrence: National Assoc. for Music Therapy, 1959. Print.

Siegel, Elaine V. *Dance-Movement Therapy: Mirror of Our Selves.* New York: Human Sciences, 1984. Print.

Walsh, Fintan. *Theatre and Therapy.* Basingstoke: Palgrave, 2013. Print.

Robin Franck; updated by Martha Oehmke Loustaunau

SEE ALSO: Group therapy; Humanistic psychology; Person-centered therapy; Play therapy; Psychoanalytic psychology; Psychotherapy: Children; Psychotherapy: Goals and techniques.

Myers-Briggs personality type indicator

TYPEOFPSYCHOLOGY: Consulting;Counseling;Occupational; Organizational; Personality; Social

The Myers-Briggs Personality Type Indicator (the MBTI) is a popular, theory-based assessment designed to measure personality preferences. Based on Carl Jung's theory of psychological types, the MBTI measures four dimensions of personality: Extraversion vs. Introversion (EI), Sensing vs. Intuition (SN), Thinking vs. Feeling (TF), and Judging vs. Perceiving (JP). From scores on these bipolar dimensions, 16 personality types can be identified, each as a four-letter code (e.g., INTP). The MBTI has been used in personality research, and has been widely used in industry and business to measure employees' personality preferences and tendencies, with the stated aim of improving relationships in the workplace.

KEY CONCEPTS
- Bipolar scales
- Construct validity
- Personality
- Personality vreferences
- Preference Clarity Index (PCI)
- Reliability

INTRODUCTION

In the early 1940s, Katharine Cook Briggs and her daughter, Isabel Briggs Myers, developed a survey to identify personality preferences. The purpose of the instrument was to make Jung's (1923) theory of psychological types understandable, and to "put Jung's theory to practical use" (e.g., Myers & McCaulley, 1985, p. iii). By describing the unique characteristics of individuals, those individuals could gain insight into themselves and others.

Their survey was eventually published as the Myers-Briggs Type Indicator (MBTI) in 1962 by Educational Testing Service (ETS) for use in research. In 1975, it was published by Consulting Psychologists Press, Inc., (now named simply "CPP") for more general use in counseling and employment settings. Besides the MBTI itself, extensive information related to the instrument is availablefrom the CPP website (www.cpp.com), such as interpretative information, example computer reports, up-to-date pricing, and so forth. The CPP website describes the MBTI as "the best known and most trusted personality assessment tool available today."

As stated earlier, the authors' approach was based on their interest in utilizing psychologist Carl Jung's analytic theory of psychological types. In his book, *Psychological Types* (1923), Jung theorized that we come to know the world in four primary ways: sensing (knowing via the senses), intuition (intuiting knowledge), feeling (the emotional part), and thinking (abstract thinking). Another aspect of personality Jung described was the now-familiar notion of extraversion versus introversion. These concepts became operationalized as three of the bipolar scales of the MBTI: Extraversion vs. Introversion (EI), Sensing vs. Intuition (SN), Thinking vs. Feeling (TF). Briggs and Myers added a fourth dimension that they felt was implicit in Jung's theory: Judging vs. Perceiving (JP).

THE FOUR BIPOLAR SCALES

The MBTI consists of a large set of two-choice survey items that feed into four bipolar scales. Form M contains 93 items, and is the standard version of the instrument. The more recently developed Form Q contains those same 93, plus an additional 51 for a total of 144 items. The extra items on Form Q yield more detailed information about the individual (i.e., five "facets" for each of the four bipolar scales). The forms are available in both online and print formats. The four basic scales are now described in more detail.

First, the Extraversion vs. Introversion Scale has to do with one's source of energy. A person with an Extraversion (E) preference or attitude indicates a focus on the outside world. One's attention is toward other people and things in their environment. Such individuals are drawn to action, and communication with others. In contrast, an Introversion preference (I) indicates a focus on a more quiet, internal world of impressions and ideas. Jung's (and the MBTI's) descriptions of these two preferences are broader than every-day notions of the "extravert" and "introvert."

The Sensing vs. Intuition Scale (SN) has to do with the way information is taken in. These two were termed "irrational functions" by Jung, meaning they were not directed by rational thinking. An individual with a Sensing preference focuses on the "here and now," and basic information is taken in through the senses (e.g., visual, auditory, etc.). Individuals with an Intuition preference use insight (e.g., hunches, etc.) to perceive relationships and meanings. They tend to focus on the big picture and the future.

The Thinking vs. Feeling Scale (TF) has to do with ones style of decision-making. As the name suggests, it indicates whether decisions are made based on either thinking or feeling. Individuals with a Thinking preference use logic to make rather impersonal, objective decisions. Those with a Feeling preference make decisions based on values and on more subjective evaluations -- for example, weighing evidence and making decisions reflecting group values.

Finally, Myers' and Briggs' Judging vs. Perceiving Scale (JP) deals with attitudes and behaviors toward the outer world. Individuals with a Judging preference like order (e.g., structure and organization). They tend to be decision makers and planners. In contrast, those with a Perceiving preference are more flexible, open, curious, and spontaneous in facing life.

Based on one's item choices related to these four bipolar dimensions, 16 possible four-letter personality types can result (e.g., ESFP, INTP, etc.), each with a unique interpretation. The four-letter code is the primary outcome that defines one's personality type. A variety of different MBTI profile score reports are available from CPP. Beyond the profile reports, extensive interpretative information is available from a variety of sources, including the MBTI test Manual (Myers & McCaulley, 1993), Introduction to Type (Myers, 1998), the CPP website, and the "Myers & Briggs Foundation" website. Suffice it to say that effective use of the MBTI requires knowledge of Jungian theory, as well as details concerning its interpretation beyond the scope of this entry.

The MBTI provides a "preference clarity index" (pci) for each of the four identified preferences. With values and descriptive adjectives ranging from 0 - 5 (Slight), 5-10 (Moderate), 15-25 (Clear), to 25-30 (Very Clear), the pci indicates how clearly one has selected that pole over the other on that scale. This information is reported by way of a bar graph, with bar lengths reflecting the degree of clarity obtained for each of the four preferences.

RELIABILITY AND VALIDITY

Theory underlying the MBTI suggests that one's personality types or preferences are relatively stable over time. In this regard, various reliability studies indicate that the MBTI classifications have acceptable levels of reliability. For example, studies have demonstrated that each of the four scales of Form M have internal consistency estimates of .90 or higher. As another example, the manual for Form M describes a study that examined test-retest reliability over a four-week period. In comparing examinees' four-letter codes from the first test to the second administration, 65% had the same four-letter code, and the rest were similar in terms of three of the four letters. Overall, Hess (2003) suggests that the MBTI "demonstrates a comforting degree of stability of classification" (p. 613).

Numerous lines of evidence for validity have been established by way of factor analysis, behavioral observations, and correlations with other criteria, such as personality measures. For example, factor analysis of the MBTI suggests that the four preference scales correspond to four of the Big Five personality traits (i.e., Openness to Experience, Conscientiousness, Extraversion, and Agreeableness). Also, the MBTI tends to correlate with other personality tests, such as the California Psychological Inventory, the Eysenck Personality Questionnaire, and Rotter's Locus of Control Scale. These correlations provide convergent evidence for construct validity. Furthermore, according to Lanning

(2003), even if one does not "believe" in the preference types as "real entities, there is value in using the types as descriptive labels" (p. 615). The MBTI has been extensively revised over the years, with recent versions utilizing modern test-development techniques, such as basing norms on a representative national sample, and using item response theory (IRT) to select test items.

A PRACTICAL, USER-FRIENDLY MEASURE OF PERSONALITY

The MBTI is a theory-based measure of personality preferences or types that is widely used in the business world and in research. It is designed as an instrument to help individuals gain insight into their particular personality "type," and the personality types of others. In a business setting, it can be used to improve communication, and to facilitate career development, team building, decision-making, conflict resolution, and so forth. Yet, the makers of the MBTI are quick to acknowledge its limitations. For example, the scales are not meant to measure traits or behaviors per se. Further, the MBTI is not intended to be a predictive device, and should "never be used for hiring, screening or to dictate life decisions" (CPP website). Those limitations aside, the MBTI is nevertheless a practical measure of personality preferences that may be helpful in a variety of counseling, business and research settings. The instrument is well supported by ancillary materials available from the CPP website and other sources. Translated into over 20 languages, the MBTI is administered to over one million individuals each year.

BIBLIOGRAPHY

Hess, A. K. (2003). *Review of the Myers-Briggs Type Indicator Step II (Form Q)*. In B. S. Plake, J. C. Impara, & R. A. Spies (Eds.) The fifteenth mental measurements yearbook (pp. 612-613).

Lincoln, NE: Buros *Institute of Mental Measurements. The Mental Measurements Yearbook* (MMY) is a trusted reference book on tests that provides descriptions of tests, as well as objective critiques by knowledgeable reviewers, such as the one referenced here.

Jung, C. G. (1923). *Psychological types: Or, the psychology of individuation*. Princeton: Princeton University Press. Carl Jung's book in which he discusses his analytic theory of psychological types.

Lanning, K. (2003). *Review of the Myers-Briggs Type Indicator Step II (Form Q)*. In B. S. Plake, J. C. Impara, & R. A. Spies (Eds.) The fifteenth mental measurements yearbook (pp. 614-616). Lincoln, NE: Buros Institute of Mental Measurements. Another critique by a knowledgeable reviewer published in the MMY.

Myers, I. B. (1998). *Introduction to Type: A Guide To Understanding Your Results on the Myers-Briggs Type Indicator*. Sunnyvale, CA: Consulting Psychologists Press, Inc. Revised by Linda K. Kirby and Katharine D. Myers, this brief book provides descriptions of the 16 types.

Myers, I. B., & McCaulley, M. H. (1993). *Manual: A Guide to the Development and Use of the Myers-Briggs Type Indicator*. Sunnyvale, CA: CPP, Inc. The manual for users of the MBTI. It includes details regard its development, and guidelines for its use.

Saunders, F. W. (1995), Katharine and Isabel: *Mother's Light, Daughter's Journey*. Boston: Nicholas Brealey Publishing. A biography of the mother-daughter team that created the MBTI: Katharine Cook Briggs and Isabel Briggs Myers.

Russell N. Carney

SEE ALSO: Measurement; Personality disorders; Personality traits; Personality type; Psychometrics.

N

Narcissistic personality disorder (NPD)

TYPE OF PSYCHOLOGY: Personality; Psychopathology

Narcissistic personality consists of a constellation of traits that include an exaggerated sense of self-importance, a preoccupation with being admired, and a lack of empathy for the emotions of other people. Narcissistic personality disorder is a long-standing, inflexible way of behaving that has developed from childhood.

KEY CONCEPTS
- Entitlement
- Grandiosity
- Perspective-taking ability
- Temperament

INTRODUCTION

A person with a narcissistic personality shows a pattern of grandiosity, which is manifested by a strong tendency to overestimate one's abilities and accomplishments. Together with this grandiosity is a central feature of entitlement. This produces an exaggerated sense of self-importance and preoccupation with being admired. People with a narcissistic personality expect other people to give them their undivided attention and admiration. It is their belief that unlimited success, power, intelligence, and beauty are due them regardless of their actual accomplishments. Their behavior is marked with repeated self-references and bragging. These actions make them the center of attention, and they fully expect that others comply with their fantasy of entitlement.

Narcissistic personality disorder is one of the psychiatric disorders described by the American Psychiatric Association. The behaviors associated with the condition are persistent and lead to difficulties in maintaining mutually respectful and satisfying interpersonal relationships.

POSSIBLE CAUSES

An additional central feature of the narcissistic personality relates to the inability to take the perspective of others. Persons with this personality cannot empathize with the feelings of others, since it is only their own emotions that are important. Although very young children have this narcissistic tendency, it usually disappears through the course of development as they acquire perspective-taking ability. This capacity allows people to look at the world through the eyes of other people. With perspective-taking ability, a person can sympathize with the hardships endured by others and empathetically feel the pain of and commiserate with the joy felt by others. Children who do not show the typical pattern of emotional development grow to become adult narcissistic personalities. As adults, these individuals often take advantage of others to achieve their own goals and become arrogant and snobbish toward other people. Envy is found among persons with a narcissistic personality, as they resent the success of others.

Basic personality traits or temperaments are factors in the development of narcissistic personality disorder. Temperament emerges early in infancy and affects how the child interacts with the environment. Some infants show shyness or are inhibited around novel situations, while others are outgoing and playful. Such temperaments are an early foundation for the development of an adult personality. Genetics may play a role in the formulation of these infant temperaments or character traits. The maladaptive style of the narcissistic personality may evolve from a disturbed parent-child attachment due to the particular early temperament found in the infant. It has also been argued that larger cultural and societal factors can encourage narcissistic tendencies, and that the increase in diagnoses of narcissistic personality disorder in the twenty-first century may be attributable to the influences of contemporary society, but researchers remain divided on the validity of this theory.

DIAGNOSIS

A diagnosis of narcissistic personality disorder requires that a person shows a pervasive pattern of grandiosity, need for admiration, and lack of empathy beginning in early adulthood. Grandiosity produces a sense of unlimited power and intelligence and the feeling that only successful, high-status persons are worthwhile as friends and associates. The narcissistic personality disorder is described by an exaggerated sense of self-importance, a preoccupation with fantasies of unlimited success, a belief in being special, an exploitative style toward other people, a sense of entitlement, and arrogance. Formal diagnosis of narcissistic personality disorder by mental health professionals is often difficult because the diagnostic criteria are inferred from behavior rather than through direct observation. Personality characteristics exist on a continuum from normal to pathological. It is difficult to determine at what point particular behavioral tendencies have become the sign of a psychiatric disorder. In an attempt to address this difficulty, a major revision of the personality disorders category which would have eliminated NPD was proposed for the fifth edition of the Diagnostic and Statistical Manual of Mental Disorders (DSM); however, many clinicians objected to it, and in the end the diagnostic categories for personality disorders were not changed from those in the previous edition of the DSM.

TREATMENT AND IMPACT

The narcissistic personality disorder is resistant to the traditional methods used for treatment. Patients do not believe that they need to change and typically enter treatment only at the insistence of someone else. Persons with narcissistic personality disorder put responsibility for treatment on other people and will avoid being the focus of therapy. Individual psychotherapy (talk therapy) and group therapy have been used for persons with this disorder. The psychotherapy approach is called cognitive behavior therapy. This therapy assumes that problem behaviors are caused by faulty ways of thinking about the environment and other people, and the focus of treatment is on the modification of the troublesome beliefs. However, psychotherapy and even the use of medications such as antidepressants have been found to be of limited value for persons with narcissistic personality disorder. No treatment has yet produced a cure. Because people with this disorder seldom seek therapy themselves, they may become involved with treatment in conjunction with another person's therapy.

The negative impact of the disorder often falls on the family and friends of persons with a narcissistic personality. A narcissistic spouse may cause great difficulty in a marriage through constant demands and expectations of admiration. Conflicts may emerge when these expectations are not realized. A parent with narcissistic personality disorder may prevent a child from receiving adequate care and nurturance, as personal demands for attention dominate the child's needs.

BIBLIOGRAPHY

Blais, M. "Content Validity of the DSM-IV Borderline and Narcissistic Personality Disorder Criteria Sets." Comparative Psychiatry 38 (1997): 31–37. Print.

Campbell, W. Keith, and Joshua D. Miller. The Handbook of Narcissism and Narcissistic Personality Disorder: Theoretical Approaches, Empirical Findings, and Treatments. Hoboken: Wiley, 2011. Print.

Golomb, M., M. Fava, and J. Rosenbaum. "Gender Differences in Personality Disorders." American Journal of Psychiatry 152 (1995): 579–82. Print.

Kernberger, O. "A Psychoanalytic Theory of Personality Disorders." Major Theories of Personality Disorder, ed. J. F. Clarkin and M. Lenzenweger. New York: Guilford, 2005. Print.

Lanier, Paul, Sarah Bollinger, and Robert F. Krueger. "Advances in the Conceptualization of Personality Disorders: Issues Affecting Social Work Practice and Research." Clinical Social Work Journal 41.2 (2013): 155–62. Print.

Paris, Joel. "Modernity and Narcissistic Personality Disorder." Personality Disorders: Theory, Research, and Treatment 5.2 (2014): 220–26. Print.

Ronningstam, E. Identifying and Understanding the Narcissistic Personality. New York: Oxford UP, 2005. Print.

Ronningstam, E., and M. Lyons. "Changes in Pathological Narcissism." American Journal of Psychiatry 152 (1995): 253–57. Print.

Frank J. Prerost

SEE ALSO: Addictive personality and behaviors; Antisocial personality disorder; Borderline personality disorder; Genetics and mental health; Histrionic personality disorder; Intimacy; Multiple personality; Personality disorders; Personality theory; Power.

Narcolepsy

DATE: 1950's forward
TYPE OF PSYCHOLOGY: Biological bases of behavior

Narcolepsy is a condition that causes daytime sleepiness and frequent lapses into sleep at inappropriate times.

KEY CONCEPTS

- Antidepressant drugs
- Cataplexy
- Epilepsy
- Hypnagogic hallucinations
- Multiple sleep latency test (MSLT)
- Nocturnal polysomnogram
- Rapid eye movement (REM)
- Sleep apnea
- Sleep paralysis

INTRODUCTION

Narcolepsy, an often misunderstood disorder, frequently intrudes on the daily lives of those with the disorder, with disturbing results. Children under the age of ten are seldom diagnosed with narcolepsy; its symptoms often manifest in adolescence, although sometimes not until the forties. About half of narcoleptics who end up in treatment remember that their symptoms date to their teens even though they did not seek professional help until long after the onset of the condition.

The most usual age of onset is between fifteen and thirty years. Because many cases develop during adolescence, when young people are experiencing growth spurts and drastic hormonal changes, the tendency to experience excessive daytime sleep episodes is often dismissed as merely a normal part of growing up. In many instances, this is actually the case. Diagnosis frequently is made difficult because the symptoms of narcolepsy mimic those of other unrelated disorders.

Initially narcolepsy may be minimally disruptive to a person's daily activity, but it progresses rapidly to the point that those with the condition may regularly lapse into sleep several times a day. In one extreme case, a male patient lapsed into sleep up to two hundred times a day. Obviously such lapses, lasting from a few seconds to an hour or more, interfere significantly with a person's ability to hold a job and may cause people to be accident prone, sometimes limiting their ability to work with machinery or causing them to have their drivers' licenses revoked.

Sharon L. Merritt and others have studied the socioeconomic implications of narcolepsy. Their findings show that narcoleptics are severely handicapped in their ability to contribute meaningfully to society, although some means have been found to control and remedy their conditions at least minimally. To date, medical science has not found a means of reversing narcolepsy entirely, although means of managing the condition have been employed with limited success.

FREQUENCY

Narcolepsy is a relatively infrequent disorder that occurs in less than one-half of 1 percent of the general population in the United States. Two antigens, DR2 and DQ1, are associated with narcolepsy. DR2 is found in 100 percent of all Japanese narcoleptics, in more than 90 percent of whites with the disorder, and in about 60 percent of narcoleptic African Americans.

Some researchers suggest that there are three or four narcoleptics for every ten thousand people in the general population. Given this statistic, one would expect to find between fifteen hundred and two thousand narcoleptics in a country the size of Israel. Instead, according to reliable statistics, there are thought to be just twelve to fifteen narcoleptics in the entire country.

Of the young people conscripted into Israel's armed forces, no cases of narcolepsy have been detected. Further research conducted at the Montefiore Sleep Center in New York City, which is located in a city with a large Jewish population, revealed that almost no Jewish patients had sought treatment at the center. For some inexplicable reason, it appears that narcolepsy does not occur in Jews. Scientists are unable to explain why.

DSM-IV-TR CRITERIA FOR NARCOLEPSY (DSM CODE 347)

Irresistible attacks of refreshing sleep occurring daily over at least three months

Presence of one or both of the following:

- cataplexy (brief episodes of sudden bilateral loss of muscle tone, most often in association with intense emotion)
- recurrent intrusions of elements of rapid eye movement (REM) sleep into the transition between sleep and wakefulness, as manifested by either hypnopompic or hypnagogic hallucinations or sleep paralysis at beginning or end of sleep episodes

Disturbance not due to direct physiological effects of a substance or another general medical condition

---

SYMPTOMS

The most apparent symptom of narcolepsy is continuing sleepiness that causes those suffering from the disorder to lapse into sleep unexpectedly, sometimes while they are in the middle of a conversation or are engaged in some activity such as driving an automobile. All at once, their eyes glaze over, and rapid eye movement (REM), which in most people occurs about ninety minutes after they fall sleep, may be observed as soon as sleep overtakes the subjects. They fall asleep, sometimes for a matter of seconds but not infrequently for an hour or more. It can be difficult to rouse them from these sleep episodes, and on emerging from them, they may seem disoriented and often have little memory of what they were doing when they fell asleep.

The symptoms of narcolepsy may closely resemble those of epilepsy, although the two conditions usually are unrelated.Epilepsy, narcolepsy versusEpilepsy can cause tremors that are absent in most cases of narcolepsy, although rapid eye movement may accompany both conditions. Some people also confuse narcolepsy with sleep apnea, which causes those suffering from it to stop breathing for extended periods while they are sleeping. Sleep apnea is not a form of narcolepsy.

In the 1880's, the French physician who was a pioneer in studying narcolepsy and who named the disorder, Jean-Baptiste-Édouard Gélineau, noted that in epileptics, a muscular collapse frequently occurs, causing subjects to fall down, after which they sleep. The reverse is true in narcoleptics, whose collapse is caused by sleep and occurs following the sleep their narcolepsy has caused.

About 90 percent of those suffering from narcolepsy experience excessive Sleepsleepiness during the day, and such daytime sleeping may interfere with normal sleep patterns at night. About three-quarters of such patients also experience cataplexy, a sudden loss of muscle tone brought on by laughter, anger, excitement, or some other emotional demand. Cataplexy can cause one's legs to give way, resulting in the person's falling down. The axial and facial muscles may also be affected, rendering facial expression impossible.

About one-third of those suffering from narcolepsy experience hypnagogic hallucinations as they are falling asleep or immediately after awakening. This manifestation, which may include terrifying dreams, is frequently accompanied by REM. About one-quarter of narcolepsy patients experience sleep paralysis either on going to asleep or immediately on awakening. These conditions make it impossible for those experiencing them to move for several minutes.

About 15 percent of narcoleptics experience all four of the symptoms noted above. Often those who suffer from narcolepsy accept it as normal for many years before they seek help to deal with the condition. They think that it is part of their natural sleep pattern to take short naps during the day, and they adjust to the condition, although such an adjustment is not easy. Often such people are considered lazy or unmotivated, so a degree of shame may accompany the manifestations of their conditions.

CAUSES

Little reliable medical information about narcolepsy existed until the development of sleep clinics, where sleep recordings are made of people with sleep disorders. Professor Mary Carskadon of Brown University has devised a multiple sleep latency test (MSLT) that monitors the daily sleepiness levels of subjects who attempted to fall asleep in a dark, soundproof room during daylight hours. Subjects who had seven hours of sleep the night before usually take fifteen to seventeen minutes to fall asleep when confined to the soundproof room, whereas narcoleptics fall asleep almost immediately.

In sleep clinics, patients are attached to machines that produce nocturnal polysomnograms as they sleep. These polysomnograms provide valuable information about the normal phases of sleep, particularly about REM activity. Normally, REM sleep does not occur until people have been sleeping for approximately ninety minutes. In narcoleptics, however, REM sleep occurs as soon as they fall asleep.

Most people are unaware of the events and many of the dreams that occur during REM sleep, whereas narcoleptics who fall into REM sleep immediately on going to sleep during the daylight hours are very much aware of the events that occur as they drift off into sleep.

Genetic factors are thought to play some role in the development of narcolepsy. Research has revealed that if a family has one narcoleptic in it, others in the family are likely to be affected by it. First-degree relatives are forty times more likely to develop the disorder than people in the general population. It has been established, however, that if one identical twin suffers from the disorder, in 25 percent of all cases, the other twin does not. Such seemingly conflicting information has led to confusion regarding the causes of narcolepsy.

Further confusion has occurred with the discovery that most narcoleptics have a common genetic marker in their blood, the leukocyte antigen DR2. Seemingly this discovery could pave the way for developing blood tests capable of detecting narcolepsy or a genetic tendency for the condition, because this antigen is found in all but about 1 percent of all narcoleptics. Further research, however, has determined that the presence of DR2 in the blood of African American subjects was insufficient to draw conclusions about it as a foolproof genetic marker.

Narcolepsy has been associated with the Kleine-Levin syndrome, diagnosed in the 1930's, in which young people experience prolonged and excessive sleepiness and extreme overeating. When this syndrome occurred, its subjects would sleep almost continuously for three or four consecutive days and experienced extreme behavioral changes. In time, these behaviors would diminish and patients would return to normal for an extended period.

The hypothalamus, an organism in the brain that controls a person's drives and the activity of the central nervous system, is so small and inaccessible that it is virtually impossible to study it directly. However, because the hypothalamus controls the secretion of hormones, scientists can study its functions indirectly. Some early research has determined that reductions in the amount of prolactin and the gonadotropins, both of which are secretions of the hypothalamus, may be associated with the Kleine-Levin syndrome.

TREATMENT

Current treatments for narcolepsy are admittedly inadequate. Those suffering from the disorder are encouraged to take regular naps, but this solution is far from effective, because subjects are already lapsing into sleep during the day. Some physicians think that regularizing the nap time will help control the involuntary lapses that characterize the condition, but there is little evidence to support such a contention.

Along with regular napping, stimulant drugs are generally prescribed for subjects, who often take additional stimulants in the form of coffee or caffeinated soft drinks. To control cataplexy, which can lead to falls and to injury, physicians sometimes prescribe antidepressants. Narcoleptics are encouraged to avoid alcoholic beverages and recreational drugs, to eat balanced meals, and to exercise regularly.

Most treatments for narcolepsy have involved stop-gap measures that have not worked well in the long term. Considerable study is being undertaken in an effort to find means of controlling the hormonal output of the

hypothalamus, which may be at the heart of dealing with the disorder.

BIBLIOGRAPHY

Balch, Phyllis, and James F. Balch. *Prescription for Nutritional Healing.* 3d ed. New York: Avery, 2000. Examines treating some of the major symptoms of narcolepsy through diet.

Bazil, Carl W. "Parasomnias, Sleep Disorders, and Narcolepsy." *In Imitations of Epilepsy,* edited by Peter W. Kaplan and Robert S. Fisher. 2d ed. New York: Demos Press, 2005. Bazil, in sixteen pages, relates narcolepsy to a number of similar disorders and discusses the reasons that the condition often remains undiagnosed for many years.

Kellerman, Henry. *Sleep Disorders: Insomnia and Narcolepsy.* New York: Brunner/Mazel, 1981. One of the more venerable sources that deals with narcolepsy. Kellerman's presentation remains cogent and accurate.

Lavie, Peretz. *The Enchanted World of Sleep.* Translated by Anthony Berris. New Haven, Conn.: Yale University Press, 1996. An accessible text that devotes its final chapter, "Narcolepsy: Reversal of the Natural Order," to narcolepsy and, in nine pages, presents a highly informative overview of the condition.

Merritt, Sharon L. "Narcolepsy and Daytime Sleepiness: The Impact on Daily Life." *In Sleep Psychiatry,* edited by Alexander Z. Golbin, Howard M. Kravitz, and Louis G. Keith. New York: Taylor and Harris, 2004. Chapter 9 is devoted to presenting a number of practical considerations relating to narcolepsy, which can intrude on every aspect of a person's daily life.

Scammell, Thomas E. "Narcolepsy and Other Neurological Sleep Disorders." *In Principles of Molecular Medicine,* edited by Marschall S. Runge and Cam Patterson. Totowa, N.J.: Humana Press, 2006. In seven carefully considered pages, Scammell presents a lucid account of narcolepsy, relating it to other sleep disorders.

R. Baird Shuman

SEE ALSO: Caffeine and mental health; Dreams; Hallucinations; Hormones and behavior; Insomnia; Sleep; Sleep apnea; Stimulant medications.

National Institute of Mental Health (NIMH)

DATE: Founded on April 14, 1949
TYPE OF PSYCHOLOGY: Biological bases of behavior; Cognition; Developmental psychology; Personality; Social psychology

At the conclusion of World War II, a confluence of numerous factors, including a heightened awareness of the benefits of preventive psychological treatment, led to the formation of the National Institute of Mental Health. Robert H. Felix pushed for a comprehensive federal plan to codify American psychological philosophy and technique, which led to the National Mental Health Act signed into law by President Harry S. Truman in July, 1946.

KEY CONCEPTS

- Community Mental Health Act
- Community mental health centers
- Mental illness
- National Institutes of Health
- National Mental Health Act
- Neuroinformatics

INTRODUCTION

Forged from the general optimism and sense of responsibility engendered by the New Deal notion that the federal government was invested in the mental health of its citizenry and based on the findings of psychologists witness to the mental health dilemmas presented by World War II, the National Institute of Mental Health (NIMH) emerged as the primary institutional representation of the National Mental Health Act (NMHA) of 1946. In 1944, Robert H. Felix, a psychiatrist and head of the U.S. Public Health Service Division of Mental Hygiene, began work on a proposal for a federally funded mental health organization, which eventually led to the creation and implementation of the NMHA. From 1946 to 1949, NIMH was a subdivision of the US Public Health Service before it became a part of the National Institutes of Health (NIH), an organization under the umbrella of the US Department of Health and Human Services.

Felix—a gregarious and dedicated leader who served as NIMH's first director from 1949 to 1964—believed in research and community-based prevention to ensure the psychological well-being of the general populace. His ideology coincided with that of congressional leaders and Surgeon General Thomas Parran, Jr., and Felix had little difficulty gaining support, both financially and philosophically, for the direction in which he took NIMH. Felix emphasized federal intervention into localized community mental health centers, where the effectiveness of services could be assessed and psychological techniques could be tested. During this time, university psychologists, initially leery of federal financial intervention, were granted millions of dollars for research by NIMH. In this way, NIMH greatly influenced and supported advances in multidisciplinary approaches to mental health. NIMH heightened the profile of psychiatrists but also relied on the research of those in behavioral and social sciences to gain a comprehensive understanding of the etiology of mental illness and to develop treatment options.

NIMH AFTER FELIX

By 1963, NIMH had become the leading financial supporter of academic psychology research. That same year, President John F. Kennedy, in an attempt to deinstitutionalize mental health care facilities, persuaded Congress to pass the Community Mental Health Act, which set up Community Mental Health Centers (CMHC), administered by NIMH. After Kennedy was killed and Felix retired, President Lyndon B. Johnson expanded the focus of NIMH to issues such as urban social problems, poverty, and drug and alcohol abuse, to conform to his Great Society initiatives. In 1967, because of its dual focus on research and community service, NIMH split from the NIH and became part of the Public Health Service, joining the Health Services and Mental Health Administration (HSMHA) the following year. The research division of NIMH eventually rejoined the NIH in 1992.

Stanley F. Yolles, who presided as NIMH director from 1964 to 1970, rescinded power to Bertram S. Brown, who oversaw a period of transition for the organization. The HSMHA folded, forcing NIMH to rejoin the NIH temporarily. Not until President Jimmy Carter took power in 1976 did NIMH regain presidential support, as the president's wife, Rosalynn, endorsed the CMHC program, boosting the profile of NIHM. In the 1980s, however, President Ronald Reagan drastically cut back funding for programs within NIMH, deemphasizing the federal government's role in mental health care.

THE DECADE OF THE BRAIN AND BEYOND

In the 1980s, NIMH shifted its research focus to the burgeoning psychiatric thesis that a connection existed between neurology and genetics and the causes of mental illness. This coincided with George H. W. Bush's

1990 Presidential Proclamation 6158, which announced the 1990s as the Decade of the Brain. Meanwhile, NIMH played down long-held beliefs about the nature of mental illness, specifically the primary contribution of environmental factors. In 1993, NIMH initiated the Human Brain Project to support the developing field of research known as neuroinformatics. Clinical neuroscience research became the primary undertaking of NIMH as the organization moved into the twenty-first century.

In 2002, Tom Insel, a psychiatrist and neuroscientist, became the director of NIMH and further promoted the exploration of links between brain functioning and mental instabilities such as bipolar disorder and schizophrenia. The institute emphasized that brain research, including the study of disparities that exist between normal brain functioning and the processes associated with abnormal functioning, conformed to NIMH's original vision of preventive and curative mental health care. Using the brain's biology as the cornerstone of research into the nature of mental illness, NIMH supplemented its focus by examining class, culture, and epidemiological issues. All these approaches were aimed at improvements in federally funded mental health care.

BIBLIOGRAPHY

Coghlan, Andy, and Sara Reardon. "Psychiatry Divided as Mental Health 'Bible' Denounced." *New Scientist*. Reed Business Information, 3 May 2013. Web. 29 May 2014.

Felix, Robert H. *Mental Illness: Progress and Prospects*. New York: Columbia UP, 1967. Print.

Grob, Gerald N. "Creation of the National Institute of Mental Health." *Public Health Reports* 3.4 (July/August, 1996): 378–381. Print.

Kahn, Ada P., and Jan Fawcett. *The Encyclopedia of Mental Health*. 3d ed. New York: Facts On File, 2007. Print.

Kemp, Donna R. *Mental Health in America: A Reference Handbook*. Santa Barbara: ABC-Clio, 2007. Print.

Pickren, Wade E., and Alexandra Rutherford. *A History of Modern Psychology in Context*. Hoboken: Wiley, 2010. Print.

Pickren, Wade E., and Stanley F. Schneider, ed. *Psychology and the National Institute of Mental Health: A Historical Analysis of Science, Practice, and Policy*. Washington, DC: Amer. Psychological Assn., 2005. Print.

Thornicroft, Graham. *Oxford Textbook of Community Mental Health*. Oxford: Oxford UP, 2011. Print.

Christopher Rager

SEE ALSO: American Psychiatric Association; American Psychological Association.

Native Americans/Alaskan Natives and mental health

TYPE OF PSYCHOLOGY: Developmental psychology; Multicultural psychology; Psychotherapy; Social psychology; Stress

Native Americans and Alaskan Native populations are especially affected by behavioral health and substance abuse issues. They experience one of the highest rates of suicide. Native Americans and Alaskan Natives frequently contend with issues that prevent them from receiving quality medical care, such as cultural barriers, geographic isolation, stigma and mistrust of treatment, and lack of financial resources.

KEY CONCEPTS
- Caste-like minorities
- Cultural proficiency
- Holistic approach
- Immigrants
- Inner curriculum

INTRODUCTION

The federal Bureau of Indian Affairs (BIA) identifies an individual as Indian if there is legal demonstration of at least one-fourth Indian heritage. Generally, the term "Native Americans" includes American Indians, Eskimos, and Aleuts. Many of those termed Native Americans prefer to view their ethnicity in terms of their tribe. Due to a tendency to place all Native Americans and Alaskan Natives into one large classification, much of the literature is based on generalizations from one or two specific tribes and ignores the vast diversity of the cultures included.

Many sociologists follow John Ogbu's categorization of two kinds of minorities: oppressed immigrant groups, who assimilated into the dominant society after two or three generations, and caste-like groups, whose social status rarely changes. Caste-like minorities include groups who either were brought to the United States against their will or were subjugated because of European migration to North America. Ogbu's perspective calls attention to the centuries of legalized racism a minority group has experienced, such as confinement to reservations. Groups most often included in the second category are African Americans and Indian Americans. Opponents of this concept question whether data exist to support the categories.

MENTAL HEALTH ISSUES

The percentage of Native Americans or Alaskan Natives aged eighteen or older who reported a major depressive episode in 2007 was 9.2. This compared with 2.9 for Asians, 6.1 for African Americans, 6.3 for Hispanics, and 8.1 for whites. Native American and Alaskan Natives also have disproportionately high death rates from unintentional injuries and suicide.

The National Survey on Drug Use and Health (NSDUH) concluded that Native Americans and Alaskan Natives suffer disproportionately from substance use disorders compared with other racial groups in the United States. The survey found that in 2012, 12.7 percent of Native Americans or Alaska Natives aged twelve or older used illicit drugs, compared with 11.3 percent for blacks, 9.2 percent for whites, and 8.3 percent for Hispanics. Similarly, 30.2 percent of Native Americans or Alaska Natives reported engaging in binge or heavy alcohol use, compared with 23.9 percent for whites, 23.2 percent for Hispanics, and 20.6 percent for blacks. However, rates of drug and alcohol abuse vary extensively among tribes. The myth that Native Americans have a lower tolerance for alcohol is not substantiated.

CULTURAL VALUES

Knowledge of traditional cultural values of Native Americans and Alaskan Natives can be helpful to mental health personnel. At the same time, it is important to remember the great variation that exists because of differences between and within groups and that every culture contains all the possible values.

Minority group members may feel resentful or defensive because of past treatment of their ethnic group. This can immobilize or impede them in present-day functioning or contribute to depression. Messages about success within the traditional American value system tend to overlook the fact that successful performance for individuals rests on a foundation of mental health.

Increasingly, mental health centers and professionals are employing a holistic approach to mental health by combining primary and mental health care. This view is more consistent with the traditional view of the interrelationship between the mind and the body held by Native Americans and Alaskan Natives, as well as with the value they place on the overall harmony of life.

THE MENTAL HEALTH PROFESSION

Barriers to cultural competence on the part of mental health professionals include a sense of entitlement and a lack of awareness of the need to adapt. This sense of entitlement suggests that standards provided by their professional training or their own life experiences should motivate clients and emanates from the assumption that the successes the mental health practitioner has enjoyed are available to everyone else in the same way. The lack of awareness of the need to adapt overlooks the client's "inner curriculum," which is the primary influence in the healing process. Although the concept was designed to be applied to the classroom, it is as important in the mental health care setting. Mental health settings that are aware of the inner curriculum provide services that are based on the following assumptions:

- Individual characteristics influence change by the client.
- Cultural identity is to be valued and included.
- Culture serves as a framework for sense making.
- Change is influenced by self-interpretation and self-directedness.
- Clients respond to provisions for individualization.

When possible, both Western and the traditional healing techniques of Native Americans and Alaskan Natives should be used. When both are available in mental health clinics, clients are more comfortable seeking mental health services.

BIBLIOGRAPHY

Lee, Wanda M. L., et al. *Introduction to Multicultural Counseling for Helping Professionals.* 3rd ed. New York: Routledge, 2014. Print.

Lyon, William S. *Encyclopedia of Native American Healing.* Santa Barbara, Calif.: ABC-CLIO, 1996. Print.

McAuliffe, Garrett, et al., eds. *Culturally Alert Counseling: A Comprehensive Introduction.* 2nd ed. Thousand Oaks: Sage, 2013. Print.

Ogbu, John. *Minority Education and Caste: The American System in Cross-Cultural Perspective.* New York: Academic, 1978. Print.

Suzuki, Lisa A., and Joseph G. Ponterotto. *Handbook of Multicultural Assessment: Clinical, Psychological, and Educational Applications.* 3rd ed. San Francisco: Jossey, 2008. Print.

Lillian J. Breckenridge

SEE ALSO: Alcohol dependence and abuse; Crosscultural psychology; Cultural competence; Culture and diagnosis; Culture-bound syndromes; Genetics and mental health; Help-seeking; Multicultural psychology; Prejudice; Substance use disorders; Suicide.

Nearsightedness and farsightedness

TYPE OF PSYCHOLOGY: Sensation and perception

Nearsightedness and farsightedness result from an inability of the lens of the eye to focus the image of far or near objects on the retina. In the inherited form of the disability, the eyeball is too long or short in the anterior-posterior direction to allow correct focusing by the lens. In the form of the disability that is related to age, the lens becomes too inflexible to focus nearby objects.

KEY CONCEPTS
- Emmetropia
- Hyperopia
- Laser-assisted in situ keratomileusis (LASIK)
- Myopia
- Photorefractive keratectomy (PRK)
- Presbyopia
- Refractive surgery

INTRODUCTION
Several disabilities affecting vision involve defects in the lens or cornea or the focusing mechanism of the eyes. By far the most common of these disabilities are nearsightedness and farsightedness, the inability to focus the eyes on objects that are either far from or close to the viewer.

Light reflected or originating from distant objects enters the eye in essentially parallel rays. In a person with normal vision, the lens of the eye brings these rays to a point of focus on the retina. The focusing creates an image of distant objects on the retina, much like the image focused by a film or slide projector on a screen. The image focused on the retina by the lens of the eye, however, is inverted and greatly reduced in size. The image of a person's head and shoulders at a distance of twenty feet from the viewer, for example, is focused upside down on the retina in a spot only a half millimeter wide.

Many people suffer from disabilities in vision caused by an inability to focus on near or far objects. In such people, the distance between the lens and retina of the eye is too long or short to allow correct focusing. When the distance from the lens to the retina is too long, the point of focus of the lens falls in front of the retina when parallel rays from distant objects enter the eye. Such people cannot focus clearly on distant objects and are said to be nearsighted or myopic. When the distance between the lens and the retina is too short, the diverging rays from near objects are focused on a point that would fall behind the retina. Individuals with this disability cannot focus on nearby objects and are said to be farsighted or hyperopic. An individual with normally shaped eyeballs, who is neither nearsighted nor farsighted, is emmetropic. Myopia and hyperopia are inherited conditions in many individuals.

Another form of farsightedness, presbyopia, occurs with advancing age and results from a gradual loss of flexibility in the lens with advancing age. The lens of the eye differs from the lens of an optical device such as a telescope or camera in being flexible and able to change in surface curvature. Instead of focusing primarily by moving the lens forward or backward with respect to the retina, the eye contracts small muscles surrounding the lens, the ciliary muscles, to change the curvature of the lens, thereby changing its focal length. (The focal length is the distance from the center of the lens to the point of focus.)

LENSES AND FOCUS
The focusing process, first worked out by Hermann von Helmholtz, has some characteristics that at first seem unexpected. If the fully flexible lens of a young person were removed from the eye, it would assume an approximately spherical shape, with the maximum possible surface curvature. In this form, the lens would have maximum converging or focusing power. This is a result of the fact that the lens consists of a jellylike internal substance enclosed and held under pressure by a tough but elastic surface capsule. A spherical shape would allow the lens to assume a conformation of minimum surface area per volume.

In the eye, the lens is placed under constant tension by fibers that radiate from the lens and attach to the sides of the eye. These nonelastic fibers stretch the lens into a maximally flattened state. In this form, the lens has minimum converging or focusing power. When in its fully flattened form, the lens is considered relaxed. In a person with normal vision, the parallel light rays reflected from distant objects are brought to a point of perfect focus on the retina by the relaxed lens.

Light rays reflected from objects closer than about six meters diverge too widely to be focused on the retina by the relaxed lens. In response, a group of ciliary muscles surrounding the lens contracts. These muscles collectively form a sphincter, in a form similar to the pupil of the eye or to the lips compressed to form the letter O. Contraction of the ciliary muscles has the effect of opposing the zonular fibers, compressing the lens and allowing it to assume a more spherical shape. This increases the converging power of the lens, allowing the diverging rays reflected from nearby objects to be brought to a point of perfect focus on the retina.

There is a limit to the ability of the lens to round up under the action of the ciliary muscles, so that objects held too closely cannot be clearly focused. As individuals age, several interacting factors modify this ability. One factor is the consistency of the lens, which becomes less flexible with age and loses its ability to round up under the action of the ciliary muscles. Other factors, analyzed by Jane F. Koretz and George H. Handelman, include growth of the lens and changes in the tension and arrangement of the zonular fibers. These combined factors have the effect of moving the limit of nearest vision steadily farther from the eye—that is, of making the individual more farsighted—as the individual ages. In a newborn baby, the lens is so flexible that objects placed as close as seven centimeters can be clearly focused. In young children, the nearest focusing distance lengthens to about eight and one-half centimeters. By the twenties to thirties, the point of nearest focus has extended to about ten to fifteen centimeters. By age forty, the point of clearest focus has receded to about twenty-two centimeters for the average person. By this time, most people need glasses or contact lenses to converge light strongly enough to see nearby objects in clear focus. By age fifty, the nearest point of focus lies at about forty centimeters, so that objects must be held at arm's length to be seen clearly without the aid of glasses. By age seventy, the point of nearest focus has receded to hundreds of centimeters. (These figures are for people who are neither nearsighted nor farsighted in their twenties and thirties.)

DIAGNOSIS

To test an individual's eyes for nearsightedness or farsightedness, the ability of the lens to accommodate, or change in focus, must be eliminated. Otherwise, the condition of nearsightedness or farsightedness might be hidden by the eye's ability to change its focus. For example, in mild farsightedness, in which the fully relaxed lens would focus light rays slightly behind the retina, the ciliary muscles can easily contract enough to bring the rays into focus on the retina. As a result, the farsightedness will pass undetected. This is an undesirable condition, because in such persons the ciliary muscles are under a constant state of contraction, which can lead to eyestrain and headaches.

To eliminate accommodation as a source of error, drops are usually added to paralyze the ciliary muscles temporarily. The point of focus of the fully relaxed lens can then be accurately determined. The ability of the eye to accommodate and conceal inherent nearsightedness or farsightedness is one of several reasons that it is not advisable to correct faulty vision by trying on the glasses available at drugstores and department stores until a pair is found that apparently provides clear vision.

TREATMENT

Nearsightedness and farsightedness have been problems for the human population since long before recorded history. In ancient times, people noticed that glass spheres, or a spherical bottle filled with water, could magnify objects and make them more clearly visible. Crude lenses of this type were probably used, at least by farsighted persons, to provide a partial correction from the earliest times. More highly developed, handheld lenses correcting for nearsightedness and farsightedness were used during the early history of both Europe and China; by the fourteenth century, the first eyeglasses had been invented in Italy. Credit for this invention is generally given to Alessandro di Spina of Florence, Italy. A portrait painted in Italy in 1352 is the first known depiction of a person wearing eyeglasses.

Nearsightedness and farsightedness can be corrected by lenses placed in front of the eye or directly on the cornea. For correction of farsightedness, a converging lens is placed in front of the eye. This lens bends parallel rays reflected from distant objects into converging pathways. Because the rays are now converging rather than parallel, the lens can bring the rays to focus precisely on the retina rather than behind the lens. For the correction of nearsightedness, a diverging lens is placed in front of the eye. The diverging rays are focused precisely on the retina rather than off the retina, as they would be in the uncorrected eye. The degree of convergence or divergence needed to correct for farsightedness or nearsightedness is usually determined simply by trial and error, by the selection of progressively stronger or weaker lenses until the correcting lens that gives maximal visual acuity is found.

In 1784, Benjamin Franklin invented bifocals by combining lenses correcting for near and far vision. The lenses were cut in half, placed one above the other, and held in a common frame. By the early twentieth century, bifocals were cut from a single piece of glass. In more recent years, trifocals have allowed correction for near, intermediate, and far vision. The ultimate correction is now obtained by multifocal lenses, which have a complex surface curvature that increases the power of the lens continuously from the top to the bottom. The top of the lens corrects for distant vision and the bottom for near vision. By tilting the head, the wearer can find a point on the lens that gives clear vision for any distance between near and far vision.

Because eyeglasses are fixed in place on the head, they cannot move with the eyes. As a consequence, the distance from the eye to the lens changes as the eyeball rotates. This change in distance is compensated for by a difference in curvature in the front and back of the eyeglass lens, so that the power of the lens varies from the center to the edges. The correction is imperfect even in modern glasses, so that objects viewed through off-center regions of the lenses appear distorted and slightly out of focus. This has the effect of reducing the clarity of peripheral vision. To compensate for this deficiency, most persons wearing glasses learn to turn the head instead of the eyes to view objects in the periphery. Eyeglasses present another problem because they are located several centimeters from the lens of the eye. Because of their position, lenses correcting for nearsightedness or farsightedness have the effect of changing the size or magnification of the image.

Whether the correcting lens is placed a few centimeters in front of the eye, as it is in glasses, or directly on the cornea, as it is in contact lenses, makes essentially no difference to the correction of nearsightedness or farsightedness. Contact lenses, however, have the advantage of automatically correcting astigmatism caused by defects in the curvature of the cornea. Because the cornea has a curved surface, it acts as a fixed lens and contributes to the focus of the eye. In corneal astigmatism, the cornea, rather than having a spherical shape, is slightly flattened or rounded too greatly in one direction over the surface. The effect makes one region of the cornea converge light rays more strongly than other regions. As a result, not all parts of the field of view can be placed in focus. If a series of lines radiating from a point is viewed by an astigmatic individual, some of the lines are seen in focus and some out of focus. Usually, the in-focus and out-of-focus lines are ninety degrees apart. When a contact lens is placed over the cornea, the contact lens, in effect, becomes the cornea. Because a contact lens is constructed with a perfectly spherical surface curvature, any astigmatism caused by imperfections in the cornea is relieved. Because most astigmatism is corneal, rather than caused by imperfections in the lens of the eye, contact lenses are usually effective in eliminating astigmatism as well as nearsightedness.

Since contact lenses are seated directly on the cornea of the eyes, they turn with the eye. As a result, they provide a wide field of undistorted view comparable to normal vision. Because they are placed close to the lens of the eye, in a position that is essentially the same as the cornea itself, they correct for nearsightedness and farsightedness without significantly affecting the size of the image. The several advantages of contact lenses are offset for many persons, however, by their greater expense and irritation of the eyes.

REFRACTIVE SURGERIES
Newer state-of-the-art vision correction is available to the nearsighted, the farsighted, and the astigmatic in the form of refractive surgery. Refractive surgeries include all procedures that reduce refractive errors, correcting myopia, hyperopia, and astigmatism. Currently, there are many refractive procedures available to those with impaired vision.

Photorefractive keratectomy (PRK) has been used since 1989, when clinical trials began. This procedure employs a laser to modify the curvature of the cornea, thereby correcting nearsightedness, farsightedness, or astigmatism.

Laser-assisted in situ keratomileusis (LASIK) is a newer type of refractive surgery, which was first studied in clinical trials in 1995. Using a microkeratome, the surgeon creates a thin layer of cornea that can be folded back. The laser correction is then applied underneath the flap. When this technique is used, there is little scarring, recovery of vision is quick, and minimal pain occurs.

There are currently many new procedures being evaluated by the Food and Drug Administration (FDA) for treatment of nearsightedness and farsightedness. These procedures include intraocular rings and laser thermokeratoplasty. Which procedure is best for any individual depends on the subject's age, type and degree of refractive error, and the risks and benefits for each person as well as the subject's personal circumstances.

BIBLIOGRAPHY

Brint, Stephen F., Corrine Kuypers-Delinger, and D. Kennedy. *The Laser Vision Breakthrough: Everything You Need to Consider Before Making the Decision.* Rocklin, Calif.: Prima, 2001. This book, coauthored by the first U.S. surgeon to perform LASIK, gives a detailed account of laser vision correction. It includes a discussion of everything from pre-op examination to follow-up care, detailing pros and cons of the procedure.

Masland, Richard H. "The Functional Architecture of the Retina." *Scientific American* 255 (December, 1986): 102-111. This clearly written article describes the types of cells in the retina and how they are arranged and organized into a system functioning in light absorption and the transmission of nerve impulses. Outlines the author's research in tracing the shapes of individual retinal nerve cells and shows how his and other techniques will eventually lead to a complete three-dimensional reconstruction of the organization of the retina. Many diagrams and photos, including both light and electron microscope pictures, illustrate the text.

Neisser, Ulric. "The Process of Vision." *Scientific American* 259 (September, 1988): 204-214. Analyzes the interaction between the retinal image and the brain in the perception of visual images, including factors that affect visual perception, such as memory and attention. Clearly and simply written; includes interesting illustrative examples. Demonstrates that what is perceived in vision is vastly more complex than the initial image projected on the retina.

Schnapf, Julie L., and Denis A. Baylor. "How Photoreceptor Cells Respond to Light." *Scientific American* 256 (April, 1987): 40-47. Explains the techniques used to detect and record the responses to stimulation by single rods and cones in the retina, and the patterns in which the photoreceptors respond to light absorption. Describes the differences between rods and cones, and outlines the roles of cones in color vision. Clearly and simply written, with a wealth of illustrations, some in full color.

Sherwood, Lauralee. *Human Physiology: From Cells to Systems.* 6th ed. Pacific Grove, Calif.: Brooks/Cole, 2009. This college physiology text outlines the structure and function of the human visual system from the receptors in the eye through the thalamus and the occipital lobe of the brain. This topic is clearly explained in a chapter on "special senses."

Slade, Stephen G., R. N. Baker, and D. K. Brockman. *The Complete Book of Laser Eye Surgery.* New York: Bantam Books, 2002. A complete guide to the state-of-the-art refractive procedures currently being used to correct myopia, hyperopia, presbyopia, and astigmatism. This book answers questions on LASIK, PRK, and other new surgical options.

Vander, Arthur, James Sherman, and Dorothy Luciano. *Human Physiology: The Mechanisms of Body Function.* 8th ed. Boston: McGraw-Hill, 2001. Chapter 9 of this college physiology text, entitled "The Sensory Systems," includes a clear overview of the human visual system as it normally functions.

Stephen L. Wolfe; updated by Robin Kamienny Montvilo

SEE ALSO: Brain structure; Pattern vision; Sensation and perception; Vision: Brightness and contrast; Vision: Color; Visual system.

Nervous system

TYPE OF PSYCHOLOGY: Biological bases of behavior; Language; Learning; Memory; Sensation and perception

The nervous system represents the interconnections of cells that recognize and coordinate the senses of the body. The nervous system is divided into two major components: the central nervous system, which includes the brain and spinal cord, and the peripheral nervous system, which communicates impulses to and from the regions of the body.

KEY CONCEPTS

- Central nervous system
- Endocrine system
- Endorphins and enkephalins
- Limbic system
- Neuron
- Neurotransmitters
- Peripheral nervous system

INTRODUCTION

The functions of the human nervous system are in many ways analogous to that of a computer. The brain receives information in the form of stimuli from the senses open to the outside world. Within the brain are specific regions, analogous to programs, that interpret the stimuli and allow for a response. More specifically, such responses take the form of physiological or behavioral changes. Some of these stimuli result from activation of tissues or organs within the endocrine system,Endocrine system a network of glands that secrete hormones directly into the bloodstream for regulation of target organs.

The functional unit of the nervous system is the neuron,Neurons a cell that receives or sends information in the form of electrical impulses. The major component of the neuron is the cell body, the portion that contains the nucleus and most of the internal organelles. Two major forms of neurons are found within the nervous system: sensory neurons, which transmit the impulse toward the central nervous system (brain and spinal cord), and motor neurons, which receive impulses from the brain or spinal cord and transmit the impulse to muscles or other tissues.

Depending on the type of neuron, a variety of processes may emanate from the cell body. Axons transmit the impulse away from the cell body and toward the target cell or tissue. Dendrites receive the impulse from other neurons or other sources of stimuli. The actual nerve consists of bundles of thousands of axons wrapped within a form of connective tissue.

The surface of a resting, or unstimulated, neuron has a measurable electrical potential across the membrane. When the nerve is stimulated, whether mechanically such as by pressure or electrically as in the sense of sight, an influx of electrically charged ions such as sodium occurs; the result is referred to as an action potential. The electrical discharge flows along the axon until it reaches the end of the neuron. Eventually the resting potential is restored, and the neuron may again undergo stimulation.

At its tip, the axon divides into numerous terminal branches, each with a structure called a synaptic bulb on the end. Within the bulb are vessels containing chemicals called neurotransmitters, molecules that transmit the electrical signal from one neuron to another, or to target tissues such as those in the endocrine system.

There exist within the nervous system a large number of different forms of neurons, many of which respond to different types of neurotransmitters. Alterations in production of these chemicals, or in the ability of nerves to respond to their stimuli, form the physiological basis for a variety of psychological problems.

CENTRAL NERVOUS SYSTEM

The central nervous systemCentral nervous system is composed of two principal structures: the brain and the spinal cord. The brain is one of the largest organs in the body, weighing on average about three pounds and consisting of one trillion neurons by early adulthood.

The brain is subdivided into four major functional areas. The cerebrum, the largest portion of the brain, regulates sensory and motor functions. The convolutions characteristic of the human brain represent the physical appearance of the cerebrum. The brain stem connects the brain with the spinal cord, carrying out both sensory and motor functions. The diencephalon consists of the thalamus, the relay center for sensory functions entering the cerebrum, and the hypothalamus, which controls much of the peripheral nervous system activity and regulates endocrine processes. The fourth portion of the brain is the cerebellum, the rear of the brain where voluntary muscle activity is controlled.

PERIPHERAL NERVOUS SYSTEM

The peripheral nervous systemPeripheral nervous system consists of the sensory receptors, such as those that recognize touch or heat in the skin or visual stimuli in the retina of the eye, and the nerves that communicate the stimuli to the brain. The peripheral nervous system is often subdivided into two parts, according to function: the somatic portion, which recognizes stimuli in the external environment such as on the skin, and the autonomic portion, which recognizes changes in the internal environment, such as hormone or mineral concentrations in the bloodstream.

The somatic portion of the peripheral nervous system in humans consists of twelve pairs of nerves that originate in the brain and that transmit sensory input from the body. For example, nerve endings in the retina of the eye transmit images to the brain; sensory fibers in the face transmit impulses affecting the skin or teeth. An additional thirty-one pairs of nerves emerge from the spinal cord, subdivide into branches, and innervate various regions of the body.

The autonomic nervous system maintains homeostasis, or constancy, within the body. For example, receptors measure heart rate, body temperature, and the activity of hormones within the bloodstream and tissues. Any abnormality or change results in a signal sent to the brain.

The most notable of the functions of the autonomic nervous system occur in the sympathetic and parasympathetic systems. The sympathetic arm of the system is primarily associated with the stimulation of tissues and organs. For example, during times of stress, hormones are released that increase the heart rate, constrict blood vessels, and stimulate the sweat glands, a phenomenon often referred to as "fight or flight." By contrast, the parasympathetic system counteracts these effects, decreasing the heart rate, dilating blood vessels, and decreasing the rate of sweating.

ROLE OF NEUROTRANSMITTERS

Neurons communicate with one another through the release of neurotransmitters, chemical substances that transmit nerve impulses between nerve cells. Numerous types of neurotransmitters have been identified. Some of these transmitters act to excite neurons, while others inhibit neuronal activity. The particular type of transmitter is synthesized within the cell body of the neuron, travels along the axon, and is released into the space between neurons, known as the synapse.

Among the most prominent neurotransmitters involved in the excitation of neurons is acetylcholine. Acetylcholine The same transmitter bridges the junctions between nerves and skeletal muscles as well as glandular tissues in the body. In the brain, acetylcholine bridges the synapses between neurons throughout the central nervous system. The amino acids glutamic acid and aspartic acid are also known to be involved in excitation of some neurons within the brain. The neurotransmitter serotonin is released mainly within the brain stem, where it appears to regulate activities such as sleep, moods, and body temperature.

Certain neurotransmitters serve in the inhibition of neuronal activity. The most common of these is gamma-aminobutyric acid (GABA),Gamma-aminobutyric acid found primarily in the diencephalon region of the brain. Here GABA acts to reduce the activity within the region. Antianxiety drugs such as Valium or Librium appear to work by enhancing the activity of GABA, resulting in the relaxation of skeletal muscles. Antidepression compounds such as fluoxetine (Prozac) and sertraline (Zoloft) appear to function through blockage of serotonin uptake by neurons.

ENDORPHINS AND THE PLACEBO EFFECT

People who receive treatments with agents that possess no pharmacological activity for various illnesses or conditions have often been known to show improvement. Such a reaction is called the placebo effect. Whether the placebo effect is real has long been controversial. A 1955 study published in the prestigious *Journal of the American Medical Association* was the first significant report that the effect was real. More recent work has suggested the placebo effect may be sometimes more myth than reality. Nevertheless, there is evidence that such an effect may indeed occur and may be associated with forms of neurotransmitters called endorphinsEndorphins (endogenous morphines) and enkephalins. Endorphins and enkephalins represent a class of neurotransmitterlike chemicals called neuropeptides, small molecules that consist of between two and forty amino acids.

Enkephalins, discovered in 1975, block pain impulses within the central nervous system in ways similar to the drug morphine. The second class of molecules, subsequently called endorphins, was discovered soon afterward. They appear to act through suppression of pain impulses through suppression of a chemical called substance P. Substance P is released by neurons in the brain, the result of pain impulses from receptors in the peripheral nervous system. By inhibiting the release of substance P, these neuropeptides suppress sensory pain mechanisms. In support of a physiological basis for the placebo effect, patients treated with the endorphin antagonist naloxon produced no discernable response to placebo treatment.

Endorphins have been shown to play a role in a wide variety of body functions, including memory and learning and the control of sexual impulses. Abnormal activity of endorphins has been shown to play a role in organic psychiatric dysfunctions such as schizophrenia and depression. Deficits in endorphin levels have been observed to correlate with aggressiveness; endorphin replacement therapy results in the diminishment of such behavior. Abnormal levels of endorphins in the blood have also been found in individuals suffering from behavioral disorders such as anorexia or obesity.

LIMBIC SYSTEM AND EMOTIONS

The limbic systemLimbic system is the label that applies to regions of the diencephalon such as the thalamus and hypothalamus that are associated with behaviors such as emotions, learning, and sexual behavior. Stimulation of various areas within the limbic system during surgery has resulted in the patient feeling a variety of conflicting emotions, such as happiness and pleasure or fear and depression, depending on the area being tested.

Some of these emotions or behaviors are associated with survival. For example, stimulation of certain areas results in feelings of rage or sexual excitement. Such patterns of behavior, accompanied by increased heart rate and blood pressure, have suggested that the limbic system plays a role in the fight-or-flight phenomenon.

Neurotransmitters such as serotonin and dopamine are believed to play roles in these behaviors. The effects of recreational drugs on behaviors and emotions may in part be due to the similarity of action between these drugs and neurotransmitters. For example, the high associated with amphetamine use or abuse may result from stimulation of these neurotransmitters. Cocaine blocks the movement of dopamine, resulting in the continual activation of neurons that use dopamine as a neurotransmitter. The addiction associated with cocaine results from alterations in the affected neurons, resulting in an increase in need for stimulation by these pathways.

The disorder schizophrenia may also be the result of impaired transmission of dopamine. The symptoms of schizophrenia—hallucinations or delusions—may be decreased through the use of drugs that inhibit dopamine release. Likewise, drugs that stimulate dopamine activity increase the severity of symptoms.

BIBLIOGRAPHY

Becker, J., S. Breedlove, and D. Crews. *Behavioral Endocrinology.* 2d ed. Cambridge, Mass.: MIT Press, 2002. Emphasis is on the role of the endocrine system and neurotransmitters on physiology of the nervous system, as well as effect on behaviors.

"The Brain." *Scientific American* 241 (September, 1979). The issue was devoted entirely to the nervous system. Though new information has subsequently become available, the issue remains an excellent general source for the subject. Excellent photographs and diagrams are included in the articles.

Kolb, Bryan, and Ian Q. Whishaw. *An Introduction to Brain and Behavior.* 2d ed. New York: Worth, 2006. Textbook on the subject. In addition to thorough coverage of brain structure and function, the authors describe the role of neurophysiology and behavior.

Sherwood, Lauralee. *Human Physiology: From Cells to Systems.* 6th ed. Pacific Grove, Calif.: Brooks/Cole, 2009. Drawing on recent experimentation, the author provides extensive background material for those chapters that explain the function of the nervous system. The text includes comprehensive details, but tables and diagrams clarify the material and provide numerous examples.

Richard Adler

SEE ALSO: Adrenal gland; Brain damage; Brain structure; Endocrine system; Endorphins; Gonads; Hormones and behavior; Neurons; Neuropsychology; Neurotransmitters; Pituitary gland; Psychobiology; Reticular formation; Sensation and perception; Senses; Sex hormones and motivation; Split-brain studies; Synaptic transmission; Synesthesia; Thyroid gland; Visual system.

Neurons

TYPE OF PSYCHOLOGY: Biological bases of behavior

The basic cellular units of the nervous system are glial cells and neurons. Thinking, emotions, and behavior are made possible by electrochemical messages transmitted from one location to another—a process that is accomplished only by neurons.

KEY CONCEPTS
- Action potential
- Axon
- Dendrite
- Long-term potentiation
- Myelin
- Neuron
- Resting potential
- Soma
- Synapse

INTRODUCTION

In the latter part of the nineteenth century, there were two competing theoretical approaches toward explaining the composition of the brain. The reticular theory, championed by the Italian scientist Camillo Golgi, proposed that the brain consisted of a dense, netlike structure of nerve wires with no individual cells. The neuron doctrine, as advocated by the Spanish scientist Santiago Ramón y Cajal, asserted that the brain was composed of individual cells, just like other structures of the body, and that these cells were separated from one another by small gaps. The best microscopic views of that era could not provide evidence to determine which theory was correct, and a contentious debate ensued.

Ironically, it was a staining technique developed by Golgi in the late 1800s that enabled Ramón y Cajal eventually to demonstrate the existence of individual cells in the brain, confirming the neuron doctrine. Ramón y Cajal called these cells neurons, nerve cells that are specialized to receive information and electrochemically transmit it to other cells. In 1906, the gaps between these neurons were termed "synapses" by Charles Sherrington, who deduced many of the properties of synaptic functioning.

NEURONAL STRUCTURE AND TYPES

There are an estimated one trillion neurons in the human nervous system, with somewhere around one hundred billion in the brain. Neurons share many of the same features as other cells. For example, they are surrounded by a membrane, have a nucleus that contains the chromosomes, are provided metabolic energy by mitochondria, and synthesize proteins at sites called ribosomes. What makes neurons structurally different from other cells is a unique tripartite structure.

Most neurons contain a soma, many dendrites, and only one axon. The soma or cell body is a rounded swelling of the neuron that contains the cell nucleus. Electrical messages, also called impulses or action potentials, are collected in the soma, which, in turn, may cause the discharge of electricity to another cell.

Input to the soma usually comes from dendrites. Most neurons have many of these branching fibers whose surface is lined with receptors specialized to receive impulses. Some dendrites have small outgrowths called spines, which increase the places available for connection to other cells.

The axon is a thin fiber, usually longer than the dendrites, that is specialized to send messages from the soma to other cells. Axons have many branches, each of which enlarges at the tip, forming the terminal end bulb. It is from this end bulb that chemicals are released into the synaptic cleft (gap).

Neurons can be distinguished from one another in several ways. Axonal length is long in projection neurons, but short or even absent in local neurons. The function of neurons is different in sensory neurons, which are specialized to detect physical information from the environment, and in motor neurons, which are specialized to activate muscles and glands. A third function of neurons, found in interneurons, is to communicate only with other neurons. The direction of the neural impulse is toward a structure in afferents, away from a structure in efferents, and within a structure in intrinsic neurons. Finally, neurons can be distinguished on the basis of polar dimensions. Unipolar neurons carry a message in one direction only, bipolar neurons convey an impulse in two directions, and multipolar neurons can transmit information in many directions.

THE RESTING POTENTIAL

Each neuron has the capability of producing an electrical charge called the resting potential. Neurons in their resting (nondischarging) state generate voltage by creating an imbalance of positive (sodium, potassium, and calcium) and negative (chloride) electrically charged particles called ions. Four factors contribute to this ion imbalance between the inside and the outside of the neuron's membrane. First, the membranes of neurons have small gaps in them called ion channels. Potassium and chloride ions pass through these channels more readily than sodium ions, resulting in more negative ions on the inside of the neuron than on the outside. Second, the sodium-potassium pump forces three sodium ions out of the neuron for every two potassium ions allowed inside the cell, resulting in less positively charged ions inside the neuron. Third, proteins on the inside of the neuron carry a negative charge. Finally, the gradient balance between entropy—ions will move toward a place of less density—and enthalpy—ions will move toward a place of opposite electrical charge—results in a further negatively charged environment inside the neurons. Combining these four factors together yields approximately a −70 millivolt resting potential for each neuron. In other words, the neuron is like a battery that carries a charge of −70 millivolts.

THE ACTION POTENTIAL

Stimulation from the environment or other neurons can disturb the balance that creates the neuron's resting potential and produce a reversal of electrical polarity that leads the neuron to discharge an electrical impulse. This process is called the action potential and occurs in three phases. The first phase begins with a depolarization—a reduction of the electrical charge toward zero—of the neuron. When this depolarization is sufficient to cause the neuron to be approximately 10 to 15 millivolts less negative, the threshold of excitation is reached and the sodium ion gates, responding to the voltage change, will be opened. This results in a sudden influx of positively charged ions resulting in a reversal of polarity. One millisecond after the sodium gates open, they immediately shut, cutting off the sodium influx, and the gates cannot be opened for another millisecond or so, ending the first phase of the process.

The second phase begins with the opening of the potassium ion channels. Because the inside of the neuron is now positively charged and dense with potassium ions, the positively charged potassium ions flow out of the neuron. Unlike the sodium gates, the potassium gates do not snap shut quickly, and this results in fewer potassium ions inside the neuron than during the resting state. The net effect is that the second phase produces a hyperpolarization, which means that the neuron has an increased charge of approximately −110 millivolts.

In the third phase, the sodium and potassium gates return to their normal conditions, restoring the ion flow conditions that create the resting potential. As a result of the action potential, slightly more sodium ions and slightly fewer potassium ions are found in the neuron at the beginning of the third phase. The sodium-potassium pump eventually corrects this small imbalance and restores the original resting potential conditions.

Between the peak of the action potential and the restoration of the resting potential, the neuron resists generating an action potential. This resistance of refractory period is first absolute—it is impossible for an action potential to occur—and then relative—action potentials can happen, but require stronger-than-normal stimulation.

AXONAL CONDUCTION

In motor neurons, but not all interneurons or sensory neurons, the action potential begins where the axon exits the soma, a place called the axon hillock. Basically, each point along the axon regenerates the sodium-ion influx as it travels down the axon like a ripple caused by throwing a stone in a pond. Because the sodium-ion gates snap shut shortly after they open, the action potential will not travel back to the soma and the impulse is ensured to move toward the synapse. Unlike the small ripple on the pond, the traveling wave down the axon does not diminish in size or velocity and is independent of the size of the stimulus that generates it. This axonal (not dendritic or somatic) phenomenon is called the all-or-none law.

The speed of the impulse down the axon is affected by two factors. First, the larger the diameter of the axons, the more rapidly the impulse is transmitted. Second, many axons are covered with an insulating material called myelin. In myelinated axons, neural impulses "jump" from one break in the myelin sheath—called a node of Ranvier—to another break, resulting in conduction speeds of up to 270 miles per hour. This node-to-node jumping, called saltatory conduction, is much faster than conduction in unmyelinated axons, which produces speeds of only 2 to 22 miles per hour.

SYNAPTIC TRANSMISSION

Because a small gap separates one neuron from another, the traveling electrical charge down the axon cannot affect the next neuron electrically: The "wire" is cut. What allows the gap to be bridged is a chemical process that can be described as a sequence that begins with presynaptic events (what occurs in the sending neuron) and ends with postsynaptic events (what occurs in the receiving neuron).

Presynaptically, when the action potential reaches the terminal end bulb, it opens ion channels for calcium ions that then enter the axon. Calcium activates tiny bubbles called vesicles, which contain chemicals called neurotransmitters. The neurotransmitters are chemicals synthesized in the somas of sending neurons that will cause changes in receiving neurons. The activated vesicles will then excrete neurotransmitters into the synaptic cleft. These chemicals will diffuse across the cleft to the postsynaptic neuron. The total process takes approximately two milliseconds.

Postsynaptically, neurotransmitters attach to places on the receiving neuron called receptors. Different receptors are specialized to pick up different kinds of neurotransmitters. Additionally, most of the many kinds of neurotransmitters will have several different types of receptors with which they can interact. Once the neurotransmitter activates the receptor, it may have an excitatory effect, making the postsynaptic cell more likely to produce an impulse, or an inhibitory effect, making the receiving neuron less likely to generate an action potential. Although most neurotransmitters are predominantly excitatory or inhibitory, the ultimate effect of the neurotransmitter depends on the particular receptor. Furthermore, neurotransmitters can alter the activity of the postsynaptic neuron iontropically, by opening ion gates (a quick but brief process), or metabotropically, by initiating metabolic changes (a slow but long-lasting process). Neurotransmitters that do not bind to receptors are usually reabsorbed into the presynaptic neuron or enzymatically broken down, thereby preventing overactivity of the postsynaptic neuron.

Most neurons are on the receiving end of input from many other neurons. How often a synapse is activated (temporal summation), how many innervating synapses are activated (spatial summation), what neurotramsitters are released, and what receptors are involved all combine to determine whether a neuron will produce an action potential.

BRAIN, MIND, AND NEURON

The synaptic network that links neurons is a dynamic system that is highly responsive to the organism's experience. The more synapses are stimulated, the more efficient they become in their activity. Furthermore, repeated synaptic stimulation increases the number of synapses and induces dendritic branching. This phenomenon, called long-term potentiation, is the neuronal substrate of learning. Long-term potentiation is one reason that those who frequently engage in intellectually stimulating habits, such as reading, develop denser brains than less intellectually stimulated individuals. In other words, an active mind makes for a better brain.

BIBLIOGRAPHY

Barnes, Jim. *Essential Biological Psychology*. London: SAGE, 2012. Print.

Huguenard, John, David A. McCormick, and Gordon M. Shepherd. *Electrophysiology of the Neuron: An Interactive Tutorial/Book and Disk*. New York: Oxford UP, 1997. Print.

Kalat, James W. *Biological Psychology*. 10th ed. Belmont: Wadsworth/Cengage Learning, 2009. Print.

Levitan, Irwin B., and Leonard K. Kaczmarek. *The Neuron: Cell and Molecular Biology*. 3d ed. New York: Oxford UP, 2002. Print.

Liljefors, Max. *Atomized Body: The cultural Life of Stem Cells, Genes, and Neurons*. Lund: Nordic Academic, 2012. Print.

McKim, William A. *Drugs and Behavior: An Introduction to Behavioral Pharmacology*. 6th ed. Upper Saddle River: Prentice, 2007. Print.

Nicholls, John G., A. Robert Martin, Paul A. Fuchs, and Bruce G. Wallace. *From Neuron to Brain*. Sunderland: Sinauer, 2001. Print.

Strominger, Norman L., Rovert J. Demarest, Lois B. Laemle, and Charles Robert Noback. Noback's *Human Nervous System: Structure and Function*. 7th ed. New York: Humana, 2012. Print.

Paul J. Chara, Jr.

SEE ALSO: Adrenal gland; Brain damage; Brain structure; Endocrine system; Endorphins; Gonads; Hormones and behavior; Nervous system; Neuropsychology; Neurotransmitters; Pituitary gland; Psychobiology; Reticular formation; Sensation and perception; Senses; Sex hormones and motivation; Split-brain studies; Synaptic transmission; Synesthesia; Thyroid gland; Visual system.

Neuropsychology

TYPE OF PSYCHOLOGY: Biological bases of behavior

Neuropsychology is the study of the relationship between the brain and behavior. It has provided insights into the workings of the normal brain as well as innovations for diagnosing and assisting individuals with an injury to or disease of the brain..

KEY CONCEPTS

- Alzheimer's disease
- Brain imaging
- Dysfunction
- Lesion
- Process approach
- Rehabilitation
- Standard battery approach

INTRODUCTION

Neuropsychology studies the relationships between brain functions and behaviors. It examines both human and animal nervous systems and tries to link biological organization and function of the nervous system to cognitive processing and behavior. Both healthy and damaged neural systems are examined. Although neuropsychology can be divided into a number of specialty areas, breaking the field into the branches of clinical neuropsychology and experimental neuropsychology serves to classify the primary types of work in which neuropsychologists are involved. This distinction is not absolute, of course.

CLINICAL NEUROPSYCHOLOGY

Clinical neuropsychology involves the clinical testing of individuals who suffer from brain dysfunction, either developmental (genetic or chromosomal) or, more often, acquired (brain damage). Developmental disorders include Turner and Down syndromes; acquired disorders can be caused by problems such as fetal alcohol syndrome, brain lesions caused by tumors, cerebral vascular accidents (strokes), or head trauma.

Although neuropsychological evaluations once relied almost exclusively on paper-and-pencil tests to identify the probable location of a brain lesion and the resulting deficits, localization of lesions is typically handled through computerized brain imaging techniques such as computed tomography (CT) or magnetic resonance imaging (MRI). Clinical neuropsychologists primarily assess a patient's cognitive and behavioral deficits and describe the individual's level of functioning. They are often involved in planning treatments and rehabilitation programs. Because damage to the same brain area may affect two individuals differently, it is vital that clinical neuropsychologists assess the effect of the lesion on the patient's daily functioning at work, at home, and in social contexts. Furthermore, it is important that the evaluation consider the patient's strengths in addition to weaknesses or impairments. Intact abilities can assist the patient in coping and compensating for the loss of other functions.

BRAIN TESTING
Clinical neuropsychologists typically take one of two approaches with patients, the standard battery approach or the process approach. The standard battery approach is the older of the two and involves administering the same set of neurological tests to every patient. These tests typically demand different mental or cognitive abilities, which involve various regions of the brain. These different cognitive abilities are commonly referred to as cognitive domains and include functions such as attention, memory, perception, movement, language, and problem solving. A number of comprehensive test batteries have been created to assess these different skills, but two commonly used ones are the Halstead-Reitan and the Luria-Nebraska.

The process approach to clinical neuropsychology tailors the testing to the patient. It requires neuropsychologists to spend more one-on-one time with patients, and the tests chosen for each case can vary considerably. Essentially, neuropsychologists try to develop a hypothesis about the patient's problems, then test it, and either accept or reject that hypothesis.

Each approach has its costs and benefits. The standard battery approach is cheaper and easier to use and teach. The process approach better recognizes the individuality of patients and can give a more comprehensive picture of an individual.

EXPERIMENTAL NEUROPSYCHOLOGY
Experimental neuropsychology focuses on answering theoretical questions in the laboratory rather than solving clinical or practical problems in the outside world. Because of the invasive nature of their questions, experimental neuropsychologists often use animals rather than humans in their research. Only after a line of research has been proven safe and effective is it verified, wherever possible, with a human sample.

More than with most fields of psychology, advances in neuropsychology are determined by the technology available to researchers. An experimental neuropsychologist is usually familiar with the techniques of neurosurgery, primarily on animals, and with a variety of techniques, such as the staining of neurons, that help in examining brain structure. Neuropsychologists will certainly be familiar with electroencephalography (EEG), a recording of the brain's electrical activity, and they often use direct electrical stimulation of the brain, at very low levels of current, in research. They commonly use brain imaging devices such as the CT or MRI. A high degree of technological expertise is demanded of the neuroscientist, but the result has been a rapid increase in knowledge about the relationship between the brain and behavior.

Although the daily routines of clinical and experimental neuropsychologists are quite different, their work often intertwines. The insights of experimental neuropsychologists often improve clinicians' ability to assess and treat individuals with neurological impairment. Similarly, clinicians' descriptions of interesting patients often open the road for further theoretical investigation by experimental neuropsychologists.

PRACTICE AND THEORY
Overall, the field of neuropsychology has been useful in solving a number of practical problems as well as more theoretical ones. For example, clinical neuropsychological procedures have been applied in the assessment and treatment of individuals suspected of having Alzheimer's disease. This disease is virtually impossible to confirm without removing and inspecting a sample of brain tissue under the microscope for the structural abnormalities that characterize the disorder. Therefore, a final diagnosis must wait until after the person's death, at autopsy. However, neuropsychological test procedures have contributed dramatically to the accurate diagnosis of probable Alzheimer's disease in still living individuals. A person with such a diagnosis is said to have senile dementia of the Alzheimer's type (SDAT).

To family members of the Alzheimer's patient, memory problems are often the first sign of trouble. However, a careful examination usually reveals subtle difficulties with language, problem solving, and visual-spatial activities such as navigating in the neighborhood or at home. Clinical neuropsychologists can investigate such problems by using a variety of pencil-and-paper tests to measure specific cognitive and behavioral functions. The patient is then tested serially at six-month intervals, and the overall pattern of test scores across time is evaluated. If the patient displays a pattern of declining performance across two or more cognitive domains (for example, memory and language), a diagnosis of dementia is supported. In addition, neuroimaging techniques such as the MRI are used to evaluate potential structural damage to the brain. Brain scans cannot reveal the microscopic plaques and tangles of neural tissue that characterize Alzheimer's, but they can reveal large-scale neuron loss and can be used to eliminate other possible causes for the symptoms, such as a tumor or stroke.

Along with the measurement of various cognitive functions, neuropsychology also seems particularly well equipped to investigate other aspects of Alzheimer's. Although a patient's performance on a test battery is certainly helpful, other factors must be considered in diagnosing the disorder. For example, depression, hallucinations, delusions, and verbal or physical outbursts are often common with the disease. Because of this diverse collection of psychological and behavioral symptoms, clinical neuropsychology may be the best source of services for such patients.

A rapidly expanding field of endeavor for modern neuropsychologists involves work with recovery and rehabilitation efforts for brain-injured patients. The primary purpose is to reeducate and retrain brain-injured individuals for reentry into job and home settings, which usually means working with both the patient and the family. Often, people with brain injuries do not struggle equally in all cognitive domains. They may, for example, have particular problems with attention or language. Clinical neuropsychologists focus their efforts on the affected domain, bringing in other specialists as needed for physical, occupational, or speech therapy.

Generally, rehabilitation involves intensive exposure to situations involving the problematic cognitive task. For example, automobile accidents often result in damage to the frontal areas of the brain. Such patients typically lack appropriate social skills and have problems with planning and organizing their behaviors. Rehabilitation efforts might entail placement in group situations in which social skills can be practiced. Specific activities might include working on conversation skills, role-playing a job interview or asking for a date, or working on a group project. Individual sessions with the patient might be better suited for the treatment of the organizational and planning deficits experienced by frontal patients. Here, the neuropsychologist might teach the patient to use a diary for planning the week's activities. Increasingly, computer technology is being used in rehabilitation, either to assist with training simulations, or to act as an actual prosthetic aid for tasks such as speech production.

Although neuropsychologists often assist patients in acquiring compensation strategies to work around their particular difficulties, there are other rationales for rehabilitative efforts. Many researchers believe that practicing an impaired function assists the healing brain in the recovery of that function. There appears to be a six-to twelve-month period immediately after a brain injury when the brain is developing pathways around the damaged tissue. Many believe that during this critical period, it is important to engage the patient in those activities most compromised by the injury. Therefore, if the injury took a major toll on memory abilities, the patient should be exposed to exercises and activities that demand remembering.

In general, neuropsychology has tremendous applied value for persons who have sustained a neurological insult such as a stroke or brain injury. Furthermore, it is useful in the initial assessment and accurate diagnosis of a given neurological disorder, as well as in the continued care and treatment of individuals with known brain pathology.

BRAIN STUDY

The term neuropsychology appears to have been coined by Sir William Osler, sometimes called the father of modern medicine, in an address at Johns Hopkins Hospital in 1913. The field really began to expand, however, after Donald O. Hebb, often called the father of neuropsychology, published *The Organization of Behavior: A Neuropsychological Theory* (1949). This book introduced Hebb's concept of neural networks, which remains a unifying theme for modern neuropsychologists. The 1970s and 1980s were a particularly explosive time in the development of neuropsychology, with many new training programs springing up. Funding for all subfields of neuroscience increased dramatically when the US Congress designated the 1990s as the Decade of the Brain.

Although the field is relatively young, neuropsychology's underpinnings can be traced back thousands of years. Ancient peoples from both Europe and the Americas engaged in trephination, the cutting of holes in the skull, presumably as a treatment for some sort of physical or behavioral problem. Ancient Egyptian and Greek writings also describe the results of brain injury, including the behaviors of patients. A theory of brain functioning was put forth in the nineteenth century by Franz Gall, the founder of phrenology, who thought specific areas of the brain were responsible for specific behavioral traits, and that brain abilities could be "read" by studying the shape of people's skulls.

Although phrenology was eventually discredited, the nineteenth century also produced Paul Broca, a pioneer in the study of brain anatomy. Broca demonstrated that a lesion of the left frontal lobe of the brain disrupted speech production. Inspired by Broca's work, some researchers became consumed with localizing all cognitive functions to a discrete part of the brain. These scientists became known as localizationists. In contrast, investigators who believed that all areas of the brain were equally involved in all cognitive abilities were labeled equipotentialists. A third group, known as interactionists, suggested that basic cognitive functions were relatively localized but interacted to allow for complex cognitive processes. This perspective was derived from the late nineteenth century research of John Hughlings Jackson and remains a prominent view in the twenty-first century.

The twentieth century witnessed a steady accumulation of knowledge concerning the relationships between brain and behavior. Much of this knowledge developed out of the need to assist soldiers who had sustained brain injuries in the two world wars. In treating these individuals, much was learned about the role of specific brain regions in carrying out various behaviors. A major contribution to the neurosciences in the twentieth century was made by the Soviet neuropsychologist Aleksandr Luria, whose systematic study of brain-injured people contributed tremendously to the process of assessing and localizing brain dysfunction.

This wealth of new knowledge has given clinical psychologists a much more sophisticated understanding of how best to treat patients with behavioral difficulties. It has also removed some of the stigma attached to mental illness or dysfunction. The lay public seems more willing to tolerate atypical behavior from an individual with physical damage to the brain than from a patient labeled as mentally ill.

The future appears to be full of promise for the field of neuropsychology. Although it may be years, if ever, before a complete understanding of the brain is achieved, the steady growth in new knowledge and new applications for that knowledge has already enriched the lives of countless human beings with brain dysfunctions. New insights into diseases such as Alzheimer's promise to help many more people. Furthermore, as an understanding

of the brain's effects on behavior grows, the diverse subfields of psychology are bound ever closer together.

BIBLIOGRAPHY

Chatterjee, Anjan. *The Roots of Cognitive Neuroscience: Behavioral Neurology and Neuropsychology*. Oxford: Oxford UP, 2014. Print.

Finger, Stanley. *Origins of Neuroscience: A History of Explorations into Brain Function*. New York: Oxford UP, 2001. Print.

Glozman, Janna. *Developmental Neuropsychology*. New York: Routledge, 2013. Print.

Koffler, Sandra, et al., eds. *Neuropsychology*. New York: Oxford, 2013. Print.

Kolb, Bryan, and Ian Q. Whishaw. *Fundamentals of Human Neuropsychology*. 6th ed. New York: Worth, 2006. Print.

LeDoux, Joseph. *Synaptic Self: How Our Brains Become Who We Are*. New York: Penguin, 2003. Print.

Luria, Aleksandr Romanovich. *The Working Brain: An Introduction to Neuropsychology*. New York: Basic, 1976. Print.

Sacks, Oliver. *The Man Who Mistook His Wife for a Hat*. Rpt. New York: Simon, 2006. Print.

Zillmer, Eric A., Mary V. Spiers, and William Culbertson. *Principles of Neuropsychology*. 2nd ed. Belmont: Wadsworth, 2007. Print.

Jeffery B. Allen; updated by Charles A. Gramlich

SEE ALSO: Alzheimer's disease; Brain damage; Brain structure; Cognitive psychology; Computer models of cognition; Dementia; Elders' mental health; Nervous system; Neurons; Neurotransmitters; Parkinson's disease; Psychosurgery; Split-brain studies.

Neurotic disorders

TYPE OF PSYCHOLOGY: Consciousness; Personality; Psychopathology; Psychotherapy

Neurotic disorders are defined by the form and type of symptoms that become manifest. The various neurotic disorders include anxiety neurosis, depressive neurosis, obsessive-compulsive neurosis, phobic neurosis, and hysterical neurosis. These disorders are the result of unconscious mental conflict and are shaped by early experience, coupled with innate temperament.

KEY CONCEPTS

- Anxiety
- Depression
- Emotional conflict
- Hysteria
- Mental conflict
- Obsessive compulsiveness
- Oedipus complex
- Phobia
- Psychoanalytic psychotherapy
- Transference

INTRODUCTION

Neurosis is a general term used to describe various forms of mental disorders that involve symptoms of anxiety, depression, hysteria, phobia, and obsessive compulsiveness. The Scottish physician and researcher William Cullen first used the term during the eighteenth century. At that time, a whole range of symptoms and diseases were referred to as neurotic and were thought to be organically based, with specific, localized points (for example, digestive neurosis). The Austrian psychiatrist Sigmund Freud coined the term psychoneurosis to denote and describe his discovery that neurotic disorders do not have localized organic origins but are psychological in nature and caused by early emotional trauma, the results of which are psychological and emotional conflict. Based on his research into neurotic disorders with colleague and physician Josef Breuer, Freud created the theory and mental health discipline of psychoanalysis. The psychoanalytic understanding of mental disorders is based on the observation that early life experience, in combination with an individual's biological givens, affects later emotional development and that many of the sources of one's psychological symptoms (for example, unhappiness and anxiety) stem from early experiences with parents and other caregivers. These early interpersonal experiences, coupled with one's early temperament, have emotional consequences that are largely unconscious in nature.

The symptomatology associated with various neurotic disorders, then, stems from emotional conflicts originating in early life. Although the sources of these conflicts are unconscious, the consequences of this unrecognized emotional turmoil lead to various psychological symptoms.

EARLY CONCEPTION OF NEUROTIC DISORDERS

During the end of the nineteenth century and the early part of the twentieth century, Freud described the two broad types of neuroses: transference neuroses and narcissistic neuroses. He thought that patients with psychotic symptoms or severe depression were incapable of forming a relationship with their treating psychoanalyst; they were narcissistic, autistic-like, and consequently unable to be helped by psychotherapeutic means. He believed that patients with hysterical, phobic, or obsessive-compulsive symptoms, however, were capable of developing an emotional tie to the analyst. He referred to the special nature of the patient-doctor relationship as transference and referred to patients with hysterical, phobic, or obsessive-compulsive symptoms as suffering from transference neuroses. These patients were amenable to "the talking cure."

Freud first began to formulate his theory of psychoneurosis, his discovery that symptoms had psychological meaning, after studying in France with the famous French neurologist Jean-Martin Charcot, who demonstrated that patients' symptoms under hypnosis could be displaced or eliminated. For example, a woman with an arm paralysis could be hypnotized and the paralysis transferred from one arm to another. This observation, coupled with his experience of treating sexually repressed upper-middle-class patients in the late nineteenth and early twentieth centuries in Vienna, led Freud to the conclusion that neurotic symptoms stem from early sexual wishes and desires that were unacceptable and therefore rendered unconscious. Psychological defense mechanisms such as repression are used to eliminate unacceptable thoughts or feelings or painful inner emotional conflicts.

Freud believed that around the age of three or four, the child wanted to possess the parent of the opposite sex and get rid of the same-sex parent (the Oedipus complex in boys, the Electra complex in girls). Because of basic physical limitations and fear of retaliation, these desires had to be repressed. Unresolved sexual conflict and less-than-successful repression of these wishes and desires led to the various forms of neurotic symptoms. These symptoms represented repressed sexual conflict that was striving for release and gratification ("the return of the repressed"). The particular symptom both symbolized and disguised the nature of the conflict. The specific fixation point at which the individual's sexual development was arrested dictated the "choice" of a particular neurotic disorder or symptom. Heightened sexual pleasure was localized at three bodily areas, corresponding to three different stages of development. The three stages of childhood sexuality were labeled oral, anal, and phallic, with the Oedipus complex culminating at the phallic stage of development. Healthy negotiation of these stages and the Oedipus complex dictated normal heterosexual relationships. Fixation or arrest during these stages of development culminated with problems in intimate heterosexual relationships as an adult as well as in the development of neurotic symptomatology.

The symptoms associated with hysterical neurosis have been recognized since antiquity. They include unstable and tense emotional experience, hypochondrias, overreaction to external demands, sexual conflict coupled with heightened flirtatiousness toward the opposite sex, and lack of psychological insight. Hysterical neurosis may lead to a conversion of anxiety into physical symptoms.

Freud also discovered that the hysteric's predominant mode of defense against conflict and distress is repression. With repression, an individual is unable consciously to remember or experience disturbing feelings, thoughts, or wishes. In hysterical neurosis, unacceptable thoughts and feelings have been eliminated from consciousness via this mechanism of defense. The presence, however, of a neurotic symptom reflects the fact that repression was incomplete. Unacceptable anger at a loved one, for example, will be repressed from consciousness, but one may be left with the symptom of paralysis of the arm. A psychological conflict is converted into a physical symptom.

The obsessive neurotic is seen as utilizing his or her intellect excessively, so as to avoid emotional conflicts or experience. These individuals, therefore, will excessively ruminate, be hyperrational, and avoid their emotions completely. They use the defense mechanism of intellectualization and also of reaction formation, whereby one behaves the opposite of what one truly but unacceptably feels. The obsessive neurotic, therefore, may be overly kind and rational toward someone at whom she or he is enraged but also loves.

Freud also wrote about phobia as a neurosis whereby an individual uses the defense mechanism of displacement, transferring a danger that is internal (castration anxiety, for example) onto an external danger that symbolizes the inner anxiety. Castration anxiety due to Oedipal conflict may lead to a displacement of that fear onto an external danger, with the phobic child, for example, manifesting a seemingly irrational fear of being bitten by a horse.

CONTEMPORARY UNDERSTANDING

Modern psychoanalytic understanding of neurotic disorders is broader than the early Freudian classifications of hysteria, obsessive-compulsiveness, and phobia, with less emphasis on sexual conflict as the sole causative feature. Conflicts involving a range of early emotions and impulses are seen as implicated in the development of neurotic disorders. Modern psychoanalysts use scientific approaches to enhance theory and practice. The University of Michigan research psychoanalyst Howard Shevrin, for example, has provided empirical brain-based evidence for the presence of unconscious psychological conflict and has enhanced the understanding of the role of unconscious conflict in the formation of psychological symptoms.

Sexuality and aggression continue to be seen as essential driving forces that shape development and are central factors in the construction of neurotic symptoms. Additionally, the modern psychoanalyst considers factors associated with later points of development, when examining neurotic symptomatology.

The developing child is seen as possessing immature intellectual, emotional, and imaginative capacities. He or she is faced with managing inner fears as well as with negotiating relationships with primary caretakers. Frustration and conflict inevitably emerge, and patterns of emotional experience, fantasy, and behavior develop in response to these early experiences. Modern psychoanalysis emphasizes the position that character, behavior, and the imagination of the child all reflect, in part, solutions to the inevitable conflicts experienced by the child as a result of his or her wishes, urges, and fantasies that are unacceptable to caretakers and also ambivalently felt by the child (hateful feeling toward one's mother, for example). Emotional conflict, guilt, and self-condemnation inevitably result to some degree or other and necessitate the mobilization of various psychological defense mechanisms, including repression. Fears, wishes, and thoughts that are unacceptable and censored take on a dangerous, forbidding dimension. These unresolved, repressed thoughts and feelings lead to the creation of unconscious fantasies that are in conflict with the more conscious self and may cause seemingly senseless or unreasonable emotional turmoil. For example, a young boy who is frightened, ashamed, and guilt-ridden by his hateful impulses toward his father will repress these urges. As an adult, he may inexplicably feel like a "monster" (an unconscious fantasy of himself when angry) whenever he naturally asserts himself, without consciously understanding why self-expression is so difficult.

Modern psychoanalysis differentiates a range of neurotic disorders within two broad classifications: symptom neurosis and character neurosis. The symptom neuroses are specific and tied to specific symptoms. Hysterical neurosis, obsessive neurosis, depressive neurosis, and anxiety neurosis all reflect underlying emotional conflicts but are manifested through different symptoms. For example, the hysteric converts emotional turmoil into somatic complaints. The obsessive is emotionally cut off from self and others and is ritualistic, while the depressive is sad, with chronic self-esteem problems. The anxiety neurotic ruminates and may have a specific irrational fear (phobia).

With symptom neurosis, the neurotic is distressed and the symptoms are ego-dystonic; that is, the symptoms are felt to be alien, unwanted, and foreign to the self. With character neurosis, however, symptoms are not present and the character neurosis is reflected by maladaptive and enduring personality patterns of behavior and experience that, although neurotic, are accepted features of the individual's self or identity (ego-syntonic). Others may perceive an obsessive neurotic personality, for example, as unemotional and excessively avoidant of feelings, but he or she will see himself as objective and fastidious. The hysterical neurotic personality will view himself or herself as spontaneous and not excessively emotional, whereas the depressive neurotic personality may realize he or she is always depressed, but believe that it is for good reasons. Because the neurotic pattern of behavior is ego-syntonic, neurotic personalities are more difficult to treat.

PSYCHOANALYTIC TREATMENT

Psychoanalytic psychotherapy seeks not only to relieve current symptoms but also to deal with root emotional conflicts and causes of the symptoms or behavioral patterns. Because the sources of one's conflicts, symptoms, and behavior patterns are essentially unconscious, and because defenses have been constructed to help one adapt as effectively as possible, psychoanalytic treatment takes time, is intensive, and lasts from one to three or more years. The therapeutic relationship that develops is intimate and intense. The psychoanalyst and patient collaborate in the exploration of the patient's symptoms and style of relating. This leads to the patient becoming aware of his or her underlying sources of conflict, not only intellectually but also emotionally. The emotional understanding occurs predominantly through the understanding of feelings, thoughts, and fantasies that arise out of the realistic and unrealistic (transference) dimensions of the therapeutic relationship. It is through the relationship that the patient can reexperience, in the here and now, how his or her inner conflicts and unconscious difficulties have been creating symptoms and dysfunctional repetitive patterns of behavior. The analyst and patient work together to understand how and why certain wishes and desires, feelings, thoughts, and unconscious fantasies have developed and contribute to the patient's emotional and behavioral difficulties. Over the course of treatment, the patient's capacity for emotional integration improves, as does his or her capacity to function without self-defeating behaviors, emotions, and thoughts.

BIBLIOGRAPHY

Boag, Simon. *Freudian Repression, the Unconscious, and the Dynamics of Inhibition.* London: Karnac, 2012. Print.

Bowlby, Rachel. *Freudian Mythologies: Greek Tragedy and Modern Identities.* New York: Oxford UP, 2007. Print.

Doctor, Ronald M., Ada P. Kahn, and Christine Adamec. *The Encyclopedia of Phobias, Fears, and Anxieties.* New York: Facts on File, 2008. Print.

Fenichel, Otto. *The Psychoanalytic Theory of Neurosis.* New York: Routledge, 2010. Digital file.

Kligman, D. *The Development of Freud's Theories: A Guide for Students of Psychoanalysis.* Madison: International Universities P, 2001. Print.

Mitchell, L. S., and M. Black. *Freud and Beyond: A History of Modern Psychoanalysis.* New York: Basic, 1995. Print.

Moore, B., and E. Fine. *Psychoanalytic Terms and Concepts.* New Haven: Yale UP, 1994. Print.

Phillips, Adam. *Becoming Freud: The Making of a Psychoanalyst.* New Haven: Yale UP, 2014. Print.

Sandler, J., A. Holder, C. Dare, and A. Dreher. *Freud's Model of the Mind: An Introduction.* Madison.: International Universities P, 1997. Print.

Westen, D. "The Scientific Legacy of Sigmund Freud: Toward a Psychodynamically Informed Psychological Science." *Psychological Bulletin* 124.3 (1998): 331–71. Print.

Richard Lettieri

SEE ALSO: Anxiety disorders; Defense mechanisms; Depression; Ego defense mechanisms; Freud, Sigmund; Freudian psychology; Hysteria; Obsessivecompulsive disorder;

Oedipus complex; Phobias; Psychoanalytic psychology and personality: Sigmund Freud; Women's psychology: Sigmund Freud.

Neurotransmitters

DATE: 1920 forward
TYPE OF PSYCHOLOGY: Biological bases of behavior

Neurotransmitters are chemicals that are synthesized and released by neurons and cause a response in target cells.

KEY CONCEPTS
- Excitatory
- Inhibitory
- Neuron
- Receptor
- Synapse

INTRODUCTION
In the late 1880s and the early 1900s, Santiago Ramón y Cajal and Charles Sherrington, respectively, demonstrated that there is a gap separating one neuron (nerve cells that transmit and store information) from another, which Sherrington called the synapse. Their work was extended by Otto Loewi, who proved in 1920 that neurons send messages across the synaptic gap using chemicals. By the 1950s, the principle that neurons communicate with one another through chemicals was well established, stimulating both a search for new neurotransmitters and new drugs for psychiatric and other medicinal uses.

The early view was that a presynaptic (sending) neuron discharges only one kind of neurotransmitter across the synaptic cleft to a postsynaptic (receiving) neuron. However, later researchers found that not only are multiple neurotransmitters released in most synapses, but neurotransmitters can be discharged from nonsynaptic neuronal membranes and postsynaptic neurons can send chemical messages to presynaptic cells. Furthermore, the idea that thoughts, feelings, and behavior can be reduced to specific neuronal chemicals is overly simplistic. Neurotransmitter effects depend on a combination of the type of neurotransmitter, what kind of receptor (a transmitter-activated protein molecule) picks up the neurotransmitter, and where in the nervous system the chemicals are released. For example, drug addiction has been linked with high amounts of dopamine at D2 receptors in the mesolimbic system.

Although what is known about neurotransmitters is complex and somewhat hard to grasp, there are three general principles that clarify matters. First, neurotransmitters can be distinguished from one another by the thoughts, feelings, and behaviors with which they are most prominently associated. Second, neurotransmitters can be classified into a handful of categories based on their chemical structure. Third, most neurotransmitters tend to have either an excitatory (activating) or inhibitory (deactivating) effect on affected cells.

SMALL MOLECULE NEUROTRANSMITTERS
The first neurotransmitter discovered was acetylcholine. Acetylcholine is the primary neurotransmitter for stimulating muscles (atropine and botulism block its effects) and conveying information in the parasympathetic nervous system. In the central nervous system, acetylcholine promotes rapid eye movement (REM) sleep and is critical for learning: Foods high in choline—a precursor of acetylcholine—boost learning; low acetylcholine levels inhibit learning, such as in Alzheimer's disease.

Several small molecule transmitters are amines (substances containing NH2, an amino group). Four amines tend to have arousing effects. Dopamine is essential for experiencing pleasure and has been implicated in almost any kind of addiction. Low levels of dopamine are associated with depression, restless leg disorder, and Parkinson's disorder; very high levels are associated with schizophrenia and impulsiveness. Epinephrine and norepinephrine are related: Norepinephrine plays a primary role in arousal, vigilance, active emotions, and emotional memories. Stimulant drugs, such as amphetamines, activate norepinephrine pathways. Most norepinephrine receptors accept epinephrine, which is the primary neurotransmitter in the sympathetic nervous system. Histamine conducts itching sensations, and its release by mast cells causes the red flaring typical in allergic reactions. Unlike the other amines, higher levels of serotonin tend to induce a calming effect, reducing impulsivity and decreasing appetite. Low levels are linked with depression (selective serotonin reuptake inhibitors, or SSRIs, form a category of antidepressants that increase serotonin), increased aggression (including suicide), and sudden infant death syndrome. Many hallucinogenic drugs (for example, lysergic acid diethylamine, or LSD, and 3,4-methylenedioxy-N-methylamphetamine, known as MDMA or Ecstasy) appear to work by interacting with serotonin.

The three most prevalent neurotransmitters are amino acids (substances containing amino and carboxyl groups). Almost all synaptic excitation requires glutamate; almost all synaptic inhibition necessitates gamma-aminobutyric acid (GABA) in the brain or glycine in the spinal cord and lower brain areas. Glutamate is essential for learning; however, an overrelease can precipitate amnesia and neuronal death. Too much glutamate is also implicated in diseases of white matter (loss of myelin), such as multiple sclerosis; not enough glutamate is associated with schizophrenia. GABA has a sedative effect on the nervous system: Benzodiazepines, barbiturates, and alcohol bind on GABA receptors. Lack of GABA and glycine overactivates the nervous system and can induce disorders such as epilepsy (GABA deficits) and lockjaw (glycine deficits).

PEPTIDES

The largest group of neurotransmitters—several dozen—are peptides (amino acid chains). Two peptides have a complementary effect: Substance P is the main carrier of pain; beta endorphins decrease pain. Beta endorphins and enkephalins belong to a family of opiate chemicals produced by the brain that typically increase pleasure but may inhibit learning.

Neuropetides play a role in many basic drives, including drinking (vasopressin), eating (neuropeptide Y), and sexuality (oxytocin). Oxytocin, the hormone that is involved in uterine contractions and lactation, also serves as the bonding neurotransmitter. Higher levels of oxytocin stimulate and help to maintain pair bonding, parenting, and other prosocial behaviors.

LIPIDS, NUCLEOTIDES, AND GASES

The brain not only produces opioids but also cannabis-like lipids called endocannabinoids. One of these chemicals, anandamide, helps to regulate the release of several small molecule transmitters. Endocannabinoids appear to interact with opioids to produce pleasurable effects, and, as with the opioids, overrelease may interfere with learning.

Adenosine, a nucleotide involved in sleep production, is also released by the nervous system's other main cell type: glia. Caffeine has excitatory effects because it blocks adenosine receptors.

Two water-soluble gases, nitric acid and carbon monoxide, are neurotransmitters that can be released from any neuronal area, unlike all other neurotransmitters. Both neurotransmitters modulate the activity of other neurotransmitters and play a role in metabolic processes. Nitric oxide also dilates blood vessels: Erectile dysfunction drugs enhance the activity of nitric oxide.

BIBLIOGRAPHY

Bohlen und Halbach, Oliver von, and Rolf Dermietzel. *Neurotransmitters and Neuromodulators: Handbook of Receptors and Biological Effects*. Hoboken: Wiley, 2006. Print.

Carlson, Neil R. *Foundations of Physiological Psychology*. 7th ed. Boston: Allyn, 2008. Print.

Ingersoll, R. Elliott, and Carl F. Rak. *Psychopharmacology for Helping Professionals: An Integral Perspective*. Belmont.: Thomson, 2006. Print.

Julien, Robert M., Claire D. Advokat, and Joseph E. Comaty. *A Primer of Drug Action*. 12th ed. New York: Worth, 2011. Print.

Kandel, Eric R. *Principles of Neural Science*. 5th ed. New York: McGraw, 2013. Print.

Lajtha, Abel, and E. Sylvester Vizi, eds. *Handbook of Neurochemistry and Molecular Neurobiology: Neurotransmitter Systems*. 3rd ed. New York: Springer, 2008. Print.

Paul J. Chara, Jr.

SEE ALSO: Antianxiety medications; Antidepressant medications; Antipsychotic medications; Brain structure; Drug therapies; Nervous system; Neuropsychology; Psychopharmacology.

Nicotine dependence

TYPE OF PSYCHOLOGY: Psychopathology; Psychotherapy; Sensation and perception; Stress

Unlike many damaging addictive pursuits (other than the consumption of alcohol), the use of tobacco is legal in most cultures. Cigars, cigarettes, pipe tobacco, and chewing tobacco contain many chemicals, but the active, addictive ingredient in all of them is nicotine, which can create a craving in many people that is as acute (and as difficult to break) as that for heroin, cocaine, or other drugs.

KEY CONCEPTS

- Acetylcholine receptors
- Adrenaline
- Neurotransmitters

- *Nicotiana tabacum*
- Nicotine

INTRODUCTION

Nicotine produces a temporary mood-altering "lift," or "buzz," that encourages continued use and helps produce an addictive craving. The body receives nicotine (and other addictive substances) through receptors in the brain. Dependence increases slightly each time the drug is used, leading to more intense addiction. Thus, although going without the drug is easier for younger people, the addiction becomes more trenchant with age. Going without nicotine causes withdrawal symptoms, including irritability and anxiety, that vary in intensity and duration among individuals.

HISTORY AND HEALTH RISKS

The smoking of tobacco once was deemed healthy. Nicotine was named for the tobacco plant *Nicotiana tabacum*, which itself was named after Jean Nicot de Villemain, a French ambassador who imported it to Portugal in 1560 as a medicine.

Until the 1950s, university lecture halls were built with ashtrays, and indoor smoking was commonplace. The newsroom of the New York Times, for example, contained so many chain smokers (people who smoke one cigarette after another) in the 1930s that by the end of the workday janitors used push brooms to sweep away a carpet of butts an inch or two deep.

In 1963, however, the US Surgeon General issued a report linking smoking with a large number of health problems, including heart disease, stroke, and cancer. Since then, even the inhalation of tobacco effluvia from other people's lungs, so-called passive (or secondhand) smoking, especially by children, has been associated with health risks. The nicotine itself usually does not cause health risks. Other substances in tobacco, including tar and various chemicals, do most of the damage. As of 2012, about 18 percent of adults in the United States smoked tobacco, according to the Centers for Disease Control and Prevention. The percentage using tobacco was higher in other countries, such as China and Russia.

PHYSICAL AND PSYCHOLOGICAL CUES

Nicotine reaches the brain within seven to ten seconds after inhalation. One of the major symptoms of nicotine dependence (addiction) is an inability to go without smoking, even after serious attempts to stop. Other symptoms of addiction, according to the Mayo Clinic,

include anxiety, irritability, restlessness, difficulty concentrating, depressed mood, frustration or anger, increased hunger, insomnia, and constipation or diarrhea.

Continued use of tobacco even in the face of serious health problems is another obvious sign of serious addiction. Some people have been known to continue smoking even after lung-cancer surgery. Some people defend their "freedom" to smoke, as if engaging in addictive behavior could be defended as an exercise of free choice. Studies have found that a propensity to smoke may be related to genetic makeup. In other words, smoking behavior can be inherited, to a degree. Some people do not experience pleasure from the use of nicotine and are unlikely to continue its use after experimenting.

Beginning smoking at a young age increases the chances of serious and intense addiction later in life. Nicotine binds to nicotinic acetylcholine receptors in the brain, increasing levels of neurotransmitters that play a role in the brain's regulation of mood and behavior. Nicotine provides many people's brains with a shot of dopamine, a neurotransmitter, producing a brief sense of euphoria and relaxation that rewards continued use, reinforcing the physiological addiction of the drug. Use of nicotine also increases the flow of the stimulating hormone adrenaline (epinephrine). Nicotine also increases heart rate by about twenty beats per minute and elevates blood pressure, as it constricts arteries.

The combustion of tobacco provokes release of more than sixty cancer-causing chemicals. According to the American Lung Association, smoking plays a role in 90 percent of lung-cancer cases among men (80 percent among women), as well as in cases of emphysema and chronic bronchitis. It also aggravates asthma. Smoking plays a major role in cancers of the mouth, esophagus, larynx, and throat (pharynx). It plays a role in other pathologies in the kidneys, bladder, stomach, pancreas, cervix, stomach, and other parts of the body. It can increase the risk of impotence and infertility.

Tobacco dependence is a physical process that also brings into play psychological cues. A smoker's desire to increase his or her nicotine level may be linked to well-established daily rituals, such as morning coffee, drinking alcohol at a bar, or free time between tasks at work. Certain friends may provoke an urge to smoke. Smoking also can be associated with specific locations, such as a particular automobile. Stress can raise anxiety levels and lead to smoking. The smell of burning tobacco can increase the desire to use it. People who experience depression, schizophrenia, and other mental illnesses

Photo: iStock

Web. 22 May 2014.

Di Giovanni, Giuseppe. *Nicotine Addiction: Prevention, Health Effects, and Treatment Options.* Hauppauge: Nova Science, 2012. eBook Collection (EBSCOhost). Web. 22 May 2014.

Johnson, Bankole A. *Addiction Medicine: Science and Practice.* New York: Springer, 2011. eBook Collection (EBSCOhost). Web. 22 May 2014.

Koskinen, Charles J. *Handbook of Smoking and Health.* New York: Nova Science, 2011. eBook Academic Collection (EBSCOhost). Web. 22 May 2014.

Kozlowski, Lynn T., Jack E. Henningfield, and Janet Brigham. *Cigarettes, Nicotine, and Health: A Biobehavioral Approach.* Thousand Oaks: Sage, 2001. Print.

Wagner, Eric F., ed. *Nicotine Addiction among Adolescents.* New York: Haworth, 2000. Print.

Bruce E. Johansen

are, statistically speaking, more likely to smoke tobacco. Abusers of alcohol and illegal drugs also smoke in higher proportion than do other people. However, tobacco use has been studied as a treatment for schizophrenia, as well as for attention-deficit hyperactivity disorder (ADHD) and Parkinson's disease.

Products designed to help smokers quit using tobacco have become a multibillion-dollar industry worldwide. In some countries, smoking tobacco remains legal for adults, but the places where people can smoke have become limited. In the Netherlands, for example, the smoking of tobacco has become illegal in some cafés where the use of marijuana is allowed. California was the first US state to ban smoking in all enclosed work areas, doing so in 1995.

SEE ALSO: Addictive personality and behaviors; Alcohol dependence and abuse; Caffeine and mental health; Genetics and mental health; Substance use disorders.

Nonverbal communication and social cognition

TYPE OF PSYCHOLOGY: Language

Nonverbal communication describes all the wordless messages that people exchange, either intentionally or unintentionally. It plays an important role in the way people interact and is the primary means for communicating emotion, forming impressions, and communicating about relationships.

KEY CONCEPTS

- Chronemics
- Haptics
- Kinesics
- Leakage
- Olfaction
- Paralanguage

BIBLIOGRAPHY

Benowitz, Neal L., ed. *Nicotine Safety and Toxicity.* New York: Oxford UP, 1998. Print.

Bock, Gregory, and Jamie Goode, eds. *Understanding Nicotine and Tobacco Addiction.* Hoboken: Wiley, 2006. Print.

David, Sean P., Jennifer B. McClure, and Gary E. Swan. "Nicotine Dependence." *Handbook of Psychology. Vol. 9.* 2nd ed. 149–81. Hoboken: Wiley, 2013. PsycINFO.

- Proxemics
- Violation of expectations

INTRODUCTION

Most researchers accept Ray Birdwhistell's approximation that nonverbal communication accounts for at least 60 to 70 percent of what humans communicate to one another, although psychologist Albert Mehrabian estimates that as much as 93 percent of the emotional meaning of messages is transmitted nonverbally. Studies have shown that nonverbal messages are generally more believable than verbal ones; when verbal and nonverbal messages contradict one another, most people believe the nonverbal. Nonverbal communication is at least as important as verbal communication; however, the formal study of nonverbal communication is still in its infancy when compared to verbal communication.

Charles Darwin's *The Expression of the Emotions in Man and Animals* (1872) was one of the first studies to associate nonverbal behaviors of humankind with other species and to emphasize its function of indicating mood, attitude, and feeling. His research initiated the modern study of nonverbal communications, an interdisciplinary field that calls on scholars from linguistics, anthropology, sociology, physical education, physiology, communication, and psychology. The early works on nonverbal communication tended to be speculative, anecdotal, and tentative, but by 1960, major works began emerging that organized and synthesized the existing data from these diverse fields. Theoretical issues became clarified, and many methodological problems were solved.

IMPLICIT COMMUNICATION CODES

One of the most influential researchers in the nonverbal communication area has been Mehrabian, who calls this "implicit communication" because it is usually done subtly; people are generally not aware of sending or receiving nonverbal messages. Mehrabian found that nonverbal communication is used to communicate attitudes, emotions, and preferences, especially the following four: pleasure/displeasure; arousal/nonarousal; dominance/submissiveness; and liking/nonliking.

Each of these emotions is associated with a cluster of nonverbal actions that is communicated in one of seven different codes. Codes are organized message systems consisting of a set of symbols and the rules for their use. The eight nonverbal codes are physical appearance (especially height and body type); kinesics (the study of body movements, gestures, posture, and facial expressions); proxemics (the use of space as a special elaboration of culture); haptics (the study of touch and touching); chronemics (the study of how people use and structure time); olfactics; paralanguage (tone, pitch, accents, emphases, yawns, voice qualities, rate of speaking, and pauses) and silence; and artifacts (objects, such as clothing, jewelry, furniture, and cars, that are associated with people).

FUNCTIONS

Joseph DeVito and Michael Hecht state that nonverbal messages perform seven important functions. First, they provide information; this can occur deliberately or through leakage, as when a person reveals that he or she is lying by talking overly fast and in short sentences. Second, they regulate interaction, by telling people when to begin a conversation, whose turn it is to speak, and when the conversation is over. Kinesics, especially eye contact, is the main code used for this function. Third, nonverbal communication is the primary means of expressing emotions. Researchers have identified the nonverbal cues used in expressing the basic emotions of happiness, surprise, fear, anger, sadness, disgust, contempt, and interest. Paul Ekman and Wallace Friesen found that the expression and interpretation of emotions is universal; therefore, the nonverbal expression of emotion is probably biologically determined.

The fourth function of nonverbal communication is in exercising social control. Nonverbal messages of power and dominance can be used to control people and events. Fifth, nonverbal communication helps to accomplish specific tasks or goals (such as hitchhiking using the familiar hand gesture). Sixth, nonverbal messages are very important in telling the listener how to interpret a message; for example, sarcasm is signaled through paralanguage, and kinesics help to communicate empathy, as when the speaker leans forward and touches the listener while giving bad news. Finally, nonverbal messages present a person's self-image. Physical appearance is usually the major code used in forming first impressions; artifacts such as clothing, office furniture, hairstyle, and glasses can be used to create a variety of self-images. Paralanguage, such as a squeaky voice or a certain accent, may also help to create a particular image of a person.

CHARACTERISTICS

Just as verbal messages are often misunderstood, so are nonverbal messages. Three characteristics of nonverbal communication are important in understanding the potential for confusion that may exist in both sending and interpreting nonverbal messages. First, nonverbal communication is different from nonverbal behavior. Nonverbal communication consists of messages that are symbolic, that stand for something other than themselves. Nonverbal behavior does not stand for anything else. For example, if a listener avoids eye contact with a speaker because of an emotional response to the message or to the person, or if the speaker interprets the action that way, the action is nonverbal communication. If the listener avoids eye contact because the sun is in her eyes, and the speaker does not interpret it as meaningful, then the action is nonverbal behavior.

Second, nonverbal communication activity is rule-guided. These rules are arbitrary and unwritten; they are learned by observing others. Breaking these rules can provoke unpleasant emotional reactions; for example, staring at someone in an elevator can result in hostility. Because the nonverbal rules are arbitrary and may change from situation to situation (such as at home versus on the job), it is important to be a careful observer and learn the rules before acting.

The third characteristic is that nonverbal communication is strongly influenced by culture. Although all cultures interpret some nonverbal behaviors (such as smiling) in the same way, they also differ from one another in interpreting other nonverbal messages, such as proxemics. Many cultures, for example, allow a closer standing distance than does the culture of the United States, and this difference can often result in misunderstandings. Hand gestures that are innocent in one culture may be highly offensive in another.

INTERPERSONAL RELATIONSHIPS
Nonverbal communication has been used to examine almost every aspect of human behavior. Two of the most widely researched areas are interpersonal relationships and nonverbal communication in the workplace.

Nonverbal communication plays an important role in initiating, maintaining, and terminating relationships. One study identified fifteen cues that express a woman's interest in dating; almost all of these were nonverbal cues, including high amounts of eye contact, smiling, forward lean, shoulder orientation, close (about 45 centimeters, or 18 inches) proximity, and frequent touching. The men and women participants all agreed that a woman who displays these cues to a man is probably interested in dating him. More than two-thirds of the males surveyed said they prefer women to use these nonverbal messages to convey their interest in dating; less than one-third said they preferred a verbal approach. A similar study observed flirting behavior in a singles bar and catalogued fifty-two different nonverbal acts; the most frequently occurring were eye gaze, forward lean, smiles, and touch.

Nonverbal cues are also used to develop and maintain relationships. On dates, sexual intimacy is regulated by nonverbal cues, and increasing intimacy is marked through intimate physical contact. Desmond Morris, in his book *Intimate Behaviour* (1971), suggested twelve stages of contact in animal courtship that he believes apply generally to human beings: eye to body, eye to eye, voice to voice, hand to hand, arm to shoulder, arm to waist, mouth to mouth, hand to head, hand to body, mouth to breast, hand to genitals, and genitals to genitals. Finally, nonverbal cues are involved in relationship termination. There are many nonverbal signs that a relationship is ending, including chronemics (less time spent together), less touching and mutual eye contact, and fewer smiles.

UNDERSTANDING POWER IN THE WORKPLACE
Nonverbal communication on the job can determine who is hired, promoted, and fired. Power plays an important role in business organizations, and, as Mehrabian demonstrated, nonverbal communication is the implicit communication system through which power is manifested. The nonverbal codes that are most often used in communicating power are physical appearance, artifacts, kinesics, proxemics, haptics, and chronemics.

A person's height and physical size are important components of power and status. Research shows that taller men get better jobs, are paid larger salaries, and are perceived as having more status; overweight people have more problems getting hired and being accepted by colleges. Attractive people are more persuasive than unattractive people and are more likely to receive assistance and encouragement. Body shape is associated with a wide range of personality characteristics: For example, mesomorphs (bony, muscular, athletic) are identified as being dominant, confident, and adventurous; ectomorphs (tall, thin, fragile) with being shy, tense, and awkward; and endomorphs (soft, round, fat) with being dependent, sluggish, and sympathetic. People make these judgments unconsciously, and the impressions are usually difficult to overcome.

Artifacts function as symbols of power in four ways: First, they are symbols of the power structure within the organization; second, individuals who have access to them may rise to more powerful positions in the formal power structure; third, certain artifacts may be the actual rewards that maintain the organization through material reinforcement; and finally, artifacts of power may produce self-expectancies that actually cause the individual to act in a more powerful manner. Some examples of artifacts that symbolize power are large corner offices, reserved parking places, and expensive company cars and office furnishings. Clothing is an artifact that helps others determine a person's status, credibility, and persuasiveness; for example, in one study, job interviewers rated applicants who dressed in darker colors as more competent than applicants with the same qualifications who dressed in light colors. Kinesic postures and positions correspond to organizational positions in that superiors tend to be more kinesically expansive than subordinates. One kinesic sign of power is upright posture; another is a comfortable, relaxed seated position with the legs crossed, arms asymmetrically placed, and body leaning sideways and reclining slightly.

Numerous dominance and submission messages are sent via facial expressions because they convey emotional states and evaluations better than any other part of the body; the human face is capable of more than 250,000 different expressions. Among both primates and humans, smiling is a submissive gesture often displayed to appease a dominant aggressor. Eye gaze is another indicator of power; many researchers have found that higher-status persons look more when speaking and look less when listening than do lower-status persons. Apparently the high-status individual has both the ability and the prerogative to maintain visual attentiveness while speaking but is not obligated to reciprocate eye contact when listening. These gaze patterns during interactions may severely undercut or augment an individual's power.

In proxemics, as Nancy Henley points out in *Body Politics: Power, Sex, and Nonverbal Communication* (1979), dominant animals and dominant humans follow the same pattern: They control greater territory; they are free to move in territory belonging to others; subordinates yield space to them when approached, or in passing; they are accorded greater personal space; and they take up more space with their bodies and possessions. Haptic behavior is the most intimate form of nonverbal communication. Power and control are communicated through the initiation of touch. Empirically, touchers have been found to be significantly more dominant than recipients of touch, higher-status persons more frequently will touch lower-status persons, and direct poking with an index finger is a dominant act.

ROLE IN HUMAN DEVELOPMENT

Nonverbal communication was of interest primarily to elocutionists until 1872, when Darwin published his findings. Darwin aroused interest in nonverbal communication among researchers in many different fields, especially psychology. Nonverbal communication is of particular interest to the field of psychology for two reasons: its role in the development of human personality and its usefulness in treating patients with psychological disturbances.

Nonverbal communication, especially touch, plays an essential role in human development. Of the available forms of communication, haptics is the first form developed in infants. Babies explore their own bodies and their environment through touch. Psychologically, the infant, through self-exploration, begins the process of achieving self-identity, environmental identity, security, and well-being. The development of healthy individuals seems related to the amount of touch they receive as infants; for example, tactile deprivation has been associated with learning problems and lack of trust and confidence.

RELATIONSHIP WITH DISORDERS

Clinical psychologists have become increasingly interested in the relationship between psychological disorders and nonverbal behavior, and they have relied on a knowledge of the behavioral symptoms of maladjustment in diagnosing and treating psychological problems. Sigmund Freud believed that a patient's physical actions were at least as important as verbal actions in communicating the sources of psychological trauma.

Wilhelm Reich used relaxation exercises with his obsessive-compulsive patients; his belief was that actions and feelings are connected, and if feelings cannot be changed through discussions and insight, maybe they can be modified by simply changing a person's postures, gestures, and facial and vocal expressions. More recently, Reich's premise has been elaborated extensively by action-oriented therapies such as dance or body-awareness therapy. In some cases, the therapist tells the client to express different emotions through movement. By observing these movements, the therapist is able to find out which emotions the client typically and easily conveys and which he or she has trouble expressing. The latter are symptomatic of a more general difficulty, and the client is encouraged to express these particular feelings in movements. The improved ability to express such feelings in action can then provide the stimulus for a more explicit discussion of feelings.

OLFACTORY RESEARCH

In the 1990s, psychologists and other nonverbal researchers became interested in the role of olfaction (the study of how people use and perceive odors) and olfactory memory in affecting mood and behavior and in improving the learning process. They found that strong fragrances such as musk can cause mood changes. Synthetic aroma chemicals that are often used seem to be the culprit, but researchers have not yet discovered why smelling these chemicals would cause a person's mood to change. Researchers also discovered that olfaction affects behavior; for example, workers exposed to stimulating scents such as peppermint set higher goals and were more alert and productive than workers who were not exposed to the scents.

Finally, olfactory memory seems to play a role in learning. In one study, fragrance was sprayed in the classroom while the professor was lecturing. When students were tested, the same fragrance was sprayed. Students in the experimental group scored much higher and seemed to retain more of the knowledge than did students in the control group, who had not smelled the fragrance. The area of olfaction appears to be a promising one for nonverbal communication researchers.

BIBLIOGRAPHY

Gorman, Carol Kinsey. *The Nonverbal Advantage: Secrets and Science of Body Language at Work.* San Francisco: Berrett, 2008. Print.

Guerrero, Laura, Joseph A. DeVito, and Michael L. Hecht, eds. *The Nonverbal Communication Reader.* 3rd ed. Prospect Heights: Waveland, 2008. Print.

Hall, Judith, and Mark L. Knapp, eds. *Nonverbal Communication.* Boston: De Gruyter, 2013. Print.

Harper, Robert Gale, Arthur N. Wiens, and Joseph D. Matarazzo. *Nonverbal Communication: The State of the Art.* New York: Wiley, 1978. Print.

Henley, Nancy M. *Body Politics: Power, Sex, and Nonverbal Communication.* New York: Simon, 1986. Print.

Hickson, Mark L., Don W. Stacks, and Nina-Jo Moore. NVC, *Nonverbal Communication: Studies and Applications.* 4th ed. Los Angeles: Roxbury, 2002. Print.

Knapp, Mark L., and Judith A. Hall. *Nonverbal Communication in Human Interaction.* 8th ed. Belmont: Wadsworth, 2013. Print.

Matsumoto, David Ricky, Mark G. Frank, and Hyi Sung Hwang. *Nonverbal Communication: Science and Applications.* Thousand Oaks: Sage, 2013. Print.

Mehrabian, Albert. *Silent Messages: Implicit Communication of Emotions and Attitudes.* 2nd ed. Belmont: Wadsworth, 1981. Print.

Ting-Toomey, Stella. *Communicating across Cultures.* New York: Guilford, 1999. Print.

Karen Anding Fontenot

SEE ALSO: Attraction theories; Couples therapy; Emotional expression; Emotions; Facial feedback; Self-presentation; Strategic family therapy; Power; Workplace issues and mental health.

Nutrition and mental health

DATE: 1950s forward
TYPE OF PSYCHOLOGY: Biological bases of behavior

Nutrition potentially relieves symptoms associated with psychological conditions, enhances brain functioning, and might prevent some mental illnesses. Vitamin and mineral deficiencies impede brain development and can cause mental disorders. Mental illnesses often interfere with people consuming nutritious foods.

KEY CONCEPTS

- Amino acid
- Brain function
- Fatty acid
- Mineral
- Neurotransmitter
- Nutrient
- Omega-3
- Orthomolecular psychiatry
- Vitamin

INTRODUCTION

Nutrition is the acquisition of nutrients from foods to provide energy and maintain physiological systems and functions. In antiquity, the Greek physician Hippocrates prescribed certain foods to heal medical problems. Since then, health care providers have accepted the concept that food can aid in the treatment of some physical ailments. By the early twentieth century, some medical professionals had developed theories that nutrients obtained during digestion and distributed in blood might also be useful in alleviating mental illnesses by adjusting brain chemistry. Medical guides suggested that poor nutrition and toxins in food could be associated with mental disorders. After scientists discovered many vitamins in the 1920s, articles appeared in medical journals describing experiments into the use of vitamins, especially B and C, and minerals, such as manganese, as treatments to ease psychological symptoms.

During the 1950s, pharmaceutical companies increased the manufacturing of drugs for various psychological therapies and encouraged mental health professionals to prescribe them. Most physicians chose pharmaceuticals rather than nutrients to treat mental disorders. Research investigating how nutrition might help mental health was minimal in the following decades because of insufficient funding and interest. People who supported the use of nutrition to achieve mental health pointed out that studies had linked deficiencies in nutrients and unbalanced diets to various brain development problems. They argued that food influences brain structure and performance and that access to or deprivation of nutrients shapes mental health. Most scientific research in this field, however, has been too inconclusive to convince skeptics that nutrition has a valid role in mental health prevention or treatment.

Photo: iStock

ORTHOMOLECULAR RESEARCH

Some psychiatrists who were reluctant to rely on antipsychotic medications, including Canadian Abram Hoffer, tested theories that nutrients might aid patients experiencing mental disorders. In 1952, Hoffer initiated clinical trials in which he gave schizophrenic patients niacin (vitamin B3). Pleased by the results, he treated several thousand schizophrenics with nutritional therapies, using vitamin C and riboflavin, among other substances. With his colleague Humphry Osmond, Hoffer wrote "The Biochemistry of Mental Disease," which the *Canadian Medical Association Journal* printed in 1961. The next year, Hoffer and Osmond published *Niacin Theory in Psychiatry*. In 1963, their report, "Massive Niacin Treatment in Schizophrenia: Review of a Nine-Year Study," appeared in *Lancet*.

Other scientists recognized that naturally occurring vitamins and minerals in foods might be healthier treatments than prescription medicines, which posed such risks as side effects and physical reactions. In April, 1968, Nobel Prize-winning chemist Linus Pauling published "Orthomolecular Psychiatry" in *Science*, introducing the term "orthomolecular" to refer to using natural rather than manufactured resources for medical purposes. Pauling suggested that adjusting brain chemistry naturally with nutrients might help mental processes. Acceptance of orthomolecular practices at that time was hindered by many psychiatrists having minimal knowledge regarding nutrition.

In 1973, the American Psychiatric Association (APA) Task Force on Vitamin Therapy in Psychiatry criticized the use of vitamins and orthomolecular techniques. The task force's report targeted the work of Hoffer and Osmond, stating that their experiments testing vitamins for psychiatric treatment lacked scientific controls. The APA also denounced psychiatrists who accepted the popular media promoting orthomolecular studies. Hoffer and Osmond prepared a response defending their methods, which was published by the Canadian Schizophrenia Foundation in 1976. Other groups dismissed orthomolecular therapies for mental illnesses. The National Institute of Mental Health's Research Advisory Committee and the American Academy of Pediatrics noted the dangers of consuming too many vitamins.

Hoffer and Osmond continued their orthomolecular treatments for psychiatric diseases. Some mental health professionals recognized the importance of vitamin B to memory and cognition, particularly in geriatric patients.

Many, however, continued relying on tranquilizers to calm schizophrenics. Patients became aware of alternatives described in popular health guides published in the 1970s, 1980s, and 1990s. Many of those books used words such as psychonutrient, psychodietetics, and psychochemical, and promoted the use of vitamins and nutrients to solve common psychological complaints, especially depression. Some authors recommended herbal aids such as St. John's wort and gingko biloba.

At the start of the twenty-first century, mental health professionals disagreed as to whether nutrition could be credited with bringing about psychological improvements in patients, and the quantity of research examining nutrition and neurochemistry expanded. Many psychologists recognized the importance of nutrition in maintaining physical health. Some psychologist believed that nutrition could also help sustain mental health. Critics suggested that other factors, such as endorphins released when eating delicious food or dining with friends, had greater effects on patients' moods than nutrition did. Skeptics noted that many studies evaluating nutrition and mental health used supplements rather than food to test participants. They also pointed out that nutrition therapies relied on patients' eating correctly. Some researchers have continued investigating in this field in search of scientific validation for their theories concerning nutrition's role in influencing brain biochemistry. Future research may involve scientific trials to advance knowledge of people's unique genetic and metabolism factors and enable nutrients to be better used in psychotherapy.

NUTRITIONAL BALANCE
Nutrition is the primary source of vitamins, fatty acids, carbohydrates, phytonutrients, minerals, and proteins consisting of amino acids crucial to health but which human bodies cannot manufacture. Scientists have determined that approximately 60 percent of a typical human brain consists of fatty acids, including omega-3 fatty acids, which are considered essential for the brain to function normally. Researchers have linked consumption of fish, seeds, and nuts, which contain omega-3 fatty acids, to several mental health benefits. Toddlers whose mothers ate fish while pregnant often display better brain development than their peers whose mothers did not eat fish. Clinical studies suggest that omega-3 fatty acids improve focus in people with attention disorders. These fatty acids were also shown to ease panic attacks and stabilize moods.

Nutrients enable central nervous system neurotransmitters, most of which are amino acids, to send impulses to nerve cells. Amino acids create chemicals in the brain that balance moods, so an amino acid shortage can alter neurotransmitters' actions. For example, the amino acid tryptophan manufactures serotonin, which helps minimize depression and agitation. Tryptophan is found in poultry, cheese, soy, and other proteins. A tryptophan deficiency can contribute to depressed or angry moods.

Researchers hypothesize that because omega-3 fatty acids regulate serotonin activity in brains, they might alleviate depression better than antidepressants. The Royal College of Psychiatrists recognizes that omega-3 fatty acids may aid patients with schizophrenia, bipolar disorders, or mood disorders but warned against relying on them independent of pharmaceuticals.

Research suggests that people who do not consume or do not have access to nutritious foods experience mental impairment. Some scientists, such as Michael A. Crawford of the Institute of Brain Chemistry and Human Nutrition at London Metropolitan University, associate the rise in the number of mental disorders, including schizophrenia, depression, Alzheimer's disease, and attention-deficit hyperactivity disorder (ADHD), since the mid-twentieth century with reduced fish consumption and increased consumption of processed foods. Processed foods often contain omega-6 fatty acids and other substances, including additives, refined sugar, and saturated fat, which can impair cognitive abilities. Physiological processes, especially in brains, suffer when diets are draw mainly from convenience foods rather than from foods prepared using fresh ingredients.

Researchers affiliated with the Mental Health Foundation (MHF) in the United Kingdom stated in the foundation's 2006 report, *Feeding Minds: The Impact of Food on Mental Health*, that changes in how livestock and crops are cultivated and converted into food have resulted in the loss of important vitamins, fats, and minerals, and that the pesticides and hormones used leave harmful chemicals in the food. The foundation's researchers found that a nutrient-deficient diet with added omega-6 fatty acids has a negative impact on mental health. An affiliated group, Sustain, distributed the report, *Changing Diet, Changing Minds: How Food Affects Mental Health, Well-Being, and Behaviour*, seeking to improve farming techniques to produce healthful foods and to influence consumers' attitudes regarding nutrients.

In April, 2006, the nonprofit Food for the Brain program started educating British schoolchildren about the need to eat nutritiously and avoid junk foods for good mental health. Participants learned about nutrients necessary to maintain healthy brains for desired thinking skills, behavior, and resiliency to such mental conditions as depression. Several studies observed that children and teenagers who ate breakfasts representing varied food groups exhibited better moods than peers who consumed sugary foods or did not eat breakfast.

MENTAL DISORDERS AND NUTRITION

Some scientists have hypothesized that foods can cause mental disorders. Since the 1960's, researchers have noted that people with an allergy to gluten, a protein in grains, sometimes exhibit psychological distress. In 2004, the *British Medical Journal* reported that some schizophrenics are gluten intolerant. Researchers looked at whether gluten, usually associated with celiac disease, might be a factor causing schizophrenia. They found that removing gluten from schizophrenics' diets often eased symptoms. Psychologist Patrick Holford, who studied with Hoffer and Pauling, served as director of the Institute for Optimum Nutrition and the Brain Bio Centre. He recognized that food allergies could impair mental health. The Brain Bio Centre devised nutritional plans for patients, based on physical examinations to identify nutritional vulnerabilities. These plans were designed to use appropriate foods, with nutrients recommended for specific mental conditions, to balance brain biochemistry.

Mental health professionals often monitor patients with mental disorders to ensure that they eat healthful foods. Caregivers note any distorted ideas that mentally ill patients may have that could interfere with therapeutic nutrition. People with eating disorders are often affected by nutrient deficiencies, and their psychiatric treatment includes the restoration of adequate nourishment to their body and brain. Mental illness affects how aware people are of their own nutritional needs as well as those of any one who depends on them. Clinical trials have demonstrated that some mothers with mental disorders neglect their children's nutrition, both before and after birth.

Malnourishment intensifies some mental health concerns. Deficiencies of zinc are often associated with ADHD. Diets insufficient in iodine damage brains and can cause mental retardation. Malnutrition deprives pregnant women of crucial nutrition and is usually detrimental to prenatal brain development. In 2004, the United Nations Children's Fund estimated that each year insufficient vitamins and minerals result in the deaths of one million children and in impaired mental abilities in twenty million youths. Approximately 250,000 infants are born with defects each year. The Micronutrient Initiative reported that iodine deficiencies annually result in eighteen million infants displaying symptoms of mental retardation. Adults also suffer, with iodine deficiencies affecting approximately 700 million people in 2006. Health professionals realized that fortifying salt with iodine and enriching flour with thiamine, riboflavin, or niacin could prevent some nutritional dilemmas.

BIBLIOGRAPHY

Bottomley, Alan, and Jane McKeown. "Promoting Nutrition for People with Mental Health Problems." *Nursing Standard* 22.49 (13 Aug. 2008): 48–55. Print.

Christensen, Larry. *Diet-Behavior Relationships: Focus on Depression.* Washington: APA, 1996. Print.

Dunne, Annette. "Food and Mood: Evidence for Diet-Related Changes in Mental Health." *British Journ. of Community Nursing.* Nutrition Supplement, Nov. 2012: S20–24. Print.

Hoffer, Abram. *Vitamin B-3 and Schizophrenia: Discovery, Recovery, Controversy.* Kingston: Quarry Press, 1999. Print.

Holford, Patrick. *Optimum Nutrition for the Mind.* Bergen: Basic Health Publications, 2004. Print.

Kaplan, Bonnie J., Susan G. Crawford, Catherine J. Field, and J. Steven A. Simpson. "Vitamins, Minerals, and Mood." *Psychological Bulletin* 133. 5 (September 2007): 747–60. Print.

Leyse-Wallace, Ruth. *Nutrition and Mental Health.* Boca Raton: Taylor, 2013. Print.

Logan, Alan C. *The Brain Diet: The Connection Between Nutrition, Mental Health, and Intelligence.* Rev. ed. Nashville: Cumberland House, 2007. Print.

Null, Gary. *The Food-Mood Connection: Nutritional and Environmental Approaches to Mental Health and Physical Well-Being.* Rev. ed. New York: Seven Stories, 2008. Print.

Oddy, Wendy H. "Fatty Acid Nutrition, Immune, and Mental Health Development Through Childhood." *Frontiers in Nutrition Research.* eEd. Julie D. Huang. New York: Nova Science, 2006. Print.

Rahman, Atif, Vikram Patel, Joanna Maselko, and Betty Kirkwood. "The Neglected 'M' in MCH Programmes— Why Mental Health of Mothers Is Important for Child Nutrition." *Tropical Medicine & International Health* 13.4 (April 2008): 579–83. Print.

Terry, Nicola. "Food and Mood." *Therapy Today* 25.1 (2014): 14–18. Print.

Elizabeth D. Schafer

SEE ALSO: Anorexia nervosa and bulimia nervosa; Antipsychotic medications; Brain structure; Caffeine and mental health; Drug therapies; Eating disorders; Obesity; Psychopharmacology.

O

Obesity

TYPE OF PSYCHOLOGY: Biological bases of human behavior; Developmental; Family; Health; Social

KEY CONCEPTS
- Adiponectin
- Binge eating disorder
- Emotional eating
- Epigenetics
- Leptin
- Ghrelin

INTRODUCTION

The Centers for Disease Control (CDC) estimates that one-third of Americans are obese. Obesity is determined by having a body mass index (BMI) over 30 kg/m2 which is a calculation based on height and weight. Although obesity appears to be a physical condition, the root cause is almost always psychological in nature. Obese people tend to suffer from issues such as depression, eating disorders, sleep deprivation, anxiety, or stress. Of course there are biological factors that come into play as well such as hormonal imbalances, genetics, inflammation, and slowed metabolic processes. Generally, psychological issues compound physiological conditions that predispose people to becoming obese. Once a person is obese a sense of hopelessness to reverse the condition is also quite common. Awareness of the psychological connection to obesity is growing, and therapy is starting to be incorporated more and more frequently in attempts to treat the obesity epidemic in our country.

THE EFFECT OF GENETICS ON OBESITY

Obesity does not happen overnight and usually develops from a combination of factors. Biological conditions play a major role in becoming obese. Some people are predisposed to gaining weight based on epigenetics, or gene expression. Epigenetics plays a role in the size, number, and regional distribution of fat cells in the body. A person's resting metabolic rate and set point theory are also determined by genetics. The set point theory states that the body will slow down or speed up metabolism in order to maintain a certain predisposed weight.

BIOLOGICAL AND HORMONAL CAUSES OF OBESITY

In addition to genetics, hormones also play a major role in the potential to become obese. For example, the body's cells may become insulin resistant. Insulin is secreted by the pancreas when blood sugar levels rise after eating a meal. Typically this stimulates uptake of glucose into the cell which causes blood sugar levels to go down and signals the brain to stop eating. Insulin resistance prevents this entire process, resulting in high blood sugar levels and the brain not knowing it is time to stop eating. A lack of production of a hormone called adiponectin may also contribute to obesity. Adiponectin is made by fat cells to help improve insulin function and uptake; therefore low levels will result in the potential for obesity. Leptin is a hormone produced by fat cells which senses energy stores and signals the brain to decrease intake. Therefore, low leptin levels may result in weight gain. Lastly, ghrelin, the "hunger hormone" increases appetite and typically decreases after a meal. High levels of ghrelin may also result in weight gain.

ENVIRONMENTAL CAUSES OF OBESITY

Certain environmental factors may also contribute to obesity. Low income may result in people buying less expensive foods which are high in fat, sugar, and sodium and low in healthy nutrients. Fast food restaurants are notorious for offering unhealthy menu items that are cheap and convenient. Low income areas usually have a plentitude of fast food chains and convenience stores. This creates a struggle for people who want to eat healthy but just do not have physical or monetary access to healthier food choices. Some people living in low income areas do not have adequate transportation to travel to other locations to buy food. Sixty percent of Americans are food insecure; they lack reliable access to a sufficient quantity of affordable, nutritious food. An obese individual may be suffering from malnutrition even though he or she appears to be well-nourished.

PSYCHOSOCIAL CAUSES OF OBESITY

Emotional Eating. The etiology for obesity is usually a combination of genetic, biological, environmental, and psychological risk factors. People suffering from psychological issues such as depression and anxiety have a greater tendency to lose control of their eating patterns and lack the motivation to exercise regularly. People may also engage in emotional eating which refers to using food as a coping mechanism when they feel sad, lonely, angry, or anxious. Emotional eating often results in people not understanding why they are gaining weight since they feel disconnected and distracted during the eating process. Eating under distress results in a vicious cycle where the person feels guilty for the behavior but keeps resorting to it for the short-term pleasure. A genetic predisposition for weight gain and slowed metabolism, along with an environment lacking healthy snacks, may create the perfect storm for obesity to ensue.

Eating Disorders. Although eating disorders have a stigma of only defining food deprivation diseases such as anorexia nervosa and bulimia, eating excessive amounts of food is also considered to be a disordered eating pattern. Binge eating disorder (BED), or "mindless eating," occurs when people overeat at meals, engage in frequent snacking on high calorie foods, and/or secretly eat at night. BED is currently included in the Diagnostic and Statistical Manual of Mental Disorders (DSM-5) and is characterized by recurrent episodes of eating during a discrete period of time. This overeating occurs at least two days a week over a six month period. People with BED consume large quantities of food, quantities much larger than most people eat during a similar amount of time. People with BED also lack a sense of control during the episodes and typically feel guilt or distress following these episodes. One major difference between BED and other eating disorders such as anorexia and bulimia is that BED is not associated with any regular compensatory behaviors such as fasting, purging, or excessive exercise. Therefore, people suffering from BED become overweight and obese.

THE PSYCHOSOCIAL IMPACT OF OBESITY

American society has become obsessed with doing whatever is necessary to have the perfect body. Cultural ideals such as "thin is in" and "skinniness is next to godlessness" can be extremely disheartening for an overweight individual. Obese individuals are extremely aware of society's negative views about their condition, resulting in feelings of shame and humiliation in their own skin. A viscous cycle may begin where people feel that they are overweight because they eat and they eat because they are overweight. Obese individuals may refrain from

social gatherings for fears that people are judging their food choices against their size. They may also feel embarrassed to attend events because they are worried people will make fun of them. In short, obesity may result in psychosocial isolation. Human beings that do not receive positive nurturing from friends and family may have increased risk for depression, anxiety, and loneliness.

SELF-MANAGEMENT

Current political campaigns are aimed at obesity prevention. This is an interesting concept because obesity is a measure of size; therefore obesity prevention literally can be interpreted as "size prevention." This clearly does not make sense. Obesity prevention is not the answer. The answer is actually balancing energy intake with physical activity. Although the diet industry has made billions of dollars from the suggestion that gaining weight may be prevented by taking a tiny pill, unfortunately it is not that simple. A lifestyle adjustment is absolutely imperative for an individual to lose weight and maintain his or her new physique. "Obesity prevention" can only occur when people listen to the hunger and satiety cues of their own bodies. Meeting with a registered dietitian to determine an appropriate meal plan may be an excellent start to learning how to eat a well-balanced diet while meeting appropriate nutrient and energy requirements. In addition, an exercise physiologist can help customize an attainable exercise regimen. Lastly, when an individual feels hopeless and depressed, a therapist may help overcome some of the mental health issues presenting barriers to a healthy lifestyle.

BIBLIOGRAPHY

Carr, D., & Friedman, M.A. (2005). "Is Obesity Stigmatizing? Body Weight, Perceived Discrimination, and Psychological Well-being in the United States. *Journal of Health and Social Behavior*, 46(3), 244-259.

Greenberg, I., Perna, F., Kaplan, M., & Sullivan, M. (2005). "Behavioral and Psychological Factors in the Assessment and Treatment of Obesity Surgery Patients". *Obesity Research*, 13(2), 244-249.

Stunkard, A., Grace, W., & Wolff, H. (1955). "The Night-Eating Syndrome: A Pattern of Food Intake Among Certain Obese Patients". *American Journal of Medicine*, 19, 78-86.

Swencionis, C., & Rendell, S. (2012). "The Psychology of Obesity". *Abdominal Imaging*, 37(5), 733-737. DOI: 10.1007/s00261-012-9863-9

Dawn Ortiz

SEE ALSO: Binge eating; Diet; Eating disorder; Health; Impulse control.

Observational learning and modeling therapy

TYPE OF PSYCHOLOGY: Learning; Personality; Psychotherapy

Many behaviors are acquired through observing the behaviors of others, and this phenomenon, known as observational learning, has been the subject of extensive scientific theorizing and research. Modeling therapies are a major application of observational learning theory and principles. These therapies primarily have been used to alleviate skill deficits that are associated with psychiatric disorders and to treat fear and anxiety.

KEY CONCEPTS

- Imitation
- Modeling
- Skills training
- Vicarious consequences
- Vicarious extinction
- Vicarious punishment
- Vicarious reinforcement

INTRODUCTION

Observational learning refers to acquiring information and changing one's behaviors as a consequence of having observed another's behaviors. It is a major form of learning for humans and primates (hence the expression, "Monkey see, monkey do"). Humans can and do acquire the gamut of behaviors they are capable of performing through observational learning, including verbal and motor skills, attitudes, preferences, values, body language and mannerisms, and emotional responses such as fear. Whereas many behaviors can be learned through Pavlovian and instrumental conditioning, frequently they are acquired more quickly through observational learning. Moreover, it is doubtful that some behaviors, such as language skills, could be acquired without observational learning.

Observational learning requires two parties: a model who explicitly or implicitly demonstrates some behavior and an observer who is exposed to the demonstration. The components of the model's behavior are known as modeling cues, which can be either live or symbolic. Live modeling occurs when the model is physically present; symbolic modeling occurs when the model is not physically present, as in movies, books, television, and any oral description of a person's behaviors. For instance, myths and fairy tales provide archetypal models of roles (such as mother and hero) and values (such as loyalty and honesty) that constitute the fabric of human existence.

STAGES

There are three sequential stages of observational learning: exposure, acquisition, and acceptance. First, the observer must be exposed to a model. Every day, people are exposed to countless models, but they pay attention to and remember only a small subset of those modeling cues. The second stage involves the observer's learning (acquiring) the modeling cues and storing them in memory. If the second stage is reached, observational learning has taken place. However, this does not necessarily mean that the observer's behaviors will change because of the acquired modeling cues. In fact, people act on relatively few of the modeling cues that they acquire.

If one's behavior changes based on modeling cues one has acquired, this occurs in the third stage of observational learning, which is called acceptance because one accepts a model's behaviors as a guide for one's own. Acceptance can consist of imitation, which involves acting as the model has, or counterimitation, which involves acting differently than the model has. In each case, the outcome can be direct or indirect. Thus, acceptance can take one of four forms, illustrated by a child observing a parent putting coins in a street beggar's cup.

In direct imitation, the observer copies or does virtually the same thing as the model has done (for example, the child puts change in a beggar's cup). In direct counterimitation, the observer does virtually the opposite of what the model did (the child passes by a beggar without donating change). With indirect imitation, the observer generalizes the model's behavior and acts in a similar, but not exactly the same, way (at school the child donates a toy to a fund for needy children). With indirect counterimitation, the observer generalizes from the model's behavior and acts differently, but not exactly the opposite way (the child does not donate to the toy fund).

During exposure, observers are exposed not only to the model's behavior but also to the consequences of the model's behavior. These consequences influence the observer indirectly or vicariously, which is why they are known as vicarious consequences. Vicarious reinforcement refers to a positive or favorable outcome for the model's behaviors, and vicarious punishment refers to a negative or unfavorable outcome. Vicarious consequences influence both the acquisition and acceptance stages of observational learning. By focusing the observer's attention on the model's actions, vicarious consequences enhance acquisition. In the acceptance stage, vicarious reinforcement increases the likelihood that the observer will imitate the model's actions, whereas vicarious punishment increases the likelihood that the observer will counterimitate. These effects occur because observers believe that they are likely to receive similar consequences for imitating the model.

There are other factors than vicarious consequences that can influence acceptance. For example, in general, imitation is more likely to occur when observers perceive models to be similar to themselves, prestigious, competent, and attractive (factors that are well known to the advertising industry).

SCIENTIFIC RESEARCH

The formal, scientific study of observational learning was begun in 1941 with the publication of *Social Learning and Imitation* by Yale University psychologist Neal E. Miller and sociologist John Dollard. However, their studies and theorizing essentially were restricted to direct imitation. It was psychologist Albert Bandura at Stanford University who spearheaded the broad study of observational learning with the publication in 1963 of a small but highly influential book titled *Social Learning and Personality Development* (coauthored by Canadian psychologist Richard H. Walters).

Among Bandura's most influential investigations is the now-classic Bobo doll study. Nursery school boys and girls were shown a five-minute modeling film depicting an adult engaging in discrete, novel, aggressive acts toward an adult-sized inflated plastic Bobo doll (shaped like a bowling pin). The physically aggressive acts (for example, hitting Bobo with a mallet) were accompanied by verbal expressions of aggression ("Soceroo . . . stay down"). One group of children saw the model reinforced for her aggressive behaviors, a second group saw the model punished, and a third group saw her receive no consequences. Next, to ascertain the degree to which the children in each group would spontaneously imitate the model (a measure of acceptance), each child was left alone in a room with a Bobo doll and a variety of toys, including all those used by the model in her assault of Bobo. The child was observed unobtrusively from behind a one-way glass. Following this free-play period, the experimenter reentered the room and offered the child

juice and stickers as incentives for showing the experimenter what the model had done (a measure of acquisition). The incentives were given to overcome any inhibitions the child might have had for acting aggressively (which is not socially acceptable behavior).

The results of the experiment showed that all of the children learned more aggressive behaviors than they spontaneously performed, and this was especially true for the children exposed to vicarious punishment. Bandura's study supported the critical distinction between the behaviors one learns from models (acquisition) and the behaviors one subsequently engages in (acceptance). Moreover, one of the most remarkable findings of the study was that many of the children engaged in precisely the behaviors they observed the model perform (direct imitation). Subsequently, the effects of violence in television programs on the aggressive behaviors of children and adolescents have been studied extensively. Not surprisingly, the general findings have been that viewing television violence is related to and can be the cause of aggressive behaviors.

Prosocial behaviors also are influenced by modeling. For example, psychologists James Bryan and Mary Ann Test demonstrated that exposure to a model engaging in altruistic behavior in a naturalistic setting would increase imitation for people who observe the model. In one study titled "Lady in Distress: A Flat Tire Study," a college-aged woman stood beside her Ford Mustang that had a flat left rear tire and a spare tire leaning against the car. In the modeling period, a quarter of a mile before reaching the disabled Mustang, motorists passed another car with a flat tire and a man changing the tire as a woman looked on. In the control period, the modeling scene was absent. The presence of the model significantly increased the number of motorists who stopped to offer assistance. In another of Bryan and Test's naturalistic experiments titled "Coins in the Kettle," once every sixty seconds a man approached a Salvation Army kettle outside a large department store and donated money. The first twenty seconds after the model made his donation was considered the modeling period and the third twenty-second period after the modeling sequence was considered the no-modeling period. Donations occurred significantly more often in the modeling periods than in the no-modeling periods.

MODELING THERAPIES

A major practical application of modeling theory and principles has been to provide psychotherapy and remediation for psychiatric disorders and other problem behaviors. Modeling therapies have primarily been used for two problems: to alleviate skill deficits that are associated with psychiatric disorders and to treat fear and anxiety. Modeling also is employed extensively in training psychotherapists.

TREATMENT OF SKILL DEFICITS

Modeling is a major component of skills training; other components include direct instruction, behavior rehearsal, feedback, prompting (providing cues as to how to perform a behavior), and shaping (being reinforced for closer and closer approximations of a behavior). Modeling often is essential, because direct instruction may not convey the subtleties of complex skills ("seeing" the behavior may be necessary) and prompting and shaping may not be adequate. One of the earliest applications of skills training was in teaching language and other social skills to children who completely lacked these skills. In the eighteenth century, Jean-Marc-Gaspard Itard attempted to socialize the Wild Boy of Aveyron, a child who grew up without human contact. More recently, in the 1960s, psychologist Ivar Lovaas pioneered the most successful treatment yet developed for ameliorating some of the massive social skills deficits shown by children with autism. Modeling has played an essential role in this treatment, although children with autism often have not learned to imitate in the course of their development. Accordingly, they must first be taught to imitate, which is accomplished through prompting and shaping. Other clinical populations that have serious social skill deficits and have benefited from skills training include children who rarely interact with peers or interact inappropriately (for example, only aggressively); children and adolescents with physical and language disabilities; people of all ages who are not acting assertively in their lives; hospitalized adults with schizophrenia; and the elderly in nursing homes.

Self-modeling is a unique technique in which clients serve as their own models of adaptive behaviors. Self-modeling capitalizes on the similarity of the model and the observer, which enhances imitation. Developed by psychologist Peter Dowrick, the technique involves preparing a videotape of the client performing the desired behavior (such as appropriately approaching peers and asking them to play a game) and then having the client watch the videotape. Because the client is having difficulty performing the behavior, various "tricks" are used to create the videotape. For instance, clients may be assisted in performing the behavior by the therapist's prompting and modeling the behaviors off-camera, but the final video does not show the assistance. When sustaining a behavior is the problem, brief segments of the client engaging in the behavior are taped and then strung together so that the final videotape shows the client performing the behavior for an extended period.

TREATMENT OF FEAR AND ANXIETY

Fear or anxiety may consist of an emotional component and a behavioral component; the former involves anticipation of negative consequences (such as getting into an accident while driving in traffic) while the latter involves a skill deficit (not knowing how to drive in traffic). Both of these issues can be dealt with when a model performs a feared behavior (such as demonstrating how to drive in traffic) with no negative consequences occurring (the model does not have an accident). This process, known as vicarious extinction, is facilitated by a coping model who, like the observer, is initially fearful and incompetent. The coping model engages in the fear-evoking behavior and gradually becomes less fearful and more competent. Both live and symbolic models are suitable.

The use of a live coping model is illustrated by participant modeling in which the therapist first demonstrates the fear-evoking behavior for the client and then encourages and physically guides the client in performing it. One case involved a forty-nine-year-old woman who had been intensely afraid of crossing streets for ten years and, as a consequence, had withdrawn from social interactions almost completely. The therapist first crossed a street with little traffic while the woman watched. Then, in graduated steps, the therapist, with her arm around the woman's waist, walked with the woman across the street. This was repeated until the woman felt comfortable. With each crossing, the therapist decreased the amount of physical contact with the client until the therapist just walked beside and then behind the woman. Finally, the therapist gradually reduced the distance she accompanied the woman across the street until the woman was able to cross on her own.

FILM AND VIDEO MODELING

Although live modeling can be customized to the client and can be highly efficacious, it may not be cost-effective in terms of therapist time. Symbolic modeling in the form of films and videos, once they are made, can be shown to many people with little or no therapist time required. A major application of film or video modeling has been in the prevention and treatment of fear of medical and dental procedures.

This work was begun by psychologist Barbara Melamed in the 1970s with her modeling film *Ethan Has an Operation*. The sixteen-minute film depicts the experiences of a seven-year-old boy who is about to have surgery to repair a hernia. In its fifteen scenes, the film shows all of the events children who undergo elective surgery are likely to encounter, from admission to discharge. These included Ethan having blood samples taken; the surgeon and anesthesiologist's preoperation consultation with Ethan; Ethan being separated from his mother when wheeled to the operating room; the operating room with all its potentially frightening machines; and Ethan being in the recovery room. Ethan serves as a coping model who initially exhibits apprehension and fear and then gradually copes with these emotions and successfully goes through each stage of the surgical process. The film has been demonstrated to reduce children's anxiety as well as behavioral problems related to surgery.

Ethan Has an Operation has been widely distributed, and in one survey it was estimated that one-third of all pediatric hospitals in the United States use modeling films to prepare children for surgery and related medical procedures. Other specific modeling films for children, adolescents, and adults have been designed to target fear and distress related to specific medical procedures ranging in severity from receiving an injection to undergoing a bone marrow transplant. Similar films have been produced to help children and adults cope with dental procedures, such as having one's teeth cleaned for the first time. Other, less expensive forms of symbolic modeling, such as coloring books that depict children undergoing medical and dental procedures, have been published. In all cases, coping models are used.

EVALUATION

In general, modeling therapies have been shown to be at least as effective as alternative treatments with which they have been compared; in some cases, such as in reducing children's fears, they are more effective. Modeling therapies are very efficient interventions and sometimes can result in significant changes after only one or two exposures to appropriate models. A number of factors may account for this. Modeling is simultaneously able to teach clients adaptive behaviors, prompt and motivate their performing them, and reduce anxiety clients have about engaging in the adaptive behaviors (such as fear of being rebuffed when acting assertively). Reinforcement need not be administered, because observational learning can occur without reinforcement. Standard symbolic modeling in the form of films or videos and pamphlets can be used with many clients, thereby rendering such interventions highly cost-effective once they have been produced. Nonprofessional change agents, such as parents, can easily be trained to administer modeling treatments at home. Finally, therapists can instruct clients to expose themselves, on their own, to natural models, people in their everyday environments who would serve as good exemplars because they exhibit the adaptive behaviors that would benefit the clients.

Clients consider modeling therapies to be an acceptable form of treatment. Because modeling is inherently subtle and unintrusive, clients do not feel manipulated or coerced, as they might in more directive forms of therapy. When clients feel freer and in control of their treatment, they are more likely to change.

BIBLIOGRAPHY

Bandura, Albert. *Social Foundations of Thought and Action: A Social Cognitive Theory*. Englewood Cliffs: Prentice, 1986. Print.

Bandura, Albert, and Richard H. Walters. *Social Learning and Personality Development*. New York: Holt, 1963. Print.

Fryling, Mitch J., Cristin Johnston, and Linda J. Hayes. "Understanding Observational Learning: An Interbehavioral Approach." *Analysis of Verbal Behavior* 27.1 (2011): 191–203. Print.

Hearold, Susan. "A Synthesis of 1,043 Effects of Television on Social Behavior." *Public Communication and Behavior*. Ed. George Comstock. New York: Academic, 1986. Print.

Hoppitt, William. *Social Learning: An Introduction to Mechanisms, Methods, and Models*. Princeton: Princeton UP, 2013. Print.

Hughes, Claire. *Social Understanding and Social Lives*. New York: Psychology, 2011. Print.

Lovaas, O. Ivar. *The Autistic Child: Language Development through Behavior Modification*. New York: Irvington, 1980. Print.

Striefel, Sebastian. *How to Teach through Modeling and Imitation*. 2nd ed. Austin: Pro-Ed, 1998. Print.

Michael D. Spiegler

SEE ALSO: Anxiety disorders; Bandura, Albert; Bobo doll experiment; Learning; Observational methods; Phobias; Punishment;

Qualitative research; Social learning: Albert Bandura; Violence and sexuality in the media; Violence: Psychological causes and effects.

Observational methods

TYPE OF PSYCHOLOGY: Psychological methodologies

Humans are poor observers: they omit, overemphasize, and distort various aspects of what they have seen. Observational methods in psychology have been devised to control or to eliminate this problem. These methods increase the accuracy of observations by reducing the effects of perceptual distortion and bias. The development of this methodology has been central to the evolution of scientific psychology..

KEY CONCEPTS
- Behavioral taxonomy
- Interrater reliability
- Operational definition
- Reliability
- Validity

INTRODUCTION

Humans have tremendous difficulty making accurate observations. Different people will perceive the same event differently; they apply their own interpretations to what they see. One's perception or recollection of an event, although it seems accurate, may well be faulty. This fact creates problems in science, because science requires objective observation.

In large part, this problem is eliminated through the use of scientific instruments to make observations. Many situations exist, however, in which the experimenter is still the recorder. Therefore, methods must be available to prevent bias, distortion, and omission from contaminating observations. Behavior may be observed within natural settings. When using naturalistic observation, scientists only watch behavior; they do not interfere with it.

HISTORY OF RESEARCH

The need for an observational methodology that ensures objective data became apparent early in the history of scientific psychology. In fact, in 1913, John B. Watson, an early American behaviorist, stated that for psychology to become a science at all, it must eliminate the influence of subjective judgment. Watson's influence caused psychology to shift from the subjective study of mental processes to the objective study of behavior. Shifting the focus to behavior improved the reliability of observation dramatically. Behavior is tangible and observable. In the 1920s, the operational definition—a description of behavior in terms that are unambiguous, observable, and easily measured—was introduced. Through using such definitions, communication between psychologists improved greatly. Psychologists were then able to develop experiments that met the scientific criterion of repeatability. Repeatability means that different researchers must be able to repeat the experiment and get similar results.

It soon became apparent, however, that this was not enough. It was discovered that the expectations of researchers biased their observations. This was true even when observations were focused on operationally defined behavior. Methods had to be developed to eliminate these effects, and this led to the development of techniques to reduce or control for experimenter bias. The technique of interrater reliability is an example of one such method. Using observers uninformed about the researchers' expectations also reduces experimenter bias.

In 1976, Robert Rosenthal reported results that showed that subject expectations can also contaminate observational data. It was found that simply observing subjects alters their behavior. How it changes depends on the subjects' interpretation of the situation and their motivation. If subjects could discover what the experimenters' expectations were, they could decide to help or to hinder the progress of the research. This type of reactivity severely contaminates the accuracy of observational data. Although this is a problem associated primarily with human research, animals also react to observers. This is why it is important to allow sufficient time for animals under observation to habituate to one's presence. Efforts to refine and improve observational methodology continue. Attention is now primarily directed at developing equipment to automate the observational process. The goal is to improve objectivity by removing the experimenter from the situation altogether.

BEHAVIORAL TAXONOMY

To make observation as accurate and objective as possible, researchers use behavioral taxonomy. A behavioral taxonomy is a set of behavioral categories that describe the behavior of the subjects under study. To develop a behavioral taxonomy, the experimenter must first spend time simply watching the population of interest. The observer's presence will alter the subjects' behavior at first. Organisms are reactive, so their initial behavior in the presence of an observer is not typical. Once they become accustomed to being observed, however, behavior returns to normal. This initial observation period, called the habituation period, is important for two reasons. First, it allows the subjects time to become accustomed to the observer's presence. Second, the researcher learns about the subjects by observing them in as many different situations as possible. During this time a diary is kept. Behaviors and their possible functions are jotted down as they are seen. This diary would not be entirely accurate. The observer might distort how often a behavior occurred or perhaps overemphasize interesting behaviors. To overcome these problems, a behavioral taxonomy must be developed.

The taxonomy will include several behavioral categories. Each category describes a specific behavior. During observation, when the behavior is seen, the category is scored. Categories can be either general or specific. Broad categories permit very consistent, and hence reliable, scoring of behavior, but they are less precise. Specific categories are more precise but make scoring behavior more difficult and less reliable. Whether categories of behavior are general or specific, there are three criteria that all taxonomies must meet: A taxonomy must be clearly defined, mutually exclusive, and exhaustive.

All categories within the behavioral taxonomy must be operationally defined. Operationally defining a category means that one will describe, in concrete terms, exactly what one means by the category name. Operational definitions are used to indicate exactly what one must see to score the category. This serves to eliminate subjective judgment when scoring observations. It also permits scientists to communicate precisely about which behaviors are being studied.

DETERMINING RELIABILITY AND VALIDITY

The next step is to determine whether category definitions are reliable and valid. The term "reliable" refers to whether the definitions permit one to score the behavioral category consistently. To determine whether a definition is reliable, interrater reliability is established. This tells whether two independent observers agree in scoring behavioral categories. If the rate of agreement is high, the category is reliable. For the taxonomy itself to be reliable, all its categories must be reliable. Validity is established when one can show that one is really measuring what one thinks one is. This is very important, as

it is not unusual to infer the function of a behavior, only to discover later that the behavior served an entirely different purpose. One way to establish validity is to show a relationship between the category definition and independent assessments of the same behavior.

EXCLUSIVE AND EXHAUSTIVE CATEGORIES

Once taxonomic categories are clearly defined, one must be sure that they are mutually exclusive. This means that each behavior one observes should fit into one, and only one, category; there should be no overlap of meaning between categories. With overlap, the observer will get confused about which behavioral category to score. Such a judgment is subjective, and it will reduce the reliability of the taxonomy and objectivity of the observations.

Finally, the categories should be exhaustive. This means that the categories, as a group, must cover all the behaviors capable of being demonstrated by subjects. Ideally, there should be no behavior that cannot be scored. If the categories are not exhaustive, one will get a distorted idea of how often a particular behavior occurs. Taxonomy must not be developed so as to overrepresent behaviors one finds interesting. Mundane behaviors must be included as well. In this way one can calculate how often each behavior occurs. Although efforts to develop an exhaustive taxonomy must be made, in reality this is impossible. New behaviors will invariably be seen throughout the course of extended observation. To control for this problem, observers will include a category entitled "other." In this way, one can score a behavior even if one has never seen it before. By examining the number of times the "other" category is scored, one can get an idea of how exhaustive the taxonomy is.

TAXONOMY APPROACHES

In measuring behavior with a taxonomy, one can take several approaches. For example, one could use a clock to measure how long each behavior is observed. Using a duration approach is most useful when low-frequency, high-duration behavior is present. One could also quantify how often each behavioral category is scored. The frequency approach is most useful for scoring high-frequency, short-duration behaviors. One could use either the duration or the frequency approach separately or combine the two. Finally, the length and number of observational periods must be determined. In general, the more observational periods used, the better. With respect to length, the observational period must be long enough to permit adequate observation of behavior, but short enough so that one does not become tired and miss important behavior.

APPLIED RESEARCH

An applied example of behavioral taxonomy is its use by researchers to describe monkey behavior. The first step would be to spend many days watching the monkeys' behavior. During this time, the observers would be writing down, in diary form, the behaviors that they see. They would also indicate the function they believe that each behavior serves. The monkeys may appear disturbed or agitated during these initial observations; as time goes by, however, their behavior would become less agitated and they would pay less attention to the observers' presence. Here one can see the importance of the habituation period. If observers had begun recording behavior from the start, they would probably have described the monkeys inaccurately in some respect.

With the information acquired during the habituation period, the researchers would begin to develop a behavioral taxonomy. They must decide how general or specific the categories in the taxonomy will be. This depends primarily on their purpose. If the categories must be very sensitive to change in behavior, they should be specific. If not, broader categories can be used. Once categories are selected, they are operationally defined. A category for aggression, for example, could be operationally defined as "grabbing and shaking the cage fence while maintaining eye contact with the experimenter." Note that this definition is clear and concrete. That is, it is based on observable behavior.

In developing the list of behavioral categories, researchers must be sure they are mutually exclusive and exhaustive. To be mutually exclusive, categories must be defined so there is no overlap in meaning between them. To illustrate, the vocalization category might be defined as "any discernible vocal output." It would be unlikely, however, that this category would be mutually exclusive. For example, what if a monkey showed aggression, but while doing so was also vocalizing? Would this be scored as an instance of aggression or vocalization? Because these categories are not mutually exclusive, one would not know. When this occurs, at least one of the categories must be redefined. The listing of categories must also be exhaustive. Observers must form a category for every possible behavior the monkeys might show; also, an "other" category must be included.

Once category definitions have been developed, it must be determined whether they are reliable, valid,

mutually exclusive, and exhaustive. This can be determined by having two observers score monkey behavior using the taxonomy. If interrater agreement is high (above 85 percent agreement), the definitions can be considered reliable. If it is low, researchers will revise the necessary category definitions. These observers can also determine if categories are mutually exclusive and exhaustive. They are mutually exclusive if observers found no confusion about which category to score. They are exhaustive if they did not need to score the "other" category. Finally, to establish the validity of category definitions, researchers could ask people familiar with monkey behavior to describe what they would expect to see within each of the categories. If their descriptions agree with the researchers' definitions, there is some evidence that the taxonomy is valid.

With the taxonomy developed, the researchers must decide how many observational periods to use and how long each period will be. In general, the more observational periods used, the more reliable the results. Twenty observational periods is adequate to produce reliable data in most cases. In deciding how long the observational period should be, the purpose of the study must be considered. If high-frequency behavior that falls into very specific categories is being observed, a short observational period should be used. For example, if eye blinks are being counted, the observational period should be no longer than two minutes. Any longer than this and observers would get tired and make inaccurate observations. On the other hand, if low-frequency behavior that is scored in broader categories (for example, tool use) is being watched, longer observational periods should be used.

Finally, researchers must decide how behavior will be quantified. They can measure how long each category of behavior is seen, how often each category of behavior is seen, or both. If they are interested in how much of the monkeys' time is spent engaging in each behavior, they will use the duration approach. If, on the other hand, researchers are more interested in determining the likelihood that a particular behavior will occur, they will use the frequency approach.

With an appropriately developed behavioral taxonomy, the behavior of the monkeys can be described accurately and objectively. Researchers can make statements about the likelihood of various behaviors, what the behaviors mean, and how much time the monkeys spend engaged in each type of behavior. From this information, they obtain an in-depth understanding of the monkeys. For example, through the use of behavioral taxonomies it is known that rhesus monkeys have a dominance hierarchy, are very social, can show tool use and other creative adaptations of behavior when necessary, and show rudimentary forms of communication.

IMPLICATIONS FOR OTHER FIELDS

Humans simply do not record events like video cameras. At the scientific level, much care has to be used to ensure that observations are accurate and objective. Understanding how human limitations affect observational capabilities has important implications beyond the field of psychology—for example, in law. Tremendous weight is placed on eyewitness testimony in a court of law. Even though eyewitness accounts are probably biased, distorted, and imperfect, the courts recognize them as the best evidence available. Because of what has been learned about the human capacity to make accurate and objective observations, people are well advised to evaluate eyewitness testimony very carefully.

BIBLIOGRAPHY

Bakeman, Roger. *Observing Interactions: An Introduction to Sequential Analysis.* 2nd ed. New York: Cambridge UP, 1997. Print.

Bordens, Kenneth S., and Bruce B. Abbott. *Research Design and Methods: A Process Approach.* 7th ed. Boston: McGraw, 2008. Print.

Comer, Jonathan S., and Philip C. Kendall, eds. *The Oxford Handbook of Research Strategies for Clinical Psychology.* New York: Oxford UP, 2013. Print.

Coolican, Hugh. *Research Methods and Statistics in Psychology.* 6th ed. New York: Psychology, 2014. Print.

Leahey, Thomas. *A History of Psychology: Main Currents in Psychological Thought.* 7th ed. Englewood Cliffs: Prentice Hall, 2007. Print.

Nestor, Paul G., and Russel K. Schutt. *Research Methods in Psychology.* 2nd ed. Thousand Oaks: Sage, 2015. Print.

Alan J. Beauchamp

SEE ALSO: Animal experimentation; Archival data; Case study methodologies; Complex experimental designs; Data description; Experimental psychology; Experimentation: Ethics and subject rights; Experimentation: Independent, dependent, and control variables; Eyewitness testimony; Field experimentation; Hypothesis development and testing; Qualitative research; Quasi-experimental designs; Sampling; Scientific methods; Statistical significance tests; Survey research: Questionnaires and interviews; Withinsubject experimental designs.

Obsessive-compulsive disorder

TYPE OF PSYCHOLOGY: Psychopathology

Obsessions and compulsions are the cardinal features of a chronic anxiety disorder known as obsessive-compulsive disorder. The identification of repetitive, anxiety-provoking thoughts known as obsessions and of associated compulsive, ritualistic behaviors is critical in the diagnosis and assessment of this debilitating condition.

KEY CONCEPTS

- Anxiety
- Checking ritual
- Cleaning ritual
- Compulsions
- Fear of contamination
- Obsessions
- Response prevention

INTRODUCTION

Obsessive thinking and urges to engage in ritualistic compulsive behaviors are common phenomena that most individuals experience to some extent throughout their lives. It is not uncommon, for example, for a person to reexperience in his or her mind involuntary, anxiety-provoking images of circumstances surrounding a traumatic accident or embarrassing moment. Similarly, behaviors such as returning home to make sure the iron is turned off or refusing to eat from a spoon that falls on a clean floor represent mild compelling rituals in which many persons engage from time to time. It is only when these patterns of obsessive thinking and behaving become either too frequent or too intense that they may escalate into a distressing clinical condition known as obsessive-compulsive disorder.

According to the American Psychiatric Association's *Diagnostic and Statistical Manual of Mental Disorders: DSM-IV-TR* (rev. 4th ed., 2000), the primary feature of this disorder is the presence of distressing obsessions or severe compulsive behaviors that interfere significantly with a person's daily functioning. Although diagnosis requires only the presence of either obsessions or compulsions, they typically are both present in obsessive-compulsive disorder. In most cases, persons with this diagnosis spend more time on a daily basis experiencing obsessive thinking and engaging in ritualistic behaviors than other constructive activities, including those pertaining to occupational, social, and family responsibilities. Therefore, it is not uncommon for obsessive-compulsive patients also to experience severe vocational impairment and distraught interpersonal relationships.

OBSESSIONS

The word "obsession" comes from the Latin word obsidere ("to besiege") and can be defined as a recurrent thought, impulse, idea, or image that is intrusive, disturbing, and senseless. Among the most common types are themes of violence (for example, images of killing a loved one), contamination (for example, thoughts of catching a disease from a doorknob), and personal injury or harm (for example, impulses to leap from a bridge). Obsessional doubting is also characteristic of most patients with obsessive-compulsive disorder, which leads to indecisiveness in even the most simple matters such as selecting a shirt to wear or deciding what to order at a restaurant. The basic content of obsessive thinking distinguishes it from simple "worrying." Worrying involves thinking about an event or occurrence that may realistically result in discomfort, embarrassment, or harm and has a likely probability of occurring; obsessive thinking is typically recognized by the patient as being senseless and not likely to occur. An example of a worry is thinking about an event that possesses a strong likelihood of occurring, such as failing a test when one has not studied. Imagining that one might leap from the third-floor classroom during the exam, a highly unlikely event, is considered an obsession. Furthermore, because the obsessive-compulsive patient is aware that these intrusive thoughts are senseless and continuously attempts to rid the thought from his or her mind, obsessive thinking is not delusional or psychotic in nature. Although both delusional and obsessive patients may experience a similar thought (for example, that they have ingested tainted food), the obsessive patient recognizes that the thought is unlikely and is a product of his or her mind and struggles to get rid of the thought. The delusional patient adheres to the belief with little to no struggle to test its validity.

COMPULSIONS

Most obsessive-compulsive patients also exhibit a series of repetitive, intentional, stereotyped behaviors known as compulsions, which serve to reduce the anxiety experienced from severe obsessive thinking. The most common forms include counting (for example, tapping a pencil three times before laying it down), cleaning (for example, hand washing after shaking another person's hand), checking (for example, checking pilot lights several times a day), and ordering (for example, arranging pencils from longest to shortest before doing homework). Compulsions are different from simple habits in that attempts to resist urges to engage in them result in a substantial increase in anxiety, eventually forcing the patient to engage in the compelling behavior to reduce the tension. Urges to engage in simple habits, on the other hand, can often be resisted with minimal discomfort. Furthermore, most habits result in deriving some degree of pleasure from the activity (for example, shopping, gambling, drinking), while engaging in compulsive behaviors is rarely enjoyable for the patient. Compulsions must also be distinguished from superstitious behaviors, such as an athlete's warm-up ritual or wearing the same "lucky" shoes for each sporting event. In contrast to superstitious people, who employ their rituals to enhance confidence, obsessive-compulsive patients are never certain their rituals will result in anxiety reduction. This typically forces these patients continually to expand their repertoire of ritualistic behaviors, searching for new and better ways to eliminate the anxiety produced by obsessive thinking.

It is estimated that approximately 2 percent of the adult population in the United States—a larger percentage than was once believed—has at some time experienced obsessive-compulsive symptoms severe enough to warrant diagnosis. Typically, obsessive-compulsive symptoms begin in adolescence or early adulthood, although most patients report symptoms of anxiety and nervousness as children. Regarding early developmental histories, many obsessive-compulsive patients report being reared in very strict, puritanical homes. The disorder occurs equally in males and females, although cleaning rituals occur more frequently among women. Although the course of the disorder is chronic, the intensity of symptoms fluctuates throughout life and it occasionally has been reported to remit spontaneously. Because of the unusual nature of the symptoms, obsessive-compulsive patients often keep their rituals hidden and become introverted and withdrawn; as a result, the clinical picture becomes complicated by a coexisting depressive disorder. It is typically the depression that forces the patient to seek psychological help.

ETIOLOGY AND TREATMENTS

Because of the distressing yet fascinating nature of the symptoms, several theoretical positions have attempted to explain how obsessive-compulsive disorder develops. From an applied perspective, each theoretical position has evolved into a treatment or intervention strategy for eliminating the problems caused by obsessions and compulsions. According to psychoanalytic theory, as outlined by Sigmund Freud in 1909, obsessive-compulsive rituals are the product of overly harsh toilet training that leaves the patient with considerable unconscious hostility, primarily directed toward an authoritarian caregiver. In a sense, as uncomfortable and disconcerting as the obsessions and compulsive behaviors are, they are preferable to experiencing the intense emotions left from these childhood incidents. Obsessions and compulsions permit the patient to avoid experiencing these emotions. Furthermore, obsessive-compulsive symptoms force the patient to become preoccupied with anxiety-reduction strategies that prevent them from dealing with other hidden impulses, such as sexual urges and desires. Based on the psychoanalytic formulation, treatment involves identifying the original unconscious thoughts, ideas, or impulses and allowing the patient to experience them consciously. In his classic case report of an obsessive patient, Freud analyzed a patient known as the "rat man," who was plagued by recurrent, horrifying images of a bucket of hungry rats strapped to the buttocks of his girlfriend and his father. Although periodic case reports of psychoanalytic treatments for obsessive-compulsive disorder exist, there is very little controlled empirical work suggesting the effectiveness of this treatment approach.

Behavioral theorists, differing from the psychoanalytic tradition, have proposed that obsessive-compulsive disorder represents a learned habit that is maintained by the reinforcing properties of the anxiety reduction that occurs following ritualistic behaviors. It is well established that behaviors that are reinforced occur more frequently in the future. In the case of compulsive behaviors, the ritual is always followed by a significant reduction in anxiety, therefore reinforcing the compulsive behavior as well as the preceding obsessive activity. Based on the

---

DSM-IV-TR CRITERIA FOR OBSESSIVE-COMPULSIVE DISORDER (DSM CODE 300.3)

Either obsessions or compulsions

Obsessions defined by all of the following:
- recurrent and persistent thoughts, impulses, or images experienced, at some time during disturbance, as intrusive and inappropriate and cause marked anxiety or distress
- thoughts, impulses, or images not simply excessive worries about real-life problems
- attempts made to ignore or suppress thoughts, impulses, or images, or to neutralize them with some other thought or action
- recognition that thoughts, impulses, or images are product of his or her own mind (not imposed from without, as in thought insertion)

Compulsions defined by both of the following:
- repetitive behaviors (hand washing, ordering, checking) or mental acts (praying, counting, repeating words silently) that individual feels driven to perform in response to an obsession or according to rules that must be applied rigidly
- behaviors or mental acts aimed at preventing or reducing distress or preventing some dreaded event or situation; behaviors or mental acts either are not connected in a realistic way with what they are designed to neutralize or prevent or are clearly excessive

At some point, individual recognizes obsessions or compulsions as excessive or unreasonable; this does not apply to children

Obsessions or compulsions cause marked distress, are time-consuming, or interfere significantly with normal routine, occupational or academic functioning, or usual social activities or relationships

If another Axis I disorder is present, content of obsessions or compulsions not restricted to it

Disturbance not due to direct physiological effects of a substance or general medical condition

Specify if with Poor Insight (most of the time during current episode, obsessions and compulsions not recognized as excessive or unreasonable)

behavioral perspective, an intervention strategy called response prevention, or flooding, Flooding was developed to facilitate the interruption of this habitually reinforcing cycle. Response prevention involves exposing the patient to the feared stimulus (for example, a doorknob) or obsession (for example, an image of leaping from a bridge) to create anxiety. Rather than allowing the patient to engage in the subsequent compulsive activity, however, the therapist prevents the response (for example, the patient is not permitted to wash his or her hands). The patient endures a period of intense anxiety but eventually experiences habituation of the anxiety response. Although treatments of this nature are anxiety provoking for the patient, well-controlled investigations have reported significant reductions in obsessive thinking and ritualistic behavior following intervention. Some estimates of success rates with response prevention are as high as 80 percent, and treatment gains are maintained for several years.

Theories emphasizing the cognitive aspects of the obsessive-compulsive disorder have focused on information-processing impairments of the patient. Specifically, obsessive-compulsive patients tend to perceive harm (for example, contamination) when in fact it may not be present and to perceive a loss of control over their environment. Although most individuals perceive a given situation as safe until proved harmful, the obsessive-compulsive patient perceives situations as harmful until proved safe. These perceptions of harm and lack of control lead to increased anxiety; the belief that the patient controls his or her life or the perception of safety leads to decreased anxiety. Accordingly, compulsive rituals represent a patient's efforts to gain control over his or her environment. Cognitive interventions aim to increase the patient's perception of control over the environment and to evaluate realistically environmental threats of harm. Although cognitive approaches may serve as a useful adjunct to behavioral treatments such as response prevention, evidence for their effectiveness when used in treating obsessions and compulsions is lacking.

Finally, biological models of obsessive-compulsive disorder have also been examined. There is some indication that electrical activity in the brain during information processing, particularly in the frontal lobes, is somewhat slower for obsessive-compulsive patients in comparison with other people. For example, metabolic activity of the frontal brain regions measured using positron emission tomography (PET) scans differentiates obsessive-compulsive patients from both normal people and depressive patients. Further, a deficiency in certain neurotransmitters (for example, serotonin and norepinephrine) has been implicated in the etiology of the disorder. Several interventions based on the biological model have been employed as well. Pharmacotherapy, using antidepressantAntidepressantsobsessive-compulsive disorder medications that primarily act to facilitate neurotransmitter functioning (for example, clomipramine), has been shown to be effective in treating from 20 to 50 percent of obsessive-compulsive patients. More drastic interventions such as frontal lobotomies have been reported in the most intractable cases, with very limited success.

Among the interventions employed to rid patients of troublesome obsessions and compulsions, response prevention holds the most promise. Because of the intensity of this treatment approach, however, the cost may be substantial, and many patients may not immediately respond. A number of predictors of poor treatment response to behavioral interventions (characteristic of those most refractory to treatment) have been identified. These include a coexisting depression, poor compliance with exposure/response-prevention instructions, the presence of fears that the patient views as realistic, and eccentric superstition. In these cases, alternative forms of treatment are typically considered (for example, pharmacotherapy).

PREVALENCE AND RESEARCH

Obsessions and compulsions represent human phenomena that have been a topic of interest for several centuries; for example, William Shakespeare's characterization of the hand-washing Lady Macbeth has entertained audiences for hundreds of years. Prior to the first therapeutic analysis of obsessive-compulsive disorder, then called a neurosis—Freud's description of the "rat man"—obsessive thoughts were commonly attributed to demoniac influence and treated with exorcism. Freud's major contribution was delivering the phenomenon from the spiritual into the psychological realm. Although initial case reports employing psychoanalysis were promising, subsequent developments using behavioral and pharmacological formulations have more rapidly advanced the understanding of the phenomenology and treatment of this unusual condition. In addition, with the public revelation that certain prominent individuals such as the aircraft designer and film producer Howard Hughes suffered from this condition, the prevalence estimates of this disorder have steadily increased. Although a number of patients have sought help for this debilitating disorder since the time it was first clinically described, it has been confirmed that this problem is far more prevalent than initially thought. The increase is probably related not to an actual increase in incidence but to individuals becoming more willing to seek help for the problem. Because of the increasing number of individuals requesting help for problems relating to obsessions and compulsions, it is becoming more and more important to foster the maturation of appropriate treatment strategies to deal with this disorder.

Further, it has become increasingly important to understand the manifestation of obsessions and compulsions from a biological, psychological, and socio-occupational level. Ongoing investigations are examining the biological makeup of the nervous systems peculiar to this disorder. Research examining the specific information-processing styles and cognitive vulnerabilities of obsessive-compulsive patients is also being conducted. Both response-prevention and biochemical-intervention strategies (for example, clomipramine) are deserving of continued research, primarily in examining the characteristics of obsessive-compulsive patients that predict treatment efficacy with either form of intervention. Finally, early markers for this condition, including childhood environments, early learning experiences, and biological predispositions, require further investigation so that prevention efforts can be provided for individuals who may be at risk for developing obsessive-compulsive disorder. With these advances, psychologists will be in a better position to reduce the chronic nature of obsessive-compulsive disorder and to prevent these distressing symptoms in forthcoming generations.

BIBLIOGRAPHY

American Psychiatric Association. *Diagnostic and Statistical Manual of Mental Disorders: DSM-IV-TR.* Rev. 4th ed. Washington, D.C.: Author, 2000. The DSM-IV-TR provides specific criteria for making psychiatric diagnoses of obsessive-compulsive disorder and other anxiety disorders. Brief summaries of research findings regarding each condition are also provided.

Clark, David A. *Cognitive-Behavioral Therapy for OCD.* New York: Guilford Press, 2007. This book offers guidelines on the assessment of obsessive-compulsive disorder and presents a variety of effective treatments, based on patient models.

Emmelkamp, Paul M. G. *Phobic and Obsessive Compulsive Disorders: Theory, Research, and Practice.* New York: Plenum, 1982. A somewhat dated but classic work outlining the importance of behavioral strategies in overcoming obsessive-compulsive, as well as phobic, conditions.

Hyman, Bruce M., and Troy Dufrene. *Coping with OCD: Practical Strategies for Living Well with Obsessive-Compulsive Disorder.* Oakland, Calif.: New Harbinger, 2008. This resource, designed for those who are struggling with obsesseive-compulsive disorder, describes the condition in layperson's terms and advises sufferers on how to deal with the depression, shame, and blame that usually accompanies it.

Jenike, Michael A., Lee Baer, and William E. Minichiello. *Obsessive-Compulsive Disorders: Theory and Management.* 2d ed. Littleton, Mass.: PSG, 1990. A comprehensive overview of the topic that does not burden the reader with intricate details of analysis. Readable by the layperson. Covers the topic thoroughly.

Mavissakalian, Matig, Samuel M. Turner, and Larry Michelson. *Obsessive-Compulsive Disorders: Psychological and Pharmacological Treatment.* New York: Plenum, 1985. An exceptionally well-written text based on a symposium held at the University of Pittsburgh. Issues pertaining to etiology, assessment, diagnosis, and treatment are covered in detail.

Rachman, S. J. "Obsessional-Compulsive Disorders." *In International Handbook of Behavior Modification and Therapy,* edited by Alan S. Bellack, Michel Hersen, and Alan E. Kazdin. 2d ed. New York: Plenum, 1990. Rachman's work using behavioral strategies with obsessive-compulsive patients is unparalleled. No bibliography would be complete without a contribution from Rachman, one of the most respected authorities in the field.

Steketee, Gail, and Andrew Ellis. *Treatment of Obsessive-Compulsive Disorder.* New York: Guilford, 1996. A comprehensive resource for mental health professionals. Covers behavioral and cognitive approaches, biological models, and pharmacological therapies.

Turner, S. M., and L. Michelson. "Obsessive-Compulsive Disorders." *In Behavioral Theories and Treatment of Anxiety,* edited by Samuel M. Turner. New York: Plenum, 1984. Summarizes information regarding diagnostic issues, assessment strategies, and treatment interventions for obsessive-compulsive disorder. Provides an excellent review of intervention efforts employing response prevention and clomipramine.

Kevin T. Larkin and Virginia L. Goetsch

SEE ALSO: Abnormality: Biomedical models; Antidepressant medications; Anxiety disorders; Aversion therapy; Cognitive therapy; Drug therapies; Implosion; Intervention; Personality disorders; Systematic desensitization.

Oedipus complex

TYPE OF PSYCHOLOGY: Biological bases of behavior; Developmental psychology; Emotion; Memory; Personality; Psychopathology; Psychotherapy; Social psychology

Oedipus, a character from Greek mythology who inadvertently killed his father and married his mother, became a model comparison figure for Sigmund Freud as he began the recognition of infantile sexuality and the Oedipus complex during his period of self-analysis, starting in 1897..

KEY CONCEPTS
- Abandonment
- Aggression
- Depression
- Family dynamics
- Guilt
- Incest
- Infantile sexuality
- Murder
- Psychoanalysis
- Rage
- Self-mutilation
- Suicide

INTRODUCTION

The classic presentation of the myth of Oedipus is the play *Oidipous Tyrannos* (c. 429 BCE; *Oedipus Tyrannus,* 1715), by the Greek playwright Sophocles. The play begins when Laius, ruler of Thebes, is told he will one day be murdered by a son. When Jocasta, his wife, gives birth to a son, the couple orders him killed. Instead, the baby is abandoned, then found and adopted by Polybus, king of Corinth. The boy, named Oedipus, grows up believing Polybus is his biological father.

As an adult, Oedipus is told that he is fated to kill his father and, in an attempt to evade the prophecy, leaves Corinth. On the road, he meets an old man driving a wagon who refuses to move and let Oedipus pass. In a rage, Oedipus kills Laius, not aware that he is Oedipus's biological father.

The throne of Thebes is now vacant, and through a series of circumstances Oedipus becomes king of Thebes and marries the widow of the former king—his biological mother, Jocasta. The two have four daughters. Thebes is then beset with a terrible plague. Oedipus vows to save his kingdom and puts a curse on the person who must have committed the sin that has caused the plague. Through an entanglement of circumstances and the confession of Polybus, Oedipus learns the truth about his murder of his father and his marriage to his mother, Jocasta. When Jocasta hangs herself in shame, Oedipus takes the brooches from her dress and thrusts the pins into his eyes, blinding himself so he cannot see the evil around him. Oedipus is taken to Mount Cithaeron, where he was originally abandoned, and left to die as the gods originally intended.

OEDIPUS IN THE HUMAN PSYCHE

Sigmund Freud, the Austrian founder of psychoanalysis, first turned his attention to the Oedipus myth while undertaking his own self-analysis in the late 1890s, as he was attempting to puzzle out the dynamics of infant sexuality. After studying the Oedipus myth, Freud believed he had gained insight into the human mind, revealing a basic tenet of the human psyche based on persons dealing with family dynamics. Freud believed all male children deal with aggression toward their fathers and dream of making love to their mothers at some point in their development. Freud felt that Oedipus was the perfect model for this example because of his extreme behaviors.

Improper infantile sexual feelings that are not dealt with cause neuroses that affect daily life. These neuroses can cause disabilities later on. However, historical data now prove incestuous behaviors are extremely rare in all societies worldwide. Psychiatrists have dismissed much of what Freud had to say on the subject.

Diagnosing this complex is difficult in the light of psychological research since Freud first used the term and began treatment using psychoanalysis. Versions of what might still be termed Oedipal conflicts may be found in psychiatric patients exhibiting sexual disorders as a result of childhood incestuous experiences. Serial murderers most often have suffered abnormal sexual experiences, and case histories show that child molesters were often sexually abused as children. However, the idea that the incestuous relations between children and adults are the result of (unconscious) desire on the part of the child is now discredited. Most references to the Oedipus complex now take place in the realm of literary studies.

BIBLIOGRAPHY

Bergmann, Martin S. "The Oedipus Complex and Psychoanalytic Technique." *Psychoanalytic Technique* 30.6 (2010): 535–40. Print.

Blazina, Chris. "Mythos and Men: Toward New Paradigms of Masculinity." *The Journal of Men's Studies* 5.4 (May, 1997): 285–95. Print.

Blum, Harold P. "Adolescent Trauma and the Oedipus Complex." *Psychoanalytic Inquiry* 30.6 (2010): 548–56. Print.

Kulish, Nancy, and Deanna Holtzmann. *A Story of Her Own: The Female Oedipus Complex Reexamined and Renamed.* Lanham: Aronson, 2008. Print.

Nicolson, Paula. "Oedipus At Work: A Family Affair?" *Psychodynamic Practice* 18.4 (2012): 427–40. Print.

Sophocles. *The Oedipus Cycle.* Trans. Dudley Fitts and Robert Fitzgerald. San Diego: Harvest, 1987. Print.

Young, Robert M., ed. *Oedipus Complex: Ideas in Psychoanalysis.* New York: Totem, 2001. Print.

Virginiae Blackmon

SEE ALSO: Ego, superego, and id; Freud, Sigmund; Freudian psychology; Men's mental health; Penis envy; Psychoanalytic psychology and personality: Sigmund Freud; Psychosexual development.

Operant conditioning therapies

TYPE OF PSYCHOLOGY: Psychotherapy

Operant conditioning therapies are based on the assumption that operant behavior is shaped by its consequences; therapists use reinforcement, extinction, punishment, and discrimination training to overcome behavioral problems. Operant conditioning techniques have been applied to individual and group behavior in a variety of settings, including hospitals, prisons, schools, businesses, and homes..

KEY CONCEPTS

- Aversive stimulus
- Discrimination training
- Extinction
- Negative punishment
- Operant conditioning
- Positive punishment
- Positive reinforcement
- Successive approximations

INTRODUCTION

Behavior therapy uses principles of learning to modify human behavior. One orientation within behavior therapy is the operant conditioning approach, also called behavior modification. This approach modifies operant behavior by manipulating environmental consequences. The term "operant" refers to voluntary or emitted behavior that operates on the environment to produce consequences. The basic premise of operant conditioning is that operant behavior is controlled by its consequences. What happens to an individual after he or she performs some behavior determines the likelihood of that behavior being repeated. Pleasant or reinforcing consequences strengthen behavior, while unpleasant or punishing consequences weaken behavior.

THERAPEUTIC APPROACHES

There are several characteristics that distinguish the operant approach to therapy. One is the manner in which clinical problems are conceptualized and defined. Traditional psychotherapy tends to view disturbed behavior as a symptom of an internal psychological conflict; the goal of therapy is to help the individual gain insight into this inner problem. Therapists with an operant orientation, however, view maladaptive behavior as the problem itself. They believe that just as normal or adaptive behavior is shaped by environmental consequences, so, too, is abnormal or maladaptive behavior. Therefore, by carefully arranging events in the client's environment, it should be possible to modify maladaptive behavior and help the client learn more appropriate ways of behaving.

The behavior therapist defines problems in terms of specific behaviors that can be observed and quantified. Behavioral excesses involve too much of a specific behavior that can be specified in terms of frequency, intensity, or duration. Chain-smoking, overeating, and physically abusing another person are examples of behavioral excesses. The opposite difficulty is a behavioral deficit. In the case of a behavioral deficit, a behavior either does not occur or occurs at an extremely low rate. A man who cannot feed or dress himself and a child who rarely talks to other children exhibit behavioral deficits. Still other behaviors are problematic because they are inappropriate when performed in a particular setting. Taking one's clothes off in public or laughing during a solemn funeral service illustrates behavioral inappropriateness.

Behavioral monitoring is an integral component of operant conditioning therapies. The problem behavior is first observed and recorded as it naturally occurs in a variety of settings, and no attempt is made to modify the behavior. The therapist, a parent, a teacher, a spouse, a peer, or the client may conduct the observation and record the behavior. This part of the behavior modification program, which is called baseline observation, provides a record of where and when the behavior occurred as well as information about its topography or form, such as duration and intensity. Behavioral measures are often plotted on a graph to provide a visual record of behavior. The baseline data are used to define the problem or target behavior as precisely as possible. The client and therapist also define the desired changes in this target behavior and set up specific behavioral goals to be met during treatment.

TREATMENT TECHNIQUES

Operant techniques that are appropriate for modifying the target behavior are then selected. Therapists begin by selecting the least intrusive and restrictive procedures demonstrated to be effective for treating a specific problem. Since these techniques are based on years of experimental research and evaluation, it is possible for therapists to define explicitly their methods and their rationale to the client. This degree of precision, rarely found in traditional psychotherapy, makes it easier for clients and those working with clients to understand and to implement therapeutic procedures.

Behavioral observation continues throughout the treatment phase of the modification program. Behavior is monitored on a regular basis, and changes from the baseline level are recorded. Examination of this ongoing record of behavioral progress allows both therapist and client to evaluate the effectiveness of the treatment at any given time. If behavior is not changing in the desired direction or at the desired pace, the treatment program can be altered or adjusted.

Behavior modifiers often include a follow-up phase as part of the modification program. After termination of treatment, the client may be contacted on a periodic basis to assess whether treatment gains are being maintained. Behavior therapists have discovered that generalization of behavior changes from the therapeutic setting to the natural environment does not occur automatically. An increasing emphasis is being placed on incorporating procedures to facilitate behavior transfer into modification programs. Some therapists have reduced their reliance on tangible reinforcers, such as food or toys, and have stressed the use of social and intrinsic reinforcers, such as positive attention from others and personal feelings of

pride and mastery. These are the kinds of reinforcers that are likely to maintain positive behavioral changes in the client's natural setting. Therapists also devote attention to training individuals who will interact with the client after the termination of treatment in the effective use of operant procedures.

Ethical guidelines are followed when conducting a behavior modification program. Because behavior therapists insist on explicit definition of problem behaviors and treatment methods, this approach facilitates public scrutiny of ethical conduct. Educating the client in the rationale and application of procedures greatly reduces the possibility that operant conditioning techniques will be used in an exploitive or harmful fashion.

POSITIVE REINFORCEMENT

The treatment of behavioral deficits typically involves the application of positive reinforcement techniques. Positive reinforcement increases the frequency of a response by immediately following the response with a favorable consequence. If the desired behavior does not occur at all, it can be developed by using the shaping procedure. In shaping, successive approximations—responses that more and more closely resemble the desired response—of the desired behavior are reinforced. Wayne Isaacs, James Thomas, and Israel Goldiamond provided an impressive demonstration of the use of shaping to reinstate verbal behavior in a schizophrenic patient who had been mute for nineteen years. Chewing gum was used as the positive reinforcer, and gum delivery was made contingent first on eye movements in the direction of the gum, then on lip movements, then on any vocalization, and finally on vocalizations that increasingly approximated actual words. Within six weeks, the patient was conversing with the therapist.

Positive reinforcement is also used to strengthen weak or low-frequency behaviors. Initially, the desired behavior is placed on a continuous reinforcement schedule in which each occurrence of the behavior is followed by reinforcer delivery. Gradually, an intermittent schedule can be introduced, with several responses or a time interval required between successive reinforcer deliveries.

Since people get tired of the same reinforcer and different people find different commodities and activities reinforcing, a token economy system provides another means of programming positive reinforcement. A system that delivers tokens as rewards for appropriate behaviors can be used with a single individual or a group of individuals. Tokens are stimuli such as check marks, points, stickers, or poker chips, which can be accumulated and later exchanged for commodities and activities of the individual's choosing. Tokens can be delivered on a continuous or intermittent schedule of reinforcement and are often accompanied by praise for the desired behavior. Ultimately, the goal of the program is to fade out the use of tokens as more natural social and intrinsic reinforcers begin to maintain behavior.

EXTINCTION AND PUNISHMENT PROCEDURES

Extinction and punishment procedures are used to treat behavioral excess. If the reinforcer that is maintaining the excessive behavior can be identified, an extinction program may be effective. Extinction is a procedure that is used to eliminate a response by withholding the reinforcer following performance of the response. A classic demonstration of extinction is a study by Carl Williams designed to eliminate intense tantrum behavior at bedtime in a twenty-one-month-old child. Observation revealed that parental attention was reinforcing the tantrums, so the parents were instructed to put the child to bed, close the bedroom door, and not return to the child's room for the rest of the night. This extinction procedure eliminated the tantrums in seven nights. Tantrums were then accidentally reinforced by the child's aunt, and a second extinction procedure was instituted. Tantrums were reduced to a zero level by the ninth session, and a two-year follow-up revealed that no further tantrums had occurred.

Punishment procedures decrease the frequency of a response by removing a reinforcing stimulus or by presenting an aversive stimulus (a painful or unpleasant event) immediately following the response. Removal of a positive reinforcer contingent on performance of the target behavior is called negative punishment or response cost. Some token economy systems incorporate a response cost component, and clients lose tokens when specified inappropriate behaviors are performed. In another form of negative punishment, time-out or sit-out, an individual is moved from a reinforcing environment to one that is devoid of positive reinforcement for a limited amount of time. For example, a child who misbehaves during a classroom game might be seated away from the other children for a few minutes, thereby losing the opportunity to enjoy the game.

The most intrusive behavior-reduction technique is positive punishment, which involves the presentation of an aversive stimulus contingent on performance of the undesirable behavior. This procedure is used only when other procedures have failed and the behavioral excess is injurious to the client or to others. Thomas Sajwaj and his colleagues employed a positive punishment procedure to reduce life-threatening regurgitation behavior in a six-month-old infant. Within a few minutes of being fed, the infant would begin to bring up the milk she had consumed, and regurgitation continued until all the milk was lost. Treatment consisted of filling the infant's mouth with lemon juice immediately following mouth movements indicative of regurgitation. Regurgitation was reduced to a very low level after sixteen lemon-juice presentations.

Extinction and punishment techniques can produce side effects that include aggressive behavior and fear, escape, and avoidance responses. These can be reduced by combining behavior-reduction procedures with a program of positive reinforcement for desirable alternative behaviors. In this way, the behavioral excess is weakened and the client is simultaneously learning adaptive, socially approved behaviors.

STIMULUS-DISCRIMINATION TRAINING

Behaviors that are labeled as inappropriate because of their place of occurrence may be treated using stimulus-discrimination training. This involves teaching the client to express a behavior in the presence of some stimuli and not express the behavior in the presence of other stimuli. For a preschooler who takes his clothes off in a variety of public and private places, discrimination training might involve praising the child when he removes his clothes in his bedroom or the bathroom and using extinction or punishment when clothing removal occurs in other settings. Verbal explanation of the differential contingencies also helps the client learn discrimination.

EVOLUTION OF RESEARCH

Operant conditioning therapies evolved from the laboratory research of B. F. Skinner. In 1938, Skinner published *The Behavior of Organisms,* which outlined the basic principles of operant conditioning that he had derived from the experimental study of the effects of environmental consequences on the lever-pressing behavior of rats. This work stimulated other psychologists to analyze operant behavior in many animal species.

Most early studies with human subjects were designed to replicate and extend this animal research, and they served to demonstrate that operant techniques exerted similar control over human behavior. A literature of operant principles and theory began to accumulate, and researchers referred to this approach to learning as the experimental analysis of behavior.

Some of these human demonstrations were conducted in institutional settings with patients who had not responded well to traditional treatment approaches. The results of such studies suggested that operant procedures could have therapeutic value. In 1959, Teodoro Ayllon and Jack Michael described how staff members could use reinforcement principles to modify the maladaptive behaviors of psychiatric patients. In the 1960s, Sidney Bijou pioneered the use of operant procedures with mentally disabled children, and Ivar Lovaas developed an operant program for autistic children.

The 1960s also saw applications in noninstitutional settings. Operant techniques were introduced into school classrooms, university teaching, programs for delinquent youth, marriage counseling, and parent training. Universities began to offer coursework and graduate training programs in the application of operant principles. By the late 1960s, the operant orientation in behavior therapy became known by the terms behavior modification and applied behavior analysis.

During the 1970s, many large-scale applications were instituted. Psychiatric hospitals, schools, prisons, and business organizations began to apply operant principles systematically to improve the performances of large groups of individuals. Another important trend that began in the 1970s was an interest in the self-modification of problem behaviors. Numerous books offered self-training in operant procedures to deal with problems such as smoking, drug abuse, nervous habits, stress, sexual dysfunction, time management, and weight control.

INTEGRATION WITH BEHAVIORAL MEDICINE

Since the 1980s, operant conditioning therapies have become an integral component of behavioral medicine. Reinforcement techniques are being used in the treatment of chronic pain, eating and sleeping disorders, cardiovascular disorders, and neuromuscular disorders. Operant procedures are also effective in teaching patients adherence to medical instructions and how to make healthy lifestyle changes.

Behavior modifiers continue to direct attention toward public safety and improvement of the physical environment. Therapists are evaluating the effectiveness of operant procedures to combat crime, reduce traffic accidents, and increase the use of seat belts, car pools,

and public transportation. Programs are being designed to encourage energy conservation and waste recycling.

Throughout the history of its development, behavior modification has emphasized the use of operant conditioning principles to improve the quality of life for individuals and for society as a whole. Behavior therapists actively support efforts to educate the public in the ethical use of operant techniques for social betterment.

BIBLIOGRAPHY

Karoly, Paul, and Anne Harris. "Operant Methods." Helping People Change: A Textbook of Methods. Ed. Frederick H. Kanfer and A. P. Goldstein. 4th ed. Boston: Allyn, 1991. Print.

Kazdin, Alan E. Behavior Modification in Applied Settings. 7th ed. Long Grove: Waveland, 2013. Print.

Martin, Garry, and Joseph Pear. Behavior Modification: What It Is and How to Do It. 8th ed. Upper Saddle River: Prentice-Hall, 2009. Print.

Mazur, James. E. Learning and Behavior. 7th ed. Boston: Pearson, 2013. Print.McSweeney, Frances K., and Eric S. Murphy, eds. The Wiley Blackwell Handbook of Operant and Classical Conditioning. Malden: Wiley, 2013. Print.

Watson, David L., and Roland G. Tharp. Self-Directed Behavior: Self-Modification for Personal Adjustment. 9th ed. Belmont: Wadsworth, 2007. Print.

Linda J. Palm

SEE ALSO: Aversion therapy; Behaviorism; Conditioning; Habituation and sensitization; Implosion; Learned helplessness; Learning; Pavlovian conditioning; Phobias; Punishment; Reflexes; Systematic desensitization; Time-out.

Optimal arousal theory

TYPE OF PSYCHOLOGY: Motivation

Optimal arousal theory suggests that arousal prompts human behavior. Arousal theorists hypothesize that each human has a level of arousal at which he or she generally performs best and that the individual strives to maintain that level of arousal in much the same way that the body homeostatically controls its temperature.

KEY CONCEPTS
- Construct
- Hedonic

- Homeostatic
- Motivation
- Reticular activating system

INTRODUCTION

Optimal arousal theory is a "push" or internal motivation theory. Arousal, like drive, is thought to energize and direct behavior. Arousal theory enjoys some advantages over drive theory, however; it is able to explain behavior that continues at the same level and intensity or increases, and it is not a hypothetical construct but a measurable phenomenon. A construct can be defined as a formal concept representing the relationships between variables such as motivation and behavior. The latter fact permits empirical testing.

Arousal is both physiological and behavioral in its makeup. The physiological component is generally objective and measurable; the psychological component is subjective and observable. The central nervous system controls physiological arousal. The brain stem, for example—particularly the reticular activating system (RAS)—controls levels of consciousness from coma or deep sleep to complete wakefulness, while the cerebral cortex (the outer layer of the brain that controls complex voluntary functions such as thinking, reasoning, motor coordination, memory, and language), in coordination with the RAS and by way of the autonomic nervous system and the endocrine system, provides for moment-to-moment, "gut-level" differences in levels of arousal. According to various theorists, moment-to-moment differences in arousal relate to the type, intensity, quality, and effectiveness of individual behavior, including stable aspects of behavior that make up a significant part of individual personality.

The individual's arousal level at any given moment is a function of stimulation (in the near past and the present), the individual's baseline (resting) level of arousal, and his or her stimulus sensitivity. A stimulus is whatever impinges on and is processed by any of the senses (for example, the warmth of a campfire on one's skin or the sound of a car horn in one's ears). The effects of stimulation are generally cumulative, persist over time, and have a direct effect on behavior.

THEORETICAL PERSPECTIVES

The Yerkes-Dodson law provides a starting point for understanding the arousal-behavior relationship. According to that early twentieth century law, there is an inverted-U relationship between motivation and performance;

that is, as motivation increases, performance improves up to some point at which performance is maximized. Thereafter, increases in motivation lead to decreases in performance. Thus, the peak of the inverted U is analogous to the point of diminishing marginal returns.

Since arousal is a motivational concept, it is a simple matter to replace the motivation of the Yerkes-Dodson law with arousal, a substitution that was formalized by Donald O. Hebb in 1955. D. E. Berlyne developed this relationship further when he proposed that each individual has an optimal level of arousal (OLA) at which he or she typically feels and performs best and that each individual engages in activities that are calculated to maintain the OLA in a homeostatic (referring to the maintenance of balance or equilibrium in bodily processes) manner.

Arousal both prompts and is the consequence of behavior; for example, a person who is experiencing a low level of arousal is motivated to engage in behavior that has a high stimulus value—that will result in increased overall arousal approaching the optimum. People with chronically low resting levels of arousal will tend to be able to tolerate noise, crowds, excitement, and the like. An individual with a chronically high resting level of arousal, however, will tend to engage in behavior of modest to low stimulus value to avoid exceeding or deviating from his or her OLA. Such individuals tend to engage in more solitary pastimes, avoid noise, avoid crowds, and shun sensation-seeking behavior. According to Hans Eysenck, these differences in behavior, which are attributable to differing resting levels of arousal—particularly cortical arousal—are the hypothetical basis for the dimension of personality called extroversion.

ROLE OF TIME AND CIRCUMSTANCES

An individual is, however, more than a simple product of his or her mean resting arousal level. Time and circumstances can cause any individual at any given moment to be above or below the OLA and engage in behavior that is either typical or atypical. An extrovert, for example, might feel overwhelmed or become too busy and consequently seek a period of atypical peace and solitude. In addition, while some theorists have posited a single OLA for all behavior, others espouse the idea that there is a separate OLA for each possible behavior, including tasks or problems with different degrees of difficulty. Certain latter-day theorists have noted cogently that the extremes of arousal have both positive and negative hedonic values; that is, low arousal corresponds to boredom or relaxation depending on the situation, and high arousal similarly corresponds to either anxiety or excitement.

Arousal is, in summary, a ubiquitous, continuous, and persistent aspect of human life. It has the theoretical potential to affect—to a greater or lesser extent—virtually all behavior. Practical interests in the arousal-behavior link cover a variety of topics, including the role of arousal in performance, decision making, moods and emotions, and personality formation.

EFFECT ON TASK PERFORMANCE

Arousal affects performance in several ways: It affects how well one is able to complete difficult tasks, perform in the presence of others, and make effective decisions. In the first case, research has generally supported the idea that people perform difficult tasks best at moderate levels of arousal (at the peak of the inverted U), although it is possible to perform easy or moderately difficult tasks effectively over a wider range of arousal. For example, when taking an important examination, one will likely be able to answer easy test questions correctly even if one is very tired, relaxed, or anxious, whereas one will probably find more complex test items difficult to answer if one is only moderately tired or anxious. As a matter of fact, challenging questions often induce the very arousal that interferes with answering them expeditiously and correctly.

The mere presence of others seems to add another measure of difficulty to task performance. Since 1898, social psychologists have studied a phenomenon known as social facilitation. Social facilitation is the tendency of people to perform easy or well-learned tasks more effectively and difficult or poorly learned tasks less effectively in the presence of one or more other persons. Robert B. Zajonc has posited that the mere presence of others (whether they pay attention to the performer or not) is stimulating, hence arousing, and that it is this increase in arousal that causes social facilitation effects. Thus, the presence of others might facilitate the performance of a runner but impair the performance of someone attempting to solve a complex crossword puzzle or pass a difficult exam.

AROUSAL AND DECISION-MAKING RESEARCH

Because life is full of pressure-filled and arousing moments and because there is always a demand for people who can remain coolheaded and effective under stressful conditions, researchers have been very interested in the relationship between arousal and decision mak-

ing. In 1959, J. A. Easterbrook observed that increasing arousal leads to an increasing restriction of cues (stimuli/information), perhaps as a result of a narrowing of attention to essential information. Continued increases in arousal may, however, begin to narrow attention too much and thus interfere with the proper consideration of essential information. Thus, according to the combined results of several researchers, increased arousal actually facilitates the decision-making process up to a point by focusing attention on relevant information and eliminating distraction caused by extraneous detail. Increases in arousal beyond that point begin to screen out crucial information and impair decision making. Again, the Yerkes-Dodson law applies. From a practical standpoint, it seems that practice and training best enable an individual to counteract the effects of increased arousal on decision making.

RELATIONSHIP TO EMOTION

Though emotion theorists and scholars differ regarding the precise process of human emotion, they hold at least one belief in common: Autonomic nervous system arousal is central to the experience of emotion. Autonomic arousal provides the subjective physical coloring of the experience of emotion. Therefore, even the novice should not be surprised that there is an interplay between emotion and other arousal-related phenomena. For example, Dolf Zillmann noted that people who had been riding bicycles for exercise and who were angered after they ceased exercising displayed an anger that was considerably greater than might otherwise have been expected considering the circumstances. Physical exercise activates the sympathetic nervous system. After one finishes exercising, the sympathetic nervous system returns to its normal level of activation at a measured pace; thus, for some time after the completion of exercise, one is in a state of decreasing neural arousal. If one is angered during this period, the neural arousal "piggybacks" the arousal generated as the result of becoming angry, causing the anger to be inappropriately intense. This piggybacking of residual neural arousal on subsequently induced emotional arousal, which Zillmann calls the excitation-transfer process, provides a plausible explanation for the human tendency to overemote occasionally about trifling matters or events.

Individuals manifest stable differences in mean arousal level as a function of their typical arousal levels' proximity to their OLAs. People who are chronically overaroused have only a modicum of room for increased arousal before they exceed their optimal level, while those who are chronically underaroused seem to engage almost constantly in stimulus-seeking behavior. It is reasonable to posit that enduring differences in mean arousal levels lead to more or less stable patterns of behavior that are predictable and intended to optimize arousal. Thus, individual differences in baseline arousal and sensitivity to further arousal may lead to personality formation in the way that Eysenck suggests.

Eysenck has hypothesized that extroversion is composed of two first-order factors: sociability and impulsivity. Extroversion, sociability, and impulsivity are supposed to relate to arousal negatively and linearly, which suggests, for example, that the less aroused a person typically is, the more sociable and impulsive he or she will be; the more aroused someone is, the less sociable and more controlled he or she will be. Eysenck's theory has inspired considerable research that has yielded illuminating and theory-consistent results. In addition to a large body of research that, when synthesized, finds substantial support for the predicted relationships between various indices of physiological arousal and extroversion, other experimental studies provide theory-consistent results such as the ability of extroverts to tolerate significantly higher levels of noise and pain than introverts and the ability of introverts to detect audio or video signals at a significantly lower intensity threshold than extroverts (an indication of greater stimulus sensitivity). Such findings have useful applications in determining individual occupational and situational suitability.

NEWER RESEARCH
Though the inverted U of the Yerkes-Dodson law was an early twentieth century conceptualization, it was not until the 1950s that arousal theory emerged to adopt the inverted U. Following the 1949 discovery of the reticular formation's "arousing" function, a number of arousal theories of motivation, including Hebb's, were developed. All these theories incorporated the idea that the human being could be underaroused or overaroused. The reticular activating system, in conjunction with the cerebral cortex, was viewed as the homeostatic mechanism for maintaining a balance—or optimal level—of arousal. As a result, optimal arousal theory had a describable and measurable theoretical basis.

The early arousal theories touted a simplified notion of the relationship between indices of arousal and human behavior. There was a tendency to believe that virtually any of a variety of measures of physiological arousal would correlate well with behavioral measures of arousal as well as with one another. The results of research sometimes confirmed and sometimes contradicted this simplistic approach. Behavioral-level measures of arousal were not always well conceptualized: The central nervous system clearly did not act in simple unison with arousal. The results of research varied with the particular choice of cortical or autonomic arousal measure. Using heart rate as a measure, for example, has generally resulted in equivocal results in the study of the relationship between extroversion and arousal. This probably does not mean that the theory is invalid. The heart rate apparently has no simple relationship with cortical arousal. In addition, problems were caused by the design of the behavior measures, the types of experimental activity in which the subjects were engaged, the time of day, and the simplified notion that too much and too little arousal take on only negative hedonic (associated with the seeking of pleasure and the avoidance of pain) significance.

The results of research through the early 1970s suggested that arousal theory had validity but contradicted the simple theoretical connection between behavior and physiology that had been postulated. Such research has led to the modification of some theories and the formation of others. Eysenck, for example, shifted his theoretical focus from chronic or resting levels of arousal underlying extroversion to differences in underlying arousal potential (for example, stimulus sensitivity). Michael J. Apter, on the other hand, offered a new theoretical formation that accounts for the dual hedonic nature of high and low arousal. Apter posited two biological arousal systems, the telic and paratelic, which are roughly equivalent to introversion and extroversion and which underlie the dual metamotivational states. The future of optimal arousal theory seems to lie with the further development of theories that account for the ambiguities of past research, the apparent complexities of biological arousal systems, and the revision of behavioral-level arousal measures to fit the data that have been gathered.

BIBLIOGRAPHY
Apter, Michael J. *Reversal Theory: The Dynamics of Motivation, Emotion, and Personality.* 2nd ed. Oxford: Oneworld, 2007. Print.

Apter, Michael J., David Fontana, and Stephen J. Murgatroyd. *Reversal Theory: Applications and Developments.* Hillsdale: Erlbaum, 1985. Print.

Berlyne, D. E. *Conflict, Arousal, and Curiosity.* New York: McGraw, 1960. Print.

Evans, Phil. *Motivation and Emotion*. New York: Routledge, 1989. Print.

Eysenck, Hans. *Personality, Genetics, and Behavior*. New York: Praeger, 1982. Print.

Freeman, Erin, et al. "Extraversion and Arousal Procratination: Waiting for the Kicks." *Current Psychology* 30.4 (2011): 375–82. Print.

Geen, R. G. "Human Motivation: New Perspectives on Old Problems." *The G. Stanley Hall Lecture Series.* Vol. 4. Washington: APA, 1984. Print.

Pfaff, Donald. *Brain Arousal and Information Theory: Neural and Genetic Mechanisms*. Cambridge.: Harvard UP, 2006. Print.

Schmidt, Barbara, Patrick Mussel, and Johannes Hewig. "I'm Too Calm—Let's Take a Risk! On the Impact of State and Trait Arousal on Risk Taking." *Psychophysiology* 50.5 (2013): 498–503. Print.

Shah, James Y., and Wendi L. Gardner, eds. *Handbook of Motivation Science*. New York: Guilford, 2008. Print.

Ronald G. Ribble

SEE ALSO: Brain structure; Decision making; Emotions; Hormones and behavior; Motivation; Nervous system; Neurons.

Organizational behavior and consulting

DATE: 1880s forward

TYPE OF PSYCHOLOGY: Cognition; Learning; Motivation; Personality; Social psychology; Stress

Organizational behavior, the scientific study of human behavior in organizations, is a subspecialty within management. It is a multidisciplinary field that draws on findings from psychology, sociology, anthropology, public administration, economics, and other behavioral sciences. Those who study organizational behavior seek to uncover truths about people in organizations and also work with organizations to enhance performance and the quality of the members' work life.

KEY CONCEPTS
- Classical organizational theory
- Human relations movement
- Leadership
- Organizational citizenship behavior
- Organizational culture
- Organizational design
- Organizational development
- Organizational injustice
- Scientific management
- Worker motivation

INTRODUCTION

According to the organizational behavior division of the Academy of Management, organizational behavior examines human behavior in organizations from multiple perspectives, including those of organizational members, organizational groups, and the entire organization. The scientific study of organizational behavior has led to the development of techniques and strategies that can improve the functioning and productivity of organizations, whether large, profit-driven corporations or small nonprofit groups. This had led to the creation of organizational behavior consulting groups, which strive to improve organizational structure from a behavioral viewpoint.

HISTORY

American mechanical engineer Frederick Winslow Taylor initiated the scientific study of organizational behavior in the 1880s, when his experiments uncovered the keys to worker productivity. Taylor called his approach scientific management, and based on his finding, he created the piece-rate pay system to improve worker motivation.

German economist and sociologist Max Weber argued that bureaucracy was the most efficient method to organize jobs and workers. He was aware, however, that bureaucracies can limit workers through their rigid rules. His work in this area formed the basis of classical organizational theory.

Scientific management took a mechanized view of human behavior; however, many researchers thought that the emotional and social side of work was also important and developed theories along these lines. The work of sociologist Elton Mayo in this vein contributed to the human relations movement. Researchers have shifted between rational approaches, such as psychologist Herbert Simon's work on bounded rationality in human decision making, and nonrational approaches, such as psychologist Daniel Kahneman's studies of errors in human judgment. Simon won the Nobel Prize in Economics in 1978 for his work, as did Kahneman in 2002.

WORKER ATTITUDES AND BEHAVIORS

The performance of an organization depends on the performance of each of its members. Therefore, researchers in this area explore various dimensions of job performance. Job performance is primarily measured by successful achievement of the worker's duties. Other job performance measures include organizational citizenship behavior (behaviors that go above and beyond a worker's duties), employee withdrawal (tardiness, absenteeism, and turnover), and workplace deviance (the worst form being workplace violence).

When job performance suffers, so does the organization. When workers perceive that they are being treated unjustly by their organization, they respond negatively. Organizational injustice may take many forms: distributive, procedural, interpersonal, or informational. Violations of the workers' psychological contract may cause them to mentally withdraw. Worker attitudes, such as job satisfaction and organizational commitment, also influence job performance measures.

Researchers have developed many theories of work motivation. Content theories, such as Abraham Maslow's hierarchy of needs theory, explore what motivates workers. Process theories—such as equity theory, expectancy theory, and goal-setting theory—examine how to motivate workers.

Organizational professionals not only help their organizations create a committed, motivated, high-performing workforce but also seek to improve work-life quality for employees. Work stress can impair workers' mental and physical health and prevent a workforce from functioning optimally. Exploring causes of stress, such as work-life conflicts, and creating interventions, such as flextime, lead to humanizing and healthy practices on the part of the organization.

GROUP BEHAVIOR

Groups exert enormous influence on their members because they control powerful social-emotional rewards. By studying group processes, organizational professionals help organizations build stronger teams that support organizational goals. Maintaining harmony and the appropriate level of cohesiveness within groups are two problems faced by any organization.

Even within the best teams, conflicts emerge. Although conflict can be healthy, when it becomes personal, it can destroy group functioning. Intergroup conflict occurs even more often than intragroup conflict. Consultants help organizations manage and resolve their conflicts in healthy ways. They also teach negotiation skills so that workers can achieve win-win solutions.

People are prone to many nonrational tendencies, which, unfortunately, tend to multiply in group situations. One example is groupthink, in which the group's need for cohesion and harmony overrides quality decision making. Organizational consultants can help organizations limit these tendencies.

LEADERSHIP AND COMMUNICATION

Researchers have developed many theories of leadership. They explore leader traits and behaviors, and the situations in which certain leader traits and behaviors thrive. Consultants use these theories, and others, to develop better leaders.

However, no matter the quality of the leadership, if the organization's goals and strategies are not communicated to its workforce, little can be achieved. Communication is the lifeblood of any organization. However, effective communication is difficult because errors occur on the part of the sender and the receiver. Consultants help organizations overcome these limitations.

ORGANIZATIONAL PERSPECTIVES

Since Weber's groundbreaking research on bureaucracy, new ideas have emerged on organizational design. Two examples are matrix organizations, which are organized more around projects than functional departments, and modular organizations, which outsource many noncore functions.

Organizational culture influences organizational behavior. Each organization has its own culture, driven by the values and assumptions of its members. Often members of an organization are unaware of the values and assumptions that guide their behavior. If organizations are made aware of their values (such as through the creation of a mission statement), they can better live up to them.

Beginning with German-born psychologist Kurt Lewin's action research, organizational professionals have developed various interventions that improve organizational functioning. Collectively, these are called organizational development. Organizational consultants have helped organizations better achieve their goals; however, they have also been criticized for producing results that do not last within an organization. Some consultants have therefore extended their involvement, advising on change and then providing follow-up.

BIBLIOGRAPHY

Greenberg, Jerald, and Robert A. Baron. *Behavior in Organizations*. 9th ed. Upper Saddle River: Pearson, 2008. Print.

Johnson, C. Merle, and Terry A. Beehr, ed. *Integrating Organizational Behavior Management with Industrial and Organizational Psychology*. New York: Routledge, 2013. Print.

Koppes, Laura L., ed. *Historical Perspectives in Industrial and Organizational Psychology*. New York: Psychology, 2014. Digital file.

Morgan, Gareth. *Images of Organization*. Thousand Oaks: Sage, 2006. Print.

Nahavandi, Afsaneh, et al. *Organizational Behavior*. Thousand Oaks: Sage, 2015. Print.

Silverthorne, Colin P. *Organizational Psychology in Cross-Cultural Perspective*. New York: New York UP, 2005. Print.

Staw, Barry M. *Psychological Dimensions of Organizational Behavior*. 3rd ed. Upper Saddle River: Pearson, 2004. Print.

Vandeveer, Rodney C., and Michael L. Menefee. *Human Behavior in Organizations*. 2nd ed. Columbus: Pearson, 2009. Print.

George B. Yancey

SEE ALSO: Cooperation, competition, and negotiation; Field theory: Kurt Lewin; Group decision making; Groups; Hierarchy of needs; Humanistic psychology; Industrial and organizational psychology; Lewin, Kurt; Motivation; Motivation: Intrinsic and extrinsic; Work motivation; Workplace issues and mental health.

P

Pain

TYPEOFPSYCHOLOGY: Biologicalbasesofbehavior;Sensation and perception

Pain is an extremely important sensation or perception, warning a person of actual or potential injury or disease. Chronic pain may debilitate and distress a person far beyond the condition that triggered it. Theories of pain and analgesia have provided an understanding of diverse psychological phenomena, ranging from phantom limb pain to the placebo effect, and led to new psychological and biological treatments for both acute and chronic pain.

KEY CONCEPTS
- Analgesia
- Endorphin
- Nociceptor
- Opiate
- Placebo effect
- Primary afferent neuron
- Receptor

INTRODUCTION

Pain is the physical or mental suffering caused by injury or disease. It is characterized variously as a sensation of pricking, burning, aching, stinging, or soreness. It is a highly individual and plastic (changeable) experience, influenced by factors such as drugs, surgery, hypnosis, fear, joy, stress, social ritual, status, sex, social interaction, and even culture. Pain is not a uniquely human experience; it is common to almost all animals.

Pain sensations may be triggered by a wide variety of stimuli—anything that causes tissue injury (for example, intense heat or cold, excessive pressure or stretching, cutting or piercing). Tissue injury is not required, however. For example, damaging X and gamma radiation causes tissue injury but not pain, while touching the eyeball or eardrum causes pain without tissue injury. Furthermore, psychological states can cause pain in the absence of tissue injury. Examples include stress manifesting as stomach pain or memories of a trauma experienced as recurring pain in an involved body part. Some

rare individuals are born without the ability to feel pain and often injure themselves severely without knowing it.

The pain experience begins with the primary afferent neurons. Their specialized receptor endings, the free nerve endings, are triggered by painful stimuli and send their messages to the spinal cord via two distinct bundles of fibers: A delta and C fibers. The A delta fibers, most sensitive to mechanical pressure and damaging heat, are associated with the sensation of sharp, pricking pain. The C fibers (polymodal nociceptors), most sensitive to chemical stimuli, are associated with long-lasting, burning pain. When stimulated, these fibers release multiple neurotransmitter, including Substance P and glutamate, onto secondary neurons in the dorsal horn of the spinal cord. Finally, there are small interneurons, which run between dorsal horn neurons and release opioids, GABA (an inhibitory neurotransmitter), and other chemicals to decrease the pain signal.

These secondary dorsal horn neurons then transmit pain signals to the brain. One component of this system, the neo- or lateral spinothalamic tract (pathway), carries messages to the thalamus and may enable a person to localize sharp or acute pain. The thalamus is a set of structures in the forward part of the brain (forebrain) that receives and forwards messages from all sensory systems.

Another component, the paleospinothalamic (or spinoreticular) tract, carries pain messages to the brain stem (lower brain) reticular formation, with only a few cells going to the thalamus. Since the reticular formation is responsible for maintaining wakefulness and alertness, pain and other noxious (dangerous) stimuli may alert a person via this pathway. Paleospinothalamic fibers, also called multireceptive or wide dynamic range Nociceptorsnociceptors, react to both noxious and nonnoxious stimuli, and may be responsible for carrying the diffuse pain messages of chronic pain.

A third component, the spinotectal tract, sends fibers to the midbrain (middle brain), especially an area called the periaqueductal gray. Both the periaqueductal gray and the thalamus connect to the limbic system, an area of the brain associated with emotions. Scientists suspect that limbic input influences the emotional part of the pain experience.

Pain messages are sent finally to the cortex (the highest forebrain area): from the forebrain thalamus to specific areas of the cortex; from the midbrain reticular formation to the cortex in a diffuse, nonspecific way; and from the midbrain periaqueductal area to the cortex indirectly, through connections with the limbic system.

A simple ascending model of the pain system, however, does not account for a variety of human pain experiences. For example, rubbing an injured limb can reduce pain, as can strong emotions. To account for such phenomena, in 1965, Ronald Melzack and Patrick Wall postulated a "gating mechanism" within the spinal cord that would prevent pain signals from traveling from the spinal cord to the brain. Rubbing the skin would presumably close the gate. Most important, Melzack and Wall hypothesized that the brain itself could send signals down to the spinal cord to close the gate directly, thus shutting off pain messages at their source.

Although incorrect in its details, this theory was of great significance because it drew attention to the psychological aspects of pain—the role of emotion and motivation in the pain experience—and integrated these psychological aspects with the traditional, purely sensory account of pain. It also encouraged scientists to look for descending components of the pain system. It is now known that the pain signal is heavily modified by descending tracts at the spinal cord level. Under conditions of external threat, injury, or emotional stress, descending tracts from the brain release opioids and hormones, such as cortisol, that decrease the pain signal that is perceived. This phenomenon may be observed in wounded soldiers who continue to function under fire with minimal perception of pain until the attack ceases. Two of the most important of these tracts use the neurotransmitters norepinephrine and serotonin to reduce the pain signal. These tracts malfunction in people with depression, increasing their experience of pain.

PAIN RESEARCH

Basic animal research has been successfully applied to the treatment of pain in people. For example, in experiments with rats, electrical stimulation of the periaqueductal gray made the animals less sensitive to pain. When other brain areas were similarly stimulated, no such pain reduction occurred. Subsequently, electrical stimulation techniques for both the brain and spinal cord were developed to reduce chronic pain in human patients. Former Alabama governor George Wallace, crippled with chronic pain by an attacker's bullet, had electrodes implanted over the pain pathways in his spinal cord. Using a dorsal column stimulator, a cigarette-pack-sized device, he was able to send small amounts of electrical current into the spinal cord. Pain relief occurred without the undesirable drowsiness and constipation associated with painkilling drugs such as morphine. Similarly, cancer patients with chronic pain can sometimes gain relief with electrical stimulation delivered through electrodes implanted directly into their brains. Unfortunately, the effects of electrical brain and spinal cord stimulation are relatively short-lived, and, like traditional, addictive painkilling medications, their analgesic effects tend to lessen with time.

Pain research has led to a better understanding of Acupunctureacupuncture, a technique used for centuries in China to relieve pain. Acupuncturists insert fine needles through the skin and rotate them. The specific points stimulated, however, do not correspond to any known neural pathways. For this reason, Western physicians categorically rejected this approach as unscientific for many years. During the 1960's, however, American scientists visited China and observed painless surgery using only acupuncture anesthesia in awake patients. Convinced that the phenomenon was real, they began searching for new explanations.

Animal research provided an answer. Two groups of rats were first given a painful (but not injurious) heat stimulus to their tails. The control group was then given acupuncture stimulation to relieve the pain. The experimental group was first treated with naloxone and then given acupuncture. Naloxone is a substance that acts in the brain as an opiate antagonist; that is, it can bind to the brain receptor sites normally reserved for the body's own opiates and thus block the normal action of the opiates. Pain was reduced in the control but not in the experimental group, suggesting that acupuncture analgesia is mediated by an endogenous opiate analgesia system. With this new understanding, acceptance of the technique for the management of pain has grown significantly. Some clinics now offer this noninvasive method of pain relief to women during labor.

External events and even mental states can affect the experience of pain. Soldiers severely injured during battle often fail to notice the injury until long after the battle is over, and patients given a sugar pill (a placebo) for pain often obtain relief. Basic research has provided further insights into the mechanisms by which this occurs.

In one laboratory study, rats were placed in a steep-walled container filled with cold water from which escape was impossible. They had to swim to avoid drowning. After a few minutes, they were removed from the water and their pain thresholds were tested using a heat stimulus applied to their tails. The thresholds were found to be significantly elevated (they felt less pain) for several hours compared to before the swim. Thus, environmental stressors were shown to produce pain relief. Other studies have shown that some of the analgesic effects of stress (and the placebo effect) result from the release of endogenous opiates. If the opiate antagonist naloxone is given to the rats before they are exposed to cold-water stress, the elevation in their pain thresholds is blocked.

Researchers have also found that stress, opiate analgesia, and immunity are related. Large doses of the drug morphine can suppress immunity. Moreover, stress can trigger the release of endorphins both to reduce pain and to suppress the immune system (by reducing the number of natural killer cells released from the spleen).

PAIN STUDY

The study of pain must have emerged from the human desire to eliminate it. Various folk remedies for pain have existed since the time of Scribonius Largus, the Roman physician who used electric eels to reduce pain, often killing his patients in the process. Formal scientific study of the causes and treatment of pain, however, was practically unknown until the 1970's. Progress in this area was hampered by several factors. Researchers were reluctant to acknowledge that studies of animal pain might be relevant for the study of human pain, particularly since human pain appeared to be so plastic. Adequate techniques for accurately measuring pain in humans or animals were also slow to develop. Interest in pain research reached critical mass in 1974, leading to the appearance of Pain, the first journal entirely dedicated to reporting pain research. The 1970's also brought two key discoveries in pain research: Neurochemist Candace Pert found opiate receptors in the rat brain, and neurochemist Choh Li subsequently identified endogenous opiates (endorphins and enkephalins).

In 1971, psychologist Huda Akil discovered that brain stimulation with electrical current or opiates could reduce pain in animals. This finding, taken together with the discovery of endogenous opiates and their receptors, quickly led scientists to realize that in addition to the well-known ascending pathways that mediated pain, there were also descending, perhaps opiate-related, pathways that could modify pain. This realization revolutionized the study of pain, focusing attention sharply on the interaction between ascending and descending pain systems.

Interest in pain research and treatment received a further boost in the 1980's, when the World Health Organization, under its chief Jan Stjermsward,Stjermsward, Jan launched a series of major initiatives to increase international awareness of pain, improve training in pain management, and provide access to pain medication in underserved countries.

Psychologists have been concerned with pain from both the clinical and basic research perspectives. Pain as a topic has supplied the context and motivation for much productive interdisciplinary work. The efforts of molecular biologists, pharmacologists, electrophysiologists, neurochemists, neurosurgeons, biomedical engineers, and computer modelers, as well as physiological and clinical psychologists, have combined to propel the investigation of pain ahead at a rapid rate.

Psychologists have had a profound impact on the study of pain by other scientists and, in turn, have been influenced by them. They have carefully documented the behavioral phenomena to be explained (for those seeking to understand the chemistry and anatomy of pain), such as phantom limb pain (pain seeming to come from a limb that has been removed), analgesia associated with sex and defeat, the placebo effect, the "high" of the long-distance runner, the modifiable pain of childbirth, the analgesic effects of stress, and the role of emotions, cognition, and motivation in modifying sensory experience. Psychologists have also provided the sophisticated psychophysical techniques needed to assess pain, and framed the behavioral questions to be considered by nonbehavioral researchers. Psychologists have been at the forefront in developing behavioral and biological techniques to manage pain.

Reciprocally, neurochemical, neurophysiological, and neuroanatomical studies have guided psychologists toward a new understanding of how behavioral systems are organized in the brain. Opiate receptors of various types have been identified in many brain areas, not only those associated with pain. They appear to have a broad range of behavioral functions, ranging from the regulation of food intake to sex, emotion, vision, hearing, biological rhythms, aggression, and sleep.

Fortunately, advances in the study of pain have had a rapid and direct impact on human health. They have already revolutionized the medical treatment of pain and have also contributed to the improved psychological treatment of pain. Ultimately, a more coherent picture of the complex interactions of pain and the cognitive, emotional, and motivational systems of the brain will emerge, and with it a more enlightened approach to both the biological and psychological treatments of pain.

BIBLIOGRAPHY

Basbaum, Allan J., and Thomas M. Jessell. "The Perception of Pain." *In Principles of Neural Science,* edited by Eric R. Kandel and James H. Schwartz. 5th ed. New York: McGraw-Hill, 2006. An excellent neuroscience text geared toward the upper-level undergraduate, graduate student, or professional, with detailed chapters on neuroanatomy, neurophysiology, and other cutaneous senses (touch), in addition to the well-written and clear pain chapter. Extensive bibliography, pictures and diagrams, and subject and name indices, bring the reader quickly to seminal research in the field.

Melzack, Ronald, and Patrick D. Wall. *The Challenge of Pain.* 3d ed. New York: Penguin, 1996. A detailed and thorough treatment of the subject for a nontechnical audience, written by major theorists in the field. Discusses types of clinical pain, physiological mechanisms, the evolution of pain theories, and pain control techniques. Contains references, glossary, index, and illustrations.

_____, eds. *Textbook of Pain.* 4th ed. New York: W. B. Saunders, 2000. A 1,588-page textbook with exhaustive coverage of all aspects of pain physiology and treatment.

Neal, Helen. *The Politics of Pain.* New York: McGraw-Hill, 1978. Discusses pain from the patient's rather than the scientist's point of view. Explores the religious, psychological, and cultural aspects of pain; neglect of pain in children; the cancer industry; patient activism in the face of medical ignorance and unwillingness to respond to patients' pain; and the role of pharmaceutical companies. Dated in some respects, but places pain research and clinical practice in their proper political, social, and economic contexts.

Waldman, Steven D. *Atlas of Common Pain Syndromes.* 2d ed. Philadelphia: Saunders/Elsevier, 2008. Highlights common pain syndromes, with illustrations that depict symptoms and anatomy, and describes various options for testing and treatment.

Nancy Oley; updated by Elizabeth Haase

SEE ALSO: Biofeedback and relaxation; Emotions; Endorphins; Nervous system; Pain management; Placebo effect; Psychosomatic disorders; Sensation and perception; Senses; Touch and pressure.

Pain management

TYPE OF PSYCHOLOGY: Biological bases of behavior; Cognition; Emotion; Sensation and perception; Stress

Pain is not simply a physical sensation; it also has important psychological components, including attention and the significance of the injury to the person. In addition, various secondary reinforcers may serve to sustain the pain experience. Psychological approaches to pain management take these factors into account. These approaches include hypnosis, biofeedback, operant conditioning, and the cognitive behavioral therapy.

KEY CONCEPTS

- Acute pain
- Biofeedback
- Chronic pain
- Cognitive behavioral therapy
- Hypnosis
- Psychopharmacology
- Reinforcement
- Secondary reinforcers

INTRODUCTION

Contemporary attempts to define pain specify the inclusion of both physiological and psychological components. That is, at least in higher species, pain is not simply a function of bodily damage alone. The amount and quality of pain are also influenced by a number of psychological factors. These include the focus of one's attention, one's thoughts concerning the pain (including one's understanding of its consequences), one's culture, and the degree to which one feels that one can, at least partially, control the pain. These elements, originating from the cortex, thalamus, and limbic system, modulate pain in the body via descending neural tracts in the spinal cord.

The interaction of psychology and physiology is demonstrated by the phenomenon of stress-induced analgesia. Stress brought on by swimming in cold water, by running a marathon, or perhaps by being wounded in battle results in the production of the body's own chemical pain suppressors, the endorphins (endogenous morphines), to help suppress the pain.

The influence of psychological factors on pain is also demonstrated in research on the effects of placebos. Although not all people respond to placebos, about one-third do obtain relief comparable to the effects of the drug presumed to be administered. Research has shown that the pain suppression effect of a placebo is influenced by several factors. These include the assumed strength of the drug being administered as well as the dosage—that is, two placebo capsules produce twice the effect of one capsule. Factors that have been found to influence the level of placebo analgesia include the level of anxiety of the patient (anxious persons are more responsive) and the doctor-patient relationship. The placebo effect may, in some cases, be mediated by the production of endorphins.

Cognitive factors may also be critical in the perception and control of pain. In a classic study conducted by Richard Nisbett and Stanley Schachter, participants were given a pill that presumably contained a drug. Some of the participants were led to believe that this drug would produce pain-associated sensations: heart palpitations, breathing irregularities, and butterflies in the stomach. That is, they were led to believe that the pill they had taken would cause the same physical reactions as a painful stimulus. Other participants were led to believe that the drug would produce pain-irrelevant effects such as an itching sensation, numb feet, and possibly a mild headache. After taking the pill, participants received electric shocks. Those participants who had received the pain-relevant instructions were able to tolerate four times as much shock as those in the pain-irrelevant condition, suggesting that intellectual knowledge of what to expect decreased how much the shocks "hurt." This study clearly indicates that people's attributions and thoughts can influence the experience of pain.

The importance of cognition to the experience of pain is also demonstrated by a study conducted by Philip Zimbardo and others. These researchers found that those participants in their study who were led to believe they had little justification for experiencing pain not only reported less pain but actually experienced less pain (as reflected by galvanic skin response) than those who had greater justification.

A number of cultural differences have also been found with respect to the experience of pain. These differences indicate the importance of expectations—that is, whether one has learned that a particular experience is painful—on the experience of pain. Using childbirth as an example, Americans expect labor and delivery to be painful. Yet, as Ronald MelzackMelzack, Ronald mentions in his book *The Puzzle of Pain* (1973), women in many other cultures have much less distress during childbirth. In some cultures, it is the husband who gets in bed and moans and groans as if in pain. Even in Scandinavia, which enjoys a standard of living comparable to that of the United States, women are far less likely to require medication when delivering a child than are American or English women.

The meaning of the situation is also a critical psychological variable influencing the experience of pain. A dramatic example of the importance of this was observed on the battlefields of World War II. Although many of the casualties had experienced considerable physical trauma, only a minority complained of enough pain to require morphine, even though they were sensitive enough to feel the pain of an injection. The vast majority of persons experiencing similar injury in civilian life, however, do require morphine. The difference is the significance of the event. For soldiers, the injury meant that they would be sent home—not whole, perhaps, but at least alive.

Finally, pain states can be caused by or modulated by many psychiatric illnesses. Somatoform disorder is an illness in which the patient has pain in at least six body organs, none of which show tissue injury. In Conversion disordersconversion disorders, patients develop physical symptoms such as blindness, paralysis, or paresthesias (painful tingling in the limbs) in response to a stress—again, without physical injury. Patients with major depression develop a general increase in pain sensitivity, as well as more acute pains such as headaches and backaches, due to dysregulation of neurotransmitters that play a role in both pain and depression. Psychotic illnesses and anxiety disorders can also be associated with pain states.

PAIN MANAGEMENT TECHNIQUES

Several techniques have been found to be effective for the management of acute or recurring pain. Two of these are hypnosis and biofeedback.

Hypnosis has been found to be effective as the sole or supplementary anesthetic for a variety of painful procedures, including tooth extractions, surgery, and childbirth. Two important factors influencing the effectiveness of hypnosis in pain relief are the patient's ability to be hypnotized and the therapist's ability to elicit responses appropriate and adequate to bring about useful perceptual alterations. According to Josephine Hilgard, the best candidates for hypnosis are those people who have a rich imagination, enjoy daydreaming, and can generate vivid mental images. Hypnotic management of pain includes specific suggestions of dissociation (reducing emotional involvement), distraction, changing interpretation of body signals, displacing pain to a different body part, or suggestions of numbness.

Psychologists have used biofeedback management to help people control recurrent pain. The object of this technique is for the person to learn to use higher mental processes to regulate physiological functioning. To do this, the person must learn to discriminate subtle internal cues associated with desired physiological changes and reproduce these cues at will. Biofeedback also facilitates the learning of relaxation, which may reduce chronic pain involving muscle contraction. Biofeedback encourages involvement (therefore, distraction) and provides the person with a coping strategy. The effect is to increase the person's perception of his or her control of the pain.

The most frequent use of biofeedback involves the use of electromyography (EMG) for reducing muscle tension associated with a variety of conditions, including tension headache, chronic back pain, and muscle tension pain in the neck and shoulders. EMG measures the electrical activity of muscle fibers, thus serving as an index of muscle contraction or relaxation. EMG can be effective if the pain is in the muscle being monitored (rather than referred pain) and is sufficiently close to the surface that the muscle activity can be sensed.

Temperature feedback is used to assist people who suffer from vascular (migraine) headaches. A thermometer is put on the index finger and the person is told that blood is flowing to the periphery, or that his or her hand is warming. The effect of this is to bring about the suggested change and, thus, reduce pressure within the blood vessels surrounding the brain, which, in turn, reduces pain.

BEHAVIORAL APPROACHES

Psychological approaches have also been adapted to help people deal with chronic pain. These include operant and cognitive behavioral approaches.

The object of the operant approach is to reduce the excessive disability associated with the pain problem, rather than to reduce the pain itself. The first step in this procedure is one of confrontation and education, that is, to convince the person that he or she can do more even if the pain continues. Typically, it is the family that serves as the primary reinforcer of disability and activity. Therefore, their cooperation and involvement are essential if this approach is to be effective in the long term. The most common reinforcers used in the treatment are praise and attention. Rest may also be used as a reinforcer following the completion of activities. Undesirable behaviors, such as talking about the pain or screaming, are not rewarded with attention. Desired behaviors are broken down into small increments. The pain patient is encouraged to do more and more over time. This gradually results in the person being able to engage in more normal activities. As activity increases, there is a progressive withdrawal from pain medications.

The focus of the cognitive behavioral approach is to convince the person that the pain is at least partially under his or her control. The person is provided with a range of coping skills to help deal with maladaptive thoughts and noxious sensations that may contribute to the suffering. In contrast to the behavioral approach, the cognitive approach does not view the person as passive. Instead, it places emphasis on the fact that people are active processors of their environment. This approach generally employs relaxation training, either for its direct effects (the reduction of arousal) or for its cognitive effect (distraction). Deliberate attempts to distract are also employed. This may involve having the person listen to an interesting talk show rather than to music; it may involve having the person engage in an activity that requires close attention and thus serves to direct his or her attention outward. This approach also uses cognitive restructuring. First, the therapist elicits the unique thoughts and feelings the individual associates with pain—for example, that his or her continued pain signals a life-threatening condition. The therapist then attempts to elicit competing thoughts from the person, perhaps that the pain has always subsided in the past and will this time as well. In addition, coping imagery is often employed. This involves having the person imagine he or she is becoming anxious and is beginning to experience pain. The person then is asked to imagine himself or herself successfully coping with the pain using the techniques that have been learned.

PHARMACEUTICAL TREATMENTS

Medications are used to augment psychological management strategies. Over-the-counter nonsteroidal anti-inflammatory drugs such as acetaminophen, aspirin, and stronger prescription drugs like them are the most widely used pain medications. The World Health Organization recommends that they be used throughout a pain treatment. For more severe pain, such as cancer pain, long-acting opiate drugs, such as oxycodone, morphine sulfate, and methadone, are added. Shorter-acting opiates are then added for pain that "breaks through" this core treatment.

Antidepressant drugs are commonly used to treat pain. Since the 1960's, tricyclic antidepressants such as amitriptyline and imipramine have been shown to be beneficial adjuvants to a pain treatment. These medicines act on noradrenergic pathways. Serotonin reuptake inhibitor drugs, such as paroxetine and citalopram, are effective for pain because of their action on serotonin receptors in inflamed tissue, the descending serotonergic tract of the spinal cord, and the serotonergic neurons that modulate opiate pathways in the periaqueductal gray. Many other types of medicine, acting on the multiple systems that modulate pain, are also used in pain control.

NECESSITY OF PAIN RESEARCH

With the exception of a very few individuals, every person occasionally experiences acute pain. This may be the result of a toothache, cuts or bruises received while engaging in an athletic event, or countless other sources of injury. In addition, tens of millions of people in the United States, and probably hundreds of millions of people around the world, suffer from the effects of chronic pain, lower-back pain, arthritis, and various forms of headache. Migraine headaches alone are thought to cost up to seventeen billion dollars in lost productivity annually. In addition to the financial costs, untreated pain has a host of negative health consequences, including lower immune function, increased tumor growth, and the health consequences of self-medication through substance abuse.

Despite these deleterious effects, pain remains an underrecognized and undertreated social problem. On medical wards, up to half of patients suffer with untreated pain. Reasons include patient stoicism and fears of addiction, and doctors' lack of pain management training. Although studies have repeatedly shown that pain treatment does not lead to addiction, fears persist. Psychological methods of pain control can help lessen fears of dependency on medication and enhance appropriate medication use.

Pain management is a truly interdisciplinary concern. Future development will be dependent on the cooperation of people in the fields of neurology, neurosurgery, psychology, psychiatry, and many other disciplines. This cooperation will undoubtedly result in an increased understanding of pain and a reduction of human suffering, and will also facilitate efforts to gain a better understanding of the interaction of mind and body.

BIBLIOGRAPHY

Barber, Joseph, and Cheri Adrian, eds. *Psychological Approaches to the Management of Pain.* New York: Brunner/Mazel, 1982. A compilation of selections, written by authorities from both research and applied areas, concerned with psychology of pain control. Major topics include the use of hypnosis (including self-hypnosis) for the control of pain, the management of acute pain, and the treatments used in interdisciplinary pain clinics.

Benzon, Honororio T., James P. Rathmell, Christopher L. Wu, et al. *Raj's Practical Management of Pain.* 4th ed. Philadelphia: Mosby-Elsevier, 2008. Although designed for the medical professional, this resource contains information on treating a variety of conditions, including orofacial pain, phantom pain, postoperative pain, and AIDS.

Bresler, David E., and Richard Trubo. *Free Yourself from Pain.* New York: Awareness Press, 1999. Discusses the nature and control of pain, as well as a number of both traditional and unconventional therapies used in pain management. Numerous self-help forms are included.

Hiesiger, Emile, and Kathleen Brady. *Your Pain Is Real: Free Yourself from Chronic Pain with Breakthrough Medical Discoveries.* New York: HarperCollins, 2002. Neurologist and pain management specialist Hiesiger seeks to empower the chronic pain sufferer. Similar in content to *The Pain Relief Handbook* but more recent.

Nown, Graham, and Chris Wells. *The Pain Relief Handbook: Self-Help Methods for Managing Pain.* New York: Firefly Books, 1998. A comprehensive layman's guide to understanding and managing chronic pain, with illustrations and an elaborate resource guide.

Raj, P. Prithi, Leland Lou, Serdar Erdine, et al. *Interventional Pain Management: Image-Guided Procedures.* Philadelphia: W. B. Saunders, 2007. Several experts in pain management offer descriptions of and their opinions of various interventions designed to relieve the suffering of those in chronic pain. Includes a helpful section on implantable devices.

Robert D. Johnson; updated by Elizabeth Haase

SEE ALSO: Antidepressant medications; Attention; Biofeedback and relaxation; Hypnosis; Meditation and relaxation; Pain; Psychosomatic disorders; Stress: Physiological responses; Zimbardo, Philip.

Panic attacks

DATE: 1980–
TYPE OF PSYCHOLOGY: Psychopathology

Panic attacks are the defining symptoms of panic disorder, which is classified as an anxiety disorder. Panic attacks are associated with depression and substance use disorders and are more common in women than in men. Panic attacks are treated most effectively with medication and cognitive behavioral therapy.

KEY CONCEPTS
- Agoraphobia
- Antidepressant
- Anxiety disorders
- Cognitive behavioral theory
- Co-occurring disorders
- Fight-or-flight response
- Genetic predisposition
- Panic disorder

INTRODUCTION
Panic attacks are the defining symptoms of panic disorder, a painful psychiatric condition that affects 2.7 percent of, or roughly 6 million, Americans each year. Panic disorder is classified under the rubric of anxiety disorders in the American Psychiatric Association's *Diagnostic and Statistical Manual of Mental Disorders*, 5th Edition (2013) the standard nomenclature for mental illness, which is used to diagnose and categorize disorders for the purpose of treatment, research, and insurance reimbursement. Untreated panic attacks can significantly diminish the quality of a person's life, resulting in marital and social dysfunction, unemployment, and a heavy reliance on government entitlement programs such as Social Security income or disability insurance. Research has shown that a large percentage of people with panic disorder are also suicidal, depressed, or alcohol- or drug-dependent.

PRIMARY SYMPTOMS AND DIAGNOSIS
Panic attacks are overwhelmingly severe episodes of extreme fear that occur repeatedly, without warning, and under harmless circumstances. The episodes usually last for fifteen to twenty minutes and are typically experienced as waves of symptoms that encompass a wide variety of physical manifestations. These include heart palpitations, hot flashes or sudden chills, numbness or tingling sensations, chest pain or discomfort, choking sensations, sweating, trembling, dizziness or light-headedness, shortness of breath or hyperventilation, and abdominal distress or nausea. The psychological manifestations of panic attacks include powerful feelings of imminent danger, impending doom, or dread; paralyzing terror; an urgent need to escape from a situation; a sense of depersonalization or derealization; and a fear of losing control, "going crazy," or dying.

People with panic disorder are frequently convinced that they are suffering from a serious medical illness or emergency, such as a heart attack, respiratory problem, or thyroid irregularity; therefore, they often visit the emergency room or the doctor's office desperately seeking relief from their symptoms. They are usually subjected to a battery of medical tests that reveal no identifiable, underlying medical condition to which their symptoms can be attributed.

AGORAPHOBIA
Panic attacks are so uncomfortable that they cause those who experience them to fear the next attack. Out of this worry, people start to avoid places or circumstances that they believe were involved in or caused previous episodes of panic. For example, if an attack occurred in a car, the person might avoid driving or driving alone. If an attack occurred in a shopping mall or sports arena, the person might stop frequenting such places. When attacks occur in a variety of settings, people with panic disorder can experience a complication known as agoraphobia, which means the fear of open spaces, but their concern actually derives from the more deep-seated fear of having another panic attack. Chronic anticipatory anxiety and avoidance behavior prevent people with panic disorder from enjoying many opportunities for travel or recreation. In extreme cases, they become homebound for decades, simply in an attempt to avoid a future panic attack.

WHO IS AFFECTED AND WHY
The exact cause of panic attacks is unknown. However, researchers believe that they stem from a malfunction in the brain's fight-or-flight response, which is located in the part of the brain known as the locus coeruleus. Like most mental illnesses, panic disorder is best explained

by a combination of biological, psychological, and social factors.

Studies show that panic attacks are, in part, genetically determined. Having a first-degree relative (a parent or sibling) with the condition increases an individual's chances of also having the condition. In addition, panic disorder is more common among identical twins than it is among fraternal twins, suggesting a genetic predisposition to the illness.

Women are two times more likely than men to suffer from panic attacks. Although panic attacks can strike anyone at any time in their lives, the first stages of the onset of panic disorder usually occur during late adolescence and early adulthood. First episodes are also common among people in their mid-thirties. Panic attacks are often precipitated by major life events or stressors, such as leaving home to attend college, getting married, having a first child, beginning a new career, or losing a loved one. They can also follow a serious illness.

TREATMENT OPTIONS

Panic attacks are treated with a combination of medications and psychotherapy. The medications most commonly used are in the benzodiazepine and antidepressant families. Because of their short-lived effects and great potential for addiction and overdose, benzodiazepines, such as lorazepam (Ativan), alprazolam (Xanax), and clonazepam (Klonopin), are prescribed for only a limited period and never for a patient with a history of suicide attempts or substance abuse or dependence disorders. These medications also cause drowsiness and cannot be taken with alcohol—in fact, they can be fatal when mixed in high doses and large quantities with alcohol. People with panic disorder are prone to self-medicate with drugs and alcohol in an attempt to control their attacks. Such a strategy can exacerbate the severity and frequency of panic attacks and creates another problem for the patient, namely, a co-occurring substance use disorder.

The first antidepressants used to treat panic disorder belong to the category of psychiatric medications known as tricyclic antidepressants. The most popular is imipramine, which is used in larger doses to treat depression and in smaller doses to treat panic disorder. Imipramine is effective in relieving the symptoms of panic disorder, but its side effects, including dry mouth, constipation, urinary retention, and dizziness when arising from a sitting or prone position, are unpleasant for many patients.

In addition, imipramine is contraindicated for a subset of patients with a certain type of heart problem.

With the advent of fluoxetine (Prozac) and other selective serotonin reuptake inhibitors (SSRIs)—paroxetine (Paxil) and sertraline (Zoloft)—the tricyclic antidepressants were no longer considered frontline medications in the treatment of depression or panic disorder. SSRIs were touted over the tricyclic antidepressants because of their excellent side effect profiles and extremely low risk of overdose. Like the tricyclic antidepressants, the SSRIs are effective in treating panic disorders and present no risk for addiction. However, SSRIs have other types of unpleasant side effects, such as weight gain and sexual side effects that include impotence, the inability to achieve orgasm, and retrograde ejaculation in which semen is ejected backward into the bladder.

To avoid the hazards associated with taking medications, many people opt for talk therapy as a way to manage their panic attacks. Several techniques have been used successfully to control panic attacks alone or in combination with medications. One method teaches patients to practice progressive muscle relaxation, which involves tensing and relaxing each part of their bodies while listening to instructions provided by their therapists, soothing music, or pleasant background sounds. Progressive relaxation is usually employed with deep breathing exercises or meditation strategies. These methods result in overall anxiety reduction, which lowers the likelihood of a panic attack. Patients can also use relaxation exercises when they feel an attack is imminent, thereby "flowing through" and short-circuiting the attack before it becomes full-blown. Gaining a sense of mastery over the attacks makes them less likely to reoccur, and when they do, they are less severe in their intensity.

The most widely used psychotherapy in the treatment of panic attacks is cognitive behavioral therapy. For example, cognitive restructuring is a process in which patients reframe or reinterpret the experience of panic. Teaching patients that panic attacks, albeit unpleasant, are not dangerous or harmful physically (for example, that they are not harbingers of heart attacks) can help significantly diminish anxiety or ruminations about future attacks. Another cognitive behavioral technique is interoceptive exposure, in which a patient allows the therapist to trigger or induce the symptoms of a panic attack in a controlled and safe setting, such as the doctor's office. The patient learns to experience symptoms without fearing them or allowing them to progress to a full-blown panic attack. Another effective method to control panic disorder involves the systematic, in vivo exposure of patients to the real-world situations that they associate with panic attacks (for example, flying, driving, shopping, and leaving the house) while teaching them to stay relaxed in those situations. Practicing the ability to remain panic-free allows the patient to return to formerly threatening places or circumstances without the fear of experiencing a panic attack.

BIBLIOGRAPHY

Bandelow, Borwin, Katharina Domschke, and David Baldwin. *Panic Disorder and Agoraphobia.* New York: Oxford UP, 2013. Print.

Barlow, David H., et al. "Cognitive-Behavioral Therapy, Imipramine, or Their Combination for Panic Disorder: A Randomized Controlled Trial." *Journal of the American Medical Association* 283.19 (2000): 2529–36. Print.

Burns, David D. *When Panic Attacks: The New Drug-Free, Anxiety Therapy That Can Save Your Life.* New York: Random, 2006. Print.

Ehring, Thomas, and Paul M. G. Emmelkamp. *The Wiley Handbook of Anxiety Disorders.* Malden: Wiley, 2014. eBook Collection (EBSCOhost). Web. 22 May 2014.

Eaton, William, et al. "Panic and Panic Disorder in the United States." *American Journal of Psychiatry* 151.3 (1994): 413–20. Print.

Hyman, Bruce M., and C. Pedrick. *Anxiety Disorders.* Minneapolis: Lerner, 2005. Print.

Marshall E. C., et al. "Panic Attacks and Physical Health Problems in a Representative Sample: Singular and Interactive Associations with Psychological Problems, and Interpersonal and Physical Disability." *Journal of Anxiety Disorders* 22.1 (2008): 78–87. Print.

Stahl, Bob, and Wendy Millstine. *Calming the Rush of Panic: A Mindfulness-Based Stress Reduction Guide to Freeing Yourself from Panic Attacks and Living a Vital Life.* Oakland: New Harbinger, 2013. eBook Collection (EBSCOhost). Web. 22 May 2014.

Torterolo, Angela D., and Jose K Levin. "Panic Disorder: Symptoms, Treatment, and Prevention." *Psychology Research Progress.* New York: Nova Science, 2012. eBook Collection (EBSCOhost). Web. 22 May 2014.

Arthur J. Lurigio

SEE ALSO: Agoraphobia and panic disorders; Antianxiety medications; Antidepressant medications; Anxiety disorders; Cognitive behavior therapy; Drug therapies; Fear; Generalized anxiety disorder; Genetics and mental health; Psychopharmacology.

Paranoia

TYPE OF PSYCHOLOGY: Psychopathology

Paranoia is a term that has been generally used by the public to indicate any type of suspiciousness. Professionals reserve the use of the term for persons showing extreme suspicion of other people and their motives. The level of suspiciousness is delusional. Paranoia was once used as a diagnosis, but currently the diagnosis of delusional disorder has been developed to signify delusional paranoia.

KEY CONCEPTS

- Delusional disorder
- Delusional system
- Erotomanic type
- Grandiose type
- Jealous type
- Paranoid social cognition
- Persecutory type
- Repression
- Schizophrenia
- Somatic type

INTRODUCTION

Paranoia is defined as a psychiatric disorder in which a person has a group of false beliefs or delusions. The person with paranoia cannot be argued out of believing that the delusions are true. Usually when paranoia is present, a network or system of interconnecting false beliefs is present in the person's mind. Paranoia is no longer used as a diagnosis. Today when a person has been found to show paranoia, a diagnosis of delusional disorder is made.

The use of the term "paranoia" has a long history that extends back to the ancient Greeks and Romans. The word "paranoia" derives from the Greek words meaning "beside" and "mind." The Greeks and Romans used the term to describe a wide variety of mental disorders, and their use does not reflect the current utilization of the term.

During the 1800's, paranoia began to be defined by experts in the field of psychiatry as a mental condition influencing how a person conceptualized the surrounding environment. In 1863, Karl Kahlbaum used the term "paranoia" to describe a state of partial insanity that affected the intellect, but not other areas of mental functioning. In the view of Kahlbaum, a person with paranoia held a group of false beliefs to be true. Emil Kraepelin expanded on this concept by characterizing paranoia as a condition with a persistent delusional system of false belief that a person held to be true despite evidence to the contrary. Eugen Bleuler believed that paranoia was a distinct but rare psychiatric disorder.

Sigmund Freud wrote that paranoia developed from homosexual impulses that caused a person great distress. Because of the anxiety, the person would use repression to force the impulses into the unconscious mind. Once in the unconscious mind, the threatening impulses would show themselves in the form of suspiciousness and fear of being persecuted. Today the ideas of Freud are useful only as suggestions of how the unconscious may affect behavior, but the sexual connotations are no longer seen as significant in the development of paranoia.

EXTENT OF THE PROBLEM

Paranoia or delusional disorder has been found to be a rare condition, with an annual incidence of one to three new cases per 100,000 persons each year in the United States. Usually the age of onset for the disorder is around forty, but persons have been diagnosed with the condition from adolescence to late adulthood. Females show a slight edge in the number of persons diagnosed with delusional disorder. In general, it is believed that the condition is unreported because few people with delusional disorder seek professional help.

DIAGNOSIS

It can be difficult to diagnose paranoia because of the imprecise nature of the symptoms. Many people believe ideas that cannot be proven empirically or that are definitely false. To assist with the diagnosis of paranoia, the psychiatric community suggests that formal identification of delusions requires consideration of the beliefs and ideas in a person's own community. If the community would label a belief as preposterous, then paranoia can be considered as a diagnosis.

For a diagnosis of delusional disorder to be made, the false beliefs must not appear to be bizarre. This means that the delusional ideas could be possible. For example, a person believing a flying hamburger is attempting to devour him would have a bizarre delusion. Bizarre delusions are usually associated with schizophrenia, which is a severe psychiatric disorder in which a person loses reasoning capacity, has a severe disruption in mood

state, shows disorganized speech, and may experience hallucinations.

Delusional disorder exists in the form of different types that indicate the content of the delusions. The persecutory delusional disorder type is found when a person falsely believes that someone is spying, stalking, or spreading false rumors about him or her. Sometimes the person with a persecutory type of delusional disorder can be dangerous to others, threatening or carrying out acts of violence. The jealous delusional disorder type is found when a person is convinced that a sexual partner is unfaithful. The grandiose delusional disorder type believes that he or she has unusual powers, talents, or a special relationship with someone with a celebrity status. Another type of delusional disorder is the erotomanic delusional disorder type. This type involves the false belief that someone of high status or importance is in love with the delusional person. The somatic delusional disorder type has an extreme belief that he or she has some physical illness or medical condition.

POSSIBLE CAUSES

The causes of delusional disorder are not known, but delusional disorder appears to develop slowly over a period of time. The person who develops the disorder usually has a group of personality characteristics including being standoffish, unfriendly, and emotionally cold. Usually a pattern emerges in which the person blames others for his or her failures and disappointments. This leads to a paranoid social cognition as a constant interpretation of the world.

TREATMENT

There is no one treatment for persons with delusional disorder. It has been found that once the delusional system has been established, it is extremely difficult to remove or modify it. For psychotherapy to be effective, a relationship needs to be developed between the patient and the therapist. However, communication with a person who has a delusional disorder is difficult, and such a patient will usually refuse offers of medication. The group of drugs called antipsychotic medications, including haloperidol and pimozide, are often tried for treatment, but the medications are usually not taken with any regularity. Many persons with this disorder are hospitalized if they become a threat to other people, but once the person renounces the delusion, he or she will be discharged. The long-term prognosis for the successful treatment of delusional disorder has been poor.

DSM-IV-TR CRITERIA FOR PARANOIA

DELUSIONAL DISORDER (DSM CODE 297.1)

Nonbizarre delusions (involving situations occurring in real life, such as being followed, poisoned, infected, loved at a distance, or deceived by spouse or lover, or having a disease) of at least one month's duration

Symptoms for schizophrenia not met; tactile and olfactory hallucinations may be present if related to delusional theme

Apart from impact of delusion(s) or its ramifications, functioning not markedly impaired and behavior not obviously odd or bizarre

If mood episodes have occurred concurrently with delusions, their total duration has been brief relative to duration of delusional periods

Disturbance not due to direct physiological effects of a substance or general medical condition

Type based on predominant delusional theme:
- Erotomanic Type: Delusions that another person, usually of higher status, is in love with individual
- Grandiose Type: Delusions of inflated worth, power, knowledge, identity, or special relationship to deity or famous person
- Jealous Type: Delusions that individual's sexual partner is unfaithful
- Persecutory Type: Delusions that person (or someone to whom person is close) is being malevolently treated in some way
- Somatic Type: Delusions that person has some physical defect or general medical condition
- Mixed Type: Delusions characteristic of more than one of above types but no one theme predominates
- Unspecified Type

PARANOID PERSONALITY DISORDER (DSM CODE 301.0)

Pervasive distrust and suspiciousness of others such that their motives are interpreted as malevolent, beginning by early adulthood and present in variety of contexts

Indicated by four or more of the following:
- suspects, without sufficient basis, that others are exploiting, harming, or deceiving him or her
- preoccupied with unjustified doubts about loyalty or trustworthiness of friends or associates
- reluctant to confide in others because of unwarranted fear that information will be used maliciously against him or her
- reads hidden demeaning or threatening meanings into benign remarks or events
- persistently bears grudges (unforgiving of insults, injuries, or slights)
- perceives attacks on his or her character or reputation not apparent to others and quick to react angrily or counterattack
- has recurrent suspicions, without justification, regarding fidelity of spouse or sexual partner

Does not occur exclusively during course of schizophrenia, a mood disorder with psychotic features, or another psychotic disorder and not due to direct physiological effects of a general medical condition

(SCHIZOPHRENIA) PARANOID TYPE (DSM CODE 295.30)

Type of Schizophrenia involving preoccupation with one or more delusions or frequent auditory hallucinations

None of the following is prominent:
- disorganized speech
- disorganized or catatonic behavior
- flat or inappropriate affect

BIBLIOGRAPHY

Chadwick, Paul, Max J. Birchwood, and Peter Trower. *Cognitive Therapy for Delusions, Voices, and Paranoia.* New York: John Wiley & Sons, 1996. Written for psychologists and therapists, offers guidelines for diagnosing paranoia and delusional disorders and analyzes the usefulness of cognitive therapy for dealing with them.

Gabbard, G., S. Lazar, and D. Spiegel. "The Economic Impact of Psychotherapy: A Review." *American Journal of Psychiatry* 154 (1997): 147-155. This is a study on the benefits of attempting psychological treatment with persons who have delusional disorder. Although it is a difficult process, the long-term benefits are significant.

Kantor, Martin. *Understanding Paranoia: A Guide for Professionals, Families, and Sufferers.* Westport, Conn.: Praeger, 2008. Insightful resource for the layperson. The author describes vividly the workings of the paranoid mind, in an attempt to help sufferers and their family members, friends, and colleagues understand paranoid behavior.

Kinderman, P., and R. Bentall. "Causal Attributions in Paranoia and Depression: Internal, Personal, and Situational Attributions for Negative Events." *Journal of Abnormal Psychology* 106 (1997): 341-345. The underlying cognitive processes found in delusional disorder are reviewed. The authors discuss how the delusional person generalizes small negative events to a broader context.

Kramer, M. "Paranoid Cognition in Social Systems: Thinking and Acting in the Shadow of Doubt." *Personality and Social Psychology Review* 4 (1998): 251-275. The author provides an excellent description of the cognitive framework used by paranoid individuals to interpret the world. This is a good source to understand how the delusional person thinks.

Munro, Alistair. *Delusional Disorder: Paranoia and Related Illnesses.* New York: Cambridge University Press, 1999. A thorough overview of the current thinking on paranoia. Reviews the classic literature and considers the 1987 DSM-III-R revisions of the diagnosis of paranoia.

Oltmanns, Thomas, and Brendan Maher, eds. *Delusional Beliefs.* New York: John Wiley & Sons, 1988. A collection of papers from a number of disciplines on delusional disorders.

Siegel, Ronald K. *Whispers: The Voices of Paranoia.* New York: Touchstone, 1996. A psychopharmacologist relates the delusional beliefs of paranoids, attempting to communicate the experience of suffering from paranoid disorders.

Frank J. Prerost

SEE ALSO: Antipsychotic medications; Cognitive psychology; Drug therapies; Fear; Hallucinations; Jealousy; Kraepelin, Emil; Personality disorders; Psychoanalytic psychology and personality: Sigmund Freud; Psychopharmacology; Schizophrenia: Background, types, and symptoms.

Parental alienation syndrome (PAS)

DATE: 1960s forward

TYPE OF PSYCHOLOGY: Biological bases of behavior; Developmental psychology; Emotion; Motivation; Personality; Psychopathology; Psychotherapy; Social psychology; Stress

Parental alienation syndrome is the systematic denigration of one parent by the other with the intent of alienating the child against the other parent, with no justification. The purpose of the alienation is usually to gain or retain custody.

KEY CONCEPTS

- Abandonment fear
- Absent parent
- Arbitration/family counseling
- Brainwashing/programming
- Discussed alienation
- Dysfunctional families
- Gender-specific political issues
- Joint custody laws
- Physical abuse
- Systematic denigration

INTRODUCTION

Parental alienation syndrome (PAS) has arisen primarily in the context of child custody in divorce actions. Divorcing parents getting joint custody find that the interactions that must take place in transferring the child between households further complicate emotions for both parents. There is an ongoing confusion in both the legal and the medical professions as to the syndrome's nature and dimensions and how PAS can be detected. The courts have four main criteria to guide attorneys in establishing PAS.

Criterion I must show active blocking of access or contact between the child and the absent parent for the protection of the child.

Criterion II establishes that permanent termination of visitation has occurred as the result of accusations of physical abuse against the absent parent.

Criterion III establishes that a positive relationship existed between the child and the absent parent before the divorce or separation, but has severely deteriorated since then. Healthy established parental relationships do not erode naturally.

Criterion IV establishes that the alienating parent is

creating a fear-based environment, causing a child to fear abandonment by the resident parent.

These criteria seem easy to identify separately. However, when coupled with actual court cases, absolutes of the human behaviors involved are difficult to establish.

POSSIBLE CAUSES

Courts have become the arena for determining what the legal system believes to be "the best interest of the child" because PAS arises primarily from child-custody disputes. Parents who initiate PAS seem to be psychologically stuck in the first stage of child development, when survival skills are learned. The initiating parent needs total control of his or her environment and the people in it. These parents expect emotional recompense for any attempt on their part to please other people; they do not know how to give and are not likely to obey court rules because they do not play by the rules. Through many studies, these traits have been shown to be intergenerational in dysfunctional families. PAS can be a very effective tool in obtaining complete custody. Numerous motivations are involved, such as a desire for money in the form of child support, or because the alienating parent wants to remarry and not have the first spouse in the picture.

DIAGNOSING PARENTAL ALIENATION SYNDROME

Actual diagnosis of PAS in a legal proceeding is left to a mental health professional. The diagnosis by a physician or psychologist called to testify might be presented in clinical terms that are not always clear to the layman, especially to the emotionally biased parents involved. The diagnosis is therefore open to interpretation and argument by opposing attorneys. There is an ongoing argument among medical professionals regarding whether PAS is a syndrome (a number of symptoms occurring together, constituting a distinct clinical picture) or a disorder (a disruption or interference with normal functions or established systems). Further complicating the issue is the fact that PAS does not appear in the *Diagnostic and Statistical Manual of Mental Disorders* or in the World Health Organization's *International Statistical Classification of Diseases* and many clinicians do not accept it as a legitimate diagnosis.

One parent turning a child against another parent is not a complicated concept on its own. Historically, however, PAS has been hard to prove because of the unpredictable, often untruthful human behaviors involved.

There is also attempted PAS, when the legal criteria are not met, but the parent has tried, without success, to alienate the child from the other parent.

TREATMENT OPTIONS

Arbitration by a family counseling specialist must be ordered before court proceedings begin. False accusations can psychologically damage a child for life. As adults, these children often seek out the alienated/absent parent, only to find that the accusations were unfounded. If severe guilt and emotional distress do exist, professional help is recommended immediately.

CONTROVERSY

PAS has not been received uncritically in the fields of psychology and law. Many psychology experts consider it lacking in scientific basis, noting that the original publications about PAS were self-published and that subsequent publications in peer-reviewed journals have been anecdotal case studies. As of 2014, no large-scale, repeatable, falsifiable clinical studies of PAS had been made. Neither the American Medical Association nor the American Psychiatric Association recognizes PAS, and the American Psychological Association declines to give a position on it due to the lack of data.

In the legal realm, courts in Canada and the United Kingdom have decided that a diagnosis of PAS is not admissible in a custody case; courts in the United States may still accept it, but its lack of support from the psychiatric and psychological community complicates its use in custody battles.

Additionally, some child advocacy and women's groups have raised concerns that Gardner's formulation of PAS demonizes mothers (whom he labeled as the alienating parent in the vast majority of cases) and enables the dismissal of legitimate instances of child abuse. Some therapists and clinicians working with children in divorce situations also take issue with PAS's placement of the blame solely on one parent, believing that often both parents contribute to the problems.

BIBLIOGRAPHY

Baker, Amy J. *Adult Children of Parental Alienation Syndrome: Breaking the Ties That Bind.* New York: Norton, 2007. Print.

Bond, Richard. "The Lingering Debate over the Parental Alienation Syndrome Phenomenon." *Journal of Child Custody* 4.1–2 (2008): 35–54. Print.

Bow, James N., Jonathan W. Gould, and James R.

Flens. "Examining Parental Alienation in Child Custody Cases: A Survey of Mental Health and Legal Professionals." *American Journal of Family Therapy* 37.2 (2009): 127–45. Print.

Clawar, S. S., and B. V. Rivlin. *Children Held Hostage: Dealing with Programmed and Brainwashed Children.* Chicago: Amer. Bar Assn., 1991. Print.

Crary, David. "Parental Alienation Not a Mental Disorder, American Psychiatric Association Says." *Huffington Post.* TheHuffingtonPost.com, 21 Sep. 2012. Web. 29 May 2014.

Emery, Robert E. "Parental Alienation Syndrome: Proponents Bear the Burden of Proof." *Family Court Review* 43.1 (2005): 8–13. Print.

Gardner, Richard A. *Parental Alienation Syndrome.* 2d ed. Cresskill: Creative Therapeutics, 2000. Print.

Gardner, Richard A. "Should Courts Order PAS Children to Visit or Reside with the Alienated Parent?" *The American Journal of Forensic Psychology* 19.3 (2001): 61–106. Print.

Moskovitch, Deborah. *The Smart Divorce: Proven Strategies and Valuable Advice from One Hundred Top Divorce Lawyers, Financial Advisers, Counselors, and Other Experts.* Chicago: Chicago Review, 2007. Print.

Turkat, Ira Daniel. "Questioning the Mental Health Expert's Custody Report." *American Journal of Family Law* 7 (1993): 175–177. Print.

Virginiae Blackmon

See Also: Children's mental health; Family life: Adult issues; Family life: Children's issues; Law and psychology; Parenting styles; Teenagers' mental health.

REFERENCE
Not to be taken from this
room

Kirtland Community College Library
4800 W. Four Mile Rd.
Grayling, MI 49738
989.275.5000 x 1246